DATE DUE

			PRINTED IN U.S.A.

Literature Criticism from 1400 to 1800

Guide to Gale Literary Criticism Series

When you need to review criticism of literary works, these are the Gale series to use:

If the author's death date is:	You should turn to:

After Dec. 31, 1959
(or author is still living)

CONTEMPORARY LITERARY CRITICISM

for example: Jorge Luis Borges, Anthony Burgess,
William Faulkner, Mary Gordon,
Ernest Hemingway, Iris Murdoch

1900 through 1959

TWENTIETH-CENTURY LITERARY CRITICISM

for example: Willa Cather, F. Scott Fitzgerald,
Henry James, Mark Twain, Virginia Woolf

1800 through 1899

NINETEENTH-CENTURY LITERATURE CRITICISM

for example: Fedor Dostoevski, Nathaniel Hawthorne,
George Sand, William Wordsworth

1400 through 1799

LITERATURE CRITICISM FROM 1400 TO 1800
(excluding Shakespeare)

for example: Anne Bradstreet, Daniel Defoe,
Alexander Pope, François Rabelais,
Jonathan Swift, Phillis Wheatley

SHAKESPEAREAN CRITICISM

Shakespeare's plays and poetry

Antiquity through 1399

CLASSICAL AND MEDIEVAL LITERATURE CRITICISM

for example: Dante, Homer, Plato, Sophocles, Vergil,
the Beowulf Poet

Gale also publishes related criticism series:

CHILDREN'S LITERATURE REVIEW

This ongoing series covers authors of all eras. Presents criticism on authors and author/illustrators who write for the preschool through high school audience.

SHORT STORY CRITICISM

This series covers the major short fiction writers of all nationalities and periods of literary history.

ISSN 0740-2880

Volume 7

Literature Criticism from 1400 to 1800

Excerpts from Criticism of the Works
of Fifteenth-, Sixteenth-, Seventeenth-, and
Eighteenth-Century Novelists, Poets, Playwrights,
Philosophers, and Other Creative Writers, from
the First Published Critical Appraisals
to Current Evaluations

Guest Introduction:
"Men of Letters as Statists:
Locke, Montesquieu, Hume, Burke"
by Russell Kirk

James E. Person, Jr.
Editor

Robin DuBlanc
Associate Editor

Gale Research Company
Book Tower
Detroit, Michigan 48226

STAFF

James E. Person, Jr., *Editor*

Robin DuBlanc, *Associate Editor*

James P. Draper, Jay P. Pederson, *Senior Assistant Editors*

Claudia Loomis, Peter Wehrli, *Assistant Editors*

Jeanne A. Gough, *Permissions and Production Manager*

Lizbeth A. Purdy, *Production Supervisor*
Kathleen M. Cook, *Assistant Production Coordinator*
Suzanne Powers, Jani Prescott, Lee Ann Welsh, *Editorial Assistants*

Linda M. Pugliese, *Manuscript Coordinator*
Donna Craft, *Assistant Manuscript Coordinator*
Jennifer E. Gale, Maureen A. Puhl, Rosetta Irene Simms, *Manuscript Assistants*

Victoria B. Cariappa, *Research Supervisor*
Maureen R. Richards, *Research Coordinator*
Mary D. Wise, *Senior Research Assistant*
Joyce E. Doyle, Kevin B. Hillstrom, Karen D. Kaus, Eric Priehs,
Filomena Sgambati, Laura B. Standley, *Research Assistants*

Janice M. Mach, *Text Permissions Supervisor*
Kathy Grell, *Text Permissions Coordinator*
Susan D. Battista, *Assistant Permissions Coordinator*
Mabel E. Gurney, Josephine M. Keene, *Senior Permissions Assistants*
Eileen H. Baehr, H. Diane Cooper, Anita L. Ransom, Kimberly F. Smilay, *Permissions Assistants*
Melissa A. Kamuyu, Martha A. Mulder, Lisa M. Wimmer, *Permissions Clerks*

Patricia A. Seefelt, *Picture Permissions Supervisor*
Margaret A. Chamberlain, *Assistant Permissions Coordinator*
Collen M. Crane, *Permissions Assistant*
Lillian Tyus, *Permissions Clerk*

Library of Congress Catalog Card Number 83-20504
ISBN 0-8103-6106-X
ISSN 0740-2880

Computerized photocomposition by
Typographics, Incorporated
Kansas City, Missouri

Printed in the United States

Contents

Preface

"If I have seen farther," wrote Sir Isaac Newton, echoing Fulbert of Chartes and commenting on his own indebtedness to the sages who preceded him, "it is by standing on the shoulders of giants," a statement as applicable to ourselves today as it was to Newton and his world. Many of the political and intellectual foundations of the modern world can be found in the art and thought of the fifteenth through eighteenth centuries. During this time the modern nation-state was born, the sciences grew tremendously, and many of the political, social, economic, and moral philosophies that are influential today were formulated. The literature of these centuries reflects this turbulent time of radical change: the period saw the rise of drama equal in critical stature to that of classical Greece, the birth of the novel and personal essay forms, the emergence of newspapers and periodicals, and significant achievements in poetry and philosophy. Much of modern literature reflects the influence of these centuries' developments. Thus the literature of this period provides insight into the universal nature of human experience, as well as into the life and thought of the past.

Literary criticism can also give us insight into the human condition, as well as into the specific moral and intellectual atmosphere of an era, for the criteria by which a work of art is judged reflect contemporary philosophical and social attitudes. Literary criticism takes many forms: the traditional essay, the book or play review, even the parodic poem. Criticism can also be of several kinds, including descriptive, interpretive, textual, appreciative, and generic, among others. Collectively, the range of critical response helps us understand a work of art, an author, an era.

Scope of the Series

Literature Criticism from 1400 to 1800 (LC) is designed to serve as an introduction to the authors of the fifteenth through eighteenth centuries and to the most significant commentators on these authors. The works of the great poets, dramatists, novelists, essayists, and philosophers of those years are considered classics in every secondary school and college or university curriculum. Because criticism of this literature spans a period of up to six hundred years, an overwhelming amount of critical material confronts the student. To help students locate and select criticism on the works of authors who died between 1400 and 1800, *LC* presents significant passages from the most noteworthy published criticism on authors of these centuries. Each volume of *LC* is carefully compiled to represent the critical heritage of the most important writers from a variety of nationalities. In addition to major authors, *LC* also presents criticism on lesser-known writers whose significant contributions to literary history are reflected in continuing critical assessments of their works.

The need for *LC* among students and teachers of literature of the fifteenth through eighteenth centuries was suggested by the proven usefulness of Gale's *Contemporary Literary Criticism (CLC), Twentieth-Century Literary Criticism (TCLC),* and *Nineteenth-Century Literature Criticism (NCLC),* which excerpt criticism of creative writing from the nineteenth and twentieth centuries. Because of the different time periods covered, there is no duplication of authors or critical material between any of Gale's literary criticism series. For further information about these series, readers should consult the Guide to Gale Literary Criticism Series preceding the title page of this volume. Here, the reader will note that there is a separate Gale reference series devoted to Shakespearean studies. For though belonging properly to the literary period covered in *LC,* William Shakespeare has inspired such a tremendous and ever-growing corpus of secondary material that the editors have deemed it best to give his works the extensive critical coverage best served by a separate series, *Shakespearean Criticism.*

Each author entry in *LC* provides an overview of major criticism on an author. Therefore, the editors include approximately twelve authors in each 550-page volume (compared with approximately forty authors in a *CLC* volume of similar size) so that more attention may be given each author. Each author entry represents a historical survey of the critical response to an author's work: early criticism is presented to indicate initial responses, later selections represent any rise or decline in the author's literary reputation and describe the effects of social or historical forces on the work of an author, and retrospective analyses provide students with a modern view. The length of an author entry is intended to represent the author's critical reception in English or foreign criticism in translation. Articles and books that have not been translated into English are therefore excluded. Every attempt has been made to identify and include excerpts from the seminal essays on each author's work, and to include recent critical commentary providing modern perspectives on the writer. An author may appear more than once in the series because of the great quantity of critical material available, or because of a resurgence of criticism generated by such events as an author's anniversary celebration, the republication of an author's works, or the publication of a newly translated work.

Organization of the Book

An author entry consists of the following elements: author heading, biographical and critical introduction, list of principal works, excerpts of criticism (each followed by a bibliographical citation), and an additional bibliography for further reading. Also, most author entries reproduce author portraits and other illustrations pertinent to the author's life and career.

- The *author heading* consists of the author's full name, followed by birth and death dates. The unbracketed portion of the name denotes the form under which the author most commonly wrote. If an author wrote consistently under a pseudonym, the pseudonym will be listed in the author heading, with the real name given in parentheses on the first line of the biographical and critical introduction. Also located at the beginning of the introduction to the author entry are any name variations under which an author wrote, including transliterated forms for authors whose native languages use nonroman alphabets. Uncertain birth or death dates are indicated by question marks.

- The *biographical and critical introduction* contains background information designed to introduce the reader to an author and to the critical discussion surrounding his or her work. Parenthetical material following many of the introductions provides references to biographical and critical reference series published by Gale, including *Children's Literature Review, Dictionary of Literary Biography, Something about the Author,* and *Yesterday's Authors of Books for Children.*

- Most *LC* entries include *portraits* of the author. Many entries also contain illustrations of materials pertinent to an author's career, including selected holographs of manuscript pages, title pages, letters, or representations of important people, places, and events in an author's life.

- The *list of principal works* is chronological by date of first book publication and identifies the genre of each work. In the case of foreign authors whose works have been translated into English, the title and date of the first English-language edition are given in brackets following the foreign-language listing. Unless otherwise indicated, dramas are dated by first performance, not first publication.

- *Criticism* is arranged chronologically in each author entry to provide a useful perspective on changes in critical evaluation over the years. All titles by the author featured in the critical entry are printed in boldface type to enable the user to ascertain without difficulty the works being discussed. Also for purposes of easier identification, the critic's name and the composition or publication date of the critical work are given at the beginning of each excerpt. Unsigned criticism is preceded by the title of the source in which it appeared. When an anonymous essay has been attributed to a critic, the critic's name appears in brackets at the beginning of the excerpt and in the bibliographical citation. Publication information (such as publisher names and book prices) and parenthetical numerical references (such as footnotes or page and line refrences to specific editions of works) have been deleted at the editor's discretion to provide smoother reading of the text.

- Critical essays are prefaced by *explanatory notes* as an additional aid to students using *LC*. The explanatory notes may provide several types of useful information, including: the reputation of a critic, the importance of a work of criticism, the specific type of criticism (biographical, psychoanalytic, structuralist, etc.), the intent of the criticism, and the growth of critical controversy or changes in critical trends regarding an author's work. In some cases, these notes cross-reference the work of critics who agree or disagree with each other. Dates in parentheses within the explanatory notes refer to a book publication date when they follow a book title and to an essay date when they follow a critic's name.

- A complete *bibliographical citation* designed to facilitate location of the original essay or book by the interested reader follows each piece of criticism.

- The *additional bibliography* appearing at the end of each author entry suggests further reading on the author. In a few rare cases it includes essays for which the editors could not obtain reprint rights.

An appendix lists the sources from which material in each volume has been reprinted. It does not, however, list every book and periodical consulted in the preparation of the volume.

Cumulative Indexes

Each volume of *LC* includes a cumulative index to authors listing all the authors that have appeared in *Contemporary Literary Criticism, Twentieth-Century Literary Criticism, Nineteenth-Century Literature Criticism,* and *Literature Criticism from 1400 to 1800,* along with cross-references to the Gale series *Children's Literature Review, Authors in the News, Contemporary Authors, Contemporary Authors Autobiography Series, Contemporary Authors Bibliographical Series, Dictionary of Literary Biography, Something about the Author, Something about the Author Autobiography Series,* and *Yesterday's Authors of Books for Children.* Readers will welcome this cumulative author index as a useful tool for locating an author within the various series. The index, which includes authors' birth and death dates, is particularly valuable for those authors who are identified with a certain period but whose death dates cause them to be placed in another, or for those authors whose careers span two periods. For example, Wyndham Lewis is found in *TCLC,* yet a writer often associated with him, T. S. Eliot, is found in *CLC.*

Each volume of *LC* also includes a cumulative nationality index, in which authors' names are arranged alphabetically under their respective nationalities and followed by the numbers of the volumes in which they appear. In addition, each volume of *LC* includes a cumulative title index which cites works under critical consideration, followed by the volume and page number where the criticism can be found.

Acknowledgments

No work of this scope can be accomplished without the cooperation of many people. The editors especially wish to thank the copyright holders of the excerpts included in this volume, the permissions managers of many book and magazine publishing companies for assisting us in locating copyright holders, and Anthony Bogucki for assistance with copyright research. We are also grateful to the staffs of the Detroit Public Library, the Library of Congress, University of Detroit Library, University of Michigan Library, and Wayne State University Library for making their resources available to us. Finally, the editors wish to thank Russell Kirk for contributing his fine introductory essay "Men of Letters as Statists: Locke, Montesquieu, Hume, Burke." This, a short study of four men whose writings are often cited as having influenced the framers of the United States Constitution, is a timely work in light of recent celebrations of the Constitution's bicentennial.

Suggestions Are Welcome

Readers who wish to suggest authors to appear in future volumes, or who have other suggestions, are cordially invited to write the editor.

Additional Authors to Appear
in Future Volumes

Abravenel, Isaac 1437-1508
Abravenel, Judah 1460-1535
Addison, Joseph 1672-1719
Agricola, Johannes 1494?-1566
Akenside, Mark 1721-1770
Alabaster, William 1567-1640
Alarcón y Mendoza, Juan Rúiz
   1581-1634
Alberti, Leon Battista 1404-1472
Alembert, Jean Le Rond d' 1717-1783
Amory, Thomas 1691?-1788
Anton Ulrich, Duke of Brunswick
   1633-1714
Aretino, Pietro 1492-1556
Ascham, Roger 1515-1568
Aubigne, Théodore Agrippa d'
   1552-1630
Aubin, Penelope 1685-1727?
Aubrey, John 1620-1697
Bâbur 1483-1530
Bacon, Sir Francis 1561-1626
Bale, John 1495-1563
Barber, Mary 1690-1757
Baretti, Giuseppi 1719-1789
Barker, Jane 1652-1727?
Bartas, Guillaume de Salluste du
   1544-1590
Baxter, Richard 1615-1691
Bayle, Pierre 1647-1706
Beaumarchais, Pierre-Augustin Caron
   de 1732-1799
Beaumont, Francis 1584-1616
Belleau, Rémy 1528-1577
Berkeley, George 1685-1753
Bessarion, Johannes 1403-1472
Bijns, Anna 1493-1575
Bisticci, Vespasiano da 1421-1498
Blackmore, Sir Richard 1650-1729
Boccalini, Traiano 1556-1613
Bodin, Jean 1530-1596
Bolingbroke, Henry St. John
   1678-1751
Boyle, Roger 1621-1679
Bradford, William 1590-1657
Brant, Sebastian 1457-1521
Breitinger, Johann Jakob 1701-1776
Breton, Nicholas 1545-1626
Broome, William 1689-1745
Browne, Sir Thomas 1605-1682
Bruni, Leonardo 1370-1444
Bruno, Giordano 1548-1600
Buffon, George-Louis Leclerc, Comte
   de 1707-1788

Burgoyne, John 1722-1792
Burnet, Gilbert 1643-1715
Burton, Robert 1577-1640
Butler, Samuel 1612-1680
Byrd, William, II 1674-1744
Byrom, John 1692-1763
Calderón de la Barca, Pedro 1600-1681
Camden, William 1551-1623
Campion, Thomas 1567-1620
Carew, Richard 1555-1620
Carew, Thomas 1594-1640
Carver, Jonathan 1710-1780
Casanova di Seingalt, Giacomo
   Girolamo 1725-1798
Castiglione, Baldassare 1478-1529
Castillejo, Cristobalde 1492-1550
Cavendish, William 1592-1676
Caxton, William 1421?-1491
Centlivre, Susanna 1667?-1723
Chapman, George 1560-1634
Chartier, Alain 1390-1440
Christine de Pisan 1365?-1431?
Cibber, Colley 1671-1757
Cleveland, John 1613-1658
Collyer, Mary 1716?-1763?
Colonna, Vittoria 1490-1547
Commynes, Philippe de 1445-1511
Condillac, Etienne Bonnot, Abbé de
   1714?-1780
Cook, James 1728-1779
Corneille, Pierre 1606-1684
Cortés, Hernán 1485-1547
Cotton, John 1584-1652
Courtilz de Sandras, Gatiende
   1644-1712
Cowley, Abraham 1618-1667
Cranmer, Thomas 1489-1556
Crashaw, Richard 1612-1649
Crébillon, Prosper Jolyot de 1674-1762
Cruden, Alexander 1701-1770
Curll, Edmund 1675-1747
Dampier, William 1653-1715
Daniel, Samuel 1562-1619
Davenant, Sir William 1606-1668
Davidson, John 1549?-1603
Da Vinci, Leonardo 1452-1519
Day, John 1574-1640
Dekker, Thomas 1572-1632
Delany, Mary Pendarves 1700-1788
Denham, Sir John 1615-1669
Dennis, John 1657-1734
Deloney, Thomas 1543?-1600?
Descartes, René 1596-1650

Desfontaines, Pierre François Guyot,
   Abbé 1685-1745
Diaz del Castillo, Bernal 1492?-1584
Diderot, Denis 1713-1784
Donne, John 1572-1631
Drayton, Michael 1563-1631
Drummond, William 1585-1649
Du Guillet, Pernette 1520?-1545
Dunbar, William 1460?-1520?
Elyot, Thomas 1490-1546
Emin, Fedor ?-1770
Erasmus, Desiderius 1466-1536
Etherege, Sir George 1635-1691
Eusden, Laurence 1688-1730
Evelyn, John 1620-1706
Fabyan, Robert ?-1513
Fairfax, Thomas 1621-1671
Fanshawe, Lady Anne 1625-1680
Fanshawe, Sir Richard 1608-1666
Farquhar, George 1678-1707
Fénelon, François 1651-1715
Fergusson, Robert 1750-1774
Ficino, Marsillo 1433-1499
Fletcher, John 1579-1625
Florian, Jean Pierre Claris de
   1755-1794
Florio, John 1553?-1625
Fontaine, Charles 1514-1565
Fontenelle, Bernard Le Bovier de
   1657-1757
Fonvizin, Denis Ivanovich 1745-1792
Ford, John 1586-1640
Foxe, John 1517-1587
Franklin, Benjamin 1706-1790
Froissart, Jean 1337-1404?
Fuller, Thomas 1608-1661
Galilei, Galileo 1564-1642
Garrick, David 1717-1779
Gascoigne, George 1530?-1577
Gay, John 1685-1732
Gibbon, Edward 1737-1794
Gildon, Charles 1665-1724
Glanvill, Joseph 1636-1680
Góngora y Argote, Luis de 1561-1627
Gosson, Stephen 1554-1624
Gottsched, Johann Christoph
   1700-1766
Gower, John 1330?-1408
Graham, Dougal 1724-1779
Greene, Robert 1558?-1592
Griffith, Elizabeth 1727?-1793
Guarini, Giambattista 1538-1612
Hakluyt, Richard 1553-1616

Hall, Edward 1498-1547
Harrington, James 1611-1677
Hartley, David 1705-1757
Helvetius, Claude Arien 1715-1771
Henslowe, Philip ?-1616
Herbert, George 1593-1633
Herrick, Robert 1591-1674
Heywood, Thomas 1574-1641
Hobbes, Thomas 1588-1679
Hogarth, William 1697-1764
Holbach, Paul Heinrich Dietrich 1723-1789
Holinshed, Raphael ?-1582?
Hooker, Richard 1544-1600
Hooker, Thomas 1586-1647
Howard, Henry, Earl of Surrey 1517-1547
Hung Sheng 1646-1704
Hutcheson, Francis 1694-1746
Ibn Khaldun, Abd al-Rahman ibn Muhammad 1332-1406
Iriarte, Tomas de 1750-1791
Isla y Rojo, José Francisco de 1703-1781
James I, King of Scotland 1394-1437
Johnson, Samuel 1709-1784
King, William 1662-1712
Knox, John 1514?-1572
Kochanowski, Jan 1530-1584
Kyd, Thomas 1558-1594
La Bruyére, Jean de 1645-1696
La Fontaine, Jean de 1621-1695
Langland, William 1330?-1400
La Rochefoucauld, Francois de 1613-1680
Law, William 1686-1761
Lessing, Gotthold Ephraim 1729-1781
L'Estrange, Sir Roger 1616-1704
Let-we Thon-dara 1752-1783
Littleton, Sir Thomas 1422-1481
Lo Kuan-Chung c.1400
Lodge, Thomas 1558-1625
Lope de Vega 1562-1635
Lopez de Ayala, Pero 1332-1407?
Lovelace, Richard 1618-1657
Loyola, Ignacio de 1491-1556
Luther, Martin 1483-1546
Lydgate, John 1370?-1452
Lyly, John 1554-1606
Lyttleton, George 1709-1773
MacDomhnaill, Sean Clarach 1691-1754
Machiavelli, Niccolò 1469-1527
Macpherson, James 1736-1796
Maitland, Sir Richard 1496-1586
Malory, Sir Thomas ?-1471
Mandeville, Bernard de 1670-1733
Marat, Jean Paul 1743-1793
Marie de l'Incarnation 1599-1672
Marlowe, Christopher 1564-1593
Marston, John 1576-1634
Massinger, Philip 1583-1640
Mather, Cotton 1663-1728

Mather, Increase 1639-1723
Metastasio, Pietro 1698-1782
Michelangelo Buonarrotti 1475-1564
Middleton, Thomas 1580-1627
Milton, John 1608-1674
Molière 1622-1673
Montagu, Lady Mary Wortley 1689-1762
Montaigne, Michel Eyquem, Seigneur de 1533-1592
Montfort, Hugo von 1357-1423
More, Henry 1614-1687
More, Sir Thomas 1478-1535
Morton, Thomas 1575-1647
Muret, Marc-Antoine de 1526-1585
Nashe, Thomas 1567-1601
Nawa i 1441-1501
North, Sir Thomas 1535?-1601?
Norton, Thomas 1532-1584
Oldham, John 1653-1683
Otway, Thomas 1652-1685
Pade-tha-ya-za 1684-1754
Painter, William 1540?-1594
Paracelsus 1493-1541
Parr, Catharine 1512-1548
Pascal, Blaise 1623-1662
Pasek, Jan Chryzostom 1636-1701
Peele, George 1556-1596
Pembroke, Mary Sidney, Countess of 1561-1621
Penn, William 1644-1718
Pepys, Samuel 1633-1703
Pétursson, Halligrímur 1614-1674
Pico della Mirandola, Giovanni 1463-1494
Pix, Mary 1666-1720
Poliziano, Angelo 1454-1494
Quarles, Francis 1592-1644
Quevedo y Villegas, Francisco Gomez de 1580-1645
Racine, Jean 1639-1699
Raleigh, Sir Walter 1552-1618
Reuter, Christian 1665-1712
Revius, Jacobus 1586-1658
Reynolds, Sir Joshua 1723-1792
Rochester, John Wilmot, Earl of 1648-1680
Rojas Zorilla, Francisco de 1607-1648
Roper, William 1498-1578
Rousseau, Jean-Jacques 1712-1788
Rowe, Elizabeth 1674-1737
Rowe, Nicholas 1674-1718
Rutherford, Samuel 1600?-1661
Sackville, Thomas 1536-1608
Saint-Simon, Louis de Rouvroy 1675-1755
Sannazaro, Jacopo 1458-1530
Santeuil, Jean Baptiste de 1630-1697
Savage, Richard 1696-1742
Savonarola, Girolamo 1452-1498
Scarron, Paul 1610-1660
Scott, Sarah 1723-1795
Selden, John 1584-1654

Sévigné, Madame de 1626-1696
Sewall, Samuel 1652-1730
Shadwell, Thomas 1642-1692
Shaftesbury, Anthony Ashley Cooper, Earl of 1671-1713
Shenstone, William 1714-1763
Shirley, James 1596-1666
Sidney, Sir Philip 1554-1586
Sigüenza y Góngora, Carlos de 1645-1700
Skelton, John 1464?-1529
Smith, Adam 1723-1790
Smith, Captain John 1580-1631
Spee, Friedrich von 1591-1635
Sprat, Thomas 1635-1713
Stanhope, Philip 1694-1773
Steele, Sir Richard 1672-1729
Suckling, Sir John 1609-1642
Swedenborg, Emanuel 1688-1772
Takeda Izumo 1690-1756
Tasso, Bernardo 1494-1569
Taylor, Edward 1645-1729
Taylor, Jeremy 1613-1667
Temple, Sir William 1629-1699
Tencin, Madame de 1682-1749
Testi, Fulvio 1593-1646
Thomas à Kempis 1380?-1471
Thomson, James 1700-1748
Tourneur, Cyril 1570-1626
Traherne, Thomas 1637-1674
Trai, Nguyen 1380-1442
Tristan 1601-1655
Trotter, Catharine 1679-1749
Tyndale, William 1494?-1536
Urquhart, Sir Thomas 1611-1660
Ussher, James 1581-1656
Vasari, Giorgio 1511-1574
Vaughan, Henry 1621-1695
Vaughan, Thomas 1622-1666
Vico, Giambattista 1668-1744
Villiers, George 1628-1687
Villon, François 1431-1463
Voltaire 1694-1778
Waller, Edmund 1606-1687
Walton, Izaak 1593-1683
Warburton, William 1698-1779
Warner, William 1558-1609
Warton, Thomas 1728-1790
Webster, John 1580-1638
Weise, Christian 1642-1708
Wesley, John 1703-1791
Whetstone, George 1544?-1587?
White, Gilbert 1720-1793
Wigglesworth, Michael 1631-1705
Williams, Roger 1603-1683
Winckelman, Johann Joachim 1717-1768
Winthrop, John 1588-1649
Wyatt, Sir Thomas 1503-1542
Wycherley, William 1640?-1716
Yuan Mei 1716-1797
Zólkiewski, Stanislaw 1547-1620
Zrinyi, Miklos 1620-1664

Readers are cordially invited to suggest additional authors to the editors.

Guest Introduction

Men of Letters as Statists:
Locke, Montesquieu, Hume, Burke
by Russell Kirk

During the century that elapsed between the "Glorious" Revolution of 1688 and the Jacobins' execution of Louis XVI in 1793, four men of letters dominated British and American political thought; and their influence still may be discerned on either side of the Atlantic near the end of the twentieth century. John Locke, the grandfather of liberalism; the Baron de Montesquieu, the philosopher of constitutional order; David Hume, the empirical skeptic; Edmund Burke, the conservative reformer: these men's writings are quick yet.

Of the four, only Burke entered upon the hurly-burly of political practice, and that at first with reluctance. "In politics the professor always plays the comic role," Nietzsche instructs us. None of these four was a professor, nor yet strictly a closet philosopher; still, Burke excepted, they were men of theory. Locke could affect the public affairs of his time only through his uncertain influence first upon Lord Shaftesbury and later upon William of Orange and the Princess Mary. Montesquieu, though a high magistrate of Bordeaux, found himself powerless to arrest the drift of public affairs in France, and could only observe and reflect during his two years' residence in England. Hume held public offices from time to time, but no very important one, preferring conviviality and folios to the labors of statecraft. As for Burke, during nearly all of his eminent political career he was a leader of the opposition, not an architect of the grand policies of the United Kingdom and the Empire.

So the power exerted by these four men—for this is true of Burke also—was principally the power of the pen, not the power of office or of intrigue. As John Taylor, the "Water Poet", had put it at the beginning of the seventeenth century—

> Pens are most dangerous tools, more sharp by odds
> Than swords, and cut more keen than whips or rods.

In politics, the pen's power may work ruinous mischief, as well as considerable good. Whatever may be thought of the long-run effects of the several ideas of these four writers, all four were gentlemen of good character and high motives. They were political philosophers, but not ideologues: for ideology, aspiring to take the Terrestrial Paradise by storm, did not afflict the world until the coming of the Jacobins in the French Revolution.

However virtuous an author's intentions, and no matter how skillfully written his books, those writings do not work alterations in the civil social order unless their publication coincide with favorable circumstances—that is, readers must find in such books certain ideas and images pertinent to the discontents or the urgent necessities of the age. Locke, Montesquieu, Hume, and Burke moved men's minds because they dealt with questions of the first importance in their own generation.

Locke's *Treatises of Government* served as an apology for the Whig's ascendancy during most of the eighteenth century. Montesquieu's *Spirit of Laws,* published when the future signers of the Declaration of Independence and the future framers of the American Constitution were young men or boys, gave the infant United States a textbook on ordered liberty. Hume's *Political Discourses* and the six volumes of his *History of England* opened many eyes to the empirical understanding of political reality. Burke's *Reflections on the Revolution in France,* and his later writings, upheld "the chartered rights of Englishmen" and the Christian understanding of the human condition, against fanatic utopianism.

Yet these books would not have been widely read and learnedly commented upon down to our own day unless they had been more than tracts for their authors' times. In the pages of Locke, Montesquieu, Hume, and Burke, every generation has found insights of enduring power, applicable to epochs and circumstances very different from those encountered by any of those men of letters. Important writings in the discipline of politics must possess some relevence to the society in which they are written; but also they must possess qualities that confer permanence.

With these considerations in mind, I think it of some interest to examine succinctly the enduring reputations of Locke, Montesquieu, Hume, and Burke as statists—a word that in their times signified political theorists—and to ask how consonant their present "relevance" is with the original aim and repute of each of these writers. A great author's disciples at two or three centuries' remove sometimes venerate an ikon of their long-buried mentor without much regard for what the departed man of genius actually believed and wrote.

*　　*　　*　　*　　*

In politics, it was the object of John Locke, toward the end of the seventeenth century, to prevent any Catholic claimant from ascending the throne of England; to assure the domination of Parliament by the Whig landed magnates; to advance England's commercial interests. Locke was anything but a leveller and a democrat. He did argue that the majority of a people should rule; but to understand that contention, one must remember that a "people", in seventeenth- and eighteenth-century usage, signified the responsible, educated, propertied part of the general population: the word carried then no connotation of universal suffrage. The two *Treatises of Government* constitute an endeavor to justify these ends by rational argument.

But this actual, historical Locke is not the philosopher long described in American textbooks, at both high-school and college levels. There Locke has been sketched piously as the forerunner of twentieth-century liberalism in the United States—or, on the other hand, frowned upon as the intellectual ancestor of laissez-faire capitalism, the selfish defender of private property. Both academic friends and academic adversaries of Locke, in the twentieth century, have instructed the rising generation that Locke has dominated the America mind since the very beginning of the eighteenth century.

Or such was the textbook declaration until very recently. It was an error, this notion, leading historians now pronounce. (Some time will be required for the authors and editors of textbooks to become aware of what genuine historians have concluded, in this instance as in others.) Clinton Rossiter, for example, in his *Seedtime of the Republic* (1953) observes that Locke was little read and less quoted by Americans on the eve of the Revolution. Locke is not mentioned at all in the records of the Constitutional Convention or in the Federalist Papers.

The conventional textbooks have represented Locke as a zealot for absolute liberty and total toleration of all religious or irreligious opinions. But in truth, anyone who has read Locke attentively (which textbook authors clearly have not done, most of them) knows that the Whig philosopher was well aware of the need for restraints upon claims of liberty, lest liberty become license. And as for what Burke later called "a licentious toleration"—why, a principal reason for the overthrow of James II had been the King's Toleration Act, which had relieved Papists as well as Dissenters. Locke makes it exceeding clear that the government of England must not tolerate Roman Catholics.

Locke's concept of the social compact did have some influence upon Thomas Jefferson, John Adams, and others. But today there probably does not exist anywhere in the United States a professor of history or of politics or of anthropology who would try to maintain the truth of Locke's notion that at some time all human beings lived without government, and then made a solemn compact so that property might be secure. This is a thesis patently absurd, if taken literally; and Locke's principal biographer, Maurice Cranston, writes that Locke himself did mean it literally. This social-contract argument was demolished presently by Hume, and then by Burke.

This is not to say that it has become pointless to read Locke's writings. All sorts of ideas circulating in our era were first given clear expression by Locke; his name always will loom large in the history of ideas.

But it is a mistake to regard Locke as a colossus who still, for good or ill, bestrides America. Louis Hartz, of Harvard, in 1955 published a book, *The Liberal Tradition in America,* pleading with Americans to purge themselves of "irrational Lockianism", which Hartz regarded as the source of a multitude of evils, from colonial times to the present. People like Professor Hartz start at shadows, while the clear and present dangers to American society in the closing years of the twentieth century come from a quarter that does not resemble in the least the moderate Anglicanism and Whig complacency that formed Locke's setting.

An "irrational Lockianism", nevertheless, really does exist in certain American circles—curiously enough, among persons who regard themselves as the leading lights of logicalism. Take, for examples, two recent writers on jurisprudence, whose books have received much solemn attention: John Rawls, the author of *A Theory of Justice* (1971), and Robert Nozick, the author of *Anarchy, State, and Utopia* (1974). These writers, though disagreeing in much, both take as the fundamental premise of their whole argument John Locke's hypothesis of a "state of nature" for mankind, out of which arose the social compact. Rawls and Nozick explicitly affirm that their concept of justice rests upon this footing. They do not trouble themselves to explain why, nor do they endeavor to answer the critics who, ever since the middle of the eighteenth century, have reduced Locke's social compact to dust. Rawls and Nozick simply take John Locke as irrefutable Absolute Authority.

Although Locke was not easily moved to mirth, such an irony surely would have made him smile wryly. The great rationalist Locke converted, three centuries later, into an ikon of modern abstract liberalism! The great questioner of accepted authorities converted into an Unquestionable Authority himself! Two abstract philosophical writers on jurisprudence, who brush aside the actual origins of human societies and laws, declaring in substance, "In erring reason's spite, one truth is clear: what John Locke says is right!"

After this fashion, the imperial intellects of yesteryear sometimes suffer caricature at the hands of their latter-day devotees. Poor John Locke!

*   *   *   *   *

Charles Louis de Secondat, Baron de Montesquieu, has stood high in reputation ever since the publication of his *Persian Letters* in 1721. His theory of the influence of geography and climate upon societies has been much debated; but his political doctrine of separation of powers has prevailed, in theory, in the Western world, and has been woven into the formal written constitutions of many countries—although the practice of that concept is another matter.

The Bicentenary of the Constitution of the United States has revived some scholarly interest in Montesquieu. His name, more than any other, emerges from Madison's notes on the Constitutional Convention and the pages of the Federalist Papers: nobody at the Convention disputed Montesquieu's authority. For Montesquieu heartily approved the British Constitution—on which America's constitution was founded, for the most part; and the separation of powers, together with other checks upon governors, had prevailed in the constitutions of most of the thirteen original states. It was not that the delegates to the Constitutional Convention at Philadelphia modelled their document upon Montesquieu's scheme; rather, they cited the authority of Montesquieu as an endorsement of what they had meant to do anyway. Montesquieu seemed to the gentlemen assembled at Philadelphia almost a contemporary authority (which Locke distinctly did not seem); for Montesquieu had died only twenty-two years before Congress adopted the Articles of Confederation. His recognition of the healthy power of custom and habit, and his defense of local liberties, accorded well with the conservative inclinations and necessities of 1787.

As the persuasive advocate of constitutional order, with effective checks upon the executive power especially, and as the defender of what has come to be called federalism (as opposed to centralization), Montesquieu is approved today by both conservatives and liberals. Nevertheless, the great democratic powers of the United States and Britain have been drifting away from Montesquieu's principles for a good long while. As for the French, the nation that Montesquieu tried to dissuade from the politics of centralized power, his *Spirit of Laws* never has borne fruit among them.

The separation of powers that Montesquieu thought he found in Britain was shifting even during the French observer's lifetime. By the end of the eighteenth century, Parliament clearly was supreme; by the end of the nineteenth century, Parliament was chosen by the mass electorate; near the end of the twentieth century, Britain is governed, in effect, by a committee of the House of Commons, with no real checks remaining upon what the House of Commons may do. As for that "depository of laws" so desired by Montesquieu, an independent system of courts of law as a distinct and separate branch of government—why, that never really did exist in Britain, Montesquieu notwithstanding; and the British judiciary never has acquired any sort of power to impede acts of Parliament, constitution or no constitution.

In the United States, the systematic separation of powers conforms faithfully—or perhaps excessively—to Montesquieu's principles of good government. But that separation, joined with constitutionally devised checks and balances, more than once has come near to paralyzing the federal government at an hour of crisis, the executive force and the Congress being at loggerheads. And for a century and a quarter, the system called federalism, dividing sovereignty between the state governments and the general government, has been decaying—during the past half century, crumbling very rapidly.

An independent "depository of laws", so emphasized by Montesquieu as essential to the separation of powers, the United States certainly retains. The Supreme Court, indeed, is vastly more powerful, presumably, than ever

Montesquieu fancied the judicial branch of government might become; it has taken unto itself, over the decades, an authority that even James Madison and Alexander Hamilton never expected or desired the Court to assume. What Montesquieu seems to have had in mind as an independent judicial branch of government was the jury system (unknown in France, then or now), rather than what has been reproached by its American critics as "the reign of Nine Old Men": an oligarchy of justices, arbitrary as the ephors of ancient Sparta.

Montesquieu's search for a political structure that would join sufficient power in the government with security for a reasonable freedom—an argument carried further by Burke, in the latter half of the eighteenth century—remains his principal value for statists at the close of the twentieth century. Were the United States to hold a second constitutional convention, Montesquieu's name might echo again; it would deserve to; but his teachings would be less well understood than they were in 1787.

*　　*　　*　　*　　*

High above Edinburgh, in the Calton Hill Burying Ground, looms massive and ungnawed by time a Roman round tower designed by Robert Adam, the greatest of Scottish architects. This is the monument to David Hume, the greatest of Scots philosophers. Nearby stands the gigantic obelisk commemorating Scots Jacobins hanged for subversion. There could not be sepulchral neighbors more incongruous.

For Hume, though popularly reputed an atheist, was a defender of things long established. His essay on miracles may have worked powerfully to undermine the Christianity of the eighteenth and nineteenth centuries; yet Hume himself, something of a fideist, wanted no revolution in church or state.

In practical politics he was a Scots Tory—which was not the same as being an English Tory. In his *History of England* he wrote that the triumph of the Whig party had "proved destructive to the truth of History, and . . . established many gross falsehoods." In this he has been sustained by a whole school of twentieth-century historians, Sir Herbert Butterfield in particular.

Only Montesquieu was more frequently cited at the Constitutional Convention of 1787 than was Hume, and Hume's actual influence upon leading delegates' minds seems to have been greater than Montesquieu's. Hume had died in 1776, seven weeks after the Declaration of Independence; a revised edition of his *History* had been published in 1778, and most educated Americans had read those six volumes, or some part of them, for that lively work had no scholarly competitors at the time.

It is curious that a good many American historical writers, during the nineteenth and twentieth centuries, said little about Hume's strong influence upon the Americans of the Revolutionary and Constitutional periods. In very recent years, however, Hume has been restored to his dignity by such well-known historians as Forrest McDonald and Irving Brant. A new American edition of his *History* was published in 1982 through 1983 by Liberty Classics.

Hume confirmed the framers of the Constitution in convictions which the French *philosophes*—so far as those writers had been read in America—had not seriously shaken: the beneficent influence of custom and habit, and the power of self-interest among human motives. Custom, he wrote, "is the greatest guide of human life. It is that principle alone which renders our experience useful to us, and makes us expect, for the future, a similar train of events with those which have appeared in the past. Without the influence of custom, we should be entirely ignorant of every matter of fact beyond what is immediately present to the memory and senses." And elsewhere, "Habits, more than reason, we find in everything to be the governing principle of mankind." Self-interest, though necessary to human survival, must be hedged: thus arose the institutions of justice, Hume argues. The Constitution of 1787, drawn up by men well aware of their own self-interest, is full of curbs upon that sort of self-interest which would injure the public interest.

Hume is of the very small number of those formal philosophers who, through lucidity and charm of literary style, attract readers who otherwise would grow impatient at treatises on human nature, ethics, and political theory. Men of affairs of his time read him because he wrote in such lively fashion, and were persuaded by him, Whigs though they were and Tory though he was called.

Hume was buried secretly in 1776, and Burke buried secretly in 1797—though for different reasons. Hume feared that his corpse might be disinterred and violated by rough zealots of the Kirk, given to Edinburgh riots; Burke thought that very possibly triumphant Jacobins might treat his remains as they had dealt with dead adversaries in

France. But neither in Scotland nor in England did the civil social order crumble into what Burke called "the antagonist world of madness, discord, vice, confusion, and unavailing sorrow."

The books of those two masterful men of letters, indeed, had more than a little to do with the preservation of order, justice, and freedom on either side of the Atlantic. Talented writers on politics sometimes do successfully oppose their pens, "more sharp by odds than swords," to revolutionary pikes.

*   *   *   *   *

Edmund Burke's name, like that of Locke, does not appear in Madison's notes on the Constitutional Convention, nor in the Federalist Papers. But it was not that the Framers had failed to read Burke. He had been the most eloquent parliamentary opponent of George III's colonial policies; he had been parliamentary agent for the Province of New York; his great speech on conciliation with the colonies, 1775, was known to every American who took any interest in public affairs; and throughout the Revolution—indeed, throughout 1787 and 1788—Burke edited *The Annual Register,* the most reliable source in the English language for information about public affairs throughout the world, including American affairs.

It was not from ignorance of Burke's speeches and writings, then, that his name was not uttered in the old State House at Philadelphia, in 1787. Rather, the delegates to the Constitutional Convention did not quote any British writer or speaker then living. Burke was a leader of party, very much alive, and able to retort if he should disagree with what might be attributed to him at the Convention.

Edmund Burke's greater achievements, indeed, occurred after the framing and ratification of the Constitution of the United States. As Lord Percy of Newcastle puts it, "His party pamphlets have been taken as sound history, while his anti-revolutionary philosophy has been dismissed as a crochet of old age and declining powers. This is almost the exact reverse of the truth. Burke was a Whig partisan, no more reliable as a witness to contemporary fact than any other party politician. But, as other such politicians have not seldom been shocked into statesmanship by war, he was shocked into philosophy by, first, the American Revolution and, then, the French Revolution."

Beginning in 1790, when Burke's *Reflections on the Revolution in France* appeared, Burke's American reputation and influence were vastly renewed in the United States. "Mr. Burke's book" was discussed by American political leaders, among them Alexander Hamilton, John Adams, John Quincy Adams, and many among the fifty-five men who had framed the Constitution. John Marshall and Joseph Story, among American jurists, were much influenced by Burke's later writings. Presently Southerners, among them John Randolph of Roanoke and John C. Calhoun, were won over by Burke's arguments.

Throughout the nineteenth century, Burke was quoted and cited by American writers and politicians—James Russell Lowell was an especial admirer—and Burke's famous *Speech on Conciliation* was carefully studied in most American high schools as an example of rhetoric, down to the early decades of the twentieth century. Several complete editions of Burke's works were published in the United States. During the first three or four decades of the nineteenth century, Burke was well known in France, the Austrian system, and the German states, also—though after the European revolutions of 1848, attention to Burke's writings diminished.

British interest in Burke's ideas and career continued, little diminished, well into the twentieth century. But in America, during the closing decade of the nineteenth century and the first half of the twentieth century, Burke seemed nearly forgotten. Woodrow Wilson, in 1901, published an essay showing that Burke's opposition to the French Revolution was consistent with Burke's earlier politics; but the politicians of that time, Wilson aside, said little of Burke on either side of the Atlantic. In 1915, the American critic Paul Elmer More devoted the first chapter of his book *Aristocracy and Justice* to a discussion of Burke's significance. He mentioned on his first page that, he having shown a copy of a new book on Burke's thought to a New York clubman, his acquaintance had remarked merely, "Ah, Burke! He's dead, is he not?"

More and his fellow-critic Irving Babbitt endeavored to remind Americans of Burke's importance; they waked no great response at the time. One might have expected the First World War, and particularly the Russian Revolution, to bring about a renewal of Americans' interest in the statesman-philosopher, the founder of conservative politics: parallels between the French and Russian revolutions, and between Europe's situation after the success of the Jacobins and Europe's prospects after the success of the Bolsheviki, were sufficiently obvious. Yet there did not occur, between the two World Wars, any very conspicuous reference to Burke and his thought among either scholars or practical politicians.

After the Second World War, however, this indifference to Burke vanished. The dread power of the Communist, Nazi, and Fascist ideologies—so many examples of what Burke had called "armed doctrine"—induced historical and political scholars, serious publicists, some political leaders, and a good many "common readers" to look about for some body of ideas or some form of political imagination that might defend the permanent things (in T. S. Eliot's phrase) of the human condition. This renewal of close attention to Burke's thought was far stronger in America than in Britain. One British scholar who had published a book on Burke, Alfred Cobban, seemed positively annoyed at the Americans' enthusiasm for Burke; he complained to an acquaintance that "In America Burke is being used for political purposes." Edmund Burke, a professional politician, naturally would have been gratified to find his principles put to some political use nearly two centuries later—rather than carved up as material for doctoral dissertations merely.

In the United States, during the 1950s and 1960s, more than a score of serious books on Burke and his ideas and his times were published. Marxist attacks on Burke, by way of reply, began to appear in the 1970s, although more in Britain than in America.

*   *   *   *   *

Were they able to behold our civilization, presumably Locke, Montesquieu, Hume, or Burke would be dismayed. Beginning about 1750, the first Industrial Revolution smashed the cake of custom in Britain, and presently in western Europe and North America. The Britain of 1790, when *Reflections on the Revolution in France* was published, differed little from the Britain of 1689, when Locke brought out his *Two Treatises of Government*. The world of 1989 is a far cry from the world of 1689, however—and more's the pity, in a good many ways.

The gigantic changes in social patterns, technology, and the outward appearance of things have been paralleled by radical intellectual alterations. The climate of opinion that prevailed in Britain and America about 1787 to 1790—a temperate climate much influenced by the ideas of Locke, Montesquieu, Hume, and Burke—was broken in upon by the hurricane of the French Revolution. Ever since, political philosophy has yielded ground to fanatic ideology, and religion has been assailed by scientism. After two centuries during which the doctrines of Rousseau, Bentham, Darwin, Marx, and Freud have been everywhere disseminated, how much significance remains to the writings of Locke, Montesquieu, Hume, and Burke? Are their books so much cultural debris, soon to be swept into the dust-bin of antiquarianism?

No: not if human nature is a constant. The powerful minds of those four famous men of letters still can teach us much. They did not play the comic role in politics, even though this or that notion of theirs may seem absurd by hindsight. They are the giants on whose shoulders we moderns stand. Or, as my old friend T. S. Eliot put it in his first great essay—"Some one said: 'The dead writers are remote from us because we *know* so much more than they did.' Precisely, and they are that which we know."

We discard Locke's theory of a primitive state of nature; but we still can profit from his arguments for reason in politics and religion.

We discern difficulties in the application of Montesquieu's doctrine of separation of powers; but we are the beneficiaries of his endeavor to reconcile the claims of authority and the claims of freedom.

We may be vexed by Hume's complacency, thinking him Mr. Know-All; but we would be intellectually poorer, were we deprived of his realistic analysis of human motives and his understanding of the foundations of the civil social order.

We may reproach Bruke for intemperate partisanship, much of his career; but we know that, as even Harold Laski put it, Burke's writings form "the permanent manual of political wisdom without which statesmen are as sailors on an uncharted sea."

Whatever their foibles and flaws, Locke, Montesquieu, Hume, and Burke were true *statists,* joining to a philosophical habit of mind a good apprehension of the social circumstances into which they were born. All possessed in high degree that rather mysterious power of insight which we call political imagination. All four were centric, rather than eccentric, men of genius. All have been misrepresented somewhat, from time to time, by their latter-day panegyrists or detractors; but the remedy for that is to read or re-read attentively, with one's own critical eye, the basic writings of these writers on order, justice, and freedom. Anyone who has studied sympathetically these four great men of letters, differing though they do one with another in much, will be armored against the assaults of totalist ideologues.

Russell (Amos) Kirk is an American man of letters who is best known as one of the major rejuvenators of twentieth-century conservative thought in the United States. This position was established primarily on the strength of his seminal study *The Conservative Mind: From Burke to Santayana* (1953)—subtitled in later editions "From Burke to Eliot"—which is one of the most widely discussed works of political theory written in the twentieth century. *The Conservative Mind* traces and explains the rise and flow of Anglo-American conservatism from its wellspring in Edmund Burke through such political and literary notables as John Adams, Sir Walter Scott, Orestes Brownson, George Santayana, and T. S. Eliot. In addition, Kirk has published biographies of John Randolph of Roanoke, Robert Taft, and Burke; four volumes of literary and social essays (the best-known being *Enemies of the Permanent Things: Observations of Abnormality in Literature and Politics,* 1969); five volumes of supernatural fiction (of which the novel *Old House of Fear,* 1961, is said to have revitalized the genre of Gothic fiction); and a colorful historical survey of ideas and institutions, *The Roots of American Order* (1974); among several other books. He edited *The Portable Conservative Reader* (1982) and was the founding editor of the quarterlies *Modern Age* and the *University Bookman.* From 1955 to 1980 he contributed a regular column on the state of American education, "From the Academy," to William F. Buckley, Jr.'s magazine *National Review.* A former professor or distinguished visiting professor at numerous colleges and universities throughout the United States, Kirk, along with his wife, Annette, has written extensively on education, and both have long championed the need for academic excellence—notably in his book *Decadence and Renewal in the Higher Learning: An Episodic History of American Universities and Colleges since 1953* (1978) and in her contribution to the 1983 study *A Nation at Risk* as a member of the National Commission on Excellence in Education. Historian Forrest McDonald has called Russell Kirk "the American Cicero," and of his primary contribution to American social and political thought one anonymous reviewer has spoken for many other critics from a wide variety of belief systems in acknowledging that Kirk convincingly demonstrates "that conservatives are not old fogies or Colonel Blimps, but men who wrestle with eternal problems of life, morals and politics and possess as much intellectual depth and integrity as their radical opponents." Kirk resides in Mecosta, Michigan.

(For further reference, please see: Louis Filler, "The Wizard of Mecosta: Russell Kirk of Michigan," in *Michigan History,* vol. 63, September-October 1979; Don Herron, "The Crepuscular Romantic: An Appreciation of the Fiction of Russell Kirk," in *The Romantist,* no. 3, 1979; John East, "Russell Kirk," in *The American Conservative Movement,* 1986; and Henry Regnery, "Russell Kirk: Conservatism Becomes a Movement," in *Memoirs of a Dissident Publisher,* (1979.)

Edmund Burke

1729-1797

Irish-born English essayist, political writer, and philosopher.

Widely recognized as the founder of modern Anglo-American conservatism, Burke is considered by many the most important and influential English statesman and political writer of the eighteenth century. In his speeches and essays he addressed all the major issues of his time, including the precepts of the American and French revolutions, the two-party political system, principles of economic reform, and the rights of government versus the rights of the individual. To each issue Burke brought the dramatic eloquence of a professional orator, the cool rationalism of a classical logician, the confident prescience of a social prophet, and the moral fervor of a Christian polemicist. Despite his lack—indeed, rejection—of any systematized theory to answer the political problems he faced, his writings continue to shape and illumine both conservative and liberal responses to major contemporary dilemmas. Such works as *Speech on Moving His Resolutions for Conciliation with the Colonies, Reflections on the Revolution in France,* and *A Letter from the Right Honourable Edmund Burke to a Noble Lord* stand as testaments to one of the most remarkably original and powerful voices in the history of political thought.

Born in Dublin to middle-class parents of different faiths—his father an Anglican attorney and his mother a staunch Roman Catholic—Burke was a sickly child who spent much of his boyhood reading and studying, to the near-exclusion of any outside pursuits. Although raised in his father's faith, he developed an early appreciation for the plight of oppressed Irish Catholics. In his teens he attended a Quaker boarding school in County Kildare before entering Trinity College in Dublin in 1744. During his years at Trinity, Burke demonstrated a proclivity for poetry, history, mathematics, and logic. He vigorously participated in literary coffeehouse gatherings and eventually formed a debating society, in which he honed his rhetorical skills. He also launched and edited a literary review/social issues weekly titled the *Reformer,* which went through thirteen numbers before folding. After receiving his bachelor of arts degree in 1748, Burke remained at Trinity for some time to continue work on an independent study of human responses to aesthetics, a field which had interested him since his first reading of the anonymous first-century Greek treatise *On the Sublime.* Revised and expanded several years later and published as *A Philosophical Enquiry into the Origin of Our Ideas of the Sublime and Beautiful,* Burke's study anticipates the nineteenth-century Romantic interest in the Gothic. Burke's first publication of consequence was political in scope, however, foreshadowing his eventual resolve to make politics his career. Published in 1748 and entitled *A Free Briton's Advice to the Free Citizens of Dublin,* this four-pamphlet series displays Burke's command of Roman history while counseling Irish citizens on the electoral process.

Satisfying both his own inclination to move to London and his father's desire that he become a barrister, Burke began law studies at the Middle Temple in 1750. To augment his study there, he attended meetings of various debating clubs as well as a school of elocution. However, Burke gradually began neglecting his studies, to his father's bitter disappointment, and entered a six-year period of relative withdrawal from so-

ciety. During this time, biographers believe, he was frequently ill, directionless, and intensely self-searching. He arose from this inertia in 1756 and anonymously published *A Vindication of Natural Society.* Labeled by Carl B. Cone "the opening blast in his long campaign against the enemies of the traditional order of things in western Europe," this work cleverly imitates the style of recently deceased Tory leader Henry St. John Bolingbroke, attacks Jean-Jacques Rousseau's *Discours sur l'origine et les fondements de l'inégalité parmi les hommes* (1755) and satirizes Bolingbroke's promotion of a natural society ruled by instinct and individual judgment rather than tradition, religious institutions, and ingrained cultural mores. Among conservative intellectual circles the work was much admired, but several reviewers and the public at large failed to recognize Burke's satiric intent, and some even mistook the work for another of Bolingbroke's posthumous writings. Therefore, Burke added an explanatory preface to his *Vindication* the following year.

With the publication of his aesthetic treatise in 1757, Burke's intellectual and literary abilities were quickly made apparent to London literary circles. By the end of the decade he was closely acquainted with several of the leading figures of the time, including David Garrick, Oliver Goldsmith, Elizabeth Montagu, Samuel Johnson, and David Hume. By the time he launched the weekly conversational society The Club in 1764 with Johnson and Joshua Reynolds, Burke was being commended by Johnson as "the first man everywhere," and his intimates believed him capable of succeeding brilliantly at anything he chose to do. Having no intention of resuming his legal training, Burke sought to support himself and his wife, whom he married in 1757, by applying his literary and scholarly talents. Contracting with publisher Robert Dodsley in 1758, he agreed to compile a yearly review of world affairs and noteworthy publications entitled the *Annual Register,* which he edited for 31 years. It is very probable that Burke wrote the entire journal through the year 1765, though this has not been proven conclusively. But the historical articles he indeed contributed remain primary sources for the study of mid- to late-eighteenth-century English life. Burke also contracted with Dodsley to write a survey of English history, but he abandoned this project by 1760 after having written some 90,000 words.

By this time, though still desirous of a literary career, Burke had turned to politics as a means of insuring financial security and public advancement. Following a failed attempt to obtain a foreign consulship, he secured employment with William Hamilton, serving as his private secretary and adviser from 1759 to 1764. In 1761 Burke accompanied Hamilton, then named Chief Secretary of Ireland, to Dublin, where Burke's indignation over the oppression of Irish Catholics peaked. The difficulty of effecting reform in Ireland, and the machinations of legislators in general, disgusted Burke and led him to confide in a friend that he hoped to remain aloof from "crooked politicks." No longer in Hamilton's service and having twice failed to obtain official agentries, Burke aligned with the second Marquis of Rockingham, who had marshaled the largest and most powerful Whig faction in England—the faction which was, at the time, the least threatening in its conservative ideology and practices to the viability of the Crown. (Although the English Tory party is commonly understood as emblematically conservative, the Whig establishment of Burke's time more closely embodied the principles of modern-day conservatism than did the authoritarian opposition. It was not until the early nineteenth century that the Tory party began evolving, through considerable absorption of "New" Whig principles, into its present form.) In 1765, Rockingham and his supporters received cautious royal favor and established a new government; as Rockingham's private secretary, Burke had at last attained a position of power. Although Rockingham's administration was short-lived, Burke remained among the most prominent framers of Whig theory and legislation throughout the rest of his career. Shortly after his secretarial appointment, Burke was elected to the House of Commons by the voters of Wendover. (In later elections, he assumed the seats of Bristol and Malton). He immediately made a mark as a forcible, accomplished speaker. Yet, for his loyalty to Rockingham (whose political career remained stormy until his death in 1782), Catholic leanings, and common, Irish heritage, Burke was forced to battle almost continual opposition. He therefore accumulated comparatively little power, no wealth, only minor offices, and few political victories. Although he desperately yearned to devote himself fully to literary endeavors, he never achieved this goal; as Russell Kirk has written, it was "not until he had become hotly entangled in the struggles over American and Indian affairs, and in domestic reform" that he found, "with Cicero, that the career of the statesman may provide occasions and themes for the moral imagination and the literary genius."

Burke's first major political work, the 1770 essay *Thoughts on the Cause of the Present Discontents,* was inspired by mounting tension between the Whigs and George III, who sought to restore a measure of autonomy to the Crown and to fortify his own Tory party, both of which had been checked severely since the Glorious Revolution of 1688 and the passage of the Bill of Rights the following year. During the mid-1770s Burke turned his attention to another issue: growing tensions in colonial America regarding the issue of taxation without representation. Burke set out to alleviate the conflict while protecting both the rights of Americans and the interests and integrity of the British Empire. In *Speech on American Taxation, Speech on Moving His Resolutions for Conciliation with the Colonies,* and *Letter . . . to the Sheriffs of Bristol,* Burke displayed what scholars deem an enviable command of colonial history and a prudent sympathy for American grievances, as well as a willingness to undertake appropriate governmental reform to heal the British-American rift. Although his speeches and writings directly stimulated American revolutionary leaders to urge a public call to arms (and, in addition, his political principles significantly shaped the constitutional theories espoused by James Madison, John Jay, and Alexander Hamilton in *The Federalist* (1787-88) a decade later), Burke abhorred violent, radical change and was seriously disillusioned by the onset of the American Revolution.

Burke's most significant appointment to office came with Rockingham's being made paymaster general in the year of his death, 1782. Burke urged serious economic reform within the English government to quell abuses of the system as well as to control a mounting national deficit. A version of Burke's economic bill passed into law the same year and became, according to many, his chief legislative success. As member of a committee appointed to investigate imperial impropriety in India, Burke entered into perhaps his most ardent and sustained battle for the rights of British subjects. In 1787, he served as the principal force behind the impeachment of Warren Hastings, India's governor general, which led to a highly publicized, eight-year trial ending in Hastings's acquittal. Although his failure to implicate Hastings in administrative abuses devastated Burke, his efforts have been recognized as some of the most imaginative, powerful, and self-revelatory—if highly emotional—oratory of his career. Following the outbreak of the French Revolution in 1789, Burke took upon himself the security and defense of the tradition, government, and constitution of Britain in his most praised and enduring work, *Reflections on the Revolution in France.* This work, like later ones on the same subject, produced an irreparable division between Burke and several of his Whig colleagues, especially his longtime friend and then-Whig leader, Charles James Fox. *Reflections,* which eventually proved a prophetic vision of France's future, won wide European support but also engendered serious counterattacks, in particular, Mary Wollstonecraft's *A Vindication of the Rights of Men in a Letter to the Right Honourable Edmund Burke; Occasioned by His "Reflections on the Revolution in France"* (1790) and Thomas Paine's *The Rights of Man: Being an Answer to Mr. Burke's Attack on the French Revolution* (1791-92). Burke retired from Parliament in 1794, after having labored intensely for a variety of unpopular, unsuccessful causes; perhaps his greatest disappointment was his largely ineffectual, though long-standing, attempt to promote greater toleration of Catholics throughout Great Britain. He continued to write on such topics as Irish rights, economic reform, and the disintegration of French society for the rest of his life. In 1797 he died at Beaconsfield, Buckinghamshire, and is buried there in an unknown, unmarked grave.

"If there is one recurrent theme in Burke's letters, speeches, and writings," claims Harvey C. Mansfield, Jr., "it is his emphasis on the moral and political evils that follow upon the intrusion of theory into political practice.'' Burke, indeed, despised all abstract thought when applied to political situations. He believed that to solve specific problems, well-reasoned, historically founded solutions, applied with prudence, were required. Thus Burke considered Rousseau, for his love of abstraction and reverence for theoretical human rights, an ''insane Socrates''; likewise, he esteemed Charles-Louis de Secondat, Baron de La Brède et de Montesquieu for his conservative view of tradition and deep respect for the British Constitution, calling him "the greatest genius, which has enlightened this age.'' Burke has been credited with two major contributions to politics: his exposition, in *Thoughts on the Cause of the Present Discontents,* of the structure and function of political parties; and his well-defined blueprint—apparent throughout his works, but found particularly in his *Reflections*—of the fundamental principles of political conservatism. Burke conceived of party as a vehicle by which, above all, constitutional integrity could be maintained in the legislative process; parties represented the necessary link between king and Parliament, serving as a check to misguided power and as a means toward sound governing. Regarding his conservative principles: custom, convention, continuity, presumptive virtue (a trust in the capability of the aristocracy to rule, albeit policed by the good judgment of the common classes), and the tenets of the British Constitution, dominated and directed all his thought. Still, Burke remained amenable to gradual change and always sympathetic to the rights and needs of the people. His system succeeds, according to Woodrow Wilson, because: "There is no element of speculation in it. It keeps always to the slow pace of inevitable change, and invents nothing, content to point out the accepted ways and to use the old light of day to walk by."

A major charge levied against Burke since the publication of his writings on France is that he was inconsistent in the moral and political values he espoused. Several commentators have claimed that Burke, while once an ardent defender of the individual rights of the Irish, Americans, and Indians, abandoned his praiseworthy efforts during the French Revolution to defend the royalty, the aristocracy, and the grand French tradition instead. Henry Thomas Buckle, for example, asserted that with the furor of the time, Burke's emotional nature overstepped the bounds of reason, the harsh inveighing of the *Reflections* proving that Burke had suffered a profound deterioration of mind and worldview. Other critics, however, have objected to this view of Burke's career, vindicating Burke for his consistent approach toward governmental reform. According to these writers, Burke believed that what occurred in America, Ireland, and India was simply the assertion of the legitimate rights held by British subjects against the depredations of a burgeoning, increasingly repressive government which sought to deny those rights it was bound to defend. The American War for Independence, he wrote, was ''a revolution not made, but prevented.'' On the other hand, Burke held that the French Revolution saw the accession of rootless and ruthless ideology, and that custom, convention, and continuity, along with their religious underpinnings, were eradicated so that the mob, guided only by speculation and abstract reason, might rule. The tenets of the French National Assembly to which Burke reacted so vehemently were those that unequivocally renounced all the institutions and customs upon which ordered European society had relied for centuries. For Burke, as for his mentor Cicero, reform was advisable only when favored by the majority, and then only provided such reform could be executed through careful refinement, not endangerment, of existing social struc-

tures. Perhaps the most telling indictment of this philosophic position was written by John MacCunn: ''As a gospel for his age, or for any age, it has the fatal defect that, in its rooted distrust of theories and theorists, it finds hardly any place for political ideals as serious attempts to forefigure the destinies of a people as not less Divinely willed than its eventful past history or present achievement. And, by consequence, it fails to touch the future with the reformer's hope and conviction of better days to come.'' Despite this charge, Burke's theories are among the most prevalent that modern-day politicians, conservative and liberal, have used to guide their legislative decisions.

Apart from political and philosophical evaluations of his work, Burke has received encomiums for the sheer ascendancy of his oratory and the inimitable style of his prose. His writings on America have been considered models of rhetorical eloquence: his *A Letter from the Right Honourable Edmund Burke to a Noble Lord,* according to W. Somerset Maugham, "the finest piece of invective in the English language,'' and his *Reflections,* one of the most impassioned and inspired documents in the history of the English essay. Although Burke has been faulted for an excessive emotionalism that hindered his philosophic purposes, his supporters suggest that he habitually combined beautifully metaphorical language with resounding moral statement to express his inmost philosophic convictions. Consequently, he is regarded not only as a vastly influential political philosopher but as an equally influential orator and prose writer.

What, finally, was Burke's contribution to English letters? Many critics see it as an astonishingly broad and enduring one, affirming that he addressed all the major issues of his day not only in a lofty, imaginative prose unparalleled in the latter eighteenth century, but by means of explicitly stated concepts which have remained valid to a host of succeeding writers and politicians. Among these figures may be counted Sir Walter Scott, Alexis de Tocqueville, and T. S. Eliot. Given his philosophic training, political vocation, oratorical powers, and literary talents, Burke's achievements have necessarily spanned several fields. As Kirk has written, ''He enlivened political philosophy by the moral imagination; he shored up Christian doctrine; he stimulated the higher understanding of history; he enriched English literature by a mastery of prose that makes him the Cicero of his language and nation. And to the modern civil social order, he contributed those principles of ordered freedom, preservation through reform, and justice restraining arbitrary power, which transcend the particular political struggles of his age.''

PRINCIPAL WORKS

A Free Briton's Advice to the Free Citizens of Dublin (essay) 1748

A Vindication of Natural Society; or, A View of the Miseries and Evils Arising to Mankind from Every Species of Artificial Society (essay) 1756

A Philosophical Enquiry into the Origin of Our Ideas of the Sublime and Beautiful (essay) 1757

*The Annual Register (journal) 1759-65

An Essay towards an Abridgement of the English History (unfinished history) 1760

Thoughts on the Cause of the Present Discontents (essay) 1770

Speech on American Taxation, April 19, 1774 (essay) 1775

*This journal was edited by Burke through 1789, and may have been written entirely by him through 1765.

†This work was written in 1795.

‡This is an ongoing, multi-volume series published by Oxford University Press.

OLIVER GOLDSMITH   (essay date 1757)

[*Goldsmith is considered one of the most important writers of the Augustan age. He distinguished himself during his lifetime as an expressive narrative poet, but has since been acclaimed for two major literary works:* The Vicar of Wakefield (1766), *a novel which pioneered the use of the protagonist as narrator, and* She Stoops to Conquer (1733), *a drama written in reaction to the sentimental and moralistic comedic tradition, and one which greatly influenced later works written for the English stage. As original members of one of the earliest and most prestigious London literary societies, The Club, Goldsmith and Burke shared a professional admiration for one another's accomplishments. In the following excerpt from a review originally published in 1757 in the* Monthly Review, *Goldsmith offers an exacting, yet largely favorable reading and appraisal of* Philosophical Enquiry into the Origin of Our Ideas of the Sublime and Beautiful. *Goldsmith also wrote a well-known, lightly satirical poetic portrait of Burke, which is reprinted in the excerpt by Ralph Waldo Emerson (1835).*]

There are limits prescribed to all human researches, beyond which if we attempt to explore, nothing but obscurity and conjecture lie before us, and doubts instead of knowledge must terminate the enquiry. The genius, not the judgment, of an Author may appear in the too abstracted speculation; he may contribute to the amusement, but seldom to the instruction of the Reader. His illustrations may perplex, but not enlighten the mind; and, like a microscope, the more he magnifies the object, he will represent it the more obscurely.

There is, perhaps, no investigation more difficult than that of the passions, and other affections resulting from them. The difference of opinion among all who have treated on this subject, serves to convince us of its uncertainty. Even the most eminent Philosophers have sometimes taken novelty, not truth, for their conductor; and have destroyed the hypothesis of their predecessors without being able to establish their own. It often happens, indeed, that while we read the productions of such a philosopher, tho' we condemn the Reasoner, we admire the Writer. Yet still learning, taste, and perspicuity, can lay claim but to a subordinate degree of esteem, when they are employed in contradicting truth, or in the investigation of inextricable difficulties.

Our Author [Edmund Burke] thus, with all the sagacity so abstruse a subject requires; with all the learning necessary to the illustration of his system; and with all the genius that can render disquisition pleasing; by proceeding on principles not sufficiently established, has been only agreeable when he might have been instructive. He rejects all former systems, and founds his philosophy [in *A Philosophical Enquiry into the Origin of Our Ideas of the Sublime and Beautiful*] on his own particular feelings. (pp. 27-8)

The Author first enquires into the affections of the sublime and beautiful, in their own nature; he then proceeds to investigate the properties of such things in nature as give rise to these affections: and lastly, he considers in what manner these properties act to produce those affections, and each correspondent emotion.

All our passions have their origin in *self-preservation,* and in *society;* and the ends of one or the other of these, they are all calculated to answer. The passions which concern Self-preservation, and which are the most powerful of all the passions, turn mostly on pain, or danger. For instance, the ideas of pain, sickness, and death, fill the mind with strong emotions of horror; but life, and health, tho' they put us in a capacity of being affected with pleasure, make no such impression by the simple enjoyment.

When danger or pain immediately affect us, they are simply terrible, and incapable of giving any delight; but when the idea of pain or danger is excited, without our being actually in such circumstances as to be injured by it, it may be delightful, as every one's experience demonstrates. This pleasing sensation arising from the diminution of pain, and which may be called hereafter *delight,* is very different from that satisfaction which we feel without any pain preceding it, which may be, in the sequel, termed *positive pleasure,* or simply, pleasure. *Delight* acts by no means so strongly as *positive pleasure;* since no lessening, even of the severest pain, can rise to pleasure, but the mind still continues impressed with awe; a sort of tranquility shadowed with horror. When we have suffered from any violent emotion, the mind naturally continues in something like the same condition, even after the cause which first produced it has ceased to operate; as the fashion of the countenance, and the gesture of the body, in those who have just escaped some imminent danger, sufficiently indicate.

Whatever excites this delight, whatever is fitted in any sort to excite the ideas of pain and danger, without their actual existence, whatever is in any sort terrible, or is conversant about terrible objects, or operates in a manner analogous to terror, is the source of the sublime; (i.e.) it is productive of the strongest emotion the mind is capable of feeling. [Goldsmith adds in a footnote: "Our Author by assigning terror for the only source of the sublime, excludes love, admiration, &c. But to make the sublime an idea incompatible with those affections, is what the general sense of mankind will be apt to contradict. It is certain, we can have the most sublime ideas of the Deity, without imagining him a God of terror. Whatever raises our esteem of an object described, must be a powerful source of sublimity; and esteem is a passion nearly allied to love: Our astonishment at the sublime as often proceeds from an increased love, as from an increased fear. When after the horrors of a tempestuous night, the Poet hails us with a description of the beauties of the morning, we feel double enjoyment from the contrast. Our pleasure here must arise from the beautiful or the sublime. If from the beautiful, then we have a positive pleasure, which has had its origin, contrary to what the Author advances, in a diminution of pain. If from the sublime, it is all we contend for, since here is a description which, though destitute of terror, has the same effect that any increase of terror could have produced."]

The second head to which the passions are referred, in relation to their final cause, is society. There are two kinds of society; the first is the society of the sex; the passion belonging to which is called love: it contains a mixture of lust, and its object is the beauty of women. The other is the great society with man, and all other animals; the passion subservient to which is likewise called love; but this has no mixture of lust, tho' its object be beauty. The passions belonging to the preservation of the individual, which are capable of affecting us with the strong emotions of the sublime, turn wholly on pain and danger, but those of society, on our desire of enjoyment; hence, as the sublime had its rise in pain, so beauty has its source in positive pleasure.

The passion caused by the great and sublime in *nature,* when these causes operate most powerfully, is astonishment: by which all the motions of the soul are suspended, with some degree of horror. Whatever also is terrible with regard to sight, is sublime, whether this cause of terror be endued with greatness of dimensions or not: for it is impossible to look on any thing as trifling, or contemptible, that may be dangerous. To heighten this terror, obscurity, in general, seems necessary. When we know the full extent of any danger, when we accustom our eyes to it, a great deal of the apprehension vanishes. Thus in Pagan worship, the idol is generally placed in the most obscure part of the temple; which is done with a view of heightening the awe of its adorers. Wherefore it is one thing to make an

idea clear, and another to make it affecting to the imagination. Nay, so far is clearness of imagery from being absolutely necessary to influence the passions, that they may be considerably operated upon, as in music, without presenting any image at all. Painting never makes such strong impressions on the mind as description, yet painting must be allowed to represent objects more distinctly than any description can do; and even in painting, a judicious obscurity, in some things, contributes to the proper effect of the picture. Thus in reality, clearness helps but little towards affecting the passions; as it is, in some measure, an enemy to all enthusiasm whatsoever.

All general privations are great, because they are terrible; as vacuity, darkness, solitude, silence. Greatness of dimension is a powerful cause of the sublime. Infinity is another source; though, perhaps, it may be resolved into magnitude. In all objects where no boundary can be fixed to the eye, as in the inside of a rotund, there must necessarily arise the idea of greatness. Another source of greatness is difficulty. When any work seems to have required immense force and labour to effect it, as in Stonehenge, the idea is grand. Magnificence, too, or a great profusion of any things which are splendid or valuable in themselves, is sublime. (pp. 28-32)

With respect to feeling, the idea of bodily pain in all the modes and degrees of labour, anguish, torment, is productive of the sublime; and nothing else in this sense can produce it. Hence every cause of the sublime, with reference to the senses, evinces that the sublime is an idea belonging to self-preservation: that it is therefore one of the most affecting we have: that its strongest emotion is an emotion of distress, and that no positive or absolute pleasure belongs to it.

Beauty is that quality, or those qualities, of bodies by which they cause love, or some passion similar to it. This idea cannot arise from proportion, since in vegetables and animals there is no standard by which we can measure our ideas of proportion; and in man, exact proportion is not always the criterion of beauty; neither can it arise from fitness, since, then, all animals would have beauty; for every one seems best adapted to its own way of living; and in man, strength would have the name of beauty, which, however, presents a very different idea. Nor is it the result of perfection, for we are often charmed with the imperfections of an agreeable object. Nor, lastly, of the qualities and virtues of the mind; since such rather conciliate our esteem than our love. Beauty, therefore, is no creature of reason, but some merely sensible quality acting mechanically upon the human mind, by the intervention of the senses. . . . In sounds, the most beautiful are the soft and delicate; not that strength of note required to raise other passions, nor notes which are shrill, or harsh, or deep. It agrees best with such as are clear, even, smooth, and weak. Thus there is a remarkable contrast between the beautiful and the sublime: sublime objects are vast in their dimensions; beautiful ones comparatively small. Beauty should be smooth and polished; the Great rugged and negligent. Beauty should not be obscure; the Great ought to be dark and gloomy. Beauty should be light and delicate; the Great ought to be solid, and even massive.

The Author comes next to consider, in what manner the sublime and beautiful are produced. As the sublime is founded on pain and terror, which are but different degrees of an unnatural tension of the nerves; whatever produces this tension must be productive also of the sublime; but how any species of delight can be derived from a cause so apparently contrary to it, deserves to be considered.

As the body by inactivity contracts disorders, so labour is necessary to prevent those evils. Labour is an exertion of the contracting power of the muscles, and as such resembles pain, (which consists in tension or contraction) in every thing but degree. Thus, as common labour, which is a mode of pain, is the exercise of the grosser; a mode of terror is the exercise of the finer parts of the system. In this case, if the pain or terror be so modified as not to be actually noxious, they are capable of producing delight, since they serve to put the machine into motion. In visual objects, the eye labours to take in their great dimensions; and by a parity of reasoning, we may extend this to every sense in its reception of sublimity. Darkness has, by general consent of mankind, and perhaps by its own painful operation on the sensory, been accounted terrible; too great a dilatation of the pupil of the eye, caused by darkness, may be offensive to the mind, as being primarily so to the organs of the body; and hence this sensation is so well fitted to produce sublimity. [In a footnote Goldsmith adds: "The muscles of the uvea act in the contraction, but are relaxed in the dilatation of the ciliary circle. Therefore, when the pupil dilates, they are in a state of relaxation, and the relaxed state of a muscle, is its state of rest. In an amaurosis, where these muscles are never employed, the pupil is always dilated. Hence darkness is a state of rest to the visual organ, and consequently the obscurity which he justly remarks to be often a cause of the sublime, can affect the sensory by no painful impression; so that the sublime is often caused by a relaxation of the muscles, as well as by a tension."]

Beauty, as we may gather from the attitude of any person beholding a beautiful object, arises from a quite contrary cause to the sublime, viz. from an universal relaxation of the nervous system. Hence smoothness, which has no asperities to vellicate the parts, nor cause a sensation of pain, is beautiful. Sweets also, which, when reduced to their proper salts, assume a globular figure, and may be called the smooth in taste, must consequently relax, that is, be beautiful to the sense which they respectively affect. Smallness and colour may be accounted for on the same principles.

Thus have we given an abstract of the more material parts of a performance, which seems to have cost the Author much study and attention; and which, with all the charms of stile, is branched out more extensively on the subject than any modern work of this kind, within our recollection. A Writer who endeavours to penetrate beyond the surface of things, though he may be sometimes too minute, and at others even erroneous, will, however, clear the way for succeeding Adventurers; and perhaps make even his errors subservient to the investigation of truth. If we have, in a very few instances, attempted to point out any mistake or oversight in this very agreeable Author's principles; not a captious spirit of controversy, but a concern for truth, was the motive: and the ingenious Enquirer, we are persuaded, is too much a philosopher to resent our sometimes taking a different course in pursuit of the game he has started. (pp. 32-5)

Oliver Goldsmith, "'A Philosophical Enquiry into the Origin of Our Ideas of the Sublime and Beautiful','' in his Collected Works of Oliver Goldsmith, *Vol. I, edited by Arthur Friedman, Oxford At the Clarendon Press, Oxford, 1966, pp. 27-35.*

SAMUEL JOHNSON (conversation date 1769)

[*Critic, essayist, poet, and lexicographer, Johnson was one of the principal English literary figures of the eighteenth century.*

His Dictionary of the English Language *(1755) helped standardize English spelling, while his moralistic criticism strongly influenced the literary taste of the time. His analytical writings, which are characterized by sound judgment, generally promote the theory that a work of literature should be evaluated chiefly on its ability to please and instruct the reader. This theory is also reflected in a number of Johnson's more casual remarks, many of which were recorded by the Scottish man of letters James Boswell in* The Life of Samuel Johnson, LL.D. *(1791). In the following excerpt from this work, Boswell relates Johnson's favorable opinion—originally offered in the presence of Boswell, Oliver Goldsmith, and Arthur Murphy at a dinner party in 1769—of* A Philosophical Enquiry into the Origin of Our Ideas of the Sublime and Beautiful.]

Johnson proceeded: "The Scotchman [Henry Home, Lord Kames] has taken the right method in his *Elements of Criticism.* I do not mean that he has taught us any thing; but he has told us old things in a new way." MURPHY. "He seems to have read a great deal of French criticism, and wants to make it his own; as if he had been for years anatomising the heart of man, and peeping into every cranny of it." GOLDSMITH. "It is easier to write that book, than to read it." JOHNSON. "We have an example of true criticism in Burke's *Essay on the Sublime and Beautiful;* and, if I recollect, there is also Du Bos; and Bouhours, who shews all beauty to depend on truth. There is no great merit in telling how many plays have ghosts in them, and how this Ghost is better than that. You must shew how terrour is impressed on the human heart.—In the description of night in Macbeth, the beetle and the bat detract from the general idea of darkness,—inspissated gloom."

Samuel Johnson, in an excerpt from The Life of Samuel Johnson *by James Boswell, 1791. Reprint by E. P. Dutton & Co., 1976, p. 367.*

MARY WOLLSTONECRAFT   (essay date 1790)

[*Wollstonecraft, an eighteenth-century English author, is best known for her* A Vindication of the Rights of Woman *(1792), now considered the first great feminist manifesto. In the following excerpt from one of the most vehement contemporary refutations of* Reflections on the Revolution in France, *Wollstonecraft castigates Burke for exalting the propertied classes and distorting natural human rights.*]

SIR,

It is not necessary with courtly insincerity, to apologise to you for thus intruding on your precious time, not to profess that I think it an honour to discuss an important subject with a man whose literary abilities have raised him to notice in the state. I have not yet learned to twist my periods, nor, in the equivocal idiom of politeness, to disguise my sentiments, and imply what I should be afraid to utter: if, therefore, in the course of this epistle, I chance to express contempt, and even indignation, with some emphasis, I beseech you to believe that it is not a flight of fancy; for truth, in morals, has ever appeared to me the essence of the sublime; and, in taste, simplicity the only criterion of the beautiful. But I war not with an individual when I contend for the *rights of men* and the liberty of reason. You see I do not condescend to cull my words to avoid the invidious phrase, nor shall I be prevented from giving a manly definition of it, by the flimsy ridicule which a lively fancy has interwoven with the present acceptation of the term. Reverencing the rights of humanity, I shall dare to assert them; not intimidated by the horse laugh that you have raised, or waiting till time has wiped away the compassionate tears which you have elaborately laboured to excite. (pp. 1-2)

The birthright of man, to give you, Sir, a short definition of this disputed right, is such a degree of liberty, civil and religious, as is compatible with the liberty of every other individual with whom he is united in a social compact, and the continued existence of that compact.

Liberty, in this simple, unsophisticated sense, I acknowledge, is a fair idea that has never yet received a form in the various governments that have been established on our beauteous globe; the demon of property has ever been at hand to encroach on the sacred rights of men, and to fence round with awful pomp laws that war with justice. But that it results from the eternal foundation of right—from immutable truth—who will presume to deny, that pretends to rationality—if reason has led them to build their morality and religion on an everlasting foundation—the attributes of God?

I glow with indignation when I attempt, methodically, to unravel your slavish paradoxes, in which I can find no fixed first principle to refute; I shall not, therefore, condescend to shew where you affirm in one page what you deny in another; and how frequently you draw conclusions without any previous premises:—it would be something like cowardice to fight with a man who had never exercised the weapons with which his opponent chose to combat, and irksome to refute sentence after sentence in which the latent spirit of tyranny appeared.

I perceive, from the whole tenor of your **Reflections,** that you have a mortal antipathy to reason; but, if there is any thing like argument, or first principles, in your wild declamation, behold the result:—that we are to reverence the rust of antiquity, and term the unnatural customs, which ignorance and mistaken self-interest have consolidated, the sage fruit of experience: nay, that, if we do discover some errors, our *feelings* should lead us to excuse, with blind love, or unprincipled filial affection, the venerable vestiges of ancient days. These are gothic notions of beauty—the ivy is beautiful, but, when it insidiously destroys the trunk from which it receives support, who would not grub it up?

Further, that we ought cautiously to remain for ever in frozen inactivity, because a thaw, whilst it nourishes the soil, spreads a temporary inundation; and the fear of risking any personal present convenience should prevent a struggle for the most estimable advantages. This is sound reasoning, I grant, in the mouth of the rich and short-sighted.

Yes, Sir, the strong gained riches, the few have sacrificed the many to their vices; and, to be able to pamper their appetites, and supinely exist witout exercising mind or body, they have ceased to be men.—Lost to the relish of true pleasure, such beings would, indeed, deserve compassion, if injustice was not softened by the tyrant's plea—necessity; if prescription was not raised as an immortal boundary against innovation. Their minds, in fact, instead of being cultivated, have been so warped by education, that it may require some ages to bring them back to nature, and enable them to see their true interest, with that degree of conviction which is necessary to influence their conduct. (pp. 7-11)

[On] what principle Mr. Burke could defend American independence, I cannot conceive; for the whole tenor of his plausible arguments settles slavery on an everlasting foundation. Allowing his servile reverence for antiquity, and prudent attention to self-interest, to have the force which he insists on, the slave trade ought never to be abolished; and, because our ignorant forefathers, not understanding the native dignity of man, sanctioned a traffic that outrages every suggestion of

reason and religion, we are to submit to the inhuman custom, and term an atrocious insult to humanity the love of our country, and a proper submission to the laws by which our property is secured.—Security of property! Behold, in a few words, the definition of English liberty. And to this selfish principle every nobler one is sacrificed. (pp. 23-4)

There appears to be such a mixture of real sensibility and fondly cherished romance in your composition, that the present crisis carries you out of yourself; and since you could not be one of the grand movers, the next *best* thing that dazzled your imagination was to be a conspicuous opposer. Full of yourself, you make as much noise to convince the world that you despise the revolution, as Rousseau did to persuade his contemporaries to let him live in obscurity.

Reading your **Reflections** warily over, it has continually and forcibly struck me, that had you been a Frenchman, you would have been, in spite of your respect for rank and antiquity, a violent revolutionist; and deceived, as you now probably are, by the passions that cloud your reason, have termed your romantic enthusiasm an enlightened love of your country, a benevolent respect for the rights of men. Your imagination would have taken fire, and have found arguments, full as ingenious as those you now offer, to prove that the constitution, of which so few pillars remained, that constitution which time had almost obliterated, was not a model sufficiently noble to deserve close adherence. And, for the English constitution, you might not have had such a profound veneration as you have lately acquired; nay, it is not impossible that you might have entertained the same opinion of the English Parliament, that you professed to have during the American war.

Another observation which, by frequently occurring, has almost grown into a conviction, is simply this, that had the English in general reprobated the French revolution, you would have stood forth alone, and been the avowed Goliah of liberty. But, not liking to see so many brothers near the throne of fame, you have turned the current of your passions, and consequently of your reasoning, another way. Had Dr. Price's sermon not lighted some sparks very like envy in your bosom, I shrewdly suspect that he would have been treated with more candour; nor is it charitable to suppose that any thing but personal pique and hurt vanity could have dictated such bitter sarcasms and reiterated expressions of contempt as occur in your **Reflections.** (pp. 108-10)

[Among] all your plausible arguments, and witty illustrations, your contempt for the poor always appears conspicuous, and rouses my indignation. (p. 142)

I know, indeed, that there is often something disgusting in the distresses of poverty, at which the imagination revolts, and starts back to exercise itself in the more attractive Arcadia of fiction. The rich man builds a house, art and taste give it the highest finish. His gardens are planted, and the trees grow to recreate the fancy of the planter, though the temperature of the climate may rather force him to avoid the dangerous damps they exhale, than seek the umbrageous retreat. Every thing on the estate is cherished but man;—yet, to contribute to the happiness of man, is the most sublime of all enjoyments. But if, instead of sweeping pleasure-grounds, obelisks, temples, and elegant cottages, as *objects* for the eye, the heart was allowed to beat true to nature, decent farms would be scattered over the estate, and plenty smile around. Instead of the poor being subject to the griping hand of an avaricious steward, they would be watched over with fatherly solicitude, by the man whose duty and pleasure it was to guard their happiness, and shield from rapacity the beings who, by the sweat of their brow, exalted him above his fellows. (pp. 144-46)

You mourn for the empty pageant of a name, when slavery flaps her wing, and the sick heart retires to die in lonely wilds, far from the abodes of men. Did the pangs you felt for insulted nobility, the anguish that rent your heart when the gorgeous robes were torn off the idol human weakness had set up, deserve to be compared with the long-drawn sigh of melancholy reflection, when misery and vice are thus seen to haunt our steps, and swim on the top of every cheering prospect? Why is our fancy to be appalled by terrific perspectives of a hell beyond the grave?—Hell stalks abroad;—the lash resounds on the slave's naked sides; and the sick wretch, who can no longer earn the sour bread of unremitting labour steals to a ditch to bid the world a long good night—or, neglected in some ostentatious hospital, breathes his last amidst the laugh of mercenary attendants.

Such misery demands more than tears—I pause to recollect myself; and smother the contempt I feel rising for your rhetorical flourishes and infantine sensibility.

• • • • •

Taking a retrospective view of my hasty answer, and casting a cursory glance over your *Reflections,* I perceive that I have not alluded to several reprehensible passages, in your elaborate work; which I marked for censure when I first perused it with a steady eye. And now I find it almost impossible candidly to refute your sophisms, without quoting your own words, and putting the numerous contradictions I observed in opposition to each other. This would be an effectual refutation; but, after such a tedious drudgery, I fear I should only be read by the patient eye that scarcely wanted my assistance to detect the flagrant errors. It would be a tedious process to shew, that often the most just and forcible illustrations are warped to colour over opinions *you* must *sometimes* have secretly despised; or, at least, have discovered, that what you asserted without limitation, required the greatest. (pp. 152-54)

[Amongst your] contradictions, you blame the National Assembly for expecting any exertions from the servile principle of responsibility, and afterwards insult them for not rendering themselves responsible. Whether the one the French have adopted will answer the purpose better, and be more than a shadow of representation, time only can shew. In theory it appears more promising.

Your real or artificial affection for the English constitution seems to me to resemble the brutal affection of some weak characters. They think it a duty to love their relations with a blind, indolent tenderness, that *will not* see the faults it might assist to correct, if their affection had been built on rational grounds. They love they know not why, and they will love to the end of the chapter.

Is it absolute blasphemy to doubt of the omnipotence of the law, or to suppose that religion might be more pure if there were fewer baits for hypocrites in the church? But our manners, you tell us, are drawn from the French, though you had before celebrated our native plainness. If they were, it is time we broke loose from dependance—Time that Englishmen drew water from their own springs; for, if manners are not a painted substitute for morals, we have only to cultivate our reason, and we shall not feel the want of an arbitrary model. Nature will suffice; but I forget myself:—Nature and Reason, acording

to your system, are all to give place to authority; and the gods, as Shakespeare makes a frantic wretch exclaim, seem to kill us for their sport, as men do flies.

Before I conclude my cursory remarks, it is but just to acknowledge that I coincide with you in your opinion respecting the *sincerity* of many modern philosophers. Your consistency in avowing a veneration for rank and riches deserves praise; but I must own that I have often indignantly observed that some of the *enlightened* philosophers, who talk most vehemently of the native rights of men, borrow many noble sentiments to adorn their conversation, which have no influence on their conduct. They bow down to rank, and are careful to secure property; for virtue, without this adventitious drapery, is seldom very respectable in their eyes—nor are they very quicksighted to discern real dignity of character when no sounding name exalts the man above his fellows.—But neither open enmity nor hollow homage destroys the intrinsic value of those principles which rest on an eternal foundation, and revert for a standard to the immutable attributes of God. (pp. 155-59)

> *Mary Wollstonecraft, in her* A Vindication of the Rights of Men in a Letter to the Right Honourable Edmund Burke; Occasioned by His "Reflections on the Revolution in France," *1790. Reprint by Scholars' Facsimiles & Reprints, 1960, 159 p.*

HORACE WALPOLE   (letter date 1791)

[*An English author, politician, and publisher, Walpole is best known for his memoirs and voluminous correspondence, which provide revealing glimpses of life in England during the last half of the eighteenth century. In the following excerpt from a letter to Mary Berry, a minor literary figure and a friend, Walpole upholds the intent and (for the most part) the execution of Burke's writings on the French Revolution.*]

Burke has published another pamphlet against the French Revolution [*A Letter from Mr. Burke, to a Member of the National Assembly, in Answer to some Objections to his Book on French Affairs*], in which he attacks it still more grievously [than he had in *Reflections on the Revolution in France*]. The beginning is very good, but it is not equal, nor quite so injudicious as parts of its predecessor; is far less brilliant, as well as much shorter; but were it ever so long, his mind overflows with such a torrent of images, that he cannot be tedious. His invective against Rousseau is admirable, just and new. Voltaire he passes almost contemptuously. I wish he had dissected Mirabeau too: and I grieve that he has omitted the violation of the consciences of the clergy; nor stigmatized those universal plunderers, the National Assembly, who gorge themselves with eighteen *livres* a day, which to many of them would three years ago have been astonishing opulence. (p. 277)

> *Horace Walpole, in a letter to Mary Berry on May 26, 1791, in his* Horace Walpole's Correspondence with Mary and Agnes Berry and Barbara Cecilia Seton, Vol. I, *edited by W. S. Lewis and A. Dayle Wallace, Yale University Press, 1944, pp. 272-79.*

THOMAS PAINE   (essay date 1791)

[*An English-born American journalist and political philosopher, Paine exerted a powerful influence on the course of political thought in America, England, and France during the years spanning the American and French Revolutions. His pamphlet* Common Sense *(1776) is an eloquent defense of the principles of liberty, sovereignty, and human rights, and his* The American

Crisis papers (1776-83) were instrumental in bolstering American confidence during the turbulent years of the Revolution. Paine is also remembered for defending the rights of the common individual in his The Rights of Man *(1791-92), a two-volume work written in direct response to Burke's* Reflections. *Although the work was highly popular and struck a sympathetic chord throughout America and Europe, the threat it posed for the British government served to alienate Paine from his native England. Paine was tried in absentia and found guilty of seditious writing, however, for in 1792 he journeyed to France to assume an active role in the Revolution. Greeted as a hero, Paine was given French citizenship and participated in the writing of a new constitution for the country. However, he soon fell out of favor with the more radical elements of the Revolution because, despite his fervent antimonarchism, he opposed the execution of the French royal family. Stripped of his citizenship, Paine was imprisoned and threatened with execution, but was eventually released. The most controversial of Paine's works,* The Age of Reason *(1794-95), represents a rationalistic critique of Christianity's supernatural aspects, and earned him the reputation of irreligious radical, though in actuality he held deistic beliefs similar to those of some of the Founding Fathers. In the following excerpt from the first section of his two-part* The Rights of Man, *Paine counters the conservative philosophic content of* Reflections on the Revolution in France *with a liberal manifesto of human rights, democratic government, and constitutional reform.*]

Among the incivilities by which nations or individuals provoke and irritate each other, Mr. Burke's [*Reflections on the Revolution in France*] is an extraordinary instance. Neither the people of France, nor the National Assembly, were troubling themselves about the affairs of England, or the English Parliament; and why Mr. Burke should commence an unprovoked attack upon them, both in Parliament and in public, is a conduct that cannot be pardoned on the score of manners, nor justified on that of policy.

There is scarcely an epithet of abuse to be found in the English language, with which Mr. Burke has not loaded the French Nation and the National Assembly. Everything which rancour, prejudice, ignorance or knowledge could suggest, is poured forth in the copious fury of near four hundred pages. In the strain and on the plan Mr. Burke was writing, he might have written on to as many thousands. When the tongue or the pen is let loose in a phrenzy of passion, it is the man, and not the subject, that becomes exhausted.

Hitherto Mr. Burke has been mistaken and disappointed in the opinions he had formed of the affairs of France; but such is the ingenuity of his hope, or the malignancy of his despair, that it furnishes him with new pretences to go on. There was a time when it was impossible to make Mr. Burke believe there would be any Revolution in France. His opinion then was, that the French had neither spirit to undertake it nor fortitude to support it; and now that there is one, he seeks an escape by condemning it.

Not sufficiently content with abusing the National Assembly, a great part of his work is taken up with abusing Dr. Price (one of the best-hearted men that lives) and the two societies in England known by the name of the Revolution Society and the Society for Constitutional Information.

Dr. Price had preached a sermon on the 4th of November, 1789, being the anniversary of what is called in England the Revolution, which took place 1688. Mr. Burke, speaking of this sermon, says, ''The political Divine proceeds dogmatically to assert, that by the principles of the Revolution, the people of England have acquired three fundamental rights:

1. To choose their own governors.
2. To cashier them for misconduct.
3. To frame a government for ourselves.''

Dr. Price does not say that the right to do these things exists in this or in that person, or in this or in that description of persons, but that it exists in the *whole;* that it is a right resident in the Nation. Mr. Burke, on the contrary, denies that such a right exists in the Nation, either in whole or in part, or that it exists anywhere; and, what is still more strange and marvellous, he says, ''that the people of England utterly disclaim such a right, and that they will resist the practical assertion of it with their lives and fortunes.'' That men should take up arms and spend their lives and fortunes, *not* to maintain their rights, but to maintain they have *not* rights, is an entirely new species of discovery, and suited to the paradoxical genius of Mr. Burke.

The method which Mr. Burke takes to prove that the people of England have no such rights, and that such rights do not now exist in the Nation, either in whole or in part, or anywhere at all, is of the same marvellous and monstrous kind with what he has already said; for his arguments are that the persons, or the generation of persons, in whom they did exist, are dead, and with them the right is dead also. To prove this, he quotes a declaration made by parliament about a hundred years ago, to William and Mary, in these words: ''The Lords Spiritual and Temporal, and Commons, do, in the name of the people aforesaid [meaning the people of England then living], most humbly and faithfully *submit* themselves, theirs *heirs* and *posterities,* for EVER.'' He also quotes a clause of another act of Parliament made in the same reign, the terms of which, he says, ''bind us [meaning the people of that day], our *heirs* and our *posterity,* to *them,* their *heirs* and *posterity,* to the end of time.'' (pp. 9-11)

It requires but a very small glance of thought to perceive that altho' laws made in one generation often continue in force through succeeding generations, yet that they continue to derive their force from the consent of the living. A law not repealed continues in force, not because it *cannot* be repealed, but because it *is not* repealed; and the non-repealing passes for consent.

But Mr. Burke's clauses have not even this qualification in their favour. They become null, by attempting to become immortal. The nature of them precludes consent. They destroy the right which they *might* have, by grounding it on a right which they *cannot* have. Immortal power is not a human right, and therefore cannot be a right of Parliament. (pp. 15-16)

Mr. Burke's book has the appearance of being written as instruction to the French Nation; but if I may permit myself the use of an extravagant metaphor, suited to the extravagance of the case, It is darkness attempting to illuminate light. (p. 16)

I know a place in America called Point-no-Point, because as you proceed along the shore, gay and flowery as Mr. Burke's language, it continually recedes and presents itself at a distance before you; but when you have got as far as you can go, there is no point at all. Just thus it is with Mr. Burke's three hundred and fifty-six pages. It is therefore difficult to reply to him. But as the points he wishes to establish may be inferred from what he abuses, it is his paradoxes that we must look for his arguments.

As to the tragic paintings by which Mr. Burke has outraged his own imagination, and seeks to work upon that of his readers, they are very well calculated for theatrical representation, where facts are manufactured for the sake of show, and accommodated to produce, through the weakness of sympathy, a weeping effect. But Mr. Burke should recollect that he is writing history, and not *plays*, and that his readers will expect truth, and not the spouting rant of high-toned exclamation.

When we see a man dramatically lamenting in a publication intended to be believed that *"The age of chivalry is gone! that The glory of Europe is extinguished for ever! that the unbought grace of life* (if any one knows what it is), *the cheap defence of nations, the nurse of manly sentiment and heroic enterprise is gone!"* and all this because the Quixote age of chivalry nonsense is gone, what opinion can we form of his judgment, or what regard can we pay to his facts? In the rhapsody of his imagination he has discovered a world of windmills, and his sorrows are that there are no Quixotes to attack them. But if the age of Aristocracy, like that of Chivalry, should fall (and they had originally some connection), Mr. Burke, the trumpeter of the order, may continue his parody to the end, and finish with exclaiming: *"Othello's occupation's gone!"*

Notwithstanding Mr. Burke's horrid paintings, when the French Revolution is compared with the Revolutions of other countries, the astonishment will be that it is marked with so few sacrifices; but this astonishment will cease when we reflect that *principles*, and not *persons*, were the meditated objects of destruction. The mind of the nation was acted upon by a higher stimulus than what the consideration of persons could inspire, and sought a higher conquest than could be produced by the downfall of an enemy. Among the few who fell there do not appear to be any that were intentionally singled out. They all of them had their fate in the circumstances of the moment, and were not pursued with that long, cold-blooded, unabated revenge which pursued the unfortunate Scotch in the affair of 1745. (pp. 22-3)

[Mr. Burke] has libelled in the most unprovoked manner, and in the grossest stile of the most vulgar abuse, the whole representative authority of France, and yet Mr. Burke takes his seat in the British House of Commons! From his violence and his grief, his silence on some points and his excess on others, it is difficult not to believe that Mr. Burke is sorry, extremely sorry, that arbitrary power, the power of the Pope and the Bastille, are pulled down.

Not one glance of compassion, not one commiserating reflection that I can find throughout his book, has he bestowed on those who lingered out the most wretched of lives, a life without hope in the most miserable of prisons. It is painful to behold a man employing his talents to corrupt himself. Nature has been kinder to Mr. Burke than he is to her. He is not affected by the reality of distress touching his heart, but by the showy resemblance of it striking his imagination. He pities the plumage, but forgets the dying bird. Accustomed to kiss the aristocratical hand that hath purloined him from himself, he degenerates into a composition of art, and the genuine soul of nature forsakes him. His hero or his heroine must be a tragedy-victim expiring in show, and not the real prisoner of misery, sliding into death in the silence of a dungeon. (p. 24)

I cannot consider Mr. Burke's book in any other light than a dramatic performance; and he must, I think, have considered it in the same light himself, by the poetical liberties he has taken of omitting some facts, distorting others, and making the whole machinery bend to produce a stage effect. Of this kind is his account of the expedition to Versailles. He begins this account by omitting the only facts which as causes are known to be true; everything beyond these is conjecture even in Paris;

and he then works up a tale accommodated to his own passions and prejudices.

It is to be observed thoughout Mr. Burke's book that he never speaks of plots *against* the Revolution; and it is from those plots that all the mischiefs have arisen. It suits his purpose to exhibit the consequences without their causes. It is one of the arts of the drama to do so. If the crimes of men were exhibited with their sufferings, the stage effect would sometimes be lost, and the audience would be inclined to approve where it was intended they should commiserate.

After all the investigations that have been made into this intricate affair (the expedition to Versailles), it still remains enveloped in all that kind of mystery which ever accompanies events produced more from a concurrence of awkward circumstances than from fixed design. While the characters of men are forming, as is always the case in Revolutions, there is a reciprocal suspicion, and a disposition to misinterpret each other; and even parties directly opposite in principle will sometimes concur in pushing forward the same movement with very different views, and with the hopes of its producing very different consequences. A great deal of this may be discovered in this embarrassed affair, and yet the issue of the whole was what nobody had in view.

The only things certainly known are that considerable uneasiness was at this time excited at Paris by the delay of the King in not sanctioning and forwarding the decrees of the National Assembly, particularly that of the *Declaration of the Rights of Man*, and the decrees of the *fourth of August*, which contained the foundation principles on which the constitution was to be erected. The kindest, and perhaps the fairest conjecture upon this matter is, that some of the ministers intended to make remarks and observations upon certain parts of them before they were finally sanctioned and sent to the provinces; but be this as it may, the enemies of the Revolution derived hope from the delay, and the friends of the Revolution uneasiness. (pp. 34-5)

Before anything can be reasoned upon to a conclusion, certain facts, principles, or data, to reason from, must be established, admitted, or denied. Mr. Burke, with his usual outrage, abuses the *Declaration of the Rights of Man*, published by the National Assembly of France as the basis on which the constitution of France is built. This he calls "paltry and blurred sheets of paper about the rights of man." Does Mr. Burke mean to deny that *man* has any rights? If he does, then he must mean that there are no such things as rights anywhere, and that he has none himself; for who is there in the world but man? But if Mr. Burke means to admit that man has rights, the question then will be: What are those rights, and how came man by them originally?

The error of those who reason by precedents drawn from antiquity, respecting the rights of man, is that they do not go far enough into antiquity. They do not go the whole way. They stop in some of the intermediate stages of an hundred or a thousand years, and produce what was then done, as a rule for the present day. This is no authority at all. If we travel still farther into antiquity, we shall find a direct contrary opinion and practice prevailing; and if antiquity is to be authority, a thousand such authorities may be produced, successively contradicting each other; but if we proceed on, we shall at last come out right; we shall come to the time when man came from the hand of his Maker. What was he then? Man. Man was his high and only title, and a higher cannot be given him. (pp. 40-1)

We are now got at the origin of man, and at the origin of his rights. (p. 41)

Though I mean not to touch upon any sectarian principle of religion, yet it may be worth observing that the genealogy of Christ is traced to Adam. Why then not trace the rights of man to the creation of man? I will answer the question. Because there have been upstart Governments, thrusting themselves between and presumptuously working to *un-make* man.

If any generation of men ever possessed the right of dictating the mode by which the world should be governed for ever, it was the first generation that existed; and if that generation did it not, no succeeding generation can show any authority for doing it, nor can set any up. The illuminating and divine principle of the equal rights of man (for it has its origin from the Maker of man) relates, not only to the living individuals, but to generations of men succeeding each other. Every generation is equal in rights to the generations which preceded it, by the same rule that every individual is born equal in rights with his contemporary. (p. 42)

It is not among the least of the evils of the present existing Governments in all parts of Europe that man, considered as man, is thrown back to a vast distance from his Maker, and the artificial chasm filled up by a succession of barriers, or sort of turnpike gates, through which he has to pass. I will quote Mr. Burke's catalogue of barriers that he has set up between Man and his Maker. Putting himself in the character of a herald, he says: *We fear God—we look with* AWE *to kings— with affection to Parliaments—with duty to magistrates—with reverence to priests, and with respect to nobility.* Mr. Burke has forgotten to put in *"chivalry."* He has also forgotten to put in Peter.

The duty of man is not a wilderness of turnpike gates, through which he is to pass by tickets from one to the other. It is plain and simple, and consists but of two points. His duty to God, which every man must feel; and with respect to his neighbour, to do as he would be done by. If those to whom power is delegated do well, they will be respected; if not, they will be despised; and with regard to those to whom no power is delegated, but who assume it, the rational world can know nothing of them. (pp. 43-4)

> *Thomas Paine, "Rights of Man: Part the First," in his* The Rights of Man, *J. M. Dent & Sons Ltd., 1915, pp. 1-138.*

WILLIAM COBBETT   (essay date 1797)

[*Cobbett was one of the most notable and prolific English essayists of his time. His interests were broad and included economics, linguistics, politics, and rural life; this last interest inspired one of Cobbett's most entertaining works,* Rural Rides *(1830). He was profoundly affected by the outbreak of the French Revolution and fled for a time to America to express the traditional principles to which he, like Burke, adhered. Cobbett was a bitter antagonist, in particular, of Thomas Paine, and criticized Paine's egalitarian philosophy in his monthly the* Political Censor. *In his later journals,* Porcupine's Gazette and Daily Advertiser *and the* Weekly Political Register, *Cobbett made a name for himself as a formidable, splendid prose writer, who wrote (often under the pseudonym Peter Porcupine) upon the leading political and social issues in eighteenth- and early nineteenth-century America, England, and Europe. In the following excerpt from an essay originally published in* Porcupine's Gazette and Daily Advertiser *shortly after Burke's death, Cobbett defends the honor and achievement of Burke, concluding with an extract from Thomas Townshend's* A Summary Defence of the Rt. Hon. Edmund Burke in Two Letters *(1796).*]

The exit of this great man, the most eloquent of orators, and the profoundest of statesmen; the ornament of his country, and the prop of sinking liberty, morality, and religion: this cruel stroke of the ruthless destroyer has, as might be expected, called forth the exulting malice of the still more ruthless sons of *liberty* and *equality.* When the eagle falls from his lofty perch, birds of ignoble flight insultingly flutter from their hidden roosts; the owl hoots, and the buzzard croaks for joy.

The literary buzzard, through whose foul vehicle Mr. Burke's death was first communicated to the public, takes the following malicious peck at his memory: *"Our obituary of this week,"* says he, *"announces the exit of* Edmund Burke, *the great, but eccentric orator and author, at one time the* redoubted champion of public liberty, *and in the evening of his life* ITS VENAL AND DETERMINED FOE."

Most certainly the memory of Edmund Burke stands in need of no defence; yet, gratitude for the pleasure and instruction I have derived from his Herculean, invaluable, and immortal labours, impels me, and will ever impel me, as long as I have the means, to give publicity to whatever may tend to the shame and confusion of his base and remorseless calumniators.

With this motive it is, that I shall here subjoin a defence of Mr. Burke's *consistency,* from the letters of *Thomas Townsend, Esq.* It may not be amiss to observe previously, that the charge of *inconsistency* is the only one which his vile slanderers ever think of bringing against him.

This is the old worn-out monotone string on which they are everlastingly harping. It has for years past been the *Alpha* and *Omega* of all the seditious paragraphs, pamphlets, and harangues of the scribbling and spouting Jacobins of Britain.

"But," says Mr. Townsend,

> in all he said and did respecting America, there was not a single sentiment, impliedly or directly, savouring of the savage eccentricities which are broached with so much rage by modern theorists. There were no allusions to visionary doctrines of government; no abstract imaginary rights; no wanderings through infinite space, to jostle upon new expedients in legislation. In no one page of his writings at that period, can be found any chimerical designations for the perfection of human nature; in none of his volumes can you discover man unfledged, and plucked of all his habitudes, modes of mind, and disposition of heart— standing an abstract *crop,* a rifled metaphysical thing, to be forged and hammered into any fantastic shape to which the decree of a Convention may doom him. Till Mr. Burke can be convicted of slumbering in his mind, and having his dreams disturbed with the *incubus* of theory, and his fancy swarming with all sorts of monstrous phantoms of government, I must defy you, or any man, be he who he will, to prove his dereliction of his principles.
>
> (pp. 103-05)

In defending the laws and liberties of his country, he has shown that monarchy, religion, nobility, and freedom, are the well-twisted strands of the cable which hold the political bark: no one of them can sustain, in the mighty whirl of State tempests, the trust consigned to it; it will yield like a cobweb; but,

"The Impeachment; or, The Father of the Gang Turn'd King's Evidence" by James Gillray, 1791. Burke is depicted denouncing Sheridan and Fox as "abettors of Revolutions." The Parliamentary debate that inspired this cartoon ended Burke's longtime friendship with Fox.

whilst we keep them in the close-blended twist which
the cautious zeal of our ancestors has given them,
and have found hearts aboard, the winds may rise,
and the waters roll in harmless sublimity.

(p. 108)

William Cobbett, "The Death of Burke," in his Porcupine's Works, Vol. VII, *Cobbett and Morgan, 1801,
pp. 103-08.*

WILLIAM HAZLITT (essay date 1808)

*[An English essayist, Hazlitt was one of the most important critics
of the Romantic age. He was a deft stylist, a master of the prose
essay, and a leader of what was later termed "impressionist
criticism"—a form of personal analysis directly opposed to the
universal standards of critical judgment accepted by many eighteenth-century critics. For Hazlitt the ideal of any critical endeavor is not an ultimate judgment regarding works of literature;
instead, the critic serves as a guide to help determine the reader's
response to certain works, or passages within those works. A
journalist who wrote for the general public and who lived from
the proceeds of his pen, he was acutely aware of the abstract
nature of literature as well as the limitations of his audience in
understanding questions of aesthetics and style. For this reason
Hazlitt purposely made his criticism palatable by frequently using
illustrations, digressions, and repetition. In the following excerpt
from an essay originally published in his* The Eloquence of the
British Senate *(1808), he esteems Burke's powers as a logician
and stylist.]*

The only limits which circumscribed [Burke's] variety were
the stores of his own mind. His stock of ideas did not consist
of a few meager facts, meagerly stated, or half a dozen com-
mon-places tortured in a thousand different ways: but his mine
of wealth was a profound understanding, inexhaustible as the
human heart, and various as the sources of nature. He, therefore, enriched every subject to which he applied himself, and
new subjects were only the occasions of calling forth fresh
powers of mind which had not been before exerted. It would,
therefore, be in vain to look for the proof of his powers in any
one of his speeches or writings: they all contain some additional
proof of power. In speaking of Burke, then, I shall speak of
the whole compass and circuit of his mind . . . ; to do otherwise
would be like the story of the man who put the brick in his
pocket, thinking to show it as the model of a house. . . . But
who can bind Proteus, or confine the roving flight of genius?

Burke's writings are better than his speeches, and indeed his
speeches are writings. But he seemed to feel himself more at
ease, to have a fuller possession of his faculties in addressing

the public, than in addressing the house of commons. Burke was *raised* into public life; and he seems to have been prouder of this new dignity than became so great a man. For this reason most of his speeches have a sort of parliamentary preamble to them: there is an air of affected modesty, and ostentatious trifling in them: he seems fond of coquetting with the house of commons, and is perpetually calling the speaker out to dance a minuet with him, before he begins. There is also something like an attempt to stimulate the superficial dulness of his hearers by exciting their surprise, by running into extravagance; and he sometimes demeans himself by condescending to what may be considered as bordering too much upon buffoonery, for the amusement of the company. Those lines of Milton were admirably applied to him by some one—"The elephant to make them sport wreathed his proboscis lithe." The truth is, that he was out of his place in the house of commons; he was eminently qualified to shine as a man of genius, as the instructor of mankind, as the brightest luminary of his age: but he had nothing in common with that motley crew of knights, citizens, and burgesses. He could not be said to be "native and endued unto that element." He was above it; and never appeared like himself but when, forgetful of the idle clamours of party, and of the little views of little men, he appealed to his country, and the enlightened judgment of mankind.

I am not going to make an idle panegyric on Burke, (he has no need of it;) but I cannot help looking upon him as the chief boast and ornament of the English house of commons. What has been said of him is, I think, strictly true, that "he was the most eloquent man of his time: his wisdom was greater than his eloquence." (pp. 331-32)

I do not say that his arguments are conclusive: but they are profound and *true,* as far as they go. There may be disadvantages and abuses necessarily interwoven with his scheme, or opposite advantages of infinitely greater value, to be derived from another order of things and state of society. This, however, does not invalidate either the truth or importance of Burke's reasoning; since the advantages he points out as connected with the mixed form of government are really and necessarily inherent in it; since they are compatible in the same degree with no other; since the principle itself on which he rests his argument (whatever we may think of the application) is of the utmost weight and moment; and since, on which ever side the truth lies, it is impossible to make a fair decision without having the opposite side of the question clearly and fully stated to us. This Burke has done in a masterly manner. He presents to you one view or face of society. Let him, who thinks he can, give the reverse side with equal force, beauty, and clearness. It is said, I know, that truth is *one;* but to this I cannot subscribe, for it appears to me that truth is *many.* There are as many truths as there are things and causes of action, and contradictory principles at work in society. In making up the account of good and evil, indeed, the final result must be one way or the other; but the particulars on which that result depends are infinite and various.

It will be seen from what I have said, that I am very far from agreeing with those who think that Burke was a man without understanding, and a merely florid writer. There are two causes which have given rise to this calumny; namely, that narrowness of mind which leads men to suppose that the truth lies entirely on the side of their own opinions, and that whatever does not make for them is absurd and irrational; secondly, a trick we have of confounding reason with judgment, and supposing that it is merely the province of the understanding to pronounce

sentence, and not to give in evidence, or argue the case; in short, that is a passive, not an active faculty. Thus there are persons who never run into any extravagance, because they are so buttressed up with the opinions of others on all sides, that they cannot lean much to one side or the other; they are so little moved with any kind of reasoning, that they remain at an equal distance from every extreme, and are never very far from the truth, because the slowness of their faculties will not suffer them to make much progress in error. These are persons of great judgment. The scales of the mind are pretty sure to remain even when there is nothing in them. In this sense of the word, Burke must be allowed to have wanted judgment, by all those who think that he was wrong in his conclusion. This accusation of want of judgment, in fact, only means that you yourself are of a different opinion. But if, in arriving at one error, he discovered a hundred truths, I should consider myself a hundred times more indebted to him than if, stumbling on that which I consider as the right side of the question, he had committed a hundred absurdities in striving to establish his point. I speak of him now merely as an author, or as far as I and other readers are concerned with him; at the same time, I should not differ from any one who may be disposed to contend that the consequences of his writings, as instruments of political power, have been tremendous, fatal, such as no exertion of wit, or knowledge, or genius, can ever counteract or atone for.

Burke also gave a hold to his antagonist by mixing up sentiment and imagery wih his reasoning; so that being unused to such a sight in the region of politics, they were deceived, and could not discern the fruit from the flowers. Gravity is the cloak of wisdom: and those who have nothing else, think it an insult to affect the one without the other, because it destroys the only foundation on which their pretensions are built. The easiest part of reason is dulness: the generality of the world are therefore concerned in discouraging any example of unnecessary brilliancy that might tend to show that the two things do not always go together. Burke in some measure dissolved the spell. It was discovered, that his gold was not the less valuable for being wrought into elegant shapes, and richly embossed with curious figures: that the solidity of a building is not destroyed by adding to it beauty and ornament; and that the strength of a man's understanding is not always to be estimated in exact proportion to his want of imagination. His understanding was not the less real, because it was not the only faculty he possessed. He justified the description of the poet,

> How charming is divine philosophy!
> Not harsh and crabbed, as dull fools suppose,
> But musical as is Apollo's lute!

Those who object to this union of grace and beauty with reason, are in fact weak-sighted people, who cannot distinguish the noble and majestic form of Truth from that of her sister Folly, if they are dressed both alike! But there is always a difference even in the adventitious ornaments they wear, which is sufficient to distinguish them.

Burke was so far from being a gaudy or flowery writer, that he was one of the *severest* writers we have. His words are the most like things; his style is the most strictly suited to the subject. He unites every extreme and every variety of composition; the lowest and the meanest words and descriptions with the highest. He exults in the display of power, in showing the extent, the force, and intensity of his ideas; he is led on by the mere impulse and vehemence of his fancy, not by the affectation of dazzling his readers by gaudy conceits or pompous images. He was completely carried away by his subject. He had no other object but to produce the strongest impression on his reader, by giving the truest, the most characteristic, the fullest, and most forcible description of things, trusting to the power of his own mind to mould them into grace and beauty. He did not produce a splendid effect by setting fire to the light vapours that float in the regions of fancy, as the chemists make fine colours with phosphorus, but, by the eagerness of his blows, struck fire from the flint, and melted the hardest substances in the furnace of his imagination. The wheels of his imagination did not catch fire from the rottenness of the materials, but from the rapidity of their motion. One would suppose, to hear people talk of Burke, that his style was such as would have suited the *Lady's Magazine;* soft, smooth, showy, tender, insipid, full of fine words without any meaning. The essence of the gaudy or glittering style consists in producing a momentary effect by fine words and images brought together, without order or connection. Burke most frequently produced an effect by the remoteness and novelty of his combinations, by the force of contrast, by the striking manner in which the most opposite and unpromising materials were harmoniously blended together; not by laying his hands on all the fine things he could think of, but by bringing together those things which he knew would blaze out into glorious light by their collision. The florid style is a mixture of affectation and common-place. Burke's was a union of untameable vigour and orginality.

Burke was not a verbose writer. If he sometimes multiplies words, it is not for want of ideas, but because there are no words that fully express his ideas, and he tries to do it as well as he can by different ones. He had nothing of the *set* or formal style, the measured cadence, and stately phraseology of Johnson and most of our modern writers. This style, which is what we understand by the *artificial,* is all in one key. It selects a certain set of words to represent all ideas whatever, as the most dignified and elegant, and excludes all others as low and vulgar. The words are not fitted to the things, but the things to the words. Every thing is seen through a false medium. (pp. 337-40)

Burke was altogether free from the pedantry which I have here endeavoured to expose. His style was as original, as expressive, as rich and varied, as it was possible; his combinations were as exquisite, as playful, as happy, as unexpected, as bold and daring, as his fancy. If any thing, he ran into the opposite extreme of too great an inequality, if truth and nature could ever be carried to an extreme.

Those who are best acquainted with the writings and speeches of Burke, will not think the praise I have here bestowed on them exaggerated. . . . But the full proof must be sought in his works at large, and particularly in the **Thoughts on the Discontents**; in his **Reflections on the French Revolution**; in his **Letter to the Duke of Bedford**; and in the **Regicide Peace**. The two last of these are perhaps the most remarkable of all his writings, from the contrast they afford to each other. The one is the most delightful exhibition of wild and brilliant fancy, that is to be found in English prose, but it is too much like a beautiful picture painted upon gauze; it wants something to support it: the other is without ornament, but it has all the solidity, the weight, the gravity, of a judicial record. It seems to have been written with a certain constraint upon himself, and to show those who said he could not *reason,* that his arguments might be stripped of their ornaments without losing any thing of their force. It is certainly, of all his works, that in which he has shown most power of logical deduction, and the only one in which he has made any important use of facts.

In general, he certainly paid little attention to them: they were the playthings of his mind. He saw them as he pleased, not as they were; with the eye of the philosopher or the poet, regarding them only in their general principle, or as they might serve to decorate his subject. This is the natural consequence of much imagination; things that are probable are elevated into the rank of realities. To those who can reason on the essences of things, or who can invent according to nature, the experimental proof is of little value. This was the case with Burke. In the present instance, however, he seems to have *forced* his mind into the service of facts: and he succeeded completely. His comparison between our connexion with France or Algiers, and his account of the conduct of the war, are as clear, as convincing, as forcible examples of this kind of reasoning, as are any where to be met with. Indeed, I do not think there is any thing in Fox, (whose mind was purely historical,) or in Chatham, (who attended to feelings more than facts,) that will bear a comparison with them.

Burke has been compared to Cicero—I do not know for what reason. Their excellencies are as different, and indeed as opposite, as they well can be. Burke had not the polished elegance, the glossy neatness, the artful regularity, the exquisite modulation of Cicero: he had a thousand times more richness and originality of mind, more strength and pomp of diction. (pp. 340-41)

It may be asked whether Burke was a poet. He was so only in the general vividness of his fancy, and in richness of invention. There may be poetical passages in his works, but I certainly think that his writings in general are quite distinct from poetry; and that for the reason before given, namely, that the subject matter of them is not poetical. The finest parts of them are illustrations or personifications of dry abstract ideas; and the union between the idea and the illustration is not of that perfect and pleasing kind as to constitute poetry, or indeed to be admissible, but for the effect intended to be produced by it; that is, by every means in our power to give an animation and attraction to subjects in themselves barren of ornament, but which, at the same time, are pregnant with the most important consequences, and in which the understanding and the passions are equally interested.

I have heard it remarked by a person, to whose opinion I would sooner submit than to a general council of critics, that the sound of Burke's prose is not musical; that it wants cadence; and that instead of being so lavish of his imagery as is generally supposed, he seemed to him to be rather parsimonious in the use of it, always expanding and making the most of his ideas. This may be true if we compare him with some of our poets, or perhaps with some of our early prose writers, but not if we compare him with any of our political writers, or parliamentary speakers. There are some very fine things of Lord Bolingbroke's on the same subjects, but not equal to Burke's. As for Junius, he is at the head of his class; but that class is not the highest. He has been said to have more dignity than Burke. Yes, if the stalk of a giant is less dignified than the strut of a petit-maitre. I do not mean to speak disrespectfully of Junius, but grandeur is not the character of his composition; and if it is not to be found in Burke, it is to be found nowhere. (p. 342)

William Hazlitt, "Edmund Burke," in The Analectic Magazine, *April, 1815, pp. 330-42.*

JEREMY BENTHAM (essay date 1817)

[*An English philosopher, legal theorist, and political economist, Bentham is known for his* Introduction to Principles of Morals and

Legislation (1789), his most famous work and the one in which he enunciated the concept of utilitarianism: that is, the pursuit by government of the greatest happiness for the greatest number of people. Bentham's writings on this and other subjects greatly influenced James Mill and his son John Stuart Mill, who modified Bentham's theories, codifying and popularizing his revised system in his Utilitarianism *(1863). In the following excerpt from an essay originally published in 1817 in the* Pamphleteer, *Bentham condemns Burke as a self-serving economic reformer.]*

Needy as well as ambitious—dependent by all his hopes on a party who beheld in his person the principal part of their intellectual strength—struggling, and with prospects every day increasing, against a ministry whose popularity he saw already in a deep decline, [Burke], from this economical scheme of his, *bill* and *speech* together, [*Speech . . . on Presenting, on the 11th of February 1780—a Plan for the Better Security of the Independence of Parliament and the Economical Reformation of the Civil and Other Establishments*], proposed to himself, on this occasion, two intimately connected, though antagonizing objects; viz. immediate depression of the force in the hands of the adversary, and at the same time the eventual preservation and increase of the same force in the hands of the assailants, in the event of success, which on the like occasions are, by all such besiegers, proposed to themselves, and, according to circumstances, with different degrees of skill and success pursued.

For the more immediate of the two objects, viz. *distress of the enemy,* it was, that the bill itself was provided; and to this object nothing could be more dexterously or happily adapted. Opposition it was certain of: and whatsoever were the event, advantage in some degree was sure. Suppose the opposition completely successful, and the whole plan of retrenchment thrown out together: here would be so much reputation gained to the promoters of the measure, so much reputation lost to the opponents of it. Suppose the plan in any part of it carried, in proportion to the importance of the part so carried, the reputation of its supporters would receive an ulterior increase: while that of its opponents, the weakness betrayed by them increasing in proportion to the conquests thus made upon them, would, in the same proportion, experience an ulterior decrease.

But as it is with the war of hands, so it is with the war of words. No sooner is the conquest effected, than the weakness of the vanquished becomes in no inconsiderable degree the weakness of the conquerors—of the conquerors, who from assailants are become possessors. To this eventual weakness an eventual support was to be provided.

To this service was his *speech* directed and adapted. . . .

Such in truth were the two objects thus undertaken to be recommended—recommended at one and the same time—to public favour: a practical measure (a measure brought forward by his bill)—a measure of practice, and in the same breath a set of *principles* with which, necessary as they were to the main and ulterior purpose, the measure, so far as it went, was in a state of direct repugnancy.

The problem, therefore, with which his ingenuity had to grapple, was—so to order matters, as that the economical measure should be pursued, and even if possible carried, with as little prejudice as possible to the necessary anti-economical principles. (p. 282)

[Of] principles really favourable to frugality and public probity—of principles in which waste and corruption would equally have found their condemnation, in whatever hands—in the hands of

whatever party—the matter of waste and means of corruption were lodged,—of any such principles the prevalence would, by its whole amount, have been in a proportionable degree unfavourable to the orator's bright and opening prospects. Once in possession of the power he was aiming at, the only principles suitable to his interests, and thence to his views, would be such principles as were most favourable to the conjunct purposes of waste and corruption. So far as was practicable, his aim would therefore be, and was—to preserve for use the principles of waste and corruption in the event of his finding himself in possession of the matter and the means—to preserve them in undiminished, and, if possible, even in augmented force.

For this purpose, the only form of argument which the nature of the case left open to him was, that of *concession* or admission. Such, accordingly, . . . was the form embraced by him and employed.

By the portion, comparatively minute as it was, of the mass of the matter of waste and corruption, of which his bill offered up the sacrifice, his *frugality* and *probity* were to stand displayed by the vast, and as far as depended upon his exertions, the infinite mass preserved—preserved by the principles let drop, and as it were unwillingly, and as if wrung from him by conviction in his *speech,* his *candour,* his *moderation,* his *penetration,* his *discernment,* his *wisdom,*—all these virtues were, in full galaxy, to be made manifest to an admiring world.

All this while, an argument there was, by which, had there been any lips to urge it, this fine-spun web, with purity at the top and corruption at bottom, might have been cut to pieces. If of the precious oil of corruption a widow's cruise full, and that continually drawn upon, be so necessary as you have been persuading us to believe, why, by any such amount as proposed, or by any amount, seek to reduce it?

True: *had there been any lips to urge it.* But, that there were no such lips, was a fact of which he had sufficient reason to be assured: to urge it, probably enough, not so much as a single pair of lips:—to listen to it, most assuredly, not any sufficient number of ears: and where ears to listen and eyes to read are wanting, all the lips in the world to speak with, all the hands in the world to write, would, as was no secret to him, be of no use.

Thus, then, by the craft of the rhetorician, were a set of principles completely suited to his purpose—principles by a zealous application of which, anything in the way in question, howsoever pernicious, might be done—anything, however flagrantly pernicious defended—collected together as in a magazine ready for use: a magazine, too, the key of which was in his own pocket, and with an adequate assurance, that, on the part of no enemy whom he and his need care for, would any attempt ever be made to blow it up. (p. 283)

As to the principles thus relied upon by the orator, they will be seen to be all of them reducible to this one, viz. that as much of their property as, by force or fraud, or the usual mixture of both, the people can be brought to part with, shall come and continue to be at the disposal of him and his;—and that, for this purpose, the whole of it shall be and remain a perpetual fund of premiums, for him who on each occasion shall prove himself most expert at the use of those phrases by which the imaginations of men are fascinated, their passions inflamed, and their judgments bewildered and seduced; whereupon he—this orator—whose expertness in those arts being really superior to that of any man of his time (to which perhaps might be added, or any *other* time) could not but by himself be felt to be so, would in this perpetual *wrestling-match* or *lottery*—call it which you will—possess a fairer chance than could be possessed by any other adventurer, for bearing off some of the capital prizes. (pp. 283-84)

In writing, no man ever weighed his words in nicer scales; no author ever blotted more, to find, for each occasion, a set of words that shall comprehend two meanings—one for *attack,* another in case of necessity for *retreat* and *self-defence;* such throughout is the study of the rhetorician, whom devotion to a party reduced to that species and degree of servitude, with which sincerity is incompatible.—In this sinister art, no man ever laboured more—no man surely ever made a greater proficiency—no man, one may venture to say, ever made so great a proficiency, as this Edmund Burke.

Here [in his **Speech**] we have a picture (shall we say?) or a plan of Machiavelism, sketched out by his own hand. In itself it is but a loose sketch, for by anything like a complete and correct draught, too much would have been brought to view. But in its exact shape, no small part, and in outline the whole, was already in his own breast. Nor, so far as concerned his own portrait, was it from fancy, but from the looking-glass, that he drew.

The treasury bench—the castle of mis-rule—stood before him. Sham-economy, an instrument of "Young Ambition," the ladder by which it was to be scaled. Already the ladder was in his hand. A bill for *"independence"* and so forth—and for *"economical reformation"* and so forth—was the name—the wordy name—he had found for it.

At the end of a long contest, the ladder performed its service. But when the fortress was in his hands, a buttress was deemed necessary to enable him to maintain his ground. The buttress fell, and he in it, and along with it; the buttress fell, and great was the fall thereof.

And what was this buttress? Few readers can be at a loss for it.

Four years after, when under the pressure of the mass of corruption, in the bands of the secret advisers of the crown they betook themselves for relief, he and his party, not to the legitimate influence of the people, as it would have been manifested in an equalized representation, accompanied with the exclusion of dependent votes, but *to a counter-mass* of corruption, to be drawn from the East Indies—it was to the *"fallacious show of disinterestedness"* made by this his *Economy Bill,* already carried and turned into an act, that he trusted for that blind support, which he had looked for at the hands of a supposed blinded people. The result is known to everybody.

As to the picture we here see him drawing, it was, at the time of his thus drawing it, half history, half prophecy: the prophetic part left unfinished, as everything in the shape of prophecy must necessarily be.

The picture dramatized, the characters and other objects in it might stand as follows:—

1. *"Ambitious man,"* Edmund Burke.

2. *"Fallacious show of disinterestedness:"* the show made by this *economy bill* of his, with the inconsiderable retrenchments (£60,000 a-year, or some such matter) effected by it.

3. *"Competitors run down"* by means of it (in addition to the force derived from other sources, such as the unpopularity and ill success of the American war, together with the exertions of arbitrary vengeance in the case of Wilkes, &c.) Lord North and his ministry then in power, with the secret advisers of the crown for their support.

4. Instrument attempted to be made *for the "fixing himself in power,"* Burke's East India bill: a steadiment, containing in it a sort of pump, contrived for drawing from the East Indies the matter of *wealth,* to be applied in the character of matter of *corruption,* by hands of his own choice, to the purpose of engaging a sufficient number of workmen for the fixing him and his party as above, to wit, with such a force of resistance as it should not be in the power of the secret advisers of the crown, with all the assistance they could get from the people, to overcome.

As to the particular *"course,"* which, for the purpose of reaping the fruits of his conquest, had this machinery of his succeeded, it might have happened to him to take, and with the word *indemnity* in his mouth, the quantity of public money he might *have claimed,*—so it is, that his grand instrument of steadiment and *"fixation"* having failed, all these, together with so many other *quondam* future contingencies, remain in darkness inscrutable. But, supposing the indemnity no more than *"ten times"* the amount of the sacrifice, still would it have fallen short, as anybody may see, of the ground prepared for it by this his speech.

Some years after, viz. about the year 1790, a decent quantity of public money, even though not in office, he did contrive to get: but forasmuch as for this donation there was a pretence made out of a pamphlet, with the help of which the embers of war between Britain and France were blown into a flame, and, for security against anarchy, the good people of Great Britain driven, as far as by his pious endeavours they could be driven, into the arms of despotism, so it was, that the bread of *sinecure*—the sacred *shew-bread,* destined and appropriated to the chief priests of the temple of corruption—was not, any part of it, profaned and diverted to this use: reward in the ordinary shape of *pension* being regarded as applicable to, and sufficient for, this ordinary service. (pp. 299-300)

Money is a good thing—a very good thing indeed: and, if it were not a good thing, scarce would anything else be; for there are few good things which a man may not get by means of it—get, either in exchange for it, or (what is still better) even without parting with it.

But the misfortune is, that from us the people, for paying orators of the class of Edmund Burke, it is not to be had without our being forced to part with it: and if the orator suffer in case of his not having it—in case of his never having got so much of it as he could have wished, we the people, who, after having had it, find ourselves, for the use and benefit of the orator, forced to part with it, suffer still more.

Thence it is, that if there be anything else, which, the people not feeling themselves forced to part with it, the orator can persuade himself to be satisfied with, so much the better. Upon this plan, everybody is satisfied—orator and people both: whereas, upon the orator's plan, only one of the parties is satisfied, viz. the orator—the orator, who is the agent and spokesman of *the ruling few;* while the other party, viz. we the people, are suffering and grumbling, and as it should seem not altogether without reason; for we are *the many;* and in our number consists our title to regard: a very unpretending title, but not the less a good and sufficient one. (p. 301)

Jeremy Bentham, "Official Aptitude Maximized—Expense Minimized: Defence of Economy against Burke," in his The Works of Jeremy Bentham, Vol. V, *William Tait, 1843, pp. 282-301.*

SAMUEL TAYLOR COLERIDGE (essay date 1817)

[*An English poet and critic, Coleridge was central to the English Romantic movement and is considered one of the greatest literary critics in the English language. Besides his poetry, his most important contributions include his formulation of Romantic theories, his introduction of the ideas of the German Romantics to England, and his Shakespearean criticism, which overthrew the last remnants of the Neoclassical approach to Shakespeare and focused on the dramatist as a masterful portrayer of human character. In a portion of his* Biographia Literaria *not excerpted here, Coleridge asserts that "in Mr. Burke's writings indeed the germs of almost all political truths may be found." In the following excerpt, he attests to Burke's pervasive influence on English politics.*]

[If] unanimity grounded on moral feelings has been among the least equivocal sources of our national glory, that man deserves the esteem of his countrymen, even as patriots, who devotes his life and the utmost efforts of his intellect to the preservation and continuance of that unanimity by the disclosure and establishment of principles. For by these all opinions must be ultimately tried; and (as the feelings of men are worthy of regard only as far as they are the representatives of their fixed opinions) on the knowledge of these all unanimity, not accidental and fleeting, must be grounded. Let the scholar who doubts this assertion refer only to the speeches and writings of Edmund Burke at the commencement of the American war, and compare them with his speeches and writings at the commencement of the French revolution. He will find the principles exactly the same and the deductions the same; but the practical inferences almost opposite in the one case from those drawn in the other; yet in both equally legitimate and in both equally confirmed by the results. Whence gained he this superiority of foresight? Whence arose the striking difference, and in most instances even the discrepancy between the grounds assigned by him, and by those who voted with him, on the same question? How are we to explain the notorious fact that the speeches and writings of Edmund Burke are more interesting at the present day than they were found at the time of their first publication; while those of his illustrious confederates are either forgotten, or exist only to furnish proofs that the same conclusion which one man had deduced scientifically *may* be brought out by another in consequence of errors that luckily chanced to neutralize each other. It would be unhandsome as a conjecture, even were it not, as it actually is, false in point of fact, to attribute this difference to deficiency of talent on the part of Burke's friends, or of experience, or of historical knowledge. The satisfactory solution is that Edmund Burke possessed and had sedulously sharpened that eye which sees all things, actions and events in relation to the laws that determine their existence and circumscribe their possibility. He referred habitually to principles. He was a scientific statesman; and therefore a seer. For every principle contains in itself the germs of a prophecy; and as the prophetic power is the essential privilege of science, so the fulfilment of its oracles supplies the outward and (to men in general) the only test of its claim to the title. Wearisome as Burke's refinements appeared to his parliamentary auditors, yet the cultivated classes throughout Europe have reason to be thankful that

————he went on refining,
And thought of convincing, while they thought of dining.

Our very sign-boards (said an illustrious friend to me) give evidence that there has been a Titian in the world. In like manner not only the debates in parliament, not only our proclamations and state papers, but the essays and leading paragraphs of our journals are so many remembrancers of Edmund Burke. Of this the reader may easily convince himself, if either by recollection or reference he will compare the opposition newspapers at the commencement and during the five or six following years of the French revolution with the sentiments and grounds of argument assumed in the same class of journals at present, and for some years past. (pp. 104-06)

Samuel Taylor Coleridge, in an extract from his Biographia Literaria; or, Biographical Sketches of My Literary Life and Opinions, *1817. Reprint by J. M. Dent & Sons Ltd., 1975, pp. 104-06.*

[THOMAS DE QUINCEY] (essay date 1828)

[*An English critic and essayist, De Quincey chronicled his own life and his addiction to opium in his best-known work,* Confessions of an English Opium Eater *(1822). He contributed reviews to a number of London journals and earned a reputation as an insightful if occasionally long-winded literary critic. In the twentieth century, some critics still disdain·the digressive qualities of De Quincey's writing, though many find that his essays display an acute psychological awareness. In the following excerpt from a survey of rhetoric and orators, he emphasizes Burke's preeminence as a rhetorician.*]

All hail to Edmund Burke, the supreme writer of his century, the man of the largest and finest understanding! Upon that word, *understanding*, we lay a stress: for oh! ye immortal donkeys, who have written "about him and about him," with what an obstinate stupidity have ye brayed away for one third of a century about that which ye are pleased to call his "fancy." Fancy in your thoats, ye miserable twaddlers! as if Edmund Burke were the man to play with his fancy, for the purpose of separable ornament. He was a man of fancy in no other sense than as Lord Bacon was so, and Jeremy Taylor, and as all large and discursive thinkers are and must be: that is to say, the fancy which he had in common with all mankind, and very probably in no eminent degree, in him was urged into unusual activity under the necessities of his capacious understanding. His great and peculiar distinction was that he viewed all objects of the understanding under more relations than other men, and under more complex relations,. According to the multiplicity of these relations, a man is said to have a *large* understanding; according to their subtlety, a *fine* one; and in an angelic understanding all things would appear to be related to all. Now, to apprehend and detect moral relations, or to pursue them steadily, is a process absolutely impossible without the intervention of physical analogies. To say, therefore, that a man is a great thinker, or a fine thinker, is but another expression for saying that he has a *schematizing* (or, to use a plainer but less accurate expression, a figurative) understanding. In that sense, and for that purpose, Burke is figurative: but understood, as he *has* been understood by the long-eared race of his critics, not as thinking in and by his figures, but as deliberately laying them on by way of enamel or after ornament,—not as *incarnating*, but simply as *dressing* his thoughts in imagery,—so understood, he is not the Burke of reality, but a poor fictitious Burke, modelled after the poverty of conception which belongs to his critics. (pp. 899-900)

[Thomas De Quincey], "Elements of Rhetoric," in Blackwood's Edinburgh Magazine, *Vol. XXIV, No. CXLVII, December, 1828, pp. 885-908.*

Thomas Babington Macaulay, "Southey's 'Collo-quies on Society'," in The Edinburgh Review, *Vol. L, No. C, January, 1830, pp. 528-65.*

THOMAS BABINGTON MACAULAY (essay date 1830)

[*Macaulay was a distinguished historian, essayist, and politician of mid-nineteenth-century England. For many years he was a major contributor of erudite, highly opinionated articles to the* Edinburgh Review. *Besides these essays, collected in* Critical and Historical Essays *(1843), his most enduring work is his five-volume* History of England from the Accession of James II *(1849-61), which, despite criticism of its strong bias toward the Whig party, is esteemed for its consummate rhetorical and narrative prose. According to Richard Tobias, Macaulay was a writer who "feared sentiment and preferred distance, objectivity, dispassionate vision. Yet withal, he was a brilliant writer who . . . is still capable of moving a reader by sheer verbal excitement." In the following excerpt from a review of Robert Southey's* Sir Thomas More; or, Colloquies on the Progress and Prospects of Society *(1829), Macaulay discusses the juxtaposition of reason and emotionalism in Burke's character.*]

[Mr. Burke] possessed an understanding admirably fitted for the investigation of truth,—an understanding stronger than that of any statesman, active or speculative, of the eighteenth century,—stronger than every thing, except his own fierce and ungovernable sensibility. Hence, he generally chose his side like a fanatic, and defended it like a philosopher. His conduct, in the most important events of his life,—at the time of the impeachment of Hastings, for example, and at the time of the French Revolution,—seems to have been prompted by those feelings and motives, which Mr Coleridge has so happily described:

> Stormy pity, and the cherish'd lure
> Of pomp, and proud precipitance of soul.

Hindostan, with its vast cities, its gorgeous pagodas, its infinite swarms of dusky population, its long-descended dynasties, its stately etiquette, excited in a mind so capacious, so imaginative, and so susceptible, the most intense interest. The peculiarities of the costume, of the manners, and of the laws, the very mystery which hung over the language and origin of the people, seized his imagination. To plead in Westminster Hall, in the name of the English people, at the bar of the English nobles, for great nations and kings separated from him by half the world, seemed to him the height of human glory. Again, it is not difficult to perceive, that his hostility to the French Revolution principally arose from the vexation which he felt, at having all his old political associations disturbed, at seeing the well-known boundary-marks of states obliterated, and the names and distinctions with which the history of Europe had been filled for ages, swept away. He felt like an antiquarian whose shield had been scoured, or a connoisseur, who found his Titian retouched. But however he came by an opinion, he had no sooner got it, than he did his best to make out a legitimate title to it. His reason, like a spirit in the service of an enchanter, though spell-bound, was still mighty. It did whatever work his passions and his imagination might impose. But it did that work, however arduous, with marvellous dexterity and vigour. His course was not determined by argument; but he could defend the wildest course by arguments more plausible, than those by which common men support opinions which they have adopted, after the fullest deliberation. Reason has scarcely ever displayed, even in those well-constituted minds of which she occupies the throne, so much power and energy as in the lowest offices of that imperial servitude. (pp. 528-29)

RALPH WALDO EMERSON (lecture date 1835)

[*Emerson was one of the most influential figures of the nineteenth century. An American essayist and poet, he founded the Transcendental movement and shaped a distinctly American philosophy embracing optimism, individuality, and mysticism. His philosophy stresses the presence of ongoing creation and revelation by a god apparent in everything and everyone, as well as the essential unity of all thoughts, persons, and things in the divine whole. In the following excerpt from the text of a lecture delivered in 1835, he discusses Burke's intellectual nature and philosophical heritage, political causes, oratory, and social influence.*]

The great variety of [Burke's] accomplishments, the superiority of his genius to all competitors at that time or before or since in the same walks, and the nearness of our position even at this hour to him and the events which he studied, make it difficult to speak of him with confidence as a man whose claims Time the judge has considered and decided. Certainly it is not in the formal biographies of him that his merits have been determined. I can almost call a biography the admirable satire in Goldsmith's "Retaliation" which with the allowance to be made for satire, embodies so much truth in every line and word, that, trite as it is, I shall be pardoned for repeating it.

> Here lies our good Edmund whose genius was such
> We scarcely can praise it or blame it too much
> Who born for the Universe narrowed his mind
> And to party gave up what was meant for mankind. . .
> Though equal to all things for all things unfit
> Too nice for a statesman, too proud for a wit,
> For a patriot too cool for a drudge disobedient
> And too fond of the right to pursue the expedient
> In short twas his fate unemployed or in place sir
> To eat mutton cold, and cut blocks with a razor.

The great contemporaries of this man who cooperated with him and outran him in the race of power and personal consideration in society he has long already left behind. The once sunbright names of Fox and Pitt and Sheridan have become pale and faint. Burke once interested the politician as a supporter or opposer of these men. They now derive all their interest from their relation to him. They now plead their rival pretensions before a very different tribunal from the people of London or the majority of the Parliament. There is no caprice and no chance in the final award upon human merit. A dim, venerable Public decides upon every work and upon every man. When a new book or a new man emerges into consequence a sort of perplexity, an uneasy waiting for judgment appears in the minds of the spectators and most in those who are the oracles of the day, but the new pretender presently takes his true place by a force which no furtherance can help and no opposition can hinder, namely, by the real importance of his doing and thinking to the constant mind of man.

It may be that the very perceptible connexion between the events which Burke influenced and those amidst which we live, does not suffer us yet to escape from all optical illusion, exaggerating this or that part of characters related to the American and French Revolutions, yet we shall endeavor to ascend to that verdict which is formed or forming upon his life in the permanent public opinion.

It has rarely happened in history that a philosopher by genius should be called to take any important part in the administration of affairs. Not only a prejudice often envenomed is against them among vulgar minds, but for the most part their own incapacity for action and strong disinclination to business forbids. The emperor Marcus Aurelius is an eminent and almost solitary example within the period of certain history of a philosopher on a throne. (pp. 185-86)

Nicholas Machiavel, who in the beginning of the sixteenth century served the Florentine state with great ability in various employments for many years chiefly at foreign courts and gave on some occasions valuable advice at home, is another example of a philosopher engaged in politics. But the Florentine territory was so narrow and its foreign relations so unimportant that his influence is too small to be taken into the account of European history.

Lord Bacon is the first conspicuous example of modern times of the philosopher in action. He certainly possessed an eminent ability in both kinds. To him was given a sight like that of an archangel into the Present and the Future. He saw things before they were yet out of the doors of their causes, and has left the most remarkable generalizations of the history of literature, of science, and even of social man that are on record. He is in a long series of generations the great Secretary of philosophy. At the same time he was all too skilful in much meaner arts. He was by taste and by practice a cunning statesman, preferring on every occasion the expedient to the right and very adroit in the use of all means to petty ends. (p. 187)

Edmund Burke, another philosopher who entered the House of Commons in 1765, has some points of resemblance to . . . these men. He had the piety of the Roman Emperor, a sentiment of reverence to virtue that was omnipresent with him and pervaded and exalted every thing he did or said. But by position and by genius he had an intellect infintely more comprehensive and minutely informed. He saw all things from his own point of view but in a glance that shot so far and grasped so much that particular objects still seemed to occupy their proportionate place, and whilst he magnified them they did yet not break the harmony of nature. The concerns of the Roman Empire great as they were cannot vie in complexity or extent with those of the British Government at this period. Despotism is simple and as yet the people were governed as a mass and did not insist on being considered as individuals.

He can even be compared to Bacon in some of Bacon's excellences. As wonderful was his mastery of language; as minute his observation upon manners, trades, arts, ceremonies; as great his address in the dispatch of business; as perfect the dependence of his imagination upon his Understanding, so far as composition is concerned. Not so masculine a judgment as Bacon who never multiplies words. Burke is diffuse. He cannot deny himself the pleasure of fully expanding all the particulars. Bacon draws his grand designs. Every word is as essential as a figure in a date. Burke draws his design and finishes and decorates and gilds every head. (Bacon's Political Tracts are much inferior to Burke's.) With Bacon in literature, with Bacon as an observer and legislator for the human intellect, Burke can never compare. Then Bacon seems to be merely a mouth for the soul of the World. But in the House of Commons and in the part taken by them in public affairs, the advantage is forever with Burke, not only as it seems to me in the sincerity with which the latter acted, but in the enlargement of his view and the fitness and grace of his execution. Bacon treats particular affairs like a lawyer, devises expedients, and considers all the facts; Burke treats his business as a piece of the world,

and quitting temporary expedients seeks to harmonize it with the whole constitution of Society.

Bacon's philosophy deserts him in business. His general remarks sound formal and pedantic. Burke actually applies his philosophy in good faith to the point in question. He was favored . . . by the immensity of the province he had to govern. The government administered by the leaders of opinion [of] the English House of Commons in the close of the eighteenth century was so vast, so complicated by the variety of gross interests and still more by the resistless importance of individuals, that it had really become of importance to a philosopher on its own account. In the other cases the philosopher might forsake his study to get the profit and rank of a part in government. Now, the public business had arisen to that dignity as to solicit the philosopher. It offered him a field for his study, a work worthy of his faculties, to introduce method into so great masses of facts and to second the natural efforts at organization of time and wealth by the direct application of principles.

This is the position which he occupies in the last age, the *philosophical politician*, not a man who, quoting Latin and German, Aristotle and Hume, acted with a total disregard to general principles,—but one who, drawing from the same fountain with these theorists, brought principles to bear upon the public business of England.

But this view is subject to some limitations. Mr. Burke was never a philosopher in the highest nor in the lowest use of that term. He was never of the French School or the recent English Schools of politics, neither agrarian nor Utopian. He did not propose to satisfy the wishes of the majority as they are, with one class, nor to legislate for human nature as it ought to be, with Plato and Rousseau. He did not establish his theory of government in his chambers and then go into Parliament with the design to make the experiment of it on the British nation. He did not begin at this end. But led by a strong delight which he took in watching public affairs he spent his days in the gallery of the House of Commons long before he was a member of that body and studying intensely, as was his habit, the course of business, and the characters of public men, he soon became a proficient and afterwards a master in the facts. But nothing could come out of his mind in the state in which it went in. His mental activity quickened and arranged without transforming every fact, every event. Things fell in his mind into associations of a new and natural kind. That which he saw disordered, assumed order in his own thought.

And all men were amazed to see how rapidly the most heterogeneous business took in his own mind a certain shape of proportion and yet without misrepresentation or neglect of any parts. I speak now not of particular instances, though there are several in point, but of the general character of his usefulness: That it is a characteristic of this man's wisdom, that he did not take his theory as a basis, and force the facts into a conformity thereto, but he took the facts as the base and reduced them by the illumination of his genius into the best order which they themselves admitted, and, as it always seemed when he announced it, a natural and perfect order.

The light therefore in which he appears to us is as the Conservative of modern times; but this in an exalted and quite peculiar sense, the teacher of order, peace, and elegance; the adorner of existing institutions, but, combining therewith a fire of affection, and a depth of virtuous sentiment that add heroism to his wisdom.

But almost the uniform tendency of men of thought coupled with ardent temper has been to the freest institutions; has been democratic rather than royalist. What made Burke who, even in opposition, is yet conservative, lean so strongly to establishments?

There are many elements which appear in the life of Burke, that serve to explain this determination of his character, and show why his love of liberty and his fondness for theory, did not produce their usual effect by making him a radical Reformer.

And first, his exquisite Taste. As a general observation I suppose it will hold, that men of fine taste are not fond of revolutions. As Fontenelle said, "I hate War, for it spoils conversation," so, Taste is pacific; the objects on which it is conversant only collect themselves in quiet and stable communities. Books, poems, the drama, learning, architecture, painting, sculpture, elegant society, fine manners, of all these was Edmund Burke very fond and in them all very skilful. Calm times and monarchy have always been observed to favor them, and he looked with affection to the historical names and renowned laws of his country, under whose shadow he had found them. The particular regard he gave to these objects, demonstrates his attachment. He wrote a Theory of Taste. He was the intimate friend of Sir Joshua Reynolds and of Barry. He has been supposed to have given assistance to the former in his lectures; to the latter he gave advice which seems to show his eye for art to have been equal to his ear for eloquence.

Moreover not the least of his talents was his skill in conversation. He taxed the powers of Johnson, who declared that Burke was the only great man whose conversation was equal to his reputation, adding that "no man could talk with him under an archway during a shower, without finding him out." And England has probably never contained more brilliant circles than at that moment. (pp. 188-91)

The affectionate, childlike sweetness of this man's temper which endeared to him his friends, his neighbors, his countrymen, naturally inclined him to take favorable views of the laws and the historical institutions of the state. May I add the remark made to me by an ingenious friend upon Burke's strong partiality for Establishments: That as in every civilized country a man is exalted by the courtesy and respect he pays to woman, so Burke felt that the wise and influential citizen is exalted by the honor he pays to whatever venerable or elegant institutions exist in the land. It was a chivalrous feeling which led him freely to bestow a protection which he might have withheld.

Meantime it was the natural effect of the same elevation of his sentiments that he was no vulgar conservative. Believing that in the British Constitution rightly administered would be found within this boundary a remedy for every mischief he was found a steadfast friend of liberty, of humanity, the redresser of wrong. The British House of Commons whilst Burke was in it was an asylum of the earth. Every cause of humanity found in him its lover and defender. The terrors of the Constitution he turned against every cruelty and selfishness. (pp. 193-94)

The oppression by the Crown of the Americans stimulated him to his great exertions in their behalf. He was member for Bristol. A proposition to revise some oppressive restrictions on the trade of Ireland, he advocated earnestly. Bristol which with other trading towns found its own advantage in this oppression, called upon him to maintain her views. Mr. Burke refused to comply, and in consequence lost his reelection. The East Indians had been cruelly oppressed by the Company. Burke never ceased to fill the House with his indignation and entreaty until

at last the Governor was impeached and the opportunity given him to open the whole enormous history of Indian tyranny. So was it with his voice of warning against the contagious spirit of the French Revolution until he had turned the tide of public sentiment.

On all these, on all his questions he squandered himself as if each were his own cause. Never labor hindered him, never fear, never pride. (p. 195)

Such were the traits [which] swayed his mind originally and habitually towards the side of the existing order and at the same time made him from first to last a wise reformer. He brought to the service of his country the lights of his philosophy, the almost novel ability of treating business according to higher laws than the rules of office or the interests of party, and the additional aid of an industry as indefatigable. The effects were proportionate. By an insight into principles he foretold with eloquent boldness the course and issue of the measures he opposed. Nobody regarded the prediction until day after day and month after month still fulfilled them. This abstract metaphysician soon became the oracle of the House upon the whole subject of Commerce. Adam Smith declared that Mr. Burke was the only man who had arrived at his conclusions without previous communication. The House soon found that in the hands of this wonderful person who rivalled Shakspear in his fancy and a banker or tradesman in his acquaintance with details every business became a text of political and economical philosophy; the Ministers and the Opposition were alike instructed and did not fail to profit continually of the lesson, though they neglected their teacher. His influence over the great leaders of the Whig Party was unbounded especially over Mr. Fox. For his wisdom and his labor and his fervor gave him a habitual ascendency. He is the author of the measures which they often conducted to an end. Finally on the outbreak of the French Revolution he foresaw and foretold not only the whole course but almost the single incidents with such memorable accuracy that he seems ever to speak on secret information, and he sounded such an alarm through England and the World [in his *Reflections on the Revolution in France*] that he raised up everywhere a hostile party and did more than any except the atrocities of the French themselves to destroy the influence of revolutionary principles in England. (pp. 195-96)

It is said of Demosthenes that when one day his voice failing him, the people hissed, he exclaimed, "Ye are to judge of players indeed by the clearness and tuneableness of their voice but of orators by the gravity and excellence of their sentences." Mr. Burke, whose voice was harsh, and whose action was not graceful but forcible, and who gave a half support never, but threw his whole soul into his cause, might have well put in the same plea against the occasional caprice and weariness of his audience. There is even a striking parallelism in the anecdotes related of the effect produced by these two. Philip of Macedon in a moment of enthusiasm on hearing the report of one of his speeches from an earwitness exclaimed, "Had I been there, I too should have declared war against myself." And Warren Hastings attested by a similar confession the force of Burke's harrowing description of the crimes of the monster Debi Sing by whom he charged the Governor General with having been bribed. "For half an hour," said Mr. Hastings, "I looked up at the orator in a reverie of wonder, and during that space I actually felt myself the most culpable man on earth." And the existing report of that speech is singular in all recorded eloquence for the horror and indignation it awakens.

I think that the evidence remaining on this subject warrants us in believing that there were moments in Mr. Burke's life when he did embody the idea of eloquence, when he did fill the ear and mind and heart of his hearers and produce the perfect triumph of the orator which consists in the oneness of his audience. And I must say that when such a man as he was, accomplished this end by such means as he used, then was shown an art that soared above all the praise of Demosthenes or of any civil orator.

But I confess I see no strong resemblance between the Athenian and the Englishman. The points of difference admit of being more strongly marked. The obvious character of Demosthenes is his abstemiousness. King Philip said that his orations were soldiers. Mr. Burke's might be called, wise men. And as much more effective as is a soldier than a wise man is this world in coming directly to his end, that is the difference between the success of Burke and that of Demosthenes. (pp. 198-99)

Whether or not Mr. Burke judged wisely in the part he took on the French Revolution is the question on which most persons according as they answer it fix their views on him. That he judged wisely for his own time and country will be by most conceded. No doubt he was unconsciously biased by his taste and imagination. When he espoused the cause of liberty in America, America was empty of all things that could dazzle his love of right, no establishments, no privileges. But in Europe the same question was not simple but complicated with ruin to ancient institutions, laws, nobility, priesthood, and crown. And these [were] menaced and uprooted with such ferocity in France that I suppose the boldest lover of freedom if he love virtue also might well hesitate to decide between the continuance of tyranny and the outrageous abuses of freedom. (p. 201)

Ralph Waldo Emerson, "Biography: Edmund Burke," in his The Early Lectures of Ralph Waldo Emerson: 1833-1836, Vol. I, *Cambridge, Mass.: Harvard University Press, 1959, pp. 183-201.*

HENRY THOMAS BUCKLE   (essay date 1857)

[*An English historian, Buckle is remembered for his unfinished* The History of Civilization in England *(1857-61), in which he intended to review the whole of English history by means of an exacting, scientific methodology. John M. Robertson, editor of a later edition of this work, has capsulized Buckle's significance in the following statement: "Where Darwin definitely brought within the scope of scientific law the phenomena of biology, as previous pioneers had done those of geology and astronomy, Buckle began anew the most complicated and difficult task of all—the reduction to law of the phenomenon of social evolution." In the following excerpt from the 1857 introduction to his* History, *Buckle forwards what has been termed a utilitarian estimation of Burke's political significance. Buckle, however, emphasizes Burke's betrayal, during the French Revolution, of his humanitarian, utilitarian principles.*]

[In Burke's] hands nothing was barren. Such was the strength and exuberance of his intellect that it bore fruit in all directions, and could confer dignity upon the meanest subjects, by showing their connexion with general principles, and the part they have to play in the great scheme of human affairs.

But what has always appeared to me still more remarkable in the character of Burke is the singular sobriety with which he employed his extraordinary acquirements. During the best part of his life, his political principles, so far from being speculative, were altogether practical. This is particularly striking, because he had every temptation to adopt an opposite course.

He possessed materials for generalization far more ample than any politician of his time, and he had a mind eminently prone to take large views. On many occasions, and indeed whenever an opportunity occurred, he showed his capacity as an original and speculative thinker. But the moment he set foot on political ground, he changed his method. In questions connected with the accumulation and distribution of wealth, he saw that it was possible, by proceeding from a few simple principles, to construct a deductive science available for the commercial and financial interests of the country. Further than this he refused to advance, because he knew that, with this single exception, every department of politics was purely empirical, and was likely long to remain so. Hence it was that he recognized in all its bearings that great doctrine which even in our own days is too often forgotten, that the aim of the legislator should be, not truth, but expediency. Looking at the actual state of knowledge, he was forced to admit that all political principles have been raised by hasty induction from limited facts; and that therefore it is the part of a wise man, when he adds to the facts, to revise the induction, and, instead of sacrificing practice to principles, modify the principles that he may change the practice. Or, to put this in another way, he lays it down that political principles are at best but the product of human reason; while political practice has to do with human nature and human passions, of which reason forms but a part; and that, on this account, the proper business of a statesman is to contrive the means by which certain ends may be effected, leaving it to the general voice of the country to determine what those ends shall be, and shaping his own conduct, not according to his own principles, but according to the wishes of the people for whom he legislates, and whom he is bound to obey.

It is these views, and the extraordinary ability with which they were advocated, which make the appearance of Burke a memorable epoch in our political history. We had, no doubt, other statesmen before him who denied the validity of general principles in politics; but their denial was only the happy guess of ignorance and they rejected theories which they had never taken the pains to study. Burke rejected them because he knew them. It was his rare merit that, notwithstanding every inducement to rely upon his own generalizations, he resisted the temptation; that, though rich in all the varieties of political knowledge, he made his opinions subservient to the march of events; that he recognized as the object of government, not the preservation of particular institutions, nor the propagation of particular tenets, but the happiness of the people at large; and, above all, that he insisted upon an obedience to the popular wishes which no statesman before him had paid, and which too many statesmen since him have forgotten. Our country, indeed, is still full of those vulgar politicians against whom Burke raised his voice; feeble and shallow men, who, having spent their little force in resisting the progress of reform, find themselves at length compelled to yield; and then, so soon as they have exhausted the artifices of their petty schemes, and by their tardy and ungraceful concessions have sown the seed of future disaffection, turn upon the age by which they have been baffled; they mourn over the degeneracy of mankind; they lament the decay of public spirit; and they weep for the fate of a people, who have been so regardless of the wisdom of their ancestors as to tamper with a constitution already hoary with the prescription of centuries.

Those who have studied the reign of George III. will easily understand the immense advantage of having a man like Burke to oppose these miserable delusions; delusions which have been fatal to many countries, and have more than once almost ruined our own. They will also understand that, in the opinion of the king, this great statesman was at best but an eloquent declaimer, to be classed in the same category with Fox and Chatham; all three ingenious men, but unsafe, unsteady, quite unfit for weighty concerns, and by no means calculated for so exalted an honour as admission into the royal councils. In point of fact, during the thirty years Burke was engaged in public life, he never once held an office in the cabinet; and the only occasions on which he occupied even a subordinate post, were in those very short intervals when the fluctuations of politics compelled the appointment of a liberal ministry.

Indeed, the part taken by Burke in public affairs must have been very galling to a king who thought everything good that was old, and everything right that was established. For, so far was this remarkable man in advance of his contemporaries, that there are few of the great measures of the present generation which he did not anticipate and zealously defend. Not only did he attack the absurd laws against forestalling and regrating, but, by advocating the freedom of trade, he struck at the root of all similar prohibitions. He supported those just claims of the Catholics which, during his lifetime, were obstinately refused; but which were conceded, many years after his death, as the only means of preserving the integrity of the empire. He supported the petition of the Dissenters, that they might be relieved from the restrictions to which, for the benefit of the Church of England, they were subjected. Into other departments of politics he carried the same spirit. He opposed the cruel laws against insolvents, by which, in the time of George III., our statute-book was still defaced; and he vainly attempted to soften the penal code, the increasing severity of which was one of the worst features of that bad reign. He wished to abolish the old plan of enlisting soldiers for life; a barbarous and impolitic practice, as the English legislature began to perceive several years later. He attacked the slave-trade; which, being an ancient usage, the king wished to preserve, as part of the British constitution. He refuted, but, owing to the prejudices of the age, was unable to subvert, the dangerous power exercised by the judges, who, in criminal prosecutions for libel, confined the jury to the mere question of publication; thus taking the real issue into their own hands, and making themselves the arbiters of the fate of those who were so unfortunate as to be placed at their bar. And, what many will think not the least of his merits, he was the first in that long line of financial reformers to whom we are deeply indebted. Notwithstanding the difficulties thrown in his way, he carried through parliament a series of bills by which several useless places were entirely abolished, and, in the single office of paymaster-general, a saving effected to the country of 25,000*l.* a year.

These things alone are sufficient to explain the animosity of a prince whose boast it was that he would bequeath the government to his successor in the same state as that in which he had received it. There was, however, another circumstance by which the royal feelings were still further wounded. The determination of the king to oppress the Americans was so notorious that when the war actually broke out it was called ''the king's war;'' and those who opposed it were regarded as the personal enemies of their sovereign. In this, however, as in all other questions, the conduct of Burke was governed, not by traditions and principles such as George III. cherished, but by large views of general expediency. Burke, in forming his opinions respecting this disgraceful contest, refused to be guided by arguments respecting the right of either party. He would not enter into any discussion as to whether a mother-country has the right to

tax her colonies, or whether the colonies have a right to tax themselves. Such points he left to be mooted by those politicians who, pretending to be guided by principles, are in reality subjugated by prejudice. For his own part, he was content to compare the cost with the gain. It was enough for Burke that, considering the power of our American colonies, considering their distance from us, and considering the probability of their being aided by France, it was not advisable to exercise the power; and it was therefore idle to talk of the right. Hence he opposed the taxation of America, not because it was unprecedented, but because it was inexpedient. As a natural consequence, he likewise opposed the Boston-Port Bill, and that shameful bill to forbid all intercourse with America, which was not inaptly called the starvation plan; violent measures by which the king hoped to curb the colonies, and break the spirit of those noble men, whom he hated even more than he feared.

It is certainly no faint characteristic of those times that a man like Burke, who dedicated to politics abilities equal to far nobler things, should during thirty years have received from his prince neither favour nor reward. But George III. was a king whose delight it was to raise the humble and exalt the meek. His reign, indeed, was the golden age of successful mediocrity; an age in which little men were favoured, and great men depressed; when Addington was cherished as a statesman, and Beattie pensioned as a philosopher; and when, in all the walks of public life, the first conditions of promotion were, to fawn upon ancient prejudices, and support established abuses.

This neglect of the most eminent of English politicians is highly instructive; but the circumstances which followed, though extremely painful, have a still deeper interest, and are well worth the attention of those whose habits of mind lead them to study the intellectual peculiarities of great men.

For, at this distance of time, when his nearest relations are no more, it would be affectation to deny that Burke, during the last few years of his life, fell into a state of complete hallucination. When the French Revolution broke out, his mind, already fainting under the weight of incessant labour, could not support the contemplation of an event so unprecedented, so appalling, and threatening results of such frightful magnitude. And when the crimes of that great revolution, instead of diminishing, continued to increase, then it was that the feelings of Burke finally mastered his reason; the balance tottered; the proportions of that gigantic intellect were disturbed. From this moment, his sympathy with present suffering was so intense, that he lost all memory of the tyranny by which the sufferings were provoked. His mind, once so steady, so little swayed by prejudice and passion, reeled under the pressure of events which turned the brains of thousands. And whoever will compare the spirit of his latest works with the dates of their publication, will see how this melancholy change was aggravated by that bitter bereavement from which he never rallied, and which alone was sufficient to prostrate the understanding of one in whom the severity of the reason was so tempered, so nicely poised, by the warmth of the affections. Never, indeed, can there be forgotten those touching, those exquisite allusions to the death of that only son who was the joy of his soul and the pride of his heart, and to whom he fondly hoped to bequeath the inheritance of his imperishable name. Never can we forget that image of desolation, under which the noble old man figured his immeasurable grief. ''I live in an inverted order. They who ought to have succeeded me, have gone before me. They who should have been to me as posterity, are in the place of ancestors. . . . The storm has gone over me, and I lie like one of those old oaks which the late hurricane has scattered about me. I am stripped of all my honours; I am torn up by the roots, and lie prostrate on the earth.''

It would perhaps be displaying a morbid curiosity, to attempt to raise the veil, and trace the decay of so mighty a mind. Indeed, in all such cases, most of the evidence perishes; for those who have the best opportunities of witnessing the infirmities of a great man, are not those who most love to relate them. But it is certain that the change was first clearly seen immediately after the breaking out of the French Revolution; that it was aggravated by the death of his son; and that it became progressively worse till death closed the scene. In his *Reflections on the French Revolution*; in his *Remarks on the Policy of the Allies*; in his *Letter to Elliot*; in his *Letter to a Noble Lord*; and in his *Letters on a Regicide Peace,* we may note the consecutive steps of an increasing, and at length an uncontrollable violence. To the single principle of hatred of the French Revolution, he sacrificed his oldest associations and his dearest friends. Fox, as is well known, always looked up to Burke as to a master, from whose lips he had gathered the lessons of political wisdom. Burke, on his side, fully recognized the vast abilities of his friend, and loved him for that affectionate disposition, and for those winning manners, which, it has often been said, none who saw them could ever resist. But now, without the slightest pretence of a personal quarrel, this long intimacy was rudely severed. Because Fox would not abandon that love of popular liberty which they had long cherished in common, Burke publicly, and in his place in parliament, declared that their friendship was at an end; for that he would never more hold communion with a man who lent his support to the French people. At the same time, and indeed the very evening on which this occurred, Burke, who had hitherto been remarkable for the courtesy of his manners, deliberately insulted another of his friends, who was taking him home in his carriage; and, in a state of frantic excitement, insisted on being immediately set down, in the middle of the night in a pouring rain, because he could not, he said, remain seated by a ''friend to the revolutionary doctrines of the French.''

Nor is it true, as some have supposed, that this mania of hostility was solely directed against the criminal part of the French people. It would be difficult, in that or in any other age, to find two men of more active, or indeed enthusiastic benevolence, than Condorcet and La Fayette. Besides this, Condorcet was one of the most profound thinkers of his time, and will be remembered as long as genius is honoured among us. La Fayette was no doubt inferior to Condorcet in point of ability; but he was the intimate friend of Washington, on whose conduct he modelled his own, and by whose side he had fought for the liberties of America; his integrity was, and still is, unsullied; and his character had a chivalrous and noble turn, which Burke, in his better days, would have been the first to admire. Both, however, were natives of that hated country whose liberties they vainly attempted to achieve. On this account, Burke declared Condorcet to be guilty of ''impious sophistry;'' to be a ''fanatic atheist, and furious democratic republican;'' and to be capable of ''the lowest as well as the highest and most determined villanies.'' As to La Fayette, when an attempt was made to mitigate the cruel treatment he was receiving from the Prussian government, Burke not only opposed the motion made for that purpose in the House of Commons, but took the opportunity of grossly insulting the unfortunate captive, who was then languishing in a dungeon. So dead had he become on this subject, even to the common instincts of our nature, that, in his place in parliament, he could

find no better way of speaking of this injured and high-souled man, than by calling him a ruffian: ''I would not,'' says Burke,—''I would not debase my humanity by supporting an application in behalf of such a horrid ruffian.''

As to France itself, it is ''Cannibal Castle;'' it is ''the republic of assassins;'' it is ''a hell;'' its government is composed of ''the dirtiest, lowest, most fraudulent, most knavish, of chicaners;'' its National Assembly are ''miscreants;'' its people are ''an allied army of Amazonian and male cannibal Parisians;'' they are ''a nation of murderers;'' they are ''the basest of mankind;'' they are ''murderous atheists;'' they are ''a gang of robbers;'' they are ''the prostitute outcasts of mankind;'' they are ''a desperate gang of plunderers, murderers, tyrants, and atheists.'' To make the slightest concessions to such a country in order to preserve peace, is offering victims ''on the altars of blasphemed regicide;'' even to enter into negotiations is ''exposing our lazar sores at the door of every proud servitor of the French republic, where the court-dogs will not deign to lick them.'' When our ambassador was actually in Paris, he ''had the honour of passing his mornings in respectful attendance at the office of a regicide pettifogger;'' and we were taunted with having sent a ''peer of the realm to the scum of the earth.'' France has no longer a place in Europe; it is expunged from the map; its very name should be forgotten. Why, then, need men travel in it? Why need our children learn its language? and why are we to endanger the morals of our ambassadors, who can hardly fail to return from such a land with their principles corrupted, and with a wish to conspire against their own country.

This is sad, indeed, from such a man as Burke once was; but what remains shows still more clearly how the associations and composition of his mind had been altered. He who, with humanity not less than with wisdom, had strenuously laboured to prevent the American war, devoted the last few years of his life to kindle a new war, compared to which that with America was a light and trivial episode. In his calmer moments, no one would have more willingly recognized that the opinions prevalent in any country are the inevitable results of the circumstances in which that country had been placed. But now he sought to alter those opinions by force. From the beginning of the French Revolution, he insisted upon the right, and indeed upon the necessity, of compelling France to change her principles; and, at a later period, he blamed the allied sovereigns for not dictating to a great people the government they ought to adopt. Such was the havoc circumstances had made in his well-ordered intellect, that to this one principle he sacrificed every consideration of justice, of mercy, and of expediency. As if war, even in its mildest form, were not sufficiently hateful, he sought to give to it that character of a crusade which increasing knowledge had long since banished; and loudly proclaiming that the contest was religious rather temporal, he revived old prejudices in order to cause fresh crimes. He also declared that the war should be carried on for revenge as well as for defence, and that we must never lay down our arms until we had utterly destroyed the men by whom the Revolution was brought about. And, as if these things were not enough, he insisted that this, the most awful of all wars, being begun, was not to be hurried over; although it was to be carried on for revenge as well as for religion, and the resources of civilized men were to be quickened by the ferocious passions of crusaders, still it was not to be soon ended; it was to be durable; it must have permanence; it must, says Burke, in the spirit of a burning hatred, be protracted in a long war: ''I speak it emphatically, and with a desire that it should be marked, in a *long* war.''

It was to be a war to force a great people to change their government. It was to be a war carried on for the purpose of punishment. It was also to be a religious war. Finally, it was to be a long war. Was there every any other man who wished to afflict the human race with such extensive, searching, and protracted calamities? Such cruel, such reckless, and yet such deliberate opinions, if they issued from a sane mind, would immortalize even the most obscure statesman, because they would load his name with imperishable infamy. For where can we find, even among the most ignorant or most sanguinary politicians, sentiments like these? Yet they proceed from one who, a very few years before, was the most eminent political philosopher England has ever possessed. To us it is only given to mourn over so noble a wreck. More than this no one should do. We may contemplate with reverence the mighty ruin; but the mysteries of its decay let no man presume to invade, unless, to use the language of the greatest of our masters, he can tell how to minister to a diseased mind, pluck the sorrows which are rooted in the memory, and raze out the troubles that are written in the brain.

It is a relief to turn from so painful a subject, even though we descend to the petty, huckstering politics of the English court. And truly, the history of the treatment experienced by the most illustrious of our politicians is highly characteristic of the prince under whom he lived. While Burke was consuming his life in great public services, labouring to reform our finances, improve our laws, and enlighten our commercial policy,—while he was occupied with these things, the king regarded him with coldness and aversion. But when the great statesman degenerated into an angry brawler; when, irritated by disease, he made it the sole aim of his declining years to kindle a deadly war between the two first countries of Europe, and declared that to this barbarous object he would sacrifice all other questions of policy, however important they might be;—then it was that a perception of his vast abilities began to dawn upon the mind of the king. Before this, no one had been bold enough to circulate in the palace even a whisper of his merits. Now, however, in the successive, and eventually the rapid decline of his powers, he had fallen almost to the level of the royal intellect; and now he was first warmed by the beams of the royal favour. Now he was a man after the king's own heart. Less than two years before his death there were settled upon him, at the express desire of George III., two considerable pensions; and the king even wished to raise him to the peerage, in order that the house of Lords might benefit by the services of so great a counsellor. (pp. 259-69)

Henry Thomas Buckle, "Outline of the History of the English Intellect from the Middle of the Sixteenth to the End of the Eighteenth Century," in Introduction to the History of Civilization in England, *revised edition, 1904. Reprint by Albert and Charles Boni, 1925, pp. 189-285.*

MATTHEW ARNOLD (essay date 1864)

[Arnold is considered one of the most influential authors of the later Victorian period in England. While he is well known today as a poet, in his own time he asserted his greatest influence through his prose writings. Arnold's forceful literary criticism, which is based on his humanistic belief in the value of balance and clarity in literature, significantly shaped modern theory. In the following excerpt from an essay originally published in 1864

in the National Review, *Arnold upholds Burke as a politician of ideas and thus as one of the greatest of English political thinkers.]*

[The French Revolution's] movement of ideas, by quitting the intellectual sphere and rushing furiously into the political sphere, ran, indeed, a prodigious and memorable course, but produced no such intellectual fruit as the movement of ideas of the Renaissance, and created, in opposition to itself, what I may call an *epoch of concentration*. The great force of that epoch of concentration was England; and the great voice of that epoch of concentration was Burke. It is the fashion to treat Burke's writings on the French Revolution as superannuated and conquered by the event; as the eloquent but unphilosophical tirades of bigotry and prejudice. I will not deny that they are often disfigured by the violence and passion of the moment, and that in some directions Burke's view was bounded, and his observation therefore at fault, but on the whole, and for those who can make the needful corrections, what distinguishes these writings is their profound, permanent, fruitful, philosophical truth, they contain the true philosophy of an epoch of concentration, dissipate the heavy atmosphere which its own nature is apt to engender round it, and make its resistance rational instead of mechanical.

But Burke is so great because, almost alone in England, he brings thought to bear upon politics, he saturates politics with thought; it is his accident that his ideas were at the service of an epoch of concentration, not of an epoch of expansion; it is his characteristic that he so lived by ideas, and had such a source of them welling up within him, that he could float even an epoch of concentration and English Tory politics with them. It does not hurt him that Dr Price and the Liberals were displeased with him; it does not even hurt him that George the Third and the Tories were enchanted with him. His greatness is that he lived in a world which neither English Liberalism nor English Toryism is apt to enter;—the world of ideas, not the world of catchwords and party habits. So far is it from being really true of him that he "to party gave up what was meant for mankind," that at the very end of his fierce struggle with the French Revolution, after all his invectives against its false pretensions, hollowness, and madness, with his sincere conviction of its mischievousness, he can close a memorandum on the best means of combating it, some of the last pages he ever wrote,—the *Thoughts on French Affairs*, in December 1791,—with these striking words:—

> The evil is stated, in my opinion, as it exists. The remedy must be where power, wisdom, and information, I hope, are more united with good intentions than they can be with me. I have done with this subject, I believe, for ever. It has given me many anxious moments for the last two years. *If a great change is to be made in human affairs, the minds of men will be fitted to it; the general opinions and feelings will draw that way. Every fear, every hope will forward it; and then they who persist in opposing this mighty current in human affairs, will appear rather to resist the decrees of Providence itself, than the mere designs of men. They will not be resolute and firm, but perverse and obstinate.*

That return of Burke upon himself has always seemed to me one of the finest things in English literature, or indeed in any literature. That is what I call living by ideas: when one side of a question has long had your earnest support, when all your feelings are engaged, when you hear all round you no language but one, when your party talks this language like a steam-engine and can imagine no other,—still to be able to think, still to be irresistibly carried, if so it be, by the current of thought to the opposite side of the question, and, like Balaam, to be unable to speak anything *but what the Lord has put in your mouth*. I know nothing more striking, and I must add that I know nothing more un-English. (pp. 8-10)

The notion of the free play of the mind upon all subjects being a pleasure in itself, being an object of desire, being an essential provider of elements without which a nation's spirit, whatever compensations it may have for them, must, in the long run, die of inanition, hardly enters into an Englishman's thoughts. It is noticeable that the word *curiosity,* which in other languages is used in a good sense, to mean, as a high and fine quality of man's nature, just this disinterested love of a free play of the mind on all subjects, for its own sake,—it is noticeable, I say, that this word has in our language no sense of the kind, no sense but a rather bad and disparaging one. But criticism, real criticism, is essentially the exercise of this very quality; it obeys an instinct prompting it to try to know the best that is known and thought in the world, irrespectively of practice, politics, and everything of the kind; and to value knowledge and thought as they approach this best, without the intrusion of any other considerations whatever. This is an instinct for which there is, I think, little original sympathy in the practical English nature, and what there was of it has undergone a long benumbing period of check and suppression in the epoch of concentration which followed the French Revolution. (pp. 10-11)

> *Matthew Arnold, ''The Function of Criticism at the Present Time,'' in his* Essays Literary & Critical, *E. P. Dutton & Co., 1906, pp. 1-25.*

SIR LESLIE STEPHEN (essay date 1876)

[*Stephen is considered one of the most important English literary critics of the late Victorian and early Edwardian era. In his criticism, which was often moralistic, Stephen argued that all literature is nothing more than an imaginative rendering, in concrete terms, of a writer's philosophy or beliefs. It is the role of criticism, he contended, to translate into intellectual terms what the writer has told the reader through character, symbol, and plot. Stephen's analyses often include biographical judgments of the writer. As he once observed, ''The whole art of criticism consists in learning to know the human being who is partially revealed to us in his spoken or his written words.'' In the following excerpt, Stephen outlines the essential traits of Burke's political thought, emphasizing in particular his views of the American and French revolutions.*]

No English writer has received, or has deserved, more splendid panegyrics than Burke. To do justice to his multifarious activity, or to estimate accurately the influence which he exerted upon contemporary history, would involve a course of enquiry alien to [my] purpose. . . . I must try, however, to disengage his leading principles from the writing in which they are embedded, and to exhibit their relation to other systems of speculation. Considered simply as a master of English prose, Burke has not, in my judgment, been surpassed in any period of our literature. Critics may point to certain faults of taste; the evolution of his thought is sometimes too slow; his majestic march is trammelled by the sweep of his gorgeous rhetoric; or his imagination takes fire, and he explodes into fierce denunciations which shock the reader when the excitement which prompted them has become unintelligible. But, whatever blemishes may be detected, Burke's magnificent speeches stand alone in the language. They are the only English speeches which may still be read with more than an historical interest

when the hearer and the speaker have long been turned to dust. His pamphlets, which are written speeches, are marked by a fervour, a richness, and a flexibility of style which is but a worthy incarnation of the wisdom embodied in them. It matters little if we dissent from his appreciations of current events, for it is easy to supply the corrective for ourselves. The charge of over-refinement sometimes brought against him is in great part nothing more than the unconscious testimony of his critics that he could see farther than themselves. To a certain degree it is, perhaps, well founded. His political strategy was a little too complex for the rough give-and-take of ordinary partisans. His keen perception of the tendencies of certain politics led him to impute motives to their advocates for which their stupidity rather than their morality incapacitated them. When, for example, we are told that the Court party persecuted Wilkes in order to establish a precedent tending to show 'that the favour of the people was not so sure a road as the favour of a Court, even to popular honours and popular trusts,' we may prefer the simpler explanation founded on the blunted instincts of obtuse rulers. It was doing them too much honour to attribute to them any design beyond that of crushing an antagonist by the weapons readiest at hand. The keen intelligence which thus sometimes takes the form of excessive ingenuity is more frequently revealed by passages in which profound wisdom is concentrated in a single phrase. We should not ask how we got into the American difficulty, was the cry of the hand-to-mouth politicians, but how we are to get out of it. That is to say, is Burke's comment, 'we are to consult our invention, and reject our experience.' 'Nobody will be argued into slavery' is another phrase from the same speech, which compresses into half-a-dozen words the confutation of the special pleading and pettifogging of antiquarian lawyers, which the so-called practical men mistook for statesmanlike reasoning. 'I know no method,' he says elsewhere, 'of drawing up an indictment against a whole people;' but lawyers thought that nothing was beyond the reach of their art. His later writings are equally fertile. 'Art is man's nature' sums up his argument against the Rousseau school of theorists; and here is another phrase which might serve as text for a political treatise. On occasions of this nature, he says, 'I am most afraid of the weakest reasonings, because they discover the strongest passions.' Not to multiply instances, I quote one more passage of great significance in regard to Burke's method. 'From this source,' he says, speaking of history, 'much political wisdom may be learnt; that is, learnt as habit, not as a precept, and as an exercise to strengthen the mind, not as a repertory of cases and precedents for a lawyer.'

Such sayings, which occur in profusion, illustrate the most marked peculiarity of Burke's mind—the admirable combination of the generalising faculty with a respect for concrete facts. His theorising is always checked and verified by the test of specific instances, and yet in every special case he always sees a general principle. . . . [If] he is at times too visionary and at times too condescending to the men with whom he was unequally yoked, he contributed the most elevating influence of contemporary politics, and was the one man who accurately gauged the breadth and depth, though he may have partly misunderstood the direction, of the great political movements of his time.

The greatness of Burke as a thinker cannot be adequately appreciated without noticing the nobility of his moral nature. It is not from want of human feeling so much as from want of imaginative power that we are generally so dead to the sorrows and sufferings of the great mass of our fellow-creatures. Beneath the rough crust of Johnson and the versatile talent of Goldsmith lay hearts as true and tender as that of Burke. Hume possessed an intellect still more penetrative, though he had little enough of imaginative power. But Burke stands alone in his generation for the combination of width of view with deepness of sympathy. Thinking of the mass, he never forgets the individual. . . . Few stories are sadder, to us who are accustomed to estimate a man's happiness by his last days, and to see good fortune only in immediate success, than the story of Burke's bereaved old age, when the son whom he loved most tenderly had died before him, and the cause to which he had devoted a life was tottering. Yet he had the right to remember that, throughout life he had, with one doubtful exception, taken the generous side. The exception—namely, his assault on the French Revolution—placed him for once on the side of the oppressors, and therefore brought him the reward denied to his earlier labours. Yet no opponent will now impute to him, even in that case, sordid motive or blunted sensibility. He had defended the Americans against the blundering tyranny of George III., and the dogged stupidity of that part of the nation of which the dull king was the fit representative. He had denounced the penal laws which nearly drove Ireland to follow the American precedent. He had laboured with surpassing industry in the ungrateful task of curbing English brutality in India. He had defended the rights of his countrymen at home as well as protested against the abuses of their power abroad. He had opposed the petty tyranny engendered by the corrupt government of a servile aristocracy; he had denounced the numerous abuses which flourished under the congenial shade of jobbery in high places. If once or twice an irritable temperament led him to sanction mere factious intrigue, his voice had always been the most powerful and the least selfish on the side of honour, justice, and mercy. It is the least of his merits that his views of political economy were as far in advance of his time as his view of wider questions of policy; but the fact deserves notice as a proof that, if an orator by temperament, he laid the foundations of his intellectual supremacy deep in the driest and most repulsive of studies. (pp. 219-23)

["**Economical Reform**"] is a most admirable specimen of lucid exposition. Its purpose is defined in the opening sentences. 'What, I confess, was uppermost with me; what I bent the whole force of my mind to, was the reduction of that corrupt influence, which is itself the perennial spring of all prodigality and of all disorder; which loads us more than millions of debt; which takes away vigour from our arms, wisdom from our councils, and every shadow of authority and credit from the most venerable parts of our constitution.' The power of corruption enjoyed under the old system lay at the root of all our political evils. (p. 236)

Burke would not have touched one recognised branch of the royal prerogative or have removed one privilege of the peerage. He would renovate and strengthen the old system. He would enable its practice to conform to its theory; and, by enforcing publicity and sweeping away the malpractices of backstairs intrigue, would stimulate the leaders of the people to adopt an attitude worthy of their exalted position. He would cherish most tenderly every institution which tended to preserve the historical dignity of the constitution, whilst removing the morbid growths which had accumulated in darkness and stagnation. A different spirit, however, was beginning to stir the political surface; and the method by which Burke encountered it can best be expounded by his attitude towards the American and the French Revolutions. (pp. 236-37)

[Burke had laid down in *Present Discontents*] one great principle in the American controversy. 'When popular discontents have been very prevalent,' he says, 'it may well be affirmed and supported that there has been found something amiss in the constitution or in the conduct of government. The people have no interest in disorder. When they do wrong, it is their error and not their crime. But with the governing part of the state it is far otherwise. They certainly may act ill by design as well as by mistake.' . . . During the American troubles, Burke adhered steadily to this view. The French Revolution exposed the theory to a more trying test. Burke had proclaimed the responsibility of rulers to their subjects, and declared that discontent was a sufficient proof of misgovernment. The French people were about to enforce responsibility by the guillotine, and to justify their actions as a revolt against intolerable oppression. Would Burke apply the same test in this case? Would he admit that the force of the explosion testified to the severity of the previous compression? A people, he had said, was free when it thought itself free. Would that view justify the French, who showed most unmistakably that they considered themselves to be slaves? Should Burke, therefore, approve of this as of the former revolt, and agree with his political friends that a new era of liberty and happiness was dawning upon the world? The writings on the eloquence and wisdom of which his reputation chiefly rests gave an answer to these questions which scandalised many of his former friends, and have exposed him to the imputations of inconsistency, if not of political apostasy. And yet they are but expansions of the doctrines which he had previously expounded.

The outbreak of the French Revolution affected Burke's imagination with extraordinary force. He saw in it something strange, abnormal, and tremendous. . . . Burke looked upon the Revolution with that kind of shudder with which man acknowledges the presence of a being believed to be supernatural. All ordinary rules seemed to be suspended. The earth trembled, and the strongest barriers gave way. No wonder if, in presence of the spectre, Burke's whole nature, already worn by many failures, disappointments, and vexations, reeled under the excitement. Nowhere, indeed, is his intellectual power more marked than in the outpourings of his anti-revolutionary wrath. But the eloquence passes into virulence. The *Reflections* published in 1790 are still philosophical in tone, though shot with gorgeous rhetoric; but, as the horror increases, his passion rises, till, in the letters on a *Regicide Peace* . . . , he seems almost to be foaming at the mouth, and to be speaking with the fury of inspiration rather than with the energy of earthly apprehension.

In January 1791 he already regards the leaders as mere quacks and impostors, and the people as madmen, who, 'like other madmen,' must be subdued in order to be cured. The Revolution, a few months later, is declared to be 'a foul, monstrous thing, wholly out of the course of moral nature;' it was 'generated in treachery, frauds, and falsehood, hypocrisy, and unprovoked murder.' As he goes on he strains his whole power of invective to gratify the vehemence of his hatred. Jacobinism is incarnate evil; it is atheism by establishment; it makes a 'profane apotheosis of monsters whose vices and crimes have no parallel amongst men.' Jacobins are animated by 'determined hostility to the human race.' They have deliberately established a system of manners 'the most licentious, prostitute, and abandoned that ever have been known, and at the same time the most coarse, rude, savage, and ferocious.' . . . One seems to see the face of the orator convulsed; he pants, struggles, and grasps for utterance, and in the whirlwind of his passion tears all propriety and common sense to rags. If words could blast, the French revolutionists would have been scorched and shrivelled by his fury.

Why did the wisest politician of the day thus throw the reins on the neck of his eloquence? Something must be set down to the excitement of the struggle; something to the pain inflicted by the sharp severance of all ties; much, in the later writings, to the consequences of the cruel domestic loss which shadowed his declining years with so deep a gloom. The actual atrocities of the Revolution increased his horror, but from the very first he saw the glare of hell in the light which others took to herald the dawn of the millennium. Nor, indeed, can it be doubted that Burke's antipathy to the Revolution was based upon a profound and reasoned conviction of the utter falsity of its leading principles. Good steady-going Whigs might fancy that the French were merely a set of interesting converts to the doctrines of the Petition of Right and the Revolution of 1688. Men like Priestley and Price fancied that reason was revealing itself to mankind, and dispersing the antiquated prejudices of centuries. Burke's insight was deeper and truer. He saw with the revolutionists that the phenomenon did not signify a mere adjustment of an old political balance, and the adoption of a few constitutional nostrums. A new doctrine was spreading from the schools into the mass of the people, and threatening the very foundations of the old social order. Moreover, he saw through the flimsy nature of the logic which it was supposed to embody; and recognised the emptiness of the predictions of an instant advent of peace, justice, and goodwill. He had weighed Rousseau's metaphysics and found them grievously wanting; and what to others appeared to be a startling revelation of new truths was to him a fitful rehabilitation of outworn fallacies. (pp. 242-45)

The equality of mankind was the fundamental dogma of the revolutionary creed. That dogma was equivalent to justifying the absolute disorganisation of the old society. It condemned all subordination, whether to rightful superiors or to arbitrary despots. It involved the levelling of all the old institutions, however important the part which they played in the social machinery. It explicitly swept aside as irrelevant and immoral all arguments from experience and expediency. It regarded prescription, not as the sacred foundation of all social rights, but as a mischievous superstition. It attacked the historical continuity of the race, and proposed first to make a *tabula rasa* of all existing organisation, and then to construct society anew on purely *a priori* grounds. Pure arithmetic was to take the place of observation, and the constitution to be framed without the least reference to the complex internal structure of the nation. The most valuable part of Burke's writings are the passages, full of both of wisdom and eloquence, in which he exposes the fallacy of this fanatical creed. The very simplicity of the new schemes condemned them sufficiently, for it proved them to have been constructed without reference to the primary data of the problem. 'The nature of man,' he says [in his *Reflections*], 'is intricate; the objects of society are of the greatest possible complexity; and therefore no simple disposition or direction of power can be suitable either to man's nature or to the quality of his affairs.' To neglect to take into account the forces by which men are bound together in the constituent elements of society is a fatal error. . . . In fact, the revolutionary ideas embodied the formal contradictory to that truth, the full appreciation of which was Burke's greatest title to speculative eminence, and which guided his wisest reflections. To him a nation was a living organism, of infinitely complex structure, of intimate dependence upon the parts, and to be treated by politicians in obedience to a careful observation of the laws of

its healthy development. To them a nation was an aggregate of independent units, to be regulated by a set of absolute *a priori* maxims. (pp. 247-49)

[To the charge of inconsistency], Burke had, up to a certain point, a triumphant and conclusive answer, which is given in the ***Appeal to the Old Whigs***. The revolutionary ideas were radically opposed in every detail to the principles which he had spent a life in proclaiming. His defence of the colonies, even his attacks upon the royal prerogative, were absolutely free from any revolutionary tendency. His efforts had been directed to maintaining the 'equipoise' of the constitution. It is only on the theory that a man who approves of one is bound to approve of all revolts, or that a man who opposes the corrupt influence of any power must be opposed to its existence, that the charge could be made at all plausible. Burke's horror of the Revolution indeed gives to his later utterances upon the British Constitution an exaggerated tone. When, in his ***Appeal from the New to the Old Whigs,*** he invokes the authority of the managers of the Sacheverel trial, one feels a little scandalised by his excessive reverence for those rather questionable fathers of the true political church. His faith becomes superstitious, and his catchword prescription covers something like a defence of absolute stagnation. His favourite revolution of 1688 is justified as a strictly defensive revolution, in which the people and not the king represented adherence to the established order; and Burke ignores the fact that it really involved a transfer of power. But though, under the stress of terror and the influence of old age, Burke's conservatism became stronger as well as more emphatically expressed, the change did not seriously affect the substance of his creed. His whole conception of political science is radically unaltered, and his method shows the same characteristic peculiarities. His position in the narrow limits of political party may have changed, but as a thinker he insists upon the same principles, applies the same tests, and holds to the same essential truths. (pp. 249-50)

One question might have revealed the weakness of a theory which seems to have imposed upon him, as upon his readers, more by the power with which it is stated than by the force of the arguments alleged. Jacobinism, he said, and with perfect truth, was partly the offspring of philosophical atheism; and to what was the atheism owing? That question could hardly be answered by a thinker content to rest the claims of religious, as of political faith, upon prescription. Prescription, once questioned, is but a foundation of sand. Burke could not or would not see that the old ideas were perishing. So long as men could be warned off the sacred ground, an appeal to prescription might be in place. But the attempt had long been hopeless. The creeds were rotten; and therefore the 'dry rot' could sap the old supports and render the crash inevitable. And, as Burke refused to face this difficulty in the sphere of religion, he was equally unsound in the sphere of politics. A religious creed resting on prescription is analogous to a political creed which renounces responsibility. The rulers who objected to change could appeal to no satisfactory ground of reverence. The divine-right theory was dead; and therefore to claim the reverence due only to divinely appointed rulers was to invite destruction. In the face of this, a power relying upon the mere force of prejudice, the revolutionary doctrines had a tremendous advantage; their dogmas might be erroneous, but they were dogmas. The revolutionists asserted, with the fervour of new converts, that laws ought to be reasonable; that social arrangements should be in conformity with justice; that all power should be administered for the good of the people. True, these doctrines were mixed with an element of utterly delusive metaphysics; and therefore the attempt to carry them into practice led to cruel disappointment. Burke's obstructive creed had not that positive element which was required to meet the destructives effectually. Delivered, indeed, to a people full of stubborn conservatism, comparatively careless of general ideas, and frightened by the catastrophe of France, it served to give courage to the party of resistance. But, as yet, men's minds were left in the hopeless dilemma between doctrines which would destroy all authority and doctrines which would support all authority not flagrantly intolerable. (pp. 251-52)

Sir Leslie Stephen, "Political Theories: Burke," in his History of English Thought in the Eighteenth Century, *Vol. II, 1876. Reprint by John Murray, 1927, pp. 219-52.*

AUGUSTINE BIRRELL   (essay date 1886)

[*Birrell was an English statesman and essayist. Although his political career was always his primary interest, he earned a reputation for reflective humor, insightful observation, and judicious pronouncement in such collections of miscellaneous essays and literary criticism as* Obiter Dicta *(1884) and* Et Cetera *(1930) and in his critical biographies of Charlotte Brontë, William Hazlitt, and Andrew Marvell. Birrell's writing style—scholarly, personal, and socially conscious—led to the coinage of the verb "to birrell," defined as: "to comment on life in a combination of irony and kindly mordancy, with apparent irrelevance, but with actual point." In the following excerpt from an essay orginally published in an 1886 issue of the* Contemporary Review, *Birrell stresses Burke's imaginative practicality, comparing his place in the political realm with Cardinal Newman's in the religious.*]

[It] was Burke's peculiarity and his glory to apply the imagination of a poet of the first order to the facts and the business of life. Arnold says of Sophocles:

He saw life steadily, and saw it whole.

Substitute for the word "life" the words "organised society," and you get a peep into Burke's mind. There was a catholicity about his gaze. He knew how the whole world lived. Everything contributed to this: his vast desultory reading; his education, neither wholly academical nor entirely professional; his long years of apprenticeship in the service of knowledge; his wanderings up and down the country; his vast conventional powers; his enormous correspondence with all sorts of people; his unfailing interest in all pursuits, trades, manufactures,—all helped to keep before him, like motes dancing in a sunbeam, the huge organism of modern society, which requires for its existence and for its development the maintenance of credit and of order. Burke's imagination led him to look out over the whole land: the legislator devising new laws, the judge expounding and enforcing old ones, the merchant despatching his goods and extending his credit, the banker advancing the money of his customers upon the credit of the merchant, the frugal man slowly accumulating the store which is to support him in old age, the ancient institutions of Church and University with their seemly provisions for sound learning and true religion, the parson in his pulpit, the poet pondering his rhymes, the farmer eyeing his crops, the painter covering his canvases, the player educating the feelings. Burke saw all this with the fancy of a poet, and dwelt on it with the eye of a lover. But love is the parent of fear, and none knew better than Burke how thin is the lava layer between the costly fabric of society and the volcanic heats and destroying flames of anarchy. He trembled for the fair frame of all established things, and to his horror saw men, instead of covering the thin surface with the

concrete, digging in it for abstractions, and asking fundamental questions about the origin of society, and why one man should be born rich and another poor. Burke was no prating optimist: it was his very knowledge how much could be said against society that quickened his fears for it. There is no shallower criticism than that which accuses Burke in his later years of apostasy from so-called Liberal opinions. Burke was all his life through a passionate maintainer of the established order of things, and a ferocious hater of abstractions and metaphysical politics. The same ideas that explode like bombs through his diatribes against the French Revolution are to be found shining with a mild effulgence in the comparative calm of his earlier writings. I have often been struck with a resemblance, which I hope is not wholly fanciful, between the attitude of Burke's mind towards government and that of Cardinal Newman towards religion. Both these great men belong, by virtue of their imaginations, to the poetic order, and they both are to be found dwelling with amazing eloquence, detail, and wealth of illustration on the varied elements of society. Both seem as they write to have one hand on the pulse of the world, and to be for ever alive to the throb of its action; and Burke, as he regarded humanity swarming like bees into and out of their hives of industry, is ever asking himself, How are these men to be saved from anarchy? whilst Newman puts to himself the question, How are these men to be saved from atheism? Both saw the perils of free inquiry divorced from practical affairs.

"Civil freedom," says Burke, "is not, as many have endeavoured to persuade you, a thing that lies hid in the depth of abstruse science. It is a blessing and a benefit, not an abstract speculation; and all the just reasoning that can be upon it is of so coarse a texture as perfectly to suit the ordinary capacities of those who are to enjoy and of those who are to defend it."

"Tell men," says Cardinal Newman, "to gain notions of a Creator from His works, and if they were to set about it (which nobody does), they would be jaded and wearied by the labyrinth they were tracing; their minds would be gorged and surfeited by the logical operation. To most men argument makes the point in hand more doubtful and considerably less impressive. After all, man is not a reasoning animal, he is a seeing, feeling, contemplating, acting animal."

Burke is fond of telling us that he is no lawyer, no antiquarian, but a plain, practical man; and the Cardinal, in like manner, is ever insisting that he is no theologian—he leaves everything of that sort to the Schools, whatever they may be, and simply deals with religion on its practical side as a benefit to mankind.

If either of these great men has been guilty of intellectual excesses, those of Burke may be attributed to his dread of anarchy, those of Newman to his dread of atheism. Neither of them was prepared to rest content with a scientific frontier, an imaginary line. So much did they dread their enemy, so alive were they to the terrible strength of some of his positions, that they could not agree to dispense with the protection afforded by the huge mountains of prejudice and the ancient rivers of custom. The sincerity of either man can only be doubted by the bigot and the fool. (pp. 179-82)

Wordsworth has been called the High Priest of Nature. Burke may be called the High Priest of Order—a lover of settled ways, of justice, peace, and security. His writings are a storehouse of wisdom, not the cheap shrewdness of the mere man of the world, but the noble, animating wisdom of one who has the poet's heart as well as the statesman's brain. Nobody is fit to govern this country who has not drunk deep at the springs of Burke. "Have you read your Burke?" is at least as sensible a question to put to a parliamentary candidate, as to ask him whether he is a total abstainer or a desperate drunkard. Something there may be about Burke to regret, and more to dispute; but that he loved justice and hated iniquity is certain, as also it is that for the most part he dwelt in the paths of purity, humanity, and good sense. May we be found adhering to them! (p. 183)

Augustine Birrell, "Edmund Burke," in his The Collected Essays & Addresses of the Rt. Hon. Augustine Birrell: 1880-1920, Vol. I, *Charles Scribner's Sons, 1923, pp. 155-83.*

WOODROW WILSON   (essay date 1896)

[A political scientist and president of Princeton University before becoming the twenty-eighth president of the United States, Wilson published a number of studies on American history and political theory, of which A History of the American People *(1902) and* Constitutional Government in the United States *(1908) are notable examples. His writings on the social and ideological division between the North and South which culminated in the Civil War are often considered his most accomplished;* Division and Reunion, 1829-1889 *(1893) is deemed the most important such study. In the following excerpt, Wilson examines Burke's consistently conservative approach to four key political issues and comments on the statesman's literary qualities.]*

Four questions absorbed the energies of Burke's life and must always be associated with his fame. These were, the American war for independence; administrative reform in the English home government; reform in the government of India; and the profound political agitations which attended the French Revolution. Other questions he studied, deeply pondered, and greatly illuminated, but upon these four he expended the full strength of his magnificent powers. There is in his treatment of these subjects a singular consistency, a very admirable simplicity of standard. It has been said, and it is true, that Burke had no system of political philosophy. He was afraid of abstract system in political thought, for he perceived that questions of government are moral questions, and that questions of morals cannot always be squared with the rules of logic, but run through as many ranges of variety as the circumstances of life itself. "Man acts from adequate motives relative to his interest," he said, "and not on metaphysical speculations. Aristotle, the great master of reasoning, cautions us, and with great weight and propriety, against this species of delusive geometrical accuracy in moral arguments, as the most fallacious of all sophistry." And yet Burke unquestionably had a very definite and determinable system of thought, which was none the less a system for being based upon concrete, and not upon abstract premises. It is said by some writers (even by so eminent a writer as Buckle [see excerpt dated 1857]) that in his later years Burke's mind lost its balance and that he reasoned as if he were insane; and the proof assigned is, that he, a man who loved liberty, violently condemned, not the terrors only,—that of course,— but the very principles of the French Revolution. But to reason thus is to convict one's self of an utter lack of comprehension of Burke's mind and motives: as a very brief examination of his course upon the four great questions I have mentioned will show.

From first to last Burke's thought is conservative. Let his attitude with regard to America serve as an example. He took his stand, as everybody knows, with the colonies, against the mother country; but his object was not revolutionary. He did not deny the legal right of England to tax the colonies (*we* no longer deny it ourselves), but he wished to preserve the empire, and he saw that to insist upon the right of taxation would be irrevocably to break up the empire, when dealing with such a people as the Americans. He pointed out the strong and increasing numbers of the colonists, their high spirit in enterprise, their jealous love of liberty, and the indulgence England had hitherto accorded them in the matter of self-government, permitting them in effect to become an independent people in respect of all their internal affairs; and he declared the result matter for just pride. (pp. 141-43)

> The question with me is, not whether you have a right to render your people miserable, but whether it is not your interest to make them happy. It is not what a lawyer tells me I *may* do, but what humanity, reason, and justice tell me I *ought* to do. . . . Such is steadfastly my opinion of the absolute necessity of keeping up the concord of this empire by a unity of spirit, though in a diversity of operations, that, if I were sure that the colonists had, at their leaving this country, sealed a regular compact of servitude, that they had solemnly abjured all the rights of citizens, that they had made a vow to renounce all ideas of liberty for them and their posterity to all generations, yet I should hold myself obliged to conform to the temper I found universally prevalent in my own day, and to govern two million of men, impatient of servitude, on the principles of freedom. I am not determining a point of law; I am restoring tranquillity: and the general character and situation of a people must determine what sort of government is fitted for them. That point nothing else can or ought to determine.
>
> (pp. 147-48)

Here you have the whole spirit of the man, and in part a view of his eminently practical system of thought. The view is completed when you advance with him to other subjects of policy. He pressed with all his energy for radical reforms in administration, but he earnestly opposed every change that might touch the structure of the constitution itself. He sought to secure the integrity of Parliament, not by changing the system of representation, but by cutting out all roots of corruption. He pressed forward with the most ardent in all plans of just reform, but he held back with the most conservative from all propositions of radical change. (pp. 148-49)

> Time is required to produce that union of minds which alone can produce all the good we aim at. Our patience will achieve more than our force. If I might venture to appeal to what is so much out of fashion in Paris,—I mean to experience,—I should tell you that in my course I have known, and, according to my measure, have coöperated with great men; and I have never yet seen any plan which has not been mended by the observations of those who were much inferior in understanding to the person who took the lead in the business. By a slow, but well sustained progress, the effect of each step is watched; the good or ill success of the first gives light to us in the second; and so, from light to light, we are conducted with safety, through the whole series. . . . We are enabled to unite into a consistent whole the various anomalies and contending principles that are found in the minds and affairs of men. From hence arises, not an excellence in simplicity, but one far superior, an excellence in composition. Where the great interests of mankind are concerned through a long succession of generations, that succession ought to be admitted into

some share in the counsels which are so deeply to affect them.

It is not possible to escape deep conviction of the wisdom of these reflections. They penetrate to the heart of all practicable methods of reform. Burke was doubtless too timid, and in practical judgment often mistaken. Measures which in reality would operate only as salutary and needed reformations he feared because of the element of change that was in them. He erred when he supposed that progress can in all its stages be made without changes which seem to go even to the substance. But, right or wrong, his philosophy did not come to him of a sudden and only at the end of his life, when he found France desolated and England threatened with madness for love of revolutionary principles of change. It is the key to his thought everywhere, and through all his life.

It is the key (which many of his critics have never found) to his position with regard to the revolution in France. He was roused to that fierce energy of opposition in which so many have thought that they detected madness, not so much because of his deep disgust to see brutal and ignorant men madly despoil an ancient and honorable monarchy, as because he saw the spirit of these men cross the Channel and find lodgment in England, even among statesmen like Fox, who had been his own close friends and companions in thought and policy; not so much because he loved France as because he feared for England.... He hated the French revolutionary philosophy and deemed it unfit for free men. And that philosophy is in fact radically evil and corrupting. No state can ever be conducted on its principles. For it holds that government is a matter of contract and deliberate arrangement, whereas in fact it is an institute of habit, bound together by innumerable threads of association, scarcely one of which has been deliberately placed. It holds that the object of government is liberty, whereas the true object of government is justice; not the advantage of one class, even though that class constitute the majority, but right equity in the adjustment of the interests of all classes. It assumes that government can be made over at will, but assumes it without the slightest historical foundation. For governments have never been successfully and permanently changed except by slow modification operating from generation to generation. It contradicted every principle that had been so laboriously brought to light in the slow stages of the growth of liberty in the only land in which liberty had then grown to great proportions. The history of England is a continuous thesis against revolution; and Burke would have been no true Englishman, had he not roused himself, even fanatically, if there were need, to keep such puerile doctrine out.

If you think his fierceness was madness, look how he conducted the trial against Warren Hastings during those same years: with what patience, with what steadiness in business, with what temper, with what sane and balanced attention to detail, with what statesmanlike purpose! Note, likewise that his thesis is the same in the one undertaking as in the other. He was applying the same principles to the case of France and to the case of India that he had applied to the case of the colonies. He meant to save the empire, not by changing its constitution, as was the method in France, and so shaking every foundation in order to dislodge an abuse, but by administering it uprightly and in a liberal spirit.... Good government, like all virtue, he deemed to be a practical habit of conduct, and not a matter of constitutional structure. It is a great ideal, a thoroughly English ideal; and it constitutes the leading thought of all Burke's career.

In short ..., this man, an Irishman, speaks the best English thought upon the essential questions of politics. He is thor-

oughly, characteristically, and to the bottom English in all his thinking. He is more liberal than Englishmen in his treatment of Irish questions, of course; for he understands them, as no Englishman of his generation did. But for all that he remains the chief spokesman for England in the utterance of the fundamental ideals which have governed the action of Englishmen in politics. (pp. 152-58)

A man of sensitive imagination and elevated moral sense, of a wide knowledge and capacity for affairs, he stood in the midst of the English nation speaking its moral judgments upon affairs, its character in political action, its purposes of freedom, equity, wide and equal progress. It is the immortal charm of his speech and manner that gives permanence to his works. Though his life was devoted to affairs with a constant and unalterable passion, the radical features of Burke's mind were literary. He was a man of books, without being under the dominance of what others had written. He got knowledge out of books and the abundance of matter his mind craved to work its constructive and imaginative effects upon. It is singular how devoid of all direct references to books his writings are. The materials of his thought never reappear in the same form in which he obtained them. They have been smelted and recoined. They have come under the drill and inspiration of a great constructive mind, have caught life and taken structure from it. Burke is not literary because he takes from books, but because he makes books, transmuting what he writes upon into literature. It is this inevitable literary quality, this sure mastery of style, that mark the man, as much as his thought itself. Every sentence, too, is steeped in the colors of an extraordinary imagination. The movement takes your breath and quickens your pulses. The glow and power of the matter rejuvenate your faculties.

And yet the thought, too, is quite as imperishable as its incomparable vehicle. (pp. 159-60)

Woodrow Wilson, "The Interpreter of English Liberty," in his Mere Literature, and Other Essays, *Houghton Mifflin Company, 1896, pp. 104-60.*

JOHN MacCUNN   (essay date 1913)

[In the following excerpt, MacCunn regrets Burke's lack of idealism.]

When a statesman finds himself face to face with ideals he detests, it is never enough to meet them by criticism and invective. Even when ideals may be false and fanatical, they will seldom, if they have once found lodgment in the popular mind, be driven from the field till they are met by some rival ideal strong and attractive enough to oust them from their tenancy. The forward-struggling spirit of man, especially of masses of men chafing under obstructions, is not to be won by negations. So long as reason and imagination keep their hold on life, mankind will cleave to whatever plan or project seems to satisfy that craving for betterment which lies deep in, at any rate, all Western peoples. Hence the familiar remark—it is what Maine said of the 'broken-down theories' of Bentham and Rousseau— that ideals may survive long after their brains are out. They do survive, and they will continue to survive, if there be no counter-ideal to supersede them.

It is here that Burke is lacking. One may not say that he has no ideal to offer; and indeed it has been said a hundred times that the constitution he worshipped was not the constitution as it was, but a glorified picture of it as it shaped itself in his soaring imagination. Nor is the reader to be envied who can rise from his pages without having found an ideal. But it is an ideal that has the defects of its qualities. For, when all is said, the political imagination of Burke spent its marvellous force almost wholly in two directions. In the one direction it conjured up with the vividness of actual vision the disasters which radical reforms, so easy to initiate, and so hard to control, might carry in their train: in the other it lavished its powers in glorifying the present as a legacy of priceless practical value inherited from the ever-memorable past. The result is splendid, and it is an incomparably richer thing than the ideals of Rousseau or Paine or Price or Godwin. But it has limitations which these escaped. As a gospel for his age, or for any age, it has the fatal defect that, in its rooted distrust of theories and theorists, it finds hardly any place for political ideals as serious attempts to forefigure the destinies of a people as not less Divinely willed than its eventful past history or present achievement. And, by consequence, it fails to touch the future with the reformer's hope and conviction of better days to come.

> The echoes of the past within his brain,
> The sunrise of the future on his face,

—they are both the attributes of all great statesmanship. But if the sunrise of the future ever irradiates the pages of Burke, it is all too quickly to be quenched, at best in the clouds that veil the incalculable future, and at worst in the incendiary smoke of revolutionary fires. It is this that leaves our gratitude not unmixed with regrets. For Burke is no ordinary statesman, from whom it is enough to expect, that, if he look beyond the present at all, he should see no further than the next practical step in advance. Nor is he to be judged as such. It would do him wrong being so majestical. He is a political genius of the first order; and just because he is so great it is impossible to withhold from him the tribute of wishing for more than he has actually given. No one had it in him as he had to give his country a comprehensive and satisfying political ideal. He had the knowledge, the imagination, the experience; and, not least, he had the religious faith which, when it strikes alliance with the idealising spirit, makes all the difference between ideals that are but subjective dreams and ideals which are beliefs that nerve to action. Nor is the reader who has felt the power and fascination of his pages to be blamed if he falls to wondering how much of the strife and embitterment of the nineteenth century might have been averted, if this master in politics had given the reins to his imagination as freely and sympathetically in looking forward to posterity as in looking backward to ancestors. But it was not in that path he was to walk. Somehow, though not . . . without reasons, his faith failed him. It was strong enough to make the course of history divine, to consecrate the legacy of the past, to intensify the significance and the responsibilities of the present. But it could not inspire an ideal of constitutional and social progress. 'Perhaps,' he once remarked, with even more than his wonted distrust of thought divorced from actuality, 'the only moral trust with any certainty in our hands is the care of our own time.'

The result is that we find in Burke's writings the presence of two things, and the absence of a third. We find an unfaltering faith in the presence of a 'Divine tactic' in the lives of men and nations. We find also an *apologia* such as has never been equalled, for the existing social and political system as it has come to be by the long toil of successive generations. What we do not find, and are fain to wish for, and most of all from a thinker to whom the happiness of the people was always paramount, is some encouragement for the hope that the 'stupendous Wisdom' which has done so much in the past, and

even till now, will not fail to operate in the varieties of untried being through which the the State, even the democratic State, must pass in the vicissitudes and adventures of the future. (pp. 268-72)

John MacCunn, in his The Political Philosophy of Burke, *Longmans, Green and Co., 1913, 272 p.*

PAUL ELMER MORE   (essay date 1914)

[*More was an American critic who, along with Irving Babbitt, formulated the doctrine of New Humanism in early twentieth-century American thought. The New Humanists were strict moralists who adhered to traditional conservative values in reaction to an age of scientism and artistic self-expression. In regard to literature, they considered a given work's implicit reflection of support for the classic ethical norms of as much importance as its aesthetic qualities. More was particularly opposed to Naturalism, which he believed accentuated the animal nature of humans, and to any literature, such as Romanticism, that broke with established classical tradition. His importance as a critic derives from the rigid coherence of his ideology, which polarized American critics into hostile opponents of New Humanism (such as Van Wyck Brooks, Edmund Wilson, H. L. Mencken) or devoted supporters (such as Norman Foerster, Stuart P. Sherman, and, to a lesser degree, T. S. Eliot). He is especially esteemed for the philosophical and literary erudition of his multi-volume* Shelburne Essays *(1904-21). In the following excerpt from an essay which originally appeared in the* Unpopular Review *in 1914, More discusses the role of imagination in Burke's philosophy.*]

Despite some tincture of the so-called "enlightenment," which few men of that age could entirely escape, Burke had a deep distrust of the restive, self-seeking nature of mankind, and as a restraint upon it he would magnify the passive as opposed to the active power of what is really the same human nature. This passive instinct he called "prejudice"—the unreasoning and unquestioning attachment to the family and "the little platoon we belong to in society," from which our affection, coincident always with a feeling of contented obligation, is gradually enlarged to take in the peculiar institutions of our country; "prejudice renders a man's virtues his habits, . . . through just prejudice his duty becomes a part of his nature." Prejudice is thus the binding force which works from below upwards; the corresponding force which moves from above is "prescription"—the possession of rights and authority which have been confirmed by custom. In other words, Burke believed that the only practical way of ensuring a natural aristocracy was by the acceptance of a prescriptive oligarchy; in the long run and after account had been taken of all exceptions—and he was in no wise a blind worshipper of the Whig families which then governed England—he believed that the men of light and leading would already be found among, or by reason of their preëminence would be assumed into, the class of those whose views were broadened by the inherited possession of privilege and honours.

He so believed because it seemed to him that prejudice and prescription were in harmony with the methods of universal nature. Sudden change was abhorrent to him, and in every chapter of history he read that the only sound social development was that which corresponded to the slow and regular growth of a plant, deep-rooted in the soil and drawing its nourishment from ancient concealed sources. In such a plan prejudice was the ally of the powers of time, opposing to all visionary hopes a sense of duty to the solid existing reality and compelling upstart theory to prove itself by winning through long resistance. And with the force of time stood the kindred force of order and subordination personified in privilege. "A disposition to preserve, and an ability to improve, taken together," would be Burke's standard of a statesman; "everything else is vulgar in the conception, perilous in the execution." In passages of a singular elevation he combines the ideas of Hobbes on the social contract with those of Hooker on the sweep of divine universal law, harmonizing them with the newer conception of evolutionary growth. "Each contract of each particular State," he says,

> is but a clause in the great primeval contract of eternal society, linking the lower with the higher natures, connecting the visible and invisible world, according to a fixed compact sanctioned by the inviolable oath which holds all physical and all moral natures, each in their appointed place. And thus, too, our political system is placed in a just correspondence and symmetry with the order of the world, and with the mode of existence decreed to a permanent body composed of transitory parts; wherein, by the disposition of a stupendous wisdom, moulding together the great mysterious incorporation of the human race, the whole, at one time, is never old, or middle-aged, or young, but, in a condition of unchangeable constancy, moves on through the varied tenor of perpetual decay, fall, renovation, and progression. Thus, by preserving the method of nature in the conduct of the State, in what we improve, we are never wholly new; in what we retain, we are never wholly obsolete.

If we look below these ideas of prejudice and privilege, time and subordination, for their one animating principle, we shall find it, I think, in the dominance of the faculty of the imagination. Nor did this imaginative substructure lying beneath all of Burke's writings and speeches, from the early essay on the *Sublime and Beautiful* to his latest outpourings on the French Revolution, escape the animadversion of his enemies. Tom Paine made good use of this trait in *The Rights of Man* [see excerpt dated 1791], which he issued as an answer to the *Reflections*. "The age of chivalry is gone," Burke had exclaimed at the close of his famous tirade on the fall of Marie Antoinette.

> Now all is changed. All the pleasing illusions, which made power gentle, and obedience liberal, which harmonized the different shades of life, and which, by a bland assimilation, incorporated into politics the sentiments which beautify and soften private society, are to be dissolved by this new conquering empire of light and reason. All the decent drapery of life is to be rudely torn off. All the superadded ideas, furnished from the wardrobe of a *moral imagination*. . . .

To this Paine retorted with terrible incision. Ridiculing the lamentation over the French Queen as a mere sentimental rhapsody, he catches up Burke's very words with malign cunning:

> Not one glance of compassion, not one commiserating reflection, that I can find throughout his book, has he bestowed on those who lingered out the most wretched of lives, a life without hope in the most miserable of prisons. It is painful to behold a man employing his talents to corrupt himself. Nature has been kinder to Mr. Burke than he has been to her. He is not affected by the reality of distress touching his heart, but by the showy resemblance of its striking his imagination. He pities the plumage, but forgets the dying bird.

Now there is an element of truth in Paine's charge, but there is distortion also. To say that Burke had no thought for the oppressed and the miserable is a wanton slander, disproved by abundant passages in the very *Reflections* and by his whole career. . . . But it is the fact nevertheless, construe it how one will, that in the ordinary course of things Burke's ideas of government were moulded and his sentiment towards life was coloured by the vivid industry of his imagination, and that he thought the world at large controlled by the same power. I doubt if analysis can reach a deeper distinction between the whole class of minds to which Burke belongs and that to which Paine belongs than is afforded by this difference in the range and texture of the imagination.

And in this Burke had with him the instinct of his people, while in a way transcending it; for a good deal of what we regard as the British character depends on just the excess of imagination over a rather dull sensibility and sluggish intelligence. This, if we look into it, is what Bagehot signalized as the saving dulness of England and what Walpole meant by attributing to "the good sense [note the contrast of *sense* and sensibility] of the English that they have not painted better."

It was this same quality that inspired Burke's great comparison of the French excitability with the British stolidity: "Because half a dozen grasshoppers under a fern make the field ring with their importunate chink whilst thousands of great cattle, reposed beneath the shadow of the British oak, chew the cud and are silent, pray do not imagine that those who make the noise are the only inhabitants of the field." In its higher working, when sensibility and intelligence are also magnified, the imagination, no doubt, is the source of the loftier English poetry and eloquence, but in the lower range, which we are now considering, it is rather a slow, yet powerful and endearing, visualization of what is known and familiar; it is the beginning of that prejudice for existing circumstances and actual relations which Burke exalted as the mother of content. And with content it produces a kind of egotistic satisfaction in the pomps and privileges which pass before the eye, giving to the humble a participation in things wherein they have no material share. . . . Thus, too, the imagination is an accomplice of time as well as of the law of subordination; indeed, its deepest and noblest function lies in its power of carrying what was once seen and known as a living portion and factor of the present, and there is no surer test of the quality of a man's mind than the degree in which he feels the long-remembered past as one of the vital and immediate laws of his being. So it is that the imagination is the chief creator and sustainer of the great memorial institutions of society, such as the Crown and the Church and the other pageantries of State, which are the very embodiment of prescription, as it were the soul of tradition taking form and awful authority among the living. How deeply Burke felt this prescriptive right of the imagination no one need be told; nor is it necessary to quote the familiar passages in which he likens the British monarchy, with its bulwark of nobility, to "the proud keep of Windsor, rising in the majesty of proportion, and grit with the double belt of its kindred and coeval towers," or calls on the Church to "exalt her mitred front in courts and parliaments." There is the true Burke; he knew, as Paine knew, that the support of these institutions was in their symbolic sway over the imaginations of men, and that, with this defence undermined, they would crumble away beneath the aggressive passions of the present, or would remain as mere bloodless vanities. He thought that the real value of life was in its meaning to the imagination, and he was not ashamed to avow that the fall and tragedy of kings, because they bore in their person the destiny of ancient institutions, stirred him more profoundly than the sufferings of ordinary men.

It is perfectly easy for a keen and narrow intelligence to ridicule Burke's trust in the imagination, but as a matter of fact there is nothing more practical than a clear recognition of its vast domain in human affairs—it was Napoleon Bonaparte who said that "imagination rules the world." Burke is not dead; his pages are an inexhaustible storehouse of inspiration and wisdom. But it is true nevertheless, that his ideas never quite freed themselves from their matrix, and that in his arguments the essential is involved in the contingent. Though he saw clearly enough the imperfections of the actual union of a prescriptive and a natural aristocracy, he was not able, with all his insight, to conceive the existence of the latter alone and by virtue of its own rights. He cried out that the age of chivalry was gone; he saw that the age of prescription, however it might be propped up for a time, was also doomed, not only in France but in his England as well, and with that away there was nothing for his imagination but an utter blank. (pp. 13-21)

Paul Elmer More, "Natural Aristocracy," in his Aristocracy and Justice: Shelburne Essays, ninth series, *Houghton Mifflin Company, 1915, pp. 1-38.*

HAROLD J. LASKI (essay date 1920)

[*A controversial figure with strongly held Marxist views, Laski was a noted English political scientist and author who, as a popular lecturer and teacher, maintained a large following of students throughout his career. In addition, he was an outspoken and active participant in the British Labour Party, advocating labor reforms that were in line with his socialist thought. While lecturing at several universities in the United States, he became an astute observer of the American social and political scene, as reflected in his works* The American Presidency (1940), American Democracy (1948), *and* Reflections on the Constitution (1951). *In an assessment of Laski, Edmund Wilson stated that he was "not only a well-equipped scholar and an able political thinker but a fighter for unpopular ideals whose career as a whole is an example of singularly disinterested devotion." In the following excerpt, Laski delineates the shortcomings of Burke's political system, but concludes with a high estimation of Burke's achievement.*]

Criticism of Burke's theories can be made from at least two angles. It is easy to show that his picture of the British Constitution was remote from the facts even when he wrote. Every change that he opposed was essential to the security of the next generation; and there followed none of the disastrous consequences he had foreshadowed. Such criticism would be almost every point just; and yet it would fail to touch the heart of Burke's position. What is mainly needed is analysis at once of his omissions and of the underlying assumptions of what he wrote. Burke came to his maturity upon the eve of the Industrial Revolution; and we have it upon the authority of Adam Smith himself that no one had so clearly apprehended his own economic principles. Yet there is no word in what Burke had to say of their significance. The vast agrarian changes of the time contained, as it appears, no special moment even for him who burdened himself unduly to restore the Beaconsfield estate. No man was more eager than he that the public should be admitted to the mysteries of political debate; yet he steadfastly refused to draw the obvious inference that once the means of government were made known those who possessed the knowledge would demand their share in its application. He did not see that the metaphysics he so profoundly distrusted was itself the offspring of that contemptible worship of expediency which Balckstone generalized into a legalistic jargon. Men never move to the adumbration of general right until the conquest of po-

litical rights has been proved inadequate. That Burke himself may be said in a sense to have seen when he insisted upon the danger of examining the foundations of the State. Yet a man who refuses to admit that the constant dissatisfaction with those foundations his age expressed is the expression of serious ill in the body politic is wilfully blind to the facts at issue. No one had more faithfully than Burke himself explained why the Whig oligarchy was obsolete; yet nothing would induce him ever to realize that the alternative to aristocratic government is democracy and that its absence was the cause of that disquiet of which he realized that Wilkes was but the symptom.

Broadly, that is to say, Burke would not realize that the reign of political privilege was drawing to its close. That is the real meaning of the French Revolution and therein it represents a stream of tendency not less active in England than abroad. In France, indeed, the lines were more sharply drawn than elsewhere. The rights men craved were not, as Burke insisted, the immediate offspring of metaphysic fancy, but the result of a determination to end the malignant wrong of centuries. A power that knew no responsibility, war and intolerance that derived only from the accidental caprice of the court, arrest that bore no relation to offence, taxation inversely proportionate to the ability to pay, these were the prescriptive privileges that Burke invited his generation to accept as part of the accumulated wisdom of the past. It is not difficult to see why those who swore their oath in the tennis-court at Versailles should have felt such wisdom worthy to be condemned. Burke's caution was for them the timidity of one who embraces existent evils rather than fly to the refuge of an accessible good. In a less degree, the same is true of England. The constitution that Burke called upon men to worship was the constitution which made the Duke of Bedford powerful, that gave no representation to Manchester and a member to Old Sarum, which enacted the game laws and left upon the statute-book a penal code which hardly yielded to the noble attack of Romilly. These, which were for Burke merely the accidental excrescences of a noble ideal, were for them its inner essence; and where they could not reform they were willing to destroy.

The revolutionary spirit, in fact, was as much the product of the past as the very institutions it came to condemn. The innovations were the inevitable outcome of past oppression. Burke refused to see that aspect of the picture. He ascribed to the crime of the present what was due to the half-wilful errors of the past. The man who grounded his faith in historic experience refused to admit as history the elements alien from his special outlook. He took that liberty not to venerate where he was unable to comprehend which he denied to his opponents. Nor did he admit the uses to which his doctrine of prescription was bound to be put in the hands of selfish and unscrupulous men. No one will object to privilege for a Chatham; but privilege for the Duke of Grafton is a different thing, and Burke's doctrine safeguards the innumerable men of whom Grafton is the type in the hope that by happy accident some Chatham will one day emerge. He justifies the privileges of the English Church in the name of religious well-being; but it is difficult to see what men like Watson or Archbishop Cornwallis have got to do with religion. The doctrine of prescription might be admirable if all statesmen were so wise as Burke; but in the hands of lesser men it becomes no more than the protective armour of vested interests into the ethics of which it refuses us leave to examine.

That suspicion of thought is integral to Burke's philosophy, and it deserves more examination than it has received. In part it is a rejection of the Benthamite position that man is a reasoning animal. It puts its trust in habit as the chief source of human action; and it thus is distrustful of thought as leading into channels to which the nature of man is not adapted. Novelty, which is assumed to be the outcome of thought, it regards as subversive of the routine upon which civilization depends. Thought is destructive of peace; and it is argued that we know too little of political phenomena to make us venture into the untried places to which thought invites us. Yet the first of many answers is surely the most obvious fact that if man is so much the creature of his custom no reason would prevail save where they proved inadequate. If thought is simply a reserve power in society, its strength must obviously depend upon common acceptance; and that can only come when some routine has failed to satisfy the impulses of men.

But we may urge a difficulty that is even more decisive. No system of habits can ever hope to endure long in a world where the cumulative power of memory enables change to be so swift; and no system of habits can endure at all unless its underlying idea represents the satisfaction of a general desire. It must, that is to say, make rational appeal; and, indeed, as Aristotle said, it can have virtue only to the point where it is conscious of itself. The uncritical routine of which Burke is the sponsor would here deprive the mass of men of virtue. (pp. 258-64)

[Burke] thought of the people—it was obviously a generalization from his time—as consistently prone to disorder and checked only by the force of ancient habit. Yet he has himself supplied the answer to that attitude. "My observation," he said in his **Speech on the East India Bill,** "has furnished me with nothing that is to be found in any habits of life or education which tends wholly to disqualify men for the functions of government." We can go further than that sober caution. We know that there is one technique only capable of securing good government and that is the training of the mass of men to interest in it. We know that no State can hope for peace in which large types of experience are without representation. Indeed, if proof were here wanting, an examination of the eighteenth century would supply it. Few would deny that statesmen are capable of disinterested sacrifice for classes of whose inner life they are ignorant; yet the relation between law and the interest of the dominant class is too intimate to permit with safety the exclusion of a part of the State from sharing in its guidance. Nor did Burke remember his own wise saying that "in all disputes between the people and their rulers the presumption is at least upon a par in favor of the people"; and he quotes with agreement that great sentence of Sully's which traces popular violence to popular suffering. No one can watch the economic struggles of the eighteenth and nineteenth centuries or calculate the pain they have involved to humble men, without admitting that they represent the final protest of an outraged mind against oppression too intolerable to be borne. Burke himself, as his own speeches show, knew little or nothing of the pain involved in the agrarian changes of his age. The one way to avoid violent outbreak is not exclusion of the people from power but their participation in it. The popular sense of right may often, as Aristotle saw, be wiser than the opinion of statesmen. It is not necessary to equate the worth of untrained commonsense with experienced wisdom to suggest that, in the long run, neglect of common sense will make the effort of that wisdom fruitless.

This, indeed, is to take the lowest ground. For the case against Burke's aristocracy has a moral aspect with which he did not deal. He did not inquire by what right a handful of men were to be hereditary governors of a whole people. Expediency is no answer to the question, for Bentham was presently to show how shallow was that basis of consent. Once it is admitted that the personality of men is entitled to respect institutional room must be found for its expression. The State is morally stunted where their powers go undeveloped. There is something curious here in Burke's inability to suspect deformity in a system which gave his talents but partial place. He must have known that no one in the House of Commons was his equal. He must have known how few of those he called upon to recognize the splendor of their function were capable of playing the part he pictured for them. The answer to a morally bankrupt aristocracy is surely not the overwhelming effort required in its purification when the plaintiff is the people; for the mere fact that the people is the plaintiff is already evidence of its fitness for power. Burke gave no hint of how the level of his governing class could be maintained. He said nothing of what education might accomplish for the people. He did not examine the obvious consequences of their economic status. Had his eyes not been obscured by passion the work of that States-General the names in which appeared to him so astonishing in their inexperience, might have given him pause. The "obscure provincial advocates . . . stewards of petty local jurisdictions . . . the fomenters and conductors of the petty war of village vexation" legislated, out of their inexperience, for the world. Their resolution, their constancy, their high sense of the national need, were precisely the qualities Burke demanded in his governing class; and the States-General did not move from the straight path he laid down until they met with intrigue from those of whom Burke became the licensed champion.

Nor is it in the least clear that his emphasis upon expediency is, in any real way, a release from metaphysical inquiry. Rather may it be urged that what was needed in Burke's philosophy was the clear avowal of the metaphysic it implied. Nothing is more greatly wanted in political inquiry than discovery of that "intuition more subtle than any articulate major premise" which, as Mr. Justice Holmes has said, is the true foundation of so many of our political judgments. The theory of natural rights upon which Burke heaped such contempt was wrong rather in its form than in its substance. It clearly suffered from its mistaken effort to trace to an imaginary state of nature what was due to a complex experience. It suffered also from its desire to lay down universal formulae. It needed to state the rights demanded in terms of the social interests they involved rather than in the abstract ethic they implied. But the demands which underlay the thought of men like Price and Priestley was as much the offspring of experience as Burke's own doctrine. They made, indeed, the tactical mistake of seeking to give an unripe philosophic form to a political strategy wherein, clearly enough, Burke was their master. But no one can read the answers of Paine [see excerpt dated 1791] and Mackintosh, who both were careful to avoid the panoply of metaphysics, to the **Reflections,** without feeling that Burke failed to move them from their main position. Expediency may be admirable in telling the statesmen what to do; but it does not explain the sources of his ultimate act, nor justify the thing finally done. The unconscious deeps which lie beneath the surface of the mind are rarely less urgent than the motives that are avowed. Action is less their elimination than their index; and we must penetrate within their recesses before we have the full materials for judgment. (pp. 265-70)

[Burke's] very defects are lessons in themselves. His unhesitating inability to see how dangerous is the concentration of property is standing proof that men are over-prone to judge the rightness of a State by their own wishes. His own contempt for the results of reasonable inquiry is a ceaseless lesson in the virtue of consistent scrutiny of our inheritance. His disregard of popular desire suggests the fatal ease with which we neglect the opinion of those who stand outside the active centre of political conflict. Above all, his hostility to the Revolution should at least make later generations beware lest novelty of outlook be unduly confounded with erroneous doctrine.

Yet even when such deduction has been made, there is hardly a greater figure in the history of political thought in England. Without the relentless logic of Hobbes, the acuteness of Hume, the moral insight of T. H. Green, he has a large part of the faculties of each. He brought to the political philosophy of his generation a sense of its direction, a lofty vigour of purpose, and a full knowledge of its complexity, such as no other states-man has ever possessed. His flashes of insight are things that go, as few men have ever gone, into the hidden deeps of political complexity. Unquestionably, his speculation is rather that of the orator in the tribune than of the thinker in his study. He never forgot his party, and he wrote always in that House of Commons atmosphere which makes a man unjust to the argument and motives of his opponent. Yet, when the last word of criticism has been made, the balance of illumination is immense. He illustrates at its best the value of that party-system the worth of which made so deep an impression on all he wrote. He showed that government by discussion can be made to illuminate great principles. He showed also that allegiance to party is never inconsistent with the deeper allegiance to the demand of conscience. When he came to the House of Commons, the prospects of representative government were very dark; and it is mainly to his emphasis upon its virtues that its victory must be attributed. Institutional change is likely to be more rapid than in his generation; for we seem to have reached that moment when, as he foresaw, "they who persist in opposing that mighty current will appear rather to resist the decrees of Providence itself than the mere designs of men." The principles upon which we proceed are doubtless different from those that he commended; yet his very challenge to their wisdom only gives to his warning a deeper inspiration for our effort. (pp. 278-80)

> *Harold J. Laski, "Burke," in his* Political Thought in England: From Locke to Bentham, *Henry Holt and Company, 1920, pp. 213-80.*

IRVING BABBITT (essay date 1924)

[*With Paul Elmer More, Babbitt was one of the founders of the New Humanism movement which arose during the second decade of the twentieth century. The New Humanists were strict moralists who held to traditional conservative cultural values in reaction to an age of scientism and artistic self-expression. They believed, as regards literature, that the implicit support for the classic ethical norms reflected in a given work of art should be of as much importance as its aesthetic qualities. They were particularly opposed to Naturalism, which they believed accentuated the animal nature of humans, and to any literature, such as Romanticism, that broke with established classical tradition. Besides Babbitt and More, other prominent New Humanists included Norman Foerster and T. S. Eliot, although the latter's conversion to Christianity angered Babbitt, whose concept of humanism substituted faith in humanity for faith in God. The author of several books propounding his philosophy, Babbitt was more a theorist than a literary critic; most of the New Humanist criticism was written by More, Eliot, and—until the mid-1920s—Stuart P. Sherman. In the following excerpt, Babbitt discusses the imaginative foundations of Burke's political theory, differentiates Burke from Jean-*

Jacques Rousseau, and gauges the viability of Burke's thought in the modern world.]

[Burke] saw how much of the wisdom of life consists in an imaginative assumption of the experience of the past in such fashion as to bring it to bear as a living force upon the present. The very model that one looks up to and imitates is an imaginative creation. A man's imagination may realize in his ancestors a standard of virtue and wisdom beyond the vulgar practice of the hour; so that he may be enabled to rise with the example to whose imitation he has aspired. The forms of the past and the persons who administer them count in Burke's eyes chiefly as imaginative symbols. In the famous passage on Marie Antoinette one almost forgets the living and suffering woman to see in her with Burke a gorgeous symbol of the age of chivalry yielding to the age of "sophisters, economists, and calculators." There is in this sense truth in the taunt of Tom Paine that Burke pities the plumage and forgets the dying bird [see excerpt dated 1791]. All the decent drapery of life, Burke complains of the new philosophy, is to be rudely torn off. "All the superadded ideas, furnished from the wardrobe of a moral imagination, . . . are to be exploded as a ridiculous, absurd, and antiquated fashion."

The apostles of the rights of man were, according to Burke, undermining the two principles on which everything that was truly civilized in the European order had for ages depended: the spirit of religion and the spirit of a gentleman. The nobility and the clergy, who were the custodians of these principles and of the symbols that embodied them and ministered to the moral imagination, had received in turn the support of the learned. Burke warns the learned that in deserting their natural protectors for Demos, they run the risk of being "cast into the mire and trodden under the hoofs of a swinish multitude."

Burke is in short a frank champion of aristocracy. It is here especially, however, that he applies flexibly his Christian-Platonic, and humanistic principles. He combines a soundly individualistic element with his cult of the traditional order. He does not wish any static hierarchy. He disapproves of any tendency to deal with men in classes and groups, a tendency that the extreme radical shares with the extreme reactionary. He would have us estimate men, not by their hereditary rank, but by their personal achievement. "There is," he says, "no qualification for government but virtue or wisdom, actual or presumptive. Wherever they are actually found, they have in whatever state, condition, profession or trade, the passport of Heaven to human place and honor." He recognizes, to be sure, that it is hard for the manual worker to acquire such virtue and wisdom for the reason that he lacks the necessary leisure. The ascent of rare merit from the lower to the higher levels of society should, however, always be left open, even though this merit be required to pass through a severe probation.

In the same fashion, Burke would admit innovations in the existing social order only after a period of severe probation. He is no partisan of an inert traditionalism. His true leader or natural aristocrat, as he terms him, has, in his adjustment of the contending claims of new and old, much of the character of the "trimmer" as Halifax has described him. "By preserving the method of nature in the conduct of the state, in what we improve we are never wholly new; in what we retain, we are never wholly obsolete." "The disposition to preserve, and ability to improve, taken together, would be my standard of a statesman." In such utterances Burke is of course simply giving the theory of English liberty at its best, a theory almost too familiar for restatement. In his imaginative grasp of all that is involved in the task of mediating between the permanent and the fluctuating element in life, the Platonic art, as one may say, of seeing the One in the Many, he has had few equals in the field of political thinking.

Burke is, however, in one important respect highly un-Platonic, and that is in his attitude toward the intellect. His distrust of what we should call nowadays the intellectual may be variously explained. It is related in some respects to one side, the weak side, one is bound to add, of Christianity. "A certain intemperance of intellect," he writes, "is the disease of the time, and the source of all its other diseases." He saw so clearly the dangers of this abuse that he was led at times, as the Christian has at times been led, to look with suspicion on intellect itself. And then he was familiar, as we are all familiar, with persons who give no reasons at all, or the wrong reasons, for doing the right thing, and with other persons who give the most logical and ingenious reasons for doing the wrong thing. The basis for right conduct is not reasoning but experience, and experience much wider than that of the individual, the secure possession of which can result only from the early acquisition of right habits. Then, too, there is something specifically English in Burke's disparagement of the intellect. The Englishman, noting the results of the proneness of a certain type of Frenchman to reason rigorously from false or incomplete premises, comes to prefer his own piecemeal good sense and proclivity for "muddling through." As Disraeli told a foreign visitor, the country is governed not by logic but by Parliament. In much the same way Bagehot in the course of a comparison between the Englishman and the Frenchman in politics, reaches the semihumorous conclusion that "in real sound stupidity the English are unrivaled."

The antiintellectual side of Burke reminds one at times of the antiintellectual side of Rousseau: when, for instance, he speaks of "the happy effect of following nature, which is wisdom without reflection and above it." The resemblance is, however, only superficial. The wisdom that Rousseau proclaimed was not *above* reflection but *below* it. A distinction of this kind is rather meaningless unless supported by careful psychological analysis. Perhaps the first contrast between the superrational and the subrational is that between awe and wonder. Rousseau is plainly an apostle of wonder, so much so that he is probably the chief single influence in the "renascence of wonder" that has resulted from the romantic movement. The romantic objection to intellect is that by its precise analysis and tracing of cause and effect, it diminishes wonder. Burke, on the other hand, is fearful lest an indiscreet intellectual activity may undermine awe and reverence. "We ought," he says, "to venerate where we are unable presently to understand." As the best means of securing veneration, Burke leans heavily upon habit, whereas the romantics, from Rousseau to Walter Pater, are no less clearly hostile to habit because it seems to lead to a stereotyped world, a world without vividness and surprise. To lay stress on veneration meant for Burke, at least in the secular order, to lay stress on rank and degree; whereas the outstanding trait perhaps of the state of nature projected by Rousseau's imagination, in defiance of the actual facts of primitive life so far as we know them, is that it is equalitarian. This trait is common to his no-state and his all-state, his anarchistic and his collectivistic utopia. The world of the *Social Contract,* no less than that of the *Second Discourse,* is a world without degree and subordination; a world in which no one looks up to anyone else or expects anyone to look up to him; a world in which no one (and this seems to Rousseau very desirable) has either to command or to obey. (pp. 127-32)

[The] modern political movement may be regarded in its most significant aspect as a battle between the spirit of Rousseau and that of Burke. Whatever the explanation, it is an indubitable fact that this movement has been away from Burke is and toward Rousseau. "The star of Burke is manifestly fading," Lecky was able to write a number of years ago, "and a great part of the teaching of the *Contrat Social* is passing into English politics." Professor Vaughan . . . , the editor of the recent standard edition of Rousseau's political writings, remarked in his introduction, apparently without awakening any special contradiction or surprise, that in the essentials of political wisdom Burke is "immeasurably inferior to the man of whom he never speaks but with scorn and loathing; to the despised theorist, the metaphysical madman of Geneva."

Burke will be cherished as long as anyone survives in the world who has a perception of the nature of true liberty. It is evident, however, that if a true liberalism is to be successfully defended under present circumstances, it will not be altogether by Burke's method. The battle for prejudice and prescription and a "wisdom above reflection" has already been lost. It is no longer possible to wave aside the modernists as the mere noisy insects of an hour, or to oppose to an unsound activity of intellect mere stolidity and imperviousness to thought—the great cattle chewing their cud in the shadow of the British oak. (pp. 139-40)

> *Irving Babbitt, "Burke and the Moral Imagination,"*
> *in his* Democracy and Leadership, *1924. Reprint by*
> *Liberty Classics, 1978, pp. 121-40.*

ALFRED COBBAN   (essay date 1929)

[*An English historian and educator, Cobban was an authority on French history and the history of political thought. In the following excerpt, he examines Burke's modification of the principles of law propounded by John Locke.*]

In a sense Burke represents the culmination of Lockian political theory; he is also the leading figure in the revolt against eighteenth-century politics, for although, in some respects, Hume had anticipated him, both in quality and quantity his political thinking is so much incomparably greater than Hume's that our study of the revolt must necessarily begin with Burke. (pp. 37-8)

Burke has held rather a dubious position in the history of political thought. A political philosopher who is also a practical politician is apt to be regarded as somewhat of an anomaly and to be treated accordingly by other politicians during his life and by philosophers after his death. Of Burke we may say that had he been less of a theorist he would have met with higher rewards in his Parliamentary career, while had he been a less violent partisan his political ideas might have been granted a juster appreciation by those who studied them in the subsequent century. So intermingled with advocacy of party policy is his exposition of political principles, that those who set out to treat him as a theorist in the light of pure reason have generally ended by applauding or denouncing him as a politician in the light of latter-day politics. Mostly it has been applause, but of rather a self-regarding nature. In a political way of speaking, all things to all men, to Liberals such as Morley, Burke has seemed a Gladstonian who went wrong towards the end of his days; while to Conservatives like Lord Hugh Cecil the vision has been revealed of the great Whig as spiritually one with Disraeli and Young England. It is obvious that any account of Burke's theories which begins with assumptions of this nature is unlikely to give an unbiased view, though the temptation to label him in some such way is great, for even his own contemporaries did not know quite what to make of him. (pp. 38-9)

Burke is the greatest of the followers of Locke; he it was who filled in the somewhat sketchy outlines of the *Treatise on Government* and worked out the theoretical elaboration which explained, justified, or condemned the many expedients which practical politicians had devised in putting the principles of 1688 into operation. But Burke also it was who, not only in the **Reflections** but long before the French Revolution, wrote of the political relation in language Locke would never have dreamed of using. It is not true that Burke changed his opinions fundamentally at the time of the Revolution or at any other time, but it is true that an inconsistency runs right through his thought. The extent of his divergence from Locke will be made clear if we take for study in the first place just those aspects in which Burke might be assumed to follow him.

What, we will ask, has Burke to say about the fundamental principles which the famous *Second Treatise* lays down? Does he simply accept them on the authority of Locke, or does he attempt to work out a fresh theoretical basis for himself? As he nowhere devotes a work specifically to questions of theory, it has sometimes been assumed that the former alternative is the true one. But if he does not ever definitely set out to treat of theoretical issues, Burke is all the time being brought up against them and compelled, willingly or unwillingly, to offer some answer; and the incidental discussions and *obiter dicta* resulting are often more valuable than a set treatise would have proved. For whatever he himself may say and believe as to his undeviating allegiance to Locke, actually he diverges in some most significant respects from his teacher. Let us take these fundamental principles in turn.

The basic political conception of Locke was that embodied in the theory of the Social Contract, which, of course, was introduced primarily for the purpose of making possible the transition from a state of nature to the social state. Now the object according to Locke of this transition was the inauguration of the rule of law—a conception to which the *Second Treatise on Government* continually appeals, and which is perhaps the political principle nearest the heart of England. When FitzJames Stephen declares that by his reverence for the rule of law Burke is nearer to Montesquieu than to the English tradition, he forgets that before Montesquieu was Locke, from whom it is that Burke as well as Montesquieu derives this element in his theory; before Locke, indeed, were Coke and Hooker, with behind them the centuries-old traditions of feudal and common law.

But does Law mean quite the same to the later thinker as to Locke? Times change and words and phrases remain, but they bear more often than not a new meaning to a new age. Locke and Burke appeal with equal constancy to the ideal of law, but is it to the same law that they are appealing? A comparison of the two soon shows that Locke, who hardly ever refers to the judicial power of the actual State, continually invokes the Law of Nature, for the enforcement of which he regards political society as formed, and clearly bases his most important arguments on this conception; whereas Burke makes use of it but rarely, and when he does talk of the Law of Nature seems to have something different in his mind. To discuss fully what the term meant to Locke would be to enter into pathless wilds of controversy; it is evident, however, that it was really a pseudo-philosophical conception, and could be taken as equivalent to the "law of reason"—though what that might mean in its turn beyond a law of common sense it would be difficult to say. On the other hand the law of which Burke talks is not a rationalized law of nature but a supra-rational law of God—that law "by which we are knit and connected in the eternal frame of the universe, out of which we cannot stir". In just the same way his Contract is not the prosaic Social Contract of Locke, but "the great primeval contract of eternal society, linking the lower with the higher natures, connecting the visible and invisible world".

Burke's conception of law presents itself thus on a much more exalted plane than Locke's, but when we come to the actual application of the theory the reverse is the case; for whereas Locke uses his law of nature merely as a philosophical basis for the political principles he is anxious to set up, Burke passes directly from divine law to the positive laws of man. Although in the eternal law Will and Reason coincide, because of the restless will and impious passions of mankind, he argues, temporal laws are necessary to preserve the same coincidence on earth. Just government, he echoes Locke, can never be at the disposition of individual will. Above it, Locke had claimed, are the precepts of natural law; Burke says, in different phraseology, because all power is from God, by the very fact of being thus delegated it should be exercised in accordance with divine law; that it is so exercised is his conclusion in most cases. Human laws being merely declaratory of God's in his opinion, the respect which to begin with he attributes to the Law of God is thus passed on to positive human laws; and so it naturally follows that when he thinks of the authority of law it is with reference generally to some definite code and lawcourts. When he declared dramatically in the indictment of Hastings, "Let him fly where he will from law to law;—law (I thank God) meets him everywhere", Burke had in front of his mind not the ever-present and unchanging law of nature, but the innumerable local laws of human society. This dissolution of Locke's Law of Nature into two distinct but closely allied concepts—the law of God and the laws of men—very largely reverses its function. The law of God is perfect, but its contents cannot easily be specified; the laws of men have quite definite contents but are very far from perfect. By linking them together so ingeniously Burke is able to justify all the ordinances of the latter on the authority of the former. Thus the idea of Law which for Locke in the form of the Law of Nature had been a ground of revolution is transformed into an essentially conservative doctrine.

True, it can be said that Burke is absolutely impartial in his application of the idea of law, and that although he starts from divine obligation and not from natural right, a despotic constitution remains to him just what it had been to Locke, a contradiction in terms. The arguments that Locke had used against James II he is equally willing to turn against George III. Again, shameful as he considered the incidental tyrannies of Hastings's rule in India, the attempt to defend these by a claim of immunity from law, the attempt to erect arbitrary violence into a principle, he rightly accounts the impeached Governor-General's most heinous crime. But on whichever side it may chance to arise the principle of despotism is always the enemy. Locke had denounced the tyranny of a King—Burke places tyranny and unprovoked rebellion on an equality: he refuses to recognize either absolute monarchy or absolute democracy as a legitimate form of government. In his Revolution pamphlets he condemns the lawless tyranny of the mob; in his Indian speeches he passes judgment on the despotism of a ruler with equal severity. According to his lights he fought against lawlessness wherever he found it, whether in a king's treatment of a colony, a governor's oppression of a conquered country, great States lording it over small, or revolutionary mobs governing by caprice.

The important point to be noted, however, is that this admirable result, although comprising a most triumphant vindication of the rule of law, and impressing it as a constitutional maxim firmly on the British people, was not in the last resort based on the same theoretic foundations as Locke's equally famous protest against Stuart tyranny. This fact becomes clearer when we go behind the Law of Nature in search of Natural Rights, as—the idea of law being meaningless unless it is taken as defending some definite rights—we necessarily must. Locke, like Rousseau, bases his case on the natural and inalienable rights of man. Burke, on the other hand, refuses even to speculate on the subject of natural rights, reserving them in his theory only as a final recourse against despotism. . . . (pp. 40-5)

[Just] as Burke's rule of law is different from Locke's, so are his natural rights: in fact, it is only with very considerable qualifications that he can be said to belong to the natural right school of thought. He declares in orthodox fashion that natural rights are sacred, but adds that he puts little value on attempts to codify them. . . . Unlike Locke and the revolutionists, the only catalogue of rights he will draw up is one of legal rights. Natural rights, he definitely states, are at the formation of society abrogated and replaced by civil rights, to which henceforth man is confined, because as soon as any restriction whatever is admitted on the abstract rights of man, society passes into the realm of expediency. Burke's theory of the change is that political authority must be admitted to be an artificial derogation from the natural equality of man, but that it can be justified on grounds of utility; natural rights are at best abstract rights, the rights men can look for from government are their own advantages. Hence political questions are related primarily not to natural rights or wrongs, nor even to truth and falsehood, but to the positive good and evil of actual men and women.

The whole of Burke's career is a commentary on that text. His first great political crusade exposed it clearly: his objection to the English Government's American policy was that it had been determined by considerations of rights instead of according to the actual circumstances. On the other hand, he rejected equally the abstract demands put forward by the extremists on the colonists' side. In marginal notes to Pownall's book on the colonies he remarks: "Whatever they (the colonists) claim under the laws of Nature has nothing to do with our positive constitution". His criticism of Chatham, as later of the French Revolutionaries, was that he allowed himself to be governed too much by general maxims. For himself as he boasted to the Sheriffs of Bristol, "I never ventured to put your solid interests on speculative grounds". To sum up, Burke is, in the broad sense and with far more consistency than Locke, a utilitarian. (pp. 45-6)

[The] system of natural rights which Locke had retained as the framework of his political theory is practically discarded by Burke, who lets a conscious and noble utilitarianism provide its own justification. Such were Burke's views on the ends of political society, and on its nature his views are equally in advance of Locke's. The contractual theory being an essential element in the Whig political scheme, Burke naturally accepted it unquestioningly, but once inside his mind it was to undergo a strange metamorphosis. Its function in Locke had been to effect the transformation of natural into civil rights, and so to bridge the gap between the state of nature and the political state; which it did by setting up with general consent a government to enact and enforce the necessary laws in the ways

"A Uniform Whig" by James Gillray: A political cartoon dated 16 November 1791. Drawn to satirize Burke's self-acknowledged political consistency, Gillray depicts Burke as an opportunist siding with the court of George III, lured by the prospect of financial gain.

and for the purposes prescribed by the social contract. The government thus formed gave society its only element of unity. (p. 49)

[Without] abandoning the contractual theory in so many words, [Burke] tacitly drops it when he regards every man as necessarily born into political obedience, and as becoming, when he grows to adult years, automatically a full member of the body politic and subject to all the ensuing obligations. The justification that Burke would have given, if the need for one had ever presented itself to him, would have been that he could not conceive of the individual as a moral and rational being apart from society, by which he is shaped and conditioned and endowed with moral personality. Not merely a particular code of morality, but his very conscience and sense of duty are bestowed on him by society. A humble respect for the dictates of the social conscience is the least he can offer in return; to refuse to accept his due position in society with all its implications would be to renounce obedience not merely to a particular code, but to all moral law and utterly to cast off the yoke of duty. What room is left in a society regulated on this principle for the individual liberty, the right of resistance, in a word, the atomism of Locke's political philosophy? The only possible conclusion is that Burke has outgrown Locke; he has finally destroyed the system of natural law and contract, not by denying it, but in the only way in which an idea of value should ever be destroyed, by absorbing such parts of it as are fitted to be carried on and reintegrating them into the fabric of a fresh construction. (pp. 52-3)

Burke's principal interest in the Whig Revolution is as a final settlement, not as a precedent; there is a great deal more desire to preserve than to progress apparent here. Natural rights and the social contract being put on one side, perhaps stored up in some Lockian heaven, he is left with legal rights and the actual Constitution: these are his grand concern. The British Constitution is the solid foundation on which all his theorizing is built, and the ark of his adoration. (p. 58)

> *Alfred Cobban, in his* Edmund Burke and the Revolt against the Eighteenth Century: A Study of the Political and Social Thinking of Burke, Wordsworth, Coleridge and Southey, *The Macmillan Company, 1929, 280 p.*

W. SOMERSET MAUGHAM (essay date 1950-51)

[*Maugham was an English dramatist, short story writer, and novelist who is considered a skilled, cynical satirist. Best known for his autobiographical novel* Of Human Bondage *(1915), he also achieved popular success with such plays as* Caesar's Wife *(1922),* The Breadwinner *(1930), and* Our Betters *(1923). In the following excerpt from an essay originally published in the* Cornhill Magazine, *he admiringly explores the literary texture, technique, and antecedents of Burke's prose.*]

I had not read Burke since I was very young; I read then *On Conciliation with the Colonies* and *On the Affairs with America*; perhaps owing to my youth I did not find the matter very interesting, but I was deeply affected by the manner and I retained the recollection, vivid though vague, of a splendid magniloquence. I have now read these speeches once more, and of the more important writings of Burke besides, and in the following pages I wish to submit to the reader the reflections that have occurred to me. (p. 125)

English is a difficult language to write, and few authors have written it consistently with accuracy and distinction. The best way of learning to do this is to study the great masters of the past. Much of what Burke wrote has no longer, except perhaps to the politician, a pressing interest; indeed, I believe that almost all that he has to say of value to the average reader now could be put into one volume of elegant extracts; and for my part I must confess that I could never have brought myself to read his voluminous works with such care if I had not hoped to gain something from them that would enable me to write more nearly as I wish to. (pp. 127-28)

I think there are few writers who write well by nature. Burke was a man of prodigious industry and it is certain that he took pains not only over the matter of his discourse, but over the manner. . . . A glance at the *Origin of Our Ideas of the Sublime and Beautiful* is enough to show that Burke's style was the result of labour. Though this work, praised by Johnson, turned to account by Lessing and esteemed by Kant, cannot now be read with great profit it may still afford entertainment. In arguing that perfection is not the cause of beauty, he asserts:

> Women are very sensible of this; for which reason they learn to lisp, to totter in their walk, to counterfeit weakness, and even sickness. In all this they are guided by nature. Beauty in distress is much the most

affecting beauty. Blushing has little less power; and modesty in general, which is a tacit allowance of imperfection, is itself considered as an amiable quality, and certainly heightens every other that is so. I know it is in everybody's mouth, that we ought to love perfection. This is to me a sufficient proof that it is not the proper object of love.

Here is another quotation:

> When we have before us such objects as excite love and complacency, the body is affected so far as I could observe, much in the following manner: The head reclines something on one side, the eyelids are more closed than usual, and the eyes roll gently with an inclination to the object; the mouth is a little opened, and the breath drawn slowly, with now and then a long sigh; the whole body is composed, and the hands fall idly to the sides.

This book is supposed to have been first written when Burke was nineteen and it was published when he was twenty-six. I have given these quotations to show the style in which he wrote before he submitted to the influence which enabled him to become one of the masters of English prose. It is the general manner of the middle of the eighteenth century and I doubt whether anyone who read these passages would know who was the author. It is correct, easy and flowing; it shows that Burke had by nature a good ear. . . . He was not a melodious writer as Jeremy Taylor was in the seventeenth century or Newman in the nineteenth; his prose has force, vitality and speed rather than beauty; but notwithstanding the intricate complication of many of his sentences they remain easy to say and good to hear. I have no doubt that at times Burke wrote a string of words that was neither and in the tumult of his passion broke the simple rules of euphony which I have indicated. An author has the right to be judged by his best.

I have read somewhere that Burke learnt to write by studying Spenser and it appears that many of his gorgeous sentences and poetical allusions can be traced to the poet. He himself said that: 'Whoever relishes and reads Spenser as he ought to be read, will have a strong hold of the English language.' I do not see what he can have acquired from that mellifluous but (to my mind) tedious bard other than that sense of splendid sound of which I have just been speaking. He was certainly never influenced by the excessive use of alliteration which (again to my mind) makes the *Faerie Queene* cloying and sometimes even absurd. It has been said, among others by Charles James Fox, who should have known, that Burke founded his style on Milton's. I cannot believe it. It is true that he often quoted him and it would be strange indeed if with his appreciation of fine language Burke had failed to be impressed by the magnificence of vocabulary and grandeur of phrase in *Paradise Lost;* but the *Letters on a Regicide Peace,* on which, such as it is, the evidence for the statement rests, were written in old age: it seems improbable that if Burke had really studied Milton's prose for the purpose of forming his own its influence should not have been apparent till he had one foot in the grave. Nor can I believe, as the *Dictionary of National Biography* asserts, that he founded it on Dryden's. I see in Burke's deliberate, ordered and resonant prose no trace of Dryden's charming grace and happy-go-lucky facility. There is all the difference that there is between a French garden of trim walks and ordered parterres and a Thames-side park with its coppices and its green meadows. For my part I think it more likely that the special character of Burke's settled manner must be ascribed to the robust and irresistible example of Dr. Johnson. I think it was from him that Burke learnt the value of a long intricate sentence, the potent force of polysyllabic words, the rhetorical effect of balance and the epigrammatic elegance of antithesis. He avoided Johnson's faults (small faults to those who like myself have a peculiar fondness for Johnson's style) by virtue of his affluent and impetuous fancy and his practice of public speaking. (pp. 128-32)

His style, it must be obvious, is solidly based on balance. Hazlitt stated that it was Dryden who first used balance in the formation of his sentences. That seems an odd thing to say since one would have thought that balance came naturally to anyone who added two sentences together by a copulative: there is balance of a sort when you say: 'He went out for a walk and came home wet through'. Dr. Johnson on the other hand, speaking of Dryden's prose, said: 'The clauses are never balanced, nor the periods modelled: every word seems to drop by chance, though it falls in its proper place.' Thus do authorities disagree. Burke was much addicted to what for want of a better word I will call the triad; by this I mean the juxtaposition of three nouns, three adjectives, three clauses to reinforce a point. Here are some examples: 'Never was cause supported with more constancy, more activity, more spirit.'—'Shall there be no reserve power in the Empire, to supply a deficiency which may weaken, divide or dissipate the whole?'—'Their wishes ought to have great weight with him: their opinion, high respect; their business, unremitted attention.'—'I really think that for wise men this is not judicious; for sober men, not decent; for minds tinctured with humanity, not mild or merciful.' Burke had recourse to this pattern so often that in the end it falls somewhat monotonously on the ear. It has another disadvantage, more noticeable perhaps when read than when heard, that one member of the triad may be so nearly synonymous with another that you cannot but realise that it has been introduced for its sound rather than for its sense.

Burke made frequent use of the antithesis, which of course is merely a variety of balance. Hazlitt says it is first found in *The Tatler*. I have discovered no marked proof of this in an examination which I admit was cursory; there are traces of it, maybe, but adumbrations rather than definite instances. You can find more striking examples in the *Book of Proverbs.* . (pp. 142-43)

The antithetical style is vastly effective, and if it has gone out of common use it is doubtless for a reason that Johnson himself suggested. Its purpose is by the balance of words to accentuate the balance of thought, and when it serves merely to tickle the ear it is tiresome. (p. 143)

Now, the vogue of the antithesis had a marked effect on sentence structure, as anyone can see for himself by comparing the prose of Dryden, for example, with that of Burke. It brought into prominence the value of the period. I may remind the reader that a period is a sentence in which the sense is held up until the end: when a clause is added after a natural close the sentence is described as loose. The English language does not allow of the inversions which make it possible to suspend the meaning, and so the loose sentence is common. To this is largely due the diffusiveness of our prose. When once the unity of a sentence is abandoned there is little to prevent the writer from adding clause to clause. The antithetical structure was advantageous to the cultivation of the classical period, for it is obvious that its verbal merit depends on its compact and rounded form. I will quote a sentence of Burke's.

> Indeed, when I consider the face of the kingdom of France; the multitude and opulence of her cities; the useful magnificence of her spacious high roads and bridges; the opportunity of her artificial canals and navigations opening the conveniences of maritime communication through a solid continent of so immense an extent; when I turn my eyes to the stupendous works of her ports and harbours, and to her whole naval apparatus, whether for war or trade; when I bring before my view the number of her fortifications, constructed with so bold and masterly a skill, and made and maintained at so prodigious a charge, presenting an armed front and impenetrable barrier to her enemies upon every side; when I recollect how very small a part of that extensive region is without cultivation, and to what complete perfection the culture of many of the best productions of the earth have been brought in France; when I reflect on the excellence of her manufactures and fabrics, second to none but ours, and in some particulars not second; when I contemplate the grand foundations of charity public and private; when I survey the state of all the arts that beautify and polish life; when I reckon the men she has bred for extending her fame in war, her able statesmen, the multitude of her profound lawyers and theologians, her philosophers, her critics, her historians and antiquaries, her poets and her orators, sacred and profane; I behold in all this something which awes and commands the imagination, which checks the mind on the brink of precipitate and indiscriminate censure, and which demands that we should very seriously examine, what and how great are the latent vices that could authorise us at once to level so spacious a fabric with the ground.

The paragraph ends with three short sentences.

I should like to point out with what skill Burke has given a 'loose' structure to his string of subordinate clauses, thus further suspending the meaning till he brings his period to a close. Johnson, as we know, was apt to make periods of his subordinate clauses, writing what, I think, the grammarians call an extended complex, and so lost the flowing urgency which is characteristic of Burke. I should like to point out also what a happy effect Burke has secured in this compound sentence by forming his different clauses on the same plan and yet by varying cadence and arrangement avoiding monotony. He used the method of starting successive clauses with the same word, in this case with the word *when*, frequently and with effectiveness. It is of course a rhetorical device, which when delivered in a speech must have had a cumulative force, and shows once more how much his style was influenced by the practice of public speaking. I do not know that there is anyone in England who is capable now of writing such a sentence; perhaps there is no one who wants to; for, perhaps from an instinctive desire to avoid the 'loose' sentences which the idiosyncrasy of the language renders so inviting, it is the fashion these days to write short sentences. Indeed not long ago I read that the editor of an important newspaper had insisted that none of his contributors should write a sentence of more than fourteen words. Yet the long sentence has advantages. It gives you room to develop your meaning, opportunity to constitute your cadence and material to achieve your climax. Its disadvantages are that it may be diffuse, flaccid, crabbed or inapprehensible. The stylists of the seventeenth century wrote sentences of great length and did not always escape these defects. Burke seldom failed, however long his sentence, however elaborate its clauses and opulent his 'tropes', to make its fundamental structure so solid that you seem to be led to the safety of the full stop by a guide who knows his business and will permit you neither to take a side-turning nor to loiter by the way. Burke was careful to vary the length of his sentences. He does not tire you with a succession of long ones, nor, unless with a definitely rhetorical intention, does he exasperate you with a long string of short ones.

He has a lively sense of rhythm. His prose has the eighteenth-century tune, like any symphony of Haydn's, though with a truly English accent, and you hear the drums and fifes in it, but an individual note rings through it. It is a virile prose and I can think of no one who wrote with so much force combined with so much elegance. If it seems now a trifle formal, I think that is due to the fact that, like most of the eighteenth-century writers, he used general and abstract terms when we are now more inclined to use special and concrete ones. This gives a greater vividness to modern writing, though at the cost perhaps of concision. (pp. 145-48)

Dr. Johnson has told us that in his day nobody talked much of style, since everybody wrote pretty well. 'There is an elegance of style universally diffused,' he said. Burke was outstanding. His contemporaries were impressed, as well they might be, by his command of words, his brilliant similes, his hyperboles and fertile imagination, but did not invariably approve. Hazlitt relates a conversation between Fox and Lord Holland on the subject of his style. It appears that this

> Noble Person objected to it as too gaudy and mere-tricious, and said that it was more profuse of flowers than fruit. On which Mr. Fox observed, that though this was a common objection, it appeared to him altogether an unfounded one; that on the contrary the flowers often concealed the fruit beneath them; and the ornaments of style were rather a hindrance than an advantage to the sentiments they were meant to set off. In confirmation of this remark, he offered to take down the book and translate a page anywhere into his own plain, natural style; and by his doing so, Lord Holland was convinced that he had often missed the thought from having his attention drawn off to the dazzling imagery.

It is instructive to learn that Noble Persons and Eminent Politicians were interested in such questions in those bygone days and with such amiable exercises beguiled their leisure. But of course if his lordship's attention was really drawn off the matter of Burke's discourse by the brillancy of the manner, it is a reflection on his style. For the purpose of imagery is not to divert the reader, but to make the meaning clearer to him; the purpose of simile and metaphor is to impress it on his mind and by engaging his fancy make it more acceptable. An illustration is otiose unless it illustrates. Burke had a romantic and a poetic mind such as no other of the eighteenth-century masters of prose possessed, and it is this that gives his prose its variegated colour; but his aim was to convince rather than to please, to overpower rather than to persuade, and by all the resources of his imagination not only to make his point more obvious, but by an appeal to sentiment or passion to compel acquiescence. I don't know when Mr. Fox held his conversation with the Noble Lord, but if the *Reflections on the French Revolution* had then appeared he might well have pointed to it to refute his lordship's contention. For in that work the decoration so interpenetrates the texture of the writing that it becomes part and parcel of the argument. Here imagery, metaphor and simile fulfil their function. The one passage that leaves me doubtful is the most celebrated of all, that in which Burke tells how he saw Marie Antoinette at Versailles: 'and surely never lighted on this orb, which she hardly seemed to touch, a more delightful vision.' It is to be found in anthologies, so I will not quote it, but it is somewhat high flown to my taste.

But if it is not perfect prose it is magnificent rhetoric; magnificent even when it is slightly absurd: 'I thought ten thousand swords must have leapt from their scabbards to avenge even a look that threatened her with insult'; and the cadence with which the paragraph ends is lovely:

> The unbought grace of life, the cheap defence of nations, the nurse of manly sentiment and heroic enterprise is gone! It is gone, that sensibility of principle, that chastity of honour, which felt a stain like a wound, which inspired courage whilst it mitigated ferocity, which ennobled whatever it touched, and under which vice itself lost half its evil, by losing all its grossness.

(pp. 150-52)

As the quotations I have given plainly show, Burke made abundant use of metaphor. It is interwoven in the substance of his prose as the weavers of Lyons thread one colour with another to give a fabric the shimmer of shot silk. Of course like every other writer he uses what Fowler calls the natural metaphor, for common speech is largely composed of them, but he uses freely what Fowler calls the artificial metaphor. It gave concrete substance to his generalisations. He used it to enforce a statement by means of a physical image; but unlike some modern writers, who will pursue the implications of a metaphor like a spider scurrying along every filament of its web, he took care never to run it to death. (pp. 152-53)

On the other hand Burke used the simile somewhat sparingly. Modern writers might well follow his example. For of late a dreadful epidemic has broken out. Similes are clustered on the pages of our young authors as thickly as pimples on a young man's face, and they are as unsightly. A simile has use. By reminding you of a familiar thing it enables you to see the subject of the comparison more clearly or by mentioning an unfamiliar one it focuses your attention on it. It is dangerous to use it merely as an ornament; it is detestable to use it to display your cleverness; it is preposterous to use it when it neither decorates nor impresses. (Example: 'The moon like a huge blanc-mange wobbled over the tree-tops.') When Burke used a simile it was generally, as might be expected, with elaboration. (p. 153)

I have harped upon the fact that Burke's style owed many of its merits to his practice of speaking in public; to this it owed also such defects as a carping critic might find in it. There is more than one passage in the famous speech on the Nabob of Arcot's Debts when he asks a long series of rhetorical questions. It may have been effective in the House of Commons, but on the printed page it is restless and fatiguing. To this may be ascribed his too frequent recourse to the exclamatory sentence. 'Happy if they had all continued to know their indissoluble union, and their proper place! Happy if learning, not debauched by ambition, had been satisfied to continue the instructor, and not aspired to be the master.' Something of an old-fashioned air he has by his frequent use of an inverted construction, a mode now seldom met with; he employs it to vary the monotony of the simple order—subject, verb, object—and also to emphasise the significant member of the sentence by placing it first; but such a phrase as 'Personal offence I have given them none' needs the emphasis of the living voice to appear natural. On the other hand it is to his public speaking, I think, that Burke owed his skill in giving to a series of quite short sentences as musical a cadence and as noble a ring as when he set himself to compose an elaborate period with its pompous train of subordinate clauses; and this is shown nowhere to greater advantage than in the *Letter to a Noble Lord*.

Here a true instinct made him see that when he was appealing for compassion on account of his age and infirmities and by reminding his readers of the death of his beloved and only son, he must aim at simplicity. The passage is deeply moving:

> The storm has gone over me; and I lie like one of those old oaks which the late hurricane has scattered about me. I am stripped of all my honours, I am torn up by the roots, and lie prostrate on the earth . . . I am alone. I have none to meet my enemies in the gate. Indeed, my lord, I greatly deceive myself, if in this hard season I would give a peck of refuse wheat for all that is called fame and honour in the world. This is the appetite but of a few. It is a luxury, it is a privilege, it is an indulgence for those who are at their ease. But we are all of us made to shun disgrace, as we are made to shrink from pain, and poverty, and disease. It is an instinct; and under the direction of reason, instinct is always in the right. I live in an inverted order. They who ought to have succeeded me have gone before me. They who should have been to me as posterity are in the place of ancestors. I owe to the dearest relation (which ever must subsist in memory) that act of piety, which he would have performed to me; I owe it to him to show that he was not descended, as the Duke of Bedford would have it, from an unworthy parent.

Here the best words are indeed put in the best places. This piece owes little to picturesque imagery, nothing to romantic metaphor, and proves with what justification Hazlitt described him as, with the exception of Jeremy Taylor, the most poetical of prose-writers. I hope it will not be considered a literary conceit (a trifling, tedious business) when I suggest that in the tender melody of these cadences, in this exquisite choice of simple words, there is a foretaste of Wordsworth at his admirable best. If these pages should persuade anyone to see for himself how great a writer Burke was I cannot do better than advise him to read this *Letter to a Noble Lord.* It is the finest piece of invective in the English language and so short that it can be read in an hour. It offers in its brief compass a survey of all Burke's dazzling gifts, his formal as well as his conversational style, his gift for epigram and for irony, his wisdom, his sense, his pathos, his indignation and his nobility. (pp. 154-57)

> *W. Somerset Maugham, "After Reading Burke," in his* The Vagrant Mood: Six Essays, *1952. Reprint by Kennikat Press, 1969, pp. 123-57.*

LEO STRAUSS   (essay date 1953)

[*A German-born American philosopher, historian, and political scientist, Strauss wrote important studies on such figures as Thomas Hobbes, Benedictus de Spinoza, Plato, and Niccolò Machiavelli. In the following excerpt, Strauss discusses the fundamental ideas and values contained in Burke's political writings.*]

Burke did not write a single theoretical work on the principles of politics. All his utterances on natural right occur in statements *ad hominem* and are meant to serve immediately a specific practical purpose. Accordingly, his presentation of political principles changed, to a certain degree, with the change of the political situation. Hence he might easily appear to have been inconsistent. In fact, he adhered throughout his career to the same principles. A single faith animated his actions in favor of the American colonists, in favor of the Irish Catholics, against Warren Hastings, and against the French Revolution. In accordance with the eminently practical bent of his thought, he stated his principles most forcefully and most clearly when

such a statement was most urgently needed, i.e., when these principles were attacked both most intransigently and most effectively—after the outbreak of the French Revolution. The French Revolution affected his expectations in regard to the future progress of Europe; but it hardly affected, it hardly did more than confirm, his views of what is right or wrong both morally and politically.

The practical character of Burke's thought partly explains why he did not hesitate to use the language of modern natural right whenever that could assist him in persuading his modern audience of the soundness of a policy which he recommended. He spoke of the state of nature, of the rights of nature or of the rights of man, and of the social compact or of the artificial character of the commonwealth. But he may be said to integrate these notions into a classical or Thomistic framework. (pp. 295-96)

Burke admits that the purpose of civil society is to safeguard the rights of man and especially the right to the pursuit of happiness. But happiness can be found only by virtue, by the restraints "which are imposed by the virtues upon the passions." Hence the subjection to reason, to government, to law, or "the restraints on men, as well as their liberties, are to be reckoned among their rights." Man can never act "without any moral tie," since "men are never in a state of total independence of each other." Man's will must always be under the dominion of reason, prudence, or virtue. Burke therefore seeks the foundation of government "in a conformity to our duties" and not in "imaginary rights of men." Accordingly, he denies the contention that all our duties arise from consent or from contract.

The discussion regarding the "imaginary rights of men" centers on the right of everyone to be the sole judge of what is conducive to his self-preservation or to his happiness. It was this alleged right which seemed to justify the demand that everyone must have some share, and, in a sense, as large a share as anyone else, in political power. Burke questions this demand by going back to the principle on which the alleged basic right is founded. He grants that everyone has a natural right to self-preservation and to the pursuit of happiness. But he denies that everyone's right to self-preservation and to the pursuit of happiness becomes nugatory if everyone does not have the right to judge of the means conducive to his self-preservation and to his happiness. The right to the satisfaction of wants or to the advantages of society is therefore not necessarily a right to participation in political power. For the judgment of the many, or "the will of the many, and their interest, must very often differ." Political power or participation in political power does not belong to the rights of man, because men have a right to good government, and there is no necessary connection between good government and government by the many; the rights of man, properly understood, point toward the predominance of the "true natural aristocracy" and therewith to the predominance of property and especially landed property. In other words, everyone is indeed able to judge properly of grievances by his feelings, provided that he is not seduced by agitators into judging of grievances by his imagination. But the causes of grievances "are not matters of feeling, but of reason and foresight; and often of remote considerations, and of a very great combination of circumstances, which (the majority) are utterly incapable of comprehending." Burke therefore seeks the foundation of government not in "imaginary rights of men" but "in a provision for our wants, and in a conformity to our duties." Accordingly, he denies that natural right by itself can tell much about the legitimacy of a given constitution: that constitution is legitimate in a given society which is most suitable to the provision for human wants and to the promotion of virtue in that society; its suitability cannot be determined by natural right but only by experience.

Burke does not reject the view that all authority has its ultimate origin in the people or that the sovereign is ultimately the people or that all authority is ultimately derived from a compact of previously "uncovenanted" men. But he denies that these ultimate truths, or half-truths, are politically relevant. "If civil society be the offspring of convention, that convention must be its law." For almost all practical purposes, the convention, the original compact, i.e., the established constitution, is the highest authority. Since the function of civil society is the satisfaction of wants, the established constitution derives its authority less from the original convention or from its origin than from its beneficent working through many generations or from its fruits. (pp. 297-99)

Burke does not deny that under certain conditions the people may alter the established order. But he admits this only as an ultimate right. The health of society requires that the ultimate sovereignty of the people be almost always dormant. He opposes the theorists of the French Revolution because they turn "a case of necessity into a rule of law" or because they regard as normally valid what is valid only in extreme cases. "But the very habit of stating these extreme cases is not very laudable or safe." Burke's opinions, on the other hand, "never can lead to an extreme, because their foundation is laid in an opposition to extremes."

Burke traces the extremism of the French Revolution to a novel philosophy. "The old morality" was a morality "of social benevolence and of individual self-denial." The Parisian philosophers deny the nobility of "individual self-restraint" or of temperance or of "the severe and restrictive virtues." They recognize only the "liberal" virtues: "a virtue which they call humanity or benevolence." Humanity thus understood goes well with dissoluteness. It even fosters it; it fosters the loosening of the marriage bonds and the substitution of the theater for the church. In addition, "the same discipline which . . . relaxes their morals," "hardens their hearts": the extreme humanitarianism of the theorists of the French Revolution necessarily leads to bestiality. For that humanitarianism is based on the premise that the fundamental moral facts are rights which correspond to the basic bodily wants; all sociability is derivative and, in fact, artificial; certainly, civil society is radically artificial. Hence the virtues of the citizen cannot be grafted "on the stock of the natural affections." But civil society is assumed to be not only necessary but noble and sacred. Accordingly, the natural sentiments, all natural sentiments, must be ruthlessly sacrificed to the alleged requirements of patriotism or of humanity. The French revolutionists arrive at these requirements by approaching human affairs in the attitude of scientists, of geometricians or of chemists. Hence, they are, from the outset, "worse than indifferent about those feelings and habitudes, which are the support of the moral world." They "consider men in their experiments, no more than they do mice in an air pump, or in a recipient of mephitic gas." Accordingly, "they are ready to declare that they do not think two thousand years too long a period for the good that they pursue." "Their humanity is not dissolved. They only give it a long prorogation. . . . Their humanity is at their horizon—and, like the horizon, it always flies before them." It is this "scientific"

attitude of the French revolutionists or of their teachers which also explains why their dissoluteness, which they oppose as something natural to the conventions of earlier gallantry, is "an unfashioned, indelicate, sour, gloomy, ferocious medley of pedantism and lewdness."

Burke opposes, then, not merely a change in regard to the substance of the moral teaching. He opposes likewise, and even primarily, a change in regard to its mode: the new moral teaching is the work of men who think about human affairs as geometricians think about figures and planes rather than as acting men think about a business before them. It is this fundamental change from a practical to a theoretical approach which, according to Burke, gave the French Revolution its unique character.

"The present revolution in France seems to me . . . to bear little resemblance or analogy to any of those which have been brought about in Europe, upon principles merely political. It is a revolution of doctrine and theoretic dogma. It has a much greater resemblance to those changes which have been made upon religious grounds, in which a spirit of proselytism makes an essential part." The French Revolution, therefore, has a certain resemblance to the Reformation. Yet "this spirit of general political faction," or this "armed doctrine," is "separated from religion" and is, in fact, atheistic; the "theoretic dogma" guiding the French Revolution is purely political. . . . The success of the French Revolution can be explained only by that one among its features which distinguishes it from all parallels. The French Revolution is the first "philosophic revolution." It is the first revolution which was made by men of letters, philosophers, "thoroughbred metaphysicians," "not as subordinate instruments and trumpeters of sedition, but as the chief contrivers and managers." It is the first revolution in which "the spirit of ambition is connected with the spirit of speculation."

In opposing this intrusion of the spirit of speculation or of theory into the field of practice or of politics, Burke may be said to have restored the older view according to which theory cannot be the sole, or the sufficient, guide of practice. He may be said to have returned to Aristotle in particular. But, to say nothing of other qualifications, one must add immediately that no one before Burke had spoken on this subject with equal emphasis and force. One may even say that, from the point of view of political philosophy, Burke's remarks on the problem of theory and practice are the most important part of his work. He spoke more emphatically and more forcefully on this problem than Aristotle in particular had done because he had to contend with a new and most powerful form of "speculatism," with a political doctrinairism of philosophic origin. That "speculatist" approach to politics came to his critical attention a considerable time before the French Revolution. Years before 1789, he spoke of "the speculatists of our speculating age." It was the increased political significance of speculation which, very early in his career, most forcefully turned Burke's attention to "the old quarrel between speculation and practice."

It was in the light of that quarrel that he conceived his greatest political actions: not only his action against the French Revolution but his action in favor of the American colonists as well. In both cases the political leaders whom Burke opposed insisted on certain rights: the English government insisted on the rights of sovereignty and the French revolutionists insisted on the rights of man. In both cases Burke proceeded in exactly the same manner: he questioned less the rights than the wisdom of exercising the rights. In both cases he tried to restore the genuinely political approach as against a legalistic approach. Now he characteristically regarded the legalistic approach as one form of "speculatism," other forms being the approaches of the historian, the metaphysician, the theologian, and the mathematician. All these approaches to political matters have this in common—that they are not controlled by prudence, the controlling virtue of all practice. Whatever might have to be said about the propriety of Burke's usage, it is here sufficient to note that, in judging the political leaders whom he opposed in the two most important actions of his life, he traced their lack of prudence less to passion than to the intrusion of the spirit of theory into the field of politics. (pp. 299-304)

Burke's political theory is, or tends to become, identical with a theory of the British constitution, i.e., an attempt to "discover the latent wisdom which prevails" in the actual. One might think that Burke would have to measure the British constitution by a standard transcending it in order to recognize it as wise, and to a certain extent he undoubtedly does precisely this: he does not tire of speaking of natural right, which, as such, is anterior to the British constitution. But he also says that "our constitution is a prescriptive constitution; it is a constitution whose sole authority is that it has existed time out of mind" or that the British constitution claims and asserts the liberties of the British "as an estate especially belonging to the people of this kingdom, without any reference whatever to any other more general or prior right." Prescription cannot be the sole authority for a constitution, and therefore recourse to rights anterior to the constitution, i.e., to natural rights, cannot be superfluous unless prescription by itself is a sufficient guaranty of goodness. Transcendent standards can be dispensed with if the standard is inherent in the process; "the actual and the present is the rational." What could appear as a return to the primeval equation of the good with the ancestral is, in fact, a preparation for Hegel. (p. 319)

Among the great theoretical writings of the past, none seems to be nearer in spirit to Burke's statements on the British constitution than Cicero's *Republic*. The similarity is all the more remarkable since Burke cannot have known Cicero's masterpiece, which was not recovered until 1820. Just as Burke regards the British constitution as the model, Cicero contends that the best polity is the Roman polity; Cicero chooses to describe the Roman polity rather than to invent a new one, as Socrates had done in Plato's *Republic*. These contentions of Burke and of Cicero are, if taken by themselves, in perfect agreement with the classical principles: the best polity being essentially "possible," it could have become actual at some place and at some time. One should note, however, that, whereas Burke assumed that the model constitution was actual in his time, Cicero assumed that the best polity had been actual in the past but was no longer actual. Above all, Cicero made it perfectly clear that the characteristics of the best polity can be determined without regard to any example, and especially to the example of the Roman polity. In the respect under discussion, there is no difference between Cicero and Plato in particular; Plato commenced a sequel to his *Republic,* namely the *Critias,* in which the "invented" polity of the *Republic* was to be shown to have been actual in the Athenian past. The following agreement between Burke and Cicero seems to be more important: just as Burke traced the excellence of the British constitution to the fact that it had come into being "in a great length of time" and thus embodies "the collected reason of ages," Cicero traced the superiority of the Roman polity to the fact that it was not the work of one man or of one generation but of many men and many generations. Cicero calls the way

in which the Roman order developed into the best polity, "some natural road." Still, "the very idea of the fabrication of a new government" did not fill Cicero, as it did Burke, "with disgust and horror." If Cicero preferred the Roman polity, which was the work of many men and many generations, to the Spartan polity, which was the work of one man, he did not deny that the Spartan polity was respectable. In his presentation of the origins of the Roman polity, Romulus appears almost as the counterpart of Lycurgus; Cicero did not abandon the notion that civil societies are founded by superior individuals. It is "counsel and training" as opposed to chance that Cicero understands to be the "natural road" by which the Roman polity reached its perfection; he does not understand the "natural road" to be processes unguided by reflection.

Burke disagreed with the classics in regard to the genesis of the sound social order because he disagreed with them in regard to the character of the sound social order. As he saw it, the sound social or political order must not be "formed upon a regular plan or with any unity of design" because such "systematical" proceedings, such "presumption in the wisdom of human contrivances," would be incompatible with the highest possible degree of "personal liberty"; the state must pursue "the greatest variety of ends" and must as little as possible "sacrifice any one of them to another, or to the whole." It must be concerned with "individuality" or have the highest possible regard for "individual feeling and individual interest." It is for this reason that the genesis of the sound social order must not be a process guided by reflection but must come as close as possible to natural, imperceptible process: the natural is the individual, and the universal is a creature of the understanding. Naturalness and free flowering of individuality are the same. Hence the free development of the individuals in their individuality, far from leading to chaos, is productive of the best order, an order which is not only compatible with "some irregularity in the whole mass" but requires it. There is beauty in irregularity: "method and exactness, the soul of proportion, are found rather prejudicial than serviceable to the cause of beauty." The quarrel between the ancients and the moderns concerns eventually, and perhaps even from the beginning, the status of "individuality." Burke himself was still too deeply imbued with the spirit of "sound antiquity" to allow the concern with individuality to overpower the concern with virtue. (pp. 321-23)

*Leo Strauss, "The Crisis of Modern Natural Right,"
in his* Natural Right and History, *The University of
Chicago Press, 1953, pp. 252-323.*

CHARLES PARKIN   (essay date 1956)

[In the following excerpt, Parkin analyzes Burke's conceptions of prescription and the moral order in English society.]

[While] Burke's thought is by design a response to immediate contingencies, it is in no sense an uncontrolled or arbitrary response, but always, in his own eyes, under the guidance of moral principles, which certainly, to be real, must be reinterpreted, rediscovered, and reaffirmed in an infinity of specific and unique situations, but which represent themselves unchanging truths of human life and community. So that while Burke's political thought, viewed in one aspect, is hardly more than a reaction to the revolution of ephemeral political chance and even personal fortune, it yet always leans toward a still centre of the most general and absolute belief. His ideas carry all the marks and associations of their origin, but they converge on a core of moral certainty freed finally from the relative and the contingent. (p. 3)

[For Burke, the] supreme wisdom of the statesman is to apprehend the moral reason and make it fruitful in the present. He must seek for it by a careful attention to the heritage of tradition and the wisdom of antiquity; but this is as a guide rather than as a rule to him. The appeal to the record of the settled order of the world is only the preliminary to co-operation with it now. The politician is the philosopher in action; though he must not lose sight of principle, he is to be guided by circumstances. A sphere of discretion and prudence must be left to him. True prudence is a caution and modesty which springs from his sense of the immense moral trust in his hands, not a complexional timidity, a false, reptile prudence, of trivial maxims, which is afraid to venture beyond the tried and familiar. The statesman must be aware that he stands in an arena of change and that he cannot stem the flux by an unthinking defence of the traditional order. *Stare super vias antiquas* [''to stand on the ancient ways''] must not be interpreted to preclude all improvement. Change is the essence of political life as of all nature. There is bound to be change, it is even necessary for survival; a state without the means of change is without the means of conservation. We must all obey the great law of change. For the statesman, this means distinguishing the live forms of human activity from those which are obsolete and rigidified, and in guiding them toward a harmony. His materials are the general energies of nature, the powers growing wild from the rank productive force of the human mind. He has to manage and tend these, to refine them, to extract from this vital confusion true moral relations. This is his attempt to grasp the immanent Providential order; but he cannot succeed in it if he is more concerned to preserve the achievement of the past than to reaffirm the *spirit* of that achievement. But of course, on the other hand, he is not to think too highly of legislation, or overestimate its creative power, for this brings the danger of attempting to impose an order in human affairs instead of eliciting one from them.

Reform and renovation are an integral aspect of the political scene. In the flux of human relations, institutions which originally satisfied genuine social needs may be left without live purpose or function, and thus superfluous or even constricting new aspirations and forms of expression. But when the reason of establishments has gone, it is absurd to preserve the burden of them. Antiquity and prescription are not powerful enough titles to preserve inveterate abuse; it is no defence of a pernicious system that it is an inheritance from the past. This is a comprehensive and undiscriminating adhesion to the prescriptive order, as though it had been an unconscious and unwilled growth. It forgets that the most ancient institutions were at one time the product of human deliberation responding to needs, and that they have always been subject to modification according to changing exigencies. To imagine otherwise is to turn a rational principle into an idle and vulgar superstition. The British constitution has admitted many revisions in order to reaffirm its principles in changed circumstances; and it has always been bettered by these corrections.

The statesman must therefore be prepared to undertake political reformation, in response to the great law of change which is operative in human affairs. However, if this is to be a preservation of the higher moral order in the flux of human relations, it must not be arbitrary or total or destructive change; it should be reform designed to re-embody unchanging moral principles in new circumstances, the preservation of a balance

of permanence and contingency. It is therefore a fundamental requirement of political reformation that it should combine the two principles of conservation and correction. (pp. 124-26)

A wise legislator, instead of trying to carry through complete reform at once, will often be content with establishing a correct social principle, which will fructify in time; in this way he cooperates with the natural order instead of trying to impose his schemes of improvement upon it. This is safe and permanent reform, because it respects the past and looks to the future. It will be achieved by men who realise that they are fallible, and that their compass in political change must be the higher moral order. They will eschew both the obstinacy which rejects all improvement and the levity which is disgusted with everything of which it is in possession. Their moderation will be at the opposite pole from indecision or fear. They will be respectful of the social heritage, and solicitous to preserve it alive. This dual capacity, a disposition to preserve, and an ability to improve, taken together, are the standard of a statesman.

A genuine sense of the moral achievement of our ancestors, in statesmen and in communities, must be inseparable from the awareness of the moral challenge of the present. The reason for our respect for the wisdom of antiquity must preclude us from surrendering ourselves wholly to its tutelage. What is venerated in the past is not just a human wisdom whose operation has ceased with the disappearance of its possessors, and whose works must therefore be preserved intact. It is the evidence of a superhuman wisdom, and this does not languish or fail. The same eternal order which has given value and significance to human relations in the past must be potential in the life of each generation. If this is so, it is a misinterpretation of Burke's appeal to Prescription to regard it, as Cobban does, as an admission of ignorance, a counsel of pessimism, a lack of faith in the future, which leaves a blind attachment to tried usages as the only guide into the unknown. Belief in the embodiment of the Providential order in the past is inseparable from belief in its latent presence in the present; the two convictions stand or fall together. The moral order is not only visible in the achievement of the past: it is immanent in our own lives and we are called upon to discern it and to co-operate with it. This is where we most directly encounter it. Therefore Burke's maintenance of the principle of Prescription, powerful though it is, is not merely not advanced in a spirit of despair or pessimism, but is not intended as his final article of belief. The moral order cannot be fully experienced through our sense of its presence in the traditional order. It confronts us in our own situation and circumstances. It requires a complete and live response; veneration for the wisdom of antiquity does not dispense with the need for a creative moral effort in each generation. Indeed, too literal and servile a deference to the heritage of the past will defeat its own ends, because the spirit of that wisdom will be lost, leaving only lifeless precept and habit. It is the nature of the higher reason that it cannot be possessed through its former embodiments; it can only be preserved by being rediscovered and relived. To imagine that it can be embalmed in an unchanging way of life is to misconceive its essence. It is to ignore its presence where it is most immediately presented to us, in our own unique circumstances. Of course, in the nature of things, the present movement of Providence, though a real thing, is indefinable, because it is all-embracing; it cannot be categorised by the abstract reason because it is deeper than the range of conscious understanding. But it can be felt, if sought with humility and a wide vision, and responded to. It is not superficial, however, and cannot be found without difficulty. Its presence demands a live response, and makes necessary a creative moral effort. This is the 'practicable virtue' which God has put within our reach; the appeal to the practicable here is not simply a confinement to what is in practice already. A community cannot retain moral worth if it is content with the mechanical and unfelt prolongation of a traditional way of life. Burke's conception of the historical process suggests a more exacting and more satisfying human situation, because it implies an encounter with the eternal moral order of each generation in its turn. (pp. 128-30)

> *Charles Parkin, in his* The Moral Basis of Burke's Political Thought: An Essay, *Cambridge at the University Press, 1956, 145 p.*

PETER J. STANLIS (essay date 1958)

[An American scholar of English literature and an authority on Robert Frost, Stanlis is also recognized as one of the world's foremost Burke scholars. In addition to publishing several works on Burke, he founded the Burke Newsletter *in 1959 and continues to contribute to this periodical, now titled the* Eighteenth Century: Theory and Interpretation. *Of Stanlis's* Edmund Burke and the Natural Law, *Russell Kirk commented: "Dr. Stanlis's book does more than any other study of this century to define Burke's position as philosopher, relating the convictions of Burke to the great traditions of Christian and classical civilization." In the following excerpt from this work, Stanlis assesses Burke's conception of the natural law, concluding with a discussion of Burke's relevance to twentieth-century politics.]*

The Natural Law is fundamental in Burke's conception of man and civil society. As principle or as the spirit of prudence, Natural Law permeates his view of Church and State and all international relations; it transcends all national, geographical, and historical considerations, all religious and political loyalties, all man-made legal systems and forms of government. It achieves this higher moral synthesis without in any way violating the right reason or true interests of man. But the Natural Law is also evidenced consistently in the negative side of Burke's thought; it supplied the moral and legal weapons for his attacks on various eighteenth-century radical theories and innovations, and on existing abuses in government. From his **"Tract on the Popery Laws"** (1761?) to the last of his *Letters on a Regicide Peace* (1797), Burke conceived of the Natural Law as an ethical norm by which to judge the social and political behavior of men. . . . [In] every period of his political life, from before his entrance into parliament through the crisis of the French Revolution, he consistently appealed to the Natural Law for the standard of redress against tyranny, chaos, and injustice.

Burke's faith in the Natural Law secured him firmly to the most vital ethical and political traditions of Europe, so that he was able to ride out the storm of ideas that swept over Europe during the last half of the eighteenth century. The appeals of deism and pantheism in religion left him untouched. His faith that the basic principles of Natural Law were self-evident to right reason, and that man had inherent rights by virtue of his innate spiritual nature, made him skeptical of the whole tradition of Locke's empiricism and rationalism. To Burke the revolutionary conception of an idyllic "state of nature," whether historical or hypothetical, was a childish and dangerous illusion, and led directly to such theories as the revocable social contract.

Burke was always convinced that no civilization, however just, could long survive the application of the revolutionary abstract "rights of man" to civil society. He was equally untouched by Rousseauist and other eighteenth-century theories of "sen-

sibility," simplicity, and primitivism. The moral calculus of Bentham and the utilitarians likewise was wholly rejected by Burke. In short, from the beginning to the end of his life he remained a Christian humanist, an Anglican who recognized that the particular revelations of Scripture were supplemented by Church tradition and by the historical continuity of man as a corporate rational being living under the general sovereignty of the Natural Law. Burke's theological consistency as a Christian paralleled his political consistency as a humanist adherent of the Natural Law. In his religion and politics, man as a corporate being was obliged to recognize and submit to the superiority of God's law, whether perceived as revelation or through right reason. The persistent antithesis to divine law and man's corporate reason was the arbitrary will or power of men. (pp. 231-33)

Throughout Burke's career there is ample evidence of his profound respect for the corporate will of the English people when it functioned within constitutional forms and according to the principles of the Natural Law. In his *Thoughts on the Cause of the Present Discontents* . . . , Burke had stated that the constitutional forms of government were themselves a product of the people's will: "Although government is an institution of Divine authority . . . its forms, and the persons who administer it, all originate from the people." In the same year he confessed: "I reverentially look up to the opinion of the people, and with an awe that is almost superstition." In 1780 Burke expressed his complete faith in the positive will of the people as against any negative will that might circumscribe it: "It would be a dreadful thing if there were any power in this country of strength enough to oppose with effect the general wishes of the people." In his *Speech on the Economical Reform* . . . , Burke defined the relationship between the general national will and the will of parliament, and of both to the Natural Law: "The desires of the people, when they do not militate with the stable and eternal rules of justice and reason (rules which are above us and above them) ought to be as a law to the House of Commons." Veneration for popular will was a deep and abiding conviction of practical policy with Burke, but it was not the final test of conscience for legislators, nor the ultimate moral basis of government:

> When we know, that the opinions of even the greatest multitudes are the standard of rectitude, I shall think myself obliged to make those opinions the masters of my conscience. But if it may be doubted whether Omnipotence itself is competent to alter the essential constitution of right and wrong, sure I am that such *things*, as they and I, are possessed of no such power. No man carries further than I do the policy of making government pleasing to the people. But the widest range of this politic complaisance is confined within the limits of justice. I would not only consult the interest of the people, but I would cheerfully gratify their humours. We are all a sort of children that must be soothed and managed. . . . I would bear, I would even myself play my part in any innocent buffooneries, to divert them. But I never will act the tyrant for their amusement. If they will mix malice in their sports, I shall never consent to throw them any living, sentient creature whatsoever, no, not so much as a kitling, to torment.

There was certainly nothing in Burke's conception of political sovereignty under the Natural Law which in any way prevented the corporate will of the people from fulfilling the just ends of government.

After 1789 Burke's faith in the Natural Law and in constitutional political sovereignty came into direct conflict with a fundamental dogma of the French Revolution—that the general will of the people at large was the sole legitimate criterion for making changes in society and the only allowable basis for sovereignty in government. The anonymous author of *The Political Crisis* (London, 1791) summarized this cardinal principle in the revolutionists' creed: "The people have an undoubted right . . . to alter the government when they think fit, for any cause, or for no cause at all; if they will it, it is sufficient." This "right" exists because "mankind are a law to themselves."

Burke's rejection of this theory of popular sovereignty forms a major theme in his attacks on the French Revolution. . . . Since Natural Law contained the moral norms of every nation, and constitutional law established its legal and political norms, *every* form of sovereign power had to be exercised within these necessary limits. The great object of law was to make ruling authority morally responsible to the citizens at large, and ultimately to "the one great Master, Author, and Founder of society," God himself. Thus, by "subjecting . . . occasional will to permanent reason," good order, liberty and justice would prevail. Nothing was more dangerous, Burke contended, than to say that any power was above the law, or that power made rather than followed law. This cardinal principle applied to *every* form of government, to democracy quite as much as to monarchy. Actually, because responsibility was more dispersed under a democracy, and therefore harder to assess, Burke held that those who composed the collective sovereignty under a democracy should be particularly impressed with the principle that they act in trust to God and the people. Abuses of power exercised with the apparent consent of the people at large were particularly difficult to redress. It is important to note that in appealing to the Natural Law, "that eternal, immutable law," against the claims of arbitrary will centered in popular sovereignty, Burke used the phrase "in which will and reason are the same." Like St. Thomas Aquinas and Hooker before him, Burke recognized that in the nature of God there was the perfect fusion of will and reason or power and law. While Burke subordinated man's will to the ethical norms of right reason, he also knew that man's corporate right reason was capable of conforming to the Natural Law. Under these conditions, Burke believed profoundly that the voice of the people was as the voice of God.

Implicit throughout Burke's strong objections to the revolutionary theory of popular sovereignty was his principle that the Natural Law supplied the moral basis of all political sovereignty, regardless of the *form* of government under which power was exercised. Since government was a trust for the entire nation, Burke denied that a present numerical majority had any absolute rights of sovereignty. The revolutionary theory that the majority will could reconstruct the whole social order according to each impulse of the heart's desire was completely contrary to Burke's faith in historical continuity, moral prudence, legal prescription, the restrictive safeguards of constitutional law, and above all the ethical norms of Natural Law and the moral inviolability of the divine contract.

In his *Thoughts on French Affairs* . . . , Burke resumed his earlier attack on the revolutionary theory of popular sovereignty. He noted that the Jacobins no longer restricted themselves to France, but applied their new "political dogma" to all the countries of Europe. . . . Burke's last three works on domestic affairs, [*The Present State of Affairs, The Conduct of the Minority,* and *Letter to a Noble Lord*] . . . , reveal that his greatest fear was that an English-French revolution might establish a government centered in absolute arbitrary popular will. To combat this possibility he defended the "sovereign reason" of the British constitution as a prescriptive instrument grounded upon the Natural Law. (pp. 238-41)

Once it is clearly understood that Burke applied his belief in the Natural Law and his principle of political sovereignty with complete impartiality to every ruler and every form of government, the problem of his consistency, which has harassed all his interpreters sine 1789, should perplex no one. Without once mentioning the Natural Law or political sovereignty, Woodrow Wilson sensed the true answer to Burke's consistency: "He was applying the same principles to the case of France and to the case of India that he had applied to the case of the colonies" [see excerpt dated 1896]. The key to Burke's consistent love of liberty and justice under a political sovereignty based on the Natural Law is contained in such statements as the following: "If I were to describe slavery, I would say with those who hate it, it is living under will, not under law." This principle applied equally to the Americans and the Irish living under the monarchical arbitrary will of George III, to the people of India under Hastings' oligarchical arbitrary will, and to the French under the democratic "general will" of the National Assembly. Burke opposed Price, Priestley, Paine, and other English radical reformers, and the revolutionists in France, on exactly the same grounds on which he had opposed Hastings and George III. (p. 245)

There is little doubt that Burke's intense moral integrity is the chief source of his greatness as a political thinker. Among a great variety of religious and political thinkers, from his own era to the present, Burke has enjoyed a supreme reputation for political knowledge and wisdom. On their tour of the Hebrides, Dr. Johnson once said to Boswell: "I do not grudge Burke being the first man in the House of Commons, for he is the first man everywhere." The "new Whig" Charles James Fox admitted that Burke had taught him more about politics than he had learned from all the books he had ever read and all that experience of the world had taught him. Burke's erstwhile opponent James Mackintosh said that "his works contain an ampler store of political and moral wisdom than can be found in any other writer whatever." After his disillusionment in the French Revolution, Wordsworth admitted that "Burke was . . . by far the greatest man of his age." William Hazlitt, whose faith in the French Revolution remained unshaken, even made it a test of the good sense of its proponents that they had to admit the greatness of Burke as a man and political thinker. Macaulay pronounced Burke "the greatest man since Milton." (p. 246)

The whole of Burke's political career is profoundly instructive in the moral wisdom of Christian statesmanship. No one has defined the just relationship between mother country and colony better than Burke. No one has made a better case for individual and minority corporate rights under constitutional law. No English writer has so ably defended historical continuity and legal prescription as the wise and just method for social growth. In all these and many related matters Burke saturated politics with thought and provided the model for applying first principles to practical affairs. However, his reply to the totalitarian challenge of the French Revolution has a special significance to twentieth-century man. We too are confronted with Jacobin types of popular collectivism which would make society and the state everything and the individual nothing. We have witnessed the rise of impersonal leviathan states, claiming the sanction of the popular will, in which every local corporate interest and every personal human right is extinguished or exists solely at the discretion of a centralized sovereign power. This cosmic struggle between the might of the state and the natural rights of man as man is the central conflict to be resolved during the second half of the twentieth century. If the commonwealth of Christian Europe is to survive and form the ethical norms of civilization throughout the world, all men but particularly Americans will have to learn the great lessons in Burke's political philosophy.

To a very considerable degree contemporary man is the heir of the same elements in the "Enlightenment" which Burke opposed throughout his life. The eighteenth-century rationalists who constructed a priori social projects, based on infallible mathematics and moral computation, without reference to history or to human nature, find their familiar counterparts among the sophisters, economists, and calculators of our century. Burke's philosophy is the best cure for the complex satanic disease of the soul that deludes fallen man to the Faustian illusion of superman. Neither a cynic nor a despairing pessimist, Burke was fully aware of the sins and moral paradoxes which resulted from man's moral and intellectual pride. He spent his life opposing all theories which presupposed an idyllic primitive or simple state of nature, because such naïve optimism about the natural goodness of "natural" man was destructive of the ethical norms of civilization and the Natural Law. He perceived that the Encyclopedists and later the Jacobins, in their unbounded confidence in logical reason, science, and progress, pointed toward the Reign of Terror and political despotism. He knew there was no harder heart to be found anywhere than that of a refining metaphysician and logician. On grounds of morality, social utility, or abstract "truth," a convinced and zealous utopian, bent upon reshaping civilization on a scientific basis, could justify even mass murder. By degrees inhumane methods become the systematic and necessary means for superhuman ends. Political reforms that begin in abstract and unrestricted liberty end in absolute and unlimited despotism. A doctrine of popular sovereignty, interpreted by the majority counted by the head, will produce perfect anarchy until, interpreted by Napoleon, it will produce perfect tyranny. A homogenized *vox populi,* in servitude to a bureaucratic elite disguised as *vox Dei* and fed with journalist slogans on liberty, equality, and fraternity, becomes sooner or later a cannibal state that eats its weaker young and makes war on its neighbors. All this Burke perceived in revolutionary France, and his analysis is profoundly instructive beyond the events which provoked him. In the later political writings of Burke, contemporary lovers of constitutional democracy will find effective armor and powerful weapons against every form of totalitarianism. (pp. 247-49)

To a world in which secular rulers make ultimate appeals to nationalism, race, class interest, social utility, descriptive science, popular will, and so on, in which subjects are told they must give up civil liberty to enjoy economic security, and in which the rights of private conscience are treated with contempt, Burke will always have much to say. The destiny of free men may depend largely upon their ability to understand and choose wisely between the philosophies of Caesar and Cicero, between "the fanatics of popular arbitrary power" and "a manly, moral regulated liberty" based upon constitutional law and Natural Law. Throughout Western history the Natural Law has played a vital role in the dramatic struggle to preserve and extend the traditions of civil and religious liberty, and men

who wish to gain fresh insights into its applied principles will have their faith in liberty renewed by turning to the political writings of Edmund Burke. (p. 250)

Peter J. Stanlis, in his Edmund Burke and the Natural Law, *The University of Michigan Press, 1958, 311 p.*

C. P. COURTNEY   (essay date 1959)

[*In the following excerpt from a study written in 1959, Courtney summarizes the influence of Montesquieu's thought on Burke's political sensibility.*]

In one of his earliest writings Burke refers to Montesquieu as 'the greatest genius which has enlightened this age'; and in one of his late works he concludes with a magnificent eulogy of Montesquieu as 'a genius not born in every country, or every time'. However, Burke did more than simply admire the great French thinker: he found in him sustenance for his own thought; and, indeed, it has long been commonplace to consider Burke as Montesquieu's disciple. The purpose of the present study is to examine in some detail the nature and extent of this influence of one great thinker on another.

Any study of the thought of Edmund Burke must face the problem of the protean nature of Burke's activities. He is writer, politician, propagandist, orator, and philosopher; and his subject matter is as wide and varied as such combined careers would suggest, ranging from America to India, and from polite literature to political philosophy. The consequence of this is that anyone who wishes to see Burke steadily and to see him whole cannot hope to do so by approaching him merely from the standpoint of one narrow specialized discipline. This has perhaps not always been sufficiently understood by Burke scholars, and it is all too common to find studies of his thought consisting of a rather rigid systematizing of *obiter dicta* culled in a haphazard fashion from different parts of his writings and speeches with a complete disregard of chronology and of the practical nature of the political issues with which Burke was dealing. Such accounts of his thought normally assume *a priori* that Burke never changed his mind on anything, that he was perfectly consistent throughout his long and varied career, and that we only have to look and we shall find in him a systematic philosophy. Such studies, by disregarding the active politician, and by forgetting that politicians are rarely, if ever, disinterested philosophers, tend to idealize Burke, to see in him nothing but the sublime and beautiful philosopher of liberalism and conservatism, whose wisdom on England, Ireland, America, India and France, would have made a new heaven and a new earth if it had not been for the influence of evil men like George III, Lord North, Warren Hastings, and the French revolutionaries. Such studies usually select from Burke those passages that will confirm the students' own prejudices: thus positivists see in him a positivist, conservatives a conservative, and Catholics regard him as a writer in the tradition of Aquinas. If, on the other hand, we turn away from political philosophers to historians, we shall find a picture of Burke which is so different that we might wonder whether we are still dealing with the same person. To them he is often merely a crafty politician, an Irish adventurer who curried favour with the great, and whose private life was involved in financial scandals. They believe that on most of the great political problems of the time he was lacking in the wisdom of a Chatham, a Warren Hastings, or a Pitt; and they show little interest in his interpretation of the French Revolution. (pp. ix-x)

[In the *Abridgment of English History*] Burke proclaims Montesquieu the greatest genius of the age, and copies his historical method as well as his theory of the origin of the British constitution. In this work Burke takes the writing of history seriously, and had thought of writing a history of English law, a task which Hale had attempted. It was Burke's interest in English Common Law and its traditions which led him to dislike the unhistorical reasoning of Rousseau, and led him to admire the achievement of Montesquieu. In him Burke found a competent legal historian who had succeeded in a field where the English—even Hale—had failed. The English legal historians were better antiquarians than historians; but in Montesquieu Burke found that the genetic method, which the English had used in a fumbling way, was raised to the status of an historical method, making history a scientific discipline. Burke's attempt to apply this method to English history is rather unsure, leading him into rather vague hypotheses; but the *Abridgment* is a work of promise, and if Burke had not deserted scholarship for politics his achievement in this field might have been very great indeed.

As a politician Burke was confronted with various practical issues demanding solutions not normally to be found in works of political theory. However, Burke proved an excellent propagandist, and was clever in adapting the wisdom of Montesquieu to the purposes of propaganda for the Rockinghams. In the years 1765-70 Burke was concerned with the problem of the working of the British constitution, and the relationship between the King and Parliament. The sources of his ideas on this . . . [are] found in the friction which came about, for various reasons, between George III and Lord Rockingham; and we . . . [know] that the Rockinghams were led to assume an attitude contrary to the letter and spirit of the constitution as described by Montesquieu. Nevertheless, in his pamphlet, *The Present Discontents,* Burke makes use of ideas he found in Montesquieu: ideas on the importance of governing a people according to their temper and character, and ideas on the nature and principle of despotism. In his speeches on America we [find] a further use of Montesquieu's ideas, Burke applying to the American colonies the historical method he had learned while writing the *Abridgment.* However, at the same time, Burke's ideas on the British constitution were developing in a way which led him into unconstitutional doctrines certainly owing nothing to Montesquieu. In his speeches on India and on the impeachment of Warren Hastings we find a further application of Montesquieu's historical method for a political end.

It is in his works on the French Revolution that Burke reaches his full stature as a thinker. . . . [It] is difficult to find precise sources for his writings at this time, as he was drawing mainly on a rich and fertile mind which had accumulated political wisdom over years as writer and politician. Burke, confronted with arguments of natural right, turned to arguments which appeal to history and tradition, and most of these arguments, in one form or another, had been used in the seventeenth century against the exponents of absolute monarchy. Burke's spiritual ancestors are the exponents of English Common Law who believed that political systems should be based not on theories of the sovereign will or social contract, but on the ancient constitution and tradition. In Montesquieu Burke found a thinker whose mind was of this same historical and legal cast, who despised theories of social contract and natural right, who revered the ancient institutions and laws of France. The similarity of Burke's ideas in his writings on the French Revolution to the ideas of Montesquieu is to be explained not entirely in

terms of direct influence, but also, and especially, by the similarity of English and French conservative and legal thought. Burke's only direct debt to Montesquieu at this time is when he analyses the spirit of the French constitution. In Montesquieu he saw not so much a writer to be imitated, as a fellow-worker in the great cause of defending civilization and the old order against theories which would sweep all established institutions away. The enemies of Montesquieu were the enemies of Burke; and the criticisms levelled against Montesquieu by the revolutionaries were also applicable to Burke. Above all both Burke and Montesquieu revered the British constitution, which the revolutionaries considered a monument of superstition and ignorance. It is chiefly as the defender of the British constitution that Burke, at this time, admires Montesquieu. Montesquieu had spent twenty years writing the *Esprit des lois,* and his considered judgement was that the British constitution was the greatest monument to liberty. Burke had spent twenty years in politics, and he likewise puts the British form of government before all others. His political theory is, in the last resort, a defence of this constitution.

Burke's last political cause was the cause of his native country, and here the influence of Montesquieu is slight. Burke did not apply Montesquieu's historical method to an analysis of the Irish problem in the same way as he had applied it to America and India. This may be because after 1789 he no longer believed that human affairs could be explained in this way. The Irish problem was essentially one of imperial relationships, on which Montesquieu was not an authority at this time. Burke shared Montesquieu's views on the injustice and cruelty of penal laws; but he did not share the views on legislative union which Montesquieu had expressed to Lord Charlemont.

Without the influence of Montesquieu the works of Burke would certainly be poorer. In his early literary period it is mainly the *Abridgment of English History* which we owe to the inspiration of Montesquieu. Between 1765 and 1789 the influence of Montesquieu helped Burke to become a great propagandist, especially when dealing with the problems of America and India. After 1789 the direct influence of Montesquieu is slight, but he was in Burke's eyes a model of all that was greatest in the *Ancien régime* discredited at the time of the Revolution. In France Montesquieu was being attacked because he had defended the French and British constitutions. It is Burke who, in a sense, defends Montesquieu and continues the tradition for which the great French thinker stood. (pp. 181-84)

> *C. P. Courtney, in an introduction and conclusion to his* Montesquieu and Burke, *Basil Blackwell, 1963, pp. ix-xv, 181-84.*

JEFFREY HART   (essay date 1967)

[*Hart is an American educator and essayist who is a senior editor of the conservative biweekly* National Review, *to which he contributes book reviews and a column on the state of American education, ''The Ivory Foxhole.'' In the following excerpt, he discusses Burke's conception of the basis and limits of personal freedom.*]

[In our time Burke] has come to be read not merely as one among a large number of other important figures in the history of political thought, but as a thinker of intense, of special, contemporary relevance. Burke is our contemporary, he is an *issue,* in a way that Locke is not, and Leibniz is not, and even Mill is not. (p. 221)

In part, of course, Burke is a beneficiary of the revival of critical and scholarly esteem for eighteenth-century writing generally, and especially of eighteenth-century writing on the conservative side. Like Dryden and Pope and Swift and Johnson, he speaks, we see, for civilization, for a high and elegant and traditional civilization, and this is welcome to us in our age of cultural democratization, and corruption of manners. In part, too, Burke is a beneficiary—as is conservative thought generally—of the fact that in the world arena today America is irreversibly a conservative nation, with everything to gain from the maintenance of order and nothing from its dissolution. Yet neither of these reasons quite accounts for the atmosphere of passion and polemic that surrounds the subject of Burke. Attitudes toward him among otherwise sober-seeming scholars tend to suggest total commitment—for him, or against him. Individuals whom one would never suspect of much capacity for feeling transform themselves when the question of Burke is up. And this . . . is because Burke was the first to recognize the deep moral division of the West, which was just then opening up, and which today, across the board, is decisive for our moral, political, and metaphysical opinions: and because Burke, having recognized the division and defined its doctrinal grounds, took sides. (pp. 221-22)

In his parliamentary career Burke had fought for the independence of parliament against what he thought to be the unconstitutional influence of the Crown. In economic matters, Burke was reformist as against the older mercantilist economic theory; he inclined to the theories of Adam Smith, who said, indeed, that Burke was the only man in England who really understood him. Burke's reformist politics even involved him in some friendly friction with his associates in Dr. Johnson's circle, who were very largely Tories. (Dr. Johnson, you will recall, remarked only half-playfully that the first Whig was the Devil, and that Patriotism—by which he meant the so-called Patriot political group, that is, the critics of George III, and not what we mean today by patriotism—was "the last refuge of a scoundrel.") Burke was the friend of Dr. Johnson, but he was the friend and political ally of the reformers—of Sir Philip Francis (the probable author of the Junius letters), of Sheridan, of Charles James Fox. Jeremy Bentham had read with approval and copiously annotated his reformist speeches; and Burke was admired from afar by Tom Paine. If we could transport the pre-French Revolutionary Burke to our own times we would consider him a moderate and a reformer, humanitarian in his sympathies; he was, as against politics, half in love with philosophy and literature; but the French Revolution did occur: and it changed all this. Burke's principles did not change, but the deep transformation of the world cast him into an entirely different role. (pp. 222-23)

The focus of the *Reflections* is on final political things. We do not go to it for a definitive account of the economic conditions of France in 1789, or for a character sketch of Marie Antoinette, or for an apt account of the members of the Assembly. We do go to it for Burke's insight into the intellectual and spiritual issues. For the French Revolution seemed momentous to Burke not because of its violence, or because it threatened the peace of Europe: these things were derivative. Burke was, as he says, "alarmed into reflection" by what he considered a "revolution of doctrine and theoretic dogma," by emotions which, it seemed to him, would render impossible any stable and settled condition of society, and which would issue, indeed, in *permanent* revolution. As he says, near the beginning of the *Reflections*, in a sentence which reverberates in the mind like the opening bars of a great and dark symphony, this was "a great crisis,

not of the affairs of France alone, but of all Europe, perhaps of more than Europe."

I think the best way of stating Burke's fundamental objection to the Revolution would be to say that it turned on a definition of "freedom"—that for Burke, freedom was a concrete and historical thing, the actual freedoms enjoyed by actual Englishmen: they enjoyed the historic rights of *Englishmen*. What revolutionary theory proposed, he thought, was a freedom that was abstract and unhistorical: not the rights of Englishmen but the Rights of Man. For Burke, there was no such thing as an abstract man, and to evoke one, as Rousseau had done in the famous first sentence of *The Social Contract,* was to construct a battering ram against all normal social relationships: "Man is born free," said Rousseau, "but everywhere he is in chains." (p. 224)

The theoreticians of the Revolution proposed, as Taine put it, to strip from man his artificial garments, all those fictitious qualities that made him "ecclesiastic or layman, noble or plebeian, sovereign or subject, proprietor or proletarian." Only when these fictions had been stripped away could "natural man" make his appearance—spontaneous, innocent, and free. Nor, we may note, was this hope defeated by the actual results of the Revolution; there is, indeed, a sense in which it cannot *be* defeated, historically, since it is fundamentally unhistorical. Long after the French Revolution, the poet Shelley could hope for another, culminating revolution which would transcend completely the "masks" of actual social existence:

> The loathesome mask has fallen, the man remains
> Scepterless, free, uncircumscribed, but man
> Equal, unclassed, tribeless, and nationless,
> Exempt from awe, worship, degree, the king
> Over himself; just, gentle, wise; but man
> Passionless? no, yet free from guilt or pain.

At the center of Burke's *Reflections* is an explicit recognition of this dream, and a powerful attack upon it. Adopting the familiar metaphor of *clothes,* Burke describes in this way the guiding impulse of the Revolution:

> All the decent drapery of life is to be rudely torn off. All the superadded ideas, furnished from the wardrobe of a moral imagination, which the heart owns and the understanding ratifies as necessary to cover the defects of our naked, shivering nature, and to raise it to dignity in our estimation, are to be exploded. . . .

In Burke's metaphor, clothes—what he calls "the decent drapery of life"—correspond to Shelley's "loathesome mask" and to Rousseau's "chains"; that is, they are our actual social roles. When they are stripped away, there remains "our naked shivering nature"—or in Shelley's terms, "man . . . scepterless, free"; or in Rousseau's terms, man "free" as he supposedly was when he was born.

At the center of the *Reflections,* then, is this issue: if indeed that "self" does exist, can it really be divested of its "artificial" attributes, and if it can be, will its nakedness be productive of joy? Burke was one of the first to understand that the spirit of the Revolution—and, as I wish to insist, the spirit of revolutionary modernity (which is not here a merely chronological concept)—was at its roots characterized by a hatred of the very idea of *society*. He knew that the defense of what the *philosophes* called "appearances" or "masks" is the defense of society itself, that the reality of society consists of appearances, of "roles." The natural man of revolutionary theory is only a myth, though a powerful one, and a destructive one—for the critique of roles, of forms, the assault upon Rousseau's "chains" . . . has issued, precisely because natural man is a fiction, not in a more intense experience of selfhood but in the experience of emptiness, disgust, and alienation, in a deep hatred of the actual circumstances of social life, in a deep hatred, indeed, for historical existence itself; that is to say, in the special anger of the revolutionary spirit, which we daily feel all around us. (pp. 225-27)

Burke views man as naturally involved with links, and he considers that as those links dissolve, man's identity does too.

One such link in Burke's thought is the link in time. "People will not look forward to posterity," he says in the *Reflections,* "who never look back to their ancestors," and he thinks that men isolated from their past are little better than "flies of a summer." A man's sense of his place in a succession of generations gives him an awareness of being located in a coherent chronology which is not just a sequence of mechanical clock-minutes or calendar days. The past is not anonymous, and so neither will the future be. "Respecting your forefathers," he said to the revolutionaries, "you would have been taught to respect yourselves." Clearly, his position here is correct. We know from the work of modern sociologists and psychologists the role the father plays in the formation of identity, and Freud has a great deal to say about the father's role with regard to ego and superego formation; that is, with the establishing of identity and of principles. The father's own identity, in turn, is the result of his own ancestry. Groups in which the family structure is weak, or the father's sense of identity uncertain, or in which the father is actually likely to desert the family—as in the case of the American Negro at the present time—tend to be characterized by identity "crises" and deep uncertainty about goals and values. As Burke argues repeatedly in the *Reflections,* imaginative awareness of the links between himself and his past prevents the individual from feeling that his existence is arbitrary, or, in the fashionable term, absurd.

Another link, in Burke's thought, is the link to one's contemporaries: to the family, first of all, but extending beyond that to the neighborhood and the region, and thence to the nation and the civilization. Burke characteristically moves outward, from the immediate to the more remote, insisting upon the importance of the group closest to the individual: "To be attached to the subdivision, to love the little platoon we belong to in society, is the first principle (the germ, as it were) of public affections. It is the first *link* [my italics] in the series by which we proceed towards a love to our country, and to mankind." Concerned to protect the various groups to which the individual is most immediately linked, and which help to constitute his identity, Burke characteristically refuses to begin in the abstract, unhistorical way with Mankind or the Brotherhood of Man. (pp. 231-32)

Still another link, for Burke, was the link to place. A man's identity is very much involved with his attachment to place, his sense of himself as associated with a geographic locality. The length of time he has lived there has much to do with the strength of such local feeling, as do the distinctive characteristics of the place itself: Burke was attached to the "irregularities" of things, and instinctively rejected a uniformitarian idea of "reason." But the link to place also has much to do with ownership: the man who owns his house is likely to have a deeper imaginative involvement with the neighborhood than one who does not. And here we may observe that Burke, drawing upon Locke, perhaps, but also on his own common sense, put a very high valuation on the protection of property.

He did not make that grotesque but familiar distinction between property rights and human rights, but viewed property as a human right. It is not, after all, a vegetable or a mineral right.

In proportion as such links as these were dissolved, Burke thought, man's identity would be dissolved as well. The links prevented him from floating away psychologically as a kind of angry abstraction, or, to put it another way, from resembling, psychically, those odd modern sculptures, composed of coat hangers, tin cans, and stove bolts. And we may indeed suppose that much of the distinctive pain of modern existence does proceed from the assault that has been carried forward against such links. They sometimes have been weakened or broken, of course, by historical developments of a nonideological character—by industrialization, by urbanization, by the widening possibilities of geographical and social mobility. But the point to be made here is that the bad effects of these developments have been intensified, rather than moderated, by the ideology Burke fought. A moral assault as well has been conducted on these natural links, a moral assault that would seem to have as its intention the isolation of the individual, the reduction of him to a "free" self. Think of the deeply antidomestic implications of progressive pressure for sexual freedom and for relaxed divorce laws and for more abortions. Or the implications of the advocacy, by R. H. Tawney, on moral grounds, of a 100 percent death tax.

I would like to turn now to the matter which plays a very important role in Burke's political thought; it is, like the links I have been talking about, a psychological point primarily, but also, like them, it issues in a political principle. For Burke's politics, like any genuinely conservative politics, places a high valuation on *habit.* "Prejudice," he says in the *Reflections,* "renders a man's virtues his habit, and not a series of unconnected acts. Through just prejudice, his duty becomes a part of his nature." This high valuation of habit proceeds from an awareness of the complexity of social life, and from the elementary observation—though Burke was the first to make it; in a sense *he* was the discoverer of the unconscious—that habit performs complex tasks with greater ease and efficiency than does the conscious reason. The daily tasks that we perform most easily (we say, usually, that we perform them "naturally"), from tying our shoes to handling the day's social encounters, we perform habitually. If we were forced to think them through analytically, our activities would come rapidly to a halt. There is a sense, indeed, in which it is really habit, paradoxically enough, that renders one free, since freedom actually is experienced only as a quality of an activity. One is free to do this or that; one is not "free" in an abstract way apart from activity. (pp. 232-34)

[The] sort of society advocated throughout Burke's works operates to strengthen the element of habit in social role. Wealth, property, and power are not to pass with great rapidity from one hand to another. He opposed mobility rapid enough to endanger social habit. "I do not hesitate to say," he wrote in the *Reflections,* "that the road to eminence and power from obscure condition ought not to be made too easy, nor a thing too much of course. If rare merit be the rarest of all things, it ought to pass through some sort of probation." In the society thus adumbrated, a man might be a solider, a merchant, a landholder, or a nobleman, and would expect to remain one. His sense of himself would be that his identity was to a considerable degree "given" rather than willed. But in a more fluid condition of society this is much less the case. Individuals become to a much greater degree free to create themselves, become, in Don Quixote's marvellous phrase, the children of their deeds rather than the children of their actual parents. But to the extent that careers are open to talents, to the extent, that is, that one's social role is the result of one's own talent and will, one's identity must be experienced as *arbitrary.* One might just as well have willed something else. And when identity thus partakes of the quality of the willed and the arbitrary, it is experienced as a kind of mask, or even as a lie. One's roles seem absurd, perhaps even hateful. The self comes to stand in an ironic or antagonistic relationship to all its social manifestations. Perhaps this is one reason why the literature of the Enlightenment, responding at once to actual conditions of increasing social mobility, but also to the ideological assumption that mobility is simply *good,* has as one of its central themes the critique of roles and appearances. Even such ostensibly conservative writers as Swift and Goldsmith shock conventional views by examining society through the wrong end of a telescope or from the perspective of a Chinaman.

Nevertheless, as Burke saw, there is an intimate connection between habit and ease, and this applies as much to society at large as to the individual. The vast majority of its activities, from delivering the mail to running a legislature, go forward smoothly so long as they follow habitual procedures. It is the habits of society—its customs, institutions, and prejudices—that embody the results of its historical experience and enable it to function and preserve its coherence in the present. It was one of Burke's great accomplishments as a political philosopher to show that Hobbes and Locke erred in assigning to reason rather than to habit the function of maintaining the stability of a society. Habit, to be sure, is not an appropriate instrument for dealing with *novel* experience; but on that very account, as Burke saw, a society is better off if it can absorb novelty in small and manageable amounts. (pp. 234-35)

The emphasis in Burke's writing upon man in his historical existence and his denigration of "abstract" speculation have led many to suppose that his thought is pragmatic in character, and informed by no permanent principles. John Morley, for example, who wrote a good short book on Burke during the nineteenth century, was of this opinion [see Additional Bibliography]. But this view is quite mistaken and ignores the special way in which Burke made use of history.

Burke considered that an "eternal law" is discoverable in history. Men, he says, "attain to the moral reason in their collective experience, they realize and embody it in their stable social relations and organization." For Burke, that is to say, the moral law is eternal and universal, though men cannot, because of their limited reason, apprehend it directly. The moral law does, however, acquire concrete existence and so may be apprehended, historically—in man's stable (and the word is crucial) social arrangements. The stability of those arrangements demonstrates that the moral law is being obeyed. Thus there exists for Burke two sources of our knowledge of the "eternal law"—Christian revelation and our historical experience. From this perspective, novel theories of government and human nature, though they may be the product of brilliant thinkers, can scarcely compare in validity either with revelation or with institutions that have been the creation of many generations. Such novel theories are presumptuous in attempting to set up as rivals of "eternal law," and their inadequacy is proved by the catastrophes that result when they are used as principles of government.

When the statesman acts in conformity with the eternal law, Burke thinks, *tranquility* is fostered in society. Running through

his work is a vocabulary indicative of a set of fundamental polarities. On the one hand are the qualities to be desired in society: stability, public tranquility, peace, quiet, order, harmony, regularity, unity, decorum. Opposed to these are the symptoms of social disease: discord, contradiction, confusion, violence, excess, the need for coercion. The task of the statesman is to promote "tranquility."

The attitudes and doctrines that informed the French Revolution, Burke thinks, make tranquility impossible. Asserting against an actual society rights derived from a mythical state of nature, and celebrating a freedom equally mythical—"man is born free"—the theorists wielded a weapon to which any society would be vulnerable. Against such demands, he said, "no agreement is binding; these admit no temperament and no compromise; anything withheld is so much fraud and injustice." On the other hand, the rights Burke was defending were rights he had known as historical facts. It was those rights that he put in the path of a permanent shattering of tranquility, a permanent revolution. (pp. 236-38)

In his splendid brief study of Piero della Francesca, Bernard Berenson speaks of a quality to be found in many of the greatest portraits that date from before the nineteenth century. A kind of silence surrounds those figures, he says; they do not gesture or grimace at us from the canvas. A portrait by Piero or Botticelli, Velasquez or Murillo, Reynolds or Gainsborough, seems to say that the existence of its subject in no way appeals to *our* presence before the canvas. Those dukes and cardinals and princesses and statesmen take their existence as a matter of course. They are *there,* self-contained; their being is concrete, actual, accepted. And it may be that sense of being which really is in harmony with the deepest intuitions of the West about the proper mode of the human, for it is that sense which comes to us from the oldest and most continuous of our moral traditions—from Plato and Aristotle, Cicero, Aquinas, Hooker, Elyot, Samuel Johnson, Burke; and so, in politics, it is to Burke that we logically turn as we seek to reconstitute that tradition in the teeth of another revolution. (p. 238)

Jeffrey Hart, "Burke and Radical Freedom," in The Review of Politics, *Vol. 29, No. 2, April, 1967, pp. 221-38.*

RUSSELL KIRK (essay date 1967)

[*An American historian, political theorist, novelist, journalist, and lecturer, Kirk is one of America's most eminent conservative intellectuals. His works have provided a major impetus to the conservative revival that has developed since the 1950s. The* Conservative Mind *(1953), one of Kirk's early books, describes conservatism as a living body of ideas "struggling toward ascendancy in the United States"; in it Kirk traces the roots and canons of modern conservative thought to such important predecessors as Burke, John Adams, and Alexis de Tocqueville. Founder of the conservative quarterlies* Modern Age *and the* University Bookman, *Kirk has long been a trenchant critic of the decline of academic standards in American public schools and universities. His* Decadence and Renewal in the Higher Learning *(1978), in particular, is a forceful denunciation of the "academic barbarism" which he states has replaced the traditional goals of higher education—wisdom and virtue—with the fallacious ones of "utilitarian efficiency" and innovative forms of education. The result, in Kirk's view, is that "the higher learning in America is a disgrace." Kirk's detractors have sometimes been skeptical of the charges he levels against liberal ideas and programs, accusing him of a simplistic partisanship. His admirers, on the other hand, point to the alleged failure of liberal precepts—in particular those*] *applied in the universities—as evidence in support of Kirk's ideas and criticism. In the following excerpt, Kirk underscores the influence and preeminence of Burke's political conservatism.*]

[The] resurrection of Burke is a product of modern discontents. Uncertain of the dogmas of liberalism (which Santayana knew for a mere transitory phase), disillusioned with Giant Ideology, the modern serious public is willing to give Burke a hearing. Burke's ideas interest nearly anyone nowadays, including men bitterly dissenting from his conclusions. If conservatives would know what they defend, Burke is their touchstone; and if radicals wish to test the temper of their opposition, they should turn to Burke. Having done this, some conservatives may find that their previous footing was insecure; while some radicals may acknowledge that the position of traditionalists is tenable, or that Burke, too, was a liberal—if liberalism be in any degree associated with ordered freedom.

At a New York club, about 1913, Paul Elmer More happened to mention Burke's name; and a companion inquired, "Burke? He's dead, is he not?" In spirit, Burke is stirring once more. Some there are who wish Burke were immured forever in his tomb. Not long ago, a British scholar professed his sorrow that, in America today, "Burke is being used for political purposes." This gentleman would prefer to keep Burke as a kind of cadaver, out of which doctoral dissertations might be carved. (Burke himself, one may remark, would have been amused and vexed at the notion that a dead master of politics never should influence the living: as statesman and as rhetorician, he intended his speeches and writings for immediate *use*—and for use by the rising generation and by posterity, if useful they might be found. The closet theoretician, the abstract metaphysician, the "drydocked" scholar, Burke cordially detested.)

Burke expected to be disinterred—though not, perhaps, after the fashion in which he has been raised up in the middle of the twentieth century. Fearing that triumphant Jacobins would treat his corpse as Cromwell's had been dishonored at the Restoration—that his head and limbs might be impaled on some Temple Bar—he left instruction for his body to be buried secretly, somewhere in Beaconsfield church or churchyard, and to this day no man knows the precise spot where Burke lies.

Yet Burke has been invoked in all honor, because he is one of those giants who (in the phrase of the medieval Schoolmen) support us upon their shoulders, one of those dead who walk. Burke endures as part of a great continuity and essence. He offers an alternative to the dreary doctrines of ideology in the mass age. (pp. 17-19)

Notwithstanding his strong influence on the course of British and international affairs during his political career, it is as a man of thought and of the pen that Burke lives for us today. Nothing, we are told, is deader than dead politics. Although Burke was a chief architect of the modern political-party system, it is not as a partisan leader that we find him interesting two centuries later. In the end, undoing Goldsmith's criticism of himself [see Goldsmith's poem quoted in the Emerson excerpt dated 1835], Burke gave to mankind what he owed to party. (p.28)

God willed the state, Burke declared, for man's benefit; men must not venture to trade upon the petty bank and capital of their private rationality, but should venerate where they do not presently understand, and abide by the wisdom of their ancestors, the winnowed and filtered experience of the human spe-

cies. Life being short and experience limited, the individual—even the wisest man of his age—is comparatively foolish; but through the experience of man with God, and through the experience of man with man, over thousands of years, the species has a wisdom, expressed in prejudice, habit, and custom, which in the long run judges aright.

This faith is at the antipodes from the sort of Whiggery that Yeats assailed. The "levelling, rancorous, rational sort of mind", the mind of the "sophisters, economists, and calculators" whom Burke detested, never would quote from memory, as did Burke, this passage from Richard Hooker: "The reason first why we do admire those things which are greatest, and second those things which are ancientest, is because the one are the least distant from the infinite substance, the other from the infinite continuance, of God."

The party which Burke, with Rockingham, had forged to maintain the constitution fell into ruin under the impact of the French Revolution. Yet without his having expected it, after his death Burke became the intellectual founder of a new and more powerful party, the Conservative—a fusion of Tories and conservative Whigs—which now endures as the oldest coherent political party in the fluctuating twentieth-century world.

Though this might be distinction enough for any man, it is only a lesser aspect of the achievement of Burke. His influence, with the defeat of Napoleon, spread far beyond Britain to most of western Europe, and the architects of European reconstruction lived by his maxims, to the best of their understanding. Directly or by a kind of intellectual osmosis, he permeated American political thought and action. He enlivened political philosophy by the moral imagination; he shored up Christian doctrine; he stimulated the higher understanding of history; he enriched English literature by a mastery of prose that makes him the Cicero of his language and nation. And to the modern civil social order, he contributed those principles of ordered freedom, preservation through reform, and justice restraining arbitrary power, which transcend the particular political struggles of his age. Against the fanatic ideologue and the armed doctrine, the great plagues of our time, Burke's wisdom and Burke's example remain a powerful bulwark.

The philosopher in action, Burke knew, can alter the whole course of nations, for good or ill. We are not governed by mere Fate and Fortune; no inexorable destiny rules nations. "I doubt whether the history of mankind is yet complete enough, if ever it can be so, to furnish grounds for a sure theory of the internal causes which necessarily affect the fortune of a State." The ways of Providence are mysterious, but we need not bow down before theories of historical determinism, which a twentieth-century writer, Gabriel Marcel, calls "that armed ghost, the 'meaning' of history."

Private thoughts and individual actions, Burke pointed out in the Fourth Letter of the *Regicide Peace,* may alter profoundly the apparent great drift of the times. "The death of a man at a critical juncture, his disgust, his retreat, his disgrace, have brought innumerable calamities on a whole nation. A common soldier, a child, a girl at the door of an inn, have changed the face of fortune, and almost of Nature." [Kirk adds in a footnote: "Burke's 'common soldier' is Arnold of Winkelried, the Swiss who broke in upon the spears at Sempach; his child is Hannibal, taking at the age of twelve his oath to make undying war upon Rome; his girl at the inn is Joan of Arc."] Burke himself, in his almost solitary opposition of 1790, did incalculably much to exorcise the revolutionary spirit of the age, which his most enlightened contemporaries had mistaken for the irresistible genius of the future.

The prophecies of the Jacobins and their kind, Burke understood, are of the sort which work their own fulfillment—if honest men credulously accept the ideologue's dogmatic assertions. But if possessed of principle, resolution, and moral imagination, men may unite to restrain the enemies of order and justice and freedom. To precisely that unending labor of curbing arbitrary will and arbitrary appetite, Burke devoted his life. Because corruption and fanaticism assail our era as sorely as they did Burke's time, the resonance of Burke's voice still is heard amidst the howl of our winds of abstract doctrine. (pp. 208-11)

> *Russell Kirk, in his* Edmund Burke: A Genius Reconsidered, *Arlington House, 1967, 255 p.*

C. B. MACPHERSON   (essay date 1980)

[*Macpherson is a Canadian scholar who has written widely on the history of political philosophy. In the following excerpt, he analyzes the capitalist theory of Burke and evaluates his relevance for twentieth-century political and economic reformers.*]

[The] central Burke problem which is still of considerable interest in our own time is the question of the coherence of his two seemingly opposite positions: the defender of a hierarchical establishment, and the market liberal. This question, I suggest, transcends the debate, which claimed most attention a few decades ago, as to whether he was a utilitarian or a Natural Law man. It raises more acutely the relevance of Burke's work to one of the main political debates in Western societies in the late twentieth century. And it suggests a final question for our consideration: how far, if at all, can Burke properly be enlisted by conservatives or liberals today? (p. 7)

Burke was a close student of economic affairs and commercial policy from early on in his political career. He took that to be part of his duty as a Member of Parliament, and there is plenty of evidence of his industry in that regard, notably the detailed economic analysis of the *Observations.* . . . He recommended himself to his Bristol constituency in the 1770s partly on the ground of his knowledge of commercial principles. His case for a more lenient British policy towards the American colonies, and towards Ireland, and his sustained attack on the East India Company, were similarly based. (p. 51)

Burke's preference in the matter of commercial policy was always for free trade, provided that diplomatic and strategic considerations did not call for some abatement from that principle, as he thought they did in the case of the English Navigation Acts. International commerce could, and when feasible and desirable should, be an instrument of economic warfare. Commercial treaties, as with France in 1787, should be made not on short-run grounds of immediate economic advantage, but on long-run grounds of their probable effect in weakening or strengthening a rival nation. Burke's position on this, arrived at independently, coincided with Adam Smith's proviso about *laissez-faire:* defence is more important than opulence.

But about the virtue of *laissez-faire* at home Burke had no doubts. A competitive, self-regulating market economy was the ideal. It was the most efficient system of production. It was the most equitable system of distribution of the whole product. It was a necessary part of the natural order of the universe. It was, even, divinely ordained, which set the seal on its being both necessary and equitable.

The system Burke saw as natural and necessary, and praised as efficient and equitable, was not a simple market economy in which independent small producers—peasants and craftsmen—exchanged their products to mutual advantage. It was a specifically capitalist economy. The motor of his system was the desire for accumulation. The mechanism was the employment of wage-labour by capital so as to yield a profit to the capitalist. It was *this* system that Burke held to be natural, necessary and equitable. The evidence for this is clear, though not often noticed or given much weight by Burke's admirers. Only after we have examined it will we be in a position to appreciate his extraordinary theoretical achievement.

The desire to accumulate, which Burke took to be natural, at least in those who had some capital already, was the source of every state's prosperity:

> Monied men ought to be allowed to set a value on their money; if they did not, there could be no monied men. This desire of accumulation, is a principle without which the means of their service to the state could not exist. The love of lucre, though sometimes carried to a ridiculous, sometimes to a vicious excess, is the grand cause of prosperity to all states. In this natural, this reasonable, this powerful, this prolifick principle . . . it is for the statesman to employ it as he finds it, with all its concomitant excellencies, with all its imperfections on its head. It is his part, in this case, as it is in all other cases, where he is to make use of the general energies of nature, to take them as he finds them. . . .

There is nothing the matter with avarice: the more avaricious the employer is, the more he must take care of his labourers:

> But if the farmer is excessively avaricious?—why so much the better—the more he desires to increase his gains, the more interested is he in the good condition of those, upon whose labour his gains must principally depend. . . .
>
>   (pp. 53-4)

Burke had no patience with modish talk about 'the labouring poor', nor with plans for the relief of the able-bodied poor:

> Hitherto the name of poor (in the sense in which it is used to excite compassion) has not been used for those who can, but for those who cannot labour—for the sick and infirm; for orphan infancy; for languishing and decrepid age: but when we affect to pity as poor, those who must labour or the world cannot exist, we are trifling with the condition of mankind. . . .

Not only must the able-bodied poor work, to keep the world going: they must do so, Burke held, as wage-labourers, selling their labour as a commodity for a wage determined by impersonal market forces. That was necessary because that was the source of the profit which was the source of the capital which kept the world going. In Burke's view, as we shall now see, the wage relation was not only necessary but also natural, and therefore equitable.

Burke did not always distinguish between the capitalist as a mere receiver of interest or rent and the capitalist as a risk-taking enterpriser, but he was clear that the mainspring of the whole productive system was the profit to be made by employing wage-labour, which must be treated simply as a commodity in the market:

> Labour is a commodity like every other, and rises or falls according to the demand. This is in the nature of things. . . .

(pp. 55-6)

[The] principle on which he was most insistent was, that in those years when the market did not treat the wage-earners well, even to the point that wages were less than bare subsistence, the state should not intervene:

> But what if the rate of hire to the labourer comes far short of his necessary subsistence, and the calamity of the time is so great as to threaten actual famine? Is the poor labourer to be abandoned to the flinty heart and griping hand of base self-interest, supported by the sword of law, especially when there is reason to suppose that the very avarice of farmers themselves has concurred with the errours of government to bring famine on the land?
>
> In that case, my opinion is this. Whenever it happens that a man can claim nothing according to the rules of commerce, and the principles of justice, he passes out of that department, and comes within the jurisdiction of mercy. In that province the magistrate has nothing at all to do: his interference is a violation of the property which it is his office to protect. . . .

(p. 57)

State regulation of wages or intervention in the labour market, then, was not only useless but was also unjust. It was 'the rules of commerce' that were 'the principles of justice'. Burke's distributive justice, like Hobbes's a century and a half earlier, was the justice of the market. (p. 58)

If things were hard on the labourer, as they sometimes were, that was simply a temporary incident in the working of a divinely-ordained natural order. It is the duty of governments and of all thinking men

> manfully to resist the very first idea, speculative or practical, that it is within the competence of government, taken as government, or even of the rich, as rich, to supply to the poor, those necessaries which it has pleased the Divine Providence for a while to with-hold from them. We, the people, ought to be made sensible, that it is not in breaking the laws of commerce, which are the laws of nature, and consequently the laws of God, that we are to place our hope of softening the Divine displeasure to remove any calamity under which we suffer, or which hangs over us. . . .

Whatever one may think of Burke's theology, one need not doubt his certainty that the laws of the market were divinely ordained. Nor need one doubt that it was because of his political economy that he found no difficulty in accepting that ordination, and recommending it to his readers. The central assumption of his political economy is strikingly like Adam Smith's 'invisible hand', though Burke's assumption is more obtrusively theological:

> the benign and wise Disposer of all things . . . obliges men, whether they will or not, in pursuing their own selfish interests, to connect the general good with their own individual success. . . .

(pp. 58-9)

Burke's paradigm case was the relation between the employing farmer and the agricultural labourer. The relation he saw was a curious blend of free contract and customary status, and this brings us close to the heart of his vision of the social universe. The interests of the employing farmer and the labourer were identical: their contracts could not be onerous to either, for if they were, the contracts would not be made:

> . . . in the case of the farmer and the labourer, their interests are always the same, and it is absolutely impossible that their free contracts can be onerous to either party. It is in the interest of the farmer, that his work should be done with effect and celerity: and that cannot be, unless the labourer is well fed, and otherwise found with such necessaries of animal life, according to his habitudes, as may keep the body in full force, and the mind gay and cheerful. . . .

But this identity of interests operated only because the wage relation was part of a natural chain of subordination, which Burke, following his beloved ancient writers, saw as extending from the employing farmer, through his human employees, to his cattle, and finally to his ploughs and spades. . . . The mutual advantage of the farmer and the labourer depends on their acceptance of this natural and just chain of subordination.

This is but a particular case of a more general rule which Burke had laid down in the *Reflections,* a rule which is the heart of his political economy. Speaking there of the need for capital accumulation, which as we have already seen was the starting-point of his political economy, he wrote:

> To be enabled to acquire, the people, without being servile, must be tractable and obedient. The magistrate must have his reverence, the laws their authority. The body of the people must not find the principles of natural subordination by art rooted out of their minds. They must respect that property of which they cannot partake. They must labour to obtain what by labour can be obtained; and when they find, as they commonly do, the success disproportioned to the endeavour, they must be taught their consolation in the final proportions of eternal justice. Of this consolation, whoever deprives them, deadens their industry, and strikes at the root of all acquisition as of all conservation. He that does this is the cruel oppressor. . . .

With this we have the crucial point of Burke's political economy. Accumulation is essential. It is possible only if the body of the people accept a subordination which generally short-changes them. That subordination is natural and customary: the common people will accept it if they are not seduced by art. It is right that they should accept it, for it is in tune with 'the final proportions of eternal justice'. The seductive art that Burke feared was of course the egalitarian propaganda of the French revolutionists and their English supporters, which would undo the whole fabric of the natural, customary and just social order of subordination of ranks.

Everyone sees that Burke had always been a defender of a traditional, inherited social order of subordination of ranks. What has not generally been seen is that the traditional order which he cherished was not simply any hierarchical order but a capitalist one. His case against the French principles was the same as his case against the Speenhamland principle: both would destroy traditional society by destroying the prerequisite condition of capitalist accumulation, that is, a submissive wage-earning class.

The argument that the wage relation is equitable is quite clear and can be put, as Burke did put it, either on utilitarian or on Natural Law grounds. The utilitarian argument runs: continuous capital accumulation is a prerequisite of civilisation; accumulation (in any but a slave or servile society, which is unacceptable) requires a wage-labour force whose wage leaves a profit for the capital which employs it; that can be assured if and only if the determination of wages is left to the impersonal market forces of supply and demand; those market forces, being impersonal, are neither arbitrary nor based on physical force, and are therefore equitable; therefore what must, and may in good conscience, be upheld, is the capitalist order, in spite of the hardship it sometimes inflicts on the labouring poor.

On Natural Law grounds the argument is shorter but shakier: what is divinely ordained must be equitable, the wage-labour/capital relation is part of the divinely ordained natural order, therefore it is equitable. The minor premise here, that the capitalist order is part of the divine and natural order, is not self-evident: indeed, at least until the end of the sixteenth century most writers and preachers would have treated it as nonsense. But Burke needed the natural and divine law because he had to show not only that the capitalist order was just but also that it was naturally acceptable to the working class. The whole structure of society, Burke insisted, depended on their submissiveness. And he estimated that they would remain submissive if they were protected from the "rights of man" principles by a counter-barrage of Christian Natural Law principles.

Burke was more astute than most of his contemporaries in seeing that a revival of Christian Natural Law was just what was needed. To make use of it, indeed, its content had to be changed, for it had on the whole been sharply critical of market morality. Its concept of justice, both distributive and commutative, had been based on customary norms and had been used to defend the medieval and early modern society, a society of custom and status, against the encroachments of the market.

Was Burke, then, doing violence to the old Natural Law in turning it to the support of the capitalist market order? Was his assumption that the capitalist order was the traditional order an outrageous one? I think not. For capitalist behaviour and capitalist morality, which had been making inroads on the earlier society throughout the sixteenth century, had got the upper hand in England by the middle of the seventeenth. The property law and the political institutions needed for full capitalist order development were well in place when they were confirmed by the Whig Revolution in 1689. So by Burke's time the capitalist order *had in fact been* the traditional order in England for a whole century. And it had become so by inserting itself inside an older hierarchical order without altering either the political forms—King, Lords and Commons remained—or the most fundamental class gradation, that between owners, enterprisers and labourers.

So there is nothing surprising or inconsistent in Burke's championing at the same time the traditional English hierarchical society and the capitalist market economy. He believed in both, and believed that the latter needed the former. (pp. 59-63)

His genius was in seeing that the capitalist society of the late eighteenth century was still heavily dependent on the acceptance of status. Contract had not replaced status: it was dependent on status. Burke's historical view was, for his time at least, more valid than the view of nineteenth-century analysts such as Sir Henry Maine, which is still apt to be taken as the received wisdom, namely, that the movement of the last few centuries had been a movement from status to contract. Burke saw that, down to his own time, such movement as there had been was not from status to contract but from status to status, that is, from a feudal status differentiation, which rested on military capacity, to what we should now call an internalised status differentiation, which rested on nothing more than habit and tradition, that is, on the subordinate class continuing to accept its traditional station in life. With no more solid basis than that, it could easily be undermined. Burke, recognising that fragility, had no recourse except to enlist Christian Natural Law in its aid. And this did no violence to the Christian Natural Law. It had always upheld a traditional social order against any threats. Now the content of the social order had changed, and in England it had changed long enough ago that the new content had already become traditional. So the Natural Law could now appropriately be used to defend the new traditional social order against new threats, the more so since the new content utilised the old forms.

Thus Burke is not to be condemned for twisting Christian Natural Law through a hundred and eighty degrees, but is to be commended for having seen that society had moved through the same arc. This, however, does not exonerate those who present Burke as a pure Christian Natural Law man without seeing that he had put a new bourgeois content into Natural Law. That misses Burke's real insight. And it begs the question of how useful a return to Burke would be in the late twentieth century. (pp. 69-70)

What use can properly be made of him now by those who are seeking to retain or revive moral values in late twentieth-century Western societies in the face of the dangers by which they now seem to be beset? At first sight, not much use. For in spite of the persuasive efforts of a few economists such as Milton Friedman, it is no longer politically realistic for conservatives to try to take us back to a pure *laissez-faire* market economy; and liberal theorists who have accepted the modified capitalism of the welfare state do not seem to have much to gain from Burke's appeal to tradition.

Of course Burke's insistence on the rule of law, on constitutional versus arbitrary government, and on the respect due to property, is agreeable to both conservatives and liberals. And his case for letting a 'natural aristocracy' interpret and implement the real will of the people would be welcome enough to both; though they might not be willing to avow it, it is not too far from the idea of meritocracy to which they both subscribe in some measure. The real difficulty seems to lie in Burke's idea of distributive justice: the just distribution of the national product is that which the free market allots to those who enter the market from positions of class domination and subordination. That concept of justice cannot now be accepted or avowed by either conservatives or liberals; and it seems to be especially obnoxious to welfare-state liberals, since they start from the postulate of equal natural rights.

Nevertheless, the most renowned current liberal theory of distributive justice, namely John Rawls's *A Theory of Justice* (1971), is not fundamentally different from Burke's. Rawls accepts the welfare-state distribution up to a certain limit, but the limit is set on precisely the same principle as Burke's zero limit. Rawls holds that state interference with the market, intended to be in the interests of the poor, must stop short of the point at which it would make everybody, including the poor, worse off; and that that point is reached when the degree of interference would discourage enterprisers from continuing their work of maximising efficient production. This, as we have seen, was also Burke's position. The only difference is that Burke argued that *any* interference would have this effect, whereas the twentieth-century liberals have learned from experience that capitalist enterprise is still very active when it has to contend with the present quite substantial amount of state interference. The difference is not one of principle but of empirical judgement.

It appears, then, that if current liberals were to point this out they might well enlist Burke, the more readily in view of Burke's lifelong insistence that circumstances alter cases and that statesmen and projectors should always devise their policies in the light of changing circumstances.

But the risks of enlisting Burke in this way would be considerable, for the change in circumstances between his time and ours is [considerable]. . . . The liberal task now is different from Burke's task. His was to persuade the English (and European) ruling class to resist any ideas which would weaken the still prevailing working-class acceptance of the established hierarchical order. He did not have to speak to the working class, nor did he do so. Now, however, the main liberal task is to legitimate the presently established modified capitalist order, or some variant of it, in the eyes of a somewhat politically conscious and quite strongly organised Western working class. And this has to be done in quite changed international circumstances. (pp. 71-3)

To sum up: twentieth-century democrats, both liberal and conservative, share with Burke, the non-democrat, the perception that what is at stake is the legitimation of a social order, and that this is ultimately a question of moral values. They share, also, some of Burke's most general moral values. But if they heed Burke's warning about the vital necessity of adjusting principles to concrete circumstances, they must think twice about recruiting him. By his insistence on the importance of circumstances Burke ruled himself out of court for the late twentieth century. (p. 74)

> *C. B. Macpherson, in his* Burke, *Hill and Wang, 1980, 83 p.*

HARVEY C. MANSFIELD, JR.　(essay date 1984)

[*In the following excerpt, Mansfield examines Burke's opposition to political theory and his approval of prudence and prescription.*]

Burke is known today as the philosopher of "conservatism." But he has not yet shared much in the revival of American conservatism in the 1980s. Of the two schools of thought that have been identified in that revival, traditionalism and libertarianism, Burke is very much with the former. Although he favored the freeing of commerce wherever possible, contributed his *Thoughts and Details on Scarcity* . . . to the new school of political economy, and was an admiring friend of Adam Smith, he so opposed unhampered individual freedom, theoretical systems of self-interest, and the influence of new property that he surrounded and enveloped the abstract free economy of political economists with the traditions of the British constitution. But of course these traditions—"establishments," Burke called them—are far from the provisions of the American constitution, and even farther . . . from the planned character of the American constitution. Such are the obstacles to Burke's influence in American politics today. (p. 3)

If there is one recurrent theme in Burke's letters, speeches, and writings, it is his emphasis on the moral and political evils that follow upon the intrusion of theory into political practice. It is theory as such that he rejects; his emphasis on the evils of intrusive theory is not balanced by a compensating reliance on sound theory that men would need as a guide to their politics. Sound theory, to him, would seem to be self-denying theory. Although Burke may occasionally refer to "the pretended philosophers of the hour," thus implying the existence of another sort, he is usually content to denounce philosophers, meta-

physicians, and speculators as such without making a point of what might seem to be the vital distinction among them. In a famous passage in *A Letter to a Member of the National Assembly* . . . , he attacks Rousseau—"the philosopher of vanity," "a lover of his kind but a hater of his kindred"—in terms no philosopher had flung publicly at another, until a decline of decorum in this matter occurred in the nineteenth century. In that place Burke distinguishes "modern philosophers," which expresses "everything that is ignoble, savage and hard-hearted," from "the writers of sound antiquity" whom Englishmen continue to read more generally, he believes, than is now done "on the continent." But Burke does not propose that ancient authors be adopted, even remotely, as guides to show the way out of the crisis into which modern philosophers have brought all mankind. Reading them is not so much the cause as the effect of English good taste, something that is sadly lacking "on the continent." Considering Burke's hostility to the intrusion of philosophy in politics, yet recalling too that Burke does not merely despair at the growing influence of philosophy, the problem of his political philosophy would seem to be to design a theory that never intrudes into practice. Our question in assessing it is: can theory serve solely as a watchdog against theory and never be needed as a guide?

The harms done by theory to sound practice had been under Burke's eye from the first. His first publication, *A Vindication of Natural Society* . . . , was a satire showing the absurd political consequences of Bolingbroke's theory, and in the early pamphlets on party, *Observations on a Late Publication Intituled "The Present State of the Nation"* . . . and *Thoughts on the Cause of the Present Discontents* . . . , he argued against the factious effects of a theoretical preference for "men of ability and virtue" over parties composed of gentlemen acting together publicly in mutual trust. In his speeches opposing British policy in America, he attacked the government's insistence on the rights of taxation and sovereignty without regard to consequence or circumstance as a speculative, legalistic reliance on "the virtue of paper government." For lawyers with their concern for rights and forms do not have regard to the actual exercise of formalities, substitute legal correctness for prudent policy, and seek to generalize in the manner of law—which is also that of theory. In a speech given in 1785, Burke was already denouncing "the speculatists of our speculating age." But it was in the French Revolution that the evils of speculation in politics became visible in their full extent and as a whole. Burke was surprised by the outbreak of that revolution, but he had been prepared by every major concern of his previous career in politics to identify it as a philosophical revolution, the first "*complete* revolution," a "revolution in sentiments, manners and moral opinions" that reached "even to the constitution of the human mind." The French Revolution displayed and summed up all the evils of speculative politics. (pp. 4-5)

[Burke] does not offer a theoretical clarification and reconstruction which would meet the revolutionaries on their own ground. Instead, he attempts to stand on the ground and stay within the realm of political practice, insofar as possible. His writings proposing action are much richer in political wisdom—hence seemingly more "theoretical"—than those of ordinary statesmen even when reminiscing, yet they are also much more circumscribed and circumstantial than treatises which are intended to interest theorists: thus, fullsome for historians, meager for philosophers. He once said: "The operation of dangerous and delusive first principles obliges us to have recourse to the true ones"—thereby admitting the necessity of such recourse, by contrast to ordinary statesmen, and declaring his reluctance, against the habit of theorists.

Yet the first principles to which Burke has recourse do not appear to be first principles. Instead of providing theoretical clarification, he asserts that direction of human affairs belongs to prudence; and instead of establishing what might be the best or legitimate state, he celebrates the genius of the British constitution. Burke's political philosophy emerges from the elaboration of these two things, prudence and the British constitution. They may not be the first, grounding principles, but they are surely the principles Burke puts forward to claim our attention before all others.

Prudence, Burke says, is "the god of this lower world," since it has "the entire dominion over every exercise of power committed into its hands." Prudence is "the first of all the virtues, as well as the supreme director of them all." This means, in particular, that "practical wisdom" justly supersedes "theoretic science" whenever the two come into contention. The reason for the sovereignty of prudence is in the power of circumstances to alter every regularity and principle. "Circumstances (which with some gentlemen pass for nothing) give in reality to every political principle its distinguishing color and discriminating effect." Burke emphasizes that the prudence he speaks of is a "moral prudence" or a "public and enlarged prudence" as opposed to selfish prudence, not to mention cleverness or cunning. But he does not say how to be sure of the morality of prudence. If prudence is supreme, it must reign over morality; but if prudence can be either moral or selfish, it would seem to require the tutelage of morality. Aristotle, when facing this problem, was led to understand prudence as the comprehensive legislative art, and then to subordinate that to theory. Burke makes a different disposition. Instead of pursuing an inquiry into the first principles or ends of prudence, which necessarily leads beyond prudence, he distinguishes within prudence between "rules of prudence" available to ordinary statesmen and "prudence of a higher order." Rules of prudence are not mathematical, universal, or ideal; but they are nonetheless rules, Burke says grandly, "formed upon the known march of the ordinary providence of God," that is, visible in human experience. But as these rules are sovereign over all theoretical rights or metaphysical first principles, so higher prudence, the prudence of prudence, can suspend the rules of prudence when necessary.

This distinction within prudence, by which Burke attempts to secure the morality of prudence without subverting its sovereignty, corresponds to a distinction he draws between presumptive virtue and actual virtue: "There is no qualification for government but virtue and wisdom, actual or presumptive." Presumptive virtue and wisdom are the lesser, probable virtue that can be presumed in well-bred gentlemen of prominent families born into situations of eminence where they are habituated to self-respect; to the "censorial inspection of the public eye"; to taking a "large view of the wide-spread and infinitely diversified combinations of men and affairs in a large society"; to having leisure to reflect; to meeting the wise and learned as well as rich traders; to military command; to the caution of an instructor of one's fellow citizens thus acting as a "reconciler between God and man"; and to being employed as an administrator of law and justice. Actual virtue, such as Burke's own perhaps, is higher but more dubious; it must intervene when the rules of prudence fail, but it must not rule ordinarily lest society fall victim to the instability of men of ability. The idea of presumptive virtue presumes ability, not

the highest but ordinarily sufficient, in men of property; at the same time it presumes at least instability, and sometimes immorality, in those who have nothing but ability, and rather than being born and bred in an elevated condition they must rise to eminence by means that may not be moral and should not be exemplary. No country can reject the service of those with actual virtue, but "the road to eminence and power, from obscure condition, ought not to be made too easy." When that road is made too easy, too many follow it, and men of actual virtue are encouraged to display their ability rather than their virtue, and are crowded out by new men who have cleverness and little property, as happened in the French Revolution. Actual virtue therefore must be kept subordinate ordinarily to presumptive virtue, while being allowed, after due probation, the right of intervention in an emergency, such as the French Revolution, when men of presumptive virtue are confronted with an event so astonishing that they do not know how to react.

Thus Burke solves the problem of prudence within prudence: he keeps moral prudence distinct from mere cleverness, yet maintains its sovereignty over clever theorists except for occasional interventions by higher prudence. (pp. 8-10)

It is the ruling characteristic of Burke's political philosophy as well as the guiding theme of his politics to avoid the ground on which theory and practice converge. Founding, which prior to Burke had been considered by all political thinkers to be the essential political act, is for him a nonevent. The making of a constitution can never be "the effect of a single instantaneous regulation." It cannot happen, and it is wrong to try to make it happen.

In complete disagreement with Tocqueville, Burke does not consider that democracy is a possible regime. The people cannot rule; they are the passive element in contrast to the "active men in the state." Though the people may be led by a vicious oligarchy of some kind, it should be led by a "true natural aristocracy," by ministers who "are not only our natural rulers, but our natural guides." Thus, for Burke, one cannot choose between democracy and aristocracy, nor can there be a democratic or an aristocratic age, as for Tocqueville; nature has made the many incapable of governing themselves. "A perfect democracy is . . . the most shameless thing in the world," because each person's share of responsibility is so small that he does not feel it, and because public opinion which should restrain government is in the case of democracy nothing but the people's self-approbation. Responsible government is capable of shame, perhaps more than anything else; it is defending what one has had to do rather than taking credit for what one has chosen to do. No aristocracy, any more than a democracy, can rule long or well without the sense of a power above it; the lack of this sense is what makes democracy impossible as well as shameless. Only in an attenuated sense, therefore, is any human government, even a true natural aristocracy, a kind of self-government. Government is so far from a matter of choice, of choosing a form of rule, that it is a "power out of ourselves."

Fundamentally, government is not ruling; it is changing, reforming, balancing, or adjusting. Government is not nourished, as Aristotle thought, by claims to rule asserted by democrats and oligarchs in defense (and exaggeration) of their equality and inequality to others. The people do not claim to rule of their own accord; only when inflamed by a few do they believe they want to rule. And aristocrats, however natural, are bred to their eminence, which they accept rather than demand.

As far as Burke is from the Aristotelian sense of rule—government by human choice, art, and political science—he does not rush into theocracy and grasp at divine right in order to keep governments under control by shame. To make it certain that government has a human origin, Burke adopts the language of contract from modern theorists. But since government by contract might seem calculated, if not chosen, for convenience—in effect, a matter of arbitrary will or pleasure, not of judgment—he stresses the great differences between ordinary contracts "taken up for a little temporary interest" and the social contract that establishes the state. The latter contract is a "partnership in all science; a partnership in all art; a partnership in every virtue, and in all perfection." And it is a contract made between the living, the dead, and those to be born—that is, a contract not in the power of the present generation but in trust for the past and the future. (pp. 11-13)

Natural rights, which Burke deprecatingly calls "metaphysic rights," do not come to us directly, but "like rays of light which pierce into a dense medium, are, by the laws of nature, refracted from their straight line." Taking a cue from this famous remark, we might say that for Burke laws of nature are laws of refraction. They are laws describing the ways in which men, making their own conventions, constitutions, or property, imitate or follow nature as nature conducts itself without reference to humans. For example . . . , men making constitutions imitate nature in finding harmony through the struggle of its discordant powers and permanence through the rise and fall of its transitory parts. "Art is man's nature," Burke says, in reproach of the modern philosophers who place the "state of nature" outside civil society. Art (not choice) is nature's special gift to humans, but the gift is not used in a manner to preserve human specialness. All society is artificial, yet all artifice is according to natural law; the gift of art must be given back to nature. One wonders whether prudence is after all sovereign for Burke, if it must operate "under that discipline of nature."

The sovereign rule of prudence is also a rule *for* prudence. It is prescription, "this great fundamental part of natural law," which describes the manner of growth of property and constitutions and lays down the method of inheritance. Strange to say, prescription before Burke was never considered to be unequivocally part of natural law, for it was not thought to be applicable in public law. Burke borrowed the concept from Roman law, in which prescription gives title to property without a deed by long-continued use or takes it away despite a deed after long-continued disuse. This rule of private law was transformed by Burke into a rule of public law applicable to constitutions (not merely to the law of nations). Thus, a rule of private property becomes *the* rule for government, "the most solid of all titles, not only to property, but, which is to secure that property, to government"; "a title which is not the creature, but the master, of positive law," "the sacred rules of prescription." If the problem of theory's intrusion into practice is the theme of Burke's political philosophy, prescription is his special discovery—one must say, since he could not abide the word "innovation," his grand reform. It was merely a description of the working of the British constitution, he claimed; but as theory it was certainly new. Indeed, Burke had, he said, "a very full share" in the passage of the Nullum Tempus Act of 1769, by which he attempted to establish prescription as public law in Britain. Burke made this claim proudly in his splendid self-defense against the Duke of Bedford, *A Letter to a Noble Lord,* but he did not similarly advertise the theoretical reform which justified the legal novelty (which went against

the authority of Blackstone). Nor did he remark that prescription became public law in 1769 not through prescription but by statute. That not merely *a* title, but the *most solid* title to property comes from long use rather than a deed implies that government, which issues deeds, is bound by long-continued practices rather than by principles. Property by prescription implies government without a founding or a theory: the best claim to rule comes not from establishing one's own claim as best but by securing the abandonment of rival claims. Yet it required a theory to show this, and even if Burke had tread softly to introduce it, even if his theory had fit neatly the shape of fact, it cannot be denied that his theory intrudes upon the prudence of statesmen. (pp. 19-20)

[For Burke], prescription is a "great fundamental part of natural law." He does not quite say it is *the* fundamental part, and he does not specify the full content of natural law in the manner of more theoretical theorists such as Aquinas or Hobbes. He is satisfied that natural law be understood as a law beyond and above human legislation; he does not require that human law be seen as application of natural law. In the debate between Cicero and Hobbes as to whether "men have a right to make what laws they please," Burke is on the side of Cicero in denying this. He then says that "all human laws are, properly speaking, only declaratory; they may alter the mode and application, but have no power over the substance of original justice." But since Burke has imported prescription into natural law itself, and has said little to establish the substance of original justice, it seems in effect that the mode and application, more than the substance, of natural law is to guide practice. Natural law is more means than ends because prescription, in order to exclude violent, comprehensive change, prevents the ends of politics from appearing in politics unrefracted by materials and circumstances. Prescription is prudence crystallized in theory. As such it is censor to the rest of natural law, so that natural law can speak in its own voice only "the principle of a superior law." Human liberty is so far from opposed to the principle of a superior will that it cannot survive without one. Although society is the product of a contract among men, men cannot live freely if they are free to make a new contract in every generation. Each generation must regard its liberties as an "entailed inheritance," as its property precisely because those liberties were not created by it. One may venture to conclude that at the center of Burke's political philosophy is the British constitution, not natural law. Natural law is the ground, but only because a constitution, made by accidents, needs a ground. However admirable it may be, the British constitution is not, for Burke, the rational state. But the ground of the constitution must be unseen and unfelt lest it upset the constitution that rests on it.

Here one might object that we are forgetting the "laws of commerce," which Burke, in a passage in his *Thoughts and Details on Scarcity* . . . , once equated, to the disgust of Karl Marx, with the "laws of nature, and consequently the laws of God." The laws of commerce, it would seem, promote too much novel enterprise to be held accountable to the principle of prescription. That is so, except insofar as prescription welcomes and justifies private enterprise without deeds or charters from the government. But the mobile property of merchants, together with the active abilities that create it, could be held in check and kept in balance, Burke believed, by the establishment of landed property and by the rule of gentlemen. With some basis in English experience, and some degree of hope, he joined together the supremacy of the landed interest, which he rightly said was recommended by "the practical politics of antiquity'' (particularly Aristotle and Cicero), with a statement that could not be found, except as satire or disapproval, in ancient writers: "The love of lucre, though sometimes carried to a ridiculous, sometimes to a vicious, excess, is the grand cause of prosperity to all states.'' (pp. 21-2)

Burke, the champion of gentlemanly prudence, spent his political life beyond the limits of gentlemanly prudence, looking ahead to what his party could not see, urging it on to unaccustomed activity on uncongenial ground. One should say also that he devoted himself to securing and improving the boundaries of gentlemanly prudence, to keeping out subversive speculators and refashioning constitutional practices, such as party and impeachment, that would facilitate the rule of gentlemen. Having helped to found his party—by giving it a doctrine and a soul rather than by directing it—he abandoned it after the French Revolution and then attacked it. His colleagues could not see the difference between the American Revolution and the French; they did not appreciate the uniqueness of the latter event, the most complete revolution ever known. Burke's political philosophy centers on the defense of an actual constitution rather than the contruction of an imaginary one. His theme is the sufficiency—rather, the perfection—of gentlemanly prudence. But his defense of his beloved gentlemen reveals their limitations, perhaps better than any revolutionary attack. For the revolutionaries found no suitable replacement for gentlemen; nor indeed have we, though we have sought among bureaucrats, technocrats, and democrats. One could almost define "gentlemen" by adding up everything that is lacking in bureaucrats, technocrats, and democrats. Burke's admiring view of them is clearer than that of their critics; the defects of gentlemen are to be seen in the need for his own contribution to their defense. That contribution went well beyond warning them of perils they were too dull to sense and arousing them with fine phrases. Using what he once called "the seasonable energy of a single man," Burke tried to fortify the rule of gentlemen so as to make them less liable to subversion and attack. The result in the nineteenth century was both to fix them in place, immobile in their newly philosophical prejudice (the conservatives), and to loosen their attachments, trusting in the promise that reform would be the means of their conservation (the liberals). Somewhat unwillingly, Burke bears testimony to the necessary imperfection of politics in the very midst of his inspiring speeches and noble deeds. (pp. 26-7)

> *Harvey C. Mansfield, Jr., in an introduction to* Selected Letters of Edmund Burke *by Edmund Burke, edited by Harvey C. Mansfield, Jr., The University of Chicago Press, 1984, pp. 1-27.*

CHRISTOPHER REID (essay date 1985)

[*In the following excerpt, Reid examines the relationship between the development of literary technique in Burke's writings and the political circumstances that prompted them.*]

Literary appreciations of Burke have from the very outset been tinged with regret, as if he had somehow been too fine a writer to soil his hands in the mire of party politics. The rebuke which Goldsmith administered in his poem "Retaliation" [quoted in the excerpt by Emerson dated 1835], when he accused his friend of being one

> Who, born for the Universe, narrow'd his mind,
> And to party gave up, what was meant for mankind
>
> (ll. 31-2)

established a way of understanding Burke's writings and career which has never quite lost its force in literary study. A variation of this attitude has been to value his works in so far as they failed, or are supposed to have failed, to secure practical political objectives. Political defeat can then be seen as almost a prerequisite for a literary triumph. In these responses to Burke one senses the embarrassment literary criticism sometimes suffers when faced by works written for specific occasions and with a view to obtaining particular ends. Such works do not obviously fulfil the criteria of permanence and universality which are so often held to distinguish literature worthy of serious critical attention, a category from which works of political argument, with their concern for immediate issues and possibilities of action, have generally been excluded. If Burke's political writings have been regarded as exceptional, it has usually been on the grounds that, unlike the works of other controversialists of his time, they are universal in their application and appeal.

There may not, on the face of it, appear to be anything particularly contentious in this assessment. Some works, after all, are simply more serious, interesting and durable than others. Yet in seeking to emphasise what is of permanent value in Burke's writings it is easy to detach them from the crises and contingencies which lent them their particular urgency, form and colour. Such an approach would no doubt succeed in highlighting their most humane, liberal and rational elements, those which may continue to move, inspire or make us think. The outcome, however, would be a highly selective reading of Burke, one which would risk misrepresenting his historical role and even his literary manner. For in the works on which his reputation now largely rests, the counter-revolutionary tracts of the 1790s, humanity and sympathy are at a premium. These writings reverberate with an extraordinary rhetorical violence. Burke came early to the conclusion that the revolution in France should be crushed by military force. In his last years it was largely in urging this course of action that he exercised his formidable literary talents. (pp. 3-4)

The ***Thoughts on the Cause of the Present Discontents*** is perhaps the most even and controlled political work Burke ever published. It is, as he put it himself, "a piece of Gentlemanlike Hostility" in which the polemic observes the decorum of reasoned debate. Together with the two celebrated parliamentary speeches on America, it established Burke's reputation as a liberal and rational Whig, a principled opponent of the excessive and unconstitutional use of state power. The writings of the 1790s, however, were seen almost from the moment of their publication as initiating a sharp break in Burke's thinking about politics. His long campaign against the allegedly improper political influence of the Court gave way to a more urgent and vehement polemical effort, designed to mobilise all the forces of the state against the Antichrist of innovation. The tone of his economic writing also changed. In the 1770s it was characterised by the optimistic and even heroic view of commerce presented in the works on America; in the 1790s by the grim and punitive "realism" of the scarcity tract [***Thoughts and Details on Scarcity***]. And in the ***Reflections,*** with its conception of society as an organism to which the individual is attached by the indissoluble ties of nature, custom and birth, Burke broke decisively with the liberal Whig creed of social contract and natural right. The causes, extent and significance of these changes have been at the centre of the debate about the alleged "inconsistency" of Burke's political thought. (p. 215)

[Yet, considered] outwardly, in terms of genre, Burke's political writing, across a period of almost thirty years, shows little evidence of radical change. Throughout this period he continued to work within the literary forms—notably the parliamentary speech and the "private" letter—appropriate to a "closed" political culture. At the same time, however, we can see in his work an attempt to adapt those forms, not so much because he wished to create a new public, along Wilkite lines, but because he felt the need to reach an existing one more effectively. The *Thoughts* is a case in point. Concealed within the pamphlet are elements of a relatively closed form of address. It was originally conceived in the form of a letter to a retired member of parliament . . . [and] Burke at one point makes plain his assumption that he is addressing an audience of propertied men. Yet for the most part, and notwithstanding its partisan objects and origins, the pamphlet rises above the mode of direct appeal to interested parties. Its language of principle encourages a broad range of response to Burke's political argument. The same can be said of the parliamentary speeches he published. Burke retains the authority and prestige of the original form, but submits his case to the judgment of a wider audience—the political nation "out of doors", as parliamentarians of the period liked to put it.

Within these customary forms of argument there are important shifts of tone and emphasis which bear more directly on the question of Burke's consistency. The most important change occurs in the *Reflections* of 1790, where the intended audience is at least as wide as it had ever been in Burke, but where the form of address is more narrowly pedagogic and the style more diverse, emotive and unstable. The address to "a very young gentleman at Paris" establishes a literary relationship based on an assertion of authority rather than on the rational exchange of views among equals. The important general propositions about politics which Burke makes in the course of the pamphlet retain something of this mood of instruction. As Williams . . . puts it [in *Writing in Society* (1983)], Burke's address to the young Depont "permits the decisive tone of the reflections, from settled wisdom (English politics) to inexperience (French politics)". It is evident that more than a question of mere "style" is at stake here. The manner of address shapes and informs both the argument and the outlook of the *Reflections*. The connection is made explicit when, in a discussion of the National Assembly's alleged mismanagement of the armed forces of France, Burke pours scorn on "the fantastick vagaries of these juvenile politicians." . . . The youth of the correspondent who had asked for Burke's views on the revolution in France paves the way for a general charge of callow ineptitude. Burke was to make further use of the address to a younger man in other works of the 1790s. In the *Letter to a Noble Lord* he exploits the Duke of Bedford's political inexperience—"Let me tell my youthful censor . . ." . . .—for rhetorical advantage. In the *Letter to William Elliot* and the *Letters on a Regicide Peace* he speaks as a dying prophet to a younger generation, urging his disciples into action in defence of a ruling class which he saw as dangerously complacent. There is, then, a nice irony in the fact that in *A Vindication of Natural Society*, the parody of Bolingbroke's philosophy which Burke published at the very beginning of his literary career, he should have anticipated the rhetoric of the master/pupil relationship which he was to use so effectively in his final years ("You are, my Lord, but just entering into the world; I am going out of it," . . . he announces to the imaginary addressee of the *Vindication*). Broadly speaking, then, there is a development of manner in which the appeal to a common experience, shared by writer, reader and addressee, which characterised the earlier works, gives way to a more peremptory mode of argument in the writings of the 1790s. (pp. 216-18)

[This] development in address is linked to some significant changes in political idiom. It is as if the conventions of polite argument, whereby an exchange of views can take place even between those who disagree, have been rendered obsolete by the threat of the French Revolution. The old questions, and the old manner of disputing them, no longer seem important. Burke's tendency towards violence in debate, which had sometimes shocked his milder-mannered parliamentary colleagues even in pre-revolutionary days, becomes increasingly pronounced. In seeking to communicate his sense of crisis he alternates rapidly between the twin extremes of fierce denunciation and sentimental acts of homage. When he writes in this strain, it is in a language consonant with his earlier concept of the sublime—a language which operates primarily on the passions, and which presents the affairs of the political world in terms of an imagery of apocalypse. In this way the style of Burke's political writing in the 1790s is significantly less "parliamentary", less imbued with the historical and secular idioms of the House of Commons, than the earlier work. Instead the French Revolution is experienced within a framework of ideas and images which are often frankly religious in origin. This is the language—of increasing importance in the 1790s—which has been seen as evidence of Burke's allegiance to the principles of Natural Law, according to which the social and economic system he sought to uphold is understood as a temporal expression of the divine order of things. (p. 218)

[Central] to his endeavour in the 1790s is a certain attitude towards, knowledge of, and engagement in the realm of feeling. Burke succeeds in his ideological task in so far as he is able to induce the reader to live out, and experience as "true," the values and beliefs of the dominant culture of his time. For that reason the rhetorical appeal to the reader's sensibility, by means of which Burke activates a host of ideological and cultural attachments, is as important—and as open to analysis—as the mode of rational argument.

The question I have raised here is initially a question of reading (in what terms and at what levels of significance should a political discourse such as Burke's be read?), but it is also inescapably a question of Burke's historical role (what were the conditions which required the changed and charged manner of the *Reflections*?). As such it relates directly to the long debate on the meaning of his career. The Burke who emerges from most discussions of this problem is somehow less troubling and troubled a figure than his writings, in their complex interplay of competing attitudes and feelings, usually suggest. This is true even of Macpherson who provides a convincing explanation of Burke's ideological role without always indicating how tense and contradictory, historically, that role was. In Macpherson's view, what unifies the various phases and campaigns of Burke's career is his work as a political economist and his commitment to the principle of a self-regulating capitalist market [see excerpt dated 1980]. What occurred in the 1790s was a change in style rather than substance. Burke's use of the language of Christian Natural Law was not a reversion to a traditional conservatism but a brilliant rhetorical manoeuvre, made necessary by the revolutionary threat to property, and designed to sanctify the operations of the market. Burke saw that in Britain the capitalist order had, by his time, become "traditional". His achievement was that he was able to revive the Christian Natural Law, once hostile to the morality of the market, by providing it with a new capitalist content.

Macpherson's suggestive and provocative analysis is a useful corrective to the view that by 1790 Burke had become an anachronism, an ideological Canute striving vainly to stem the tides of change. But although it is true to say that Burke consistently championed the cause of the "free" market, it should be added that he did so from a particularly exposed and increasingly unstable position. As a consequence of his own social experience and political career, Burke owed allegiance to two closely allied classes: the landed and politically dominant aristocracy, and the professional, mercantile and manufacturing bourgeoisie. Although both of these classes could certainly be described in Burke's period as "capitalist", there were significant differences in their modes of social, economic and cultural life. The tension of Burke's position, as one whose task was to articulate and reconcile these differences, is expressed most memorably in the *Letter to a Noble Lord,* but its influence is not confined to that work. It also accounts for Burke's surprisingly impassioned denunciations of the conduct of ambitious new men in India. When, in the *Speech on the Nabob of Arcot's Debts,* he described Paul Benfield with revealing irony as "a specimen of the new and pure aristocracy created by the right honourable gentleman [Pitt], as the support of the crown and constitution, against the old, corrupt, refractory, natural interests of this kingdom," Burke showed how fearful he was that this unbridled (because unattached) ambition which he so well understood could threaten the stability of the alliance between classes. The outraged aristocratic humanism of this speech, and its attack on middle-class administrators and adventurers whose origins were not unlike those of Burke himself, clearly anticipates the anti-Jacobin rhetoric of the 1790s. The corollary of this vein of denunciation, of course, is Burke's reverence for tradition, a deeply rooted sentiment which is occasionally elevated to theoretical status in the language of Natural Law.

Considered from this point of view, the more memorable rhetorical episodes of the *Reflections* and other works of the 1790s can be seen as a genuine expression of cultural alarm, the true language of a man *plus royaliste que le roi* who had staked his career on the continued hegemony of the landowning class. It is the dominance of a specifically agrarian form of capitalism, and the social and cultural life which arises from it, that Burke is concerned to uphold. Thus in the *Reflections* he laments a situation in which the "landed interest" of France has fallen prey to a metropolitan alliance forged between the "monied interest" and a set of insubordinate literary men. In making his defence of property Burke puts forward arguments which he claimed were broadly consistent with political principles he had held throughout his career. It is true that the *Reflections* does not mark a complete break in his discourse. For one thing, the elevated but distinctly unhyperbolical mode of the *Thoughts* did not altogether disappear in the 1790s. For another, as I have just suggested, elements of the anti-Jacobin rhetoric are clearly present in the earlier work. Yet the general change in manner is unmistakable. The position Burke was defending may have been the same, but it had to be defended in different terms in order to meet a new and more sinister threat. "New things in a new world! I see no hopes in the common tracks," Burke declares in the *Letter to William Elliot,* a pamphlet which combines cultural nostalgia and political realism in a way which is characteristic of his final works. The circumstances of the 1790s called for an experiment in ideology, a more urgent and wide-ranging response than before. At the same time those circumstances (including the break with the Foxite Whigs) led to Burke's political isolation and exposure, a pressure which brought the instability of his social role increasingly into the open. (pp. 219-22)

As the representative of a mature and distinguished literary culture—the culture of Johnson, Hume and Gibbon—he had at his command a rich moral and historical vocabulary with which to articulate his sense of crisis. In his response to the French Revolution, and in its most characteristic literary effects—its moments of excess and illumination, its sudden shifts of tone, temper and style—Burke realised the potential and released the accumulated pressures of this social and cultural experience. He was empowered to conduct his uncompromising defence of privilege in a language which was, for the most part, more elaborate, audacious and animated than the discourse of English radicalism. Only Blake, who belonged to a tradition of which Burke was probably unaware, lived out the crisis of the 1790s more completely and proved a more powerful interpreter of his times. It is in performing a similar role, though with an entirely different set of assumptions, that Burke still claims our attention. Few would now read him as a "philosopher", as the author of a coherent theory which contains political lessons of timeless worth. Yet his works offer more than a case of simple expediency, tricked out in a rhetoric which can be conveniently stripped away. The rhetoric, indeed, embraces Burke's whole response. It is the very art and impulse of his work, the shaping spirit of a political discourse in which he communicates a complex experience of history. (p. 223)

> Christopher Reid, in his Edmund Burke and the Practice of Political Writing, *St. Martin's Press, 1985, 238 p.*

RUSSELL KIRK   (essay date 1985-86)

[*In the following excerpt, Kirk affirms Burke's formative influence on the United States Constitution.*]

Burke was the most eloquent champion of the English constitution, and the most mordant adversary of the several French constitutions of the Revolutionary era. He touches upon constitutional questions from his earliest political speeches to his final publications. And yet Burke never did or wrote anything about the Constitution drawn up at Philadelphia in 1787.

So my choice of theme may surprise some people. Burke's name is not to be found in the recorded proceedings of that Convention at Philadelphia, nor is it mentioned in the pages of *The Federalist.* After the year 1782 and American independence, Burke scarcely mentions North American affairs in his speeches, his publications, his correspondence. Then why assert that the great Whig politician, who never visited the Thirteen Colonies, somehow may be associated with that highly successful political device the federal constitution of the American Republic?

I have my reasons. First, because the general frame and substance of the Constitution of the United States accords with the political principles of the Rockingham Whigs, whose manager and intellectual chief Burke was. The framers of the American constitution borrowed deliberately and liberally from the English constitution. According to Sir Henry Maine in his *Popular Government,* the American framers took for their model the English constitution as it stood between 1760 and 1787— the years when Burke loomed so large in the House of Commons.

I do not suggest that everything in the original Constitution of the United States would have been thoroughly approved by Edmund Burke. . . . Yet for the most part, the constitution agreed upon at Philadelphia not only was derived from the eighteenth-century British constitution, but was derived more precisely from the idea of that English constitution which Burke himself had enunciated so ringingly from his ***Thoughts on the Present Discontents*** to his ***Speech on Moving Resolutions for Conciliation with the Colonies***. In substance, the Constitution of the United States was an amended version of what Burke called "the chartered rights of Englishmen." (pp. 3-4)

Burke never had favored American separation from the British Empire; the Declaration of Independence struck him a sore blow; nevertheless, doubtless the large majority of delegates to the Convention at Philadelphia regarded Burke as a friend to America. Burke's constitutional doctrines, during those five years of vehement opposition to the King's Friends, had been intertwined with his denunciations of the folly of taxing Americans against their will. So it is not surprising that Burke's concept of a just constitution had come to be taken for granted by most of the delegates to Philadelphia.

Moreover, the Philadelphia delegates' understanding of the causes and course of the War of Independence had been formed by Burke himself through a medium quite distinct from his speeches. For also Burke was the editor of ***The Annual Register***, the London publication that printed every year a detailed account of the Revolution in the Thirteen Colonies—the only such reporting available on either side of the Atlantic. Assuming the ***Register***'s editorship when the publication was founded, Burke continued editorial supervision down to 1789, when he retired from that labor. Much of the writing and editing of some articles was done by subordinates, from time to time; but those subordinates were Rockingham Whigs, Burke's friends and disciples. The whole political tone of the ***Register*** was Burke's. And probably every delegate at Philadelphia in 1787 had read the ***Register***, with its interpretations of the war and related constitutional controversies, in its annual volumes from 1765 to 1785 (and perhaps the newly-published volume for 1786); indeed, they had available then no other systematic and tolerably impartial analysis of military and political events during those years. In this fashion, quite aside from his oratory in the House of Commons, Burke exercised through serious journalism an ascendancy over the minds of leading Americans of the Revolutionary and Constitutional eras an influence greater than is obtained over the American people two centuries later by the most famous publicist of our day. (pp. 4-5)

Let us descend to particulars. In what respects would the new Constitution of the United States have satisfied Edmund Burke—if he had not been too busy in 1787 even to notice that Constitution in the pages of his ***Annual Register***?

First, the Constitution did not break with the established institutions and customs of the American people: it was a healthy growth, an enlargement of a political structure of which the foundations had been laid early in the seventeenth century—or earlier still, in medieval England. As James Bryce would point out nearly a century later, the new federal constitution had for precedent and source the colonial charters or constitutions. Those basic laws were altered somewhat with the coming of American independence; but some of them not altered greatly. The colonial constitution of Massachusetts was transmuted into the state constitution of 1780 without radical change; and, as Bryce remarks, the Constitution of Massachusetts "profoundly influenced the Convention that prepared the Federal Constitution in 1787."

Second, the Constitution recognized and incorporated a body of historical experience far older than the North American colonies: the constitutional development of England, the coun-

try with the highest degree of both freedom and order during the eighteenth century. Many parallels between the old British constitution and the new American constitution are obvious enough. Sir Henry Maine points out somewhat wittily that the Convention's delegates conferred upon the president of the United States powers precisely of the sort which George III claimed for the kingly office—despite all their previous lamentations about royal usurpation of power.

Third, the Constitution rejected *a priori* theories of government, settling for politics as the art of the possible. As Sir William Holdsworth puts in it his *History of English Law*, "The political theory of the Declaration of Independence which dwelt upon the equality of men, their unalienable rights to life, liberty, and the pursuit of happiness, and their right to resist a tyrannical government, retired into the background. The founders of the American constitution recognized with Burke that such theories, however well they might be suited to a period of revolution, were of very little help in a period of reconstruction. They therefore abandoned the democratic theories of Paine and Rousseau, and went for inspiration to that eighteenth-century British constitution with which they were familiar."

It may be added that besides rejecting Paine and Rousseau, the Framers ignored John Locke. Gottfried Dietze, who has written the best book about *The Federalist*, suggests that "Locke is the philosopher to whom the authors of *The Federalist* are most indebted for an exposition of constitutionalism and free government." I dissent. Locke's influence upon the Declaration of Independence is sufficiently obvious, though Jefferson was somewhat awkward about confessing that indebtedness; yet Locke is not mentioned in *The Federalist*. Why not? He was sufficiently removed in time to be cited without difficulty. It appears to me that Locke was omitted deliberately, as indeed Burke usually avoided reference to the first great Whig thinker. There is Whiggery in the Constitution, and the echo of the Glorious Revolution—though this latter chiefly in the first nine amendments. But I find this the later Whiggery of Burke, not the early Whiggery of Locke. To the Framers, as to Burke, Locke's first principles had become suspect. *The Second Treatise of Civil Government* no longer could be accounted a true historical account of the origins of society, nor could its reliance upon the law of nature be accepted by the serious statist. Despite Locke's frequent quotations from Richard Hooker, he did not really echo that great divine in his understanding of natural law, and still less did he follow Hooker back to Aquinas and the other Schoolmen. When Burke, a century after Locke wrote, found it necessary to oppose a revolution on the same grounds that Locke had used to justify a revolution, he appealed not to the "law of nature" that Locke understood, but rather to the richer natural-law tradition of Hooker, the Scholastics of the fourteenth century, and Cicero. Besides, Locke, with his fantastic scheme for organizing the colony of Carolina, was not precisely the sort of constitutionalist required for drawing up a practical instrument of government for a new nation. The realist Hume was far more to the Framers' taste. Let me add that Professor Dietze expresses more perceptively than does any other commentator the strong influence of Hume upon the authors of *The Federalist*. It is worth mentioning in this connection that Hume, sixty years after the publication of Locke's *Second Treatise*, made mincemeat of Locke's theory that men, at any remote period, ever joined themselves in a formal compact for their common welfare.

Fourth, the Constitution of the United States put strong constraints upon arbitrary power. It distinctly limited the operations of the general government; it preserved state and local powers for the most part, avoiding the curse of centralization for which Burke was to reproach the French revolutionaries; it recognized a form of natural aristocracy in the United States senate; it established the Congress as a body of true *representatives,* not delegates, according to Burke's famous speech on declining the poll at Bristol. (pp. 6-8)

Nowadays there is much talk of a Second Constitutional Convention in these United States. If merely two more state legislatures should pass resolutions calling for such a convention, with the purpose of drawing up an amendment to provide for a balanced federal budget, presumably that gathering would come to pass.

Just as the Convention of 1787 swept away the Articles of Confederation altogether—even though not convened for that express purpose—so a Convention of 1987, say, could deal so summarily as it might like with the present Constitution of the United States. All sorts of voices would be heard at such a convention; all sorts of interests would clash hotly there. Great error would be possible, irremediable error; one may even conceive of the drafting of a constitution quite new—and perhaps destined to last no longer than the constitutions of Zaire or Kampuchea.

Whether we Americans are to have a second constitutional convention or not, we would do well to renew our knowledge of the constitutional wisdom of Edmund Burke and of the authors of *The Federalist,* and that of other eminent practical statesmen of 1787. Burke's unfinished *Fourth Letter on a Regicide Peace,* his last published work, terminates with the fragment of a sentence: ''There is no such Euthanasia for the British Constitution. . . .'' Here Burke refers to an early essay by David Hume, in which the speculative Scot suggested that in the fullness of time the decaying British Constitution might die an easy death from inanition, a case of euthanasia, ''gently expiring without a groan in the paternal arms of a mere Monarchy.'' The end of the Constitution would not be painless, Burke declared: not if Jacobin France, or Jacobins within Britain, should gain the mastery. The end would be terrible, a destruction of Britain's civil social order by merciless fanatics.

Nor would there by any euthanasia for the Constitution of the United States, if we Americans should lose the great grim contest with the Soviet power, more formidable and more ruthless than ever the Jacobin power was. Or if we were to undo our Constitution ourselves, on plausible grounds, substituting for it some frame of government purportedly suited to the Age of the Computer—why, before long we would discover that a nation's passage from a venerable old order to a hard glittering new order cannot be painless.

For today we may say of the Constitution of the United States, which has endured very nearly two centuries, what Burke said of the British constitution in 1791:

> It is no simple, no superficial thing, nor to be estimated by superficial understandings. An ignorant man, who is not fool enough to meddle with his clock, is however sufficiently confident to think he can safely take to pieces, and put together at his pleasure, a moral machine of another guise, importance, and complexity, composed of far other wheels, and springs, and balances, and counteracting and co-operating powers. Men little think how immorally they act in rashly meddling with what they do not understand. Their delusive good intention is no sort of excuse for their presumption. They who truly mean well must

be fearful of acting ill. The British constitution may have its advantages pointed out to wise and reflecting minds; but it is of too high an order of excellence to be adapted to those which are common. It takes in too many views, it makes too many combinations, to be so much as comprehended by shallow and superficial understandings. Profound thinkers will know it in its reason and spirit. The less inquiring will recognize it in their feelings and their experience. They will thank God they have a standard which, in the most essential point of this great concern, will put them on a par with the most wise and knowing. . . . We ought to understand it according to our measure; and to venerate where we are not able presently to comprehend.

Amen to that. Should there come to pass a Constitutional Convention of 1987, it should be opened with prayer, and the prayer should be followed by a solemn public reading of that passage from *An Appeal from the New to the Old Whigs.* For we have learned how to transplant human hearts, after a fashion, precariously; but constitutions, the hearts of nations, remain unresponsive to sudden surgery. (pp. 10-11)

Russell Kirk, ''Edmund Burke and the Constitution,'' in The Intercollegiate Review, *Vol. 21, No. 2, Winter, 1985-86, pp. 3-11.*

ADDITIONAL BIBLIOGRAPHY

Barry, Liam. *Our Legacy from Burke.* Clarke's Bridge, Ireland: Paramount Printing House, 1952, 235 p.
General survey and literary exegesis of Burke's major works.

Baumann, Arthur A. *Burke: The Founder of Conservatism.* London: Eyre and Spottiswoode, 1929, 171 p.
General study of Burke's career, to which is appended a commentary on the current state of the British political system, followed by the complete text of Burke's *Letter to a Noble Lord.*

Bevan, Ruth A. *Marx and Burke: A Revisionist View.* La Salle, Ill.; Open Court Publishing Co., 1973, 197 p.
Compares the empirical outlooks and sociopolitical thought of Karl Marx and Burke, evaluating their respective relevance to contemporary politics.

Bormann, Dennis R. ''The 'Uncontested Term' Contested: An Analysis of Weaver on Burke.'' *Quarterly Journal of Speech* LVII, No. 3 (October 1971): 298-305.
Attacks the position taken by Richard M. Weaver (see citation below) that Burke's argumentative methods were faulty and essentially sprang from a nonconservative mind.

Boulton, James T. Introduction to *A Philosophical Enquiry into the Origin of Our Ideas of the Sublime and Beautiful,* by Edmund Burke, edited by James T. Boulton, pp. ix-cxxvii. Notre Dame, Ind.: University of Notre Dame Press, 1968.
Excellent study of the *Enquiry,* focusing on Burke's conception of taste, the sublime, and the beautiful, with commentary on the influence of the work.

Browning, Reed. ''The Origin of Burke's Ideas Revisited.'' *Eighteenth-Century Studies* 18, No. 1 (Fall 1984): 57-71.
Finds Burke's political views grounded in the writings of Cicero and the established platforms of the Court Whigs.

Bryson, Lyman; Barzun, Jacques; and Van Doren, Mark. ''Edmund Burke and Thomas Paine.'' In *The New Invitation to Learning,* edited by Mark Van Doren, pp. 368-83. New York: Random House, 1942.
Three-part conversation on Burke's and Paine's theories regarding political progress and reform.

Colum, Padraic. "Burke and the Present Order." *The Saturday Review of Literature* X, No. 11 (30 September 1933): 141-42.
> Tribute to Burke's conception of an ordered society founded upon tradition.

Cone, Carl B. *Burke and the Nature of Politics*. 2 vols. Lexington: University of Kentucky Press, 1957-64.
> Highly regarded political biography of Burke.

Conniff, James. "Edmund Burke's Reflections on the Coming Revolution in Ireland." *Journal of the History of Ideas* XLVII, No. 1 (January-March 1986): 37-59.
> Detailed examination of Burke's reformist attitudes toward the Irish Constitution and political structure.

Copeland, Thomas Wellsted. "Edmund Burke and the Book Reviews in Dodsley's *Annual Register*." *PMLA* 57, No. 2 (June 1942): 446-68.
> Speculative study of Burke's literary proclivities and critical opinions based on his probable authorship of numerous reviews for the *Annual Register*.

———. *Our Eminent Friend Edmund Burke: Six Essays*. New Haven: Yale University Press, 1949, 251 p.
> Six biographically centered essays, ranging from "Boswell's Portrait of Burke" to "Burke, Paine, and Jefferson," which point out gaps of information in Burke biographical scholarship.

———. "Johnson and Burke." In *Statesmen, Scholars, and Merchants: Essays in Eighteenth-Century History Presented to Dame Lucy Sutherland*, edited by Anne Whiteman, J. S. Bromley, and P. G. M. Dickson, pp. 289-303. Oxford: Clarendon Press, 1973.
> Explores Burke's and Samuel Johnson's powers as conversationalists.

Dicey, A. V. "Burke on Bolshevism." *The Nineteenth Century and After* LXXXIV, No. 494 (August 1918): 274-87.
> Considers Burke's writings in light of what they say of modern English government and the advent of bolshevism in Russia.

Dreyer, Frederick. "Edmund Burke: The Philosopher in Action." *Studies in Burke and His Time* XV, No. 2 (Winter 1973-74): 121-42.
> Contends that Burke upheld principles of natural justice over the laws of the state recurrently during his career. For a conflicting view, see the citation below by Peter J. Stanlis.

The Eighteenth Century: Theory and Interpretation. XX—. (1979—). Formerly *Studies in Burke and His Time* (1973-79); originally *The Burke Newsletter* (1959-73). Published three times a year, this periodical presents articles on British, American, and European culture during the era 1660 to 1800.

Fennessy, R. R. *Burke, Paine, and the Rights of Man: A Difference of Political Opinion*. The Hague: Martinus Nijhoff, 1963, 274 p.
> Closely examines the politico-philosophical controversy of Burke and Paine, focusing in particular on the "rights of man" doctrine espoused by Paine and rejected by Burke.

Hale, Edward E., Jr. Introduction to *Speech on Conciliation with America*, by Edmund Burke, pp. v-xxviii. New York: University Publishing Co., 1907.
> Presents an historical overview of colonial times and briefly studies Burke's rhetorical style, calling him "the greatest prose writer of the eighteenth century."

Hamm, Victor M. "Burke and Swift." *Thought* XLVIII, No. 188 (Spring 1973): 107-19.
> Reviews comparisons which have been made of these two writers and provides an overview of their common influences, thought, and stylistic traits.

Hart, Jeffrey. "Burke and Pope on Christianity." *The Burke Newsletter* VIII, No. 3 (Spring 1967): 702.
> Asserts the personal relevance of Christianity in Burke's life. See the citation by Harvey C. Mansfield, Jr. below for an opposing viewpoint.

Himmelfarb, Gertrude. "Edmund Burke." In her *Victorian Minds*, pp. 3-31. New York: Alfred A. Knopf, 1968.

Two essays presented as alternative ways of approaching Burke. The first (pp. 3-14), originally published in 1953, regards Burke's political temper as one "bordering on hysteria" when facing proposals for reform. The second (pp. 14-31), written fifteen years later, serves as a critical reconsideration of the first, focusing on the text of *Reflections* and discovering in Burke's thought an underlying, conciliatory liberalism.

Hoffman, Ross J. S. *Edmund Burke, New York Agent*. Philadelphia: American Philosophical Society, 1956, 632 p.
> Studies Burke's political activites during the years 1760 through 1776, particularly those years during which Burke served as agent to the New York General Assembly (1771 to 1775). Hoffman provides a wealth of pertinent letters and other material stemming from this period which shed light on Burke's thoughts on the problems of colonial America.

James, Regina. "Edmund Burke's Indian Idyll." *Studies in Eighteenth-Century Culture* 9 (1979): 3-13.
> Explores the imaginative color of Burke's writings and speeches on India.

Kaufman, Pamela. "Burke, Freud, and the Gothic." *Studies in Burke and His Time* XIII, No. 3 (Spring 1972): 2179-92.
> Explores the affinities between Gothic fable, the writings of Sigmund Freud, and Burke's *A Philosophical Enquiry into the Origin of Our Ideas of the Sublime and Beautiful*.

Kirk, Russell. "Burke and the Politics of Prescription." In his *The Conservative Mind: From Burke to Eliot*, 7th rev. ed., pp. 11-61. Washington: Regnery Books, 1986.
> Discusses Burke's political career and the relevance of his theories to the philosophy of conservativism.

Kramnick, Isaac. *The Rage of Edmund Burke: Portrait of an Ambivalent Conservative*. New York: Basic Books, 1977, 225 p.
> Explores Burke's dichotomous political role as ardent bourgeois reformer and humble servant of the aristocracy.

McGoldrick, James E. "Edmund Burke as Christian Activist." *Modern Age* 17, No. 3 (Summer 1973): 275-86.
> General overview of Burke's political career, which McGoldrick contends was informed by a markedly Christian outlook.

Macknight, Thomas. *History of the Life and Times of Edmund Burke*. 3 vols. London: Chapman and Hall, 1858.
> In-depth study of Burke's political career.

Mahoney, Thomas H. D. *Edmund Burke and Ireland*. Cambridge: Harvard University Press, 1960, 413 p.
> Political survey which reveals the prominence of Burke's role in Irish affairs throughout his career.

Mansfield, Harvey C., Jr. *Statesmanship and Party Government: A Study of Burke and Bolingbroke*. Chicago: University of Chicago Press, 1965, 281 p.
> In-depth study of the ideological differences between Bolingbroke and Burke, particularly Bolingbroke's disdain for and Burke's pioneering advocacy of partisan government.

———. "Burke on Christianity." *Studies in Burke and His Time* IX, No. 2 (Winter 1968): 864-65.
> Asserts Burke's philosophical distance from Christianity, opposing the viewpoint taken by Jeffrey Hart (see citation above).

May, Gita. "Diderot and Burke: A Study in Aesthetic Affinity." *PMLA* LXXV, No. 5 (December 1960): 527-39.
> Discusses *A Philosophical Enquiry into the Origin of Our Ideas of the Sublime and Beautiful* as it pertains to Denis Diderot's thoughts on aesthetics.

Morley, John. *Burke*. 1879. Reprint. London: Macmillan, 1936, 220 p.
> A standard survey of Burke's career and literary achievement. Along with Henry Thomas Buckle's study (see excerpt dated 1857), it established a utilitarian interpretation which dominated Burke criticism until twentieth-century studies by Kirk, Stanlis, and others superseded it.

Namier, L. B. ''The Character of Burke.'' *The Spectator* 201, No. 6808 (19 December 1958): 895-96.
    Employing Burke's private letters, asserts Burke's political fallibility, due to a troubled personality plagued with contradictoriness.

O'Brien, Conor Cruise. ''An Anti-Machiavel: Edmund Burke.'' In his *The Suspecting Glance*, pp. 33-49. London: Faber and Faber, 1972.
    Text of a 1969 lecture in which O'Brien discusses Burke's Irish Catholicism and contrasts Burke's thought to that of Niccolò Machiavelli.

O'Gorman, Frank. *Edmund Burke: His Political Philosophy*. Bloomington: Indiana University Press, 1973, 153 p.
    Historical, rather than philosophical, approach to Burke's political development.

Osborn, Annie Marion. *Rousseau and Burke: A Study of the Idea of Liberty in Eighteenth-Century Political Thought*. London: Oxford University Press, 1940, 272 p.
    Biographical and evaluative study which discusses the essential philosophic differences between Jean-Jacques Rousseau and Burke, yet notes their shared admiration for the theories of Montesquieu.

Paulson, Ronald. ''Burke, Paine, and Wollstonecraft: The Sublime and the Beautiful.'' In his *Representations of Revolution (1789-1820)*, pp. 57-87. New Haven: Yale University Press, 1983.
    Examines imagery, metaphor, and ideas concerning human rights in the thought of Burke, Thomas Paine, and Mary Wollstonecraft.

Perry, Bliss. Introduction to *Selections from Edmund Burke*, by Edmund Burke, pp. iii-xxiv. New York: Henry Holt and Co., 1896.
    Appreciative estimate of Burke's career. Perry writes: ''Much of the noblest English literature is the offspring of the conservative temper, and in all that literature there is no writing with a clearer claim than Burke's to be ranked among the permanent literature of the world.''

Priestley, Joseph. *Letters to the Rt. Hon. Edmund Burke Occasioned by His Reflections on the Revolution in France*. Birmingham: Thomas Pearson, 1791, 152 p.
    Prominent attack on Burke's *Reflections on the Revolution in France*.

Prior, James. *Memoir of the Life and Character of the Right Hon. Edmund Burke*. 2 vols. Rev. ed., 1854. Reprint. New York: Burt Franklin, 1968.
    Considered the best nineteenth-century biography of Burke. Volume two contains a literary analysis of his works.

Raleigh, Walter. ''Burke.'' In his *Some Authors: A Collection of Literary Essays, 1896-1916*, pp. 317-32. Oxford: Oxford University Press, Clarendon Press, 1923.
    Discusses Burke as a great political writer, but finds fault with his perception of the French Revolution.

Sharma, G. N. ''Samuel Butler and Edmund Burke: A Comparative Study in British Conservatism.'' *The Dalhousie Review* 53, No. 1 (Spring 1973): 5-29.
    Compares Burke's and Butler's philosophic concepts of human thought and behavior.

Stanlis, Peter J. ''A Preposterous Way of Reasoning: Frederick Dreyer's Edmund Burke: The Philosopher in Action.'' *Studies in Burke and His Time* XV, No. 3 (Spring 1974): 265-75.

Contradicts points made by Frederick Dreyer (see citation above), asserting that Burke's application of natural law principles was limited, and always based upon solid historical contexts.

————, ed. *The Relevance of Edmund Burke*. New York: P. J. Kenedy & Sons, 1964, 134 p.
    Contains the following essays: ''Edmund Burke in the Twentieth Century,'' ''Edmund Burke and the Legal Order,'' ''Burke as a Reformer,'' and ''Burke as a Practical Politician.''

————, ed. *Edmund Burke: The Enlightenment and the Modern World*. Detroit: University of Detroit Press, 1967, 129 p.
    Seven symposium essays treating various aspects of Burke's career and thought. Of special note is the comparative essay by Harvey C. Mansfield, Jr. entitled ''Burke and Machiavelli on Principles in Politics.''

Todd, William B. *A Bibliography of Edmund Burke*. Surrey, England: St. Paul's Bibliographies, 1982, 316 p.
    Comprehensive bibliography—spanning the years 1748 to 1827—of works by Burke, works falsely attributed to him, and various Burkean imitations and parodies.

Weaver, Richard M. ''Edmund Burke and the Argument from Circumstance.'' In his *The Ethics of Rhetoric*, pp. 55-84. Chicago: Henry Regnery Co., 1953.
    Analyzes Burke's ad hoc method of argumentation in his writings. See the citation above by Dennis R. Bormann for direction to an opposing view.

Weston, John C., Jr. ''The Ironic Purpose of Burke's *Vindication* Vindicated.'' *Journal of the History of Ideas* XIX, No. 3 (June 1958): 435-41.
    Affirms the ironic content of *A Vindication of Natural Society*.

White, James Boyd. ''Making a Public World: The Constitution of Language and Community in Burke's *Reflections*.'' In his *When Words Lose Their Meaning: Constitutions and Reconstitutions of Language, Character, and Community*, pp. 192-230. Chicago: University of Chicago Press, 1984.
    Considers the partnership of language and legal thought in *Reflections*. White states: ''Burke's purpose in the *Reflections* is not to communicate ideas that are already perfectly statable in existing languages but to make a language in which new ideas and new sentiments can be expressed, a new constitution established, in the text and in the world: a language he wishes his reader first to learn and then to own and use.''

Wilkins, Burleigh Taylor. *The Problem of Burke's Political Philosophy*. Oxford: Oxford University Press, Clarendon Press, 1967, 262 p.
    Comprehensive analysis of Burke and the degree to which his philosophy is informed by natural law theories. Wilkins concludes that ''Burke's political philosophy was a conservative version of the natural law and not a denial of the natural law in the name of either history or utility.''

Wilson, Woodrow. ''Edmund Burke and the French Revolution.'' *The Century Magazine* LXII, No. 5 (September 1901): 784-92.
    Defense of Burke's antipathy for the French Revolution and tribute to his prudence and farsightedness.

Young, G. M. ''Burke.'' In his *Today and Yesterday: Collected Essays and Addresses*, pp. 83-109. London: Rupert Hart-Davis, 1948.
    Appreciative survey of Burke's career.

Benvenuto Cellini

1500-1571

Italian autobiographer, essayist, and poet.

Although an acclaimed sculptor and, in the words of his contemporary Michelangelo, "the greatest goldsmith of whom the world has ever heard," Cellini is best known as the author of *Vita di Benvenuto Cellini (Life of Benvenuto Cellini)*, an autobiographical history that has survived with his material works of art but far eclipsed them in fame and importance. The *Life*—a chronicle of violent passions versus reverence for beauty, simplicity juxtaposed with cunning, and egocentrism paralleled only by the author's unwavering belief in God's special approval and support—describes an individual of marked contrasts, a man critically deemed wholly representative of that remarkable age in which he lived: the Italian Renaissance. John H. Jenkins, in his book *Works of Genius* (1974), has called Cellini "a magnificent Renaissance man—a genius and a thief, a great artist and a murderer, and author of a great autobiography that will live forever."

The son of a Florentine musician and maker of instruments, Cellini was governed by his father's special interests until, drawn during adolescence toward design, he became apprenticed to a goldsmith. His predisposition to volatility surfaced in a brawling incident at sixteen, for which he was briefly banished to Siena. He then wandered about Pisa and Bologna before entering the service of a goldsmith in Rome in 1519. After two years he returned to Florence, but soon fled to avoid prosecution for involvement in another affray—this one resulting in murder—one of a string of such incidents which occurred sporadically throughout his lifetime. Cellini lived in Rome from 1523 to 1540. During his years there his craftsmanship in portrait medallions, coins, and jewelry was sought by many prominent churchmen, including popes Clement VII and Paul III, the latter of whom imprisoned the artisan on suspicion of theft. While incarcerated, Cellini underwent a religious conversion which involved several dramatic visions and which convinced him that his relationship to God was a privileged one. He spent the five years following 1540 in Paris and Fontainebleau pursuing sculpting and architectural projects for Francis I, whose patronage, like that of all his supporters, he ultimately found unsatisfactory. This, coupled with his becoming embroiled in certain intrigues at court, caused him to leave France.

Cellini's truly creative period began in 1545 with his return to Florence. Under commissions given by Duke Cosimo de' Medici, he executed a celebrated bust of his patron, several statues in marble depicting classical themes, and his most ambitious effort, the bronze *Perseus,* receiving undisputed acclaim for these and other works. His success, however, was soon adulterated by mounting differences with Cosimo, particularly in matters of payment, and by rivalries with other craftsmen. It was not until age fifty-eight that Cellini, drawing on the venerable tradition inherited from such diverse models as St. Augustine's *Confessions* and Plutarch's *Lives,* began to compose the *Life,* in which he recorded his observations and the colorful incidents of his life. Dictated to an apprentice in his workshop, Cellini's *Life* was composed with the intent to render thanks to his Creator (who had, he believed, vouchsafed divine sanction of his actions) and to publish his own excellence as a man

BENVENUTO   CELLINI
FIORENTINO   OREFICE,
E SCULTORE   ECCELLENTE.
nacque nel MD.   mori nel MDLXX.

and artist. The narrative is divided into two parts: the first recalls Cellini's childhood, early education, and events anticipating his vivid religious conversion while imprisoned by Pope Paul III; the second addresses his greatest artistic achievements, particularly the casting of the *Perseus,* but breaks off abruptly in 1562. The *Life* thus preserves intact Cellini's image of personal and aesthetic triumph, for his last years were attended by misfortunes. During the 1560s, ill health and financial problems noticeably reduced Cellini's creativity, though he did at this time write significant treatises on the goldsmith's art and on sculpture. He died in his native Florence in 1571.

Infrequently has a personal history transmitted the very essence of an individual, particularly one as vigorous as Cellini, and with even less frequency has an author, quite unintentionally, managed to convey in his memoirs the unmistakable flavor of an era: Cellini's *Life,* scholars contend, succeeds in both areas. Scrutinized by a wide spectrum of critical commentators, the *Life* has been deemed an arresting autobiography and its author no less than spellbinding. Moreover, many have suggested that it is Cellini's checkered career that generally lends the work great reading appeal, adding that the artist's genius—however firmly grounded—would little interest readers today were not the rogue in him conspicuous. Stuart P. Sherman has declared Cellini "no piddling, hole-in-the-corner scamp, but a fine, full-bodied, full-passioned, expressive villain who did things in the grand style." It is exactly this incredible gusto, critics have concurred, that evokes our admiration of the man's spirit even while we shrink from his deeds. Despite his utter self-absorption, he was so completely natural and unpremeditated that the reader cannot help but be fascinated with such a gargantuan will. Furthermore, critics note that Cellini's ungoverned will, though trafficking in transgressions contemptible in modern eyes, was measurably at variance with neither contemporary secular values nor existing religious practice. If compelled to assault or kill, Cellini (twice pardoned for murder with the purported papal assurance that men like himself were exempt from the law) felt wholly justified by a Renaissance God, whose respect for His keen and determined servant he never doubted.

Infused with the author's unblushing candor, inviolable spirit, and overwhelming confidence, the *Life* reflects the lusty, intrepid temperament of the time. An anonymous reviewer for the *Academy* rhapsodized of the *Life:* "It leaves the reader's imagination full of sound, life, and colour . . . of fair galleries cool with the breath of marble, and of streets simmering with packed humanity; of the clash of arms and the click of the trowel, and the reverberation of imperial salutes." And John Addington Symonds, whose scholarship on Cellini is extensive, has unequivocally insisted that nowhere else, "whether in the frescoes of the Sistine Chapel or on Palladian palace fronts, in Ariosto's cantos or in Machiavelli's dissertations, do we find the full character of the epoch so authentically stamped." Like others, Symonds endorsed Cellini's felicitous portraiture, more implied than overt, of the vast gallery of personages with whom he was acquainted, all without "attempting to do more than record his recollection of what happened to himself in commerce with men of all sorts . . . exactly as our best authorities in their more colourless and cautious style present them to our fancy." Symonds has also praised Cellini's literary style as one echoing not "the finest, highest, purest accents of the Renaissance," but one as unvarnished as casual conversation, "attaining unsurpassable vividness of narration by pure simplicity."

As the *Life* was circulated in manuscript for nearly two centuries, its impact as a personal and historical document was greatly deferred. Soon after its publication in 1728, however, Cellini's memoirs became one of the most widely read works of its genre, a work later translated by Johann Wolfgang von Goethe and adapted for the opera by Hector Berlioz. Cellini is, then, remembered for a legacy he himself would have considered less significant than works fashioned out of bronze or marble. His was the plain speech of one remarkable—certainly notorious—individual who, above all, embodied an age made almost palpable by the narrative he artlessly constructed. Summarizing for many, Symonds has concluded: "From the pages of [Cellini's *Life*] the Genius of the Renaissance, incarnate in a single personality, leans forth and speaks to us."

PRINCIPAL WORKS

Due trattati uno intorno alle otto principale arti dell oreficeria. L'altro in materia dell'arte della scultura . . . (essays) 1568
    [*The Treatises of Benvenuto Cellini on Goldsmithing and Sculpture,* 1898]
*Vita di Benvenuto Cellini, orefice e scultore fiorentino, da lui medesimo scritta . . . (autobiography) 1728
    [*Life of Benvenuto Cellini,* 1771; also published as *Memoirs of Benvenuto Cellini, a Florentine Artist, Written by Himself,* 1822; and *Autobiography,* 1956]

Opere. Vita, trattati, rime, lettere. (autobiography, essays, poetry, and letters) 1968

*This work was written between 1558 and 1562.

THE LIFE OF BENVENUTO CELLINI, A FLORENTINE ARTIST (essay date 1828)

[*In the following excerpt, an anonymous critic comments on the attraction of Cellini's memoirs as autobiography and a mirror of the age.*]

The life of a man of genius by himself can scarcely fail to be interesting under any circumstances; but in regard to Cellini, the peculiar sphere in which he moved, and the period in which he lived, unite with his own wild and wayward eccentricities, to give a charm to his personal adventures, which has been acknowledged not only in his own country and language, but throughout Europe. His employment by the Popes Clement VII and Paul III, by Francis I, the Emperor Charles V, the Grand Dukes Alexander and Cosmo de'Medici,—with most of whom he held frequent communion and conversation,—bring all these personages before the eyes of the reader [of the *Memoirs of Benvenuto Cellini*], and give him the best of all possible insight into the social spirit of the age. His sketches of the papal conduct and manners are especially curious and interesting. His own high character as an artist also brought him in contact or acquaintance with the kindred men of genius of his day, including Michael Angelo, Titian, Julio Romano, and nearly the whole of the leading painters and sculptors who were his contemporaries. Nor is the attraction lessened by the jealousy and spirit of competition which frequently guides his pen; for however such feelings might warp his inclinations, Cellini was one of those children of impulse, who usually display all the springs of action by which they are guided, whether they intend it or not. Looking to his warm, reckless, and impetuous notions, the life of such a man would be a romance in any age; it was peculiarly so in his own.

It is impossible not to perceive in these remarkable memoirs, that, deeply imbued with the superstition and credulity of the times, Cellini gives several marvellous anecdotes which prove both that he sometimes imposed upon himself, and was frequently imposed upon by the simplicity or imposture of others. A warm imagination, undisciplined by much either of education or reflection, will readily account for this tendency in the early part of the sixteenth century, without affecting his veracity on less extraordinary occasions. It is of less moment to admit, that the picture which this gifted artist draws of himself is not always calculated to excite our admiration. Even as delineated by his own hand, he appears to have been one of the most petulant, capricious, and revengeful, men of genius on record; and he was evidently treated by the majority of his great employers as a wayward child. It is to be feared, that the manner in which more than one life was sacrificed to his revenge merits no other name than assassination; and the little difficulty with which he obtained pardon and absolution, affords a curious example of papal justice, and of the lax police which has for so many ages been the opprobrium of Italy. All this, however, adds to the curiosity of the work, as descriptive of a singular variety in human nature; and taken altogether, the *Memoirs of Cellini* are now generally admitted to be among the most interesting and amusing pieces of self-biography extant. (pp. v-viii)

An introduction to The Life of Benvenuto Cellini, a Florentine Artist, Vol. I *by Benvenuto Cellini, translated by Thomas Nugent, Whittaker, Treacher, and Arnot, 1828, pp. v-viii.*

S.G.C. Middlemore, The Phaidon Press, 1944, pp. 171-76.

JACOB BURCKHARDT   (essay date 1860)

[*Burckhardt was a Swiss historian whose best-known work,* Die Cultur der Renaissance in Italien *(1860;* The Civilization of the Period of the Renaissance in Italy, *1878), is a classic analysis of the period. In the following excerpt from that work, he commends Cellini's memoirs within the range of early Italian autobiography.*]

[Autobiography in the fifteenth century] takes here and there in Italy a bold and vigorous flight, and puts before us, together with the most varied incidents of external life, striking revelations of the inner man. Among other nations, even in Germany at the time of the Reformation, it deals only with outward experiences, and leaves us to guess at the spirit within from the style of the narrative. It seems as though Dante's *Vita Nuova,* with the inexorable truthfulness which runs through it, had shown his people the way.

The beginnings of autobiography are to be traced in the family histories of the fourteenth and fifteenth centuries, which are said to be not uncommon as manuscripts in the Florentine libraries—unaffected narratives written for the sake of the individual or of his family, like that of Buonaccorso Pitti.

A profound self-analysis is not be looked for in the *Commentaries* of Pius II. What we here learn of him as a man seems at first sight to be chiefly confined to the account which he gives of the different steps in his career. But further reflexion will lead us to a different conclusion with regard to this remarkable book. There are men who are by nature mirrors of what surrounds them. It would be irrelevant to ask incessantly after their convictions, their spiritual struggles, their inmost victories and achievements. Æneas Sylvius lived wholly in the interest which lay near, without troubling himself about the problems and contradictions of life. His Catholic orthodoxy gave him all the help of this kind which he needed. And at all events, after taking part in every intellectual movement which interested his age, and notably furthering some of them, he still at the close of his earthly course retained character enough to preach a crusade against the Turks, and to die of grief when it came to nothing.

Nor is the autobiography of Benvenuto Cellini [*Life of Benvenuto Cellini*], any more than that of Pius II founded on introspection. And yet it describes the whole man—not always willingly—with marvellous truth and completeness. It is no small matter that Benvenuto, whose most important works have perished half finished, and who, as an artist, is perfect only in his little decorative speciality, but in other respects, if judged by the works of him which remain, is surpassed by so many of his greater contemporaries—that Benvenuto as a man will interest mankind to the end of time. It does not spoil the impression when the reader often detects him bragging or lying; the stamp of a mighty, energetic, and thoroughly developed nature remains. By his side our northern autobiographers, though their tendency and moral character may stand much higher, appear incomplete beings. He is a man who can do all and dares to do all, and who carries his measure in himself. Whether we like him or not, he lives, such as he was, as a significant type of the modern spirit. (pp. 173-74)

Jacob Burckhardt, "Biography," in his The Civilization of the Renaissance in Italy, *translated by*

FRANCESCO DE SANCTIS   (essay date 1870)

[*A nineteenth-century Italian literary critic and educator, De Sanctis is regarded as a critical innovator whose work provided the basis for modern Italian literary criticism. Fusing the existing critical criterion of "form" with the additional criterion of "idea," he created an aesthetic approach to literature in which the critic considers a work of art in and of itself, rather than how it relates to such factors as biography and history. It has been suggested that De Sanctis's major work,* Storia della letteratura italiana *(1870;* History of Italian Literature, *1931), in its attempt to provide a historical perspective of Italian literature, insolubly conflicts with the author's critical method of appraising works of literature apart from circumstances. Be that as it may, the* History *remains an influential, very highly regarded work of criticism. In the following excerpt from this study, De Sanctis describes Cellini's character and its relation to his autobiography.*]

The last of [the sixteenth-century Italian] adventurers of literature was Benvenuto Cellini, who died in 1571. An extremely rich nature, genial and uncultivated, Cellini is a compendium of the Italian of that period unmodified by culture. There is something of Michelangelo in his nature and something of Aretino, fused together; or rather, he is the rough, primitive, homespun material that produced both Aretino and Michelangelo.

He was a pleasing and conscientious artist; art was his god, his morality, his law, his right. He thought that an artist like himself was above the law, that "men like Benvenuto, unique in their profession, do not require to be bound by the laws." And he wandered from court to court, seeking adventures, armed with a rapier and a musket, and argued with his weapons as well as with his tongue, which was no less deadly in its thrusts. If he happened to meet his enemy he ran him through without waiting to argue; and if the man died, then the worse for him, for "one does not stab by agreement." When he was thrown into prison he thought it an "infamy," and lamented that they had done him "a villainous wrong." And he was as bigoted as a lay-sister and as superstitious as a brigand. He believed in miracles, in devils, and in incantations, and when he happened to have need of God and the saints he remembered their existence, chanted psalms and prayers, and went on pilgrimages. Of moral sense he had none; right and wrong were the same to him, and he often boasted of crimes he had not committed. A liar, a braggart, audacious, impudent, gossiping, dissolute, overbearing, beneath his false appearance of independence he was really the servant of whosoever paid him. And with it all he was extremely pleased with himself, and felt that he was the equal of any one, with the exception only of the "very divine" Michelangelo, as he called him. Extremely robust physically and richly endowed with inner life, this knight errant dictated his own biography, painting himself freely with all those fine characteristics we have mentioned, never doubting for a moment that he was raising a monument of glory to himself. These qualities spring out from his pages spontaneously, with the vivacity of natural forces, with a literary style as clear-cut and decided as the chiselling of his statues. (pp. 634-35)

Francesco De Sanctis, "Torquato Tasso," in his History of Italian Literature, Vol. 2, *translated by Joan Redfern, 1931. Reprint by Basic Books, Inc., Publishers, 1960, pp. 621-67.*

VITA

DI

BENVENUTO CELLINI

OREFICE E SCULTORE FIORENTINO,

DA LUI MEDESIMO SCRITTA,

Nella quale molte curiofe particolarità fi toccano apparte-
nenti alle Arti ed all' Iftoria del fuo tempo,
tratta da un'ottimo manofcritto, e

DEDICATA

ALL'ECCELLENZA DI MYLORD

RICCARDO BOYLE

Conte di Burlington, e Cork, Vifconte di Dungarvon,
Barone di Clifford, e di Lansborough, Baron Boyle
di Brog Hill, Lord Teforiere d' Irlanda, Lord
Luogotenente di Weftriding in Yorkshire,
ficcome della Città di York, e Cavaliere
della Giarrettiera.

IN COLONIA

Per Pietro Martello.

Title page of the first edition of Cellini's Life, *1728.*

JOHN ADDINGTON SYMONDS (essay date 1877)

[*Symonds was an English poet, historian, and critic who wrote
extensively on Greek and Italian history and culture; he also made
several highly praised translations of Greek poetry and the literature of the Italian Renaissance. In the following excerpt, he
extols Cellini's memoirs as an autobiography and historical
document.*]

Few names in the history of Italian art are more renowned than
that of Benvenuto Cellini. This can hardly be attributed to the
value of his extant works; for though, while he lived, he was
the greatest goldsmith of his time, a skilled medallist and an
admirable statuary, few of his many masterpieces now survive.
The plate and armour that bear his name, are only in some rare
instances genuine; and the bronze 'Perseus' in the Loggia de'
Lanzi at Florence remains almost alone to show how high he
ranked among the later Tuscan sculptors. If, therefore, Cellini
had been judged merely by the authentic productions of his
art, he would not have acquired a celebrity unique among his
fellow-workers of the sixteenth century. That fame he owes to
the circumstance that he left behind him at his death a full and
graphic narrative of his stormy life [*Life of Benvenuto Cellini*].
The vivid style of this autobiography dictated by Cellini while
still engaged in the labour of his craft, its animated picture of
a powerful character, the variety of its incidents, and the amount
of information it contains, place it high both as a life-romance

and also as a record of contemporary history. . . . The sack of
Rome, the plague and siege of Florence, the humiliation of
Clement VII., the pomp of Charles V. at Rome, the behaviour
of the Florentine exiles at Ferrara, the intimacy between Alessandro de' Medici and his murderer, Lorenzino, the policy of
Paul III., and the method pursued by Cosimo at Florence, are
briefly but significantly touched upon—no longer by the historian seeking causes and setting forth the sequence of events,
but by a shrewd observer interested in depicting his own part
in the great game of life. Cellini haunted the private rooms of
popes and princes; he knew the chief actors of his day, just as
the valet knows the hero; and the picturesque glimpses into
their life we gain from him, add the charm of colour and reality
to history.

At the same time this book presents an admirable picture of
an artist's life at Rome, Paris, and Florence. Cellini was essentially an Italian of the Cinque-cento. His passions were the
passions of his countrymen; his vices were the vices of his
time; his eccentricity and energy and vital force were what the
age idealised as *virtù*. Combining rare artistic gifts with a most
violent temper and a most obstinate will, he paints himself at
one time as a conscientious craftsman, at another as a desperate
bravo. He obeys his instincts and indulges his appetites with
the irreflective simplicity of an animal. In the pursuit of vengeance and the commission of murder he is self-reliant, coolly
calculating, fierce and fatal as a tiger. Yet his religious fervour
is sincere; his impulses are generous; and his heart on the whole
is good. His vanity is inordinate; and his unmistakable courage
is impaired, to Northern apprehension, by swaggering bravado.
(pp. 320-22)

As a man, Cellini excites more interest than as an artist. . . .
It has been well said that the two extremes of society, the
statesman and the craftsman, find their point of meeting in
Machiavelli and Cellini, inasmuch as both recognise no moral
authority but the individual will. The *virtù* extolled by Machiavelli is exemplified by Cellini. Machiavelli bids his prince
ignore the laws; Cellini respects no tribunal and takes justice
into his own hands. The word conscience does not occur in
Machiavelli's phraseology of ethics; conscience never makes
a coward of Cellini, and in the dungeons of S. Angelo he is
visited by no remorse. If we seek a literary parallel for the
statesman and the artist in their idealisation of force and personal character, we find it in Pietro Aretino. In him, too,
conscience is extinct; for him, also, there is no respect of King
or Pope; he has placed himself above law, and substituted his
own will for justice. With his pen, as Cellini with his dagger,
he assassinates; his cynicism serves him for a coat of armour.
And so abject is society, so natural has tyranny become, that
he extorts blackmail from monarchs, makes princes tremble,
and receives smooth answers to his insults from Buonarroti.
These three men, Machiavelli, Cellini, and Aretino, each in
his own line, and with the proper differences that pertain to
philosophic genius, artistic skill, and ribald ruffianism, sufficiently indicate the dissolution of the social bond in Italy. They
mark their age as the age of adventurers, bandits, bullies,
Ishmaelites, and tyrants. (pp. 350-51)

> *John Addington Symonds, '' 'Life of Benvenuto Cel-
> lini','' in his* Renaissance in Italy: The Fine Arts,
> *Vol. III, 1877. Reprint by Peter Smith, 1967, pp.
> 320-51.*

AUGUSTINE BIRRELL (essay date 1884)

[*Birrell was an English statesman and essayist. Although his political career was always his primary interest, he earned a rep-*

utation for reflective humor, insightful observation, and judicious pronouncement in such collections of miscellaneous essays and literary criticism as Obiter Dicta *(1884) and* Et Cetera *(1930) and in his critical biographies of Charlotte Brontë, William Hazlitt, and Andrew Marvell. Birrell's writing style—scholarly, personal, and socially conscious—led to the coinage of the verb "to birrell," defined as: "to comment on life in a combination of irony and kindly mordancy, with apparent irrelevance, but with actual point." In the following excerpt from an essay originally published in 1884, he seeks to determine the attraction of Cellini's autobiography.]*

What a liar was Benvenuto Cellini!—who can believe a word he says? To hang a dog on his oath would be a judicial murder. Yet when we lay down his *Memoirs* and let our thoughts travel back to those far-off days he tells us of, there we see him standing, in bold relief, against the black sky of the past, the very man he was. Not more surely did he, with that rare skill of his, stamp the image of Clement VII. on the papal currency than he did the impress of his own singular personality upon every word he spoke and every sentence he wrote.

We ought, of course, to hate him, but do we? A murderer he has written himself down. A liar he stands self-convicted of being. Were anyone in the nether world bold enough to call him thief, it may be doubted whether Rhadamanthus would award him the damages for which we may be certain he would loudly clamour. Why do we not hate him? Listen to him:

> Upon my uttering these words, there was a general outcry, the noblemen affirming that I promised too much. But one of them, who was a great philosopher, said in my favour, "From the admirable symmetry of shape and happy physiognomy of this young man, I venture to engage that he will perform all he promises and more." The Pope replied, "I am of the same opinion"; then calling Trajano, his gentleman of the bed-chamber, he ordered him to fetch me five hundred ducats.

And so it always ended; suspicions, aroused most reasonably, allayed most unreasonably, and then—ducats. He deserved hanging, but he died in his bed. He wrote his own memoirs after a fashion that ought to have brought posthumous justice upon him, and made them a literary gibbet, on which he should swing, a creaking horror, for all time; but nothing of the sort has happened. The rascal is so symmetrical, and his physiognomy, as it gleams upon us through the centuries, so happy, that we cannot withhold our ducats, though we may accompany the gift with a shower of abuse. (pp. 322-24)

You open his book—a Pharisee of the Pharisees. Lying indeed! Why, you hate prevarication. As for murder, your friends know you too well to mention the subject in your hearing, except in immediate connection with capital punishment. You are, of course, willing to make some allowance for Cellini's time and place—the first half of the sixteenth century and Italy. "Yes," you remark, "Cellini shall have strict justice at my hands." So you say as you settle yourself in your chair and begin to read. We seem to hear the rascal laughing in his grave. His spirit breathes upon you from his book—peeps at you roguishly as you turn the pages. His atmosphere surrounds you; you smile when you ought to frown, chuckle when you should groan, and—O final triumph!—laugh aloud when, if you had a rag of principle left, you would fling the book into the fire. Your poor moral sense turns away with a sigh, and patiently awaits the conclusion of the second volume. (pp. 325-26)

That such a man as this encountered suffering in the course of his life, should be matter for satisfaction to every well-regulated

mind; but, somehow or another, you find yourself pitying the fellow as he narrates the hardships he endured in the Castle of S. Angelo. He is so symmetrical a rascal! (p. 327)

He tells lies about other people; he repeats long conversations, sounding his own praises, during which, as his own narrative shows, he was not present; he exaggerates his own exploits, his sufferings—even, it may be, his crimes; but when we lay down his book, we feel we are saying good-bye to a man whom we know.

He has introduced himself to us, and though doubtless we prefer saints to sinners, we may be forgiven for liking the company of a live rogue better than that of the lay-figures and empty clock-cases labelled with distinguished names, who are to be found doing duty for men in the works of our standard historians. What would we not give to know Julius Cæsar one half as well as we know this outrageous rascal? The saints of the earth, too, how shadowy they are! Which of them do we really know? (p. 328)

On laying down his *Memoirs,* let us be careful to recall our banished moral sense, and make peace with her, by passing a final judgment on this desperate sinner, which perhaps, after all, we cannot do better than by employing language of his own concerning a monk, a fellow-prisoner of his, who never, so far as appears, murdered anybody, but of whom Cellini none the less felt himself entitled to say:

> I admired his shining qualities, but his odious vices
> I freely censured and held in abhorrence.

> (p. 329)

Augustine Birrell, "A Rogue's Memoirs," in his The Collected Essays & Addresses of the Rt. Hon. Augustine Birrell: 1880-1920, Vol. 2, *1922. Reprint by Charles Scribner's Sons, 1923, pp. 319-29.*

JOHN ADDINGTON SYMONDS   (essay date 1888)

[In the following excerpt from an introduction to his 1888 translation of Cellini's autobiography, Symonds addresses the style and descriptive range of the work.]

A book which the great Goethe thought worthy of translating into German with the pen of *Faust* and *Wilhelm Meister,* a book which Auguste Comte placed upon his very limited list for the perusal of reformed humanity, is one with which we have the right to be occupied, not once or twice, but over and over again. It cannot lose its freshness. What attracted the encyclopædic minds of men so different as Comte and Goethe to its pages still remains there. This attractive or compulsive quality, to put the matter briefly, is the flesh and blood reality of Cellini's self-delineation. A man stands before us in his *Memoirs* unsophisticated, unembellished, with all his native faults upon him, and with all his potent energies portrayed in the veracious manner of Velasquez, with bold strokes and animated play of light and colour. No one was less introspective than this child of the Italian Renaissance. No one was less occupied with thoughts about thinking or with the presentation of psychological experience. Vain, ostentatious, self-laudatory, and self-engrossed as Cellini was, he never stopped to analyse himself. He attempted no artistic blending of *Dichtung und Wahrheit;* the word "confessions" could not have escaped his lips; a *Journal Intime* would have been incomprehensible to his fierce, virile spirit. His autobiography is the record of action and passion. Suffering, enjoying, enduring, working with restless activity; hating, loving, hovering from place to place as impulse moves him; the man presents himself dramatically by his deeds and spoken words, never by his ponderings or meditative broodings. It is this healthy externality which gives its great charm to Cellini's self-portrayal and renders it an imperishable document for the student of human nature.

In addition to these solid merits, his life, as Horace Walpole put it, is "more amusing than any novel." We have a real man to deal with—a man so realistically brought before us that we seem to hear him speak and see him move; a man, moreover, whose eminently characteristic works of art in a great measure still survive among us. Yet the adventures of this potent human actuality will bear comparison with those of Gil Blas, or the Comte de Monte Cristo, or Quentin Durward, or Les Trois Mousquetaires, for their variety and ever-pungent interest.

In point of language, again, Cellini possesses an advantage which places him at least upon the level of the most adroit romance-writers. Unspoiled by literary training, he wrote precisely as he talked, with all the sharp wit of a born Florentine, heedless of grammatical construction, indifferent to rhetorical effects, attaining unsurpassable vividness of narration by pure simplicity. He was greatly helped in gaining the peculiar success he has achieved by two circumstances; first, that he dictated nearly the whole of his *Memoirs* to a young amanuensis; secondly, that the distinguished academical writer to whose correction he submitted them refused to spoil their ingenuous grace by alterations or stylistic improvements. While reading his work, therefore, we enjoy something of that pleasure which draws the folk of Eastern lands to listen to the recitation of Arabian Nights' entertainments. (pp. xi-xiii)

The most convincing proofs of Cellini's trustworthiness are not . . . to be sought in . . . minor details. I find them far stronger and far more abundant in the vast picture-gallery of historical portraits which he has painted. Parini, while tracing the salient qualities of his autobiography, remarked: "He is peculiarly admirable in depicting to the life by a few salient touches the characters, passions, personal peculiarities, movements and habits of the people with whom he came in contact."

Only one who has made himself for long years familiar with the history of Cellini's period can appreciate the extraordinary vividness and truth of Cellini's delineation. Without attempting to do more than record his recollection of what happened to himself in commerce with men of all sorts, he has dramatised the great folk of histories, chronicles, and diplomatic despatches exactly as our best authorities in their more colourless and cautious style present them to our fancy. He enjoyed the advantages of the alcove and the ante-chamber; and without abusing these in the spirit of a Voltaire or a valet, he has greatly added to our conception of Clement VII., Paul III., Francis I., and Cosimo de' Medici, Grand Duke of Tuscany. Clement driven to his wits' end for cash during the sack of Rome; Paul granting favours to a cardinal at the end of a copious repast, when wine was in his head; Francis interrupting the goldsmiths in their workshop at the Petit Nesle; Cosimo indulging in horse-play with his buffoon Bernardone—these detach themselves, as living personages, against the grey historic background. Yet the same great people, on more ceremonious occasions, or in the common transactions of life, talk, move, and act precisely as we learn to know them from the most approved documentary sources. (pp. xxxviii-xxxix)

It was not only in dealing with the greatest actors on the world's stage that Cellini showed this keen fidelity to fact. His portraits

of the bestial Pier Luigi Farnese, of the subtle and bizarre Lorenzino de' Medici, of the Ferrarese minister Giliolo, of the Florentine majordomo Ricci, of the proud Comte de St. Paul, correspond exactly to what we learn otherwise about them, adding slight significant touches from private information. Madame D'Etampes and the Duchess Eleanora of Tuscany move across his pages as they lived, the one with the vivacity of an insolent king's mistress, the other with the somewhat sickly and yet kindly grandeur of the Spanish consort to an astute Italian prince. Lesser folk, with whom we are equally acquainted through their writings or biographical notices, appear in crowds upon a lower plane. Bembo, in his polished retreat at Padua; Torrigiano, swaggering about the Florentine workshops; Giulio Romano, leading the debauched society of Roman artists; Maitre Roux, in his Parisian magnificence; Alamanni, the humane and gentle nobleman of letters; Sansovino, expanding at ease in Venetian comfort; old Michel Angelo, with his man Urbino, in their simple Roman dwelling; Bandinelli, blustering before the Duke of Florence in a wordy duel with Cellini, which Vasari also has reported—all these, and how many more besides, are portrayed with an evident reality, which corresponds in each particular to the man as he is otherwise revealed to us by independent evidence. Yet Cellini had no intention of describing such folk for our benefit. As they happened to cross his life, so he sketched them with sharp, pungent quill-strokes, always thinking more about his own affairs than their personality. Nothing inspires a firmer confidence in his accuracy as an observer and his veracity as a narrator than the undesigned corroboration given to his portraits by masses of external and less vivid testimony. (pp. xl-xli)

[We have] to regard Cellini as the composer of one of the world's three or four best autobiographies, and next as the most eminent exponent of the later Italian Renaissance in craftsmanship of several kinds.

It would be superfluous to quote authorities upon the high esteem in which the *Memoirs* are held, both for their style and matter, by Italians. Baretti's emphatic eulogy can hardly be called exaggerated: "*The Life of Benvenuto Cellini,* written by himself in the pure and unsophisticated idiom of the Florentine people, surpasses every book in our literature for the delight it affords the reader."

In truth, without multiplying passages of panegyric, I am confident that every one who may have curiously studied Italian history and letters will pronounce this book to be at one and the same time the most perfect extant monument of vernacular Tuscan prose, and also the most complete and lively source of information we possess regarding manners, customs, ways of feeling, and modes of acting in the sixteenth century. Those who have made themselves thoroughly familiar with Cellini's *Memoirs,* possess the substance of that many-sided epoch in the form of an epitome. It is the first book which a student of the Italian Renaissance should handle in order to obtain the right direction for his more minute researches. It is the last book to which he should return at the close of his exploratory voyages. At the commencement he will find it invaluable for placing him at the exactly proper point of view. At the end he will find it no less invaluable for testing and verifying the conclusions he has drawn from various sources and a wide circumference of learning. From the pages of this book the Genius of the Renaissance, incarnate in a single personality, leans forth and speaks to us. Nowhere else, to my mind, whether in the frescoes of the Sistine Chapel or on Palladian palace fronts, in Ariosto's cantos or in Machiavelli's dissertations, do we find the full character of the epoch so authentically stamped. That is because this is no work of art or of reflection, but the plain utterance of a man who lived the whole life of his age, who felt its thirst for glory, who shared its adoration of the beautiful, who blent its paganism and its superstitions, who represented its two main aspects of exquisite sensibility to form and almost brutal ruffianism. We must not expect from Cellini the finest, highest, purest accents of the Renaissance. He does not, as an artist, transport us into the heavens of Michel Angelo and Tintoretto. He has nothing of Ariosto's golden melody or Tasso's romantic love-chant. He cannot wield Aretino's lash or Machiavelli's scalpel of analysis. But his *Memoirs* enable us to comprehend how those rarer products of the Italian genius at a certain point of evolution were related to the common stuff of human nature in the race at large. For students of that age he is at once more and less than his illustrious contemporaries; less, inasmuch as he distinguished himself by no stupendous intellectual qualities; more, inasmuch as he occupied a larger sphere than each of them singly. He touched the life of that epoch at more points than any person who has left a record of his doings. (pp. lvi-lviii)

The literary merits of Cellini's autobiography demand a passing notice. Notwithstanding the plebeian simplicity of his language, he has described some scenes with a dramatic vigour and a richness of colouring rarely to be found upon the pages of romance or history. Among these I would call attention to the Roman banquet, during which Diego, dressed magnificently like a woman, won the homage of assembled artists; to the conjuration in the Coliseum; Cecchino's deathbed; Benvenuto's vision of the sun while lying sick and hopeless in his dungeon; the phantom of Charon which haunted him throughout a lingering fever; the exhibition of his Jupiter in the great gallery of Fontainebleau; the Parisian law-court; and the long episode of his casting the bronze Perseus. His memory was so tenacious that he could present the incidents of bygone years, with all their circumstances, just as though his eye were on the object. Without conscious effort he communicates the atmosphere, the local colour, the specific feeling of each place he visited. Ferrara has a different note from Florence, Rome from Paris, in his narrative. Yet it is clear that he never took thought about word-painting. The literary result is not attained by external touches of description, but by the vigorous reproduction of a multitude of impressions made upon his eagerly observant nature. (pp. lix-lx)

Having already touched upon his power of portrait-painting with the pen, I need not return to that topic. It should, however, be remarked that his method of sketching men resembles his treatment of things and places. There is very little of description. The characters present themselves so vividly before our eyes because they were so clearly visible to Cellini's mind while writing, because he so firmly seized what was to him essential in their personalities, and so powerfully communicated the impression made upon his sensibilities by contact with them.

Cellini's autobiography might also be studied from the side of humour. Many passages remind us of the Florentine Novelle, notably of the old tale entitled *Il Grasso Legnaiuolo,* and of Lasca's stories about Pilucca and his mischievous companions. Take, for example, the episode of his quarrel with Bernardone, and the burlesque revenge with which he chastised that fellow's coarseness. The same note of Florentine bizarrerie distinguishes the less agreeable incident in the tavern near Chioggia. Again, how racy, how native to the soil, is that altercation

between Cellini and the old hag in a deserted street of the plague-stricken city! While posing as a hero, he was able to see the humorous side of himself also. This is shown in the passage where he relates how his good-natured housekeeper bantered him. But it is enough to have indicated these aspects of the *Memoirs.* The charm of the whole book very largely consists in a vivacity and elasticity of narrative style, which passes from grave to gay, from passion to mirth, from the serious occupations of the artist to the light amusements of the man of pleasure, without perceptible transitions, the author's own intense individuality pervading and connecting each successive mood. (pp. lx-lxii)

> *John Addington Symonds, in an introduction to* The Life of Benvenuto Cellini, Vol. I *by Benvenuto Cellini, translated by John Addington Symonds, John C. Nimmo, 1888, pp. ix-lxxxviii.*

JOHN C. VAN DYKE　(essay date 1898)

[*Van Dyke was an American art critic and librarian, the author of many books, chiefly on painting, and a frequent contributor of articles on art to the* Century *magazine. In the following excerpt, he offers favorable comments on the nature of both Cellini and his autobiography as representatives of Italian Renaissance culture.*]

From the jaunty way the Renaissance people carried their vices we might think there was some confusion of mind as to whether these vices were not virtues. Surely the moral sense of the age was not that of our time, and surely in Italian civilization the intellectual came to maturity before the ethical. Acts that we look back upon with something of a shudder, they probably never regarded as incompatible with received social usage. Indeed, the true way to get their peculiar point of view is to allow one of their number to tell about the men and manners of his time as he knew them. Fortunately, such a tale exists for us in the *Memoirs* of Benvenuto Cellini. Benvenuto himself was one of the most enlightened rascals of the advanced Renaissance. He was an accomplished goldsmith and sculptor, moving in court and ecclesiastical circles, a devout son of the Church, an impulsive bravo, a cool murderer, an individual of indifferent honesty, unbounded conceit, and unvarying fickleness, and yet to hear him tell it he is not a bad man at all. He recites his autobiography without a suspicion of apology. It is a record of which he is proud, not a defence made by a culprit. And after reading his story if we do not take sides with him we at least understand better the view of life and conduct held in the sixteenth century. The value of the book lies just here. It is an original document from which history derives and its author has not only drawn for us his own profile clear cut against the dark background of the Renaissance, but has illustrated the social and artistic life of his time. (pp. iii-v)

[Fine] artist as Benvenuto was, it may be doubted if we should have heard much about him in these days were it not for the book he left behind him. It has kept his name alive longer than his art, because it is a vivid and, in the main, a truthful picture of the times in which he lived. They were troublous times . . . , and Benvenuto at fifty-eight, looking back over his life, had reason to believe that he had cut quite a figure in his age and generation. (pp. ix-x)

When the *Memoirs* were copied, Benvenuto submitted them to Varchi, the scholar and historian. He had an idea that they were not elegant enough as literature, and needed polishing at the hands of a trained writer; but Varchi persuaded him that the simple colloquial style was worth more than academic periods. So the narrative was published as originally dictated. It was fortunate that no pedantic member of the *Literati* got at it. One of the most readable books in all literature would have been smothered in rhetoric, and the individuality of the unique Benvenuto would have been snuffed out. As it now stands, the book reads precisely as the man talked, and is graphic to the last degree. It is a book of movement, incident, life. Benvenuto was no great thinker or philosopher; he was an artist and an observer. Hence it is that there is little of introspection or of pondering or meditation in these **Memoirs**. Conscience and the moral problem do not obtrude themselves. Rousseau could confess and cry ''Mea culpa,'' but Benvenuto confesses nothing. On the contrary, he always insists that he is right. He tells the straightforward narrative of his life, and is not the least bit ashamed of it. Judging him by the lives led by his contemporaries, there was no reason why he should be. He was not better nor worse than the motley throng of popes, dukes, cardinals, artists, courtiers, cut-throats, and courtesans with whom he was associated. The contrast of splendid marble churches standing in filthy streets where the plague was bred and assassins lay in wait is not more striking than the contradictions in character during this Renaissance time. Benvenuto's tale reads like fiction as he tells of his turbulent life and describes the stage upon which he has played his part. It does not seem possible that such things could be, and yet all the while he is reciting facts—the facts of social, political, and artistic life in the sixteenth century. In that respect the book is one for all time. Edition after edition of it has been issued, and it has been translated into many tongues. Everybody praises it or blames it, but no one ignores it. It is not a book to be pushed aside; it is a book to be read. (pp. x-xi)

> *John C. Van Dyke, in an introduction to* Memoirs of Benvenuto Cellini *by Benvenuto Cellini, translated by John Addington Symonds, D. Appleton and Company, 1898, pp. iii-xi.*

C. R. ASHBEE   (essay date 1898)

[*In the following excerpt from the introduction to his translation of Cellini's writings on the manual arts—a translation "intended for the workshop . . . to bring home to English craftsmen . . . the methods and practice of the Goldsmith of the Renaissance"— Ashbee evaluates Cellini's overall craftsmanship as both a sculptor and goldsmith.*]

It is perhaps not my province as a translator to criticise the artistic merit of Cellini's work, but as my hope in placing his [**The Treatises of Benvenuto Cellini on Goldsmithing and Sculpture**] before English craftsmen is to familiarise them with his methods, I may perhaps be allowed to give a few words of warning. We must not take Cellini at his own valuation, and we must remember that he did not draw that subtle distinction between designer and executant that we nowadays are wont to do. The fact that every aesthetic criticism is inevitably biased by the style of its period must be taken into account by the student, if such criticisms as I myself, speaking as an artist, should venture to make, are to be of value to him. To Cellini's best-known critics this applies in equal measure. Vasari, Delaborde, Milanesi, Brinckman, Symonds, have each had their point of view so to speak. To some, like Vasari, it has been coloured by what the Germans call 'die Voll-Renaissance,' of which Cellini in the art of goldsmithing was undoubtedly the central figure. To others, like Delaborde, it was influenced by the Romantic Reaction of the early Nineteenth Century, and to them his work was 'an exploded myth.' Criticised from the

modern point of view—the point of view that distinguishes between goldsmith and sculptor, between craftsman & designer—we cannot rank him among the highest. There is a want of feeling for proportion in such work as we have of his, & the whole is marred by the overcrowded detail, often very exquisite in itself, of the parts; the craftsman indeed invariably overpowers the artist. Above all there is a want of spirituality in all his more important work, a want of refinement of soul, if one might so term it—a vulgarity. There is none of the 'ευηθεια of Donatello, the graciousness of Ghiberti or Duccio, the mingled strength and sweetness of Verocchio, the simple grandeur of Pisanello. Michael Angelo's manner perhaps we can trace, but of his inspiration and his self-control there is none. (p. xi)

> *C. R. Ashbee, in an introduction to* The Treatises of Benvenuto Cellini on Goldsmithing and Sculpture *by Benvenuto Cellini, translated by C. R. Ashbee, 1898. Reprint by Dover Publications, Inc., 1967, pp. ix-xiv.*

THE ACADEMY   (essay date 1899)

[*In the following excerpt, an anonymous critic uses a review of* Treatises on Goldsmithing and Sculpture *as a springboard to discuss Cellini's literary and plastic artistry in general, positing that Cellini "must be weighed as a man and a writer rather than as an artist."*]

The Renaissance was the last universal outbreak of human nature in the colloquial sense, and Benvenuto Cellini in this context has been rightly called its ultimate word and its epit-

Cellini's Perseus. *Alinari/Art Resource, New York.*

ome. This fact, and not his artistic achievement, assures him a cheerful eternity on earth. Were all the creations of his facile hand pulverised to-morrow, our impression of him would not be weakened, for his unpractised pen pictured his times and himself, the luminous point upon which all their rays were focussed, with the perfection that is attained only once in a fortunate epoch. He combines the merits of a human document of the greatest rarity with those of a unique genius who accidentally wrote one of the more excellent books among the most excellent. . . .

This is not the place to deal with the *Treatises* [*on Goldsmithing and Sculpture*] from a technical standpoint. We did not open them to learn "How to Give a Diamond its Reflector," but in the hope that they might reflect light upon Benvenuto. And they do. The fantastic, exuberant, irrepressible creature has everywhere stamped his emphatic seal. He tells us in his first sentence that "what prompted him to write, was the knowledge of how fond people are of hearing anything new," and later on that, "wishing to give God some sort of thanks for having made me the man I was, I set to write what I am now writing." Were reasons more humanly persuasive ever given for the existence of a scientific handbook? He characteristically proceeds: "Then, in the second place, I felt much troubled in mind because of all sorts of annoying things, the which I purpose in the following treatise, with due modesty, to recount." It is with a thrill of pleasure that we learn that the old bravo of the *Vita* is, as ever, ready to finger his sword hilt. But we throw up our hands at the modesty of the man who, after several lurid manslaughters, performed with infinite gusto, pointed out to the friends who had acquired the keenest relish for him, that his head had been blessed with an aureole, visible even to their disenchanted eyes!

The note of self-revelation and self-appreciation, struck so early in the book, is insisted upon again and again with such robust candour and fervid joy, that the reading of his driest technicalities is an exhilarating exercise. (p. 319)

And here recurs the idea that recurs until it convinces us as we consider Cellini—that he must be weighed as a man and a writer rather than as an artist. It is perhaps generally admitted that Cellini the artist smacks of the jeweller and of decadence, and that even Cellini the jeweller may be too Corinthian an artificer. His crowning work, the "Perseus," is indeed the figure of a "pretty man." He stands above poor trussed Medusa like a gladiator upon a vanquished rival, holding aloft the gory head with "pardonable insolence" for the applause of the thundering circus. But there is nothing elemental in the statue beyond florid youthful strength, which is the less elemental in that it is florid. There is no touch of the triumph of clear heroic serenity, no trace of the austere simplicity of great inspiration; yet it was devoutly worshipped by its creator as the masterpiece of a transcendent genius.

No; to have worked upon wax and marble is assuredly not Cellini's distinction: to have *been* "wax to receive, and marble to retain," is his felicity. It has become a commonplace to say that his reception of an impression was marvellously sharp and impersonal, and that it never grew dulled. But the singularity of these facts has perhaps never been sufficiently emphasised. It is to be found in this—that the man whose spirit was so properly his own in its self-absorption, so entirely not his own in the welter of his passions, and who saw himself purblindly in a mist of false and shifting colours, should be a medium so faithful and transparent for the transmission and record of external images. The reading of the *Autobiography* for the first

time is a milestone in one's literary experience. One cannot forget the wonderful differentiation of the units that cross its stage, or the sense of brilliant confusion that follows the final descent of the curtain. It leaves the reader's imagination full of sound, life, and colour; of the blaze of southern suns, of the crimson of cardinals, of the oppressive and blatant magnificence of popes and princes; of dusty battles and bloody treacheries; of junketings where Petronius Arbiter would have lolled an apt host and scarce have hankered after Neronian Rome; of fair galleries cool with the breath of marble, and of streets simmering with packed humanity; of the clash of arms and the click of the trowel, and the reverberation of imperial salutes. Such is the spectacle that moves in Cellini, where its flaming masses are portrayed as in a magic crystal.

Through these motley multitudes the indomitable Ego of Benvenuto winds its way, and "swims, or sinks, or wades, or creeps, or flies." Baretti, watching the progress of that turbulent soul, says: "We derive from it something of the same pleasure which we feel in contemplating a terrible wild beast who cannot get near enough to hurt us." This is true, but not entirely true. If Cellini in many moods much resembled the Pietro Torrigiano whom he has immortalised—Pietro of the terrible brows and demoniac gestures, who battered stone into statues, and statues, when he judged them better than his own, into stone—he had others as mild as that of his father, Giovanni, the architect and recluse, who delighted his soul with the music of flute and viol, and prayed God to spare his days until he should see Benvenuto the first utterer of sweet sounds in Florence. In short, Cellini is the Natural Man raised to the hundredth power, and forced into magnificent growth in the hot-bed of the Italian Renaissance. (pp. 319-20)

> *"A Natural Man," in* The Academy, *Vol. LVI, No. 1402, March 18, 1899, pp. 319-20.*

STUART P. SHERMAN (essay date 1926)

[*Sherman was, for many years, considered one of America's most conservative literary critics. During the early twentieth century, he was influenced by the New Humanism, a critical movement which subscribed to the belief that the aesthetic quality of any literary work must be subordinate to its support of traditional moral values. During ten years of service as a literary critic at the* Nation, *Sherman established himself as a champion of the long-entrenched Anglo-Saxon, genteel tradition in American letters and as a bitter enemy of literary Naturalism and its proponents. Theodore Dreiser and his chief defender, H. L. Mencken, were Sherman's special targets during the World War I era, as Sherman perceived the Naturalism they espoused to be a life-denying cultural product of America's enemy, Germany. During the 1920s, Sherman became the editor of the* New York Herald Tribune *book review section, a move that coincided with a distinct liberalization of his hitherto staunchly conservative critical tastes; in the last years of his life, he even praised his old enemies Dreiser and Mencken. In the following excerpt from an essay originally published in 1926, Sherman characterizes Cellini as larger than life.*]

That good men are not always interesting and that interesting men are not always good is a double-headed black cat of the devil which is always escaping from the moralist's bag, no matter how tight our puritan friends pull the string. He is now roaming restlessly over our housetops, caterwauling nights and causing all sorts of grotesque dreams to enter the heads of the sleeping denizens of Main Street. I suppose it is because he has been rambling over my roof that I have been prompted to re-read the autobiography of Benvenuto Cellini.

A remarkably favorable moment has arrived for presenting to our morally curious public Benvenuto Cellini, Florentine goldsmith, sculptor, soldier, courtier, and Renaissance bravo, with crimes enough to his credit to have his throat cut half a dozen times by the hangman's knife, had not friendly popes, dukes and cardinals intervened to save his fine talents for the service of art. If rogues interest us, here is a rogue worthy of our attention—no piddling, hole-in-the-corner scamp, but a fine, full-bodied, full-passioned, expressive villain who did things in the grand style.

Judged by Socratic or Christian or Puritan standards Cellini was not a good man; but his best English translator, John Addington Symonds, apologizes for him as a very tolerable specimen of the qualities which, in the Renaissance, commanded respect and admiration—not unmingled with terror. After one of his homicides, a friend of the murdered man turned to the new Pope, Paul III, and urged the inexpediency of granting pardons for acts of that sort in the first days of the papacy. The Pope, a connoisseur of the goldsmith's craft, like many of the great churchmen of the time, replied that "men like Benvenuto, unique in their profession, *stand above the law*." (pp. 218-19)

[On] the whole Benvenuto was proud of his life—including most of his acts of violence. The point is that he professed a morality which justified him, enabling him to regard the greater number of his actions as manly and virtuous and commendable in the sight of God and man. He was so little afflicted with remorse, so little ashamed of his career, that he left to the world a full and candid account of it, which ranks with the three or four greatest autobiographies in existence. Goethe so much admired it that he translated it into German. Comte listed it among the great books to be read by a reformed humanity. Our eminent American educator, Charles William Eliot, included it in the Harvard Classics.

Unquestionably acquaintance with Cellini is an educational experience: it is as educative as a couple of hours' observation of the lions and tigers in the zoölogical gardens. And it is a good book to read now that our minds have been rendered by the time-spirit singularly responsive to the interest and variety of life which it depicts. It contains everything that attracts the law-abiding citizen to rogue literature—and much more, for Cellini was much more than a rogue: he was a genius as well.

Its hero gathers up all the positive qualities in which hostile critics of the American good fellow find him deficient. He achieves the ideal toward which many of our vague, restless cravings unconsciously tend. He incarnates the leonine morality at the opposite extreme from the ovine (sheep-like). He magnificently illustrates what we hanker after when, growing faint-hearted about our modest, self-repressive democratic type of virtue, we look about for something more showy, more spontaneous, more interesting, more "aristocratic"—and begin to glorify men of large appetites and no strong inhibitions.

Do not imagine that I am undertaking to present Cellini as an abhorrent monster. The fact is that I admire and envy him in many respects enormously. I envy him his astounding literary gift—pure natural talent. An Italian critic, Baretti, has declared that "*The Life of Benvenuto Cellini*, written by himself in the pure and unsophisticated idiom of the Florentine people, surpasses every book in our literature for the delight it affords the reader." It is a masterly, enthralling narrative, packed with vital experience, every paragraph quiveringly alive from the first line to the last.

Yet writing was not this fellow's art, nor had he any discipline in it. I think his father taught him the whole mystery of rhetoric in one brief unique lesson. One day the old Giovanni called the little Benvenuto to see a salamander in the fire and at the same time administered him a resounding box on the ear—not, explained the old man, for any fault of his but merely to make him remember, with lively consciousness, that he had seen a notable sight.

Benvenuto mastered the lesson. When, at upward of fifty-eight, he dictated the story of his life he was as vividly conscious of every notable incident in it as he was of that salamander. On every occasion he had been, as we say, "all there." He followed his father's method in the recital; on every page there is something for the reader equivalent to that box on the ear—a dagger thrust or some other little fillip to make all the senses tingle.

The niggling critical sense charges Cellini with Gargantuan egotism and braggadocio, and justly. Yet how, in certain moods, one envies him the huge lustiness that often goes along with this ruddy self-satisfaction! How one envies him the immense gusto, the hot-blooded excitement, which he carried into every moment of his career!

He is pleased with everything that pertains to himself—so heartily pleased that his pleasure radiates from him and warms the heart of the reader. (pp. 220-23)

Cellini's virtues and vices were positively leonine. His fear of God was slight—he was so sure he was on the inside track. The law he took into his own hands—he was "above the law." There is no evidence that he ever weakened his initiative by respecting his neighbor. He was neither domestic nor monogamous, nor reason-professing, nor pacific. He was superstitious. He drank, lived loose and stabbed. But his devotion to his art was admirable. His self-expression was complete. His faith in himself was magnificent. To his own immense satisfaction he "proved his manhood and achieved renown."

And so in his lusty old age he washed his bloody hands and did not doubt that when he entered in to the joy of the Lord he would be saluted at the gate of death, as he had been saluted at the gate of life, cheerfully by his given name Benvenuto—"Welcome." (p. 231)

> *Stuart P. Sherman, "Benvenuto Cellini," in his* The Emotional Discovery of America and Other Essays, *Farrar & Rinehart, Incorporated, 1932, pp. 218-31.*

JEFFERSON BUTLER FLETCHER   (essay date 1934)

[*Fletcher was an American educator and poet best known for his critical studies of Dante and of the Italian Renaissance. In the following excerpt, he praises the spontaneity and individuality of Cellini's autobiography.*]

By rare good fortune, [Cellini's] autobiography—although rashly submitted to a literary friend for correction, and also not printed until 1728—has come down virtually as its author partly wrote, partly dictated, it. The literary friend, Benedetto Varchi, was a man of sense and taste, and returned the manuscript untampered with; and the eighteenth century editor was at once discreet and bold,—for it took some courage to print some passages of the book. But as it is, the spontaneity of the style exactly matches and expresses the amazing spontaneity for good and bad of the man. *Le style c'est l'homme*—as almost nowhere else in literature.

And the autobiography is to the Renaissance what the *Confessions* of St. Augustine are to the earlier Middle Ages, and what the *Confessions* of Rousseau are to later modern times. Each reveals not merely an individual experience, a temperament, a soul,—but the spirit of its age, focussed and concentrated. In and through Cellini's frank self-portrait we may see the composite photograph, as it were, of Renaissance Italy,—its serene self-confidence now and then extending and descending to *bravado* and *braggadochio*, its unaffected passion for the beautifully right a little regardless of the morally right, its elegance and chivalry, its callous cruelty.

Cellini appears, I say, altogether spontaneous. He appears to live in the moment for the moment. At any rate, only in his art does he show consistency and plan. (p. 270)

Jefferson Butler Fletcher, "Cellini—Aretino," in his Literature of the Italian Renaissance, *The Macmillan Company, 1934, pp. 268-75.*

JONATHAN GOLDBERG (essay date 1974)

[*In the following excerpt, Goldberg examines Cellini's autobiography against patterns established by its predecessors.*]

The truism that all autobiography distorts life by giving it the permanence and form of art holds in the Renaissance and earlier, but with a crucial modification. For early autobiographers, the metamorphosis of life into art does not constitute a distortion, but the means to represent a form for the self abstracted from the inchoate events of life. Although a modern autobiography might reveal a similar approach, the full weight of the disparity would emerge in comparing the kinds of forms perceived and their modes of realization. Modern autobiographers, from Rousseau on, uncover the unique design in their lives, and record a progressive path to its realization. Early autobiographers, on the other hand, find a universal design, which they perceive as a recurring pattern. Modern autobiographers discover unique selves by focusing their attention on their inner lives; early autobiographers are wont to come to self-understanding through generic models. In short, whereas modern autobiography unveils a unique, personal and private self, early autobiography presents a universal, depersonalized and public version of the self.

These differences can make early autobiographies seem untruthful and evasive to a modern reader. As Wayne Shumaker notes, with some disapproval, autobiography before the eighteenth century seems unable to confront experience directly; it presents metaphor, not reality. To read an autobiography like Cellini's with modern expectations, to pursue Cellini hoping for particularized introspection, must inevitably frustrate a reader. Like autobiographers before him, Cellini's interest lies in displaying a permanent and public version of himself, not in presenting an inner portrait. Cellini is one with early autobiographers who, to borrow Burckhardt's phrase, view the self as a work of art; indeed, autobiographers reflect Renaissance attitudes about art in revealing ideal forms of themselves. Many display such artistic self-understanding by mirroring it in other works of art. Thus, merely by providing an account of artistic endeavors, Cellini offers a reflection of himself. The most usual form to mirror the self, however, is the restatement of prose realities in the shape of verse (Cellini's **Autobiography** conforms to this pattern, introducing poems at crucial points in the narrative). Such a metamorphosis reduces the mimetic value of the narrative line for the sake of the generic forms provided by the poems, which conventionalize and universalize expe-

rience. To the autobiographer, personal events do not become less real in this metaphoric transformation. (pp. 71-2)

Cellini's subscription to such conventions differs from his forerunners perhaps only in its inevitability. His depiction of the forms shaping his life even shares with earlier autobiographies the belief that the "Idea" of the life is, in some measure, realized through him rather than by him. Such a conception points to the pervasive influence of spiritual autobiography even in so secular a life. From the first, if we take St. Augustine's *Confessions* as the cornerstone of the tradition, spiritual autobiography stresses a more than individualistic definition of the self. At the moment of his conversion, a turning to his true nature, Augustine discovers as his own the suprapersonal and generic identity of a saint. Fictions introduced at this point further establish the universal context for self-discovery. . . .

In Augustine, self-recognition coincides with an awareness of God's shaping hand. Augustine realizes an unavoidable, providential design in his life. His artistic contribution to it rests in the sacred fictions he invents to reinforce this pattern. The point at which fiction touches reality, as a modern would understand the terms, remains hazy (which events really did occur in the garden, which did not?); no value lies in its definition. The coincidence counts. (p. 73)

The assurance that God rescues those who do their utmost on their own behalf, once self-interest has been defined properly in relation to the uses of misfortune, connects Cellini's **Vita** to traditional conceptions of the self. Self-consideration moves inevitably towards cosmic considerations. If Cellini's self-scrutiny seems unsatisfactory in its objectivity, it is nonetheless true to the conception of the self that comes down from Augustine and Boethius.

Although Cellini adheres to conventional attitudes towards the self, we need not press a claim for any specific influence upon him. Cellini's is, in literary terms, a naive autobiography conditioned by conventions too pervasive to make possible the assignment of a single source. That a Renaissance autobiographer could draw quite explicitly upon autobiographical traditions and their mode of self-knowledge, and still purport to present a true version of the self, Jerome Cardan's *De Vita Propria Liber* demonstrates. The work finds its formal and thematic model in the *Meditations* of Marcus Aurelius, the book that suggests, "follow your own nature and the World-Nature (and the way of these two is one)," a key statement for the tradition of early autobiography. (pp. 74-5)

Like Cardan, Cellini portrays the suprapersonal ramifications of his identity by adopting the stance of a Christian martyr, the just man always in the right. Beleaguered by the world, Cellini maintains strong faith in God's support. . . . Like Cardan, Cellini supports this suprapersonal identity through astrological beliefs and reports of prophetic visions and dreams, even willing, for a time, to credit necromancy. (pp. 75-6)

Cellini's autobiography demonstrates that the conventions of early autobiography provide not only a version of the self but an accompanying plot as well. The plot derives from the saint's life in which recurring misfortunes are overcome by being understood as "providential." The shaping of life follows upon this understanding. The crucial plot event of conversion marks the recognition of the divine order as the basis for the events of one's life. Cardan, for instance, echoes conventional formulations when he insists that nothing casual occurs, that a logic beneath the surface of events conditions their flow. Artistically speaking, the scrutiny of life to discover and reveal these patterns means that the writer of an autobiography represents events that function prophetically or providentially, and arranges them to mark the stages in his awareness of the pattern of events. Thus, the plots of autobiographies usually offer no more than repeated patterns of misfortune and the reactions of the protagonist that display the writer's skill in the control of his life, coupled frequently (as in the case of Cellini), with the recognition of God's shaping hand.

In the *Autobiography,* Cellini maintains several narrative lines at once, interrupting each with promises of fuller revelation at the appropriate time. Events prefigure later events; Cellini's narrative imitates the patterning of Christian history that Augustine had discovered in his life. Cellini's narration does not chart a simple progress. Its rather crude and halting quality is, at least in part, an intentional effect. Only gradually does the work reveal its principle pattern. Persecution, tribulation or accidental misfortune, frequently in the form of envious intrigue directed against the artist, suggest not only the conventions of the saint's life, but identify the sacred mission with Cellini's artistry. Although Cellini insists that all he wants to present is a history of his art, seemingly irrelevant incidents constantly force themselves upon him. The emerging design of the work links supposedly separate aspects of the self. The search for patronage triggers the turbulence of his "travagliata vita" ["wretched life"] . . . ; more often than not the attempt to receive payment (a principal sign of success) initiates an inevitable series of misfortunes. In a time of deepest tribulation, a revaluation of his criteria for success occurs; the mark of newfound understanding is Cellini's vision of a Crucifixion executed in the smith's molten gold. In this vision, Cellini recognizes a providential design which his art mirrors. This unitive act of self-understanding occurs in a highly conventionalized scene of conversion, a further sign of the universal context for a fully realized self. The fictions introduced into the scene, like Augustine's sacred fictions, enhance the truth the author wishes to convey.

Before proceeding to an examination of this scene of conversion, we should recognize its place in the conventions of autobiography. For early autobiographies further conventionalize the plot line with which they convey a generic version of the self by supplying it with certain events which have immediate metaphorical value. Just as the form of events in autobiographies suggests an "I" who treads the line between unique individual and conventional archetype, the metaphors of autobiography offer a further degree of conventionalization, making more acute the overlap of truth and fiction in the work. Aside from the conventionalization of the scene of conversion, the most significant metaphorical pattern is the motif of the journey. Narrative necessity probably dictates the need for an ever-changing locale in which the autobiographer can re-enact the pattern of his martyrdom. When Cellini closes his *Autobiography* with the seemingly casual mention of an intended trip to Pisa, he invokes the continuous design of his work, the unending journey that leads him to make ever-widening circles from his native Florence, circles that move to include Rome and France as external measures of his success.

Cellini as inveterate traveller not only provides an external yardstick to measure his achievement of identity; he also allows his "I" to merge with the tradition that sees life as a pilgrimage and a journey. It hardly needs to be mentioned that the *Odyssey,* particularly as understood in the Renaissance as an allegory of the moral life, is the cornerstone of this all-pervasive metaphor.

Augustine makes typical use of the trope by measuring the inner road that led to conversion by its external reflection in the route from Carthage, to Rome, and finally to St. Ambrose in Milan. At each stopping point Augustine re-enacts the archetypal pattern governing him, that of the prodigal son; only at the end of his journey does he fulfill the pattern, at last becoming himself by realizing the eternal seed planted within. In the *Confessions,* journey as literal fact and journey as metaphor coalesce. The violation of the borderline between reality and fiction once again defines the place where truth resides.

When Cellini's journeying comes to a forced halt in prison he locates himself in a place of self-recognition made traditional not only in the prison conversion of Boethius's *Consolation* but in such classical antecedents as the *Phaedo,* for example. In the understanding of self fostered in the tradition of early autobiography, the meanings attached to the prison, from Socrates onward, are crucial: awareness of the freedom and integrity of the self despite constraints. A Renaissance autobiography that depends entirely upon this figure is Sir Thomas More's *Dialogue of Comfort Against Tribulation.* Neither the change of names nor the change in the explanation given for his imprisonment and approaching death invalidate the truth about himself that More reveals in the fictionalized dialogues between Vincent and Anthony. More undertakes the metamorphosis of real event into fiction to reveal the underlying meanings in his martyrdom. The transformation of reality into a continuous metaphor and of the events in time into a shadow of eternity signifies that a personalistic view of the self does not operate in the work.

Cellini arrives at a similar understanding of himself in his imprisonment. Three poems incorporated into this scene serve the function noted earlier of turning the inchoate events of prosaic reality into their essential form. Each poem marks a significant stage in Cellini's self-understanding. The first, a dialogue, summarizes Cellini's attempt to understand his misery in its widest context. The second records the visionary experience in which the golden sun takes on the shape of the crucified Son, and expresses Cellini's desire to turn his vision into a work of art. The third, the *capitolo,* completely recasts his prison thoughts. It clarifies Cellini's intention to permanently register the transformation of his life into art. The poems themselves demonstrate the logic of Cellini's viewpoint, moving from providential assurance to personal assurance, including the self into a larger and encompassing design and registering that awareness in the very act of making poems.

Cellini's experience in prison begins, like Boethius', with the question of the meaning of the suffering of the innocent. Confronting the problem of misfortune and the possibility of the malignancy of heaven, Cellini recognizes prison experience as an occasion for martyrdom, and he begins to glory. . . . Like Boethius, he recognizes the good fortune of his misfortune, cheerfully accepting his martyrdom to the frustration of his persecutor, Pier Luigi. From Bible reading and psalm singing, Cellini derives hope and enters into the community of the righteous. But he passes beyond even this, through visionary and prophetic experience, to emerge from prison surrounded by an aura of divine light. Outrageous as it is, the divine halo serves as one token of his conversion, a symbolic version of the course that leads Cellini from the recognition that man must suffer in imitation of Christ to his renewed assurance. Artful self-presentation does not, of course, fully define the meaning of the conversion to Cellini. He has been confirmed as an artist, given the mission of translating vision into art (as he does in the poems). Personal salvation rests in artistic fulfillment. Not surprisingly, the last work Cellini mentions in his *Vita* is the "Crucifixion." (pp. 76-80)

To read the *Autobiography* properly, we must . . . recognize that in Cellini's mode of self-understanding the true and the metaphorical are identical. From spiritual autobiography, Cellini received a plot and a mode of self-perception; from the fictional tradition of romance came a similar set of elements. Since it is the burden of fiction to present what may pass for truth, the mirroring of romance and spiritual autobiography is a key feature in the tradition behind Cellini. In Cellini's case, the mirror for autobiography is the picaresque novel. Cellini's work will always remain ambiguous, for it stands on the borderline between romance and realism. . . . Yet, had Cellini crossed those boundaries and made the attempt to tell the truth as a modern man might perceive it, he would have violated the equation of the true and the metaphorical that stood at the center of his mode of perceiving. A realistic autobiography, a novelistic autobiography, would have resulted; the great irony is, that from Cellini's perspective, such a "truthful" work would have not told the truth at all. (pp. 82-3)

Jonathan Goldberg, "Cellini's 'Vita' and the Conventions of Early Autobiography," in MLN, *Vol. 89, No. 1, January, 1974, pp. 71-83.*

GARY SCHMIDGALL   (essay date 1977)

[*In the following excerpt, Schmidgall compares Cellini's autobiography with the* Mémoires *(1870; Autobiography of Hector Berlioz, 1884) of French composer Hector Berlioz, who based the score of his opera* Benvenuto Cellini *on the artist's life.*]

[We] should pause to consider a pervasive difficulty of the memoir as a literary form, namely, the fact that truth and autobiography are almost by nature mutually exclusive. Alexander Pushkin put the problem succinctly in a letter describing his own attempted self-description (which he later burned):

> It is both tempting and pleasant to write one's mémoires. There is nobody one loves as much, or knows as well, as oneself. It is an inexhaustible subject. But it presents difficulties. It is possible not to lie; but to be sincere is a physical impossibility. The pen will sometimes stop, as a runner draws up at an abyss, before something an outsider would read with indifference.

Pushkin provides a good caveat for a reader venturing upon Cellini's *Autobiography,* which distinctly lacks an air of veracity and scrupulously avoids even the pretense of introspection or self-doubt. The events of Cellini's life are told by an author with a weakness for self-serving stage management; the characters of his friends and enemies, one instinctively feels, have passed through a roseate, self-gratifying filter. It is hard to be stern with Cellini in his fancifications, however, for he is disingenuous, even honest, about his intentions as a memoirist. The very first lines hint at the bigger-than-life artist in store for us: "No matter what sort he is, everyone who has to his credit what are or really seem great achievements, if he cares for truth and goodness, ought to write the story of his own life in his own hand. . . . I intend to tell the story of my life with a certain amount of pride." . . . No autobiography supports Pushkin's idea that one can love nobody so much as oneself better than Cellini's. It is at once an apologia and a swaggering spree of doting self-enjoyment.

Berlioz also wrote his memoir, though, unlike Cellini, he knew it would be published. It has much in common with the *Autobiography.* As with Cellini, there is nothing sanctimonious or weak-kneed about it. Berlioz warned in his preface, "I do not have the least pretension to 'appear before God, book in hand', declaring myself 'the best of men', nor to write 'Confessions'." . . . Rather, Berlioz's *Memoirs* is the apologia of a battle-scarred artistic gladiator, a relation of his "agitated and laborious career." Both memoirists are combative, uninhibited in praise and condemnation; their enemies are painted with the full palette of sarcasm, irony, ridicule, and jest. The niceties of correct chronology they leave to our more scholarly century. (pp. 155-56)

Cellini's *Autobiography* was among the first Renaissance expressions of the integrity of the individual, of fierce and proud self-esteem. One of Romanticism's central philosophers, Friedrich Schlegel, wrote that "he who has his center of gravity within himself is an artist." In musical history Berlioz, possessing this internal center of gravity, stands alongside Beethoven as one of the first musicians to assert independence from aesthetic dictates and dictators. Largely for this reason they both stood alone, belonged to their own schools. Clearly it was not Cellini's art but rather his artistic *stance* that fired the imagination of Romantics like Berlioz. It was not so much the contours of the Perseus (a flawed *chef d'œuvre,* most art historians agree) as the statue's symbolism of the artist's conquest over a grudging intellectual environment that Berlioz felt:

> Music is the most poetic, the most powerful, the most living of all arts. She ought to be the freest, but she is not yet. . . . Modern music is like the classic Andromeda, naked and divinely beautiful. She is chained to a rock on the shores of a vast sea and awaits the victorious Perseus who shall loose her bonds and break in pieces the chimera called Routine.

(p. 157)

There is considerable truth in the *Autobiography,* but it is humane rather than historical truth. The same must also be said of the Berlioz *Memoirs.* The composer developed his own persona when he took to his writing desk, and his imagination typically took hold on the slightest details. (p. 158)

To satisfy the thirst for new experiences, Romantics looked to faraway places, to eccentrics, to social outcasts, to grotesques. But above all, they looked to times that were at least artistically more free—for instance to the humanist Renaissance, that vital intellectual interregnum between the age of faith and the age of reason that was dominated by neither the ancients nor the moderns. The Romantics looked for an era as lively and promising as their own, and they naturally sensed that the times of Cellini, Rabelais, and Shakespeare suited their needs. (p. 161)

The popularity of Cellini among the new generation was to be expected, for here was a man with an encompassing egotism that drove all before it, a tenacity of feeling, and a down-to-earth quality—just what Romantics found in themselves and wanted in their art. They wanted, in short, a hero who would admit (as Cellini did in his *Treatise on Goldsmithing*), "I can't do your fine elegant manner of writing." They did not care that he lacked an inspirational artistic gravity, or even that he was a bit vulgar and trivial. They liked the turmoil and invigorating pace of Cellini's world. They were instinctively drawn to this *bandit de génie*—a man who shocked the 1830s just as he shocked the 1530s.

Giorgio Vasari, a contemporary of Cellini, described him as "in all his doings of high spirit, proud, lively, very quick to act, and formidably vehement.'' These qualities stand out in the pages of the *Autobiography* and in the score of *Cellini*. (pp. 161-62)

Gary Schmidgall, ''Hector Berlioz: 'Benvenuto Cellini','' in his Literature as Opera, Oxford University Press, 1977, pp. 149-77.

DINO S. CERVIGNI (essay date 1978)

[*In the following excerpt, Cervigni analyzes the despairing and disillusioned final section of Cellini's* Life, *and seeks to show ''to what extent it is in agreement or at variance with the main body of the narrative.''*]

The specific viewpoint of the moment in which [Cellini] wrote—characterized by past accomplishments, present condition, and self-awareness—determined the way in which he described his existence. Such a perspective should understandably emerge most clearly in the first and last pages of the work, for the beginning and the end of one's narrated world constitute significant landmarks.

Cellini critics and commentators easily place the introductory statements of the *Vita* in proper perspective. Accordingly, they envision the artist's literary undertaking as an attempt to present and vindicate his own life in the light of Renaissance *virtù*. To my knowledge, however, no one has provided a satisfactory explanation of the concluding section of the autobiography where the author, after reaching a powerful climax in the narration of his casting of the *Perseus*, rambles on aimlessly for so many pages. My purpose here is to analyze the final section of the *Vita* and to show in what way and to what extent it is in agreement or at variance with the main body of the narrative. Inasmuch as Cellini concludes on a note of despair and alienation, I believe that there is justification for considering the autobiography less Renaissance than post-Renaissance in mood, for it is the latter era that is characterized by crisis and disillusionment.

The *Vita,* as critics are quick to point out, was never really terminated, a fact no one can debate. Beyond the obvious remark that no autobiography can lead the reader to the very last moment of the writer's existence, one must reconsider the entire issue from a different angle: to what extent is Cellini able to visualize his life from a specific yet comprehensive viewpoint which might account for its entire development, indicate a meaning for the life's journey of the protagonist, and offer a coherent conclusion for the entire work? As a hero who first sets forth in search of a higher profession and always strives after nobler achievements, Cellini engages in a lifelong pursuit for glory which finds its culmination in the *Perseus*. Yet the casting of the bronze statue does not end the narration; it neither accounts for the rest of the work nor provides a comprehensive perspective for the whole autobiography. During his Roman captivity, in the middle of his life's journey, Cellini feels God's hand mark his forehead and encircle it with a halo. Such an ennobling vision, however, fails to shine throughout the journey ahead, to sustain the wayfarer's faith, or to direct him in the midst of disconcerting events. As a picaro, the protagonist displays a tremendous zest for life but comes to no conclusions. Against his wanderings, quarrels, killings, and associations with every category of human existence, Cellini counterbalances the lofty attributes of the saint and the hero. (pp. 15-16)

The narration of the events succeeding the completion of the *Perseus* and the settlement of the monetary compensation can be referred to as the epilogue of the autobiography. From the viewpoint of artistry, which many critics consider the main purpose of the *Vita,* the epilogue represents a slackening after the climactic moments that lead up to the casting of the bronze statue and to the ovation at its unveiling in the Piazza della Signoria. The marble crucifix, the last work described in the autobiography, is perhaps comparable to the *Perseus* in artistic value, but from the literary and narrative perspective it fails to inform to any degree the last pages of the book.... His vision of the crucified Christ, later his decision to reproduce him, and finally the creation of the marble crucifix correspond symptomatically to three moments of the life's story which reveal the protagonist's powerlessness when confronted by opposing forces: his inability (1) to convince the Roman judges of his innocence, (2) to win over completely Cardinal Ippolito, and (3) to have his artistry recognized by Duke Cosimo. In brief, the circumstances that surround the conception and production of the crucifix seem to indicate various moments of crisis in the artist's pursuit of success. Unable to assert himself on the basis of his human forces alone, he either lays claim to God's approval or turns into a solitary and unpatronized artist who proclaims his satisfaction in being able finally to produce the crucifix.... (p. 18)

Had Cellini terminated the narration with the account of the *Perseus* and adequately emphasized that highest culmination of his artistry, he would have composed his autobiography with a fully apologetic and explanatory outlook. On the contrary, however, he causes the narrative to linger on aimlessly in such a way that no conclusion is or possibly could be offered. One can thus infer that Cellini's failure to discover an adequate perspective caused the *Vita* to remain unfinished.

The final pages of the autobiography ... reveal the narrator-protagonist's inability to come to terms with reality and his own existence. Whereas throughout his life's journey he had fought against giants, at the very end the giants (in this case Cosimo I) refuse even to deal with him. Cellini then attacks unworthy opponents and nonexistent enemies, and is defeated! A comparison with Don Quixote imposes itself, though in reverse. The Spanish hidalgo issues forth from his castle in search of chimerical ideals; in his final return home, however, he is wiser and more profoundly aware of the true nature of reality. Cellini, on the contrary, fights real battles throughout his life and attains genuine fame. At the end of the journey, however, he becomes more disillusioned and less willing to accept reality on its own terms than he was at the beginning. (pp. 21-2)

[The] events leading to the protagonist's disillusionment in the final section reveal (1) Cellini's inability to overcome his opponents, (2) his ever-present awareness that indomitable forces always confront man, and (3) his tragic and intimate realization of personal failure, only slightly soothed by his calling upon God's justice. Consequently, a substantial agreement exists between the central body and the concluding section of the autobiography. Throughout the work the protagonist repeatedly finds himself in a critical situation, but each time the impending crisis is somehow averted until it finally sets in and ominously looms over the last pages of the narration.

The *Vita* is indeed the story of the man Cellini who issues forth to find and prove himself and, by way of searching and testing, to discover his life's meaning and his place in the world. What the hero attains, however, provides only ephemeral glory: he glimpses the substance of life, and in his youthful exuberance he believes he can forever hold onto it. The *Vita* is an art form of virile maturity: at the end of the journey, it presents the hero in his failure to attain what he has always sought. Since glory and recognition become less and less attainable, the meaning of life continues to elude the protagonist. (pp. 24-5)

At the very end of the journey, when glory disappears and the significance of life becomes elusive, Cellini's world seems to be abandoned by God. All bonds with the eternal are severed: no longer is there an ascension toward the radiant sun, as in the vision during the Roman captivity, but rather the sad contemplation of a human and crucified Christ, destined to loom over the artist's tomb. The hero reaches his lowest point when he turns into a landowner and is outwitted and defeated by the basest of all his opponents. At the end of his life's journey Cellini appears to have caught only a glimpse of life in its highest expression, a problematic hero, seeking and failing to find meaning in life and thus showing a definite estrangement from the surrounding world.

This interpretation of Cellini's *Vita* is in substantial agreement with the social and political situation of the epoch. Historians of the period argue that the collapse of civil liberties in Florence with the reinstatement of the Medici family in 1530, the subordination of most Italian states to foreign powers, and the spiritual decadence of the great European institutions (Church and Empire) effected profound changes in the ideas and ideals of the still flourishing Italian culture. The sack of Rome and the events of the years immediately following are often considered to mark the beginning of the post-Renaissance era. The period from 1530 to 1600, variously designated as late Renaissance, early Baroque, or Mannerist, is characterized by a sense of crisis, disenchantment, and alienation which affected virtually all aspects of human endeavor.

As a participant in the sack of Rome, in most of the Florentine political turbulences, and in some European wars, Cellini is imbued with the general atmosphere of the epoch. The tensions and uncertainty that characterize the time also permeate the account of his individual life. The narrator-protagonist of the *Vita* personally experiences the crisis brought about by the abatement or outright collapse of the Renaissance ideals. In his failure much more than in his success, in his attempt to achieve meaning in life and yet in his frustrations, Cellini adumbrates the experience of post-Renaissance man in his alienation from society and reality. The *Vita* thus also announces new trends in the art of narrative, trends that often portray just such an estrangement as a typical expression of modern man. (pp. 25-6)

> Dino S. Cervigni, ''Cellini's 'Vita,' or the Unfinished Story of a Disillusioned Hero,'' in Modern Language Quarterly, *Vol. 39, No. 1, March, 1978, pp. 15-26.*

DINO S. CERVIGNI (essay date 1979)

[In the following excerpt, Cervigni examines Cellini's treatment of the inanimate and human worlds in the Life.*]*

An artist by profession and a writer by natural inclination and talent, Cellini composed his autobiography during the latter part of his life. . . . More accustomed to the chisel (and the sword) than the pen, he soon gave up writing it himself and dictated—or better, narrated—his life to a thirteen-year old helper. Even more importantly, since the essence of any au-

tobiography is by nature derived and fashioned by the author's perspective at the moment of its composition, Cellini's description of his own life's journey is imbued throughout with a viewpoint characterized by a composite of past accomplishments, present conditions, and an astute, though biased, self-awareness—all of which one must take into account when interpreting and evaluating the *Vita* as either a personal apologia or a vibrant document of the times.

As one reads Cellini's *Vita,* the prodigious spontaneity and individuality which pervade the work stand out amazingly; and one is also struck by the many convergent literary traditions which contributed to its form and, in part, to its content as well. These two aspects of the autobiography, i.e., spontaneous individuality and literary influence, have not always been viewed in proper perspective throughout the history of Cellini criticism. After Antonio Cocchi first published the manuscript in 1728, Giuseppe Baretti brought it to the attention of the literary world in a few laudatory articles . . . , written in a style which typifies his expressive verve and anticipates a Romantic interpretation of the work. Goethe was another of Cellini's exceptional critics. Upon his return from his Italian journey, he translated the autobiography between 1795 and 1796, a translation followed by an appendix in which the German poet, in the light of his own poetics, views Cellini as a forerunner of both the *Sturm und Drang* movement and European Romanticism. Baretti and Goethe thus ushered in the Romantic phase of Cellini's literary fortune, a biased yet widely spread interpretation whose most illustrious representative was Francesco De Sanctis. Thereafter, in the course of the nineteenth century, the editions and translations of the *Vita* became ever more numerous. Dazzled by such characteristics as spontaneity, individuality, and the apparent violation of Renaissance rhetorical precepts, the critics and poets of the time considered Cellini a Romantic *ante litteram* and were, therefore, unable or unwilling to understand him within the proper framework of a man deeply embedded in tradition, and yet one who also foreshadowed inchoate trends. The subsequent Positivistic period, while substantially continuing the myth of Cellini as a Romantic, at the same time engaged in the scientific research of his artistic works as well as in the critical and historical annotation of his autobiography. Twentieth-century critics, spurred on by the debate between Vossler and Croce at the turn of the century, assert that they have at last superseded both the Romantic and the Positivistic shortcomings; and yet one cannot fail to notice that some of the contemporary studies are still far too often concerned with Cellini's amazing personality and thus betray a lingering influence of Romantic conceptions as well as Positivistic bias.

The *Vita,* however, can be studied as an independent entity, a literary work apart from Cellini the man and the artist. (pp. 11-14)

The *Vita* portrays not only the life's journey of the narrator-protagonist but also the world through which the traveling takes its course: a cosmos teeming with innumerable characters, animated by a myriad of incidents, and situated in a man-made setting and a God-made environment. The principal character and the countless secondary figures confront the inanimate world and frequently a struggle ensues between man and the opposing forces of nature. The protagonist in particular often feels that he is waging a war against destiny, a struggle which causes his life to become ''travagliata'' [''wretched'']. Throughout the narration, he is at times aware of a divine intervention, and yet again at times he experiences a sense of dejection. In this partial estrangement from exterior reality,

Benvenuto also engages in a conflict against most of the other characters, who thus join the forces with a destiny already battling against him.

Throughout the *Vita,* the prevalence of the human over the inanimate ambiance emerges very clearly, although the two meet at different levels and degrees of meaning. In Cellini's narrative, the non-human world loses its independence to a great extent, since it exists only insofar as it comes into contact (mostly in an unfriendly way) with the main character. On those occasions when nature seems neither amicable nor hostile, or when the protagonist is not forced to display his great *virtù,* the description of man's surroundings is kept to a minimum. At the inception of the autobiography, for instance, the narrator links an imaginary ancestor with the founding of Florence, and his name, Fiorino, with the appearance of the site strewn with flowers. The reference to the natural setting, however, is very brief. As a further illustration of this tendency, the stories of the scorpion and of the salamander, during the account of his childhood, are both placed within the framework of a man-made setting, the family house, with which the narrator is understandably very familiar; and yet, even here he offers the reader only laconic descriptive touches. On other occasions, when Benvenuto does not embark on actions of bravura, the text provides only enough information to visualize the protagonist against some background: he may be walking through the streets, working in the *bottega* ["workshop"], visiting the pope, or traveling from city to city. Only the most essential description of the inanimate environment is, therefore, characteristic of Cellini the writer, who very seldom, however, abandons his characters in a limbo of indeterminate situations.

On a few instances the writer seems to indulge in terse yet inessential remarks. . . . On a few other instances, the realization of a novel or unusual phenomenon, in fact, prompts the writer to dwell on the subject more diffusely. Illustrative of this tendency are two passages in the account of the Sack of Rome. When the enemies were about to force their way through the city walls, the young Benvenuto could hardly sit back and wait for the events to take their turn. After reaching the city walls with one of his closest friends, he not only observed the enemy army trying to force a way into Rome and many corpses lying around, but he also noticed a very thick fog. The natural phenomenon was so singular that it sprang to the fore from among the narrator's myriad recollections. The second passage relates an event, the numberless fires throughout the plundered city, which was not uncommon of itself but because of the vantage point of the protagonist who was entrusted with the defense of the highest peak of the Castel Sant'Angelo. The narrator, therefore, feels justified in describing the fiery scene on the basis of novelty, which, he adds, has always delighted him greatly.

The descriptions of natural phenomena and of the man-made environment become more detailed and extensive whenever the protagonist's *virtù* plays an important role. During the escape from the Castel Sant'Angelo, for instance, our appreciation of the prisoner's energy and valor is rendered more intense by the terse descriptive details of the fortress which cause Benvenuto's undertaking to be all the more arduous. The account, in fact, may be visualized as the struggle of the hero, who also invokes God's help, against the evil forces of his enemies, symbolized in this context by the steep walls. (pp. 113-15)

In essence, Cellini's literary treatment of the inanimate cosmos is determined by the various ways it comes into contact with the human world. Whenever the relationship holds no special momentum, the narrator provides but few essential lines; if a novel situation arises, on the other hand, Cellini tends to dwell on it more diffusely. The most extensive descriptions of nature and of a man-made setting are motivated by the writer's intent to emphasize the heroic character of the protagonist. A futile attempt would certainly be made if one were to seek any form of pastoral, let alone lyrical, viewing of nature in the *Vita.* Whereas Cellini imitates nature for his artistic purposes, his models, however, are beautiful women and handsome young men. Even while capturing their form, rarely does the artist sit back in ecstatic contemplation of the beauty of the models or of his masterpieces: he prefers, rather, either to pursue his artistic activity or to establish a more direct relationship with the models. Interaction is, therefore, the predominant mode of the characters' rapport with each other and with the external world.

His embattled existence notwithstanding, Cellini never looks beyond the world, as he experiences it, in order to find some respite in a past golden age or a future utopic condition. Some moments of the *Vita,* however, can be characterized somewhat as a longing for a happier past. Whenever a major obstacle presented itself during his final stay in Florence, Benvenuto enjoyed recalling his activity at the court of King Francis in glorious terms which idealize a bygone time—one which, in reality, was not so bereft of "mala fortuna" ["bad fortune"]. At the same time, however, the few times Benvenuto does look ahead, he seeks to foretaste the sweetness of the revenge on his enemies, as in the case of the *Perseus.* The *hic et nunc* ["here and now"], therefore, however embattled, occupies every facet of the protagonist.

Given such a prevalence of the human over the natural environment, Cellini's conception approaches the basic tenet of the Renaissance concerning man as the measure of all things—a view which can be applied to the *Vita* insofar as nature comes to life only to the extent that it establishes some relationship with the characters. At the same time, inasmuch as the external world confronts the human world in a friendly, hostile, or neutral manner, it definitely holds a position of its own. Cellini the narrator artfully manipulates the intricate constituents of reality, human and non-human, according to his purpose of describing his life's journey; but Benvenuto the protagonist needs to confront the multifarious aspects of a world which often closes ranks with the forces of "mala fortuna" to conspire against him. Thus, after stating that in the *Vita* man holds dominion over all things, one ought also to add that the human ascendancy does not go unchallenged. Indeed, from man's viewpoint, the autobiography presents a precarious situation and a state of disharmony between the human and the inanimate elements of life.

As the non-human reality becomes less significant in the literary world emerging from the *Vita,* the human cosmos gains greater prominence, coming alive through the innumerable characters who live their diverse experiences in a myriad of episodes. In relation to this aspect of narrative fiction, the literary critic distinguishes between principal and secondary characters; normally, several such characters populate the world of most narratives. In the *Vita,* however . . . , Benvenuto plays so predominant a role that he alone can be viewed as the protagonist of the work. This obvious observation, deriving logically from the autobiographical nature of the *Vita,* becomes more meaningful, however, if compared with other autobiographical works. In the *Vita nuova,* for instance, Dante's recollection of his adolescence and youth is based on the bipolar experience of the poet with Beatrice, first a living person and subsequently a heavenly ideal. In narrative fiction, the main character is always placed in close relationship with the plot. Since the *Vita* constitutes the life's journey of the protagonist, and just as no journey is without a wayfarer, so no account of a life's journey can be without the human element. In Cellini's autobiography, this binding relationship between the plot and the main character is essential, since no other figure is granted a totally independent literary life of its own, with the possible exception of Giovanni, Benvenuto's father. . . . (pp. 116-18)

The myriad secondary characters teeming within the *Vita* not only are denied a full life stature but also come to the foreground solely through their interrelationships with the protagonist. In a manner which is symptomatic of the power of Cellini's art of portraiture, the countless minor types, however, become vividly alive as poetic creations, no matter how limited their literary existence, and the reader remembers them beyond any reference to Benvenuto. At times, a word or a brief sentence suffices to create the atmosphere for an incident or to characterize a historical person forever. (p. 118)

A further quality of the minor characters, logically stemming from the previous one, consists of their being portrayed from the viewpoint of the protagonist. They are right or wrong, good or evil, great or inconsequential according to their interplay with Benvenuto. If they join forces with the "mala fortuna" opposing him, the narrator at times shows a certain sense of fairness and gives them a chance to explain their reasons. For each of theirs, however—it goes without saying—Benvenuto produces ten of his own, and his are the only cogent reasons! (pp. 118-19)

Dependent as the secondary types are upon Benvenuto for their artistic existence, one might wonder to what extent they are essential to the structure of the *Vita*. Truly, one person only is indispensable to any autobiography; moreover, it would be no easy task to determine whether Giovanni Cellini or Pope Clement or King Francis are more important than the prostitutes Benvenuto leads to his bedroom, the enemies he kills, or the rival artists he withstands vehemently. The fact remains, however, that none of the many figures and incidents which populate the *Vita* could be eliminated, unless one wants to behold a lesser Benvenuto and an impoverished narration. The writer remarks the same, more or less explicitly, at least in one instance, when he introduces Guido Guidi, a physician and a university professor, by all standards a person non-essential to the narrative. Friendly or hostile, noble or low, the narrator feels obliged to the innumerable people he has encountered and to the countless incidents he has experienced throughout his existence.

The protagonist, in fact, grows to full literary stature only through an interplay with the other figures and incidents within the multiplicity of his life's journey. In terms of a perspective of depth, therefore, only Benvenuto obtains alto-rilievo. In the background stand innumerable minor types; a certain number of figures, not so well delineated as the protagonist but more prominent than those in the background, stand midway between the two. Throughout the *Vita* one can also distinguish the descriptions of major events in the author's life from intermediate happenings or peripheral incidents. (pp. 119-20)

As we focus our attention on the secondary characters, it becomes evident that the most plausible critical interpretation consists in viewing them in terms of the three-modal perspective . . . [which can be] applied to the life's journey and to the protagonist himself, since all the figures belong either to the court or to the city or to the street. This terminology conveys first a spatial dimension. Thus, popes, kings, and dukes pertain to the court, scholars and great artists to the city, prostitutes and adventurers to the street. Because of the narrator's realistic art of portraiture, however, some of the persons belonging *per se* to the first two dimensions are depicted in a style and in a manner which lower them to the third. The same three-modal perspective applies, evidently, to the rendering of the episodes through which all the characters come to life.

Two popes, an emperor, a king, and a duke are the most prominent personages who belong to the court. (p. 120)

The two popes, the king, and the duke . . . appertain to high society, whereas their literary portraiture is rendered in terms of a realistic tendency and reveals the overriding modality of the *Vita*. Francis I alone remains on the high pedestal on which his noble rank has situated him, although not even the king who called Benvenuto "*mon ami*" ["my friend"] totally avoids the artist's animosity. Clement VII, Cosimo I, and, to a much higher degree, Paul III time and again become the victims of the literary revenge of a man who thought of himself in the highest terms but showed no mercy, in real life or in literature, toward those who held different views. While evincing a lofty and a low descriptive modality, characterized by strikingly realistic traits, these princely characters achieve a literary stature midway between the protagonist's well-rounded figure and the background types. Many more noble personages, however, populate the *Vita*, although they do not achieve the relief of those mentioned above. (pp. 128-29)

At the courts of both King Francis and Duke Cosimo, Cellini encountered formidable enemies in two women, Madame D'Etampes and Eleonora de' Medici respectively. The emerging portrait of Madame D'Etampes, perhaps better delineated than Eleonora, reveals a woman who opposes the artist because he first fails, rather inadvertently than intentionally, to pay her due homage, and thus she subsequently employs all her feminine wiles to destroy him. Eleonora de' Medici vacillates between a favorable and an unfavorable attitude toward Benvenuto, at times paralleling and at times contrasting the duke's stand. In the protagonist's mind, both women join the forces of the "mala fortuna" besetting him and both will be ultimately involved in the same judgment which God's (and Cellini's) enemies will receive.

Far less prominent than the figures analyzed above, a host of princely or noble characters form fleeting relationships with the protagonist at different levels and moments of his life's journey. In a way which is typical of Cellini's narrative art, when a high-ranking personality meets the artist but no clash arises, the narrator normally refers to him in laudatory terms. Whenever any kind of contrast ensues, however, Cellini resorts to a more savory language. Thus, because of Cardinal Salviati's depreciative remarks concerning a chalice commissioned by the pope (Salviati calls it a "cipollata"), the legate is named . . . "Cardinal bestia." To make the description even more poignant, the writer adds that the prelate looked more like an ass than a human being and that, at the artist's prompt rebuttal, he became twice as ugly as he normally was. Another cardinal, Francesco Cornaro—the unsuccessful protector of Benvenuto after the escape from the Castel Sant'Angelo—displays the touchy temper of a little bear to Cardinal Ippolito de' Medici, when the latter seeks to take the artist under his protection. (pp. 129-30)

Because of his family's origin and his artistic profession, Benvenuto Cellini belonged to that middle class which ascended the rungs of the social ladder during the latter phase of the Middle Ages and asserted itself as an economic and intellectual power during the Renaissance. One might expect, consequently, to encounter in the *Vita* as many well delineated characters from this social stratum as from the higher classes. The literary figures who appertain to the city—thus I propose to refer to those who are neither noble nor plebeian—are indeed countless, but none reaches the stature of the two popes, the king, and the duke. . . . Giovanni, Benvenuto's father, is the only exception. One might produce a socio-economic explanation for this. Totally dependent on noble and rich people for his professional activity, Cellini is deeply affected by them. Nonetheless, he encounters during his life and portrays in his autobiography a host of people who belong to his own social milieu: scholars, artists, physicians, etc. In presenting them, the narrator normally displays a twofold, mutually exclusive, descriptive technique. If the person encountered favors him or enhances his own status, Cellini refers to him in laudatory terms; on the contrary, if the acquaintance is hostile, the writer invariably portrays him in a derogatory way. Consequently, by means of Cellini's realistic art of portraiture, the character, whoever he is, often leaves his social position and joins the lower world of the rogues and the scoundrels. Because of this realistic tendency, the critic needs to examine the figures who belong to the city along with those who belong to the streets. This last dimension embraces a host of types, some known and some nameless yet all unforgettable, who are interwoven along the paths of Benvenuto's life's journey.

The following examples may serve to characterize those who hold a moderately high social position and are described in friendly, indeed encomiastic terms. . . . [For instance], Michelangelo Buonarroti receives as many ennobling titles as he could have possibly wished: "divinissimo Michelagniolo" "il divino Michelagniolo", "il gran Michelagniolo", "maraviglioso Michelagniolo", etc.; Leonardo da Vinci, whom Cellini never met, is also mentioned in an idealizing manner: "il mirabil Lionardo da Vinci," "gran Lionardo", and "il gran Lionardo da Vinci". . . . (pp. 131-32)

All of these types are situated midway between the lofty and the plebeian characters and are portrayed in an idealized fashion. Side by side with them, however, a throng of lower figures belonging to the middle class are reduced to an inferior fictional world by Cellini's personal bitterness and realistic descriptions. For example, one encounters . . . the braggadocio, the painter and sculptor Pietro Torrigiani: handsome, courageous, resembling a soldier rather than an artist, he cannot capture Benvenuto's full admiration because he does not think highly of Michelangelo. (pp. 132-33)

Intermingled among those types sketched above, another host of characters belong to the populace proper and are portrayed in an appropriate style. The prostitutes form the largest group. . . . (p. 133)

Among the more characteristic types in the low style one might mention the following: 1) a chamberlain of Clement VII, misser Benvegnato, not wholly unaccustomed to vulgar and irreverent expressions; 2) a boastful French notary and fellow traveler of Benvenuto: warned by the latter about the danger of crossing a frozen bridge on horseback, the French man spurs the animal in order to show his courage and falls headlong into the river; or 3) a paymaster, Lattanzio Gorini, whose provisions for the

workshop are as trivial as Benvenuto's plans concerning the *Perseus* are grandiose.

A few terse characteristics of cities and nationalities also seem most appropriate to close this gallery of characters and incidents. In spite of the many dissensions and rivalries which Benvenuto's fiery nature and artistic profession caused him to harvest in his native city, Florence always remained at the apex of the artist's aspirations. In a sense, he abandons all plans to return to France, where he had initiated a well-promising career, in order to assert himself also in that "mirabile Iscuola". (pp. 134-35)

Switching from cities to nationalities, one observes that Benvenuto hardly fails to disclose his feelings about the foreigners he meets. For him, the bishop from Salamanca, boastful, arrogant, capable of making threats but not of carrying them out, typifies all Spaniards. Concerning the French, the writer allows certain Milanese people at the court of Clement VII to utter the following observation: "sono uomini grossi" ("people of no culture"). In addition, during the French period, Benvenuto remarks that he no longer can stand "le ribalderie di quei franciosi" ("the rogueries of those Frenchmen"). Furthermore, we are also warned against the wiles of the Normans, since one of their businesses is to testify falsely in lawsuits. Finally, the English people are called "questi diavoli" ["those

Statue of Cellini, in the Uffizi, Florence.

devils''] at the time Benvenuto is in France and a war is raging between the two countries.

In conclusion, the human world of the *Vita,* teeming with a myriad of characters, represents every segment of society since it includes the nobility as well as countless representatives from the middle and the lower strata. As to the literary rendering, only the protagonist is a well-rounded figure, whereas all the others achieve only intermediate or low relief. At the end of this fascinating human carousel, one can very easily dismiss any question as to whether the secondary types are characterized by way of an internal analysis or an external delineation. And yet, one readily discerns the motives pulsating behind their actions: *virtù,* love, passion, hatred, greed, conceit. Indeed, roguery and wretchedness seem to characterize the human condition of the people in the *Vita* more properly than any elevated quality. Thus the question whether they might be visualized as heroes or anti-heroes has already been answered. Although this terminology is best applied to well-rounded figures, in most cases the human aspect of the secondary characters is predominantly unheroic. One could hardly view in a different perspective such types as Paul III, his son Pierluigi Farnese, Duke Cosimo I, and the countless rogues and prostitutes crossing the life's journey of Benvenuto. Indeed, one of the new literary realities emerging from the *Vita* is the representation of the lower classes alongside the higher nobility. Aside from the protagonist, who ascends from the relative obscurity of the working class or bourgeoisie to climb the social ladder, no other figure is portrayed with this kind of upward mobility. And yet, the innumerable low characters who crowd the pages of the autobiography catch the reader's attention at least as vividly as the lofty ones. At the same time, the princely characters frequently leave behind their elevated conditions and partake of the same characteristics as the plebeian types. Low realism, therefore, emerges as the most common element of all the people populating the human gallery of the *Vita.*

This human cosmos also partakes of the immense variety of everyday reality. No experience, however lofty or base, is excluded; no person, whatever his origin, is left out. And yet, everything and every one find unity in the consciousness of the experiencing and narrating ''I'': the life's journey of the protagonist, namely, the poetic rendering of Benvenuto's life experiences, embraces and unifies not only one man and one existence but also a gallery of characters and incidents. (pp. 135-36)

> *Dino S. Cervigni, in his* The ''Vita'' of Benvenuto Cellini: Literary Tradition and Genre, *Longo Editore, 1979, 184 p.*

JAMES V. MIROLLO (essay date 1987)

[In the following excerpt, Mirollo compares the autobiographical narratives of Cellini and Spanish mystic Teresa of Avila.]

At first glance the juxtaposition of Teresa of Avila and Benvenuto Cellini of Florence is bound to startle, or at the very least, to seem odd. What have the Spanish mystic and the Florentine sculptor to do with each other? Even if we note that they are both authors of celebrated autobiographies, we tend to think of them as living the lives they wrote about in totally different worlds. In fact, they were contemporaries, but they also share, as we shall see, something more than the same chronological time and generic space. (p. 54)

Teresa was born in 1515 and died in 1582. Just forty years later, on 12 March 1622, she was canonized by Pope Gregory XV (along with, among others, Ignatius Loyola and Francis Xavier). In 1726 Pope Benedict XIII instituted the Feast of the Transverberation of her Heart, to be celebrated on August 27. Teresa began writing her *vida* around 1560 and had finished it by the end of the decade. Benvenuto was born fifteen years earlier, in 1500, and died in 1571. He began writing his *vita* around 1560 and continued to write or dictate it intermittently until he broke off in 1566. Thus there was a period of several years when Teresa and Benvenuto were writing at exactly the same time! Neither of them considered writing other than an ancillary activity, and both have been praised for their utter naturalness—thereby joining Montaigne and making up a trio of sixteenth-century European authors whose colloquial styles are seen in contrast to the more formal rhetoric of their contemporaries. Both Teresa and Benvenuto took up the possibility of their candidacy for sainthood, but his canonization did not take place until well after 1728, when the rediscovery of his suppressed text initiated a process of veneration, especially among the nineteenth-century romantics who saw in him the very embodiment of the envied unbridled individualism of the Renaissance. Now, of course, that vision of the sixteenth century has faded, and Cellini is more likely to be discussed as an autobiographer or visual artist or both (a ''double talent''). (p. 55)

In contrast, the reputations they enjoyed in their own time were a source of frustration to both of them. Teresa's fame was instant, already a burden to her in her lifetime. But just as his violent behavior and frank writing posed dangers to Cellini's safety and threatened his life, her mystical transports and writing too aroused inquisitorial suspicions of both heresy and sheer fakery. While Benvenuto did not have to deal with Teresa's problem of a Jewish background and its automatic arousal of racial antagonism, he shared with her the bitterness of being targeted for charges of sexual misconduct and of brief periods of confinement or imprisonment as a result. For both writers there was a disconcerting alternation of applause for inspired creativity and denunciation for wicked eccentricity. He thought the culmination of his career and his ultimate vindication as man and artist would be a great statue of Perseus he unveiled in the Florentine piazza. While she hoped for more spiritual fruits of her labors, her ultimate fame has also become inextricably entwined with a certain controversial statue of herself, by another's hand, now to be found in a Roman church. What they shared most significantly, however, and it may well be the key to their respective personalities as well as the cause of the attitudes they aroused to themselves in their own day, was an unappeased appetite for heroism. (pp. 55-6)

Unlike Teresa, who informs the reader about her extraordinary religious experiences while deprecating herself, Cellini is unrelenting in his self-praise. Whereas *she* is concerned that her experiences and her writing may be overvalued, *he* is concerned that the reader may not realize how great he is. Her autobiography culminates in the establishment of a reformed convent in a provincial town, part of her personal war on Lutheranism through purified spirituality and more intense prayer; his autobiography culminates in the casting and unveiling of a great bronze statue of Perseus the liberator, to stand in the Loggia of the Florentine Piazza between the works of Donatello and Michelangelo, a crushing blow to the envious among his fellow artists who have belittled his skill. She attributes whatever is good in her life and works to her God; he *says* he does too, but in fact it is his *talent* that is the mainspring of his existence. She describes the life of an ascetic mystic, physically frail and psychologically hyper-tense, who nevertheless can put aside her transports and visions to deal shrewdly and energetically with the so-called real world. He prides himself on his robust health, gratifies all of his physical appetites fully, participates vigorously in the cutthroat competitive world of art production, yet can have several supernatural experiences with no sense of contradiction, *and* with no lasting or transforming effects on his attitudes and values. She can experience and analyze both human and divine love, with both the physical *and* the spiritual given their due. He narrates only incidents of gratified lust, the birth of illegitimate children, indifference to sexual partners. Though he eventually married and had a family, there is no evidence that he ever loved wife or child or any woman with the intensity of devotion he gave to the beloved mistress that was his art. Teresa became a saint thanks only in part to the power of her literary artistry. Benvenuto, a goldsmith and sculptor, today enjoys a reputation based more on his writing than on his cherished art works.

As writers, Teresa and Benvenuto are remarkably alike. They both speak in a colloquial, informal style, not scrupulous about narrative sequence, correct or clear grammar, or syntax. Even though Benvenuto dictated most of his memoirs and she wrote hers, both are notable for the homely or slangy image and phrase that occur naturally in the conversational flow. Both are argumentative and demanding, poking their fingers in our chests to make their point, directing irony and sarcasm at us as well as at their subjects, insisting in a no-nonsense way that writing is not for them a delicate craft but an annoyance, a necessary device for conveying their apologias to a skeptical if not hostile world. Each has a valued role model; for her St. Augustine, for him Michelangelo. And most important, each has an appetite for heroic action and stature that is partly inspired by the sheer size of their two predecessors. Teresa, of course, did not, and could not, even imply that she hoped to compete with St. Augustine, but Benvenuto made no bones about his life's ambition to be compared favorably to, if not to supersede, St. Buonarotti. (pp. 66-7)

Cellini tells a tale of three cities: Rome, Paris, Florence, in each of which his art achieved a temporary climax in the form of an admired work. In Rome it is the morse for the cope of Pope Clement; in Paris, the famous saltcellar for King Francis I; in Florence, the Perseus, which unlike the other two, was *not* small in size and, therefore, was more heroic, not only in bulk but also in execution. His backdrop is the turbulent world of sixteenth-century religious and political conflict, but Cellini's narrative actually moves within a smaller world dominated by the politics and economics of artistic production; he actually lives in the upwardly mobile social world of the Renaissance artist. The frustrating vagaries of the patronage system, the petty and sometimes ferocious competition among artists, the insecurity of daily life threatened everywhere by violence and disease, do not offer a promising field of heroic action. But Benvenuto, through his writing, manages to dramatize himself in this very setting as warrior and saint and, finally, as loving artist. (p. 67)

As a pioneering work of autobiography of its kind, his *vita* inevitably borrows from the previous literature of martial prowess and zealous sanctity, in order to identify and inflate the dimensions of his character and activity. This need was also a matter of his personality reacting to the situation of his gold-

smith's craft within the hierarchy of Renaissance artistic class; a sculptor enjoyed higher status than a mere jeweler. And since mental activity was superior to mere manual skill, to make one's own designs was a sign of artistic learning, talent, and stature; thus Benvenuto often insists he is not merely a craftsman executing others' ideas. In addition to competing with other artists and oneself, one must also compete with and surpass the *ancients* in order to be validated as a genuine artist for all time, no mere transient hack. Benvenuto is so obsessed with these modes of identifying and validating his talent and status that he even includes several suspicious episodes in which he has Michelangelo himself confirming them.

He would be surprised to hear it, but there was a good deal of insecurity in our arrogant author. Perhaps because the Renaissance world did *not* accept as completely as its artists did their newly won status, Cellini reveals an *arriviste* anxiety in his defensiveness about being a mere jeweler. For this reason he borrows from humanist historiography a noble military descent for his family, a precocious childhood for himself, also with some mythical touches, and from his youth on, a prodigious display of talent in music, art, and fighting. The rejection of music, the appetite for soldiering, the street brawls and homicides, the instant offense taken and the swaggering threats, the violence and brutality of his revenge on those who would sully his honor or threaten his profit—all reveal not so much the quirks of one who is essentially a committed artist as the frustrated responses of one who is not sure his profession is recognizably heroic. (pp. 67-8)

The tension in Benvenuto's life between warrior instincts and artistic activity is related to the widespread Renaissance preoccupation with the opposition of arms and letters, the reconcilement of which was an ideal and a rhetorical topos but in actuality an awkward choice. In Cellini, citizen of Florence, there is the added complication of a bourgeois association of craft with earned wealth, as might be expected given the mercantile culture and values of his city's past. Several times in his *vita,* Benvenuto couples the words *honor* (or reputation) and *profit,* and these are indeed two of the chief motives that guide his actions.

Inextricably tied in with honor and profit is a third motive, the love of bravura in artistic execution, which he identifies with the goal of beauty itself. Just as a deftly delivered thrust of the knife into the body of an enemy, followed by a swift and safe escape, is a feat of artistic proportions, so the creation of such a work as the saltcellar of Francis I, as a conquest of previously insoluble artistic problems, marks a new stage in the human achievement of beautiful art, surpassing that of the ancients. Though the rehabilitation of mannerism has raised Cellini's art works in modern estimation, it is ironic that his epic conquest, his great feat, the Perseus statue, the making of which he describes in battle terms (with Cellini the general rallying his worker troops) has not drawn as much attention recently as the famous saltcellar.

The soldier, goldsmith, sculptor, and street brawler also thought of himself as devout. He was genuinely haunted by a fear of damnation. If the casting of the Perseus is the climax of his artist's life, his supernatural experiences in prison, earlier, confirmed in a climactic way his sense of divine favor. Following the traditions of the saint's life, and remarkably like Teresa, he is lifted from the ground, visited by angels, enjoys a brief tour of the afterlife and a stupendous vision of Christ crucified—all of which Teresa also experienced. What is more, he asserts that afterward there appeared above his head a halo that could be seen under certain weather conditions, proof of his having achieved a kind of sanctity! (pp. 68-9)

The absorption in art stresses both the value and the danger in Benvenuto's account of his life. By writing, he could justify himself to a larger public able to see him whole. Instead of judging him by one work of art here, one act of violence there, one rumor about his shady behavior in still another place, the new reader of the printed book could hear it all and see the pattern of events and ponder the divine plan and favor underlying its scattered incidents. As an apologia, Cellini's autobiography served him well and *almost* convinces us. But the danger lies in its promotion of a view of art and the artist that is epitomized by the words of the Farnese Pope: ''Sappiate che gli uomini come Benvenuto, unici nella loro professione, non hanno da essere ubrigati alla legge'' (''You should know that men like Benvenuto, unique in their art, are not to be constrained by the law''). The claims that are being made here, and by the larger message of Cellini's life, for a new and exalted view of the artist, though understandable in its time and context, also heralds what would become in later times a reason for alienation, frustration, and despair at the failure of the artist to be recognized or rewarded, or even listened to, by his world.

Finally, unlike Teresa, who writes because she has been ordered to, but uses the opportunity to convince us and herself that she is both heroic saint and humble sinner, Cellini seeks our approval for his view that his life as an artist is both wholly heroic and wholly just. In this sense Teresa is closer to Montaigne, and their progeny has included all those who write about themselves to affirm their common humanity *and* its occasional possibilities for transcendence. On the other hand, Benvenuto's heirs have included Rousseau and Goethe, followed by all those artists, real and fictive, like Tonio Kröger and Stephen Dedalus, for whom the call to art is felt as a vocation that sets them apart and requires understanding, tolerance, and appreciation from their world. As matters have turned out, we have needed both Teresa and Benvenuto, not only to contrast with each other but also to remind us of how much, and what a variety of heroic stuff, we are indeed capable of when we put our minds, or our pens, to the task. (pp. 70-1)

> *James V. Mirollo, ''The Lives of Saints Teresa of Avila and Benvenuto of Florence,'' in* Texas Studies in Literature and Language, *Vol. XXIX, No. 1, Spring, 1987, pp. 54-73.*

ADDITIONAL BIBLIOGRAPHY

''A Craftsman Who Wrote.'' *The Academy and Literature* LXV, No. 1,631 (8 August 1903): 135-36.
Addresses Cellini's impact as man and artist during his own and in the present century.

Bowman, Frank. ''Of Food and the Sacred: Cellini, Teresa, Montaigne.'' *L'Esprit créateur* XVI, No. 4 (Winter 1976): 111-33.
Compares a common metaphor in the autobiographical texts of Cellini, Teresa of Avila, and Michel de Montaigne.

Bull, George. Introduction to *The Autobiography of Benvenuto Cellini,* by Benvenuto Cellini, translated by George Bull, pp. 5-11. London: Folio Society, 1966.
Places synopsis of Cellini's life and career within a historical context.

Cervigni, Dino S. ''*Lazarillo de Tormes* and the *Vita* of Benvenuto Cellini: An Inquiry into Prose Narrative and Genre.'' *Kentucky Romance Quarterly* 27, No. 4 (1980): 373-89.
Posits parallels between Cellini's autobiography and an anonymously written, fictional Spanish counterpart.

Morsberger, Robert E. ''Melville's 'The Bell-Tower' and Benvenuto Cellini.'' *American Literature* XLIV, No. 3 (November 1972): 459-62.
Claims that the protagonist of Herman Melville's short story is drawn largely from Cellini's life.

Pope-Hennessy, John. *Cellini.* New York: Abbeville Press, 1985, 324 p.
Biography drawn substantially from Cellini's autobiography and extensively illustrated with photographs of Cellini's art works.

Pyle, Gerald Jackson. ''Benvenuto Cellini: The Man and His Art.'' *The Sewanee Review* XXI, No. 1 (January 1913): 235-42.
Provides critical comments on Cellini's works as a sculptor and goldsmith.

Trollope, T. A. ''Benvenuto Cellini.'' *The Magazine of Art* V (1882): 200-06.
Biographical vignette of Cellini's life based on his autobiography and revealing several incidents indicative of the artist's colorful temperament.

Wethered, H. N. ''Cellini.'' In his *The Curious Art of Autobiography: From Benvenuto Cellini to Rudyard Kipling,* pp. 7-15. 1956. Reprint. Port Washington, N. Y.: Kennikat Press, 1973.
Characterizes Cellini through extensive quotation from his autobiography.

Wilson, Henry. Introduction to *The Life of Benvenuto Cellini, a Florentine Artist, Written by Himself,* by Benvenuto Cellini, translated by Anne MacDonell, pp. v-viii. London: J. M. Dent and Sons, 1926.
Brief sketch that paints Cellini as a man of contrasts.

Jonathan Edwards

1703-1758

American theologian, essayist, homilist, and journal writer.

A preeminent theologian of the eighteenth century, Edwards is one of the most controversial figures in American religious history. As the author of the fiery sermon, "Sinners in the Hands of an Angry God," which describes in graphic, horrific imagery the torments awaiting souls damned to hell, Edwards is viewed as the archetypal "fire and brimstone" preacher. As the author of numerous theological treatises on such subjects as freedom of the will and the nature of virtue, he is considered a highly disciplined and original thinker. Edwards has thus acquired a dual reputation, alternately dismissed as a Puritan religious fanatic and lauded as one of America's most brilliant philosopher-theologians.

Edwards was born in East Windsor, Connecticut, to a staunchly Puritan family; his father was a pastor, his mother a pastor's daughter. Tutored at home during his early childhood, Edwards displayed a precocious intellectual curiosity and an abiding interest in scientific and theological issues. Before reaching his teens he wrote a treatise on the habits of spiders as well as essays on the nature of being and the soul. In 1716, just before his thirteenth birthday, Edwards entered the Collegiate School (later Yale University) in New Haven. He graduated in 1720, remaining at college for two more years to study theology. It was during this time that Edwards experienced the climactic religious conversion which determined the course of his life and career. Although always interested in religion, he had hitherto had reservations about the validity of some aspects of Calvinist doctrine, particularly predestination, and had been unsure of his own relationship to God. The intense emotionalism of his conversion (as he later described it: ". . . there came into my soul, and was as it were diffused thro' it, a sense of the glory of the Divine Being; a new sense, quite different from any thing I ever experienced before") quelled both his intellectual and personal doubts and provided him with a mission: to dedicate himself henceforth to proclaiming and living for the glory of God.

After a short ministerial stint in New York, Edwards returned to Yale, where he became a tutor after receiving his master's degree in divinity in 1723. In 1727 he moved to Northampton, Massachusetts, where his grandfather Solomon Stoddard was pastor. Here Edwards was ordained, and here he married Sarah Pierrepont. Edwards shared his grandfather's duties as pastor until Stoddard's death in 1729 left Edwards the sole minister for the community. He remained in Northampton for several years, achieving fame and notoriety for his stern and unyielding sermons and for presiding over the series of religious revivals that swept through New England in the next few decades. The most extensive and sustained revival, known as the Great Awakening, took place in the early 1740s. Spearheaded by George Whitefield and others, the Great Awakening brought about an untold number of conversions and stimulated considerable evangelical, missionary, and philanthropic activity. Edwards applauded the spiritual fervor and atonement the revival produced, though he deplored many of its excesses, including rabid emotionalism, mass hysteria, and near riots. Nonetheless, he was himself responsible for much of the emotional frenzy and spiritual panic of the movement, for during this period

Edwards delivered many of the terrifying sermons associated with his name, including "Sinners in the Hands of an Angry God." This interlude marked the height of his influence and fame in his lifetime. In the years that followed, Edwards became increasingly embroiled in wrangles with the members of his congregation. Biographers have assigned several reasons for the dissension between Edwards and the people of Northampton, but the most telling disagreement arose over Edwards's insistence on more stringent requirements for church membership, demanding that each candidate not only make a formal declaration of faith, but that he also submit evidence of a personal experience of conversion. As both Edwards and the Northampton congregation refused to compromise, no reconciliation was possible: Edwards was relieved of his duties in 1750.

Although he received a few offers from other parishes, Edwards chose semiretirement from public life, becoming a missionary to the Housatonic Indians in the pioneer town of Stockbridge, Massachusetts. During the seven years he remained there, Edwards wrote all his important theological theses, including *The Freedom of the Will, The Great Christian Doctrine of Original Sin Defended, Concerning the End for Which God Created the World,* and *The Nature of True Virtue.* In 1757, Edwards, whose essays had attracted considerable attention, was asked to accept the presidency of Princeton University, then known as the College of New Jersey. He did so, somewhat reluctantly, early in 1758. Five weeks later, after contracting small pox from an unperfected innoculation, he died.

Any understanding of Edwards's life and thought requires a knowledge of his theological credo, that of Puritanical Calvinism. Central to his theology was his belief in the existence of a God of absolute sovereignty, whose will and grace alone can effect sinful humanity's salvation. A certain group of the elect would be arbitrarily chosen to receive God's grace while the vast majority would be doomed. Edwards was adamant in opposing what he considered the dangerous heresy of New England Arminianism, which proposed that any individual could earn God's grace through good works and adherence to Christian doctrine. He argued equally strongly against the Deists, to whom God is a kind of exalted mechanic who, having set in motion a reasonably ordered world, thereafter has left it to its own devices. To Edwards, God was a constant, all-pervasive presence in the world, and it was God alone who lent to all existence its validity. All of Edwards's work, sermons and treatises, constitutes an elucidation or defense of this religious viewpoint.

Critical assessment of Edwards has remained fairly constant throughout the centuries. Always a controversial figure in his lifetime, Edwards still provokes extreme reactions. There are many who find his life and work utterly repellent; Ludwig Lewisohn has condemned him as "a sick and corrupted soul." Others admire Edwards for his commanding intellect and philosophical perspicuity. Interestingly, those who adhere to the former view usually base their criticism on evidence from the sermons, while proponents of the latter opinion cite the theological essays. Although the beliefs incorporated in the sermons and in the treatises are in no way inconsistent, Edwards's mode of expression in the two genres was remarkably different: the sermons are noted for their intense emotionalism, the essays for their calm rationalism. Thus, while Edwards's ultimate goal of glorifying his conception of Christianity and God remained the same, in the sermons he did this by appealing to his audience's fears and credulity, in the essays by speaking to their reason.

Edwards's sermons reflect the vigor of their author and the unyielding harshness of his doctrine. Replete as they are with startling, vivid imagery, the sermons exert a powerful impression. In an isolated comment in his 1868 novel *Norwood; or, Village Life in New England,* the Congregational minister Henry Ward Beecher spoke of this impression thus: "The poems of Dante are not more complete pictures than are the sermons of Edwards, if you drop from both the instrument of language, and compare simply the picture which is left in the mind." "Sinners in the Hands of an Angry God" is the most famous of Edwards's sermons—indeed, of all his work. Critics have pronounced it a chillingly effective exercise in psychological terror. In "Sinners," Edwards graphically described humanity's utter helplessness in the face of God's implacable displeasure, relying heavily on imagery drawn from simple, everyday life. Critics have observed that Edwards's metaphors and analogies, in their very ordinariness, enhance the sermon's frightening effect. In what is perhaps his most famous and most shocking image, Edwards compared his parishioners, completely vulnerable before their unforgiving God, to a spider or other "loathsome insect" which is held for a moment over the flames before being abandoned to its doom. The status of "Sinners" and the other sermons as exercises in successful scare tactics has never been an issue, but their literary value is debatable. Some critics have contended, with Leslie Stephen,

that Edwards possessed "little faculty of literary expression," while others have agreed with Edwin H. Cady's assessment of "Sinners" as "a genuine work of literary art" which "testifies to Jonathan Edwards' right to the name of artist." Although this difference of opinion exists, Edwards's merit in strictly literary terms is not a central critical issue—the nature of his philosophy is.

Reinhold Niebuhr has eulogized Edwards as "America's first and foremost theologian," and indeed his theological treatises are inexorably logical and carefully reasoned. Some commentators, however, have contended that Edwards's theses, logical and precise as they are, nevertheless reach false conclusions because their premises, rooted in Calvinist doctrine, are assumed, not proven. But whether critics accept his premises or not, they concur that the treatises show evidence of Edwards's keen intelligence and remarkable range of knowledge. Even those who finally reject his conclusions as theologically and/ or morally repugnant have been fascinated and impressed by Edwards's masterful treatment of his subject; Mark Twain saw in *The Freedom of the Will* "the glare of a resplendent intellect gone mad." Although his conclusions invariably support his own Puritanical conception of religion, Edwards's work, commentators have noted, unmistakably evidences other modes of intellectual and philosophical thought. Edwards was significantly influenced by advances in scientific discoveries and by the formation of the scientific method. He adapted, for example, Isaac Newton's theories in the field of physics to buttress his theological arguments. In *The Freedom of the Will,* Newton's theory of cause and effect provides the backbone of Edwards's case for determinism; in tracing the choices of the will back to a necessary first cause, Edwards concluded that this first cause must be God. Although the two philosophers had little in common otherwise, Edwards was also influenced by John Locke, whose empiricism became in Edwards's theology a support to his belief in the necessity of a personal religious conversion: the true Christian is not one who merely accepts religion intellectually, but one who feels and experiences God's grace personally. The experience is thus both scientific, in the sense that it can be felt and measured empirically, and mystical, in that the experience is one of communion with a supernatural being. In exploring this mysticism (a mode of thought not usually associated with Calvinism) many critics have discovered in Edwards intimations of the transcendentalism and philosophical idealism which later characterized the thought of Ralph Waldo Emerson. Those who find traces of mystic idealism in Edwards also cite his *Personal Narrative,* which critics have described as an honest, earnest, often touching spiritual autobiography. *Personal Narrative* contains many passages to support the view of Edwards as a mystic, as one who delighted in his closeness to God, which he spoke of as "a sweet burning in my heart; an ardour of soul." Yet such sentiments are always overshadowed by Edwards's return to a stern, unyielding Puritanism: such is his "spiritual tragedy," according to Vernon Louis Parrington.

Ironically, this spiritual tragedy is what accounts for much of the continuing interest in Edwards. Were he simply a strict Puritan, commentators have noted, he would occasion little but historical interest in a world which largely finds his creed impalatable. As it is, his contradictory, often uncomfortable mélange of attitudes, his simultaneous position as scientist, mystic, and Puritanical Calvinist, is intriguing. Consequently, many who admire Edwards do so more for what he might have been than for what he was. Although Edwards is widely praised for the clarity and perception of his natural and moral philosophy, his immersion in Calvinist theology has been blamed for obscuring and thwarting his brilliance. Thus it is that the uneasy balance of Edwards's character traits and philosophical beliefs has inspired such extreme critical reaction to his work— from George Santayana's damning assessment of him in his *Character & Opinion in the United States* (1920) as "perhaps the greatest *master* in false philosophy that America has yet produced," to Charles Angoff's rueful judgment: "He had it in him to become an American Kant or Luther, but he ended his life only as a somewhat more intelligent Cotton Mather."

(See also *Dictionary of Literary Biography*, Vol. 24: *American Colonial Writers, 1606-1734*.)

PRINCIPAL WORKS

God Glorified in the Work of Redemption, by the Greatness of Man's Dependence upon Him in the Whole of It (sermon) 1731

A Divine and Supernatural Light, Immediately Imparted to the Soul by the Spirit of God, Shown to Be Both a Scriptural, and Rational Doctrine (sermon) 1734

*A Faithful Narrative of the Surprizing Work of God in the Conversion of Many Hundred Souls in Northampton, and the Neighboring Towns and Villages (essay) 1737

The Distinguishing Marks of a Work of the Spirit of God (sermon) 1741

Sinners in the Hands of an Angry God (sermon) 1741

Some Thoughts concerning the Present Revival of Religion in New England (essay) 1742

A Treatise concerning Religious Affections (essay) 1746

A Farewel-Sermon Preached at the First Precinct in Northampton After the People's Publick Rejection of Their Minister (sermon) 1750

†A Careful and Strict Enquiry into the Modern Prevailing Notions of That Freedom of Will, Which is Supposed to Be Essential to Moral Agency, Vertue and Vice, Reward and Punishment, Praise and Blame (essay) 1754

The Great Christian Doctrine of Original Sin Defended (essay) 1758

‡Personal Narrative (journal) 1765; published in *The Life and Character of the Late Reverend, Learned, and Pious Mr. Jonathan Edwards*

§Two Dissertations: I. Concerning the End for Which God Created the World. II. The Nature of True Virtue (essays) 1765

Puritan Sage: Collected Writings of Jonathan Edwards (sermons, essays, and journal) 1953

The Works of Jonathan Edwards. 7 vols. (sermons, essays, and journal) 1957-84

*This work is a revision of an unpublished letter.

†This work is commonly referred to as *The Freedom of the Will*.

‡This work was written in 1739.

§These works were written between 1755 and 1758.

[SAMUEL HOPKINS] (essay date 1764)

[*An American clergyman and author, Hopkins was Edwards's friend and disciple. In the following excerpt from an essay written*

in 1764 and first published the following year, Hopkins eulogizes Edwards.]

President Edwards, in the esteem of all the judicious, who were well acquainted with him, either personally, or by his writings, was one of the *greatest—best—*and *most useful* of men, that have lived in this age.

He discovered himself to be one of the *greatest of divines* by his conversation, preaching, and writings: one of remarkable strength of mind, clearness of thought, and depth of penetration, who well understood, and was able, above most others, to vindicate the great doctrines of Christianity.

And no one perhaps, has been in our day more universally esteemed and acknowledged to be a *bright Christian*, an eminently *good man*. His love to God and man; his zeal for God, and his cause; his uprightness, humility, self-denial, and weanedness from the world; his close walk with God; his conscientious, constant, and universal obedience, in all exact and holy ways of living: in one word, the goodness, the holiness of his heart, has been as evident and conspicuous, as the uncommon greatness and strength of his understanding.

And that this distinguished light has not shone in vain, there are a cloud of witnesses. God, who gave him his great talents, led him into a way of improving them, both by preaching and writing, which has doubtless proved the means of converting many from the error of their ways; and of greatly promoting the interest of Christ's church, both in America and Europe. And there is reason to hope, that though he is now dead, he will yet speak for a great while to come, to the great comfort and advantage of the church of Christ; that his publications will produce a yet greater harvest, as an addition to his joy and crown of rejoicing in the day of the Lord. (pp. iii-iv)

> [*Samuel Hopkins*], *in a preface to his* The Life and Character of the Late Reverend, Learned, and Pious Mr. Jonathan Edwards, *S. & E. Butler, 1804, pp. iii-vii.*

JOHN WESLEY (essay date 1774)

[*As cofounder (with his brother Charles) of Methodism, Wesley had a profound impact on life in eighteenth-century England. Ministering to the spiritual and social needs of a congregation of thousands, Wesley and his Methodist creed stimulated a wave of religious fervor throughout the country. Because of its emphasis on emotion rather than ritual and on intuitive rather than analytic thought, Methodism has been called the religious counterpart of the Romantic movement in literature. Wesley wrote tirelessly, producing numerous volumes on the history of the church, biblical commentaries, educational treatises, and translations from the classics. He also edited the works of John Bunyan, William Law, and Henry Brooke. In the following excerpt from an essay which first appeared in 1774, he affirms the absurdity of Edwards's determinism.*]

Is man a free agent, or is he not? Are his actions free or necessary? Is he self-determined in acting; or is he determined by some other being? Is the principle which determines him to act, in himself or in another? This is the question which I want to consider. And is it not an important one? Surely there is not one of greater importance in the whole nature of things. For what is there that more nearly concerns all that are born of women? What can be conceived which more deeply affects, not some only, but every child of man? (p. 459)

A late writer, in his celebrated book upon free-will [*A Careful and Strict Enquiry into the Modern Prevailing Notions of that Freedom of Will, Which is Supposed to Be Essential to Moral Agency, Vertue and Vice, Reward and Punishment, Praise and Blame*] explains the matter thus:

> The soul is now connected with a material vehicle, and placed in the material world. Various objects here continually strike upon one or other of the bodily organs. These communicate the impression to the brain; consequent on which such and such sensations follow. These are the materials on which the understanding works, in forming all its simple and complex ideas; according to which our judgments are formed. And according to our judgments are our passions; our love and hate, joy and sorrow, desire and fear, with their innumerable combinations. Now, all these passions together are the will, variously modified; and all actions flowing from the will are voluntary actions; consequently, they are good or evil, which otherwise they could not be. And yet it is not in man to direct his own way, while he is in the body, and in the world.
>
> (p. 460)

[Thus Edwards] flatly ascribes the necessity of all our actions to Him who united our souls to these bodies, placed us in the midst of these objects, and ordered that these sensations, judgments, passions, and actions should spring therefrom. (p. 463)

If all the passions, the tempers, the actions of men, are wholly independent on their own choice, are governed by a principle exterior to themselves, then there can be no moral good or evil; there can be neither virtue nor vice, neither good nor bad actions, neither good nor bad passions or tempers. The sun does much good; but it is no virtue; but he is not capable of moral goodness. Why is he not? For this plain reason, because he does not act from choice. The sea does much harm: It swallows up thousands of men; but it is not capable of moral badness, because it does not act by choice, but from a necessity of nature. If indeed one or the other can be said to act at all. Properly speaking, it does not: It is purely passive: It is only acted upon by the Creator; and must move in this manner and no other, seeing it cannot resist His will. In like manner, St. Paul did much good: But it was no virtue, if he did not act from choice. And if he was in all things necessitated to think and act, he was not capable of moral goodness. Nero does much evil; murders thousands of men, and sets fire to the city: But it is no fault; he is not capable of moral badness, if he does not act from choice, but necessity. Nay, properly, the man does not act at all: He is only acted upon by the Creator, and must move thus, being irresistibly impelled. For who can resist his will?

Again: If all the actions, and passions, and tempers of men are quite independent on their own choice, are governed by a principle exterior to themselves; then none of them is either rewardable or punishable, is either praise or blameworthy. The consequence is undeniable: I cannot praise the sun for warming, nor blame the stone for wounding me; because neither the sun nor the stone acts from choice, but from necessity. Therefore, neither does the latter deserve blame, nor the former deserve praise. Neither is the one capable of reward, nor the other of punishment. And if a man does good as necessarily as the sun, he is no more praiseworthy than that; if he does evil as necessarily as the stone, he is no more blameworthy. The dying to save your country is noway rewardable, if you are compelled thereto; and the betraying your country is noway punishable, if you are necessitated to do it.

It follows, if there be no such thing as virtue or vice, as moral good or evil, if there be nothing rewardable or punishable in the actions or passions of men, then there can be no judgment to come, and no future rewards and punishments. For might not God as well judge the trees of the wood, or the stones of the field, as man, if man was as totally passive as they? as irresistibly determined to act thus or thus? (pp. 463-64)

Such absurdities will naturally and necessarily follow from the scheme of necessity. But Mr. Edwards has found out a most ingenious way of evading this consequence: "I grant," says that good and sensible man,

> if the actions of men were involuntary, the consequence would inevitably follow,—they could not be either good or evil; nor, therefore, could they be the proper object either of reward or punishment. But here lies the very ground of your mistake; their actions are not involuntary. The actions of men are quite voluntary; the fruit of their own will. They love, they desire, evil things; therefore they commit them. But love and hate, desire and aversion, are only several modes of willing. Now, if men voluntarily commit theft, adultery, or murder, certainly the actions are evil, and therefore punishable. And if they voluntarily serve God, and help their neighbours, the actions are good, and therefore rewardable.

I cannot possibly allow the consequence, upon Mr. Edwards's supposition. Still I say, if they are necessitated to commit robbery or murder, they are not punishable for committing it. But you answer, "Nay, their actions are voluntary, the fruit of their own will." If they are, yet that is not enough to make them either good or evil. For their will, on your supposition, is irresistibly impelled; so that they cannot help willing thus or thus. If so, they are no more blamable for that will, than for the actions which follow it. There is no blame if they are under a necessity of willing. There can be no moral good or evil, unless they have liberty as well as will, which is entirely a different thing. And the not adverting to this seems to be the direct occasion of Mr. Edwards's whole mistake. (p. 467)

> *John Wesley, "Thoughts Upon Necessity," in his* The Works of John Wesley: Letters, Essays, Dialogs and Addresses, Vol. X, *1872. Reprint by Zondervan Publishing House, 1958-59, pp. 457-73.*

[WILLIAM HAZLITT]   (essay date 1829)

[*An English essayist, Hazlitt was one of the most important critics of the Romantic age. He was a deft stylist, a master of the prose essay, and a leader of what was later termed "impressionist criticism"—a form of personal analysis directly opposed to the universal standards of critical judgment accepted by many eighteenth-century critics. Hazlitt, like Samuel Taylor Coleridge before him, played a substantial role in the reinterpretation of Shakespeare's characters during the nineteenth century, and he contributed significantly to the revival of a number of Elizabethan dramatists, including John Webster and Thomas Heywood. Although he has often been considered a follower of Coleridge, he is closer in spirit and critical methodology to Charles Lamb. Like Lamb, Hazlitt utilized the critical techniques of evocation, metaphor, and personal reference—three innovations that greatly altered the development of literary criticism in the nineteenth and twentieth centuries. For Hazlitt the ideal of any critical endeavor is not an ultimate judgment regarding a work of literature; instead, the critic serves as a guide to help determine the reader's response to certain works, or passages within those works. Perhaps the most important thing to remember when reading Hazlitt is that he was a journalist writing for the general public and that he lived from the proceeds of his pen. He was acutely aware of the abstract nature of literature as well as the limitations of his audience in understanding questions of aesthetics and style. For this reason he purposely made his criticism palatable by using illustrations, digressions, and repetitions. In the following excerpt, Hazlitt praises Edwards's methods of philosophical argument.]*

Having produced [Jonathan Edwards], the Americans need not despair of their metaphysicians. We do not scruple to say, that he is one of the acutest, most powerful, and, of all reasoners, the most conscientious and sincere. His closeness and candour are alike admirable. Instead of puzzling or imposing on others, he tries to satisfy his own mind. We do not say whether he is right or wrong; we only say that his method is 'an honest 'method:' there is not a trick, a subterfuge, a verbal sophism in his whole book [*The Freedom of the Will*]. Those who compare his arguments with what Priestley or Hobbes have written on the same question, will find the one petulant and the other dogmatical. Far from taunting his adversaries, he endeavours with all his might to explain difficulties; and acknowledges that the words *Necessity, Irresistible, Inevitable,* &c., which are applied to external force, acting in spite of the will, are misnomers when applied to acts, or a necessity emanating from the will itself; and that the repugnance of his favourite doctrine to common sense and feeling, (in which most of his party exult as a triumph of superior wisdom over vulgar prejudice,) is an unfortunate stumbling-block in the way of truth, arising out of the structure of language itself. His anxiety to clear up the scruples of others, is equal, in short, to his firmness in maintaining his own opinion. (p. 131)

[*William Hazlitt*], "*American Literature—Dr. Channing,*" in The Edinburgh Review, *Vol. L, No. XCIX, October, 1829, pp. 125-44.*

LESLIE STEPHEN (essay date 1873)

[Many scholars consider Stephen the most important literary critic of the Victorian age after Matthew Arnold. He has been praised for his moral insight and judgment, as well as for his intellectual vigor. However, many others, who consider him less influential than and certainly inferior to Arnold in his contribution to English literature, argue that his work was deficient in aesthetic and formal analysis and that he failed to reconcile his moral and historical philosophies. The key to Stephen's moral criticism is his theory that all literature is nothing more than an imaginative rendering, in concrete terms, of a writer's philosophy or beliefs. It is the role of criticism, he contends, to translate into intellectual terms what the writer has told the reader through character, symbol, and event. More often than not Stephen's analysis passes into biographical judgment of the writer. As he once observed, "The whole art of criticism consists in learning to know the human being who is partially revealed to us in his spoken or his written words." Stephen's emphasis on the writer's philosophy, rather than the formal aspects of literature, has led Desmond MacCarthy to call him "the least aesthetic of noteworthy critics." In the following excerpt from an essay which first appeared in Fraser's Magazine *in 1873, Stephen discusses conflicting tendencies in Edwards's theological and metaphysical thought.]*

[Jonathan Edwards] had the fate common to men who are unfitted for the struggles of daily life, and whose philosophy does not harmonise with the dominant current of the time. A speculative recluse, with little faculty of literary expression, and given to utter opinions shocking to the popular mind, he excited little attention during his lifetime, except amongst the sharers of his own religious persuasions; and, when noticed after his death, the praise of his intellectual acuteness has generally been accompanied with an expression of abhorrence for

his supposed moral obtuseness. Mr. Lecky, for example, whilst speaking of Edwards as "probably the ablest defender of Calvinism," mentions his treatise on Original Sin as "one of the most revolting books that have ever proceeded from the pen of man." . . . That intense dislike, which is far from uncommon, for severe reasoning has even made a kind of reproach to Edwards of what is called his "inexorable logic." To condemn a man for being honestly in the wrong is generally admitted to be unreasonable; but people are even more unforgiving to the sin of being honestly in the right. The frankness with which Edwards avowed opinions, not by any means peculiar to himself, has left a certain stain upon his reputation. He has also suffered in general repute from a cause which should really increase our interest in his writings. Metaphysicians, whilst admiring his acuteness, have been disgusted by his adherence to an outworn theology; and theologians have cared little for a man who was primarily a philosophical speculator, and has used his philosophy to bring into painful relief the most terrible dogmas of the ancient creeds. Edwards, however, is interesting just because he is a connecting link between two widely different phases of thought. He connects the expiring Calvinism of the old Puritan theocracy with what is called the transcendentalism embodied in the writings of Emerson and other leaders of young America. He is remarkable, too, as illustrating, at the central point of the eighteenth century, those speculative tendencies which were most vitally opposed to the then dominant philosophy of Locke and Hume. And, finally, there is still more permanent interest in the man himself, as exhibiting in high relief the weak and the strong points of the teaching of which Calvinism represents only one embodiment. . . . The Puritan assumptions were so ingrained in his nature that the agony of mind which they caused never led him to question their truth, though it animated him to discover a means of reconciling them to reason; and the reconciliation is the whole burden of his ablest works. (pp. 281-84)

His mind, acute as it was, yet worked entirely in the groove provided for it. The revolting consequences to which he was led by not running away from his premises, never for an instant suggested to him that the premises might conceivably be false. He accepts a belief in hell-fire, interpreted after the popular fashion, without a murmur, and deduces from it all those consequences which most theologians have evaded or covered with a judicious veil.

Edwards was luckily not an eloquent man, for his sermons would in that case have been amongst the most terrible of human compositions. But if ever he warms into something like eloquence, it is when he is endeavouring to force upon the imaginations of his hearers the horrors of their position. . . . Imagine the congregation of rigid Calvinists, prepared by previous scenes of frenzy and convulsion, and longing for the fierce excitement which was the only break in the monotony of their laborious lives. And then imagine Edwards ascending the pulpit, with his flaccid solids and vapid fluids, and the pale drawn face, in which we can trace an equal resemblance to the stern Puritan forefathers and to the keen sallow New Englander of modern times. He gives out as his text, "Sinners shall slide in due time," and the title of his sermon is, **"Sinners in the Hands of an Angry God."** For a full hour he dwells with unusual vehemence on the wrath of the Creator and the sufferings of the creature. His sentences, generally languid and complex, condense themselves into short, almost gasping asseverations. God is angry with the wicked; as angry with the living wicked as "with many of those miserable creatures that He is now tormenting in hell." The devil is waiting: the fire is ready; the furnace is hot; the "glittering sword is whet and held over them, and the pit hath opened her mouth to receive them." The unconverted are walking on a rotten covering, where there are innumerable weak places, and those places not distinguishable. The flames are "gathering and lashing about" the sinner, and all that preserves him for a moment is "the mere arbitrary will and uncovenanted unobliged forbearance of an incensed God." But does not God love sinners? Hardly in a comforting sense. "The God that holds you over the pit of hell, much as one holds a spider or some other loathsome insect over the fire, abhors you, and is dreadfully provoked; He looks upon you as worthy of nothing else but to be cast into the fire; . . . you are ten thousand times as abominable in His eyes as the most hateful and venomous serpent is in ours." The comparison of man to a loathsome viper is one of the metaphors to which Edwards most habitually recurs. . . . No relief is possible; Edwards will have no attempt to explain away the eternity of which he speaks; there will be no end to the "exquisite horrible misery" of the damned. You, when damned, "will know certainly that you must wear out long ages, millions of millions of ages, in wrestling and conflicting with this Almighty merciless vengeance: and then when you have so done, when so many ages have actually been spent by you in this manner, you will know that all is but a point to what remains." Nor might his hearers fancy that, as respectable New England Puritans, they had no personal interest in the question. It would be awful, he says, if we could point to one definite person in this congregation as certain to endure such torments. "But, alas! instead of one, how many is it likely will remember this discourse in hell? It would be a wonder if some that are now present should not be in hell in a very short time, before this year is out. And it would be no wonder if some persons that now sit here in some seats of this meeting-house in health, and quiet and secure, should be there before to-morrow morning."

With which blessing he dismissed the congregation to their dinners, with such appetites as might be left to them. The strained excitement which marks this pleasing production could not be maintained; but Edwards never shrank in cold blood from the most appalling consequences of his theories. He tells us, with superlative coolness, that the "bulk of mankind do throng" to hell. . . . He sentences infants to hell remorselessly. The imagination, he admits, may be relieved by the hypothesis that infants suffer only in this world, instead of being doomed to eternal misery. "But it does not at all relieve one's reason;" and that is the only faculty which he will obey. . . . In a sermon called **"Wicked Men useful in their Destruction only"** . . . , he declares that "the view of the doleful condition of the damned will make them (the saints in heaven) more prize their own blessedness." (pp. 301-04)

Was the man who could utter such blasphemous sentiments—for so they undoubtedly appear to us—a being of ordinary flesh and blood? One would rather have supposed his solids to be of bronze, and his fluids of vitriol, than have attributed to them the character which he describes. That he should have been a gentle, meditative creature, around whose knees had clung eleven "young vipers" of his own begetting, is certainly an astonishing reflection. And yet, to do Edwards justice, we must remember two things. In the first place, the responsibility for such ghastly beliefs cannot be repudiated by anyone who believes in the torments of hell. Catholics and Protestants must share the opprobrium due to the assertion of this tremendous doctrine. Nor does Arminianism really provide more than a merely verbal escape from the difficulty. Jeremy Taylor, for example, draws a picture of hell quite as fearful and as material

as Edwards', and, if animated by a less fanatical spirit, adorned by an incomparably more vivid fancy. He specially improves upon Edwards' description by introducing the sense of smell. The tyrant who fastened the dead to the living invented an exquisite torment; "but what is this in respect of hell, when each body of the damned is more loathsome and unsavoury than a million of dead dogs, and all those pressed and crowded together in so strait a compass? Bonaventure goes so far as to say that if one only of the damned were brought into this world, it were sufficient to infect the whole earth. Neither shall the devils send forth a better smell; for, although they are spirits, yet those fiery bodies unto which they are fastened and confined shall be of a more pestilential flavour." It is vain to attempt an extenuation of the horror, by relieving the Almighty from the responsibility of this fearful prison-house. The dogma of free-will is a transparent mockery. (pp. 304-05)

The living truths in [Edwards'] theory are chained to dead fancies, and the fancies have an odour as repulsive as Taylor's "million of dead dogs." But on the truths is founded a religious and moral system which, however erroneous it may appear to some thinkers, is conspicuous for its vigour and loftiness. Edwards often shows himself a worthy successor of the great men who led the moral revolt of the Reformation. Amongst some very questionable metaphysics and much outworn—sometimes repulsive—superstition, he grasps the central truths on which all really noble morality must be based. The mode in which they presented themselves to his mind may be easily traced. Calvinism, logically developed, leads to Pantheism. The absolute sovereignty of God, the doctrine to which Edwards constantly returns, must be extended over all nature as well as over the fate of the individual human soul. The peculiarity of Edwards' mind was, that the doctrine had thus expanded along particular lines of thought, without equally affecting others. He is a kind of Spinoza-Mather; he combines, that is, the logical keenness of the great metaphysician with the puerile superstitions of the New England divine; he sees God in all nature, and yet believes in the degrading supernaturalism of the Salem witches. The object of his faith, in short, is the "infinite Jehovah". . ., the God to whose all-pervading power none can set a limit, and who is yet the tutelary deity of a petty clan; and there is something almost bewildering in the facility with which he passes from one conception to the other without the smallest consciousness of any discontinuity. . . . At the age of fifteen or sixteen he had said "God and real existence are the same; God is, and there is none else." The same doctrine is the foundation of the theories expounded in his treatises on *Virtue* and on the *End of God in Creation*. In the last of these, for example, he uses the argument (depending upon a conception familiar to the metaphysicians of the previous age), that benevolence, consisting in regard to "Being in general," must be due to any being in proportion to the degree of existence. . . . (pp. 307-08)

His metaphysical theory coincides precisely with his theological view, and is generally expressed in theological language. The love of "Being in general" is the love of God. The intellectual intuition is the reflection of the inward light, and the recognition of a mathematical truth is but a different phase of the process which elsewhere produces conversion. Intuition is a kind of revelation, and revelation is a special intuition.

One of his earliest published sermons is devoted to prove the existence of "a Divine and supernatural light, immediately imparted to the soul by the Spirit of God." . . . On that fundamental doctrine his whole theological system is based; as

Edwards's home, Northampton, Massachusetts.

his metaphysical system rests on the existence of absolute *à priori* truths. The knowledge of God sums up all true beliefs, and justifies all virtuous emotions, as the power of God supports all creation at every instant. "It is by a Divine influence that the laws of nature are upheld, and a constant concurrence of Divine power is necessary in order to our being, moving, or having a being."... To be constantly drawing sustenance from the eternal power which everywhere underlies the phenomena of the world is the necessary condition of spiritual life, as to breathe the air is the condition of physical life. The force which this conception, whether true or false, exercises over the imagination, and the depth which it gives to Edwards' moral views, are manifest at every turn. (pp. 310-11)

The strength, however, and the weaknesses of Edwards as a moralist are best illustrated from the two treatises on the *Religious Affections* and on *Original Sin*. The first, which was the fruit of his experiences at Northampton, may be described as a system of religious diagnostics. By what symptoms are you to distinguish—that was the problem which forced itself upon him—the spiritual state produced by the Divine action from that which is but a hollow mockery? After his mode of judging in concrete cases..., we are rather surprised by the calm and sensible tone of this argument. The deep sense of the vast importance of the events to which he was a witness makes him the more scrupulous in testing their real character.... Suppose, he says, that a person terrified by threats of hellfire has a vision "of a person with a beautiful countenance, smiling on him with arms open and with blood dropping down," whom he supposes to be Christ come to promise him eternal life, are we to assume that this vision and the consequent transports infallibly indicate supernatural agency? No, he replies, with equal sense and honesty; "he must have but slightly considered human nature who thinks such things cannot arise in this manner without any supernatural excitement of Divine power."... (pp. 312-13)

So far, Edwards is unassailable from his own point of view. Our theory of religion may differ from his; but at least he fully realises how profound is the meaning of the word, and aims at conquering all human faculties, not at controlling a few external manifestations. But his further applications of the theory lead him into more doubtful speculations. That Being, a union with whom constitutes true holiness, is not only to be the ideal of perfect goodness, but He must be the God of the Calvinists, who fulfils the stipulations of a strange legal bargain, and the God of the Jews, who sentences whole nations to massacre for the crimes of their ancestors. Edwards has hitherto been really protesting against that lower conception of God which is latent in at least the popular versions of Catholic or Arminian theology, and to which Calvinism opposes a loftier view. God, on this theory, is not really almighty, for the doctrine of free-will places human actions and their results beyond His control. He is scarcely omniscient, for, like human rulers, He judges by actions, not by the intrinsic nature of the soul, and therefore distributes His rewards and punishments on a system comparable to that of mere earthly jurisprudence.

He is at most the infallible judge of actions, not the universal ordainer of events and distributor of life and happiness. Edwards' profound conviction of the absolute sovereignty of God leads him to reject all such feeble conceptions. But he has now to tell us where the Divine influence has actually displayed itself; and his view becomes strangely narrowed. Instead of confessing that all good gifts come from God, he infers that those which do not come from his own God must be radically vicious. (p. 314)

[Edwards is] in the singular position of a Pantheist who yet regards all nature as alienated from God; and in the treatise on *Original Sin* he brings out the more revolting consequences of that view by help of the theological dogma of corruption. He there maintains in its fullest sense the terrible thesis, that all men are naturally in a state of which the inevitable issue is their "utter eternal perdition, as being finally accursed of God and the subjects of His remediless wrath through sin."... (pp. 315-16)

Once more, then, we are brought back to the question, How could any man hold such doctrines without going mad? or, as experience has reconciled us to that phenomenon, How could a man with so many elevated conceptions of the truth reconcile these ghastly conclusions to the nobler part of his creed? (p. 317)

[That] Edwards possessed extraordinary acuteness is as clear as it is singular that so acute a man should have suffered his intellectual activity to be restrained within such narrow fetters. Placed in a different medium, under the same circumstances, for example, as Hume or Kant, he might have developed a system of metaphysics comparable in its effect upon the history of thought to the doctrines of either of those thinkers. He was, one might fancy, formed by nature to be a German professor, and accidentally dropped into the American forests. Far away from the main currents of speculation, ignorant of the conclusions reached by his most cultivated contemporaries, and deriving his intellectual sustenance chiefly from an obsolete theology, with some vague knowledge of the English followers of Locke, his mind never expanded itself freely.... Clearing away the crust of ancient superstition, we may still find in Edwards' writings a system of morality as ennobling, and a theory of the universe as elevated, as can be discovered in any theology. That the crust was thick and hard, and often revolting in its composition, is, indeed, undeniable; but the genuine metal is there, no less unmistakably than the refuse. (pp. 320-21)

> Leslie Stephen, "Jonathan Edwards," in his Hours in a Library, Vol. I, revised edition, Smith, Elder & Co., 1909, pp. 280-321.

OLIVER WENDELL HOLMES   (essay date 1880)

[An American physician, educator, and man of letters, Holmes is noted in literary circles primarily for his minor but witty verses and for his essays, particularly those which originally appeared in the Atlantic Monthly and were collected and published as The Autocrat of the Breakfast-Table in 1858. These informal conversational essays are renowned both for their wit and for their thoughtful treatment of serious human issues. All his life Holmes rebelled against his heritage of New England Puritanism, attacking the strict creed of Calvinism in his well-known poem, "The Deacon's Masterpiece" (1858) and his novel, Elsie Venner: A Romance of Destiny (1861). In the following excerpt from an essay which originally appeared in the International Review in 1880, Holmes notes similarities between Edwards and Blaise Pascal, and surveys Edwards's essays.]

In studying the characteristics of Edwards in his life and writings, we find so much to remind us of Pascal that, if we believed in the doctrine of metempsychosis, we could almost feel assured that the Catholic had come back to earth in the Calvinist.... Each was remarkable for the precocious development of his observing and reflecting powers. Their spiritual as well as their mental conditions were parallel in many respects. Both had a strong tendency to asceticism.... Pascal and Edwards were alike sensitive, pure in heart and in life, profoundly penetrated with the awful meaning of human existence; both filled with a sense of their own littleness and sinfulness; both trembling in the presence of God and dwelling much upon his wrath and its future manifestations; both singularly powerful as controversialists, and alive all over to the *gaudia certaminis* ["delights of battle"],—one fighting the Jesuits and the other the Arminians. They were alike in their retiring and melancholy kind of life. Pascal was a true poet who did not care to wear the singing robes. As much has been claimed for Edwards on the strength of a passage here and there which shows sentiment

and imagination. But this was in his youthful days, and the "little white flower" of his diary fades out in his polemic treatises, as the "star of Bethlehem" no longer blossoms when the harsh blades of grass crowd around it. Pascal's prose is light and elastic everywhere with *esprit;* much of that of Edwards, thickened as it is with texts from Scripture, reminds us of the unleavened bread of the Israelite: holy it may be, but heavy it certainly is. The exquisite wit which so delights us in Pascal could not be claimed for Edwards; yet he could be satirical in a way to make the gravest person smile,—as in the description of the wonderful animal the traveller tells of as inhabiting Terra del Fuego, with which he laughs his opponents to scorn in his treatise on the *Freedom of the Will.* Both had the same fondness for writing in the form of aphorisms,— natural to strong thinkers, who act like the bankers whose habit it is to sign checks, but not to count out money,—and both not rarely selected the same or similar subjects for their brief utterances. (pp. 362-64)

Whether or not Edwards had ever read Pascal is not shown by any reference in his writings, but there are some rather curious instances of similar or identical expressions. Thus the words of his sermon, in which he speaks of sinners as "in the hands of an angry God," are identical in meaning with Pascal's "dans les mains d'un Dieu irrité." His expression applied to man, "a poor little worm," sounds like a translation of Pascal's "chétif vermisseau." A paragraph of his detached observations entitled "Body Infinite," reminds one of the second paragraph of the twenty-fourth chapter of Pascal's *Pensées.* These resemblances are worth noting in a comparison of the two writers. (pp. 365-66)

In his treatise, *The Great Christian Doctrine of Original Sin defended,* [Edwards] teaches that "God, in his constitution with Adam, dealt with him as a *public* person,—as the head of the human species,—and had respect to his posterity, as included in him." Again: "God dealing with Adam as the head of his posterity (as has been shown) and treating them as one, he deals with his posterity as having *all sinned in him.*" (p. 372)

By the *Work of Redemption,* of which Edwards wrote an elaborate history, a few of the human race have been exempted from the infinite penalties consequent upon being born upon this planet, the atmosphere of which is a slow poison, killing everybody after a few score of years. But "the bulk of mankind" go eventually to the place prepared for them by "Justice," of which place and its conditions Edwards has given full and detailed descriptions.

The essay on *God's Chief End in Creation* reaches these two grand results: "God aims at satisfying justice in the eternal damnation of sinners, which will be satisfied with their damnation considered no otherwise than with regard to its eternal duration. God aims to satisfy his infinite grace or benevolence by the bestowment of a good infinitely valuable because eternal."

His idea of the *Nature of True Virtue,* as expressed in his treatise with that title, is broad.... A principle of virtue is, according to Edwards, "union of heart to being, simply considered; which implies a disposition to benevolence to being, in general." This definition has been variously estimated by philosophical critics. There is something in it which reminds one of the "ether" of the physicists. This is a conceivable if not a necessary medium, but no living thing we know anything about can live in it, can fly or breathe in it, and we must leave it to the angels, with whose physiology we are not acquainted.

The full title of the work on which Edwards's reputation as a thinker mainly rests is, *A careful and strict Inquiry into the modern prevailing notions of that Freedom of the Will which is supposed to be essential to moral agency, virtue and vice, reward and punishment, praise and blame.* (pp. 373-74)

The truth is, his argument, unfolded with infinite patience and admirable ingenuity, is nothing but a careful evolution of the impossibilities involved in the idea of that old scholastic thesis best known in the popular form of the puzzle called in learned books *l'âne de Buridan*, and in common speech "the ass between two bundles of hay,"—or as Leibnitz has it, between two pastures. A more dignified statement of it is to be found at the beginning of the fourth canto of Dante's *Paradiso*. The passage is thus given in Mr. Longfellow's translation:—

> Between two viands equally removed
> And tempting, a free man would die of hunger,
> Ere either he could bring unto his teeth.

The object of Edwards was to prove that such a state of equilibrium, supposed by his Arminian opponents to be necessary to account for human freedom and responsibility, does not and cannot exist. Leibnitz had already denied its possibility without any express act of the Creator.

The reader of this celebrated treatise may well admire the sleuth-hound-like sagacity and tenacity with which the keen-scented reasoner follows the devious tracks of his adversaries; yet he can hardly help feeling that a vast number of words have been expended in proving over and over again a proposition which, as put by the great logician, is self-evident. In fact, Edwards has more than once stated his own argument with a contemptuous brevity, as if he felt that he had been paying out in farthings what he could easily hand us in the form of a shilling. (pp. 374-75)

The drift of Edwards's arguments is to show that, though we are free to *follow* our will, we are not free to *form* an act of volition, but that this of necessity obeys the strongest motive. As the natural man—that is every man since the fall of Adam—is corrupt in all his tendencies, it follows that his motives, and consequently his moral volitions, are all evil until changed by grace, which is a free gift to such as are elected from eternity according to God's good pleasure. "The doctrine of a self-determining will as the ground of all moral good and evil tends to prevent any proper exercises of faith in God and Christ in the affair of our salvation, as it tends to prevent all dependence upon them."

In spite of any general assertions of Edwards to the contrary, we find our wills tied up hand and foot in the logical propositions which he knots inextricably about them; and yet when we lay down the book, we feel as if there was something left free after all. . . . We are disposed to settle the matter as magisterially as Dr. Johnson did. "Sir," said he, "we *know* our will is free, and *there's* an end on 't." (pp. 376-77)

The *Treatise on Original Sin* deals with that subject in the usual mediæval style. (p. 382)

There are conceptions which are not only false, not only absurd, but which act as *disorganizing forces* in the midst of the thinking apparatus. . . . Edwards's powerful intellect was filled with disorganizing conceptions, like that which makes all mankind sinners thousands of years before they were born.

A chief ground of complaint against Edwards is his use of language with reference to the future of mankind which shocks the sensibilities of a later generation. There is no need of going

into all the plans and machinery of his "Inferno," as displayed in his sermons. We can endure much in the mediæval verse of Dante which we cannot listen to in the comparatively raw and recent prose of Edwards. Mr. John Morley speaks in one of his Essays of "the horrors of what is perhaps the most frightful idea that has ever corroded human character,—the idea of eternal punishment." Edwards has done his best to burn these horrors into the souls of men. (pp. 383-84)

The title of the *Treatise on the Religious Affections* might naturally lead us to expect a large expression of those tenderer feelings with which Edwards was, no doubt, naturally endowed. But in point of fact, if a sermon of Edwards is like a nail driven through a human heart, this treatise is just what clinches it. It is a sad thought how many souls it must have driven to despair. For after having equipped the underground laboratory of "revenging justice" with a complete apparatus of torture, such as to think of suggests nothing but insanity, he fills the unhappy believer's mind with so many doubts and scruples that many a pious Christian after reading it must have set himself down as a castaway. (pp. 387-88)

Edwards's system seems, in the light of to-day, to the last degree barbaric, mechanical, materialistic, pessimistic. If he had lived a hundred years later, and breathed the air of freedom, he could not have written with such old-world barbarism as we find in his volcanic sermons. (p. 395)

Again, what can be more mechanical than the God of all gods he contrived,—or accepted,—under the name of *Justice,*—a piece of iron machinery which would have held back the father's arms stretching out to embrace his son, and shed the blood of the prodigal, instead of that of the fatted calf?

What can be more utterly materialistic than to attach the idea of sinfulness and responsibility, and liability to eternal suffering in consequence, to a little organic bundle, with no more knowledge of its relations to the moral world than a marsupial embryo in the maternal pouch has of its geographical position?

And what pessimism that ever entered the mind of man has gone farther than that which taxed the imagination to the utmost for its horrors, and declared that these were but the faintest image of what was reserved for the bulk of mankind? (pp. 395-96)

[But] many lessons are to be learned from the careful study of a man, who, as Mr. Bancroft says, "sums up the old theology of New England and is the fountain-head of the new." What better comment can be made on his misdirected powers than his own remark: "A person may have a strong reason and yet not a good reason. He may have a strength of mind to drive an argument and yet not have even balances."

As we picture the scenes he described, the Divine ingenuity fitting the body and soul for the extremity of suffering, and providing new physical and chemical laws to carry torture beyond our power of imagination, friends looking on pleased, parents rejoicing and singing hallelujahs as they see their children "turned away and beginning to enter into the great furnace" where they are to "roast" forever, all natural affections utterly gone,—can we find anywhere a more striking illustration of his own words? He is speaking of the self-torturing worship of the heathen: "How powerful must be the delusions of the human mind, and how strong the tendency of the heart to carry them such a length and so to overcome the tenderest feelings of human nature!" (p. 399)

Oliver Wendell Holmes, "Jonathan Edwards," in his Pages from an Old Volume of Life: A Collection of Essays, 1857-1881, *Houghton, Mifflin and Company, 1883, pp. 361-401.*

MARK TWAIN (letter date 1902)

[*Considered the father of modern American literature, Twain broke with the genteel traditions of the nineteenth century by endowing his characters and narratives with the natural speech patterns of the common person, and by writing of subjects hitherto considered beneath the consideration of serious art. Twain is often regarded as a humorist and children's writer, though very serious subjects are treated in such perennially popular books as* The Adventures of Huckleberry Finn *(1884),* The Adventures of Tom Sawyer *(1876), and* A Connecticut Yankee in King Arthur's Court *(1889). Initially a clowning humorist, Twain matured into the role of the seemingly naive Wise Fool whose caustic sense of humor forced his audience to recognize humanity's foolishness and society's myriad injustices. Later, crushed by personal tragedy, economic hardship, and ill health, Twain turned on "the damned human race," portraying it as the totally corrupt plaything of a cruel God. In the following excerpt from a letter written in 1902 to the Rev. J. H. Twichell, whose home Twain had just visited and from whom he had received a copy of Edwards's* Freedom of the Will *to read on the journey home, Twain describes his incredulous reactions to Edwards.*]

Dear Joe,—"After compliments." From Bridgeport to New York; thence to home; and continuously until near midnight I wallowed and reeked with Jonathan in his insane debauch; rose immediately refreshed and fine at 10 this morning, but with a strange and haunting sense of having been on a three days' tear with a drunken lunatic. It is years since I have known these sensations. All through the book is the glare of a resplendent intellect gone mad—a marvelous spectacle. No, not *all* through the book—the drunk does not come on till the last third, where what I take to be Calvinism and its God begins to show up and shine red and hideous in the glow from the fires of hell, their only right and proper adornment. By God I was ashamed to be in such company.

Jonathan seems to hold (as against the Arminian position) that the Man (or his Soul or his Will) never *creates* an impulse itself, but is moved to action by an impulse *back* of it. That's sound!

Also, that of two or more things offered it, it infallibly chooses the one which for the moment is most *pleasing* to ITSELF. *Perfectly* correct! An immense admission for a man not otherwise sane.

Up to that point he could have written chapters III and IV of my suppressed "Gospel." But there we seem to separate. He seems to concede the indisputable and unshakable dominion of Motive and Necessity (call them what he may, these are *exterior* forces and not under the man's authority, guidance or even suggestion)—then he suddenly flies the logic track and (to all seeming) makes the *man* and not these exterior forces responsible to God for the man's thoughts, words and acts. It is frank insanity.

I think that when he concedes the autocratic dominion of Motive and Necessity he grants a *third* position of mine—that a man's mind is a mere machine—an *automatic* machine—which is handled entirely from the *outside,* the man himself furnishing it absolutely nothing: not an ounce of its fuel, and not so much as a bare *suggestion* to that exterior engineer as to what the machine shall do, nor *how* it shall do it nor *when.*

After that concession, it was time for him to get alarmed and *shirk*—for he was pointing straight for the only rational and possible next-station on *that* piece of road: the irresponsibility of man to God.

And he shirked. Shirked, and arrived at this handsome result:

Man is commanded to do so-and-so;

It has been ordained from the beginning of time that some men *shan't* and others *can't.*

These are to be blamed: let them be damned.

I enjoy the Colonel very much, and shall enjoy the rest of him with an obscene delight. (pp. 719-21)

Mark Twain, in a letter to Reverend J. H. Twichell in February, 1902, in his Mark Twain's Letters, Vol. II, *edited by Albert Bigelow Paine, Harper & Row, 1971, pp. 719-21.*

CARL VAN DOREN (essay date 1920)

[*Van Doren is considered one of the most perceptive American critics of the first half of the twentieth century. He was for many years a professor of English at Columbia University and served as literary editor and critic of the* Nation *and the* Century *during the 1920s. A founder of the Literary Guild and author or editor of several American literary histories, Van Doren was also a critically acclaimed historian and biographer. Howard Moss wrote of him: "His virtues, honesty, clarity, and tolerance are rare. His vices, occasional dullness and a somewhat monotonous rhetoric, are merely, in most places, the reverse coin of his excellence." In the following excerpt, Van Doren compares Edwards and Benjamin Franklin, noting the conflicting qualities they embody.*]

[The contrast between the careers of Benjamin Franklin and Jonathan Edwards] came to be so remarkable, so dramatic, that we may now regard them as protagonists and symbols of the hostile movements which strove for the mastery of their age. (Franklin, chief of the victors, we know far better than the defeated Edwards, who all his life upheld a cause which even in his youth was lost, had he but known it, and who seems on most of his pages to speak of forgotten issues in a forgotten dialect; while Franklin seems contemporaneous, fresh, full of vitality. . . . Edwards survives, so far as he may be said to survive at all, outside technical histories of Calvinism and metaphysics, chiefly as a dim figure preaching sermons full of awful imprecations and hardly at all as a remarkable scientific observer, and one of the impressive mystics of the world. Judged both of them by those of their writings which seem most intelligible and living today,—Franklin's merely utilitarian and Edwards' merely theological performances left out of account,—they are for themselves greatly important. But they grow more important when we perceive that Edwards was the resounding voice of a whole party which wanted to restore New England to the apostolic virtues of its first century, as he might have said; or to drive New England back to the dusky, witch-haunted forests wherein the first settlers had lived, body and soul, as Franklin might have preferred to put it, himself easily the first of those who led his whole country, and not merely New England, toward the blessed sun of cheerfulness and reason. (pp. ix-x)

Edwards exceeded Franklin no further in experience of God and the deeper soul of man than he was exceeded by him in experience of daily realities and human behavior; Franklin could not have written the *Personal Narrative* nor Edwards *The Way to Wealth*. (p. xx)

[Franklin was] the most completely representative and fully rounded figure which the eighteenth century produced in America and Europe.

The most completely representative—and yet Edwards too was of that age, and must be kept sight of, a flaming point in the sober background of the picture. The dream of a divine paradise faded slowly from the New England imagination, the high crystal-walled city of the Pilgrim hope melted away stubbornly before the grayer, solider towns which the sons of the Pilgrims planted. If the weapons of Edwards, his unendurable doctrines, his irresistible imprecations, were terrible, so were those of Franklin ruthless, his confidence in the material world, his sure-footed prudence, and his commonsense, which destroyed as it built. We may not withhold from Edwards the tribute of perceiving that he was tragically born out of his true century, that fate cast him with a mystic's vision into a generation which was unlearning that vision in its discovery of human dignity and self-sufficiency; nor may we forget that it was Franklin's fortune as well as his glory that the inexplicable accident of birth threw him upon a coast which he could explore, every gulf and bay and farm and city, unhaunted by any innative memories of a more illustrious region. Our sympathies are strongly with Franklin, in spite of some sentiment of pity for Edwards defeated, because we, as the sons of Franklin, naturally honor our ancestor. And yet after two hundred years, now that pious ties have ceased to bind us very closely to one rather than the other, we can see that they are not merely ancestors, not merely protagonists of an eighteenth-century conflict, but also symbols of two principles perennially contending among men. Take away from Edwards the merely doctrinal implications in his conviction that "the work of God in the conversion of one soul, considered together with the source, foundation, and purchase of it, and also the benefit, end, and eternal issue of it, is a more glorious work of God than the creating of the whole material universe," and there remains something by which the spirit of man is lifted and glorified above all the meaner dangers of life as in the revelations of the greatest prophets. Take away from Franklin some of the alloy of his earthiness, his too incessant shrewdness and his ranker appetites, and there remains the pure distillation of human experience, the quintessence of that indispensable wisdom which comes not from illumination but from the fruitful study of all that it is given to our senses and our reason to perceive. Poetry and prudence may each wonder that the other can find in his universe so much that seems important, and may each condemn the other for so great a waste of life, but mankind at large profits by their disagreements. They divide the world, but so do they multiply it. (pp. xxxiii-xxxiv)

Carl Van Doren, in an introduction to Benjamin Franklin and Jonathan Edwards: Selections from Their Writings *by Benjamin Franklin and Jonathan Edwards, edited by Carl Van Doren, Charles Scribner's Sons, 1920, pp. ix-xxxiv.*

CLARENCE DARROW   (essay date 1925)

[*Darrow was an American lawyer, social reformer, lecturer, and writer who defended many unpopular causes during his legal career. His most famous case, known as the Scopes Monkey Trial, opened the door to the teaching of biological evolution in America's public schools. In this 1925 trial, Darrow defended John Scopes, a Tennessee schoolteacher accused of teaching his stu-dents the theory of evolution, a theory bitterly opposed by Christian fundamentalists. Darrow, a self-professed agnostic, lost the case, but his brilliant cross-examination of the prosecuting attorney, William Jennings Bryan, won a public relations victory. In the following excerpt from an essay written but a few months after the trial, Darrow condemns Edwards's theology.*]

[Jonathan Edwards] was a Fundamentalist, stern and unyielding. He was filled with religious zeal and ardor and never suffered a doubt to lodge in his brain. (pp. 149-50)

He delighted in defending the most cruel dogmas and doctrines. He seemed to take joy in the thought of eternal hell for the wicked. Some of the titles of his numerous sermons show the ferocious nature of his religion: **"Future Punishment of the Wicked"**; **"Wrath Upon the Wicked to the Uttermost"**; a series entitled **"Man Naturally God's Enemies"**; **"The Misery of Unbelievers"**; **"A Warning to Professors"**; **"Of Endless Punishment."** Or take, for example, these two titles from his essays: *The Great Christian Doctrine of Original Sin Defended* and *The Justice of God in the Damnation of Sinners.* But his greatest effort, prototype of all the rest, was **"Sinners in the Hands of an Angry God."** (p. 150)

In the name of his Master who said, "Suffer little children to come unto Me," he talked of infant depravity in such language as this: "As innocent as young children seem to be to us, yet if they are out of Christ they are not in God's sight, but are young vipers, and infinitely more hateful than vipers; and are in most miserable condition as well as grown persons; and they are naturally very senseless and stupid, 'being born as the wild ass's colt' and need much to awaken them."

But enough. . . . Even cold and Puritan New Englanders could not stand this man of God. They drove him from his church for his hard and ruthless theology. (p. 151)

Who was Jonathan Edwards? Except for his weird and horrible theology, he would have filled no place in American life. His main business in the world was scaring silly women and little children and blaspheming the God he professed to adore. Nothing but a distorted or diseased mind could have produced his **"Sinners in the Hands of an Angry God."** (p. 153)

Clarence Darrow, "The Edwardses and the Jukeses," in The American Mercury, *Vol. VI, No. 22, October, 1925, pp. 147-57.*

VERNON LOUIS PARRINGTON   (essay date 1927)

[*Parrington was an American historian, critic, and educator who contributed regularly to such prestigious reference works as* Encyclopaedia Britannica *and* The Cambridge History of American Literature. *He was awarded a Pulitzer Prize for the first two volumes of his influential* Main Currents in American Thought *(1927); the third volume remained unfinished at the time of his death. In this series, Parrington composed, according to Michael O'Brien, "not a study of American literature so much as of American political thought refracted through literature." While his efforts are still widely admired today, many critics contend that his unabashedly liberal bias, and his summary literary judgments of Edgar Allan Poe, Nathaniel Hawthorne, Henry James, and others, compromise his work. In the following excerpt, Parrington explores the tension between Edwards's dual roles as philosophical idealist and reactionary Calvinist.*]

To one cardinal principle Edwards was faithful—the conception of the majesty and sufficiency of God; and this polar idea provides the clue to both his philosophical and theological systems.

Yet with this as a guide there is much that remains perplexing. There are inconsistencies in his thought as there were in his pastoral life; and we shall understand his position only when we recognize the contrary tendencies which confused him, as the inevitable consequences of a system of thought that was at once reactionary and progressive, the outcome of certain latent inconsistencies too antagonistic for any thinker to reconcile. (pp. 155-56)

In his early years, before his conversion turned him aside from his true path, setting the apologetics of the theologian above the speculations of the philosopher, Edwards gave promise of becoming a strikingly creative thinker. Following the native bent of his genius, he plunged into the study of metaphysics with such fruitful results that it seemed likely that New England Puritanism was at last to come to flower; that the mystical perception of the divine love, which had steeped the early Puritan thought in emotion and quickened it to poetry, was now to create a system of philosophy which, like transcendentalism in the next century, should adequately express the aspirations of the New England mind. There is no more interesting phase in the early history of Edwards than the transition from religious mysticism to philosophical idealism. The yearning for the knitting of the soul to Christ, as expressed in the imagery of the Song of Songs, burgeoned into a larger idealism that translated the Rose of Sharon and the Lily of the Valley into an all-pervasive spirit of divine life. In certain moods it is the mystic who cries, "My soul breaketh for the longing it hath; my soul waiteth for the Lord, more than they who watch for the morning." . . . In other moods the intellect gains ascendency over the emotions, and it is the idealistic metaphysician who speaks. With a searching curiosity that impelled him to ask what lies behind the outward semblance of things, binding them into a coherent whole and imparting to the world of experience a compelling unity, he came early to an interpretation distinctly Berkeleyan. From what source he derived it has been much debated and remains unanswered; nevertheless it is clear that it is closely related to his religious mysticism. When he inquired what lies back of the outward semblance, what is the thing in itself behind attributes and qualities, the existence of which is implicit in our perception of time and space, but which cannot be resolved into the things perceived, it was natural that he should have interpreted this *Ding an sich* ["thing in itself"] in terms of God. "Men are wont to content themselves by saying merely that it is something; but that something is *He* in whom all things consist." The world of sensation thus translates itself into a world of ideas; and this world of ideas, the expression of the divine mind, is the only reality. The more important of his early generalizations are . . . from his notes on the **"Mind"**: "Bodies have no existence of their own." "All existence is mental; the existence of all things is ideal." (pp. 156-57)

Edwards had come to such conclusions before the normal unfolding of his mind was interrupted by his conversion. From the first a strong bias toward theology had tended to warp his interest in the purely metaphysical, and with the quickening of an active religious experience, he turned to examine the dogmas which expressed his faith. The call of the churches in distress came to him, and he made ready his logic to do battle with the enemy. Against the twin tendencies that were undermining the foundations of Calvinism—Arminianism with its humanistic emphasis and deism with its mechanistic—the deepest instincts of Edwards protested. The profound God-consciousness that filled him was stirred by what seemed an infidel attack upon the divine glory and sufficiency; the mystic and

idealist was aroused to protest against a theology that conceived of religion as consisting of benevolence toward men rather than in union with God; and against a philosophy that in constructing a mechanical system was de-personalizing God into a vague First Cause, and bowing him politely out of the universe. In so great a crisis his duty seemed clear—to vindicate, not the ways of God, but God himself to men; to assert the glory and sufficiency of God even to the extent of minifying the capacities and potentialities of man.

The basis of his defense was already provided in his metaphysics, the conception of the divine idea existent in God's mind and expressed in His stable will. The needs of his polemics, however, thrust into relief the secondary rather than the primary element in his philosophy, exalting the doctrine of the divine will to the obscuring of the divine idea. How this came about is sufficiently clear in the light of the fact that in explaining the existence of evil, Calvinism fell back on determinism: the dogma of election could be fitted to the conception of a precise and stable will of God. The long feud between Arminianism and Calvinism resulted from emphasis laid upon different attributes of the Godhood. Shall God be interpreted in terms of will or love? If He is the sovereign ruler of the universe, He is also the common father; and that which broadly divides later theological systems from earlier is the shift from the former interpretation to the latter. The strategic weakness of Edwards's position lay in his assumption of the divine sovereignty as a cardinal postulate.

But in adhering to the doctrine of predetermined election by the sovereign will of God, Edwards did unconscious violence to the instincts of the mystic, that throughout his earlier speculations—and in much of his later, as well—impelled him to glorify the love of God the Father, and the sweetness of spiritual communion with Him. The practical necessities of the preacher, called upon to uphold the dogma of election in face of growing disbelief, seem to have forced him to such a position; but once having entered upon the train of speculation opened by the question of divine polity involved in "His having mercy on whom He will have mercy, while whom He will, He hardeneth," he came somewhat reluctantly to accept the doctrine of God's sovereignty as the cardinal principle of his theology, the creative source of his thinking. Thereafter he followed a path that led back to an absolutist past, rather than forward to a more liberal future. He had broken wholly with the social tendencies of his age and world. (pp. 158-59)

His celebrated work, *On the Freedom of the Will* . . . not only was his most important contribution to theology, but it was the last great defense of the conservatism that was stifling the intellectual life of New England.

The argument of this knotty book rests on a psychological rather than a metaphysical basis. Compressed into the briefest terms it runs thus: will is subject to desire, and desire follows what seems to us good; hence the determining impulse is to be sought in the impulse to seek the apparent good. The ethical import of such an argument will turn, of course, upon the character of the good which the natural man may be expected to desire. To Rousseau with his benevolent interpretation of human nature nothing is to be feared from the subjection of will to desire. Nor to the younger Edwards, feeling his way along the path of transcendentalism, rediscovering the doctrine of the inner light, was such subjection to be feared. In a remarkable sermon . . . he had expounded the thesis, "That there is such a thing as a Spiritual and Divine Light, immediately imparted to the Soul by God, of a different nature from any that is obtained by natural means.'' The divine splendor which the idealist had seen diffused through the material world the theologian was now merging with the regenerative life of the Holy Spirit which ''acts in the mind of a saint as an in-dwelling vital principle.'' It is ''a kind of emanation of God's beauty, and is related to God as the light is to the sun''; it is a new vision by means of which one may ''see the beauty and loveliness of spiritual things.'' In such a reinterpretation of the Quaker doctrine—so harshly condemned by the earlier Puritans—Edwards entered upon a train of thought that threatened to disrupt the entire Calvinistic system. He was at the dividing of the ways; he must abandon transcendentalism or the dogma of total depravity.

Instead he sought refuge in compromise, endeavoring to reconcile what was incompatible. Herein lay the tragedy of Edwards's intellectual life; the theologian triumphed over the philosopher, circumscribing his powers to ignoble ends. The field of efficiency allotted by the later theologian to this ''in-dwelling vital principle'' was no longer coextensive with the universe, but was narrowed to the little world of the elect. In the primal state of man, Edwards argued, before the sin of Adam had destroyed the harmony between creature and creator, the light which flowed from God as from a sun shone freely upon His universe, filling its remotest parts with the divine plenitude; but with the fall the harmony was destroyed, the sun was hidden, and only stray beams broke through the rifts to shine upon those whom God willed them to shine upon; all else in creation was given over to eternal darkness. And if the natural man, thus cast into sudden darkness ''as light ceases in a room when the candle is withdrawn,'' is a being whose will is impotent to his salvation, it follows that he will now be impelled as inevitably towards evil as before he was impelled towards good. Every instinct of a nature corrupt and compact of sin, and with no wish to exchange darkness for light—having no eyes for the divine glory—drives him to a blind and consuming hatred of God. He is become as a loathsome ''viper, hissing and spitting poison at God,'' the outcast and pariah of the universe. There is no drawing back from the conclusion involved in the argument; the Edwardean logic moves forward by regular steps. The punishment meted out to sin is to be measured by the excellence of which the sin is a denial. God is of infinite excellence, and denial of His excellence is therefore infinitely sinful and merits infinite punishment. As a perfectly just judge God could not decree otherwise; because of the infinite heinousness of his sin, the natural man must receive the doom of eternal damnation.

Under the rod of such logic—grotesque, abortive, unseasoned by any saving knowledge of human nature—Edwards preached that remarkable series of imprecatory sermons that sank deep into the memory of New England, and for which it has never forgiven him. (pp. 160-62)

As one follows the laborious career of this great thinker, a sense of the tragic failure of his life deepens. The burdens that he assumed were beyond the strength of any man. Beginning as a mystic, brooding on the all-pervasive spirit of sweetness and light diffused through the universe, with its promise of spiritual emancipation; then turning to an archaic theology and giving over his middle years to the work of minifying the excellence of man in order to exalt the sovereignty of God; and finally settling back upon the mystical doctrine of conversion—such a life leaves one with a feeling of futility, a sense of great powers baffled and wasted, a spiritual tragedy enacted within the narrow walls of a minister's study. . . . The greatest mind of New England had become an anachronism in a world that bred Benjamin Franklin. If he had been an Anglican like Bishop Berkeley, if he had mingled with the leaders of thought in London instead of remaining isolated in Massachusetts, he must have made a name for himself not unworthy to be matched with that of the great bishop whom he so much resembled. The intellectual powers were his, but the inspiration was lacking; like Cotton Mather before him, he was the unconscious victim of a decadent ideal and a petty environment. Cut off from fruitful intercourse with other thinkers, drawn away from the stimulating field of philosophy into the arid realm of theology, it was his fate to devote his noble gifts to the thankless task of re-imprisoning the mind of New England within a system from which his nature and his powers summoned him to unshackle it. He was called to be a transcendental emancipator, but he remained a Calvinist. (p. 165)

Vernon Louis Parrington, ''The Anachronism of Jonathan Edwards,'' in his Main Currents in American Thought: The Colonial Mind, 1620-1800, Vol. I, *1927. Reprint by Harcourt Brace Jovanovich, 1955, pp. 155-65.*

FREDERIC I. CARPENTER (essay date 1931)

[*An American educator and critic, Carpenter edited the* New England Quarterly *from 1929 to 1937. He is the author of* Emerson and Asia *(1930) and* American Literature and the Dream *(1955). In the following excerpt, he investigates what he terms Edwards's radical ''psychology of mysticism.''*]

Edwards was the last and greatest of the royal line of Puritan theologians, with regard to the symbols which he used to express his thought. But in the radical quality of his thinking Edwards was the first, if not the greatest, of a royal line of modern American mystics. (pp. 629-30)

All of Edwards's work was founded on a psychology of mysticism, which was radically different from the theology of Calvinism. The relation of the two elements appears throughout the three chief periods of his life, but the victory of mysticism was achieved only in his final period. As a boy he was a precocious idealist who made daring hypotheses concerning the nature of knowledge, before undergoing intense mystical experiences and becoming ''converted'' to a Christianity generally called Calvinism. As a man he combined the ideology of this Calvinism with a practical psychology derived directly from an acute analysis of his own religious experiences, and of his own sinful impulses. He used this composite system because it accomplished his purpose—namely, the conversion of souls. But he outgrew this system, just as Emerson was later to outgrow Boston Unitarianism. He broke with his church, but also he transcended it; for his parishioners preferred to remain on the level of the old and less strenuous Calvinistic theology. They did not object to his pictures of hell, but they did object to the high level of religious emotion which he expected them to maintain in their daily lives. So he retired to Stockbridge, and there slowly advanced from his diluted Calvinism to a mystic pantheism, which carried the seeds of the thought of many later writers. Yet he had used the phraseology of Calvinism too long, for he never quite realized the implications of his new mysticism. He never took the final steps to the end of the long trail which he had blazed through the dark forests of Mansoul.

Edwards wrote his great arguments against the freedom of the will shortly after being dismissed from his church. Then, in the following years, he wrote two speculative treatises which were not published till after his death—the more important one *Concerning the End for Which God Created the World.* In all probability he refrained from publishing these in his own lifetime because of their unorthodoxy—although they merely suggest the radical implications of his thought. Their argument runs: that God created the world to give outward expression to His own infinite fullness—that is, that God created the world out of Himself. The world exists in order to make manifest His own perfection; and the world's substance is an emanation of the divine substance. If God loves the world, it is because the world is an expression of His own perfection, and thus in loving the world, He is merely loving Himself. This is utter pantheism, and certainly no Calvinism. But how was Edwards to reconcile this mystic doctrine to his own Calvinistic conception of hell, and of man as naturally evil? If man is part of the divine substance, why is man evil? (pp. 633-35)

If God created the world by an emanation of His own Godhood, and man consists of God's own substance, then the evil in man must correspond to the evil in God. In loving the good in man, God loves His own goodness; in hating the evil in man, God hates His own iniquity. Pantheism has reached its logical conclusion in this argument which Edwards never advanced. (pp. 636-37)

Between his tragic realization of the place of evil in the scheme of things and the similar tragic realization of modern writers, such as Robinson Jeffers, lies the mystic optimism of the Transcendentalists and of Walt Whitman, who accepted evil joyfully. . . . Edwards's mystic doctrines were developed and harmonized by writers of the nineteenth century, but his tragic intensity was not reproduced until the twentieth.

The parallel between Edwards and Robinson Jeffers suggests how essentially modern Edwards's "Calvinism" was. Both he and Jeffers use violent imagery of the most terrible sort to impress man with a sense of his own utter sin and worthlessness, because, as Jeffers writes, "to forget evil calls down Sudden reminders from the clouds." It is only through a realizing sense of the utter sin of the world that the redeemed man is able to become the hero described by Jeffers, who "cast humanity, and entered in the earlier fountain." (pp. 638-39)

Edwards's most famous treatise on *Freedom of Will* was almost as radical as his later purely speculative works. It took up a position which had been maintained in his time by no notable writers except the materialists and free-thinkers such as Hobbes and Hume, whom most religious men discounted. Now Edwards, the great Christian theologian, argued to a conclusion almost identical with theirs. His seemed to be good Calvinism, but the men in the churches were disturbed. And well they might be.

Edwards argued to the apparent conclusions of Calvinistic theology, but he used the materials and the methods of a new empirical psychology, and this psychology was derived chiefly from his own experience and observation. He was merely carrying out his early resolution to trace back any conspicuously evil action till he came to the original cause of it. And by this process he found that morality was not a purely rational affair, such as Franklin imagined it, depending on the rules and prescriptions of society; but that it was essentially an impulsive, emotional process. Man was governed by his heart rather than by his head, and if man was unillumined, he could not be truly moral. Edwards had expounded this in an earlier sermon entitled **"A Divine and Supernatural Light, immediately imparted to the Soul by the Spirit of God,"** saying:

There is a twofold knowledge of good of which God has made the mind of man capable. The first, that which is merely notional; as when a person only speculatively judges that anything is [good], which, by the agreement of mankind, is called good or excellent. . . . And the other is, that which consists in a sense of the heart; as when the heart is sensible of pleasure and delight in the presence of the idea of it. In the former is exercised merely the speculative faculty, or the understanding, in distinction from the will or disposition of the soul. In the latter, the will, or inclination, or heart are mainly concerned.

The essential fact is that Edwards had already identified "the will" with "inclination" or "heart." In his later treatise he altered this definition only slightly, so that he was easily able to show how this "will" was dependent on "the previous bias and inclination" of the individual, which thus determined the apparently free choice between good and evil made by the will. In adopting this psychological definition of will, in opposition to the common-sense, or moral definition of Locke, who held that "the Will is perfectly distinguished from Desire; which in the very same action may have a quite contrary tendency from that which our Wills set us upon," Edwards was taking a radical departure. His psychology of desire traced the fruit of an action down to its roots which lay embedded in the complex of desire and impulse hidden from the light of common-sense morality. Thus human beings are not free, because their moral choices are determined by their earlier inclinations, and these inclinations (as modern psychology, following Edwards's method, has argued) are conditioned by childhood training and by inheritance, and these, in their turn, can be traced back by the necessary links of the chain of causality even into the womb. Man is not free, because his nature derives so completely from antecedent conditions.

This psychology which Edwards initiated seemed dangerous to many of his contemporaries, and in our time sounds no less radical. It tends to do away with external morality—with what merely "by the agreement of mankind, is called good or excellent." In many ways it can be compared with the modern determinism of such a writer as Theodore Dreiser, whose "biochemistry" of human affairs is frankly opposed to all the moralizing of the reformers. (pp. 639-41)

All of these parallels between Edwards and modern writers are perhaps accidental, and may be due to the inevitable recurrence of certain strains of thought in the spiritual development of a people. But one parallel is indubitable—that between Edwards and William James as historians and analysts of the mystic experience. Edwards's *Personal Narrative* of his own conversion, and his *Treatise on Religious Affections* furnished James both with material and method for his great study of *The Varieties of Religious Experience.* James quotes Edwards often throughout his book, using Edwards's material freely. . . . Edwards's method was certainly pragmatic at times, but . . . he also tried to uncover the roots of religious experience; and in this he was far more radical than James.

Edwards's *Faithful Narrative of the Surprising Work of God in the Conversion of many hundred Souls in Northampton* might well have been entitled "Varieties of Religious Experience," although there is no evidence that James used this particular work. The *Narrative* is rich in first-hand accounts of conversions, and Edwards expressly says: "here there is a vast variety, perhaps as manifold as the subjects of the operation; but yet in many things there is a great analogy in all." Although Edwards never fully formulated the "analogies," or the steps of the mystic experience, he again offered the material for the formulation, and the results, as compiled by later writers, are closely parallel to the results of James. Edwards was the first of many Americans who have been fascinated by the psychology of mysticism.

It would be superfluous to insist further on the radicalism of Edwards's thought. There is general agreement by now that he unconsciously helped lay the foundations for the American Revolution which was to come. His utter insistence on the Sovereignty of God minimized the authority of man. By nature all men were equals before the supreme God who chose whom He would to be saved. The inner illumination was all that mattered to Edwards. Indeed he noted that "There has been much talk in many parts of the country, as though the people had symbolized with the Quakers"—the Quakers who kept their hats on before kings. If the individual was supreme, and the former presbyters no longer governed the land, what was to prevent the breaking of the last bond with the past—the bond with England. . . . The preaching of Jonathan Edwards contained in itself the seeds of revolution, both for the eighteenth century, and for the twentieth. (pp. 642-44)

Frederic I. Carpenter, "The Radicalism of Jonathan Edwards," in The New England Quarterly, Vol. IV, October, 1931, pp. 629-44.

CHARLES ANGOFF (essay date 1931)

[*A naturalized American citizen born in Russia, Angoff was a prolific writer of novels, plays, short stories, and literary criticism, who is most famous for his series of novels describing the Jewish experience in American life. Also a prominent journalist, he was associated with many American newspapers and magazines, and served as editor of the* American Mercury *and the* Literary Review, *among others. In the following excerpt from an essay originally published in 1931, Angoff analyzes the tension between Edwards the philosopher and Edwards the Calvinist.*]

There is no more devastating argument against Calvinism and all it means that the life and deeds of Jonathan Edwards, the last and greatest champion of Puritanism in New England. . . . In sheer intellectual resourcefulness he was on a par with such giants as Kant, Spinoza, Hume, Pascal, and Leibnitz. . . . He was one of the world's greatest preachers in his day. He was unquestionably the clearest and most effective writer of all the Puritan divines. And yet today he is remembered mainly by his barbaric sermon, **"Sinners in the Hands of an Angry God,"** and his influence upon enlightened American thought is nil.

He had it in him to become an American Kant or Luther, but he ended his life only as a somewhat more intelligent Cotton Mather. On at least two occasions he came close to composing works of lasting metaphysical value, as witness his celebrated *Inquiry into the Modern Prevailing Notions Respecting that Freedom of the Will which is supposed to be Essential to Moral Agency* and the . . . *Treatise of Religious Affections.* But in each case, at the critical moment, Calvinism got control of his mind and ruined completely the brilliancy and logical cogency of both endeavors. Posterity has dealt harshly with his memory, as it always deals harshly with the memories of half-hearted and two-minded men. It has forgotten the giant that was in him but was never allowed full egress, and it has remembered only the pathetic, befuddled, sickly, angry Puritan, struggling in vain to stem back the new day that was being ushered in by a restless printer-contemporary, Benjamin Franklin. (pp. 289-90)

[Edwards] was surely no theological scholar. He made no contribution whatever to Biblical studies. Neither was he a kindly preacher. Hell was always in his mind, and the words of its tortures in his mouth and pen. There was no love in him for the human race; he hated all of Adam's children with a hatred bordering on the pathological. And yet it would be wrong to dismiss his preachings as the product of a disarranged mind. If he was incapable of the love of man, he was capable of the love of God and of nature, and to an extraordinary degree. The selections from his diary and from his stray observations . . . prove beyond a doubt that he was, in a way, a mystic, not a St. Francis to be sure, but a mystic nevertheless. True enough, he relegated his mysticism far to the background after his conversion, but he never disposed of it completely. (p. 302)

Edwards' real greatness lay in his philosophical studies. It is to them that he devoted his best intellectual powers. It would seem, indeed, that he was more interested in them, deep down in his heart, than in theological speculation. He never wrote one book that dealt wholly with theology, save it be *Original Sin.* To get at his ideas regarding election and redemption, one must plow through hundreds of his sermons and writings, for he comes upon them suddenly, and then rushes on to his angry imprecations against sin. But in the field of philosophy he wrote at least four books dealing almost exclusively with that subject. They were *Religious Affections, Dissertation Concerning the Nature of True Virtue, Dissertation concerning the End for Which*

The Northampton Meetinghouse, built by Edwards.

God Created the World, and *An Inquiry into the Modern Prevailing Notions Respecting that Freedom of the Will which is supposed to be Essential to Moral Agency.*

In metaphysics Edwards was, in the main, a theistic idealist. But he was never wholly clear on this point. There were times when he came perilously close to being a pagan pantheist, and there were other times when he went the whole way with Plautus. He never came to a definite stand in his metaphysics. It is plain, however, that there was a great deal of the idealist in him. (p. 303)

Edwards was an idealist, a Christian and a pagan pantheist, all in one. That he was singularly acute in the logic of his idealism does not make his contradictory position any better. The fact was that the Christian in him tended to predominate. His pantheism, for example, never approached the large-hearted pantheism of Spinoza, for whom the knowledge of God was the complete love of Him, and the supreme expression and attainment of human happiness. Not so for Edwards. . . .

Edwards' argument for the existence of God was mainly like Descartes' ontological proof, but it also had a moral element in it, which is very similar to Kant's in *The Critique of Practical Reason.* Neither Kant nor Edwards made any radical distinction between morality and religion, and to both God was essentially a moral being. Moreover, both looked upon ethics as the deepest interest in nature. (p. 305)

For Kant, however, the notion of the moral essence of the universe was got at as the result of a long and arduous process of reasoning. To Edwards it was a self-evident fact, demanding no proof. Whenver he treated of God or of His place in the universe, he never argued; he made affirmations.

Edwards' celebrated book on the freedom of the will deserves most of the encomiums that have been heaped upon it. There is a display of logical reasoning in it that is truly amazing. As a minute, persistent, tireless philosophical essay, it is one of the wonders of American thought. (p. 306)

Until toward the end, the essay is one of the most impregnable arguments for determinism ever made, and is deserving of what Dugald Steward has called it: ''a work which never was and never will be answered.'' But as he approached the end of his inquiry Edwards let flee his meticulously philosophical attitude and became the angry theologian again, and by one of the most brummagem pieces of reasoning attempted to prove that it was quite consistent with determinism for man to be a free agent when it came to the worship of God and the observance of the Calvinistic polity, and to suffer the torments of hell if he does not experience conversion and go to church regularly and submit to baptism and partake of the Sacrament of bread and adhere to all the other tenets of the Puritan church. (p. 308)

[To compare Edwards with Novalis, Spinoza, Hume, Aquinas, and Calvin] is nonsense. To be sure, if one searches his writings carefully enough, and indulges in some very fine and dubious ''interpretations,'' one can find hints in them of Hegel's philosophy of the absolute, of Schopenhauer's concept of the will as the essence of being, of Bain's psycho-physical parallelism, of James' pragmatism, of Kant's moral idealism, of Lotze's notion of the microcosm, of Leibnitz's preëstablished harmony, of Hume's skepticism, of Locke's empiricism, of Royce's curious Christian idealism, and even of Bertrand Russell's idea of neutral essences. But only hints. Just as Edwards was never the full theologian, so was he never the complete philosopher.

He always wavered between the two, though the former was generally in the ascendency. . . .

It is thus that Edwards emerges as one of the colossal tragedies in the history of American culture. He had it in him to become one of the greatest philosophers and theologians and genuine mystics of all time—an American Kant and Luther and St. Francis all in one. And on several occasions he came very close to being each of these. But every time, as he was about to make the last leap to greatness, his Calvinism intervened, and dragged him down to the state he was in immediately after his conversion—that of a stern and rabid, even though amazingly shrewd, and intellectually highly resourceful, Puritan, little better than Cotton Mather. (p. 309)

In short, he made of his intellectual life a compromise, and he paid the price of all compromisers: intellectual paralysis in his lifetime and oblivion after his death. Some disciples did carry on whatever there was definite in his teachings, but they were very few in number, and with their passing, the name of Edwards became no more than a subject of antiquarian interest. At no time did he have real lasting influence on American or world philosophical or theological thinking. Today he is not even an echo; he is no more than a word. He left nothing for posterity that is in the least vitalizing. (p. 310)

Charles Angoff, ''The Theologians—The Collapse of Puritanism as an Overt Official Force,'' in his A Literary History of the American People: From 1607 to the Beginning of the Revolutionary Period, Vol. 1, *1931. Reprint by Tudor Publishing Co., 1935, pp. 261-312.*

LUDWIG LEWISOHN　(essay date 1932)

[*A German-born American novelist and critic, Lewisohn was considered an authority on German literature, and his translations of Gerhart Hauptmann, Rainer Maria Rilke, and Jakob Wassermann are widely respected. In 1919 he became the drama critic for the* Nation, *serving as its associate editor until 1924, when he joined a group of expatriates in Paris. After his return to the United States in 1934, Lewisohn became a prominent sympathizer with the Zionist movement, and served as editor of the Jewish magazine* New Palestine *for five years. Many of his later works reflect his humanistic concern for the plight of the Jewish people. In the following excerpt, Lewisohn offers an extremely negative appraisal of Edwards's thought and works.*]

It has recently become a fashion to speak of Edwards as a man of commanding intellect. He was not that. He was a baffled poet and stylist, baffled by the moral pathology of his kind. The logical web he wove in his treatise on the *Freedom of the Will* was tight and tense. But his absurd assumptions invalidate all of his logical processes. Great minds, Spinoza, Locke, Hume, begin by breaking with the vulgar errors and delusions of their time. The faint popular memory and tradition have done quite right in neglecting Edwards' logical prowess and recollecting the sermon called **''Sinners in the Hands of an Angry God.''** There are early entries in his diary that have a mystical sweetness; there are others that show a quite enlightened psychological curiosity; there is his lovely and touching, though quite morbid description of Sarah Pierrepont, his future wife. These things fade. He fought his parishioners, determined to prevent the reading of fiction; he fed his sick soul on the eerie and ghastly conversion of little, neurotic children; he became convinced that the hysteria of the ''great awakening'' was a sign that the world's conversion to Calvinism ''may begin in America.'' The sadism of the earlier divines rises in him to a wild and poetic intensity: "The bow of God's wrath is bent and the arrow made ready on the string, and justice bends the arrow at your heart, and it is nothing but the mere pleasure of God . . . that keeps the arrow from being made drunk with your blood." One remembers Nathaniel Ward's "sword stark drunk with Irish blood." The image was a favorite one among the Puritans. Edwards marshalls the creation itself against the corruption of man. "The sun does not willingly shine upon you to give you light to serve sin and Satan; the world does not willingly yield her increase to satisfy your lusts." A baffled poet, a sick and corrupted soul. (pp. 17-18)

> Ludwig Lewisohn, "Beginnings," *in his* Expression
> in America, *Harper & Brothers, Publishers, 1932,*
> *pp. 1-57.*

OLA ELIZABETH WINSLOW (essay date 1940)

[*An American scholar, Winslow was a prominent authority on colonial religious history and an accomplished biographer of such figures as Edwards, John Eliot, Roger Williams, and John Bunyan. In the following excerpt from her Pulitzer Prize-winning biography of Edwards, Winslow characterizes his ultimate impact on American theology and culture.*]

What is [Jonathan Edwards'] greatness? In a word, it is the greatness of one who had a determining part in initiating and directing a popular movement of far-reaching consequence, and who in addition, laid the foundations for a new system of religious thought, also of far-reaching consequence. Religious leaders have often directed popular movements. Less often they have founded systems of thought. Less often still has the same leader done both. This was, in part, the distinction of Jonathan Edwards. He was a compelling preacher and also a master logician; an evangelist and also a thinker; a metaphysician on the side of the New Lights.

In both of these directions, his significance had chiefly to do with his emphasis on religion as a transforming individual experience, an emphasis he was privilged to make at one of the most favorable moments a religious leader could possibly have asked. His consequent success in what quickly became a great popular movement owed much to the hospitable time spirit, possibly more to the compulsion of his own personality and the force of his convictions; but it owed most of all to the idea itself, which really amounted to a redefinition of religion in terms of an inner, personal experience. By this new emphasis, which was really a much older emphasis, Jonathan Edwards became the initial, exciting force in a great religious crusade.

His mistake in choosing to speak through an outworn, dogmatic system instead of letting the new truth find more appropriate form of its own, was costly both to himself and to the truth he proclaimed. While he lived to speak directly, his ideas seemed more and the supporting framework less; but later, when he had gone and the traditional system came to be recognized as obsolete, his ideas seemed obsolete also. Actually, he had made substantial changes in the modified Calvinism he professed; but he had made them by way of amendment only, substituting new elements for old, and keeping the traditional phraseology, even when he had changed the meaning behind it. What he did not see was that amendment was not enough. The whole theological system needed to be demolished, most of it thrown away, and the few remaining pieces used in the formulating of a quite new order. He had already gone a long way in this direction himself, possibly further than he knew,

but not far enough to put him beyond the arid stretches of theological quibbling. The winning of many arguments became far too important. By his agility in dialectic he threw dust in the eyes of his brother intellectuals and also in his own. What he had to say did not require defence. It required only to be told. His failure to exchange a defensive warfare for leadership in a quite peaceful advance greatly limited his effectiveness in his own day. To a later judgment, it must also seriously qualify his greatness as an original thinker.

Considering the texture of his mind, one may wonder why he could not take the one more step and be free. Sometimes he did take it, but not habitually. He lacked the imagination; he lacked the mellowness and the flexibility which would have enabled him to get outside of the system and view it with enough detachment to judge it. He was on too narrow a track, and the surrounding walls were too high. For one whose thought was capable of telescopic range, and one who exhibited so large a degree of intellectual subtlety, his bondage seems almost a tragic pity. More than most men he was the prisoner of his own ideas. Yet this bondage presents no enigma. Back of it, in addition to the limitations of his personal heritage, lay three generations of Dissenting literalness, and far too many years of his own life spent in the far too industrious and too respectful study of pedestrian theologians, who trusted their hopes to logic and to logic alone. The vigor of Jonathan Edwards' moral earnestness has often enough been traced to the soil and the society from which he came. With equal reason one might say that his intellectual zeal and persistence and, in a measure, his intellectual blindness are traceable to the same sources. Among great Americans, he is perhaps the best example of one whose mind was cast strictly in the New England mold. (pp. 325-27)

What has he for a later day? Exactly what he had for his own, once his thought is taken out of the theological idiom. What is the divine sovereignty, as a conviction to live by, but the hope of a world order that can be trusted? What is eternal punishment but the insistence that right must eventually triumph over wrong, if that world order be essentially stable and just? What is "election" but the recognition that there are those who can find God and those whom no amount of teaching and leading and compelling can ever bring to a desire even to search for Him? One cannot confer sight upon the blind. What is human depravity but the reluctant notion that, left to himself, man is no credit to his kind? Certain modern novelists have called it "realism" and have written screeds which make Jonathan Edwards' view of original sin seem mild indeed. (p. 329)

Fundamentally, his beliefs were the beliefs of the great religionists of all ages. He believed that man's life is of eternal consequence. He believed that the imperfect world we see cannot be all. He believed that reality is of the spirit. He believed that there is a pathway to present peace in spite of the frustrations of life, and that man can find it, but not of himself. Had he been able to clothe these ideas in images which would have stirred men's minds as the Enfield sermon [**"Sinners in the Hands of an Angry God"**] stirred them, Emerson in his turn might have found other soil to plough.

As the details drop away, and his significance becomes clearer within the present century, the conclusion persists that as a shaping force in American culture, the man himself has been more important than anything he ever did or said or wrote. Among the great men of America, he is a lonely figure— perhaps the loneliest; and yet in spite of his severance from life as other men lived it, he stamped his personal imprint deep enough to outlast the generations. He was a man of one loyalty, and yet the total impression of his life, lived as it was without wide margins, or open spaces, or hearty human delights, is not an impression of narrowness or incompleteness. As an achievement in human living, the whole seems greater than the sum of its parts. Why, it is difficult to say, unless unity within the areas he knew helped to balance the realms he was content to let alone. By virtue of this same singleness of loyalty, there was and is no mistaking what he stood for. Even while he lived, he became the bright symbol of what he called a thousand times and more, ''the things of religion''. It has been his peculiar triumph to make that identification permanent. (pp. 329-30)

Ola Elizabeth Winslow, in her Jonathan Edwards, 1703-1758: A Biography, *The Macmillan Company, 1940, 406 p.*

ROBERT LOWELL   (poem date 1946)

[*Winner of two Pulitzer Prizes and a National Book Award, Lowell is generally considered the premier American poet of his generation. One of the original proponents of the confessional school of poetry, he frequently gave voice to his personal as well as his social concerns, leading many to consider him the prototypical liberal intellectual writer of his time. In his work he explored the contradictions in American life and the failure of Puritan ethics. A traditional stylist, he used complicated formal patterns and rhyme schemes while examining very personal topics, in contrast to the free-form style of the Beats. This concern with traditional forms culminated in his book-length sonnet sequence,* The Dolphin *(1973). Lowell was also a widely acclaimed translator and playwright as well as critic and editor. Although Lowell planned and researched a biography on Edwards, he abandoned the project when his interest waned; he did, however, compose several poems in which he addressed Edwards and his doctrines. The following poem, ''After the Surprising Conversions,'' is Lowell's response to Edwards's* A Faithful Narrative of the Surprizing Work of God in the Conversion of Many Hundred Souls in Northampton, *an account of the 1734-35 religious revival he helped to inspire. The incident to which Lowell refers in the poem is the suicide of Joseph Hawley, Edwards's uncle by marriage, who took his own life because he despaired of his soul's salvation.*]

September twenty-second, Sir: today
I answer. In the latter part of May,
Hard on our Lord's Ascension, it began
To be more sensible. A gentleman
Of more than common understanding, strict
In morals, pious in behavior, kicked
Against our goad. A man of some renown,
An useful, honored person in the town,
He came of melancholy parents; prone
To secret spells, for years they kept alone—
His uncle, I believe, was killed of it:
Good people, but of too much or little wit.
I preached one Sabbath on a text from Kings;
He showed concernment for his soul. Some things
In his experience were hopeful. He
Would sit and watch the wind knocking a tree
And praise this countryside our Lord has made.
Once when a poor man's heifer died, he laid
A shilling on the doorsill; though a thirst
For loving shook him like a snake, he durst
Not entertain much hope of his estate
In heaven. Once we saw him sitting late
Behind his attic window by a light
That guttered on his Bible; through that night
He meditated terror, and he seemed
Beyond advice or reason, for he dreamed
That he was called to trumpet Judgment Day

To Concord. In the latter part of May
He cut his throat. And though the coroner
Judged him delirious, soon a noisome stir
Palsied our village. At Jehovah's nod
Satan seemed more let loose amongst us: God
Abandoned us to Satan, and he pressed
Us hard, until we thought we could not rest
Till we had done with life. Content was gone.
All the good work was quashed. We were undone.
The breath of God had carried out a planned
And sensible withdrawal from this land;
The multitude, once unconcerned with doubt,
Once neither callous, curious nor devout,
Jumped at broad noon, as though some peddler groaned
At it in its familiar twang: ''My friend,
Cut your own throat. Cut your own throat. Now! Now!''
September twenty-second, Sir, the bough
Cracks with the unpicked apples, and at dawn
The small-mouth bass breaks water, gorged with spawn.

(pp. 60-1)

Robert Lowell, ''After the Surprising Conversions,'' in his Lord Weary's Castle, *Harcourt Brace Jovanovich, 1946, pp. 60-1.*

EDWIN H. CADY   (essay date 1949)

[*Cady is an American educator and prolific literary scholar who is the editor-in-chief of the distinguished periodical* American Literature. *He has written extensively on the works of William Dean Howells and other major American authors. In the following excerpt, Cady discusses the powerful imagery of ''Sinners in the Hands of an Angry God.''*]

From what is now increasingly apparent of Jonathan Edwards, it surprises that so quiet, academic, and sweet-natured a man could have preached sermons which broke his contemporaries down into storms of distress. Perhaps the most intriguing of these is **''Sinners in the Hands of an Angry God.''** . . . Why has it become the classic of hell-fire-and-brimstone preaching which so long shut out our view of the tender-minded and philosophic Edwards? It is perhaps too easy to lay the blame . . . on readers who would not read aright. At any rate, we are left with the fundamental question: what made the sermon so very effective? Where lie the springs of its success?

The answer, I think, is that it is in the widest sense a work of literary art. It uses all the weapons, conscious and subconscious, verbal, emotional, and sensuous, of the author at his best. (p. 61)

In the light of Edwards' reputation as polemicist one looks first to the intellectual structure of the sermon. Perhaps it is another example of his devastatingly tight, crushing logic. But a glance at the rational structure of the sermon shows it to be comparatively insignificant. In traditional form, Edwards gives his text (much more suggestive than doctrinal), four implications of the text, and ten ''observations'' upon his reading of it, before he passes on to its ''application'' to his audience. In the most simple fashion available to the Puritan homiletic tradition, the argument clusters about Edwards' ''proposition'': '''There is nohing that keeps wicked men at any one moment out of hell, but the mere pleasure of God.''' From this the argument runs: God can and should let them fall; He has already passed sentence on them; their natures are wicked, their claims on God and their powers of self-preservation worse than nothing; indeed, although God's rightful anger burns against their wickedness, nothing but His inscrutably capricious hand supports them. Let every sinner strive for grace while yet there is time. (pp. 61-2)

His aim was to stir the heart, to stimulate the soul, to turn the whole man to a devoted search for the springs of grace within him. . . . He did not lose dignity, academic poise, or logic. But he did blend thought, imagery, allusion, and personal reference in a way which can only be called organic, artistic, and poetic. (pp. 62-3)

Although thought, form, and imagery in the sermon are one, the great emotional power of the discourse comes primarily from the rich and versatile imagery. For "image" in this connection I mean a literary device by which the writer likens an inward state, that subjective fusion of sense, emotion, and recognition which we call experience, to something outward which can be used to convey approximately the same experience into the subjective inwardness of the reader. There are about twenty-five important "images" in **"Sinners in the Hands of an Angry God."** Not all of them are good: that is, artistically effective. Some are failures because they were mere clichés, others because they are not realized by the author, still others because they are somehow fumbled. But much the greater portion of them do work successfully, and their success carries Edwards' excruciatingly vivid vision alive into the minds of his hearers.

Perhaps the meaning of this can be clarified by turning first to some of Edwards' images which fail. Immersed in the highly figurative tradition both of the Bible and of seventeenth-century preaching, Edwards often thought naturally and unconsciously in metaphor—as his audience must also have done. And sometimes even so careful a stylist as he slipped into the use of outworn convention. In the second sentence of the sermon, for example, he observes that in despite of God's grace the Israelites of old by sin had "brought forth bitter and poisonous fruit." (p. 63)

Almost equally footless are the images which Edwards began to develop into means of true communication and then fumbled. Warning, for example, that there is "no security to wicked men," he noted that: "The arrows of death fly unseen at noonday; the sharpest sight cannot discern them." Like the devil as a roaring lion, the arrows of death by disease were too-familiar Biblical allusions. Edwards moved slightly toward realizing them for his listeners' imaginations but dropped the effort short of success. A failure more interesting because it is more ambitious is the metaphor which appears early in the "Application."

> There are black clouds of God's wrath now hanging directly over your heads, full of the dreadful storm, and big with thunder. . . . The sovereign pleasure of God, for the present, stays his rough wind; otherwise it would come with fury, and your destruction would come like a whirlwind, and you would be like the chaff of the summer threshing floor.

This one simply shows a failure of Edwards' imagination to carry through to artistic success a genuinely poetic impulse. In its context . . . the image is perfectly placed. It begins well, taking the storm-clouds black and pregnant with thunder as symbols of the ineffable wrath of God. But it weakens as it ceases to elaborate itself into objective terms of awe and terror. The real impulse fades out in the abstractions of "rough wind" and "whirlwind," and the scriptural clichés of chaff and threshing floor supply blank counters to fill in an imaginative void. Edwards could hardly have moved his audience with such imagery.

Inescapably, Edwards was addicted to the use of Biblical quotation and allusion with suggestive, figurative intent. Occasionally he was successful, especially with the text of his sermon. But for the most part he fails when he depends upon them rather than upon the careful, artistic elaboration of the symbols of his own imagination. An excellent case in point is section 2 of the "Application." Built around Scriptural references, it is emotionally frayed and flat in spite of Edwards' uncommon effort to heighten its effect with exclamation marks. Even the elaborate apocalyptic imagery at the end, of God trampling out the vintage of the blood of sinners, seems remote and unconvincing. This example, like the first paragraph of section 4 of the "Application," goes to show how unimpressive Edwards' message can be when the images fail to come, when his abstractions are not fleshed with the symbols of his passionate vision.

For Edwards' imagery is predominantly successful, and from its success springs the long-famed power of the sermon. By skilful timing and neat fitting into the context, he could pack even conventional images with meaning. . . . (pp. 64-5)

Yoked with the frustrated metaphor of the storm treated above, are two others, equally conventional to begin with, which grow and elaborate from within to fresh and muscular conclusions:

> The wrath of God is like great waters that are dammed for the present; they increase more and more, and rise higher and higher, till an outlet is given; and the longer the stream is stopped, the more rapid and mighty is its course, when once it is let loose . . . the waters are constantly rising, and waxing more and more mighty; and there is nothing but the mere pleasure of God, that holds the waters back, that . . . press hard to go forward. If God should only withdraw his hand from the flood-gate, it would immediately fly open, and the fiery floods of the fierceness and wrath of God, would rush forth with inconceivable fury. . . .

Here was an old image redesigned to startle Enfield out of its smugness. Every New Englander was intimate with his community's use of water power at the mill if nowhere else. The dramatic peril of floods as well as the daily power of the falling waters were familiar and exciting. And Edwards took the stuff of his hearers' own minds, raised it to the plane of his own intensity, and made his vision live in those minds. Picture, idea, and emotion existed together in the minds of speaker and listeners; the work of artistic communication had been done.

Much the same thing can be said of the accompanying image of God's wrath as an arrow bent on the creaking bow. It is a traditional picture to which is brought a sudden access of fresh terror by its notation of the vast tension of divine anger which may find shocking release when the arrow is "made drunk with your blood."

By the same token, the images which, being fresh, came most natively from Edwards' imagination and tallied most familiarly with the lives of his hearers, remain the most successful. They are individually the most memorable. Yet they are also the most organically fused with the message and the structural intent of the sermon as a whole. Like many of the images of the major poets, these of Edwards are surprisingly homely and immediate. At the very beginning, illustrating the text, "Their foot shall slide in due time," is a sort of generic picture of him that "walks in slippery places": a condition then as now realizable every New England winter. The walker is "every moment liable to fall, he cannot foresee one moment whether he shall stand or fall the next; and when he does fall, he falls at once without warning . . . without being thrown by the hand of another.'' He ''needs nothing but his own weight to throw him down.'' Then, as the thought has developed, Edwards applies it to sinners generally. ''God will not hold them up in these slippery places any longer, but will let them go; and then, at that very instant, they shall fall into destruction; as he that stands on such slippery declining ground, on the edge of a pit, he cannot stand alone, when he is let go he immediately falls and is lost.'' The fact that this has been expanded and elaborated step by step in conjunction with the four logical stages of the ''implications'' Edwards finds in his text makes it the more effective. And what member of the audience could fail to participate imaginatively, as he had often done physically, in the act of slipping to a fall? What hearer so dull that the sense of the slippery nature of worldly security did not begin to creep up the back of his mind?

Equally fresh is the ''observation'' 7 which sees ''Unconverted men walk over the pit of hell on a rotten covering, and there are innumerable places in this covering so weak that they will not bear their weight, and these places are not seen.'' And, of course, there is the climactic figure of the entire sermon, the image known to almost all literate persons, even those who have not read Edwards. To a people who lived long months by the hearth, whose leisure moments would often have been taken up in playing with the fire, it must have been horrifying to participate imaginatively (on both ends of the web) in the metaphysical *and* physical experience denoted in Edwards' saying

> The God that holds you over the pit of hell, much as one holds a spider, or some loathsome insect over the fire, abhors you, and is dreadfully provoked: . . . you are ten thousand times more abominable in his eyes, than the most hateful venomous serpent is in ours. . . .
>
> O Sinner! Consider the fearful danger you are in: it is a great furnace of wrath. . . . You hang by a slender thread, with the flames of divine wrath flashing about it, and ready every moment to singe it, and burn it asunder; and you have no interest in any Mediator, and nothing to lay hold of to save yourself, nothing to keep off the flames of wrath, nothing of your own, nothing that you ever have done, nothing that you can do, to induce God to spare you one moment.

If one had to guess the place where Edwards was forced to request silence from ''a breathing of distress, and weeping'' as Eleazar Wheelock remembered, it would be here, one supposes, beyond question. Certainly he temporarily changed direction to a more conventionally logical exposition before coming back again to the *ad hominem* attack. Much of the power of the figure is no doubt derived from its climactic position, its elaboration, and its composite admixture of other elements. But surely that all-too-empathic, homely picture of the disgusted Power, the flames, and the imminently shrivelling insect is the most potent factor.

A look at the kinds of imagery used in the sermon is revealing also. It is not surprising to find political and juridical imagery reflecting the covenant traditions of New England theology and politics. The theme of righteous king against rebellious subject is significantly used four times, including once as a sub-strand of the spider metaphor and again as the key to the whole of section 1 of the ''Application.'' The rather distantly Swiftian theme of disgust comes forward from ''We find it easy to tread on and crush a worm'' of ''observation'' 1, and ''the world would spew you out'' of the third paragraph of the ''Appli-

cation,'' to its climax in the spider metaphor. There is one sea image beside the ''great waters dammed'' figure, and a couple of swords of divine justice, including one fairly vivid ''the glittering sword is whet, and held over them.''

But the most telling images fall into three main groups: the fires of hell; the tension-pressure symbols of God's wrath; and suspension-heaviness symbols of the predicament of the sinner. Contrary to the accepted traditions about **''Sinners in the Hands of an Angry God,''** pictures of hell-fire appear to be neither its most vivid nor its most numerous images. By almost any count, fire-imagery amounts to little more than a quarter of the total of figures. Further, Edwards made surprisingly little effort to actualize fire for his audience. He used no color words and no objective heat words. Occasionally the flames ''flash'' or ''glow,'' but there is no attempt to make the reader see their infinite billows and feel their deathless, terrible pain comparable to that made in the sermon called **''The Future Punishment of the Wicked Unavoidable and Intolerable.''**

Actually, **''Sinners in the Hands of an Angry God''** is not directly concerned to create Hell imaginatively. Hell is in its picture, but only at the periphery. The focus is on the predicament of the sinner, how dreadfully he dangles *just before* he plunges to eternal agony, and while he has time to repent and be saved. The most striking and distinctive images in the work fall into two groups: (1) those which display the fearful wrath of God, and (2) those which portray dramatically (they seldom paint) the sinner shakily hanging. The tension-pressure images of wrath (those of the threatening sword, the storm, the flood, the bow, the wine-press, the grape-treading Deity) we have already examined. While they are pervasive and do much to suggest the emotional tension raised by the sermon, it is noteworthy that they are all fairly conventional, even when effectively used.

The freshest imagery, and the most essential to the peculiar success of the sermon, communicates Edwards' sense of the eerie suspension of the sinner upon almost nothing and intensifies it by adding a nightmarish feeling of his fatal weight. Dominantly these are kinesthetic, almost visceral, in their effects, rather than visual. Thus they appeal to the most fundamental human sense, one which is all too seldom commanded by writing. . . . In the third paragraph of the ''Application'' he points out with unusual kinesthetic effect:

> Your wickedness makes you as it were heavy as lead, and to tend downwards with great weight and pressure towards hell; and if God should let you go, you would immediately sink and swiftly descend and plunge into the bottomless gulf, and your healthy constitution, and your own care and prudence, and best contrivance, and all your righteousness, would have no more influence to uphold you and keep you out of hell, than a spider's web would have to stop a fallen rock.

From those points it is only a normal imaginative extrapolation to the magnificent, fearful drama of God and his loathsome, dangling spider. (pp. 65-70)

[The] secret of the effectiveness, then and since, of **''Sinners in the Hands of an Angry God''** resides first in the organic oneness of theme, image, and ''application.'' More directly, the emotional force of the sermon springs from the imagery itself, especially from the freshly imaginative, native figures which burned into the minds of his audience Edwards' vision of the horrible predicament of the sinner without grace.

Although this is not the occasion to defend Edwards from popular misconceptions, it should be apparent that he was not motivated by sadism, a rebellious libido, or any other psychiatric perversion. He was a mystic profoundly convinced of the reality of his subjective experience of God (and psychiatry has most unfortunately as yet neglected to tell us whence come creative and integrative personality forces). He was also a tender-minded pastor of the souls God and society had entrusted to him, and a responsible intellectual leader. As all these, he was faced with the problem of moving an audience left calloused, by generations of ordinary preaching, against the traditional appeals of Edwards' (and their) faith. It was his duty and his opportunity to throw all his imaginative and literary resources into the creation of a metaphysical *tour de force* which would provide profound conceptual and emotional experience for his audience so armored in ennui. His problem of expression was precisely that of a metaphysical poet: to find a means to drive out into effective form his overpowering sense of an inward reality. His problem of communication was even more exacting: to find "objective correlatives" which would carry his own experience into the minds of an audience bored with many repetitions of traditional Biblical and Puritanic conventions but otherwise unliterary. That he solved both problems brilliantly is attested both by contemporary evidence and by the eminence, savory or not, of the work ever since. By all the ordinary tests, **"Sinners in the Hands of an Angry God"** is a genuine work of literary art and testifies to Jonathan Edwards' right to the name of artist. (pp. 71-2)

> Edwin H. Cady, "The Artistry of Jonathan Edwards," in The New England Quarterly, *Vol. XXII, No. 1, March, 1949, pp. 61-72.*

PERRY MILLER (essay date 1949)

[*An American historian, Miller served for over thirty years as an instructor and professor at Harvard. The principal concern of his several published studies is America's Puritan heritage. In his two-volume* The New England Mind *(1939-54), a work noted for its thorough scholarship and wit, Miller demonstrated that the conventional view of the Puritans as purveyors of joylessness and of ruthlessly enforced moral coercion is contrary to historical fact. He is considered a pioneer in recording and interpreting the literature and culture of seventeenth-century New England. In the following excerpt, Miller explicates Edwards's arguments in* The Nature of True Virtue.]

The Nature of True Virtue is Edwards' only purely nonpolemical work; its perfection of form shows what he could have done with pure thought had he not for all his life been obliged to sacrifice himself to controversy. It takes Shaftesbury's and Hutcheson's definition of that by which, in the optimistic mechanism, the moral sense is supposed to judge: the rule of disinterested benevolence; and analyzes the internal structure of the idea. It is Edwards' supreme application of the method he learned at the beginning: "Truth consists in having perfect and adequate ideas of things.". . . The distinction which he declared the most important of all distinctions, between the speculative and the sensible, is here vindicated, for the book is not a reasoning about virtue but a beholding it. . . . He looks hard upon a conception until it yields up meaning beyond meaning, and the simulacra fall away. The book approaches, as nearly as any creation in our literature, a naked idea.

Edwards' conclusion is that what Hutcheson and the rationalists conceive as a natural possession of all mankind, the criterion of disinterested benevolence, is actually only a compounding of pleasure as against pain, nothing more than an extension of the principle of uniformity through wider and wider variety, a long-term instead of a short-term calculus, which nature can achieve unassisted by adding more and more to a column of figures. But true virtue, Edwards insists, is not a compound. It is, like the atom, a single insight; though it arises out of measurement, and recognizes the beauty "which consists in the visible fitness of a thing to its use and unity of design," it is not attained by a quantitative extension of the design. It is different in kind rather than in degree; it is an elevation of consciousness above the web of relations to the idea of relationship itself. Dr. Holmes. . . , voicing the attitude that for almost two centuries has prevented an understanding of Edwards, said that Edwards prescribed a rule of virtue more suited to angels than to flesh and blood [see excerpt dated 1880]—a statement with which, aside from the flippancy of tone, Edwards would agree. He was fully aware of how in fact humanity behave, but in his last years . . . he expanded to the full his mastery of the old Puritan disposition to expect the worst from mankind even while demanding the best, and composed a hymn to virtue which, upon the ultimate beholding, is pure intellectual beauty. (pp. 285-87)

True Virtue is all the greater a study because its composer knew that, by the absolute standard therein declared, he himself was as culpable as any.

Hence the greater part of this concentrated essay is a tracing out, with no rancor, as from an incalculable height of observation, of the manifold masquerades that self-love can resort to in the endless effort to simulate benevolence. By policy, by the craft of interest, the self will take into himself family, country, justice, conscientious righteousness, even admiration for noble deeds from which he receives no benefit, but which he can conceive as tending to his advantage "if there were opportunity and due application." Edwards called all such virtues, wherein a man loves others in "some way or other as appendages and appurtenances to himself," secondary virtue. Even in its most extended or intricate form, the secondary betrays its derivation by operating exclusively within the scheme of the objective good. It arises from a principle that unites the self to another being, "whereby the good of that other being does in a sort become his own," and must always be, in the necessary nature of a perceiving and willing being, an operative principle, even in his love to God. It is a gross misunderstanding of Edwards to conceive of him as condemning the natural goods, even the love of the self for itself, as in any sense intrinsically evil. On the contrary, when there is an agreement of desire with object, of an instinct with satisfaction, just as when the parts of a regular building agree with each other, there is a "natural beauty." But Hutcheson took this beauty for the only beauty, for the supreme test, whereas it is simply an "image" of the "cordial agreement, that consists in concord and union of mind and heart." What rationalism claims for the moral sense is true, "which is no more than to say, the more there are of different mutually agreeing things, the greater is the beauty." The pleasure men acquire from the contemplation of such beauty, especially when the tabulation makes it appear that the personal increment is slight, rests upon the nature of perceiving organisms, upon "their sensation of pleasure."

Within the frame of secondary virtue, therefore, the self-congratulatory apprehension of beauty is equated with animal delight, "immediately owing to the law God has established, or the instinct he has given." What the natural man calls virtuous and beautiful—social justice, the mother's love for her child, the happiness of those he happens to love, a regard for the public good which includes himself even when it calls upon him to sacrifice himself, ultimately even the approbation of an inward conscience that gives him invincible pleasure despite the censure of his fellows. . .—all these, analyzed into elementary terms, are no more than "the order and proportion generally observed in the laws of nature." They are reactions, like the cry of the anvil hit by the hammer, like the perpetual fall of the moon toward the earth. Though they seem virtuous, especially when most complicated, they have nothing virtuous in them beyond the seeming, and in truth are as decipherable by the laws of physics as are the motions in one arm of a lever with relation to the length and velocity of the other.

Everything that Hutcheson and the liberals ascribe to normal human nature, armed with its sensitive moral discrimination, can be resolved into the mechanics of instinct, as an insect feels out its course with its antennae, or into a scheme in the furtherance of instinct, "and may be without any principle of true virtue in the heart." In the twentieth century, to readers of Marcel Proust, it should come as no surprise that "such limited private benevolence, not arising from, not being subordinate to benevolence to Being in general, cannot have the nature of true virtue." There are men, said Edwards before Laurence Sterne was published, who will weep upon seeing a brute creature in torment, but who suffer no uneasiness whatever in knowing that thousands are slaughtered every day "at butchers' shambles in great cities." Pity, when gratifying to the ego, may not only be without benevolence, "but may consist with true malevolence, or with such ill will as shall cause men not only not to desire the positive happiness of another, but even to desire his calamity." The instincts serve for men's preservation and comfortable subsistence, which are objective and legitimate goods, for the regular satisfactions of appetite by extrinsic objects, which God by a divine constitution joined in sequences within the order of causation; but though these instincts perpetually manufacture attitudes of aversion and approbation, within the field of instinctual behavior they can be plotted by arithmetical equations only a trifle more complicated than those of the *Principia*. They can be formulated into rules as objectively beautiful, but as utterly irrelevant to moral worth, as incommensurate with the dignity of suffering and the agony of decision, as the insensate laws of motion.

So Hutcheson was correct when he identified morality with aesthetics. For Edwards, the Puritan in pioneer America, the definition of the ethical is beauty. But Hutcheson, and all utilitarians and humanitarians after him, failed to proceed from beauties to the beautiful, and so set up for perceiving beings a criterion applicable only to stones and planets. True virtue, therefore, is no law of inanimate things, but "is *that*, belonging to the *heart* of an intelligent Being, that is beautiful by a *general* beauty, or beautiful in a comprehensive view as it is in itself, and as related to every thing that it stands in connection with." The familiar process of perception still furnishes the distinction that a Hutcheson blurs: what sensation receives as the instigator of a reflex act is also received as a perception predetermined by the disposition of the agent, and according to the conception, not according to the thing, the motive compels the will. If the conception is of things as they are in themselves, without relation to the desires of the self—though all this while the self must eat and dress and marry—then in that identification of the objective and the inherent consists true virtue. No poet was more sensitive to the beauty of nature than Edwards, but he

concluded that the disinterested benevolence which is the inescapable rule of virtue among sentient beings "doth not necessarily presuppose beauty in its object." The Lockean clue, followed through the years, tested in a community that offered prototypes of almost every kind of American who was yet to figure in American history, led in the serenity of exile into realms Locke never dreamed of, into the affirmation that the beauty of holiness is one with the nature of the objective universe.

It is obvious, Edwards remarked, that none can "relish" pure beauty who has no temper for it. The coherence of his system shows that he identified the relish with the new simple idea, which is supernatural grace, and the possession of which makes certain men other (or more) than "natural" men. Yet it is remarkable that *True Virtue* contents itself with setting forth the inward beauty wholly in terms of the psychological pattern. The road out of the maze of secondary beauties up to the ideal beauty which no longer gloats upon its possessions or evaluates them in proportion to their amount of beauty, to that sight which bestows beauty on objects by regarding them, is so plain that in the simplicity of Edwards' presentation it appears open to all mankind. That it is traveled by only a few becomes a matter of biography; the determination is not from an intervention of the spirit, but from the nature of things. Man lives on the plane both of the objective good and of the inherent, not because he is both body and soul, but because he is one being, and the law of his life is that he must perceive things, yet as he perceives them, so they are and so he is. *True Virtue* can be called, if I may use the word in its primitive rather than in any of its sectarian connotations, a magnificent *humanism*. The rule of pure benevolence is implicated in every human act, so that every satisfaction of appetite, even of the lust which, within its own system, perceives the object as beautiful, has "in it some image of the true, spiritual, original beauty." By the uniformity of the cosmos, "diverse things become as it were one," and in the system of things even the fundamental distinction between the speculative and the sensible is merged into the pure beauty which is the final goal both of the reason and of the heart.

Yet this beauty is not a Platonic idea, no flame which the moth desires, no devotion to something afar from the sphere of our sorrow. It arises by discoverable processes out of motion and perception. Critics like Chauncy Whittelsey never understood Edwards, but their instinct was not far wrong when they accused him of atheism—except that they could not conceive an atheism more profoundly conscious of God than they could experience. Channing came closer to the truth when he said that by making God the only active power of the universe, Edwards annihilated the creature, became in effect a "pantheist," and obliged men at last to question whether any such thing as matter exists. Rational liberals do not want the creature annihilated, and they want matter to remain matter. I believe no one aware of recent physics and logic can be so confident as was Channing, or certainly so confident as were his colleagues and followers in liberal Protestantism, that matter is as solid as he would have it. As for annihilation of the creature, sociology and anthropology as well as history do not exactly enhance his independence of circumstance. Edwards ended the *True Virtue* with a startling recognition: "that sentiment, at least as to many particulars, by some means or other, is different in different persons, in different nations," and therefore the specific content of virtue and vice is arbitrary, being determined not by the nature of things, "but by the sentiments of men with relation to the nature of things." Edwards' scholarship, especially his anthropology, was narrow (although he could make first-hand comparative studies of English and Indian cultures); yet his experience was deep if not broad, and though he never saw a cathedral or an art gallery, never heard a symphony or an opera, out of the beauty of the world and the beauty of virtue he came to a vision of beauty for which the existence or nonexistence of matter is but a verbal quibble, a beauty which, being seen, puts the creature beyond all anxiety concerning his own annihilation. (pp. 288-93)

Perry Miller, in his Jonathan Edwards, *1949. Reprint by Meridian Books, Inc., 1959, 340 p.*

DONALD H. RHOADES (essay date 1952)

[*Rhoades is an American minister and educator. In the following excerpt, he examines intricacies of Edwards's philosophical theories of being, causation, value, and knowledge and analyzes his methodology.*]

If Jonathan Edwards had produced nothing but his Enfield Sermon, **"Sinners in the Hands of an Angry God"** . . . , he would have made his place in the realm of letters. For he was a master at a rather special kind of literature, the kind that brings the mind into the tangible presence of things usually viewed as high abstractions or florid figures of speech.

Such language hardly bespeaks the philosopher, yet such is the best-known language of America's least-known philosophical genius. If the good name of Josiah Royce has been bedeviled by a myth, that of Edwards has been set upon by a whole host of demons; he has been billed as the fiery Puritan, the sociological anachronism, the benighted provincial, fighting a rearguard skirmish against the triumphant march of reason, and, for the rest, he has been left to languish as the man nobody knows. Surely his soul can have found rest only in the serene detachment of the philosophic spirit. (pp. 135-36)

Edwards' basic philosophy falls naturally into five points—like Calvinism—or a fortress by Vauban. They are his theories of being, causation, value, and knowledge, and his methodology.

His theory of being is an idealistic monism. Reality consists of God and the emanations of God *ad extra* ["on the outside"]. Strictly, of course, it is *ad extra* only "as it were"; to keep the record clear, one must also say that anything which is not, strictly, God, is "as nothing"—that God includes all true being. Technically this is at least panentheism, if not pantheism, but from man's side, as Edwards developed the conception, it might as well be authentic theism—except in a few cases where forensic considerations become dominant.

The world is so far from being a once-for-all, deistic creation, that it is re-created, moment-by-moment, by the instant will of God. But for that instancy it would immediately lapse into nothingness. Such, for Edwards, is that same Newtonian cosmos which, for the Deists, was a practically perfect and self-sustaining mechanism.

Of the relations possible in a pluralistic scheme there are only inconsistent traces. Part-whole relationships are merely less out of order. Analogies between the divine and the human economies are tolerable only if drawn from the least personal and intimate of such human relations as involve dependence and obligation.

The theory of causation is not only integral to Edwards' system, but is central to his many discussions of the problems of human freedom, divine government, and predestination. He read Hume late in life and found him either "old stuff" or wrong. Ed-

wards' concept of "cause," in which Miller finds Newtonian influence, was an effectual denial of any genuine efficiency of antecedent causation. His own very early definition is as follows:

> Cause is that, after or upon the existence of which, or the existence of it after such a manner, the existence of another thing follows.

In his discussion of the will he can speak of one event's depending on another as its ground or reason, yet the prior event is really a means, directly used by the one ultimate Cause, rather than a proper efficiency in itself. He can speak of natural necessity as having pragmatic validity in experience, yet ever as dependent on the one true Cause.

Calvinism had asserted, without philosophical refinements, that the divine ordering operates without violence either to natural determinism or to human freedom. . . . Edwards made it clear that this was possible because violation to a system, determined or free, can properly occur only in the plane of action of that system. Injection of an external physical force into a physical system would violate the integrity of the system. But the human will does not violate the mechanics of the body in directing it. So God, in directing both the physical and the volitional, does not violate them, however deterministically he orders them. The divine predetermination operates by what Edwards calls "philosophical necessity." We are never given a really adequate definition of this concept; the nearest to such comes from the debate on the will.

> Philosophical Necessity is really nothing else than the full and fixed connection between the things signified by the subject and predicate of a proposition, which affirms something to be true. . . .

This is not too obviously helpful. However, if we understand that Edwards is really illustrating the principle that ultimately necessity is a matter of mutual implication, established, and to be "seen," as it were, immediately and simultaneously, we may begin to get his viewpoint.

He is, in effect, restoring the fulness of causation to cosmology. In spite of Aristotelian residues, the Galilean-Newtonian world practically recognized only efficient cause; indeed, scholastic arguments to God as First Cause betray an even earlier tendency so to think of the empirical world. Considering all the logical shuffling involved, in arguing from the necessity of an antecedent cause for everything, and then blandly asserting that we must assume one *un*caused Cause, one might have suspected that a cosmos with only efficient causation was not really even thinkable. Edwards reaffirms causation as ultimately one, and as presented to us as a concatenation of necessary mutual implications. The whole must be what it is, and the parts are so determined within it.

On the assumption that efficient cause is alone to be considered, religion can be saved from Deism only by abundance of miraculous interventions; apart from them, the only possible contact of God and the ongoing cosmos is way back at the beginning. The same Platonism which, by breaking the Aristotelian monopoly, helped make possible the world of Newton, was now called upon to save religion from the implications of that world.

With respect to human conduct, Edwards comes close to behaviorism, every human act being the necessary resultant of that relevant group of influences which add up to the "strongest motive." And the inward elements of this motive are as little under man's creative control as are the outward ones. For

Edwards that is as it should be, since the ultimate determination is that of God.

Irreducible good, for Edwards, is either excellency or pleasure in excellency. To be sure, he is not always consistent in thus qualifying pleasure, but his general view clearly demands it. Excellency cannot be defined, of course, but its functional aspect can be, and the definition is "consent to being." That is, excellency is the mutual implication of all reality, when that implication is considered as an act or as an attitude. Human virtue is only the human specification of this. That the ultimate determiner of man's consent is not man himself is considered irrelevant. The only important thing is that the highest good and demand of the whole is served, either directly or by compensation. Virtue and reward of human agents, or sin and punishment, seem to serve equally well.

The essentially aesthetic nature of Edwards' thinking becomes especially evident here. For him everything, in fact, which we call "good" or "evil," appears beautiful, when seen in *all* its implications. Considered by itself, evil is still evil, heinously evil, as evil as only local opposition to the infinite good and beauty can be.

Another aesthetic stumbling block for ordinary ethics appears in Edwards' compounding of the qualitative and the quantitative. A good being that is bigger than another otherwise of the same quality is therefore better. Is a bad being therefore the worse for being bigger? Not in this scheme. Anselmic feudal theory still holds. A bad being is worse the more contemptibly small it is. This is too simply stated to do Edwards full justice, but it is not unfair to his general tendency or the practical implications.

Human virtue is consent to being—absolute consent. As unconditional affirmation of objective value, this is benevolence, and benevolence is what God requires of man. But man may affirm value because it pleases him, even in a self-centered way. This is love of "complacence."

Love which is complacence is good if it has God for its ultimate object, and loves other things only for His sake; otherwise complacence is an evil. But, speaking functionally, man is benevolent only when he is also pleased. For, Edwards asserts, to be pleased, to affirm, to choose, are only different words for the same thing. Whether or not a man is pleased by the right things, depends not only upon their rightness but also on the kind of man he is. Strictly speaking, he has no option. It is a case of "love at first sight" or love never.

As we may already have suspected, there is no place here for really unconditioned good will, for *agape,* love to persons without regard to their merits or objective value. A man should love God, his fellow man, himself—each according to objective worth. Selfishness is no worse than any other disproportionate love. This follows necessarily from the command to love all things for God's sake, *i.e.,* for what they mean to God. As for God, He loves Himself supremely, and that is only being realistic with respect to the objective value of His excellency. In the last analysis, God loves His creation for its instrumental value, its value for the enhancement, as it were, of His own glory.

Edwards' theory of knowledge has already been involved in discussion of other items. The distinctive note is his thoroughgoing "sense" emphasis. We cannot call it pan-sensational, pan-sensate, or pan-sensual, for all these have misleading connotations and usages. I suggest "pan-sensistic" as being as least uncontaminated, however inadequate otherwise.

All knowledge is "sensed." That is, what is really known is presented to the mind with immediacy. The physical sense organs play their part, but their stimulation does not in itself mean our sensing anything. When we sense some item of knowledge, we sense it as idea: the reality-as-apprehended. Whether we sense color, hardness, or beauty, or even logical necessity, it is all ultimately the same. The idea emerges in (not out of) our whole-reaction to the relevant whole which we sense.

The only distinction to be made is between man's natural capacity of sensing and the "divine and supernatural light" by which we can sense the truly holy. In religious terms, this is a gift of grace, but philosophically it is just as an empirically other dimension of sensing, of becoming immediately aware.

The "idea" is thus reality-as-apprehended. It is, functionally—this is not an Edwardian term, but appropriate enough—it is, functionally, the only reality *for us*. And it is thoroughly objective, and by no means a product of irresponsible imagination, since it is determined by a concatenation of reals: the reality sensed, the sensing self, the whole—or God.

In philosophical methodology Edwards was both empirical and rationalistic. The empirical, which determined his constructive thought, was altogether prior; the rationalistic or dialectical was mostly for argumentative purposes, and these largely negative. His other use of the rationalistic method was exploratory, to suggest possible positive truth. But the only positive "proof" admitted was the final "sensed" necessity of the real or the true—its sensed *immediate* necessity.

Edwards' empiricism included scriptural and dogmatic truths so far as these are actually sensed or "tasted." Perhaps not all things could be "tasted" as being in themselves true, but they might be sensed as congruent to the tasted reality.

This is very close indeed to the current doctrine of the Word of God, as immediately confronting the spirit or mind of a man, the Word self-communicated through the written scripture or the preaching of its truth. If Edwardianism is authentic Calvinism, then the current strictures upon Neo-Orthodoxy, as being a "new modernism," may betray a lack of historical self-awareness on the part of some critics. To be sure, there were Calvinists in Edwards' own day who vehemently denied his version of Calvinism.

It is simple truth to say that Edwards had no real competitors in his own day. Both in the originality with which he reworked his materials to serve his ends, and in his power of sheer sustained intellectuality, he towered above his age, and has, indeed, few peers in any age. Occasionally one can see that he suffered in the quality of his own production, because of the lack of competent critics. He could, so to speak, "get away with murder," and now and then yielded to the temptation. The few times he stooped to an *argumentum ad hominem* only throw in sharper relief the consistently high level of his thought and writing. (pp. 139-45)

We would do him no honor by withholding what may appear to us as valid criticisms. It seems evident, on various counts, that his thought led him into what is actually a naturalistic absolutism. He could not escape the conclusion (it was practically his starting point in mature life) that whatever is, is ultimately right. All creative tension between the real and the ideal, the "is" and the "ought," is theoretically removed.

And the remaining tension, between the actual and the commanded, is haunted by a ghostly unreality, and the ethical gives place to arbitrary power and sheer submission. Man the active and living is commanded to respond to the observer's world. The moral, as distinct from the aesthetic, has no consistent place. By divorcing responsibility (man's) for acts from their actual authorship (God's)—leaving men aware, but helplessly aware that they are sinful—he made impossible any thoroughgoing ethic of obligation.

Another item is his essential reduction of the personal to impersonal categories. Person-to-person, as such, had no real place in his system. Whatever may be charged to dogmatic and logical necessities, the basic truth is that the personal was, for him, always to be subordinated to the awareness and the values realizable in isolation. He, like Kierkegaard a hundred years later, feared and distrusted the interpersonal, in part as a barrier to true objectivity.

Nor can we approve Edwards' elimination from his theories of life and values of any place for unconditional good will, the will to create values where they are not objectively evident in men, the love for persons as such which seems to be the undogmatic meaning of the Cross and of every other example of vicarious sacrifice. That his practice was far better than his theory does not validate the theory.

Edwards quite unwittingly performed a great service to religion and to philosophy in that he revealed the uneasy and pragmatic compound of empiricism, rationalism, and confessional symbolism in high Calvinism. What he could not do to validate the system as a monolithic whole, will not be done. More than any other Calvinist, he brought men to face without blinking, the full content of a too-easily-professed faith and creed. In fact, he provides us today with a case study of Calvinism, its weaknesses and its great strengths, at a time when Calvinisms of varying types are being vigorously asserted.

There is a truly modern note in the way Edwards delineated what we term existential knowledge, as something inseparable from man's whole response to the wholeness of things. His work stands as a bar of judgment upon any attempt to separate thought from life, or man from his total context, or to exalt reason, will, or feeling as sufficient for the good life.

In his failures and successes, Edwards stands like a beacon, lighting the way of truth, and warning from the very rock on which he stands. America's first philosopher is worthy of the best who have followed and who shall yet follow him. (pp. 146-47)

> *Donald H. Rhoades, "Jonathan Edwards: America's First Philosopher," in* The Personalist, *Vol. XXXIII, No. 2, April, 1952, pp. 135-47.*

PHYLLIS McGINLEY (poem date 1957)

[*McGinley was an American author best known for her light verse combining technical skill with keen insights into everyday living. Poetry editor for a time of* Town and Country, *she also wrote children's books and gained an appreciative readership with* Six Pence in Her Shoe *(1964), a collection of autobiographical essays on the satisfaction of being a wife and mother in suburban America. In "The Theology of Jonathan Edwards," a poem which first*

appeared in Harper's Magazine *in 1957, McGinley comments on Edwards's conception of a vengeful God.*]

> Whenever Mr. Edwards spake
>   In church about Damnation,
> The very benches used to quake
>   For awful agitation.
>
> Good men would pale and roll their eyes
>   While sinners rent their garments
> To hear him so anatomize
>   Hell's orgiastic torments,
>
> The blood, the flames, the agonies
>   In store for frail or flighty
> New Englanders who did not please
>   A whimsical Almighty.
>
> Times were considered out of tune
>   When half a dozen nervous
> Female parishioners did not swoon
>   At every Sunday service;
>
> And, if they had been taught aright,
>   Small children, carried bedwards,
> Would shudder lest they meet that night
>   The God of Mr. Edwards.
>
> Abraham's God, the Wrathful One,
>   Intolerant of error—
> Not God the Father or the Son
>   But God the Holy Terror.

> *Phyllis McGinley, "The Theology of Jonathan Edwards," in her* Times Three, *The Viking Press, 1961, p. 19.*

RALPH G. TURNBULL (essay date 1958)

[*In the following excerpt, Turnbull appraises the style of Edwards's sermons.*]

If "the style is the man," then Edwards' style was the result of an unfolding personality aflame with the passion of a noble heart and mind. We see him as the preacher in the hands of God. His style was the expression of deep, pent-up emotion and thought, which caught fire in the blaze of God's love and man's need of the redeeming message. It came out in the pen of a ready writer who did not parade his knowledge but delivered the message in the disciplined spiritual mind, humbled before God. (pp. 55-6)

[Edwards] endeavored to attain a modest, unadorned, plain style. In this he followed the Puritan model. As a preacher he sought to use the sermon to impress the mind and arouse the heart to action. He aimed at this by legitimate means and the plain and forthright speech of a faithful pastor was his. If he shunned the oratorical and exaggerated word, it was in the interest of divine service. The servant of the Word would not call attention to himself and detract from the glory of the Master he served.

The style of Edwards was the plain style. Each sermon was an attempt to extract from a text an axiom of theology and to dispute of this in creedal order. In procedure the text was taken apart by the method of analysis into its constituent elements, and then set out again in a proposition. After the logical analysis of Scripture the practical appeal was made by the pastor-preacher, who sought to translate the Bible into life. . . . (pp. 56-7)

If the plain style lacked adornment in pleasing phrases, nevertheless it was convincing, straightforward speech, and clearly understood in its appeal for a verdict from the hearer. Edwards' style could also be termed ''metaphysical'' and not ''witty.'' The different types of sermons in Edwards' time were classified as ''witty'' or given to word-play and quips, and as ''metaphysical'' or intellectual, less verbal character of thought without the conceits of Elizabethan learned imagery. (p. 57)

The preaching of the Northampton pastor, while it was intellectual, did not descend to the use of those learned expressions from his wide background of reading and knowledge. Sporadically, through many of the Puritan sermons, evidence of the wide reading is found, but for the most part the minister of God remembered (and Edwards in particular) that the sermons were for people who knew only English and that of the simplest. The plain man was reached by the plain style. . . .

The intellectual power in Edwards was dedicated to a humility in which he tried to hide himself, concealing knowledge. At the same time he wrote and preached with simplicity. Clarity of mind and spiritual passion were aflame together. . . . There was nothing vulgar or humorous in Edwards' sermons. All that he wrote was harnessed to one purpose, and language was the vehicle to carry truth directly and convincingly. It was the message and not the method which impressed. There was argument, persuasion, appeal, but it was not rough, although firm and stern at times. A restrained dramatic intensity is felt. . . .

For the most part his sermons were pastoral, and the style was tender, fervid, fresh, seldom controversial, and never contentious. (p. 58)

The imagery of Edwards was . . . limited and usually Biblical. . . . Metaphor and figures of speech are culled from that background. It could not be otherwise with a man steeped in the English Bible. Stories of life-interest or life-situations out of pastoral experience are generally absent, except that which deals with his own conversion and development. (p. 60)

The sermons of Edwards were unadorned, and lack what would be considered today as a useful adjunct to good preaching. (p. 61)

Without extraneous helps to catch the attention, Edwards did not use fanciful figures of speech or bookish quotations remote from colonial life. It was sufficient to announce the text and apply the doctrine from the stated proposition. He had had a rich and varied experience in spiritual truth, and this can be discerned from the texture of the sermons. He was an experimental thinker and preacher. He preached what he himself felt. Rarely does he draw from the wealth of his knowledge and reading to light up the meaning of the text. His was the art of concealment. (p. 62)

He avoided exaggerated speech, seeking always to hide himself and his erudition, so that men might look away from him to his Lord, the object of faith. (p. 63)

[Edwards] was saturated with the classic of that day, the King James Version of the Bible. His luminous quality of expression in preaching was assisted by Biblical vocabulary. His style was that of a heart warm and aglow from deep faith in and intense devotion to God. The sermons may well rank as samples of the literature of the eighteenth century. In them is pellucid English and a sustained prose of high order. There are passages that grip when read aloud, and it is not difficult to imagine how some of the sermons impressed when delivered.

Edwards had a disciplined mind and a ready pen. His force of intellect, his philosophical grasp of ideas, his knowledge of theology, and his acquaintance with the best English writers,

enabled him to write vigorously. Whatever may be thought of the imprecatory sermons, they, together with the pastoral message, were productive of action. That is a primary test of good literature. It was not some emotional disturbance in religious meetings which gave rise to those upsurgings of moral life and commitment. The reading quality of the written word was pregnant with deeps of feeling, wells of truth undefiled, and a running stream of living faith.

The sermons as literature have rhythm and balance, well-defined propositions, and marked climaxes. Novel arrangements, word-pairs, impressiveness of phrase affect us. The logical unity of thought and argument with a definite structure give the sentences a place as good literature.

Like his Puritan predecessors Edwards sought to find the pleasant word: not to delight the mind alone, but to work upon the heart. That was the goal of his preaching. Although much depended upon the personality of the preacher at the time of delivery, the sermons when read have a literary quality appealing to mind and heart. There is a poetic element pervading the prose which gives it high moments of thought and feeling. Edwards does not try for dramatic effect, unless we allow for the climax of a few of the ''hellfire'' sermons which appear more so because of their unusual conclusion.

In the sermon **''Hypocrites Deficient in the Duty of Prayer''**. . . , Edwards writes a quiet, sustained, rhythmical prose. . . . (pp. 65-6)

[Clause] after clause build up, sentence succeeds sentence, moving towards a climax. Everything to Edwards was subordinate to Scripture, and it is this spirit we find in the clear thought and forthright exposition in the sermons. (p. 66)

[Literary style] was ''varnish'' to the Puritan: it was useful, even commendable, and a good workman should know how to apply it, but his first consideration always was to secure the substance and solidity of the message. Edwards expressed his feeling for beauty in the poetic element of imaginative prose, heightened by fervent views of love and holiness of spirit. The spiritual universe dominated his thought and governed his aesthetic sense. This emotional quality was present and was wedded to spiritual affection in Christ. To Edwards, the highest and most enduring aesthetic emotion was that which was called out, not by material or natural beauty, but by holiness. This is the key to interpret his pastoral sermons. They are not all denunciatory as some have carelessly imagined. In the pastoral relationship and as an expository preacher his best preaching was suffused with this beauty and grace of the vision of God in Christ. (p. 67)

Ralph G. Turnbull, in his Jonathan Edwards: The Preacher, *Baker Book House, 1958, 192 p.*

ALFRED OWEN ALDRIDGE   (essay date 1964)

[*The editor of* Comparative Literature Studies, *Aldridge is an American educator and author. Among his studies of the eighteenth century are* Benjamin Franklin and His French Contemporaries *(1957) and* Man of Reason: Life of Thomas Paine *(1959). In the following excerpt from his study of Edwards, Aldridge explores the discrepancy between Edwards's religious and secular applications of rationalism.*]

[A] rational-supernatural dichotomy persists among Edwards' followers. Joseph Haroutunian has acutely remarked that those critics impressed by Edwards' spirituality ''have done no justice to his intelligence, and those impressed by his intelligence have been impervious to his 'sense of divine things.' " Edwards is most famous as a logician, but philosophers seem to concentrate on his idealism. Since he was the most eminent philosopher of the American enlightenment, one naturally wonders about his relationship to the broad ideals of the enlightenment concept. To what degree was he a rationalist? and to what extent did he accept the doctrine of progress?. . .

Edwards' notion of the manner by which knowledge is acquired certainly conformed with that of the scientific rationalism of the age. (p. 150)

But in addition to the processes of perception, observation, reflection and judgment implied in [his] description of reasoning, Edwards believed that knowledge may be acquired through intuition. . . . Edwards consciously made a separation between secular and religious knowledge, arguing that the world has made great progress in the former—almost none in the latter. Reason by itself provides some knowledge of religious truth, he taught, but this knowledge is entirely inadequate and must be supplemented by the more important instrument—intuition. Edwards never made the same application of a dichotomy of reason and intuition to secular knowledge and never gave a single illustration of the manner in which intuition may reveal knowledge of anything connected with the material universe. He did believe, however, that some ideas are innate: for example, the idea that every change in circumstances must have a cause. (pp. 151-52)

Strangely enough, in all his insistence upon the necessity of something greater than reason for religious knowledge, Edwards never alluded to the other anti-intellectual supposition in some of his works that the fundamental doctrines of Christianity do not require a high degree of sophistication or even literacy, but are adapted to the simplest minds, such as, for example, that of the four-year-old Phebe Bartlet.

One cannot say that Edwards belongs to the tradition of skepticism. The classical Pyrrhonists had rejected all knowledge that comes from reason or the senses, and the seventeenth-century fideists had gone through the same process of elimination in order to fall back on the authority of the Roman Catholic Church. Edwards, however, put theological knowledge and all other "articles of knowledge" in separate categories, rejecting reason in favor of revelation for theology and accepting it for everything else. (pp. 153-54)

In his formal attempt in [*Miscellaneous Observations on Important Theological Subjects*] to demonstrate that reason is inadequate to provide all men with an insight into the essential truth of religion, Edwards was faced with the problem of accounting for the sublime notions of God found in the classical philosophers, particularly in Plato and Cicero. If they did not come from reason, where did they come from since they had existed prior to the Christian tradition? Edwards in his youth had worked out an ingenious answer to this question, and he used it as the basis of most of the antideistic passages in his subsequent works. According to his solution, God had revealed the essential truths of religion to Noah, and whenever they flourished before the Christian era, they may be traced back to this source. (pp. 154-55)

That the ancient philosophers had as good a notion as they had of God, Edwards maintained, was due more to tradition that originated in divine revelation than to human invention—although reason served to keep the tradition alive. According to Edwards, experience had amply demonstrated that mankind—instead of depending on the light of nature to find out a right idea of God and his laws—had once been well acquainted with both and had gradually and at length almost universally lost sight of them, "insomuch that idolatry as bad as atheism, and wickedness worse than brutality, were established for religion and law in all countries." Edwards does not seem to have wondered why the same argument could not have been applied to his own notion of revelation—why one might not object that once revelation had been given to man it did not shed a uniform light. Why is it that certain points of history were dark—and others—such as the Reformation and the Great Awakening—glowed brightly? If Edwards were to answer—as he did not, for he never faced the problem—that God's intervention explains these periods, then he would be attributing man's knowledge neither to reason nor to revelation in the sense of Scripture tradition.

Edwards did make an attempt to answer another objection that was frequently raised by the deists: if the Scriptures were intended to convey light to all mankind so that the truths of religion could be perceived by even the weakest minds, why is it that they are filled with mysteries and apocalyptic visions? Edwards explained that the mysteries were intended to give Christian people "exercise for their pious wisdom and study" and to enable them to make progress in understanding the Scriptures "as the philosophical world makes progress in the understanding of the book of nature, and in unfolding its mysteries."

Even though Edwards could convince his readers not to believe the deists' notion that natural reason would bring about the general recognition of a divine being, he still had to dispose of the claim that revelation itself, before it can be accepted, must be submitted to the scrutiny of reason for approval or validating. He chose to examine the argument as it had been presented by one of the most brilliant of the deists, Matthew Tindal, in his *Christianity as Old as the Creation*.

Edwards' first step was to define reason as "that power or faculty an intelligent being has to judge of the truth of propositions; either immediately, by only looking on the propositions, which is judging by intuition and self-evidence; or by putting together several propositions, which are already evident by intuition, or at least whose evidence is originally derived from intuition." If one accepts this definition as a satisfactory statement of the process by which one acquires all one's ideas, one would seem to be a rationalist. Edwards obviously accepted his own statement, but he held one minor reservation concerning the universality of its application. Tindal had argued, as had Toland before him, that if reason must decide whether any pretended revelation is genuine, it must therefore pass on every doctrine and proposition contained in the pretended revelation. Edwards maintained, by a method of argument drawn partly from Locke and partly from the body of Christian apologists, that reason must indeed pass on every pretended revelation as a system, but that once the system has been accepted in general, the particular doctrines that comprised it must be exempted from scrutiny.

The essence of the deists' argument is most simply stated in a sentence in Toland's *Christianity Not Mysterious*: "There is no Mystery [or doctrine contrary to or "above" reason] in Christianity, or the most perfect Religion; and that by Consequence nothing contradictory or inconceivable, however made an article of Faith, can be contained in the Gospel, if it be really the Word of God."

Toland and Tindal relied entirely on internal evidence; they maintained that one cannot verify a system *in general* without examining and approving its particular doctrines first. Edwards relied instead on external evidence, arguing that if such supports as miracles, prophecy, and tradition furnish proof of the truth of a system, the unreasonableness of any part must be considered a sign of the weakness or limitation of human reason rather than of a fault in the general system. Despite his idealistic philosophy and his knowledge of Newtonian physics, he still fell back on traditional apologetics, prophecy and miracles, as his best proof of Christianity.

The remainder of his arguments were intended to demonstrate the deficiencies of reason. "A proposition may be evidently true," he argued, ". . . though the particular propositions that depend upon it, and follow from it, may be such, that our reason, independent of it, cannot see the truth, or can see it to be true by no other means, than by first establishing that other truth, on which it depends." As examples, Edwards argued that we accept the proposition that we may believe the testimony of history and tradition, the testimony of those we see and converse with, the testimony of our memories, and the testimony of our senses; yet many of the truths that we accept as consequences cannot be known directly by reason. Edwards was a master of arguing by analogy, although some of his parallels are not very close. One wonders whether he really overlooked the obvious fact that Toland, in objecting to the particular propositions consequent to Christianity that fail to conform to reason, would have objected equally to any proposition consequent to the testimony of those we see and converse with, or to the testimony of history, that failed to conform to reason.

Edwards similarly argued that we accept on faith a great deal of knowledge about the universe that we have not experienced and that we do not understand, for example, the effects of electricity and magnetism. Nature is full of mysteries; the further it is traced and observed, the more mysteries appear. The same is true of divine revelation, he maintained, and difficulties should not be held as arguments against it, but rather as confirmations or arguments in its favor. Furthermore, the difficulties attendant upon a revelation of spiritual nature will be vastly multiplied: the things of this world will be of a different kind from "the objects and affairs which earthly language was made to express."

Having used the method of analogy to demonstrate to his own satisfaction that God's revelation through nature involves almost the same complexity as God's revelation in the Scriptures, Edwards based his final argument on the twofold requisites of a satisfactory religious system. It must provide: "*1st,* The religion of nature, or the religion proper and needful, considering the state and relations we stand in as creatures; *2d,* The religion of a sinner, or the religion and duties proper and necessary for us, considering our state as depraved and guilty creatures, having incurred the displeasure of our Creator." However sound the logic may be in Edwards' other works, the second requirement, predicated on the doctrine of depravity in Calvinistic Christianity, the very system presumably being proved or vindicated, actually says nothing more than that no system of religion can conform to Calvinism except Calvinism.

One wonders whether, in any other realm, Edwards would have accepted general propositions from external evidence alone, without insisting that they be based on rationally acceptable subordinate propositions. (pp. 155-58)

The truth is that Edwards did not believe that the highest religious or moral knowledge comes through reason. Nor did he believe that the particular doctrines of Christianity should be expected to conform to reason. Yet, as all skeptics do, he used reason and logic to reveal the deficiencies of reason. He also used reason to demonstrate propositions that, according to his own theory, are beyond the reach of reason. . . .

Edwards is a rationalist in the sense that the best passages in his forensic works reveal extraordinary powers of logic and nearly all of his writing gives the appearance of appealing to reason; but these appearances hardly overweigh the nonrational elements. (p. 159)

> *Alfred Owen Aldridge, in his* Jonathan Edwards, *Washington Square Press, Inc., 1964, 181 p.*

CONRAD CHERRY (essay date 1966)

[*Cherry is an American professor of religious studies whose works include* Religion in the Public Domain *(1966) and* Nature and Religious Imagination *(1980). In the following excerpt from his book on Edwards's theology, he questions the accuracy of categorizing Edwards as a mystic.*]

The picture of Edwards as a curious, rather mad, eighteenth-century preacher preoccupied with hell-fire, a God of wrath, and the hatred of "all of Adam's children with a hatred bordering on the pathological" [see excerpt by Charles Angoff dated 1931] is an image that is still with us. . . . Images have a way of fixing themselves in the American consciousness, and this image of Edwards is not easily shattered. (p. 1)

Nevertheless, even when the stereotyped images are abandoned, interpreters of Edwards still feel uncomfortable with Edwards' Calvinism. To alleviate the pain of embarrassment, features of Edwards' thought are frequently searched out which "transcend" his Calvinism or which prefigure the post-Puritan era of American thought. Perhaps such a procedure would not be totally inappropriate if Edwards had not so obviously addressed himself to problems current in his eighteenth century or if he had not consciously chosen Puritan Calvinism as the framework for so much of his thought. (pp. 2-3)

For good or for ill, Edwards was a Calvinist theologian; and, as a Calvinist theologian, he claimed the heritage of his New England forefathers. . . . [His] thought was pervaded by the same visions that had caught the imagination of both Calvin and the Puritans: the sovereignty and freedom of God; the drama of history as the story both of man's tragic fallenness and of God's renewed purpose to deliver; man's frailty and unworthiness in comparison with the justice and mercy of a majestic God; the personal and social value of a disciplined, "holy" life of "practice." And though Edwards would have resisted having his thought reduced to that of his Puritan predecessors, he would have also insisted that if one learned from him *only* at the points where he departed from their thought, then one would not really learn from him at all. (p. 3)

Edwards chose to broaden, impregnate and sometimes alter his Calvinist theology, rather than transcend it. (p. 4)

Edwards has occasionally been made by his interpreters to wear the mantle of "mysticism." Christian mysticism has had a long and influential history, and the popular assumption that it was a monolithic movement marked by an overbearing penchant for ghostly, extrasocial flights into the "other world" simply will not stand the historical test. In all probability, a case could be made that Edwards—especially in his views of the Holy Spirit and spiritual knowledge—shared attitudes with some of the great Western mystics. But this is not our concern here, for those who have dressed Edwards up as a "mystic" have nothing so historically refined in mind. (p. 85)

Those interpreters in the earlier part of this century who found a mysticism in Edwards have already provoked some sound rebuttals. Lately, however, the mantle has again been placed on Edwards from a slightly different approach. The earlier interpreters proposed that Edwards inwardly rebelled against the rigid objectivism of Calvinism (though he was forced by his time outwardly to embrace many of its forms) by dwelling on the internal communication of God to the soul. And he held to an idea of the mystical absorption of the individual in the absolute, an idea existentially testified to in Edwards' record of his own religious experience. Clyde Holbrook [in his 1944 doctoral dissertation *The Ethics of Jonathan Edwards*] has correctly replied to this: (1) Edwards stressed a warm conviction of God's presence, but he remained strongly committed to the "objectivism" of Calvinism in that his new sense of God was "of God's reality and beauty standing over and beyond man and the natural world.". . . (2) Edwards' description of his conversion experience is pervaded by the idea that God lies outside man and is one on whom the converted is *dependent*, not one in whom he becomes absorbed in mystical identity. Thomas Schafer [in his 1957 dissertation *The Concept of Being in the Thought of Jonathan Edwards*] has added on this point that in Edwards' account of his personal experience of the Divine, "the infinite Being with which he seeks union always retains the element of personality; and Edwards, in his most abandoned raptures, never loses the sense of individual finite personality." Edwards' creaturely sense of sin "counteracts all tendencies toward complete identification with the divine." Edwards does record in his **Personal Narrative** that upon thought of the excellency of the Supreme Being after reading I Timothy 1:17, it occurred to him "how happy I should be, if I might enjoy that God, and be rapt up to him in heaven, and be as it were swallowed up in him forever!" And he later experienced "a kind of vision" (not unlike St. Paul's being "caught up to the third heaven") when he was "sweetly conversing with Christ, and wrapt and swallowed up in God." It is significant, however, that this reaction was initially prompted by a scriptural passage stressing God's eternity, invisibility, and immortality, and that the following part of Edwards' narrative reveals that the vision of God did not mean absorption or loss of creaturely identity, for Edwards continued to have creaturely "longings" after God even at the height of his new sense of the Divine. In all fairness to the early mystical-interpreters, it may be noted that a Neoplatonic metaphysic sometimes employed by Edwards suggests at points a monism in which the distinction between uncreated and created being is not always clear. Yet the intention of the metaphysic is to stress the manifestation of the glory of God in all creation, and this overriding intention supersedes the spelling out in any detail the relation between the identity of the Creator and the identity of the creature. Furthermore, when Edwards speaks soteriologically rather than cosmologically, the traditional Calvinist gulf between Creator and creature is clearly maintained. A typical statement is . . . : "The glory of divine power and grace is set off with the greater lustre, by what appears at the same time of the weakness of the earthen vessel. It is God's pleasure to manifest the weakness and unworthiness of the subject, at the same time that he displays the excellency of his power and the riches of his grace." Edwards apparently either did not see the possible contradiction between his Neoplatonist metaphysic and his Calvinism, or else he was willing to live with the contradiction. At any rate, there is in Edwards' thought and own life

no manifest attempt to absorb man into the divine in "mystical" identity.

Douglas J. Elwood has more recently renewed the mystical interpretation of Edwards, but with a slightly different approach [see Additional Bibliography]. He contends that Edwards' mysticism is a Spirit-mysticism that has deep roots in the Puritan tradition. Although Edwards attempts to guard against an absolute identity between God and the creature, "Edwards' mysticism reaches its height in his identification of Christian grace with the actual presence of God in the human heart." Elwood believes that there is for Edwards an internal and mystical union of God with the soul; here Edwards stresses along with certain other Puritans a personally and inwardly experienced grace rather than a grace experienced through outward means. . . . Edwards' view of the inward operation of grace never replaces an emphasis on the necessity of grace working in and through outward means. For that reason Edwards is not an heir of the Spirit-mysticism which appeared in segments of Puritan thought. As Jerald Brauer has shown, the radical Spirit-mystics of left-wing Puritanism not only shifted "from the orthodox Puritan stress on the personal operation of the Holy Spirit in salvation to the view that the Holy Spirit, in effecting man's salvation, dwells personally and substantially in a man's heart"; they also either "viewed all externals and even sacraments as things indifferent . . ." or else "repudiated all visible aspects of the Church. . . ." Edwards certainly holds that the Spirit dwells "personally" and even "substantially" in the saint's heart, but this position never leads him to a slighting of the visible means of grace. But within Elwood's rendering is a remnant of the older mystical-interpreters of Edwards. He thinks that since for Edwards *God himself* is communicated to the saint by the Spirit, there is a "union, if not in some sense identity" between God and the human soul. . . . [*Union*] between the Spirit and the soul there is; but *identity* there is not. God in his Spirit communicates himself to the saint, but He joins the saint as the saint's new principle or foundation and not as human-absorbing divinity. "Union" means for Edwards "participation." The saint participates in, but is not absorbed in, the Holy Spirit. On the basis of the new holy principle, the saint inclines in love away from self-contained experiences toward God; he does not lose his creaturely selfhood, but gains it anew in that inclination. That ecstasy of faith is not a mystical rapture in which man is cut away from the historical dimensions of his being. Rather man is constituted a faithful historical being in his standing out toward his object in love (affection) and from Love (the Spirit).

One had best leave the mantle of "mysticism" for another wearer than Edwards, for it fits him loosely at best. Even when the term "mystic" is defined broadly as "one who claims to know God through a form of spiritual inwardness," it is not strictly applicable; for in Edwards "spiritual inwardness" never replaces but complements the visible means of grace and the outward orientation of faith. (pp. 85-8)

Conrad Cherry, in his The Theology of Jonathan Edwards: A Reappraisal, *Anchor Books, 1966, 270 p.*

JORGE LUIS BORGES   (poem date 1967?)

[*An Argentine short story writer, poet, and essayist, Borges is one of the leading figures in contemporary literature. His writing is often used by critics to illustrate the modern view of literature as a highly sophisticated game. In his literary criticism, Borges is noted for his insight into the manner in which an author both represents and creates a reality with words, and the way in which*

*those words are variously interpreted by readers. With his fiction
and poetry, Borges's critical writing shares the perspective that
literary creation of imaginary worlds and philosophical speculation on the world itself are parallel or identical activities. In
the following poem, Borges records his impression of Edwards's
God.]*

> Far from the Common, far from the loud
> City and from time, which is change,
> Edwards dreams, eternal now, and comes
> Into the shadow of golden trees. Today
> Is tomorrow and yesterday. Not one
> Thing of God's in the motionless world
> Fails to exalt him strangely—the gold
> Of the evening, or of the moon.
> Content, he knows the world is an eternal
> Vessel of wrath and that the coveted
> Heaven was created for a few
> And Hell for almost all. Exactly
> In the center of the web there is
> Another prisoner, God, the Spider.

> *Jorge Luis Borges, "Jonathan Edwards (1703-1758),"
> translated by Richard Howard and César Rennert,
> in his* Selected Poems: 1923-1967, *edited by Norman
> Thomas Di Giovanni, Delacorte Press/Seymour
> Lawrence, 1972, p. 169.*

EDWARD M. GRIFFIN (essay date 1971)

*[In the following excerpt, Griffin assesses Edwards's place in
American philosophy and his importance as an American writer.]*

The glory of God. The concept appears again and again in
Edwards' work, even in the "terror" sermons such as ["**Sinners in the Hands of an Angry God**"] and **"The Justice of
God in the Damnation of Sinners."** It is the theme of the
dissertation, ***Concerning the End for Which God Created the
World,*** for in Edwards' view, God created the world in order
"that there might be a glorious and abundant emanation of his
infinite fulness of good *ad extra* ["on the outside"], or without
himself, and that the disposition to communicate himself, or
diffuse his own FULNESS, was what moved him to create the
world." To explain this emanation of goodness, Edwards returns to his favorite image of God as an infinite, inexhaustible
fountain of light. It is the controlling metaphor of the dissertation and perhaps the controlling metaphor of all Edwards'
work. It suggests a dynamic source of activity at once totally
full, yet constantly streaming and flowing. Thus God, possessing all perfections in absolute fullness, still sends out unending streams of divine and supernatural light, knowledge,
and holiness. When we speak of God's glory, we mean this
emanation. Yet the process is not one-sided. God not only
sends forth his glory, he *is glorified* by the emanation. (p. 34)

To turn to Edwards' [*History of the Work of Redemption*],
writes the contemporary historian Peter Gay, "is to leave the
familiar terrain of the modern world with its recognizable
features and legible signposts for a fantastic landscape, alive
with mysterious echoes from a distant past, and intelligible
only—if it can be made intelligible at all—with the aid of
outmoded, almost primitive maps." Other scholars, citing the
literal acceptance of scripture that informs Edwards' work, the
Calvinistic framework of his thought, and his defense of the
Puritan mode of life, agree with Gay's conclusion that, among
the intellectuals, Edwards was "the last medieval American."

They call him medieval to rebut Perry Miller's claim that he
was the first modern American. Granted, says Miller in his

1949 biography [see excerpt dated 1949], "he speaks from a
primitive religious conception which often seems hopelessly
out of touch with even his own day, yet at the same time he
speaks from an insight into science and psychology so much
ahead of his time that our own can hardly be said to have
caught up with him." Following Miller's suggestion that the
real life of Jonathan Edwards is the life of the mind, "the
interior biography," Edwards' scholars have bent their efforts
at locating that mind, so swallowed up in its studies, in a
tradition; and the choices seem to have narrowed down to
medieval or modern.

The debate appears to turn on the point that Edwards was, and
considered himself to be, a thoroughgoing, true-believing
Christian. By and large, those who call him modern believe
that he transcended his Christianity; those who call him medieval wish that he had transcended it but regret his failure to
do so. Dealing with Edwards in this way seems to lead to
stalemate. Perhaps a more fruitful approach to his symbolic
value would be to accept his Christianity and try to locate him
not as a medieval thinker or a modern intellectual but as an
American artist.

For many American artists share his fascination with the idea
that man must locate himself in relation to God. Ours is a
tradition of cosmic explorers, whose field notes have become
literary classics. Sometimes the adventurer goes no farther afield
than Walden Pond; sometimes his investigation takes him to
Mont-Saint-Michel and Chartres; in any case, the surveyors
have the common goal of mapping the realms of the divine
and the human. Their accounts of those vast territories, however, do not always tally one with the other.

Emerson, in the early nineteenth century, for instance, submitted the classic report of the transcendental party when he
found no barriers between the divine and human save those
temporary obstacles erected by society. He spoke for the party
that proclaims man's innocence and good nature and envisions
as its mythical hero the New American Adam. . . . (pp. 35-7)

Some of Edwards' modern readers, noticing the important role
of heightened sensitivity in his life and thought, regret that he
stopped short of the party of hope. If only he had not been
intellectually isolated in America (Stockbridge, yet), crippled
by his Puritan heritage, and diverted by a series of nettling
challenges to it, then he might have become, in Vernon Parrington's phrase, a "transcendental emancipator" [see excerpt
dated 1927]. But, alas, he merely wasted himself "re-imprisoning the mind of New England." Whether or not Edwards
was a transcendentalist manqué or the jailer of the New England
mind, he was certainly not a "transcendentalist emancipator."
He found a boundary between the realms of the divine and the
human and was unwilling to violate it. To him, man has no
right to encroach uninvited upon his rightful Sovereign's territory. He was terribly aware that men are the sons of the Old
Adam and carry crushing burdens of ancestry, history, and
race. He recounted the old adventure. His hero was the pilgrim,
and he knew that man could not struggle uphill to Zion by
relying on his own unique and inherent resources. Yet, even
as he recognized the imperfections of human nature and the
terrors of living in a world controlled by forces beyond human
understanding, he did not concede that the world is a perverse
joke. He did not enlist in a party of despair. Man *could* become
a "new creature," he could enjoy a ravishing experience of
transcendence, and he could enter Zion—the ***Personal Narrative***
testifies to that promise—but he needs assistance at every step.

If Edwards has affinities with any party of classic American artists, it is with that of Hawthorne and Melville. They did not share his religious doctrines, of course; but they shared his cast of mind. They also tried to locate the proper relationship between man and God. (Melville once sent a "grand, ungodly, god-like man" on precisely such an errand, and Hawthorne devoted a masterpiece to a minister who agonized over the question of whether he could "ransom" his soul.) In an optimistic age, they had their doubts about rationalists and transcendental emancipators alike. In a country yearning for simplicity and unity, they valued complexity and alternative possibilities. Melville, reviewing Hawthorne's *Mosses from an Old Manse* in 1850, finds Hawthorne strong because his stories are a rich and complicated mixture of light and shadow; the emancipators had not quite freed him of his Puritan heritage. "Certain it is," Melville remarks, "that this great power of blackness in him derives its force from its appeals to that Calvinistic sense of Innate Depravity and Original Sin, from whose visitations, in some shape or other, no deeply thinking mind is always and wholly free. For, in certain moods, no man can weigh this world, without throwing in something, somehow like Original Sin, to strike the uneven balance." Edwards, Hawthorne, and Melville, when they "weigh this world," are always aware of the uneven balance. (pp. 37-8)

[Edwards] wrote in a great variety of prose forms: treatises, sermons, histories, narrative reports, autobiography, biography, and letters. He did not try fiction as such, but his accounts in the *Faithful Narrative* of Phebe Bartlet and Abigail Hutchinson—prodigies of piety during the Northampton awakening—and his self depiction in the *Personal Narrative* demonstrate his ability to create characters. He did not try verse, but his treatises and sermons reveal a powerful grasp of rhetorical strategy and a fascination with the poetic image. He wanted to move his listeners and readers as well as instruct them, but he avoided rhetoric merely as decoration. He tried to write in a plain style that made use of figures for a purpose but not chiefly for their own sake. He drew many of his images, of course, from scripture; others he drew from natural objects, which he believed were "images and shadows" of divine things, manifestations in the natural world of God's supernatural glory. He had a good grasp for narrative strategy (witness his sense of the audience in **"Sinners"** and his **"Farewell Sermon"**) and a fine sense of timing. When his purpose was not narrative or hortatory, but expository, he displayed an extraordinary ability to manage a complicated argument in a sustained fashion. *Freedom of the Will* has long been regarded as his highest accomplishment in this vein, but for sheer expository skill in working with a complex, subtle subject, *Religious Affections* is surely a masterpiece. (p. 39)

Edwards has recaptured the interest of American scholars, artists, and students of American culture. We have learned that we can admire as well as condemn Edwards the man, for his integrity and toughness if for no other reason. We have been forced to reconsider the piety for which he was the most eloquent spokesman. It had no patience with the lukewarm formalist, and affirmed a fact the twentieth century has made brutally clear: that man should not be overly optimistic about his godly propensities. Finally, the life and works of Jonathan Edwards redirect our attention to a powerful dramatization of one of the great symbolic figures in our literature—the pilgrim, struggling in his progress but hopeful, always hopeful, of a glorious reception in Zion. (p. 40)

Edward M. Griffin, in his Jonathan Edwards, *University of Minnesota Press, Minneapolis, 1971, 46 p.*

CLYDE A. HOLBROOK   (essay date 1973)

[*Holbrook is an American clergyman, educator, and author whose theological works include* Religion, a Humanistic Field *(1963) and* The Iconoclastic Deity *(1984). In the following excerpt, he analyzes the relevance of aesthetics to Edwards's ethical system.*]

At first appearance, it seems remarkable that Edwards, usually counted both as a product and a creative mind of late Puritanism, should have fallen in with [an] aesthetic temper of mind, since popular opinion has often regarded Puritanism as rigorously ascetic and opposed to beauty in any form. The moralistic strain of late Puritanism especially has been seen to be in bitter conflict with forms of beauty which endanger the soul's duty to God and hence its salvation. What this reading of the Puritan mind sometimes forgets is the deep yearning for an ultimate beauty beyond all earthly beauties, which would crown the saints' never-ending discourse with the Creator. The Neoplatonic philosophy which informed the Cambridge Platonists and lured them toward the beautiful had also fed the springs of early Puritanism. And this tradition found its heir in Edwards. Its intuitive, penetrating grasp of realities beyond the deliverances of the senses found its counterpart in Edwards's "divine and supernatural sense." The possibility of beauty's seduction of the soul was tamed and brought within the bounds of the divine perspective when the true good of man was seen to lie in a transcendent beauty beyond that which the sensory world offered. But the rhetoric and play of images which portrayed the glorious and transcendent beauty of the saints' joyful reconciliation with God had its counterpart in the dolorous, vividly described scenes of the sinners' ultimate punishment. Here, for Edwards, was an aesthetic terminology which in embracing both the beauties of heaven and the horrors of hell was congenial to the Puritan temperament. It was not one which was satisfied to revel in nature for its own sake or in the workmanship of human hands. Rather it was a sense which pierced through a nature ever alive with signs and images of God's purposes. And the beauties wrought by man, although not without their attractive power, could only be of secondary importance at best, or at most a seduction to idolatry.

Edwards's picture, in terrifyingly vivid detail, of the fate of the sinners in the grasp of divine punishment is therefore no abrupt break with this tradition. His thought-world was one of drama to which an essentially aesthetic reading was appropriate. Neither is there a discontinuity in Edwards's thought when, in his posthumous works, he caught up in aesthetic terms his early meditations on excellence and beauty. In Edwards the Puritan aesthetic was expressed not only in terms of beauty compatible with the thought of moral sense philosophers of his century, but also as the proper medium in which to depict the entire scope of the soul's adventure as it either mounted to virtue or descended into eternal punishment. The highly imaginative language of damnation in the imprecatory sermons thus stands at the opposite pole from the placidly metaphysical language of *True Virtue* or the almost rhapsodic expressions of the *Dissertation concerning the End for which God Created the World*. The former casts theological objectivism in a starkly Calvinistic mode; the latter is suffused with a Neoplatonic perspective, but both employ a rhetoric and imagery consonant with an aesthetic consciousness. Beauty, consent, fullness of Being are balanced in the total aesthetic continuum by the images of horror, fear, and ugliness which drench the most severe of the imprecatory homilies. The concept of beauty then is not the only sign-manual indicating the aesthetic consciousness. The vision of the glorious beauty of divine Being and the beauty inherent in true virtue does not preempt the aesthetic

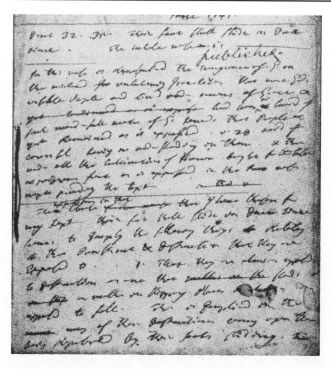

First manuscript page of one of Edwards's sermons.

field so long as Edwards's clinically unyielding gaze into the depths of hell remains in the field. (pp. 161-63)

As his major posthumous works reveal, the form which his aesthetic consciousness assumed was that of an essentially Neoplatonic ontology. However, this ontology is not developed as an exercise in aesthetics for its own sake, a rendering of beauty for the sake of beauty. Rather, the aesthetic tendency which informs the ontology is put in the service of spelling out the deepest and highest structures of religious and ethical experience, for which only the category of beauty could be conceived, as the crowning virtue for both God and man. (p. 164)

Although clearly Edwards's sensitivity to beauty can be traced in his earliest experiences and writings, he had not formulated in a systematic way a world view which could do justice both to the power and to the beauty of deity. He did render his ethical concerns within the structures of an essentially Calvinistic framework, but as he began to show in the *Religious Affections,* he was intent on providing fuller treatment of being which would encompass both the ethical and theological dimensions of human experience. To accomplish this feat, he found it necessary to adopt or readapt that type of ontology in which harmony was a ruling conception. Organic interrelatedness, rather than radical discontinuity, was to mark any outlook by which to account not only for morality but also for the relations of God, nature, and man, and even natural and moral evil. This was to be accomplished without contradicting the principle of the divine priority, that is, theological objectivism.

God therefore cannot be simply the sum total of beings in their infinite variety, as a consistent pantheism would hold. Rather he must be conceived as the ground or principle of harmony and interrelatedness among otherwise discrete beings and events. If he is to be understood as beauty or as that which beautifies, his must be a type of beauty which far excels all forms of beauty apparent in his creatures. As Edwards put it, "God is God, and distinguished from all other beings, and exalted above

'em, chiefly by his divine beauty, which is infinitely diverse from all other beauty." In respect to the moral qualities of creatures, however, there is also a beauty. The "good" and "right" take criteria, sanction, and ground in intelligibility from this structure of being which Edwards immediately intuited as both power and value. Where there is consent in personal beings to Being in general, there the good or right appears as beauty; where there is dissent, incompatibility, or lack of harmony with Being in general, then wrong and evil appear as ugliness and deformity.

Important as the category of beauty is for a full understanding of Edwards's position, it is also important to understand that the notion of beauty was not consistently maintained as the criterion of morality. Granted the difference in style and mode of expression between *True Virtue* with its normative but nonprescriptive nature, and many of the sermons with their definitely practical purpose, there remains the fact that beauty is seldom alluded to as central in the latter, whereas it continually and centrally appears in the former writings. This contention is supported in such works as *Charity and Its Fruits,* the sermons on social problems, some of the Awakening sermons, and the *History of Redemption,* where beauty is more often treated as culminating and eschatological fulfillment than it is a this-worldly possibility.

Charity and Its Fruits, one of Edwards's most practical expositions of the meaning of Christian love, serves as a test case in his use of the category of beauty. However, surprisingly enough, in the course of the sermons which make up this work, while benevolence is often mentioned, beauty, the surrogate of true virtue, is scarcely referred to. Scattered references to the love of God for his beauty and the beauty of holiness do appear, but not until Edwards speaks of the high reward of Christian love in heaven does the rhetoric of beauty appear full-blown. Beauty then comes into its own as an eschatological sanction and fulfillment of Christian love. In heaven all is to be "lovely" and "harmonious." It is a beauteous, loving place where no "unlovely persons" appear, where every saint is a "flower" in the garden of God and every soul "is as a note in some concert of delightful music, that sweetly harmonizes with every other note." Nowhere, however, is the austere language of symmetry and proportion employed as a guide to the proper expression or defining characteristic of love, as *True Virtue* maintains. The primary ethical message is couched in terms of the love of God and the neighbor, with warnings of punishment to those who fail to practice such love. The sermons which deal with civil government, the economic life, family order, and alleviation of poverty fail also to support the view that beauty is the ruling concept of all morality. God's constituted order, the principle of super- and subordination, justice, and honesty provide the moral substructure in these areas, although love is not forgotten in respect to family and as the motive for providing charity for the indigent. Edwards obviously leaned heavily upon the notion of order in these sermons, but it was an order which was not explicitly associated with beauty.

Beauty, however, is not totally missing from other representative sermons which move in the orbit of God's legalistic judgment and promise. Thus, for example, in his sermon entitled **"Ruth's Resolution,"** Edwards held forth on the theme of the glorious excellence of God, picturing him in the terms familiar to "God's Elect" as an "infinite fountain and ocean" of love. The theme of beauty appears again in **"The Peace which Christ Gives His True Followers,"** where it is associated with peace and dignity as the position of the saints. Sinners, on the other hand, fail to pursue the Christian life because they see in Christ ''no beauty nor comeliness'' which would draw their hearts to him. One of Edwards's most explicit appeals to the incentive which beauty provides is found in **"The Excellency of Christ"** where he repeatedly stresses the harmony or ''wonderful meeting of divine excellencies in Christ'' as an inducement to salvation. Ordinarily, however, Edwards's sermons indicate that the hardened sinfulness of man is too strong a power in daily life to yield easily to appeals for moral and spiritual beauty. In this respect he differs sharply from the assumptions of the British benevolence and moral sense philosophers who assumed a natural benevolent spirit in man.

The *History of Redemption* views the history of mankind and the church in the familiar Biblical pattern of judgment, punishment, reward, and renewal. Not until the climax of God's work in redemption is brought into full view does beauty provide the fitting category. At last the triumph of the saved is realized in terms of light, knowledge, praise, joy, holiness, and glory. Then the church will be united in ''one amiable society,'' and all parts of the world will be united in sweet harmony. In fact, the world will be as ''one church, one orderly, regular, beautiful society,'' a body beautiful in which all parts are ''in proportion to each other.'' Then Christ will come in his true beauty and glory, and punishment on Satan, devils, and sinners will be carried out. It is noticeable that order, discipline, and proportion are essential ingredients in the beauty which will exist at the denouement of history. But it is also clear that although beauty and excellence are God's aim in redemption, beauty is not the means by which the whole process is to be carried out. Beauty on earth and beyond history will be realized, since God cannot be frustrated in his purposes, but his means are still judgment and conversion, by which this high goal is to be realized. Thus moral beauty, as the glory of the redeemed society, was not at the same time the instrument by which the goal was to be reached. Rather, men, as the *Religious Affections* makes plain, may have only intimations of this beauty in holy affections which are distinguished by their symmetry and proportion.

A review of the evidence indicates that beauty was not the sole organizing principle about which Edwards consistently interpreted the moral and religious life, either for the individual or society. But it also becomes clear that he maintained a sense of beauty in the natural world even while he retained a spiritual and moral beauty as the height toward which the life of the redeemed aimed. Edwards was always persuaded of the reality and necessity for order, to be sure, but this order in the private and social life, although concerned aesthetically, was not uniformly identified with beauty even of the secondary type. The sinfulness of man, as well as essential human nature, made it necessary to posit a level of morality appropriate to the natural man while reserving to the elect the full vision and achievement of true virtue as beauty. In spite of his desire to view reality in an unified aesthetic fashion, Edwards had found it necessary to introduce a measure of discontinuity in moral and spiritual reality to allow for the operation of the natural moral sense. Although the concept of beauty was retained to refer to this lower order of morality, it is clear that secondary beauty partook more of ''equality and justice'' than it did of the supernatural relish for Being in general for its own sake. The distinction suggests that Edwards's appeal to beauty in both cases masked the fact that natural morality was the more basic, universally operative value in daily life, whereas true virtue or the beauty of benevolence in its comparative rarity was dif-ferentiated by valuational height rather than by comprehensive application in the common sense world. (pp. 165-70)

Edwards was to make clear the role of beauty in *True Virtue.* Whereas complacence fastened upon the beauty discoverable among consenting beings, benevolence fastened upon Being as such. Thus Being, not beauty, was to be foundational to true virtue. As he put it, even as there may be benevolence ''or a disposition to the welfare of those that are not considered beautiful,'' so in the divine nature benevolence is prior to the ''beauty of many of its objects'' as well as their existence. Beauty is the crowning category of moral value, but as Edwards's *Notes on the Mind* made explicit, beauty or excellence depends upon a proportion or harmony in being itself. Beauty used without qualification as a single term is simply vacuous without structure, and cannot therefore be employed as a model of the highest moral life. Nor is structure or proportionality simply reduced to a function of secondary virtue. It is an ingredient in Being itself. The term ''beauty'' by itself explains nothing unless it is considered not only in terms of both proportion and symmetry, but also in terms of certain spiritual and moral attitudes. Beauty is thus not simply beauty, but holiness, charity, loving kindness, glory, etc., as numerous passages of the *Religious Affections* show.

Beauty is less the underlying basis of true virtue than it is the product of harmonious relations of beings with each other and ultimately with Being itself. As such it is the teleological justification of virtue itself, for Edwards had kept his priorities clear by insisting that whatever is pleasing in ethical relations is pleasurable because of the relations themselves. Moral relations are not beautiful because they are pleasing; they are pleasing because they are beautiful, and they are beautiful because the structure of proportionality and symmetry inheres in the cordial consent in the relation to Being as such. Cordiality of consent is not itself a sufficient ground of beauty unless the structure of beauty is also present. If anything is clear about Edwards's treatment of true virtue, it is his conviction that beauty is built into the nature of being as constituted by God. It is not a sentiment first of all, but a structure of relations harmoniously proportioned, of which one is sensitively aware and appreciative. Hence Edwards describes moral beauty as ''that, belonging to the heart of an intelligent Being, that is beautiful by a general beauty, or beautiful in a comprehensive view as it is in itself, and as related to every thing that it stands in connexion with.'' Interrelationships are thus crucial. (pp. 171-72)

The principal questions which remain. . .relate to the justification Edwards found in interpreting true virtue as beauty. Can moral right or good be logically or experientially assimilated to an aesthetic good? Are there not significant differences between beauty and moral good? (p. 173)

In an aesthetic model of being it would appear that no place is left for moral or spiritual obligation unless beauty is firmly identified with the moral good and right. This alternative looks suspiciously like the ''supernaturalistic fallacy'' in which what is the case, the already extant, ordered structure of harmonious reality, determines what ought to be the case. The treatise on *True Virtue,* after all, reads like such a description of what true virtue would be like, if and when it exists. But from such a description, can any ethical responsibility be derived, even in the name of contributing to beauty?

It must first of all be clear that Edwards did not deal with this question in *True Virtue,* largely because the treatise does not purport to answer the question as to why or how one enters into true virtue. But in keeping with his aesthetic formulation of being and true virtue, an answer to the problem may be found. Edwards's vision of the beauty of the divine nature moves in a different orbit from that observed in his polemical and homiletical productions. In the latter, as we have seen, the motives for man's obedience to the divine will rest in the sovereign right of God to rule his world and the threat of everlasting punishment for those who disobey or the promise of heavenly felicity to those who do obey. Men ought to obey God because he rules by right of his power, greatness, and justice, and he provides the familiar sanctions of reward and punishment. However, in the case before us the situation is changed. It is the divine grace in Christ which transforms the fallen creature at the very center of his being so that what previously he did because he ought to, he does now from changed inclination and a renewed sense of divinity. His motivation is changed from a simple obedience to duty to a cordial consent to Being as such for its own intrinsic beauty. Cordial consent to Being not only is manifested in the symmetry and proportionality of holy affections, but marks the shift from the imperative to the indicative mood, from obligation to "relish" for the beauty which characterizes Being itself. Thus beauty draws the self to its goal in Being and reveals itself in the benevolence of the moral agent. God lures or persuades rather than commands. The rigor of moral obligation is thus converted into aspiration in response to the beauty of holiness. And "holiness comprehends all the true moral excellency of intelligent beings," as it does in God himself.

Understood in these terms, the aim of man in his new estate would seem to be that of sheer contemplation of beauty, a relatively static goal. . . . In this sense, beauty was an end in itself. However, in the broader sense of Edwards's system, the beauty ascribed to deity and the nature of true moral beauty was something more than a static condition. The vision of beauty, opened to the heart of man by grace, was itself an active principle. In figures of speech echoed later in his *God's End,* Edwards set it down in the *Religious Affections* that godliness in the heart had a direct connection with practice, even "as a fountain has to a stream, or as the luminous nature of the sun has to beams sent forth, or as life has to breathing, or the beating of the pulse, or any other vital act." Beauty is thus the nature of holy affections which provide the dynamics for moral practice, which in turn reveal the beauty inherent in the moral agent. Thus, contemplation may well have its place in the life of the "saint," but beauty does not rest in itself. It expresses or communicates itself even as the supreme instance of beauty, God, pours out his power and goodness. (pp. 175-78)

Moral beauty inheres in the interplay of intelligent beings with Being itself, even as within the Godhead, itself the Trinity, consists in the beauty of relationships among the three persons. (p. 182)

> *Clyde A. Holbrook, in his* The Ethics of Jonathan Edwards: Morality and Aesthetics, *The University of Michigan Press, 1973, 227 p.*

RUSSELL KIRK (essay date 1974)

[*An American historian, political theorist, novelist, journalist, and lecturer, Kirk is one of America's most eminent conservative intellectuals. His works have provided a major impetus to the conservative revival that has developed since the 1950s. The Conservative Mind (1953), one of Kirk's early books, describes conservatism as a living body of ideas "struggling toward ascendancy in the United States"; in it Kirk traces the roots and canons of modern conservative thought to such important predecessors as Edmund Burke, John Adams, and Alexis de Tocqueville. Founder of the conservative quarterlies* Modern Age *and the* University Bookman, *Kirk has long been a trenchant critic of the decline of academic standards in American universities:* Decadence and Renewal in the Higher Learning (1978), *in particular, is a forceful denunciation of the "academic barbarism" which he states has replaced the traditional goals of higher education—wisdom and virtue—with the fallacious ones of utilitarian efficiency and innovative forms of education. The result, in Kirk's view, is that "the higher learning in America is a disgrace." Kirk's detractors have sometimes been skeptical of the charges he levels against liberal ideas and programs, accusing him of a simplistic partisanship. His admirers, on the other hand, point to the alleged failure of liberal precepts—in particular those applied in the universities—as evidence in support of Kirk's ideas and criticism. In the following excerpt Kirk, while conceding Edwards's theological shortcomings, asserts the originality of his thought.*]

"You can't turn back the clock," we are told. Yet Edwards did just that. . . . The New England mind, which had been sliding into Deism, returned under Edwards' guidance to its old Puritan cast. (p. 340)

It will not do to think of Jonathan Edwards merely as John Calvin raised from the dead. Despite his discourses on human depravity, on divine wrath, and on the necessity for an overwhelming personal experience of conversion if a man would be saved, Edwards was a thinker of his own time, and one of remarkable originality. He had become familiar early with the writings of Sir Isaac Newton and of John Locke; he made Locke's empiricism—that is, the use of mankind's experience as proof of propositions—one prop of his renewed but reinterpreted Calvinism. As a theologian and a philosopher of creative imagination, Edwards has been called the peer of Calvin, Fénelon, Aquinas, Spinoza, and Novalis.

"His power of subtle argument," Sir James Mackintosh would write early in the nineteenth century, "perhaps unmatched, certainly unsurpassed among men, was joined, as in some of the ancient Mystics, with a character which raised his piety to fervour." All existence is mental, Edwards held—a concept which would work upon Ralph Waldo Emerson and the other American Transcendentalists, generations later. Certainly Edwards himself, the champion of Necessity and Revelation, was almost pure intellect.

God is the "being of beings," Edwards taught, the source of all benevolence. Virtue is the beauty of moral qualities, in harmony with the being of God. Goodness consists in subjugation of one's own will to God's good-will. Sinful though man is, God's design is benevolent: the misery and sinfulness that we behold about us are necessary for the contrasting existence of their opposites, happiness and virtue.

This world is a battle-ground, and we are put into it that we may contend for the good. In his most enduring work, [*Freedom of the Will*], Edwards argued that even God is bound by God's own will to pursue the good; no man is free from constraint to obey the divine will. Sin is only a negative, a vacuum—in short, sin is the absence of God, from whom all goodness radiates. "True religion in a great measure consists in holy affections," Edwards wrote in his discourse on *Religious Affections.* "A love of divine things, for the beauty and sweetness of their moral excellency, is the spring of all holy affections."

Although the severe Puritan morality was undiminished in Edwards, and although he held with Calvin that our every act is determined by some inexorable Necessity, his system won Americans by its consistency, appealing to their inherited beliefs, but adding to those doctrines a fresh persuasiveness. "Clearing away the crust of ancient superstition," Leslie Stephen says, "we may still find in Edwards' writings a system of morality as ennobling, and a theory of the universe as elevated, as can be discovered in any theology. That the crust was thick and hard, and often revolting in its composition, is, indeed, undeniable; but the genuine metal is there, no less unmistakably than the refuse" [see excerpt dated 1873]. From a nineteenth-century rationalist like Stephen, this is very high praise. (pp. 340-42)

Russell Kirk, "The New World's Christianity," in his The Roots of American Order, *Open Court, 1974, pp. 332-46.*

WILLIAM J. SCHEICK   (essay date 1975)

[*Scheick is an American educator and author, and the editor of* Texas Studies in Language and Literature. *His critical works include* The Will and the Word: The Poetry of Edward Taylor (1974) *and* The Slender Human Word: Emerson's Artistry in Prose (1978). *In the following excerpt, Scheick discusses the intent and imagery of two of Edwards's early sermons, "The Excellency of Christ" and "A Divine and Supernatural Light, Immediately Imparted to the Soul by the Spirit of God."*]

In many respects **"The Excellency of Christ"** is a typical Puritan sermon. It evinces a clear sense of organization and symmetry, which made it easy for parishioners to understand and, perhaps, to outline. It conforms to the traditional pattern of the sermon: (1) the identification of a biblical source, (2) the explication of the text, (3) the presentation of doctrine and exposition, and (4) the application or "use" of the doctrine. Based on Rev. 5: 5-6, Edwards' discourse presents the seeming paradox that Christ may be characterized as both a lion and a lamb. In developing these two polarities, Edwards constructs a chain of associations, so that Christ's union of the qualities of these two animals typifies His integration of glory and humility, majesty and meekness, equality with God and reverence toward God, and dominance and obedience, sovereignty and resignation. Furthermore, the lion typifies God as judge and the lamb represents God's creatures—both are joined in Christ. Although not distinctive in its content, this sermon does testify to Edwards' concern with structure and, as we shall see, with language and style.

Despite its reference to Christ's union of Godhead and manhood, **"The Excellency of Christ"** fails in general to extend much comfort to the listener. Unlike, say, the sermons on Christ delivered by Edward Taylor, this work hardly urges man to feel uplifted and encouraged by the dignity the Incarnation bestows on his earthly life. Instead it frequently stresses "the great distance" between God and man, less to impress the wonder of the Incarnation upon the hearer than to humble him, to reduce his sense of self-worth. The phrase "great distance" becomes a near refrain in the sermon, reinforced by remarks that "great men" are merely "bigger worms" and God is "infinitely high above you." Man is helpless with respect to the divine Will, of which he is also miserably ignorant. (pp. 18-19)

In the concluding part or application of **"The Excellency of Christ,"** Edwards somewhat soothes the feeling of insecurity aroused in his audience. Here he speaks of Christ as instrumental in narrowing the gap between God and man. . . . Herein lies an image of hope: "Any one of you that is a father or mother, will not despise one of your own children that comes to you in distress; much less danger is there of Christ despising you, if you in your heart come to him." Such consolation, however, is limited to the elect, the adopted children of God. Just who they are remains part of the mystery of the divine Will undisclosed to man. Thus Edwards' intimations of hope are not designed to abolish altogether the feeling of insecurity generated by the earlier part of the sermon. On the contrary, they underscore the fact that instead of becoming the fortunate children of a compassionate God, most men exist "in a state of exceeding great misery." (pp. 19-20)

Buttressing this impression of man's estrangement from God is Edwards' repudiation of human rational powers. If man is alienated from the very source of his being by a great distance and if he is totally dependent on an arbitrary and secret divine Will, what real help can reason offer in his search for inner identity? Edwards wrote, "Our understandings, if we stretch them never so far, cannot reach up to his divine glory." Man cannot even comprehend what the distance between him and God means because he can never know that from which he is separated. Edwards' attack on the understanding—by which he meant the composite of all of the mind's rational powers—should not be read out of context. Its limitations notwithstanding, it is a precious faculty; in fact, he explained elsewhere, the understanding is the principal faculty by which God has distinguished man from the rest of creation. It is a fundamental component of the natural image of God which men bear within them, whereby they are "akin to angels, and are capable even of knowing God, of contemplating the divine Being, and his glorious perfections, manifested in his works and in his word."

But even this remark, drawn from a later sermon [**"Wicked Men Useful in Their Destruction Only"**] when Edwards' understanding of the inner self would play a more significant role in narrowing the distance he early perceived between God and man, is finally restrained. . . . A man of his time, Edwards allowed that we may be able to learn much about the world in which we live, but as a spokesman for Puritan tradition he clung to the belief that our knowledge of the "things of religion"—knowledge attributable not to the empirical investigations of "natural reason" but to spiritual intuition—will always remain deficient, in spite of scriptural revelation, while we dwell in this world. Only the latter sort of wisdom can end the self's search for identity.

In **"The Excellency of Christ,"** then, Edwards assails any sense of security based on reason alone. He undercuts rational comfort not only explicitly but also implicitly in the language and style of the sermon. An early paragraph from the first part of the discourse, in which he is speaking of Christ, offers a good example of his technique:

> He is higher than the kings of the earth: For he is King of kings and Lord of lords. He is higher than the heavens, and higher than the highest angels of heaven. So great is he, that all men, all kings and princes, are as worms of the dust before him; all nations are as the drop of the bucket, and the light dust of the balance; yea, the angels themselves are as nothing before him. He is so high, that he is infinitely above any need of us; above our reach, that we cannot be profitable to him; and above our conceptions, that we cannot comprehend him.

Every phrase in this passage is carefully wrought. Each contributes in a progressive way to the eventual total realization that we cannot comprehend God. The images, it should be noted, initially ascend. The reader's mind is directed from the earthly realm of kings and lords, through the sky or heavens, to the realm of the angels. At this point the mind instinctively anticipates the next—we might say *logical*—step, namely now to pass on from angels to encounter something about God. But this rational expectation is frustrated, and the reader finds his thoughts suddenly thrust back to earth again, this time focusing on worms and dust. The immediate result of Edwards' management of language in this passage is an emotional or felt cognizance of our rational inability to comprehend God, an intuitive awareness reinforcing the explicit conclusion perceived by the conscious mind. The language of this passage is thoroughly appropriate to its content in that it too argues Edwards' point: the distance between God and man is indeed great, so vast that at best we can have only a fleeting experience or sense of Him in the affections of the heart. It is to the emotional level of the affections that the images of the passage finally appeal.

Edwards uses a second movement of images in the passage under discussion in order to underscore human ignorance and inadequacy. The series of images in this section recapitulates that of the first. Our attention is guided from kings and princes, to nations, to angels, and again its progress upward is abortive as we are left with the concept of "nothing." Yet, whereas the first sequence lacked any sort of resolution, abruptly returning to earth and beginning again, the second series does reach a climax. The resolution lies in the similes attached to the ascending images. Kings are likened to worms, nations to dust, and angels to nothing. Such a correlation frustrates the mind, for as each image in the second series ascends, its counterpart descends. Resolution is provided by cancelling the very terms of the statement. Reason thus balks, baffled by the paradox, and the reader realizes, at a felt, emotional level, what it means to be unable to come to terms with God, who is always "above our reach," beyond "our conceptions."

Now, too, the reader genuinely experiences the paradox of Christ's incorporation of the qualities of the lion and the lamb, how "there do meet in Jesus Christ infinite highness and infinite condescension." Edwards sought to thwart whatever sense of security men derived from their rational faculties and to communicate this to them explicitly, but also, more significantly, at the level of immediate intuition. No longer anchored on the ground of reason, they were to find themselves at sea emotionally. Cut adrift from the comforts of rationalizing about God's mercy, they were to confront the underlying currents of fear deep within the self. The fate of each of them, whether he was destined for salvation or for damnation, would remain unknown to him; what he could come to know was how helpless he was to save himself. Edwards wanted his audience to feel penetratingly, perhaps for the first time, that Christ's "majesty is infinitely awful." (pp. 20-3)

Looked at superficially, **"A Divine and Supernatural Light"** might paradoxically seem a very rational sermon about the limits of reason. The fact is, however, that underlying its formal structure and argumentation is a management of language similar in effect to that in **"The Excellency of Christ."** Edwards' language in this sermon communicates a feeling or sense of its ideas. At the simplest level Edwards reiterates a few conventional images, as for instance when he speaks of "the dawning of the light of glory in the heart" that gives "the mind peace and brightness in this stormy and dark world." He may have meant his audience to recall how they feel each dawn as the influx of life's energy returns to the gradually awakening

body; possibly he intended them to reexperience in their mind the sense of relief and renewal that comes with the dawn following a dark, stormy night. . . . The way in which such images or natural types were meant to work artistically is, I think, suggested in the following passage from the sermon: "There is a difference between having a rational judgment that honey is sweet, and having a sense of its sweetness. A man may have the former, that knows not how honey tastes; but a man cannot have the latter unless he has an idea of the taste of honey in his mind." No words can describe the taste of honey; each member of the audience must supply the context if he is to experience the meaning of the comment. It is precisely this moment of experienced or felt thought that Edwards aims for in his artistry. The attempt to elicit such inner sensations informs, we might say, the stylistic principle of decorum operative in many of his early sermons. He wishes to convey to his audience, at an emotional level, what is meant by the "inward sweetness" of grace.

Edwards recognized that images always threatened to get out of hand and might finally distract more than instruct. This is most likely why **"A Divine and Supernatural Light"** lacks the sort of imagery found in, say, **"Jesus Christ Gloriously Exalted."** Nevertheless, Edwards' principle of decorum still functions in this work with regard to style. The sentences of this discourse are declarative rather than hortatory, each projecting its meaning forward incisively. Nearly every phrase seems constructed so that its stress is not obscured by the flow of words. Edwards intensifies the effect of this technique by fashioning repeated phrases which become, in a sense, formulaic devices. In one paragraph, for example, he uses the phrase "there is a difference" twice, then adds a little more emphasis in "so there is a difference," concluding with "there is a wide difference." The outcome of such a slowly expanding formula is twofold: it lends a concreteness, a heavy seriousness, to the ideas it introduces and it tends to contribute an emotional dimension to our apprehension of the thoughts. Effective repetition of this sort becomes incantatory, somewhat hypnotic, finally communicating to an audience, at the level of feeling, a dimension which cannot, any more than it could with regard to the image of honey, be attained by mere rational comprehension.

Rhetorical control is similarly demonstrated in the conclusion of the sermon. Noting that "it is rational to suppose, that it should be beyond a man's power to obtain this knowledge and light by the mere strength of natural reason," Edwards closes the sermon by referring to four points progressively more difficult for the human mind to comprehend. He repeats first of all the simple difference between speculative knowledge and divine light; next, he contrasts secular joy with spiritual sweetness; third, he speaks of the effects of this light on the soul; and last, he refers to a "universal holiness of life," a "universal obedience" originating from "a sincere love to God, which is the only principle of a true, gracious, and universal obedience." In effect, this expanding definition progresses from the external world to the inner self. The ultimate context, the reality of God, lies within the self of the saint; with supernatural light he intuitively knows what is true and good, and, consequently, he does not require any external frame of reference provided by the world in which he lives. Special grace "assimilates the nature [of the soul] to the divine nature, and changes the soul into an image of the same glory that is beheld." This idea is what Edwards has in mind whenever he speaks of the soul as a luminary mirroring divine light. The inner self or heart becomes for him more revelatory of the divine Will than does nature.

When we consider how the ideas and techniques of many of Edwards' early sermons emphasize the inward sensation of grace as opposed to an intellectual response, we understand better why his parishioners, encouraged by their pastor, were enjoying a religious revival in Northampton. He had learned that neither a rationally governed series of steps, extended over a long period of time, nor an inflamed emotional response necessarily characterizes the drama of conversion. Generally, he concluded, the reception of grace is in fact peaceful in nature, though it always brings about, in its immediacy, a felt sensation in the heart. Edwards hoped to communicate this fact to his parishioners, not merely rationally but emotionally—as if to give them a foretaste of the experience. This is the principle of decorum functioning in the best of these early sermons: through the careful management of language and style Edwards sought to move the hearts of his audience in a way which simulated and, perhaps, prepared those same hearts for the sensation that accompanies the reception of supernatural light. (pp. 32-4)

> *William J. Scheick, in his* The Writings of Jonathan Edwards: Theme, Motif, and Style, *Texas A & M University Press, 1975, 162 p.*

TERRENCE ERDT   (essay date 1980)

[*An American educator, librarian, and author, Erdt is a student of American Puritanism. In the following excerpt, he assesses the impact of Edwards's thought on Ralph Waldo Emerson and other subsequent American writers.*]

Edwards' contribution to American literature may lie less in the artistic quality of his writings, though they occasionally exhibit estimable craftsmanship, than in the implications of his aesthetics. . . . But the question of the degree of influence the artistic implications of Edwards' system [of aesthetics] may have exerted remains to be explored. In short, a pressing question for students of early American literature is whether or not the import of art, beauty, imagination, and nature in his aesthetics significantly affected the Puritan tradition. If Edwards was known by more than just *The Freedom of the Will,* if the aesthetic character of his thought endured in Calvinist circles, then the possibility exists that his emphasis on natural beauty as a type of spiritual beauty, on the essence of regeneration as the sense of the heart or as the perception of divine beauty, entered the New England tradition and even, through currently undefined channels, eventually came to help shape the thinking of Ralph Waldo Emerson. (pp. 83-4)

The Puritan tradition as a whole, and specifically the nexus between Edwards and Emerson, still remains largely undefined. Conceivably, certain resemblances between the Calvinist and the Transcendentalist are coincidental, independent of a shared cultural background, perhaps mostly an accidental matter of personality. Both Edwards and Emerson, for instance, display a penchant for aesthetics, a curiosity as to what constitutes harmony and a wonder as to the extent it characterizes the values of both God and man. Emerson recalls passages from the [*Notes on the Mind,*] when he ponders: "It is the perpetual effort of the mind to seek relations between the multitude of facts under its eye, by means of which it can reduce them to some order." Edwards didn't for a moment dream of taking a step closer to the edge of relativism, of saying that even scientific theories and sacred theologies themselves proceed from the instinct to harmonize, yet he too emphasized that the mind orders objects by the principles of harmony. (pp. 87-8)

Some apparent connections between the thought of Edwards and that of Emerson undoubtedly owe to the careful study each made of Locke's sensationalism. The [*Essay on Human Understanding*] sculptured the thinking of both into resemblant shapes at certain points. Emerson, as had Edwards before him, regarded nature from a dual perspective, sensationalism and Puritanism, and concluded that it is ordained to furnish the mind with ideas. And he too expressed the function of nature in terms of Puritan typology, to serve emblematically as "the terminus or the circumference of the invisible world."

Certain other links between Edwards and Emerson seem to derive from Puritan principles to which each was exposed. The themes of perception and experience, for instance, stand out among the traditional Puritan conceptions that appear in the writings of both. To an extent, regeneration—according to Calvinism—verily consists of the power, entrusted through grace, to perceive the quality of mercy that lies in the Biblical promises of salvation. The ability to perceive depends upon the faculty of the will, upon the responses within its capacity. Everyone must see for him- or herself the truth embodied in Scripture in order to be saved, and the poignant realization of the Gospel promise constitutes the saint's firsthand experience, his experimental knowledge of God's wonderful mercy. Edwards redefined the doctrine somewhat, adding a dimension that endured in its appeal to the time of Emerson and beyond: the saint perceives, and so experiences, through the sense of the heart the beauty of holiness, or spirituality—ultimately the consent (harmony) of regenerate will to Being. To be sure, Emerson's system held the spiritual truths or laws perceived through regenerate vision to be more complex than what seventeenth-century Puritanism or even Edwards allowed. But the outlines of his teaching conform to Puritan tradition: "perception differs from Instinct by adding the Will. Simple percipiency is the virtue of space, not of man." Emerson emphasizes the uniqueness of the individual's point of view, or *angle of vision*. . . . As had his Puritan forefathers, Emerson preached that every man must perceive spiritual truth for himself, that without such direct, felt knowledge there is no real belief. . . . For Emerson, as for Edwards, the primary sign of divinity is beauty, and the principal motivation towards moral conduct is the apprehension of that beauty and the desire to consent to it—that is to harmonize or conform one's own will to it. . . . But of more importance, perhaps, in recognizing affinities between Edwards and Emerson is the espousal by the latter of an aesthetically structured universe, harmonized by the will of an artistically inspired God, to whom man regenerate consents through benevolence. Emerson also harkened back to the neoplatonic element in Augustinian piety and, as Edwards and numerous Puritans before, perceived a realm of primary being, consisting of divine goodness. . . . For all his supposed coldness, Emerson, as did Edwards before him, embraced passionately the conception of primary being, and as Edwards, found its primary quality to be beauty; and he too believed that all other beauty is but "the herald of inward and eternal beauty." He exclaimed, "I am thrilled with delight by the choral harmony of the whole. Design! It is all design. It is all beauty. It is all astonishment." Virtue harmonizes the soul to the realm of primary being, Emerson taught; acts of virtue possess an aesthetic dimension, one not materially different from what Edwards described in *The Nature of True Virtue,* "a true thought," he wrote, "a worthy deed, puts him [a man] at once in harmony with the real and eternal.'' Ironic it may seem, but Emerson, whose individualism some find offensive, made virtue out as requiring an effacement of self not dissimilar to what Edwards preached. . . . For Emerson the power of the individual rests entirely upon his conforming to the divine will, becoming an expression of it; only in knowing it, its laws, does one reach salvation, and hold the power that shapes the universe.

The ideal of selflessness and benevolence that Emerson describes . . . in one respect certainly was not original to Edwards; self-abnegation had long existed as a prominent facet of Calvinist culture, though as a principle it perhaps did not receive the articulation that a formal doctrine would merit. But Edwards interpreted the concept aesthetically, and something of his formulation (with, or in spite of, the help of the New Light theologians) passed into the Puritan tradition, occasionally to surface not only in the writings of Channing and Emerson, but in popular novels. In *The Minister's Wooing*, Harriet Beecher Stowe, not only a participant in but an historian of the tradition (as were Hawthorne and James), attempts to picture the vitality of Edwards' ideal:

> No real artist or philosopher ever lived who has not at some hours risen to the height of utter self-abnegation for the glory of the invisible. . . . Even persons of mere artistic sensibility are at times raised by music, painting, or poetry to a momentary trance of self-oblivion, in which they would offer their whole being before the shrine of an invisible loveliness. These hard old New England divines were the poets of metaphysical philosophy, who built systems in an artistic fervor, and felt self exhale from beneath them as they rose into the higher regions of thought. . . .

As the tone of the passage suggests, Stowe appreciated the richness of the Edwardsian aesthetic legacy, though she knew well, also, the severe mental anguish its conceptions could elicit. She perceived a moral beauty in renunciation for the sake of benevolence, as did James, who portrayed some noble as well as some pathetic ''renunciations'' of New England heroines.

The role Edwards assigned to art as a means to conceptualize spiritual sensations appears also to have become absorbed into the Puritan tradition. Art he realized could function as an *earnest*, or foreshadowing, of the sensation of spiritual beauty to be felt in heaven. . . . Stowe reveals the impact Edwards' theology had upon her when she attempts to explain the religious function of art: ''There is a ladder to heaven, whose base God has placed in human affections, tender instincts, symbolic feelings, sacraments of love, through which the soul rises higher and higher, refining as she goes, till she outgrows the human, and changes, as she rises, into the image of the divine.'' Such earthly delight is but ''the dim type, the distant shadow.'' . . . Though couched in Platonic phrasing, the substance of her comments points to Edwards; affections felt toward beauty and love of a natural order provide a glimpse of the emotions to be experienced in heaven. As Emerson noted, ''the contemplation of a work of great art draws us into a state of mind which may be called religious. It conspires with all exalted sentiments.''

In their concluding remarks, Edwards' biographers and commentators almost unfailingly express high admiration for his intelligence and sincerity and marvel at his adaptation of the New Science to his own theological ends. They praise the logical precision of his tracts and, occasionally, the economy and polish of his prose. Yet, as if by ritual, discussions of Edwards usually close on a note of ambivalence; there is dis-

appointment that he didn't break the shackles of Calvinism and escape the provincialism of the Connecticut River Valley and lead early America, intellectually, to full participation in the enlightenment. Between the lines lurks the assumption that his diet of New England Calvinism stunted his growth artistically and philosophically. Perhaps we should question the extent to which our estimation of Edwards should depend upon criteria external to his own values and purposes; but allowing the standard yardstick of achievement—influence and power—to measure his accomplishment, we may wonder if Edwards' stature isn't taller than previously suspected. He formulated an aesthetic that, certainly by implication, made large provision for art, that explicitly provided for the importance of the beauty of nature. Ideas about moral beauty, about the importance of perception, and about the signs of spiritual truth, appear in later American literature so similar to his own, that we can reasonably suppose that Edwards may have fathered them—though their precise genealogy remains a mystery. (pp. 87-93)

Terrence Erdt, in his Jonathan Edwards: Art and the Sense of the Heart, *University of Massachusetts Press, 1980, 123 p.*

BRUCE KUKLICK   (essay date 1985)

[Kuklick is an American educator and author who has written extensively on American history and philosophy. In the following excerpt, he compares Edwards's metaphysics with that of John Locke and George Berkeley and discusses Freedom of the Will.*]*

Calvinist thought in colonial America found its fullest expression in the writings of Jonathan Edwards. In his own time Edwards was recognized in the colonies and the Old World as an important figure. So penetrating was his writing that its theological biases only minimally detracted from the respect accorded him by less religious philosophers. Even they appreciated the elements of depth and tragedy in his concern for human destiny confronted by a majestic and mysterious God whose purposes were not identifiable with humanity's. Edinburgh's Dugald Stewart wrote [in *Dissertation, Exhibiting a General View of the Progress of . . . Philosophy* (1829)] that in ''logical acuteness and subtilty'' Edwards was the one American metaphysician who did ''not yield to any disputant bred in the universities of Europe.'' But for all his subtlety and acuity, Edwards was primarily an evangelical clergyman. His expositions compellingly combined unrelenting reason and poetic mysticism, and his writing was often matched by stirring revival oratory that reflected his vivid imagination and mastery of Congregational preaching. (p. 15)

Philosophy and theology were intertwined for Edwards, but even a cursory examination of his intellectual growth indicates that Calvinist divinity was not the main concern of his youth and early manhood. He mused on the problems plaguing Locke, Newton, Malebranche, and the Cambridge Platonists. His unpublished notes and connected writing suggest that his primary, sustained concern was rationalist metaphysics. In short, he had an intellectualist, philosophical interest in religion.

Edwards initially accepted Locke's distinction between primary and secondary qualities, but he also redefined the primary qualities. Apparently for Locke the primary qualities of matter inhered in the small, hard atomic particles of the Newtonian universe. Edwards argued that the primary qualities could be reduced to solidity. Then he asserted that solidity was just resistance, or the power to resist annihilation. That is, for Edwards, atoms, the material substances, were reconceived as centers of energy. But such centers of energy, being constant and active, wrote Edwards, depended upon God; or, rather, matter was nothing but the actual exertion of God's power or the expression of the law or method describing the exertion of God's power. "[T]he substance of bodies at last becomes either nothing, or nothing but the Deity acting in that particular manner in those parts of space where he thinks fit. So that, speaking most strictly, there is no proper substance but God himself. . . ."

In contrast to Berkeley, to whose work Edwards's is always compared, Edwards distinguished between secondary and primary qualities. The secondary qualities existed in the human mind, and in this sense they were mental. Human beings knew them immediately. But as the effects of substance on people, the qualities had no reality outside the perceiving minds. Primary qualities existed outside the human mind and constituted the fabric of the external world. Solidity characterized substance *independently* of human perception. But, against Locke, the primary qualities were also ideal; they were independent of individual minds but not of God's mind; in fact, they displayed his active will. "[T]he substance of all bodies," wrote Edwards, "is the infinitely exact and precise and perfectly stable idea in God's mind."

Edwards did not rest with this position, which changed in subsequent early writings. Locke and Edwards argued that the secondary qualities existed only when perceived and were less a part of the world's structure than primary qualities. Could this belief be defended? Locke also rejected direct knowledge of primary qualities, of substance and resistance, existing independently of human minds. The existence of such qualities could only be inferred. Could this inference be warranted? Edwards now argued for direct knowledge of these qualities existing outside of finite minds. Human beings at once encountered "the infinitely exact and precise and perfectly stable idea in God's mind"; they directly grasped the world of material substance, as it was. Inference was unnecessary to warrant the existence of primary qualities; they were experienced just as secondary qualities were. Moreover, secondary qualities were as much as part of the structure of things as were primary qualities. The secondary qualities, too, existed outside of human minds but not outside of God's mind. People confronted both sorts of qualities as they really existed.

In his later though still fragmentary youthful ruminations, Edwards consequently discarded the representational theory. Primary and secondary qualities were directly known. Further, Edwards continued to discount the metaphysical dualism that postulated, in addition to minds, the independent existence of material substance. Material substances were ideas in the mind of God. Edwards was an idealist, but he dissented from Berkeleyan idealism. The mental world was not a weaker image of God's ideas. When anything was known, God's ideas were experienced.

Edwards believed in *creatio continua* ["continuing creation"]. He put aside the deists' unmoved mover, who originated the world's motion and observed its movement at a remote distance. Edwards conceived God as an inexhaustible reality, an emanating light, communicating himself *ad extra* ["on the outside"] as the sun communicated its brilliance. The material world was thus not merely an idea in God's mind, but his eternal disposition, his will to display an idea. God created at every moment. The world was not an act or state of the divine consciousness, but God operating, expressing himself in finite modes and forms according to a stable purpose and by an established constitution. This was Plotinus' idea mediated into the Christian tradition by Augustine and popular among the English Puritans.

In both his early and later work Edwards availed himself of a different analogy. The world was like the moment-to-moment image in a mirror. The mirror-world depended on the objects it reflected. The images were not derived from or intrinsically connected to the immediately preceding or succeeding images. All were contingent on the objects, just as the world was produced from nothing through God's activity. Ideas in God's mind were the origin, source, and only cause of experience.

Strictly speaking, however, finite ideas were not caused by God's ideas. The finite were fragments or parts of God's ideas. Although finite ideas could not be equated with God—he was not the world—he willed a dimension of himself as the world. Certain ordered aspects of God were the world. Moreover, the human mind was just another composite of these ideas of God's. If his ideas were construed one way, they were the material world, the world of sense, of enduring objects, of structured experience. But the very same ideas could be construed as reflecting on the sense world. In this construction the order of the ideas would be different and would typify what was known as minds—the world of perception. God's mind revealed itself to us as two different orderings of one and the same aspect of his ideas. So Edwards wrote: "All existence is perception. What we call body is nothing but a particular mode of perception; and what we call spirit is nothing but a composition and series of perceptions, or an universe of coexisting and successive perceptions connected by such wonderful methods and laws."

Locke distinguished two qualities of objects, one of which existed outside of the mind. Berkeley denied that either sort of quality existed outside of mind, but he acknowledged the felt difference between what went on "in our heads" and the "perception of the world." Berkeley used Locke's dichotomy between sensation and reflection and separated two different sorts of ideas, God's and the individual's. Edwards disallowed both dualisms. Both secondary and primary qualities existed outside of finite minds but not outside of God's, and finite ideas were not weaker images of God's. To explain the felt difference he contended that the aspect of God's spirit revealed to man could be structured in two different ways. One way was the world minds knew; the other was the organization of minds knowing the world. (pp. 19-22)

• • • • •

Calvinists believed that humanity was depraved, requiring supernatural grace for salvation. At least from the end of the seventeenth century, non-Calvinists parried that individuals were not then responsible, that Calvinists ruled out free will, and that, consequently, God was the author of sin. For the Arminians, the will was not determined. Man could do good if he chose; he could respond (or not respond) to grace. Although Calvinists accepted determinism—that man sinned by nature and required supernatural grace to repent—they nonetheless believed in the will's freedom. The Catechism of the Westminster Assembly argued that natural man was "not able by his own Strength to convert himself, or to prepare himself thereunto." But the catechism also stated that "such as truly believe in Lord Jesus Christ, and love him in Sincerity, endeavoring to walk in all good Conscience before him, may, in this Life, be certainly assured that they are in a state of Grace."

In *Freedom of the Will* Edwards, too, argued for determinism, but as the full title indicated, he did not controvert freedom.

Rather, he contended against "the *modern* prevailing Notions of that Freedom of Will . . . supposed to be essential" to moral agency, virtue and vice, reward and punishment, praise and blame.

Before Edwards, Calvinists and their opponents had not thought through consistently what we now understand to be entailed by the demands of determinism and freedom. As late as 1690, when his [*Essay concerning Human Understanding*] was published, Locke juxtaposed a determinist understanding and an incompatible indeterminist notion. **Freedom of the Will** demonstrated in what sense a determinist could believe in responsibility and freedom.

Edwards contrasted freedom—what he called moral determinism—with constraint—natural determinism. People were free if they were able to do as they chose. The bride who said "I do" at the altar was free—she did as she wished. The prisoner behind bars was not free—he could not effectuate his will. How individuals got to do what they wanted was immaterial. Edwards argued that the will, like everything else, was enmeshed in a causal nexus. The will had a cause, but that it was caused had nothing to do with appraisals of freedom. The question of freedom arose when it was asked if a want or desire could be carried out. If it could, someone was morally determined but free. If it could not, someone was constrained (naturally determined) and not free.

Edwards also held that when free choices were made, people always chose to sin, and he illuminated this position by distinguishing between moral and natural ability. The sinner was naturally able to change his ways. He could, if he wanted to; but he did not want to. He was morally unable to do so. He would certainly sin. Edwards's doctrine of natural ability and moral inability at times intimated that moral determinism did not involve causality. For to argue that the sinner always sinned need not entail that the will was caused by something else. All it need entail was the perfect prediction that, given a choice, natural man would sin. At times Edwards appeared to take refuge in this ambiguity, and in one instance his son argued in this way. Might it then not be that the will was *self*-caused, the efficient cause of its own acts? That it had an inherent power to make a non-sinful moral choice? Was the will morally determined only in the sense that it was certain to sin?

Such a reading of Edwards cannot be justified because it allows that the sinner might have done otherwise than he did. This power, some theorists maintained, was essential to a genuine notion of free will. The bride at the altar had to be able to have said no were she given a second chance, be her character and circumstances the same. She had to have the ability to act contrary to the way she had acted if she were really free. For Edwards this was unacceptable. For his opponents it was necessary to genuine freedom: Edwards's distinctions between natural and moral determinism, and natural ability and moral inability, did not provide an authentic understanding of freedom.

Edwards scored more than one successful point against his antagonists, as he rendered their arguments. First of all, he pointed out, they found moral determinism and freedom compatible in the characters of Christ and God, who were both certainly virtuous and yet free. Why were freedom and determinism then not compatible in human beings?

More important, Edwards claimed that the alternative to his position was incoherent. The requisite notion of his adversaries was a spontaneous self-determination of the will, a liberty of indifference. But, Edwards argued, moral accountability and

responsibility meant predictability and behavioral regularity, a knowledge that in certain circumstances someone would act in a certain way. Unreliable conduct was just what was characterized as irresponsible. If the will had a spontaneous power, then no connection existed between causes and effect, between motives, dispositions, wants, or desires *and* what one did. Such a power did not simply justify irresponsibility, but it more accurately legitimated an unintelligible belief. A will whose choices were unconnected to motives was no will at all. Action based on such a will would be the hallmark of the irrational.

In an argument discussed repeatedly in the next 125 years Edwards said that the self-determination of the will was unintelligible and contradictory. If the will was self-determined, an act of the will prior to the act in question determined that act. But the same analysis might be made of the prior act. Then, urged Edwards, the analyst must at last reach a previous cause that was not an act of will, but a cause from which the entire sequence necessarily followed. In that case the will was not self-determined. Alternatively, it must be concluded that every act—even the first—was the effect of a prior act. That conclusion, wrote Edwards, was contradictory.

Freedom was having a will. Having a will meant possessing overriding habits, inclinations, desires, motives, and so on. God could not create free beings unless he created them in such a way that their actions would be morally determined. Human beings, through this moral determination, were certain to sin.

Edwards's position should be construed in light of his idealism. The will for Edwards was conventionally internal and consisted generically of volitions—intents, wants, desires, and feelings. In this sense, the will was coextensive with apprehensive ideas as they connected to activity in the world, Edwards's sense of the heart. His proposition "The will always is as the greatest apparent good is" was first of all a descriptive and not a casual account. The will was not so much a faculty of the self as a way of speaking about the self as a whole in its worldly engagements, a way of ordering human volitions to indicate their structure. Certain sorts would be followed by certain other sorts, and in standard cases, certain sorts would be followed by certain events in the physical world. The will was determined neither by the apparent good nor by anything else besides its own pleasure; it was neither autonomously indeterminate nor heteronomously determined by something outside itself. Rather, the will corresponded to its object, the apparent good. Each volition was an apprehension, the world as it appeared in our affectional contact with it at a given moment. The will was that part of the world with which we immediately engaged. For natural man it was a coherent body of apprehensions that justified selfish behavior, or rather selfish behavior incarnated in apprehensions.

The will synthesized the sensation and reflection revealed in action. Each volition was a disposition to act founded on the way the world appeared at a given moment; the volition was the mind's fiat. But the "letting it happen," for Edwards, occurred in a sphere beyond our immediate control, conventionally the external world. He distinguished between volition and external voluntary action, between fiat and behavior.

For Edwards will and act were mysteriously linked. Human wills were never the efficient causes of external events. The only efficient cause of these events was God. But God, for his own purposes, in certain circumstances appropriately linked the (internal) volitions with the (external) behavior that satisfied them. Freedom consisted in the effectuation of the will—the occurrence of the appropriate events in the external world. The prisoner was not free because his desire to open the door of his cell was not followed by the door's opening. The bride at the altar was free because her desire to say "I do" was followed by her saying "I do." But in each case God connected the willing and what followed. The bride was ultimately no more the efficient cause of her saying "I do" than the prisoner was *not* the efficient cause of the cell's not opening. (pp. 34-8)

The will for Edwards was just a series of volitions, of perceptual impulses (feelings, wants, desires), of *motives* to actions. Each of these, he held, was linked to the one following it. One motive determined the next. Similarly, a given motive was determined by its predecessor. But determination was again not efficient causation. The train of volitions was only connected in the way events in the natural world were connected. Given the predecessor volition, the sucessor could be certainly predicted. Given an occurrence of a certain type, God willed that an occurrence of another type would follow. The motive dominant in the will at a certain time was such that God efficaciously caused its succeeding volition. God produced the motive on the occasion of a preceding volition. There was a certainty in the serial appearance of the members of this chain of volitions, but no one of them ever (efficiently) caused any of the others.

Edwards's analysis combined the efficient causality of the deity and what he called philosophical necessity—the certainty of the connection of volition and volition, or volition and act. The realm of human freedom lay in the "occasional" nature of this kind of necessity: specifically with the moral determinism that connected volitions, and volitions and acts; and the natural ability that postulated action if motive were present. In effect, Edwards preserved freedom by maintaining two distinct spheres—that of the infinite (with God's efficient causality) and that of the finite (with occasional causality). This dualism did not obscure the fact that only God was causally efficacious, nor did it falsify the truth that man had free will any more than the truth that fire burned. An accurate analysis of freedom had two prerequisites. First, Edwards noted the difference between the natural order and the moral order, that is, between connections among objects *and* connections among volitions, and between volitions and objects. Second, he recognized that these orders were so arranged that it was certain that human beings would have selfish volitions and that selfish acts or further selfish volitions would follow on them. Finally, however, we must note that both internal and external—mind and world—were for Edwards simply divergent arrays of those aspects of God's ideas that human beings knew. (pp. 38-9)

> Bruce Kuklick, "Jonathan Edwards: Philosopher and Pastor" and "Jonathan Edwards: Theologian," in his Churchmen and Philosophers from Jonathan Edwards to John Dewey, Yale University Press, 1985, pp. 15-26, 27-42.

STEPHEN R. YARBROUGH   (essay date 1986)

[In the following excerpt, Yarbrough explicates Edwards's views on moral authority and divine communication through nature and grace.]

Throughout his life Jonathan Edwards worked on a treatise entitled a *Rational Account of the Main Doctrines of the Christian Religion Attempted.* He managed to finish very little of it. To get an idea of what he had intended to say, we have to reconstruct it from bits and pieces of materials not published in his lifetime and fill in the gaps with published works and our own conjectures.

The *Account* apparently tries to prove the unity of history, nature, and theology by way of a new kind of rhetoric. The treatise was also to be somewhat polemical: according to Perry Miller [in his introduction to his edition of *Images or Shadows of Divine Things*], Edwards was "highly resolved not to let science itself, as a mere description of phenomena, take the place of a philosophy or theology of nature."

We are, Edwards believed, persuaded to a right and proper understanding of the world by an encompassing rhetorical process of which science, though important, is only a single aspect. The problem with science, as with any discipline whose immediate aim is not obviously the illumination of the moral dimension of our lives, is that its ends tend to supplant the properly ultimate ends of God. In Edwards's view the origins and grounds of discourse determine its ends; thus the aim of rhetoric (had Edwards used this term) should be to reveal the possibility and explicate the means of God's communication with man. For the problem is not that communication among men is impossible without its being originated in God, but that it *is* possible. Coherent and rational visions of the world *can* be accomplished in a Godless society, yet they may damn the beings who live by them.

Edwards's basically Lockean position, which has been argued and reargued, is that words refer to ideas rather than to things themselves, that complex ideas are built from simple ideas which are themselves sensible, that men have the same sense organs with approximately the same capacities, and therefore that language can serve as the basis for a coherently organized society—for through language we can have certainty of nature "not only *as great* as our frame can attain to, but *as our Condition needs.*" To Edwards, however, man's needs go well beyond those enabling him to deal pragmatically with nature and to maintain a stable society precisely because "our condition," first and foremost, is that of fallen creatures. The world's languages are in a state of Babel: men born into societies whose languages are in such a state are destined to damnation because they cannot receive the Word.

Puritan theology asserted that God gave His Word to the children of Abraham (and the Puritans counted themselves among this small number), so that they might live within a social order that could prepare them to receive grace and eventual regeneration. The problem, of course, was that the Bible is as subject to multiple interpretation as any other text, as the dissension among the Protestants themselves forcefully demonstrated.

A paradox arose here. The Word was a necessary preparation for receiving grace, yet one's interpretation of the Word was suspect unless one had received grace. This paradox lies at the very center of Puritan theology, yet as far as I can determine, it was never stated explicitly. (pp. 395-96)

The right understanding of language must rest upon the rock that no Puritan saint could afford to deny—the experience of a saving grace. Accordingly, the Puritan conception of grace had to be formulated in such a way that it could perform this function within a theory of language. . . .

The question of what Edwards believed grace is and how it functions must be answered if we are to understand his view of language. Those who have asserted Edwards's Lockeanism, most notably Perry Miller [in an essay in his *Critical Essays on Jonathan Edwards*, edited by William J. Scheick; see Additional Bibliography] and Michael Colacurcio [in his *Puritan Influences in American Literature* (1979)], have argued that to Edwards grace functions as a "new simple idea." (p. 396)

In Edwards's theology grace is not understood as a "new simple idea." It adds no new element to experience; rather, it alters our experience by altering the perspective of our experience. Thus Edwards describes the effects of grace much as Kant will describe the effects of assuming the aesthetic standpoint. Like the aesthetic, the standpoint of grace provides a sort of universal position, a common ground on which all men can agree. Just as one can be assured of perceiving beauty when seeing it, so one can be assured of perceiving the effects of grace when in a state of grace. Thus, like the aesthetic standpoint, grace confers authority upon the individual within it. But of course the authority of the saint is not like what Kant conceived for the artist: God alone is the moral artist. The saint can merely appreciate His masterpieces—His Nature and His Word. Yet the saint's appreciation confers an authority upon him that goes well beyond that of the aesthete, for his perception of the right order of nature and his grasp of the right order of language establish his authority with regard to the word of God and therefore with regard to society.

Consider the following statement from a too little regarded thesis of Edwards entitled *On the Medium of Moral Government—Particularly Conversation*: "By all that we see and experience, the *moral* world and the *conversible* world, are the same thing. . . ." This passage exemplifies Edwards's view that rhetorical and moral authority issue from the same ground. Yet beyond this it contends that what can be said and what can be judged are identical. To put it another way, the world one apprehends is determined by the words one speaks. This notion lies at the center of Edwards's concerns. (pp. 397-98)

Edwards's argument in [*The Insufficiency of Reason as a Substitute for Revelation*] is, for all its length, a simple one. After defining reason as "that power or faculty an intelligent being has to judge the truth of propositions", he argues that the truth of any proposition in a chain of argument will always depend upon the truth of the proposition which precedes it. Original propositions will always depend upon some sort of experience, so that rational statements are only as valid as the experience grounding the original propositions. Experience is then classified into various sorts of "testimonies," including the testimonies of the senses, the memory, and history or tradition. (p. 398)

Edwards can easily conclude that revelation is a kind of testimony subsumed under the heading of history and tradition, and that the difficulties attending revelation are the very sort of difficulties one might expect to have concerning messages from God. In short man has no reason not to accept revelation.

Next, Edwards turns to argue that revelation is necessary. To summarize briefly his conclusions: Inasmuch as we are creatures, as creatures the light of nature alone can *possibly* give what must be known of the moral. But it is highly improbable, since the light of nature does not have "a *sufficiency of tendency* actually to reach the effect" or else it would have reached that effect, whereas the facts show that it has not. Furthermore, inasmuch as we are sinners, as sinners we cannot be led to what we need to know of religion by the light of nature "in any sense whatsoever." . . . Why not? Edwards does not explain here.

The explanation, of course, lies in the Calvinist doctrine of original sin. (pp. 398-99)

The important thing to note here is that original sin is defined as a shift in point of view from the infinite and divine to the finite and human. The proof of original sin is that men "come into the world mere *flesh*." . . . The horizon of man's perception is reduced because of his bodily existence, so that the result of original sin is "self-love"—man can constitute his world and its values only from their relations to himself. Edwards's doctrine of revealed religion, and consequently his entire moral philosophy and (our concern here) his theory of language, are guided by his conception of man as a sinner: man as a finite being.

But Edwards saw man as a finite being with an infinite purpose. The nature of man's end, indeed the end of all creation, Edwards consistently conceived in terms of communication: "The great and universal end of God's creating the world was to communicate himself. God is a communicating being." God's own essence defines Him as a communicating being. . . . The highest end of finite man, therefore, is to become able to be a recipient of communication from God.

Precisely how man can receive communication from God is the subject of *On the Medium of Moral Government*. Its point is that if conversation is to serve as such a medium, there must

The Edwards Memorial in First Church, Northampton.

be a social authority in the form of speakers who have been partially restored to the original point of view that was removed by Adam's sin.

Edwards begins by distinguishing between "God's *moral* government of his creatures, that have an understanding and will, and his general government of providential disposal." The latter refers to the operation of the material world. . . . [Since] the relationships among God and man and the world as material are sustained by God, inasmuch as the testimony of the senses is reliable, man is capable of understanding the material world. . . . Science and man's reason are adequate instruments for understanding the material world.

The moral world, however, is a different matter. Here, even when the objects of perception are the same as those of the material world, the relationships with which the perceiver is concerned are different. Moral perception is concerned with the objects' relationships to one another within a whole of value. Just as things are *beautiful* insofar as they maintain a proportionate or symmetrical bearing toward the other objects considered along with them, beings are *excellent* (the analog of beautiful) insofar as they reflect the totality of the spiritual realm within which men judge them. *Consent*, the relationship holding between spiritual beings, is one being's recognition of another's status as spiritual and as within a spiritual totality. Thus the greater the totality of the spiritual world within which a being is consented to, and the greater totality to which the being consented to consents, the greater the excellency; or, as Edwards says, "The more the Consent is, and the more extensive, the greater is the Excellency." . . . The highest of all possible excellencies is summed up in Edwards's famous phrase, "consent to Being in general." (pp. 399-400)

[Man] has been reduced by original sin to judging all relationships in terms merely of his own being—his own ends and aims. Since the relationships that hold in the moral world are relations of proportion, of part to whole, perspective is everything; and since the whole exists in terms of God's communication with Himself, man is by necessity doomed, unless God extends His communication to him.

Edwards's conception of unregenerate man is indeed that of the poor spider dangling helplessly over the flames. Man is unable by his own fallen essence to perceive the excellency of being in general or even to perceive that his final end should be to receive communication from God. Yet God has determined that man shall live within a moral government, and therefore it is necessary that he should receive communication from God. . . . (pp. 400-01)

Differentiating between "*mere cogitation*" and "*apprehension*," Edwards sees that most of the time we recognize the relations among things by recognizing the relations among the signs that refer to them. But when we do so we are not necessarily affected by them—that is, we ourselves do not change because our attitude toward the things has not changed. When we apprehend, however, we change in our attitude toward the things, so that the very appearances of the things change as well. For this reason Edwards calls the same differentiation one between "merely speculative" and "sensible" knowledge. . . . This differentiation extends "to all the knowledge we have of all objects whatsoever." . . . (p. 401)

Interpretation, then, can take place at two distinct levels. When Edwards applies this differentiation to the end for which man was created—to receive communication from God—it becomes clear that man can receive that communication in two ways.

The first is a preparatory communication, by a sign, i.e., through revelation. The second is an apprehension of the meaning of that same sign through grace. Another possibility is God's direct inspiration, the inspiration that produced revelation in the first place. Thus, the "extraordinary influence of the Spirit of God in inspiration imparts speculative knowledge to the soul, but the ordinary influence of God's Spirit communicates only a sensible knowledge of those things that the mind had a speculative knowledge of before." . . . Since knowledge of revelation without apprehension has . . . been classified by Edwards as a kind of speculative knowledge . . . , man *as an individual* clearly has no way of knowing before receiving grace what knowledge is or is not truly revelation or how to gauge the relevance of a true revelation.

Here Edwards's categorization of revelation as a kind of history or tradition takes on its full significance. He makes it clear in the fourteenth section of *On the Medium of Moral Government* that the kind of thoughts that people can think, indeed the kinds of phenomena that they can experience, are determined by the traditions they receive. . . . Unquestionably, without the testimony of visible saints to confirm the validity of the tradition, based upon the authority of their own conversion experience, the unconverted may very well accept a tradition that will prepare for them a way straight to hell. Edwards's view is clear: without first accepting the true tradition—the revealed Word—and without a knowledge of his intended final end, people have little chance of preparing themselves for that end.

The pilgrims' preparatory journeys toward their destined communion with the Father, consequently, are less individual than social acts. The possibility of the sinner's salvation is founded on the fact that human nature is a social nature, since language, as conversation, is sustained by society through the speech and actions of the visible saints. Only through language, as the Word of God, can sinners perceive relationships as God would have them seen. Moral behavior is for Edwards, then, a product of rhetorical forces: "The *ground* of moral behavior, and all moral government and regulation, is society, or mutual intercourse and social regards. The special medium of union and communication of the members of the society, and the being of society as such, is conversation." . . . Though finite human beings can judge the material world with some certainty insofar as the testimony of the senses and the framework of reason are trustworthy, they can judge the moral world with certainty only insofar as the testimony of tradition is sound. Here Edwards is obviously getting very close to a notion of cultural relativity. Perhaps he would have been forced into such a position if he had not already had the doctrine (and his experience) of grace ready at hand to authenticate revelation. Yet even the experience of grace does not *absolutely* confirm the Gospel to be the Word of God. . . . According to Edwards, only by inference do we suppose the Gospel to be the true Word of God.

This inference, though obvious, is extremely important for our understanding of Edwards's thought: grace can ground neither statements of apodeictic truth, such as mathematical proofs, nor empirically valid assertions of scientific truth; rather, grace supports statements which induce persuasion and conviction. Grace is a seat of rhetorical authority in exactly the same way as, to the rationalists whom Edwards opposed, such as the Earl of Shaftesbury, taste would be a seat of rhetorical authority. In other words we might say, without stretching the facts too far, that the effect of a saint's receiving grace would be analogous to a barbarian's receiving taste. The one who had once seen the forms of the world in a material, grasping, self-serving way now begins to see the order and proportion of God's great art.

Even after grace, of course, one remains a finite being but with an essence no longer of *radical* finitude.... [For] Edwards, as with Berkeley, anything is *as* it is perceived. Once one believes and is allowed by grace to apprehend God's communication through nature, one's perception of oneself changes; therefore the person changes, becoming a saint. In *The Nature of True Virtue* we find that the primary result of grace is a shift in the direction of one's perception from consent to beings in particular to consent to Being in General, which is at the same time a shift of motives from love of self to love of God. In **"A Divine and Supernatural Light"** we find that grace is accompanied by an intensification of one's appreciation of speculative truths of divine things. For our purpose now, however, what grace does not do is more interesting.

"This spiritual light," writes Edwards, "is not the suggesting of any new truths or propositions not contained in the word of God." ... When unregenerate man becomes saint, the Word remains the same, though his relationship toward the Word changes.... (pp. 401-03)

[It] seems best to infer ... that neither the Word nor the world changes but that the perspective of the recipient of grace changes, so that although nothing new is perceived in the Word or the world, they seem to be of a piece, a unified, coherent, and beautiful work of the Master Artist.

God's two chief means of communication with man, nature and revelation, were coherent because they were unified. Edwards described this conjunction between natural structure and Biblical scripture by advancing his new typology, one which went beyond the traditional interpretation of Old Testament events in view of their New Testament fulfillment, to include also the interpretation of revelatory statements in view of natural facts. The saints could communicate this correspondence to listeners as yet unconverted, thus preparing them for grace, only if the Word and the world were the same for regenerate and unregenerate alike. Therefore, Edwards could not have understood grace as a new Lockean idea. Such ideas are derived from sensory experience, so that the world would have to change before the saint could receive such an idea. The work of the ministry could not be effective if the spiritual truths the preacher spoke about were not visible in the world in which the congregation lived.

Finally we begin to understand the full significance of the short passage with which we began: "By all that we see and experience, the *moral* world, and the *conversible* world, are the same thing...." Conversation—language—brings into being those relationships which are in fact the moral world. Language itself is sustained by society, which in turn received the Word from tradition—the Bible as interpreted by the exemplary speech and behavior of the saints. (pp. 404-05)

Although Edwards undoubtedly drew his conceptions of the material world from the science of his day, he very likely drew his views on spiritual matters from a deeper, more reliable wellspring of Puritan thought. Edwards must have recognized the fundamental differences of attitude one must assume in order to shift from viewing the scholastic world of spirit to viewing the empirical world of matter. It is no wonder, then, that in many ways Edwards's work foreshadows the categorical understanding of transcendental philosophy. Very shortly, Kant would describe the aesthetic standpoint in terms of a capacity to see form as purposiveness when there is no apparent purpose.

Edwards defined the moral standpoint in terms of a capacity to see in form a very special purpose. Only God's grace could confer this capacity. It was as unlearned as it was undeserved. Yet once conferred, grace brought a man's vision back into focus, so that he saw as a unity both Scripture and Nature communicating God's harmonious, proportionate, beautiful work of art. This communication gave the Puritan saint his authority to interpret and to teach. (p. 408)

> *Stephen R. Yarbrough, "Jonathan Edwards on Rhetorical Authority," in* Journal of the History of Ideas, *Vol. XLVII, No. 3, July-September, 1986, pp. 395-408.*

ADDITIONAL BIBLIOGRAPHY

Blankenship, Russell. "The Flowering of the Colonial Mind." In his *American Literature as an Expression of the Natural Mind*, pp. 116-38. New York: Henry Holt and Co., 1931.
    Appraises Edwards within the context of American Puritanism and evaluates his significance as a mystic theologian.

Brooks, Van Wyck. "'Highbrow' and 'Lowbrow'." In his *America's Coming of Age*, pp. 3-38. New York: B. W. Huebsch, 1924.
    Consideration of Edwards and Benjamin Franklin as prototypes of the American character.

Canby, Henry Seidel. "The Colonial Background." In his *Classic Americans: A Study of Eminent American Writers from Irving to Whitman*, pp. 3-66. New York: Russell & Russell, 1959.
    Includes a consideration of Edwards's character and writing. Canby praises his subject as "a saint and a genius."

Carse, James. *Jonathan Edwards & the Visibility of God*. New York: Charles Scribner's Sons, 1967, 191 p.
    Interpretation of Edwards's work launched from an unusual premise. Carse proposes in his study to paint a "portrait" of Edwards, which is to be drawn against the background, not of eighteenth-century Puritan America, but of modern twentieth-century America. The study is therefore a kind of translation into modern terms of Edwards's work, as Carse believes that Edwards's importance lies not within the context of his particular historical setting, but in his continuing relevance in our times.

[Channing, William Henry]. "Edwards and the Revivalists: A Chapter of New England Ecclesiastical History." *The Christian Examiner and Religious Miscellany* XLIII (November 1847): 374-94.
    Study of revivalism in America. Channing accords due respect to Edwards's intellectual prowess, but refutes his theological conclusions.

Davidson, Edward H. "From Locke to Edwards." *Journal of the History of Ideas* XXIV, No. 3 (July-September 1963): 355-72.
    Assesses the impact of John Locke's philosophy on Edwards's thought.

Elwood, Douglas J. *The Philosophical Theology of Jonathan Edwards*. New York: Columbia University Press, 1960, 220 p.
    Examination of Edwards's spiritual and intellectual thought.

Laurence, David. "Jonathan Edwards, John Locke, and the Canon of Experience." *Early American Literature* XV, No. 2 (Fall 1980): 107-23.
    Differentiates Edwards's and Locke's conceptions of the nature of human experience and the groundings of religious faith.

Lesser, M. X. *Jonathan Edwards: A Reference Guide*. Boston: G. K. Hall & Co., 1981, 421 p.
    Comprehensive bibliography of writings about Edwards, from early eighteenth-century reactions to recent scholarly studies. Lesser precedes his bibliography with a useful overview of the major critical commentary.

Lowell, Robert. "Mr. Edwards and the Spider." In his *Lord Weary's Castle*, pp. 58-9. New York: Harcourt, Brace and Co., 1946.
  Poetic response to Edwards's image of the helpless spider held over the flames in "Sinners in the Hands of an Angry God."

———. "Jonathan Edwards in Western Massachusetts." In his *For the Union Dead*, pp. 40-4. New York: Farrar, Straus & Giroux, 1964.
  Poetic pilgrimage to Northampton highlighting the poet's attempt to understand what manner of man Edwards really was.

———. "The Worst Sinner, Jonathan Edwards' God." In his *History*, p. 73. New York: Farrar, Straus and Giroux, 1973.
  Lowell's impression, in verse, of Edwards's conception of the deity.

Miller, Perry. "Jonathan Edwards on the Sense of the Heart." *The Harvard Theological Review* XLI, No. 2 (April 1948): 123-45.
  Philosophical and critical commentary on a fragment, here transcribed, of Edwards's proposed but never completed work, *A Rational Account of the Main Doctrines of the Christian Religion Attempted*.

———. Introduction to "Benjamin Franklin, Jonathan Edwards." In *Major Writers of America, I: Bradford, Taylor, Franklin, Edwards, Irving, Cooper, Bryant, Poe, Emerson, Thoreau, Hawthorne, Longfellow, Lowell, Melville, Whitman*, edited by Perry Miller, pp. 83-97. New York: Harcourt, Brace & World, 1962.
  Contrasts Edwards and Benjamin Franklin within the context of their common Puritan society, calling the two "the pre-eminently eloquent linked antagonists in American culture."

More, Paul Elmer. "Jonathan Edwards." In his *A New England Group and Others*, pp. 35-65. Boston: Houghton Mifflin Co., 1921.
  General discussion of Edwards which combines biographical information, explanations of Edwards's defense of Calvinism, and More's impression of Edwards's character.

Niebuhr, H. Richard. "The Kingdom of Christ" and "The Coming Kingdom." In his *The Kingdom of God in America*, pp. 88-126, 127-63. Hamden, Conn.: Shoe String Press, 1956.
  Study of the religious climate of Edwards's day.

Niebuhr, Reinhold. "Backwoods Genius." *The Nation* 169, No. 27 (31 December 1949): 648.
  Review of Perry Miller's *Jonathan Edwards* (1949). Niebuhr esteems Edwards but considers Miller's conception of Edwards's modernity misguided.

Parkes, Henry Bamford. *Jonathan Edwards: The Fiery Puritan*. New York: Minton, Balch & Co., 1930, 271 p.
  Biography which attempts to recreate Edwards's world and emotions as well as his thoughts and deeds.

Richards, I. A. Review of *Images or Shadows of Divine Things*, by Jonathan Edwards. *The New England Quarterly* XXII, No. 3 (September 1949): 409-11.
  Review of Perry Miller's edition of Edwards's collection of notes, *Images and Shadows of Divine Things*.

Rogers, Henry. "An Essay on the Genius and Writings of Jonathan Edwards." In *The Works of Jonathan Edwards*, by Jonathan Edwards, edited by Edward Hickman, pp. i-lii. London: F. Westley & A. H. Davis, 1834.
  Defines the chief characteristics of Edwards's intellect and closely analyzes his major works.

Scheick, William J., ed. *Critical Essays on Jonathan Edwards*. Boston: G. K. Hall & Co., 1980, 310 p.
  Compendium of twenty-six essays, including studies by C. C. Goen, Joseph A. Conforti, and Wayne Lesser. The book is divided into four sections, providing essays on the topics of biography (both factual and interpretative), aspects of Edwards's thought, Edwards's theology in relation to preceding and succeeding thinkers, and literary criticism of Edwards's writing.

Stein, Stephen J. "Providence and the Apocalypse in the Early Writings of Jonathan Edwards." *Early American Literature* XIII, No. 3 (Winter 1978-79): 250-67.
  Posits that Edwards's *Theological Miscellanies, Notes on Scripture*, and *Notes on the Apocalypse* share a common concern with "theological and literary order in the Apocalypse relating to the theme of providence."

Watts, Emily Stipes. "The Neoplatonic Basis of Jonathan Edwards' True Virtue." *Early American Literature* X, No. 2 (Fall 1975): 179-89.
  Postulates that Edwards's *The Nature of True Virtue* was heavily influenced by Henry More's *Enchiridion Ethicum*.

Wendell, Barrett. "Jonathan Edwards." In his *A Literary History of America*, pp. 83-91. New York: Charles Scribner's Sons, 1917.
  Asserts that Edwards's theology was at odds with his society.

David Hume

1711-1776

Scottish philosopher, essayist, historian, critic, and auto-biographer.

Hume is considered an outstanding figure in world philosophy. He was a major promoter of what he called a "mitigated" form of philosophical skepticism—the doctrine that true knowledge is uncertain—and a profound explorer of the human mind. He wrote extensively on causation and perception, formulated theories of knowledge and ideas, and wrote at length on moral, political, and religious issues. Also a prolific historian, he wrote an important multivolume history of England. Above all else a man of reason who aimed to shed light on the reasoning process itself, Hume was, in the words of his friend, Scottish economist Adam Smith, a man of "the most severe application, the most extensive learning, the greatest depth of thought, and a capacity in every respect the most comprehensive."

Hume's life was decidedly an intellectual and literary one. He was born on his family's estate at Ninewells in Berwickshire, the son of Joseph Home, a lawyer, and Katherine Falconer Home, an ardent Calvinist. Hume was of a distinguished family, and proud of it: in his short autobiography, *The Life of David Hume, Esq., Written by Himself*, composed four months before his death, Hume noted that on his father's side the family was "a branch of the Earl of Home's or Hume's," and that his mother was "the daughter of Sir David Falconer, President of the College of Justice." Joseph Home died during David's infancy: most of Home's estate passed to David's older brother, John, leaving David a small patrimony of fifty pounds per annum—too little ever to offer financial independence. David remained at Ninewells until age twelve, when he went with John to the University of Edinburgh. The boys remained there for nearly three years, but, as was then common, left without degrees. Although the Edinburgh curriculum probably included some philosophy, all that is known for certain about David's studies is what he himself recorded, that he "passed through the ordinary Course of Education with Success."

Hume returned to Ninewells intending to study law, but soon, as he related, he found in himself "an insurmountable Aversion to anything but the pursuits of Philosophy and General Learning." Around age eighteen a "new scene of thought" opened to him, and he began the work which became his *Treatise of Human Nature*. The *Treatise* was written mostly at La Flèche in Anjou, France, where Hume had temporarily retired in 1734, the better to manage on his fixed income and to recover from protracted ill health. Back in London in 1737 and with his completed *Treatise* in hand, Hume searched long for a publisher, eventually signing a contract for an edition of a thousand copies of the work's first two books, "Of the Understanding" and "Of the Passions." Publication of the third book, "Of Morals," was delayed for over a year. Hume was deeply disappointed by the reception of his anonymously issued study. As he later wrote, "Never Literary Attempt was more unfortunate than my Treatise. It fell *dead-born from the Press....*" In an effort to promote the work, *An Abstract of a Late Philosophical Performance, Entituled, "A Treatise of Human Nature"*—an essay almost surely by Hume himself—was brought out anonymously in 1740. Within two years, however, Hume's desire to disown the style, if not the substance, of the *Treatise*

was reflected in his *Essays, Moral and Political* in which, remaining anonymous, he described himself as a "new Author." This work, unlike the *Treatise*, was a considerable success: readers were numerous and critics were favorable, and Hume was pleased with the money he made. On the strength of this success he solicited a professorship at Edinburgh but, probably owing to the perception among some members of the university that the *Treatise* was philosophically unsound, was unsuccessful in his bid. Hume lowered his sights and was made tutor to the insane Marquis of Annandale. He found this position extremely disagreeable, but it gave him time to begin his *Philosophical Essays concerning Human Understanding* (more commonly known by its later title, *Enquiry concerning Human Understanding*) and probably to write *Three Essays, Moral and Political*, both of which he issued in 1748, the latter under his own name.

Henceforth Hume was a known, if not yet famous, thinker and writer. He was called to serve as a military judge-advocate, traveled as an aide-de-camp to Turin, and began a correspondence with the French political philosopher Charles-Louis de Secondat, Baron de La Brède et de Montesquieu. At the same time, Hume was becoming markedly controversial: his work attracted adverse criticism—mostly on religious grounds, for he was an avowed atheist—but he decided "never to reply to anybody." By 1751 he was settled in Edinburgh. He was made librarian of the Advocates Library there, and availed himself of the books in his charge to write his *History of England*. After a slow start the work became a huge success in Britain and abroad: Hume found himself financially independent and was courted by London and Edinburgh society. He went to Paris in 1763 as secretary to the British ambassador, and was received with thunderous acclaim. Persons of the highest rank and distinction competed for his favor, flattering him shamelessly. He left Paris for London in 1766, taking Jean-Jacques Rousseau with him. But Rousseau, who was testy, unpredictable, and paranoid, cruelly embarrassed Hume by falsely accusing him of all kinds of misdeeds, and the two quarreled publicly and in print before Rousseau's sudden departure. Back in Edinburgh in 1769, Hume had a great house built for himself and worked on his *Dialogues concerning Natural Religion,* which was published posthumously. Sixteen months after having been, as he wrote, "struck with a disorder in my bowels" in 1775, he died peacefully at home.

Hume's works are for the most part philosophical, historical, or religious. Hume set out his theory of knowledge in two studies: Book I of the *Treatise of Human Nature* and the later, more considered, *Enquiry concerning Human Understanding.* Like John Locke, whose philosophy he knew well, but against the teaching of René Descartes, Hume denied the existence of innate ideas. He maintained that beliefs are not based on reason, because reason is grounded only on the inadequate data of experience. Reason may be certain only in mathematics, making the existence of demonstrative knowledge based on reason and experience impossible. The identification of causes and effects, Hume argued, results from reason, but such identification does not approach certainty and is not strictly rational. Instead, it is the result of imagination, and may be misleading. According to Hume, "natural instincts" make up for the inadequacy of experience and reason in matters of causal inference. Through habitual association—that is, through our observation of apparent causal relationships—a *feeling* of causality is all that is possible, not absolute knowledge of the *fact* of causality. In a word, the inference of causes results not from rational detection but from the observation of habitual relationships. Here Hume differed from Locke, who believed that causal power could be observed internally. Hume went on in both the *Treatise* and the *Enquiry* to consider the nature of belief and the process of cognition. No type of reason or empirical observation, he argued, will yield what passes for knowledge unless it is based on experience. But, he continued, it is natural, right, and essential to believe that causal relationships do exist, have always existed, and will continue to exist in the future. This is Hume's "mitigated" skepticism: a denial not of belief but of evidence.

Hume's moral philosophy, which is set out in Book III of the *Treatise* and in the *Enquiry concerning the Principles of Morals,* is as original as his theory of knowledge. Recognizing that moral distinctions are felt, not judged, Hume defined morality as those qualities that are approved (1) in whomsoever they exist and (2) by practically everyone. He judged the merits of these qualities by their utility and agreeableness. Utility, he argued, involves the fitness of anything to serve a good end. When utility involves a concern or regard for the well-being of others—as it does in the case of justice, for instance—it is an example of what Hume termed "public utility." Equally, utility may involve qualities primarily useful to those who have them (as opposed to qualities primarily useful to others) but which are not the result of self-love. These qualities include honesty, truthfulness, diligence, and frugality. Hume also recognized qualities which are felt as pleasant by their owners regardless of who the owners happen to be. This type of moral utility is evident, for example, in acts of benevolence, which

are instrinsically attractive *and* serve others. Finally, Hume isolated a type of morality in those qualities which are approved simply because they are agreeable or attractive to others. Such qualities include modesty and good manners. Although Hume's concern with utility has suggested to a few critics a utilitarian or Benthamite concern with the greatest good for the greatest number, Hume appears to have had no such concern. Rather, his system of moral philosophy is generally acknowledged to be essentially eudaemonistic: it holds that the highest goal is happiness and personal well-being.

Hume's historical and religious works reflect in some degree their author's philosophy, but for the most part they are independent of it. Hume attempted in his ambitious *History of England* to outdo his predecessors in comprehensiveness, attention to detail, impartiality, and judiciousness. By the standards of the time, he was successful on all counts. Nevertheless, many critics—chiefly the modern ones—note that the *History* is marked by a strong prejudice against the Whigs and, especially in the later volumes, by an obsession with the English attitude toward Scotland, an attitude generally dismissive and, to Hume's mind, at best condescending. The work's most notable advance is its strong emphasis on social and literary events as opposed to military and political ones—a far cry from some earlier chronicles of kings, conflicts, and councils. Hume's religious skepticism is evident in his essay "Of Miracles" and the expansive *Dialogues concerning Natural Religion.* Searching for the "origin of religion in human nature," Hume maintained that the premises for religious argument are faulty, illogical, unauthoritative, and inconclusive. Noting the general uncertainty of causes, he concluded his exposition of "The Natural History of Religion" with these words: "The whole is a riddle, an ænigma, an inexplicable mystery." Hume also wrote on political economics, most prominently on interest rates, protectionism, the circulation of money, and the nature of wealth. Unlike Adam Smith, his junior, he did not work out a system of economics, but his writings in this area are considered lucid and well-reasoned.

Evidence for Hume's reputation among his contemporaries is copious and authoritative. Once in the public eye, Hume quickly acquired a coterie of admirers and disciples, including Adam Smith and the historian Edward Gibbon. He was, however, fair game for a host of detractors as well. Indeed, the most striking feature of Hume criticism—both then and now—is the extent of disagreement. Early critics praised and pummeled the philosophical and historical works alike. "In a word," wrote the Comtesse de Boufflers to Hume, "[*The History of Great Britain, under the House of Stuart*] is a rich mine of morality and of instruction, presented in colours so bright, that we believe we see them for the first time." Equally, Immanuel Kant and Rousseau extolled Hume and his writings extravagantly, the former crediting Hume's philosophical works with inspiring his own, the latter declaring: "Mr. Hume is the truest philosopher that I know and the only historian that has ever written with impartiality. . . . He has measured and calculated the errors of men while remaining above their weaknesses." Notwithstanding such favorable reviews, James Beattie and Joseph Priestley wrote full-length attacks on Hume's logic, reasoning, and philosophical principles, and Thomas Gray said this about Hume's philosophical works: "I have always thought David Hume a pernicious writer, and believe he has done as much mischief here [in England] as he has in his own country."

Nineteenth-century critical views of Hume's works generally reflected those of the eighteenth century, but with the addition of more penetrating analysis of Hume's historical and philosophical methods. Hume's historical works retained their earlier prominence and were edited, reedited, and reissued throughout the century, but now serious critical challenges were advanced—and by distinguished thinkers and historians at that. Thomas Jefferson declared that "Hume's [*History of England*], were it faithful, would be the finest piece of history which has ever been written by man," adding the serious charges that Hume "suppressed truths, advanced falsehoods, forged authorities, and falsified records." Jefferson's was a strong statement of a fairly common theme: Hume's historical prejudices. Another critic, Friedrich von Schlegel, found more to praise than to reprove in Hume's works, but he located faults nevertheless, including what he considered Hume's partisan imposition of his own "narrow principles and views of things not perfectly just." Still, Hume's works—historical and philosophical alike—had their champion in Hume's first important biographer, John Hill Burton, and in the latter part of the century Thomas H. Huxley honored Hume with a careful, largely commendatory exposition of his philosophy.

Commenting on Hume's historical works, the twentieth-century critic Lytton Strachey claimed that Hume's "cast of mind was in reality ill-fitted for the task he had undertaken." This assessment of Hume's *History of England* echoed the nineteenth-century train of thought, but Strachey's rigorous and highly favorable review of Hume's philosophy represents a new departure altogether, one which helped open an era in Hume studies. Strachey said of Hume and his character that "no mortal being was ever more completely divested of the trammels of the personal and the particular, none ever practised with a more consummate success the divine art of impartiality." Strachey continued: "With astonishing vigour, with heavenly lucidity, Hume leads one through the confusion and the darkness of speculation." Similarly, Huntington Cairns called Hume's *Treatise of Human Nature* "the greatest single work in the whole range of English philosophy," and Isaiah Berlin claimed this of Hume: "No man has influenced the history of philosophical thought to a deeper and more disturbing degree." Critics of this century are by no means united in unqualified admiration of Hume, however; some have questioned his method, while others have faulted his motivation and results. Still, the twentieth-century critical consensus holds that Hume was a profound and serious thinker, a pioneer in the field of human cognition, and a historian who recognized how broadly his field could be defined. These achievements few critics deny him, in spite of their occasional disagreement with his determinations.

Hume is renowned today for shedding light on how human beings think, successfully propounding a penetrating and original system of moral philosophy, producing a monumental history of England, and making important contributions to political and religious theory. Most importantly, he forced men to think about thinking itself: to ask how and why their thoughts were as they were, and to accept no conclusion in this regard too lightly. No longer was it possible for philosophers and others to take cognitive matters for granted, for Hume helped establish searching analysis as the standard of inquiry, and such has been the standard ever since. Near the end of the eighteenth century, Immanuel Kant claimed that Hume "first interrupted my dogmatic slumber," giving his speculative philosophy "a quite new direction." Since Kant's day Hume's influence has increased, not waned, and Hume is recognized today as one of his country's greatest sages, as a renowned philosopher, and as a thinker of world importance.

PRINCIPAL WORKS

A Treatise of Human Nature: Being An Attempt to Introduce the Experimental Method of Reasoning into Moral Subjects. 3 vols. (essay) 1739-40

†*An Abstract of a Book Lately Published, Entituled, "A Treatise of Human Nature," wherein the Chief Argument of That Book Is Farther Illustrated and Explained* (essay) 1740

Essays, Moral and Political. 2 vols. (essays) 1741-42

A Letter from a Gentleman to His Friend in Edinburgh (essay) 1745

‡*Philosophical Essays concerning Human Understanding* (essays) 1748

Three Essays, Moral and Political, Never before Published (essays) 1748

A True Account of the Behaviour and Conduct of Archibald Stewart, Esq. (essay) 1748

An Enquiry concerning the Principles of Morals (essay) 1751

The Petition of the Grave and Venerable Bellmen (or Sextons) of the Church of Scotland, to the Hon. House of Commons (essay) 1751

Political Discourses (essays) 1752

§*Essays and Treatises on Several Subjects*. 4 vols. (essays) 1753-56

‖*The History of Great Britain, Vol. I: Containing the Reigns of James I. and Charles I.* (history) 1754; also published as *The History of Great Britain, under the House of Stuart*, 1759

Four Dissertations (essays) 1757

‖*The History of Great Britain, Vol. II: Containing the Commonwealth, and the Reigns of Charles II. and James II.* (history) 1757

‖*The History of England, under the House of Tudor*. 2 vols. (history) 1759

‖*The History of England, from the Invasion of Julius Caesar to the Accession of Henry VII*. 2 vols. (history) 1762

Exposé succinct de la contestation qui s'est élevée entre M. Hume et M. Rousseau (essay) 1766

[*A Concise and Genuine Account of the Dispute between Mr. Hume and Mr. Rousseau*, 1766]

The Life of David Hume, Esq., Written by Himself (autobiography) 1777

#*Two Essays* (essays) 1777

Dialogues concerning Natural Religion (dialogues) 1779

Original Letters of David Hume, Relative to J. J. Rousseau (letters) 1799

The Letters of David Hume. 2 vols. (letters) 1932

**"An Historical Essay on Chivalry and Modern Honour" (essay) 1947; published in journal *Modern Philology*

New Letters of David Hume (letters) 1954

*This work contains the essays "Of the Understanding," "Of the Passions," and "Of Morals."

†Hume's authorship of this work is not universally recognized.

‡This work is a revision of Book I of *A Treatise of Human Nature*, with the addition of the essay "Of Miracles."

§This work is the first collected edition of Hume's essays and treatises. In this work *Philosophical Essays concerning Human Understanding* is called *Enquiry concerning Human Understanding*.

‖These works were published as *The History of England, from the Invasion of Julius Caesar to the Revolution in 1688* in 1762.

#This work contains the essays, ''Of Suicide'' and ''Of the Immortality of the Soul,'' originally intended for publication in *Four Dissertations* but withdrawn in proof.

**This work is the first complete text of what is believed to be Hume's earliest extant essay.

THE HISTORY OF THE WORKS OF THE LEARNED (essay date 1739)

[*In the following excerpt from an anonymous review of* A Treatise of Human Nature, *the critic or critics—for it has been argued that the review is the work of two persons, the final ''conciliatory'' paragraph being the work of the journal's editor, not the primary commentator—outline the central tenets of Hume's philosophy. Hume himself described the review as ''somewhat abusive.''*]

I Do not recollect any Writer in the *English* Language who has framed a System of human Nature, morally considered, upon the Principle of this Author, which is that of Necessity, in Opposition to Liberty or Freedom. (p. 353)

[Having] made it appear, that our simple Impressions are prior to their correspondent Ideas, a very few Instances excepted, Method seems, our Author says, to require we should examine our Impressions, before we consider our Ideas. But after informing us that Impressions may be divided into two kinds, those of *Sensation* and those of *Reflexion,* and briefly illustrating both sorts, he gives us to understand, that it will be necessary to reverse that Method, which at first Sight seems most natural; and, in order to explain the Nature and Principles of the human Mind, give a particular Account of Ideas, before we proceed to Impressions.

In Pursuance of this Resolution, he goes on: First, to describe and distinguish the Ideas of the Memory and Imagination: Secondly, to explain the Connexion or Association of Ideas: Thirdly, to assign their several other Relations: Fourthly, to define and fix the true Essence of Modes and Substances: And Fifthly, to determine the Nature of abstract Ideas. On all these Heads, a Man, who has never had the Pleasure of reading Mr. *Locke*'s incomparable Essay, will peruse our Author with much less Disgust, than those can who have been used to the irresistible

Ninewells House, Hume's birthplace.

Reasoning and wonderful Perspicuity of that admirable Writer. (p. 359)

I proceed to say a Word or two of the second and third Sections [of volume II of *A Treatise of Human Nature*]. In the former we have somewhat about *Probability,* and *the Idea of Cause and Effect.* In the latter we are told, *Why a Cause is always necessary.* All manner of Persons, that have any Antipathy to the Argument *à Priori* for the Existence of God, may repair to this latter Section, where they will have the Satisfaction of seeing it utterly demolished. This Writer has here destroy'd the Foundation of it, and so there's an End of the whole Fabrick. Dr. *Clarke,* and one *John Locke,* Esq; whom he particularly names, two of the most superficial Reasoners, were, as well as many others, so weak as to fancy, that *whatever begins to exist, must have a Cause of Existence;* nay, *Hobbes* himself, as much an Atheist as we believe him, was of this Opinion: Every one knows, how he, and the greater men afore named, pretended to evince the Proposition; but our Author pronounces all they produced for that Purpose fallacious, sophistical, and frivolous; and he really thinks it unnecessary to employ many Words in shewing the Weakness of their Arguments.

But, tho' our Author has quite erased the Argument *à Priori* for the Divine Existence, I would willingly hope, he has no Intention of weakening this fundamental Truth, that *there is some one necessary, eternal, independent Being;* nor does he directly assert a *Thing may come into Being without a Cause;* only he will have *Experience* to be the sole Road by which we can arrive at the Certainty of this *Thesis, Whatever has began to exist, must have had a Cause of its Existence.* And that *Experience* will lead us thereunto, is what, I fancy, our Author aims at proving, in some ensuing Sections. I would be more positive upon this Point if I could; but having run over the Sections referr'd to (13 in Number) in order to know whether this were the real Scope of them, I acknowledge I cannot understand them enough to pronounce dogmatically: Nor is it to be wonder'd at, if I am at a Loss in this Matter, seeing any Man must be so, who is not bless'd with an extraordinary Penetration; according to our Author's own Acknowledgement of the relative Obscurity of this Part of his Argument. (pp. 377-78)

In the second Section [of the Fourth Part] he considers Scepticism with regard to the Senses. And here he inquires into the Causes which induce us to believe in the Existence of Body: And his Reasonings on this Point he begins with a Distinction which will contribute, he assures us, very much to the perfect understanding of what follows. We ought, as he says, to examine apart those two Questions, which are commonly confounded together, *viz. Why we attribute a* CONTINUED *Existence to Objects, even when they are not present to the Senses?* and *why we suppose them to have an Existence* DISTINCT *from the Mind and Perception.* Upon a very careful Scrutiny, he rejects what has commonly been offered for the Solution of these *Queries,* and proposes one of his own; which, as he apprehends, very clearly and satisfactorily accounts for what is contained in them.

Glad would I be, could I present my Readers with the Sentiments of so profound and accurate a Genius as we are now dealing with, upon one of the most abstruse and perplexing Topicks in all Metaphysicks; but alas! they are of too wide an Extent for the Compass of this Article: However, we will endeavour to introduce some Specimens thereof, whereby we shall at least see how happy a Talent he has for surmounting those Difficulties, which have proved the *ne plus ultra* of many others.

"After a little Examination we shall," he says,

find, that all those Objects to which we attribute a continued Existence, have a peculiar *Constancy,* which distinguishes them from the Impressions, whose Existence depends upon our Perception. Those Mountains, and Houses, and Trees, which lie at present under my Eye, have always appeared to me in the same Order; it is so also with my Bed and Table, my Books and Papers; and when I lose Sight of them by shutting my Eyes, or moving my Head, I soon after find them recur upon me without the least Alteration. This is the Case with all the Impressions, whose Objects are supposed to have an external Existence; and is the Case with no other Impression, whether gentle or violent, voluntary or involuntary.

This Constancy, however, is not so perfect as not to admit of very considerable Exceptions. Bodies often change their Position and Qualities, and after a little Absence or Interruption may become hardly knowable. But in these Changes they preserve a *Coherence,* and have a regular Dependence on each other, which produces, very reasonably, the Opinion of their continued Existence.—This *Coherence* therefore in their Changes, is one of the Characteristics of external Objects, as well as their Constancy.

(pp. 385-87)

• • • • •

[This] Writer deals mightily in *Egotisms;* he is no less notable for Paradoxes. . . . [In] the fifth Section, which I am now entering upon, there are at least half a Dozen, enough to stagger any Man who has not a strong Head-piece. The Title of this Section is, "Of the Immateriality of the Soul." And the Intention of it is to shew, that the Immateriality of the Soul is a nonsensical Expression, and the Belief of it a most horrible Heresy. The Author begins with telling us, that the intellectual World, though involved in infinite Obscurities, is not however perplexed with any such Contradictions as in the foregoing Pages he has proved to attend every System concerning external Objects, and the Idea of Matter, which we fancy so clear and determinate. There are indeed certain Philosophers, as he complains, who, envious of this good Quality in the Subject, would fain load it with those Absurdities from which it is naturally free. These troublesome Gentlemen are the curious Reasoners concerning the material or immaterial Substances, in which they suppose our Perceptions to inhere. But, to put an effectual Stop to their Impertinence, he has set them a Question, which he very well knows is sufficient entirely to employ them till Doom's-day, and that is, in a few Words, *What they mean by Substance and Inhesion?* Some of the Difficulties which will obstruct the Response of this *Query,* he has very fairly set down, and he as fairly warns his Antagonists that he will keep them strictly to the Point, and that it will be in vain for them to think of shuffling; for if any should attempt to evade the foresaid Difficulties, by saying, that the Definition of a Substance is *something which may exist by itself,* and that this Definition ought to satisfy us, he presently whips about, to their Confusion, and observes, "That this Definition agrees to every thing that can possibly be conceived; and never will serve to distinguish Substance from Accident, or the Soul from its Perceptions." For thus he reasons. "Whatever is clearly conceived may exist; and whatever is clearly conceived after any manner, may exist after the same manner." (pp. 393-94)

[The purpose of this article is] to make the *Treatise* it refers to more generally known than I think it has been; to bring it, as far as I am able, into the Observation of the Learned, who are the proper Judges of its Contents, who will give a Sanction to its Doctrines, where they are true and useful, and who have Authority to correct the Mistakes where they are of a different Nature; and lastly, to hint to the ingenious Writer, whoever he is, some Particulars in his Performance, that may require a very serious Reconsideration. It bears indeed incontestable Marks of a great Capacity, of a soaring Genius, but young, and not yet thoroughly practised. The Subject is vast and noble as any that can exercise the Understanding; but it requires a very mature Judgment to handle it as becomes its Dignity and Importance; the utmost Prudence, Tenderness and Delicacy, are requisite to this desirable Issue. Time and Use may ripen these Qualities in our Author; and we shall probably have Reason to consider this, compared with his later Productions, in the same Light as we view the *Juvenile* Works of *Milton,* or the first Manner of a *Raphael,* to other celebrated Painter. (p. 404)

> *A review of "A Treatise of Human Nature," in* The History of the Works of the Learned, *Vol. II, November & December, 1739, pp. 353-90; 391-404.*

DAVID HUME?   (essay date 1740)

[*In the following excerpt from the anonymously published* Abstract of a Book Lately Published, Entituled, "A Treatise of Human Nature"—*a work widely attributed to Hume himself—the critic defends the argument of* A Treatise of Human Nature *and comments on the work's critical reception.*]

The work [*A Treatise Human Nature*], of which I here present the Reader with an abstract, has been complained of as obscure and difficult to be comprehended, and I am apt to think, that this proceeded as much from the length as from the abstractedness of the argument. If I have remedy'd this inconvenience in any degree, I have attain'd my end. The book seem'd to me to have such an air of singularity, and novelty as claim'd the attention of the public; especially if it be found, as the Author seems to insinuate, that were his philosophy receiv'd, we must alter from the foundation the greatest part of the sciences. Such bold attempts are always advantageous in the republic of letters, because they shake off the yoke of authority, accustom men to think for themselves, give new hints, which men of genius may carry further, and by the very opposition, illustrate points, wherein no one before suspected any difficulty.

The Author must be contented to wait with patience for some time before the learned world can agree in their sentiments of his performance. 'Tis his misfortune, that he cannot make an *appeal to the people,* who in all matters of common reason and eloquence are found so infallible a tribunal. He must be judg'd by the FEW, whose verdict is more apt to be corrupted by partiality and prejudice, especially as no one is a proper judge in these subjects, who has not often thought of them; and *such* are apt to form to themselves systems of their own, which they resolve not to relinquish. I hope the Author will excuse me for intermeddling in this affair, since my aim is only to encrease his auditory, by removing some difficulties, which have kept many from apprehending his meaning. (pp. 3-4)

> *David Hume?, in a preface to his* An Abstract of a Treatise of Human Nature: 1740, A Pamphlet Hitherto Unknown, *1938. Reprint by Cambridge University Press, 1965, pp. 3-4.*

DAVID HUME   (letter date 1751)

[*In the following excerpt from a letter to his friend and confidant Sir Gilbert Elliot of Minto, Hume comments on his* Philosophical

Essays concerning Human Understanding *and* Treatise of Human Nature.]

I believe the *Philosophical Essays* contain every thing of Consequence relating to the Understanding, which you woud meet with in the *Treatise*; & I give you my Advice against reading the latter. By shortening & simplifying the Questions, I really render them much more complete. *Addo dum minuo* ["more may come from less."] The philosophical Principles are the same in both: But I was carry'd away by the Heat of Youth & Invention to publish too precipitately. So vast an Undertaking, plan'd before I was one and twenty, & compos'd before twenty five, must necessarily be very defective. I have repented my Haste a hundred, & a hundred times.

> *David Hume, in a letter to Gilbert Elliot of Minto in March or April, 1751, in his* The Letters of David Hume, Vol. I, *edited by J. Y. T. Greig, Oxford at the Clarendon Press, Oxford, 1932, p. 158.*

HYPPOLYTE DE SAUJON, COMTESSE DE BOUFFLERS (letter date 1761)

[*An outspoken eighteenth-century French admirer of Hume's works, the Comtesse de Boufflers was probably the prime cause of Hume's sojourn in France during the 1760s. She introduced Hume to the leading French personalities of the day, and her efforts to promote Hume's reputation were tireless. For years she and Hume corresponded candidly and often; they talked intimately when they were together, and, it has been suggested, may have been lovers for a time. "You have saved me," Hume once wrote to her, "from a total indifference towards everything in human life." In the following excerpt from her first letter to Hume, she extols the style and lessons of Hume's* History of the Stuarts.]

For a long time, Sir, I have struggled with conflicting sentiments. The admiration which your sublime work has awakened in me and the esteem with which it has inspired me for your person, your talents, and your virtue, have frequently aroused the desire of writing to you, that I might express those sentiments with which I am so deeply smitten. Considering, however, that I am unknown to you, that my approbation will seem pointless to you, and that reserve and even privacy are more suitable to my sex, I am timid of being accused of presumption and of allowing myself to be known to my own disadvantage by a man whose good opinion I shall always regard as the most flattering and the most precious of blessings. Nevertheless, although the reflections I have made on this subject appeared to have much force, an irresistible inclination rendered them unavailing; and I can only add one further instance to a thousand others to justify the truth of that remark which I read in your *History of the Stuarts*: "Men's views of things are the result of their understanding alone: their conduct is regulated by their understanding, their temper, and their passions."

Thus, when my reason tells me I ought to remain silent, my enthusiasm prevents me from following its authority.

Though a woman and of no advanced age, and despite the dissipated life one leads in this country, I have always loved reading; and there are few good books in any language or of any kind that I have not read, either in the original or in translation. And I can assure you, Sir, with unquestionable sincerity, that I have found none which, in my judgment, unites so many perfections as yours. I know no words to express how I felt while reading that work. I was moved, transported, and the emotion which it engendered is, in some manner, painful in its continuance. It elevates the soul and fills the heart with sentiments of humanity and benevolence. It enlightens the mind by showing that true happiness is closely united with virtue and discovers, by the same light, what is the end, the sole end, of every reasonable being. In the midst of the calamities which, on all sides surrounded Charles I, we see peace and security shining brightly and accompanying him to the scaffold; whereas trouble and remorse, the inseparable attendants of crime, follow the steps of Cromwell, even to the throne. Your book also teaches how the best of things are liable to abuse, and the reflections made on this subject ought to increase our vigilance and diffidence in ourselves. It animates the reader with a noble emulation; it inspires love of liberty; and it teaches, at the same time, submission to the government under which we are obliged to live. In a word, it is a rich mine of morality and of instruction, presented in colours so bright, that we believe we see them for the first time.

The clearness, the majesty, the touching simplicity of your style delight me. Its beauties are so striking that, despite my ignorance of the English language, they cannot escape me. You are, Sir, a wonderful painter. Your pictures have a grace, a naturalness, an energy surpassing the reaches of the imagination.

But how can I express the effect produced upon me by your divine impartiality? I would that I had, on this occasion, your own eloquence with which to express my thought! In truth, I believed that I had before my eyes the work of some celestial being, free from human passions, who, for the sake of mankind, has deigned to write the history of these latter times.

I dare only add that in all the products of your pen, you show yourself a perfect philosopher, a statesman, an historian of genius, an enlightened political scientist, a true patriot.

All these sublime qualities are so far above the understanding of a woman, that it is fitting I should say little about them; and I have already great need of your indulgence for my heresies against prudence and propriety, by the excess of my veneration for your attainments. This I pray you, Sir, and, at the same time, the most profound secrecy. The step I have taken is perhaps extraordinary. I fear that I shall be reproached for it; and I would be grieved if the sentiment which prompted it should not be recognised. (pp. 425-26)

> *Hyppolyte de Saujon, Comtesse de Boufflers, in a letter to David Hume on March 13, 1761, in* The Life of David Hume *by Ernest Campbell Mossner, second edition, Oxford at the Clarendon Press, Oxford, 1980, pp. 425-26.*

JEAN-JACQUES ROUSSEAU (letter date 1762)

[*Rousseau was a French philosopher and essayist who has often been called "the father of Romanticism" because of the influence he exerted on William Wordsworth and Percy Bysshe Shelley in England and on Johann von Schiller and Immanuel Kant in Germany. Though he was by no means a literary critic in the strict sense, his ideas of individual freedom, of the supremacy of emotion over reason, of the goodness of the primitive human being as opposed to the civilized one, and of the benefits of "natural" education, permeate late-eighteenth- and the whole of nineteenth-century literature. In the following excerpt from a letter to the Comtesse de Boufflers, he praises Hume's philosophical and historical method, comparing it with his own.*]

Mr Hume is the truest philosopher that I know and the only historian that has ever written with impartiality. He has not loved truth more than I have, I venture to believe; but I have sometimes put passion into my researches, and he has put into his only wisdom and genius. Pride has often led me astray by my aversion for what was evil or what seemed so to me. I have hated despotism in the republican and intolerance in the theist. Mr Hume has said: here is what makes intolerance, and here is what makes despotism. He has seen from all points of view what passion has let me see only from one. He has measured and calculated the errors of men while remaining above their weaknesses.

> *Jean-Jacques Rousseau, in an extract of a letter to Madame la Comtesse de Boufflers on August 20, 1762, in* The Life of David Hume *by Ernest Campbell Mossner, second edition, Oxford at the Clarendon Press, Oxford, 1980, p. 507.*

THOMAS REID (essay date 1764)

[*Reid helped found the Scottish school of common-sense philosophy and wrote a work often cited as the most important defense of common-sense thinking,* An Inquiry into the Human Mind, on the Principles of Common Sense *(1764). By "common sense" Reid meant the beliefs common to rational beings as such. He held that philosophy was best pursued by the methods of the physical sciences, and followed John Locke in his appeal to experience, observation, and induction in cognitive study. But Reid did not accept Locke's (and later Hume's) assumption that what is immediately perceived is something that exists only as part of the perceptual situation in which it figures, and maintained that while Hume himself had wisely attempted to apply scientific method to his study of the human mind, he had been misled into skepticism by his acceptance of René Descartes's "ideal system" and its powerful attacks on the whole problem of certainty. Reid therefore rejected Hume's skepticism, following common sense in his acceptance of existence independent of perception. In the following excerpt from* An Inquiry into the Human Mind, *Reid ironically considers the foundation of Hume's skepticism.*]

The present age, I apprehend, has not produced two more acute or more practised in [the philosophical study of the knowledge of the human mind], than the Bishop of Cloyne, and the author of the ***Treatise of Human Nature***. The first was no friend to scepticism, but had that warm concern for religious and moral principles which became his order: yet the result of his inquiry was a serious conviction, that there is no such thing as a material world; nothing in nature but spirits and ideas; and that the belief of material substances, and of abstract ideas, are the chief causes of all our errors in philosophy, and of all infidelity and heresy in religion. His arguments are founded upon the principles which were formerly laid down by Des Cartes, Malebranche, and Locke and which have been very generally received.

And the opinion of the ablest judges seems to be, that they neither have been, nor can be confuted; and that he hath proved, by unanswerable arguments, what no man in his senses can believe.

The second proceeds upon the same principles, but carries them to their full length; and as the Bishop undid the whole material world, this author, upon the same grounds, undoes the world of spirits, and leaves nothing in nature but ideas and impressions, without any subject on which they may be impressed.

It seems to be a peculiar strain of humour in this author, to set out in his introduction, by promising with a grave face, no less than a complete system of the sciences, upon a foundation entirely new, to wit, that of human nature; when the intention of the whole work is to shew, that there is neither human nature nor science in the world. It may perhaps be unreasonable to complain of this conduct in an author, who neither believes his own existence, nor that of his reader; and therefore could not mean to disappoint him, or to laugh at his credulity. Yet I cannot imagine, that the author of the ***Treatise of Human Nature*** is so sceptical as to plead this apology. He believed, against his principles, that he should be read, and that he should retain his personal identity, till he reaped the honour and reputation justly due to his metaphysical *acumen*. Indeed he ingeniously acknowledges, that it was only in solitude and retirement that he could yield any assent to his own philosophy; society, like day-light, dispelled the darkness and fogs of scepticism, and made him yield to the dominion of Common Sense. Nor did I ever hear him charged with doing any thing, even in solitude, that argued such a degree of scepticism, as his principles maintain. Surely if his friends apprehended this, they would have the charity never to leave him alone.

Pyrrho the Elean, the father of this philosophy, seems to have carried it to greater perfection than any of his successors; for if we may believe Antigonus the Carystian, quoted by Diogenes Laertius, his life corresponded to his doctrine. And therefore, if a cart run against him, or a dog attacked him, or if he came upon a precipice, he would not stir a foot to avoid the danger, giving no credit to his senses. But his attendants, who, happily for him, were not so great sceptics, took care to keep him out of harm's way; so that he lived till he was ninety years of age. Nor is it to be doubted, but this author's friends would have been equally careful to keep him from harm, if ever his principles had taken too strong a hold of him.

It is probable the ***Treatise of Human Nature*** was not written in company; yet it contains manifest indications, that the author every now and then relapsed into the faith of the vulgar, and could hardly, for half a dozen pages, keep up the sceptical character.

In like manner, the great Pyrrho himself forgot his principles on some occasions; and is said once to have been in such a passion with his cook, who probably had not roasted his dinner to his mind, that with the spit in his hand, and the meat upon it, he pursued him even into the market-place.

It is a bold philosophy that rejects, without ceremony, principles which irresistibly govern the belief and the conduct of all mankind in the common concerns of life; and to which the philosopher himself must yield, after he imagines he hath confuted them. Such principles are older, and of more authority, than Philosophy: she rests upon them as her basis, not they upon her. If she could overturn them, she must be buried in their ruins; but all the engines of philosophical subtility are too weak for this purpose; and the attempt is no less ridiculous, than if a mechanic should contrive an *axis in peritrochio* to remove the earth out of its place; or if a mathematician should pretend to demonstrate, that things equal to the same thing, are not equal to one another.

Zeno endeavoured to demonstrate the impossibility of motion; Hobbes, that there was no difference between right and wrong; and this author, that no credit is to be given to our senses, to our memory, or even to demonstration. Such philosophy is justly ridiculous, even to those who cannot detect the fallacy of it. It can have no other tendency, than to shew the acuteness of the sophist, at the expence of disgracing reason and human nature, and making mankind Yahoos. There are other prejudices against this system of human nature, which, even upon a general view, may make one diffident of it.

Des Cartes, Hobbes, and this author, have each of them given us a system of human nature; an undertaking too vast for any one man, how great soever his genius and abilities may be. There must surely be reason to apprehend, that many parts of human nature never came under their observation; and that others have beens stretched and distorted, to fill up blanks, and complete the system. Chrystopher Columbus, or Sebastian Cabot might almost as reasonably have undertaken to give us a complete map of America.

There is a certain character and style in nature's works, which is never attained in the most perfect imitation of them. This seems to be wanting in the systems of human nature I have mentioned, and particularly in the last. One may see a puppet make variety of motions and gesticulations, which strike much at first view; but when it is accurately observed, and taken to pieces, our admiration ceases; we comprehend the whole art of the maker. How unlike is it to that which it represents; what a poor piece of work compared with the body of a man, whose structure the more we know, the more wonders we discover in it, and the more sensible we are of our ignorance! is the mechanism of the mind so easily comprehend, when that of the body is so difficult? Yet by this system, three laws of association, joined to a few original feelings, explain the whole mechanism of sense, imagination, memory, belief, and of all the actions and passions of the mind. Is this the man that nature made? I suspect it is not so easy to look behind the scenes in nature's work. This is a puppet surely, contrived by too bold an apprentice of nature, to mimic her work. It shews tolerably by candle-light, but brought into clear day, and taken to pieces it will appear to be a man made with mortar and a trowel. The more we know of other parts of nature, the more we like and approve them. The little I know of the planetary system; of the earth which we inhabit; of minerals, vegetables, and animals; of my own body, and of the laws which obtain in these parts of nature; opens to my mind grand and beautiful scenes, and contributes equally to my happiness and power. But when I look within, and consider the mind itself which makes me capable of all these prospects and enjoyments; if it is indeed what the *Treatise of Human Nature* makes it, I find I have been only in an inchanted castle, imposed upon by spectres, and apparitions. I blush inwardly to think how I have been deluded; I am ashamed of my frame, and can hardly forbear expostulating with my destiny: Is this thy pastime, O Nature, to put such tricks upon a silly creature, and then to take off the mask, and shew him how he hath been befooled? If this is the philosophy of human nature, my soul enter thou not into her secrets. It is surely the forbidden tree of knowledge; I no sooner taste of it, then I perceive myself naked, and stript of all things, yea even of my very self. I see myself, and the whole frame of nature, shrink into fleeting ideas, which, like Epicurus's atoms, dance about in emptiness.

But what if these profound disquisitions into the first principles of human nature, do naturally and necessarily plunge a man into this abyss of scepticism? May we not reasonably judge so from what hath happened? Des Cartes no sooner began to dig in this mine, than scepticism was ready to break in upon him. He did what he could to shut it out. Malebranche and Locke, who dug deeper, found the difficulty of keepoing out this enemy still to increase; but they laboured honestly in the design. Then Berkeley, who carried on the work, despairing of securing all, bethought himself of an expedient: By giving up the material world, which he thought might be spared without loss, and even with advantage, he hoped, by an impregnable partition, to secure the world of spirits. But, alas! the *Treatise of*

Human Nature wantonly sapped the foundation of this partition, and drowned all in one universal deluge. (pp. 33-40)

> Thomas Reid, in an introduction to An Inquiry into the Human Mind, on the Principles of Common Sense, 1764. Reprint by Gray, Maver, & Co., 1817, pp. 17-43.

FRANÇOIS MARIE AROUET DE VOLTAIRE (essay date 1764)

[*A French philosopher and man of letters, Voltaire was a major figure of the eighteenth-century European Enlightenment, a movement in which reason and empiricism markedly superseded reliance on prescription, faith, and authority. As a man of diverse and intense interests, Voltaire wrote prolifically on many subjects and in a variety of genres, always asserting the absolute primacy of personal liberty—be it intellectual, social, religious, or political. Consequently, he opposed religious traditions and political organizations that he believed thwarted or curtailed individual freedom. Voltaire's most valuable contribution to literature is usually considered his invention of the philosophical* conte, *or tale, in which the story is a vehicle for an ethical or philosophical message; the most famous of these* contes *is the highly regarded* Candide (1759). *In the following excerpt from a review originally published in French in 1764, Voltaire extols the impartiality of Hume's* History of England.]

Nothing can be added to the fame of [David Hume's *History of England*], perhaps the best ever written in any language. . . . Mr Hume, in his *History,* is neither parliamentarian, nor royalist, nor Anglican, nor Presbyterian—he is simply judicial. . . . The fury of parties has for a long time deprived England of a good historian as well as of a good government. What a Tory wrote was disowned by the Whigs, who, in their turn, were given the lie by the Tories. Rapin Thoiras, a foreigner, alone seemed to have written an impartial history; yet prejudice sometimes stains the truths that Thoiras relates. Whereas in the new historian we find a mind superior to his materials; he speaks of weaknesses, blunders, cruelties as a physician speaks of epidemic diseases.

> François Marie Arouet de Voltaire, in an extract of a review of "History of England," in The Life of David Hume by Ernest Campbell Mossner, second edition, Oxford at the Clarendon Press, Oxford, 1980, p. 318.

JOHN DICKINSON (essay date 1768)

[*Dickinson was an eighteenth-century American statesman and political writer. He was a member of the first and second Continental Congresses, and his writings are credited with having a major influence on American political thought before the Revolution. Conciliatory by nature, however, and fearful of civil war, he cast his vote against the Declaration of Independence in 1776. He is best known for the serially published* Letters from a Farmer in Pennsylvania to the Inhabitants of the British Colonies (1767-68), *an economic and legal study in which he applied the political philosophy of John Locke to questions concerning English taxation. In the following excerpt from this work, he credits Hume with promoting constitutional checks in government.*]

No free people ever existed, or can ever exist, without keeping, to use a common, but strong expression, "the purse strings," in their own hands. Where this is the case, *they* have a *constitutional check* upon the administration, which may thereby be brought into order *without violence:* But where such a power is not lodged in the *people,* oppression proceeds uncontrouled in its career, till the governed, transported into rage, seek redress in the midst of blood and confusion.

The elegant and ingenious Mr. *Hume,* speaking of the *Anglo Norman* government, says—''Princes and Ministers were too ignorant, to be themselves sensible of the advantage attending an equitable administration, and there was no established council or *assembly,* WHICH COULD PROTECT THE PEOPLE, and BY WITHDRAWING SUPPLIES, regularly and PEACEABLY admonish the king of his duty, and ENSURE THE EXECUTION OF THE LAWS.''

Thus this great man, whose political reflections are so much admired, makes *this power* one of the foundations of liberty.

The *English* history abounds with instances, proving that *this* is the proper and successful way to obtain redress of grievances. How often have kings and ministers endeavoured to throw off this legal curb upon them, by attempting to raise money by a variety of inventions, under pretence of law, without having recourse to parliament? And how often have they been brought to reason, and peaceably obliged to do justice, by the exertion of this constitutional authority of the people, vested in their representatives?

The inhabitants of these colonies have, on numberless occasions, reaped the benefit of this authority lodged *in their assemblies.* (pp. 364-65)

> John Dickinson, *''Letters of a Farmer in Pennsylvania, 1768,'' in his* The Writings of John Dickinson: Political Writings, 1764-1774, Vol. I, *edited by Paul Leicester Ford, The Historical Society of Pennsylvania, 1895, pp. 277-406.*

JAMES BEATTIE (essay date 1770)

[*Beattie was a Scottish poet and philosophical writer whose immensely popular poem* The Minstrel *(1771-74)—which traced the development of the poet in the early stages of civilization—is considered an early manifestation of English Romanticism. His* Essay on the Nature and Immutability of Truth, in Opposition to Sophistry and Scepticism *(1770) caused quite a controversy in his own time. A philosophical essay based on social rather than metaphysical arguments, the work vigorously defends orthodox Christian beliefs against the rationalism of Hume. It includes what might be called an official doctrine of pre-Romanticism, particularly in its evocation of primitivism and natural beauty. Beattie was championed by his contemporaries as the defender of Christianity and the poet of a new era. His critical and philosophical works are marked by a lively style and, at times, an artificial manner. On this last point William Cowper once remarked that Beattie was the only writer whose philosophical works were ''diversified and embellished by a poetical imagination that makes even the driest subject and the leanest a feast for epicures.'' In the following excerpt from* An Essay on the Nature and Immutability of Truth, *Beattie disputes the soundness of Hume's philosophical method.*]

Mr Hume, more subtle, and less reserved, than any of his predecessors, hath gone still greater lengths in the demolition of common sense; and reared in its place a most tremendous fabric of doctrine; upon which, if it were not for the flimsiness of its materials, engines might easily be erected, sufficient to overturn all belief, science, religion, virtue, and society, from the very foundation. He calls this work, **A Treatise of Human Nature; being an attempt to introduce the experimental method of reasoning into moral subjects.** This is, in the style of Edmund Curl, a *taking title-page;* but, alas! ''Fronti nulla fides!'' The

whole of this author's system is founded on a false hypothesis taken for granted; and whenever a fact contradictory to that false hypothesis occurs to his observation, he either denies it, or labours hard to explain it away. This, it seems, in his judgement, is experimental reasoning!

He begins his book with affirming, That all the perceptions of the human mind resolve themselves into two classes, impressions, and ideas; that the latter are all copied from the former; and that an idea differs from its correspondent impression only in being a weaker perception. Thus, when I sit by the fire, I have an impression of heat, and I can form an idea of heat when I am shivering with cold; in the one case I have a stronger perception of heat, in the other a weaker. Is there any warmth in this idea of heat? There must, according to this doctrine; only the warmth of the idea is not quite so strong as that of the impression. For this author repeats it again and again, that ''an idea is by its nature weaker and fainter than an impression, but is in every other respect'' (not only similar, but) ''the same.'' Nay, he goes further, and says, that ''whatever is true of the ''one must be acknowledged concerning the other;'' and he is so confident of the truth of this maxim, that he makes it one of the pillars of his philosophy. To those who may be inclined to admit this maxim on his authority, I would propose a few plain questions. Do you feel any, even the least, warmth, in the idea of a bonfire, a burning mountain, or the general conflagration? Do you feel more real cold in Virgil's Scythian winter, than in Milton's description of the flames of hell? Do you acknowledge that to be true of the idea of eating, which is certainly true of the impression of it, that it alleviates hunger, fills the belly, and contributes to the support of human life? If you answer these questions in the negative, you deny one of the fundamental principles of this philosophy. We have, it is true, a livelier perception of a friend when we see him, than when we think of him in his absence. But this is not all: every person of a sound mind knows, that in the one case we believe, and are certain, that the object exists, and is present with us; in the other we believe, and are certain, that the object is not present: which, however, they must deny, who maintain, that an idea differs from an impression only in being weaker, and in no other respect whatsoever.

That every idea should be a copy and resemblance of the impression whence it is derived;—that, for example, the idea of red should be a red idea; the idea of a roaring lion a roaring idea; the idea of an ass, a hairy, long-eared, sluggish idea, patient of labour, and much addicted to thistles; that the idea of extension should be extended, and that of solidity solid;—that a thought of the mind should be endued with all, or any, of the qualities of matter,—is, in my judgement, inconceivable and impossible. Yet our author takes it for granted; and it is another of his fundamental maxims. Such is the credulity of Scepticism!

If every idea be an exact resemblance of its correspondent impression, (or object, for these terms, according to this author, seem to amount to the same thing);—if the idea of extension be extended, as the same author allows;—then the idea of a line, the shortest that sense can perceive, must be equal in length to the line itself; for if shorter, it would be imperceptible; and it will not be said, either that an imperceptible idea can be perceived, or that the idea of an imperceptible object can be formed:—consequently the idea of a line a hundred times as long, must be a hundred times as long as the former idea; for if shorter, it would be the idea, not of this, but of some other shorter line. And so it clearly follows, nay it admits of demonstration, that the idea of an inch is really an inch long; and that of a mile, a mile long. In a word, every idea of any particular extension is equal in length to the extended object. The same reasoning holds good in regard to the other dimensions of breadth and thickness. All ideas, therefore, of solid objects, must be (according to this philosophy) equal in magnitude and solidity to the objects themselves. Now mark the consequence. I am just now in an apartment containing a thousand cubic feet, being ten feet square, and ten high; the door and windows are shut, as well as my eyes and ears. Mr HUME will allow, that, in this situation, I may form ideas, not only of the visible appearance, but also of the real tangible magnitude of the whole house, of a first-rate man of war, of St Paul's cathedral, or even of a much larger object. But the solid magnitude of these ideas is equal to the solid magnitude of the objects from which they are copied: therefore I have now present with me an idea, that is, a solid extended thing, whose dimensions extend to a million of cubic feet at least. The question now is, Where is this thing placed? for a place it must have, and a pretty large one too. I should answer, In my mind; for I know not where else the ideas of my mind can be so conveniently deposited. Now my mind is lodged in a body of no great dimensions, and my body is contained in a room ten feet square, and ten feet high. It seems then, that, into this room, I have it in my power at pleasure to introduce a solid object a thousand, or ten thousand, times larger than the room itself. I contemplate it a while, and then, by another volition, send it a-packing, to make way for another object of equal or superior magnitude. Nay, in no larger vehicle than a common post-chaise, I can transport from one place to another, a building equal to the largest Egyptian pyramid, and a mountain as big as the peak of Teneriff.—Take care, ye disciples of HUME, and be very well advised before ye reject this mystery as impossible and incomprehensible. It seems to be geometrically deduced from the principles, nay from the first principles, of your master.

Say, ye candid and intelligent, what are we to expect from a logical and systematic treatise founded on a supposition that leads into such absurdity? Shall we expect truth? then must it not be inferred by false reasoning?—Shall we expect sound reasoning? then must not the inferences be false?—Indeed, though I cannot much admire this author's sagacity on the present occasion, I must confess myself not a little astonished at his courage. A witch going to sea in an egg-shell, or preparing to take a trip through the air on a broom-stick, would be a surprising phenomenon; but it is nothing to Mr Hume, on such a bottom "launching out into the immense depths of philosophy."

To multiply examples for the confutation of so glaring an absurdity, is ridiculous. I therefore leave it to the reader to determine, whether, if this doctrine of solid and extended ideas be true, it will not follow, that the idea of a roaring lion must emit audible sound, almost as loud and as terrible, as the royal beast in person could exhibit;—that two ideal bottles of brandy will intoxicate as far at least as two genuine bottles of wine;—and that I must be greatly hurt, if not dashed to pieces, if I am so imprudent as to form only the idea of a bomb bursting under my feet. For has not our author said, that "impressions and ideas comprehend all the perceptions (or objects) of the human mind; that whatsoever is true of the one must be acknowledged concerning the other; nay, that they are in every respect the same, except that the former strike with more force than the latter?"

The absurdity and inconceivableness of the distinction between objects and perceptions, is another of our author's doctrines. "However philosophers may distinguish (says he) betwixt the objects and perceptions of the senses;—this is a distinction which is not comprehended by the generality of mankind." Now how are we to know, whether this distinction be conceived and acknowledged by the generality? If we put the question to any of them, we shall find it no easy matter to make ourselves understood, and, after all, perhaps be laughed at for our pains. Shall we reason *a priori* about their sentiments and comprehensions? this is neither philosophical nor fair. Will you allow me to reckon myself one of the generality? Then I declare, for my own part, that I do comprehend and acknowledge this distinction, and have done so ever since I was capable of reflection.

Suppose me to address the common people in these words: "I see a strange sight a little way off; but my sight is weak, so that I see it imperfectly; let me go nearer, that I may have a more distinct sight of it."—If the generality of mankind be at all incapable of distinguishing between the object and the perception, this incapacity will doubtless discover itself most, when ambiguous words are used on purpose to confound their ideas; but if their ideas on this subject are not confounded even by ambiguous language, there is reason to think, that they are extremely clear, distinct, and accurate. Now I have here proposed a sentence, in which there is a studied ambiguity of language; and yet I maintain, that every person, who understands English, will instantly, on hearing these words, perceive, that by the word *sight* I mean, in the first clause, the thing seen; in the second, the power, or perhaps the organ, of seeing; in the third, the perception itself, as distinguished both from the percipient faculty, and from the visible object. If one of the multitude, on hearing me pronounce this sentence, were to reply as follows: The sight is not at all strange; it is a man on horseback: but your sight must needs be weak, as you are lately recovered from sickness: however, if you wait a little, till the man and horse, which are now in the shade, come into the sunshine, you will then have a much more distinct sight of them:"—I would ask, Is the study of any part of philosophy necessary to make a man comprehend the meaning of these two sentences? Is there any thing absurd or unintelligible, either in the former or in the latter? Is there any thing in the reply, that seems to exceed the capacity of the vulgar, and supposes them to be more acute than they really are? If there be not, and I am certain there is not, here is an unquestionable proof, that the vulgar, and indeed all men whom metaphysic has not deprived of their senses, do distinguish between the object perceived, the faculty perceiving, and the perception or impulse communicated by the external object to the mind through the organ of sensation. What though all the three are sometimes expressed by the same name? This only shows, that accuracy of language is not always necessary for answering the common purposes of life. If the ideas of the vulgar are sufficiently distinct, notwithstanding, what shall we say of that philosopher, whose ideas are really confounded by this inaccuracy, and who, because there is no difference in the signs, imagines that there is none in the things signified! That the understanding of such a philosopher is not a vulgar one, will be readily allowed; whether it exceeds, or falls short, let the reader determine.

This author's method of investigation is no less extraordinary than his fundamental principles. There are many notions in the human mind, of which it is not easy perhaps to explain the origin. If you can describe in words what were the circumstances in which you received an impression of any particular notion, it is well; he will allow that you may form an idea of it. But if you cannot do this, then, says he, there is no such notion in your mind; for all perceptions are either impressions or ideas; and it is not possible for us so much as to conceive any thing specifically different from ideas and impressions: now all ideas are copied from impressions: therefore you can have no idea nor conception of any thing of which you have not received an impression.—All mankind have a notion of power or energy. No, says he; an impression of power or energy was never received by any man; and therefore an idea of it can never be formed in the human mind. If you insist on your experience and consciousness of power, it is all a mistake: his hypothesis admits not the idea of power; and therefore there is no such idea.—All mankind have an idea of self. That I deny, says our author; I maintain, that no man ever had, or can have, an impression of self; and therefore no man can form any idea of it. If you persist, and say, that certainly you have some notion or idea of yourself: My dear Sir, he would say, you do not consider, that this assertion contradicts my hypothesis of impressions and ideas; how then is it possible it should be true!

But though the author deny, that I have any notion of *self,* surely he does not mean to affirm, that I do not exist, or that I have no notion of myself as an existent being. In truth, it is not easy to say what he means on this subject. Most philosophical subjects become obscure in the hands of this author; for he has a notable talent at puzzling his readers and himself: but when he treats of consciousness, of personal identity, and of the nature of the soul, he expresses himself so strangely, that his words either have no meaning, or imply very great absurdity. "The question," says he, "concerning the substance of the soul is unintelligible."—Well, Sir, if you think so, you may let it alone.—No; that must not be neither. "What we call a *mind,* is nothing but a heap or collection of different perceptions (or objects) united together by certain relations, and supposed, though falsely, to be endowed with perfect simplicity and identity.—If any one, upon serious and unprejudiced reflection, thinks he has a different notion of himself, I must confess I can reason with him no longer. All I can allow him is, that he may be in the right as well as I, and that we are essentially different in this particular. He may perhaps perceive something simple and continued, which he calls *himself;* though I am certain there is no such principle in me. But setting aside some metaphysicians of this kind,"—that is, who feel and believe that they have a soul,—"I may venture to affirm of the rest of mankind, that they are nothing but a bundle or collection of different perceptions, which succeed each other with inconceivable rapidity, and are in a perpetual flux and movement.—There is properly no simplicity in the mind at one time, nor identity in different [times], whatever natural propension we may have to imagine that simplicity and identity.—They are the successive perceptions only that constitute the mind."

If these words have any meaning, it is this: My soul (or rather that which I call my soul) is not one simple thing, nor is it the same thing to-day it was yesterday; nay, it is not the same this moment it was the last; it is nothing but a mass, collection, heap, or bundle, of different perceptions, or objects, that fleet away in succession, with inconceivable rapidity, perpetually changing, and perpetually in motion. There may be some metaphysicians, to whose souls this description cannot be applied; but I am certain, that this is a true and complete description

of my soul, and of the soul of every other individual of the human race, those few metaphysicians excepted.

That body has no existence, but as a bundle of perceptions, whose existence consists in their being perceived, our author all along maintains. He now affirms, that the soul, in like manner, is a bundle of perceptions, and nothing else. It follows, then, that there is nothing in the universe but impressions and ideas; all possible perceptions being by our author comprehended in those two classes. This philosophy admits of no other existence whatsoever, not even of a percipient being, to perceive these perceptions. So that we are now arrived at the height of human wisdom; at that intellectual eminence, from whence there is a full prospect of all that we can reasonably believe to exist, and of all that can possibly become the object of our knowledge. Alas! what is become of the magnificence of external nature, and the wonders of intellectual energy, the immortal beauties of truth and virtue, and the triumphs of a good conscience! Where now the warmth of benevolence, the fire of generosity, the exultations of hope, the tranquil ecstasy of devotion, and the pang of sympathetic delight! All, around, above, and beneath, is one vast vacuity, or rather an enormous chaos, encompassed with darkness universally and eternally impenetrable. Body and spirit are annihilated; and there remains nothing (for we must again descend into metaphysic) but a vast collection, bundle, mass, or heap, of impressions and ideas.

Such, in regard to existence, seems to be the result of this theory of the understanding. And what is this result? If the author can prove, that there is a possibility of expressing it in words which do not imply a contradiction, I will not call it nonsense. If he can prove, that it is compatible with any one acknowledged truth in philosophy, in morality, in religion natural or revealed, I will not call it impious. If he can prove, that it does not arise *from common facts misrepresented,* and *common words misunderstood,* I shall admit that it may have arisen from accurate observation, candid and liberal inquiry, perfect knowledge of human nature, and the enlarged views of true philosophic genius. (pp. 157-69)

> *James Beattie, "On the Nature and Immutability of Truth, in Opposition to Sophistry and Scepticism," in his* Essays, *Garland Publishing, Inc., 1971, pp. 140-346.*

THOMAS GRAY   (letter date 1770)

[Gray is widely considered the most important poet of mid-eighteenth-century England. He remains particularly distinguished for his "Elegy Written in a Country Churchyard" (1751), whose eloquent evocation of the natural world and profound contemplation of death, greatly influenced such Romantics as Samuel Taylor Coleridge and Percy Bysshe Shelley. Gray's poetry in general reveals an emotionally sensitive, yet scholarly and exacting, approach to verse; consequently, the best of his work is considered unsurpassed in artful fusion of content and form. Gray is also esteemed—beside Horace Walpole and William Cowper— as one of the consummate letter-writers of his century. In addition to gracefully expressed sentiment and perspicuous observation of life, his letters (in the words of R. W. Ketton-Cremer) "contain some of the most intelligent literary criticism of the time." In the following excerpt from a July, 1770 letter to the Scottish poet and essayist James Beattie, who had earlier in the year attacked Hume's philosophy in his Essay on the Nature and Immutability of Truth, *Gray negatively assesses Hume's philosophical writings.]*

I will not enter at present into the merits of your *Essay on Truth*, because I have not yet given it all the attention it deserves, though I have read it through with pleasure: besides I am partial, for I have always thought David Hume a pernicious writer, and believe he has done as much mischief here as he has in his own country. A turbid and shallow stream often appears to our apprehensions very deep. A professed sceptic can be guided by nothing but his present passions (if he has any) and interests; and to be masters of his philosophy we need not his books or advice, for every child is capable of the same thing, without any study at all. Is not that *naïveté* and good humour, which his admirers celebrate in him, owing to this, that he has continued all his days an infant, but one that has unhappily been taught to read and write? That childish nation, the French, have given him vogue and fashion, and we, as usual, have learned from them to admire him at second hand. (pp. 288-89)

> Thomas Gray, in a letter to James Beattie on July
> 2, 1770, in his The Letters of Thomas Gray, Vol.
> III, edited by Duncan C. Tovey, G. Bell and Sons,
> Ltd., 1912, pp. 287-89.

EDWARD GIBBON   (letter date 1773)

[*Best known as the author of* The History of the Decline and Fall of the Roman Empire *(1766-88), Gibbon is considered one of England's foremost historians and a historical theorist of the first rank. Early in life a devoted admirer of Hume's philosophical essays, the young Gibbon paid tribute to Hume in 1758 when he informed his father, "I am . . . to meet . . . the great David Hume." In the following excerpt from a letter to his friend John Holroyd, who was then traveling in Scotland, Gibbon compares Hume's historical works with those of William Robertson.*]

You tell me of a long list of Dukes, Lairds, and Chieftains of Renown to whom you are recommended; were I with you, I should prefer one David to them all. When you are at Edinburgh, I hope you will not fail to visit the Stye of that fattest of Epicurus's Hogs [David Hume], and inform yourself whether there remains no hope of its recovering the use of its right paw. There is another animal of *great*, though not perhaps of *equal*, and certainly not of *similar* merit, one Robertson; has he almost created the new World? Many other men you have undoubtedly seen, in the country where you are at present, who must have commanded your esteem. But when you return, if you are not very honest, you will possess great advantages over me in any dispute concerning Caledonian merit. (p. 190)

> Edward Gibbon, in a letter to J. B. Holroyd on Au-
> gust 7, 1773, in his Private Letters of Edward Gibbon
> (1753-1794), Vol. I, edited by Rowland E. Prothero,
> John Murray, 1896, pp. 190-92.

ADAM SMITH   (letter date 1776)

[*Smith was an eighteenth-century Scottish economist whose* Inquiry into the Nature and Causes of the Wealth of Nations *(1776) is considered the foundation of classical economics. By emphasizing the virtues of the free market, Smith anticipated—some say created—nineteenth-century liberalism, the Free Trade movement, and a large part of capitalist doctrine as we know it. In the following excerpt from his* "account of the behaviour of our late excellent friend, Mr. Hume, during his last illness," *addressed to Hume's literary executor, William Strahan, shortly after Hume's death, Smith describes Hume's mien and character.*]

[Mr. Hume's temper] seemed to be more happily balanced, if I may be allowed such an expression, than that perhaps of any other man I have ever known. Even in the lowest state of his fortune, his great and necessary frugality never hindered him from exercising, upon proper occasions, acts both of charity and generosity. It was a frugality founded not upon avarice, but upon the love of independencey. The extreme gentleness of his nature never weakened either the firmness of his mind or the steadiness of his resolutions. His constant pleasantry was the genuine effusion of good nature and good humour, tempered with delicacy and modesty, and without even the slightest tincture of malignity, so frequently the disagreeable source of what is called wit in other men. It never was the meaning of his raillery to mortify; and therefore, far from offending, it seldom failed to please and delight, even those who were frequently the objects of it; there was not perhaps any one of all his great and amiable qualities which contributed more to endear his conversation. And that gayety of temper, so agreeable in society, but which is so often accompanied with frivolous and superficial qualities, was in him certainly attended with the most severe application, the most extensive learning, the greatest depth of thought, and a capacity in every respect the most comprehensive. Upon the whole, I have always considered him, both in his lifetime and since his death, as approaching as nearly to the idea of a perfectly wise and virtuous man as perhaps the nature of human frailty will permit. (pp. xxiv-xxv)

> Adam Smith, in a letter to William Strahan on No-
> vember 9, 1776, in Selections from: An Enquiry con-
> cerning Human Understanding and A Treatise of Hu-
> man Nature by David Hume, Open Court, 1966, pp.
> xvii-xxv.

JOSEPH PRIESTLEY   (essay date 1780)

[*Priestley was an eighteenth-century English polymath: theologian, clergyman, and chemist, he was the discoverer of oxygen, wrote numerous important scientific works, and was a founding member of the Unitarian Society in 1791. Described by Samuel Taylor Coleridge as "Patriot, and Saint, and Sage," he was also known as "Gunpowder" Priestley for his comments about setting gunpowder "under the old building of error and superstition." Radically nonconformist and markedly a man of reason, he is credited with first suggesting, in his* Essay on the First Principles of Government *(1768), the Benthamite idea of "the greatest happiness of the greatest number" as the criterion of moral goodness. In the following excerpt from his* Letters to a Philosophical Unbeliever *(1780), a work largely directed against Hume's* Dialogues concerning Natural Religion, *he refutes Hume's atheism. For an analysis of Priestley's argument, see the Richard H. Popkin entry in the Additional Bibliography.*]

[You wish] to know distinctly what I think of *Mr. Hume's posthumous* **Dialogues on Natural Religion**; because, coming from a writer of some note, that work is frequently a topic of conversation in the societies you frequent.

With respect to *Mr. Hume's metaphysical writings* in general, my opinion is, that, on the whole, the world is very little the wiser for them. For though, when the merits of any question were on his side, few men ever wrote with more perspicuity, the arrangement of his thoughts being natural, and his illustrations peculiarly happy; yet I can hardly think that we are indebted to him for the least real advance in the knowledge of the human mind. Indeed, according to his own very frank confession, his object was mere *literary reputation*. It was not the *pursuit of truth*, or the advancement of virtue and happiness;

Engraving of Jean-Jacques Rousseau (''The Savage Man''), Hume, and Voltaire, made in 1766 at the suggestion of James Boswell.

and it was much more easy to make a figure by disturbing the systems of others, than by erecting any of his own. All schemes have their respective weak sides, which a man who has nothing of his own to risk may more easily find, and expose.

In many of his **Essays** (which, in general, are excessively wire-drawn) Mr. Hume seems to have had nothing in view but to *amuse* his readers, which he generally does agreeably enough; proposing doubts to received hypotheses, leaving them without any solution, and altogether unconcerned about it. In short, he is to be considered in these **Essays** as a mere *writer* or *de-claimer,* even more than Cicero in his book of Tusculan Questions.

He seems not to have given himself the trouble so much as to read *Dr. Hartley's Observations on Man,* a work which he could not but have heard of, and which it certainly behoved him to study. The doctrine of *association of ideas,* as explained and extended by Dr. Hartley, supplies materials for the most satisfactory solution of almost all the difficulties he has started, as I could easily shew if I thought it of any consequence; so that to a person acquainted with this theory of the human mind, *Hume's Essays* appear the merest trifling. Compared with Dr. Hartley, I consider Mr. Hume as not even a child.

Now, I will frankly tell you, that this last performance of Mr. Hume has by no means changed for the better the idea I had before formed of him as a metaphysical writer. The dialogue

is ingeniously and artfully conducted. Philo, who evidently speaks the sentiments of the writer, is not made to say all the good things that are advanced, his opponents are not made to say any thing that is very palpably absurd, and every thing is made to pass with great decency and decorum.

But though Philo, in the most interesting part of the debate, advances nothing but common-place objections against the be-lief of a God, and hackneyed declamation against the plan of providence, his antagonists are seldom represented as making any satisfactory reply. And when, at the last, evidently to save appearances, he relinquishes the argument, on which he had expatiated with so much triumph, it is without alledging any sufficient reason; so that his arguments are left, as no doubt the writer intended, to have their full effect on the mind of the reader. Also though the debate seemingly closes in favour of the theist, the victory is clearly on the side of the atheist. I therefore shall not be surprised if this work should have a considerable effect in promoting the cause of atheism, with those whose *general turn of thinking,* and *habits of life,* make them no ill-wishers to that scheme.

To satisfy your wishes, I shall recite what I think has most of the appearance of strength, or plausibility, in what Mr. Hume has advanced on the atheistical side of the question. . . . (pp. 124-28)

With respect to the general argument for the being of God, from the marks of design in the universe, he says, ''Will any man tell me, with a serious countenance, that an orderly universe must arise from some thought and art, like the human, because we have experience of it. To ascertain this reasoning, it were requisite that we had experience of the origin of worlds, and it is not sufficient, surely, that we have seen ships and cities arise from human art and contrivance.''

Now, if it be admitted that there are marks of design in the universe, as numberless fitnesses of things to things prove beyond all dispute, is it not a necessary consequence, that if it had a cause at all, it must be one that is capable of design? Will any person say that an eye could have been constructed by a Being who had no knowledge of optics, who did not know the nature of light, or the laws of refraction? And must not the universe have had a cause, as well as any thing else, that is finite and incapable of comprehending itself?

We might just as reasonably say, that any particular ship, or city, any particular horse, or man, had nothing existing superior to it, as that the visible universe had nothing superior to it, if the universe be no more capable of comprehending itself than a ship, or a city, a horse, or a man. There can be no charm in the words *world* or *universe,* so that they should require no cause when they stand in precisely the same predicament with other things that evidently *do* require a superior cause, and could not have existed without one.

All that Mr. Hume says on the difficulty of stopping at the idea of an uncaused Being, is on the supposition that this uncaused Being is a *finite one,* incapable of comprehending itself, and, therefore, in the same predicament with a ship or a house, a horse or a man, which it is impossible to conceive to have existed without a superior cause. ''How shall we satisfy ourselves,'' says he, ''concerning the cause of that Being whom you suppose the author of nature.—If we stop and go no farther, why go so far, why not stop at the material world. How can we satisfy ourselves without going on in infinitum.—By supposing it to contain the principle of order within itself, we really assert it to be God, and the sooner we arrive at that Divine Being, so much the better. When you go one step beyond the mundane system, you only excite an inquisitive humour, which it is impossible ever to satisfy.''

It is very true, that no person can satisfy himself with going backwards *in infinitum* from one thing that requires a superior cause, to another that equally requires a superior cause. But any person may be sufficiently satisfied with going back through finite causes as far as he has evidence of the existence of intermediate finite causes; and then (seeing that it is absurd to go on *in infinitum* in this manner) to conclude that; whether he can comprehend it or not, there *must* be some *uncaused intelligent Being,* the original and designing cause of all other Beings. For otherwise, what we *see* and *experience* could not have existed. It is true that we cannot conceive *how* this should be, but we are able to acquiesce in this ignorance, because there is no *contradiction* in it. (pp. 124-31)

What Mr. Hume says with respect to the *origin of the world . . . ,* which I think unworthy of a philosopher, and miserably trifling on so serious a subject, goes intirely upon the idea of the supreme cause resembling such beings as do themselves require a superior cause, and not (which, however, *must* be the case) a Being that can have no superior in wisdom or power. I, therefore, think it requires no particular animadversion. (p. 133)

In reading *Mr. Hume's life,* [*The Life of David Hume, Esq., Written by Himself*], one might be surprised to find no mention of a *God,* or of a *providence,* which conducted him through

it; but this cannot be any longer wonderful, when we find that, for any thing he certainly believed to the contrary, he himself might be the most considerable Being in the universe. His maker, if he had any, might have been either a careless playful infant, a trifling forgetful dotard, or was, perhaps, dead and buried, without leaving any other to take care of his affairs. All that he believed of his maker was, that he was capable of *something like design,* but of his own comprehensive intellectual powers he could have no doubt.

Neither can we think it at all extraordinary that Mr. Hume should have recourse to *amusing books* in the last period of his life, when he considered the author of nature himself as never having had any serious object in view, and when he neither left any thing behind him, nor had any thing before him, that was deserving of his care. How can it be supposed that the man, who scrupled not to ridicule his maker, should consider the human race, or the world, in any other light than as objects of ridicule, or pity. And well satisfied might he be to have been so fortunate in his passage through the world, and in his easy escape out of it, when it was deserted by its maker, and was continually exposed to some unforeseen and dreadful catastrophe. How poor a consolation, however, must have been his *literary fame,* with such gloomy prospects as these!

What Mr. Hume says with respect to the deficiency in the proof of the *proper infinity* of the divine attributes, and of a probable *multiplicity of deities,* all goes on the same idea, viz. that the ultimate cause of the universe is such a Being as must himself require a superior cause; whereas, nothing can be more evident, how incomprehensible soever it may be, than that the Being which has existed from eternity, and is the cause of all that does exist, must be one that *cannot* have a superior, and therefore must be infinite in knowledge and power, and consequently . . . can be but *one.* (pp. 134-36)

[Speaking of causes and effects, Mr. Hume says,

> In] like manner as a tree sheds its seeds into the neighbouring fields, and produces other trees; so the great vegetable the world, or this planetary system, produces within itself certain seeds, which being scattered into the surrounding chaos, vegetate into new worlds. A comet, for instance, is the seed of a world, and after it has been fully ripened by passing from sun to sun, and star to star, it is at last tossed into the unformed elements, which every where surround this universe, and immediately sprouts up into a new system.
>
> Or, if we should suppose this world to be an *animal,* a comet is the *egg* of this animal; and in like manner as an ostrich lays its egg in the sand, which, without any farther care, hatches the egg, and produces a new animal; so———Does not a plant or an animal, which springs from vegetation or generation, bear a stronger resemblance to the world than does any artificial machine, which arises from reason and design?

Had any friend of religion advanced an idea so completely absurd as this, what would not Mr. Hume have said to turn it into ridicule. With just as much probability might he have said that Glasgow grew from a seed yielded by Edinburgh, or that London and Edinburgh, marrying, by natural generation, produced York, which lies between them. With much more probability might he have said that *pamphlets* are the productions of large *books,* that *boats* are young *ships,* and that *pistols* will grow into great *guns;* and that either there never were any first towns, books, ships, or guns, or that, if there were, they had no makers.

How it could come into any man's head to imagine that a thing so complex as this world, consisting of land and water, earths and metals, plants and animals, &c. &c. &c. should produce a seed or egg, containing within it the elements of all its innumerable parts, is beyond my power of conception.

What must have been that man's knowledge of philosophy and nature, who could suppose for a moment, that a comet could possibly be the seed of a world? Do comets spring from worlds, carrying with them the seeds of all the plants, &c. that they contain? Do comets travel from sun to sun, or from star to star? By what force are they tossed into the *unformed elements,* which Mr. Hume supposes every where to surround the universe? What are those elements? and what evidence has he of their existence? or, supposing the comet to arrive among them, whence could arise its power of vegetating into a new system?

What Mr. Hume objects to the arguments for the *benevolence* of the Deity is such mere cavilling, and admits of such easy answers, that I am surprised that a man whose sole object was even *literary reputation* should have advanced it. (pp. 139-42)

It is pretty clear to me, that Mr. Hume was not sufficiently acquainted with what has been already advanced by those who have written on the subject of the being and attributes of God. Otherwise he either would not have put such weak arguments into the mouth of his favourite Philo, or would have put better answers into those of his opponents. It was, I imagine, his dislike of the subject that made him overlook such writers, or give but little attention to them; and I think this conjecture concerning his aversion to the subject the better founded, from his saying that "there is a gloom and melancholy remarkable in all devout people."

No person really acquainted with true devotion, or those who were possessed with it, could have entertained such an opinion. What Mr. Hume had seen, must have been some miserably low superstition, or wild enthusiasm, things very remote from the calm and sedate, but chearful spirit of rational devotion.

Had he considered the nature of true devotion, he must have been sensible that the charge of gloom and melancholy can least of all apply to it. Gloom and melancholy certainly belong to the system of atheism, which entirely precludes the pleasing ideas of a benevolent author of nature, and of a wise plan of providence, bringing good out of all the evil we experience; which cuts off the consoling intercourse with an invisible, but omnipresent and almighty protector and friend, which admits of no settled provision for our happiness, even in this life, and closes the melancholy scene, such as Mr. Hume himself describes it, with a total annihilation.

Is it possible to draw a more gloomy and dispiriting picture of the system of the universe than Mr. Hume himself has drawn in his tenth dialogue? No melancholy religionist ever drew so dark a one. Nothing in the whole system pleases him. He finds neither *wisdom*, nor *benevolence*. (pp. 145-47)

In the scriptures the Divine Being is represented as "encouraging us to cast all our "care upon him who careth for us." The true christian is exhorted to *rejoice evermore,* and especially to *rejoice in tribulation,* and persecution for righteousness sake. Death is so far from being a frightful and disgusting thing, that he triumphs in it, and over it. *O death, where is thy sting? O grave, where is thy victory?*

Would any person hesitate about chusing to *feel* as these writers felt, or as Mr. Hume must have done. With his views of things, the calmness and composure with which, he says, he faced death, though infinitely short of the *joyful expectation* of the christian, could not have been any thing but affectation. If, however, with his prospects he really was as calm, placid, and chearful, as he pretends, with little reason can he charge any set of *speculative principles* with a tendency to produce gloom and melancholy. If *his* system did not produce this disposition, it never can be in the power of *system* to do it.

Notwithstanding I have differed so much from Mr. Hume with respect to the principles of his treatise, we shall, in words, at least, agree in our conclusion. For though I think the being of a God, and his general benevolence and providence, to be sufficiently demonstrable, yet so many cavils may be started on the subject, and so much still remains, that a rational creature must wish to be informed of concerning his maker, his duty here, and his expectations hereafter, that what Mr. Hume said by way of cover and irony, I can say with great seriousness, and I do not wish to say it much otherwise, or better.

"The most natural sentiment," he says,

> which a well-disposed mind will feel on this occasion, is a longing desire and expectation, that heaven would be pleased to dissipate, at least alleviate, this profound ignorance, by affording some more particular revelation to mankind, and making discoveries of the nature, attributes, and operation of the divine object of our faith. A person seasoned with a just sense of the imperfection of natural reason will fly to *revealed truth* with the greatest avidity. To be a philosophical sceptic is, in a man of letters, the first and most essential step towards being a sound believing christian.
>
> (pp. 149-51)

Joseph Priestley, "An Examination of Mr. Hume's 'Dialogues on Natural Religion'," in his Letters to a Philosophical Unbeliever, *Garland Publishing, Inc., 1974, pp. 124-51.*

IMMANUEL KANT (essay date 1783)

[*A highly influential German philosopher, Kant propounded—in his* Kritik der reinen Vernunft *(1781;* Critique of Pure Reason, *1929) and other works—a system in which knowledge is derived from both the senses and the reasoning processes of the mind. Holding that one cannot arrive at absolute truth through reason alone, Kant allowed that reason serves principally in the construction of moral laws and works toward an ultimate good, all of which must be predicated on faith in a moral author of the world. In the following excerpt from an essay originally published in 1783, he examines Hume's conception of cause and effect and discloses his philosophical debt to Hume.*]

Since the *Essays* of Locke and Leibniz, or rather since the origin of metaphysics so far as we know its history, nothing has ever happened which could have been more decisive to its fate than the attack made upon it by David Hume. He threw no light on this species of knowledge, but he certainly struck a spark by which light might have been kindled had it caught some inflammable substance and had its smouldering fire been carefully nursed and developed.

Hume started chiefly from a single but important concept in metaphysics, namely, that of the connection of cause and effect (including its derivatives force and action, and so on). He challenged reason, which pretends to have given birth to this concept of herself, to answer him by what right she thinks anything could be so constituted that if that thing be posited, something else also must necessarily be posited; for this is the meaning of the concept of cause. He demonstrated irrefutably that it was perfectly impossible for reason to think *a priori* and by means of concepts such a combination, for it implies necessity. We cannot at all see why, in consequence of the existence of one thing, another must necessarily exist or how the concept of such a combination can arise *a priori*. Hence he inferred that reason was altogether deluded with reference to this concept, which she erroneously considered as one of her own children, whereas in reality it was nothing but a bastard of imagination, impregnated by experience, which subsumed certain representations under the law of association and mistook a subjective necessity (habit) for an objective necessity arising from insight. Hence he inferred that reason had no power to think such combinations, even in general, because her concepts would then be purely fictitious and all her pretended *a priori* cognitions nothing but common experiences marked with a false stamp. In plain language, this means that there is not and cannot be any such thing as metaphysics at all.

However hasty and mistaken Hume's inference may appear, it was at least founded upon investigation, and this investigation deserved the concentrated attention of the brighter spirits of his day as well as determined efforts on their part to discover, if possible, a happier solution of the problem in the sense proposed by him, all of which would have speedily resulted in a complete reform of the science.

But Hume suffered the usual misfortune of metaphysicians, of not being understood. It is positively painful to see how utterly his opponents, Reid, Oswald, Beattie, and lastly Priestley [see excerpts by Reid, Beattie, and Priestley, dated 1764, 1770, and 1780], missed the point of the problem; for while they were ever taking for granted that which he doubted, and demonstrating with zeal and often with impudence that which he never thought of doubting, they so misconstrued his valuable suggestion that everything remained in its old condition, as if nothing had happened. The question was not whether the concept of cause was right, useful, and even indispensable for our knowledge of nature, for this Hume had never doubted; but whether that concept could be thought by reason *a priori*, and consequently whether it possessed an inner truth, independent of all experience, implying a perhaps more extended use not restricted merely to objects of experience. This was Hume's problem. It was solely a question concerning the *origin*, not concerning the *indispensable* need of using the concept. Were the former decided, the conditions of the use and the sphere of its valid application would have been determined as a matter of course.

But to satisfy the conditions of the problem, the opponents of the great thinker should have penetrated very deeply into the nature of reason, so far as it is concerned with pure thinking—a task which did not suit them. They found a more convenient method of being defiant without any insight, namely, the appeal to *common sense*. It is indeed a great gift of God to possess right or (as they now call it) plain common sense. But this common sense must be shown in action by well-considered and reasonable thoughts and words, not by appealing to it as an oracle when no rational justification for one's position can be advanced. To appeal to common sense when insight and science fail, and no sooner—this is one of the subtle discoveries of modern times, by means of which the most superficial ranter can safely enter the lists with the most thorough thinker

and hold his own. But as long as a particle of insight remains, no one would think of having recourse to this subterfuge. Seen clearly, it is but an appeal to the opinion of the multitude, of whose applause the philosopher is ashamed, while the popular charlatan glories and boasts in it. I should think that Hume might fairly have laid as much claim to common sense as Beattie and, in addition, to a critical reason (such as the latter did not possess), which keeps common sense in check and prevents it from speculating, or, if speculations are under discussion, restrains the desire to decide because it cannot satisfy itself concerning its own premises. By this means alone can common sense remain sound. Chisels and hammers may suffice to work a piece of wood, but for etching we require an etcher's needle. Thus common sense and speculative understanding are each serviceable, but each in its own way: the former in judgments which apply immediately to experience; the latter when we judge universally from mere concepts, as in metaphysics, where that which calls itself, in spite of the inappropriateness of the name, sound common sense, has no right to judge at all.

I openly confess my recollection of David Hume was the very thing which many years ago first interrupted my dogmatic slumber and gave my investigations in the field of speculative philosophy a quite new direction. I was far from following him in the conclusions at which he arrived by regarding, not the whole of his problem, but a part, which by itself can give us no information. If we start from a well-founded, but undeveloped, thought which another has bequeathed to us, we may well hope by continued reflection to advance farther than the acute man to whom we owe the first spark of light.

I therefore first tried whether Hume's objection could not be put into a general form, and soon found that the concept of the connection of cause and effect was by no means the only concept by which the understanding thinks the connection of things *a priori*, but rather that metaphysics consists altogether of such concepts. I sought to ascertain their number; and when I had satisfactorily succeeded in this by starting from a single principle, I proceeded to the deduction of these concepts, which I was now certain were not derived from experience, as Hume had attempted to derive them, but sprang from the pure understanding. This deduction (which seemed impossible to my acute predecessor, which had never even occurred to anyone else, though no one had hesitated to use the concepts without investigating the basis of their objective validity) was the most difficult task which ever could have been undertaken in the service of metaphysics; and the worst was that metaphysics, such as it is, could not assist me in the least because this deduction alone can render metaphysics possible. But as soon as I had succeeded in solving Hume's problem, not merely in a particular case, but with respect to the whole faculty of pure reason, I could proceed safely, though slowly, to determine the whole sphere of pure reason completely and from universal principles, in its boundaries as well as in its contents. This was required for metaphysics in order to construct its system according to a safe plan. (pp. 5-9)

Immanuel Kant, in an introduction to his Prolegomena to Any Future Metaphysics, *edited and translated by Lewis White Beck, The Liberal Arts Press, 1951, pp. 3-12.*

JOHN WESLEY   (sermon date 1790)

[As cofounder (with his brother Charles) of Methodism, Wesley had a profound impact on life in eighteenth-century England.

Ministering to the spiritual and social needs of a congregation of thousands, Wesley and his Methodist creed stimulated a wave of religious fervor throughout the country. Because of its emphasis on emotion rather than ritual and on intuitive rather than analytic thought, Methodism has been called the religious counterpart of the Romantic movement in literature. Wesley wrote tirelessly, producing numerous volumes on the history of the church, biblical commentaries, educational treatises, and translations from the classics. He also edited the works of John Bunyan, William Law, and Henry Brooke. In the following excerpt from his 1790 sermon "On the Deceitfulness of the Human Heart," Wesley censures Hume's religious opinions.]

[Who can discover the deceitfulness of the human heart] in all the disguises it assumes, or trace it through all its latent mazes? And if it be so difficult to know the heart of a good man, who can know the heart of a wicked one, which is far more deceitful? No unregenerate man, however sensible, ever so experienced, ever so wise in his generation. And yet these are they who pique themselves upon "knowing the world," and imagine they see through all men. Vain men! One may boldly say, they "know nothing yet as they ought to know." Even that politician in the late reign neither knew the heart of himself or of other men, whose favourite saying was, "Do not tell me of your virtue, or religion; I tell you, every man has his price." Yes, Sir R———; every man like you; every one that sells himself to the devil.

Did that right honourable wretch, compared to whom Sir R——— was a saint, know the heart of man,—he that so earnestly advised his own son, "never to speak the truth, to lie or dissemble as often as he speaks, to wear a mask continually?" that earnestly counselled him, "not to debauch *single women*," (because some inconveniences might follow,) "but always married women?" Would one imagine this grovelling animal ever had a wife or a married daughter of his own? O rare Lord C———! Did ever man so well deserve, though he was a Peer of the realm, to die by the side of Newgate? Or did ever book so well deserve to be burned by the common hangman, as his *Letters*? Did Mr. David Hume, lower, if possible, than either of the former, know the heart of man? No more than a worm or a beetle does. After "playing so idly with the darts of death," do you now find it a laughing matter? What think you now of Charon? Has he ferried you over Styx? At length he has taught you to know a little of your own heart! At length you know, it is a fearful thing to fall into the hands of the living God!

One of the ablest champions of infidelity (perhaps the most elegant and the most decent writer that ever produced a system of religion without being in the least obliged to the Bible for it) breaks out in the fulness of his heart, "Who would not wish that there was full proof of the Christian Revelation; since it is undoubtedly the most benevolent system that ever appeared in the world!" Might he not add a reason of another kind,—Because without this man must be altogether a mystery to himself? Even with the help of Revelation, he knows exceeding little; but without it, he would know abundantly less, and nothing with any certainty. Without the light which is given us by the oracles of God, how could we reconcile his greatness with his meanness? While we acknowledged, with Sir John Davis,—

> I know my soul has power to know all things;
>   Yet is she blind, and ignorant of all;
> I know I'm one of nature's little kings;
>   Yet to the least and vilest things in thrall.

Who then knoweth the hearts of all men? Surely none but He that made them. Who knoweth his own heart? Who can tell

the depth of its enmity against God? Who knoweth how deeply it is sunk into the nature of Satan? (pp. 341-42)

> *John Wesley, "On the Deceitfulness of the Human Heart," in his* The Works of John Wesley, *Vol. VII, 1872. Reprint by Zondervan Publishing House, 1958-59, pp. 335-43.*

JAMES BOSWELL AND SAMUEL JOHNSON   (essay date 1791)

[Critic, essayist, poet, and lexicographer, Johnson was one of the principal English literary figures of the eighteenth century. His Dictionary of the English Language *(1755) helped standardize English spelling, while his moralistic criticism strongly influenced the literary taste of his time. His analytical writings, which are characterized by sound judgment, generally promote his theory that a work of literature should be evaluated chiefly on its ability to please and instruct the reader. This theory is also reflected in many of his more casual remarks recorded by the Scottish diarist and man of letters James Boswell, who actively pursued Johnson's company and left as a record of their acquaintance* The Life of Samuel Johnson, LL.D. *(1791), a pioneering biography combining life history with anecdote, observation, and dialogue. In the following excerpt from this work, Boswell relates Johnson's comments concerning Hume's prose style, position on miracles, religious opinions, statements about death, and apparent atheism.]*

[On Wednesday, July 20, 1763], Mr. Johnson, Mr. Dempster, and my uncle Dr. Boswell, who happened to be now in London, supped with me. . . . (pp. 270-71)

[The conversation] turned upon Mr. David Hume's style. JOHNSON. "Why, Sir, his style is not English; the structure of his sentences is French. Now the French structure and the English structure may, in the nature of things, be equally good. But if you allow that the English language is established, he is wrong. My name might originally have been Nicholson, as well as Johnson; but were you to call me Nicholson now, you would call me very absurdly." (p. 272)

Next morning I found [Dr. Johnson] alone. . . . (p. 274)

I mentioned Hume's argument against the belief of miracles, that it is more probable that the witnesses to the truth of them are mistaken, or speak falsely, than that the miracles should be true. JOHNSON. "Why, Sir, the great difficulty of proving miracles should make us very cautious in believing them. But let us consider; although GOD has made Nature to operate by certain fixed laws, yet it is not unreasonable to think that he may suspend those laws, in order to establish a system highly advantageous to mankind. Now the Christian Religion is a most beneficial system, as it gives us light and certainty where we were before in darkness and doubt. The miracles which prove it are attested by men who had no interest in deceiving us; but who, on the contrary, were told that they should suffer persecution, and did actually lay down their lives in confirmation of the truth of the facts which they asserted. Indeed, for some centuries the heathens did not pretend to deny the miracles; but said they were performed by the aid of evil spirits. This is a circumstance of great weight. Then, Sir, when we take the proofs derived from prophecies which have been so exactly fulfilled, we have most satisfactory evidence. Supposing a miracle possible, as to which, in my opinion, there can be no doubt, we have as strong evidence for the miracles in support of Christianity, as the nature of the thing admits." (pp. 275-76)

[On another occasion I told Dr. Johnson] that a foreign friend of his, whom I had met with abroad, was so wretchedly perverted to infidelity, that he treated the hopes of immortality with brutal levity; and said, "As man dies like a dog, let him lie like a dog." JOHNSON. "*If* he dies like a dog, *let* him lie like a dog." I added, that this man said to me, "I hate mankind, for I think myself one of the best of them, and I know how bad I am." JOHNSON. "Sir, he must be very singular in his opinion, if he thinks himself one of the best of men; for none of his friends think him so."—He said, "No honest man could be a Deist; for no man could be so after a fair examination of the proofs of Christianity." I named Hume. JOHNSON. "No, Sir; Hume owned to a clergyman in the bishoprick of Durham, that he had never read the New Testament with attention."— I mentioned Hume's notion, that all who are happy are equally happy; a little Miss with a new gown at a dancing-school ball, a General at the head of a victorious army, and an orator, after having made an eloquent speech in a great assembly. JOHNSON. "Sir, that all who are happy, are equally happy, is not true. A peasant and a philosopher may be equally *satisfied*, but not equally *happy*. Happiness consists in the multiplicity of agreeable consciousness. A peasant has not capacity for having equal happiness with a philosopher." I remember this very question very happily illustrated in opposition to Hume, by the Reverend Mr. Robert Brown, at Utrecht. "A small drinking-glass and a large one, (said he,) may be equally full; but the large one holds more than the small." (p. 315)

[When Dr. Johnson and I were alone one time in 1769], I introduced the subject of death, and endeavoured to maintain that the fear of it might be got over. I told him that David Hume said to me, he was no more uneasy to think he should *not be* after his life, than that he *had not been* before he began to exist. JOHNSON. "Sir, if he really thinks so, his perceptions are disturbed; he is mad; if he does not think so, he lies. He may tell you, he holds his finger in the flame of a candle, without feeling pain; would you believe him? When he dies, he at least gives up all he has." BOSWELL. "Foote, Sir, told me, that when he was very ill he was not afraid to die." JOHNSON. "It is not true, sir. Hold a pistol to Foote's breast, or to Hume's breast, and threaten to kill them, and you'll see how they behave." BOSWELL. "But may we not fortify our minds for the approach of death?"—Here I am sensible I was in the wrong, to bring before his view what he ever looked upon with horror; for although when in a celestial frame of mind in his "Vanity of Human Wishes," he has supposed death to be "kind Nature's signal for retreat," from this state of being to "a happier seat," his thoughts upon this awful change were in general full of dismal apprehensions. (pp. 377-78)

[Once in 1777] I mentioned to Dr. Johnson, that David Hume's persisting in his infidelity, when he was dying, shocked me much. JOHNSON. "Why should it shock you, Sir? Hume owned he had never read the New Testament with attention. Here then was a man who had been at no pains to enquire into the truth of religion, and had continually turned his mind the other way. It was not to be expected that the prospect of death would alter his way of thinking, unless GOD should send an angel to set him right." I said, I had reason to believe that the thought of annihilation gave Hume no pain. JOHNSON. "It was not so, Sir. He had a vanity in being thought easy. It is more probable that he should assume an appearance of ease, than so very improbable a thing should be, as a man not afraid of going (as, in spite of his delusive theory, he cannot be sure but he may go), into an unknown state, and not being uneasy at leaving all he knew. And you are to consider, that upon his own principle of annihilation he had no motive to speak the truth." (pp. 113-14)

James Boswell and Samuel Johnson, in The Life of Samuel Johnson, 2 Vols. *by James Boswell, 1791. Reprint by Dent, 1976, 638 & 646 p.*

FRIEDRICH VON SCHLEGEL   (lecture date 1812)

[*Schlegel was a German novelist, playwright, classicist, orientalist, and critic whose critical works are noted for their depth, originality, and range. In the following excerpt from an 1812 Vienna lecture, he examines what he considers the skeptical and prejudicial character of Hume's historical works.*]

Of all the works connected with elegant literature which the English produced during the last century, by far the most important are their great historical writings. They have, in this department, surpassed all the other European nations; they had, at all events, the start in point of time; and have become the standard models both in France and in Germany. The first place is, I believe, universally given to David Hume. But however salutary may be the spirit of scepticism in the conduct of historical researches, I am strongly of opinion that this spirit, when it is not confined to events alone, but extends its doubts to all the principles of morality and religion, is by no means becoming in a great national historian, and will, in the end, diminish in a very considerable measure the influence which the native genius of this singular man might well have entitled him to maintain over the minds of his countrymen.

Narrow principles and views of things not perfectly just, are, I am free to confess, in my estimation, much better fitted for a great historian than no principles at all, and a deadening want of feeling, warmth, and passion. When these are removed, the only remaining means of creating interest in a historical work is the love of opposing the ruling opinions and of paradoxy. The leaning to this species of opposition is most evident in Hume. However praiseworthy and salutary it might be, that such a writer as Hume was, should take up a set of opinions opposed to those of the Whigs—a party in his day, as well as in our own, possessed of perhaps too much influence over the lierature of England—and should represent a most important part of the British history with a predilection for the unfortunate house of Stuart, and the principles of the Tories; it is evident, that had he written without any such views, he might have attained to an eminence far beyond that which he has reached, and descended to posterity not as the first of all party writers of history, but as the author of a truly great national work, the spirit and excellence of which should have been equally admired and appreciated by all the English. In his treatment of the elder periods of the English history, he is quite unsatisfactory and meagre; he had no love for its antiquities, and could not transport himself back into the spirit of remote ages. (pp. 330-31)

Friedrich von Schlegel, in a lecture in 1812, in his Lectures on the History of Literature: Ancient and Modern, *translated by J. G. Lockhart, 1818. Reprint by J. & H. G. Langley, 1841, pp. 322-41.*

RICHARD WHATELY   (essay date 1819)

[*Whately was an English clergyman, essayist, theologian, and political theorist. He is best known for his first published work, the anonymously issued* Historic Doubts Relative to Napoleon Buonaparte *(1819), a rollicking, chiding attempt to show that on Hume's principles the existence of Napoleon could not be admitted "as a well-authenticated fact." In the following excerpt from the text and notes of this work, Whately endeavors to debunk Humean skepticism.*]

[A peculiar circumstance in the history of Napoleon Buonaparte] is that when it is found convenient to represent him as defeated, though he is by no means defeated by halves, but involved in much more sudden and total ruin than the personages of real history usually meet with; yet, if it is thought fit he should be restored, it is done as quickly and completely as if Merlin's rod had been employed. He enters Russia with a prodigious army, which is totally ruined by an unprecedented hard winter (everything relating to this man is *prodigious* and *unprecedented)*. Yet in a few months we find him entrusted with another great army in Germany, which is also totally ruined at Leipsic—making, inclusive of the Egyptian, the third great army thus totally lost; yet the French are so good-natured as to furnish him with another, sufficient to make a formidable stand in France. He is, however, *conquered, and presented with the sovereignty of Elba* (surely, by the bye, some more *probable* way might have been found of disposing of him, till again wanted, than to place him thus on the very verge of his ancient dominions). Thence he returns to France, where he is received with open arms, and enabled to lose a fifth great army at Waterloo; yet so eager were these people to be a sixth time led to destruction that it was found necessary to confine *him* in an island some thousand miles off, and to quarter foreign troops upon *them,* lest they should make an insurrection in his favour. Does anyone believe all this and yet refuse to believe a miracle? Or rather, what is this but a miracle? Is it not a violation of the laws of nature?—for surely there are moral laws of nature as well as physical, which, though more liable to exceptions in this or that particular case, are no less *true as general rules* than the laws of matter, and therefore cannot be violated and contradicted *beyond a certain point,* without a miracle.

This doctrine, though hardly needing confirmation from authority, is supported by that of Hume; his [**"Of Liberty and Necessity"**] is, throughout, an argument for the doctrine of "Philosophical Necessity," drawn entirely from the general uniformity observable in the course of nature with respect to the principles of *human conduct,* as well as those of the material universe—from which uniformity, he observes, it is that we are enabled, *in both cases,* to form our judgments by means of *Experience.* "And if," says he, "we would explode any forgery in history, we cannot make use of a more convincing argument, than to prove that the actions ascribed to any person, are directly contrary to the course of nature. . . . The veracity of Quintus Curtius is as suspicious when he describes the supernatural courage of Alexander, by which he was hurried on singly to attack multitudes, as when he describes his supernatural force and activity, by which he was able to resist them. So readily and universally do we acknowledge a *uniformity in human motives and actions, as well as in the operations of body'.*" (pp. 26-7)

Accordingly in [**"Of Miracles"**] his use of the term "miracle," after having called it "a transgression of a law of nature," plainly shows that he meant to include *human* nature. "No testimony," says he, "is sufficient to establish a miracle, unless the testimony be of such a nature that its falsehood would be more miraculous than the fact which it endeavours to establish." The term "prodigy" also (which he all along employs as synonymous with "miracle") is applied to testimony, in the same manner, immediately after. "In the foregoing reasoning we have supposed . . . that the falsehood of that testimony

would be a kind of *prodigy.*" Now, had he meant to confine the meaning of "miracle" and "prodigy" to a violation of the laws of *matter,* the epithet "*miraculous,*" applied even thus hypothetically to *false testimony,* would be as unmeaning as the epithets "green" or "square"; the only possible sense in which we can apply to it, even in imagination, the term "miraculous," is that of "highly improbable"—"contrary to those laws of nature which respect human conduct"; and in this sense he accordingly uses the word in the very next sentence. "When anyone tells me that he saw a dead man restored to life, I immediately consider with myself whether it be more *probable* that this person should either deceive or be deceived, or that the fact which he relates should really have happened. I weigh the one *miracle* against the other." (pp. 27-8)

Perhaps it was superfluous to cite authority for applying the term "miracle" to whatever is "highly improbable," but it is important to students of Hume to be fully aware that *he* uses those two expressions as synonymous; since otherwise they would mistake the meaning of that passage which he justly calls "a general maxim worthy of our attention." (p. 28)

> *Richard Whately, in his* Historic Doubts Relative to Napoleon Bonaparte, *edited by Ralph S. Pomeroy, Scholar Press, 1985, 124 p.*

THOMAS JEFFERSON   (letter date 1825)

[*The third president of the United States, Jefferson is best known as a statesman whose belief in natural rights, equality, individual liberties, and self-government found its fullest expression in the American Declaration of Independence. A skilled writer noted for his simple yet elegant prose, he profoundly influenced the direction of American politics, inspiring generations of American and other followers. In the following excerpt from a letter to an unnamed member of the University of Virginia faculty, Jefferson describes both the merits and faults of Hume's historical works.*]

Hume's, were it faithful, would be the finest piece of history which has ever been written by man. Its unfortunate bias may be partly ascribed to the accident of his having written backwards. His maiden work was the *History of the Stuarts.* It was a first essay to try his strength before the public. And whether as a Scotchman he had really a partiality for that family, or thought that the lower their degradation, the more fame he should acquire by raising them up to some favor, the object of his work was an apology for them. He spared nothing, therefore, to wash them white, and to palliate their misgovernment. For this purpose he suppressed truths, advanced falsehoods, forged authorities, and falsified records. All this is proved on him unanswerably by Brodie. But so bewitching was his style and manner, that his readers were unwilling to doubt anything, swallowed everything, and all England became Tories by the magic of his art. His pen revolutionized the public sentiment of that country more completely than the standing armies could ever have done, which were so much dreaded and deprecated by the patriots of that day.

Having succeeded so eminently in the acquisition of fortune and fame by this work, he undertook the history of the two preceding dynasties, the Plantagenets and Tudors. It was all-important in this second work, to maintain the thesis of the first, that "it was the people who encroached on the sovereign, not the sovereign who usurped on the rights of the people." And, again, chapter 53d, "the grievances under which the English labored [to wit: whipping, pillorying, cropping, imprisoning, fining, &c.,] when considered in themselves, without regard to the Constitution, scarcely deserve the name, nor were they either burthensome on the people's properties, or anywise shocking to the natural humanity of mankind." During the constant wars, civil and foreign, which prevailed while these two families occupied the throne, it was not difficult to find abundant instances of practices the most despotic, as are wont to occur in times of violence. To make this second epoch support the third, therefore, required but a little garbling of authorities. And it then remained, by a third work, to make of the whole a complete history of England, on the principles on which he had advocated that of the Stuarts. This would comprehend the Saxon and Norman conquests, the former exhibiting the genuine form and political principles of the people constituting the nation, and founded in the rights of man; the latter built on conquest and physical force, not at all affecting moral rights, nor even assented to by the free will of the vanquished. The battle of Hastings, indeed, was lost, but the natural rights of the nation were not staked on the event of a single battle. Their will to recover the Saxon constitution continued unabated, and was at the bottom of all the unsuccessful insurrections which succeeded in subsequent times. The victors and vanquished continued in a state of living hostility, and the nation may still say, after losing the battle of Hastings,

> What though the field is lost?
> All is not lost; the unconquerable will
> And study of revenge, immortal hate
> And courage never to submit or yield.

The government of a nation may be usurped by the forcible intrusion of an individual into the throne. But to conquer its will, so as to rest the right on that, the only legitimate basis, requires long acquiescence and cessation of all opposition. The Whig historians of England, therefore, have always gone back to the Saxon period for the true principles of their constitution, while the Tories and Hume, their Coryphæus, date it from the Norman conquest, and hence conclude that the continual claim by the nation of the good old Saxon laws, and the struggles to recover them, were "encroachments of the people on the crown, and not usurpations of the crown on the people." Hume, with Brodie, should be the last histories of England to be read. If first read, Hume makes an English Tory, from whence it is an easy step to American Toryism. But there is a history, by Baxter, in which, abridging somewhat by leaving out some entire incidents as less interesting now than when Hume wrote, he has given the rest in the identical words of Hume, except that when he comes to a fact falsified, he states it truly, and when to a suppression of truth, he supplies it, never otherwise changing a word. It is, in fact, an editic expurgation of Hume. Those who shrink from the volume of Rapin, may read this first, and from this lay a first foundation in a basis of truth. (pp. 1094-96)

> *Thomas Jefferson, in a letter on October 25, 1825, in his* The Complete Jefferson, *edited by Saul K. Padover, Duell, Sloan & Pearce, Inc., 1943, pp. 1094-96.*

JOHN HILL BURTON   (essay date 1846)

[Burton was a prominent nineteenth-century Scottish lawyer, historian, and biographer who wrote the first major biography of Hume. In the following excerpt from this work, he considers Hume's minor essays.]

Some of the subjects of [*Essays, Moral and Political*] were not less untrodden at the time when they appeared, than they are

hackneyed in the present day. Of these may be cited, **"The Liberty of the Press;" "The Parties of Great Britain;" "The Independency of Parliament."** When they are compared with the *Craftsman,* with *Mist's Journal,* and with the other periodicals of the day, which had set the example of discussing such subjects, these essays as little resemble their precursors, as De Lolme's "Remarks on the British Constitution" do the articles in a daily London party paper. Whatever he afterwards became, Hume was at that time no party politician. He retained the Stoic severity of thought with which . . . he had sixteen years previously invested himself; and would allow the excitements or rewards of no party in the state to drag him out of the even middle path of philosophical observation. There is consequently a wonderful impartiality in these essays, and an acuteness of observation, which to the reader, who keeps in view how little the true workings of the constitution were noticed in that day, is not less remarkable. (p. 137)

It has often been observed, that foreigners have been the first to remark the leading peculiarities of the British constitution, and of the administration of justice in this country, in a manner rational and unimpassioned, yet so as to give them greater prominence, and a more full descriptive development than they obtain from our own impassioned party writers—an observation attested by the character which the works of Montesquieu and De Lolme held in the preceding century, and those of

First page of Hume's essay "Of Suicide," showing Hume's handwritten corrections.

Thierry, Cottu, Meyer, and Raumer, have obtained in the present. The reason of this superiority is to be sought in the circumstance that the acuteness of these foreign observers was not obscured, or their feelings excited, by any connexion with the workings of the systems they have described; and the isolation from active life in which Hume was placed, appears to have in some measure given him like qualifications for the examination of our political institutions. He expresses a general partiality for the monarchical government of Britain, but it is a partiality of a calm utilitarian character, which would not be inconsistent with an equally great esteem for a well-ordered republic. On his philosophical appreciation of its merits, the monarchy has no stronger claims than these—that to have an individual at the head of the government who is merely the name through which other persons act, and who is not amenable to any laws, while the real actors are personally responsible for what they do in his name, is an expedient arrangement. That it is very convenient to have some fixed criterion such as the hereditary principle, which shall obviate the trouble and danger of a competition for this elevated station. But that these are all recommendations on the ground of expediency, which may be outweighed by others, and the misconduct of a weak or tyrannical prince will justify an alteration in that arrangement, which convenience only, and the avoidance of occasions for turbulence and anarchy, have sanctioned. (pp. 139-40)

Perhaps the most ambitious of the essays, and those on which the author bestowed most of his skill and attention, are **"The Epicurean," "The Stoic," "The Sceptic,"** and **"The Platonist."** These are productions of the imagination, suggested apparently by the style and method of *The Spectator.* There is no attempt either to support or to attack the systems represented by the names of the essays, nor is there a description or definition of them; but on each occasion a member of one of these celebrated schools speaks in his own person, and describes the nature of the satisfaction that he finds in his own code of philosophy, as a solution of the great difficulty of the right rule of thought and action. **"The Epicurean"** takes a flight of imagination beyond that of Hume's other works. It departs from the cold atmosphere of philosophy, and desires to fascinate as well as enlighten. But though it possesses all the marks of a fine intellect, the reader is apt to feel how far more sweetly and gracefully the subject would have been handled by Addison, to whose department of literature it seems rightly to belong. The follower of Epicurus is not represented, as indulging in that gross licentiousness, as wallowing in that disgusting "style" which the representations of Diogenes Laertius, and others, have impressed on the vulgar associations with the name of that master. On the other hand, the picture is far from embodying what many maintain to be the fundamental precept of Epicurus, that happiness being the great end sought by man, the proper method of reaching it is by the just regulation of the passions and propensities. (pp. 141-42)

Hume, who was not correcting errors, or instructing his readers in the true meaning of terms, or appreciation of characters, draws in **"The Epicurean"** a picture of one who is not gross or grovelling in his pleasures, and who restrains himself lest he should outrun enjoyment; but whose ruling principle is still that of the voluptuary.

The reader expects to find an attempt to draw his own picture in **"The Sceptic;"** but it is not to be found there. The sceptic of the essays is not a man analyzing the principles of knowledge, to find wherein they consist, but one who is dissatisfied with rules of morality, and who, examining the current codes

one after another, tosses them aside as unsatisfactory. It is into **"The Stoic"** that the writer has thrown most of his heart and sympathy; and it is in that sketch that, though probably without intention, some of the features of his own character are portrayed. (pp. 142-43)

John Hill Burton, in his Life and Correspondence of David Hume, *Vol. I, 1846. Reprint by Burt Franklin, 1967, 480 p.*

SIR JAMES FITZJAMES STEPHEN (essay date 1867)

[*Stephen was an English judge and essayist who wrote extensively for the* Saturday Review, *the* Cornhill Magazine, *and the* Pall Mall Gazette. *An expert in criminal law and evidence, he is best known for his* General View of the Criminal Law of England *(1863), an early attempt to link criminal law with social science. In the following excerpt from an essay originally published in 1867, he argues that Hume was not a true skeptic.*]

Hume's [*Essays and Treatises on Several Subjects*] are far more characteristic than his *History of England,* and give his readers much more insight into his mind. They are of very various degress of merit; and those which constitute, in the common editions, the first part, which were originally published by themselves when their author was quite a young man, are greatly inferior to those which belong to the second part, published ten years afterwards. Some have about them a sort of debating-society air, and all convey the impression that the author is feeling his way and learning his business, and that he has not yet discovered, either the true direction of his powers, or the real bearing of his views.

With the Essays in the second part it is quite different. They are open to many and very serious objections, but when they are considered either in an artistic or an intellectual point of view, they are entitled to the very highest praise. They are perfect models of quiet, vigorous, and yet graceful composition, as full of thought as any writings need to be, yet never so much compressed as to impose needless labour on the reader. As to their intellectual merits, it is almost superfluous to praise them. They are the most complete, the most powerful, and, in essentials, though not always in language, the most accurate pieces of mental workmanship which the last century produced in Scotland. They contain the germ of all the most active and fruitful speculations of our own day; and it is curious, in reading them over, to see how very little subsequent speculation has added to a great part of what Hume wrote.

Perhaps the most remarkable feature about the *Essays* is the substantial identity of the vein of thought which runs through a variety of subjects that are apparently, and at first sight, unconnected with each other. The subjects of the *Essays,* in the order in which they stand, are—political economy, politics, metaphysics, morals, and theology. In short, Hume handles successively, and in the inverse order of their interest, most of the subjects which possess what, in these days, is sometimes decribed as a 'human' interest—the subjects, that is, which relate directly to the concerns, the thoughts, the duties, and the prospects of mankind. Some of these topics are widely remote from each other. For instance, there is little apparent relation between an inquiry into the populousness of ancient nations, and an inquiry into the nature of benevolence or justice; but, if they are read continuously, it will be found that a certain unity of thought and method pervades the whole, and that the subjects in question were by no means chosen at random, or without a more or less distinct conception of the common method in which all were to be considered.

The great characteristic of this common vein of thought has sometimes been called scepticism. Hume himself often employs the word, and, apparently, was not altogether averse to it. The somewhat sluggish good nature of his temperament led him to enjoy the formal and avowed repudiation of responsibility for the world and its prospects. He liked to push it all on one side, and to say, in the concluding words of his Essay *On the Natural History of Religion,* 'The whole is a riddle, an enigma, an inexplicable mystery. Doubt, uncertainty, suspense of judgment appear the only result of our most accurate scrutiny concerning this subject.' (pp. 369-71)

Mere scepticism—the bare power of collecting doubts and difficulties from all quarters upon all subjects—can never, from the nature of the case, exercise much permanent influence on mankind. A mere cloud-compeller is, as a rule, no more than an intellectual juggler, whose feats rapidly pall upon the spectators, especially when they get to see how they are done. Hume was much more than this. Under his scepticism and indifference lay a set of doctrines which are open to serious objection, and which are certainly incomplete, but which are as far from scepticism as light from darkness.

He was in truth what we should now call a Positivist, and the real gist of his scepticism is not to throw contempt on all human knowledge, but to throw contempt on particular sets of popular opinions which in his days were even more influential than they are in our own. Whatever may be the subject on which Hume is inquiring, he always propounds some distinct opinion, and that opinion is always founded on facts. His scepticism ends not in universal doubt, but in an attempt, and in many cases a very successful attempt, to show what are the foundations, and, in part at least, what are the limits of real knowledge, and what phrases, professing to convey information, are in reality darkening counsel by words without understanding.

It appears to have been his greatest delight to show the ambiguities and contradictions latent in common words and modes of thought, and carefully and accurately to limit the degree of information which they do really afford. His analysis of the word 'power,' his inquiries into the nature of money, of interest, of causation, of justice, and many other subjects, are all conducted on the same principles. By applying all sorts of tests and putting every imaginable case, he ultimately arrives, not, as he sometimes affected to do, at mere doubt and difficulty, but at some result, involved, it may be, and implied in the common views of the subject, but generally supposed to form but a small and perhaps an unimportant part of the teaching contained in the established phraseology.

Hume, in fact, deserves to be regarded by no means as a sceptic, but as the founder, at least in this country, of the least sceptical and most positive of all schools of thought. (pp. 372-73)

[Hume's] metaphysics, which have been described as so sceptical, are in truth little more than an attempt, by extreme simplicity in thinking and in the use of terms, to lay the foundation of a fruitful and really scientific treatment of the subject. We start, he says, with sensible impressions. Our reflections on these impressions are our ideas. You might suppose that these ideas or thoughts followed each other at random, but as a fact they do not. They suggest each other, or are associated, and this association falls into certain shapes—namely, resemblance, contiguity, and causation; which last is afterwards explained in the most celebrated essays of the whole volume to

be a form of contiguity—namely, constant, and, as Mr. Mill afterwards added, unconditional sequence. The general result is, that metaphysics, in so far as they are sound, are based, not on reasoning, but on observed facts; or, to quote one of the pregnant sentences which are so characteristic of Hume— 'All inferences from experience, therefore, are effects of custom, not reasoning.' (p. 377)

Sir James Fitzjames Stephen, "Hume's Essays," in his Horae Sabbaticae: Reprint of Articles Contributed *to "The Saturday Review," second series, Macmillan and Co., 1892, pp. 367-85.*

SIR LESLIE STEPHEN   (essay date 1876)

[*Many scholars consider Stephen the most important English literary critic of the Victorian age after Matthew Arnold. He has been praised for his moral insight and judgment, as well as for his intellectual vigor. Some scholars, however, who consider Stephen's contribution to English literature to be less influential than Arnold's, argue that Stephen's work is deficient in aesthetic and formal analysis and fails to reconcile its author's moral and historical philosophies. The key to Stephen's moral criticism is his theory that all literature is nothing more than an imaginative rendering, in concrete terms, of a writer's philosophy or beliefs. It is the role of criticism, he contends, to translate into intellectual terms what the writer has told the reader through character, symbol, and event. More often than not, Stephen's analysis passes into biographical judgment of the writer rather than the work. As he once observed, "The whole art of criticism consists in learning to know the human being who is partially revealed to us in his spoken or his written words." Stephen's emphasis on the writer's philosophy, rather than the formal aspects of literature, has led Desmond MacCarthy to call him "the least aesthetic of noteworthy critics." In the following excerpt, Stephen examines the method and motives of Hume's philosophical and theological works, focusing on the author's* Dialogues concerning Natural Religion *and his skeptical approach to theology.*]

[Hume's] scepticism in metaphysics seems at times to be but half sincere, as scepticism must be which not only disputes certain dogmas, but throws doubt upon the validity of the reasoning process itself. The so-called scepticism of the theological essays is not in this sense sceptical; it admits the validity of reason in its own sphere, but seeks to demonstrate that theology lies outside of that sphere. In the metaphysical writings Hume throws doubts upon the validity of our belief in the invariable order of the universe. His theological writings are made more cogent by admitting that fundamental truth. The doubts which he expounds are not the mere playthings of philosophical fancy, which vanish when we leave the closet for the street. They are strong convictions seen from another side; and are as dogmatic, in one sense, as the theologian's in the opposite sense. From his various writings, the *Treatise on Human Nature,* the *Dialogues on Natural Religion,* the *Philosophical Essays,* and the *Natural History of Religion,* we may frame a complete and logically co-ordinated system of argument. J. S. Mill, the most distinguished of Hume's recent disciples, left behind him an essay upon theism, discussing the same vital problems with the advantage afforded by familiarity with subsequent speculation. Though more symmetrically arranged, it scarcely includes a single argument not explicitly stated or clearly indicated by Hume. It is marked, however, by one quality, curiously absent from Hume's colourless logic. A pathetic desire to find some remnant of truth in the ancient dogmas breathes throughout its pages, and is allowed to exercise a distorting influence upon its conclusions. In Hume there is no trace of such a sentiment. As a rule, he neither scoffs, nor sneers, nor regrets. The dogma under discussion seems neither to attract nor to repel him. Here and there we may trace too complacent a sense of his ingenuity, or a desire to administer a passing rebuff to the confidence of men like Warbuton; but the stream of his logic is generally as unruffled and limpid as though he were discussing a metaphysical puzzle unrelated to human passion, or undertaking an historical enquiry into the truth of some doubtful legend. This strange calmness is characteristic of the man and of his age; it is only possible to a consummate logician, arguing at a time when theology, though living amongst the masses, was being handed over by thinkers to the schools. We have in his pages the ultimate expression of the acutest scepticism of the eighteenth century; the one articulate English statement of a philosophical judgment upon the central questions at issue. (pp. 311-12)

[Hume's whole philosophy] is the antithesis of the doctrine upon which reposed the ontological proof of Descartes, or the more familiar cosmological proof represented by Clarke. His scepticism is one continuous assault upon the validity of their methods; and the direct application is made, though with some veil of reticence, in the fourth part of the *Treatise of Human Nature,* and more explicitly in the posthumous *Dialogues on Natural Religion.* Abandoning the high *a priori* road, divines might betake themselves to the 'physico-theological' argument, generally described as the argument from final causes. A prolonged and most ingenious discussion of this theory forms the main substance of the *Dialogues.* Reasoners, again, who doubted the soundness of this mode of argument, or shrank from raising the fundamental questions involved, might retire to the moral argument, which, in one shape or other, has the strongest influence with many minds. The theory of the 'categorical imperative,' and the deduction of theology as a regulative principle of conduct, was not known to English thinkers, but it has a close affinity to the ethical doctrine of Clarke, and is represented to some extent in Butler's doctrine of the conscience. Hume's morality, if accepted, strikes at the root of this theory; and the application to Butler's argument is sufficiently indicated in the essay upon **"A Particular Providence and a Future State."** Finally, abandoning all strictly philosophical arguments, the divine might fall back upon the historical argument. He might appeal to experience at large, as showing that the idea of a supreme Deity must have been supernaturally implanted in men's minds, or to the particular experience embodied in the history of revelation. The answers to these arguments are given by Hume in the *Natural History of Religion,* and in that **"Essay on Miracles,"** which alone excited any vehemence of controversy. (pp. 313-14)

[Whatever] the value of Hume's reasonings, he has, at least, the high merit of having unflinchingly enquired into the profoundest of all questions, and of having dared to give the result of his enquiries without fear or favour. The want of intellectual courage displayed by his contemporaries is doubtless pardonable, in one sense. We cannot judge harshly of men who feared to injure a doctrine which, true or false, seemed to afford the only lasting consolation to suffering humanity, and the only sound basis for morality. But, in another sense, no cowardice is ever pardonable, for it is never pardoned by facts. Want of candour brings an inevitable penalty upon the race, if not upon the individual. The hollowness in theory and the impotence in practice of English speculation in the last half of the century, is but the natural consequence of the faint-heartedness which prevented English thinkers from looking facts in the face. The huge development of hypocrisy, of sham beliefs, and indolent scepticism, is the penalty which we have had to pay for our

not daring to meet the doubts openly expressed by Hume, and by Hume alone.

Hume's scepticism cuts away the very base of ontological proof. The mind, according to him, is unable to rise one step beyond sensible experience. It can separate and combine the various 'impressions' and 'ideas;' it is utterly unable to create a single new idea, or penetrate to an ultimate world of realities. The 'substance' in which the qualities of the phenomenal world are thought to inhere is a concept emptied of all contents, and a word without a meaning. The external world, which supports the phenomena, is but a 'fiction' of the mind; the mind, which in the same way affords a substratum for the impressions, is itself a fiction; and the divine substance, which, according to the Cartesians, causes the correlation between these two fictions, must—that is the natural inference—be equally a fiction. Impressions and ideas, combining and separating in infinite variety, being the sole realities; the bond which unites, and the substratum which supports them, must be essentially unknowable, for knowledge itself is but an association of ideas. Dismiss these doubts, attempt to frame ontological propositions, and the fallacy manifests itself afresh in the futility of the dogma which emerges. Under the form of examining Bayle's criticism upon the 'hideous hypothesis' of Spinoza, Hume exhibits the inevitable antinomies, which beset the reason in its endeavour to soar beyond experience, and, therefore, on his assumption, to transcend itself. Metaphysicians had insisted upon the utterly disparate character of mind and matter. The two could not be brought into relation, except by the verbal explanation of the divine power. It was only necessary, then, to exhibit this antithesis, to show that the doctrine was inconceivable. Mind cannot be resolved into matter, therefore materialism is absurd. But neither can mind be brought into contact with matter, unless mind be itself extended. Therefore spiritualism is equally absurd. The external universe, said Bayle, in answer to Spinoza, in all its complex variety, cannot be a simple indivisible substance. Neither, then, can the soul, whose ideas, by the hypothesis, reflect every conceivable modification of the external universe, be a simple indivisible substance. Whatever may be said of the assumed object, may be said of the impression by which it is represented. Matter and motion, it was argued again, however varied, could still be nothing but motion and matter. Hume's theory of causation destroys the argument. Causes and effects are but names for conjoined phenomena, and we cannot assert *a priori* that any two phenomena will or will not be conjoined. No position of bodies can produce motion, any more than it can produce thought; for, turn it which way you will, it is still but a position of bodies. As thought and motion are, in fact, constantly united, motion may be, and on Hume's definition it actually is, the cause of thought. We must either assert that causal connection between two objects exists only where we can perceive the logical nexus between their ideas, or we must admit that uniform conjunction implies a causal relation. In the first case, there can be no 'cause or productive principle' in the universe, not even the Deity himself. For we have no 'idea' of the Deity, except from impressions, each of which appears to be an independent entity, and, therefore, includes no efficacy. If we still assert the Deity to be the one cause which supplies this defect, he must be the cause of every action, virtuous or vicious; and we fall into Pantheism. If we admit that uniform connection is sufficient to establish cause, we must then admit that anything may be the cause of anything; and the argument against Materialism vanishes. Nominally retorting upon Bayle the objections to Spinozism, Hume is really extending Bayle's scepticism beyond its immediate purpose; and bringing out the contradictions which inevitably beset the attempt to treat of absolute substances supposed to exist in perfect simplicity and independence of all relations. His argument was shrouded by a thin veil of reticence, and the defects of style which mar the early treatise: and it dealt with considerations too abstract to impress the ordinary reasoner. In the posthumous *Dialogues* he comes to closer quarters with the popular theology.

The *Dialogues* are prefaced by an apology for adopting that form of argument. The true motives are obvious enough. Theologians might indulge in demonstrations. The sceptic finds it convenient to create personages to whose utterances he is not obviously pledged. Moreover, the form of the Dialogue itself implies an argument. The sceptic Philo mediates between the rigidly orthodox Demea and the more amenable Cleanthes. Demea and Cleanthes represent, in fact, two opposite schools of theology, and Philo finds in each of them an ally in his assault upon the other. [We may notice] the antithesis between Clarke and Waterland, or between Browne and Berkeley. When each divine accused his brother of sanctioning the first principles of Atheism, so keen an observer as Hume was not likely to overlook the advantage to himself. He could stand aside, like Faulconbridge in *King John,* and watch France and Austria shoot in each other's faces. Demea, in fact, represents the *a priori* school, who at once assert the existence of God and exhaust themselves in assertions of the utter inconceivability of his attributes. Cleanthes, relying upon the argument from final causes, is forced to admit a certain analogy between the Divine workman whose purpose is revealed in his work, and the human observer who can understand his designs. The agreement of theologians is an agreement to use a common name, but the name covers radically inconsistent conceptions. The arguments of the anthropomorphist for a limited Deity tell against the ontological argument for an infinite Deity. The worship of nature can be no more made to square with the worship of Jehovah than with the worship of the supreme artisan. Hume is least antipathetic to the least exalted conception. He has a common ground with the reasoner from design, and resents the metaphysical arrogance which at once admits that its dogmas are unintelligible, and insists upon their acceptance. There is hope of a definite issue between ourselves and a reasoner who accepts our method. Between the *a priori* school and Hume's the opposition was vital, though in practice the ontologists might frame a theology of a more neutral tint than that of their rivals.

In the *Dialogues,* Hume deals briefly with the *a priori* argument. Assuming the truth of his philosophy, it falls, as we have seen, to the ground. He states, however, distinctly the main ground of the difficulties to which it is exposed. Admitting ostensibly the necessity of a belief in God, he quotes Malebranche, and adds that he might have quoted any number of philosophical divines in favour of the utter inconceivability of the divine nature. We call God a spirit to signify that he is not matter; but without venturing to imply that his nature has any resemblance to ours. We attribute to him thought, design, knowledge; but such words are used in a sense indefinitely distant from that which they bear when applied to mankind. Cleanthes, the advocate of final causes, asks Demea—the representative of the *a priori* theorists—how this doctrine differs from that of the sceptics or atheists, who declare the first cause to be unknown and unintelligible? Men, he says, who assert that God can have no attributes corresponding to human ideas, that he is absolutely simple and immutable, are in fact atheists without knowing it. 'A mind whose acts and sentiments and ideas are not distinct and successive; one that is wholly simple

and totally immutable, is a mind which has no thought, no reason, no will, no sentiment, no love, no hatred; or, in a word, is no mind at all.' The ontologists may prove the existence of God; but God with them means pure Being—a blank, colourless, and useless conception.

But can it be proved? Hume lays down as a principle that it is evidently absurd to demonstrate a matter of fact, or to prove it by any arguments *a priori*. 'Nothing is demonstrable, unless the contrary implies a contradicion. Nothing that is distinctly conceivable implies a contradiction. Whatever we conceive as existent, we can also conceive as non-existent. There is no being, therefore, whose non-existence implies a contradiction. Consequently, there is no being whose existence is demonstrable. I propose this argument as entirely decisive, and am willing to rest the whole controversy upon it.' This, in fact, is Hume's retort to the ontological argument of Descartes. It anticipates the more elaborate analysis of the same argument by Kant; and though it may need development, seems to be substantially unanswerable. Reid characteristically admits its validity in regard to all truths concerning existence, excepting 'only the existence and attributes of the Supreme Being, which is the only necessary truth we know regarding existence.' It is impossible, however, to assign a clear logical ground for this judicious exception. The Cartesian proof is really a subtile mode of begging the question. It is contradictory to speak of non-existing existence; and, therefore, if God be defined as the existing Being, his existence is, of course, necessary. But to transmute this logical necessity into an objective necessity is a mere juggle. It proves that God exists, *if* he exists; which is indeed a true, but not a fruitful, proposition. The argument, in fact, proves nothing, or simply asserts the apparently identical proposition that all existence exists. Every being which exists is known as related to and limited by other existences. From our experience of a particular existence, we may advance by help of such relations to other existences, beyond our immediate experience. But an existence, proved by *a priori* argument, and therefore independent of all relations to the facts of experience, can be nothing but the totality of all existence. The conclusion must be as wide as the premisses. From an argument, independent of all experience, we must infer an existence which does not affect experience, or which affects all experience equally. It has been attempted to revive the ontological argument thus assailed by Hume and Kant; but their criticism is at least decisive against its original form.

The 'cosmological' argument attempts to amend this plea by introducing a datum from experience. Something, it is admitted, exists; therefore, there is a necessary existence. Hume scarcely distinguishes this from the ontological argument with which, as Kant says, it is ultimately identical. In a short passage, however, he touches the vital point. Clarke had argued that matter could not be the self-existent Being, because any particle of matter might be conceived to be annihilated or altered. But it is equally possible, as Hume rejoins, to imagine the Deity to be non-existent, or his attributes to be altered. If that be impossible in fact, it is impossible in virtue of some unknown and inconceivable attributes, which may, therefore, be capable of union with matter. Or, if we put the argument into the more familiar form of the 'first cause,' we are falling into another fallacy. To ask for the cause of an eternal succession is absurd, for cause implies priority of time. In the everlasting chain each link is caused by the preceding, and causes the succeeding. But the whole requires a cause? To call it a whole is an act of the mind which implies no difference in the nature of things. If I could show the cause of each individual in a collection of twenty particles, it would be absurd to ask for the cause of the whole twenty. That is given in giving the particular causes. Hume sees, in fact, that the conception of causality which compels us to bind together all things as mutually conditioned by each other, cannot, without a logical trick, be transferred to the totality of being. If applicable at all, it would produce an infinite series; for, having determined the cause of the whole, we should have to ask for the cause of the cause. The application of the principle is in its very nature incapable of ever leading to an ultimate conclusion. It suggests only an infinite progression, reminding us once more of Locke's famous illustration of the Indian philosopher and his world-supporting elephant. (pp. 314-20)

It may still be asked, what was Hume's real belief? Did his theoretical scepticism follow him into actual life? That is a question for a biographer rather than for the historian of thought. There is a famous saying which has been attributed to the first Lord Shaftesbury, to Garth, to Humboldt, and probably to others. What is your religion? The religion of all sensible men. And what is the religion of all sensible men? Sensible men never tell. Hume quotes a similar saying of Bacon's. Atheists, says the philosopher, have now-a-days a double share of folly; for, not content with saying in their hearts that there is no God, they utter it with their lips, and are 'thereby guilty of multiplied indiscretion and imprudence.' Hume so far adopted these precepts of worldly wisdom that he left his most outspoken writings for posthumous publication. Yet Hume said enough to incur the vehement indignation both of the truly devout and of the believers in the supreme value of respectability. It is impossible to suppose that the acutest reasoner of his time would have considered his most finished work as a mere logical play, or that he should have encountered obloquy without the justification of sincerity. I have, therefore, no doubt that Hume was a sceptic in theology, that he fully recognised the impossibility of divining the great secret, and that he anticipated this part of what is now called the positive philosophy. Yet, as a true sceptic, he probably did not expect that the bulk of mankind would ever follow him in his conclusions. He felt that, although a rational system of theology capable of affecting men's lives be an impossibility, his own denial of its validity did not quite destroy the underlying sentiment. Though the old bonds were worthless, some mode of contemplating the universe as an organised whole was still requisite. A vague belief, too impalpable to be imprisoned in formulæ or condensed into demonstrations, still survived in his mind, suggesting that there must be something behind the veil, and something, perhaps, bearing a remote analogy to human intelligence. How far such a belief can be justified, or, if justified, made the groundwork of an effective religion, is a question not precisely considered by Hume nor to be here discussed. We may be content to respect in Hume the most powerful assailant of the pretentious dogmatism and the timid avoidance of ultimate difficulties characteristic of his time. (pp. 341-42)

> *Sir Leslie Stephen, "David Hume," in his* History of English Thought in the Eighteenth Century, *Vol. I, 1876. Reprint by John Murray, 1927, pp. 309-43.*

THOMAS H. HUXLEY   (essay date 1878)

[*A celebrated agnostic and freethinker, Huxley was a scientist and essayist who wrote widely on physiology, natural history, and philosophy. In the following excerpt from an essay originally published in 1878, he explores the development of Hume's theology.*]

Hume seems to have had but two hearty dislikes: the one to the English nation, and the other to all the professors of dogmatic theology. The one aversion he vented only privately to his friends; but, if he is ever bitter in his public utterances, it is against priests in general and theological enthusiasts and fanatics in particular; if he ever seems insincere, it is when he wishes to insult theologians by a parade of sarcastic respect. One need go no further than the peroration of the **"Essay on Miracles"** for a characteristic illustration. (p. 165)

[It is obvious that in **"Essay on Miracles"**] Hume, adopting a popular confusion of ideas, uses religion as the equivalent of dogmatic theology; and, therefore, he says, with perfect justice, that "religion is nothing but a species of philosophy." Here no doubt lies the root of his antagonism. The quarrels of theologians and philosophers have not been about religion, but about philosophy; and philosophers not unfrequently seem to entertain the same feeling towards theologians that sportsmen cherish towards poachers. "There cannot be two passions more nearly resembling each other than hunting and philosophy," says Hume. And philosophic hunters are given to think, that, while they pursue truth for its own sake, out of pure love for the chase (perhaps mingled with a little human weakness to be thought good shots), and by open and legitimate methods; their theological competitors too often care merely to supply the market of establishments; and disdain neither the aid of the snares of superstition, nor the cover of the darkness of ignorance.

Unless some foundation was given for this impression by the theological writers whose works had fallen in Hume's ways, it is difficult to account for the depth of feeling which so good-natured a man manifests on the subject. (pp. 166-67)

[Hume] seems to have had a theology of his own; that is to say, he seems to have thought (though, as will appear, it is needful for an expositor of his opinions to speak very guardedly on this point) that the problem of theism is susceptible of scientific treatment, with something more than a negative result. His opinions are to be gathered from the eleventh section of the *Inquiry* . . . , from the *Dialogues concerning Natural Religion* . . . , and from the *Natural History of Religion*. . . .

In the first two pieces, the reader is left to judge for himself which interlocutor in the dialogue represents the thoughts of the author; but for the views put forward in the last, Hume accepts the responsibility. Unfortunately, this essay deals almost wholly with the historical development of theological ideas; and, on the question of the philosophical foundation of theology, does little more than express the writer's contentment with the argument from design. (p. 169)

[Hume] appears to have sincerely accepted the two fundamental conclusions of the argument from design; firstly, that a Deity exists; and, secondly, that He possesses attributes more or less allied to those of human intelligence. (p. 170)

[It cannot be said that Hume's] theological burden is a heavy one. But, if we turn from the *Natural History of Religion*, to the [*Treatise of Human Nature*], the *Inquiry*, and the *Dialogues*, the story of what happened to the ass laden with salt, who took to the water, irresistibly suggests itself. Hume's theism, such as it is, dissolves away in the dialectic river, until nothing is left but the verbal sack in which it was contained.

Of the two theistic propositions to which Hume is committed, the first is the affirmation of the existence of a God, supported by the argument from the nature of causation. In the *Dialogues*,

Philo, while pushing scepticism to its utmost limit, is nevertheless made to say that—

> . . . .where reasonable men treat these subjects, the question can never be concerning the *Being*, but only the *Nature* of the Deity. The former truth, as you will observe, is unquestionable and self-evident. Nothing exists without a cause, and the original cause of this universe (whatever it be) we call God, and piously ascribe to him every species of perfection.

The expositor of Hume, who wishes to do his work thoroughly, as far as it goes, cannot but fall into perplexity when he contrasts this language with that of the sections of the third part of the *Treatise*, entitled, "Why a Cause is Always Necessary" and "Of the Idea of Necessary Connexion."

It is there shown at large that, "every demonstration which has been produced for the necessity of a cause is fallacious and sophistical"; it is affirmed, that "there is no absolute nor metaphysical necessity that every beginning of existence should be attended with such an object" [as a cause]; and it is roundly asserted, that it is "easy for us to conceive any object to be non-existent this moment and existent the next, without conjoining to it the distinct idea of a cause or productive principle." So far from the axiom, that whatever begins to exist must have a cause of existence, being "self-evident," as Philo calls it, Hume spends the greatest care in showing that it is nothing but the product of custom, or experience.

And the doubt thus forced upon one, whether Philo ought to be taken as Hume's mouthpiece even so far, is increased when we reflect that we are dealing with an acute reasoner; and that there is no difficulty in drawing the deduction from Hume's own definition of a cause, that the very phrase, a "first cause," involves a contradiction in terms. (pp. 172-74)

Now the "first cause" is assumed to have existed from all eternity, up to the moment at which the universe came into existence. Hence it cannot be the sole cause of the universe; in fact, it was no cause at all until it was "assisted by some other principle"; consequently the so-called "first cause," so far as it produces the universe, is in reality an effect of that other principle. Moreover, though, in the person of Philo, Hume assumes the axiom "that whatever begins to exist must have a cause," which he denies in the *Treatise*, he must have seen, for a child may see, that the assumption is of no real service.

Suppose Y to be the imagined first cause and Z to be its effect. Let the letters of the alphabet, *a, b, c, d, e, f, g,* in their order, represent successive moments of time, and let *g* represent the particular moment at which the effect Z makes its appearance. It follows that the cause Y could not have existed "in its full perfection" during the time *a—e,* for if it had, then the effect Z would have come into existence during that time, which, by the hypothesis, it did not do. The cause Y, therefore, must have come into existence at *f,* and if "everything that comes into existence has a cause," Y must have had a cause X operating at *e,* X a cause W operating at *d;* and so on, *ad infinitum.*

If the only demonstrative argument for the existence of a Deity, which Hume advances, thus literally, "goes to water" in the solvent of his philosophy, the reasoning from the evidence of design does not fare much better. If Hume really knew of any valid reply to Philo's arguments in . . . the *Dialogues,* he has dealt unfairly by the reader in concealing it. . . . (pp. 174-76)

It is obvious that, if Hume had been pushed, he must have admitted that his opinion concerning the existence of a God, and of a certain remote resemblance of his intellectual nature to that of man, was an hypothesis which might possess more or less probability, but, on his own principles, was incapable of any approach to demonstration. And to all attempts to make any practical use of his theism; or to prove the existence of the attributes of infinite wisdom, benevolence, justice, and the like, which are usually ascribed to the Deity, by reason, he opposes a searching critical negation.

The object of the speech of the imaginary Epicurean in the eleventh section of the *Inquiry,* entitled "Of a Particular Providence and of a Future State," is to invert the argument of Bishop Butler's *Analogy.*

That famous defence of theology against the *a priori* scepticism of Freethinkers of the eighteenth century, who based their arguments on the inconsistency of the revealed scheme of salvation with the attributes of the Deity, consists, essentially, in conclusively proving that, from a moral point of view, Nature is at least as reprehensible as orthodoxy. If you tell me, says Butler, in effect, that any part of revealed religion must be false because it is inconsistent with the divine attributes of justice and mercy; I beg leave to point out to you, that there are undeniable natural facts which are fully open to the same objection. Since you admit that nature is the work of God, you are forced to allow that such facts are consistent with his attributes. Therefore, you must also admit, that the parallel facts in the scheme of orthodoxy are also consistent with them, and all your arguments to the contrary fall to the ground. Q. E. D. In fact, the solid sense of Butler left the Deism of the Freethinkers not a leg to stand upon. Perhaps, however, he did not remember the wise saying that "A man seemeth right in his own cause, but another cometh after and judgeth him." Hume's Epicurean philosopher adopts the main arguments of the *Analogy,* but unfortunately drives them home to a conclusion of which the good Bishop would hardly have approved. (pp. 179-81)

[The Freethinker said that] the attributes of the Deity being what they are, the scheme of orthodoxy is inconsistent with them; whereupon Butler gave the crushing reply: Agreeing with you as to the attributes of the Deity, nature, by its existence, proves that the things to which you object are quite consistent with them. To whom enters Hume's Epicurean with the remark: Then, as nature is our only measure of the attributes of the Deity in their practical manifestation, what warranty is there for supposing that such measure is anywhere transcended? That the "other side" of nature, if there be one, is governed on different principles from this side?

Truly on this topic silence is golden; while speech reaches not even the dignity of sounding brass or tinkling cymbal, and is but the weary clatter of an endless logomachy. One can but suspect that Hume also had reached this conviction; and that his shadowy and inconsistent theism was the expression of his desire to rest in a state of mind, which distinctly excluded negation, while it included as little as possible of affirmation, respecting a problem which he felt to be hopelessly insoluble.

But, whatever might be the views of the philosopher as to the arguments for theism, the historian could have no doubt respecting its many-shaped existence, and the great part which it has played in the world. Here, then, was a body of natural facts to be investigated scientifically, and the result of Hume's inquiries is embodied in the remarkable essay on the *Natural History of Religion.* Hume anticipated the results of modern investigation in declaring fetishism and polytheism to be the form in which savage and ignorant men naturally clothe their ideas of the unknown influences which govern their destiny. . . . (pp. 183-84)

The doctrine that you may call an atheist anybody whose ideas about the Deity do not correspond with your own, is so largely acted upon by persons who are certainly not of Hume's way of thinking and, probably, so far from having read him, would shudder to open any book bearing his name, except the *History of England,* that it is surprising to trace the theory of their practice to such a source.

But on thinking the matter over, this theory seems so consonant with reason, that one feels ashamed of having suspected many excellent persons of being moved by mere malice and viciousness of temper to call other folks atheists, when, after all, they have been obeying a purely intellectual sense of fitness. As Hume says, truly enough, it is a mere fallacy, because two people use the same names for things, the ideas of which are mutually exclusive, to rank such opposite opinions under the same denomination. If the Jew says, that the Deity is absolute unity, and that it is sheer blasphemy to say that He ever became incarnate in the person of a man; and, if the Trinitarian says, that the Deity is numerically three as well as numerically one, and that it is sheer blasphemy to say that He did not so become incarnate, it is obvious enough that each must be logically held to deny the existence of the other's Deity. Therefore; that each has a scientific right to call the other an atheist; and that, if he refrains, it is only on the ground of decency and good manners, which should restrain an honourable man from employing even scientifically justifiable language, if custom has given it an abusive connotation. While one must agree with Hume, then, it is, nevertheless, to be wished that he had not set the bad example of calling polytheists "superstitious atheists." It probably did not occur to him that, by a parity of reasoning, the Unitarians might justify the application of the same language to the Ultramontanes, and *vice versâ.* (pp. 186-87)

> *Thomas H. Huxley, in his* Hume with Helps to the Study of Berkeley: Essays, *D. Appleton and Company, 1894, 319 p.*

CHARLES S. PEIRCE (essay date 1901)

[*Peirce was an American philosopher and scientist. Called "the most original thinker of his generation" by William James and "the most versatile, profound, and original philosopher that the United States has ever produced" by Philip P. Wiener, Peirce achieved his principal renown in such technical areas as logic and science. He also wrote numerous articles and essays on more general philosophical subjects, and one of these, entitled "How to Make Our Ideas Clear" (1878), introduced the term "pragmatism" to philosophy. In the following excerpt from a 1901 study prepared for his colleague S. P. Langley, Peirce expounds Hume's conception of the laws of nature and comments on his argument against miracles.*]

[In his argument against miracles] Hume falls into an error which is very characteristic of the kinds of mistake which the Ockhamists frequently commit, and particularly of their conception of laws of nature. Namely, he thinks that when a man is led to expect a certain sort of result in a given case, because it is, on the whole, more comfortable to the analogous instances in his past experience than the opposite result would be, those single experiential instances, or "experiments," as he calls them, can logically be "balanced" against one another, as if they were independent "evidences." But this is not so. The single instances though they may be evidences in the ordinary sense of the word are not "evidences," in the sense his

argument requires. If I do not know what balls have been put into an urn, the drawing of a ball and finding it to be blue, affords me no assurance that any definite proportion of future drawings (and no more) will be of blue balls. This blunder has been committed, even by great mathematicians; but nobody but Hume ever fell into the manifest absurdity of holding the single instances to be *independent* "evidences." Were that the case, a man who merely knew of a certain urn of balls that a hundred white drawings had been made from it, would, in the absence of all information in regard to the black drawings, be entitled to a definite intensity of "belief" in regard to the next drawing, and not only so, but the degree of this "belief" would remain quite unaffected by the further information that the number of black drawings that had ever been made from the urn was zero!

It must not be supposed that because a sign that anything is a fact is highly convincing, therefore that sign must be an "evidence," in the sense here required. An "evidence," in what we are bound to take as Hume's meaning, is an argument from which it *necessarily* follows that a given sort of result must happen in the long run just so often, neither more nor less. Past experience is no "evidence" of future experience, because it is quite conceivable that the arrangements of the universe should change. Nor is there any sense in speaking of "evidence" of any single event; for "evidence" only shows how often a certain *kind* of event occurs. In short, "evidence" properly relates only to a purely hypothetical state of things, which quite *other* kinds of reasons may induce us to believe approximately agrees with the real state of things.

It is proper here to explain the analogy between Hume's erroneous assumption that the single instances of an induction are *independent* "evidences," and the opinion he and his followers entertain that when an event occurs in accordance with a law of nature, there is no real "necessity" in it. I do not accuse them of saying that there is no necessity in such an occurrence in *any* sense. On the contrary, they are fond of calling themselves "necessitarians." In the strict scholastic sense, necessity, as all the old logics containing the doctrine of modals explain, is a species of universality. To say that an event is necessary, in the strict sense, means that it not only does happen, but would happen under *all* circumstances. In this sense, the Humists are not peculiar in denying that any experiential knowledge is necessary. Almost all philosophers agree to that. In the usual sense of every-day life, that is necessary which would happen under all circumstances *that would ordinarily be considered.* Thus, we do not say that the alteration of day and night is necessary, because it depends upon the circumstance that the earth continually rotates. But we do say that by virtue of gravity every body near the surface of the earth *must* be continually receiving a component downward acceleration. For that will happen under all circumstances we are likely to take into account. Nor do Hume or his followers dream of denying that. But what they mean when they say there is no "necessity" in gravitation is that every "event" which gravitation formulates is in reality totally *independent* of every other; just as Hume supposes the different instances of induction to be *independent* "evidences." One stone's falling has no real connection with another's fall. The fact that the acceleration, which is what gravitation consists in, is continual, would make it necessary for such theorists to suppose time to be composed of discrete instants; and, of course, the Ockhamist doctrine that nothing really *is* but individual objects is contrary to any true continuity. The objection to Hume's conception of a Law of Nature is that it supposes the universe to be utterly unintelligible, while, in truth, the only warrant for any hypothesis must be that it renders phenomena intelligible. The Humists are very fond of representing their conception of a law of nature as a scientific result; but unfortunately metaphysics has not yet reached the scientific stage, and when it shall at length be so far matured, every indication today is that it will be a metaphysics as far as possible from this fourteenth-century Ockhamism. Anybody who maintains that there is any sense (except the strict scholastic sense) in which it is a result of science that a law of nature is not necessary, may at least be required to explain very distinctly just what that sense is; and to avoid the imputation of insisting upon a truism, he will probably vouchsafe to tell us who are the philosophers of the present day with any following who hold the contrary opinion.

The treatises on probabilities, which are written exclusively in the interest of the mathematical developments, and are weak upon their logical side, treat testimonies as "evidences" to be balanced along with and against one another. That is to say, they think that the character of a witness, etc., will in itself afford an absolute assurance that he will falsify just one in so often, neither more nor less. This seems to be absurd. How often he will answer wrongly depends on how the questions are put. If they are so put as to be answered by "yes" or "no," mere haphazard answers will, *we are told*, be half the time right; but a person who should answer correctly half the questions in such a book as *Mangnall's Historical Questions*, would not have answered at random. If it be said that what is meant is the ordinary course of questions in the long run, I doubt very much whether there is any long run in such a case. This phrase implies a series of ratios converging (though irregularly) toward a definite value. There is no necessity that there should be such a convergence; and if there is not, there is no long run and no such thing as probability in the case.

Without going deeper into the discussion, I will only say that if I am right in contending that there is no such thing as the numerical "veracity" of a witness; that the idea is essentially absurd; then, whether I am right or not in maintaining that a similar remark holds good of the "credibility" of a narrative, taken in itself, Hume's argument is hopelessly wrong and past all mending. But if I am wrong in both respects, then with the proper definitions, there can be no doubt that his method of "balancing evidences" is profound and excellent, and that his argument does refute all very extraordinary histories. (pp. 308-12)

The fathers of the church defined a miracle as a performance so far beyond ordinary human powers as to show that the agent must have had extraordinary super-human aid. This definition, which contains nothing about laws of nature or anything else, of a metaphysical character, would have suited Hume's purpose to admiration. He would have said, here we have two alternatives before us; either we have to believe that falsity has in some way crept into the testimony, or we have to believe that a man did something which all experience is against the possibility of his having done. Which is the more likely? Since experience is the only source of knowledge, we ought to accept the former alternative, which is quite comfortable to experience, rather than the latter, which is altogether against it. This is Hume's argument, unmodified. It thus appears that that argument does not require any particular view to be taken of the regularities of phenomena or of the nature of a miracle—further than that it is something opposed to all experience.

Hume did not employ the patristic definition, because that definition was no longer usual. He simply adopted the defi-

nition of Aquinas, translating *ordo naturae* by the phrase "laws of nature," which had been familiar in England for more than two generations.

It, no doubt, seemed to Hume preferable to allow the current definition of a miracle to stand, rather than to perplex the main question by disputing this point. And yet, were that usual definition accepted, either in its original sense or in the sense which the Cartesians and others among Hume's contemporaries would put upon it, it ought logically to preclude the admission of Hume's argument. For it is a vital postulate of that argument that experience is absolutely the sole source of our knowledge; while by the "order of nature" the scholastic realists had understood something like thought, or reasonableness, really active in shaping the phenomena of the cosmos. But to grant that there is such an energizing reasonableness is to give some hope that the inborn light of man's reason may contribute something to knowledge. Now if any place for such hope be allowed, then in cases where experience seems to be wholly in default, as (apart from the gospel narratives) it seems to be wholly in default as to what would happen if the Son of God commanded a man to rise from the dead, then we shall inevitably resort, in such cases, to that inward "light of nature," to the discomfiture of Hume's argument. It thus appears that a strictly Ockhamist conception of the world, and consequently of the laws of nature, is presupposed in Hume's argument. (pp. 315-16)

Charles S. Peirce, "The Laws of Nature and Hume's Argument against Miracles," in his Values in a Universe of Chance: Selected Writings of Charles S. Peirce (1839-1914), *edited by Philip P. Wiener, Doubleday & Company, Inc., 1958, pp. 289-316.*

ERNEST ALBEE (essay date 1902)

[*Albee was an American philosopher and psychologist whose best-known study,* A History of English Utilitarianism (1902), *was described by Ernest Sutherland Bates in 1928 as "one of the few American contributions to the history of philosophy." In the following excerpt from this work, Albee outlines Hume's system of ethics in* A Treatise of Human Nature *and* Inquiry concerning the Principles of Morals *and assesses Hume's contribution to utilitarianism.*]

[So] far as formative influences are concerned, Hume seems to have taken his starting-point in Ethics from those who, like Shaftesbury and Hutcheson, had maintained the existence of a 'moral sense'.

This is by no means to say that Hume was himself a 'Moral Sense' philosopher. Quite as much as anything else, his object was to show that what the 'Moral Sense' writers had professed to explain by merely referring to a supposed 'faculty,' could really be explained in a scientific way, according to the most general principles of human nature. Still, his primary contention was that morality was founded, not on 'reason,' as he expressed it, but on 'sentiment'; that our starting-point in ethical discussions must always be the fact of our approval of moral actions—a fact which could not, by any possibility, be explained on purely rational principles. In emphasising 'feeling' at the expense of 'reason,' Hume was clearly with the 'Moral Sense' writers, and it is fair to assume that he was historically, as well as logically, related to them in this respect. (p. 91)

In both the [*Treatise of Human Nature*] and the [*Inquiry concerning the Principles of Morals*]—though the order of exposition in the two works differs otherwise, in certain respects—

Hume begins with the fact of moral approbation. He first shows—in the *Treatise* at considerable length; in the *Inquiry* more briefly, but perhaps as convincingly—that moral approbation cannot ultimately be founded upon principles of mere reason. After thus clearing the ground, he attempts to explain our approbation of moral conduct by referring, not to a supposed 'moral sense,' but to what he assumes to be the springs of human action and the determining effects of human experience.

Now the important difference between the standpoint of the *Treatise* and that of the *Inquiry* . . . consists in the radically different answers given in the two works to the question: What are the springs of action—the fundamental tendencies of human nature? In the *Treatise,* these are held to be (1) egoism, (2) limited altruism, and (3) 'sympathy'. The relation between them is difficult to state in a few words—indeed, so far as 'sympathy' is concerned, difficult to state at all—but Hume's position in the *Treatise* apparently is that human nature is essentially egoistic. As regards altruism, he holds distinctly that we have no particular love for our fellow-beings as such. Our limited altruism manifests itself only in the case of those standing to us in the closest relations of life, and in a way which does not permit us to suppose that it is an original principle of human nature, strictly co-ordinate with the self-regarding tendency.

At this point Hume employs the rather mysterious principle of 'sympathy'. For him, in his earlier work, as for many of the later empiricists, 'sympathy' is produced through the 'association of ideas'. His peculiar mode of explanation is as follows—the point being to show that in this case an 'idea' is practically converted into an 'impression'. The 'impression of ourselves' is particularly vivid, and by 'association' it happens that a corresponding (though of course not equal) vividness is imparted to that which relates to ourselves. But other human beings are *similar* to ourselves. This relation of 'similarity' makes us vividly conceive what concerns them, the other relations of 'contiguity' and 'causation' [*i.e.,* kinship here] assisting in the matter. Thus our idea of another's emotion may become so vivid as to give rise to the same emotion in ourselves. In spite of its obvious ingenuity, this explanation of 'sympathy' is far from being satisfactory. One readily sees that for Hume, as for the Associationist school in general, 'sympathy' is left in a condition of unstable equilibrium, liable at a touch to be precipitated into egoism pure and simple.

This aspect of Hume's system, in its earlier form, is the more confusing for the reason that he never seriously attempts to state the relation between our derived 'sympathy' and our fundamental self-regarding tendency. The result is a degree of theoretical confusion that can only be appreciated by those who have read the *Treatise* with considerable care. It should be observed that one does not here refer to the inevitable ambiguity of the words 'egoism' and 'altruism,' as ordinarily used, but rather to the fact that Hume professes to explain—almost in the sense of explaining away—what we ordinarily understand by (general) 'sympathy,' without anywhere telling us exactly what he claims to have reduced it to.

If Hume's treatment of 'sympathy' were the same in the *Inquiry concerning the Principles of Morals* as in Book III. of the *Treatise*—which is apparently the careless assumption of those who regard his position in the two works as identical—we should need to examine the mysterious principle considerably in detail. As a matter of fact, however, Hume seems to have been keenly aware that his earlier treatment of 'sympathy' was a mistake, and a bad one; and he gives us what he would probably have

regarded as the best possible antidote in what he says on the same subject in the *Inquiry.* There he means by the word 'sympathy' nothing essentially different from the general benevolent tendency, the degree of which he shows his good judgment in not attempting to define, but which he regards as the foundation of the historical development of morality.

The significance of this change can hardly be overrated. It does away at once with an almost indefinite amount of theoretical confusion, and puts Hume on the right track just where his historical, but not logical, successors—Tucker, Paley, and Bentham—were destined to go astray. Nor must it for a moment be supposed that Hume is here going to the other extreme, and contending for the existence of a perfectly differentiated 'altruism' in our human nature, as opposed to an equally differentiated 'egoism'—as Hutcheson, for example, had mistakenly done. He rather shows that, in the last resort, this distinction resolves itself into an abstraction, and holds, in language which Butler himself would have had to commend: "Whatever contradiction may vulgarly be supposed between the *selfish* and *social* sentiments or dispositions, they are really no more opposite than selfish and ambitious, selfish and revengeful, selfish and vain." And one is almost startled at the agreement with Butler, when he immediately adds: "It is requisite that there be an original propensity of some kind, in order to be a basis to self-love, by giving a relish to the objects of its pursuit; and none more fit for this purpose than benevolence or humanity".

To conclude, then: in place of the three quasi-distinct (but by no means co-ordinate) principles—egoism, limited altruism, and 'sympathy'—which had been assumed in the *Treatise,* we have 'sympathy,' in the ambiguous sense first explained, struck out in the *Inquiry,* and a human nature there assumed which, as Hume sometimes has occasion to show, necessarily implies at least a certain degree of the benevolent tendency, alongside of the equally essential self-regarding tendency—the two becoming differentiated, in so far as they do become differentiated at all, only in the course of human experience. (pp. 94-7)

No account of Hume's ethical system . . . can afford to neglect the admirable Conclusion to the *Inquiry,* in which he takes a comprehensive view of the issues which have been raised and met separately, and makes a final plea for the validity of his general position. Like most of the preceding chapters, or 'sections,' the Conclusion is divided into two parts. The first and more important part of the argument attempts in outline a sort of natural history of morals, while the second part gives an account of the ground of moral obligation. It will be found that the second part is too much of the nature of an *argumentum ad hominem,* and fails to do justice to the spirit of the first part, to which latter we shall principally direct our attention.

Hume begins by arguing that, whatever philosophers may teach, we never actually continue to approve of any quality in human nature, which does not at least appear to be either useful or agreeable to ourselves or others. The apparent approval of celibacy, fasting, penance, etc., is to be attributed to superstition and false religion, and it is important to notice that, in the course of a healthy intellectual and moral development, such fictitious virtues are gradually transferred to the opposite column, and placed in the catalogue of vices. So far we have little but a reaffirmation of the author's general position, marred somewhat by his continued use of the artificial division . . . of moral actions into those which give pleasure either directly or indirectly to oneself or others. But now Hume pertinently points out that he has avoided becoming entangled in the wearisome dispute concerning the degrees of benevolence or self-love which prevail in human nature. "It is sufficient for our present purpose," he says, "if it be allowed, what surely, without the greatest absurdity cannot be disputed, that there is some benevolence, however small, infused into our bosom." No matter how faint these generous sentiments may be thought to be, they must at any rate direct the determinations of our mind where everything else is equal, and "produce a cool preference of what is useful and serviceable to mankind, above what is pernicious and dangerous".

The result is most important: "A *moral distinction*, therefore, immediately arises; a general sentiment of blame and approbation; a tendency, however faint, to the objects of the one, and a proportionable aversion to those of the other". Avarice, ambition, vanity, and all the other passions which are commonly, though improperly, comprised under the general head of 'self-love,' are to be ruled out as wholly inadequate to explain our original recognition of moral distinctions, not because they are too weak, but because they have not a 'proper direction' for that purpose. They wholly fail to explain that principle of objectivity which we demand and recognise in moral judgments. This implies some sentiment which is at once common to all mankind, and so comprehensive as to extend to all mankind, no matter how remote from ourselves in space or time. Nothing but the sentiment of humanity, here insisted upon, can reasonably be regarded as the ultimate cause of the all-important phenomenon which we are attempting to explain. An important auxiliary sentiment, however, which does much to re-enforce our strictly moral sentiments, is to be found in that very love of fame, which has so often been regarded as a merely selfish passion. This tends to make us regard our own conduct objectively, and to keep alive in us the highest ideals; and it further begets in noble natures that habit of self-reverence which is the surest guardian of every virtue.

As already indicated, the second part of the Conclusion, concerning the ground of moral obligation, is hardly in the spirit of the first part. There the common feeling of humanity had been treated as the ultimate ground of our recognition of moral distinctions; here one would naturally expect Hume to take the same principle as a starting-point, from which to revise the conception of moral obligation. As a matter of fact, however, he mainly contents himself with commending his system to those who hold the selfish theory of the moral motive rather than his own. The principal question considered, then, is how far morality is for the interest of the individual, abstractly considered, although in the course of this very argument he makes the highly significant remark, already quoted, that "whatever contradiction may vulgarly be supposed between the *selfish* and *social* sentiments or dispositions, they are really no more opposite than selfish and ambitious, selfish and revengeful, selfish and vain".

Returning still again to his artificial classification of the virtues, he does not, of course, have to prove that the virtues which are such because they conduce either directly or indirectly to the pleasure of the individual agent are for the individual's selfish interest, for that follows from the definitions themselves. And he points out that it is really superfluous to prove that the 'companionable virtues,' *i.e.*, those 'immediately agreeable to others,' like good manners and wit, decency and genteelness, are more desirable than the contrary qualities. The only real problem arises in the case of justice, the typical virtue of the remaining class, *i.e.*, the class of virtues 'useful to others'. That 'honesty is the best policy' is a good general rule; but how about the possible exceptions, where a man may seem to be the loser by his integrity? Hume practically admits that he has no arguments of a strictly logical kind with which to meet this real or supposed difficulty, but rather lays stress upon the inward peace of mind, consciousness of integrity, etc., which, as he says, "are circumstances very requisite to happiness, and will be cherished and cultivated by every honest man, who feels the importance of them". It will readily be seen that this appeal to our moral consciousnes hardly meets the theoretical difficulty—the self-imposed difficulty of eighteenth century individualism—which was to show that morality was for the advantage of the moral agent, not as a social being, with no interests wholly separate from those of society, but rather as an isolated centre of self-interest. The only logical solution, from that point of view, was that of the so-called 'Theological Utilitarians,' who frankly depended upon the doctrine of rewards and punishments after death.

Such was Hume's system as actually worked out by himself. When we come to compare it with that of Gay—his only predecessor who had stated the Utilitarian principle in a perfectly unambiguous form—we see at once what an important advance had been made in the development of ethical theory. Gay's system had been as frankly individualistic, in its way, as that of Hobbes; but, at the same time, it had avoided those offensive paradoxes of the earlier doctrine, which had undoubtedly kept many from appreciating the plausibility of the egoistic position. Indeed, it would be quite unfair to put Gay and his successors (*i.e.*, those Utilitarian writers who maintained the egoistic character of the motive of the moral agent) in the same category with Hobbes. Gay and the others never employed egoism as a means by which to vilify human nature, but rather seem to have regarded it as a tempting device for simplifying ethical theory. Moreover, they partly succeeded in disguising its essentially unlovely character by supposing the development of a derived 'sympathy' through the 'association of ideas.' Hume had at first allowed himself to use 'association' in much the same way; but the very fact that his explanations in the *Treatise* are so much less clear than those of Gay in the *Dissertation*, suggests a lack of certainty in his own mind as to the validity of the method. . . . (pp. 107-11)

Taken by itself, Hume's recognition and defence of original altruism could not be regarded as an important contribution to English Ethics. From the time of Cumberland to that of Shaftesbury and Hutcheson, there had never been wanting those who, from one point of view or another, opposed the egoistic position of Hobbes. But of all those moralists, Cumberland alone can properly be termed a Utilitarian, and even he . . . had carried through 'the perfection of mind and body' as a principle parallel to that of 'the greatest happiness of all'. Hume, then, was the first to hold the Utilitarian doctrine in its unmistakable form and at the same time to admit, and defend, the altruistic tendencies of human nature.

Gay had vigorously, and more or less successfully, opposed the 'Moral Sense' theory, as held by Shaftesbury and Hutcheson. While, however, he was greatly in advance of those writers in clearness and simplicity of ethical theory, he by no means equalled them in his grasp of the fundamental facts of our moral experience. Hume was as sure as Gay had been that we must not explain the phenomena of our moral life by referring them, or any part of them, to a special faculty like the 'moral sense'; but he took a much broader view of human nature than Gay had done, and, from first to last, attributed more importance to the part played by the affective side of our nature in the formation of moral judgments. In fact, he has sometimes been misjudged on account of this very catholicity of treatment. . . . [There] are even those who hold that he never quite departed from the 'Moral Sense' theory. I can only regard this view as a serious mistake. We have seen again and again, that, while he always begins with the fact of moral approbation, as applying to a particular class of actions, it is his special endeavour to show how this approbation arises, according to the recognised principles of human nature. With all his faults as a philosopher and as a moralist, Hume was far too scientific, both in his ideals and his methods, to be guilty of any flagrant form of 'faculty psychology'.

We can only speculate as to just what Hume's system might have become, if the author had given up his artificial and somewhat misleading classification of the virtues. It is fair to remark, however, that, if he had been more thorough in his revision of the third book of the *Treatise,* and had definitely shown, what certainly was implicit in his system, that all the virtues are such because they conduce to 'the greatest happiness of the greatest number,' he would have stated the Utilitarian principle practically in its modern form. As it was, he freed the doctrine from the unfortunate dogma that the motive of the moral agent is always, in the last resort, egoistic. This was a distinct advantage upon Gay, which, however, was wasted upon Tucker, Paley, and Bentham, all of whom reproduce the position of the *Dissertation.* Even as stated to-day, the 'greatest happiness' theory does seem likely to be accepted as the final word of Ethics: but it would hardly be too much to claim that the *Inquiry concerning the Principles of Morals,* with all its defects and shortcomings, is the classic statement of English Utilitarianism. (pp. 111-12)

Ernest Albee, "David Hume," in his A History of English Utilitarianism, *Swan Sonnenschein & Co., Ltd., 1902, pp. 91-112.*

GEORGE SAINTSBURY (essay date 1904)

[*Saintsbury was an English literary historian and critic. Hugely prolific, he composed histories of English and European literature as well as numerous critical works on individual authors, styles, and periods. In the following excerpt, he studies Hume as literary critic.*]

The position of Hume in regard to literary criticism has an interest which would be almost peculiar if it were not for something of a parallel in Voltaire. If the literary opinions of the author of the *Enquiry into Human Nature* stood alone they would be almost negligible; and if he had worked them into an elaborate treatise, like that of his clansman Kames, this would probably, if remembered at all, be remembered as a kind of "awful example." In their context and from their author, however, we cannot quite "regard and pass" Hume's critical observations as their intrinsic merit may seem to suggest that we should do: nay, in that context and from that author, they constitute a really valuable document in more than one relation.

It cannot be said that Hume does not invite notice as a critic; on the contrary, his title of *Essays: Moral, Political, and Literary* seems positively to challenge it. Yet his actual literary utterances are rather few, and would be almost unimportant but for the considerations just put. He tells us that criticism is difficult; he applies (as Johnson did, though differently) Fontenelle's remark about "telling the hours"; he illustrates from Holland the difference of excellence in commerce and in literature. He condemns—beforehand, and with the vigour and acuteness which

we should expect from him—the idea of Taine, the attempt to account for the existence of a particular poet at a particular time and in a particular place. He is shocked at the vanity, at the rudeness, and at the loose language of the ancients. He approaches, as Tassoni and Perrault had approached, one of the grand *cruces* of the whole matter by making his Sceptic urge that "*beauty* and worth are merely of a relative nature, and consist of an agreeable sentiment produced by an object on a particular mind"; but he makes no detailed use or application whatever of this as regards literature. His Essay on **"Simplicity and Refinement in Writing"** is psychology rather than criticism, and he uses his terms in a rather curious manner. At least, I myself find it difficult to draw up any definitions of these qualities which will make Pope the *ne plus ultra* of justifiable Refinement, and Lucretius that of Simplicity; Virgil and Racine the examples of the happy mean in both; Corneille and Congreve excessive in Refinement, and Sophocles and Terence excessive in Simplicity. The whole is, however, a good rationalising of the "classical" principle; and is especially interesting as noticing, with slight reproof, a tendency to too great "affectation and conceit" both in France and England—faults for which *we* certainly should not indict the mid-eighteenth century. The Essay **"On Tragedy"** is more purely psychological still. And though **"On the Standard of Taste"** is less open to this objection, one cannot but see that it is Human Nature, and not Humane Letters, in which Hume is really interesting himself. The vulgar censure on the reference to Bunyan is probably excessive; for it is at least not improbable that Hume had never read a line of *The Pilgrim's Progress,* and was merely using the tinker's name as a kind of type-counter. But this very acceptance of a conventional judgment—acceptance constantly repeated throughout the Essay—is almost startling in context with the *alleszermalmend* ["crush everything"] tendency of some of its principles. A critic who says that "It is evident that none of the rules of composition are fixed by reasonings *a priori,*" is in fact saying "Take away that bauble!" in regard to Neo-classicism altogether; and though in the very same page Hume repeats the orthodox cavils at Ariosto, while admitting his charm on the next, having thus set up the idol again, he proceeds once more to lop it of hands and feet and tumble it off its throne by saying that "if things are found to please, they cannot be faults; let the pleasure which they produce be ever so unexpected and unaccountable." The most dishevelled of Romantics, in the reddest of waistcoats, could say no more.

In his remarks upon the qualifications and functions of the critic, Hume's anthropological and psychological mastery is evident enough: but it is at least equally evident that his actual taste in literature was in no sense spontaneous, original, or energetic. In comparing him, say, with Johnson, it is not a little amusing to find his much greater acquiescence in the conventional and traditional judgments. Indeed, towards the end of his essay Hume anticipates a later expression of a perennial attitude of mind by declaring, "However I may excuse the poet on account of the manners of his age, I never can relish the composition," and by complaining of the want of "humanity and decency so conspicuous" even sometimes in Homer and the Greek tragedies. That David, of all persons, should fail to realise—he did *not* fail to perceive—that the humanity of Homer *was* human and the decency of Sophocles *was* decent, is indeed surprising.

Such things might at first sight not quite dispose one to regret that, as he himself remarks, "the critics who have had some tincture of philosophy" have been "few," for certainly those who have had more tincture of philosophy than Hume himself have been far fewer. But, as is usually the case, it is not the fault of philosophy at all. For some reason, natural disposition, or want of disposition, or even that necessity of clinging to *some* convention which has been remarked in Voltaire himself, evidently made Hume a mere "church-going bell"—pulled by the established vergers, and summoning the faithful to orthodox worship—in most of his literary utterances. Yet, as we have seen, he could not help turning quite a different tune at times, though he himself hardly knew it. (pp. 159-62)

> George Saintsbury, "Aesthetics and Their Influence," in his A History of Criticism and Literary Taste in Europe from the Earliest Texts to the Present Day: Modern Criticism, Vol. III, *William Blackwood & Sons Ltd.*, 1904, pp. 141-70.

ALFRED NORTH WHITEHEAD (essay date 1922)

[*Whitehead was an Anglo-American mathematician, philosopher, and educator. He is best known as coauthor with Bertrand Russell of the three-volume* Principia Mathematica *(1910-13), in which the authors argue that the principles of mathematics can be deduced from those of logic by symbolic reasoning. In the following excerpt from an essay originally published in 1922, Whitehead focuses on Hume's theory of "necessary connexion amongst events."*]

Hume accepts, without question, space and time as reigning throughout nature. It is in fact the very basis of his celebrated analysis of the idea of necessary connexion amongst events. He says [in Essay VII of his *Philosophical Essays concerning Human Understanding*, "**Of the Idea of Necessary Connexion**"]:

> It appears, then, that this idea of necessary connexion amongst events arises from a number of similar instances, which occur, of the constant conjunction of these events, nor can that idea ever be suggested by any one of these instances, surveyed in all possible lights and positions. But there is nothing in a number of instances, different from every single instance, which is supposed to be exactly similar; except only, that after a repetition of similar instances, the mind is carried by habit, upon the appearance of one event, to expect its usual attendant and to believe, that it will exist.
>
> This connexion, therefore, which we *feel* in the mind, or customary transitive of the imagination from one object to its usual attendant, is the sentiment or impression, from which we form the idea of power or necessary connexion.
>
> (p. 133)

You will notice that in this passage "the constant conjunction" of events and the "attendance" of one event on another must mean spatio-temporal contiguity, or else the whole point of his explanation of the idea of causation is lost. Accordingly the spatio-temporal character of nature is a presupposition of Hume's philosophy. I am not making any objection to Hume's assumption: far from it, I am claiming his support. What Hume says of the history of Europe is true of any set of events. "They have still a species of unity, amidst all their diversity." They obtain this "species of unity" in virtue of their joint inclusion within some definite four-dimensional region of space and time. (pp. 133-34)

Hume, it may be said, provides a standard of normality by reference to what is usual, so that, according to him, the repeated impact of the usual on our minds automatically produces

a judgment according to this standard. In fact, the essence of Hume's doctrine is our expectation of the usual. I have already quoted his own statement of this doctrine, and will now repeat it:

> But there is nothing in a number of instances, different from every single instance, which is supposed to be exactly similar; except only, that after a repetition of similar instances, the mind is carried by habit, upon the appearance of one event, to expect its usual attendant, and to believe, that it will exist.

I am myself accepting Hume's doctrine, and am merely investigating the presuppositions which it involves. My point is, that this doctrine will not suffice to discriminate dreams from actual occurrences. Some dreams are very usual, and some occurrences are very rare. For example, my dream of hovering has been much more usual in my experience than my first-hand experience of glaciers. Why (on Hume's principle) would I turn my hoverings out of nature, and retain my excursions on glaciers? Surely it is very arbitrary. But it may be said that other people have been on glaciers, and it is their concurrent testimony which we trust. I am afraid that, if you read Hume carefully, this argument will not hold. I do not understand how other people's experience can "carry" my mind "by habit." Furthermore, it is probable that among the twelve hundred million people now existing, not to speak of previous ages, there have occurred many more dreams of hovering than excursions on glaciers. Indeed, I do not know how to conduct such an extensive census of other people's experience, and still less do I see how to obtain the information in time to make it of use in the quick bustle of daily life. (p. 140)

The space-time continuum is not the sole basis of uniformity in nature. If it were so, induction would be impossible. It is here that we find the weakness in Hume's, and in some other, philosophies. Hume explains a ground for the origin of our instinctive trust in induction. But unfortunately his explanation does not disclose any rational explanation of this trust. The rational conclusion from Hume's philosophy has been drawn by those among the lilies of the field, who take no thought for the morrow. Hume admits this conclusion. He writes [in Essay XII, "**Of the Academic or Sceptical Philosophy**"]:

> The sceptic, therefore, had better keep in his proper sphere, and display those philosophical objections, which arise from more profound researches. Here he seems to have ample matter of triumph; while he justly insists, that all our evidence for any matter of fact, which lies beyond the testimony of sense or memory, is derived entirely from the relation of cause and effect; that we have no other idea of this relation than that of two objects, which have been frequently conjoin'd together; that we have no arguments to convince us, that objects, which have, in our experience, been frequently conjoin'd, will likewise, in other instances, be conjoined in the same manner; and that nothing leads us to this inference but custom or a certain instinct of our nature; which it is indeed difficult to resist, but which, like other instincts, may be fallacious or deceitful.
>
> (pp. 142-43)

Hume runs away from his own conclusion: he adds:—

> On the contrary, he (a Pyrrhonian) must acknowledge, if he will acknowledge anything, that all human life must perish, were his principles universally and steadily to prevail.
>
> (p. 143)

I wonder how Hume knows this: it must be that there is some element in our knowledge of nature which his philosophy has failed to take account of. Bertrand Russell adopts Hume's position. He says:—

> If, however, we know of a very large number of cases in which A is followed by B and few or none in which the sequence fails, we shall in *practice* be justified in saying 'A causes B,' provided we do not attach to the notion of cause any of the metaphysical superstitions that have gathered about the word (*Analysis of Mind,* Lecture V, Causal Laws).

Again I should like to know how Russell has acquired the piece of information which he has emphasized by italics—"we shall in *practice* be justified, etc."

I do not like this habit among philosophers, of having recourse to secret stores of information, which are not allowed for in their system of philosophy. They are the ghost of Berkeley's "God," and are about as communicative.

I do not conceive myself to have solved the difficulty which puzzled Hume. But I wish to point out the direction in which, as I believe, the complete solution will be found. In an extract, already quoted, he has stated the issue with his usual clearness:—

> But there is nothing in a number of instances, different from every single instance, which is supposed to be exactly similar; except only, that after a repetition of similar instances, the mind is carried by habit, upon the appearance of one event, to expect its usual attendant, and to believe, that it will exist.

Hume's philosophy found nothing in any single instance to justify the mind's expectation. Accordingly he was reduced to explaining the origin of the mind's expectation otherwise than by its rational justification. It follows, that, if we are to get out of Hume's difficulty, we must find something in each single instance, which would justify the belief. The key to the mystery is not to be found in the accumulation of instances, but in the intrinsic character of each instance. When we have found that, we will have struck at the heart of Hume's argument. (pp. 143-44)

> *Alfred North Whitehead, "Uniformity and Contingency," in his* Essays in Science and Philosophy, *Philosophical Library, 1947, pp. 132-48.*

LYTTON STRACHEY   (essay date 1928)

[*Strachey was an English biographer, critic, essayist, and short story writer. He is best known for his biographies* Eminent Victorians *(1918),* Queen Victoria *(1921), and* Elizabeth and Essex: A Tragic History *(1928). Critics agree that these iconoclastic reexaminations of historical figures revolutionized the course of modern biographical writing. Strachey's literary criticism is also considered incisive. In the following excerpt from an essay originally published in 1928, Strachey examines Hume's* Treatise of Human Nature *and describes the merits and faults of Hume's historical works.*]

In what resides the most characteristic virtue of humanity? In good works? Possibly. In the creation of beautiful objects? Perhaps. But some would look in a different direction, and find it in detachment. To all such David Hume must be a great saint in the calendar; for no mortal being was ever more completely divested of the trammels of the personal and the particular, none ever practised with a more consummate success the divine art of impartiality. And certainly to have no axe to grind is something very noble and very rare. It may be said to be the antithesis of the bestial. A series of creatures might be

constructed, arranged according to their diminishing interest in the immediate environment, which would begin with the amoeba and end with the mathematician. In pure mathematics the maximum of detachment appears to be reached: the mind moves in an infinitely complicated pattern, which is absolutely free from temporal considerations. Yet this very freedom—the essential condition of the mathematician's activity—perhaps gives him an unfair advantage. He can only be wrong—he cannot cheat. But the metaphysician can. The problems with which he deals are of overwhelming importance to himself and the rest of humanity; and it is his business to treat them with an exactitude as unbiassed as if they were some puzzle in the theory of numbers. That is his business—and his glory. In the mind of a Hume one can watch at one's ease this superhuman balance of contrasting opposites—the questions of so profound a moment, the answers of so supreme a calm. And the same beautiful quality may be traced in the current of his life, in which the wisdom of philosophy so triumphantly interpenetrated the vicissitudes of the mortal lot. (pp. 139-40)

[During his years in France, Hume] composed his *Treatise of Human Nature,* the masterpiece which contains all that is most important in his thought. The book opened a new era in philosophy. The last vestiges of theological prepossessions—which were still faintly visible in Descartes and Locke—were discarded; and reason, in all her strength and all her purity, came into her own. It is in the sense that Hume gives one of being

A

TREATISE

OF

Human Nature :

BEING

An ATTEMPT to introduce the experimental Method of Reasoning

INTO

MORAL SUBJECTS.

Rara temporum felicitas, ubi fentire, quæ velis ; & quæ fentias, dicere licet.   TACIT.

BOOK I.

OF THE

UNDERSTANDING.

LONDON:
Printed for JOHN NOON, at the *White-Hart,* near *Mercer's-Chapel* in *Cheapfide.*
MDCCXXXIX.

Title page of A Treatise of Human Nature, *1739.*

committed absolutely to reason—of following wherever reason leads, with a complete, and even reckless, confidence—that the great charm of his writing consists. But it is not only that: one is not alone; one is in the company of a supremely competent guide. With astonishing vigour, with heavenly lucidity, Hume leads one through the confusion and the darkness of speculation. One has got into an aeroplane, which has glided imperceptibly from the ground; with thrilling ease one mounts and mounts; and, supported by the mighty power of intellect, one looks out, to see the world below one, as one has never seen it before. In the *Treatise* there is something that does not appear again in Hume's work—a feeling of excitement—the excitement of discovery. At moments he even hesitates, and stands back, amazed at his own temerity.

> The *intense* view of these manifold contradictions and imperfections in human reason has so wrought upon me, and heated my brain, that I am ready to reject all belief and reasoning, and can look upon no opinion even as more probable or likely than another. Where am I, or what? From what causes do I derive my existence, and to what condition shall I return? Whose favour shall I court, and whose anger must I dread? What beings surround me? and on whom have I any influence, or who have influence on me? I am confounded with all these questions, and begin to fancy myself in the most deplorable condition imaginable, environed with the deepest darkness, and utterly deprived of the use of every member and faculty.

And then his courage returns once more, and he speeds along on his exploration. (pp. 141-43)

The *History* was a great success; many editions were printed; and in his own day it was chiefly as a historian that Hume was known to the general public. After his death his work continued for many years the standard history of England, until, with a new age, new fields of knowledge were opened up and a new style of historical writing became fashionable. The book is highly typical of the eighteenth century. It was an attempt—one of the very earliest—to apply intelligence to the events of the past. Hitherto, with very few exceptions (Bacon's *Henry the Seventh* was one of them) history had been in the hands of memoir writers like Commines and Clarendon, or moralists like Bossuet. Montesquieu, in his *Considérations sur les Romains,* had been the first to break the new ground; but his book, brilliant and weighty as it was, must be classed rather as a philosophical survey than a historical narration. Voltaire, almost exactly contemporary with Hume, was indeed a master of narrative, but was usually too much occupied with discrediting Christianity to be a satisfactory historian. Hume had no such *arrière pensée* ["hidden motive"]; he only wished to tell the truth as he saw it, with clarity and elegance. And he succeeded. In his volumes—especially those on the Tudors and Stuarts—one may still find entertainment and even instruction. Hume was an extremely intelligent man, and anything that he had to say on English history could not fail to be worth attending to. But, unfortunately, mere intelligence is not itself quite enough to make a great historian. It was not simply that Hume's knowledge of his subject was insufficient—that an enormous number of facts, which have come into view since he wrote, have made so many of his statements untrue and so many of his comments unmeaning; all that is serious, but it is not more serious than the circumstance that his cast of mind was in reality ill-fitted for the task he had undertaken. The virtues of a metaphysician are the vices of a historian. A generalised, colourless, unimaginative view of things is admirable

when one is considering the law of causality, but one needs something else if one has to describe Queen Elizabeth.

This fundamental weakness is materialised in the style of the *History*. Nothing could be more enchanting than Hume's style when he is discussing philosophical subjects. The grace and clarity of exquisite writing are enhanced by a touch of colloquialism—the tone of a polished conversation. A personality—a most engaging personality—just appears. The cat-like touches of ironic malice—hints of something very sharp behind the velvet—add to the effect. "Nothing," Hume concludes, after demolishing every argument in favour of the immortality of the soul, "could set in a fuller light the infinite obligations which mankind have to divine revelation, since we find that no other medium could ascertain this great and important truth." The sentence is characteristic of Hume's writing at its best, where the pungency of the sense varies in direct proportion with the mildness of the expression. But such effects are banished from the *History*. A certain formality, which Hume doubtless supposed was required by the dignity of the subject, is interposed between the reader and the author; an almost completely latinised vocabulary makes vividness impossible; and a habit of *oratio obliqua* ["speaking obliquely"] has a deadening effect. We shall never know exactly what Henry the Second said—in some uncouth dialect of French or English—in his final exasperation against Thomas of Canterbury; but it was certainly something about "a set of fools and cowards," and "vengeance," and "an upstart clerk." Hume, however, preferred to describe the scene as follows: "The King himself being vehemently agitated, burst forth with an exclamation against his servants, whose want of zeal, he said, had so long left him exposed to the enterprises of that ungrateful and imperious prelate." Such phrasing, in conjunction with the Middle Ages, is comic. The more modern centuries seem to provide a more appropriate field for urbanity, aloofness and common sense. The measured cynicism of Hume's comments on Cromwell, for instance, still makes good reading—particularly as a corrective to the *O, altitudo!* sentimentalities of Carlyle. (pp. 144-47)

> Lytton Strachey, "Six English Historians: Hume,"
> in his Portraits in Miniature and Other Essays, *Harcourt, Brace and Company, 1931, pp. 139-51.*

JOHN LAIRD   (essay date 1932)

[*Laird was a Scottish moral philosopher who wrote widely on ethics, metaphysics, and the works of Hume and Thomas Hobbes. In the following excerpt, he surveys Hume's literary criticism.*]

[It] is abundantly clear, even from the *Treatise,* that Hume had a desultory but active interest in the relations between his philosophical theory and the philosophy of the arts. Thus he said that the sentiments in poetry or in music were analogous to the sensation of belief because of their vivacity, that a certain verisimilitude heightened artistic effect, and drew upon the steadier principles of association, although, in general, the 'agility and unsteadiness' of the imagination was the decisive factor in all artistry; and that a man's genius consisted in the range of his associations. Concerning smaller matters, Hume said that cider, *teste* ["as shown by"] Philips, might be a poetical theme, although beer could not be—with which may be compared his statement that Sannazarius made a mistake in trying to adapt pastoral poetry to the pursuits of fishermen. He also said that the rules of art forbade abrupt transitions and that a certain executive and even physiological ease (e.g. in pronunciation) had subtle consequences for the literary art.

Hume's purely literary essays (apart from those that were withdrawn) dealt with **"Eloquence"**, **"Tragedy"** and **"Simplicity and Refinement in Writing"**, together with a letter to the *Critical Review* (never re-published) concerning Wilkie's *Epigoniad*. (Hume's eventual repudiation of Macpherson's *Ossian* was based, in the main, upon historical improbabilities.)

Of these essays, the first deplored the decay of eloquence in modern times—the dispute between the ancients and the moderns had not subsided in Hume's day—and the second tried to improve upon the theories of the Abbé Dubos and of Fontenelle in the analysis of the way in which the dramatist's art converted the painful themes of tragedy into something stimulating and subtly delightful. It contained, as we might expect, a severe criticism of the English stage for its 'shocking images' and its 'mingled brains and gore.' The third essay was, on the whole, the most important. Accepting Addison's dictum that 'fine writing consists of sentiments which are natural without being obvious' and the canon of the imitation of nature in the straitest sense of 'copying,' the essay pleaded for a judicious blend of refinement with simplicity and gave the outlines of a scale of what was permissible in this regard by putting Pope and Lucretius at opposite extremities, and Virgil and Racine in the middle. It contained the curious statement, 'It is sufficient to run over Cowley once; but Parnell, after the fiftieth reading, is as fresh as at the first'—a severe test for the *Hermit* and its polished company. . . . (pp. 276-77)

From Hume's *Essays,* perused generally, we extract the information that Swift was the first British author to write polite prose, that 'Sprat, Locke and even Temple' knew too little of the rules of art, and that 'Bacon, Harrington and Milton' (in his prose works) were 'altogether stiff and pedantic.' We also learn that Waller was inferior to Horace; and we find Hume quoting from Tasso in Italian. In one of the essays subsequently withdrawn Hume said that 'England must pass through a long gradation of its Spencers, Johnsons, Wallers, Drydens before it arrive at an Addison or a Pope', that Milton was a 'divine poet' and that 'Of the Greek poets that remain, Homer alone seems to merit this character [of *greatness*]: of the Romans, Virgil, Horace and Lucretius: of the English, Milton and Pope: Corneille, Racine, Boileau and Voltaire of the French: and Tasso and Ariosto of the Italians.' Something may also be gleaned from the *Enquiry* with its admiration for Boileau and Longinus and its admiration of the 'elegant and judicious poet' Armstrong, . . .—as well as Virgil.

In general the frigidity and portentous correctness of Hume's opinions on these matters strongly suggest that Dr. Carlyle was right when he said that Hume's taste was 'a rational act rather than the instantaneous effect of fine feeling'. Hume deduced from his preconceived idea that (certain) classical standards, together with the French models that he believed to conform to these classical standards, were all that good taste could mean. But Hume's occasional and very terse comments upon literature in his *History* are the most important evidence in this matter.

From the *History* we learn that, in Hume's maturest opinion, neither literature nor general philosophy was the finest flower of civilization, that distinction being reserved for mathematics and natural philosophy. Galileo and, perhaps, even Kepler were greater than Bacon. We also learn that as late as 1641 learning was 'rude as yet.'

Indeed, Spenser seems to have been the first of the English poets that Hume considered worthy of a paragraph, and Spenser, Hume said, deserved a place on 'the shelves', not on 'the table'. Hume further stated that the 'first English writers' in the reigns of Elizabeth and of James 'were possessed of great genius before they were endowed with any degree of taste.' Therefore it had to be said of Shakespeare that, although often felicitously inspired, 'a reasonable propriety of thought he cannot for any time uphold.' Again, Ben Jonson's 'rude art' was rightly eclipsed by Shakespeare's 'rude genius'; and 'some flashes of wit and ingenuity' in Donne's satires were 'totally suffocated and buried by the hardest and most uncouth expression that is any-where to be met with.'

With time, Hume believed, improvement came. Waller was 'the first refiner of English versification.' Milton's 'poems are admirable, though liable to some objections; his prose writings disagreeable, though not altogether defective in genius. . . . More concise than Homer, more simple than Tasso, more nervous than Lucretius; had he lived in a later age, and learned to polish some rudeness in his verses; had he enjoyed better fortune, and possessed leisure to watch the returns of genius in himself, he had attained the pinnacle of perfection and borne away the palm of epic poetry.' But Cowley was 'extremely corrupted by the bad taste of his age.' Contrariwise Denham's *Cooper's Hill* deserved high commendation. (pp. 277-79)

The coming of the later age which Milton so unfortunately had missed, was retarded, according to Hume, by the licentiousness of Charles II's reign (when the sciences flourished, but literature did not). Hume indeed spoke almost as a Puritan when he mentioned Dryden, Rochester and Wycherley, although he quoted from Dryden's *Absalom and Achitophel* and from his *Aurungzebe*, and said of him 'amidst this great number of loose productions, the refuse of our language, there are found some small pieces, his "Ode to St. Cecilia," the greater part of *Absalom and Achitophel*, and a few more, which discover so great genius, such richness of expression, such pomp and variety of numbers, that they leave us equally full of regret and indignation, on account of the inferiority, or rather great absurdity of his other writings'. (p. 279)

Hume's judgments concerning his literary contemporaries in Britain were undoubtedly biased by his enthusiasm over the revival of letters in Scotland, and by his prejudice against the English. Congratulating Gibbon upon the excellence of the *Decline and Fall*, he said: 'I own that if I had not previously had the happiness of your personal acquaintance, such a performance, from an Englishman in our age, would have given me some surprise. You may smile at this sentiment but . . . I no longer expected any valuable production ever to come from them.' And Hume's generosity towards his literary friends in Scotland, doubtless explained, to some extent, his vigorous advocacy of the exceptional merits of Home's *Douglas* and of Wilkie's *Epigoniad*. Hume spoke with all the authority of Edinburgh behind him when he told Home that his *Douglas* possessed 'the true theatric genius of Shakespear and Otway, refined from the unhappy barbarism of the one, and licentiousness of the other.' Nevertheless, Hume's admiration of these pieces was not merely a parochial assertion that Edinburgh, with the Rev. John Home for its poet, and the Rev. Dr. Robertson for its historian, was giving the lead to all Europe. Hume sincerely believed that these Scottish authors had imitated the classical correctness and delicacy at least as judiciously as the French, and therefore that their fame was secure. Of himself, Hume said: 'I make my work very concise, after the manner of the ancients.' To John Home he wrote: 'For God's sake read Shake-spere, but get Racine and Sophocles by heart. It is reserved to you, and you alone, to redeem our stage from the reproach of barbarism.'

A word may be said of Dr. Johnson's opinion of Hume's literary style: 'Why, Sir, his style is not English; the structure of his sentences is French. Now the French structure and the English structure may, in the nature of things, be equally good. But if you allow that the English language is established, he is wrong' [see excerpt dated 1791].

Assuming that these statements were intended to apply to Hume's later works, particularly the *History* (for there is no evidence that Johnson had studied the *Treatise* carefully if at all), they were probably just. It was dangerous to imitate the ancients through the help of the French; and it is further to be remembered that, according to the universal testimony of his contemporaries, Hume, whether or not he *wrote* English, never *spoke* it in his life. The only tongue he could speak (for his colloquial French was indifferent) was a very broad Scots, in his native dialect of the Merse. Even Scottish ladies, like Lady Murray, ridiculed his talk about his *byeuks*. (pp. 280-81)

Pronunciation, no doubt, is one thing; style and vocabulary quite another; and Hume's nervous anxiety about Scotticisms—'I wonder', said Johnson, 'that *he* should find them'—might have been all that followed from his odd predicament. But it is entirely possible, and indeed not unlikely, that Hume wrote English almost as a man writes a foreign language. (p. 281)

> *John Laird, in his* Hume's Philosophy of Human Nature, *E. P. Dutton and Company Inc., 1932, 312 p.*

NORMAN KEMP SMITH (essay date 1941)

[*Smith was a Scottish-American academic and philosopher whose* The Philosophy of David Hume: A Critical Study of Its Origins and Central Doctrines *(1941) is considered an essential treatment of its subject. In the following excerpt from this work, he comments on Hume's distinction between the "object" and "subject" of pride and humility and outlines his first formulation of the principles of association.*]

To mark the relation between the self and the passions Hume speaks [in *A Treatise of Human Nature*] of the self as being the 'object' of pride and humility: we should have expected him rather to say their 'subject'. This latter term he employs to denote what, in his view, is no less essential to the production of the passions, and yet has likewise to be distnguished from them, viz. their exciting cause. That this cause is not to be equated with the self is obvious. Since pride and humility are contrary to one another they cannot find their sufficient cause in what is common to both. We have therefore to distinguish between their *cause* and their *object*, i.e. between that which excites them and that to which they direct the view when excited. It is, Hume declares, on the presentation to the mind of the idea of the cause that both pride and humility first begin to be produced. And the passion, when excited, turns our view to another idea, which is that of the self.

> Here then is a passion plac'd betwixt two ideas, of which the one produces it, and the other is produc'd by it. The first idea, therefore, represents the *cause*, the second the *object* of the passion.

Within the idea of the cause Hume further distinguishes between the *quality* which operates in generating the passion, and the *subject* in which the quality is placed. The quality may be simple, but the subject has in all cases to be complexly conceived, and one of its invariable components or accompaniments is the idea of the self. For what are the qualities which excite pride? Either (1) some valuable quality *belonging to the self,* such as wit, good-sense, learning, courage, justice, or (2) some bodily endowments or dexterity *belonging to the self,* such as beauty, strength, address in dancing or fencing, or (3) whatever is *in the least allied or related to us,* such as our children, relations, houses, gardens, clothes, our country, and even indeed our climate. In all three types of instance, it will be noted, the 'quality' exists in a something, a 'subject', which stands related to the self, either as in some manner constituting it or as casually related to it, as a possession or dependent. Thus when a beautiful house arouses pride in the owner of the house, the quality which excites the passion is its beauty, the *subject* of the quality is the house "considered as his property or contrivance". And the subject, *as thus complexly conceived,* is, Hume points out, no less essential than the quality. Beauty merely as such, when not located in something thus related to us, will cause pleasure but not pride. The relation to the self—as a factor in the *cause*—is required in order that the 'subject' besides arousing pleasure, may likewise, in and through this pleasure, arouse pride. The opposite qualities, in a 'subject' similarly conceived, arouse the idea of humility.

The self, according to the account which Hume is here giving of pride and humility, thus enters into the passion in two ways: (1) as integral to the 'subject' which *excites,* i.e. produces, the passion; and (2) as being the 'object' to which the passion, *when excited,* at once leads the mind. The idea of the self is thus, on the one hand, a factor in the complex 'subject' of pride, and on the other, by itself alone, its object.

Besides thus insisting on the complex constitution of the 'cause', Hume also dwells upon the four-stage sequence whereby (1) starting from the idea of this complex 'subject', into which the idea of the self enters as a component, the mind is carried (2) in and through a separate 'sensation of pleasure or pain' and (3) through the consequent passion of pride or humility, (4) back to the idea of the self. The four stages, he insists, are distinct and separate—the sensation of pleasure for instance is, he maintains, distinct from the passion of pride, just as truly as the passion, in itself simple, is distinct both from its exciting 'subject' and from its 'object'. And it is because he regards these stages as distinct that he is committed to the task of explaining why the steps thus follow in sequence, and how in so doing they combine to support and reinforce one another.

First in order he takes the last stage in the sequence. It can, he asserts, be disposed of quite briefly. It is by "an *original* quality or primary impulse" that the passion of pride (or humility), on being excited, leads the mind to view the idea of the self. That the passion has this effect is an ultimate quality of our human nature, and must be accepted as such. It is, he adds, the *distinguishing* characteristic of these particular passions.

> For this I pretend not to give any reason; but consider such a peculiar direction of the thought as an original quality.

> Unless nature had given some original qualities to the mind, it cou'd never have any secondary ones; because in that case it wou'd have no foundation for action, nor cou'd ever begin to exert itself. Now these qualities, which we must consider as original, are such as are most inseparable from the soul, and can be resolv'd into no other: And such is the quality, which determines the object of pride and humility.

In how naïvely realistic a manner, using physiological analogies, Hume was content to approach his problems in these sections in Parts i and ii of Book II is even more than usually evident in the following passage:

> That we may comprehend this the better, we must suppose, that nature has given to the organs of the human mind, a certain disposition fitted to produce a peculiar impression or emotion, which we call *pride:* To this emotion she has assign'd a certain idea, *viz.* that of *self,* which it never fails to produce. This contrivance of nature is easily conceiv'd. We have many instances of such a situation of affairs. The nerves of the nose and palate are so dispos'd, as in certain circumstances to convey such peculiar sensations to the mind: The sensations of lust and hunger always produce in us the idea of those peculiar objects, which are suitable to each appetite. These two circumstances are united in pride. The organs are so dispos'd as to produce the passion; and the passion, after its production, naturally produces a certain idea. All this needs no proof. 'Tis evident we never shou'd be possest of that passion, were there not a disposition of mind proper for it; and 'tis as evident, that the passion always turns our view to ourselves, and makes us think of our own qualities and circumstances.

Hume adopts a very different attitude in regard to the three earlier stages in the generation of these passions. For whereas it is, he says, *natural* (in the sense of being an ultimate characteristic of our human nature to be thus self-conscious) that pride should fix the view of the mind upon the self, there can be no such natural connexion between it and the endlessly varied *causes,* many of which are products of human manufacture. It cannot, for instance, be by any quite direct and immediate provision of human nature that a fine escritoire, on first invention, is enabled to generate pride. On any such assumption, we should have to postulate in the human mind 'a monstrous heap of principles', and moral philosophy would be condemned to remain in the same condition as astronomy prior to Copernicus.

It is as delivering moral philosophy from this evil estate that Hume proceeds to give, in Book II, Part i, Section 4, what would appear to have been his *first* formulation of the principles of association. They are represented as taking a threefold form. (1) In the association of *ideas:* and here also in threefold form, as the principles of resemblance, contiguity, and causality.

> 'Tis impossible for the mind to fix itself steadily upon one idea for any considerable time; nor can it by its utmost efforts ever arrive at such a constancy. . . . The rule by which [our thoughts] proceed, is to pass from one object to what is resembling, contiguous to, or produc'd by it.

(2) In the association of *'impressions',* by which Hume here intends to signify only the 'passions'.

> All resembling impressions are connected together, and no sooner one arises than the rest immediately follow. Grief and disappointment give rise to anger, anger to envy, envy to malice, and malice to grief again, till the whole circle be compleated. In like manner our temper, when elevated with joy, naturally throws itself into love, generosity, pity, courage, pride, and the other resembling affections.

In the case of the passions, no less than of ideas, changeableness is, Hume insists, essential to our human nature; and when it changes, the change, so far as it is determined by inward causes, is from any one passion to what (especially as regards agreeableness or the reverse) most resembles it.

> And to what can it so naturally change as to affections or emotions, which are suitable to the temper, and agree with that set of passions, which then prevail? 'Tis evident, then, there is an attraction or association among impressions, as well as among ideas; tho' with this remarkable difference, that ideas are associated by resemblance, contiguity, and causation; and impressions only by resemblance.

(3) In what (adapting Hume's own phraseology) may be entitled *the principle of concurrent direction:* as when independent processes of association (of ideas and of passions), in leading to the same 'object', assist and forward each other.

> Thus a man, who, by any injury from another, is very much discompos'd and ruffled in his temper, is apt to find a hundred subjects of discontent, impatience, fear, and other uneasy passions; especially if he can discover these subjects in or near the person, who was the cause of his first passion. Those principles, which forward the transition of ideas, here concur with those, which operate on the passions; and both uniting in one action, bestow on the mind a double impulse.

On applying these principles to account for the manner in which pride and humility are caused, Hume, returning upon his steps, again remarks (1) that each of the two passions is "determn'd by an original and natural instinct" to have the self as its object; and (2) that it is of the very being and essence of pride to be pleasant and of humility to be painful.

> Thus pride is a pleasant sensation, and humility a painful; and upon the removal of the pleasure and pain, there is in reality no pride and humility.

Hume, it may be noted, is not here gong back upon his previous assertion, that the immediate causal antecedent of pride is a *separate* sensation of pleasure, and in the case of humility a *separate* sensation of pain. What he is here pointing out is that pride, in itself, is likewise pleasant, and humility likewise painful, and that to this extent there is resemblance between them and their antecedents.

Hume next proceeds to correlate these two properties of the passions with the two corresponding properties of the supposed causes. Corresponding to the fact that each passion has the self as its object is the no less certain fact that the cause, to be effective, must itself have a relation to the self; and corresponding to the fact that each passion is essentially in itself pleasant or painful is the manner in which the cause produces a pleasure or a pain independently of the passion. There is thus a double relation of association, involving both ideas and impressions, and consequently a double impulse in which the ideas and the impressions assist and reinforce one another. The 'subject', which excites the passion, is related, *causally,* to the 'object' (i.e. the self) to which the passion *quâ* passion turns the view of the mind; and the sensation of pleasure or pain which the 'subject' separately produces is related *by way of resemblance* to the sensation of the passion. The first association between the 'subject' of the passion and its 'object' is an association of *ideas;* the other association, between the pleasure or pain and the passion, is an association of *impressions.* The former association is in terms of causality, reinforced, it may be by contiguity, and even perhaps also by resemblance; the latter association is wholly one of resemblance. In both pride and humility the relation to the self, alike in the 'subject' and the 'object', continues the same; it is the initiating sensations of pleasure or pain that are contrasted. (pp. 180-86)

One of the main points upon which Hume dwells in . . . later sections is the thesis, of which he makes such extensive use in his ethics, that owing to the primary constitution of our human nature the quality of the 'subject' which arouses any one of the indirect passions is *immediately* pleasing or painful on "the very view and contemplation" of it. This is the case, for instance, with the virtues and vices that arouse in us pride and love, or humility and hatred.

> The uneasiness and satisfaction are not only insep-
> arable from vice and virtue, but constitute their very
> nature and essence. To approve of a character is to
> feel an original delight upon its appearance. To dis-
> approve of it is to be sensible of an uneasiness.

So also with the intellectual virtues, e.g. the talent of pleasing by our wit, good humour or any other accomplishment.

> 'Tis plainly nothing but a sensation of pleasure from
> true wit, and of uneasiness from false, without our
> being able to tell the reasons of that pleasure or uneas-
> iness. The power of bestowing these opposite sen-
> sations is, therefore, the very essence of true and
> false wit; and consequently the cause of that pride
> or humility, which arises from them.

Similarly with beauty and deformity, with external advantages and disadvantages, in our natural endowments and possessions. (p. 188)

> *Norman Kemp Smith, in his* The Philosophy of David
> Hume: A Critical Study of Its Origins and Central
> Doctrines, *Macmillan and Co., Limited, 1941, 568 p.*

LEWIS MUMFORD   (essay date 1944)

[*Mumford is an American sociologist, historian, philosopher, and critic whose primary interest is in the relationship between the modern individual and the environment. In the following excerpt from an essay originally published in 1944, he considers the nihilistic implications of Hume's concept of reason and passion.*]

[It] is in the apparently innocent lucubrations of David Hume that the real Reign of Terror began: the beginnings of a nihilism that has reached its full development only in our own times. In his *Enquiry on Human Understanding* the assault upon historic filiations and human reason reached a pitch of cool destructiveness. Hume used the technical processes of reason to sap its very foundations. He was far more radical in his attack than Rousseau, far more devastating than d'Holbach or La Mettrie.

Hume's essential doctrine was the autonomy of raw human impulse and the absolutism of raw sensation. In analyzing cause and effect, he broke down the rational connection between human events to a bald sequence of abstract sensations in time. That, however, was a mere refinement of Locke's analysis of sensations as the building-stones of "ideas," and in terms of isolated sense experience Hume's description was the most accurate report possible of the operation of one agent upon another. But Hume went much further. A passion, for him, was an original existence: it did not derive from any sense impression or copy any other existence: impulses were primordial in a fashion that was not true for any response to the outer world. "When I am angry," Hume wrote, "I am actually possessed with passion, and in that emotion have no more reference to any other object than when I am thirsty or sick,

or more than five feet high. It is impossible, therefore, that this passion can be opposed by, or be contradictory to truth or reason."

According to this principle, Hume went on to show, there are only two ways in which any affection can be called unreasonable: first, when a passion is founded on the belief in the existence of objects which do not really exist, as when fear in the dark is based upon the supposition of a non-existing brute lying in wait in the bushes, or when, in carrying out a passion, we choose means insufficient for the end. "Where a passion is neither founded on false suppositions nor chooses means insufficient for the end, the understanding can neither justify it nor condemn it. It is not contrary to reason to prefer the destruction of the whole world to the scratching of my finger."

One could not caricature this doctrine if one wanted to. In the last sentence Hume has done so beyond further challenge: it stands self-condemned. But if one pursues the implications of this philosophy, one sees that this imperturbable philosopher has arrived at a position of absolute nihilism: Turgeniev's Bazarov, in *Fathers and Sons,* is a mere amateur in moral devastation by comparison. For Hume not merely confirms the absolutism of sensations—and completely overlooks the mediation of sensations through symbols—but he completes this work with an absolutism of brute impulse: he unites a despotism of the outer world with a despotism of the ego, or rather, of the id. Life as he pictured it was life in the raw—with a rawness the most primitive savage never exhibited. In his own plain words, the passions that possess man are above reason and beyond reason.

Hume's philosophy rejects the social background; it refuses to admit the social interpretation of events or the social (symbolic) nature of their analysis; it turns its back upon social responsibilities; it shows human beings as living in a moment-to-moment continuum in which the appetites alone have an unqualified claim to existence, and in which no impulses can be called good or bad, rational or irrational, since every impulse that is founded on the existence of real objects and is pursued with appropriate means is *ipso facto* reasonable. Raskolnikov's murder of the old woman for her money, like Hitler's wiping out of the center of Rotterdam, are both in Hume's creed entirely reasonable affairs—though Hitler's invasion of Russia would be unreasonable because it chose means that were insufficient to its end.

This erroneous conclusion necessarily overtakes every theory that excludes values from the fundamental substratum of all human experience: Hume's office was to make the error so openly that it becomes a classic clarification. Since value is integral to all human experience, a theory that eliminates value as a primary ingredient inevitably smuggles it back again by making sensations or impulses, as such, the seat of value; whereas value comes into existence through man's primordial need to distinguish between life-maintaining and life-destroying processes, and to distribute his interests and his energies accordingly. Here lies the main function of reason: that of relating and apportioning the facts of experience into an intelligible and livable whole. Reason inter-connects events that Hume analytically tears apart: for the purest sensation, the most immediate passion, takes place in a world of values, logical order, moral duties, social institutions, by which sensation and impulse are modified, into which they are integrated. Reason is as fundamental a part of the human equipment as bones, skin, viscera, nerves: by a constant process of relation and apportionment, by suppressing this impulse and by encouraging that, it maintains man's self and his community in a state of psychic wholeness. (pp. 183-85)

Hume's mission was simply to carry the current atomism to its logical conclusion: the world became a dissociated flux of sensations and the self became a magma of impulses that might occasionally erupt into life without following any orderly channels in descent. No society could manifestly exist on such irrational, ultra-nominalist premises. If Hume's ideological disintegration was far more complete than the social disintegration, that was partly because it was easier to explain away reason than to live for a day without having some recourse to it. (pp. 185-86)

In practice, one must add, Hume recoiled from his own strict analysis. Having used his logic to dissolve all the connections of cause and effect, to remove value from sensation, to dissociate impulse from purpose, Hume cast doubt upon the very instruments he had used to accomplish this astonishing result—and so recoiled into the world of history and social convention. No one would have been more distressed than Hume if anyone had taken his metaphysics seriously; actually nothing alarmed him more than raw impulse. One remembers with a smile his discomfort over Rousseau's tearful demonstration of gratitude for being rescued from his persecutors by Hume: "My dear sir! my dear sir!" (p. 186)

Lewis Mumford, "Hume: Nihilistic Atomism," in his Interpretations and Forecasts, 1922-1972: Studies in Literature, History, Biography, Technics, and Contemporary Society, *Harcourt Brace Jovanovich, 1973, pp. 183-86.*

BERTRAND RUSSELL (essay date 1945)

[*A respected and prolific author, Russell was an English philosopher and mathematician known for his support of humanistic concerns. Two of his early works,* Principles of Mathematics *(1903) and* Principia Mathematica *(1910-1913), written with Alfred North Whitehead, are considered classics of mathematical logic. His philosophical approach to all his endeavors discounts idealism or emotionalism and asserts a progressive application of his "logical atomism," a process whereby individual facts are logically analyzed. Russell's humanistic beliefs often centered around support of unorthodox social concerns, including free love, undisciplined education, and the eradication of nuclear weapons. His staunch pacifism during World War I led to a six-month imprisonment and began a history of political and social activism which culminated when, at the age of eighty-nine, he was again jailed for his active participation in an unruly demonstration advocating unilateral nuclear disarmament. After the incident Russell stated: "What I want is some assurance before I die that the human race will be allowed to continue." Regarding Russell, biographer Alan Wood has written:"He started by asking questions about mathematics and religion and philosophy, and went on to question accepted ideas about war and politics and sex and education, setting the minds of men on the march, so that the world could never be quite the same as if he had not lived." In recognition of his contributions in a number of literary genres, Russell was awarded the Nobel Prize for literature in 1950. In the following excerpt from his* History of Western Philosophy, *in which he approaches philosophy "not as the isolated speculations of remarkable individuals, but as both an effect and a cause of the character of the various communities in which different systems flourished," Russell outlines the major tenets of the first book of* A Treatise of Human Nature, *focusing on Hume's conception of causation, perception, and induction.*]

[David Hume] is one of the most important among philosophers, because he developed to its logical conclusion the em-

pirical philosophy of Locke and Berkeley, and by making it self-consistent made it incredible. He represents, in a certain sense, a dead end: in his direction, it is impossible to go further. To refute him has been, ever since he wrote, a favourite pastime among metaphysicians. For my part, I find none of their refutations convincing; nevertheless, I cannot but hope that something less sceptical than Hume's system may be discoverable. (p. 659)

Hume's *Treatise of Human Nature* is divided into three books, dealing respectively with the understanding, the passions, and morals. What is important and novel in his doctrines is in the first book, to which I shall confine myself.

He begins with the distinction between "impressions" and "ideas." These are two kinds of perceptions, of which *impressions* are those that have more force and violence. "By ideas I mean the faint images of these in thinking and reasoning." Ideas, at least when simple, are like impressions, but fainter. "Every simple idea has a simple impression, which resembles it; and every simple impression a correspondent idea." "All our simple ideas in their first appearance are derived from simple impressions, which are correspondent to them, and which they exactly represent." Complex ideas, on the other hand, need not resemble impressions. We can imagine a winged horse without having ever seen one, but the *constituents* of this complex idea are all derived from impressions. The proof that impressions come first is derived from experience; for example, a man born blind has no ideas of colours. Among ideas, those that retain a considerable degree of the vivacity of the original impressions belong to *memory*, the others to *imagination*.

There is a section (Book I, Part I, Sec. VII) "Of Abstract Ideas," which opens with a paragraph of emphatic agreement with Berkeley's doctrine that "all general ideas are nothing but particular ones, annexed to a certain term, which gives them a more extensive significance, and makes them recall upon occasion other individuals, which are similar to them." He contends that, when we have an idea of a man, it has all the particularity that the impression of a man has. "The mind cannot form any notion of quantity or quality without forming a precise notion of degrees of each." "Abstract ideas are in themselves individual, however they may become general in their representation." This theory, which is a modern form of nominalism, has two defects, one logical, the other psychological. To begin with the logical objection: "When we have found a resemblance among several objects," Hume says, "we apply the same name to all of them." Every nominalist would agree. But in fact a common name, such as "cat," is just as unreal as the universal CAT is. The nominalist solution of the problem of universals thus fails through being insufficiently drastic in the application of its own principles; it mistakenly applies these principles only to "things," and not also to words.

The psychological objection is more serious, at least in connection with Hume. The whole theory of ideas as copies of impressions, as he sets it forth, suffers from ignoring *vagueness*. When, for example, I have seen a flower of a certain colour, and I afterwards call up an image of it, the image is lacking in precision, in this sense, that there are several closely similar shades of colour of which it might be an image, or "idea," in Hume's terminology. It is not true that "the mind cannot form any notion of quantity or quality without forming a precise notion of degrees of each." Suppose you have seen a man whose height is six feet one inch. You retain an image of him, but it probably would fit a man half an inch taller or shorter. Vagueness is different from generality, but has some of the same characteristics. By not noticing it, Hume runs into unnecessary difficulties, for instance, as to the possibility of imagining a shade of colour you have never seen, which is intermediate between two closely similar shades that you have seen. If these two are sufficiently similar, any image you can form will be equally applicable to both of them and to the intermediate shade. When Hume says that ideas are derived from impressions which they *exactly* represent he goes beyond what is psychologically true.

Hume banished the conception of *substance* from psychology, as Berkeley had banished it from physics. There is, he says, no *impression* of self, and therefore no idea of self (Book I, Part IV, Sec. VI). "For my part, when I enter most intimately into what I call *myself,* I always stumble on some particular perception or other, of heat or cold, light or shade, love or hatred, pain or pleasure. I never catch *myself* at any time without a perception, and never can observe anything but the perception." There may, he ironically concedes, be some philosophers who can perceive their selves; "but setting aside some metaphysicians of this kind, I may venture to affirm of the rest of mankind, that they are nothing but a bundle or collection of different perceptions, which succeed each other with inconceivable rapidity, and are in a perpetual flux and movement."

This repudiation of the idea of the Self is of great importance. Let us see exactly what it maintains, and how far it is valid. To begin with, the Self, if there is such a thing, is never perceived, and therefore we can have no idea of it. If this argument is to be accepted, it must be carefully stated. No man perceives his own brain, yet, in an important sense, he has an "idea" of it. Such "ideas," which are inferences from perceptions, are not among the logically basic stock of ideas; they are complex and descriptive—this must be the case if Hume is right in his principle that all simple ideas are derived from impressions, and if this principle is rejected, we are forced back on "innate" ideas. Using modern terminology, we may say: Ideas of unperceived things or occurrences can always be defined in terms of perceived things or occurrences, and therefore, by substituting the definition for the term defined, we can always state what we know empirically without introducing any unperceived things or occurrences. As regards our present problem, all psychological knowledge can be stated without introducing the "Self." Further, the "Self," as defined, can be nothing but a bundle of perceptions, not a new simple "thing." In this I think that any thoroughgoing empiricist must agree with Hume.

It does not follow that there is no simple Self; it only follows that we cannot know whether there is or not, and that the Self, except as a bundle of perceptions, cannot enter into any part of our knowledge. This conclusion is important in metaphysics, as getting rid of the last surviving use of "substance." It is important in theology, as abolishing all supposed knowledge of the "soul." It is important in the analysis of knowledge, since it shows that the category of subject and object is not fundamental. In this matter of the ego Hume made an important advance on Berkeley.

The most important part of the whole Treatise is the section called "Of Knowledge and Probability." Hume does not mean by "probability" the sort of knowledge contained in the mathematical theory of probability, such as that the chance of throwing double sixes with two dice is one thirty-sixth. This knowledge is not itself probable in any special sense; it has as much certainty as knowledge can have. What Hume is concerned

with is uncertain knowledge, such as is obtained from empirical data by inferences that are not demonstrative. This includes all our knowledge as to the future, and as to unobserved portions of the past and present. In fact, it includes everything except, on the one hand, direct observation, and, on the other, logic and mathematics. The analysis of such "probable" knowledge led Hume to certain sceptical conclusions, which are equally difficult to refute and to accept. The result was a challenge to philosophers, which, in my opinion, has still not been adequately met.

Hume begins by distinguishing seven kinds of philosophical relation: resemblance, identity, relations of time and place, proportion in quantity or number, degrees in any quality, contrariety, and causation. These, he says, may be divided into two kinds: those that depend only on the ideas, and those that can be changed without any change in the ideas. Of the first kind are resemblance, contrariety, degrees in quality, and proportions in quantity or number. But spatio-temporal and causal relations are of the second kind. Only relations of the first kind give *certain* knowledge; our knowledge concerning the others is only *probable*. Algebra and arithmetic are the only sciences in which we can carry on a long chain of reasoning without losing certainty. Geometry is not so certain as algebra and arithmetic, because we cannot be sure of the truth of its axioms. It is a mistake to suppose, as many philosophers do, that the ideas of mathematics "must be comprehended by a pure and intellectual view, of which the superior faculties of the soul are alone capable." The falsehood of this view is evident, says Hume, as soon as we remember that "all our ideas are copied from our impressions."

The three relations that depend not only on ideas are identity, spatio-temporal relations, and causation. In the first two, the mind does not go beyond what is immediately present to the sense. (Spatio-temporal relations, Hume holds, can be perceived, and can form parts of impressions.) Causation alone enables us to infer some thing or occurrence from some other thing or occurrence: "'Tis only *causation*, which produces such a connexion, as to give us assurance from the existence or action of one object, that 'twas followed or preceded by any other existence or action."

A difficulty arises from Hume's contention that there is no such thing as an *impression* of a casual relation. We can perceive, by mere observation of A and B, that A is above B, or to the right of B, but not that A causes B. In the past, the relation of causation had been more or less assimilated to that of ground and consequent in logic, but this, Hume rightly perceived, was a mistake.

In the Cartesian philosophy, as in that of the Scholastics, the connection of cause and effect was supposed to be necessary, as logical connections are necessary. The first really serious challenge to this view came from Hume, with whom the modern philosophy of causation begins. He, in common with almost all philosophers down to and including Bergson, supposes the law to state that there are propositions of the form "A causes B," where A and B are classes of events; the fact that such laws do not occur in any well-developed science appears to be unknown to philosophers. (pp. 660-64)

Hume begins by observing that the power by which one object produces another is not discoverable from the ideas of the two objects, and that we can therefore only know cause and effect from experience, not from reasoning or reflection. The statement "what begins must have a cause," he says, is not one that has intuitive certainty, like the statements of logic. As he puts it: "There is no object, which implies the existence of any other if we consider these objects in themselves, and never look beyond the ideas which we form of them." Hume argues from this that it must be experience that gives knowledge of cause and effect, but that it cannot be merely the experience of the two events A and B which are in a causal relation to each other. It must be experience, because the connection is not logical; and it cannot be merely the experience of the particular events A and B, since we can discover nothing in A by itself which should lead it to produce B. The experience required, he says, is that of the constant conjunction of events of the kind A with events of the kind B. He points out that when, in experience, two objects are constantly conjoined, we do *in fact* infer one from the other. (When he says "infer," he means that perceiving the one makes us expect the other; he does not mean a formal or explicit inference.) "Perhaps, the necessary connection depends on the inference," not vice versa. That is to say, the sight of A causes the expectation of B, and so leads us to believe that there is a necessary connection between A and B. The inference is not determined by reason, since that would require us to assume the uniformity of nature, which itself is not necessary, but only inferred from experience.

Hume is thus led to the view that, when we say "A causes B," we mean only that A and B are constantly conjoined in fact, not that there is some necessary connection between them. "We have no other notion of cause and effect, but that of certain objects, which have been *always conjoined* together. . . . We cannot penetrate into the reason of the conjunction."

He backs up his theory with a definition of "belief," which is, he maintains, "a lively idea related to or associated with a present impression." Through association, if A and B have been constantly conjoined in past experience, the impression of A produces that lively idea of B which constitutes belief in B. This explains why we *believe* A and B to be connected: the percept of A *is* connected with the idea of B, and so we come to think that A is connected with B, though this opinion is really groundless. "Objects have no discoverable connexion together; nor is it from any other principle but custom operating upon the imagination, that we can draw any inference from the apperance of one to the experience of another." He repeats many times the contention that what appears to us as necessary connection among *objects* is really only connection among the ideas of those objects: the mind is *determined* by custom, and "'tis this impression, or *determination,* which affords me the idea of necessity." The repetition of instances, which leads us to the belief that A causes B, gives nothing new in the object, but in the mind leads to an association of ideas; thus "necessity is something that exists in the mind, not in objects." (pp. 664-66)

Hume is commonly accused of having too atomic a view of perception, but he allows that certain relations can be perceived. "We ought not," he says, "to receive as reasoning any of the observations we make concerning *identity,* and the relations of *time* and *place;* since in none of them the mind can go beyond what is immediately present to the senses." Causation, he says, is different in that it takes us beyond the impressions of our senses, and informs us of unperceived existences. As an argument, this seems invalid. We believe in many relations of time and place which we cannot perceive: we think that time extends backwards and forwards, and space beyond the walls of our room. Hume's real argument is that, while we sometimes perceive relations of time and place, we

never perceive causal relations, which must therefore, if admitted, be inferred from relations that can be perceived. The controversy is thus reduced to one of empirical fact: Do we, or do we not, sometimes perceive a relation which can be called causal? Hume says no, his adversaries say yes, and it is not easy to see how evidence can be produced by either side.

I think perhaps the strongest argument on Hume's side is to be derived from the character of causal laws in physics. It appears that simple rules of the form "A causes B" are never to be admitted in science, except as crude suggestions in early stages. The causal laws by which such simple rules are replaced in well-developed sciences are so complex that no one can suppose them given in perception; they are all, obviously, elaborate inferences from the observed course of nature. I am leaving out of account modern quantum theory, which reinforces the above conclusion. So far as the physical sciences are concerned, Hume is *wholly* in the right: such propositions as "A causes B" are never to be accepted, and our inclination to accept them is to be explained by the laws of habit and association. These laws themselves, in their accurate form, will be elaborate statements as to nervous tissue—primarily its physiology, then its chemistry, and ultimately its physics.

The opponent of Hume, however, even if he admits the whole of what has just been said about the physical sciences, may not yet admit himself decisively defeated. He may say that in psychology we have cases where a causal relation can be perceived. The whole conception of cause is probably derived from volition, and it may be said that we can perceive a relation, between a volition and the consequent act, which is something more than invariable sequence. The same might be said of the relation between a sudden pain and a cry. Such views, however, are rendered very difficult by physiology. Between the will to move my arm and the consequent movement there is a long chain of causal intermediaries consisting of processes in the nerves and muscles. We perceive only the end terms of this process, the volition and the movement, and if we think we see a direct causal connection between these we are mistaken. This argument is not conclusive on the general question, but it shows that it is rash to suppose that we perceive causal relations when we think we do. The balance, therefore, is in favour of Hume's view that there is nothing in *cause* except invariable succession. The evidence, however, is not so conclusive as Hume supposed.

Hume is not content with reducing the evidence of a causal connection to experience of frequent conjunction; he proceeds to argue that such experience does not justify the expectation of similar conjunctions in the future. For example: when I see an apple, past experience makes me expect that it will taste like an apple, and not like roast beef; but there is no rational justification for this expectation. If there were such a justification, it would have to proceed from the principle "that those instances, of which we have had no experience, resemble those of which we have had experience." This principle is not logically necessary, since we can at least conceive a change in the course of nature. It should therefore be a principle of probability. But all probable arguments assume this principle, and therefore it cannot itself be proved by any probable argument, or even rendered probable by any such argument. "The supposition, *that the future resembles the past,* is not founded on arguments of any kind, but is derived entirely from habit. The conclusion is one of complete scepticism." . . . (pp. 668-70)

The ultimate outcome of Hume's investigation of what passes for knowledge is not what we must suppose him to have desired. The sub-title of his book is: "An attempt to introduce the experimental method of reasoning into moral subjects." It is evident that he started out with a belief that scientific method yields the truth, the whole truth, and nothing but the truth; he ended, however, with the conviction that belief is never rational, since we know nothing. After setting forth the arguments for scepticism (Book I, Part IV, Sec. I), he goes on, not to refute the arguments, but to fall back on natural credulity. (pp. 670-71)

Hume's philosophy, whether true or false, represents the bankruptcy of eighteenth-century reasonableness. He starts out, like Locke, with the intention of being sensible and empirical, taking nothing on trust, but seeking whatever instruction is to be obtained from experience and observation. But having a better intellect than Locke's, a greater acuteness in analysis, and a smaller capacity for accepting comfortble inconsistencies, he arrives at the disastrous conclusion that from experience and observation nothing is to be learnt. There is no such thing as a rational belief: "If we believe that fire warms, or water refreshes, 'tis only bcause it costs us too much pains to think otherwise." We cannot help believing, but no belief can be grounded in reason. Nor can one line of action be more rational than another, since all alike are based upon irrational convictions. This last conclusion, however, Hume seems not to have drawn. Even in his most sceptical chapter, in which he sums up the conclusions of Book I, he says: "Generally speaking, the errors in religion are dangerous; those in philosophy only ridiculous." He has no right to say this. "Dangerous" is a causal word, and a sceptic as to causation cannot know that anything is "dangerous."

In fact, in the later portions of the *Treatise,* Hume forgets all about his fundamental doubts, and writes much as any other enlightened moralist of his time might have written; he applies to his doubts the remedy that he recommends, namely "carelessness and inattention." In a sense, his scepticism is insincere, since he cannot maintain it in practice. It has, however, this awkward consequence, that it paralyses every effort to prove one line of action better than another.

It was inevitable that such a self-refutation of rationality should be followed by a great ouburst of irrational faith. The quarrel between Hume and Rousseau is symbolic: Rousseau was mad but influential, Hume was sane but had no followers. Subsequent British empiricists rejected his scepticism without refuting it; Rousseau and his followers agreed with Hume that no belief is based on reason, but thought the heart superior to reason, and allowed it to lead them to convictions very different from those that Hume retained in practice. German philosophers, from Kant to Hegel, had not assimilated Hume's arguments. I say this deliberately, in spite of the belief which many philosophers share with Kant, that his *Critique of Pure Reason* answered Hume. In fact, these philosophers—at least Kant and Hegel—represent a pre-Humian type of rationalism, and can be refuted by Humian arguments. The philosophers who cannot be refuted in this way are those who do not pretend to be rational, such as Rousseau, Schopenhauer, and Nietzsche. The growth of unreason throughout the nineteenth century and what has passed of the twentieth is a natural sequel to Hume's destruction of empiricism.

It is therefore important to discover whether there is any answer to Hume within the framework of a philosophy that is wholly or mainly empirical. If not, there is no intellectual difference between sanity and insanity. The lunatic who believes that he is a poached egg is to be condemned solely on the ground that

Hume (left) meets Jean-Jacques Rousseau, in an engraving by T. Holloway published around 1766.

he is in a minority, or rather—since we must not assume democracy—on the ground that the government does not agree with him. This is a desperate point of view, and it must be hoped that there is some way of escaping from it.

Hume's scepticism rests entirely upon his rejection of the principle of induction. The principle of induction, as applied to causation, says that, if A has been found very often accompanied or followed by B, and no instance is known of A not being accompanied or followed by B, then it is probable that on the next occasion on which A is observed it will be accompanied or followed by B. If the principle is to be adequate, a sufficient number of instances must make the probability not far short of certainty. If this principle, or any other from which it can be deduced, is true, then the causal inferences which Hume rejects are valid, not indeed as giving certainty, but as giving a sufficient probability for practical purposes. If this principle is not true, every attempt to arrive at general scientific laws from particular observations is fallacious, and Hume's scepticism is inescapable for an empiricist. The principle itself cannot, of course, without circularity, be inferred from observed uniformities, since it is required to justify any such inference. It must therefore be, or be deduced from, an independent principle not based upon experience. To this extent, Hume has proved that pure empiricism is not a sufficient basis for science. But if this one principle is admitted, everything else can proceed in accordance with the theory that all our knowledge is based on experience. It must be granted that this is a serious departure from pure empiricism, and that those who are not empiricists may ask why, if one departure is allowed, others are to be forbidden. These, however, are questions not directly raised by Hume's arguments. What these arguments prove—and I do not think the proof can be controverted—is that induction is an independent logical principle, incapable of being inferred either from experience or from other logical principles, and that without this principle science is impossible. (pp. 672-74)

> Bertrand Russell, *"Modern Philosophy: Hume,"* in his A History of Western Philosophy, and Its Connection with Political and Social Circumstances from the Earliest Times to the Present Day, *Simon & Schuster, 1945, pp. 659-74.*

C. S. LEWIS (essay date 1947)

[*Lewis is considered one of the foremost Christian and mythopoeic authors of the twentieth century. Indebted principally to George MacDonald, G. K. Chesterton, Charles Williams, and the writers of ancient Norse sagas, he is regarded as a formidable logician and Christian polemicist, a perceptive literary critic, and—perhaps most highly—as a writer of fantasy literature. Also a noted academic and scholar, Lewis held posts at Oxford and Cambridge, where he was an acknowledged authority on medieval and Renaissance literature. A traditionalist in his approach to life and art, he opposed the modern critical movement toward biographical and psychological interpretation, preferring to practice and propound a theory of criticism that stresses the author's intent rather than the reader's presuppositions and prejudices. In the following excerpt, he evaluates Hume's essay "Of Miracles."*]

Ever since Hume's famous [essay **"Of Miracles"**] it has been believed that historical statements about miracles are the most intrinsically improbable of all historical statements. According to Hume, probability rests on what may be called the majority vote of our past experiences. The more often a thing has been known to happen, the more probable it is that it should happen again; and the less often the less probable. Now the regularity of Nature's course, says Hume, is supported by something better than the majority vote of past experiences: it is supported by their unanimous vote, or, as Hume says, by "firm and unalterable experience." There is, in fact, "uniform experience" against Miracle; otherwise, says Hume, it would not be a Miracle. A miracle is therefore the most improbable of all events. It is always more probable that the witnesses were lying or mistaken than that a miracle occurred.

Now of course we must agree with Hume that if there is absolutely "uniform experience" against miracles, if in other words they have never happened, why then they never have. Unfortunately we know the experience against them to be uniform only if we know that all the reports of them are false. And we can know all the reports to be false only if we know already that miracles have never occurred. In fact, we are arguing in a circle.

There is also an objection to Hume which leads us deeper into our problem. The whole idea of Probability (as Hume understands it) depends on the principle of the Uniformity of Nature. Unless Nature always goes on in the same way, the fact that a thing had happened ten million times would not make it a whit more probable that it would happen again. And how do we know the Uniformity of Nature? A moment's thought shows that we do not know it by experience. We observe many reg-

ularities in Nature. But of course all the observations that men have made or will make while the race lasts cover only a minute fraction of the events that actually go on. Our observations would therefore be of no use unless we felt sure that Nature when we are not watching her behaves in the same way as when we are: in other words, unless we believed in the Uniformity of Nature. Experience therefore cannot prove uniformity, because uniformity has to be assumed before experience proves anything. And mere length of experience does not help matters. It is no good saying, "Each fresh experience confirms our belief in uniformity and therefore we reasonably expect that it will always be confirmed"; for that argument works only on the assumption that the future will resemble the past—which is simply the assumption of Uniformity under a new name. Can we say that Uniformity is at any rate very probable? Unfortunately not. We have just seen that all probabilities depend on *it*. Unless Nature is uniform, nothing is either probable or improbable. And clearly the assumption which you have to make before there is any such thing as probability cannot itself be probable.

The odd thing is that no man knew this better than Hume. [**"Of Miracles"**] is quite inconsistent with the more radical, and honourable, scepticism of his main work.

The question, "Do miracles occur?" and the question, "Is the course of Nature absolutely uniform?" are the same question asked in two different ways. Hume by sleight of hand, treats them as two different questions. He first answers "Yes," to the question whether Nature is absolutely uniform; and then uses this "Yes" as a ground for answering, "No," to the question, "Do miracles occur?" The single real question which he set out to answer is never discussed at all. He gets the answer to one form of the question by assuming the answer to another form of the same question.

Probabilities of the kind that Hume is concerned with hold inside the framework of an assumed Uniformity of Nature. When the question of miracles is raised we are asking about the validity or perfection of the frame itself. No study of probabilities inside a given frame can ever tell us how probable it is that the frame itself can be violated. Granted a school time-table with French on Tuesday morning at ten o'clock, it is really probable that Jones, who always skimps his French preparation, will be in trouble next Tuesday, and that he was in trouble on any previous Tuesday. But what does this tell us about the probability of the time-table's being altered? To find that out you must eavesdrop in the masters' common-room. It is no use studying the time-table.

If we stick to Hume's method, far from getting what he hoped (namely, the conclusion that all miracles are infinitely improbable) we get a complete deadlock. The only kind of probability he allows holds exclusively within the frame of uniformity. When uniformity is itself in question (and it is in question the moment we ask whether miracles occur) this kind of probability is suspended. And Hume knows no other. By his method, therefore, we cannot say that uniformity is either probable or improbable; and equally we cannot say that miracles are either probable or improbable. We have impounded *both* uniformity *and* miracles in a sort of limbo where probability and improbability can never come. This result is equally disastrous for the scientist and the theologian; but along Hume's lines there is nothing whatever to be done about it. (pp. 101-04)

> C. S. Lewis, *"On Probability,"* in his Miracles: A Preliminary Study, *1947. Reprint by Macmillan Publishing Co., Inc., 1978, pp. 100-07.*

HUNTINGTON CAIRNS (essay date 1949)

[Cairns was an American lawyer, educator, editor, and author who wrote widely on the law and the fine arts. Often described as a Renaissance man, he worked in a variety of intellectual disciplines, interweaving them with the single, complex thread of his rational philosophy. Cairns is perhaps best known for his many writings on legal history, including Legal Philosophy from Plato to Hegel *(1949), a work described by the leading German jurist Hans Kelsen as especially successful in illustrating a coherent connection between society and the law. In the following excerpt from this work, Cairns discusses Hume's theory of social justice and elucidates his statements concerning the origin and nature of rules of law.]*

[In *A Treatise of Human Nature*] Hume was at great pains to prove that justice was not a natural but only an artificial virtue, and his [1896 editor L. A. Selby-Bigge] is of the opinion "it is pretty plain that he meant to be offensive in doing so." It is difficult to perceive on what basis this extraordinary appraisal rests. By the time Hume had come to write [*An Enquiry concerning Human Understanding* and *An Enquiry concerning the Principles of Morals*] he was so perplexed by the multitudinous senses of the word "natural" that he was inclined to dismiss the question as "vain" and "verbal"; nevertheless, he did not depart from his position. It is obvious, of course, that Hume was raising one of the oldest problems in the history of jurisprudence, and one upon which he had decided views—whether right was right by nature or only by convention and enactment. From the Sophists to his beloved Cicero and to Hooker the question had been endlessly discussed and it would be fruitless to speculate upon the source which suggested it to his mind. But that he handled the matter with what he felt was the deference due the theological and moral atmosphere of his time is clear from the reservations which he attached to his ultimate conclusion.

Justice according to Hume, is approved because of its utility, and this recognition of its necessity is discovered by reason; but inasmuch in Hume's theory "reason is and ought to be the slave of the passions" the approval we bestow upon justice must be due to something other than reason. Hume therefore raises the question: Why does utility please? We are able through reason to understand the utility of justice in promoting human happiness. What is that to me? Perhaps the application of justice will result in an increase of general human happiness, but bring only misery to the individual. Hume answers this problem by observing that the ultimate ends of human actions can never, in any case, be accounted for by reason, but recommend themselves entirely to the sentiments and affections of mankind, without any dependence on the intellectual faculties. Reason is not alone sufficient to produce any moral blame or approbation. Utility is only a tendency to a certain end; and were the end totally indifferent to us, we should feel the same indifference towards the means. It is requisite that a sentiment should here display itself, in order to give a preference to the useful above the pernicious tendencies. This sentiment can be no other than a feeling for the happiness of mankind, and a resentment of their misery; since these are the different ends which virtue and vice have a tendency to promote. Here therefore reason instructs us in the several tendencies of actions, and humanity makes a distinction in favor of those which are useful and beneficial. Thus sympathy with the public interest is the source of the moral approbation which attends justice. We begin therefore with the proposition that justice, although an artificial virtue, owes its moral approval to a feeling.

Hume initiated his argument in the usual manner of the period. He began with a quest for the First Origin, and inasmuch as the discovery of that elusive condition defies, in the nature of things, the customary historical analysis, he fell back upon invention. He assumed that man in a solitary condition was ill equipped by nature to secure food, clothes and shelter. It is through society alone that he is able to supply his needs. But in order to form society, it is necessary not only that it be advantageous, but also that men be sensible of its advantages. However, it is impossible, in their wild uncultivated state, that by study and reflection alone, they should ever be able to attain this knowledge. Fortunately another necessity exists which may justly be regarded as the first and original principle of human society. This necessity is the sexual drive which unites man and woman and preserves their union until a new tie takes place in their concern for their common offspring. This new concern becomes also a principle of union between the parents and offspring, and forms a more numerous society. In time, custom and habit operate on the impressionable minds of the children, make them sensible of the advantages which they may reap from society, and fashion them by degrees for it.

This view of the origin of society is deceptively plausible and has had many adherents. However, it may be answered on several grounds. If taken in a strict historical sense, it is completely speculative and may therefore be dismissed. If taken as a logical reconstruction, it is inconsistent with many of the facts of ethnology, on the basis of which alternative theories of greater plausibility can be constructed. Thus, as [Robert Briffault maintains in *The Mothers: A Study of the Origins of Sentiments and Institutions* (1927)], the primitive social instincts of humanity, which constitute the bond that knits that primitive social group and actuates its collective mentality, thus affording the conditions of all human mental and social development may not be the sexual instincts; they may be the maternal instincts and the ties of kinship that derive directly from their operation. This hypothsis would account for the fact that in many societies the family group, in the patriarchal sense, does not exist. Finally, if Hume's theory is taken as a sociological concept, the comparable but more complex theory of Aristotle, recently revived by Mead, promises greater usefulness. Man is by nature a social animal, said Aristotle; but he alone of all animals possesses the power of speech which means that nature has fitted him for a social life. He is the best of all animals when perfected, but he can realize perfection only in society; therefore society is philosophically prior to the individual in the sense that the whole is prior to the part; it is also prior in time in the sense that the individual is not complete until he becomes a part of it. Without society and the elements it adds to man's personality, he would be either a "beast or a God." As Rousseau was later to remark, one becomes a man by being a citizen.

Hume argued that there are three different species of good of which we are possessed: the internal satisfaction of our minds, the external advantages of our body, and the enjoyment of such possessions as we have acquired by our industry and good fortune. We are perfectly secure in the enjoyment of the first; someone may tear the second from us, but it can be of no advantage to him. The last only is both exposed to the violence of others, and may be transferred without suffering any loss or alteration; at the same time, there is not a sufficient quantity of them to supply every one's desires and necessities. The fact that a society has come into being is not sufficient to protect these goods, the proper care of which is the chief advantage of society. Our natural uncultivated ideas of morality would, in fact, increase the hazards which attend ownership. The remedy, then, is not derived from nature, but from artifice; or more properly speaking, nature provides a remedy through reason for what is irregular in sentiment. For when men, from their early education in society, have become sensible of the infinite advantages that result from it; and when they have observed that the principal disturbance arises from those goods, which Hume calls external, and from their looseness and easy transition from one person to another; they must seek for a remedy, by putting those goods, as far as possible, on the same footing with the fixed and constant advantages of the mind and body. This can be done after no other manner, than by a convention entered into by all the members of the society to bestow stability on the possession of those external goods, and leave everyone in the peaceable enjoyment of what he may acquire. This convention is not of the nature of a promise; for promises themselves arise from human conventions. It is only a general sense of common interest; and this sense all the members of the society express to one another, and it induces them to regulate their conduct by certain rules. Two men who pull the oars of a boat do it by an agreement or convention, although they have never given promises to each other. After the convention is entered into there immediately arise the ideas of justice and injustice; and then those of property, right and obligation.

To avoid giving offense, Hume remarks he must observe, when he denies justice to be a natural virtue, he makes use of the word *natural,* only as opposed to *artificial.* In another sense of the word, as no principle of the human mind is more natural than a sense of virtue, so no virtue is more natural than justice. Mankind is an inventive species; and where an invention is obvious and absolutely necessary, it may as properly be said to be natural as any thing that proceeds immediately from original principles, without the intervention of thought or reflection. However, Hume observes, although the rules of justice are artificial, they are not arbitrary.

Here Hume has set forth what in its elements is the accepted sociological theory of today. He has described the process through which societary control is formed, and he has correctly emphasized the fact that culture traits, such as the rules of law, are all ultimately the product of invention. Translated into contemporary terms, we have first an *emotion* of approval or disapproval in a *particular* case; second, a *judgment* of approval or disapproval constituting a generalization as to the desirability of cases of this type; third, *folkways, mores,* and *usages,* informal non-institutionalized embodiments of previously formed judgments of approval or disapproval, but generally understood and commonly accepted as applying to all cases of this *general class;* finally, accepted *institutions,* culminating in *law,* the formal crystallization of the previously formed judgments of approval or disapproval, into *express statutes,* with definite penalities for violation. Hume's account of the formation of the rules of laws is plainly enough the forerunner of the present day hypothesis. Moreover, he centered his whole account upon the crucial element—that rules of law come into existence through the process of invention. They are inherited from one generation to another, and they are also borrowed from other cultures. But at some stage they had to be originated, and it was this fact which, in his insistence upon invention, Hume always kept in view.

Nowhere did Hume attempt a formal analysis of the nature of law, but it is clear from his text that he thought of it as embracing at least three elements. There was first the general system of morality, which he termed "equity," that guided the judges in the decision of cases. Again, he thought of law in the sense in which jurists now speak of the "legal order"—the regime which adjusts relations and orders conduct by the systematic and orderly application of the force of a politically organized society. Thus he writes, "We are, therefore, to look upon all the vast apparatus of our government, as having ultimately no other object or purpose but the distribution of justice, or in other words, the support of the twelve judges." Hume's vocabulary is not clear and at times he seems to define justice as meaning "property." However, for the most part he treated the two ideas as distinct concepts, and in any event he was perhaps using the term "property" in the broad sense employed by Locke and which embraced the individual's rights to life, liberty and health. Finally, he thought of law in its customary sense as a body of precepts. Thus Hume distinguished many of the separate ideas which jurists now find in the concept "law."

Political obligation, or submission to authority, was founded by Hume on the interest which all men have in the security and protection afforded by political society. He believed that on the strict observance of what he termed the three fundamental laws of nature—that of the stability of possession, of its transference by consent, and of the performance of promises—depended entirely the peace and security of human society. These laws are antecedent to government and are supposed to impose an obligation before the duty of allegiance to civil magistrates has been thought of. Upon the first establishment of government Hume is willing to admit that it derives its obligation from the three laws of nature, and in particular from the one concerning the performance of promises. Men would naturally promise their first magistrates obedience, and a promise is therefore the original sanction of government, and the source of the first obligation to obedience. Although the rules of justice are sufficient to maintain any society, men soon discover in advanced societies that a further element must be added if the rules are to be observed. They therefore establish government as a new invention to attain their ends; by a more strict execution of justice they preserve the old or procure new advantages. Our civil duties are therefore connected with our natural duties, and the former are chiefly invented for the sake of the latter. Thus the principal object of goverment is to constrain men to observe the laws of nature. However, the law of nature with respect to the performance of promises is only comprised along with the rest; and its exact observance is to be considered as an effect of the institution of government, and not the obedience to government as an effect of the obligation of a promise. Although the object of our civil duties is the enforcement of our natural duties, yet the first (in time, not in dignity or force) motive of the invention is nothing but self-interest. But the interest in obeying government is separate from that in the performance of promises, and we must therefore allow a separate obligation. To obey the civil magistrate is requisite to preserve order and concord in society. To perform promises is requisite to beget mutual trust and confidence in the common offices of life. The ends, as well as the means, are perfectly distinct; nor is the one subordinate to the other.

Hume's solution of the problem of why men obey the law is essentially a sociological and not an ethical one. It is also the basis of most later thinking on the subject, which has not contributed an analysis which has taken the question much further. Hume's theory, simply stated, is that society is an advantageous condition, and for society to function properly it is to everyone's advantage to obey the rules that permit the attainment of that end. Contemporary thought would add to this statement, as the program of a sound political theory, the conditions that the rules which the government establishes command obedience by virtue of their quality, and that the formation of the rules be accomplished on the basis of the widest possible participation. The first condition presupposes the establishment of some standard of values which political theory has yet to propose; the second begs the question since participation rarely results in unanimity, and with a situation short of that the fact of the government of the dissenters by the majority must still be accounted for. Other elements than self-interest have been suggested as the basis of obedience—utility, which is merely a generalization of Hume's idea; and habit, which Hume himself allowed for. Hume also admitted the right of revolution on the argument that if interest first produces obedience to government, the obligation to obedience must cease, whenever the interest ceases in any great degree and in a considerable number of instances. That is to say, whenever the civil magistrate carries his oppression so far as to render his authority perfectly intolerable, we are no longer bound to submit to it. The cause ceases; the effect must also cease. However, he rejected as an absurdity the mediaeval doctrine of passive obedience, which had its origin in the right of the Christian minority to resist, at least passively, the actions of an unchristian or heretical authority. We must, he insisted, make allowances for resistance in the more flagrant instances of tyranny and oppression.

In Montesquieu's theory of law Hume found an account which appeared sound to him, and he adopted it in its essential aspects. In general he thought that the authority of civil laws extends, restrains, modifies, and alters the rules of natural justice according to the particular convenience of each community. The laws have, or ought to have, a constant reference to the constitution of government, the manners, the climate, the religion, the commerce, the situation of each society. However, Hume observed that Montesquieu's premises for this conclusion differed from his own. Montesquieu supposed that all right was founded upon certain relations, which was a system, in Hume's opinion, which would never be reconciled with true philosophy. It excluded all sentiment and pretended to found everything on reason; it has therefore, Hume observed, not wanted followers in this philosophic age. He argued that the inference against Montesquieu's basic theory was short and conclusive. Hume admitted that property was dependent on civil laws; civil laws are allowed to have no other object but the interest of society: This therefore must be allowed to be the sole foundation of property and justice, not to mention that our obligation itself to obey the magistrate and his laws is founded on nothing but the interests of society. If our ideas of justice are not in accord with those of the civil law, this is a confirmation, he insists, of his theory. A civil law which is against the interest of society, loses all its authority, and men judge by the ideas of natural justice which are conformable to those interests. Civil laws also sometimes, for useful purposes, require a ceremony or form to a deed; and where the formality is not observed, the legal consequences may be contrary to justice; but one who takes advantage of such chicanery is not commonly regarded as an honest man. Thus, the interests of society require that contracts be fulfilled; and there is not, Hume thought, a surer material article either of natural or civil justice; but the omission of a trifling circumstance will often, by law, invalidate a contract, *in foro humano* ["before the tribunal of mankind"], but not *in foror conscientiae* ["before the tribunal of conscience"]. In these cases the magistrate is supposed only to withdraw his power of enforcing the right, not to have altered the right. Where his intention extends to the right, and is con-

formable to the interests of society, it never fails to alter the right—a clear proof, Hume believed, of the origin of justice and property as he had expounded it. (pp. 375-84)

Huntington Cairns, "Hume," in his Legal Philosophy from Plato to Hegel, *The Johns Hopkins Press, 1949, pp. 362-89.*

ISAIAH BERLIN   (essay date 1956)

[*Berlin is an English philosopher, historian, and political thinker whose many studies of European intellectual life are widely known and respected. In the following excerpt, he probes Hume's analyses of knowledge, causation, induction, and identity.*]

Hume's philosophical writings need little interpretation. He is, with the possible exception of Berkeley, the clearest philosophical writer in an age of exceptional clarity, and he may claim to be the greatest and most revolutionary (in the history of ideas these are almost synonymous terms) of British philosophers. His particular conception of philosophy as an empirical "science of man" is the true beginning of modern philosophy, which, in essence, is the history of the development of, and opposition to, his thought. The "science of man" is to be conducted by the methods of the natural sciences: observation and generalization. Philosophy to become properly scientific must dispense with methods of its own; these are to be exposed as shams and illusions.

The "observations" required for Hume's theory of knowledge are, apparently, to be conducted mainly in the field of introspective psychology, from which indeed his philosophizing is often scarcely distinguishable. "Men's behaviour in company, in affairs and in their pleasures" is more relevant to the account of "The Passions" and to moral philosophy, as discussed in Books II and III of [*A Treatise of Human Nature*], than to Hume's theory of knowledge and criticism of metaphysics. (pp. 163-64)

Hume divides "the contents of the mind," all labeled indiscriminately "ideas" by Locke and Berkeley, into two classes, "impressions" and "ideas." The impressions are intended to be the immediately given data of sense and of introspection, while the ideas are the images of memory and imagination. Hume avoids the trap, into which Locke falls, of distinguishing impressions (of sense) from ideas by their respective sources, the impressions "coming from bodies without us." Rather he distinguishes them—and indeed, having once adopted a strictly epistemological approach (i.e. that of giving an inventory of mental data, not of some unknown external reality), he must do so if he is to avoid a vicious circle—by an intrinsic quality of impressions that is not shared by ideas, namely force and liveliness. The distinction is, as Hume himself notes, unsatisfactory; images seen in a hallucination or in the dreams of delirium may be far more "forceful" and "lively" than any sense-experience.

Next he establishes that every simple idea that we have is a copy of a simple impression and that, while we may form complex ideas which do not copy any impression, these are built up from simple ideas which are copies of impressions. Finally he proves that the impressions are temporally prior to the ideas which resemble them: first, by the simple fact of observation that they come earlier in time; and, secondly, by the argument that, while we may have impressions without subsequently having any resembling idea, we never have a (simple) idea without having previously had a resembling impression. This is Hume's statement of the empiricist thesis. It is a piece of descriptive psychology: all complex ideas are built up of simple ideas; all simple ideas are copies of previously experienced simple impressions; thus all our ideas are ultimately derived from impressions. It is characteristic of the genetic approach of the time that Hume should prove not (what would seem to be required) that sense experience and introspection are logically necessary for the existence of our ideas, but rather that they are temporally prior.

The famous case of the intermediate shade of blue—where, contrary to this doctrine, I can imagine a new shade (i.e., one not previously given in sense experience) if the two shades adjacent to it in a continuous scale of colours have been seen by me—is a symptom of the weakness both of Hume's atomistic sensationalism and more generally of the whole psychological and genetic approach to philosophy.

Hume's treatment of philosophy as if it were a none too precise natural science, the results of which are established by observation and induction, is very noticeable in [Book I, "Of the Understanding," Part I, "Of Ideas, Their Origin, Composition, Connexion and Abstraction."] This is, no doubt, why he is so unconcerned at the exception to his general law, and also about the unsatisfactoriness of distinguishing impressions from ideas by the criterion of "liveliness." He does not expect to be able to prove his generalizations to be irrefutably true as one proves a theorem in mathematics. The world is a rich amalgam, not a Cartesian system; it has no precise frontiers; the lines we draw over it must be our own invention: propositions about it cannot be expected to be more than correct-on-the-whole. (pp. 165-67)

[Hume], in common with all other pre-Kantian empiricists, confounds logic with genetic psychology, and distinguishes a priori from other truths by a supposed psychological fact about the way in which we come to know them.

He correctly places the propositions of arithmetic and algebra amongst a priori truths, giving as his reason that these are strictly deduced from intuitively known truths. What intuition is, is left obscure.

In the *Treatise,* Hume does not regard geometry as a priori. The matter is discussed at length in Part II, where he [concludes that] . . . the steps of deductive reasoning by which we prove a theorem from the axioms of geometry are indeed infallible; but the axioms, themselves being "drawn from the appearances of things," are not, particularly because we have not (as we have in arithmetic and algebra for numbers) a precise standard of equality for extension in space. Nevertheless, geometry is much superior to the rest of our empirical knowledge because these axioms, though not fully certain, "depend on the easiest and least deceitful appearances."

Hume is absolutely correct so far as applied geometry, i.e., geometry regarded as describing the properties of actual objects in space, is concerned. We have no absolutely precise criterion of equality, say, of length in two real lines; indeed it is doubtful whether it makes sense to talk of absolute equality without reference to measuring instruments and their degrees of error. Pure geometry, however, is not a description of empirical properties of space; it has nothing to do with the behavior of foot rules, surveyor's chains or theodolites. It is a system of purely abstract relations—a logical pattern applicable to a range of utterly heterogeneous subject matter, as is shown by the fact that "interpretations" (i.e. uses or applications) other than the spatial can be found for it. In an obscure passage in Hume's

later work *The Enquiry into Human Understanding* there is a hint that he realized this distinction, and was prepared to assign pure geometry where it belongs, namely to the region of the a priori.

Hume's analysis of causation, and his consequent posing of the problem of induction, is his most important, as it is his most celebrated, contribution to the theory of knowledge. It occupies almost the whole of the long Part III of the *Treatise*. Kant's stupendous effort to deal with its consequences inaugurated modern philosophy. The failure to provide an answer to Hume's problem (attempts to do so have filled many volumes) has been called a scandal to philosophy.

Hume begins by stressing the importance of the relation of cause and effect. It is the only relation that enables us to reason to the existence of any object, or the occurrence of any event, beyond our present immediate impressions; but for it, we should have no ground for believing in anything beyond our own present immediate experience. He then proceeds to examine a single instance of cause and effect. The example which he uses, and which we may as well keep in mind, is that of one billiard ball striking another and thereby causing the second ball to move. In such a case, where we say that an event A has caused an event B, what do we mean? In the first place, says Hume, that A and B were spatially contiguous; secondly, that A occurred immediately before B. But these, though necessary, are not sufficient, conditions of causation; obviously we do not say of every pair of spatially contiguous events of which one occurs immediately before the other that the one is the cause of the other. If you touch a table with your finger and immediately after feel a pain in it, you do not assume that the first event is necessarily the cause of the second, which might well have occurred without it. A third condition must be fulfilled: there must be a necessary connection.

Having analyzed the idea of causation into its component ideas, those of contiguity, priority in time, and necessary connection, Hume devotes the rest of Part III to an investigation of the most obscure and by far the most important of the three, the idea of necessary connection.

As always, when an obscure idea is being clarified, Hume's investigation is dominated by the genetic question: "From what impression is the idea derived?" The argument is complex and pursues a sinuous course, as Hume "beats about all the neighbouring fields." Accordingly it seems to me best to give a summary of it in modern language.

Let us consider a particular instance of "A causes B." First, says Hume, the connection is not one of logical entailment: for "There is no object which implies the existence of any other." Hume tends to substitute a psychological criterion for logical entailment, and asks whether we can conceive of an A not followed by a B; but this is not the point he means to make: whether or not A and B are psychologically distinct (this may differ from one individual to another), they either are or are not so used that the proposition "An A has occurred not immediately followed by a B" is self-contradictory. If it is not, then what makes us think that it states a *necessary* relation? Now, no doubt, we do sometimes utter propositions of the form "A causes B" where the contradictory of "A causes B" is self-contradictory, i.e., where the proposition "A causes B" is analytic; but this is neither the most frequent nor the historically basic use of the word "cause." And, of course if all our causal propositions were analytic in this way, and followed from definitions and the like, then, taken as a whole, tracing connections between them would become a sort of lexico-graphical game like exchanging counters for each other according to fixed rules; and such games give us no information about the world. Hence Hume's point remains: there are many, and those the most important, causal propositions where the connexion between A and B is *not* logical.

But if the connection is not logical, then it must be empirical. But, as Hume emphasizes, there is nothing observable in any one instance except the mere sequence of events. The one billiard ball rolls up to the other, the two are in contact, the second moves on; there is nothing observable here that can be called a necessary connection. And to talk of one event being "produced" by the other is merely to coin a synonym for being "caused"—the very matter under discussion; nor do such other words as "power," "efficacy," "creation," "agency," etc., advance the inquiry. (It may be observed that words like "force," as used in mechanics, do not denote *unobservable* links between objects; they are shorthand ways of referring to the observed or observable regularities of *observed* phenomena. The anthropomorphic overtones of such terms may indeed be misleading, and have led to various forms of the "pathetic fallacy," but they are not relevant to mechanics.) In a word, the idea of a non-logical necessary connection—a link between two events at one observable and necessary—is unintelligible.

Hume goes on to note a third characteristic which distinguishes the cases of spatial contiguity and temporal succession where we call the sequence causal, from those where we do not: in the former the sequence is *regular,* i.e., has often been observed to occur and *never* been observed to fail. This Hume calls "constant conjunction." According to Hume this is not, of course, a "real," external, necessary connection between events—an item in the world; but it provides the key to the psychological explanation of why we think of some events as necessarily connected, although this thought turns out to embody an illusion. (Today we should, if we accepted Hume's analysis of causation, be more inclined to say that constant conjunction, together with contiguity and temporal succession, constituted the criterion for the correct use of the word "cause".) Hume's explanation is this: When events of type A have been constantly observed without fail to be conjoined with events of type B, a habitual association is set up in the imgination so that whenever we observe a new A, the idea of a B arises in the mind with an overwhelming force, this force being itself an introspectively observable feeling. This feeling of force we now illegitimately project into the external world, and imagine a "force" or "power" as pushing and pulling events or objects in the world. As for the psychological machinery—irresistible association, liability to externalize inner compulsions which themselves seem, prima facie, forms of causation, psychological rather than physical, Hume does not analyze these concepts. If we are to escape a vicious circle whereby external causation is explained away by internal causation, we must assume that Hume regards such processes as themselves merely regularities, themselves observable, "brute facts,"—the ultimate terminus at which enquiry must, of necessity, stop.

Hume's analysis of our use of the word "cause" is inadequate also in other ways. We do not use the word "cause" in the description of every regularity to be found in the world; for example, in statements of the laws of astronomy or modern physics, the word "cause" may never appear. It is only in cases which fulfill certain specifiable conditions that we feel inclined to talk of one event as causing another. Moreover, observed constant conjunction is not always the main ground

for detecting "causal influence"—it is often reinforced and overshadowed by our deductions from accepted scientific theories; and these theories are often accepted not on the basis of regularities alone. Finally Hume's psychological explanation of the illusion of "real" binding connections in the world is certainly not the whole truth. Such an idea seems traceable no less to animistic projections on to the inanimate world, e.g., the sensation of effort of will, and, perhaps most of all, of musuclar effort.

But this criticism does not detract from the crucial importance of Hume's discovery, which consists in the uncovering of the problem of induction. If all our general statements about the world were causal (and they are not), and if the word "cause" stood for some metaphysically binding cement between events, such that the one not merely never did, but *could not,* happen without the other in any circumstances, there would be no problem of induction. Our general statements would be "metaphysically" guaranteed to the hilt for unobserved as for observed cases. But Hume shows that the word "cause" does not stand for any such impalpable entity, and thus reveals to the view a hitherto largely unnoticed problem, namely that we seem to claim to know, yet never in principle do know for certain, that any generalization based upon observed instances of phenomena remains true when extrapolated to cover unobserved instances, whether in the past or the future.

If we are to know facts which we do not observe with a certainty resembling that of our deductive—say mathematical—knowledge; if the statements of physics are to be impregnable like those of, say, geometry, what we need is an absolute guarantee for the principle of induction "that unobserved instances resemble observed instances." Hume rightly concludes that we cannot obtain this guarantee anywhere—that we neither know, nor can know, any principle which makes induction as certain as deduction. Nor—and here he shows more perspicacity than many of his successors in this field—can we without circularity show such a principle to be even probable: "probability is founded on the presumption of a resemblance betwixt those objects of which we have had experience and those of which we have had none; and therefore it is impossible this presumption can arise from probability." Probability rests on the unbolsterable principle of induction, and cannot itself be used to bolster it up. This is the basis of the notorious "skepticism" of Hume and later philosophers. This attitude has either been accepted with pessimistic resignation or else attacked as craven or fallacious. Yet it is difficult to see good reason for either attitude: for the skepticism in question is skeptical only of the possibility of turning induction into a species of precisely what it is not—deduction; and this is not a rational ambition. Hume himself is largely to blame: in common with his contemporaries, he regarded deduction as the only authentic form of true reasoning; and therefore attributed our inferences from cause to effect to the "imagination," the source of irrational processes. If we are to be wholly rational we must have a "justificaton" of induction. But what could "justify" it? The search for a guarantee is a demand for a world in which events or objects are linked by "objective" necessary connections; if Hume has shown anything he has shown that this notion is not intelligible, and rests on a confusion of logical machinery with the facts of experience, a wish that the symbols of logic or mathematics or grammar should possess objective counterparts. This craving for a metaphysical system is one of the most obsessive of all the fantasies which has dominated human minds. (pp. 184-90)

Hume begins his contribution to the philosophical question of the self with an attack on the notion of self as substance, the doctrine, held for example by Descartes and Leibniz and their followers, that there exists a single unitary soul-substance persisting always the same through time, underlying all our "impressions and ideas" and in which these latter "inhere"—bearing, in fact, the same sort of relation to our impressions and ideas as does Locke's material substratum to the qualities of bodies. Against this time-honored view Hume argues as follows:

(1) What is *meant* by the expressions "substance" and "inhesion"? These expressions have never been satisfactorily explained.

(2) How can we find out anything about this substance? We cannot have an impression of it. For an impression could only be an impression of the substance by resembling it. But the very starting point of those who believe that the soul is a substance is that impressions are utterly unlike substances, and it is for this reason that impressions require a substance in which to "inhere." (It will be remembered that Berkeley, who believed in a substantive soul, declared that we have no "*idea*" of it, but only a "relative notion.")

(3) Argument (2) is logical, being designed to show the logical impossibility of our having an impression of a substance called soul. Hume reinforces this with an empirical argument, an appeal to experience. In Chapter V he taunts the substance theorists: "Is it [the impression of the soul-substance] pleasant or painful or indifferent? Does it attend us at all times or only at intervals?" and so on. In Chapter VI he makes a more formidable point: he says that when we look within we never in fact come upon any such ideas as that of a single unitary self, continuing the same throughout our lives. On the contrary, we only meet, as always, with some *particular* perception or other or a cluster of them; and these numerous particular perceptions "succeed each other with an inconceivable rapidity."

(4) It was argued by the old metaphysicians that only substances are (logically) capable of "existing by themselves" and therefore there must be a soul-substance in which impressions inhere. To this Hume replies that, since he can conceive of impressions "existing by themselves," it must be logically possible that they should so exist; so that on this definition of substance, impressions themselves turn out to be substances, and certainly have no need of a further substance to prop them up.

He concludes that "the question concerning the substance of the soul is wholly unintelligible." He can find no such entity: only collections of data, a stream—or several parallel streams—of thoughts, images, feelings, perceptions, loosely connected. The mind is nothing but "a bundle or collection of different perceptions." And so he is left with the problem of explaining what it is that makes us "collect together" certain perceptions and not others as the history of any one single mind. Following his treatment of the notion of material things, he similarly disperses minds or selves. And where we should today be inclined to say that Hume was trying to establish the criterion for correctly describing cerain ideas as belonging to the mental history of a particular person, he regards himself as providing a psychological explanation for our tendency fictitiously to ascribe identity to a set of wholly discrete impressions and ideas, since we have a "natural propension . . . to imagine that simplicity and identity" which in reality does not exist. (pp. 238-39)

[Absolute] identity, in the logical or mathematical sense, has no relevance to the identification of things or persons. It cannot have, for the good empirical reason that we do often utter such statements as: "The Mr. Jones I saw yesterday is the same (person) as the Mr. Jones I knew in London five years ago," or "The table on which I am now writing is the same (table) as the one that has been in my study for fifteen years," or "The chestnut tree in the square is the same (tree) as has been there for two hundred years." And we call some of these statements *true* and others *false*. It follows that we have criteria for the correct use of such statements. In no empirical case will these criteria amount to the absolute identity of Hume; and in different empirical cases (different sorts of objects) the criteria are, as a matter of fact, of different kinds and of different degrees of elasticity and vagueness. Thus where Hume supposes that he is overthrowing the metaphysics of substance in favor of the (equally indemonstrable) metaphysics of sense data, and is, in addition, giving a psychological explanation of our fictitious ascription of (metaphysical) identity to non-identical (empirical) objects of various sorts, he is in fact performing the more useful, in appearance less exciting, task of giving the criteria for the correct use of the expression "the same as," applied to different classes of objects.

Hume explains the "fictitious ascription of identity" as being due to the imagination, which passes so smoothly over the ideas of the separate perceptions that it comes to think of them as not a rain of discrete data, but rather a single "uninterrupted and invariable" object. Finally to justify itself, as it were, it "feigns" some soul or self or substance, which really would, if it existed, be a single unchanging object. As usual, the principles of association by which the imagination is led to this deceptively smooth transition are resemblance, contiguity, and causation, though, in this case, Hume says, contiguity plays little part.

Hume's own constructive "theory of the self" is not satisfactory, as he himself realizes. . . . In particular, he is in some confusion as to whether memory *produces* or *discovers* personal identity, i.e., whether or not some memory relation between the discrete impressions and ideas constitutes the meaning or part of the meaning of the expression "the same as" as applied to persons, or whether, rather, it is by means of memory that we find out that several discrete impressions and ideas "belong" to the history of the "same" person. It is not clear that these two questions are as distinct as Hume thought them. Be that as it may, he has failed to give us a satisfactory account of what it is in a set of impressions and ideas that makes it the sort of "bundle" that we call the history of a single person and not of several persons at once, or of none. (pp. 239-41)

Two other important and neglected doctrines of Hume's should be noticed. . . . (p. 243)

(1) That an object may exist, and yet be nowhere. Hume himself makes but a poor use of this dictum. He tries to show by means of it that our idea that, e.g., the taste of an olive is spatially conjoined with the actual extended body, the olive, must be an illusion, since the taste, being a perception, cannot properly be said to be anywhere in space. But he is forgetting, that on his view, the extension, bulk, etc., of the olive are no more and no less our perceptions than is the taste, and that he has not explained what he means by "somewhere in space." However, despite the fact that Hume makes use of the dictum only to land himself in inconsistency, it is, as so often with his *aperçus*, of first-rate importance. It is logically absurd to talk of a mind (and a fortiori an idea "in" a mind) being *some-*

where. Spatial predicates do not apply to minds or ideas. And, with this discovery, Hume liberates us from the Cartesian picture, shared to some extent by Locke, of the mind literally situated within the brain, a picture according to which, just as light rays in a mechanical way produce physical changes in the eyes, the optic nerves and finally the brain, so—the last link in the causal chain—the brain in a quasi-mechanical way produces ideas in the mind.

(2) It had been held by, e.g., certain Cartesians, that matter and motion on the one hand and ideas on the other are so different in kind that it is impossible that either should leap over the gulf to "cause" the other. Hume points out that once we realize that cause is nothing but regularity, "constant conjunction," there can be no a priori reason why anything should not cause anything else. The importance of his principle that there are no impassable "natural" barriers between kinds of things or events, and that no causal connections between any sorts of events can ever be ruled out a priori, remains worthy of notice even in the twentieth century. (pp. 243-44)

> Isaiah Berlin, *"David Hume," in his* The Age of Enlightenment: The Eighteenth Century Philosophers, *edited by Isaiah Berlin, Houghton Mifflin Company, 1956, pp. 162-260.*

F. L. LUCAS   (essay date 1959)

[*Lucas was an English man of letters who is best known as the editor of John Webster's works and as a literary critic. In addition to his position as poetry critic of the* New Statesman, *he wrote several noteworthy works, including* Authors, Dead and Living *(1926) and* The Decline and Fall of the Romantic Ideal *(1936). Lucas wrote extensively on classical Greek literature, and his poetic ideal stressed, according to John Sparrow, "the proper appreciation of the relation between form and matter, feeling and its artistic expression, which inspired alike the poetry and the criticism of the Greeks." Noted for what another critic termed the "eighteenth-century" qualities of the "bluff common sense and man-of-the-world manners" in his criticism, Lucas was antagonistic to modernist trends in poetry and criticism, a position which frequently placed him at odds with his scholarly adversary and fellow Cambridge don, F. R. Leavis. In the following excerpt, Lucas investigates Hume's skepticism and comments on his ethics, politics, and historical viewpoint.*]

Imagine Dr Johnson kicking a large, grey stone to refute Berkeley. He has a *feeling,* an impression of what he calls his foot coming in contact with what he calls a stone—a thing appearing to have certain qualities such as size, greyness, and hardness. Such impressions Hume calls 'impressions of sensation'.

Suppose Dr Johnson *thinks* of the episode in bed that night. The 'impressions of sensation' are no longer present to him; but, from them, he still has 'ideas' of the situation. Suppose he also has a *feeling* that he would rather not do it again, because it hurt his toe; this, in Hume's terminology, would be an 'impression of reflexion'.

But both 'ideas', and 'impressions of reflexion', follow on original 'impressions of sensation'. For Hume, this sequence is invariable.

True, one may have an 'idea' of the Heavenly Jerusalem, paved with gold and walled with precious stones, without ever having had any such 'impression of sensation'; but this imaginary vision is compounded from actual impressions, in past experience, of cities, gold, and precious stones. Without having seen a horse one could never conceive a centaur. Even the

Deity of many popular conceptions is a compound concept, anthropomorphic in mind, and often in body too, with certain valued human qualities magnified *ad infinitum.*

In short, Hume does not believe in innate ideas.

But even the evidence of the senses about any external reality remains inadequate and contradictory. Seeing is *not* believing. Locke had maintained that bodies really possessed in themselves 'primary qualities'—solidity, extension, figure, motion, or rest; although 'secondary qualities'—'colours, tastes, smells, sounds, etc.'—were only in the percipient.

But Hume, following Berkeley, argued that we had no more logical grounds for belief in the objective existence of primary qualities than of secondary. Dr Johnson was merely *seeming* to kick what *seemed* a solid stone with what *seemed* a solid foot. For aught we know, all our perceptions are insubstantial pageants, as shadowy as Satan's vision of Death—

> What seem'd his head
> The likeness of a Kingly Crown had on.

Further, the term 'impression' suggests something that presses. But we can never know what it is that causes our 'impressions of sensation'. What, indeed, do we mean by 'cause'? Dr Johnson, if the stone hurt his toe, thought that the impact 'caused' the pain. But all he really knew was that (A) the impression of impact was followed by (B) the impression of pain. We can never see any intrinsic reason why A should 'cause' B—why, for example, violent impacts are usually painful. That belief is simply based on custom or experience. Adam could acquire it only by experience; and every infant does acquire it only by experience.

And, again, if we expect that A, having always 'caused' B, will continue to 'cause' it, this too is only because custom or experience is followed by a belief in the uniformity of natural laws. Yet why should natural law be assumed *always* uniform? No doubt, we have always observed unimpeded apples to fall downwards; but we cannot *know* for certain that the next apple we see will not rocket upwards. 'Let the course of things be allowed hitherto ever so regular, that alone, without some new argument or inference, proves not that for the future it will continue so.'

But if causation is not established as a certainty, then we can be absolutely sure of nothing except arithmetic and algebra (and, to a lesser degree, of geometry; for geometry involves certain axioms). 'All the objects of human reason or inquiry may naturally be divided into two kinds, to wit, *Relations of Ideas,* and *Matters of Fact.* Of the first kind are the sciences of Geometry, Algebra, and Arithmetic.' But 'all reasonings concerning matters of fact seem to be founded on the relation of *Cause and Effect.*'

We only believe, for example, in the existence of Julius Caesar because we believe that he caused certain impressions and ideas in his contemporaries, which caused them to make certain records in writing and sculpture; which caused others in turn to copy them; which, by a long chain of similar causation, causes certain impressions and ideas in ourselves. Indeed we can only believe in the objective existence of the pikestaff plain before our noses if we believe that there is some external object there which *causes* our impression of it.

I will to move my little finger; and I believe this *causes* it to move. But if I have had a stroke, it may not move. And even if it does move, I can only say that certain changes in my nerves and muscles appear to follow my volition, and to be followed in turn by the appearance of movement in what appears to be my finger.

One cannot even be certain of the existence of what is called one's 'self'. 'For my part, when I enter most intimately into what I call *myself*, I always stumble on some particular perception or other, of heat or cold, light or shade, love or hatred, pain or pleasure. I never can catch *myself* at any time without a perception, and never can observe anything but the perception.' In fact, we seem to be 'nothing but a bundle or collection of different perceptions, which succeed each other with an inconceivable rapidity'.

> We are such stuffe
> As dreames are made on.

Dr Johnson, in fine, is now reduced to saying, if he would speak with certainty—(though he would doubtless have perished sooner than agree)—'What *seemed* myself *seemed* to kick what *seemed* a stone with what *seemed* my foot.'

Having thus undermined the certainty of external reality, of causation, and even of the self, leaving nothing but 'impressions' and 'ideas', and pure mathematics, Hume had reached a position of considerable scepticism. And yet, in the words of Russell [see excerpt dated 1945], these sceptical conclusions, 'are equally difficult to refute and to accept. The result was a challenge to philosophers, which, in my opinion, has still not been adequately met.' This seems a sufficiently remarkable achievement for a young man only in his twenties, over two hundred years ago.

So, by laborious reasoning, Hume has reached a complete doubt not unlike what Montaigne had arrived at by nonchalant commonsense. One may picture them together in that tower at Montaigne whose rafters were crowded with inscribed mottoes of the sceptics. . . . (pp. 30-4)

[Hume] has, I take it, two quite different standpoints; first, in logical theory, an extreme scepticism; second, for practice, a 'mitigated' scepticism, which provisionally assumes, as a working hypothesis, the truth of causation and natural laws, though these cannot be proved.

And why not? It works very well to act *as if* such things were true; and it does not work at all well to act *as if* they were not. I do not see why Hume should be accused of inconsistency, because, having suspended his judgement on the ultimate facts, he refused to suspend all thought and action in the practical world of appearances.

'Strictly logical reasoning,' he might have answered, 'leads us only into chaos—into Cimmerian darkness and Serbonian bogs. Vain to build metaphysical structures on that quaking mire. Doubt swallows the phenomenal world—causation and natural law—even the human self. Uncertainty of uncertainties, all is uncertainty. Man finds himself like an osprey that has clawed a fish too large for it, and is dragged down by its quarry to sunless and suffocating abysses; perforce he must let go and return to the surface. Superficial it may be: but there only can he breathe. To demand total certainty, I have argued, is to find total scepticism. You may think my arguments a mere battle with shadows. But in *my* day men thought they could *prove* things like the existence of God. It was against such dogmatisms that I fought; not, it seems, wholly in vain.

'And so in this world of Maya—of illusion—let us go our ways content with the flickering lantern of "mitigated scepticism". Let us provisionally assume causation to be true, things and people to be real. We shall find that even this "mitigated scepticism" leads us to new scepticisms about such matters as ethics or aesthetics; but also to some probabilities.'

Thus, having accepted the existence of causes as a working hypothesis, Hume now proceeds to work it hard. And so, paradoxically enough, this thinker who had previously questioned all causation, now argues from it against the freedom of the will. A man is, of course, often free to do what he wills; but he is not free to will what his will shall be; his impulses are as much determined as the colour of his eyes. So Freud also was to conclude. Try as one may even to think of a number at random, one's choice seems determined by subconscious causes.

Similarly, if causation be supposed to exist, miracles become as dubious as the freedom of the will. A miracle is an infraction of the seeming uniformity of natural laws. Belief in this uniformity is based on infinite numbers of observations. But that men should deceive, or be deceived, in their testimony is certainly not contrary to natural law—indeed it is constantly occurring. Therefore it is not reasonable to believe any testimony that a miracle occurred, unless the falsehood of that testimony would be a miracle greater still.

So too with the idea of a perfectly wise and just Providence. It has often been argued that the Universe is so like an artefact as to imply an artificer. But, first, says Hume, this analogy is weak. We have small experience of creations of Universes. Secondly, even if the analogy be admitted, it is still not reasonable to attribute to any cause more qualities than are implied by its effect. Now the world seems far from perfect in its working, or in its justice; there is therefore no rational ground for arguing greater perfections in its First Cause, than would suffice to produce so imperfect a work. A faulty product suggests a faulty workman.

Similar doubts attend the immortality of the soul. . . . He argues, for a number of reasons, against the soul's survival; though, as so often, he ends with the ironic profession that reason must bow to faith and revelation. 'Nothing could set in a fuller light the infinite obligations which mankind have to Divine revelation; since we find that no other medium could ascertain this great and important truth.'

I own that I find these perfunctory genuflexions of Hume's, like Voltaire's, a little tedious. I do not see that they could shield him much from the fury of the orthodox; especially as he elsewhere expresses himself with what, for that period, seems shattering audacity. If, on the other hand, all this art had not a precautionary purpose, I do not much like it for its own sake.

Having grown, however, this formidable hedge of sceptical thistles for the bafflement of metaphysicians and theologians, Hume turned to cultivate a harvest of his own in fields less rocky and forbidding—ethics, politics, literature, history. It seems to me part of his shrewdness that, two centuries ago, he already realized the paramount importance of psychology. 'Human nature is the only science of man; and yet has been hitherto the most neglected.' Even in his philosophical titles this sound preoccupation appears—*A Treatise of Human Nature*—*An Enquiry concerning Human Understanding*. Unluckily for him, psychology was, as yet, hardly born. Indeed, psychology without an understanding of the Unconscious was foredoomed to be as limited as geography before Copernicus, Columbus, and Magellan. Hume had indeed shown that reason played a far smaller part than supposed, in our notions of the external world; but even he could not realize, also, how much less than supposed was the part played by conscious reason in our own internal world of sensation, emotion, and thought.

True, he saw through the common idea of the eighteenth century (which still remains a too common idea of ours about the eighteenth century) that reason conquers passion. When, he argues, such a conquest seems to occur, what really happens is that, aided by reason, a *calmer,* but more steadfast desire overcomes a more violent one. The real conflict within us is a civil war between antagonistic *desires.* (pp. 38-41)

[Although] Hume, not knowing the Unconscious, could not fully realize how fantastically our desires, impulses, and emotions may fool our reason, and even our senses, still one should recall his comment on popular religions through the ages: 'You will scarcely be persuaded that they are anything but sick men's dreams: Or perhaps will regard them more as the playsome whimsies of monkeys in human shape, than the serious positive dogmatical asseverations of a being who dignifies himself with the name of rational.' Anyway, if in ethics Hume tended, perhaps, to be a little *too* rational, he was to receive a shrewd lesson from Rousseau, when that sick mind distorted his warmest kindness into the blackest treachery.

What, then, of ethics? What makes actions or qualities seem to us meritorious or the reverse? Hume, as one would expect, does not believe in absolute moral goods and evils. Ethics is

Hume's bookplate.

based, for him, partly on reason, which judges consequences; partly on feeling—above all, the feeling of *sympathy.* Men, one might put it, are moral because they are gregarious. A herd of cattle that spent all their days in butting and trampling one another would have an existence both nasty and short.

What we regard as personal merits, says Hume, are qualities agreeable or useful to their possessor, or else agreeable or useful to those associated with him. These are the qualities that win our approbation. And the ultimate *sanctions* of ethics, though not always the conscious motives or ends, are pleasure and pain.

There was a general tendency in the eighteenth century—Montesquieu and Herder are wise exceptions—to underestimate the diversities of human thought and feeling from age to age, and from land to land. This, for example, is one of the defects of Hume's or Gibbon's history then, as of Shaw's historic plays since; they are too prone to picture the people of the past as differing from us merely in their clothes and their superficial conventions. Hume himself . . . tends to underestimate the diversity and relativity of aesthetic tastes. But in ethics at least he is clear enough about the relativity of morals. *A Dialogue* amusingly and convincingly brings out how an honest and respectable citizen of fifth-century Athens would seem in eighteenth-century Paris an absurd and criminal monster; and how an *honnête homme* from eighteenth-century Paris would have seemed no less odious to fifth-century Athens. All the same, he continues, these ethical differences can be largely explained by different social conditions and needs; whereas such fundamentally valuable qualities as wisdom, courage, kindness were honoured then as now. (pp. 43-4)

One of Hume's most recent expounders has objected to his dispraise of humility. But by humility Hume meant a sense of inferiority towards those one meets. He does not mean Newton's sense of human insignificance before the Universe. Now if a man really feels constantly inferior to those he meets, his state seems to me unpleasant and unhealthy; and, if he does not really feel so, why pretend? Modesty forms part of courtesy; but that is quite another story. The tale of the pious Jesuit Barcena whose humility was such that he gave up his chair even to the devil, when that personage honoured his cell with a visit, is, I admit, charming; but, for me, it is the charm of a quaint absurdity. If one took it seriously, I suspect that the holy man was guilty both of heresy, and of a kind of inverted arrogance, in supposing that his iniquity surpassed even Satan's. But, of course, if he had given up his chair on the principle—'All possible politeness even to the worst of enemies', in that case the holy man would have my full admiration.

For Hume, then, the motive force of moral action springs from a sense of human sympathy; which it is socially desirable, and often pleasant, to obey. (Perhaps it would be truer to say that it often proves painful to disobey. The pains of a bad conscience are, I think, a much more frequent and cogent influence than the pleasures of a good one—except for prigs.) Hume also recognizes the reinforcing effect, here, of moral training in early years. But, living when he did, he could not know the full importance of that early environment—how it can build up, from the influence of those respected, admired, or revered in childhood, a kind of shadowy monitor, the superego; not wholly conscious and, indeed, partly unconscious; a power that can punish transgressions not only by mental conflicts and self-frustrations, but even by physical maladies; so that, for example, young women who flout their upbringing by setting out to imitate Ninon de l'Enclos, can thwart themselves by frigidity; or men who have gained forbidden successes, can punish themselves by illness or 'accidents'. Nemesis and the Erinyes dwell often within ourselves.

But, with these provisos, Hume's ethics seem to me sound. (pp. 45-6)

In politics, as one would expect, Hume remained a man of the centre, and was attacked by both sides accordingly; just as Montaigne became, in his own phrase, a Guelf for the Ghibellines, and a Ghibelline for the Guelfs. True to his family tradition, Hume regarded the revolution of 1688 as justified, and the Hanoverian succession as a blessing. 'So long and so glorious a period no nation almost can boast of. Nor is there another instance in the whole history of mankind, that so many millions of people have, during such a space of time, been held together, in a manner so free, so rational, and so suitable to the dignity of human nature.' The difference between sensible men of both parties has really, he thinks, been far slighter than it seemed.

> A Tory, therefore, since the Revolution, may be defined in a few words, to be *a lover of monarchy, though without abandoning liberty; and a partisan of the family of Stuart:* As a Whig may be defined to be *a lover of liberty, though without renouncing monarchy; and a friend to the settlement in the Protestant line.*

This sounds sane enough.

Tory though Hume might be called, there is no nonsense in him about St Charles the Martyr, or the beauties of passive obedience. On the other hand, he rejected as mythical the Whig theory of an original social contract; he disliked the 'fanaticism' of the Puritans, if possible, even more than the 'superstition' of Laud. And he was no democrat; he cared far more for freedom of thought and speech than for the 'liberty' of John Wilkes and his 'factious Barbarians'. 'So much Liberty,' Hume thought in 1769, 'is incompatible with human society. And it will be happy, if we can escape from it without falling into a military Government, such as Algiers or Tunis.'

In fine, he seems to me a practical and utilitarian psychologist, opposed both to political legalism and to political mysticism; too sceptical to be impressed by talk either of the natural rights of men, or of the divine right of kings; sharing Burke's distrust of 'violent innovations', but without the later Burke's tendency to vapour about 'divine tactics'. (pp. 53-4)

No doubt Hume's history has failed to endure monumentally like Gibbon's. It is rare for the brilliant to remain laborious, or for the laborious to remain brilliant. Razors are bad for cutting rocks. The plump Scots philosopher was probably too indolent, too unwilling to stir from his sofa for a piece of research, too philosophically inclined to doubt whether such minutiae as torment modern scholars, really matter. In Hume, for example, one is somewhat startled to read, of fourteenth-century France and England, that 'the government of the two kingdoms was at that time pretty much alike'. Again, as already noted, both Hume and Gibbon suffered from that strange eighteenth-century obsession with human uniformity from China to Peru. 'Nor are the earth, water, and other elements, examined by Aristotle and Hippocrates, more like those which at present lie under our observation, than the men, described by Polybius and Tacitus, are to those who now govern the world.' With the classical world that seems not wholly untrue. But this tendency of Hume's grew more distorting the further he went back into the medieval twilight. Actually, the men

described by Gregory of Tours or Matthew of Paris seem to me often as incomprehensibly different from ourselves, as if they came from another planet. (pp. 55-6)

[As Hume] grew older, he did make alterations towards the Tory side. But not exclusively towards that side. Even in its final form his account of the seventeenth century, the most contentious period he treated, seems to me very fairly balanced. If Hume grew somewhat more Tory, that tendency is natural enough with age; and this is not simply because men grow more timid, and enfeebled swimmers welcome with less exhilaration the prospects of a deluge. There is also the factor that an observant person tends, the longer he lives, to grow more and more convinced of the folly and hysteria of men, the obscurity and complexity of things. Most revolutionaries are minds not fully adult. A few revolutions have been both necessary and beneficial, like the English Revolution of 1688. Some have been beneficial, though not really necessary, like the American Revolution of 1775. (Only a minority wanted it, and it could have been won without any war by merely waiting a generation or two.) But most revolutions seem to me to have cost an extortionate amount of needless suffering. Well might Hume distrust them. (p. 57)

> *F. L. Lucas, "David Hume," in his* The Art of Living, Four Eighteenth-Century Minds: Hume, Horace Walpole, Burke, Benjamin Franklin, *Cassell, 1959, pp. 1-78.*

RUSSELL KIRK (essay date 1961)

[*An American historian, political theorist, novelist, journalist, and lecturer, Kirk is one of America's most eminent conservative intellectuals. His works have provided a major impetus to the conservative revival that has developed since the 1950s. The* Conservative Mind (1953), *one of Kirk's early books, describes convervatism as a living body of ideas "struggling toward ascendancy in the United States"; in it Kirk traces the roots and canons of modern conservative thought to such important predecessors as Edmund Burke, John Adams, and Alexis de Tocqueville. Founder of the conservative quarterlies* Modern Age *and the* University Bookman, *Kirk has long been a trenchant critic of the decline of academic standards in American public schools and universities. His* Decadence and Renewal in the Higher Learning (1978), *in particular, is a forceful denunciation of the "academic barbarism" which he states has replaced the traditional goals of higher education—wisdom and virtue—with the fallacious ones of "utilitarian efficiency" and innovative forms of education. The result, in Kirk's view, is that "the higher learning in America is a disgrace." Kirk's detractors have sometimes been skeptical of the charges he levels against liberal ideas and programs, accusing him of a simplistic partisanship. His admirers, on the other hand, point to the alleged failure of liberal precepts—in particular those applied in the universities—as evidence in support of Kirk's ideas and criticism. In the following excerpt, Kirk analyzes Hume's criticism of reason and comments on the immediate and long-range influence of his philosophy.*]

The great philosophical systems are perennial. Hume was in the line of the Greek Sceptics, or the medieval Nominalists: his pleasure was to puncture balloons. The biggest balloon that came his way was John Locke, whom he undoes thoroughly in [*An Enquiry concerning Human Understanding.*] Reason with a Roman R, pure rationality as the guide to morals and politics, dominated the first half of the eighteenth century, and Locke was the great champion and exponent of this system. Pure Reason never recovered from Hume's needleprick, and Kant carried on Hume's criticism; but philosophical systems last a long while, in the public consciousness, long after they have been mortally wounded, so that journalists like Tom Paine were crying up the Age of Reason well into the nineteenth century, and Reason has its worshippers still.

"Religion is irrational, theism is permissible only in utter attenuation: oh for a revelation! but not, if you please, the one we are supposed to have had already." So Basil Willey sums up Hume's theology. The thread of Hume's discourse runs thus. Locke did not understand the nature of innate ideas. They do exist; they form, indeed, our human nature, which we know through the study of history; and it is these innate ideas, or impressions, which guide us through life. The knowledge we pick up in life is fragmentary, and necessarily imperfect because of the imperfection of our senses; these are vast realms of which we can know nothing; and we do not form our judgements upon the basis of logically-arranged accumulations of experience, but rather attach these experiences to general ideas. Those ideas are produced from "impressions"; but the origin of impressions is inexplicable. We cannot say whether they arise immediately from the object, or are produced by the creative power of the mind, or are derived from God. The imagination, rather than mere experience-knowledge, is the source of whatever wisdom we have. And no one can account for the existence of the imagination in individuals, varying so greatly: it is literally *genius,* though Hume does not say so.

What we learn in this world we learn through custom, repeated experiences, rather than pure Reason. "Our reason never does, nor is it possible that it should upon any supposition, give us an assurance of the continued and distinct existence of body." Education really is the accumulated custom of the race. The ways of society are not the products of reason, but of the customary experience of the species, beginning with small family-groups and growing upward into the state. It is perilous to meddle, on principles of pure rationality, with valuable social institutions that thus are natural developments, not logical schemes. All religion is irrational; it is derived from Revelation and Faith; it cannot be sustained by logical argument, which only betrays Christianity to its enemies. (This was the stand of the Nominalists.) In nature are vast mysteries which we cannot possibly apprehend. There are no metaphysical or supernatural sanctions for morality; reason only reveals a universe in which the great mysterious powers have no regard for human good or evil; no, our morality—which Hume was sedulous to uphold—is obedience to the rules of approbation and disapprobation by our fellows; and the standard of morality is shown to us by the study of history, and its arbiters are men of strong sense and delicate sentiment, whose impressions force themselves upon the wills of their fellow-men.

A moderate scepticism of this sort, Hume declared, is the only real defence of Christianity, morality, and established social institutions. Follow Nature, not a vain illusory Reason; understand the nature of man, and be guided accordingly; we cannot know more; our intellects are puny. "Mankind are so much the same, in all times and places, that history informs us of nothing new or strange in this particular. Its chief use is only to discover the constant and universal prnciples of human nature." This chain of argument is formed with consummate skill and power, and expressed with an urbane good humour. The effect of Hume's books, joined to the general influence of similar reflections by other men, began very promptly to change the climate of opinion among advanced thinkers, so that the *philosophes,* after the middle of the eighteenth century, turned reluctantly away from pure reason and busied themselves with history, political reform, and scholarly concerns that did not aspire to perfect knowledge of universals.

As a congenital Tory, Hume had every desire to preserve the pleasant society of the eighteenth century, of which he was an ornament. He did not desire to alter the established morality of the age, nor to destroy religious faith, nor to make any radical change in social institutions. Revolutionaries of every description, he said, the civil magistrate justly puts on the same footing with common robbers. He was well aware of the inflammatory power of certain concepts, once they have been vulgarized, and said so. "Why rake into those corners of nature, which spread a nuisance all around?" The obsession of *philosophes* with abstract reason, *a priori* systems, and dialectics tends towards this. "Truths which are *pernicious* to society, if any such there are, will yield to errors, which are salutary and *advantageous.*" It is quite possible to reason ourselves out of virtue and social enjoyment. "The passion for philosophy, like that for religion, seems liable to this inconvenience, that, though it aims at the correction of our manners, and extirpation of our vices, it may only serve, by imprudent management, to foster a predominant inclination, and push the mind, with more determined resolution, towards that side which already *draws* too much, by the bias and propensity of the natural temper." Nor had a man ought to let his speculations disturb the even tenor of his ways: Hume himself postponed the publication of his ***Natural History of Religion*** until his death, to spare himself the fury of outraged orthodoxy.

Yet, in the long run, Hume's ideas had their revolutionary consequences. It was sufficient unto his time that the gentleman and the scholar, like Hume himself, should set the standard of taste and morality; their approbation secured the substantial emulation of the mass of men. But when the gentleman and the scholar ceased to fix the tone of life, the fate of morality became in question; transcendent sanction lacking, and deference from the crowd gone, every appetite might be indulged. It was sufficient unto his time that moderate scepticism should chasten the presumption of established churches: those churches seemed very secure indeed, with the mob on their side, so that when Hume died, in 1776, it was found prudent to set a watch by his grave on the Calton Hill for eight days, lest the Edinburgh zealots for religion wreak their vengeance on the sceptic's corpse. But a time would come when faith would go out of the masses, and revelation would be forgotten: and then religion might need the Schoolmen's bulwark of reason.

And though Hume's books undid Locke and the French philosophers of pure rationality, philosophical systems and their refutations work their way only slowly to the congnizance of the great public. By the last decade of the century, Reason was enthroned in Notre Dame, and *a priori* notions were applied to the governance of great states, and the Rights of Man triumphed over custom and prudence. That urbane, leisurely, orderly world of Hume's was submerged in France and much of the rest of Europe; it has been sinking ever since; and what remains of it now is in peril everywhere. Whether human nature, as Hume described it, can endure the assault of modern armed doctrines is now a question ominously debated by the philosophers of our own century.

Two hundred and fifty years after Hume's birth, we live in a society—what with his dislike of all things vulgar—the sage of Ninewells would have despised. And yet our era was of Hume's making, in part. In France, d'Alembert and Turgot were Hume's intimates: the great rationaliser and the great centralizer, the advocates of radical social reform and democracy, who reaped the whirlwind—curious friends for the champion of customary ways and Stuart causes.

At home, Hume found for his disciple Adam Smith, the philosopher of the new industrial and commercial order that would give the quietus to the old rural Scotland of which Hume was patriotically proud. In England, Jeremy Bentham, "the great subversive", took his ethics straight from Hume—Bentham, whose jurisprudence and political utilitarianism led to a domination that would have been more repugnant to Hume than the ascendancy of the Whigs whom he mauled so cavalierly.

It was in 1776, the year of *The Wealth of Nations* and of the Declaration of Independence, that Hume went to his grave on the Calton. In his will he left a sum for the repair of a bridge near Ninewells, specifying that the work must not injure the aspect of a charming old quarry which he had admired for years. Despite all his causticity, to the last Hume stood by ancient usage, prescription, old sights and ways, and refined taste. As the sardonic critic of fashionable delusions, and as the exemplar of scholarly candour, Hume ought to endure. The Whigs, with their abundant preferment to bestow upon men of letters, he once wrote to the Earl of Balcarres, do not rest content with *small* lies. And Hume never condescended to tell any big ones. (pp. 10-14)

        Russell Kirk, "Hume and His Heirs," in New Saltire, *No. 2, November, 1961, pp. 9-14.*

H. R. TREVOR-ROPER (essay date 1963)

[*Trevor-Roper is a renowned English authority on sixteenth- and seventeenth-century English and European history, espionage in the twentieth century, and the Second World War, especially the private and public lives of Adolf Hitler, Martin Bormann, and Joseph Goebbels. Also a noted historical theorist, he has edited the works of Edward Gibbon and Thomas Babington Macaulay. In the following excerpt, he describes Hume's historical method and motivation.*]

David Hume was the greatest of British philosophers. He was also an important figure in the development of the social sciences. We do not often think of him as a historian. Yet when he died, in 1776, he was better known as a historian than as a philosopher. He was the first, and for long the most famous, of the so-called 'philosophical historians' in Britain, of whom the second was William Robertson, now unjustly neglected, and the third Edward Gibbon. We now recognise Gibbon as by far the greatest; but Gibbon himself, all his life, bowed modestly before the other two. (p. 89)

Yet Hume, unlike Gibbon, became a historian almost by accident. In 1752, after a great electoral battle which he has described in one of his most entertaining letters, he was elected Librarian of the Advocates' Library in Edinburgh, and there, sitting among those 30,000 volumes, he suddenly saw his opportunity. 'You know', he wrote to a friend, 'that there is no post of honour in the English Parnassus more vacant than that of History. Style, judgement, impartiality—everything is wanting to our historians'; and so he decided to fill the vacant throne. He would write the history of England. No sooner had he decided than he set to work. Beginning at 1603, his pen moved briskly forward; and as he wrote he became entranced with the subject. 'The more I advance in my undertaking', he wrote, 'the more I am convinced that the History of England has never yet been written, not only for style, which is notorious to all the world, but also for matter; such is the ignorance and partiality of our historians. Rapin, whom I had an esteem for, is totally despicable. . . .' Rapin—a French Huguenot who had been taken up by Dutch William, lived in Germany, and wrote

in French—was the fashionable historian of the time; he was the official historian of his triumphant patrons, the English whigs.

For in the 1750s the whigs still had it all their own way. As Hume himself wrote, 'for a course of near seventy years, almost without interruption' they had 'enjoyed the whole authority of the government, and no honours nor offices could be obtained but by their countenance and protection'. This whig victory, he admitted, had been 'advantageous to the state'; but unfortunately the whigs had not been content with political triumph: they had 'assumed a right to impose upon the public their account of all particular transactions, and to represent the other party [*i.e.* the tories] as governed entirely by the lowest and most vulgar prejudices'. In fact the whigs had established the doctrine that the English constitution, even before 1688, was 'a regular plan of liberty', and that the whigs, and they alone, had been the faithful champions of this constitution, the devoted idealists of liberty. Hume's researches in the Advocates' Library convinced him that this doctrine was 'ridiculous', and in his first volume, which was published in 1754 and covered the reigns of James I and Charles I, he offered what he considered a juster, more 'moderate view'.

Like all historians, Hume considered himself entirely impartial. 'I may be liable to the reproach of ignorance', he wrote, 'but I am certain of escaping that of partiality.' After all, why should he be partial? He was a foreigner, a Scotsman, happily outside the factious party politics of England for which he always expressed the greatest contempt. He was also a social philosopher, with a new point of view: a point of view from which politics receded into the interstices left by social and economic laws. And in religion he was a sceptic—'that notorious infidel', as Johnson and Boswell called him—for whom religion too receded into its social context. For all these reasons he felt himself outside and above the stale and vulgar battles of whig and tory, Church and Dissent. (pp. 89-91)

Neither Hume nor any of the 'philosophical historians' of the eighteenth century wrote vivid history. They did not seek, as their sucessors after the Romantic movement did, to plunge back, bodily and mentally, into the past. Archaic language, local colour—these devices for bringing the reader himself into the scenes of history never occurred to them. They sat in Edinburgh, or London, or Lausanne and wrote about remote, unvisited countries and distant, disagreeable centuries in the cool style of the eighteenth century. The idea that they should become part of the past, wear its clothes, sink into its conventions, sympathise with its bigotries, would have shocked them. A rational man, living in 'the full light and freedom of the eighteenth century', might look back into the Dark Ages, but only an idiot or a monk would seek to plunge back into them. History, the philosophical historians believed, was an intellectual exercise: it required a modern mind, and should be expressed in modern language. They aimed at social analysis, not description of antique costume, elegant paraphrase, not quotation of bizarre texts. No doubt this makes them less vivid than their successors, but it has its advantages. Too many of those successors plunged back only into the clothes, not the mind, of the past: and today the judicious mind of the eighteenth century often seems more modern as well as more humane than the misplaced sympathies of the nineteenth. Hume, Robertson and Gibbon are more modern than Motley or Freeman, more humane than Macaulay or Froude.

Apart from this general point, we must remember that Hume was not an Englishman, but a Scot. This was of great significance, because the coming of the Enlightenment, which he represented, was very different in Scotland and in England. In both countries, as in all Europe, the Enlightenment was largely the triumph of lay reason over clerical bigotry. But the bigots in the two countries were different. In England they were tory parsons; therefore the English Enlightenment wore 'whig' colours. In Scotland they were the ministers of the 'whiggamore' Kirk; therefore Scottish Enlightenment was a tory movement. Hume's 'toryism' is an obvious result of this fact. He had himself had plenty of trouble from the bigots of the Kirk, and he could never accept the easy English orthodoxy that men who opposed the Stuarts, or were oppressed by them, were thereby necessarily friends of liberty or truth. (pp. 93-4)

Looking at the past without the customary whig blinkers, and with the new social spectacles, [Hume] saw that no party, political or religious, had a monopoly of political or intellectual virtue. Historical situations were created by objective social laws, and individual human beings interpreted or failed to interpret those laws. So, in each volume of his history, he wrote a short section on social history; he periodically deduced or applied social formulae; and he treated historical characters not, like his whig predecessors (or even the greatest of his whig successors, Macaulay), as heroes or villains but as individuals to whom, within this general framework, it was easier to be just, because he sought not to take sides but to explain. He was, he thought, impartial. And indeed, in personal matters, he was impartial. His bias, if he had one, was in a different field, in the philosophy that lay behind his history and informed it throughout.

For Hume was not only a social historian who, by his freedom from whig prejudices, redressed the balance of history: he was also, in his whole social outlook, a conservative. This is very clear when we consider his treatment of religion. Basically, Hume considered that all religious doctrines were equally untrue. This being so, different religions must be judged by their social usefulness. But how is social usefulness defined? It might be defined as social challenge. If Hume had been a radical, he might well have defined it thus, and then he would have excused incidental religious fanaticism when it clearly represented such a challenge. But in fact he defined it otherwise. For him, as for Gibbon, a good Church was one which does not trouble men with too much doctrine, which forwards, or at least does not oppose, art and letters, and which, preferably, is governed by laymen: in other words, an established Church which has accepted the society around it and become settled, civilised and worldly. So we find him preferring the Renaissance Popes to the 'enraged and fanatical Reformers'. 'That delicious country where the Roman pontiff resides', he wrote, 'was the source of all modern art and refinement and diffused on its superstition an air of politeness which distinguishes it from the gross rusticity of other sects.' And in the seventeenth century we find him excusing 'the mild humane Charles' whose 'inoffensive liturgy'—*i.e.* the Anglican Prayer Book—was so unreasonably assailed by the philistine Scotch clergy. Of Archbishop Laud, the architect of that fatal policy, Hume might admit that he showed, in his narrow-minded clericalism, 'the intemperate zeal of sectary', but he adds, ''tis sufficient vindication to observe that his errors were the most excusable of all those which prevailed during that zealous period'. Words such as these can hardly have been welcome in Woburn or Chatsworth, far less in Galloway or Fife; but we can see why it was that the infidel philosopher was encouraged to persevere in his historical studies by the primates of the Established Church in England and Ireland. (pp. 97-8)

H. R. Trevor-Roper, "Hume as a Historian," in David Hume: A Symposium, *edited by D. F. Pears, Macmillan & Co. Ltd., 1963, pp. 89-100.*

JOHN VALDIMIR PRICE (essay date 1969)

[*Price is an American scholar and educator who has written widely on Hume's life and works. In the following excerpt, he surveys Hume's political and economic writings.*]

Hume's political thought is something of a trial for the average reader since his ideas cannot be conveniently fitted into any prescribed political ideology. In addition, the reader has to contend with an eighteenth-century vocabulary that does not always convey a concept amenable to modern standards of classification. Much of Hume's political practicality derives from his moral persuasions, and he is prone to refer to social virtues as "artificial" and as distinct from "natural" virtues—the uniquely personal ones. The *Enquiry concerning the Principles of Morals* devotes some sections to considerations of moral acts involved in the social and political spheres, and almost all of the 1741-42 essays with political titles are permeated with moral judgments.

While an essay like **"The Sceptic"** gives the impression of a person unwilling to make judgments about the habits and peculiarities of others, we later find that Hume has no qualms about depicting the French government of Henry III as one filled with "oppression, levity, artifice on the part of the rulers; faction, sedition, treachery, rebellion, disloyalty on the part of the subjects. . . ." In the same essay, **"That Politics may be Reduced to a Science,"** Hume asserts that a republican and free government whose checks and controls had little effect, and which also "made it not the interest, *even of bad men,* to act for the public good," would be absurd (my italics). Apparently, man must worry about the public good and upgrade it before he can turn his attention to the improvement of individual morality.

To neglect the principles of decency and morality is a common failing, as Hume observes in **"Of the First Principles of Government."** "When men act in a faction, they are apt, without shame or remorse, to neglect all the ties of honour and morality, in order to serve their party. . . ." These same men, however, should they form their faction on a principle of right or morality, could be unswervingly stubborn in their devotion to justice or equity. Still, the reader cannot escape Hume's implication that justice and equity derive, not from noble motives, but from a convenient rallying-point. The state will thus have a function in the formation of public morality. Virtue and a strong sense of morality, the foremost requirements for happiness, are not formed by the hard-shelled admonitions of religion or by the most subtle and refined principles of philosophy; virtue and general morality in a state "must proceed entirely from the virtuous education of youth, the effect of wise laws and institutions." Peace and security in life derive from good government instead of from an abundance of material possessions and comforts. The benefits of good government and the morality of man are interdependent.

If this insistence upon a moral basis for governments seems to suggest that Hume accepted the idea of a "social contract," which he called the "original contract," then I must point out that Hume tentatively embraced the idea in the *Treatise* and quickly abandoned it. In the *Treatise,* he asserts that "government, *upon its first establishment,* wou'd naturally be suppos'd to derive its obligation from those laws of nature, and, in particular, from that concerning the performance of promises.'' Yet he accepts only a part of the social-contract theory by maintaining ''that tho' the duty of allegiance be at first grafted on the obligation of promises, and be for some time supported by that obligation,'' it later becomes independent of all contracts. A formation of government upon this basis stems from the intrusion of change, such as the acquisition of wealth or power, among a body of people, requiring that some sort of human promises be made to supplement natural law.

Hume's concept of the usefulness and value of the ''original contract'' had itself changed when the essay **''Of the Original Contract''** appeared in *Three Essays, Moral and Political,* then in the third edition of *Essays, Moral and Political.* In this edition Hume admits only a rough idea of a theory attributing the origin of government to an original contract. He affirms that one cannot deny that government was formed by an original contract if this meant that men, living in the woods or deserts, voluntarily gave up their native liberty to accept certain conventions whose obviousness precluded any necessity of placing them in a formal document. Any original contract proceeded from the native equality, or something close to it, of men; or they would not otherwise willingly have abandoned their will to the authority of an established government.

In a paragraph which Hume added to the posthumous edition of these essays, he argues that even this sketchy consent was imperfect and could not have been effective in establishing a regular administration. The exercises of authority required by such primitive forms of government, in which a tribe might be ruled by a chief of some kind, were unique; they had no established or preordained rules but were guided by the exigencies of each emergency. And, of course, the more this chief exercised his authority, the more accustomed people became to submitting to it. Thus, he acquired some control over them and established the custom of submission to authority.

Hume apparently had more trouble with this political concept— the origin of a government—than with any other. He quickly disposed of the idea that government arose from the will of a Deity by pointing out the pettiness into which the concept of rule by divine right extended. The formation of government had to be accounted for somehow since it was a human and not a divine institution; Hume could never free himself from the idea that some kind of agreement or inclination among people created at least the rudiments of government.

The only essay added to the posthumous 1777 edition was titled **''Of the Origin of Government''** and dealt with the same problem. In it, Hume alleges that, given some kind of temporary original agreement, the origin of a government was slow and erratic, that it did not spring into being by the agreement of men. For one thing (and Hume's moral sense inserts itself into the argument here), ''such is the frailty or perverseness of our nature! [*sic*] it is impossible to keep men, faithfully and unerringly, in the paths of justice.'' The incurable weakness of human nature tempts man into anti-social action. Even if the original cause of government had been some kind of contract, it would never have long subsisted because one man, or many, would be tempted to break the agreement for some private advantage. To circumvent large-scale anti-social action, man must establish the concept of obedience in order to support justice.

Accounting for the origin of government, Hume discovers that it must arise from the interplay of political forces, from the consolidation of habit, and from the human inclination to order

and power. In fact, men ruled by the love of power can be instrumental in shaping a government. The force of their personalities and devotion to ''their'' state impose a kind of order upon other men by subordinating the wills of others to that of one leader. This interplay of political forces involves authority and liberty in perpetual opposition, although neither one can prevail for long, if a government is to be established and to survive.

Indeed, neither liberty nor authority can or should gain dominance. Liberty represents the perfection of a civil society, but, paradoxically, authority is necessary for it to exist, to insure that the partitions of power are justly administered. Justice itself, among other desiderata associated with liberty, may be suspended should some alien force threaten the welfare of a government which has emerged from various political forces that shaped it into something stable and reliable.

When discussing the various ways in which liberty takes shape in the world, Hume points out (in this same essay) that a sultan, while the master of the life and fortune of any one of his subjects, could not increase their taxes, any more than the French monarch, who can impose new taxes at will, could regulate and decide the lives of his subjects. The various ways in which liberty was regarded throughout the world was a topic of perennial interest to Hume, and one of the essays of 1741 bore the title **''Of the Liberty of the Press.''** In it, Hume remarks that nothing would more astonish the foreign visitor to England than the liberty of the press and the journalistic censure attendant upon every decision made by the crown or by Parliament. To Hume's mind, the mixed form of government, one neither totally monarchical nor entirely republican, accounts for this liberty more than any fact. So long as the republican part of England's government can prevent its being overwhelmed by the monarchical, the liberty of the press will be allowed to continue, for liberty of the press is one of the strongest props of republicanism.

Hume's attitude toward what he called a ''mixed form of government'' was one of his most enlightened but one also misunderstood by those in his century who wanted him classified as either Tory or Whig, so that they could pelt him with ready-made refutations. Hume found the mixed government of Britain to be predominantly republican although held in check by a strong monarchical tradition. Although he altered his opinion in later life, in 1741 he saw the power of the crown increasing, after a long period when popular government was ideologically and politically powerful. The wealth of the monarchy, however, militated against the continued preeminence of republicanism.

In answering the question of his essay **''Whether the British Government inclines more to Absolute Monarchy, or to a Republic,''** Hume prefers, in abstract, a monarchy to a republic in Great Britain. If the present form of mixed government is to come to an end—and Hume hopes that it will continue, even while recognizing that all governments have some terminus— he hoped it would come in the form of absolute monarchy, ''the true *Euthanasia* of the British constitution.'' Why? The dangers of popular government are far more terrible. The kind of republic Britons might get upon the dissolution of the present form is not the ''fine imaginary republic, of which a man may form a plan in his closet,'' and indeed which Hume outlined in **''Idea of a Perfect Commonwealth,''** but one unlikely to have any respect for justice and liberty. Hume suggests that it is better to let a new government form itself by whatever forces shape it under an absolute monarch than to permit a totally republican form to degenerate into anarchy. For this reason, Hume is frequently lined up with the Tories, who, if truth be said, would at the very least suspect the motives of a man who denied their divine-right theory as an account of the formation of monarchical government.

Toward the end of his life, however, in 1775, Hume had come to think that republicanism was sometimes the best form of government. In a letter to his nephew, also named David Hume, he judged that modern practices had corrected all the traditional, historical abuses associated with monarchies. He confessed his preference: "[Republicanism] is only fitted for a small State: And any Attempt towards it can in our [Country], produce only Anarchy, which is the immediate Forerunner of Despotism" (words in brackets are conjectures by Greig). Another immediate forerunner of despotism is revolution since it overthrows established governments and seeks to start anew. Hume is almost always on the side of an established government, assuming it is not tyrannical; and he prefers to keep it rather than substitute one uncertainty for a greater. But Hume also admired the revolution in the American colonies, thought it justified, and confessed, also in 1775, to Baron Mure of Caldwell, that "I am an American in my Principles."

What is the reader to make of these seeming inconsistencies and others like them which compose Hume's political essays? The suggestion I can offer is only speculative, but such a solution seems preferable to an accusation of inconsistency and political illiteracy against Hume. Basically, Hume was a political theorist and not a politician. Custom and the frame of his mind led him into a skeptical analysis of conventional political wisdom; instead of continuing the principles beyond the a priori precepts of certain political ideologies, Hume tried to substitute an empirical methodology in both politics and economics. The essay **"Of the Populousness of Antient Nations"** is an excellent example of an attempt to fuse historical inquiry, skeptical doubts, and empirical conclusions.

As a philosopher, Hume found himself more at home with the theoretical constructs of political science, than with the popular sentiments that over-simplified the complications of a continually emerging government. The **"Idea of a Perfect Commonwealth"** leaves no doubt that Hume was basically libertarian and that his personal preference was for a government that insured a high degree of individual liberty. Yet personal preferences, regardless of their propinquity, were expendable if the exigencies of government demanded it. Hume's function was to raise doubts, to propose alternatives, and to say the unpopular when necessary. To others belong the tasks of mollifying the populace and administering the nation's polity.

The extent and the effectiveness of Hume's economic thought are not necessarily indicated by the quantity of his writings on economics. He wrote only nine essays that, strictly speaking, could be called economic essays: **"Of Commerce," "Of Luxury," "Of Money," "Of Interest," "Of the Balance of Trade," "Of the Balance of Power," "Of Taxes," "Of Public Credit,"** and **"Of the Jealousy of Trade."** All were published in 1752 in his *Political Discourses*, except the last-named, which was published in 1758. Hume's discussion of economics is neither systematic nor thorough; nevertheless, his ideas on economics have been thought to be among the most valuable written in the eighteenth—or any—century.

Since Hume was a contemporary of and advisor to Adam Smith, almost any discussion of Hume's economic thought is immediately compared to Smith's. Basically, Hume and Smith are

in sympathy so far as the methodology of economic inquiry is concerned, although Smith's inquiries are much more developed. Smith is less concerned than Hume with the psychology of human beings involved in economic transactions, and Smith often assumes the "universal psychology" attributed to every man, regardless, as the saying goes, of race, creed, or color. In contrast, Hume considers variations in men's behavior; and his economic ideas belong most properly in the pattern of his other thoughts.

Hume is a transitional figure in the movement from mercantilist economic theory to classical economic theory, and he cannot be said to belong to either school. He was one of the first writers to demonstrate the interrelations of economic theory and economic practice and their further relation with social and political events. Briefly, for Hume, economics is the science of explaining the way in which money, trade, taxes, public credit, and commerce are produced by the changes in human wants, which are, in turn, affected by environment.

"Of Commerce," generally regarded as Hume's most important economic essay, contains the outlines of his economic psychology, or the relationship between the state and the individual. He asserts what is commonly allowed, that "The greatness of a state, and the happiness of its subjects, how independent soever they may be supposed in some respects, are commonly allowed to be inseparable with regard to commerce; and as private men receive greater security, in the possession of their trade and riches, from the power of the public, so the public becomes powerful in proportion to the opulence and extensive commerce of private men."

Hume admits that some exceptions may be admitted to this rule because of the variations in behavior patterns. Historically speaking, Hume continues, the state is greatest when its "superfluities" are used to increase public welfare; but, I hasten to add, Hume does not have in mind a "welfare state." Instead, he is following the psychological ideas suggested in his other works, that economic matters develop less from arbitrary laws of cause and effect, but from attitudes, customs, experiences, and habits. In keeping with his view in the *Treatise* that the passions are more often the "springs" of behavior than reason, Hume makes the passions the starting point of his economic theory. This procedure removed economics from the politics of mercantilism and centered it in the "science of human nature."

For Hume, labor is the ultimate source of wealth, and passions are the ultimate source of labor. Therefore, the passions are the ultimate source for the wealth and productions of the world. Passions, however, do not necessarily govern the way in which wealth is used. For example, poverty can occur when the means for attaining economic advantages are so simple and expedient that men are led into indolence, as they are in the Mediterranean countries. When economic advantages are not easily attained, men must have some potential profit before embarking on the dangers concomitant with production: "Men must have profits proportionable to their expense and hazard." Throughout his essays, of course, Hume puts the psychology of economics in historical perspective; transactions involving capital or labor are obviously affected by the culture in which they occur.

Commerce, which arises from the pleasure of profits and the luxury they can bring, is not estimable exclusively in monetary terms: "Money is not, properly speaking, one of the subjects of commerce. . . ." While Hume's monetary theory is in places ambiguous, it is, as the preceding sentence would suggest, dominantly classical. That is, Hume argues that the supply of money is unimportant since the prices of goods will always be proportionable to the actual quantity of money. Money, like a priori ideas, has no intrinsic value. The public may receive advantage from a greater supply of money, but it does so only during wars and in trade with other countries. Money by itself does not increase trade; and those countries accumulating the greatest wealth usually have the greatest expense.

Thus, their accumulation of money or wealth gives them no special advantage in commerce because the greater expenses producing that wealth make it possible for other countries to undersell them. Nor is the domestic happiness of the state increased by the quantity of its money. If the policy of the state works to increase the quantity of money, the result is desirable: it "keeps alive a spirit of industry in the nation, and encreases the stock of labour, in which consists all real power and riches." As he had done in his earlier writings, Hume insists on the subtle distinctions necessary in economics between causes and effects: money is not a cause of plenty and happiness, but it can be an effect of labor and industry.

"Of Public Credit" is likely to be of more interest to the casual reader than most of Hume's other economic essays because Hume is specifically interested in the problems arising from and associated with the public, or national, debt. Hume's ironic opposition to the accumulation of public debt to be paid off by other generations would give aid and comfort to modern conservatives opposed to "deficit financing": "it seems pretty apparent, that the ancient maxims [saving great sums against any public exigency] are, in this respect, more prudent than the modern; even though the latter had been confined within some reasonable bounds, and had ever, in any instance, been attended with such frugality, in time of peace, as to discharge the debts incurred by an expensive war."

Hume, like many of his latter-day counterparts, thinks that ministers of state and politicians are unlikely to exercise restraint in borrowing, a position pretty well borne out by historical evidence. Incorporating sociological analysis and historical perspective, he suggests that the increase of the public debt will, as a matter of course, lead to bankruptcy and to political deterioration. Hume ascribes the inclination towards a mounting public debt to the "natural progress of things"; from a knowledge of the natures of men and politicians, Hume suggests two possible consequences of an increasing debt. One would result in what he calls the "natural death" of public credit, as a result of governmental overextension; another consequence would be the "violent death" of public credit as a result of an inability or reluctance to accept voluntary bankruptcy and the subsequent submission of the state to a conqueror.

The relations of a state to its neighbors form the subject of two essays containing some of Hume's most original thought. **"Of the Balance of Trade"** is an exposition of the inadequacy of mercantilist attempts to increase the internal quantity of money or commodities by imposing artificial limits on international trade. Hume argues that the amount of currency or cash in a country tends toward an equilibrium as a result of a balance between its exports and imports. Free trade prevents the escalation of prices out of proportion to the prices asked in other countries. In a series of rhetorical questions, Hume doubts the ability of a country to maintain a disproportion between its supply of money and its labor and commodities. He specifically questions the ability of a state to lose its labor and industry and yet retain its gold and silver; it need never fear losing its currency so long as its industry and labor are maintained.

Six years later, in **"Of the Jealousy of Trade,"** Hume was to reject the protectionist theory of international trade agreements, although he had conceded the necessity of tariffs in the earlier essay. No nation was likely to have its domestic industry damaged by the prosperity of neighbors, but Hume said he wished to go farther and to observe "that where an open communication is preserved among nations, it is impossible but the domestic industry of every one must receive an encrease from the improvements of the others." Although the reader finds some evidence for Hume's doubts about the effectiveness of this principle, he can never doubt the moral outlook of Hume's economics, which found unlikely the proposition that a nation's wealth, commodities, and industry would be increased by its conquest of neighboring states.

Hume's economic views are neither easy to summarize nor to relate to modern problems. Perhaps his most important contribution to economic thought was the insistence that man ought to reason as subtly and as abstrusely on economics as he did on other branches of "moral science." That was the contention of the opening paragraphs in **"Of Commerce,"** and Hume followed his own suggestion conscientiously. He never ignored the role of custom and habit in shaping economic changes; in fact, custom and habit were the source of all economic change. History and psychology were the means by which he attempted economic analyses, and he focused attention upon both the myths of economics, as well as upon the general principles to be derived from study of domestic and international transactions. His inquiry into economics relied upon the same tools he used to inquire into human understanding and into the principles of morals. (pp. 72-81)

> *John Valdimir Price, in his* David Hume, *Twayne Publishers, Inc., 1969, 174 p.*

LEO BRAUDY (essay date 1970)

[Braudy is an American literary and film critic. In the following excerpt, he explores Hume's historical intentions, method, and style.]

Clarendon found continuity in his own life and the easy commerce between his private and his public duty. Bolingbroke obviated the problem by concentrating on exempla and easily detaching them from their place in the past. Hume makes the problem of coherence the center of his attempt to write history. He immediately grasps the need to define the role of the historian and his relation to the materials that the past offers. Bolingbroke's scattered comparisons between the literary man and the interpreter of history become a guiding principle of Hume's practice. But while Bolingbroke's literary analogies emphasized the act of "translating" past events into present practice, Hume's refer to the more inclusive issues of style, theme, and structure. Going beyond Bolingbroke, he considers the writing of history to be first of all a literary problem. His experimentations with literary method finally lead him to researches into the unique nature of the past. But when he begins his *History of England,* he says that the motive that most animated him to write was the desire for "literary fame." Style was at least as important a concern as matter: "The more I advance in my undertaking, the more I am convinced that the History of England has never yet been written, not only for style, which is notorious to all the world, but also for matter; such is the ignorance and partiality of all our historians."

In his early writings Hume's emphasis on the structural interrelation of history and fiction is close in form to Bolingbroke's.

He says in *An Enquiry Concerning Human Understanding*: "The PELOPONNESIAN war is a proper subject for history, the siege of ATHENS for an epic poem, and the death of ALCIBIADES for a tragedy." Hume here cares little about the criterion of verifiable facts that would make a distinction between fiction that deals with a historical subject and history itself. The principles of coherence in both draw upon similar literary methods: "The unity of action . . . which is to be found in biography or history, differs from that of epic poetry, not in kind, but in degree." Without a design any literary production "would be like the ravings of a madman." And historical "design," like literary design, depends first of all on a continuity of time and a contiguity of space: "All events, which happen in [a] portion of space, and period of time, are comprehended in this design, tho' in other respects different and unconnected. They have still a species of unity, amidst all their diversity."

The historian refines this abstract "species of unity" by discovering lines of cause, tracing them from their origins to their "most remote consequences." The better his penetration of causes and "the more unbroken the chain is," the better the historian, for the study of causes is not only "the most satisfactory" part of reading history, but also "the most instructive; since it is by this knowledge alone, we are enabled to control events, and govern futurity." Such an optimism about the control that knowledge can give over events befits the philosophical *Enquiry*. Here Hume is also optimistic about dispelling the claim that chance rules history. He denies chance an operative role and calls it only "our ignorance of the real cause of any event. . . ." The coherence of this more Bolingbrokian approach to history lies not in history's special nature, but in the control of the historian, who traces causes and discerns the general principles of human nature. By the end of his *History*, however, Hume feels satisfied if historical knowledge has succeeded in "humanizing the temper and softening the heart." Although he does not want to personalize the historian, history has become a study which is valuable in itself for its ability to extend sympathies and perceptions beyond the immediate.

Hume gradually discovers in the course of writing his *History* that history is a problem with unique terms, rather than a mere adjunct to moral philosophy or political science. As the volumes flow on and Hume moves backward in his search for the shape of English history, he tries out themes, experiments with style, and investigates new possibilities for narrative structure. He gradually will become more and more disenchanted with some of the structural techniques he has imported either from past historiographical practice or from his own philosophical precepts. But Hume begins to write history within a tradition that defines public event and public personality to be the basic elements of history. His first discussions of character are, therefore, overstated in both the exactness of their formulation and his claim for their causal relevance. (pp. 31-4)

Hume may believe in the centrality of human character to the understanding of history, but he also appreciates how the "character" as a device of literary organization can be more binding than liberating. Hume's most obvious uneasiness in the *History* appears when he must follow previous historiographers in narrative techniques like the literary "character." However it changed in expression, Hume's interest in the role of character in events does persist throughout his *History*. His practice becomes the realization of Bolingbroke's injunction that "Man is the subject of every history; and to know him well, we must see him and consider him, as history alone can present him to us, in every age, in every country; in every state, in life and in death." (p. 34)

The movement of Hume's *History* . . . often results from a tension between the demands of sympathetic character analysis and those of detached narrative. As the uniformity of human character "in all ages, and in almost all countries," becomes a topic insufficient to support a six-volume history, so the received tradition of public narrative is found similarly wanting. Hume introduces stately denunciations of the dull repetitions of military battles, martyrdoms, and revolutions that spot histories. History has become a problem for Hume. He can experiment with different types of narrative. In the early volumes he is uncomfortable when he finds it necessary to break the narrative flow; he continually apologizes for digressions. As he says in the Tudor volumes, he wishes to avoid "as much as possible the style of dissertation in the body of his History." This discomfort does not vanish by the medieval volumes, but by then Hume has found new strength in the form of chronological narrative.

Because of Hume's emphasis on chronological structure, events often seem isolated within his history, connected only by the meditative, unhurried flow of Hume's narration and the consecutive pages. The method seems almost doggedly anti-dramatic, as if Hume were attempting, for all his emphasis on style, to develop a rhetoric of truth, which does not dazzle by effects and arrangement, but presents his facts and generalizations only through the clearest medium possible. His narrative voice, except for a few one-sentence outbursts, mainly in the Stuart volumes, is careful and measured. No search for inevitable causal chains disturbs the serenity of his detachment. In place of concentration on a few main themes, Hume concentrates on the chronological flow of events and the power of his narrative voice as the contemplator of history *en philosophe*. In his balanced sentences and juxtaposed contraries we sense no irrepressible movement except the flow of time.

Hume's concern with the literary and philosophical problems of narrative structure expands his concept of cause in history. As Hume goes further into the *History*, he emphasizes more and more that causes, especially both causes in character and in the development of society, can never necessarily imply their effects. He continually points out plausible effects that never materialize and unlooked-for ones that do. His tone is impartial and moderate, and the standard of his *History* is the need to avoid extremes. Both his method and his observations counsel moderation and balance by insisting on the gradual but insistent accretions of time. He corrects the work of past historians and emends his own in order to balance possible prejudice. It is notorious that he said more of his revisions favored the Tories than the Whigs. But this was less a concession to party than, as he also said, an effort to be above party and to rid himself of the "plaguy whig prejudices" with which he began the work. As Gibbon writes, "Mr. Hume told me that in correcting his history he always laboured to reduce superlatives and soften positives."

Both Hume's expansive view of cause and his effort at narrative detachment are in great part reactions to the work of the party-historians whom he detested. Whether Whig or Tory, they partook of what Herbert Butterfield has called "the whig interpretation of history": studying the past "with direct and perpetual reference to the present," mistaking an imposition of interpretation as an actual line of cause, overdramatizing the agency of "friends" or "enemies" at the expense of complex process, and generally assuming a "false continuity" in events that can justify whatever contemporary position the "Whig" historian is defending. Like the Whig historians, Hume is often interested in passing moral verdicts on past action, but not such verdicts as were defined by contemporary controversy. He is the historian above party, and in the medieval volumes he continually ridicules both sides of the eighteenth-century political arguments that drew upon equally biased interpretations of early English history. Such arguments were born in the era of the civil wars, when each side used historical examples to justify its own position. Hume believed that the time had come when these events could be viewed with detachment. He was too sanguine; he was attacked by almost everyone. But gradually the impulses behind Hume's impartiality, detachment, balance, and praise of moderation become the mainspring of his *History*. In the Stuart volumes he makes firm and usually unqualified adjudications of rights and wrongs. In the later volumes, as his sense of the complexity of the accumulating causes of history becomes more refined, Hume's desire to make ethical judgments grows weaker. The urge to judge individual action becomes secondary to his effort to understand that essential part of history that is expressed in the unimpeded flow of time. Even though general themes like the growth of law and the relation between the ruler and the constitution become stronger methods of organization in the medieval volumes, the *History* never really coheres thematically. There are no overall movements and few short summaries of what Hume was "shown." Hume experiments with different kinds of coherence. But, perhaps perversely, he rests with the coherence of space and time he recommended in the *Enquiry* and in the hard-won detachment of his own narrative voice. Hume's focus is upon specific situations and what caused them, rather than great historical movements. His examination of causes is more proximate than long range. Even the Stuart volumes, with their apparent theme of progress of liberty in England as the result of the interaction of kingly prerogative and parliamentary privilege, deal with larger themes only sporadically.

As Hume more firmly demonstrates our inability to move from historical causes to their effects, he also emphasizes the problematic relation of the historical past to future action. Hume in his *History,* like Voltaire, often takes the opportunity to exhibit human foolishness and cruelty. But it also gradually emerges into a recognition of the complexity of circumstances and the confusion of motives, an appreciation scarcely to be found in Voltaire or Bolingbroke. Hume's sections on economic and cultural history exhibit his efforts to translate a feeling for the immediate context of action into an appreciation for the special quality of a historical era. Throughout the *History* there is a growing realization of the inadequacy and perhaps the irrelevancy of the didactic role of history envisioned by Bolingbroke. Hume includes very few references to contemporary society beyond remarks about political controversialists who wrongly draw upon history for their arguments. Hume has become more at ease with the variety of history and begins to evolve more flexible forms to deal with his material.

In the Stuart volumes, Hume has as yet made no real break with past historians. Despite his emphasis on cultural and economic history, he still writes the history of great figures engaged in military and political events. Successive volumes show him, however, more and more dissatisfied with these methods of organization. Finally, by the medieval volumes, the process of writing itself has uncovered a new rationale and new methods for the contemplation of history. Through his problems in centering history on great personages, Hume has learned to appreciate the need in the study of history to emphasize the gradual growth and continuity of law, rather than the eruptions and idiosyncrasies of personality. He associates the evils of

Hume's personal seal.

system with the evils of political bias, and attempts to make his own narrative voice stand in place of specifically formulated moral and political standards. In short, he abandons the systematic treatment of history in much the same way that he abandoned the systematic treatment of philosophy. In his commitment to the narrative of history and the exploration of his own stance as historian, he points toward a method that might encompass both structure and chance, established institutions and human innovations. In the process of writing history and testing literary methods for its presentation, he comes to discover something of its unique nature. (pp. 35-9)

> *Leo Braudy, "Hume: The Structure of the Past," in his* Narrative Form in History and Fiction, *Princeton University Press, 1970, pp. 31-90.*

G. E. M. ANSCOMBE (essay date 1973)

[*Anscombe is a distinguished English academic and philosopher who has written on ethics, religion, politics, and the philosophy of mind. In the following excerpt from an essay originally published in 1973, she analyzes Hume's conception of the grounds for belief.*]

Section IV of Part III of Book 1 of the *Treatise* is a doubly unusual piece of philosophical writing for Hume. Read very casually, all seems uncommonly smooth and acceptable. A little attention, and it collapses. Revision is incontrovertibly needed to secure coherence. The needed revision then reveals the position as incredible.

The topic is our belief in matters falling outside our own experience and memory:

> When we infer effects from causes, we must establish the existence of these causes . . . either by an immediate perception of our memory or senses, or by an inference from other causes; which causes we must ascertain in the same manner either by a present impression, or by an inference from their causes and so on, until we arrive at some object which we see or remember. 'Tis impossible for us to carry on our inferences *in infinitum*, and the only thing that can stop them, is an impression of the memory or senses, beyond which there is no room for doubt or enquiry.

Now this is a credible account of a kind of *prognosis* from what is seen or remembered. That once noted, what must be our astonishment on observing that in illustration Hume invites us

> To chuse any point of history, and consider for what reason we either believe or reject it. Thus we believe that Caesar was kill'd in the senate-house on the *ides* of *March;* and that because this fact is established on the unaminous testimony of historians. . . . Here are certain characters and letters . . . the signs of certain ideas; and these ideas were either in the minds of such as were immediately present at that action; or they were deriv'd from . . . testimony . . . and that again from another testimony . . . 'till we arrive at . . . eye witnesses and spectators of the event. 'Tis obvious all this chain of argument or connexion of causes and effects is at first founded on those characters or letters, which are seen or remember'd.

This is not to infer effects from causes, but rather causes from effects. We must, then, amend: "When we infer effects from causes *or* causes from effects", etc. For historical belief:

> When we infer causes from effects, we must establish the existence of those effects, either by perception or by inference from other effects; which effects we must ascertain in the same manner by a present impression or by an inference from their effects and so on, until we arrive at an object which we see or remember.

For Hume, the relation of cause and effect is the one bridge by which to reach belief in matters beyond our present impressions or memories. (That is why the Section "On the Idea, or Belief" is in the middle of the Part which we would think of as the Part on cause.) But also, cause and effect are inferentially symmetrical.

The historical example is an inference of the original cause, the killing of Caesar, from its remote effect, the present perception of certain characters or letters. The inference goes through a chain of effects of causes which are effects of causes, etc. What is its starting-point? It is natural to say the starting-point is the present perception.

But that cannot be a sufficient exegesis! For what on this account has become of the argument that we cannot go on *in infinitum*? The end of the chain is now the death of Caesar or the perception of its eyewitnesses, not our perception. But it has to be our perception. What is in question isn't a chain nailed at both ends, but a cantilever.

The impossibility of running up with our inferences *in infinitum* was not occasioned by our incapacity or exhaustion. The chain of inference has to stop or else "there wou'd be no belief nor evidence. And this actually is the case with all *hypothetical*

arguments; there being in them neither any present impressions, nor belief of a real existence".

"'Tis impossible for us to carry on our inference *in infinitum*" means: *the justification of the grounds of our inferences cannot go on in infinitum.* Where we have chains of belief on grounds believed on grounds . . . we must come to belief which we do not base on grounds. The argument here is that there must *be* a starting point of the inference to the original cause, not that inference must terminate. Indeed, one reason why this passage of Hume's seems fairly ordinary and acceptable at first sight is, that he strikes one as just making this point, together with the one that the starting-point must be perception.

Does our original amendment "When we infer effects from causes, or causes from effects . . ." still stand? Yes, it must. But Hume is arguing not merely that we must have a starting-point, but that we must *reach* a starting-point in the justification of these inferences. He would have been clearer if he had said, not "we cannot carry our inferences on *in infinitum*" but "we cannot trace them back *in infinitum*". But as we have said, cause and effect are taken by him to be inferentially symmetrical. So for him the tracing back is inference too. But note that it must be purely *hypothetical* inference.

Let us see what this looks like in the case in hand.

Let

p = Caesar was killed.
q = There were [at least ostensible] eyewitnesses of Caesar's killing.
r = There was testimony from the eyewitnesses.
s = There were records made, deriving from the testimony.
t = There are characters and letters to be seen which say that Caesar was killed.

We must suppose that we start (how?—but let that not delay us) with the mere idea of Caesar's death. Perhaps we really do infer an effect from it as cause: "There will have been chaos and panic in the Senate when Caesar was killed." But "we must establish the existence of this cause". As we have seen, this will not be as (at the beginning) Hume suggests, by deriving it as an effect from a cause; we shall rather have to derive it as a cause from an effect. So we reason—and here our reasoning must be "purely suppositious and hypothetical"—: if p, then q, if q then r, then s; if s, then t. Not all these hypothetical propositions are equally convincing, but only this is a chain of inferences through causes and effects such as Hume envisages. It terminates in something that we perceive. That is the last consequent. We can assert this consequent. Now we go in the other direction: since t, s; since s, r; and so on back to p.

So Hume's thesis falls into four parts. First, a chain of reasons for a belief must terminate in something that is believed without being founded on anything else. Second, the ultimate belief must be of a quite different character from the derived beliefs: it must be perceptual belief, belief in something perceived, or presently remembered. Third, the immediate justification for a belief p, if the belief is not a perception, will be another belief q, which follows from, just as much as it implies, p. Fourth, we believe by inference through the links in a chain of record.

There is an implicit corollary: when we believe in historical information belonging to the remote past, we believe that there has been a chain of record.

Hume must believe all this: otherwise he could not, however confusedly, cite the chain of record back to the eyewitnesses as an illustration of the chain of inferences *via* cause and effect, with which we cannot run up *in infinitum*.

But it is not like that. *If* the written records that we now see are grounds of our belief, they are first and foremost grounds for belief in Caesar's killing, belief that the assassination is a solid bit of history. Then our belief in that original event is a ground for belief in much of the intermediate transmission.

For let us ask: why do we believe that there were eyewitnesses of that killing? Certainly for no other reason than that we believe it happened. We infer *q* from *p*, not *p* from *q*. I have heard that the Rabbis held that the 600,000 witnesses to the crossing of the Red Sea must be credited. 600,000 witnesses! That's a lot. But now: why does anyone believe there were 600,000 witnesses?—Because he believes that 600,000 passed through. And let us make no mistake: it is not otherwise for belief in there having been eyewitnesses to Caesar's assassination.

Compare one's belief in the spatio-temporal continuity of the existence of a man whom one recognizes and identifies as a man seen last week. We don't believe in the identity because we believe in the spatio-temporal continuity of a human pattern from now here to then there. It is the other way about—On the other hand a proof of a *break* in the continuity—a proof that this man was in New York in between, while that man was not—would destroy our belief in the identity. *Mutatis mutandis* the same holds for the chain of transmission of historical information.

It is so also with proper names. In using proper names that we take to be the names of people we don't know, or people in the remote past, we implicitly depend on an 'apostolical succession' of users of these names—or linguistic transforms of them—going back to original users, who knew the people. We do not, and usually could not, *trace* the chain of use of the name. But a discovery that a name belonged originally to a period later than the life-time of the supposed bearer of the name at any rate reduces the status of the name: it becomes equivalent to some set of definite descriptions.

Belief in recorded history is on the whole a belief *that there has been* a chain of tradition of reports and records going back to contemporary knowledge; it is not a belief in the historical facts by an inference that passes through the links of such a chain. At most, that can very seldom be the case.

All this is not just catching Hume out in a mistake. That would not be very interesting or important. The mistake—which I think it is now not a bit of patronizing superiority *more hodierno* ["after today's manner"] to refer to as such—has the rare character of being easily demonstrated while yet it touches the nerve of a problem of some depth. It is a lot more difficult to see what to say, than it is to point clearly to error in Hume.

One of the rare pieces of stupidity in the writings of Wittgenstein concerns this matter:

> That it is thinkable that we may yet find Caesar's body hangs directly together with the sense of a proposition about Caesar. But so too does the possibility of finding something written, from which it emerges that no such man ever lived, and his existence was made up for particular ends.
>
> (*Philosophische Bemrkungen*, IV, 56)

What document or inscription could be evidence that Julius Caesar never existed? What would we *think* for example of an inscription saying "I, Augustus Caesar, invented the story of the divine Julius so that Caesars should be worshipped; but he never existed"? To ask a question Wittgenstein asked much later: what would get judged by what here?

Take something a bit less extreme: a document recounting a conversation about siege-engines between Caesar and Archimedes. We will suppose that the document itself gets acknowledged by experts in such matters as a genuine old MS. Dispute exists, perhaps, whether it was made in the tenth or eleventh century and it comes under much critical scrutiny. (It is no Piltdown skull.) The Hellenicity or Latinity is authentically ancient; it seems reasonable to place the writing of it in the first century BC. The style is such as might fit, if possible, with its being a piece of historical writing. (Xenophon's *Cyropaedeia* is an example of such writing.) The content proves it to be fictitious.

It might well be that the discovery of such a piece would compel some adjustment in our picture of what was 'on' in the literature of the time. It could not force an adjustment in our idea of the relative dates of Archimedes and Caesar.

Of course Wittgenstein doesn't tell us from what character of document that could 'emerge'. I do not believe he could.

If you go to an expert on Julius Caesar, you will find he is an expert on whether Caesar conducted such and such negotiations with Pompey or when he wrote his books, for example. Not on whether Caesar existed. Contrast an expert on King Arthur.

I was taught, I think, that when Lucretius was first published during the Renaissance, the *De Rerum Natura* was suspected of being a forgery; but its Latinity and the absence of 'giveaways' won its acceptance. That means that there were standards by which to judge. The ancient Latinity of Horace, Ovid, Virgil, Cicero and Caesar was such a standard, itself known by tradition and never subject to question. The attempt to construct a serious doubt whether we have writings of Cicero—how could it find a ground from which to proceed?

We know about Caesar from the testimony of ancient historians, we even have his own writings! And how do you know *that* those are ancient historians, and these, works of Caesar? You were told it. And how did your teachers know? They were told it.

We know it from being taught; not just from explicit teaching, but by its being implicit in a lot else that we are taught explicitly. But it is very difficult to characterize the peculiar solidity involved, or its limits. It wasn't an accident that Hume took the killing of Caesar as his example; he was taking something which existed in his culture, and exists in ours, with a particular logical status of one *kind* of certainty. And yet he got a detail wrong! And yet again, that detail's being right would not be an important aspect of what he knew. I mean, if he had been careful, he could have called that in question; he could even perhaps have called the date in question (*might* it not have been a false accretion?)—but that that man, Caesar, existed and that his life terminated in assassination: this he could call in question only by indulging in Cartesian doubt. (pp. 86-90)

I once asked an expert on Galen how he knew that his subject existed. His reaction was to consider the hypothesis that Galen did not exist. "It wouldn't do, you know," he said; "we know too much about him—" and went on to mention Galen's connection with Marcus Aurelius as an example. The response was surely a correct one. *What* does the hypothesis amount to in face of our information about the time? But if all that is irrelevant—as we could have no reason for doubting the existence of Caesar, say, but continuing to believe in Cicero and Pompey—then the effect of the hypothesis is to make a vacuum in which there is nothing by which to judge anything else.

The hypothesis about Galen is merely one that 'won't do'! That is: one can relate him to better known historical matters. But in face of such an hypothesis about Caesar one would have to ask: "What am I allowed to count as evidence, then?"

People 'in history', as we say, are not in any case hypotheses which we have arrived at to explain certain phenomena. No more than is the fact of my birth or the existence of my great-grandmothers . . . Though I have never given the question any thought before this, I know I had more than one. Do I know I had four? I would have said so. But not in the sense that the hypothesis that one of my grandfathers was a half brother, say, of the other is such that the supposition of its truth involves destroying bases and standards for discovering any historical facts at all.—And so also about people 'in history' there are gradations; and there is the possibility of discovering that some obscure supposed historical figure is probably mythical, or is a conflation or the like. Things get corrected or amended because of inconsistencies. But not everything can be put up for checking. Neurath's image is of a ship which we repair—and, I suppose, build on to—while it is afloat: if this suggests that we can go round tapping every plank for rottenness, and so we might end up with a wholly different ship, the analogy is not good. For there are things that are on a level. A general epistemological reason for doubting one will be a reason for doubting all, and then none of them would have anything to test it by. (pp. 91-2)

> G. E. M. Anscombe, "Hume and Julius Caesar,"
> in her From Parmenides to Wittgenstein, *University*
> *of Minnesota Press, 1981, pp. 86-92.*

KEITH E. YANDELL (essay date 1976)

[*Yandell is an American academic and scholar who has written on metaphysics, religion, and the history of philosophy. In the following excerpt, he discusses Hume's religious opinions.*]

Hume opens his *Natural History of Religion* by distinguishing "two questions . . . which challenge our attention, to wit, that concerning [religion's] foundation in reason, and that concerning its origin in human nature." The *Dialogues* are mainly concerned with the first question, although . . . the last part of the *Dialogues*, which has caused such consternation among commentators, deals with the second. The *Natural History* but touches on the first question and concentrates on the second. Therefore it is the *Natural History* which one must regard as Hume's *locus classicus* with respect to his views concerning religion, for it is there that he most fully relates religion to human nature. (p. 112)

[The] fundamental question to ask in attempting to understand Hume's views on religion is "How is religious belief related to human nature?" This question leads us immediately into the doctrines of the *Natural History* where he writes "The whole frame of nature bespeaks an intelligent author. . . ." Nonetheless, belief in an author of nature is not absolutely universal, and even where such belief prevails there is no single account of the nature of the author. Given these facts, Hume suggests a conclusion:

It would appear, therefore, that this preconception springs not from an original instinct or primary impression of nature, such as gives rise to self-love, . . . since every instinct of this kind has been found absolutely universal in all nations and ages, and has always a precise determinate object, which it inflexibly pursues.

It follows that the "first religious principles must be secondary; such as may easily be perverted by various accidents and causes, and whose operation too, in some cases, may, by an extraordinary concurrence of circumstances, be altogether prevented." What is denied in this passage is less to be stressed than what is affirmed: namely, that there are "religious first principles" built into human nature, though not so indelibly and lucidly imprinted that they may not be blurred or erased. Nor is this passage unique.

> The universal propensity to believe in invisible, intelligent power, if not an original instinct, being at least a general attendant of human nature, may be considered as a kind of mark or stamp, which the divine workman has set upon his work. . . .

If all men have this propensity to minimal theism, what interferes with its operation? The answer to this question is implicit in the distinction between religion's "foundation in [human] reason" and its "origin in human nature." It is Hume's contention that acceptance of theism is a product of man's *rational* capacities; the propensity to theism is a propensity of reason. (pp. 112-13)

As a propensity of reason, the propensity to minimal theism is a less fundamental portion of human nature than are propensities of the imagination. Propensities of the imagination, which in Hume's view give rise to beliefs in external objects and causal connections, have these features: (*a*) they are universally efficacious in bringing about the beliefs toward which they are propensities; and (*b*) the belief to which they give rise is always the *same* belief with little or no variation. In line, however, with reason's role in Hume as the "slave of the passions," the propensity to minimal theism is often thwarted or perverted by other propensities. (p. 113)

[One] factor (not a propensity) which, Hume claims, thwarts the propensity to minimal theism at lower stages of mental evolution is a law of progression in thought from the lower to the higher. Much at least of his argument that monotheism is late in the history of religion rests on the *a priori* claim that the earlier stages of human thought are too crude to have seized upon anything so rarified. This claim, however, is peripheral to our present interests.

Another factor is more relevant. There is, Hume asserts, a quite different source of religious belief from the actualization of a propensity of reason. Put succinctly: men are unaware of the causes which control their fate, but are filled with hope and fear about these causes. This combination of ignorance, hope, and fear unites with other natural propensities to create religious beliefs other than simple minimal theism:

> [In] all nations, which have embraced polytheism, the first ideas of religion arose not from a contemplation of the works of nature, but from a concern with regard to the events of life, and from the incessant hopes and fears, which actuate the human mind.

Hume lists several natural propensities, besides that toward minimal theism, which operate to produce religious belief.

[The] imagination, perpetually employed on the same subject [the unknown causes of human destiny], must labour to form some particular and distinct idea of them.

Men would not be led to raise questions as to the causes of their pleasures and pains "were it not for a propensity in human nature, which leads into a system, that gives them some satisfaction." Thus there is a propensity to seek a satisying system of interpretation for the events of human life.

There is also a universal propensity of mankind to "conceive all beings like themselves, and to transfer to every object, those qualities, with which they are familiarly acquainted. . . ." This propensity to anthropomorphize both deities and natural objects is not assigned to any "faculty."

There is still another propensity to concentrate our attention on perceivable objects.

And thus, however strong men's propensity to believe invisible, intelligent power in nature, their propensity is equally strong to rest their attention on sensible, visible objects; and in order to reconcile these opposite inclinations, they are led to unite the invisible power with some visible object.

Thus Hume in attributing to men a propensity to minimal theism is by no means ascribing to man's rational capacities the primary role in producing religious belief. Most religious beliefs, in his view, arise from a combination of ignorance, hope, and fear working in correlation with propensities quite distinct from the propensity to minimal theism. . . . [These] other propensities include a propensity to anthropomorphize the deity or deities, ascribing literal human passions to the object of religious devotion, thus both making the invisible, intelligent power less intelligent and also corrupting the moral influence of belief in such a power. Also noted was a propensity to concentrate on sensible objects, thus making the intelligent power visible. The net result is to produce religious beliefs which are farther from those of minimal theism than are the beliefs of avowed atheists. Thus while all men seek a satisfactory system, thereby manifesting a propensity of the imagination, following the propensity of reason toward minimal theism is only one case of providing content to such a system. Although, with certain qualifications, minimal theism is the best way of providing such content, it is not the most widely influential, being easily perverted and subjugated to propensities whose products are less noble where its operation is not altogether prevented.

With the influence of these various propensities in mind, we can now return to the propensity to minimal theism with which we began. Given that for Hume reason is an "instinct of the soul," given also that a detailed critique of the traditional attempts to justify theism of *any* sort has been offered in Parts I through IX of the *Dialogues,* it is plausible to suggest the following analysis of Hume's "natural theology passages." What Hume means when he says that "the order and frame of the universe affords [obvious and invincible] argument . . ." for the existence of an intelligent, invisible author of its design is merely this: that when men note the (at least apparent) design in nature, a propensity (of reason) to ascribe this design to an intelligent author is triggered insofar as other, competing propensities do not thwart it. In no stronger sense than this is belief in minimal theism "justified." Indeed, its *foundation in human reason is nil,* for here *justification* is in question. Its *origin in human nature* is simply the propensity which, under favorable conditions, and upon appropriate stimulus, gives rise to the belief. This account is, I believe, plainly compatible

with the doctrines of the *Natural History* and is indeed precisely what that essay intends to make clear.

One who supposes that Hume thought the argument from design a success in justifying the mitigated conclusion that the cause or causes of order in nature bear some remote analogy to human intelligence, in the sense of proving it to be more probably true than its denial, faces the obvious difficulty of making Hume more oblivious to the force of his powerful critique of that argument, at least in every formulation which he considers, than I at least would suppose possible for so astute a philosopher. But those who yield to this temptation face other difficulties as well. If Hume accepted some version of the argument from design, presumably that version has one essential premiss of the form *Since artifacts and natural objects are similar effects, they have similar causes,* and another of the form *Natural objects manifest order.* Obviously enough, the latter premiss entails *At least some natural object exists,* and presumably the relevant rationale for the former is the claim that *Like causes have like effects, and conversely.* To accept an argument is, of course, to accept its premisses as true, or as more likely true than their competitors. This, in turn, is to accept whatever those premisses entail, and whatever must be true if those premisses are known to be true. But notoriously Hume does not think that either the causal principle (*Every event must have a cause*) or the causal maxim (*Like effects, like causes* in the formulation here relevant) are either known to be true or known to be more likely true than their denials. Nor did he think it was known to be true or known to be more likely true than not that there exist any natural objects.

He does of course . . . suppose that these beliefs are "natural" and so inescapable, and in the course of the *Dialogues* Philo grants Cleanthes both the causal principle and the causal maxim. I suspect Hume has Philo do so because: (*a*) his critical say on these points is reserved for the *Treatise*; (*b*) it is a much more effective critique of the design argument if one can grant these theses and show that the argument still fails; and (*c*) as a man of common sense, Philo will ultimately have to accept them anyway. But to "accept" these claims "as a man of common sense," or in any other way which can properly be ascribed to Hume, is to grant that we cannot doubt the claims (save perhaps in moments of philosophic reflection), or perhaps doubt that they are more likely true than their competitors, not to grant that they are known to be true or known to be more likely true than their competitors. Similar remarks apply, I think, to the claim that there are natural objects, which is not questioned at all in the *Dialogues*.

One who maintains, then, that Hume accepts the argument from design, in any version which appears in the *Dialogues* or in any version which requires as essential premisses the causal principle and/or maxim and the thesis that there are natural objects (and what version of the design argument will not?) must also maintain that Hume accepts as known, or known to be more likely true than not, just those premisses. This interpretation of Hume, I should think, suffers from at least one defect—namely, it contradicts what Hume himself is notorious for having clearly maintained with respect to causality and the external world. Or it assumes that Hume forgot, or did not hold, those views when he wrote the *Dialogues*. And with that we have, I think, gone well beyond the bounds of reasonable interpretation. But if this is correct, then "at face value" interpretation of the "natural theology" passages in Hume will not do; he does not—not even in those passages—sanction the design argument. How then are we to read them? Just in the way I have suggested, with the appeal to the *Natural History* and the propensity-account of religious belief which it offers. If this interpretation also makes sense of Part XII, we may take its Humean orthodoxy as established, and this is the question we must now investigate.

A surprising switch *seems* to occur in Part XII of Hume's *Dialogues.* Philo, throughout the first eleven dialogues, has been the severe critic of all attempts to defend religion rationally. The critique of the argument from design has come mainly from his lips. Cleanthes states the crucial objection to the ontological argument, but does so saying that he will "not leave it to Philo . . . to point out the obvious weakness of this metaphysical reasoning." The implication is that Philo concurs, but that the refutation is so easy that his vast critical talents are not necessary. This role of adamant critic of natural theology makes it all the more shocking to hear from Philo a statement of faith. No interpretation of the *Dialogues* is even plausible unless it accounts for this apparent alteration in Philo's sentiments.

What is crucial, however, is that no alteration of sentiments has occurred. Rather, the topic has changed. Hume emphasizes this by having Demea, the champion of "rigorous orthodoxy," leave the scene. Demea's major positive contribution to the discussion has been to emphasize the incomprehensibility of God. Hume exploits this emphasis for his own purposes. . . . Philo, however, agrees at this point with Demea against Cleanthes. Thus a representative of an important part of Demea's position which Hume weaves into the final section is present after Demea's departure. Hence no genuine loss is sustained when alteration of theme is underlined by the departure of one of the discussants. Philo explicitly points out the change of topic in his "confession of faith." He makes his confession, not as a sceptic, but as a man of common sense. . . . Minimal theism, having no rational justification, will not be destroyed by arguments purporting to show that it has none. Just as our beliefs in causation and in external objects are not demolished by a recognition that these beliefs are utterly unfounded, so belief in minimal theism remains unscathed after a similar recognition. (pp. 114-18)

Natural religion (for Hume) is, I take it, the set of theistic beliefs which are produced by the passions and propensities he discusses in the *Natural History*. The set is of course open-ended, for as the causes and contents of human hopes and fears, and encounters with order, vary, so will the particular beliefs to which the propensities (triggered by these hopes, fears, and experiences) give rise. It is natural religion which provides the topic of Part XII, while natural theology has been the main concern of the first eleven parts. Still, Hume calls them dialogues "concerning natural religion," and given the concluding part and his introductory comments, this seems appropriate. (p. 119)

[Through Pamphilus's comments in the introduction to *Natural History of Religion*], natural religion is made to concern both the *being* and the *nature* of God, and is not distinguished from natural theology. But of course the beliefs Hume in the *Natural History* says are produced by passions and propensities concern both matters—being and nature—and in saying that "human reason has not reached any determination" concerning the divine nature Pamphilus is saying that natural theology has failed. Hume's conviction that disputes concerning competing conceptions of God are "verbal" has the effect of reducing genuine theological dispute to the question as to whether or not God exists (a point said not to be open to dispute). So, in effect,

natural theology has no legitimate office (having no foundation in human reason). Natural religion has nonetheless (a secondary) origin in human nature, and so it is among the natural phenomena which anyone who wishes to be "thoroughly acquainted with the extent and force of human understanding, and [to] explain the nature of the ideas we employ, and of the operations we perform in our reasonings" must concern himself. This concern manifests itself particularly in Part XII of the *Dialogues,* whereas the previous parts were mainly concerned to show the failure of natural theology to place any theistic belief on a firm rational foundation. This shift of concern explains the (merely apparent) shift of contentions.

It might be suggested that this interpretation makes things *too* definite. Did not Hume himself confess at the end of the *Natural History* that the "whole is a riddle, an ænigma, an inexplicable mystery. Doubt, uncertainty, suspence of judgment appear the only result of our most accurate scrutiny, concerning this subject?" How can anyone claim that Hume's views are clearly this, or that, when he himself confesses failure?

My answer is to distinguish the question as to what Hume's conclusions were from the different question as to whether Hume was (or ought to have been) satisfied with them. Condemned to a conflict of propensities which are relevant to religious belief, man's state is, if Hume is correct, less than enviable. Either blind belief which is destructive of morality or blind belief which is not: such is man's destiny with respect to religious belief. For should the propensity to deism be wed with, say, the the propensity to concentrate on sensible objects, religious beliefs arise which are detrimental to morality.

It is important in this connection to remember that according to Hume man is no better off with respect to his beliefs in an external world and in causal connections between the objects of that world. Hume writes in **"Of the Modern Philosophy"** that

> there is a direct and total opposition . . . betwixt those conclusions we form from cause and effect, and those that persuade us of the continu'd and independent existence of body. When we reason from cause and effect, we conclude, that neither colour, sound, taste, nor smell have a continu'd and independent existence. When we exclude these sensible qualities there remains nothing in the universe, which has such an [external and independent] existence.

Nonetheless we believe in an external and independent world. Thus our "natural beliefs" conflict: by reasoning from our natural belief in causal connections, we are led to the conclusion that our natural belief in an external world is false, and yet we cannot reject either belief save in the short-lived heat of philosophic reflection.

In the Appendix to the *Treatise* Hume admits that although he had hoped that his "theory of the intellectual world" would be "free from those contradictions, and absurdities, which seem to attend every explication, that human reason can give of the material world" he finds that "upon a more strict review of the section concerning *personal identity,* . . . I neither know how to correct my former opinions, nor how to render them consistent." It is, I believe, in the light of these confessions, as well as with regard to the view of religious belief which we have discussed, that we must understand the enigma passage. For surely it is not hard to see why Hume finds the matter of religion "an inexplicable mystery." The reason is simply that natural religion, as well as mathematics and natural philosophy, must rest on the "one sound foundation"—the science of man.

Given the results of investigating the explanation which human reason, he thinks, must give of beliefs concerning the material and intellectual worlds, excluding religious belief, one also finds ''an inexplicable mystery'' which makes Hume ''plead the privilege of a sceptic, and confess, that this difficulty is too hard for my understanding.'' If the enigma passage casts doubt upon the claim that the present interpretation presents Hume's views on religious matters, then the passages . . . [in the] concluding paragraphs cast equal doubt on the claim that the comments made by Hume in the *Treatise* express his own views about the ''material'' and ''intellectual'' worlds. Rather, I should think, the passages from the *Treatise* and the *Natural History* show that in the last analysis it is man himself who is for Hume ''a riddle, an ænigma, an inexplicable mystery.'' (pp. 119-21)

Keith E. Yandell, ''Hume on Religious Belief,'' in Hume: A Re-Evaluation, *edited by Donald W. Livingston and James T. King, Fordham University Press, 1976, pp. 109-25.*

IRENE COLTMAN BROWN (essay date 1981)

[*In the following excerpt, Brown comments on the theoretical and practical sides of Hume's skepticism and outlines the principles underlying Hume's historical writings.*]

David Hume said he was a Whig, but a very sceptical one, and the sceptical Whiggishness of his historical and political writings corresponded to the scepticism of his philosophical treatises. In his revolutionary *Enquiry Concerning Human Understanding,* Hume put forward in 1748 the shocking idea that there was no logical security in the modern European's faith in cause and effect. The moderns were extremely proud of looking at the world in the light of science and reason but they only believed that the same cause would always have the same effect because so far it always had done so, and there was absolutely no guarantee that it always would. 'Our conclusions from that experience are not focussed on reason or any process of the understanding', warned Hume. We believe solely because our day-to-day experience confirms us in a certain habit of belief. 'After the constant conjunction of two objects . . . we are determined by custom alone to expect the one from the appearance of the other.' Hume did not say this was absurd, but he did say it was not certain, and it was not the result of inherent laws of thought.

'All inferences from experience, therefore, are effects of custom, not of reasoning. Custom, then, is the great guide of human life.' To know that one is captive to the past, and tied to inconclusive experience, instead of possessing an infallible key, should make one more modest and less sure that it is obvious one is right, and it should also make reflective men and women feel how very little they actually knew with certainty. People who thought that they knew the certain effects of things, when they knew no more than the past sequence of events, believed wrongly that they had knowledge of the nature of the world. Nature, suggested Hume, has left us at a great distance from all her secrets.

David Hume hoped that considerations like these could 'give us a notion of the imperfections and narrow limits of human understanding'. He realised, however, that such salutary sceptical conclusions derived from abstract reason, did clash with the every day experience of the senses that caused humanity, despite itself and reason, to accept the darkness, certain that the sun would rise again.

If such an extreme scepticism and self doubt prevailed, and no one dared to act lest they be wrong, or even dared to speak because they despaired of being right, all speech would die away, and all activity cease.

This is not, however, what happens in practice, and it is practice that the sceptic has adopted as his guide. Despite the philosophical limitations of scientific proof, humanity continues to behave as if the universe around it were ruled by general laws. Cheerfulness keeps breaking in because belief is irrepressible, but the true sceptic recognises that his convictions about the world's stability are not provided by reason but do rest on habit and the force of feeling.

Such a sceptical view of what men believe, and why they believe it, was not likely to become the burning creed of a political movement. 'Every passion is mortified by it, except the love of truth', said Hume, 'It gains no partisans.' In his *History of England* he tried in the same way to mortify the political passions; to stir up doubt, to make people see that they were victims of ancient history and prejudice when they were at their most certain and so to make them less sure they had good grounds for the use of political violence. In a letter to the great classical economist Adam Smith, Hume revealed his political and his philosophic creed when he wrote that 'faction, next to fanaticism, is of all passions the most destructive of morality'. When men were sure they were right, they formed political parties to impose their views even by force, and Hume raised Doubt as the enemy of Party which was Pride, and Philosophy against Religion which was too often Misanthropy. (pp. 40-1)

[In *A Treatise of Human Nature* Hume] hoped, like a moral Newton, to subject moral judgements to the experimental mode of reasoning. No one has better described the fear and isolation of genius and, in his conclusion to Book I, Hume said, 'I am at first affrighted and confounded with that forlorn solitude in which I am plac'd in my philosophy and fancy myself some strange uncouth monster. . . . I call upon others to join me, in order to make a company apart; but no one will hearken to me. . . . Every step I take is with hesitation, and every new reflection makes me dread an error and absurdity with my reasoning'. (p. 41)

[Hume] was sceptical even of the human capacity for scepticism, unless the private citizen could somehow escape from the dubious claims of the warring public contenders for his mind. Thus when some friends said that quite new principles of philosophy would have to be discovered now that he had demolished the old, Hume answered 'are not these Doubts by themselves very useful? Are they not preferable to blind and ignorant Assent?' Doubt made one hesitant—and 'the rage and Prejudice of Parties frightens me', he wrote. The arrogant certainty of the violently partisan made them join subversive factions within the state, like the Jacobite rebels, and sometimes it made whole nations aggressively nationalistic and vain, like the English who defeated the rebellion. Indeed, 'the English are such a mobbish people', Hume complained, 'I do not believe there is one Englishman in fifty, who, if he heard that I had broke my neck tonight would not have rejoiced with it. Some hate me because I am not a Tory, some because I am not a Whig, some because I am not a Christian, and all because I am a Scotsman'. (p. 42)

In his essay **''Of the Independency of Parliament''** Hume made the startling suggestion that a key maxim of political science was that 'every man must be supposed a knave'. Although he knew many good men in private life, he thought that men go to greater lengths to serve their party than to serve themselves. A sense of honour, and the weight of public opinion, hold back many men from criminal acts, but political parties surround a person with a small group of like-minded men all devoted to the same overriding purpose. He soon learns to seek the approval of his political associates alone, who are sure to approve everything he does for the sake of the party, and 'to despise the clamour of adversaries'. Thus, out of party loyalty, even good men can turn into rogues with a good conscience, and to Hume the danger of men being prepared to disregard the common good for party advantage was an ever-recurrent threat to good and free government. To fight for the particular against the universal was a human frailty, and he noted that most men had such a propensity for factions and parties that the smallest social division would cause them to burst into life, and that this life is so stubborn that they last long after the original difference is resolved. (pp. 42-3)

In his *History of England* that he began with the accession of the Stuarts, Hume treated the English Civil War, which had proved to Hobbes the necessity of absolute rule, as a parable of human society and of human thought. While he did not hesitate to make judgements, and in fact even to commit himself to what was best, he never lost his sense of political complexity and said it was no wonder that men of that age were divided into different parties, since 'even at this day the impartial are at a loss to decide concerning the justice of the quarrel'. Of one thing, though, Hume was certain 'and that it was religion which made any hope of peace impossible, since the spirit of enthusiasm . . . disappointed all the view of human prudence' and, their minds being clouded by religious fancies, the actors of the seventeenth-century drama did not even try to save themselves.

The roots of the Civil War, which was an extreme moment in the conflict between freedom and authority, lay in the post-feudal emancipation of thought. 'In consequence of this universal fermentation, the ideas of men expanded themselves on all sides; and the several constituent parts of the gothic governments which seem to have lain asleep for so many ages, began everywhere, to operate and encroach on each other.' At the same time both the elements of freedom and of authority in the constitution began to clamour for more room. Continental monarchies were strong enough to subdue the popular parties, and to resettle themselves on a more formidable absolutism, but in England the two sides were more evenly divided. Fearful of the new currents of freedom, the kings of England, in trying to defend themselves, became more arbitrary, while fearful of the new powers claimed by the king, the defenders of freedom became more militant. So the storm rose and 'if the republican spirit of the commons increased beyond all reasonable bounds the monarchical spirit of the court; this latter, carried to so high a pitch, tended still further to augment the former. And thus extremes were everywhere affected, and the just medium was gradually deserted by all men'.

England was faced with a critical situation, but even then human intelligence might have found a solution. The extremists, whom the outbreak of political violence brought so disastrously to the fore, were not always the major force on either side. Most men were not fanatics; they join parties, said Hume, 'they know not why; from example, from passion, from idleness,' and the prophets and the partisans of absolute power were still inconsiderable. It was true that, as Hume pointed out, the pretensions of Parliament, if successful, would have

broken the balance of the constitution and made the government quasi-republican, and that the principles and habits of the king, if not resisted, would perhaps have put the country in his absolute power, but there was a Royalism which was concerned with liberty as well as with loyalty, and constitutional monarchists who would only support the king, provided he permitted serious reforms. On the other side there was a mediating Parliamentarianism, which sought to restrain the prevailing mood of rebellion, and many who did not want to bring the country to war. Yet these philosophical moderates were swept away on the religious flood.

First in Scotland there arose a movement 'inflamed with bigotry for religious trifles and faction without a reasonable object', which in London in 1640 drowned the voice of reason. 'Noise and fury, cant and hypocrisy, formed the sole rhetoric, which during this tumult of various prejudices and passions could be heard or attended to.' The great outbreak of religious passion was a result of the liberating individualism eulogised by the Scottish enlightenment, since, in older times, religion had been rather the superstitious observance of traditional practices than the individual quest for salvation. But enthusiasts of the Reformation who preached the doctrine of peace and carried war throughout Europe, had revealed the characteristic temper of the religious mind, thought Hume, and 'barbarous and pious, traitorous and faithful, they fancied themselves favourites of heaven, while enemies of mankind'. By the outbreak of the Civil War, said Hume, 'all orders of men had drunk deep of the intoxicating poison . . . every elegant pleasure or amusement is utterly annihilated; each vice or corruption of mind is promoted . . . [and] the fanatical spirit, let loose, confounded all regards to ease, safety, interest, and dissolved every moral and civil obligation'. Those whom the gods destroy they first make mad, and, filled with religious ardour, the people of England plunged towards their own destruction.

Very little art is needed, he suggested, to foster quarrels among theologians and therefore 'a civil war must ensue; a civil war, where no party or both parties would justly bear the blame, and where the good and virtuous would scarce know what vows to form, were it not that liberty, so requisite to the perfection of human society, would be sufficient to byass [bias] their affections towards the side of its defenders'.

If he had had to take sides, Hume, though he thought the quarrel hideously deformed, and though he was Tory as to persons, and Whig as to principles, would have given his moderate support to Parliament in a war which, fuelled by religious passion, raged until both sides had learned that violence can never restore what has been threatened by violence, but must inevitably end in arbitrary rule. Thus the Civil War, being a religious explosion, was 'a singular proof both of the strength and weakness of the human mind: its widest departure from morals, and its most steady attachment to religious prejudices'.

For Hume the moral of the English Civil War was that Hobbes was wrong and that the threat to social order in modern intellectual freedom could not be contained by reinforcing political controls. Man cannot be persuaded to go back to sleep and there cannot be a return to 'the preceding state of ignorance and tranquillity'. The solution to intellectual anarchy and fanaticism must be found by the light of intelligence in the precepts of a sceptical philosophy. Hume, Tory-like, advocated 'prudent reserve'; and even suggested the benign use of habit and political illusions to dampen public feeling, and a benevolent conspiracy of philosophers not to raise up popular excitement by public political speculation. Tory-like he urged moderation on the heroes of freedom 'to extort by a gentle violence, such concessions as were requisite': but the fundamental Whiggish remedy that Hume appealed for was a philosophic spirit, 'so congenial to the human mind are religious sentiments where the temper is not guarded by a philosophical scepticism, the most cool and determined'.

Such a scepticism rests on the complexity and double nature of experience. The philosopher sees that 'from the mixt character, indeed, of Charles, arose in part the misfortunes in which England was, at this time, involved. His great political errors had raised him inveterate enemies. His eminent moral virtues had procured him zealous partisans. And betwixt the hatred of the one, and the affections of the other, was the nation agitated with the most violent convulsions'.

This attachment to nuance keeps the philosopher as a political outsider. The citizen of philosophical bent can never be a purely party man and Hume's history was denounced by Whigs for being Tory, by Tory for being Whig and by everyone for being inconsistent. But Hume delighted in mixed principles and divided views, believing that 'the heart of man is made to reconcile contradictions'. It is his protection from the fanatic, from the unthinking mob, and from inheriting unquestioningly traditional allegiances and hatreds that poison the present and allow the dead to rule the living.

Hume said John Bull's prejudices are as ridiculous as his insolence was intolerable. And England, he saw again in the peaceful era of the Hanoverian monarchy relapsing into 'Stupidity, Christianity and Ignorance'. He hoped his work would at least unsettle 'the factitious Barbarians of London' convinced that, as he said in a letter, 'What Danger can ever come from Ingenious Reasoning and Enquiry? The worst speculative Sceptic ever I knew was a much better Man than the best superstitious Devotee and Bigot'. (pp. 44-5)

Irene Coltman Brown, ''Hume's Scepticism and the Weight of History,'' in History Today, *Vol. 31, August, 1981, pp. 40-5.*

NOEL CARROLL　(essay date 1984)

[*In the following excerpt, Carroll explores Hume's understanding of taste and the mechanics of aesthetic response.*]

The crux of Hume's **"Of the Standard of Taste"** is an apparent paradox. Common sense and philosophy tell us that aesthetic taste, like gustatory taste—what Addison refers to as mental taste and sensitive taste—is subjective, while common sense also tells us that some artworks are objectively better than others. Hume calls this a paradox but refers to it in weaker terms as well, noting that the second view "opposes" the first, or that the second view only modifies or restrains the first.

The opening of the essay is devoted to developing the *de gustibus non est disputandum* ["there is no disputing about tastes"] flank of the paradox. Several considerations are brought forth in its favor. The first two are matters of observation: a) even within a small ambit of acquaintances, one can note different, conflicting aesthetic preferences; b) if one looks further afield, there are the facts of cultural relativity. Next, Hume argues that much of the apparent agreement in aesthetic discourse is based on a linguistic mirage. That is, everyone appears to agree that, for example, elegance is good. Yet, when it comes to selecting the elegant objects, there is no consensus. It merely seems that people agree in matters of taste because they use the same general terms for commendation and condemnation.

"But when critics come to particulars, this seeming uniformity vanishes. . . ." This is contrasted to science where Hume feels that disagreement rages over general terms and that once disagreements about such general terms are settled the application of said terms to particulars is straightforward. Hume also analogizes the behavior of aesthetic terms to that of moral terms. Everyone applauds virtue and abhors vice, but there is grand diversity in establishing who and what is virtuous and evil. The illusion of agreement in moral discourse, and by extension in aesthetic discourse, is, in part, accounted for by Hume by the fact that such terms have commendation and condemnation as central elements of their meaning. Everyone uses the same terms to recommend or to praise certain actions and objects, but they differ on which actions and objects they single out for recommendation and blame. Hume does not dwell on this proto-emotivist interpretation in **"Of the Standard of Taste"** but only briefly introduces it to explain away some of the apparent counter-evidence for the thesis that there is a wide diversity of taste.

The putatively incontrovertible evidence for the diversity of preferences makes us seek a standard of taste, a rule for determining the aptness or inappropriateness of some preferences over others. But Hume says that there are important philosophical considerations that suggest that it is impossible to arrive at such a standard. These philosophical considerations, moreover, can be seen as an explanation for the lack of common agreement in matters of taste. That is, Hume's key point here—that "a thousand different sentiments, excited by the same object, are all right; because no sentiment represents what is really in the object"—can be seen as an inductive leap following from the initial premises about the diversity of aesthetic preferences as the best explanation of that apparent diversity.

For Hume, following Hutcheson, aesthetic responses, such as the intuition of beauty, are not perceptions of qualities in objects, but are subjective, i.e., in the subject. Beauty is literally in the eye of the beholder and not in external objects. Beauty is a feeling, Hume says "a sentiment," and not something in the fabric of the artwork. Thus,

> Beauty is no quality in things themselves: it exists merely in the mind that contemplates them; and each mind perceives a different beauty.

and

> All sentiment is right; because sentiment has a reference to nothing beyond itself and is always real, wherever a man is conscious of it.

In other words, we react to an artwork or a view of nature with a feeling of beauty. Our feelings, sentiments, are incorrigible. We have the reactions we have, and they are right in the sense that it is true that we respond as we respond. There are no facts of the matter apart from our liking or disliking what we apprehend. We simply feel pleasure or we don't. Our praise of the object is immediately implied by our feeling of pleasure. Since there are no facts to appeal to, each artgoer "ought to acquiesce in his own sentiment," i.e., go with the inner flow. Furthermore, there may be as many different sentiments as there are spectators, each of whom can claim that it is true that they feel as they feel but each of whom may also feel differently than every other spectator. Because the sentiments of beauty are internal to the subject, we can each talk of "my feeling of beauty" but I cannot challenge "your feeling of deformity" by invoking "my feeling of beauty." Hume analogizes aesthetic feeling and taste to gustatory feeling and taste, and says that there is no disputing either because beauty as a sentiment, like my love of Burger King, is a matter of having an individual subjective feeling rather than of observing an intersubjectively available property of objects.

Hume immediately follows this with the other wing of the paradox: Even though there is a diversity of aesthetic preferences and even though it seems, on epistemological grounds, that there is a "natural equality of tastes," we don't behave as if we believe this. We discount many people's opinions about particular artworks as ridiculous. How can we do this in the face of the evidence of subjectivism and relativism? And, can we rationalize our behavior by reference to some standard of taste?

Hume's answers to these questions are not developed in the most perspicuous manner. Often, **"Of the Standard of Taste"** seems to meander and repeat itself. But the elements of Hume's answers to these questions are clear enough. They include:

1) There are rules of art. These are not discovered by reasoning *a priori* but by observation. Artworks are composed in accordance, defiance, or in ignorance of these rules. Artworks composed in accordance with these rules, as a matter of contingent fact, have "Some particular forms or qualities from the original fabric . . . calculated to please or displease." That is, artworks that are created according to the rules of art will, given the proper standing conditions, cause approximately equivalent sentiments of beauty across spectators because everyone is constituted in roughly the same way. Given the proper circumstances, the mobilization of the rules of art will set off so many "springs" in the spectator; the analogy to mechanical causation is quite explicit. Conformity to the rules of art causes a sensation of pleasure, and that feeling is an effect that is tantamount to our praise of the object.

2) The proper standing conditions for the operation of the rules of art, as applied in a given artwork, are rarely satisfied when most of us appraise artworks. Here the idea of standing conditions is quite important because it is the fact that the proper standing conditions are so rarely secured that accounts for the diversity of tastes. That is, the diversity of tastes can be explained by the fact that in most responses to artworks, personal and circumstantial factors interfere with the operation of the relevant features of the artwork in the production of the aesthetic sentiment.

3) If we wish to ascertain the standard of taste, we should observe those people who are expert in adjusting themselves to the aesthetic situation and in bracketing intrusive circumstances when they respond to artworks. Most of us are not expert in this way; thus our reception of the aesthetic stimulus, so to speak, is fuzzy. Hume writes". . . though the principles of taste be universal and nearly if not entirely, the same in all men; yet few are qualified to give judgment on any work of art, or establish their own sentiment as the standard of beauty." Some can, however, discipline themselves so that they are properly attuned to the aesthetic stimulus; such people, namely the critics, can erect "their own sentiment" as the standard of taste. Identifying these critics is a matter of fact. They have five discernible characteristics and their pronouncements supply us with a standard of taste. Hume writes ". . . a strong sense, united to delicate sentiment, improved by practice, perfected by comparison and cleared of all prejudice, can alone entitle critics to this valuable character; and the joint verdict of such, wherever they are found, is the true standard of taste and beauty."

This account is compatible with the idea that beauty is a sentiment. Beauty is a causal effect in the subject which arises when the proper standing conditions are secured. The diversity of taste is explained by the fact that most of the time the proper standing conditions are not operative. But some people are adept at meeting the standing conditions so that they are maximally receptive to the production of the sentiment that the artwork is designed or fitted to evoke. The rest of us should follow the example of these critics and listen to their observations about how to attend to the artwork if we wish to have the appropriate sentiment raised in us. Thus, an attempt, at least, is made to bridge the gap between fact and value by making the standard of taste a matter of empirical discovery, viz., the identification of those who respond most sensitively to artworks.

Most of Hume's essay is allocated to enumerating the ways that the conditions of reception of the artwork can go awry, and to listing the ways that such mishaps can be avoided. Our appraisal of an artwork will be dubious if our perception of it is not delicate; this could happen if there was some imperfection in our sensory reception of it, or if the circumstances in which we view it are abnormal, e.g., the lighting is off, or if we inspect the artwork too hastily. At the very least, we should view the artwork with "A perfect serenity of mind, a recollection of thought, a due attention to the object." Though Hume does not say this, I suppose he would argue that we should also insure that we inspect the artwork under the proper conditions of presentation and that we don't confuse our appraisal of the object with some physical feature of our organism, for example, a fever, upset stomach, blurred eyesight, etc. Other factors that can interfere with our response to the object include envy, jealousy, and the influence of fashion. (pp. 181-83)

In **"Of the Standard of Taste,"** the notion that the aesthetic response is a simple causal effect—a sentiment consequent to a stimulus—predominates. The form of the object brings about a sensation of pleasure which itself is a judgment of approbation. Much of the current literature concerning Hume's aesthetics is devoted to isolating the causal trigger that, like Hutcheson's uniformity amidst variety, Hume thought evokes the sentiment of beauty under the proper conditions. Sympathy and utility are prime candidates here. On this view Hume held that in the right circumstances, the sentiment of beauty or deformity is excited when we meet with objects that 1) are designed to be useful or are dysfunctional, 2) objects that are evocative of or that resemble painful objects, e.g., the off-balanced paintings of *A Treatise of Human Nature* that are painful because they recall the painfulness or dysfunctionality of events like falling, and 3) objects that are immediately agreeable to others. This emphasis on the judgment of taste as an effect characterizes the aesthetic response as essentially passive and nonintellective.

Peter Jones is certainly correct in asserting [in his 1976 *Philosophical Quarterly* article "Hume's Aesthetics Reassessed"] that although Hume stresses the causal dimension of aesthetic response, Hume is also aware of the facts of "the now obscurely termed 'intentional' nature of perceptual objects. . . ." Good sense, for example, situates the artwork within the correct genre framework of expectations. However, the operation of the intellect is pictured as a condition for the pleasurable experience of the artwork rather than as an element *in* that experience. Understanding and reasoning are necessary preconditions for the proper operation of good taste but they are not part of the faculty itself nor part of its exercise. This position,

Tower designed by Robert Adam as a monument to Hume.
It stands in the Calton Hill Burying Ground, above Edinburgh.

of course, coincides with the majority opinion of Enlightenment aesthetics which traditionally treats aesthetic appreciation and pleasure as indissolubly and immediately linked in a way that precludes the operation of reasoning, while both Hume and the tradition stand in contrast with someone like Edmund Burke, who includes in the judgment of taste not only the pleasures of sense and the imagination but the conclusions of reasonings.

In the debate between Hume and Burke, my allegiance is drawn towards Burke, though not always in terms of the reasons he offers for his position. Hume portrays the aesthetic response as a passive response to the artwork, but his own account of the ideal respondents to works of art makes the aesthetic response appear far more active in nature. We must identify the category and the purpose of the artwork in order to appropriately respond to it by determining whether its parts facilitate its function, a process itself that, in turn, will require reasoning as we imaginatively postulate alternative structurings of the artwork. As well, we must attempt to identify the function and meaning of the artwork for its original audience. There is a great deal of intellection going on here. The more that understanding and interpretive reasoning are required before the right sentiment can be caused, the less persuasive it is to think that the process of aesthetic response is essentially a causal one, modeled on the notion of an unmediated perception, such as the tremor of sweetness that shocks the palate when a piece of sugar touches the tongue.

Hume says that good sense is not an essential part of taste but clearly the roles he assigns it suggest that it is operative throughout an aesthetic experience. Thus it seems likely that part of the pleasure of the aesthetic experience is grounded in the engagement of the understanding by the artwork, i.e., there are intellectual or cognitive pleasures to be had from artworks.

Many of these pleasures center around the various sorts of discoveries the spectator actively pursues in regard to the artwork. For example, we engage in frequent interpretive play when we search for often hidden meanings, symbols and themes.

Moreover, there is the cognitive pleasure derived from understanding the structural principles that make an artwork or part of one hang together. For example, we read in John Donne's "Satyre iii" that

> On a huge hill,
> Cragged and steep, Truth stands and hee that will
> Reach her, about must, and about must goe;

And what the hills suddenes resists, winne so;
Yet strive so, that before age, deaths twilight,
Thy Soule rest, for none can worke in that night.

Here, our aesthetic pleasure may not only derive from the sound and structure of the verse but also from the explicit recognition that the difficulty of the syntax is meant, by way of imitative form, to reflect the difficulty of the pursuit of truth purported by the poem. Indeed, it is often the possibility of actively discovering further correspondences between the formal choices and the subject represented that sends us back repeatedly to great works of art as well as the prospect of enriching our understanding of such a work's elaborate structure.

Understanding also plays a constitutory role in aesthetic pleasure insofar as we can derive pleasure by self-consciously observing how the structure of the artwork molds our experience of the work. Our eye is not only led pleasurably across the canvas by a series of wavy lines but we also derive pleasure from noticing that and how the wavy lines achieve this. That is, the aesthetic or appreciative response, construed broadly as our characteristic responses to, and ways of interacting with artworks rather than as an experience with its own particular quiddity or *quale,* involves active discovery, interpretation, recognition, and all the pleasures thereof. The judgment of taste, therefore, is not essentially a causal effect of the artistic stimuli on a *passive* spectator. Pleasures may also arise from the active understanding and reasoning of spectators. Were the simple causal model of aesthetic response adequate, we would have no reason to return to great artworks in the hope of experiencing them more fully and deeply. For we could only expect to experience the invariant pleasure the work delivers under the proper circumstances. That is, because Hume holds that cause and effect are uniquely linked in every case and because the judgment of taste is a causal effect of the object on a passive spectator, the theory cannot explain how it is that we normally return to great works of art expecting deeper, *different* experiences. This can be remedied, however, by including in our account of the aesthetic response the active pleasures the spectator derives by exercising his cognitive powers in relation to the artwork. (pp. 185-87)

Noel Carroll, "Hume's Standard of Taste," in The Journal of Aesthetics and Art Criticism, *Vol. XLIII, No. 2, Winter, 1984, pp. 181-94.*

JEFFREY HADDEN (essay date 1987)

[*Hadden is an associate editorial page editor of the* Detroit News. *During 1987, the bicentennial of the United States Constitution, he contributed a series of weekly essays on the background of and key figures in the Constitutional convention. In the following essay from this series, Hadden considers Hume's influence on the Framers.*]

When the Framers set about drafting a Constitution for their new nation, they looked to history—and didn't like what they saw. Efforts in classical times by free men to govern themselves, either in pure democracies or in republics, had ended in failure after failure. Republican and democratic governments in the classical era had degenerated into chaos and the people ultimately turned to absolutism.

If the Founders were to be successful in their experiment with republican government—and they were acutely conscious that it was an experiment—they would have to create a new political science, a new conception of political man.

Greeks of the classical era—in particular Plato in his *Republic*—concentrated on how government could educate and form the characters of certain men to fit them for government leadership, to serve as *disinterested* rulers who would put the common good above their own personal interests.

Subsequent thinkers traced the patterns of the rise and fall of various ancient governments, attributing the end of Greek and Roman republics to a decline in the character of their citizens. Historian Forrest McDonald, in his *Novus Ordo Seclorum: The Intellectual Origins of the Constitution*, writes that 18th-century Americans who thought about such things had a "preoccupation with the mortality of republics." Classical theory held that republican government could thrive only when citizens maintained the necessary civic virtue to put aside their selfish interests for the common good.

But while the Framers looked to the classical thinkers, they were also strongly influenced by such products of the extraordinary flowering of philosophy in 18th-century Scotland as David Hume and Adam Smith. The Scottish enlightenment took a far different view of the possibilities of human nature and the ability of government to shape it. Smith based his economic theory on the self-interest of individuals. His view is summed up in an oft-quoted passage from his *Wealth of Nations*, published in 1776: "It is not from the benevolence of the butcher, the brewer, or the baker, that we expect our dinner, but from their regard to their own self-interest."

Hume's political writings repeatedly stressed the tendency of men to be contrary, argumentative, and in the grip of their sometimes irrational political passions. In an essay published in 1741, **"That Politics May Be Reduced to a Science,"** he wrote: "There are enough of zealots on both sides who kindle up the passions of their partisans, and under pretence of public good, pursue the interests and ends of their particular faction."

Compare this with James Madison's famous *Federalist No. 10,* published some 40 years later: "As long as the reason of man continues fallible, and he is at liberty to exercise it, different opinions will be formed. As long as the connection subsists between his reason and his self-love, his opinions and his passion will have a reciprocal influence on each other. . . . The latent causes of faction are thus sown in the nature of man. . . ."

Madison's co-author of the *Federalist Papers,* Alexander Hamilton, argued at the constitutional convention: "Take mankind as they are and what are they governed by? Their passions."

A year after the ratification of the Constitution, John Adams (who wasn't at the convention but who contributed to the discussion of republican theory) wrote to his idealistic friend Sam Adams: "I am not often satisfied with the opinions of Hume, but in this he seems well founded, that all projects of government founded in the supposition or expectation of extraordinary virtue are evidently chimerical."

And yet many of the Founders wavered, as historian Gordon Wood has noted. They were still drawn to the classical ideal of the virtuous, disinterested republican. The same John Adams also wrote: "There must be a positive passion for the public good . . . or there can be no republican government, or any real liberty."

Hamilton, the self-proclaimed cynic, devoted almost his entire life to public service, and often seemed quite disappointed when men acted as he always said he expected they would. "There must be some public fools who sacrifice private to public interest," he wrote to a friend in 1795. "My vanity whispers I ought to be one of those fools. . . ."

And all of the Framers had before them the example of George Washington, who was obsessive about maintaining his integrity and never turning public office to personal advantage.

But though they yearned for their classical ideal, the Framers ultimately opted to act on what the Scottish philosophers and their own experience had taught them about human nature. They crafted a Constitution and a system of government that assumed that most men most of the time would pursue their private interests. They decided at the Philadelphia convention that they would have to take men as they are, and create a government structure that did not assume heroic virtue on the part either of the governed or the governors. Power was diffused and fractionated both within the electorate and the government. "It is vain to say that enlightened statesmen will be able to adjust these clashing interests and render them all subservient to the public good," wrote Madison in the *Federalist No. 10.* "Enlightened statesmen will not always be at the helm."

Other men at other times have sought to build governments and societies with more ambitious ideas about transforming human nature. Plato's ideal Republic, after all, was a totalitarian state. As Daniel Moynihan observes in a recent essay, the political thinkers who followed the Founders, Marx and Engels, claimed for their "wholly theoretical schema" the "designation of 'scientific socialism' and the fascination of three, perhaps four generations of Europeans and others, including not a few Americans. It was a fascination that would in time convulse continents and transform civilizations."

The political science of the Founders was more modest. It did not flatter their fellow citizens. But it has kept them free.

Jeffrey Hadden, "The Constitution and Human Nature," in The Detroit News, *April 20, 1987, p. 12A.*

ADDITIONAL BIBLIOGRAPHY

Adair, Douglass. "'That Politics May be Reduced to a Science': David Hume, James Madison, and the Tenth Federalist." In his *Fame and the Founding Fathers,* edited by Trevor Colbourn, pp. 93-106. Williamsburg, Va.: W. W. Norton for The Institute of Early American History and Culture, 1974.
    Reprints Adair's 1957 study illustrating Madison's use of Hume's "Idea of a Perfect Commonwealth" in *The Federalist,* No. 10.

Anderson, Robert Fendel. *Hume's First Principles.* Lincoln: University of Nebraska Press, 1966, 189 p.
    Examines Hume's metaphysics, focusing on his moral philosophy.

Anscombe, G. E. M. *Causality and Determination.* Cambridge: Cambridge University Press, 1971, 30 p.
    Traces major views of the connection between cause and effect, from Hume to Bertrand Russell.

———. "Times, Beginnings and Causes." *Proceedings of the British Academy* LX (1974): 253-70.
    In-depth analysis of Hume's contention that the ideas of cause and effect are evidently distinct.

Ayer, A. J. *Hume.* New York: Hill and Wang, 1980, 102 p.
    Excellent short introduction to Hume's life and works.

Barfield, Owen. Preface to his *Poetic Diction: A Study in Meaning,* 2d ed., pp. 14-38. Middletown, Conn.: Wesleyan University Press, 1984.

Contains a brief comparison of Hume's philosophy with that of John Locke.

Becker, Carl L. "The New History: Philosophy Teaching by Example." In his *The Heavenly City of the Eighteenth-Century Philosophers*, pp. 71-118. New Haven: Yale University Press, 1932.
Comments on the early reception given *Dialogues concerning Natural Religion,* focusing on why Hume "should have thought it worth while to write the work in the first place."

Broakes, Justin. "Hume and Scepticism." *The London Review of Books* 8, No. 4 (6 March 1986): 20-2.
Surveys recent studies of Hume, emphasizing the importance of recognizing opposing tendencies in his works.

Chappell, V. C., ed. *Hume*. Modern Studies in Philosophy, edited by Amelie Rorty. Garden City, N.Y.: Doubleday Anchor Books, 1966, 429 p.
Important collection of twenty-one critical essays on a variety of Humean topics. Essayists include Antony Flew, F. A. Hayek, Ernest Campbell Mossner, and George J. Nathan, among many others.

Church, Ralph W. *Hume's Theory of the Understanding*. Ithaca, N.Y.: Cornell University Press, 1935, 238 p.
Treats Hume's views of causation, substance, knowledge, and belief.

Clive, Geoffrey. "Hume's *Dialogues* Reconsidered." *The Journal of Religion* XXXIX, No. 2 (April 1959): 110-19.
Considers the historical and philosophical significance of Hume's *Dialogues concerning Natural Religion.*

Cohen, Ralph. "David Hume's Experimental Method and the Theory of Taste." *ELH* 25, No. 4 (December 1958): 270-89.
Probes Hume's method of analyzing and judging literature.

[De Quincey, Thomas]. "On Hume's Argument against Miracles." *Blackwood's Edinburgh Magazine* XLVI, No. CCLXXXV (July 1839): 91-9.
Disputes Hume's conclusions in "Of Miracles" concerning prophecy and internal miracles.

Doherty, Francis. "Sterne and Hume: A Bicentenary Essay." *Essays and Studies* n.s. 22 (1969): 71-87.
Argues that Laurence Sterne was at one with Hume on the use of the association principle and at odds with John Locke.

Draper, Theodore. "Hume & Madison: The Secrets of Federalist Paper No. 10." *Encounter* LVIII, No. 2 (February 1982): 34-47.
Describes James Madison's unacknowledged use of Hume's "Idea of a Perfect Commonwealth" in the tenth *Federalist,* concentrating on why Madison bridled at citing Hume as his inspiration and authority.

Flew, Antony. *Hume's Philosophy of Belief: A Study of His First "Inquiry."* London: Routledge & Kegan Paul; New York: Humanities Press, 1961, 286 p.
Rigorous study of Hume's *Enquiry concerning Human Understanding.*

———. Introduction to *Of Miracles*, by David Hume, pp. 1-23. La Salle, Ill.: Open Court, 1985.
Discusses Hume's aim in "Of Miracles" and considers the essay's place in Hume's work as a whole.

Force, James E. "Hume and Johnson on Prophecy and Miracles: Historical Context." *Journal of the History of Ideas* XLIII, No. 3 (July-September 1982): 463-75.
Documents Samuel Johnson's reaction to Hume's argument concerning prophecy and miracles, challenging the contention that Johnson did not blindly reject Hume's reasoning.

Grene, Marjorie. "Hume: Sceptic and Tory?" *Journal of the History of Ideas* IV, No. 3 (June 1943): 333-48.
Maintains that Hume's Tory leaning grew from and was consistent with his general philosophical views.

Hall, Roland. *Fifty Years of Hume Scholarship: A Bibliographical Guide*. Edinburgh: Edinburgh University Press, 1978, 150 p.
Useful bibliography of Hume scholarship from 1925 to 1976, with a brief survey of the main writings on Hume from 1900 to 1924.

Hobart, R. E. "Hume without Scepticism: Parts I and II." *Mind* XXXIX, Nos. 155, 156 (July 1930; October 1930): 273-301, 409-25.
Holds that Hume's doctrines concerning cause and induction are analyses of fact without skeptical consequence.

Hume Studies I— (1975—).
Semiannual journal devoted to systematic research on all aspects of Hume's life and works.

Jessop, T. E. *A Bibliography of David Hume and of Scottish Philosophy, from Francis Hutcheson to Lord Balfour*. London: A. Brown & Sons, 1938, 201 p.
Excellent primary and secondary Hume bibliography, especially useful for critical studies written before 1900.

Johnson, Oliver A. "Hume's 'True' Scepticism." *Pacific Philosophical Quarterly* 62, No. 4 (October 1981): 403-10.
Challenges the view that Hume's skepticism is epistemological, proposing instead that it is essentially psychological and that it "describes a style of living as congenial to the cognitivist as to the sceptic."

Kirk, Russell. "Eighteenth-Century Intellects: Skeptical Realism: Hume." In his *The Roots of American Order*, pp. 358-68. La Salle, Ill.: Open Court, 1974.
Outlines the major tenets of Hume's philosophy and considers Hume's influence on the American Founding Fathers.

Livingston, Donald W. "Anscombe, Hume and Julius Caesar." *Analysis* 35, No. 1 (October 1974): 13-19.
Answers G. E. M. Anscombe's response (see excerpt dated 1973) to Hume's analysis of the grounds for belief in the historicity of Julius Caesar's death.

———. "Hume and America." *The Kentucky Review* IV, No. 3 (Spring 1983): 15-38.
Assesses the influence of Hume's works on the American Founding Fathers.

———. *Hume's Philosophy of Common Life*. Chicago: University of Chicago Press, 1984, 371 p.
Comprehensive interpretation of Hume's major writings.

———, and King, James T., eds. *Hume: A Re-Evaluation*. New York: Fordham University Press, 1976, 421 p.
Excellent collection of essays treating a wide variety of Humean issues.

Maidment, H. J. "In Defence of Hume on Miracles." *Philosophy* XIV, No. 56 (October 1939): 422-33.
Refutes allegations that "Of Miracles" is seriously flawed in its reasoning and was written solely to call attention to its author.

Meyer, Paul H. "Voltaire and Hume as Historians: A Comparative Study of the *Essai sur les moeurs* and the *History of England*." *PMLA* LXXIII, No. 1 (March 1958): 51-68.
Compares the historical methods of Hume and Voltaire, noting especially the two authors' Enlightenment sensibilities.

Miller, Dickinson S. "Hume's Deathblow to Deductivism." *The Journal of Philosophy* XLVI, No. 23 (10 November 1949): 745-62.
Practical exposition of Hume's proposition that inference from experience is not deductive and is therefore a purely irrational process.

Miller, Hugh. "The Naturalism of Hume." *The Philosophical Review* XXXVIII, No. 5 (September 1929): 469-82.
Argues that Hume's philosophical outlook is the antithesis of mechanism.

Moore, G. E. "Hume's Philosophy." In his *Philosophical Studies*, pp. 147-67. London: Routledge & Kegan Paul, 1922.

General overview of Hume's philosophy, centering on the statement that all knowledge of facts, beyond the reach of observation, is founded on experience.

Mossner, Ernest Campbell. "Was Hume a Tory Historian?: Facts and Considerations." *Journal of the History of Ideas* II, No. 2 (April 1941): 225-36.
Places Hume in two camps of political theory, Whiggism and Toryism, claiming that he may not be exclusively identified with either of them.

————. "An Apology for David Hume, Historian." *PMLA* LVI, No. 3 (September 1941): 657-90.
Defends Hume against charges that he lacked historical purpose, botched the idea of social history, and simplified human psychology to the point where his character studies are valueless.

————. *The Forgotten Hume: Le bon David.* New York: Columbia University Press, 1943, 251 p.
Intimate biography of Hume, observing him "as friend and as foe, as critic and as patron, as man and as Scot."

————. "The Continental Reception of Hume's *Treatise,* 1739-1741." *Mind* LVI, No. 221 (January 1947): 31-43.
Traces early European critical reaction to Hume's *Treatise of Human Nature.*

————. "The First Answer to Hume's *Treatise:* An Unnoticed Item of 1740." *Journal of the History of Ideas* XII, No. 2 (April 1951): 291-94.
Outlines the earliest known answer to Hume's *Treatise of Human Nature,* an anonymous 1740 review published in *Common Sense; or, The Englishman's Journal.*

————. "The Religion of David Hume." *Journal of the History of Ideas* XXXIX, No. 4 (October-December 1978): 653-63.
Provocative, well-documented study of Hume's attitude toward religion.

————. *The Life of David Hume.* 2d ed. Oxford: Oxford University Press, Clarendon Press, 1980, 709 p.
Outstanding, carefully researched biography of Hume, packed with anecdote and incident and augmented by the liberal use of quotation.

Norton, David Fate. *David Hume: Common-Sense Moralist, Sceptical Metaphysician.* Princeton: Princeton University Press, 1982, 329 p.
Argues that Hume's philosophy is significantly more complex than many commentators have thought it to be.

[Oliphant, Margaret]. "Historical Sketches of the Reign of George II, No. XI: The Sceptic." *Blackwood's Edinburgh Magazine* DCXLIV, No. CV (June 1869): 665-91.
Close examination of Humean skepticism.

Peach, Bernard. "Hume's Mistake." *Journal of the History of Ideas* XLI, No. 2 (April-June 1980): 331-34.
Suggests that Hume may have admitted to the moralist Richard Price a fundamental (but presently unidentified) mistake in the argument of "Of Miracles."

Peterson, Michael L. "Reid Debates Hume: Christian versus Skeptic." *Christianity Today* XXII, No. 22 (22 September 1978): 23-6.
Surveys Thomas Reid's philosophical debate with Hume, observing that although the two men disagreed on fundamental principles, they respected each other.

Pike, Nelson. "Hume on Evil." *The Philosophical Review* LXXII (1963): 180-97.
Close study of Hume's views on evil, focusing on Parts X and XI of *Dialogues concerning Natural Religion.*

Popkin, Richard H. "David Hume: His Pyrrhonism and His Critique of Pyrrhonism." *The Philosophical Quarterly* I, No. 5 (October 1951): 385-407.
Masterly study of Hume's Pyrrhonian skepticism.

————. "Joseph Priestley's Criticisms of David Hume's Philosophy." *Journal of the History of Philosophy* XV, No. 4 (October 1977): 437-47.
Studies Joseph Priestley's attack on Hume's philosophy (see excerpt dated 1780), asserting that for the most part Priestley did not offer a well-argued or well-supported case.

Popper, Karl R. "Conjectural Knowledge: My Solution to the Problem of Induction: An Afterthought on Induction." In his *Objective Knowledge: An Evolutionary Approach,* pp. 85-101. Oxford: Oxford University Press, Clarendon Press, 1972.
Analyzes Hume's arguments concerning induction and causation.

Pottle, Frederick A. "The Part Played by Horace Walpole and James Boswell in the Quarrel between Rousseau and Hume." *Philological Quarterly* IV, No. 4 (October 1925): 351-63.
Describes Walpole's and Boswell's machinations in the quarrel between Hume and Jean-Jacques Rousseau.

Richetti, John J. "Hume." In his *Philosophical Writing: Locke, Berkeley, Hume,* pp. 183-263. Cambridge: Harvard University Press, 1983.
Approaches Hume's major works through "extraterritorial literary criticism," focusing on their principal rhetorical features.

Ring, Benjamin A. "David Hume: Historian or Tory Hack?" *North Dakota Quarterly* 36, No. 1 (Winter 1968): 50-9.
Examines the question of whether Hume was an historian of his times or a mouthpiece of the Tory politicians.

Shouse, J. B. "David Hume and William James: A Comparison." *Journal of the History of Ideas* XIII, No. 4 (October 1952): 514-27.
Sees agnosticism as simply a point of departure for Hume's investigation of belief, not as any central part or tenet of it.

Sorley, W. R. "Philosophers: David Hume." In *The Cambridge History of English Literature,* Vol. X: *The Age of Johnson,* edited by Sir A. W. Ward and A. R. Waller, pp. 363-79. New York: G. P. Putnam's Sons, 1913.
Overview of Hume's philosophical and historical career, with brief comments on his literary ambitions.

Stroud, Barry. *Hume.* The Arguments of the Philosophers, edited by Ted Honderich, No. 5. London: Routledge & Kegan Paul, 1977, 280 p.
General interpretation of the central tenets of Hume's philosophy.

Talmor, Ezra. *Descartes and Hume.* Oxford: Pergamon Press, 1980, 174 p.
Inquires how Hume could make an objective picture of man, society, and nature from purely subjective ideas.

Taylor, A. E. *David Hume & the Miraculous.* 1927. Reprint. Darby, Pa.: Folcroft Library Editions, 1972, 54 p.
Approaches Hume through his essay "Of Miracles," noting the significance of religion in Hume's life and thought.

Todd, William B., ed. *Hume and the Enlightenment: Essays Presented to Ernest Campbell Mossner.* Edinburgh: Edinburgh University Press; Austin: University of Texas Humanities Research Center, 1974, 215 p.
Contains fourteen specially commissioned essays on Hume and his works, including studies of Hume's critique of ethical rationalism, his view of reason and experience in ethics, and a primary Hume bibliography.

Ushenko, A. P. "The Problem of Causal Inference." *Philosophy of Science* 9, No. 2 (April 1942): 132-38.
Refutes Hume on causal inference, maintaining that Hume's argument is invalid unless it is assumed that mere difference in dates can affect nature's course.

Wexler, Victor G. *David Hume and the "History of England."* Memoirs of the American Philosophical Society, vol. 131. Philadelphia: American Philosophical Society, 1979, 114 p.
Close study of the composition of Hume's *History of England.*

Wheatley, Christopher J. ''Polemical Aspects of Hume's Natural History of Religion.'' *Eighteenth-Century Studies* 19, No. 4 (Summer 1986): 502-14.
> Claims that Hume's argument against the rational foundation of belief in God in *Dialogues concerning Natural Religion* was intentionally controversial and polemical.

Whelan, Frederick G. *Order and Artifice in Hume's Political Philosophy*. Princeton: Princeton University Press, 1985, 393 p.
> Delineates Hume's political views, chiefly as they illustrate the coherence of his philosophy.

Wright, John P. *The Sceptical Realism of David Hume*. Minneapolis: University of Minnesota Press, 1983, 269 p.
> Rigorous study of Hume's skepticism, emphasizing the philosopher's science of human nature.

Robert Hunter

?-1734

Scottish-born English dramatist.

Hunter wrote *Androboros,* the first play known to have been written and printed in America. A colonial administrator who recognized the practical value of political satire, he wrote his only major work in response to political and religious circumstances he found in the New World. With *Androboros,* Hunter gave birth to the American drama, signaled the advent of American political satire, appreciably furthered understanding between colonial ministers and their congregations, practically inaugurated American comic writing, and created a document of abiding interest in the history of colonial America.

Hunter's life was primarily a military and political one. He was born at Hunterston, Ayrshire, Scotland, probably during the last third of the seventeenth century. Nothing is known for certain about his boyhood and adolescence, but it has been suggested by one commentator that during his teens he may have deserted an apprenticeship to join the British army. He began to make a name for himself as a soldier around the beginning of the eighteenth century. He fought with distinction under the Duke of Marlborough in the War of the Spanish Succession and later saw action in the battle of Blenheim, possibly with the Fifth Irish Dragoons. In recognition of his model service, he was made lieutenant colonel, serving with this rank until 1707, when the Earl of Orkney, then Whig governor of Virginia, arranged his promotion to lieutenant governor of that colony. Hunter promptly left England for his new post, but, captured en route by an enemy privateer, he was forcibly detained in France, albeit in friendly, even comfortable circumstances. He used the considerable freedom allowed him to become acquainted with leading members of the French cultural establishment, eventually returning to England as part of a prisoner exchange. He arrived home thoroughly schooled in the niceties of French literature, culture, and deportment, and began to cultivate a wide circle of literary friends, one which included Jonathan Swift and Richard Steele. He was again considered for a crown appointment in America, this time apparently through the powerful influence of his wife Elizabeth, daughter of Sir Thomas Orby and widow of Brigadier General John Hay. Hunter quickly won favor: he was made captain general and governor-in-chief of New York and New Jersey in 1709, sailing for America in 1710.

Hunter's American administration is notable both for its outstanding successes and dismal failures. The new governor was entrusted with delivering to New York and then overseeing three thousand Palatine refugees who were to help produce naval stores for the British. The scheme was initially successful, but Hunter eventually found the project unmanageable and ultimately spent much of his own fortune in a vain effort to sustain it. Shortly after this fiasco, Hunter became involved in bitter factional disputes between New York and New Jersey and was beleaguered by a persistent struggle with the colonial legislatures over the control of finance. In spite of these and other difficulties and disappointments, however, he was essentially successful in most of his initiatives, especially the later ones, and won popularity by his selflessness, effectiveness as an administrator, and overall fairness—no small achievement in a place where royal officials were rarely trusted, much

less welcomed. Before July 1719, when his administration ended and he returned to England, Hunter had smoothed relations between the legislative houses, eased some serious financial problems in the colonies, helped organize strong frontier defense against the French in Canada, strengthened the New York court of chancery, and initiated—with the help of Joseph Dudley, governor of Massachusetts Bay—an express post between Albany and Boston. None of these achievements came without cost, however, for Hunter was constantly embroiled in political and religious controversy. Following his return to England, he lived in relative peace, frequently serving as a colonial-affairs consultant to the Board of Trade before being made governor of Jamaica in 1727. He died in Jamaica in 1734, having squarely and successfully confronted myriad social and economic problems during his tenure there.

Although Hunter is credited by one early critic with writing "some elegant little pieces in poetry which never appeared in his name," it is for his drama, *Androboros,* that he is remembered. The play is modeled on the Swiftian satire Hunter knew well from his London days and was intended as an indictment of troubles he experienced in his dealings with the American colonists. *Androboros* pillories two of Hunter's most vocal and irksome opponents in America (the identities of the models for the characters are provided by a handwritten key in the only known copy of the play): General Francis Nicholson, a capable but widely despised royal commissioner known for his bitter and vexatious manner, and the Reverend William Vesey, a native-born American convert to Anglicanism with whom Hunter had a falling-out over the former's illegal appointment of a minister to a church post in Jamaica, Long Island. The play's cast of characters is large. In addition to Nicholson and Vesey, who appear respectively as "Androboros" (literally, "man-eater") and "Fizle," *Androboros* showcases David Jamison, a Scottish-born religious fanatic who was appointed chief justice of the New Jersey Supreme Court in 1711; Samuel Milford, a first settler of Easthampton and a virulent opponent of Hunter on many issues; and Edward Hyde, Viscount Cornbury and later Earl of Clarendon, a venal, drunken transvestite who, as a royal official in New Jersey and New York, oversaw administrations generally accounted the worst of colonial times. The play is set, to use Hunter's own words, in the "Long Gallary in Moor-Fields," and the action is directed at exposing Nicholson's unctuousness, blasting Vesey's underhandedness, and taking to task assemblymen whose self-interest blinded them to their governor's benevolence.

Hunter exploited the major elements of traditional satire throughout *Androboros.* Blending pointed criticism with overt humor, trenchant wit, and occasional farce, he aimed at improving men and institutions, not simply debunking them, but did not shrink from the bitter, Juvenalian anger favored by many English satirists of his age. Initially hurling irony and sarcasm at individuals but later aiming more broadly, he ultimately followed Joseph Addison's dictum, to "pass over a single foe to charge all armies." The result was, according to colonial New York lieutenant governor Cadwallader Colden, that the governor's enemies "were so humorously exposed that the laugh was turned upon them in all companies and from this laughing humour the people began to be in good humour with their Governor and to despise the idol of the clergy.''

Critical notices of Hunter's literary work are neither plentiful nor especially penetrating, but among their authors are men of the greatest eminence. Swift ranked Hunter with Addison, Steele, William Congreve, and George Savile, Marquess of Halifax, and Steele himself praised Hunter for his ''humanity, justice, and honour.'' Colden attested that Hunter ''understood the Belles lettres well,'' adding that he ''had an intimacy with the distinguished men of wit at that time in England.'' Near the end of the nineteenth century, the American critic and novelist Paul Leicester Ford examined the aesthetic merits of *Androboros* and concluded: ''The piece is really dramatic; despite its politics and lack of women's parts, the characters are admirably and sharply drawn.'' Twentieth-century commentators have focused on both the literary and historical importance of the play. Oral Sumner Coad acknowledged the drama's ''ingenuity and effectiveness,'' Montrose J. Moses noted Hunter's ''venomous wit,'' and, in separate studies, Lawrence H. Leder and Brooks McNamara outlined the political and religious circumstances surrounding the play. More recently, Walter J. Meserve characterized *Androboros* as ''a fair beginning for American drama,'' and, echoing and synthesizing his predecessors' views, Julian Mates said this about the play: ''As social history, it is biting, witty, and a thoroughly worthwhile literary contribution to early Americana''—a judgment that sums up over two and one-half centuries of opinion.

During one of the darkest moments of his American administration, Hunter came face to face with a number of persistent, serious, and damaging problems, and, with characteristic wisdom and good sense, he solved them: *Androboros* lampooned Hunter's religious and political opponents, ''destroying by laughter,'' according to Leder, ''those upon whom reason had no effect.'' Critics agree that Hunter's was a singularly original and effective solution, at least for the New World. It at once initiated the American drama, inaugurated American political satire, and virtually gave birth to American comic writing. For these and other reasons, *Androboros* is a milestone in American culture, and, most commentators agree, a distinguished and enjoyable one at that.

PRINCIPAL WORK

Androboros: A B[i]ographical Farce in Three Acts, Viz. The Senate, The Consistory, and The Apotheosis (drama) [first publication] 1714

*This work was also published in an annotated critical edition in *Bulletin of the New York Public Library* in 1964.

ANTHONY HENLEY   (letter date 1708)

[*Henley was a prominent seventeenth- and early-eighteenth-century English wit and politician best known for his close friendship with Jonathan Swift and for the correspondence that grew from it. In the following excerpt from a 1708 letter to Swift, Henley recalls Swift's remark, probably made in a letter now lost, that Hunter's literary work entitles him to be ranked with George Savile, Marquess of Halifax, Joseph Addison, William Congreve, and ''the Gazetteer,'' Richard Steele.*]

The reason why your letter was so long a coming to my hands, was, its being directed to me near Winchester; and Alresford is the post-town nearest to me. If the officers should come to you, Doctor, if you want a security, that your children shall not be troublesome to the parish, pray make use of me. I will stand them all, though you were to have as many as the Holland Countess. We have had a tedious expectation of the success of the siege of Lille: the country people begin to think there is no such thing, and say the newspapers talk of it to make people bear paying taxes a year longer. I do not know how Steele will get off of it: his veracity is at stake in Hampshire. Pray desire him to take the town, though he should leave the citadel for a nest-egg. I have not the honour to know Colonel Hunter: but I never saw him in so good company as you have put him in, Lord Halifax, Mr. Addison, Mr. Congreve, and the Gazetteer. Since he is there, let him stay there. (pp. 112-13)

> *Anthony Henley, in a letter to Jonathan Swift on September 16, 1708, in* The Correspondence of Jonathan Swift, D. D., *Vol. I by Jonathan Swift, edited by F. Elrington Ball, G. Bell and Sons, Ltd., 1910, pp. 112-14.*

SIR RICHARD STEELE   (essay date 1709)

[*An Irish-born English politician, dramatist, and essayist, Steele is best known for his journalistic enterprises. Among the many periodicals he founded and edited during the eighteenth century, the two most notable are the* Tatler *and the* Spectator, *the latter a highly popular and influential daily created in collaboration with Joseph Addison. Steele was always conscious of the moral intent and effect of his essays, and though they are often diverting and amusing, their ultimate aim is the ethical improvement of the reader. As a dramatist, too, Steele was primarily a moralist; plays such as* The Tender Husband (1705) *and* The Conscious Lovers (1722) *were instrumental in effecting the transition from the decadent, cynical comedies of the Restoration to the didacticism of sentimental comedy. In the following excerpt from a 1709 issue of the* Tatler, *Steele praises Hunter—referred to here by the sobriquet ''Eboracensis''—and predicts that great things will spring from Hunter's governorship in America.*]

A man in power, who can, without the ordinary prepossessions which stop the way to the true knowledge and service of mankind, overlook the little distinctions of fortune, raise obscure merit, and discountenance successful indesert, has, in the minds of knowing men, the figure of an angel rather than a man, and is above the rest of men in the highest character he can be, even that of their benefactor. Turning my thoughts as I was taking my pipe this evening after this manner, it was no small delight to me to receive advice from Felicia [an epithet of England], that Eboracensis was appointed a governor of one of their plantations. As I am a great lover of mankind, I took part in the happiness of that people who were to be governed by one of so great humanity, justice, and honour. Eboracensis has read all the schemes which writers have formed of government and order, and been long conversant with men who have the reins in their hands; so that he can very well distinguish between chimerical and practical politics. It is a great blessing (when men have to deal with such different characters in the same species as those of free-men and slaves) that they who command have a just sense of human nature itself, by which they can temper the haughtiness of the master, and soften the servitude of the slave. ''Hæ tibi erunt artes'' [''This will be your task''; in these and in the following words from Book VI of *The Aeneid*, ''to give the nations peace, to spare the humbled and crush the rebellious,'' Vergil described the imperial destiny of Rome]. This is the notion with which those of the plantation receive Eboracensis: and as I have cast his nativity, I find it will be a record made of this person's administrations; and on that part of the shore from whence he embarks to return from his government, there will be a monument with these words: "Here the people wept, and took leave of Eboracensis, the first governor our mother Felicia sent, who, during his command here, believed himself her subject." (pp. 145-46)

> *Sir Richard Steele, in an essay in* The Tatler, *Vol. I, edited by George A. Aitken, Duckworth & Co., 1898, pp. 144-46.*

ROBERT HUNTER (essay date 1714)

[*In the following excerpt from his dedication of* Androboros *to "Don. Com. Fiz."—almost certainly the Reverend William Vesey, who appears prominently in the play under the name Fizle—Hunter presents his play and anticipates its effect on its audience.*]

Cerdo Gloucestriensis, an Author of the last Century, of great Sagacity, observ'd well, That *Runto Polimunto Plumpismenoi Raperpandico*——What d'ye stare at? This is good *Greek* for ought you know, and contains a Mystery, which shall continue so, unless you Reveal it; and so no more of that. The following *Elionophysalo Fizlical Farce* having fallen into my Hands by a most surprizing Accident, it seemeth meet unto me that it should, with all due Reverence Kiss yours. Here it lies at your Feet, take it up. Now read the first Act,——Have ye done? What's the matter Man? Have ye got the Gripes? A Plague on your Sower Faces. Bring him a Dram. What have you to do, had you to do, or ought you to have to do with the *Senate*? You smell a Rat, you say. Be it so. But compose your self, and now Read the Second Act,——How d'ye like it, ha? *O Hooo, T'churrrrrrrrrtch*, I can say that as Loud as you can do; and if you'll but leave out these Damnable *R*'s and *T*'s which make it so hard in Pronounciation, and harder in Digestion, I like it better than you do.

> *Robert Hunter, in a dedication to his* Androboros, *N.p., 1714. Reprinted in* Bulletin of the New York Public Library, *Vol. 68, No. 3, March, 1964, p. 162.*

CADWALLADER COLDEN (letter dates 1759)

[*An eighteenth-century Scottish-born American, Colden became lieutenant governor of New York after a long political career. In addition to numerous treatises on medicine, moral philosophy, and natural science, he wrote the first careful, objective study of the Iroquois Confederacy,* The History of the Five Indian Nations *(1727), and is remembered among scientists for his implied criticism of Sir Isaac Newton's theories in* Explication of the First Causes of Action in Matter, *and of the Causes of Gravitation (1745). In the following excerpt from two 1759 letters prompted by the publication of William Smith, Jr.'s* History of the Province of New York, from the First Discovery to the Year MDCCXXXII *(1757), Colden considers the merits of some unsigned writings believed to be by Hunter and describes the reception given to* Androboros *upon its publication.*]

I know not on what authority Mr Smith says that Mr Hunter when a boy was put aprentice to an Apothecary it may be on as slender authority as many other things he writes. When I knew Mr Hunter he was an exceedingly well shaped and well proportioned man tho' then advanced in years. In his younger years he had been of uncommon strength and activity. He understood the Belles lettres well and had an intimacy with the distinguished men of wit at that time in England among them

Dr Arbuthnot Queen Annes favorite physician was his most intimate and useful friend tho' he and the doctor differed greatly in their political sentiments for Mr Hunter was a Stanch Whig. He wrote some pieces in the *Tatlers*. When he was appointed Governor of New York a very high compliment was made in one of the *Tatlers* to him under the name of *Eboracensis* [see excerpt dated 1709]. He wrote some elegant little pieces in poetry which never appeared in his name. He had an exceeding pretty and entertaining manner of telling a Tale and was a most agreable companion with his intimate friends. He was fond of men of Learning and encouraged them whenever he had opportunity. In short he was a Gentleman of extraordinary abilities both natural and acquired and had every qualification requisite in a Governor. (p. 192)

• • • • •

[At one time during Mr Hunter's governorship the] Church clergy joined in the design to distress the Governor in hopes of haveing the good churchman Col Nicholson appointed governor. He had a crowd of clergymen allwise about him who were continually extolling his merits among the people and doing all in their power to lessen Mr Hunter. Mr Hunter had then a hard task. His friends in the ministry out of place his Bills to a great value protested. Mr Nicholson and the Clergy who ought to have assisted him endeavoring to undermine him and the assembly refusing to grant any support on the terms on which he could accept of it without breach of his instructions. Tho' he was at the same time so sensible of the difficulties he was under as to say to some of his friends that he expected to dye in a Jail he kept up his spirits never suffered the least dejection or diffidence of his affairs to appear in public. He kept up the dignity of the Governor without lessening the expence which attended it notwithstanding of the difficulties he was under as to money. At this time while Mr Hunter had the greatest reason to be shagreened and out of humour he diverted himself in composing a Farce with the assistance of Mr Morris which he called *Androborus* (the man eater) In this the general (Nicholson) the clergy and the assembly were so humorously exposed that the laugh was turned upon them in all companies and from this laughing humour the people began to be in good humour with their Governor and to despise the idol of the clergy. (pp. 201-02)

> *Cadwallader Colden, in letters to his son on September 25, 1759 and undated, 1759, in* Collections of the New-York Historical Society for the Year 1868, *New-York Historical Society, 1868, pp. 192-97, 197-206.*

PAUL LEICESTER FORD (essay date 1893)

[*Ford was a versatile and prolific late-nineteenth-century American novelist, scholar, and bibliographer whose rigorous studies of Thomas Jefferson and George Washington helped set a standard for biographical and historical writing. His best-known works of fiction,* The Honorable Peter Stirling and What People Thought of Him *(1894) and* Janice Meredith *(1899), reflect their author's deep knowledge of American life and history, while his pioneering bibliographical checklists of Americana retain their usefulness even today. In the following excerpt, he discusses the dramatic qualities of* Androboros.]

In 1714, Robert Hunter, Governor of New York, misliking certain political antagonists, wrote a political and personal satire on them, which he called *Androborus*, "a biographical farce in three acts," and printed it in New York City, though with the fictitious imprint of "Monoropolis," which was very bad Greek for "Fool's Town." The piece was seemingly never intended for stage production, for a part of the plot turns on so filthy an incident as to preclude its performance, even in the coarse and vulgar time of its writing. The piece is really dramatic; despite its politics and lack of women's parts, the characters are admirably and sharply drawn, and it abounds in genuine humor. The part of "Tom of Bedlam," is almost as good, in use of words, as Mrs. Malaprop, and the trick played on Androborus, of making him believe himself dead, is both quaint and effective. Altogether it cannot be ranked in cleverness by any play of American origin for many years, and it is the first both written and printed in America. (p. 8)

> *Paul Leicester Ford, in his* Some Notes towards an Essay on the Beginnings of American Dramatic Literature, 1606-1789, *1893. Reprint by Burt Franklin, 1971, 29 p.*

ORAL SUMNER COAD   (essay date 1918)

[*Coad is an American academic and scholar who has written respected works on the American stage and authoritative studies of the life and works of William Dunlap, Benjamin Franklin, and Edgar Allan Poe. In the following excerpt, he outlines the circumstances that led to the writing of* Androboros *and comments on the play's structure, characterization, satire, and action.*]

In view of the increasing attention which the dramatic literature of America is attracting, one turns with curiosity to the first play to be written and printed in this country. Its title-page reads: "**Androboros A Biographical Farce In Three Acts, Viz. The Senate, The Consistory, and The Apotheosis.** Printed at Monoropolis since 1st August, 1714." (Monoropolis means Fool's Town, which is to say New York.) . . . From the fact that the words "By Governour Hunter" have been written on the title-page in an antiquated hand, it is agreed that the author of the sketch was Robert Hunter, Governor of the Colony of New York from 1710 to 1719.

Hunter was one of the most able of the Colonial Governors, but he was not without enemies, and in **Androboros** he took occasion to pillory them ruthlessly. Before coming to America, his keen mind had won him the friendship of Addison, Steele, and other wits of his day, and in this satire he displayed a caustic and trenchant mode of attack of which the author of *The Dunciad* himself would not have been ashamed. The two persons most distinguished by the writer's ridicule were Colonel Francis Nicholson, formerly Lieutenant-Governor of the colony, and Dr. William Vesey, Rector of Trinity Church. At the very beginning of his administration Hunter, though a good Anglican, ran foul of the Established Church by refusing to obtain for it grants of land, and by a seeming lukewarmness towards its interests. Dr. Vesey, pious but bigoted, charged him with plotting to turn the control of affairs over to dissenters, and used his influence to embarrass and oppose the Governor wherever possible. Vesey's chief abettor was the arrogant and overbearing Colonel Nicholson, whom Hunter accused of attempting to usurp his power. In the spring of 1714 Vesey, at Nicholson's suggestion, went to England to secure governmental support against his antagonists. It was probably this hostile act that called forth **Androboros.** (p. 182)

[The sole surviving copy of the play, which one of its early owners, John Philip] Kemble conjectured to have been Hunter's own, contains a key to the *dramatis personæ*. From it we learn that the four main characters, Androboros (man-eater), Fizle, the Keeper of the Senate, and Solemn are disguises respectively

for Nicholson, Vesey, Hunter, and Lewis Morris, who was Hunter's ally and may have had a hand in writing the sketch.

The first two acts reflect a number of contemporary events and conditions. At the outset we find the loquacious and incompetent Senate in session under the suffrance of the Keeper, whose domineering attitude recalls Hunter's tendency to dissolve the Assembly whenever it proved unruly.

Subsequently the Senate forms itself into a Consistory, presumably for the purpose of defying the Keeper. This body, as it sits in grave deliberation, is startled by the sudden appearance of Fizle, who has intentionally besmirched his robe and comes before the Consistory, blaming the Keeper for the outrage, and threatening dire punishment with the aid of Androboros. This episode was based on one of the numerous skirmishes between Hunter and the church party. In February, 1714, Trinity Church was broken into and the vestments were torn and defiled. In proclaiming a reward for the apprehension of the culprits, the Governor took a covert fling at the reputation of Dr. Vesey by declaring that the act must have been performed by "such as are avowed enemies of religion in general, or to the civil and religious constitution of England in particular, or such as for filthy lucre, or worse purposes, may have in appearance conformed to, or complied with either, but by their unchristian and lewd conversation, and their disloyal and seditious conduct, sufficiently manifest their aversion to both." In their wrath at this attack, the churchmen addressed a condemnation of Hunter to Nicholson.

While the Consistory is discussing the indignity which Fizle has suffered, an important message is received from Androboros. Earlier in the play he had blusteringly announced his intention of making war upon the traditional enemy of his countrymen, but now his dispatch states that the expedition has been abandoned, the foe having shown his friendship by offering to resign the two poles to the New Yorkers and to retain for himself only that which lies between. For this triumph the Consistory votes Androboros a statue. In these scenes the author was lampooning Nicholson's ill-starred attempt in 1711 against the French in Canada, with whom the colonists had been frequently embroiled. This expedition, which the Colonel had strongly advocated, and in which he led the land forces, proved a failure, for after the disaster which befell the fleet he retreated without striking a blow.

In Act III the playwright beguiled himself by depicting the complete discomfiture of his opponents. The Keeper's friend, Solemn, tricks Androboros into thinking himself dead. While under this delusion, he is made the victim of much horse-play; he is knocked from a chair, he is covered with floor-sweepings, he is sprinkled with water, and he is blinded with snuff. Thus deprived of his sight, he comes charging into the Senate room and runs upon the Keeper's chair. Now Fizle has so contrived it that this seat will sink through the floor when the Keeper takes his place. But the treachery proves a boomerang, for the weight of Androboros springs the trap, and both he and Fizle are swallowed up. Solemn pronounces their obituary in these words:

> In former Ages virtuous Deeds
>   Rais'd Mortals to the blest Abodes,
> But Hero's of the Modern Breed
>   And Saints go downward to the Gods.

The sketch, which in all probability was never acted, is obviously the work of a man who was not experienced in playwriting. None the less it possesses, especially in the third act, some ingenuity and effectiveness. Delicate the humor certainly is not, but it is abundant and at times has satiric point. The misreading of Fizle's petition by Tom of Bedlam, Clerk of the Senate, is fairly typical. In place of the conventional conclusion: "And your petitioners like as they are duty Bound, shall never cease to pray," Tom reads: "And your petitioners like asses as they are, in a durty pound, shall never cease to bray."

Androboros was hardly designed to allay the quarrel which engendered it. On the contrary, the friction continued for over a year longer until a sort of armed truce was eventually declared. But the play is of interest both as a mirror of certain conditions of its time and as our first political satire in dramatic form, a type that came to be frequently employed in the Revolutionary period. (pp. 182-83)

> Oral Sumner Coad, "The First American Play," in *The Nation, Vol. CVII, No. 2772, August 17, 1918, pp. 182-83.*

MONTROSE J. MOSES   (essay date 1925)

[*Moses was a late-nineteenth- and early-twentieth-century American biographer, anthologist, and critic whose works include* The Literature of the South *(1909) and* The American Dramatist *(1911). In the following excerpt from the 1925 revision of the last-named work, he considers the value of* Androboros *as a mirror of American colonial life.*]

The characteristics which mark the drama of the colonial period are worthy of consideration, merely because they represent the interests of playwrights who began the writing of drama in America. It was Governor Robert Hunter who, in 1714, is supposed to have been the first to put his pen to paper in dramatic form. There is only one copy existent of *Androboros: A B(i)ographical Farce*. . . . The authorship of *Androboros* rests upon the name of Hunter written on the title page. He was the Royal Governor of the Colony of New York from 1710 to 1719. The play may be regarded as a muckraking diatribe against certain matters occurring in Trinity Parish, New York City. A friend of Addison and Steele, the venomous wit of Hunter played relentlessly with contemporary matters, Church politics, and colonial events. America's first satire was born of contemporary interest, and couched in language of none too polite a nature. The name *Androboros* signifies man-eater.

[All told, the first beginnings of the American drama] are more vital in their meaning if taken as social measure of the time rather than as artistic value. Their literary merit is of second-hand significance. Occasionally the eye of the colonial writer was caught by the individuality of his local surroundings. But he was an Englishman at heart. . . . All plays written by the colonists are aloof from any "national" characteristics. Because, as yet, they had had little time to nationalize, and they were still in allegiance to Great Britain. All one can hope to do with so slim a product is to call attention to its infant intentions. These intentions are of much more value than the plays themselves—which are curiosities to be prized largely as—curiosities. (p. 38)

> Montrose J. Moses, "Our Colonial Theatre," in his *The American Dramatist, third edition, Little, Brown, and Company, 1925, pp. 18-38.*

ARTHUR HOBSON QUINN   (essay date 1943)

[*A distinguished American critic, editor, biographer, anthologist, poet, and writer of short fiction, Quinn made important contri-*butions to American theater history in such works as A History of the American Drama from the Beginning to the Civil War *(1923) and* A History of the American Drama from the Civil War to the Present Day *(1927). In the following excerpt from the former work, he discusses the satirical purpose of* Androboros.]

[The first American] printed play that has survived was not acted. On the one existing copy of *Androboros, A B[i]ographical Farce in Three Acts, viz: The Senate, The Consistory and The Apotheosis,* there are written the words "By Governour Hunter," and it has been attributed to Robert Hunter, Governor of the Province of New York from 1710 to 1719. . . . Hunter was an Englishman and the play has, therefore, only an historical interest. It is a clever satire on the Senate, and on Lieutenant Governor Nicholson, who is represented, according to the key written in the unique copy in the Huntington Library, under the name "Androboros," or "man eater." Nicholson being determined to lead an attack against the Mulomachians (the French), the Senate generously notes "Negen Skillingen and Elleve Pence" for the expenses of the expedition and also passes a resolution that "he has behav'd Himself on the said Expedition with Courage, Conduct and Prudence." When the keeper, who is Hunter himself, asks why this resolution is passed before the expedition, "Aesop" replies, "By all means, lest when it is over you should have less reason for this Resolve."

Had there been any attempt made to perform *Androboros,* it would have been hard to find a theatre. He would indeed be rash, in view of the many occasions on which "the first theatre in America" has been discovered, who would attempt to fix finally a date for that event. (p. 6)

> Arthur Hobson Quinn, "The Drama and the Theatre in the Colonies," in his *A History of the American Drama from the Beginning to the Civil War, second edition, 1943. Reprint by Irvington Publishers, Inc., 1979, pp. 1-32.*

BROOKS McNAMARA   (essay date 1964)

[*McNamara is an American academic and scholar who is best known for his important study of the early American theater,* The American Playhouse in the Eighteenth Century *(1969). In the following excerpt from an earlier work, he sketches the action of* Androboros *and evaluates the play's literary merits.*]

[Something] like the full story of *Androboros* ought, perhaps, to be told, for *Androboros* is not only America's first printed play, but also our first political satire, a source document of some interest in the history of early America, and an enlightening comment on the character and personality of Robert Hunter. (p. 106)

[In his role as colonial governor of New York, Hunter] found the colonial assembly obstinate, unwilling to bend to the authority of the queen, desirous of a charter government like those found in neighboring colonies, and unwilling to vote either salaries for English officials or appropriations for government supplies. One may settle on two men, however, as the chief sources of irritation of the provincial governor—two men who . . . were assuredly the *raison d'etre* of *Androboros*—Reverend William Vesey and Francis Nicholson. (p. 109)

[The sole surviving copy of the play contains] some handwritten notes, probably put there by the literary antiquarian Thomas Coxeter, which are of singular importance in the understanding of *Androboros*. Hunter is named as the author of the piece, and the names of the individuals satirized are written opposite the name of each character in the play: Hunter is Keeper; Vesey, Fizle; and Nicholson is named as the title character, Androboros. While opinions differ, it seems reasonable to assume that *Androboros* was never performed, and it is a certainty that it never will be, for whatever humor exists in the play stems from events of a strictly parochial nature.

At the beginning of the play, Hunter turns his attention to Nicholson and the power which the lieutenant governor held over the Senate. In a few passages he succeeds in making both Nicholson and the upper house look ridiculous by making Tom of Bedlam, the type of the lunatic, clerk of the Senate, and by having Tom provide a scathing description of Androboros,

> *Tom.* Sir, it is *Old Nick-nack*, who has Paganiz'd himself with that Name, which interpreted, signifies a *Man-Eater*. He is now very far gone indeed, He talks of nothing but Battles and Seiges, tho' he never saw one, and Conquest over Nations, and Alliances with Princes who never had a being; and this Senate is mainly intended for his Reception . . .

Scene ii finds the Senate complaining about "this Plaguey *Keeper*" until they are answered by Solemn, a character conceived by Hunter to represent his friend and supporter, Lewis Morris. The scene ends on a wry note as Tom of Bedlam, with fool's eloquent logic, lays out Vesey's ultimate scheme, saying that, "He sometimes fancy'd himself to be Pope, but his Brother not relishing that as Derogatory to his Pretensions, he is now Contended [sic] to be Patriarch of the Western Empire, of which Androboros is to be Sultan . . ."

In scene iii, Androboros enters and delivers a ranting and more than slightly incoherent speech to the Senate. Coxcomb, speaking for the sheep-like assemblage, offers a vote of confidence,

> *Coxcom.* Let us Resolve to Support, Maintain, and Defend the undoubted Title of the Great *Androboros* to the Powers and Authorities he has Graciously Assum'd over this and all other like Tenements, against all Wardens, Directors, Keepers, and their Abettors.
>
> *All.* Agreed.

Finally they settle on the fact that the Keeper "ought to be dismiss't from having any further Authority over us," and in the first scene of Act II, Fizle prompts the Senate into forming itself into a Consistory as a means of defeating the Keeper, and formulates a plot to poison all minds against him.

Scene ii begins with an interesting parody on Vesey's concern over the desecration of Trinity Church, at which time a number of vestments were defiled,

> *Fizle.* O Horror! O Abomination! was ever the like seen, heard or read of!
>
> *Flip.* What's the matter?
>
> *Fizle.* As I went to Robe myself for the more decent Attendance on this Consistory I found my Robes in this Pickle! That Vestment, so Reverenc'd by the Ancient and Modern World, beskirted and Bedaub'd with what I must not name!
>
> *Aesop.* Who has done this?
>
> *Fizle.* Who has done it! Who but the known Enemies to Consistories and Long Skirts?

Fizle, of course, is putting the plot into action by having rubbed his own skirts with dung in perfect parallel to Hunter's accusation in his proclamation after the incident at Trinity Church. In scene iii, the Consistory drafts a petition to remove the

Keeper. Fizle, having finished writing the document, turns it over to Tom of Bedlam to read. Tom intentionally misreads the petition, providing a rather excellent comic scene,

> *Tom.* [Reading from the petition.] We had declared him a *Raskal*, but he had the impudence to send us packing to our Cells, though we had several *Merduous Matters* under the *Infection of our Hose*.
>
> *Mulligrub.* Hold! I do not well understand that, Read it again.
>
> *Fizle.* He cant read his own Hand; it is *Several Arduous Matters under the Inspection of our House*. Go on.
>
> *Tom.* Wherefore it is our humble and earnest Supplication, that we may be once more be put under your *Wild Distraction*.
>
> *Fizle.* Mild Direction.
>
> *Tom.* Or that the *Excrement Androboros*.
>
> *Fizle.* Excellent *Androboros*.

The scene ends in a further parody of Nicholson, striking out against an abortive expedition against the French which was headed by the lieutenant governor in 1711.

Act III provides some interesting satire and the knowledge that Hunter had great insight into Nicholson's foibles and a fair ability to apply this knowledge to a dramatic situation. Tom proposes a plot to make Androboros believe he is dead and he bases it on what would appear to be a sound psychological appraisal of the lieutenant governor,

> I'll answer for the Success of what I propose, under any Penalties you please. I'm sure he has had the Art to Dream himself into Notions every whit as absurd. His Imagination is very ductile when 'tis heated, and by a Long Practice upon't, he has made it as susceptible of Impressions from Without, as it has been of these from Within.

In a very competent little comic scene, the Keeper and Tom pretend that Androboros is dead and refuse to admit his existence when he enters the room. Moment by moment, Androboros becomes more hysterical,

> *Androb.* Sure all the World is Mad, or have a mind to make me so; I tried to get out, but the Porter lean't his Staff against my Nose, and belch't full in my Chops; a Culverine could not have done more suddain Execution than that Erruption of Barm and Tobacco Smoak.
>
> *Solemn.* When is he to be Interr'd?
>
> *Tom.* This Ev'ning, but is to lie in State here till then.
>
> *Androboros.* I made a shift to recover myself, and attempted the back passage; but in the Door of the Kitchin I was saluted with a pale of foul Water, which had like to have been succeeded by a Shovel of burning Coals, but that I made a speedy Retreat. Something's the matter, what e'er it is; I'll listen here and find out.
>
> *Keeper.* But why so suddainly? 'Tis strange so Great a Man should be bury'd with so little Ceremony.
>
> *Androb.* Bury'd said he!

The joke is continued for some time, Solemn pretending to see Androboros' ghost in a delightful parody of *Hamlet*. Solemn addresses the supposed ghost,

Angels and all the Ministers of Grace, Defend me.
Be thou a Spirit of Health or Goblin Damn'd! Bring
with the Airs from Heav'n, or Blasts from Hell, Thou
Com'st in such Questionable Shape, I'll speak to
Thee. Thanks Good Hamlet for this again,
I'll   [Softly]   call the General. Valiant *Andro-
boros*, O speak.

Androb. I tell you, ye Old Fool—

Tom of Bedlam continues to torment Androboros, playing a
series of tricks on him which culminates in Androboros being
temporarily blinded by a blast of snuff in the eyes. In the
meantime, Fizle has set a trap for the Keeper, placing his chair
on a trap door. But it is not the Keeper who falls into the chair;
the blinded Androboros finds it, sits, and together with Fizle
and Flip, sinks into the pit below as Solemn declaims,

> In former Ages virtuous Deeds
>   Rais'd Mortals to the blest Abodes
> But Hero's of the Modern Breed
>   And Saints go downward to the Gods.
>
> (pp. 112-16)

There is no attempt to state that *Androboros* is a good play.
Though it has some occasional flashes of rude wit, it is highly
topical and, in most respects, a very naive attempt at playwriting. Whatever value is to be found in *Androboros* lies in
its position as a political and social document which reveals
something of the personalities of Nicholson and Hunter and
something of the political climate of early New York. Perhaps
more justification for studying *Androboros* (if justification is
necessary) lies in its unique position in the history of American
drama, and, quite frankly, in the eternal appeal of the literary
curiosity. (p. 116)

> Brooks McNamara, "Robert Hunter and 'Andro-
> boros'," in The Southern Speech Journal, *Vol. XXX,
> No. 2, Winter, 1964, pp. 106-16.*

LAWRENCE H. LEDER (essay date 1964)

[*An American historian who specializes in the American colonial
period, Leder is an authority on colonial political theory, the
early history of New York, and the life of Robert Livingston. In
the following excerpt, he outlines the events that gave rise to*
Androboros.]

In the fall of 1714, Governor Robert Hunter of New York,
beset by more problems than he could seemingly comprehend
or solve, sought in literature an outlet for his increasing sense
of frustration. His reaction to New York politics was not uncommon among the colony's governors, but he possessed an
important and unusual advantage. Jonathan Swift, acknowledged master of satire and "no gentle critic or idle flatterer,"
ranked the Governor with Addison, Halifax, Congreve, and
Steele [see the remark by Swift in the excerpt by Henley dated
1708]. Hunter, therefore, had an outlet not available to his
predecessors or his successors, and he used it to teach his
opponents that the pen could be mightier than the sword in
cutting them down to size.

The product which emerged from Hunter's pen was *Androboros: A Biographical Farce in Three Acts,* the first play written
and printed in America. Its importance goes beyond its literary
primacy, however; it is a biting satire in which the Governor
did figuratively what he could not do literally—he pilloried
General Francis Nicholson, the Anglican clergymen in New
York and New Jersey (particularly the Reverend William Vesey), and the opposition leadership in the Assembly. They were

responsible for Hunter's unhappiness, and he retaliated by star-
ring them in his play. The consequences were best explained
by Cadwallader Colden: the Governor's enemies "were so
humorously exposed that the laugh was turned upon them in
all companies and from this laughing humour the people began
to be in good humour with their Governour and to despise the
idol of the clergy" [see excerpt dated 1759].

Hunter had arrived in New York in June 1710 to find the colony
wracked by political factionalism and intrigue, perhaps more
so than any other royal colony. The issues were so ancient that
they were almost forgotten, but the roots lay in the executions
for treason and murder of Jacob Leisler and Jacob Milborne
in 1691 and the continued persecution of their followers ever
since. Governor after governor had been either too weak or
too corrupt to do anything to eliminate this evil, and instead
played upon it for his own benefit. By joining one of the
extreme factions, the executive often found his administration
made easier and his purse fatter. Hunter insisted upon breaking
this vicious pattern, but a month after his arrival all he could
report was that "they are in no worse disposition than that I
found them in."

After three years at his self-appointed task the Governor wrote
to his friend Dean Swift:

> I thought, in coming to this country, "I should have
> hot meals, and cool drinks, and recreate my body in
> Holland sheets upon beds of down; whereas I am
> doing penance as If I was a hermit, and as I cannot
> do that with a will, believe in the long run the devil
> will fly away with me." This worthy [i e, Sancho
> Panza] was indeed but a type of me, of which I could
> fully convince you by an exact parallel between our
> administrations and circumstances. . . . The truth of
> the matter is, I am used like a dog, after having done
> all that is in the power of man to deserve better
> treatment, so that I am now quite jaded.

"Here," he added a few months later, "is the finest air to live
upon in the universe; and if our trees and birds could speak,
and our assemblymen be silent, the finest conversation too. . . .
In a word, and to be serious at last, I have spent three years
of life in such torment and vexation, that nothing in life can
ever make amends for it."

Many things caused Hunter's torment, but the most serious
was his relationship with the Assembly. His instructions from
the Crown collided directly with the wishes of the stubborn
legislators in money matters. This was nothing new, for the
Assemblymen had long since learned that no executive could
be trusted when it came to finances. Their experiences with
Benjamin Fletcher and Edward Hyde, Viscount Cornbury, gave
them ample reasons to insist on strict controls. The legislature
insisted, despite Crown instructions to the contrary, that only
it could establish a table of fees for the payment of government
officials who received their recompense by fees rather than
through salaries. The legislature also claimed that it alone could
determine the governor's salary, regardless of royal directives
about the amount to be paid. A complaisant governor, therefore, stood a better chance of receiving an adequate salary, or
even a "gift," which the Crown forbade, than one who showed
a streak of independence. The Assembly also dogmatically
denied that money bills could be amended by the governor or
council, and it refused to tempt an executive from the straight
and narrow path by voting him any long term appropriation
for the government's support.

As though these difficulties were not enough, Hunter soon found himself holding the financial bag of an experiment initiated and then dropped without warning by the Crown. Several thousand Palatinate refugees, ravaged in the Rhineland by Louis XIV and the French armies, fled to London and there posed an embarrassing problem for Queen Anne and her Whig ministers. The refugees were sent to New York with Governor Hunter in the hope that they would become self-sufficient and serve the empire by producing naval stores and populating an important colony. Before the plan could be put fully into effect, the Whigs lost power in England and were replaced by high-church Tories who had no love for dissenters of either English or foreign stock. The experiment was abandoned, but Hunter had expended £32,071 on it and received from the British government only £10,000, along with £800 from the sale of surplus goods. The balance represented funds from the Governor's own pocket and those of his friends.

Compounding these vexations was Hunter's difficulty with the Anglican ministry in New York and New Jersey. The Governor was a Church of England man in good standing—he was on friendly terms with the Bishop of London and John Chamberlayne, Secretary of the Society for the Propagation of the Gospel—but he was also a rationalist who rejected extremism in any form. The Reverend William Vesey, rector of Trinity Church, however, was a convert with a narrow and bigoted approach to ecclesiastical affairs, and he soon quarreled with Hunter over the disposition of the Queen's Farm, a valuable tract of land in New York City. It had been granted to Trinity Church by Governor Fletcher, and then reclaimed by legislative statute for the Crown's use. Vesey wanted the grant renewed permanently, but Hunter refused to do anything more than lease it. The Governor next insulted Vesey by reconditioning the old chapel in the fort for the use of the Reverend John Sharpe, chaplain to the royal troops, and attending services there.

The final rupture between Hunter and Vesey occurred over the induction of the Reverend Thomas Poyer into the vacant church in Jamaica, Long Island. The Church of England had been established in the colony by an Assembly enactment carefully worded to permit the churchwardens and vestrymen to select a minister of their own choosing. In this way congregations of dissenters would not be saddled with Anglican ministers, although the Crown ordered that all ministers assigned to parishes created by the statute must have a certificate of fitness from the Bishop of London. When the vacancy occurred, Hunter inducted Poyer who had such a certificate, but the churchwardens and vestrymen refused to oust a dissenting minister who had taken over the parish. The Governor referred the issue to Chief Justice Roger Mompesson who responded that Poyer's only recourse was a lawsuit to force the incumbent out. Hunter urged, at his own expense, that the minister undertake this action, but Poyer feared the religious complexion of the colony's courts and, at Vesey's instigation, appealed instead to the ecclesiastical authorities in London. The Anglican ministry of New York and New Jersey also sent a representation to the Earl of Clarendon, formerly Viscount Cornbury. When Hunter learned of this, he convoked a meeting of the clergy and laid the matter before them, but they persisted in their appeal to London. Some time later, however, Poyer finally followed the Governor's advice and was duly settled in his parish.

The threatened arrival of General Francis Nicholson in New York as the Royal Commissioner of Accounts, a sort of "Governor of Governors," served to unite all of Hunter's problems. The General began his investigations in Boston, and word soon reached New York that his methods were violent and his temper foul. One friend reported that "he is so violent a party man [i e, a Tory] that every man must fly very high that expects any favour or recommendation from him." Nicholson, he continued, "is a bitter Enimy of Governor Hunter and will endeavor to . . . sift his affairs . . . he swears at the very name of the palatines or companys accounts." Another gave a blunter evaluation: he "is fitter for sume Bedlam than for the post he is in."

Discontented Assemblymen, rebellious clergymen, unhappy creditors, and self-pitying politicians rallied behind Nicholson. The situation threatened to get out of hand, but Robert Hunter at this moment had the happy inspiration of lampooning the troublemakers in *Androboros,* destroying by laughter those upon whom reason had no effect. The general populace either saw the play performed or heard it read, as Colden noted, and soon began to appreciate what their Governor was trying to do. The death of Queen Anne and the collapse of the Tory cabal in London put an end to Nicholson's commission and his ability to harrass Hunter. Very soon thereafter, the Governor obtained his long-sought-for *modus vivendi* with the legislature. By 1717 he could report that there was "a perfect harmony reigning" in the province's politics and, two years later, voluntarily return to England secure in the knowledge that he was so much the master of the situation that he could select his own successor. (pp. 153-57)

Lawrence H. Leder, "Robert Hunter's 'Androboros'," in Bulletin of The New York Public Library, *Vol. 68, No. 3, March, 1964, pp. 153-60.*

WALTER J. MESERVE AND WILLAM R. REARDON (essay date 1969)

[*The author or editor of numerous important critical works, including* An Outline History of the American Drama *(1965), Studies in "Death of a Salesman" (1972), and* An Emerging Entertainment: The Drama of the American People to 1828 *(1977), Meserve is an acknowledged authority on the history of the American drama. Reardon is an American academic, critic, editor, and playwright. In the following excerpt from their* Satiric Comedies, *they discuss the farcical and satirical elements of* Androboros *and consider whether the play was ever performed.*]

One has the impression that the early American playwrights, theatre hacks as they obviously were, had great pleasure in their work. Artistry was perhaps the last thing that concerned them, and yet they possessed knowledge of their craft and certainly an understanding of theatre audiences. The theatre is always a mirror of society, but the immediacy of that reflection in eighteenth and nineteenth century American drama is startling. Let an action in Congress, a border war, or a social event occur—anything that stirred the public—and the chances for a play on the subject within a short time were reasonably good. And the play was an opportunity for commentary, satirical or otherwise. (p. viii)

Governor Robert Hunter's *Androboros* . . . has the distinction of being the first play printed in the United States. The facts behind its creation—concerning the factionalism of colonial politics in New York—are clearly described by Lawrence Leder [see excerpt dated 1964]. Hunter had been extremely angered and frustrated by certain individuals, and writing the play was his way of getting some satisfaction. Even without specific knowledge of the contemporary circumstances, however, the play is enjoyable. Considering themselves beyond the law of the land, the Assembly is a collection of incredibly self-centered imbeciles who delight in ridiculous proposals and in utter confusion. Equally obnoxious is the venal clergy. Though the adherents of common sense triumph in the play, it was a savage personal revenge for Hunter, who gave no indication that the establishment was capable of change or betterment.

Although historians of American drama and theatre have given the play only slight attention, it is certainly one of America's robust satires. No record exists of a performance of *Androboros,* and the play is usually considered a closet drama. It might, however, have been performed by Hunter and his friends, staged perhaps in a large living room under very simple conditions. Unquestionably, some people would happily have accommodated Hunter. In fact, in 1714, the very year *Androboros* was printed, Samuel Sewall was stunned at the suggestion that a play be performed in the Council Chamber in staid Boston.

The farcical effects utilized are theatrically successful. Euchred into believing that he is dead, Androboros is insulted, mocked, knocked down, belched upon, hit with foul water, poked with brooms, sprinkled with dust, sprayed with beer, blinded with snuff, and dumped into a collapsing chair. In addition to these outright farcical effects, the standard weapons of the satirist, from invective through wit, are liberally present throughout. Hunter's manipulated characters also reiterate his satirical point, because the clergy, represented by Fizle, sinks down into the trap with Androboros. Certainly there is enough theatricality in this play to make one cautious about assuming that it was not presented. (pp. ix-x)

> *Walter J. Meserve and William R. Reardon, in an introduction to* Satiric Comedies, *edited by Walter J. Meserve and William R. Reardon, Indiana University Press, 1969, pp. vii-xvi.*

WALTER J. MESERVE (essay date 1977)

[*In the following excerpt, Meserve assesses the aesthetic and historical importance of* Androboros.]

[Robert Hunter] is best known in history as the royal governor in New York and New Jersey (1710-1719) and as the governor of Jamaica from 1729 until his death, but he was also a writer of sufficient talent that Jonathan Swift ranked him with Addison, Halifax, Congreve, and Steele [see the remark by Swift in the excerpt by Henley dated 1708]. The political situation which Hunter found in New York was factional, corrupt, and sufficiently frustrating that he complained in a letter to his friend Dean Swift of the "torment and vexation" which followed his efforts to administer the colony. . . . But with a single act, showing both his literary ability as well as his political wisdom, Hunter silenced his opposition, turned the people to his point of view, and, aided by events in England, could report by 1717 a political harmony in New York.

That single act was the creation of *Androboros,* which "so humorously exposed [Hunter's enemies] that the laugh was turned upon them in all companies and from this laughing humor the people began to be in good humor with their governor and to despise the idol of the clergy" [see the excerpt by Cadwallader Colden dated 1759]. Called "A Biographical Farce in Three Acts," *Androboros* has a cast of fifteen characters, all but three of whom have counterparts in real life. It is dedicated to "Don. Com. Fiz," evidently the Reverend William Vesey, called Fizle in the dramatis personae, who first

is urged to read the play and then is broadly berated in language and fable reminiscent of Chaucer's Miller's Tale:

> And it was a most Masterly stroke of Art
> To give Fizle Room to Act his Part;
> For a Fizle restrain'd will bounce like a F——t.

The scene of the play is an asylum of sorts with a Keeper (Governor Robert Hunter), a Deputy (George Clark, secretary of the province of New York), and Tom of Bedlam, who acts as clerk to the senate which the inmates organize to receive Androboros (General Francis Nicholson), whom they consider a deliverer. Present in that body, which "disclaims all Powers, Preheminencies or Authoritys, except its own," are the Speaker (William Nichols, whom Hunter disliked but respected for his legal abilities), Coxcomb (Daniel Coxe, whom Hunter removed from the Council in 1713), Mulligrub (Samuel Mulford, Hunter's most active opponent), Doodlesack (Abraham Lakerman), who expresses himself by "Staring, Grinning and Grimacing," and Aesop (David Jamison, a close friend of Hunter), who throughout the play defends the Keeper with clever fables. When Androboros the "man-eater," a boastful, strutting creature, enters and declares himself off on another expedition, the senate resolves to defend him against "all Wardens, Directors, Keepers, and their Abettors."

Unsuccessful in their efforts as a senate to depose the Keeper, the inmates decide to become a consistory with Fizle as their leader: "This same Fizle is a Notable Fellow for the head of a Consistory, if he had but a Competent Doze of Brains; but These are so shallow that a Louse may suck 'em up without surfeiting, which renders that noble Portion of *Malice,* with which he is Liberally endow'd, of little use to the Publick." . . . It is their purpose to replace the Keeper with Lord Dinobaros (Edward Hyde, known for his venality and corrupt practices in colonial administration). Furious at having his vestment "beskirted and Bedaub'd with what I must not name," Fizle writes a letter, the major thrust of which rests in the wording of the insult he intends. Should it be ordure or, as Mulligrub insists, "Write it down so then, for a T—— is a T—— all the world over"? When word comes that Androboros has returned from his expedition, the Keeper suggests that they may "use the mighty Man according to his Deserts." In Act III, subtitled "The Apotheosis," Androboros is first ignored and then physically abused in good farcical tradition before Fizle and Flip (Adolphe Philepse)—"when Malice becomes a Moral Virtue, that Couple must be sainted"—attempt to help him by placing a chair over a trapdoor to catch the Keeper. The climax to the scene and the play comes when Androboros makes his awaited entrance, runs blindly into the chair, and sinks, Fizle and Flip falling with him, into the trap prepared for the Keeper.

Although the construction of *Andoboros* is rough and unfinished, the play has both a theatrical quality and a literary pretense which lend it some distinction. Moreover, its satire is pungent and devastating while the action and the climax are consistent with the characters and thought. Obviously a slight play, it nevertheless has wit, particularly in the lines of Solemn and the fables of Aesop, and irony to complement the robust satire. Hunter relied heavily on invective and manipulated language to gain his desired end, but he was also adept at using standard farcical effects. If the personal situation which inspired Hunter's satiric comedy has led some to discount its significance, that is unfortunate, for it is considerably more than diatribe. Rather than of importance for historical interest only, as some have contended, it is a fair beginning for American drama. (pp. 39-41)

Walter J. Meserve, "Experiments with the Drama in Colonial America," in his An Emerging Entertainment: The Drama of the American People to 1828, Indiana University Press, 1977, pp. 37-59.

JULIAN MATES   (essay date 1983)

[Mates is an American academic and scholar who has written or cowritten several studies of the American drama, including The American Musical Stage before 1800 (1962). In the following excerpt from another work, he outlines the action of Androboros.]

When he arrived as governor of N.Y. in 1710, Robert Hunter found himself at odds with all important members of the populace, from the clergy to the assembly. Upon the arrival of Gen. Francis Nicholson in N.Y. as the royal commissioner of accounts, all of Hunter's enemies rallied behind the general. Hunter, with something of a literary reputation already established, chose to satirize all of his enemies in a play, **Androborus**. Probably his friendship with Jonathan Swift was responsible for his choice of satire as a literary medium, although the success of George Villiers's satire *The Rehearsal* in 1671 may have influenced his choice of genre. It is not known whether **Androborus** was performed, but it was printed in 1714, and the resulting laughter seemed to prove the turning point in Hunter's fortunes.

The play is in three acts: The Senate, The Consistory, and The Apotheosis. The sole extant copy lists (probably in Hunter's own handwriting), next to the cast of characters, the actual person each stands for—Androborus, for example, was Gen. Francis Nicholson, and the Keeper was Hunter himself. The Keeper, his Deputy, and Tom of Bedlam conceal themselves while the Senate meets. The conversation in the play is adept; each member, with the exception of Aesop, who is constantly teaching moral lessons in verse, reveals his stupidity. Most of the first act is spent on procedural matters until Androborus (Man Eater) appears before the audience. He speaks, in almost totally garbled language, of future exploits, then struts off while the others agree to support him. The Keeper calls them hounds and sends them off to their kennels, assigning Tom to watch after them should they meet again. In the next act, the protagonists attempt to incorporate themselves into a Consistory in order to remove the Keeper. Fizle has a plan involving smearing his coat with excrement and claiming that the Keeper, in his hatred of long robes, has done it. Nothing comes of the plan. The third and final act finds the Keeper, his Deputy, and Tom preparing a scheme to convince Androborus that he is dead. The plan works until Androborus and several of the Keeper's enemies eventually drop into a vault which had been prepared for the Keeper, and the play ends.

Androborus has occasionally been listed as the first play written in America, but its value lies, rather, in other areas. As social history, it is biting, witty, and a thoroughly worthwhile literary contribution to early Americana. (pp. 802-03)

Julian Mates, "Robert Hunter" (fl. 1714-1734)," in American Writers before 1800: A Biographical and Critical Dictionary, G-P, edited by James A. Lev-

ernier and Douglas R. Wilmes, Greenwood Press, 1983, pp. 802-03.

ADDITIONAL BIBLIOGRAPHY

Davis, Peter A. "Determining the Date of Robert Hunter's *Androboros*." *Theatre Survey* XXV, No. 1 (May 1984): 95-7.
> Contends that, in spite of the evidence of its title page, *Androboros* could not have been written or printed before the middle of 1715.

Dolmetsch, Carl R. "William Byrd II: Comic Dramatist?" *Early American Literature* VI, No. 1 (Spring 1971): 18-30.
> Concludes that the Virginian William Byrd II "*could* have had something to do with the composition of [Colley Cibber's 1704 play] *The Careless Husband*," making him "in a limited way" America's first comic dramatist and thereby unsettling Robert Hunter's claim to this title.

Fiore, John D. "Jonathan Swift and the American Episcopate." *The William and Mary Quarterly* XI, No. 3 (July 1954): 425-33.
> Maintains that "a modern scholar has some trouble justifying [Jonathan Swift's and Cadwallader Colden's] praise of Hunter" (see the remark by Swift in the excerpt by Henley dated 1708 and the excerpt by Colden date 1759) on the evidence of *Androboros* alone.

Hornblow, Arthur. "The American Dramatist, 1690-1890." In his *A History of the Theatre in America, from the Beginnings to the Present Time*, Vol. II, pp. 48-73. Philadelphia: J. B. Lippincott Company, 1919.
> Reviews the early history of the American drama, noting that "from the viewpoint of dramatic construction [*Androboros*] was not without merit."

Olson, Alison Gilbert. "Governor Robert Hunter and the Anglican Church in New York." In *Statesmen, Scholars and Merchants: Essays in Eighteenth-Century History Presented to Dame Lucy Sutherland*, edited by Anne Whiteman, J. S. Bromley, and P. G. M. Dickson, pp. 44-64. Oxford: Oxford University Press, Clarendon Press, 1973.
> Studies the controversy that led to the writing of *Androboros*.

Osgood, Herbert L. "Harmony Partially Restored in New York and New Jersey under Robert Hunter, 1708-1716." In his *The American Colonies in the Eighteenth Century*, Vol. II, pp. 95-125. New York: Columbia University Press, 1924.
> Argues that Hunter wrote *Androboros* with the help of his political ally, Lewis Morris, to keep his spirits up during a troubling time.

[Todd, C. B.]. "Robert Hunter and the Settlement of the Palatines, 1710-1719." *The National Magazine*, XVII, No. 4 (February 1893): 287-309.
> Historical survey of Hunter's role in the settlement of the Palatines, including remarks on his dealings with the two principal persons lampooned in *Androboros*, Francis Nicholson and the Reverend William Vesey.

Wegelin, Oscar. "Hunter, Robert." In his *Early American Plays, 1714-1830*, edited by John Malone, pp. 59-60. 1900. Reprint. New York: Haskell House Publishers, 1968.
> Describes *Androboros* as "a severe criticism of the clergy, members, and others of Trinity Church," claiming as well Hunter's authorship of "the celebrated letter on enthusiasm, which has been ascribed to Swift."

Sarah Kemble Knight

1666-1727

American journal writer.

Knight is remembered for her lively record of a rugged journey she undertook from colonial Boston to New York at a time when long-distance travel was both difficult and perilous. This *Journal*, in addition to accurately documenting the customs, peoples, and geography of provincial New England, presaged Romantic, Gothic, and humorous American literature of the eighteenth and nineteenth centuries. Albeit a brief work, *The Journal of Madam Knight* has afforded readers of early American literature an entertaining glimpse of a charming, rustic era through the eyes of a learned and gifted writer.

Knight's life is but sketchily documented. A third-generation American, she was born in Boston into a prosperous merchant family. Biographers surmise from the high literary quality of her *Journal* that Knight benefited from a sound classical education. Around 1689 she married Richard Knight (possibly a publican or ship captain). From all accounts an unusually resourceful and independent woman for her era, "Madam" Knight, as she was respectfully known, managed a large house on Moon Street, where she took in lodgers, operated a stationery shop, witnessed legal documents, and may have conducted a writing school (said by some sources to have included Benjamin Franklin among its pupils). In October of 1704 she embarked upon a five-month journey from Boston to New Haven, Connecticut, New York City, and back, apparently to expedite the settlement of a wealthy relative's estate. The arduous trip necessitated long days of travel by horseback along unmarked, desolate roads, the occasional fording of streams and rivers by canoe, and difficult passage through heavily wooded trails. Widowed shortly after her return to Boston in March of 1705, Knight remained for several years on Moon Street, boarding lodgers and negotiating land and legal dealings. In 1714 she joined her newly married daughter in New London, Connecticut, where she apparently tended a shop in the city and oversaw landholdings in the Norwich area. Knight died in New London at the age of sixty-one.

The Journal of Madam Knight was held privately for nearly one hundred years, until journalist-editor Theodore Dwight, Jr. discovered and published what remained of the original manuscript (which has since been lost). The work attracted considerable admiration during the nineteenth century, spawning several editions as well as much speculation regarding the details of Knight's life. Among the many distinguishing characteristics of the *Journal* is the immediate, fresh quality of the accounts—a characteristic that enables the reader to share in the rigorous, eventful journey from moment to moment rather than by means of omniscient retrospective. This immediacy has been attributed to Knight's having kept fairly complete notes while on the road, which she expanded into full-fledged narration upon her return. Another quality favorably noted by readers of the journal is the humorous description of encounters with the colorful village folk of New England, including the archetypal country bumpkin and the half-socialized native Indian: characters which reappear in some of the best realistic and humorous American fiction, particularly that of Mark Twain. Commentators have also remarked in the journal Romantic and Gothic scenes—scenes similar to those later depicted by Na-

thaniel Hawthorne and Washington Irving—which vividly describe travels by night through wild, uncivilized regions. Knight's descriptions of country inns, too, are noted for their striking pictorial quality. Perhaps the most indelible narrative device is the thread of sophisticated Boston wit that runs throughout the work, providing a revealing, humorous contrast between the mean circumstances the narrator must tolerate during her journey and the refined manner of living to which she is generally accustomed. This wit is often seen to obtain its highest mark through brief passages of verse which dramatize numerous comic and pathetic situations, as well as through the narrator's mythocomic characterization of her adventures.

Virtually all commentators on Knight's *Journal* have accorded it high praise for one or more of its distinguishing features. The work's wit, charm, and engaging narration of a fascinating period in American history insure it a memorable place among travel narratives. As Peter Thorpe has written, "the *Journal* of Madam Knight is a genuine work of art and an important milestone in earlier American literature."

(See also *Dictionary of Literary Biography*, Vol. 24: *American Colonial Writers, 1606-1734.*)

PRINCIPAL WORK

**The Journal of Madam Knight*   (journal)   1825

*Written between 1704 and 1705, this work was first published with *The Journal of Rev. Mr. Buckingham* in 1825. Twentieth-century editions include *The Journal of Madam Knight* (1920) and *The Journal of Madam Knight* (1972).

THEODORE DWIGHT   (essay date 1825)

[*An American writer, Dwight was the author of several travel essays and* History of Connecticut *(1841). In addition, he served as editor of the* American Magazine and Family Newspaper, *a journal which he founded in 1845. In the following excerpt from his introduction to the first edition, in 1825, of Knight's* Journal, *Dwight praises the historical interest and intrinsic appeal of the work.*]

[*The Journal of Madam Knight*] is not a work of fiction, as the scarcity of old American manuscripts may induce some to imagine; but it is a faithful copy from a diary in the author's own hand-writing, compiled soon after her return home, as it appears, from notes recorded daily, while on the road. She was a resident of Boston, and a lady of uncommon literary attainments, as well as of great taste and strength of mind. (p. xi)

The object proposed in printing this little work is not only to please those who have particularly studied the progressive history of our country, but to direct the attention of others to subjects of that description, unfashionable as they still are; and also to remind the public that documents, even as unpretending as [*The Journal of Madam Knight*], may possess a real value, if they contain facts which will be hereafter sought for to illustrate interesting periods in our history.

It is to be regretted that the brevity of the work should have allowed the author so little room for the display of the cultivated mind and the brilliant fancy which frequently betray themselves in the course of the narrative; and no one can rise from the perusal without wishing some happy chance might yet discover more full delineations of life and character from the same practised hand. (p. xii)

The reader will find frequent occasion to compare the state of things in the time of our author with that of the present period, particularly with regard to the number of the inhabitants, and the facilities and accomodations prepared for travellers. Over that tract of country where she travelled about a fortnight, on horseback, under the direction of a hired guide, with frequent risks of life and limb, and sometimes without food or shelter for many miles, we proceed at our ease, without exposure and almost without fatigue, in a day and a half, through a well peopled land, supplied with good stage-coaches and public houses, or the still greater luxuries of the elegant steam boats which daily traverse our waters. (pp. xiii-xiv)

> *Theodore Dwight, "Introduction to 'The Journals of Madam Knight and Rev. Mr. Buckingham,'" in* The Journal of Madam Knight *by Sarah Kemble Knight, 1920. Reprint by Peter Smith, 1935, pp. xi-xiv.*

WILLIAM LAW LEARNED (essay date 1865)

[In the following excerpt, Learned stresses the freedom from Puritanical moralizing and journalistic accuracy of Knight's Journal.]

It is evident from her [*Journal*] that Madam Knight was energetic and observing; that she had some imagination and a good perception of the ludicrous. She seems also to have been free from that strict and narrow character which is generally attributed to the Puritan of early New England. She rides a few miles on Sunday, and considers the prohibition of "innocent merriment among young people," to be "rigid." She makes jokes on Mr. Devil's name, which, only a few years earlier, might have convicted her of witchcraft, if they had come to the ears of Cotton Mather. And although absent from home for five months, and a visitor with at least two or three clergymen, she gives no account of any sermon which she may have heard. Her silence in this particular may have been because there was more novelty in the matters which she narrates.

Wherever it is possible to make the test, her journal will be found accurate even in slight matters. It may therefore with good reason be relied upon in all its details. (pp. xi-xii)

> *William Law Learned, in a preface to* The Private Journal of a Journey from Boston to New York in the Year 1704 *by Sarah Kemble Knight, edited by William Law Learned, Frank H. Little, 1865, pp. iii-xii.*

ERASTUS WORTHINGTON (essay date 1891)

[In the following excerpt, Worthington notes the acute observations of colonial life in Knight's Journal.]

[The *Journal*] of Madam Knight, which was written by herself, in daily entries made during the progress of her journey from Boston to New York in 1704, has always excited interest and admiration in many readers. That this long journey was made

at so early a period in colonial history, following a path or road, which at best could only have been cut by an axe through the forest, either fording streams, or ferried in a canoe over rivers, that it was accomplished by a woman on horseback, with only such guides as she could procure from day to day, in postmen and hired out-riders, that she rode through the wilderness by night as well as by day—all these incidents would be sufficient to impart the charm of adventure to her narrative. But Madam Knight, besides being apparently insensible to the possible perils of such a journey, was a woman of superior intelligence, and an acute observer of the manner of life and speech of those whom she met, which she reproduces in her journal with a vivacity and *naivete* truly surprising. Her style and method compare favorably with those of an English classic of her day, and she gives us some pictures of life in the country inns where she tarried, which are quite as strongly drawn as an interior by some Dutch painter. (pp. 36-7)

> *Erastus Worthington, "Madam Knight's 'Journal'," in* The Dedham Historical Register, *Vol. II., No. 1, January, 1891, pp. 36-9.*

GEORGE PARKER WINSHIP (essay date 1920)

[Winship was an American scholar, librarian, and bibliographer who wrote several works on the history of the printing press. In the following excerpt, Winship commends Knight's Journal *for its unrivaled eyewitness documentation of provincial New England.]*

Madam Knight's *Journal* is the truest picture left to us of provincial New England. Ever since it was first printed in 1825 it has been the delight of those whose reading takes them below the surface of current writings about colonial times, but it has nevertheless remained one of the least familiar of contemporary sources. The reason for this may have something to do with the fact that the people described by her are not like those portrayed in most of the books about ancestral New Englanders.

The *Journal* was written midway of the hundred years during which the primitive settlements developed into readiness for independence. The writer was a lady of good family in respectable social and church standing, who was much too busy with the affairs of daily life to concern herself unduly with matters of state or of religion. It is this absorption in her immediate surroundings which gives perennial fascination to her account of a trip on horseback from Boston to New York. The people with whom she had to do on the way and the things

Knight begins her journey from Boston to New Haven, in an illustration from a 1972 edition of The Journal of Madam Knight. *Courtesy of Massachusetts Historical Society.*

they talked about were neither deacons nor Heaven, but both were typical of the period during which were established the New England characteristics which have had an influence upon the United States. (pp. iii-iv)

> *George Parker Winship, in an introduction to* The Journal of Madam Knight *by Sarah Kemble Knight, 1920. Reprint by Peter Smith, 1935, pp. iii-viii.*

TRENTWELL MASON WHITE AND PAUL WILLIAM LEHMANN (essay date 1929)

[*White was a distinguished American educator; with Lehmann he published* Writers of Colonial New England. *In the following excerpt from this work, White and Lehmann applaud the authoritative account and literary interest of Knight's* Journal.]

The diary is one of literature's most valuable adjuncts, in that in its very unaffected, informal and intimate content, it frequently holds up to the times a more accurate mirror than the formal work of the historian. In view of this, *The Journal,* kept by Mrs. Sarah Kemble Knight, a housewife of Boston, during a journey from that town to Rhode Island, Connecticut, and New York, during the winter of 1704, is particularly interesting. Keeping a daily account of her adventures, she was able to confide no small amount of personal reaction and experience in the *Journal.* It has as its most outstanding feature, perhaps, an accurate picture of the woman herself, her philosophic state of mind, her sense of humor, and her huge reservoir of common sense.

It is an amusing narrative, gaily written, for the most part, and filled with pen pictures of the country, its conditions and its inhabitants. (p. 79)

> *Trentwell Mason White and Paul William Lehmann, "Narrative and Descriptive Writers," in their* Writers of Colonial New England, *1929. Reprint by Gale Research Company, 1971, pp. 71-86.*

ROBERT O. STEPHENS (essay date 1964)

[*Stephens is a scholar of American literature who has written noted studies of Ernest Hemingway. In the following excerpt, he discusses Knight's literary pose and the mythic content of her* Journal.]

When *The Journal of Madam Knight* was first published in 1825, its editor Theodore Dwight [see excerpt dated 1825] hailed it as the "display of the cultivated mind and the brilliant fancy" of Sarah Kemble Knight, already honored in New England tradition as the schoolmistress of Benjamin Franklin and Samuel Mather. To Madam Knight's misfortune, however, the original and subsequent editors of her journal have made it a display of their predilections as well, and the result is that her account has been consistently presented as a literal diary of her 1704-1705 trip from Boston to New York rather than as an imaginative woman's odyssey through a wilderness both mythical and actual. So now the journal is most frequently placed in collections of historical writings such as Commager and Nevins' *Heritage of America* or in the "Utilitarian Writings" section of American literature anthologies. It ought, I think, to be reconsidered as a vital and creative work of the American encounter with the new world.

Introducing the work one hundred and twenty years after Madam Knight wrote it. Dwight took pains to play down any possibility that the work might be read imaginatively and, on the contrary,

emphasized the experience as a distinctively literal and local one: "This is not a work of fiction, as the scarcity of old American manuscripts may induce some to imagine; but it is a faithful copy from a diary in the author's own handwriting, compiled soon after her return home, as it appears, from notes recorded daily, while on the road." The real value of the account, he noted, was that it contained facts "to illustrate interesting periods of our history." Consulting the new nationalism of the time, he observed that such a record was an answer to those too ready to ignore local wit and to open libraries to foreign materials. Ninety-five years later in his Introductory Note to the 1920 edition, George Parker Winship could still observe that "Madam Knight's *Journal* is the truest picture left to us of provincial New England" [see excerpt dated 1920].

As editors by proxy, literary historians have similarly tended to accept the literalness of the account, and consequently characterized the *Journal* in one of three ways: either as a "refreshingly carnal, external and healthy . . . realistic picture of rural manners," a kind of proto-local colorism; as a cyptic rebellion against Puritan gloom and soberness; or as an unfortunate lapse of both taste and accuracy of observation [see Additional Bibliography entries by Moses Coit Tyler, Percy H. Boynton, and Charles Angoff]. In all cases the emphasis is on mimetic rather than mythic intentions.

What editors have overlooked are the literary implications of Madam Knight's method of writing. George Parker Winship observes that "During her journey the traveller was accustomed to set down her daily observations the last thing before retiring. There is nothing improbable in the statement that she did this in shorthand, and that her diary contained much more than appears in the printed copy." The allowable inference is that she did more than spice up the account with witty detail; the time for reflection and opportunity to revise indicate that she also selected her material and shaped it according to a pattern not apparent during day-to-day note-taking. That pattern became the myth that she worked through the realistic details. A reading of the journal in this light shows that she saw numerous parallels between her wanderings and those of Homer's Odysseus and that she chose to treat those similarities in a mock epic manner. Thus the poems and other extravagant passages are not lapses of taste but evidence of this sardonic measurement of her frontier experience against the classic odyssey. Such a reading does not negate the value of realistic detail in the account, but it does indicate that the historical value of the account is in the mythic implications rather than in the literal observations.

Within the *Journal* itself Sarah Kemble Knight assumes a Bostonian superiority to anything she might encounter in the hinterlands. Greek-like, she ranks all others according to their degrees of barbarism. That she does so in a self-mocking tone does not lessen her basic condescension or her sense of a potential Boston audience, whether public or family group. Her right to judge can be detected in her assessments of both Connecticut and New York life. After observing Connecticut yokels chew tobacco and haggle over a purchase of ribbon, she decides: "We may Observe here the great necessity and benefitt both of Education and Conversation; for these people have as Large a portion of mother witt, and sometimes a Larger, than those who have bin brought up in Cities; But for want of emprovements, Render themselves almost Ridiculos, as above." She notes also that while the Connecticut folk have essentially the same laws, church, and government as "wee in Boston,'' they are ''a little too much Independent in their principalls'' and may be laughed at for the strictness of such laws as those that forbid public kissing. If that were not irony enough, her description of New York clearly tunes to the Boston ear. Even as she acknowledges handsome treatment by New Yorkers, she damns their accomplishments with faint praise: ''The Buildings Brick Generally, very stately and high, though not altogether like ours in Boston,'' or ''The fireplace have no Jambs (as ours have) But the Backs run flush with the walls. . . .''

Out of this condescension she adopts the mock heroic technique as the proper method of characterizing her experience. She becomes imaginatively an Odysseus wandering the shores of the new world. Not that she can became purely classic: as a product of the William Bradford-John Winthrop world of Boston, she is by cultural commitment also a participant in the establishment of a New Canaan, and sometimes her allegories get mixed. But when she maintains her Odyssean identity, she sees the world through sardonic Ithacan eyes. And through such a mask she depicts hospitality customs, exotic guides, wilderness terrors, descents into the underworld, interludes of lyricism, epic games, and mock epic tales within tales. (pp. 247-49)

[In] depiction of her guides Madam Knight shows most clearly the mocking ambiguity of her epic experience. Her Teiresias from Dedham to Billings' Lodge is ambiguous John, taciturn when around his ''Limbertong'd'' wife, but loquacious and boastful while acting as guide in the wilderness. His appearance is her first hint of his character: ''His shade on his Hors resembled a Globe on a Gate post. His habitt, Hors and furniture, its looks and goings Incomparably answered the rest.'' Further in the wilderness he shows himself as both oracle and boastful knight. South of Dedham they approach a foggy swamp: ''But nothing dismay'd John: He had encountered a thousand and a thousand such Swamps, having a Universall Knowledge in the woods; and readily Answered all my inquiries, wch. were not a few.'' Nor is she surprised at this oracular talent, for she has already seen him as he must think himself to be: a noble of the wilderness whose true nature is obscured in the murkiness of Dedham society: ''Thus Jogging on with an easy pace, my Guide telling mee it was dangero's to Ride hard in the Night, (which his hors had the sence to avoid), Hee entertained me with the Adventurs he had passed by late Rideing, and eminent Dangers he had escaped, so that, Remembering the Hero's in Parismus and the Knight of the Oracle, I didn't know but I had mett with a Prince disguis'd.'' (pp. 250-51)

This readiness to caricature extends to her depiction of the ''Indian-like Animal'' who escorts her across the Paukatuk River and to her sketch of ''neighbor Polly and Jemima, a Girl about 18 years old,'' who complain their way to New London with Madam Knight.

Such concern with guides takes additional significance as she makes her descent into the underworld, for the descent reminds again that she is Puritan as well as Odyssean. Her stop at Mr. Devil's house is but the climax to a progress through the wilderness that she cannot forget is Satan's country. Thus in the ''Glorious Luminary'' passage she mocks her own fears and those of such Puritans as Cotton Mather, whose *Magnalia Christiania* of 1702 had presented the new continent as a devil-dominated land to be won by the godly. The passage, though, as she presents it, mocks the Matheresque epic idea with her classic connotations:

Now was the Glorious Luminary, with his swift Coursers arrived at his Stage, leaving poor me with the rest of this part of the lower world in darkness, with which we were soon Surrounded. The only Glimmering we now had was from the spangled Skies, whose Imperfect Reflections rendered every Object formidable. Each lifeless Trunk, with its shatter'd Limbs, appear'd an Armed Enemie; and every little stump like a Ravenous devourer.

Under the influence of such Siren-like powers she imagines herself deluded by the enchantments of the underworld and by that enchantress Cynthia, goddess of the underworld as well as of the moon. Thus, she follows her apostrophe to Cynthia with a moonlit vision of a ''Sumpteous citty, fill'd with famous Buildings and churches, with their spiring steeples, Balconies, Galleries and I know not what: Grandeurs which the stories of foreign countries had given me the Idea of.'' (p. 251)

Aware of such tricks of the mind, she both laughs and shudders at the implications of the guide's announcement that they will ''be well accommodated anon at Mr. Devills. . . .'' Relying on the effect of her moonscape delusions, she observes: ''But I questioned whether we ought to go to the Devil to be helped out of affliction. However, like the rest of Deluded souls that post to ye Infernal denn, Wee made all possible speed to this Devil's Habitation . . .''. . . . Other episodes she must endure include the encounter with the Aeolus-like hostess of the inn two miles beyond the ''habitation of cruelty.'' Once the hostess learns that the Frenchman accompanying Madam Knight is a doctor, she talks more than enough to compensate for the taciturnity of the ''old Sophister.'' And she had to flee to her own room to escape the storm of ''my Great Landly'' and ''her Talkative Guests.'' Other Odyssean encounters are the stop at Western Post and at Havens in the Narragansett country. At both places she finds sojourners enslaved by their appetites. At Western Post she is like Odysseus with the Lotus-eaters as she fails to engage a traveling companion because the tavern loafers are ''tyed by the Lipps to a pewter engine.'' At Havens she has to use enchantments to hush the quartet who argue, drink, and pound the table into the night as they contrive ''how to bring a triangle into a Square.'' Thus she scratches her conjuration:

> I ask thy aid, O Potent Rum!
> To Charm these wrangling Topers Dum.
> Thou hast their Giddy Brains possest—
> The man confounded with the Beast—
> And I, poor I, can get no rest.
> Intoxicate them with thy fumes:
> O still their Tongues till morning comes!

Post hoc or propter hoc, the talk stops.

New Haven is her Phaeacia. There she observes the epic games by the locals, in which the winner of the target shoot receives his garland: a red ribbon tied to his hatband. And ''he is Led away in Triumph, with great applause, as the winners of the Olympiak Games.'' She further carries out the Phaeacian motif by depicting the local wedding custom, analogous to Odysseus' reluctance toward Nausicia, for the bridegroom ceremonially flees the wedding and is brought back by the bridesmen. Her recitation of local color stories parallels the Odyssean tale of wandering among gods, nymphs, and giants, but here the tale is of yokels and Indians. The mockery in the narrative at this point is perhaps most evident in the description of the intricate and cautious bargaining between back country men and merchants—including at least four systems of payment—all for a piece of ribbon. (pp. 252-53)

In New York she continues the epic device of once-removed narration to provide expository background for the beginning *in medias res*. In particular she recounts the story told by her host Mr. Burroughs in which a Telemachus-like young man invokes the aid of the gods to help pay his father's debts. But in this case, the prayer is a grace said at the dinner table with his wealthy aunt, whose death would give him a fortune:

> Pray God in Mercy take my Lady Darcy
> Unto his Heavenly Throne,
> That Little John may live like a man,
> And pay every man his own.

Athena-like, the aunt comes to his aid. (p. 253)

Such mock epic devices become more scattered toward the end of the journal. In the account of the return to Boston from New York there is a definite falling away from the technique. Continued still are the concern with hospitality and the notation of contrasts between barbarians and Bostonians, but the sense of absurdity necessary for exploiting the mock epic approach is either missing or has grown too great to manage. If she can praise Governor Winthrop of Connecticut for his "wonderful civility" as a host, she nevertheless lets pass without comment such an obvious target as "Spiting Devil" bridge. Perhaps a key statement for this tendency occurs in her account of crossing a wintery river near Stratford, Connecticut: "My fears and fatigues prevented my here taking any particular observations." For she records being ill at several stops during the return. Evidently she senses the sure enough Puritan devil in the wilderness during winter, for she sounds a chastened note as she closes the journal: "I having this day bin five months from home and now I cannot fully express my Joy and Satisfaction. But desire sincearly to adore my Great Benefactor for thus graciously carying forth and returning in safety his unworthy handmaid." (pp. 253-54)

By recognizing the mythic implications of Madam Knight's *Journal*, even at the expense of its mimetic and outwardly historical impact, we are able to place the work more clearly in the fruitful tradition of colonial American, and particularly New England, literature. It is neither wholly in the utilitarian school—that limbo of critical condescension—nor in the vein of aboriginal local color writing insisted on by the new nationalists of the early republic. Seen through twentieth century eyes, the journal shares the mind of that haunted world Hawthorne pointed to in his tales of old Boston and Salem and the wilderness surrounding them. And the myth-making mind here shows itself aware of and capable of comprehending the ambiguities and ambivalences that Hawthorne was later to explore. This is indicated primarily in the tangled imagination that attempts to fuse the Homeric and Puritan world views. If the mingling is not altogether successful, it does at least afford a temporary mode of expressing the reflective woman's grasp of the wilderness as both world and underworld, local and universal, laughable and terrible. Beyond this perception is the tantalizing hint, seen particularly in the "Glorious Luminary" and "Sumpteous city" passages, that there is something both alluring and deadly in that external wilderness that mirrors the inner life, something guilty and self-destructive about the underworld mind now understood mythically by depth psychologists. This insight into the perplexities that neither a serenely dogmatic nor serenely reasonable mind perceives is what most clearly links the mind of Sarah Knight with the tradition of Nathaniel Hawthorne. The pose of Bostonian-Hellenic superiority, basic to the whole scheme, then places her both within and without that "magnetic chain of humanity" that Hawthorne

saw forged, both above the local and within the universal realms of human feeling. Identification of the individual mythic allusions is only a matter of reading, but seeing the tantalizing pattern they fall into is an indication that this innocent and rough-mannered journal has meanings that a literal reading cannot guess at. (pp. 254-55)

> *Robert O. Stephens, "The Odyssey of Sarah Kemble Knight," in CLA Journal, Vol. VII, No. 3, March, 1964, pp. 247-55.*

PETER THORPE (essay date 1966)

[*Thorpe is an American poet and professor of English. In the following excerpt, he explores Knight's ties with the picaresque tradition in her* Journal.]

From the appearance of *Lazarillo de Tormes* (c. 1554) to the close of the eighteenth century, those writings usually known as "picaresque" seem to have formed a persistent and fairly well defined tradition in Western literature. During this period the history of our culture is regularly punctuated by such picaresque or near-picaresque works as (to name a few of the more famous ones) *The Unfortunate Traveller, Don Quixote, Hudibras, Gil Blas, Moll Flanders, Roderick Random, Candide,* and volumes VII and VIII of *Tristram Shandy*. It is safe to generalize that, with a few such notable exceptions as *Huckleberry Finn*, the picaresque tradition after 1800 is less sharply defined, although some scholars—R. W. B. Lewis and Robert Alter, for example—maintain that its impulses continue noticeably even in the twentieth century literature. In any case, it is clear that the great age of picaresque places itself in those two-and-a-half centuries from *Lazarillo* to the decline of Augustanism in the later 1700s. Very near the middle of this period, American literature, though still in its infancy, made what seems to me to be a significant contribution to the picaresque tradition: the *Journal* of Sarah Kemble Knight, a brief, highly amusing and frequently incisive piece of writing which follows rather CLOSELY the customary patterns of picaresque.

Although any genre is perhaps finally elusive of definition, the patterns of picaresque are clear enough to allow certain generalizations. Always present is the element of travelling, which lends to the work a certain restless excitement and vitality. There are usually numerous episodes, but these seldom have any necessary connection with each other, except that they involve the same main character. Customarily the traveller serves as first-person narrator. He is frequently, though not always, a member of the lower classes. In any event, his travels bring him into contact with many different social groups, upon whose morals and manners he may comment, often in a witty or satirical vein. Bizarre comic situations are also a typical ingredient in picaresque, and no less common is a rakishly comic style. On the other hand, the piece may end on a serious note, for not infrequently the hero or *picaro* ("rogue") undergoes some sort of reform at the end of his travels.

According to Madam Knight's *Journal*, she was "five months from home" in her trip from Boston to New York City and back. During part of this time she sojourned with friends or relatives, but of these pauses in her travels she makes little mention. The chief emphasis is rather on the fact and act of travelling, of moving almost hurriedly from one place to the next. The first sentence of her diary tells us, without introduction or milling about, that "I begun my Journey": we are travelling at once, scarcely to pause—exept for meals, lodging and short comic scenes—until we return to Boston at the end.

The *Journal* derives much of its power and excitement from this headlong haste. It may be noted, although we are not yet formally considering style, that the language is fortified with vigorous expressions of motion. . . . (pp. 114-15)

Also picaresque is the episodic quality of the *Journal*. Although Madam Knight has numerous adventures, some of which repeat the same basic pattern, she makes no conscious effort to connect these episodes. Each one, though it may remind us of an adventure earlier in the *Journal*, seems entirely new to this vivacious Colonial writer—and, as a consequence, seems fresh to the reader. Less successful picaresque has a tendency to fall into a dull repetition of scene and action. Such a charge could be levelled at portions of *Lazarillo*, even though it is historically important. But Madam Knight's little-known diary reveals to us a narrator ever full of youthful expectancy. . . . [There] are several points in the journey at which the narrator must cross dangerous rivers. The pattern of action is basically the same, but Madam Knight's vitality makes each fording a unique and exciting experience. One crossing, in a "Cannoo," was so terrifying that it

> caused me to be very circumspect, sitting with my hands fast on each side, my eyes steady, not daring so much as to lodg my tongue a hair's breadth more on one side of my mouth then tother, nor so much as think on Lott's wife, for a wry thought would have oversett our wherey. . . .

It is the "wry thought," however, which gives the *Journal* its entertaining variety.

Another characteristic of picaresque is the use of the main character as first-person narrator, who always serves to lend coherence and order to a genre which, by its episodic nature, tends automatically to be structurally weak. In Madam Knight's *Journal*, however, we find much more consistency than we might ordinarily look for in picaresque, for we have a narrator of such brilliant force of character that she transcends the disjointed structure and pulls the variety of materials into focus. However unconnected the adventures or episodes may be, there is always in the foreground the dominant personality of Sarah Kemble Knight. Her writing does not suffer from the unconcatenated effect which one senses in, say, *The Unfortunate Traveller* and which is almost certainly caused by the subdued detachment of Jack Wilton. (pp. 115-16)

Although her grammar is slipshod—actually a virtue of her lively style—her *Journal* is laced with classical allusions and also reveals its author as the creator of some nicely chisled couplets, very much in vogue in England (but not in America) at the time. Her "tho'ts on the sight of the moon" will serve as a sample of Madam Knight's poetic art:

> Fair Cynthia, all the Homage that I may
> Unto a Creature, unto thee I pay;
> In Lonesome woods to meet so kind a guide,
> To Mee's more worth than all the world beside.
> Some Joy I felt just now, when safe got or'e
> Yon Surly River to this Rugged shore,
> Deeming Rough welcomes from these clownish Trees,
>   Better than Lodgings with Nereidees.

She was an accomplished lady, and the force of her character as first-person narrator lends strength and consistency to her picaresque *Journal*.

Another typical element in picaresque is that the narrator is frequently a member of the lower social classes. In America, however, even at the early date of 1704, much of the old

European class structure had already broken down. Madam Knight is not strictly a member of any social group, and her travels have the effect of placing her on many social levels. At one point she may be thrown in with the most abject of bumpkins, as is the case in "a merchants house," where she encounters a tobacco-spitting "tall country fellow" and his wife, who is "Jone Tawdry" to Madam Knight. At another point she is invited to "stay and take a supper" with Governor John Winthrop of Connecticut. Because she is of no class and of all classes, she is eminently qualified as an observer of society on all levels. The customary picaresque hero is restricted to the "worm's-eye view" of things, but Sarah Kemble Knight is much more versatile; and her writing, as a result, has an advantage not enjoyed by many other works in the picaresque tradition.

It is one of the functions of the picaresque hero to comment upon the morals and manners of those he meets. Madam Knight fulfills this function admirably, for she seems to have a good balance of moral indignation and amused tolerance. . . . She usually seems to have a tolerance for that which differs from her own way, provided that it does not run too strongly counter to her sense of morality, which, after all, was quite broad for that of a Bostonian born in 1666, only three years after the birth of Cotton Mather. Above all, she does not preach, either to the people she meets or to the reader. She merely relates her experiences and lets her wisdom, decency and good sense shine out as they will. And when she is morally indignant, she does not come groveling to the reader for support; rather, he is invited to draw his own conclusions. Sarah Kemble Knight knew that the world conforms to nobody's image of it, and that one must adjust himself to the shifting winds of the various settlements between Boston and New York.

Moral tolerance is usually associated with comedy, and this is very much the case in Madam Knight's *Journal*. It is pregnant with bizarre comic scenes, another common element in picaresque. At one inn, she is assigned "a little Room parted from the Kitchen by a single board partition" through which she overhears a long and tedious argument among some town drunkards about the derivation of the word "Narraganset." At another inn, a "french Doctor," with whom she has been travelling, is "entertain'd" unceasingly by a hypochondriac hostess. At still another stop, a bumpkin enters the inn, fills his pipe and sits smoking "without speaking, for near a quarter of an hower. At length the old man [i.e., the host] said how do's Sarah do?" The bumpkin's response is "as well as can be expected." This last is a species of humor which is far from extinct in America today. That these three examples occur within a few pages of each other suggests the frequency of comic scenes in Madam Knight's *Journal*. (pp. 117-19)

[The] comic style of Sarah Kemble Knight is at its highest point when it is combined with a fully worked-out comic situation. There are a number of examples in the *Journal*, two of which will be quoted in full, partly because editions are scarce and partly because their sheer virtuosity makes them pleasingly quotable. The first is an image of frontier justice (the italics are Madam Knight's):

> A negro Slave belonging to a man in ye Town, stole a hogs head from his master, and gave or sold it to an Indian, native of the place. The Indian sold it in the neighborhood, and so the theft was found out. Thereupon the Heathen was Seized, and carried to the Justices House to be Examined. But his worship (it seems) was gone into the field, with a Brother in office, to gather in his Pompions [pumpkins]. Whither

the malefactor is hurried, And Complaint made, and satisfaction in the name of Justice demanded. Their Worships cann't proceed in form without a Bench: whereupon they Order one to be Imediately erected, which, for want of fitter materials, they made with pompions—which being finished, down setts their Worships, and the Malefactor call'd, and by the Senior Justice Interrogated after the following manner. You Indian why did You steal from this man? You sho'dn't do so—it's a Grandy wicked thing to steal. Hol't Hol't, cryes Justice Junr Brother, You speak negro to him. I'le ask him. You sirrah, why did you steal this man's Hoggshead? Hoggshead? (replys the Indian,) me no stomany. No? says his Worship; and pulling off his hatt, Patted his own head with his hand, sais, Tatapa—You, Tatapa—you; all one this. Hoggshead all one this. Hah! says Netop, now me stomany that. Whereupon the Company fell into a great fitt of Laughter, even to Roreing. Silence is commanded, but to no effect: for they continued perfectly Shouting. Nay sais his worship, in an angry tone, if it be so, *take mee off the Bench.*

The second comic situation involves the familiar image of a backwoods couple at a general store (Knight's italics):

Being at a merchants house, in comes a tall country fellow, with his alfogeos [Spanish saddle bags, i.e., cheeks] full of Tobacco; for they seldom Loose their Cudd, but keep Shewing and Spitting as long as they'r eyes are open,—he advanc't to the middle of the Room, makes an Awkward Nodd, and spitting a Large deal of Aromatick Tincture, he gave a scrape with his shovel like shoo, leaving a small shovel full of dirt on the floor, made a full stop, Hugging his own pretty Body with his hands under his arms, Stood staring rown'd him, like a Catt let out of a Baskett. At last, like the creature Balaam Rode on, he opened his mouth and said: have You any Ribinen for Hatbands to sell I pray? The Questions and Answers about the pay being past, the Ribin is bro't and opened. Bumpkin Simpers, cryes its confounded Gay I, vow; and beckning to the door, in comes Jone Tawdry, dropping about 50 curtees, and stands by him: hee shows her the Ribin. *Law, You,* sais shee, *its right Gent* [genteel], do You, take it, *tis dreadful pretty.*

The above two passages show us a writer who is skilfull indeed at combining comic style and comic situation.

Although comic situation and style comprise a large portion of Madam Knight's *Journal,* approximately the final thousand words are devoid of humor of any kind. This is not surprising in that, as mentioned earlier, the picaresque hero customarily undergoes a kind of reform or moral regeneration at the end of his travels. Sarah Kemble Knight is not, of course, a rogue or *picaro* in the strict definition of the term, but her behavior parallels that of the picaresque hero in the sense that after many a rakishly frivolous narration she takes on for her closing paragraphs a serious tone. At the end of her travels she makes it clear that in spite of the carefree attitude heretofore adopted, she knows that only God's providence has brought her safely back to Boston. That last few sentences of the *Journal* suggest that the irreverent *picaro* is gone, replaced by a humble and solemn servant of the Lord:

... the next day being March 3rd wee got safe home to Boston, where I found my aged and tender mother and my Dear and only Child in good health with open arms redy to receive me, and my Kind relations and friends flocking in to welcome mee and hear the story of my transactions and travails I having this day bin

five months from home and now I cannot fully express my Joy and Satisfaction. But desire sincearly to adore my Great Benefactor for thus graciously carying forth and returning in safety his unworthy handmaid.

Such language is in marked contrast to the earlier portions of the *Journal.*

The *Journal* of Sarah Kemble Knight, then, although a short and little-read piece of literature, takes its place as a successful and significant contribution to the picaresque tradition just when that tradition was in its full flower. Madam Knight was not, of course, a conscious picaresque writer, nor did she write on the much broader scale of H. H. Brackenridge's *Modern Chivalry,* which was to appear nearly a century later. Nevertheless, the *Journal* of Madam Knight is a genuine work of art and an important milestone in earlier American literature. (pp. 120-21)

> Peter Thorpe, "Sarah Kemble Knight and the Picaresque Tradition," in CLA Journal, Vol. X, No. 2, December, 1966, pp. 114-21.

MALCOLM FREIBERG (essay date 1972)

[*In the following excerpt, Freiberg summarizes the inherent value of Knight's* Journal]

Early in October 1704, when she was midway into her thirty-ninth year, Sarah Knight had rather casually departed from Boston by horse on a journey (for vague family and business reasons) to New Haven—and in so doing entered irrevocably into American history. Following roughly the route of the present main-line Pennsylvania (the former New Haven) Railroad trains and keeping a journal of her travels, which took her ultimately to New York City (with a fortnight's stay there and even longer stops in New Haven) and which kept her from home for almost precisely five months, the redoubtable lady from Boston revealed herself as an extraordinary diarist—keenly and wittily observant, possessed of a sharp eye for local color and a sure ear for the words of others (particularly her inferiors), gently self-mocking, and quite without pretence or guile. Ever since its first publication in 1825, *The Journal of Madam Knight* has won new readers in every generation, each new generation reissuing for itself this classic account of travel and manners in the southern New England of the early eighteenth century. (pp. iv-v)

> Malcolm Freiberg, in an introduction to The Journal of Madam Knight by Sarah Kemble Knight, David R. Godine, 1972, pp. iii-vii.

WILLIAM C. SPENGEMANN (essay date 1977)

[*Spengemann is a scholar of American autobiographical literature. In the following excerpt, he defines Knight's place in the evolution of nonfiction travel literature.*]

If the development of the travel-narrative from [Christopher Columbus's *Four Voyages to the New World* to William Bradford's *History of Plimoth Plantation*] appears as a shift in the locus of authority from the traveler's home to the traveler himself, the history of the genre from [*History of Plimoth Plantation* to Richard Henry Dana's *Two Years Before the Mast*] describes the traveler's increasing susceptibility to the experiences of travel. This development figures both as a change in the apparent subject of the narrative from the things seen to the person seeing them, and as a movement of the narrator toward the experiential center of his narrative. Although Columbus does stand within his narrative to the extent that we are continually made aware of the mental processes by which he rationalizes his observations, the range of his experience is so limited by the shape of authorized belief that disturbing facts cannot really penetrate the thick shell of his self-image. A century after Columbus, at the end of the age of exploration and the beginning of the era of settlement, we find John Smith standing somewhat closer to the world he describes in *A True Relation of Virginia*, especially in those passages which recount his lone voyage up the Chickahominy River and his capture by Powhatan. And yet, even in this early captivity narrative, we detect in the narrator a certain imperviousness to his experiences. Nowhere does Smith suggest that his adventures have played any part in making him the man he is; they merely permit him to display the shrewdness and courage he brought with him from England. Unlike Bradford's history, Smith's narrative shows no formal signs that the American experiences have changed him essentially.

The traveler's movement toward the experiential center of his narrative that begins in [the second book of Bradford's *History of Plimoth Plantation*] proceeds in subsequent works of American travel with the help of literary innovations which were occurring in England around the turn of the eighteenth century, especially the increasing tendency of prose writers to create fictional characters with a distinct psychological dimension. The relationship between imaginative literature and the travel-narrative had been reciprocal from the beginning. Columbus's letter responded both to the fictitious *Travels* of John Mandeville and to the classical epics. Elizabethan accounts of exploration adopted techniques of the medieval romance, and the Elizabethan drama modeled its heroes, to some extent, on the character of the daring Elizabethan explorers. Sarah Kemble Knight's *Journal* suggests her indebtedness to such late seventeenth-century writers as John Bunyan and Aphra Behn; and, since both *Pilgrim's Progress* and Mrs. Behn's fictional autobiography were themselves influenced by travel-writing, Madame Knight's narrative may be said to close the circuit of influence. If the work of Bunyan, Mrs. Behn, Nashe, Deloney, and Defoe helped to maintain the novel's genetic relations with travel-literature in England, Madame Knight's American journal moved travel-writing itself a step closer to its artistic majority in the novels of Melville and Mark Twain.

The *Journal* evidences the author's debt to her literary contemporaries mainly in her willingness to describe fully her deepest personal reactions to her travel experiences. At times she can portray the scenery almost entirely in terms of its psychological effect on her:

> Now was the Glorious Luminar, with his swift Coursers arrived at his Stage, leaving poor me with the rest of this part of the lower world in darkness, with which wee were soon Surrounded. The only Glimmering we now had was from the spangled Skies, Whose Imperfect Reflections rendered every Object formidable. Each lifeless Trunk, with its shatter'd Limbs, appear'd an Armed Enemic; and every little stump like a Ravenous devourer. Nor could I so much as discern my Guide, when at any distance, which added to the terror.

Such passages prefigure the patently literary expressions of the natural sublime in the later travel-narratives of Bartram and Dwight, as well as Poe's occasional use of the travel-form in his psychological fictions. In Madame Knight's case, the use of these particular literary figures is largely attributable to her

method of composition. She wrote her journal from notes set down while she was traveling by land from Boston to New Haven and New York, rather than in retrospect from home. Consequently, the reader views the land of her travels from the ground, as if he were making the journey himself, instead of seeing these regions from a distance, as if he were following the route of her travels on a map.

This technique has two important effects on the narrative. It gives her descriptions an immediacy that retrospective accounts generally lack, emphasizing the traveler's spontaneous reactions to her experiences at the expense of those generalizations which a completed journey seems characteristically to elicit from travel-writers. Second, it makes the landscape emerge gradually from the traveler's accumulating perceptions, instead of placing her in a landscape which exists independent of her perceptions because it is seen whole by a retrospective narrator. "The Government of Connecticut Colony," Madame Knight says pointedly, "begins westward toward York at Stanford (as I am told) and so runs Eastward towards Boston (I mean in my range, because I dont intent to extend my description beyond my own travails)." These two effects conspire to merge external scene and internal response; the mind clothes itself in the objects of perception, and those objects become suffused with the feelings they elicit, at the same time.

While such passages of immediate perception and spontaneous inner response add a new and significant element to the literature of travel, they do not provide the entire content of the *Journal*. Sarah Knight was an educated, urbane woman, and like many Bostonians, then and now, she considered life outside Boston a diversion at best, and at worst a trial to be endured. This combination of the writer's personal involvement, facilitated by the journal form, and her habitually superior attitude toward the uncivilized world creates a continuing conflict between her more spontaneous reactions to things and her civilized evaluations of them; between the immediate impressions of a lonely, often frightened, always sensitive traveler and the wry judgments of an aloof and wittily condescending Bostonian. When she is observing backwoods America from a moral and aesthetic distance, she assumes an identity that is not contingent on her experiences. Speaking in this voice, she regards with lofty and comic disdain the government and manners of the Connecticut settlement, the mean habitations where she is forced to lodge, or the rude antics of the backwoodsmen she meets. This voice resembles, in its distance, the one assumed by Bradford in the first book of his history. It is a voice that continues to inform many travel-narratives throughout the eighteenth and nineteenth centuries. We recognize it, for example, in William Byrd's *History of the Dividing Line,* a work that reads like the account of a visit to a zoological garden; and in Francis Parkman's *The Oregon Trail,* in which the narrator grandly reports his distaste for mere emigrants and his serene contempt for the Indians he wants, inexplicably, to study. Such passages also prefigure the civilized contempt felt by the rather dandified narrator of *Roughing It* as he describes the squalid hostelries provided for passengers on the overland stage. One important quality distinguishes this voice wherever it appears: its sense of an audience, of family or friends at home. When Sarah Knight evaluates her experiences, she takes particular care to cast her remarks in an evaluative context which her fellow Bostonians can understand. In effect, she views her travels from Boston.

On the other hand, whenever she describes her immediate perceptions and her spontaneous reactions, she seems to speak only to herself, as if she were completely cut off from home and had to make sense of her experiences without the help of Boston and the standards it represents. In these passages, she assumes an identity that is contingent on its experiences, and she speaks in a voice that resembles not Byrd's or Parkman's but Hawthorne's. . . . (pp. 38-41)

When her feelings of isolation or vulnerability are particularly intense, she breaks into verse. This use of poetry to capture an unusually moving experience reminds us of Jonathan Edwards, who breaks into song when God visits him in the woods, and of Thoreau, who often interrupts his narratives with a poem when nature proves especially elevating. The mixed mode appears repeatedly in later travel-narratives as a way of expressing sublime feelings engendered by landscape, and Melville uses it with his usual originality in *Mardi*, his first avowedly fictional travel-narrative. When Madame Knight's affective states do not erupt in imaginative meditations or in verse, they often find expression in a language of innocent wonder, which sounds very much like Huck's, even in its syntactical pace: "The House . . . had Chimney Corners like ours, and they and the hearths were laid with the finest tile that I ever see, and the stair cases laid all with tile which is ever clean, and so are the walls of the kitchen which had a Brick floor." (p. 42)

The apparent conflict between what we may call the two voices of Sarah Knight's *Journal,* the disengaged Bostonian and the emotionally involved traveler, makes her narrative a crucial document in the history of American travel-writing. For the first time, two opposed attitudes toward the experiences of travel, both of them seriously entertained by the traveler-writer himself, are expressed side by side within the narrative. For Columbus, travel illustrated those truths about the shape of the world and about himself which had been revealed in Scripture and were known by the untraveled authorities. Whenever conflicting data arose on the ground, he either fit them into what was already known or else dismissed them. For the sixteenth-century explorers, travel revealed facts previously unknown, but since the nature of the world and their own characters were thought to be preordained and ultimately knowable, their job was to reveal the truths of the world and realize themselves through bold acts of exploration. The only conflict of attitudes possible here was a discrepancy between the traveler's authoritative knowledge and the homebody's ignorance. In presenting the aloof and the engaged mentalities as two aspects of the same mind, Sarah Knight continues the movement begun by Bradford, when he found himself unable either to maintain a distancing belief in the face of his experiences or to disengage himself sufficiently from those experiences to organize them into a new, coherent belief. But where Bradford had sharply separated the disengaged, comprehensive historian of book 1 from the more involved and limited annalist of book 2, Madame Knight brings these two *personae* face to face in a single narrative movement.

The presence of these two voices in the narrative raises a problem that is at once philosophical and literary: what is the relationship between the two identities represented by these two voices, and how may that relation be expressed in a narrative? Medieval travel-narratives, adopting the autobiographical form and the philosophical position of St. Augustine, had assumed that personal experience has value only insofar as it serves to illustrate revealed truth. As a result, the experiencing self remained totally subject to the knowing self, which stands above the action in the presence of eternal truth. Renaissance travel-writing argued that experience leads to truth, and organized itself around that argument. The retrospective narrator recounts those experiences which revealed the truth to him, and conveys the truth he has gained from his experience. As in earlier travel-writing, the narrator stands outside the action; but where the medieval narrator stood above his travels, the Renaissance narrator stands at the end of them. The narrative shows how the experiencing traveler became the knowing narrator by traveling. In Sarah Knight's *Journal,* however, the more distant, generalizing *persona* is no longer a retrospective narrator outside the action; it is one aspect of the traveler on the ground. And where Renaissance narratives had derived judgment from experience, the *Journal* dramatizes a progressive erosion of judgment by experience. The farther she travels from Boston and the longer she is away, the less she judges things against her original Bostonian standards and the more she gives herself up to the delights and terrors of her experiences.

Although Madame Knight does not solve the philosophical and formal problems raised by the direct confrontation of these two voices, and does not even recognize them as problems, the overall movement of the *Journal* does indicate the direction taken by later writers in pursuit of a solution. Because passages of civilized judgment give way increasingly to passages of immediate, personal involvement as the *Journal* goes along, the experiencing voice seems to arise out of the judging voice as the traveler encounters situations which do not fit her prior standards of judgment. In this respect, the two voices are linked temporally, since the judging voice precedes the experiencing voice. They are also related spatially, in that the judging voice belongs to home and the experiencing voice to the lands visited. And they are related organically, in that the journey, which proceeds through space in time, causes the absolute, judging identity to evolve, through interaction with the changing scene, into the contingent, experiencing identity. Every traveler from Columbus to John Smith had told either how his travels had confirmed his previously revealed identity or how his travels had realized his God-given potential. Sarah Knight's *Journal* tells how travel made her someone new; someone whose identity is closely tied to the scene of her transforming experiences. (pp. 42-4)

Many of the details of the *Journal* . . . contribute to our sense of Madame Knight's becoming someone new as she travels: the attention she gives to those affective states which arise from her experiences, her admission of dependence on her uncivilized guides, her expressions of unselfconscious delight in what she sees, and her conscious intention to restrict her

A wood engraving of a scene from The Journal of Madam Knight, *rendered by Michael McCurdy in 1972. Courtesy of Massachusetts Historical Society.*

remarks entirely to what she herself has seen. All of these decisions show her willingness to give the experiencing self its due, to see new lands through new eyes rather than through her settled opinions only. But none of these details indicates the extent of her change so tellingly as an entry written some four months after she left home, when her sense of herself as a Bostonian had long since begun to fade. New Rochelle, she says, "is a very pretty place well compact, and good handsome houses, clean, good and passable Rodes, and situated on a Navigable River, abundance of land well fined and Cleerd all along as wee paused, which caused in me a Love to the place, which I could have been content to live in it." The new lands have had their seductive charm, it seems, for it is difficult to imagine that she had in mind her "aged and tender mother," her "Dear and only child," and her "kind relations and friends" when she admitted her attachment to a place so far from home. Although the evolutionary theme and structure that is nascent in Madame Knight's *Journal* would take a hundred years to mature, it is important that we notice its emergence here, at the very beginnings of the modern age of prose-fiction and the dawn of the Enlightenment; for the artistic development of the travel-narrative during the next hundred years is closely tied to aesthetic theories of the eighteenth century and to the rise of the novel. (p. 44)

William C. Spengemann, "The Poetics of Adventure," in his The Adventurous Muse: The Poetics of American Fiction, 1789-1900, *Yale University Press, 1977, pp. 6-67.*

JOHN SEELYE (essay date 1977)

[*Seelye is an American novelist whose works include* The True Adventures of Huckleberry Finn *(1970), a rewriting of Mark Twain's classic according to the preferences of modern critics, and the nonfictional* Prophetic Waters: The River in Early American Life and Literature *(1977). Seelye has also published several critical studies of the works of Twain, Herman Melville, Booth Tarkington, and other American literary figures. In the following excerpt from* Prophetic Waters, *Seelye discusses Knight and her* Journal *in the context of river passage and of the social conditions of early eighteenth-century New England.*]

Boston and New York were separated by wilderness enough in 1704, and the route between was bisected by a number of treacherous streams to be crossed at hazard—whether by bridge, ferry, canoe, or on horseback. The folk of colonial New England seldom longed to go on pilgrimages, but when overland travel was mandatory, they set out not in the spring, but the fall of the year, when rivers were lowest and roads as passable as they might be. It is a wonder that Madam Knight went at all, curious that she chose to go by horseback and not by boat, but understandable that she departed Boston in early October, "to New Haven," as she thought, one of those American plans that tended to go awry on the road. (p. 302)

1704 was . . . the year in which Boston's first newspaper was published, an event which, like Madam Knight's journey, is symptomatic of the lack of communication between and within the New England colonies. But both are prophetic also of improvements soon to come, and Madam was the sort of person who would make them: like Benjamin Church she is a combination of traits which are typical of an emerging American temper, not only personal independence and enterprise, but a detectable regional pride. In most other respects, Sarah is Benjamin's antithesis, in matters of setting as well as sex, being firmly fixed in Boston, where she was at various times a school-

teacher, legal scrivener, and a keeper of shops and boarding-houses, business careers occasioned at first by her husband's long absences in England and then by his death. It was a busy life and a town life, and Knight's was likewise a business trip, symbolic in its own way of the changing New England character. Sarah is supposed to have taught young Ben Franklin his penmanship, and certainly the same blue ink colored their veins, her trip to New York, like his subsequent exodus to Philadelphia, an expression of the burgeoning Yankee spirit.

But as a humorous traveler's tale, Madam Knight's *Journal* resembles a picaresque narrative by Smollett, taking its tension from the essential disparity between town and country life. With Smollett, Sarah Knight prefers the former, whose amenities are enhanced by the ordeal of life on the road. The comic tone is established early on, her first guide after leaving the comforts of Dedham being an uncouth bumpkin "resembling a globe on a gatepost" as he rides on before her in the gloom, a Hudibrastic "shade" and the presiding genius of her voyage out: "He entertained me with the adventures he had passed by late riding, and the imminent dangers he had escaped, so that, remembering the heroes in *Parismus* and the *Knight of the Oracle,* I didn't know but I had met with a prince disguised." Despite her satirical tone, the Boston traveler is grateful for her guide's "universal knowledge in the woods," a wilderness necessity which will provide a thematic paradox throughout. Sarah's backwoods Virgil is only the first of several conductors through a dark and dangerous terrain, and he leads her safely to lodgings in Billings, the first of many rustic "Stages" where Madam will spend a night of dubious felicity, a series of advances into and out of the wilderness equivalent to [Mrs. Mary Rowlandson's "Removes" in her *The Sovereignty and Goodness of God* (1682)].

Stages there are along the way, but no stagecoaches, and some hint of the primitive level of communications at the turn of the century is given by the fact that her guides during the next leg of the journey are post riders, the eastern post turning Madam Knight over to the western post at midday. Picking her up at the western terminus of the Providence Ferry, he leads her through Rhode Island to the eastern bank of the Pawtucket, "which they generally ride through. But I dared not venture." Taking passage instead in a small and shallow canoe manned by a boy, Madam Knight, like Mrs. Rowlandson crossing the Baquaug, is at pains to avoid a soaking, "very circumspect, sitting with my hands fast on each side, my eyes steady, not daring so much as to lodge my tongue a hair's breadth more on one side than t'other," fearing that even "a wry thought would have overset our wherry." Like Mary in the wilderness, Sarah's perilous position brings to mind "Lot's wife," but Isaiah is not quoted and the closest Madam Knight comes to "Providence" while crossing over water is on the ferry of that name.

Warned by the post rider of yet another "bad river we were to ride through," Madam Knight's apprehensions are darkened by the approach of evening: "No thoughts but those of the dangerous river could entertain my imagination, and they were as formidable as various, still tormenting me with blackest ideas of my approaching fate—Sometimes seeing myself drowning, otherwiles drowned, and at the best like a holy sister just come out of a spiritual bath in dripping garments." The concluding image is baptismal, but that is not the implication, and "dying with the very thoughts of drowning," Sarah is further tormented by the transformations her lively imagination works on the forest around her: "Each lifeless trunk, with its shatter'd limbs, appear'd an armed enemy; and every little stump like a ravenous devourer.'' In this state of mind she is led to the bank of ''the hazardous river he had told me of,'' and summoning ''all the courage I was mistress of, knowing that I must either venture my fate of drowning, or be left like the Children of the Wood,'' Madam Knight ''gave reins to my nag; and sitting as steady as just before in the canoe, in a few minutes got safe to the other side, which he told me was the Narragansett Country.'' (pp. 302-05)

Safe across is not safely through and though divested of Indians by Captain Church and his courageous company, the area is wild enough still for a Boston lady, ''the way being very narrow, and on each side the trees and bushes gave us very unpleasant welcomes with their branches and boughs, which we could not avoid, it being so exceeding dark.'' To her dismay, the post rider left the weary widow behind in ''the dolesome woods, my company next to none, going I knew not whither, and encompassed with terrifying darkness; the least of which was to startle a more masculine courage.'' Doubting at this point the wisdom of her errand, Madam Knight borrows the language of the Puritan pulpit: ''my call was very questionable.'' But at the darkest moment her prospects are suddenly irradiated by an approximation of grace, ''the friendly appearance of the kind conductress of the night, just then advancing above the horizontal line. The raptures which the sight of that fair planet produced in me, caused me, for the moment, to forget my present weariness and past toils; and inspired me for most of the remaining way with very diverting thoughts.'' (p. 305)

Lapsing (as in her wont) into verse, Madam Knight pays homage to ''fair Cynthia,'' whose ''light can dissipate fears,'' whose ''bright aspect rescues from despair. . . . And a bright joy does through my soul diffuse,'' poetic diction . . . evoking an experience of grace. That her conductress is the pagan goddess who protects imperiled women recalls . . . Milton's Sabrina fair, being likewise something of a good fairy, transforming the dismal forest into ''the pleasant delusion of a sumptuous city, filled with famous buildings and churches, with their spiring steeples, balconies, galleries, and I know not what: grandeurs which I had heard of, and which the stories of foreign countries had given me the idea of.'' The protective, transformational role of Cynthia, ''the way being smooth and even, the night warm and serene,'' in effect turns the woods into a better Boston, and in the wilderness as in the town, Madam Knight lives on ''Moon Street.''

Two more ''Stages'' of discommodious accommodations brought Sarah to the Pawcatuck River, where she found the water high and her courage at its ''lowest ebb.'' Stopping by ''a little cottage just by the river, to wait the water's falling,'' Madam Knight, like Mrs. Rowlandson beside the Connecticut, sits herself down at an extreme remove from civilization. The cottage was a ''little hut,'' ''one of the wretchedest I ever saw as a habitation for human creatures,'' with ''clapboards . . . so much asunder, that the light come through everywhere.'' This ''picture of poverty,'' like Mary's experience of savagery, puts Sarah's distress into (poetic) perspective: ''Their lodgings thin and hard, their Indian fare,'' reduces her ''late fatigues'' to a ''notion or forgotten dream.'' As Mary Rowlandson went on to meet King Philip, so Madam Knight next encounters an equivalent phenomenon, a backwoods American, ''an Indian-like animal . . . who makes an awkward scratch with his Indian shoe, and a nod, sits on the block, fumbles out his black junk, dips it in the ashes, and . . . fell to sucking like a calf, without speaking, for near a quarter of an hour.''

This is the abhorred Thing Itself, Cotton Mather's Indianized Englishman, William Hubbard's borderland monster, gnawing his hunk of beef jerky in savage silence, yet ''ugly as he was,'' Madame Knight was ''glad to ask him to show me the way.'' Mary's interview with Philip marks the westernmost point of her many ''Removes,'' and Sarah is taken by her ''tattertailed guide'' to Stonington, the first ''Stage'' on her journey where she is ''very well accommodated both as to victuals and lodging,'' and the last stage of her wilderness passage. Within a day's ride of New London, Madam Knight has reentered the bounds of civilization. ''Very handsomely and plentifully treated and lodged'' in New London, she is likewise received in New Haven ''with all possible respects and civility.'' But it is New York, the western terminus of both New England and her journey, which provides her *Journal* its cosmopolitan ideal, antithesis to the varieties of backwoods and wilderness life encountered on the road.

Sarah Knight finding ''my business lying unfinished by some concerns at New York depending thereupon, my kinsman, Mr. Thomas Trowbridge of New Haven, must needs take a journey there before it could be accomplished, so I resolved to go there in company with him.'' In short, the traveler now becomes a tourist, and finds that the ''City of New York is a pleasant, well compacted place, situated on a commodious river which is a fine harbor for shipping.'' The orderly widow is also pleased by the ''very stately and high'' buildings of brick, variously colored ''and laid in checkers,'' which, ''being glazed, look very agreeable.'' The interiors are ''neat to admiration,'' the woodwork ''kept very white scoured as so is all the partitions if made of boards,'' and ''the hearth is of tiles and is as far out into the room at the ends as before the fire.'' Despite geopolitical differences the Dutch and the English share certain tidy proclivities, and the mark of Holland remains on English Manhattan, in its architecture and the conduct of business and social affairs alike. Dealt with fairly and exactly, Madam was also ''handsomely treated'' wherever she went, and it was ''with no little regret'' that she left, ''having transacted the affair I went upon and some other that fell in the way.'' (pp. 305-07)

By contrast to the checkerboard city, neighboring Connecticut is an irregular mix of moral rigidity and sloppy manners, a vast rural demonstration of ''the great necessity and benefit both of education and conversation; for these people have as large a portion of mother wit, and sometimes a larger, than those who have been brought up in cities; but for want of improvements, they render themselves almost ridiculous.'' Symbolic of the Connecticut condition is the tobacco-chewing ''tall country fellow'' who labors greatly at the purchase of little: ''Spitting a large deal of aromatic tincture, he gave a scrape with his shovel-like shoe, leaving a small shovel full of dirt on the floor, made a full stop, hugging his own pretty body with his hands under his arms, stood staring round him, like a cat let out of a basket. At last, like the creature Balaam rode on, he opened his mouth and said: Have you any ribbon for hatbands to sell I pray?'' Uncouth but not uncivil, Connecticut is a middle ground in Sarah's travels, as roadway and landscape a contrast to wild Rhode Island on the one side and civilized New York on the other. Its ungainly marriage of moral strictness and commercial opportunism is not unlike the ''pumpkin and Indian mixed bread'' and ''bare-legged punch'' which had such a disagreeable ''aspect'' and ''so awkward or rather awful a sound'' for the genteel lady from Boston. (p. 307)

Connecticut's towns are often flawed, instance Stamford, ''a well compacted town, but with a miserable meeting house,'' or Norwalk, where "the church and tavern are next neighbors," or Fairfield, which has a "spacious meeting-house and good buildings," but where the "inhabitants are litigious, nor do they well agree with their minister, who (they say) is a very worthy gentleman." Still, it is "a plentiful country for provisions of all sorts, and it's generally healthy. No one that can and will be diligent in this place need fear poverty nor the want of food and raiment." So John Smith wrote of Massachusetts nearly a century earlier, and Connecticut two generations after Hooker's arrival is still a place badly in need of improvement, its people lacking in social graces and its roads needing equivalent repairs: "As bridges which were exceeding high and very tottering and of vast length, steep and rocky hills and precipices (bugbears to a fearful female traveler)." It is understandable, therefore, that Madam Knight arrived safely back in Boston with "joy and satisfaction," giving thanks to "my Great Benefactor for thus graciously carrying forth and returning in safety His unworthy handmaiden." (pp. 307-08)

> John Seelye, "Providential Passages," in his *Prophetic Waters: The River in Early American Life and Literature,* Oxford University Press, 1977, pp. 279-309.

ANN STANFORD (essay date 1977)

[*Stanford is a scholar of American colonial literature and the author of several volumes of poetry. In the following excerpt, she culls evidence from the* Journal *to create a "portrait of Madam Knight."*]

Sarah Kemble Knight was a third-generation American, daughter of a Boston merchant. Of her husband, Richard Knight, little is known, but he seems to have been away from home when Madam Knight made her journey.... During her five months' absence, she kept a journal of her travels and those she met along the way—women and men from all social classes—innkeepers, the extremely poor, country bumpkins, ministers, middle-class travelers, the Dutch merchants of New York, and even the governor of Connecticut. All these she describes in a lively style in which passages of wry wit alternate with detailed sketches of people, places, and customs.

A portrait of Madam Knight herself emerges from these impressions—a solid, respectable, outspoken, upper-middle-class matron, whose unshakable sense of her own rank and self-worth does not deprive her of humor. Her view of the world is shrewd and lively; concern with religion has been reduced to comments on meetinghouses and ministers. She speaks wittily rather than intolerantly of other religions; when crossing a river in a canoe, she fears a wetting from which she will rise "at the best like a holy Sister Just come out of a Spiritual Bath in dripping Garments." Sunday ... is mentioned just once, as a reason for not describing the port at Milford.

Occasionally Madam Knight mingles with her wit an attempt at understanding and sympathy for those of other backgrounds. Her description of Bumpkin Simpers, who enters a store to buy a ribbon for his friend Joan Tawdry, is perhaps her most humorous, but she pauses after her ridicule to say that these people have as large a portion of "mother witt" as those brought up in the city, only they lack education and conversation.

Madam Knight apparently had both. The *Journal* includes fairly skillful original poetry that suggests acquaintance with Dryden and his contemporaries. Her practice of giving characters descriptive names may have come from reading the popular *Pilgrim's Progress*. She refers to the romances of *Parismus* and the *Knight of the Oracle* by the Jacobean Emmanuel Forde, both still popular as pamphlets much reduced from their original length. In addition, her satiric tone, her tolerant amusement with herself and the foibles of others, her reference to God as her "Great Benefactor," all suggest an acquaintance with the works of the dawning age of enlightenment. Probably through wide reading and her function as a copier and witness of legal documents, she was better educated than other women of her class and time. Moreover, Madam Knight was more independent and curious about books and the world than most of her sisters and certainly more active in affairs outside the household.

Nevertheless, she is conscious of her frailties as a woman, fearful of crossing rivers and timid when her guide outdistances her in the dark. In such travels through the night, Madam Knight foreshadows the romantic age to come. She describes the dark ride through the forest in a way that suggests the gothic scenes in Irving. And while riding among the trees after the moon has risen, she dreams of the castles and cities she has read about far away in Europe. Hers is an early example of that longing for a European civilization they have never seen that imbues Americans both in and out of literature from Irving to Henry James and beyond. (pp. 198-200)

> Ann Stanford, "Images of Women in Early American Literature," in What Manner of Woman: Essays on English and American Life and Literature, *edited by Marlene Springer, New York University Press, 1977, pp. 185-210.*

HOLLIS L. CATE (essay date 1980)

[*In the following excerpt, Cate examines the utilization and literary effect of figurative language in Knight's* Journal.]

Sarah Kemble Knight's *Journal* is more than just a factual account by a colonial American woman who took a journey from Boston to New York and thence back to Boston.... The hardships she experienced, the frights she received, the poor board and lodging she endured become for us in retrospect an epitome of one's moving from one place to another in America in the early eighteenth century. What interests us in particular, however, is that Knight, through her figurative language and her sense of humor, creatively reflects on the experiences. To the facts she adds a touch, at least, of the artist and in doing so fuses in her own subjective way language and experience. Knight had no idea that her *Journal* would reach the audience it has, but it has reached us nonetheless, and her language in it is that of a writer who made former experience come alive for herself ... and for us today. She normally set down her reflections on the same day on which the experiences occurred. Even so, in true artistic fashion she creates an interest in the event recalled in terms of what the incident becomes in her recollection of it.

Knight had to deal with many different people on her journey, and her figurative language vividly conveys to us that they neither looked nor acted like the inhabitants of her native Boston. Most of the rural people she sees either do not wish to accommodate her, or they are so repulsive she doesn't wish to deal with them. Her images, by and large, leave no doubt that *they won't do.*

At the beginning of her journey she hoped to find someone in the tavern at Dedham to show her the way to Billings, but the men were "tyed by the Lipps to a pewter engine," and apparently no guide came forward. At her lodgings in Billings she is interrogated by a young lady who runs upstairs and puts on two or three rings obviously to impress Knight, who *is* impressed, but not favorably: "But her Granam's new rung sow, had it appeared would affected me as much." Later, Knight suggests the *names* of such people won't even do. She had complained to her companion at the time of the poor accommodations along the way. Her guide points out that they would soon be lodged "at mr. Devills, a few miles further. But I questioned whether we ought to go to the Devil to be helpt out of affliction." She adds some lines of verse about lodging there. An excerpt reads: "'Tis Hell; 'Tis Hell! and Devils here do dwell: / Here dwells the Devil—surely this's Hell." Her wit would hardly allow her not to make use of such a family name in her hellish environment.

In several figurative descriptions she introduces us to rural inhabitants who are presented as beings from another world, surely from a different world from that of even early eighteenth century Boston. While she waited in a hut for the Paukataug River to fall so that she could cross, she tells us that an "Indian-like Animal came to the door, on a creature very much like himself." The "Animal" dipped his "black Junk" in the ashes of the fireplace and in eating it "fell to sucking like a calf." Offensive such a fellow might have been, but Knight knows that the creature who sucks his junk "like a calf" must be the one to show her the way, and she asks him to accompany her to Stonington, her next stop.

Her description of a country fellow at a merchant's house is much anthologized. In it Knight includes some of her most effective figurative language, which is obviously that of a creative observer:

> Being at a merchants house, in comes a tall country
> fellow, with his alfogeos full of Tobacco; for they
> seldom Loose their Cudd, but keep Chawing and
> Spitting as long as they'r eyes are open,—he advanc't
> to the middle of the Room, makes an awkward Nodd,
> and spitting a Large deal of Aromatick Tincture, he
> gave a scrape with his shovel like shoo, leaving a
> small shovel full of dirt on the floor, made a full
> stop, Hugging his own pretty body with his hands
> under his arms, Stood staring rown'd him, like a Catt
> let out of a Baskett. At last, like the creature Balaam
> Rode on, he opened his mouth and said. . . ."

[This] passage suggests the art of Mark Twain himself. Knight's description introduces us to a prototype of the American country bumpkin. Here, as she does elsewhere in other descriptions of people, Knight names or suggests one animal or another. This fellow chews like a cow, stares like a cat, and speaks like an ass. His descendants show up later not only in the fiction of Twain but also in the work of Faulkner and Erskine Caldwell. The humorists of the old Southwest knew him pretty well too.

Knight did not reserve language suggesting animality just for males. On the return trip at a house short of New Rochell she mentions being treated badly by "a surly old shee Creature, not worthy the name of woman, who would hardly let us go into her Door, though the weather was so stormy none but she would have turned out a Dogg." So the inhospitable hostess is not only transformed in Knight's recall but also more or less cursed in it as well.

Her figurative language describing food and lodging focuses on pure and simple *survival*. Her straightfaced stance (again suggesting Twain) is that she must try to survive in spite of the accomodations. Early in the journey she mentions stopping at one of the post's stages where

> . . . yᶜ woman bro't in a twisted thing like a cable,
> but something whiter; and laying it on the bord, tugg'd
> for life to bring it into a capacity to spread; wᶜʰ having
> wᵗʰ great pains accomplished, she serv'd in a dish of
> Pork and Cabbage, I suppose the remains of Dinner.
> The sause was of a deep Purple, wᶜʰ I tho't was boiled
> in her dye Kettle; the bread was Indian, and every-
> thing on the Table Agreeable to these. . . . what cab-
> bage I swallowed ser'vd me for a Cudd the whole
> day after.

As her images suggest, Knight no doubt deduced that the Pilgrims, despite their hardships, had better fare than this and in addition didn't have to pay for it. (pp. 32-3)

[Our] traveler had a particular horror of toppling in some river or other. She feels the same about the possibility of death by water on the return trip as she had on the way to New York; but her final figurative description is of safe passage across a stream, which was "rapid," and seemingly "impassable." Her account of safely reaching the opposite shore leaves us with a significant final image. Her companion, a Mr. Rogers, turned the canoe "into the swift stream and dexterously steering her in a moment wee come to the other side as swiftly passing as an arrow shott out of the Bow by a strong arm." After many days and nights on the road and after all her tribulations, she is, as if by Providence, projected unharmed to the opposite shore. She meets with one or two more difficulties, but . . . two days after her experience in the canoe, she reaches home, shaken but whole.

In the final sentence of her journal Knight gives thanks to her "Great Benefactor" for seeing her safely home. We can be sure there was no doubt in her own mind whose "strong arm" had shot her canoe across the swift stream. Whatever else happened in the two days after that, she must have known her Benefactor would not deny her, His "unworthy handmaiden," the sanctuary of home. (pp. 34-5)

> *Hollis L. Cate, "The Figurative Language of Recall in Sarah Kemble Knight's 'Journal'," in The CEA Critic, Vol. 43, No. 1, November, 1980, pp. 32-5.*

ADDITIONAL BIBLIOGRAPHY

Angoff, Charles. "Sarah Kemble Knight." In his *A Literary History of the American People*, Vol. 1: *From 1607 to the Beginning of the Revolutionary Period*, pp. 339-40. New York: Alfred A. Knopf, 1931.
    Negative appraisal of Knight's *Journal*. Angoff charges that "it says very little about the people she met and the places she passed through" and that "the poetry in it is atrocious."

Boynton, Percy H. "The Turn of the Century." In his *Literature and American Life*, pp. 69-78. Boston: Ginn and Co., 1936.
    Study of late seventeenth- and early eighteenth-century literary trends containing a brief estimation of Knight's contribution to American letters.

Deane, William R. Review of *The Journal of Madam Knight*, by Sarah Kemble Knight. *Littell's Living Age* LVII, No. 735 (26 June 1858): 963-67.
    Asserts the value of Knight's journal as an important firsthand account of an early epoch in American history.

Margolies, Alan. "The Editing and Publication of *The Journal of Madam Knight.*" *The Papers of the Bibliographical Society of America* 58 (First Quarter 1964): 25-32.

Bibliographic discussion of the first appearance of the *Journal* in 1825 and subsequent nineteenth-century editions.

Stanford, Ann. "Three Puritan Women: Anne Bradstreet, Mary Rowlandson, and Sarah Kemble Knight." In *American Women Writers: Bibliographical Essays,* edited by Maurice Duke, Jackson R. Byre, and M. Thomas Inge, pp. 3-20. Westport, Conn.: Greenwood Press, 1983.

Provides sources for further information about Knight under various headings, including bibliography, biography, and criticism.

Tyler, Moses Coit. "New England Traits in the Seventeenth Century." In his *A History of American Literature*, Vol. I: *1607-1676*, pp. 96-9. New York: G. P. Putnam's Sons, 1878.

Appreciation of Knight's *Journal* as an entertaining, realistic travel narrative of rural New England life.

John Locke

1632-1704

(Also wrote under pseudonym of Philanthropus) English philosopher, essayist, and social thinker.

Locke was an English rationalist philosopher credited with according serious consideration to issues which before had been treated only superficially. He understood the bearing of philosophy on how human beings live their lives, and his numerous and varied works dominated English thought in the first half of the eighteenth century, extending their author's influence to America, France, and beyond. His monumental and remarkably lucid *Essay concerning Human Understanding,* written to discover "the original, certainty and extent of human knowledge," furnished basic premises concerning such matters as empiricism, language, and personal identity. An important educational and religious thinker as well, Locke contributed to the understanding of a child's psychological development, and in the religious sphere advocated broad tolerance and the primacy of Christ's teachings. Locke's political and social writings, notable for their persuasive, reasoned, and circumspect proposals, have attracted wide attention, and his *Two Treatises of Government,* in which he stressed human liberty and a respect for human reason, is a milestone in the defense of representative democracy. Widely acknowledged as one of the most influential thinkers that ever lived, Locke was, in the words of the American statesman Benjamin Franklin, "the Newton of the *Microcosm.*"

Locke was born in Wrington, Somerset, to John and Agnes Keene Locke, the former a Puritan attorney and clerk to a justice of the peace, the latter from a family of Puritan tanners. Through the influence of Alexander Popham, a prominent West Country politician, Locke was sent to Westminster School, at that time under the celebrated headmaster Richard Busby, a Royalist often credited with having first set Locke on the road to liberalism. Locke's education at Westminster, which he later criticized in *Some Thoughts concerning Education,* was almost entirely in the classics, consisting mostly of rote exercises in Greek and Latin praxis. In 1652, probably thanks to the influence of Busby and others, Locke was elected to a studentship at Christ Church, Oxford, where, upon completion of the usual arts course supplemented by occasional excursions into medicine, he began six years' tenure as an Oxford tutor. Locke now regularly attended medical lectures and performed medical experiments which, scholars have suggested, early stimulated his interest in method and principle, ultimately leading to the development of much of his philosophy. In 1666 or 1667, having abandoned his early Puritanism and endangered his Oxford career by refusing to take holy orders, Locke joined the London household of Lord Ashley (Sir Anthony Ashley Cooper, created earl of Shaftesbury in 1672), a noted and outspoken champion of civil liberty. Locke served Ashley as physician, confidential adviser, and secretary, helping his employer draft a constitution for the Carolina colony, the progressive *Fundamental Constitutions of Carolina.* He began, in 1671, two early drafts of *An Essay concerning Human Understanding.*

By 1675, owing to his support of the Test Act excluding Roman Catholics from important government positions—this support was primarily political, not a breach of his customary pro-

motion of religious toleration—Shaftesbury had lost all his offices. Out of work and hoping to alleviate his asthma, Locke went to France late in the year, spending time in Montpellier, Paris, and other parts of the country, studying French science, medicine, education, religion, history, and philosophy, and noting with special interest Louis XIV's abuse of his Protestant subjects. Locke returned to England in 1678 or 1679, but soon fell under government suspicion as a supposed radical and took refuge in Holland, where, among other tasks, he revised drafts of his *Essay,* contributed several small works to his friend Jean Le Clerc's periodical *Bibliothèque universelle et historique,* and, probably as a direct result of his experiences in France, wrote a powerful defense of toleration, later published as *Epistola de tolerantia (A Letter concerning Toleration).* Back in England in 1689, Locke allied himself with the constitutional Whigs, taking on the commissionership of appeals in excise cases and, several years later, joining a new council of trade and plantations. In 1690 he published several works, most notably *An Essay concerning Human Understanding,* which, by supplying a new, plain, and careful attempt to reach epistemological truth, made its mark at once. The rest of Locke's life was spent in preparing fresh editions of his *Essay,* proposing and answering, in several works, controversial questions concerning religion, and occasionally venturing, through such pamphlet publications as *Some Considerations of the Consequences of the Lowering of Interest and Raising the Value of Money,* into economic, political, and financial controversy. His death, in 1704, came after a long illness at Oates, Essex, where, since 1691, he had made his permanent home with his friends Sir Francis and Lady Masham.

Locke's philosophy treats four principal issues: knowledge, politics, education, and religion. His theory of knowledge, set out by the "plain, historical method" in the four books of *An Essay concerning Human Understanding,* concerns the nature of knowledge and ways of judging truth. Locke rejected the concept of "innate ideas," maintaining that "there is nothing in the mind except what was at first in the sense": the mind at birth is a *tabula rasa,* a blank sheet of paper, impressionable only by environment and experience. While Locke's empiricism—his reliance on observation and experience, not system and theory—led him to conclude that knowledge is fundamentally made possible by sense perception, he maintained that sensation alone does not constitute knowledge: knowledge is the product of the perception or intuition of the intellect operating on data received from the senses. Thus he recognized intuition as but a tool or instrument; paired with demonstration, it leads to knowledge. Of the intuitive nature of knowledge he wrote: "This part of knowledge is irresistible and, like bright sunshine, forces itself immediately to be perceived, as soon as ever the mind turns its view that way; and leaves no room for hesitation, doubt or examination." Certain knowledge, however, is possible only of logical truth, not of factual truth; our knowledge of external reality is limited to knowledge of our representative ideas of it, not of the reality itself. Nevertheless, Locke affirmed—in a move seen as somewhat inconsistent but compatible with his essentially commonsense approach to philosophy—that we can have probable if not absolute certainty of our ideas, our "sensitive knowledge" of things that exist physically. Carrying his theories into his discussion of language, Locke maintained that words are "nominal essences," common signs not of physical things but of ideas of things, acting as the most significant instruments of knowledge.

Two Treatises of Government, Locke's most important work on political theory and possibly a direct reaction to contemporary events in England, is concerned with two major issues: it denies the validity of Sir Robert Filmer's 1690 defense of the divine right of kings, *Patriarcha; or, The Natural Power of Kings Asserted,* and denies the theory of absolute government, particularly as elucidated in Thomas Hobbes's *Leviathan* (1651), although this work is not explicitly mentioned. Emphasizing property and the law of nature, Locke argued that, in society, a ruler's authority is conditional rather than absolute, and individuals may rightly assume that political power will be used to preserve their property, to permit them to think as they choose and to worship as they please, and to allow them free speech. To guarantee these rights and freedoms, Locke concluded, a mixed constitution is essential, making the people sovereign above all and affording them the right to take back their support and bring down the government if it fails to honor its trust. In *Some Thoughts concerning Education,* which criticizes primary education based on the classics, Locke set out his method of educating a squire's son. He claimed that a proper education, ideally carried out by private tuition aimed at instilling useful knowledge, involves both physical and mental concerns, namely strengthening the body and imparting virtue, wisdom, and general good breeding. Locke carried this practical approach to education over to his religious works. A broad, tolerant Anglican who was opposed to religious fanaticism, Locke recognized two fundamentals of the Christian life: first, that a man accept Christ as God's Messiah, secondly,

that he follow Christ's teachings. These ideas, which are the foundation of all Locke's religious writings, are especially manifest in *The Reasonableness of Christianity,* in which Locke emphasized the need for both reason and revelation in approaching Christianity, in his letters on toleration, and in the otherwise political *Fundamental Constitutions of Carolina.*

In his day Locke enjoyed a wide and generally commendatory reputation which proved prophetic. Notwithstanding his philosophical opposition to Locke's theory of knowledge, John Norris claimed in 1690 to be "perhaps as great an Admirer of [Locke] as any of his most sworn Followers," and added that he "would not part with [*An Essay concerning Human Understanding*] for half a *Vatican.*" Five years later John Wynne acknowledged the "most agreeable and instructive entertainment" he derived from *An Essay,* and in 1711 the essayist Joseph Addison praised Locke's "admirable Reflection upon the Difference of Wit and Judgment" as "the best and most philosophical Account" of this subject he knew. Although Locke was not without his opponents—among whom the poet Matthew Prior is outstanding for his caustic and ironic denunciation of Locke's thought—eighteenth-century commentators were nearly unanimous in praising Locke. Voltaire, for instance, posited in 1733 that no one "ever had a more judicious or more methodical Genius" than Locke, stating that "Mr. *Locke* has display'd the human Soul, in the same Manner as an excellent Anatomist explains the Springs of the human Body." Among early American statesmen, who as a rule considered Locke's political thought their spiritual motivation, John Adams extolled Locke's metaphysics, claiming that Locke, "like Columbus, has discovered a new world," and Thomas Jefferson praised Locke as one of "the three greatest men that have ever lived." Nevertheless, Adams noted that Locke "astonished the world with a signal absurdity" in his "legislation for Carolina," and in England Samuel Johnson found Locke's educational theories wanting, arguing that they gave "too little to literature." With the exception of Samuel Taylor Coleridge, who objected strongly to the tenets of the *Essay,* nineteenth-century commentators on Locke's works essentially echoed eighteenth-century opinion. Leigh Hunt, remarking in 1810 that Locke "taught us to think for ourselves," called his subject "the sage who shed . . . a noble radiance on the human intellect," and in America Ralph Waldo Emerson, in spite of his mixed opinion of Locke's philosophy, wrote in his private notebook that the "history of John Locke . . . is [a] far more important part of the stock of knowledge . . . than the whole history of Poland or Hungary." Thomas E. Webb, however, though believing Locke's philosophy "for the most part, *true,*" found Locke's temperament cold, and suggested, among other criticisms, that "in his language Locke is of all Philosophers the most vague, vacillating, and various."

Stressing their subject's modernity, many twentieth-century critics have praised Locke for opening an era. Maurice Cranston, for example, saw Locke as the possessor of "the first modern mind." He claimed that, by separating philosophy from theology, Locke broke from medieval thinking, thereby providing the first modern philosophy of science. Similarly, George Santayana attributed to Locke the founding of two disciplines, modern psychology and the criticism of knowledge, and Basil Willey, in describing Locke as the founder of eighteenth- and nineteenth-century liberalism, added that Locke's prose, "like Wren's architecture . . . , is harmonious, lucid, and severe." More recently, Huntington Cairns, while generally commending Locke's works, criticized their author for losing sight of his objectives, and, in a synthetic approach,

Russell Kirk suggested that "no philosopher is more generally mentioned, and less really read, than John Locke." Nevertheless, informed critics of this century have generally found Locke's writings compelling—a fact borne out by numerous contemporary studies of Locke's scientific method, his understanding of social groupings, the relationship of his metaphysics and theology, and his concept of private property and public power.

Locke's writings, often described by scholars as eminently commonsensical in nature, cover a wide range of subjects: knowledge, belief, and understanding, moral and political principles, science, religion, economics, child-rearing, and education. This list is not complete, but gives some idea of the scope of Locke's thought. In all his works, Locke put his concern for discovering the truth before any desire for personal fame or reputation. "That which makes my writtings tolerable," he wrote, "is only this, that I never write for anything but truth and never publish anything . . . which I am not fully persuaded of myself." The success of Locke's single purpose may be measured by the extent of his fame, reputation, and influence. Recognizing that humankind's first concern is its own betterment, Locke aimed to forward human progress through rationalist philosophy, earning by his success a preeminent place in the history of philosophy.

(See also *Dictionary of Literary Biography*, Vol. 31: *American Colonial Writers, 1735-1781*.)

PRINCIPAL WORKS

"Pax regit Augusti, quem vicit Julius, orbem . . ." and "If Greece with so much mirth did entertaine . . ." (poetry) 1654; published in *Musarum Oxoniensium Helaiophoria*

The Fundamental Constitutions of Carolinas [with Anthony Ashley Cooper, 1st Earl of Shaftesbury, and others] (manifesto) 1670

A Letter from a Person of Quality, to His Friend in the Country [with Anthony Ashley Cooper, 1st Earl of Shaftesbury] (essay) 1675

Epistola de tolerantia ad clarissimum virum T.A.R.P.T.O.L.A. scripta à P.A.P.O.I.L.A. (essay) 1689

[*A Letter concerning Toleration, Humbly Submitted*, 1689]

An Essay concerning Humane Understanding (essay) 1690; also published as *An Essay concerning Human Understanding*, 1726; revised editions, 1694, 1700, and 1705

A Second Letter concerning Toleration to the Author of the Argument of the Letter concerning Toleration [as Philanthropus] (essay) 1690

Two Treatises of Government: In the Former, the False Principles and Foundation of Sir Robert Filmer, and His Followers, Are Detected and Overthrown. The Latter Is an Essay concerning the True Original, Extent, and End of Civil Government (essays) 1690

Some Considerations of the Consequences of the Lowering of Interest and Raising the Value of Money. In a Letter to a Member of Parliament (essay) 1692

A Third Letter for Toleration, to the Author of the "Third Letter concerning Toleration" [as Philanthropus] (essay) 1692

Some Thoughts concerning Education (essay) 1693; revised editions, 1695, 1699, 1705

Further Considerations concerning Raising the Value of Money. Wherein Mr. Lowndes's Arguments for It in His Late Report, concerning "An Essay for the Amendment of the Silver Coins" Are Particularly Examined (essay) 1695

The Reasonableness of Christianity, as Delivered in the Scriptures (essay) 1695

Short Observations on a Printed Paper, Intituled "For Encouraging the Coining of Silver Money in England, and After for Keeping It There" (essay) 1695

A Vindication of the Reasonableness of Christianity, &c. from Mr. Edwards's Reflections (essay) 1695

*Several Papers Relating to Money, Interest and Trade, &c. Writ upon Several Occasions and Published at Different Times (essays) 1696

A Letter to the Right Reverend Edward Ld Bishop of Worcester, concerning Some Passages Relating to Mr. Locke's Essay of Humane Understanding; in a Late Discourse of His Lordship's, in Vindication of the Trinity (essay) 1697

Mr. Locke's Reply to the Right Reverend the Lord Bishop of Worcester's Answer to His Letter, concerning Some Passages Relating to Locke's Essay of Humane Understanding . . . (essay) 1697

Mr. Locke's Reply to the Right Reverend the Lord Bishop of Worcester's Answer to His Second Letter . . . (essay) 1699

Posthumous Works of Mr. John Locke: Viz. I. Of the Conduct of the Understanding. II. An Examination of P. Malebranche's Opinion of Seeing All Things in God. III. A Discourse on Miracles. IV. Part of a Fourth Letter on Toleration. V. Memoirs relating to the Life of Anthony First Earl of Shaftesbury. To Which Is Added, VI. His New Method of a Common-Place-Book, Written Originally in French, and Now Translated into English (essays and biography) 1706

The Works of John Locke. 10 vols. (essays) 1823

Locke's Travels in France, 1675-1679, as Related in His Journals, Correspondence and Other Papers (letters, journals, and marginalia) 1953

The Correspondence of John Locke. 8 vols. (letters) 1976

*This work consists of second editions of the earlier *Some Considerations of the Consequences of the Lowering of Interest and Raising the Value of Money*, *Short Observations on a Printed Paper, Intituled "For Encouraging the Coining of Silver Money in England, and After for Keeping It There,"* and *Further Considerations concerning Raising the Value of Money*.

JOHN LOCKE   (essay date 1690)

[*In the following excerpt from his epistle to the reader of the first edition of* An Essay concerning Human Understanding, *Locke comments on his essay's origin, occasion, merits, and faults.*]

I here put into thy hands what has been the diversion of some of my idle and heavy hours; if it has the good luck to prove so of any of thine, and thou hast but half so much pleasure in reading as I had in writing it, thou wilt as little think thy money, as I do my pains, ill bestowed. Mistake not this for a commendation of my work; nor conclude, because I was pleased with the doing of it, that therefore I am fondly taken with it now it is done. He that hawks at larks and sparrows, has no less sport, though a much less considerable quarry, than he that flies at nobler game: and he is little acquainted with the subject of this treatise, the Understanding, who does not know, that as it is the most elevated faculty of the soul, so it is employed with a greater and more constant delight than any of the other. (p. 1)

If thou judgest [this treatise] for thyself, I know thou wilt judge candidly; and then I shall not be harmed or offended, whatever be the censure. For, though it be certain that there is nothing in this treatise of the truth whereof I am not fully persuaded, yet I consider myself as liable to mistakes as I can think thee; and know that this book must stand or fall with thee, not by any opinion I have of it, but thy own. If thou findest little in it new or instructive to thee, thou art not to blame me for it. It was not meant for those that had already mastered this subject, and made a thorough acquaintance with their own understandings, but for my own information, and the satisfaction of a few friends, who acknowledged themselves not to have sufficiently considered it.

Were it fit to trouble thee with the history of this *Essay*, I should tell thee, that five or six friends, meeting at my chamber, and discoursing on a subject very remote from this, found themselves quickly at a stand by the difficulties that rose on every side. After we had awhile puzzled ourselves, without coming any nearer a resolution of those doubts which perplexed us, it came into my thoughts that we took a wrong course; and that, before we set ourselves upon inquiries of that nature, it was necessary to examine our own abilities, and see what *objects* our understandings were, or were not, fitted to deal with. This I proposed to the company, who all readily assented; and thereupon it was agreed that this should be our first inquiry. Some hasty and undigested thoughts, on a subject I had never before considered, which I set down against our next meeting, gave the first entrance into this Discourse, which, having been thus begun by chance, was continued by entreaty; written by incoherent parcels; and, after long intervals of neglect, resumed again, as my humor or occasions permitted; and at last, in a retirement, where an attendance on my health gave me leisure, it was brought into that order thou now seest it.

This discontinued way of writing may have occasioned, besides others, two contrary faults, viz., that too little and too much may be said in it. If thou findest anything wanting, I shall be glad that what I have writ gives thee any desire that I should have gone further: if it seems too much to thee, thou must blame the subject; for when I put pen to paper, I thought all I should have to say on this matter would have been contained in one sheet of paper; but the further I went, the larger prospect I had: new discoveries led me still on, and so it grew insensibly to the bulk it now appears in. I will not deny but possibly it might be reduced to a narrower compass than it is; and that some parts of it might be contracted; the way it has been writ in, by catches, and many long intervals of interruption, being apt to cause some repetitions. But, to confess the truth, I am now too lazy, or too busy, to make it shorter. (pp. 2-4)

I pretend not to publish this *Essay* for the information of men of large thoughts and quick apprehensions; to such masters of knowledge I profess myself a scholar, and therefore warn them beforehand not to expect anything here but what, being spun out of my own coarse thoughts, is fitted to men of my own size, to whom, perhaps, it will not be unacceptable that I have taken some pains to make plain and familiar to their thoughts some truths, which established prejudice, or the abstractedness of the ideas themselves, might render difficult. . . . The truth is, those who advised me to publish it, advised me . . . to publish it as it is; and since I have been brought to let it go abroad, I desire it should be understood by whoever gives himself the pains to read it. I have so little affection to be in print, that if I were not flattered this *Essay* might be of some use to others, as I think it has been to me, I should have confined

Locke's birthplace in Wrington, Somerset, as it was in 1829.

it to the view of some friends, who gave the first occasion to it. My appearing therefore in print being on purpose to be as useful as I may, I think it necessary to make what I have to say as easy and intelligible to all sorts of readers as I can. And I had much rather the speculative and quick-sighted should complain of my being in some parts tedious, than that anyone, not accustomed to abstract speculations, or prepossessed with different notions, should mistake or not comprehend my meaning.

It will possibly be censured as a great piece of vanity or insolence in me, to pretend to instruct this our knowing age, it amounting to little less when I own that I publish this *Essay* with hopes that it may be useful to others. . . . I acknowledge the age we live in is not the least knowing, and therefore not the most easy to be satisfied. If I have not the good luck to please, yet nobody ought to be offended with me. I plainly tell all my readers, except half a dozen, this treatise was not at first intended for them; and therefore they need not be at the trouble to be of that number. But yet if anyone thinks fit to be angry, and rail at it, he may do it securely; for I shall find some better way of spending my time than in such kind of conversation. I shall always have the satisfaction to have aimed sincerely at truth and usefulness, though in one of the meanest ways. The commonwealth of learning is not at this time without master-builders, whose mighty designs in advancing the sciences will leave lasting monuments to the admiration of posterity: but everyone must not hope to be a Boyle or a Sydenham; and in an age that produces such masters as the great Huygenius, and the incomparable Mr. Newton, with some other of that strain, it is ambition enough to be employed as an underlaborer in clearing the ground a little, and removing some of the rubbish that lies in the way to knowledge. . . . (pp. 4-7)

John Locke, "The Epistle to the Reader," in his An Essay concerning Human Understanding, *1690. Reprint by Gateway Editions, 1956, pp. 1-9.*

JOHN NORRIS (essay date 1690)

[An English clergyman, poet, and philosopher, Norris is best remembered as a strong churchman who verbally attacked Whigs and Nonconformists. An offshoot from the school of Cambridge Platonists, he opposed the methods dominating Locke's exposition, setting out his objections to An Essay concerning Human Understanding *in the form of "a Letter to a Friend." Probably*

as a result of Norris's criticism, Locke contemptuously characterized him as "an obscure, enthusiastic man." In the following
excerpt, Norris assesses Locke's position on the existence of innate principles and the source and nature of ideas.]

SIR,

You obliged me so highly by acquainting me with the Publication of so rare a Curiosity as Mr. *Lock's* Book [*An Essay
concerning Human Understanding*], that should I dispute your
Commands when you desire my Opinion of it, I should hazard
the Credit of my *Gratitude.* . . . Without therefore any further
Demur or Delay I shall apply my self to the Task you set me,
in giving you my *Free Censure* of Mr. *Lock's* [*Essay*], which
I shall do by reflecting upon what I think most liable to Exception in the same Order as the things lie before me. (pp. 1-2)

*The Understanding like the Eye, whilst it makes us see and
perceive all other things, takes no notice of it self.* What the
Ingenious Author intends in this Period, or how to make out
any consistent Sense of it, I do not understand. For if his
meaning be, That the Understanding while it is intent upon
other things, cannot at that time take notice of it self; this
comes to no more, than that when 'tis intent upon one thing
it cannot attend to another, which is too easily and obviously
true of all *Finite* Powers to be any great Discovery. But if his
meaning be (as it rather seems, because of the Particle (All)
and the Comparison here used) that the Understanding like the
Eye, tho it maks us see all other things, yet it takes no notice
of itself, then 'tis a Contradiction to his whole following Work,
which upon this Supposition must needs be very *unaccountably*
undertaken. (p. 2)

*First I shall enquire into the Original of those Ideas which a
Man observes,* &c. But sure by all the Laws of Method in the
World, he ought *first* to have Defined what he meant by Ideas,
and to have acquainted us with their *Nature,* before he pro-
ceeded to account for their Origination. For how can any Proposition be form'd with any certainty concerning an Idea, that
it is or is not *Innate,* that it does or does not come in at the
Senses, before the meaning of the Word Idea be stated, and
the nature of the thing, at least in general, be understood? . . .
This therefore ought to have been his *first,* and indeed *main*
Business to have given us an account of the Nature of Ideas.
And yet this is not only neglected in its proper place, but wholly
omitted and passed over in deep silence; which I cannot but
remark, as a *Fundamental* defect in this Work.

In the three following Chapters our Author sets himself to prove
that there are no *Innate Principles.* But before I consider whether
there be or no, I premise this double Remarque. First, That a
thing may be false in it self, and yet not so because, or in
vertue of such an Argument. Secondly, That tho a thing be
really false, yet it may not become such a Man to deny the
Existence of it, who by some other Principles of his may be
obliged to hold the contrary. The first of these argues the Writer
guilty of *Inconsequence.* The Second of *Inconsistency.* Upon
both which Accounts this otherwise very ingenious Writer seems
in this part to be chargeable. (pp. 3-4)

His First Argument against *Innate Principles* is taken from the
want of Universal Consent. *There are,* says he, *No Principles
to which all Mankind give an universal Assent.* But in the first
place how can this Author say so, since in several places afterwards he resolves that Ready and prone Assent which is
given to certain Propositions upon the first Proposal, into the
Self-evidence of them? There are then even according to him
Self-evident Propositions. And will he say that Self-evident

Propositions are not universally assented to? How then are they
Self-evident? There must be therefore, according to him, some
Principles to which all Mankind *do* give an universal Consent.
I do not say that this proves them *Innate,* but only that there
are such Propositions.

Well, but how does he prove there are no such? Why, he
instances in some of the most Celebrated, and says that *All
Children and Ideots have not the least apprehension or thought
of them; and the want of that is enough to destroy universal
consent.* Now I always thought that Universality of Consent
had been sufficiently secured by the Consent of all, and the
Dissent of none that were capable of either. And what then
have we to do with *Ideots* and *Children?* Do any or all of these
Dissent or think otherwise? No, that he will not say, because
they think not at all, having (as he says) not the *least Apprehension or Thought of them.* (pp. 4-6)

The most therefore that this Author can mean by want of Uni-
versal Consent, is that every individual Person does not *actually*
Assent. This perhaps may be granted him from the Instance of
Ideots and *Children.* But then the Question will be about the
Consequence of his Argument, whether Actual Assent from
every Individual be necessary to the Supposition of *Innate
Principles?* Or, in other Words, whether from there not being
any Propositions to which every individual Man gives an actual
Assent, it follows that there are no Innate Truths. The Author
is of the Opinion that it does. (p. 6)

Our ingenious Author further argues against *Innate Principles*
from the *Lateness* of the Perception of such which are presumed
to be of that number, in that they are not the first that possess
the Minds of Children. *Can it be imagin'd* (says He) *that they
perceive the Impression from things without, and are at the
same time ignorant of those Characters which Nature it self
has taken care to stamp within?* This I take to be a very uncertain way of arguing. . . . For if *Nullity* of Perception will
not conclude against *Innate Principles,* much less will the *Lateness* of Perception be able to do it. And besides, there may be
many Reasons drawn from the inward, and to us unknown
Contexture of our Minds, and from the manner of that Original
Impression (if any such there be) which would also be to us
equally unknown, besides the Order of External Circumstances, that may be the Cause why these natural Characters
may not be so soon read as some others. (pp. 11-12)

Come we now to his Arguments against *Innate Practical Principles,* the first of which is from their not being universally
assented to. But what does he here mean by their not being
universally consented to? That they are not actually assented
to by every Individual whether capable or not? Or that they
are not consented to by all that judge any thing about them; If
the former, that proves nothing . . . ; If the latter, then I deny
the Proposition, and affirm that there are not only as *Certain*
but as *Uncontested* Propositions in Morality as in any other
science. But our Author demands, *Where is that Practical
Truth that is universally received?* I answer by referring him
to his own Book, where he says That this Proposition, *Where
there is no Propriety there is no Injustice,* is a Proposition as
certain as any Demonstration in *Euclid;* I add and as plain too.
It needing nothing to assure the Truth of it but only the Explication of the Terms. And I further remarque that in the same
place he says that Morality may be placed among the Sciences
capable of Demonstration. Well then, if there may be propositions demonstrated in Morality, then those Propositions must
at last be resolved into *Principles evident* and *incontestable.*
Since otherwise there can be no Demonstration. There are

therefore incontestable Principles in Morality. And he confesses as much in express terms; *I doubt not,* says he in the same place, *but from Principles as incontestable as those of the Mathematicks, by necessary Consequences, the measures of Right and Wrong might be made out to any one,* &c. Here he expressly owns incontestable Principles in Morality, that is, incontestable Truths, that is, Truths that cannot be denied, and therefore *must* be assented to. And how then can he with any tolerable *Self-Consistency* say that there are no Moral Principles universally consented to? If none are universally consented to, then all are by some contested. And yet he says there are in Morality incontestable Principles. How to adjust this I no more know, than he does to reconcile *Morality* and *Mechanism.*

His next Argument is, That *There cannot any one Moral Rule be proposed whereof a Man may not justly demand a Reason.* Well, what then? Therefore they are not *Innate.* I do not see the Consequence. Why may not the Same Proposition be Innate, and yet deducible from Reason too, as well as the same Proposition be the Object of both *Faith* and *Science?* Why may not Conclusions be Innate as well as Principles? Why may not God be supposed for a further Security of our Vertue to implant even those Practical Propositions upon our Minds, which are also capable of being demonstrated from Principles of Reason? Whether he has so done or no I do not dispute; I only say that their Dependence on Reason is no Argument that he has not. (pp. 13-16)

These are the main Arguments, and to which all that is further offered may be reduced, whereby this Author impugns the Doctrin of *Innate Principles;* and I think neither any nor all of them are sufficient for the Cause wherein they are ingaged. And I am so far from being surprized at their *Deficiency,* that I think it absolutely impossible for him or any Man else upon his Principles, to prove that there are no *Innate Truths.* For since with those of the Peripatetic School he allows that Ideas are impress'd upon the Mind from sensible Objects, he cannot (as another might) object against the *Possibility* of such Impressions. He cannot say they are capable only of a Figurative and Metaphorical Sense; Since according to him the same is litterally and really done every Day, every Hour, every Minute. No, he must grant that 'tis possible there may be such Impressions. All the Question then will be concerning the *Timing* of it, whether any of these Impressions be Original Characters or no! And why may they not be at first as well as afterwards? How can he or any man else tell (upon his Principles) whether the Author of Nature has imprinted any such or no? Or whether we brought any with us into the World or no? However that may be, I am satisfy'd 'tis impossible for any man that holds *Mental Impressions* to prove the contrary; especially if with that he allows the Possibility of *Preexistence,* which I believe no considering Man will say is Impossible.

For my part, I do as little believe there are any such things as Innate Principles strictly and properly so called, meaning by them certain Original Characters written upon or interwoven with the Mind in the very first Moment of its Being and Constitution, I say I do as little believe this as the Author himself. Not for the Reasons by him alledged, with the Cogency of which I am not satisfy'd, but because I do not allow any such thing as *Mental Impressions,* or Characters written upon the mind, which if it pretend to any thing more than Figure and Metaphor, I take to be mere *Jargon,* and unintelligible *Cant.* (pp. 18-20)

Having thus far considered our Author's Impugnation of Innate Principles, I come now to examin the Original which he gives to *Ideas.* These he derives . . . from this double Fountain, *Sensation* and *Reflection.* Especially from the Former, telling us again and again, that *the Senses let in Ideas and furnish the yet empty Cabinet.* That *the Senses convey into the mind several distinct Perceptions of things.* And that *the Senses do furnish the Soul with Ideas to think on,* with many other such Expressions.

These indeed are pretty *Smiling* Sentences. But before we go a Step further I would willingly know of the Author what kind of things these Ideas are which are thus let in at the Gate of the Senses. This indeed I expected an Account of in the beginning of the Work; but since the Author has been pleased to cast a *Shade* upon this Part, I now demand, what are these Ideas? Why you shall know that presently. *Whatsoever the Mind perceives in it self, or is the immediate Object of Perception, that I call Idea,* says he. Very good; So much my Lexicon would have told me. But this does not satisfy. I would know what kind of things he makes these ideas to be as to their *Essence* or *Nature.* Are they in the first place Real Beings or not? Without doubt Real Beings, as having Real Properties, and really different one from another, and representing things really different. Well, if Real Beings, then I demand, are they Substances, or are they Modifications of Substances? He will not say they are *Modifications.* For besides that a Modification of Substance cannot be a Representative of a Substance, there being no manner of likeness between a Substance and a Mode; if an Idea be a Modification only it cannot subsist by it self, but must be the Modification of some Substance or other, whereof also there may be an Idea; which Idea being (as is supposed) only a Mode, must have another Substance, and so on without end. As for example, If my Idea of *Figure* be only a Mode, then it must have a Substance wherein to exist as well as Figure it self, which cannot exist alone; and since of that Substance whatever it be, there may be also an Idea, which is supposed to be a Modification, this Idea must also have another Substance, and so on to Infinity. He will not therefore, I suppose, say that our Ideas are *Modifications.*

He must then say that they are *Substances.* Are they then Material Substances or Immaterial? If he says they are *Material* Substances or Corporeal Emanations from sensible Objects, I would desire him to weigh with himself, and try if he can answer, what is alledged by *M. Malebranch* against the Possibility of such Emanations. Particularly, let him tell me how this can consist with the *Impenetrability* of Bodies, which must needs hinder these Corporeal Effluvias from possessing the same *Ubi* or Point, which yet must be supposed, if these be the Representers of Objects, since there is no assignable Point where the same, and where multitudes of Objects may not be seen. This one Difficulty is enough to make this way *impassable.* (pp. 21-4)

These and a thousand more Absurdities must he wade through that will assert our Ideas to be Corporeal Effluvias derived from external Objects. It remains then that they must be *Immaterial* Substances. And so without all question they are. *All* of them as to their *Essence,* and *most* of them as to their *Representation.* (p. 26)

The short of this Argument is, If our Ideas are derived from sensible Objects, then they are Material Beings, because Matter can send forth nothing but Matter. But they are not Material Beings, for the Reasons alledg'd above. Therefore they are not derived from Sensible Objects. . . . And what does he think of the Idea of *God?* Will he say that *that* is also derived from sensible Objects? Yes: For, says he, *If we examin the Idea we have of the Incomprehensible Supreme Being, we shall find that we come by it the same way,* that is, by Sensation. But in the first place, how does this agree with what he says, *That we have the knowledge of the existence of all things without us (except only of God) by our Senses?* So then it seems we do not know the Existence of God by our Senses. No? then neither have we the Idea of him by our Senses. For if we had, why should we not know his Existence by Sensation as well as the Existence of other things, which, as he says, we know only by Sensation? For, says he, speaking of the knowledge of Existence, *We have the knowledge of our own existence by Intuition, of the existence of God by Demonstration, and of other things by Sensation.* Then it seems we do not know the Existence of God by Sensation, but that of other things we do. But why are other things known by Sensation, but only because their Ideas come in at our Senses? For I suppose he will not say that the things themselves come in at our Senses; for then what need is there of Ideas at all? And if other things are therefore known by Sensation, because their Ideas come in by the Senses, then why is not God also known by Sensation, forasmuch as his Idea according to him, comes also the same way? and yet he will not allow that God's Existence is known by Sensation; Which indeed is very true, but then he should not have said that the Idea of God comes in by the Senses. (pp. 26-9)

[Our] Author himself confesses . . . , that *Whatsoever is first of all things, must necessarily contain in it, and actually have, at least all the Perfections that can ever after exist. Nor can it ever give to another any perfection that it has not, either actually in it self, or at least in an higher degree.* God then, even according to him, is all Beings; or, has the whole Plentitude of Being. And I wonder that this Principle had not led this Sagacious Person further. I know whither it would have carried him, if he had follow'd the Clue of it. For why should we seek any further, and puzzle our selves with unintelligible Suppositions? What else *need*, and what else *can* be the immediate Object of our Understanding but the Divine Ideas, the *Omniform Essence* of God? This will open to us a plain intelligible Account of *Human Understanding*, yea of *Angelical* and *Divine* too. (pp. 30-1)

These, Sir, are the most considerable Passages that at once reading I thought liable to Reflection in this Work, which notwithstanding these few *Erratas,* I think to be a very extraordinary Performance, and worthy of the most publick Honour and Respect. And tho I do not approve of every particular thing in this Book, yet I must say that the Author is just such a kind of Writer as I like, one that has thought much, and well, and who freely Writes what he thinks. I hate your *Commonplace* Men of all the Writers in the World, who tho they happen sometimes to say things that are in themselves not only True, but considerable, yet they never write in any Train or Order of Thinking, which is one of the greatest Beauties of Composition.

But this Gentleman is a Writer of a very different Genius and Complexion of Soul, and whose Character I cannot easily give, but must leave it either to the Description of some finer Pen, or to the silent Admiration of Posterity. Only one Feature of his Disposition I am concern'd to point out, which is, that he seems to be a Person of so great Ingenuity and Candor, and of a Spirit so truly Philosophical, that I have thence great and fair Inducements to believe that he will not be offended with that Freedom I have used in these Reflections, which were not intended for the lessening his Fame, but solely for the promoting of *Truth* and *right Thinking.*

And this will justifie that part of the *Reflections,* where agreeing with the Author in the Proposition intended to be proved, I lay open the insufficiency of his Proofs. For to say that a thing is false for such Reasons, when 'tis not false for such Reasons, tho it be absolutely false, is as great an Injury to Truth, as to say a thing is false when 'tis not false. A false Inference is as much an Untruth, as a false Conclusion; and accordingly he that might reflect upon the Conclusion if false, may with as much reason reflect upon a wrong way of inferring it, tho the Conclusion it self be true. Which I mention with respect to the former part about Innate Principles, where tho I agree with the Author in the thing denied, yet I think his Reasons are not cogent.

After all, notwithstanding my dissenting from this Author in so many things, I am perhaps as great an Admirer of him as any of his most sworn Followers, and would not part with his Book for half a *Vatican.* (pp. 41-3)

John Norris, "Cursory Reflections upon a Book Call'd, 'An Essay concerning Human Understanding'," in his Christian Blessedness; or, Discourses upon the Beatitudes of Our Lord and Saviour Jesus Christ, S. Manship, 1690, pp. 1-44.*

JOHN WYNNE   (essay date 1695)

[*An English homilist and clergyman, Wynne is chiefly remembered for his "unblushing Whig propagandism" and his occasional recalcitrance in ecclesiastical affairs. Successively bishop of St. Asaph and of Bath and Wells, he published separately four sermons, but distinguished himself only through his Abridgment of Locke's "Essay concerning Human Understanding" (1696), which was commended by Locke himself. In the following excerpt from a 1695 letter to Locke, Wynne praises* An Essay concerning Human Understanding *and proposes his abridgment of it.*]

After the repeated perusal of your excellent *Essay concerning Human Understanding* (which will ever afford me the most agreeable and instructive entertainment), though I feel myself deeply impressed with motives of the greatest respect and esteem for the author, yet I am very sensible how impertinent it would be for one of my rank and condition to pretend to make any private acknowledgements for so public and universal a benefit. But having some thoughts relating to your book, which may be of advantage to the public, I make bold to offer them to you, not doubting but that your candour will pardon my presumption, though your judgment should disallow my proposal.

Ever since I had the happiness to be acquainted with your accurate *Essay,* I have been persuaded that the greatest service that could be done for the judicious and thinking part of the world, next to the composing of it, would be to bring it into vogue and credit, and thereby into common and general use. If men did not labour under inveterate prejudices and obstinate prepossessions, this might easily be effected. And yet, notwithstanding these, the truths contained in your book are so clear and evident, the notions so natural and agreeable to reason, that I imagine none that carefully reads and duly considers them, can avoid being enlightened and instructed by them. I have for some time made it my business, in my little sphere, to recommend it to all those that I have any influence over, nor did I ever meet with any, who, after an attentive and diligent perusal, complained of being disappointed in their expectation; but, on the contrary, they owned themselves to have been infinitely benefited by it. By the light which they have derived from it, they so clearly perceive how useless and insignificant our vulgar systems are, that they have resolved to trifle no longer, but to rid their hands and heads entirely of them; and in all probability it would have the same effect upon us all, if it were but read and considered by all.

Now, in order to this, I am inclined to think that it would be very useful to publish an abridgment of the book. . . . I need not represent to you the advantages of a small over a large volume; but shall only tell you that it would be of excellent use to us [in Oxford], to be put into the hands of our young men, and be read and explained to them instead of those trifling and insignificant books, which serve only to perplex and confound, instead of enlightening and improving our reason. I do not see that there is anything wanting in it to complete the third part in your division of science. I know you mention an epitome of the work in your preface; but 'tis, as I am informed, in a language not commonly understood amongst us, and too scarce to answer the end which I propose. (pp. 189-90)

> *John Wynne, in a letter to John Locke on January 31, 1695, in* The Life and Letters of John Locke, *edited by Lord King, 1884. Reprint by Burt Franklin, 1972, pp. 189-91.*

JEAN LE CLERC   (essay date 1705)

[*A Swiss lexicographer, theologian, biblical scholar, publisher, and essayist, Le Clerc knew Locke personally and published, in the Dutch periodical* Bibliothèque universelle et historique *(25 vols., 1686-93), several of Locke's earliest works. In the following excerpt from the first printed biography of Locke,* Eloge de feu Mr. Locke *(1705;* The Life and Character of John Locke, Author of the "Essay concerning Humane Understanding," *1706), Le Clerc evaluates his subject's character.*]

[John Locke was] a profound philosopher, and a man fit for the most important affairs. He had much knowledge of belles lettres, and his manners were very polite and particularly engaging. He knew something of almost everything which can be useful to mankind, and was thoroughly master of all that he had studied, but he showed his superiority by not appearing to value himself in any way on account of his great attainments. . . . In the most trifling circumstances of life, as well as in speculative opinions, he was always ready to be convinced by reason, let the information come from whomever it might. He was the most faithful follower, or indeed the slave of truth, which he never abandoned on any account, and which he loved for its own sake.

He accommodated himself to the level of the most moderate understandings; and in disputing with them, he did not diminish the force of their arguments against himself, although they were not well expressed by those who had used them. He felt pleasure in conversing with all sorts of people, and tried to profit by their information, which arose not only from the good education he had received, but from the opinion he entertained, that there was nobody from whom something useful could not be got. And indeed by this means he had learned so many things concerning the arts and trade, that he seemed to have made them his particular study, insomuch that those whose profession they were often profited by his information, and consulted him with advantage. (pp. 271-72)

If he had any defect, it was the being somewhat passionate; but he had got the better of it by reason, and it was very seldom that it did him or any one else any harm. He often described the ridicule of it, and said that it availed nothing in the education of children, nor in keeping servants in order, and that it only lessened the authority which one had over them. (p. 273)

> *Jean Le Clerc, "Le Clerc's Character of Locke," in* The Life and Letters of John Locke, *edited by Lord King, 1884. Reprint by Burt Franklin, 1972, pp. 271-76.*

JOSEPH ADDISON   (essay date 1711)

[*A prominent English statesman and man of letters, Addison, along with Richard Steele, is considered one of the most important essayists of the early eighteenth century. With Steele, he founded the influential daily the* Spectator, *which was launched with the avowed purpose of improving the morals and manners of the day. Addison's best essays, those in which he adopted the persona of the fictional country squire Sir Roger de Coverley, are trenchant, pointed observations of life, literature, and society. Didactic and moralizing, yet witty and ironic, Addison's style epitomizes the ideals of neoclassical lucidity and moderation; Samuel Johnson remarked that Addison's work is characterized by "an English style familiar but not coarse, elegant but not ostentatious." In the following excerpt from the* Spectator *No. 62 (1711), Addison evaluates Locke's distinction between wit and judgment in* An Essay concerning Human Understanding.]

Mr. *Lock* has an admirable Reflection [in his ***Essay concerning Human Understanding***] upon the Difference of Wit and Judgment, whereby he endeavours to shew the Reason why they are not always the Talents of the same Person. His Words are as follow:

> And hence, perhaps, may be given some Reason of that common Observation, That Men who have a great deal of Wit and prompt Memories, have not always the clearest Judgment, or deepest Reason. For Wit lying most in the Assemblage of Ideas, and putting those together with Quickness and Variety, wherein can be found any Resemblance or Congruity, thereby to make up pleasant Pictures and agreeable Visions in the Fancy; Judgment, on the contrary, lies quite on the other Side, In separating carefully one from another, Ideas, wherein can be found the least Difference, thereby to avoid being mis-led by Similitude, and by Affinity to take one thing for another. This is a Way of proceeding quite contrary to Metaphor and Allusion; wherein, for the most Part, lies that Entertainment and Pleasantry of Wit which strikes so lively on the Fancy, and is therefore so acceptable to all People.

This is, I think, the best and most philosophical Account that I have ever met with of Wit, which generally, though not always, consists in such a Resemblance and Congruity of Ideas as this Author mentions. I shall only add to it, by way of Explanation; That every Resemblance of Ideas is not that which we call Wit, unless it be such an one that gives *Delight* and *Surprize* to the Reader: These two Properties seem essential to Wit, more particularly the last of them. In order therefore that the Resemblance in the Ideas be Wit, it is necessary that the Ideas should not lie too near one another in the Nature of things; for where the Likeness is obvious, it gives no Surprize. . . . Mr. *Lock's* Account of Wit, with this Short Explanation, comprehends most of the Species of Wit, as Metaphors, Similitudes, Allegories, Aenigmas, Mottos, Parables, Fables, Dreams, Visions, dramatick Writings, Burlesque, and all the Methods of Allusion: As there are many other Pieces of Wit (how remote soever they may appear at first Sight from the foregoing Description) which upon Examination will be found to agree with it. (pp. 189-90)

I must not dismiss this Subject without observing, that as Mr. *Lock* in the Passage above-mentioned has discovered the most fruitful Source of Wit, so there is another of a quite contrary Nature to it, which does likewise branch it self out into several Kinds. For not only the *Resemblance*, but the *Opposition* of Ideas does very often produce Wit; as I could shew in several little Points, Turns, and Antitheses, that I may possibly enlarge upon in some future Speculation. (pp. 193-94)

Joseph Addison, "Essay No. 62," in The Spectator, *Vol. 1, by Joseph Addison, Sir Richard Steele, and others, edited by Gregory Smith, 1907. Reprint by Dutton, 1945, pp. 189-94.*

MATTHEW PRIOR   (essay date 1721?)

[*An English poet, essayist, satirist, and statesman, Prior is the author of some of the finest occasional verse in English. A shrewd observer of contemporary events, he exposed, in such works as* The Hind and the Panther, Transvers'd to the Story of the Country and the City-Mouse *(1687) and in four "Dialogues of the Dead," the philosophical, intellectual, and literary shortcomings of his age, earning himself a reputation for tact, ingenuity, and grace. In the following excerpt from his imaginary "Dialogue between Mr John Lock and Seigneur de Montaigne," written sometime before his death in 1721 but not published until 1907, Prior resurrects the French essayist Michel de Montaigne to challenge Locke's* Essay concerning Human Understanding.]

Montaigne. . . . [You] divest the Mind from . . . Human trappings, and strip off her Cloaths to shew her stark naked. The perfection therefore of your Humility would have appeared in Your giving Us a Book without any Name at all. If you had come out like the whole Duty of Man in your Language I would have said something to You. But so it is with us, we would be humble and we are proud, we fall into contrary Excesses, and are guilty of one Vice by a mistaken Design of avo[i]ding another. There is some Crany some winding Meander in every Mans brain, which he himself is the last that finds out.

Lock. It is for that very reason, good Seigneur de Montaigne, that I searched my own head, and dissected my understanding, with so great Diligence and Accuracy, that I cannot but think the Study of many Years, very usefully bestowed on that subject. I will give You some Account of it: First I found out, and explained that an Idea is the object of the Human understanding, that you may call it Idea, Phantasm, Notion, or Species.

Montaigne. Which is that any Man may speak either Greek or Latin, as he pleases; then Sir, you proceed.

Lock. O, most happily! in proving that we have no innate Speculative or Practical Principles; That Complex proceed from simple Ideas, that Ideas of reflection come later than those of Sensation, that uncompounded appearances—

Montaigne. O, Sir, I know all that as well as if I had been one of your Disciples. Two simple Ideas are the least that can possibly be allowed to make one Complex, many more may chance to be thrown into the Bargain, and a whole set of them may be resolved again into their Native Simplicity. . . . But *jerné*, Lock, what canst thou mean, if these words expressed any real things, or subsisted any where but in the Writers brain (and faith I cant tell what impression they can make the[re] neither) but if they are, I say, any thing, or can signify any thing, what matters it 3 pence if all you have said be true or no.

Lock. If you could correct that Gascon fire of Yours I would tell You that I use these terms as instruments and means to

Attain to Truth. You know the Antient Philosophers said Truth lay at the bottom of a Well.

Montaigne. It may be so, but *foy de Gentilhomme* ["on the honor of a gentleman"] you will never draw her out except your Tools are more accommodated to your Work. In short Sir, call 'em what you will, or tumble them where ever you please, they are but words, bring them together again, they will no more make things solid and usefull, than grains of Sand will make a rope.

Lock. Before we go any further, tell me truly have You read my Book quite through, and with Care?

Montaigne. Yes in good truth I have read it, and just as I read other books, with Care where they instruct me, with pleasure where they amuse me, and half asleep where they tire me. To convince You of the Truth of what I say, I will give you some of your own Axioms, almost in the order in which they lye.

Lock. With Candor I beseech You.

Montaigne. O, trust me as to that, upon my Honor. Colours come in only by the Eyes; all kind of Noises by the Ears; Tasts and Smels by the Nose and Palate; Touching from every Member (tho some indeed more sensible than others) by the Junction of two Bodies: Red is not blew; A sucking-bottle is not a Rod; A Child certainly knows that the Nurse that feeds it is neither the Catt it plays with, nor the Blackmore it is afraid of. Wormseed and Mustard are not Apples and Sugar; And there is an Essential difference between a Silly-bub & a Broomstaff.

Lock. This I tell You is only my Subtratum, the very rubbige upon which I build.

Montaigne. A House of Cards is a stronger foundation.

Lock. Hear me a little; from these plain Propositions I go on to greater Discoveries, that an Infant in the Cradle cannot make a Syllogism half so well as a Sophister in the Schools, and that a Hottentote is not so well Learned in the Bay of Sardignia as he would have been if his Friends had Educated him at Oxford or Cambridge.

Montaigne. Who the Devil did not know all these undoubted truths before You set Pen to Paper, and ever questioned them since? there are a hundred things plain in themselves that are only made Ambiguous by your Comment upon them. I hold a Stone in my hand, and ask you what it is? You tell me it is a body. I ask You what is a body? you reply it is a Substance: I am troublesome enough once more to ask You what is Substance? you look graver immediately, and inform me that it is something whose Essence consists in extension, in such manner as to be capable of receiving it in Longitude Latitude and Profundity. The Devil is in it if I am not answered. I may sooner pave the Road between London and York than have a thorow knowledge of the least Pebble in the way, except I take this Jargon in full of all Accounts. Socrates, I have some where told You, asked Memnon what was virtue? There is, replyed Memnon, the virtue of a Man, and of a Woman, of a Child, and of an aged Person, of a Magistrate, and of a Private Citizen; and as he was going on, Socrates, interrupting him, said, I am mightily obliged to your Generosity: I asked concerning one Virtue, and you have already given me half a Dozen. Now, Mr. Lock, I apprehend clearer what is meant by Understanding, than I do by your Definition of it: *The power of thinking;* and I know better what the Will is, than when I hear you call it *The power of Volition.* A Plough-Boy says to his Father, Aye, aye, I understand that as well as You; and to his Mother, I wont do it because You bid me, yet he knows not, all this while, that he hath exercised the Two great and Principal Actions of his mind, as you call them, or if that Mind had two Actions or two and Twenty.

You have heard of the Citizen turned Gentleman, Mr. Lock, who had a mind to be a Scholar, and was dabbling in Grammar. He discoursed a long time to his Wife of Regimen and Syntax, and at last asked her, Sweet heart, what is it I am talking now? on my Conscience quoth She, Husband, I think tis Nonsense. That may be he replyed, You simple Woman: But did not you know all this time that it was not Verse but Prose? Now the good Woman could not be more obliged to her Husband for this Piece of Learning then your Young Sectators are to You for the Discovery of some of those imcomparable Axioms, which you just now Quoted, when they find them amidst a heap of Metaphysical terms. How grateful are they to the Doctor, and in return for your Civility in giving them Six or Eight words together of which they can make common Sense, how joyfully do they let themselves be bambouzled thro as many Chapters? for among the variety of Errors, to which weak minds are subject, there is one very conspicuous; that they are most prone to admire what they do not perfectly understand, and are very apt to judge of the Depth of anothers thoughts by the obscurity of his Expression. Aristotle I have heard, valued himself upon having a Tallent of concealing part of his meaning, or rendring the whole Ambiguous: for which damned Affectation I most heartily hate Aristotle, and all his Imitators in this kind. I do not say Mr. Lock, that you affect this Obscurity, but I beg your Pardon, while I take the Liberty to tell You, that you often fall into it: while you are sowing Words too Plentifully, you do not always foresee what a Crop they will bear.

Lock. This is a pretty large Accusation, I hope You can make it good.

Montaigne. Why, You confess in your very preface [see excerpt dated 1690] that when you first put Pen to Paper, you thought that all you should have to say on the matter would have been contained in one Sheet of Paper, and yet, you See, You have Swelled it into a Volume. How imperfectly therefore did you judge either of the Ext[e]nt of what was to be written or of the Method in which it should be Digested. But as we say in France, the Appetite comes in Eating; so in Writing You stil found more to write. From Ideas most unexpectedly sprung Solidity, Perception, Extension, Duration, Number, and Infinity, and from these again mixed Modes, Complex and Collected Ideas of Substances, Identity, Diversity, and fifty other glorious Tresor-trouves, to which you the Master of the Soil have the only right and Property, and are entituled to dispose of them *ex mero motu & pura gratiâ* ["of your own accord and in favor"] to all Your Sectators, and Disciples, in *Secula Seculorum* ["The Age's Age"]. Now by the same way of working You might have left them Ten Volumes as well as one. Nay every Chapter might have been beaten out into a whole Book; and after Potentiality, Perceptivity, Mobility, and Motivity (which by the by You should have added to your Chapter of the Abuse of Words) You might have found out Ten thousand other Alitys and Ivitys, that would have looked equally well to the Eye in a Handsome Print, and conveyed just as much Knowlege to the Mind. Why Mr. Lock, your very Definition of Liberty, is, that it is something, which You your Self must feel; what signifies it therefore to Define it at all? Can any words out of another Mans Mouth make me understand if I feel a thing or no? Believe me, Mr. Lock, you Metaphysicians define your

Object as some Naturalists divide it, *in infinitum* ["infinitely"]: But while you are doing so, the parts become so far Separated from each other, that You lose the sight of the thing it self. Another happyness arises from all this that whenever the Writer of this sort of Mysterious Demonstration, and his Reader Disagree (as happened between You and Stillingfleet, and in a case not unlike Yours between South and Sherlock) both are in the right, and both are in the wrong: While no Man else can well Judge what either of them meant. So the Dispute only terminates as it grows forgot, and as the Property of the Bookseller in the Unsold Sheets that contained it, is transferred to his next-door Neighbors, the Grocer and the Pastry Cook.

Lock. So that You, the loosest of Writers, have no great respect for my close way of reasoning.

Montaigne. Really, Mr. Lock, I should flatter You, if I said I had. One may read your Book over as the Irishman eat Whiptcream, and when they asked him what he had been doing, he said, he had been tasting a great Nothing. All the while You wrote you were only thinking that You thought; You, and your Understanding are the *Personæ Dramatis,* and the whole Amounts to no more than a Dialogue between John and Lock.

> As I walk'd by my Self
> I talked to my Self
> And my self said unto Me.

You seem in my poor apprehension, to go to and fro upon a Philosophical Swing, like a Child upon a wooden-horse, always in motion but without any Progress; and to Act as if a Man instead of Practising his Trade should spend all his life in naming his Tools.

Lock. Pian Piano good Seigneur, one must be able to Name ones Tools before one Learns the use of them. But if a Man does not leap Hedge and Ditch, in your Opinion, he stands stock still. I begin, continue and always keep close to my subject, The Human Understanding.

Montaigne. That's the very thing I object to, I think You keep so close to Your subject, that you have spoiled Your Book. When you have set your self in your Metaphysical Goe-Cart, in order to step sure, You walk too Slow to rid any ground, and as soon as you are out of it, You commonly Mistake your way. The least things must be Demonstrated to You where no body could have doubt of them, and when ever (which is indeed most commonly) such proof is wanting, You take the whole upon trust, without the previous examination, which any other reasonable Man would make. You strain as the Proverb says, at a Gnat and swallow a Camel; not giving a just allowance to probability. You sink between two Extremes, and when You are not supported by evident Demonstration you fall into the greatest Credulity imaginable. The Identity of the same Man consists in a participation of the same continued life, by constantly fleeting particles of matter in succession, Vitally united to the same Organized body, so that an Embryo is not a Person of One and twenty; Ismael is not Socrates, Pilate is not St. Austin. Who questions any thing of this, good Mr. Lock; Yet by the way, Cæsar, who led to Battle many thousand of these Organized Bodys; Cicero, who could appease or excite them in the Senate; Bartholin, who could tell You how these Particles lay in relation to each other, and from thence what Remedies were to be applyed to the several Diseases and Violences they suffered; Spenser who could describe them all in Mythological words; and Raphael, who could imitate them in Animated Colours; All these, I say, neither thought or acted in virtue of your Definition; and if they did would not have performed any thing better in their Several Arts and Sciences. So again, the Chess-men standing upon those Squares of the Board, where we placed them, tho the Chess Board be carried out of one room into another, are stil said to remain in the same place; and the Chess-board is stil said to be in the same place it was, if it remain in the same part of the Cabin, tho perhaps the Ship it is in Sails all the while, and the Ship is stil in the same place, supposing it kept the same Distance with the part of the Neighboring Land, tho perhaps the Earth has turned round, and so both Chess-men and Board and Ship have every one changed place in respect of remoter bodies, which have kept the same distance one with another, and so on to the end of the Chapter. Who ever denyed one word of all this? and do You think now that You have explained what motion and repose is, so as to do any good to Mankind. Archimedes found out the burning-glass. Jacob Metius the Tellescope. Sanctorius the Thermometer, and Flavia Goia, the Compass, without Consulting or being guided by any sort of Verbiage like this, and I dare Swear neither Christopher Colombo, nor Francis Drake ever reasoned one half hour if their Chess-Board was in motion in relation to their Cabin, or their Cabin in regard to the Ship, all the while they were sailing round the World, and adding a fourth part to what was known of it before. (pp. 224-30)

Lock. How this Gascon runs away with things, I do not say I have the exact *Criterion Veritatis* ["mark of truth"], but I search it. I dont pretend to Infalibility, but as much as I can I endeavor to avoid Error. And since it is only by my understanding that I can judge of other things It is proper in order to that, that I make that understanding first judge of it self.

Montaigne. There is a *Je ne-scay quoy* ["I know not what"] in these words that affords me but little Satisfaction. But you

Portrait, completed by John Greenhill in 1672, of Anthony Ashley Cooper, first Earl of Shaftesbury, in his robes as Lord Chancellor.

Metaphysicians think with too much Subtilty to be pleased with what is Natural. (pp. 230-31)

Lock. Well, Sir, and what is the Result of all this?

Montaigne. That probably neither, Robin, John, Margaret, yo[u] or I, or any other five Persons alive, have either the same Ideas of the same thing, or the same way of expressing them. The difference of Temperament in the body, Hot, cold, Flegmatic or hasty, create as manifest a variety in the operations of our hands, and the conduct of our Lives; and our Conceptions may be as various as our faces, Bodies, and Senses (or sensations as you call them). If I like Assafetida, I say it has a good smell: If you cant indure a Rose, you complain it stinks. In our Taste may not I nauseate the food which you covet; and is it not even a Proverb, that what is meat to one Man is Poyson to another. If we consider even the fabrick of the Eye and the Rules of Optick, it can hardly be thought we see the same; and yet no words can express this Diversity. So that there may be as much difference between your Conceptions and mine, as there is between your Band, and my Ruff. If so, it may happen I say, that if no Mans Ideas be perfectly the same, Locks Human Understanding may be fit only for the Meditation of Lock himself. Nay further that those very Ideas changing, Lock may be led into a new Labyrinth, or sucked into another Vortex; and may write a Second Book in order to Disprove the first.

Lock. Aye now Sir I like You, We are come to the very State of the Question.

Montaigne. Are we so, my good Friend? why then 'tis just time to break off the Discourse. (p. 246)

Matthew Prior, ''Essays and Dialogues of the Dead:' A Dialogue between Mr John Lock and Seigneur de Montaigne','' in his Dialogues of the Dead and Other Works in Prose and Verse, *edited by A. R. Waller, Cambridge at the University Press, 1907, pp. 223-46.*

FRANÇOIS MARIE AROUET DE VOLTAIRE (essay date 1733)

[*A French philosopher and man of letters, Voltaire was a major figure of the eighteenth-century European Enlightenment, a movement in which reason and empiricism markedly superseded reliance on prescription, faith, and authority. As a man of diverse and intense interests, Voltaire wrote prolifically on many subjects and in a variety of genres, always asserting the absolute primacy of personal liberty—be it intellectual, social, religious, or political. Consequently, Voltaire opposed religious traditions and political organizations that he believed thwarted or curtailed individual freedom. Voltaire's most valuable contribution to literature is usually considered to be his invention of the philosophical* conte, *or tale, in which the story is a vehicle for an ethical or philosophical message; the most famous of these* contes *is the highly regarded* Candide (1759). *In the following excerpt from his* Letters concerning the English Nation, *he extols Locke's genius, wisdom, and understanding.*]

Perhaps no Man ever had a more judicious or more methodical Genius, or was a more acute Logician than Mr. *Locke,* and yet he was not deeply skill'd in the Mathematicks. This great Man could never subject himself to the tedious Fatigue of Calculations, nor to the dry Pursuit of Mathematical Truths, which do not at first present any sensible Objects to the Mind; and no one has given better Proofs than he, that 'tis possible for a Man to have a geometrical Head without the Assistance of Geometry. Before his Time, several great Philosophers had declar'd, in the most positive Terms, what the Soul of Man is; but as these absolutely knew nothing about it, they might very well be allow'd to differ entirely in opinion from one another. (p. 73)

[A] Multitude of Reasoners having written the Romance of the Soul, a Sage at last arose, who gave, with an Air of the greatest Modesty, the History of it. Mr. *Locke* has display'd the human Soul, in the same Manner as an excellent Anatomist explains the Springs of the human Body. He every where takes the Light of Physicks for his Guide. He sometimes presumes to speak affirmatively, but then he presumes also to doubt. Instead of concluding at once what we know not, he examines gradually what we wou'd know. He takes an Infant at the Instant of his Birth; he traces, Step by Step, the Progress of his Understanding; examines what Things he has in common with Beasts, and what he possesses above them. Above all he consults himself; the being conscious that he himself thinks.

I shall leave, says he, to those who know more of this Matter than my self, the examining whether the Soul exists before or after the Organization of our Bodies. But I confess that 'tis my Lot to be animated with one of those heavy Souls which do not think always; and I am even so unhappy as not to conceive, that 'tis more necessary the Soul should think perpetually, than that Bodies shou'd be for ever in Motion.

With regard to my self, I shall boast that I have the Honour to be as stupid in the Particular as Mr. *Locke*. No one shall ever make me believe, that I think always; and I am as little inclin'd as he cou'd be, to fancy that some Weeks after I was conceiv'd, I was a very learned Soul; knowing at that Time a thousand Things which I forgot at my Birth; and possessing when in the Womb, (tho' to no Manner of Purpose), Knowledge which I lost the Instant I had occasion for it; and which I have never since been able to recover perfectly.

Mr. *Locke* after having destroy'd innate Ideas; after having fully renounc'd the Vanity of believing that we think always; after having laid down, from the most solid Principles, that Ideas enter the Mind through the Senses; having examin'd our simple and complex Ideas; having trac'd the human Mind through its several Operations; having shew'd that all the Languages in the World are imperfect, and the great Abuse that is made of Words every Moment; he at last comes to consider the Extent or rather the narrow Limits of human Knowledge. 'Twas in this Chapter he presum'd to advance, but very modestly, the following Words, ''We shall, perhaps, never be capable of knowing, whether a Being, purely material, thinks or not.'' This sage Assertion was, by more Divines than one, look'd upon as a scandalous Declaration that the Soul is material and mortal. Some *Englishmen*, devout after their Way, sounded an Alarm. The Superstitious are the same in Society as Cowards in an Army; they themselves are seiz'd with a panic Fear, and communicate it to others. 'Twas loudly exclaim'd, that Mr. *Locke* intended to destroy Religion; nevertheless, Religion had nothing to do in the Affair, it being a Question purely Philosophical, altogether independent on Faith and Revelation. Mr. *Locke's* Opponents needed but to examine, calmly and impartially, whether the declaring that Matter can think, implies a Contradiction; and whether God is able to communicate Thought to Matter. But Divines are too apt to begin their Declarations with saying, that God is offended when People differ from them in Opinion; in which they too much resemble the bad Poets, who us'd to declare publickly that *Boileau* spake irreverently of *Lewis* the Fourteenth, because he ridicul'd their stupid Productions. Bishop *Stillingfleet* got the Reputation of a calm and unprejudic'd Divine, because he did not expressly

make use of injurious Terms in his Dispute with Mr. *Locke*. That Divine entred the Lists against him, but was defeated; for he argued as a Schoolman, and *Locke* as a Philosopher, who was perfectly acquainted with the strong as well as the weak Side of the human Mind, and who fought with Weapons whose Temper he knew. (pp. 76-9)

> *François Marie Arouet de Voltaire, ''On Mr. Locke,'' in his* Letters concerning the English Nation, *translated by John Lockman, 1733. Reprint by Peter Davies, 1926, pp. 73-83.*

GEORGE BERKELEY   (essay date 1734)

[*Berkeley was an eighteenth-century Anglo-Irish philosopher who pioneered a celebrated and important philosophy of sensation and perception. Deeply indebted to Locke's works for many of his own tenets but by no means in complete agreement with all Locke's precepts, Berkeley vigorously attacked the Hobbesian philosophy of materialism. His great principle is that the* esse *of material things is* percipi—*that is, the support of ideas or sensations is percipient mind. Thus ''ideas'' in Locke's sense do not represent something outside the mind. Rather, they constitute the real world, which accordingly must exist in the mind alone. In the following excerpt from an essay first published in 1710 and slightly revised in 1734, Berkeley evaluates Locke's concept of abstract ideas.*]

Whether others have [the] wonderful faculty of *abstracting their ideas*, they best can tell: for my self I find indeed I have a faculty of imagining, or representing to my self the ideas of those particular things I have perceived and of variously compounding and dividing them. I can imagine a man with two heads or the upper parts of a man joined to the body of a horse. I can consider the hand, the eye, the nose, each by it self abstracted or separated from the rest of the body. But then whatever hand or eye I imagine, it must have some particular shape and colour. Likewise the idea of man that I frame to my self, must be either of a white, or a black, or a tawny, a straight, or a crooked, a tall, or a low, or a middle-sized man. . . . To be plain, I own my self able to abstract in one sense, as when I consider some particular parts or qualities separated from others, with which though they are united in some object, yet, it is possible they may really exist without them. But I deny that I can abstract one from another, or conceive separately, those qualities which it is impossible should exist so separated; or that I can frame a general notion by abstracting from particulars. . . . Which two last are the proper acceptations of *abstraction*. (pp. 29-30)

I proceed to examine what can be alleged in defence of the doctrine of abstraction, and try if I can discover what it is that inclines the men of speculation to embrace an opinion, so remote from common sense as that seems to be. There has been a late deservedly esteemed philosopher [John Locke], who, no doubt, has given it very much countenance by seeming to think the having abstract general ideas is what puts the widest difference in point of understanding betwixt man and beast. . . . I readily agree with this learned author, that the faculties of brutes can by no means attain to *abstraction*. But then if this be made the distinguishing property of that sort of animals, I fear a great many of those that pass for men must be reckoned into their number. The reason that is here assigned why we have no grounds to think brutes have abstract general ideas, is that we observe in them no use of words or any other general signs; which is built on this supposition, to wit, that the making use of words, implies the having general ideas. From which it follows, that men who use language are able to abstract or generalize their ideas. That this is the sense and arguing of the author will further appear by his answering the question he . . . puts. 'Since all things that exist are only particulars, how come we by general terms?' *His answer is,* 'Words become general by being made the signs of general ideas.'. . . But it seems that a word becomes general by being made the sign, not of an abstract general idea but, of several particular ideas, any one of which it indifferently suggests to the mind. For example, when it is said *the change of motion is proportional to the impressed force,* or that *whatever has extension is divisible;* these propositions are to be understood of motion and extension in general, and nevertheless it will not follow that they suggest to my thoughts an idea of motion without a body moved, or any determinate direction and velocity, or that I must conceive an abstract general idea of extension, which is neither line, surface nor solid, neither great nor small, black, white, nor red, nor of any other determinate colour. It is only implied that whatever motion I consider, whether it be swift or slow, perpendicular, horizontal or oblique, or in whatever object, the axiom concerning it holds equally true. As does the other of every particular extension, it matters not whether line, surface or solid, whether of this or that magnitude or figure. (pp. 30-1)

To give the reader a yet clearer view of the nature of abstract ideas, and the uses they are thought necessary to, I shall add one more passage out of the *Essay on Human Understanding,* which is as follows. '*Abstract ideas* are not so obvious or easy to children or the yet unexercised mind as particular ones. If they seem so to grown men, it is only because by constant and familiar use they are made so. For when we nicely reflect upon them, we shall find that general ideas are fictions and contrivances of the mind, that carry difficulty with them, and do not easily offer themselves, as we are apt to imagine. For example, does it not require some pains and skill to form the general idea of a triangle (which is yet none of the most abstract comprehensive and difficult) for it must be neither oblique nor rectangle, neither equilateral, equicrural, nor scalenon, but *all and none* of these at once. In effect, it is something imperfect that cannot exist, an idea wherein some parts of several different and *inconsistent* ideas are put together. It is true the mind in this imperfect state has need of such ideas, and makes all the haste to them it can, for the conveniency of communication and enlargement of knowledge, to both which it is naturally very much inclined. But yet one has reason to suspect such ideas are marks of our imperfection. At least this is enough to shew that the most abstract and general ideas are not those that the mind is first and most easily acquainted with, nor such as its earliest knowledge is conversant about.' If any man has the faculty of framing in his mind such an idea of a triangle as is here described, it is in vain to pretend to dispute him out of it, nor would I go about it. All I desire is, that the reader would fully and certainly inform himself whether he has such an idea or no. And this, methinks, can be no hard task for any one to perform. What more easy than for any one to look a little into his own thoughts, and there try whether he has, or can attain to have, an idea that shall correspond with the description that is here given of the general idea of a triangle, which is, *neither oblique, nor rectangle, equilateral, equicrural, nor scalenon, but all and none of these at once?* (pp. 32-3)

George Berkeley, in an introduction to "A Treatise concerning the Principles of Human Knowledge," in his The Works of George Berkeley, Bishop of Cloyne, Vol. II, *edited by A. A. Luce and T. E. Jessop, Thomas Nelson and Sons Ltd., 1949, pp. 25-40.*

BENJAMIN FRANKLIN (essay date 1748)

[*Franklin was an American printer, inventor, statesman, diplomat, and author whose activities and ideas were so much of his time that he is often considered the embodiment of eighteenth-century thought and letters. Sometimes called "the wisest American," he discovered the nature of lightning and electricity and invented bifocal glasses, making his literary work seem almost incidental. But in such works as the periodical* Poor Richard's Almanack, *which started in 1733 and ran for 25 years, and* On the Slave Trade *(1790), Franklin tackled the chief moral, philosophical, and political issues of his age, helping to influence, through his genius for practicality and his balanced, humorous common sense, the whole course of his nation's development. In the following excerpt from the October, 1748 issue of* Poor Richard Improved, *he praises Locke as the master of the "little world."*]

On the 28th [of October], *Anno* 1704, died the famous John Locke, Esq; the Newton of the *Microcosm:* For, as Thomson says [see Additional Bibliography],

He made the whole *internal world* his own.

His book on the **Human Understanding,** shows it. *Microcosm,* honest reader, is a hard word, and, they say, signifies the *little world,* man being so called as containing within himself the four elements of the *greater,* &c.&c. I here explain Greek to thee by English, which, I think, is rather a more intelligible way, than explaining English by Greek, as a certain writer does, who gravely tells us, *Man is rightly called* a little world, *because he is a* Microcosm. (p. 259)

Benjamin Franklin, "Poor Richard Improved," in his The Papers of Benjamin Franklin: January 1, 1745 through June 30, 1750, Vol. 3, *edited by Leonard W. Labaree & others, Yale University Press, 1961, pp. 243-62.*

LAURENCE STERNE (novel date 1760)

[*An eighteenth-century English novelist, essayist, diarist, and sermonist, Sterne wrote* The Life and Opinions of Tristram Shandy, Gentleman *(1759-67) and* A Sentimental Journey through France and Italy *(1768), two of the most eccentric and influential works in Western literature. Deeply touched by the man he called "the sagacious Locke"—he claimed to find the explanation of his own sensibility in Locke's doctrine of ideas—Sterne maintained that Locke's influence on him could be seen "in all his pages, in all his lines, in all his expressions." In the following excerpt from* Tristram Shandy, *he interrupts the novel's narrative to comment on* An Essay concerning Human Understanding.]

Pray, Sir, in all the reading which you have ever read, did you ever read such a book as *Locke's* **Essay upon the Human Understanding**?—Don't answer me rashly,—because many, I know, quote the book, who have not read it,—and many have read it who understand it not:—If either of these is your case, as I write to instruct, I will tell you in three words what the book is.—It is a history.—A history! of who? what? where? when? Don't hurry yourself.—It is a history-book, Sir, (which may possibly recommend it to the world) of what passes in a man's own mind; and if you will say so much of the book, and no more, believe me, you will cut no contemptible figure in a metaphysic circle. (p. 85)

Laurence Sterne, in a chapter in his The Life and Opinions of Tristram Shandy, Gentleman, 9 Vols., *edited by James Aiken Work, The Odyssey Press, 1940, pp. 84-7.*

JOHN ADAMS (letter date 1760)

[*Pamphleteer, lawyer, statesman, and second president of the United States, Adams helped draft the American Declaration of Independence and was, according to Thomas Jefferson, "the pillar of its support" on the congressional floor. Essentially a conservative whose political philosophy placed him between Alexander Hamilton's federalism and Jefferson's agrarianism, Adams set out his approach to government in such works as* A Dissertation on Canon and Feudal Law *(1768) and* A Defence of the Constitutions of Government of the United States of America *(3 vols., 1787-88). In the following excerpt from a 1760 letter to the American lawyer and loyalist Jonathan Sewall, Adams comments on Locke's contribution to metaphysics.*]

In metaphysics, Mr. Locke, directed by my Lord Bacon, has steered his course into the unenlightened regions of the human mind, and, like Columbus, has discovered a new world. A world whose soil is deep and strong; producing rank and unwholesome weeds, as well as wholesome fruits and flowers. A world that is incumbered with unprofitable brambles, as well as stored with useful trees; and infested with motley savages, as well as capable of furnishing civilized inhabitants. He has shown us by what cultivation these weeds may be exterminated, and the fruits raised; the brambles removed as well as the trees grubbed; the savages destroyed as well as the civil people increased. Here is another hemisphere of science, therefore, abounding with pleasure and with profit, too, of which he had but very few, and we have many advantages for learning. (p. 53)

> *John Adams, in a letter to Jonathan Sewall in February, 1760, in his* The Works of John Adams, Second President of the United States, Vol. I, *edited by Charles Francis Adams, Little, Brown and Company, 1856, pp. 51-5.*

THE BOSTON GAZETTE (essay date 1773)

[*The following advertisement from the March 1, 1773 issue of the* Boston Gazette *announces the publication of the first American edition of Locke's* Essay concerning the True Original, Extent, and End of Civil Government *and describes this work's contents and value.*]

This Essay alone, well studied and attended to, will give to every intelligent Reader a better View of the Rights of Men and of Englishmen, and a clearer Insight into the Principles of the British Constitution, than all the Discourses on Government—The Essays in Politicks and Books of Law in our Language.—It should be early and carefully explained by every Father to his Son, by every Preceptor in our public and private Schools to his Pupils, and by every Mother to her Daughter.

> *An extract from "The Politics of Locke in England and America in the Eighteenth Century," in* John Locke: Problems and Perspectives: A Collection of New Essays, *edited by John W. Yolton, Cambridge at the University Press, 1969, p. 45.*

THOMAS JEFFERSON (letter date 1789)

[*The third president of the United States, Jefferson is best known as a statesman whose belief in natural rights, equality, individual liberties, and self-government found its fullest expression in* In Congress, July 4, 1776: A Declaration by the Representatives of the United States of America, in General Congress Assembled *(1776), commonly known as the* Declaration of Independence. *A skilled writer noted for his simple yet elegant prose, Jefferson*

profoundly influenced the direction of American politics, inspiring generations of American and other followers. In the following excerpt from a 1789 letter written to the American artist John Trumbull to commission a portrait of Locke, Francis Bacon, and Isaac Newton, Jefferson praises Locke as one of the three greatest men that ever lived.]

I have duly received your favor of the [fifth of February]. With respect to the busts & pictures I will put off till my return from America all of them except Bacon, Locke and Newton, whose pictures I will trouble you to have copied for me: and as I consider them as the three greatest men that have ever lived, without any exception, and as having laid the foundation of those superstructures which have been raised in the Physical & Moral sciences, I would wish to form them into a knot on the same canvas, that they may not be confounded at all with the herd of other great men. (pp. 939-40)

> *Thomas Jefferson, in a letter to John Trumbull on February 15, 1789, in his* Thomas Jefferson: Writings, *edited by Merrill D. Peterson, The Library of America, 1984, pp. 939-40.*

SAMUEL TAYLOR COLERIDGE (letter dates 1801?)

[*Coleridge was the intellectual center of the English Romantic movement and is considered one of the greatest literary critics in the English language. He was also the first prominent spokesman for German idealistic metaphysics in England and foreran modern psychological critics, specifically by his conception of the organic nature of literary form—a theory contending that literature derives from and is determined by inspiration rather than by external rules. Though most critics and scholars acknowledge Coleridge's importance in world literature, they also realize that much of his aesthetic philosophy and literary criticism was borrowed, and at times directly translated, from such German thinkers as Friedrich von Schelling, A. W. Schlegel, Immanuel Kant, and Johann Wolfgang von Goethe. According to René Wellek, Coleridge's complete dialectical scheme—his reconciliation of opposites—was derived primarily from German sources: for example, from Schelling Coleridge took his theory that nature exists only as it is perceived by the human consciousness, while the belief that genius resides within the imagination, whereas talent is a product of study and craftsmanship, was adopted from Kant. What makes Coleridge an imposing figure in English literary criticism is the fact that he introduced these concepts to the English-speaking world and combined them with elements of neoclassicism and English empiricism. Coleridge differs from most preceding English writers in his attempt to develop a consistent philosophy of thought, language, and knowledge from which to derive critical principles and a theory of literature. Though in his own work he failed to realize this goal, he has consistently been praised for the sincerity of his efforts. For modern critics, Coleridge's most important achievement was his attempt to fuse such variant ideas as fancy and imagination, talent and genius, mechanical and organic form, taste and judgment, and symbol and allegory, even though they believe that his efforts to create a "graceful and intelligent whole" were self-defeating and poor criteria for the actual study of literature. In the following excerpts from a series of letters addressed to his patrons the prosperous china manufacturers Josiah and Thomas Wedgwood, Coleridge, in an effort to prove Locke's high reputation to be unwarranted, criticizes* An Essay concerning Human Understanding.]

[February 18, 1801]

In my Biographical Dictionary the writer introduces Locke as "one of the greatest men that England ever produced.["] Mr. Hume, a much more competent Judge, declares that he was "really a great Philosopher." Wolf, Feder, & Platner, three Germans, the fathers or favourers of three different Systems, concur in pronouncing him to be "a truly original Genius," and Mr. Locke himself has made it sufficiently clear both in his [*Essay concerning Human Understanding*] and in his Letters to the Bishop of Worcester, that he did not regard himself as a Reformer, but as a Discoverer; not as an opposer of a newly introduced Heresy in Metaphysics, but as an Innovator upon ancient and generally received Opinions. In his dedicatory Epistle speaking of those who are likely to condemn his *Essay* as opposite to the received Doctrines, "Truth" (says he) "scarce ever yet carried it by Vote any where at *it's first appearance. New* Opinions are always suspected, and usually opposed, without any other Reason but because they are not already common. But Truth, like Gold, is not the less so, for being *newly brought out of the Mine.*" It would have been well, if Mr. Locke had stated the Doctrines which he considered as Errors in the very words of some of the most celebrated Teachers of those Doctrines & enumerated the Truths of which he considered himself as the Discoverer. A short Post script to this purpose would have brought to an easy determination the opinions of those, who (as Harris & Monboddo, for instance) believe that Mr. Locke has grossly misrepresented the ancient & received opinions, and that the Doctrines which he holds for Truths of his own Discovery are many of them erroneous & none original. Exempli gratiâ—in the very commencement of the work he says "It is an established opinion amongst some men, that there are in the understanding certain Innate Principles, some primary notions . . . , Characters as it were stamped upon the mind of man, which the Soul receives in it's very first being, and brings into the World with it." His own opinion on the contrary is that there are but two sorts of ideas and both acquired by Experience, namely, "external objects furnish the mind with ideas of sensible Qualities, which are all those different Perceptions they produce in us: and the mind furnishes the Understanding with ideas of it's own operations." Of course, as Locke teaches that the Understanding is but a Term signifying the Mind in a particular state of action, he means that the mind furnishes itself; and so he himself expresses the Thought in the preceding Paragraph, defining Ideas of Reflection by "those, which the mind gets by reflecting on it's own operations within itself." Now, it would have been well if Locke had named those who held the former Doctrines, and shewn from their own Words that the two Opinions (his and their's) were opposite or at least different. More especially, he should have given his Readers the Definition of the obscure Word "innate" in the very Language of the most accurate of such Writers as had used the Word. (pp. 68-9)

· · · · ·

[February 24, 1801]

[It appears] that Des Cartes & Locke hold precisely the same opinions concerning the original Sources of our Ideas. They both taught, nearly in the same words and wholly to the same Purpose, that the Objects of human Knowledge are either Ideas imprinted on the Senses, or else such as are perceived by attending to the passions and operations of the mind; or lastly Ideas formed by Help of Memory and Imagination, either compounding, dividing, or barely representing those originally perceived in the aforesaid ways. This proves no more, I allow, than that Mr. Locke's first Book is founded on a blunder in the History of Opinions, and that Des Cartes and Locke agree'd [*sic*] with each other in a Tenet, common to all the Philosophers before them; but it is far enough from proving the assertion . . . , that the whole System of Locke, as far [as] it was a System (i. e. made up of cohering Parts) was to be found in

the writings of Des Cartes. But even that . . . , trifling as it may seem, has led me to Reflections on the Rise & Growth of literary Reputation, that have both interested & edified me; nor can it, I suppose, be wholly without effect in the minds of any, who know or remember how much of Locke's Fame rests on the common Belief, that in overthrowing the Doctrine of Innate Ideas he had overthrown some ancient, general, & uncouth Superstition, which had been as a pillar to all other Superstitions. If you ask a person, what Sir Isaac Newton did—the answer would probably be, he discovered the universal action of Gravity, and applied it to the Solution of all the Phænomena of the Universe. Ask what Locke did, & you will be told if I mistake not, that he overthrew the Notion generally held before his time, of innate Ideas, and deduced all our knowledge from experience. Were it generally known that these Innate Ideas were Men of Straw, or scarcely so much as that—and that the whole of Mr. Locke's first Book is a jumble of Truisms, Calumnies, and Misrepresentations, I suspect, that we should give the name of Newton a more worthy associate—& instead of Locke and Newton, we should say, *Bacon & Newton*, or still better perhaps, Newton and Hartley. (p. 75)

· · · · ·

[February, 1801]

Mr. Locke would have never disgraced his *Essay* with the first Book, if he had not mistaken innasci for synonimous with connasci, whereas to be "born *in*" and to be "born *at the same time with*," are phrases of very different import. My mind is, for aught I know to the contrary, *connate* with my brain, but a staunch materialist would perhaps deny this, and affirm that the Brain was the elder of the two, and that the mind is *innate in* the brain. (p. 81)

[I] do not think the Doctrine of Innate Ideas even in Mr. Locke's sense of the Word so utterly absurd & ridiculous, as Aristotle, Des Cartes, & Mr. Locke have concurred in representing it. What if instead of innate Ideas a philosopher had asserted the existence of *constituent* Ideas. . . . In Mr. Locke there is a complete Whirl-dance of Confusion with the words *we, Soul, Mind, Consciousness,* & *Ideas*. It is *we* as far as it is consciousness, and *soul* & *mind* are only other words for *we* (and yet nothing is more common in the *Essay* than such sentences as these "I do not say there is no *Soul* in *us* because *we* are *not sensible* of it in our sleep" &—actions of our *mind* unnoticed by *us*—i.e. (according to Locke's own definition of *mind* & *we*) "actions of our *consciousness, of which our consciousness is unconscious*." Sometimes again the Ideas are coincident as objects of the mind in thinking, sometimes they stand for the mind itself, and sometimes we are the thinkers, & the mind is only the Thought-Box. In short, the Mind in Mr. Locke's *Essay* has three senses—the Ware-house, the Wares, and the Ware-house-man. . . .

· · · · ·

[Undated]

Mr. Locke's third Book is on Words; and under this head [he] should have arranged the greater number of the Chapters in his second Book. Des Cartes has said multum in parvo ["much in little"] on the subject of words. He has said the same things as Mr. *Locke;* but he has said them more perspicuously, more philosophically, & without any admixture of those errors or unintelligibilities into which Mr. Locke suffered himself to be seduced by his Essences and Abstract Ideas. (pp. 85-6)

[I think] I could make it evident, that the Cartesian is bonâ fide identical with the Berkleian Scheme, with the Difference that Des Cartes has developed it more confusedly, and interruptedly than Berkley, and probably therefore did not perceive it in his own mind with the same steadiness & distinctness. . . . So Des Cartes System is a *drossy* Berkleianism—and it is in consequence of it's dross & verbal Impurities that the System of Locke is found so completely bodied out in it. If I should not have been mistaken in this, it would follow that the famous **Essay on the human Understanding** is only a prolix Paraphrase on Des Cartes with foolish Interpolations of the Paraphrast's; the proper motto to which would be nihil hîc novi, plurimum vero superflui ["nothing new here, and in very real abundance"]. A System may have no new Truths for it's component Parts, yet having nothing but Truths, may be for that very reason a new System—which appears to me to be the case with the moral philosophy of Jesus Christ, but this, it is admitted on all hands, is not the case with Mr. Locke's **Essay**. But if it's Truths are neither new nor unaccompanied by Errors and Obscurities, it may be fairly asked, wherein does Mr. Locke's [*Essay*'s] merit consist. Certainly not in his style, which has neither elegance, spirit, nor precision; as certainly not in his arrangement, which is so defective that I at least seem always in an *eddy*, when I read him (round & round, & never a step forward) but least of all can it be in his Illustrations, which are seldom accurate to the eye, & never interesting to the Affections. I feel deeply . . . what ungracious words I am writing; in how unamiable a Light I am placing myself. I hazard the danger of being considered one of those trifling men who whenever a System has gained the applause of mankind hunt out in obscure corners of obscure Books for paragraphs, in which that System may seem to have been anticipated; or perhaps some sentence of half dozen words, in the intellectual Loins of which the System had lain Snug [?] in *homuncular* ["manikin-like"] perfection. This is indeed vile in any case, but when that system is the work of our Countryman; when the Name, from which we attempt to detract, has been venerable for a century in the Land of our Fathers and Forefathers, it is most vile. But I trust, that this can never be fairly applied to the present Instance—on the contrary I seem to myself as far as these facts have not been noticed, to have done a good work, in restoring a name, to which Englishmen have been especially unjust, to the honors which belong to it. . . . (pp. 87-8)

Berkley who owed much to Plato & Malebranche, but *nothing* to Locke, is at this day believed to be no more than a refiner upon Locke—as Hume is complimented into a refiner on Berkley. Hence Mr. Locke has been lately called the Founder of all the succeeding Systems of Metaphysics as Newton is of natural Philosophy & in this sense his Name is revered tho' his **Essay** is almost neglected. Those, who do read Mr. Locke as a part of Education or of Duty, very naturally think him a great man having been taught to suppose him the Discoverer of all the plain preadamitical Common sense that is to be found in his Book. But in general his Merit like that of a Luther, or a Roger Bacon, is not now an idea abstracted from his Books, but from History, [——?] the [——?] of Superstition: his Errors & Inaccuracies are sometimes admitted, only to be weighed against the Bullion of his Truths, but more often as in other holy Books are explained away—& the most manifest self-contradictions reconciled with each other on the plea, that so great a man was to be Judged by the general Spirit of his opinions, & not by the Dead Letters. (p. 90)

Samuel Taylor Coleridge, in letters to the Wedgwoods in 1801?, in his Coleridge on the Seventeenth

Century, *edited by Roberta Florence Brinkley, 1955. Reprint by Greenwood Press, Publishers, 1968, pp. 68-90.*

LEIGH HUNT (essay date 1810)

[*An English man of letters, Hunt encouraged and influenced several young poets, especially John Keats and Percy Bysshe Shelley. A copious and facile writer, Hunt produced volumes of poetry, critical essays, dramas, and translations, and, with his brother John, established the* Examiner, *a weekly liberal newspaper. In his critical essays, Hunt articulated the principles of Romanticism, emphasizing the poet's use of imaginative freedom and expression of personal emotions. Although his critical works were overshadowed by those of the tow most prominent English critics of the era, Samuel Taylor Coleridge and William Hazlitt, Hunt's essays are considered sensitive and generous to the fledgling writers he supported. The twentieth-century critic Clarence DeWitt Thorpe maintained that Hunt "made a constant effort when he read his authors both to get at and analyze what was uniquely good and to ferret out and characterize what was less good or downright bad. In other words, he was habitually after specific quality." In the following excerpt from an 1810 essay in the* Examiner, *written to encourage public support for a proposed monument to Locke, Hunt praises Locke's intellect and commitment to independent thinking.*]

We raise contributions for persecuted club-spouters, and for women of doubtful character, but we can afford nothing in honour of the sage who shed such a noble radiance on the human intellect and on the fame and freedom of the English character. What is it that hinders us from doing justice to such a man? [Locke] has been dead long enough to surmount the effects of ignorance, of envy, and of bigotry; he has raised our reputation in a manner at once the most innocent, most useful, and most sublime; he taught us to think for ourselves, and in so thinking to act for all mankind; it was he and the great Newton, who put to flight the dreams of former ages and opened the eyes of man to the true consciousness of his powers: even our rival neighbours could not but worship the radiant hands that dispersed their own philosophy; and shall we refuse honours to one of them? Newton, who taught us to look upwards and contemplate the glory of nature, has his monument as he ought to have; his fame was too immediate in the eyes of his countrymen to be overlooked. Locke, who taught us to look inwards and contemplate ourselves, did us more good though with less grandeur of effect, and has no monument but in the glory he bequeathed us. It is not necessary perhaps to his reputation that he should have any other;—but it is very necessary to ours. (p. 105)

It is to Locke—I do not say to Locke only, but it is to that admirable man chiefly—that English thinking has owed its freedom from jargon, from ostentation, from superficiality. The father, though not the perfecter, of definition, and the great recommender of a system of reflection at once *conscientious,* modest, and profound, there is no profession, no mode or object of learning, no mental accomplishment or personal virtue, to which he has not been of incalculable service. We are naturally too apt to refer our blessings as well as misfortunes to things or men before us; but philosophy, of all other social greatness, is that which leaves the best and most lasting influence behind it, and is acting for us long after the philosopher is dead. It is his good spirit left upon earth to counteract the baneful glories of the ambitious and the warlike, and to whisper to the mind even amidst the shouts of multitudes and the blasts of the trumpet, that there is *something* infinitely nobler than all this.

Thus there is not a day passing over our heads, in which we do not reap some solid advantage from the influence, however unacknowledged at the moment, of such men as Locke. We say to ourselves, when thinking—"This thing we see clearly," and we thank our education, or the improved state of society, for being able to see so clearly:—it was Locke who so much assisted that education and that improvement. We say to ourselves when thinking, "Thank God! nobody can deprive us of our freedom of opinion, or even dictate to us inquisitorially:"—it was Locke who asserted for us that freedom of opinion, that liberty of speech and conscience. We say to ourselves, when thinking, "France, by the help of weak opposers, has risen to a great pitch of worldly glory; but after all, the spirit of her society has not a particle of that independence which is still preserved in England:"—it was Locke, who in teaching us to distinguish false glory from true—it was Locke, and such men as himself, who, in teaching us to give up our mental liberty to no man, taught us to give up our personal liberty to no man; but to prefer even the consciousness of independence to a slavery however worshipful.—To such a man as Locke, therefore, every Englishman owes love and reverence, and not even Nelson himself, though he died on the waves bequeathing triumph to his countrymen, deserves a more glorious acknowledgment of their gratitude, than he who, dying in solitude and in silence, with no glories about him but the anticipation of heaven and the meek sublimity of departing virtue, bequeathed to his countrymen the love of what is rational. (pp. 107-08)

Leigh Hunt, *"Proposed Monument to Locke,"* in his Leigh Hunt's Political and Occasional Essays, *edited by Lawrence Huston Houtchens and Carolyn Washburn Houtchens, Columbia University Press, 1962, pp. 105-09.*

EDMUND LODGE (essay date 1835)

[*Lodge was a late-eighteenth- and early-nineteenth-century English biographer and historian whose chief work is the series of "biographical and historical memoirs" attached to his multivolume* Portraits of Illustrious Personages of Great Britain. *In the following excerpt from this work, he praises Locke's literary and philosophical achievements.*]

A more happy combination of the characters of the Christian, the scholar, and the gentleman, has perhaps never been exhibited, than in the person of this distinguished philosopher [John Locke]. Disdaining the futile speculations by which preceding writers on metaphysics had sought to veil the mysteries they were unable to comprehend, and relying solely on the original powers of his own deep and reflecting mind, it is scarcely presumptuous to say, that he brought to light perhaps all that is discoverable respecting the operations of the human understanding; and, while his talents were devoted to a work which became one of the highest ornaments of the literature of his country, his pure and virtuous life displayed the most satisfactory proof of the practical efficacy of a piety the sincerity of which was clearly proved by his efforts, not less humble than vigorous, to shew that all the parts of the Christian System were reconcilable to human reason. (p. 1)

Edmund Lodge, *"John Locke,"* in his Portraits of Illustrious Personages of Great Britain, Vol. IX, *Harding and Lepard, 1835, pp. 1-8.*

[JOHN WILSON] (essay date 1836)

[*A Scottish critic, essayist, novelist, poet, and short story writer, Wilson is best known as Christopher North, the name he often assumed when writing for* Blackwood's Edinburgh Magazine, *a Tory periodical to which he was a contributor for over twenty-five years. He is chiefly famous for his* Noctes Ambrosianae, *a series of witty dialogues originally published in* Blackwood's *between 1822 and 1835 in which contemporary issues and personalities are treated with levity, gravity, and pungent satire. Wilson is not recognized as a great critic. His criticism, which was frequently written in haste, is often deficient in wisdom, analysis, and finish. He could be severe and stinging, reserving his harshest words for gifted young writers whom he sincerely wanted to help by objectively analyzing their work. His other critical opinions are largely regarded as the projections of his varying moods. In the following excerpt from an 1836* Blackwood's *essay, with which he began his series titled "The Metaphysician," Wilson clarifies the most significant doctrines of* An Essay concerning Human Understanding.]

Locke's *Essay concerning Human Understanding* was first published at a time when the abstract, speculative, and often obscure doctrines of the scholastic logicians yet held their full sway in the science of mind. It is to be regarded as the first regular attempt to subvert the authority of those doctrines, and to establish this part of philosophy upon surer principles, as answering to those new views in physical science which were introduced by the application of Lord Bacon's method of induction to the investigation of material nature. It was, in fact, the application of that same method of induction to the investigation of mind. It is not to be wondered at, therefore, that a work, undertaken upon such grounds, by an enquirer, profound and indefatigable in his researches, ardent and sincere in the desire of truth, and of the most powerful and discriminating intellect, should have made an era in the history of philosophy, and have maintained the most marked and decisive influence upon the whole subsequent character of the science.

The first great object of Locke's enquiries was to overthrow the received opinion of innate ideas; and this he conceived would be most effectually accomplished by showing whence our ideas are derived. His work, therefore, though suggested by that particular object, takes the character of a general enquiry into the origin of human knowledge. (p. 798)

[The sum of Locke's] doctrine is this, that the mind is unconscious till it is awakened through sense; that as soon as it is affected by sensation, intelligent action begins to take place in it, variously modifying and combining these impressions; and that both from the simple sensation, and the knowledge of objects thus framed, the whole mind is set in motion, its feelings and passions called into activity; and the intelligent being now finds *a second subject* of thought and knowledge, in these acts of its own intelligence and the various affections of its own will.

The term which Locke uses to express generally the action of the mind is *operation*, to his use of which term it is necessary to call attention, because he has in some measure departed from its natural or more obvious signification; employing it to describe not merely what the word itself suggests, the intellectual acts of our mind, but its movements of feeling and passion. A peculiarity which it is the more necessary distinctly to remark, because, in the further course of his work, he draws his illustrations with such partial and almost exclusive preference from the operations of the understanding, that his reader might often feel very much in doubt with respect to some of his general propositions, whether he meant to comprehend in them or not the impassioned part of our mind, unless he remembered this enlarged sense which in the outset Locke has given to his terms. (pp. 798-99)

By the word idea, Locke understands in the first place the simple apprehension which takes place in the mind of that which is before it. Thus, when he speaks of the ideas of sensation, he makes no distinction between that idea of the sensation which the mind afterwards retains, and that first affection of which it is conscious in the moment of sensation. Accordingly, when he instances as *ideas of sensation* those of yellow, white, heat, cold, soft, hard, bitter, sweet, he must be understood as including both the first impression of the mind by the presence to its sense of the yellow, white, cold, bitter, sweet object; and also that *copy* of the impression, as it is often called, which it afterwards retains. (p. 799)

[With] respect to ideas of reflection, he considers that the notice which the mind takes of an act of understanding or feeling produces, in the very moment, the idea of that act, which idea may indeed afterwards separately be recalled, but which at first exists *with* the act or emotion itself.

These ideas, whether derived from sense or reflection, whether perceived in the presence of their object, or afterwards recalled, are either simple or complex. They are simple in their first unmixed elementary state; they are complex when the mind, by its own activity, proceeds to combine them. In distinguishing between sensation and perception, it is requisite to attend to the same difference: the difference between the simple original impressions, before the mind has begun to exert its power upon them, and its own combinations. This is all that Mr Locke means when he distinguishes our ideas into simple and complex.

Having thus grounded the origin of our knowledge in these simple ideas of sensation, and simple ideas from the mind's observation of itself, or, as he expresses it, from reflection, he proceeds to establish the office of those intellectual powers by which, from the materials thus prepared, knowledge is compounded.

The *first* in his enumeration is *perception*, concerning which it is not necessary to observe more than that he gives this name to the faculty of the mind *to take observation of what is present to it;* the old use of the term, and widely different from that fixed and limited sense to which the word is now appropriated.

The faculty by which these primary ideas are preserved for use he calls *retention,* remarking, that it implies two things—contemplation, whereby the idea is held before the mind as the subject of a more distinct and deliberate notice—and memory, by which ''we revive again in our minds those ideas which, after imprinting, have disappeared.''

Thus prepared, the mind may proceed to its intellectual work; and we have now to know the processes which he explains as constituting the whole power which it is capable of exercising over these materials of its knowledge. But it is right first to remove one of those misconceptions, which have been held even by distinguished writers, as to Locke's own notion of ideas, without which the metaphorical language he uses might easily lead into the same error. It has been imagined that Locke conceived these ideas in the mind to be something distinct from itself, and having a proper and absolute existence. Now nothing can be farther from his thoughts; for, being aware himself that there is indeed a natural tendency of the mind to take up this view, he has even thought it necessary expressly to warn his

reader against so erroneous a conception of the operations of the mind. (pp. 800-01)

[Locke's] view, that our ideas, even in memory, are nothing in themselves, but merely perceptions or *acts of the mind* renewing a former act under slight modification, was, considering the period at which Locke wrote, indeed an important and necessary step towards all just physiology of the human mind.

Thus far Locke has considered those simple ideas merely in receiving which the mind *is passive.* But having passively received them, it then begins to exert power of its own in various acts, by which, out of these simple ideas, as its materials, all others are framed. These acts are (chiefly) the three following: The first, *combining* several simple into one complex idea; the second, bringing together two simple or two complex ideas and *comparing* them, by which process all 'ideas of relation' are obtained; the third, is the act of *separating* ideas from all those which accompany them as they are presented in real existence, and thus generalizing them. To this act he gives the logical name of *abstraction;* and these *three* modes of the mind's action—combining, comparing, and separating—he conceives sufficient to account for the entire production of our most extensive and complicated knowledge, from the simple elements to which he ascribes its origin.

The complex ideas framed by the first process may, he observes, be again combined; and the combination of many complex ideas into one is still acknowledged by the mind as one idea though infinitely complex, as in the example of that one idea in which the whole of its most complex ideas are collected and combined—the universe.

This, then, is Locke's simple account of the whole process of the composition of our knowledge. But as this account so far stands merely as a *hypothesis,* and *proposes* merely but does not *establish* his system, he has occupied the chief part of his work in investigating some of those among our ideas which appear to be the most remote from such an origin, and in reducing them to their elements, and it is from the adoption of this mode of demonstrating his theory that the work is to be regarded as an example of the method of induction applied to the science of the mind.

This great undertaking of one bold and original mind changed the face of the science in this country. Till that time it was a structure of hypotheses without foundation. Locke directed men to enquire into the mind itself, on which they reasoned, and taught them to know nothing but what they found there. But he had almost done too much, for his work, overthrowing, by the power of effective and authentic science, the old systems against which it was directed, took their place in *authority.* He exhorted and guided men to enquire, and no doubt his bold example and distinguished success aroused a spirit of enquiry which has not again fallen asleep. But the great doctrines which he had himself established, which seemed to have brought forth out of the dark vacuity of the schools a whole substantial and ordered world, gave what he never intended or conceived, *the law* to science on the points which he had so laboriously investigated.

The two words, which he had singled out as comprehending the entire grounds of our knowledge, Reflection and Sensation, took possession of men's minds as if they had included all science; and his followers either accepted implicitly the doctrine which these terms described, and rested there, or sought only to push farther the principles of the same simplification.

It is something surprising to read the language of philosophers who followed him, and to observe the tone of undoubting and almost submissive assent with which they cite these doctrines, and the urgency with which they insist upon them, as containing the sum of all intellectual philosophy.

The result has been one which the author of the system did not foresee or desire. His followers, prouder in their exemption from the chains which Locke had broken than anxious themselves to tread in the painful steps of his investigations, took up his doctrines without examination; and it has happened that the authority of his name, united with a misconceived result of his speculations, has established among great numbers of his countrymen a doctrine which his work does not contain, and drawn from many writers severe animadversion upon tenets of which that work offers the confutation.

The misconception of his doctrines to which we allude is this—that there are no thoughts in our minds that are not direct copies of previous states of our mind—that the impressions made upon sense, variously compounded, make up one class, and the impressions which have commonly been referred to consciousness make up the other. So that all our thought is the representation of the external world, or the representation of the Agent Mind—a being thinking, feeling, willing, acting.

Now, this is not the doctrine of Locke. He conceives the original sources of our knowledge to be such impressions, and our complex ideas to be the combinations of such impressions; but he does nowhere limit the activity of the mind to perceiving the original ideas, and combining them into complex ones. On the contrary, he does, in the most formal manner, in describing the action of the mind upon the subjects of thought thus acquired, assert the existence of a direct and peculiar power, which, by comparing the ideas thus acquired together, obtains other ideas—namely, those of relation; such as those important and comprehensive ideas of cause and effect, duration, analogy, identity, proportion, number, and all those which he describes generally under the terms *agreement and disagreement of ideas*. (pp. 801-02)

[The] erroneous views which have been held of the principles of Locke in his own country seem nothing when compared with the wild extravagance with which they have been perverted by his followers on the Continent. If his doctrine were such as it has been frequently conceived at home, the worst charge that could be brought against it would be that it was intellectually defective—that it left some of our abstract ideas unexplained, for which it was necessary to have assigned an origin. But there is nothing in it, even as thus represented, that is dishonouring to the mind. Its own character as an intelligent nature, with intellectual powers derived from that nature alone, is distinctly asserted, as indeed it speaks from every page of his work; for the very definition of reflection includes it, in which the mind's own operations are described as original sources to it of knowledge, expressly contradistinguished from and opposed to the knowledge derived from sensation. It is something very astonishing, therefore, to find a metaphysical school established in another country professing to deduce their tenets from this system, in which the mind is in some sort excluded from the science of which it is the sole subject. Yet such is the philosophy which Condillac has deduced from that of Locke, which was eagerly received by his countrymen, and till lately was the reigning philosophy among them. Condillac refers the origin of our knowledge to sensation alone; not meaning that sensation is the only matter of knowledge to the mind on which it exercises its powers, which of itself would be sufficiently extravagant. But he represents it as constituting the mind itself, pursuing his enquiries at great length to show that all its operations, and processes, and powers, are nothing more than variations of mere sensation—a doctrine suggested perhaps by the views of Locke, but the furthest possible from resembling them.

At the same time, that there appears sufficient ground to defend Locke from the various erroneous representations to which his work has furnished the occasion, it is not to be denied that it is in some points defective and vulnerable; and that in an undertaking of such exceeding magnitude, if he has established some conclusions of great moment, as their influence on philosophy has testified, yet he did not embrace the whole subject with the same clearness of speculation, and has left much for succeeding enquirers to rectify or to supply.

The first defect that strikes us as generally characterising his essay is one to which we are made particularly sensible, by the far greater precision of language which has since been introduced into the same subjects—that is, a looseness of expression, and even an inconsistency in the use of terms, which makes it often necessary to compare his views on the same point as they are given in different places, in order to determine with certainty the precise import of his words. This is the less to be wondered at, when we remember that he had to frame his own language, in treating for the first time a very various and extensive argument of abstruse investigation. It would almost appear, however, that in his zeal to emancipate his favourite study from the tyranny of the schools, he fell into the excess of substituting for their abstract and speculative diction one borrowed too much from the familiar homeliness of common use. He endeavoured to make philosophy speak an *un*learned language; and in bringing down her speech to the plainness of common understanding, he has given up with its artificial dignity, too much of the just severity of science.

It must be admitted too that in his speculations as well, there is a defect akin to that which has been remarked in his expression, and that bold and strong in his intellectual conception, and rigorous in ascertaining the substance of his doctrine, there is sometimes a want of severe precision in the details even of thought. So that many minor inconsistencies may be remarked not only in his expression, but even as we may judge in the meaning.

There is, however, one branch of his subject which appears to be chargeable with a more serious deficiency; and in which much seems to be wanting to complete the account even of the principles of the understanding—to wit, the power of the understanding to furnish its own ideas. It must be acknowledged, that if he had treated this part of his subject with the explicitness and fulness which its importance required, he must have left it free from all ambiguity. The examination of the various parts of the essay and the comparison of them will leave no doubt that he does ascribe to the mind this power. But the fact is not decisively ascertained without this examination and comparison. There is reason therefore to imagine that he himself laboured under some hesitation and uncertainty to what extent it should be admitted; and it may be even conjectured that at one time he has gone further than at another in allowing it. If we were to offer our own conjecture on the subject, we should say that he appears to us to have entered upon his investigation with a mind full of strong convictions of the importance of those two sources of knowledge, sensation and reflection; and expecting that the part they actually bear in the composition of our knowledge would be found greater than in truth it is;

that their results would be found more independent of any additional power; but that in the progress of enquiry his view of the efficiency of the understanding itself by reasoning and judging to frame new and simple ideas was gradually enlarged; but that he never freed himself entirely from the predominance of the views under which he entered upon his examination, and consequently never saw the full extent of this power. In this respect it is that the science of the mind has so much advanced among us since the time of this Philosopher. It is in this part of philosophy that later enquirers have gone boldly on, asserting the true and native character of the intelligence, as determined by its own tendencies to produce from itself its own forms of thought, its own conceptions, its own knowledge. (pp. 804-05)

Without this principle, the utmost reverse of that dishonouring speculation which we have mentioned as prevailing in another country, there can be no true philosophy of mind, for without this the mind itself is robbed of its essential character and has lost all its original brightness. (p. 805)

[*John Wilson*], *"The Metaphysician, No. I.: On the Philosophy of Locke," in* Blackwood's Edinburgh Magazine, *Vol. XXXIX, No. CCXLVIII, June, 1836, pp. 798-805.*

JOHN STUART MILL (essay date 1843)

[*The author of* On Liberty *(1859),* Utilitarianism *(1863), and* The Subjection of Women *(1869), Mill is regarded as one of England's greatest philosophers and political economists. Educated at home under an exacting regimen designed by his father James Mill (an ardent disciple of utilitarian philosopher Jeremy Bentham), Mill became, while still in his teens, a prominent exponent of utilitarianism and a prolific essayist for the* Westminster Review. *In his early twenties, Mill suffered a "mental crisis," which he attributed to the lack of emotional and imaginative outlets in his strictly intellectual upbringing. He turned to the works of William Wordsworth and Samuel Taylor Coleridge, among others, as a means of supplying this lack, and was later instrumental in modifying the radical utilitarianism of Bentham to include the consideration of such human intangibles as idealism, emotion, and imagination. In the following excerpt, Mill discusses Locke's achievement as a philosopher.*]

Few among the great names in philosophy have met with a harder measure of justice from the present generation than Locke; the unquestioned founder of the analytic philosophy of mind, but whose doctrines were first caricatured, then, when the reaction arrived, cast off by the prevailing school even with contumely, and who is now regarded by one of the conflicting parties in philosophy as an apostle of heresy and sophistry, while among those who still adhere to the standard which he raised, there has been a disposition in later times to sacrifice his reputation in favor of Hobbes; a great writer, and a great thinker for his time, but inferior to Locke not only in sober judgment but even in profundity and original genius. Locke, the most candid of philosophers, and one whose speculations bear on every subject the strongest marks of having been wrought out from the materials of his own mind, has been mistaken for an unworthy plagiarist, while Hobbes has been extolled as having anticipated many of his leading doctrines. He did anticipate many of them, and the [doctrine of essences] is an instance in what manner it was generally done. They both rejected the scholastic doctrine of essences; but Locke understood and explained what these supposed essences really were; Hobbes, instead of explaining the distinction between essential and accidental properties, and between essential and accidental

propositions, jumped over it, and gave a definition which suits at most only essential propositions, and scarcely those as the definition of Proposition in general. (n., pp. 75-6)

John Stuart Mill, in a footnote in his A System of Logic: Ratiocinative and Inductive, *1843. Reprint by Harper & Brothers, Publishers, 1873, pp. 75-6.*

[HENRY ROGERS] (essay date 1854)

[*A nineteenth-century English poet, essayist, critic, philosopher, and philologist, Rogers was a regular contributor to the* Edinburgh Review, Good Words, *the* British Quarterly, *and other periodicals. The author of nearly fifty books and articles, he is perhaps best remembered for* The Eclipse of Faith; or, A Visit to a Religious Sceptic *(1852), a philosophical dialogue notable for its clever dialectics and adroit use of the Socratic elenchus. In the following excerpt from his 1854* Edinburgh Review *study of Locke's character and philosophy, he assesses the elements of Locke's genius.*]

Probably no philosopher of our own country—hardly any of any country—has exerted a more extensive or durable influence over the intellectual world than our illustrious countryman, John Locke. This is not owing, certainly, to the universal acceptance of all the dogmas he maintained, or to any lack of doubts and disputes as to what, on many points, *were* his dogmas. On the contrary, the criticism which has been expended on even the fundamental principles of his metaphysical theory would, as Judge Jeffreys said of the voluminous writings of Richard Baxter, 'fill a cart.'

Yet Locke has enjoyed his protracted and extensive empire not without sufficient reason. Not only has he extracted as ample a treasure of the ore of TRUTH from the mine as could fairly be expected from the efforts of a single mind; not only has he exhibited it in a form as free from error as could be hoped from the limitations of any human intellect, however powerful; but throughout his writings he breathes a *spirit* of philosophy more precious, and calculated to exert a more beneficial influence over the reader, than his philosophy itself. They are inspired by an intense love of Truth, and exhibit a rare combination of independence and caution in seeking it;—independence, in sturdily thrusting aside all authority but that of Reason; caution, in a perpetual recognition of the feebleness and ignorance of that very Reason; a profound consciousness that the highest achievement of man's wisdom will ever consist in *wisely* ascertaining within what limits alone he *can* be wise. When to these qualities we add the cogency of Locke's logic, his practical sagacity, the unusual vivacity and originality of his modes of treating abstruse subjects, we need not wonder that he is still a favourite with his countrymen, or that he continues to enjoy a European reputation. . . . We should . . . recommend to every young person, who had leisure carefully to peruse it, the . . . treatise on the ***Understanding*** itself; assured that, whatever the points in which it convinced or failed to convince, few books in any language could more effectually enamour the soul of truth, inspire a contempt of sophistry, develop and discipline the powers of the mind, train it to clearness of thought and expression, inspire it with an ambition to know wherever knowledge is possible, and, (not less signal benefit,) teach it humbly to acquiesce in ignorance where ignorance is inevitable. (pp. 383-84)

The principal characteristics of the genius of Locke are visible at once to the reader in almost every page. No author has impressed the image of his own mind more indelibly on his works, or given them a character of more perfect originality. Hence, in part, and in great part, the continued popularity they possess, and the delight and profit with which they are perused; delight and profit, as usual, often greater than can be reaped from writings less marked indeed by defects, and even by errors, but tamer in character, and less stimulating to the mind of the student. Some of his characteristics—half moral and half intellectual—have been already adverted to; his rare combination of boldness and caution, of independence and humility,—necessary complements of one another in every true philosopher. To these must be added a wonderful robustness and vigour in the logical faculty, rare sagacity, comprehensiveness and patience in the survey of whatsoever subject attracted his attention,—the characteristics of what he himself so much admired as 'a large 'round-about mind,'—a power of abstraction capable of detaining, separating, and analysing the most evanescent and complicated phenomena of thought, and great copiousness, often felicitous aptness, of homely illustrations and examples in describing and explaining them. A word or two more on two or three of the above peculiarities.

Perhaps, after all, the quality of Locke's intellect which most generally strikes the youthful reader is the force of the logical faculty, partly because it is more easily apprehended than the rest, and partly because it more continually manifests itself. Locke admired Chillingworth intensely, and often strongly reminds us of him. As with Chillingworth, the peculiar vigour of Locke's logic displays itself most in controversy. In the replies to Stillingfleet, but especially in the letters on *Toleration* (certainly the most brilliant, perhaps in his own day the most useful, of his productions,) it is impossible not to recognise the logical Milo in every page. The unhappy 'Jonas Proest,' who ventured to oppose him on the latter subject, is not so much vanquished as annihilated. Like some criminals who have been punished by being blown from a cannon's mouth, not a fragment of the unfortunate champion for persecution is to be found.

But not one of the traits of Locke indicated above—neither his logical acuteness, nor his thirst for truth, nor the sagacity with which he prosecuted his search for it,—is more marked than his habitual recognition of the narrow limits of the human faculties, and his conviction that the chief and most difficult function of a philosopher is to ascertain within what sphere men may legitimately philosophise. Profoundly feeling that there are impassable barriers which environ us on all sides, he is every where anxious to recognise the limits where philosophy must pause, the brink of those abysses and precipices on which there is no access to human hand or foot. Acknowledging without shame—rather with manly modesty—this fact of the true position of man, he never hesitates to confess his ignorance where he is ignorant, nor even in many cases his despair of ever attaining knowledge. (pp. 385-86)

Locke's love of truth, though of course essentially a moral excellence, gives an indescribable charm to all the movements of his intellect; it animates, vivifies, transfigures the most tedious processes of logic. The evident desire and longing of his soul is to arrive at truth, and that only; he spares no toil, no patience, in hunting it, nor (when he deems he has found it) in setting it forth as plainly as possible to the apprehension of others.

It is obvious that nothing could, in his judgment, make amends for missing TRUTH; he has no preconceptions which he is determined shall stand; no shame in acknowledging an error; no sinister purposes to answer. As we read him, we feel sure that neither vanity nor interest could have induced him to disguise or mutilate a truth, nor to harbour a sophism, however brilliant and however applauded by others, for one moment in his bosom. They are his own glorious words—'Whatever I write, as soon as I shall discover it not to be TRUTH, my hand shall be forwardest to throw it in the fire.'

The same reasons have made him one of the fairest of all controversial antagonists; disguising nothing, distorting nothing, garbling nothing, misquoting nothing; doing his devoir ever manfully, but knightly and honourably, and disdaining to use any weapons in the cause of truth which truth itself has not consecrated. These qualities, wherever they are found, must in the nature of things tend to give vastly augmented force to any man's logic. The intellect is more indebted to the love of truth than its worshippers generally suppose, and any aids which the understanding lends the conscience are ever faithfully repaid. (pp. 389-90)

As to the *learning* of Locke, it has, like that of Shakspeare, been most variously estimated. While some would make him almost ignorant of what his predecessors had written, and such a very Troglodyte in metaphysics that he was not properly acquainted even with such writers as Descartes or Hobbes,—others are of opinion (with Stillingfleet) that he is under vast but unconscious obligations to them. The truth lies, as usual, between the extreme estimates. To suppose that a mind so inquisitive and powerful as Locke's should not have been tolerably conversant with the principal productions of philosophers, is extravagant; to suppose that a mind so original and independent should be a servile imitator, is equally so. If any man ever thought for himself, it was Locke. He avows it everywhere, that he had faithfully endeavoured to trace the origin and analyse the composition of thought in his own mind, totally careless what might or might not be the opinions of others. His whole work bears the marks of this; and if he has erred, it is in not having sufficiently and carefully examined the opinions of others. (pp. 390-91)

Another striking characteristic of Locke, and which distinguishes him from many metaphysicians, is, that his power of external observation is almost as marked as that of introspection. It was no doubt largely developed by that study of medicine, for which he was so eminently fitted, and in which he so much excelled; but not by that only. His extensive travels, his busy public life, his practical habits, must have kept this talent in continual exercise, and more than counterpoised any undue tendency to what is apt to be the vice of great intellectual philosophers—excess of abstraction. Hence, too, as has frequently been observed, his great work is written in the style of one who had evidently seen much of life; it speaks the dialect of the world; it is familiar and colloquial beyond that of any other great work of any other philosopher in any age. A similar tact for observation is evinced in this work in a more direct way; it not only analyses the mental phenomena of man in general, but perpetually shows that the author has had a watchful and observant eye on the diversities of intellectual character which have come in his way,—that he has not only studied *man,* but *men.* In this shrewd and vigilant inspection both of general humanity and of individual character, he has some resemblance at once to Aristotle and Socrates. A little volume of weighty maxims of conduct, founded on observation of man and the world might be easily compiled from his writings; many of which would do no discredit to Bacon's *Essays,* or Pascal's *Thoughts.* (p. 392)

The union of comprehensiveness and sagacity in Locke is strikingly displayed in the variety of the subjects which employed his mind, and the success, notwithstanding, with which he treated them. On all the chief topics of importance agitated in his day he has left us his thoughts; on Religious Toleration, on Civil Government, on Education, on several questions of Economical Science, a science then in its cradle,—and on all these varied subjects, he has advanced the boundary-line of human knowledge, extricated some principles before unknown, approximated more nearly to truth in the statement of some which were disputed, and dispelled many pernicious and formidable errors. (pp. 392-93)

The understanding of Locke was, like that of so many eminent Englishmen, peculiarly *practical,* as the subjects to which he turned his attention sufficiently show. As compared with some minds of far greater harmony and variety of powers, he appears decidedly deficient; almost, we might say, truncated. The intellect absorbed to itself some of his other faculties; so that they either appear shrunk, like muscles not used, or they must have been originally feeble in comparison.

To all the forms of the Beautiful, for example, and all the fine arts, he seems to have been almost insensible. Plato is full of poetry; Aristotle could at least criticise it profoundly; Bacon is almost Shakspeare in a philosophic garb, so resplendent is his imagination, and so versatile his genius. It is curious that there is hardly a passing remark in all Locke's great work on any of the aesthetical or emotional characteristics of humanity: so that, for anything that appears, men might have nothing of the kind in their composition. (pp. 393-94)

[Locke's] sense of humour and his powers of raillery must have been very considerable. Nor had he only that dry species of logical humour (if we may use the phrase) which is often found in very close reasoners,—where fallacies and sophisms are so neatly exposed, the nut cracked and the shell thrown away with such a self-possessed air, or unexpected deductions so suddenly evolved from trivial premises, that the feat often produces much of the ludicrous surprise which is the proper effect of wit. Many of the apt anecdotes introduced into his philosophical works strongly show his sense of the ludicrous; as, for example, the well known one of the blind man, who flattered himself that at length he knew what was the colour of scarlet, namely, that it was like the sound of a trumpet;—by which Locke illustrates the impossibility of imparting the simple ideas of any sense to those who are destitute of that sense. (p. 395)

The *style* of Locke is, like himself, plain, homely, businesslike, practical; devoid, it is true, of much grace or elegance, and often copious to diffuseness, but perpetually lighted up with vivacious illustration, which tends to keep the attention of the reader alive. Considering the condition of the language when he wrote, (just feeling its way to the elegance of diction and construction at which it arrived in Addison's time,) Locke's is a very favourable specimen of English style, and, assuredly, carries away the palm from that of any preceding philosophical writer. It is true, indeed, he cannot make pretensions to that peculiar *netteté* ["clearness"]—we know not by what other name to call it—by which the French philosophic writers have been distinguished from the time of Descartes and Pascal to that of Cousin; exhibiting an admirable combination of clearness, beauty, and simplicity, to which, though we may flatter ourselves that our countrymen have not been inferior in depth or comprehensiveness, English philosophers cannot make equal pretensions. (p. 398)

But it is high time that we proceed to make our . . . remarks on Locke's Philosophy.

It is impossible to deny that the immortal *Essay* is disfigured by serious blemishes—by some errors, and many inconsistencies and ambiguities. The latter flower chiefly from that figurative and popular style which is yet one of its most attractive, as well as serviceable features; but partly also from the desultory manner in which the *Essay* was composed, and the length of time (nearly twenty years) occupied in its completion. This allowed, it is true, time for elaboration; but it also allowed time for the 'sleepy nods' which proverbially overtake a man in a 'long work;' and for those variations which are sure to characterise every large edifice when it is an aggregate of accretions. Hence the apparent, and sometimes real inconsistencies and ambiguities of expression which are found in Locke's frequent repetitions of the same or similar thoughts, and which have made it possible for critics to fight so long even over the fundamental principles of his philosophy. Of errors—some are the errors of the defective philosophy of his age which he did so much to correct; but others, as for example, his infelicitous theory of personal identity, and his gratuitous speculation as to the possibility of 'thinking matter,' are his own unchallenged and unenvied property. But whatever the faults of his book, and we have no wish to extenuate them, it may be fearlessly asked, when was an equally extensive metaphysical work,—viewed, as it ought of course to be, relatively to the age in which the author lived,—infected with less? (pp. 402-03)

Still, in spite of numerous *maculæ* ["blemishes"] the *Essay on the Understanding* is, on the whole, by far the largest and most accurate map traced, up to Locke's time, by any single mind, of the phenomena of the human consciousness; further, without denying his great obligations to previous labourers in the same field, it may be justly said, that probably no philosopher (except Aristotle) ever observed so many facts of mind not distinctly pointed out before; that none have, singly, penetrated so far into the *terra incognita* of the intellectual world, or left so carefully compiled a chart of the coasts surveyed, or in so many instances rectified and adjusted the less accurate observations of predecessors. We certainly know of no other work, even now, which so often and so distinctly arrests the surprise and attention of the youthful metaphysician by revealing to him the hitherto unrealised facts of his own consciousness; or which so often turns the vague mutter of that consciousness into articulate language; none which so often induces him to say, 'I am sensible of that—how often have I felt so and so, and never thought of it, nor had it stated to me, before.' (p. 403)

It is not the least admirable feature of the work, that with no lack of comprehensiveness, or depth, or subtlety of thought, whenever these are necessary, nearly the whole,—and it is a very unusual achievement with metaphysicians—is level to the comprehension of any reader who brings to its perusal only ordinary acuteness, and *will* bring to it but ordinary patience. Even when he does not agree with the author, he perfectly understands what he means. This is in part owing to those peculiarities of Locke's style of which we have sufficiently spoken; but quite as much to his impatience of thoughts which did not assume a sharp and definite outline to his own apprehension;—a characteristic for which, as well as for his method of appealing exclusively to consciousness as the basis of mental science, he was immeasurably indebted to the study of Descartes. His writings Locke greatly admired, and to his influence . . . he avows his signal early obligations,—much as he recoiled from many of the tenets of the Cartesian philosophy. (p. 404)

[Locke's] language, as already said, is often deficient in precision; he does not use the same terms with steadiness; and, writing in a style eminently popular for such subjects, he has availed himself very freely of colloquial and metaphorical language; language which, though in general admirably adapted to convey his meaning to the intelligence of ordinary readers, has paid the usual penalty of involving occasional obscurity. All this has been generally admitted. It may also be suspected that the self-reliant temper of Locke, on which we have already made some remarks,—his almost exclusive dependence on a profound inspection of his own consciousness, and comparative indifference to the literature and criticism of his subject,—may in some measure . . . , [have led] him to guard insufficiently against the prepossessions under which many of his readers would come to his statements, and against the ambiguity which would attach to many of the terms used differently by others, and not defined with the requisite rigour by himself. A critical acquaintance with the literature of a subject is well calculated to make a man aware of the points in which terms are liable to be misunderstood by others and to guard against their misapprehensions of them as used by himself. But a cause of obscurity (in this as in many other cases) more powerful than ignorance of the literature of the *past,* was the impossibility of anticipating the controversies of the *future;* when a more exact weighing of all the terms Locke had used would discover much that is ambiguous and fluctuating. (pp. 405-06)

But the acknowledged peculiarities of Locke's style, and especially the laxity and freedom of a popular phraseology, ought to make critics so much the more anxious to interpret him only on the principle of a scrupulous comparison and collation of seemingly inconsistent or fluctuating expressions; and most certainly ought to prevent them from taking any such apparent fluctuations of expression in contradiction to his express assertions where there is no such fluctuation to be charged. If an author has made use of expressions which seem hard to be reconciled, and susceptible of *two* meanings, we never, on that account, allow them to override an expression which is perfectly plain. As for the apparently inconsistent expressions, we endeavour, if possible, to reconcile them; if we cannot do that, we say, that the author has blundered, or has been forgetful, or careless, or what not; but we do not take the obscure and incoherent expressions wherewith to interpret such as are neither the one nor the other; nor either of two apparently inconsistent expressions as the sole and absolute criterion of his meaning. The maxim of theological critics, that passages of Scripture perfectly plain are not to be interpreted by such as are obscure, but the obscure by the plain, is a very reasonable one; and it were well if in criticism generally the same rule were fairly applied. (p. 406)

[Henry Rogers], "John Locke—His Character and Philosophy," in The Edinburgh Review, *Vol. XCIX, No. CCII, April, 1854, pp. 383-454.*

THOMAS E. WEBB (essay date 1857)

[*A nineteenth-century Anglo-Irish lawyer and man of letters, Webb wrote* The Intellectualism of Locke: An Essay *(1857), a work described by one reviewer as a "brilliant but paradoxical" attempt to show that Locke anticipated Immanuel Kant's recognition of synthetic a priori propositions. Known in his day more for his literary gifts than for his philosophical powers, Webb wrote several volumes of poetry and produced a celebrated verse translation (1880) of Johann Wolfgang von Goethe's* Faust. *In the following excerpt from* The Intellectualism of Locke, *he compares Kant's philosophy with Locke's.*]

The Philosophy of Locke was distinguished from that of Kant by an Empiric bias. In one respect, however, the Philosophy of Kant was more Empiric than that of Locke. Whatever his views on the nature of Experience, Locke recognised existence beyond its verge. But while the Englishman made Rational Certainty coextensive with the domain of Thought, the German restricted Rational Certainty to the domain of Actual Experience. Here Kant is to be compared, not with Locke, but Hume. . . . The domain of Experience, in fine, according to Kant, was an Enchanted Isle, from which the Understanding in vain attempted to escape, and all beyond was fog-bank and illusion. But Locke's Philosophy was animated by a more manly spirit. With that confidence in Reason which constant contact with reality rarely fails to produce, he reverenced its dictates as a Natural Revelation. Whatever we are necessitated to *think,* that, in his opinion, we may be said to *know.* Hence it was that he proclaimed that we have a knowledge of the World of Matter, and the Abyss of Space. Hence he proclaimed that Matter is evidently in its own nature void of thought, and that, the rights of Omnipotence reserved, the Soul is therefore Immaterial. Hence he proclaimed that the existence of God is a fact impossible to be denied, impossible to be made a theme for more than momentary doubt. Like Kant, he held that the Soul is confined to the Isle of Consciousness; like Kant, he protested against our "letting loose our thoughts into the vast Ocean of Being, as if that boundless extent were the natural possession of our Understandings." But in Locke's system the Soul is not left upon a desert shore, a desolate Ariadne, abandoned to darkness and despair. The ocean surrounds it, and the heavens stretch overhead. True, it can neither traverse the one, nor soar into the other. But its belief transcends the sphere of its Experience; and why should it gratuitously reject its own belief?

But while the Philosophy of Locke is thus advantageously contrasted with that of Kant on the subject of the reality of knowledge, there is one point with respect to which the genius of the German reached a far higher elevation of thought than that of his illustrious rival. By no Philosopher, ancient or modern, has the Moral Law been invested with such majesty as by the great Critic. Other Philosophers have recognised the eternal and immutable nature of Morality; others have recognised the universal and unconditional obligation which the mere conception of Duty is sufficient to impose. But to the eye of Kant the light of the Moral Law not only illumed the Path of Life— it lit up the Abyss of Speculation. It revealed the Freedom of the Will, the Immortality of the Soul, and the Existence of a God. . . . We *ought,* therefore we *can*—such, for instance, was the sublime enthymeme with which he demonstrated the Freedom of the Will. But far different was the case with Locke. The speculative perception of "the eternal and unalterable nature of Right and Wrong" it was the glory of his system to admit. He neither ignored the existence of these Concepts, with Hobbes, nor did he degrade them to mere Sentiments, with Hume; still less did he represent them to be the offspring of Education and Fashion, with the licentious Moralists who insulted his memory by proclaiming themselves his followers. With Cudworth and with Clarke, he placed our Moral Concepts among those "Relations" so "visibly included in the nature of our Ideas that we cannot conceive them separable by any Power whatsoever." With Cudworth and Clarke, he was the

The opening manuscript page of Locke's fifth essay on natural law, "An lex naturae cognosci potest ex hominum consensu? Negatur" ("Can the Law of Nature Be Known from the General Consent of Men? No").

assertor of an Eternal and Immutable Morality. But the legitimate influence of the Concepts of Right and Wrong upon the Will, Locke utterly ignored. It is true, he speaks of the Moral and Eternal Obligation which the Rules of Morality evidently possess. It is true, he compares the perception of Moral Obligation to the perception of Mathematical Truth. But Locke never rises to "the height of this great argument." Not only does he hold that the Will is determined by something from without; he holds that what immediately determines the Will is the uneasiness of Desire. The Desire of Happiness is with him the sole motive by which man can be influenced, and Morality is thus divested of all its Moral Power.

If on minor points we compare the two Philosophers, the advantage is wholly on the side of Kant. . . . In the case of Kant, indeed, as in the case of Bacon, the love of System frequently degenerates into an affectation of Symmetry, in which all System is violated and lost. But if the *Kritik* is disfigured by the distortions of System, Locke's *Essay* is characterized by its utter absence. Never was there so systematic a thinker whose exposition was so unsystematic. His cardinal doctrine of Relation, for instance, is to be gathered not only from his chapters on Relation, but from his chapters on Modes and Substances, nay, from the notes appended to his discussion of Simple Ideas; while the whole doctrine of Relation, as developed in the sec-

ond book, is utterly unintelligible without a constant reference to the doctrine of Intuitive Knowledge, as developed in the fourth. It is the same with his Metaphysic as with his Psychology. His doctrine of Real Existence is to be sought not only in the fourth book, but in the second and the first—nay, even among the merely logical questions which constitute the matter of the third. Its fragments are to be found scattered up and down through the whole *Essay,* like the limbs of Absyrtus, the "disjecta membra" ["scattered members"] of Ontology. Add to this that Definitions are no sooner made than they are abandoned; Divisions are no sooner laid down than they are disregarded; Doctrines are no sooner enounced than fresh elements are incidentally introduced. Locke's *Essay,* in fact, is not so much an Essay, as a collection of materials for an Essay. All the Elements of the World of Thought are there, but it presents the appearance of a world emerging from Chaos rather than that of a world developed into Creation.

Closely connected with this absence of Systematic Exposition there is another serious defect in the *Essay concerning Human Understanding,*—the absence of a truly Scientific Language. Here again Locke presents a contrast with his rival. The Scientific Language of Kant satisfies all the requirements of Science. . . . Locke objected to the coining of new words. Locke abandoned the language of the schools. Locke endeavoured to satisfy the exigencies of speculation by the use of the ordinary modes of expression. To use his own metaphor, he made Philosophy appear in the garb and fashion of the times. And what has been the consequence? A superficial and illusive clearness, which has called down the plaudits of superficial thinkers. . . . Whatever may be the merits of Locke's style in a mere literary point of view, the Philosophic Critic is constrained to admit . . . that in his language Locke is of all Philosophers the most vague, vacillating, and various. "Simple Ideas, the Materials of all our knowledge, are suggested and furnished to the Mind only by the two ways, Sensation and Reflection,"—such is the fundamental principle of Locke's Philosophy, enounced in language familiar to the most unphilosophical of readers. But what does Locke mean by "Simple Ideas"? What does he mean by "Materials of Knowledge"? What does he mean by "suggested" as distinguished from "furnished"? What does he mean by "Sensation"? What does he mean by "Reflection"? So far are these expressions from being clear, that they have been universally misunderstood; nay, they have been understood in a sense diametrically the reverse of that which they were intended to convey. It is the same with the terms "Original" and "Derived," "Complex" and "Compound," "Ideas of Comparison" and "Comparison of Ideas." Every word in Locke's Philosophy is an equivoque. Never was there such curious *in*felicity of language.

If we compare Locke and Kant with respect to what is commonly understood by Genius, we must certainly award the palm to Kant. The German Sage was not only endowed with the Spirit of the Philosopher, he was also endowed with the Spirit of the Poet. In the elevation of its tone, and the splendour of its diction, as well as in the unity of its plan, the *Kritik of the Pure Reason* is a Metaphysical Epic. We might style Kant, as Cicero styled Plato, the Homer of Philosophers. But the temperament of Locke was cold. Like his great contemporary, Newton, he possessed the power, but not the passion, of Genius. He discusses the Immortality of the Soul and the Obligations of Morality in the same spirit as he discusses the Primary and Secondary Qualities of Matter. "The Thoughts that wander through Eternity" are invested with no superhuman grandeur as they flit across his page. The austerity of his countenance is reflected in the austerity of his style. Locke was the Philosopher of the Puritans.

Even as a Philosopher the superiority of Kant to Locke can scarcely be denied. He had a clearer and more comprehensive view of the great Metaphysical Problem. He was a more systematic thinker. But in contrasting the *Essay concerning Human Understanding* with the *Kritik of the Pure Reason*, one thing should never be forgotten, and that is the diversity of the circumstances under which they were produced. . . . [While] Kant, like Socrates, had scarcely moved beyond the precincts of his native city, and, unlike Socrates, even amidst the buzz and bustle of that city, had moved self-centred and alone; Locke, from the first, had been a man of the world and a man of action. . . . Physician, Politician, Political Economist, and Philosopher,—Philosophy in his life was but an episode. The account which he gives of the composition of his great work is itself a justification of all its defects. "Begun by chance," "continued by entreaty," "written by incoherent parcels," resumed "as humour or occasions permitted" [see excerpt dated 1690]—what wonder is it if such a work reflects the agitations of his life? The agitations of his life detract from the perfection of his Philosophy, but they can only enhance our estimate of the Philosophical genius which under such circum-

stances bequeathed to posterity so proud a memorial of its power.

The defects of the *Essay concerning Human Understanding* are undeniable. Locke takes no pains to conciliate prejudice, or to guard against misapprehension. He protests against errors without sufficiently marking his recognition of the truths they embody. He inculcates truths without marking his reprobation of the errors to which they are akin. He gives undue prominence to certain elements of thought. Add to this, his exposition is confused; his language is ambiguous; his book abounds in repetition and digression. But the merits of this great work are as undeniable as its defects. It contains the first and most complete exposition of Metaphysical Science to be found in the English language. It furnishes a Philosophy which at once satisfies the exigencies of the Schools and the exigencies of common life. With a sage reserve in pronouncing on matters which lie beyond the reach of our faculties, there is an equally sage reliance upon the veracity of our faculties with reference to the matters which lie within their sphere. Locke is the Metaphysical embodiment of the good sense and practical character of the nation from which he sprung.

But the spirit of Locke's Philosophy, to adopt a phrase originally employed with reference to Descartes, is more valuable than even his Philosophy itself. There breathes throughout the *Essay* a spirit of Intellectual Independence. There breathes a spirit of Intellectual Toleration which is still more rare. . . . ["The] sacred and religious regard for Truth" inculcated by Butler, is seen conspicuous in every page of Locke. Nor has this absolute devotedness to the interests of Truth been unrewarded. The doctrine of the *Essay* may be enveloped in ambiguity, disguised by metaphor, darkened by defective exposition; but still it is, for the most part, *true*. And it is this presence of Truth, "unseen, but not unfelt," that has proved its salvation. No book has been professedly confuted so often, and with such a parade of demonstration, and yet no book has suffered so little from its professed confuters. The philosophical instinct of the ordinary reader has proved a more unerring guide than the philosophical acumen of the professed critic. Though unable to demonstrate that Locke was right, he was dissatisfied with every effort to demonstrate him wrong. He acquiesced, though he could not analyze. Hence it is that the *Essay concerning Human Understanding,* though the driest of all Metaphysical books, has also been the most popular. Hume prophesied that Addison would be read with pleasure when Locke was forgotten, yet it may be doubted whether even the *Spectator* has had a wider circulation than the *Essay*. . . . [And] to the latest posterity, when the native of a foreign land shall wish to pay homage to the philosophical genius of this country, he will speak of it as the country of Bacon and of Locke. (pp. 174-86)

Thomas E. Webb, in his The Intellectualism of Locke: An Essay, *1857. Reprint by Burt Franklin, 1973, 192 p.*

RALPH WALDO EMERSON   (essay date 1876)

[*A founder of the transcendental movement and the shaper of a distinctly American philosophy embracing optimism, individualism, and mysticism, Emerson was one of the nineteenth century's most influential figures. Through such works as* Nature *(1836),* Essays *(First Series, 1841; Second Series, 1844), and* The Conduct of Life *(1860), he preached the doctrine of the spiritual nature of reality, defending the importance of self-reliance and arguing for humanity's obedience to instinct. In the following excerpt from his* English Traits, *a collection of essays based on his English travels during 1847 and 1848, Emerson compares Locke's intellect with Francis Bacon's.*]

Bacon, in the structure of his mind, held of the analogists, of the idealists, or (as we popularly say, naming from the best example) Platonists. Whoever discredits analogy and requires heaps of facts before any theories can be attempted, has no poetic power, and nothing original or beautiful will be produced by him. Locke is as surely the influx of decomposition and of prose, as Bacon and the Platonists of growth. The Platonic is the poetic tendency; the so-called scientific is the negative and poisonous. 'Tis quite certain that Spenser, Burns, Byron and Wordsworth will be Platonists, and that the dull men will be Lockists. Then politics and commerce will absorb from the educated class men of talents without genius, precisely because such have no resistance. (pp. 239-40)

Such richness of genius [as Bacon's] had not existed more than once before. These heights could not be maintained. As we find stumps of vast trees in our exhausted soils, and have received traditions of their ancient fertility to tillage, so history reckons epochs in which the intellect of famed races bacame effete. So it fared with English genius. These heights were followed by a meanness and a descent of the mind into lower levels; the loss of wings; no high speculation. Locke, to whom the meaning of ideas was unknown, became the type of philosophy, and his ''understanding'' the measure, in all nations, of the English intellect. His countrymen forsook the lofty sides of Parnassus, on which they had once walked with echoing steps, and disused the studies once so beloved; the powers of thought fell into neglect. (p. 243)

> Ralph Waldo Emerson, ''Literature,'' in his English Traits, *revised edition, 1876. Reprint by Houghton, Mifflin and Company, 1903. pp. 232-60.*

SIR LESLIE STEPHEN   (essay date 1876)

[*Many scholars consider Stephen the most important English literary critic of the Victorian age after Matthew Arnold. He has been praised for his moral insight and judgment, as well as for his intellectual vigor. Some scholars, however, who consider Stephen's contribution to English literature to be less influential than Arnold's, argue that Stephen's work is deficient in aesthetic and formal analysis and fails to reconcile its author's moral and historical philosophies. The key to Stephen's moral criticism is his theory that all literature is nothing more than an imaginative rendering, in concrete terms, of a writer's philosophy or beliefs. It is the role of criticism, he contends, to translate into intellectual terms what the writer has told the reader through character, symbol, and event. More often than not, Stephen's analysis passes into biographical judgement of the writer. As he once observed, "The whole art of criticism consists in learning to know the human being who is partially revealed to us in his spoken or his written words." In the following excerpt from his* History of English Thought in the Eighteenth Century *(1876), Stephen discusses Locke's place in the history of philosophy and examines his theories concerning innate ideas and human morality in* An Essay concerning Human Understanding.]

The critical movement initiated by Locke and culminating with Hume reflects the national character. The strong point of the English mind is its vigorous grasp of facts; its weakness is its comparative indifference to logical symmetry. English poetry is admirable, because poetry thrives upon a love of concrete imagery; whilst Englishmen have always despised too indiscriminately the dreams of a mystical philosophy which seems to be entirely divorced from the solid basis of fact. In metaphysical speculation their flights have been short and near the ground. They have knocked pretentious systems to pieces with admirable vigour; they have been slow to construct or to accept systems, however elaborately organised, which cannot be constantly interpreted into definite statements and checked by comparison with facts. As one consequence, we perhaps underrate our own philosophical merits. Comparing Locke, or his successors, with the great German writers, we are struck by the apparently narrow, fragmentary, and inconsistent views of our countrymen. If the merit of a philosopher were to be exhaustively measured, not by the number of fruitful principles, but by the variety and order of his applications of his principles, Locke and his successors would occupy a low position. If the courage which passes over a difficulty in order to frame a system be more admirable than the prudence which refuses to proceed beyond clearly established principles, they must be content with a secondary rank. Nor is it doubtful that our dislike to pretentious elaboration often blinds us to the merit of the more daring speculators whose width of view has stimulated thought even whilst covering many fallacious generalities. Yet I believe that the merits of our shrewd and sober, if narrow and one-sided, speculation, will be more highly valued as we recognise the futility of the cloudy structures which it has dissipated.

Locke is in this sense a typical Englishman. He became the intellectual ruler of the century; and for the next two generations the English name was identified by the free-thinkers of the Continent with Locke, liberty, and philosophy. By Locke appears to have been generally meant the denial of innate ideas. And though the general impression that this denial constituted the whole sum and substance of his philosophy may be sometimes taken as a symptom that the eulogist had not got beyond the opening pages of the essay, the popular instinct was probably right. Locke objected to all the existing philosophy, as Descartes objected to the scholastic philosophy, on account of its tendency to run into mere logomachy. The method by which Descartes would escape from the old labyrinth was the rejection of all ideas not clear and all truths not self-evident. Thus would be obtained a firm basis for a mathematically coherent system. But this test, though sound in itself, was not sufficient. The discussions of the Cartesians about the relations of matter and the soul, their attempts to evolve the universe out of their own consciousness, and to pronounce upon questions incapable by their nature of being brought to any definite test, showed the source of the error. The old scholastic fallacies were reviving, and to apply an effectual remedy it was necessary to call in the test of experience. Ideas, it was plain, might be clear and coherent, and yet have no reference to facts. An imaginary world may be constructed behind the real world, which may be as symmetrical and coherent as we please. Nay, any number of such worlds may be constructed; and nobody can say which, if any, is the real one. Leibnitz's monadology may be a true system; but, also, it may not; and our faculties do not enable us to say whether it is or is not. Locke, therefore, began rightly by exorcising the spirit of false philosophy. Get rid of the ideas which do not correspond to actual facts, and of the truths which cannot be tested by experience, and philosophy will be restrained once and for ever from these fruitless and endless attempts to raise its flight above the atmosphere. The theory of innate ideas supplied the basis from which these fights were made; and Locke, therefore, rightly attacked innate ideas. In banishing them, indeed, he was really banishing more than he intended. He argued against a crude form of a theory which had in it an element of truth; and his answer could therefore not be final. The doctrine took a more refined shape, to be met again by more refined forms of Locke's arguments. For the present it is enough to say that he really aimed at the most exposed gap in his opponent's armour, and destroyed for ever the assumptions on which the older forms of ontological speculation were necessarily based.

Locke's victory was decisive and of vital importance; but he did not fully reap its fruits. His inconsistency is characteristic, and served to recommend him to his contemporaries. He fancied that the old system, or large fragments of it, might survive the attack upon its vital principle, and his uncertainty is curiously exhibited in his view of the fundamental ideas of the Cartesian cosmology. No one was less incined than Locke to attack the fundamental tenets of theology; and yet, the idea of God is with Descartes the chief instance of innate ideas, and would be in danger of disappearing with them. Now Locke . . . was profoundly sensible of the futility of theological scholasticism; indeed, it was probably that form of scholasticism which chiefly excited his indignation, as its practical effects had been most disastrous. But his was as anxious to preserve a purified and rational theology as to limit futile speculations into the inscrutable and mysterious tenets of theology. His attack upon innate ideas must not be allowed to weaken the proof of God's existence. As a philosopher he argues elaborately that we have no innate idea of God, and holds that the absence of so important an idea is a strong presumption against innate ideas generally. But as a theological philosopher, he argues that we can prove the existence of God as certainly as we can prove that the angles of a triangle are equal to two right angles. The proof upon which he chiefly insists is the proof from causation, though he, of course, admits others, and does not deny the validity even of the Cartesian proof. Cause, as Hume presently showed, was a doubtful foundation in Locke's system; but of that Locke was unconscious. His attitude towards the soul is rather more sceptical. He denies that the soul always thinks; he gave great offence by declaring that we could not tell without revelation whether the soul were immaterial or immortal; and his theory that personal identity consisted in consciousness threw a suspicion even upon the soul's unity and continuity. His theory in regard to the third great idea is, however, of more importance. His doctrine, that we have but 'an obscure and relative idea of substance in general,' is illustrated by one of those happy comparisons which Locke not unfrequently strikes out. The 'Indian and tortoise' has become a stock metaphor in our literature, and seems to imply that of absolute substance we can by no possibility know anything. But Locke accepted and developed at length the distinction between primary and secondary qualities to recognise the possibility of that kind of knowledge which he seems to disclaim. The primary qualities—solidity, extension, figure, motion, or rest, and number, according to his first numeration—are those which are inseparable from matter generally. This presently becomes identified with the proposition that the primary qualities are really in bodies, 'whether our senses perceive them or no; whereas light, heat, and secondary qualities no more exist in them than "sickness or pain" in manna.' Here, then, Locke is following the philosophy which he assailed. He, like Descartes, is trying to get outside of himself. His distinction assumes that universal perceptions must be independent not only of the constitution of this or that man, but of the constitution of man generally.

Enough has been said to exhibit the inconsistent character of Locke's position. Attacking the theory of innate ideas, he yet retains conceptions vitally associated with that theory. We know of a being who cannot be manifested through the senses, though all our knowledge comes through the senses; and, similarly, we know some qualities, not merely as they are manifested to us, but as they exist in themselves. When such contradictions run through his whole system, it is not surprising that Locke's theory of reality and truth becomes confused. It is enough to point out that, in conformity with his other views, he admits that all natural science is radically uncertain. The 'secondary' qualities being in some sense unreal, all the knowledge conversant with them must be affected by a doubt. It would be a contradiction to suppose that we could discover a 'necessary' connection between them and the primary qualities, for that connection can by its very nature be only discoverable from experience. Certainty is only derivable, as he constantly insists, from the comparison of ideas in our minds. As we can never trace the connection between the ideas and the external or primary qualities which somehow produce them, we can never obtain true knowledge in regard to the sense-given experience. 'In physical things scientifical knowledge will still be out of our reach.' We are, then, already on the road to scepticism, for it is admitted that sense gives no certainty, and yet all other avenues of knowledge are closed. Locke imagines that he has only removed the points which support useless excrescences where he has really struck at the foundations of a system. (pp. 34-8)

· · · · ·

[Locke's] attack upon the doctrine of innate ideas brought him into conflict with the intuitional school of morality. The third chapter of the first book of the [*Essay concerning Human Understanding*] is directed against the ethical application of innate ideas. The argument there stated has served several generations of a utilitarian school; and its cogency within certain limits is irresistible. The theory which he is concerned to overthrow maintains the existence of certain self-evident moral axioms, the truth of which is recognised by all human beings as soon as they are propounded. The metaphysician regards them as ultimate facts, of which no account can be given, unless he chooses to say that they are divinely implanted in the mind. Nature—the metaphysical God—has directly revealed them to all her creatures. It would seem to follow—though there is room for some dispute upon this point—that these moral axioms, whatever they may be, should be recognised throughout the world, and that the moral code of all nations, though not identical to its furthest ramifications, should at any rate comprise a central core of unvarying truth.

Locke may be mistaken in imputing these doctrines to his opponents, but his answer is interesting inasmuch as it involves the germinal principles of the various utilitarian schools. The first doctrine which he avows is common to them all. He declares that he can find no 'innate practical principles,' except 'a desire of happiness and an aversion to misery;' and these are appetites, not intellectual intuitions. 'Good or evil,' as he says in a later chapter, 'are nothing but pleasure and pain, or that which occasions pleasure or pain to us.' The one universal motive being a desire for happiness, the moral impulses must be in some way resoluble into it. An ultimate appeal, as we may say, lies to this principle from every other. There is no moral rule, urges Locke, of which we may not ask the reason, and therefore none can be innate. The rule, for example, of doing as we would be done by is susceptible of proof, and a man to whom it was proposed for the first time might fairly ask that its reasonableness should be made plain to him. Virtue is approved because visibly conducive to happiness, and conscience is merely our opinion of the conformity of actions to certain moral rules, the utility of which has been proved by experience. It is no mysterious judge laying down absolute decisions for inscrutable reasons.

This, the fundamental doctrine of Locke and of all his disciples, is in fact a first form of the primary axiom, upon which depends the possibility of reducing morality within the sphere of scientific observation. It asserts that our moral sentiments have no inscrutable or exceptional character. Its essence consists in banishing mystery from the origin of our moral instincts. If it too easily degenerated into an assertion of the absolute selfishness of human nature, the assertion that the moral sense is derivative was a necessary preliminary to all fruitful investigation of the phenomena.

The doctrine, scientific in spirit if crude in form, is supported by the scientific method of an appeal to experience. Locke insists upon the variability of the moral standard in different races and ages. The 'Tououpinambos,' for example, thought that they would merit paradise by revenge, and by eating their enemies. 'They have not so much as a name for God, and have no religion and no worship,' and these peculiarities of the Tououpinambos may be paralleled by equally stange aberrations of the moral instinct in other races. Now, though a special breach of the law may be no proof that it is unknown, a general permission to break it is a proof that it is not innate. The very recognition of any duty implies the presence in the mind of ideas of God, law, obligation, punishment, and a future life; and these ideas, so far from being universal, are not always clear and distinct, even in 'thinking and studious men.' The vast diversity of opinion which exists would be impossible if threats of Almighty vengeance were stamped in indelible characters upon the minds of all men; nor can anyone, in fact, tell us what are these 'innate practical principles' which are yet asserted to be so palpably evident. Lord Herbert's five principles, for example, are illusory. To say that repentance for sin is a duty is idle, unless you are agreed as to the particular actions which are sinful. And the attempt to evade the appeal to experience by arguing that the innate principles are dulled by education and custom is really a mode of begging the question. The argument comes simply to this; 'the principles which all men allow for true are innate; those that men of right reason admit are the principles allowed by all mankind; we, and those of our mind, are men of reason; wherefore, we agreeing, our principles are innate—which is a very pretty way of arguing and a short cut to infallibility.' The real fact is, that men, having taken up many principles on trust, and having entirely forgotten whence they came, assume them to be divinely implanted axioms; and thus 'doctrines that have been derived from no better original than the superstition of a nurse and the authority of an old woman may, by length of time and consent of neighbours, grow up to the dignity of principles in morality and religion.'

Locke brings down his logical sledgehammer on the principles of his antagonist with masculine vigour. If his objections were crudely stated, the dogmas which he smashes were at least equally crude. But it must granted that he has left little behind him but ruins. We ask, in some alarm, what then is morality? The conscience as a mysterious and independent guide is annihilated; the only motive left is self-interest; and it almost seems as if the Tououpinambos had about as much to say for themselves as the English or the Jews. Mandeville, indeed, in his denial of the real existence of virtue has simply carried Locke's method one step further. Assume that the standard of virtue is so variable that no particular duty can be singled out

as universally binding and recognised, and it is easy to infer that virtue is a mere sham.

No conclusion, of course, could be more repulsive to Locke himself, and it is curious that he did not perceive the application which might be made of his doctrines. Bending his whole energy to destroy the belief in the autocratic and irresponsible character of conscience, he never thinks of supplying its place. Apparently the need of reconstruction scarcely occurred to him. He speaks of the 'eternal and unalterable nature of right and wrong,' and he asserts emphatically that 'morality is capable of demonstration as well as mathematics.' If ethics are mathematically demonstrable, it must be possible to form a code applicable alike to Tououpinambos and Englishmen, or, at least, to assign some fixed principles from which the varying codes might be constructed. Locke would partly answer by referring to the will of God. The discussion is given in the twenty-eighth chapter of his second book, under the head of 'Moral Relations.' He there defines moral good and evil to be the conformity to 'some law,' whereby good and evil are drawn upon us by the will and power of the lawmaker. We are subject to three kinds of laws, the law of God, the civil law, and the 'law of opinion or reputation.' The law of God is enforced by the pains and penalties of the next world. Nobody can take us out of his hands. His will 'is the only true touchstone of moral rectitude; and by comparing them to his law it is that men judge of the most considerable moral good or evil of their actions; that is, whether as duties or sins they are likely to procure them happiness or misery from the hands of the Almighty.' The civil law determines men's criminality or innocence, and the 'philosophical law,' or law of opinion, varying widely in different countries, determines their virtue or vice. This, though wanting in precison, is the law by which men most frequently govern themselves; for its sanctions, vaguer than those of other laws, are more continually present to the imagination than those of the divine law, and less easily evaded than those of the civil law. These various laws may, of course, conflict as in the case of duelling, which is a sin tried by the law of God, a virtuous action by the 'law of fashion'—another synonym for the law of opinion—and a capital crime according to the civil law of some countries.

The law of God, then, is the only permanent and invariable standard; for the other laws vary—and, so far as Locke expounds his theory, vary indefinitely according to time, place, and circumstance. The law of God, too, must override the other laws in case of conflict; or, in his own language, be 'the only true touchstone of moral recititude.' How, then, is the all-important question, can this law be discovered? If God's will be concealed in impenetrable mystery, virtue would apparently become a mere arbitrary fashion. That is Mandeville's solution. If the divine will be discoverable only by revelation, Locke's theory coincides with that of the theological utilitarians. The motive is with him, as with Paley, the dread of hell and the hope of heaven. He tells us himself that the Gospel gives an absolutely pure code of morality, and for that reason he excuses himself to Molyneux for not undertaking to write a treatise on the subject. Locke, however, would not have admitted that our knowledge of morality was dependent on revelation. In fact, the whole argument of the treatise on the *Reasonableness of Christianity* implies that the heathen philosophers could discover a system approximating very closely to that directly promulgated from heaven. How, then, could they arrive at a knowledge of the divine law? What was the criterion by which they were to distinguish between moral good and evil?

The curious vacillation which runs through Locke's reasoning upon morality, and which thus makes moral truth alternately quite uncertain and mathematically demonstrable, is but one instance of the general inconsistency in his theory of reality. According to Locke . . . , our knowledge of the external world cannot be 'scientifical.' We can only know phenomena, and know that they do not correspond (except in the case of the 'primary' qualities) to the objective facts beneath them. Certainty is attained only by comparison of ideas. We may know them adequately, for they exist entirely in our minds. Hence we may obtain certainty in mathematics; we have only to compare our ideas in order to discover geometrical relations, and we know (it matters not how) that those ideas are the counterparts of external realities. The same, according to Locke, may be said of moral relations. Though he expresses himself very indistinctly, his notion seems to be that in moral questions we are reasoning about certain things of which we know 'the precise real essence,' because they are entirely 'ideas in the mind.' Thus, for example, we might compare our idea of justice with our idea of stealing, and observe that they did not correspond; whence the truth that stealing is unjust may be proved with the same certainty as the truth that three angles of a triangle are equal to two right angles. The obvious difficulty is, that this doctrine seems to make morality certain in the sense in which a verbal proposition is certain, and in that sense alone. We are merely unfolding our definition, or explaining that what we call just does not include what we call stealing. This remark was made by Berkeley. 'To demonstrate morality,' he says, in his commonplace book, 'it seems one need only make a discovery of words and see which included which. . . . Locke's instances of demonstration in morality are, according to his own rule, trifling propositions.' Locke, it is clear, never distinctly realised his own position, and whatever escape he might have attempted, it is plain that no such process as he contemplates could be reconciled with his general utilitarianism. The certainty which he would attain is not a certainty as to the tendency of actions to produce happiness. Any such theory must involve an objective element, and, on Locke's general theory, cannot be part of scientific knowledge. Here, as in the whole philosophy of which it forms a part, Locke's teaching is palpably inconsistent, and the attempt to deduce a coherent doctrine would be waste of labour. (pp. 80-6)

Sir Leslie Stephen, "The Philosophical Basis" and "Moral Philosophy" in his History of English Thought in the Eighteenth Century, *Vols. I and II, 1876. Reprint by John Murray, pp. 1-73 and 1-129.*

THOMAS FOWLER (essay date 1880)

[*Fowler was a nineteenth-century English mathematician, classicist, philosopher, historian, and editor whose distinguished career included service as president of Corpus Christi College, Oxford, as vice-chancellor of the University of Oxford, and as University Professor of Logic. The author of numerous works on the history of thought, Fowler is perhaps best remembered for his biographical monographs, including* Locke *(1880),* Francis Bacon *(1881), and* Shaftesbury and Hutcheson *(1882). In the following excerpt from* Locke, *he surveys Locke's writings on trade and finance.*]

The writings of Locke on Trade and Finance are chiefly interesting to us on account of the place which they occupy in the History of Political Economy. . . . The main positions which he endeavours to establish are three. First, interest, or the price of the hire of money, cannot, ordinarily speaking, be regulated by law, and, if it could so be regulated, its reduction below the natural or market rate would be injurious to the interests of the public. Secondly, as silver and gold are commodities not differing intrinsically in their nature from other commodities, it is impossible by arbitrary acts of the Government to raise the value of silver and gold coins. You may, indeed, enjoin by Act of Parliament that sixpence shall henceforth be called a shilling, but, all the same, it will only continue to purchase six-penny-worth of goods. You will soon find that the new shilling is only as effective in the market as the old six-pence, and hence, if the Government has taken the difference, it has simply robbed its subjects to that amount. The third position, which he only maintains incidentally in discussing the other two, is that the commercial prosperity of a country is to be measured by the excess of its exports over its imports, or, as the phrase then went, by the balance of trade. The two former of these propositions are simple, but long-disputed, economical truths. The latter is an obstinate and specious economical fallacy.

To understand Locke's contention on the first point, it must be borne in mind that in his time, and down even to the middle of the present reign, the maximum rate of interest allowable in all ordinary transactions was fixed by law. By [a 1660 statute] . . . it had been reduced from eight to six per cent. Sir Josiah Child, whose *Observations concerning Trade* had been reprinted in 1690, and who probably represented a very large amount of mercantile opinion, advocated its further reduction to four percent. He maintained, quoting the example of Holland, that low interest is the cause of national wealth, and that, consequently, to lower the legal rate of interest would be to take a speedy and simple method of making the country richer. Against this proposal Locke argued that the example of Holland was entirely beside the question; that the low rate of interest in that country was owing to the abundance of ready money which it had formerly enjoyed, and not to any legal restrictions; nay, in the States there was no law limiting the rate of interest at all, every one being free to hire out his money for anything he could get for it, and the courts enforcing the bargain. But, further, suppose the proposed law to be enacted; what would be the consequences? It would be certain to be evaded, while, at the same time, it would hamper trade, by increasing the difficulty of borrowing and lending. Rather than lend at a low rate of interest, many men would hoard, and, consequently, much of the money which would otherwise find its way into trade would be intercepted, and the commerce of the country be proportionately lessened. Excellent as most of these arguments are, Locke unfortunately stopped short of the legitimate conclusion to be drawn from them. He did not propose, as he should have done, to sweep away the usury laws altogether, but simply to maintain the existing law fixing the maximum of interest at six percent. (pp. 186-88)

On the second question, "raising the value of money," Locke's views are much clearer and more consistent than on the first. It would be impossible to state more explicitly than he has done the sound economical dictum that gold and silver are simply commodities, not differing essentially from other commodities, and that the government stamp upon them, whereby they become coin, cannot materially raise their value. As most of my readers are aware, it has been a favourite device, time out of mind, of unprincipled and impecunious governments to raise the denomination of the coin, or to put a smaller quantity of the precious metals in coins retaining the old denomination, with the view of recruiting an impoverished exchequer. There have, doubtless, been financiers unintelligent enough to suppose that this expedient might enrich the government, while it did no harm to the people. But it requires only a slight amount of reflection to see that all creditors are defrauded exactly in the same proportion as that in which the coin is debased. (pp. 189-90)

The general principle that to depreciate the coinage is to rob the creditor, and that, though you may change the name, you cannot change the thing, was quite as emphatically stated by Petty and North as by Locke. But the value of Locke's tracts consisted in their amplitude of argument and illustration, which left to the unprejudiced reader no alternative but to accept their conclusion. As he himself said in a letter to Molyneux, ''Lay by the arbitrary names of pence and shillings, and consider and speak of it as grains and ounces of silver, and 'tis as easy as telling of twenty.''

Locke had the penetration to see that the laws existing in his time against the exportation of gold and silver coin must necessarily be futile, and, while it was permitted to export bullion, could answer no conceivable purpose. . . . Nothing, as Locke says . . . , could prevent the exportation of silver and gold in payment of debts contracted beyond the seas, and it could ''be no odds to England whether it was carried out in specie or when melted down into bullion.'' But the principle on which the prohibition of exporting gold and silver coin ultimately rested seems to have been accepted by him as unhesitatingly as it was by almost all the other economists of the time. That principle was that the wealth of a nation is to be measured by the amount of gold and silver in its possession, this amount depending on the ratio of the value of the exports to that of the imports. . . . [This view forms] part of what political economists call the Mercantile Theory, which it was the peculiar glory of Adam Smith to demolish.

It is somewhat humiliating to the biographer of Locke to be obliged to confess that, in this respect, his theories on trade lag considerably behind those of an almost contemporary writer, Sir Dudley North. . . . Some of North's maxims are worthy of Adam Smith, and one wonders that, when once enunciated, they found so little currency, and were so completely ignored in both the literature and the legislation of the time. (pp. 191-92)

Some of Locke's opinions on trade and finance were undoubtedly erroneous, and it must be confessed that the little tract of Sir Dudley North supplies a better summary of sound economical doctrine than any which we can find in his writings; but then this brochure is merely a summary, with little of argument or elucidation, and perhaps it would be difficult to point to any previous or comtemporary writer whose works are, on the whole, more important in the history of economical science than those of Locke. (p. 193)

> *Thomas Fowler, in his* Locke, *Harper & Brothers, Publishers, 1880, 200 p.*

ALEXANDER CAMPBELL FRASER (essay date 1890)

[*Fraser was a nineteenth-century English philosopher, academic, and editor. An expert in logic and metaphysics, he wrote a full-length study of John Locke's life and works,* Locke *(1890), prepared the* Encyclopaedia Britannica *article on Locke (1892), and edited an elaborate edition of* An Essay concerning Human Understanding *with prolegomena and notes (1894). In the following excerpt from* Locke, *he discusses Locke's* Epistola de tolerantia.]

The *Epistola de tolerantia* has been called the most original of all Locke's works. This opinion may appear doubtful now, when its own success has made its arguments and conclusions commonplace. What when Locke wrote was a paradox, which had to work its way into the minds of men through innumerable obstructions, is the very intellectual air we breathe, so that the super-abundant argument and irony of this famous plea for liberty is apt to weary those who now try to follow its ramifications.

Yet the ''toleration'' for which Locke argued,—the idea which was the mainspring of his life from youth onwards,—then implied a complete revolution in the previously received view of human knowledge and belief. It carried in it elements of revulsion from the dogmatic or absolute point of view that was characteristic of medievalism, while it was in harmony with the critical and relative point of view that, even when Locke lived, was becoming the distinctive mark of the modern spirit,—represented by Luther and the Protestants in religious life, and by Montaigne and Descartes, Campanella and Bacon, in speculative philosophy. Free toleration implied a protest against those who, in theological and other inquiries, demand absolute certainty in questions where balanced probability alone is within reach of a human intelligence. The practice of universal toleration amidst increasing religious differences, in the room which it gives for the exercise of understanding by each person, free from everything except the reasonable restraints of experience, was perhaps at the time the most important practical application of that answer to his own memorable question, about the extent of man's knowledge of the universe, which had been forming in Locke's mind amidst the busy political life of the twenty years before he returned from Holland.

The freedom of religious opinion from political restraints, which Locke argued for, was not entirely a novelty. It had been already defended, upon various grounds, in the seventeenth century. The idea was then entering into the air. Chillingworth, Jeremy Taylor, Glanville, and other philosophical divines of the Church of England, argued for a large toleration by the State, as well as for a generous comprehension on the part of the National Church; on the ground of the natural limits and inevitable weakness of the profoundest merely human understanding of the universe, especially when men's attempts to interpret things carry them into the region of religious thought. Puritans like Owen and Goodwin, on the other hand, whose idea of ecclesiastical comprehension was narrow and dogmatic, defended liberty of different religions within the same nation; while they objected, on grounds of orthodoxy, and as members of separatist communities, to a wide comprehension within their respective sects. The ideal of liberal Anglican churchmen was that of one Church, coextensive at least with the nation, if not even with Christendom. Locke himself, exclusively attached on principle to no one religious organisation, while desirous to be in charitable sympathy with all who loved truth and lived for righteousness in each,—who had for his ideal the simple or practical Christianity of the synoptic gospels, and the ecclesiastical liberty of the apostolic age, as he interpreted it,—brought the test of a sagacious and experienced intelligence to a question which had been largely one either of academic discussion or of sectarian controversy. The intellectual freedom of each person, under whatever civil or ecclesiastical institutions, was his ideal, rather than the collective liberty of societies; for he saw that societies, whether Churches or States, often use their collective liberty to crush persons and their independent judgment. The idea of the State, however, which Locke favoured in some of his earlier unpublished writings, was not the Aristotelian, or that which has for its end the education of the entire man by one social organism. It was rather that of the Puritans, which divides the entire man and a full human life, between the State on the one hand and the Church on the other. In Locke's sober utilitarian imagination and severely argumentative mind, it must be confessed, too, that the idea of toleration lost some of the poetic beauty or philosophic grandeur which it received from Jeremy Taylor and Milton. But it was Locke who first adapted it to the wants of practical statesmen, and by his luminous reasonings carried it into the convictions of the modern world.

A deep and abiding conviction of the narrow limits of man's understanding in the sphere of religion was at the bottom of Locke's argument. While some of his abstract reasonings lead towards a mutual exclusion of the spheres of Church and State, and thus towards the dissolution of that connection between them which has been maintained in one form or another since Europe was conquered by Christianity, he was ready to accept the fact of their union in European civilisation. He only pleaded that it should rest upon a basis comprehensive enough to embrace all whose conduct was in conformity with the spirit of Christ; so that the National Church should be really the Christian nation organised to promote goodness, not to protect the verbal subtleties by which professional theologians have spoiled the simplicity of Christianity in its transmission through the ages. The recall of the national Christianity of England to early simplicity, and so from elaborate dogmas to virtuous life, would, he hoped, render nonconformity or sectarian separation unnecessary, as few would then seek to remain outside the National Church, and thus need toleration. In this respect he receded from the Puritan conception, and approached the Aristotelian and that of Hooker. In this more comprehensive conception of the Church, its functions and that of the State are inseparably blended.

Locke had found all parties and sects, as well as the Church, disposed to persecution. Government had been partial in matters of religion; and yet those who suffered from its partiality had vindicated their rights upon narrow princples, confined in their regard to the immediate interests of their own sects. He felt the need for more generous remedies than had yet been applied. "Absolute liberty, just and true liberty, equal and impartial liberty, is the thing that we stand in need of." A mutual toleration of Christians by Christians, Locke regards as "the chief characteristical mark of the true Church." Sacerdotal succession and external ritual, with that orthodoxy in which each assumes his own orthodoxy, are marks of men striving for power and empire over one another. Let one have ever so true a claim to all these things, yet, if he be destitute of charity, meekness, and goodwill towards all mankind, even to those who are not called Christians, he is still short of being a true Christian himself. He who denies not anything that the Holy Scripture teaches, cannot, he thought, be either a heretic or a schismatic. Religion is not a matter of inheritance. No person is born a member of any Church, which is a free and voluntary society. In each of the many forms of organisation which it adopts, it is only a mean to an end, and a useful mean so far as it expresses and sustains individual religion. But this may be sustained under any of its organical forms; or, in the case of some, independently of all ecclesiastical organisation. Religion lies in the individual, not in any outward organs. This was the spirit of Locke.

The harmlessness to society of most persecuted beliefs is another point insisted on in his argument for toleration by the State, as distinct from comprehension by the Church. "No man," he maintains, "is hurt because his neighbour is of a different religion from his own; and no civil society is hurt because its members are of different religions from one another." On the contrary, when we take into account the necessarily narrow extent of attainable certainties, and still more of those actually attained by each man, we see that even an encouragement of variety in individual opinion, and of the relative freedom of inquiry, may be advantageous to society, because it tends to develop the intellectual resources of mankind, and thus adds to the security for the discovery of truth. The independent activity of each mind makes it probable that a truer and deeper insight of what the lover of truth is in quest of may thus be gradually gained, and added to the previous heritage of the race. Anyhow, physical punishment, and ecclesiastical ostracism or excommunication, are, in Locke's view, unjust and even immoral means for presenting the light of truth to individual minds. Persecution merely transforms the man whom it overawes into a hypocrite. Genuine belief and insight of truth can be attained only according to those methods which are founded on the ways in which knowledge grows in a human mind; consistently with its necessary limits; and on grounds of reasonable probability. As long as a man is out of sight of good and sufficient evidence, he cannot determine his beliefs reasonably; for one cannot, without subsiding into unreasonableness, settle arbitrarily, as a matter of taste or desire, not on evidence, what opinions he should hold. Thus all Locke's pleas for universal toleration at last resolved themselves into his philosophical conclusions as to the origin and limits of the insight into realities that is within the reach of a human being of limited ideas.

But even Locke does not teach the duty of an unlimited toleration by the State. He argues for the forcible suppression of opinions that operate to the dissolution of society, or which subvert those moral rules that are necessary to the preservation of order. He even applies this principle so as to exclude from toleration all who are themselves intolerant, and who will not own and teach the duty of tolerating all other men in matters of religion—"who themselves only ask to be tolerated by the magistrate until they find that they are strong enough to seize the government, and possess themselves of the estates and fortunes of their fellow-subjects." The tyranny of the sects, which had so much scandalised Locke in his youth, was probably here in his view. The political part which, since the Restoration, Catholicism had played in Europe, and especially in England, with the recent Exclusion Bill debates, moved him also to refuse toleration to "a Church constituted upon such a bottom that all who enter into it do thereby deliver themselves up to the protection and service of another prince." He saw in the position of the Roman Church at that time, a political force, which, on grounds of public policy, it was necessary to restrain as dangerous to the newly reconstituted State. Locke also refused toleration to "all who deny the being of God." Atheism, as understood by him, means practically rejection of the principle of order or reason in the universe. "The taking away of God, though but even in thought, dissolves all." If atheism means a practical denial that reason is at the root of things, or thus immanent in the universe in which we, through our experience, participate; and that, while we seem to be living in a cosmos, we are really living in chaos,—then indeed the atheist "dissolves all"; for this atheism is universal scepticism, bound in consistency to surrender the physical and natural sciences, and even common experience, along with the ordinary rules of prudential conduct and expectation, thus making citizenship and society impossible. Thus understood, it would indeed by irreconcilable with the sanity of those who yielded to it. (pp. 90-7)

Alexander Campbell Fraser, in his Locke, *William Blackwood and Sons, 1890, 299 p.*

CHARLES A. BEARD　　(lecture date 1916)

[*Beard was one of the most influential American historians of the early twentieth century. Through his numerous works he directed the course of American historiography from the scientific formalism of his predecessors, who believed that natural law governs the course of history, toward the liberal reformism of the progressives, who viewed history as a record of social, economic, and intellectual choices made by individuals and groups, advocated political and social change based on their studies of the past, and thus sought to improve the future. Beard applied his reformist ideology to several areas of study, becoming widely recognized for his expertise in municipal government, educational development, and domestic and foreign policy. In his most famous and controversial work,* An Economic Interpretation of the Constitution of the United States *(1913), he proposed the thesis that underlies most of his works: that America's past can be best interpreted through an examination of its economic forces. Although Beard's studies have been severely criticized for their economic bias, they have nevertheless exerted a profound influence on modern historical thought. In the following excerpt from a lecture delivered in 1916, Beard notes the role of property in Locke's view of the origin and purpose of government.*]

[John Locke] was, in a serious way, the forerunner of the American and French revolutions as well as the supreme apologist for the English revolution of 1688. All the great French critics of the old régime from Voltaire to Condorcet were familiar with their Locke. . . . Everywhere in the English colonies in America, students of politics were also acquainted with the philosopher of the Glorious Revolution. From him Jefferson drew both inspiration and guidance. Parts of the Declaration of Independence are merely paraphrases of passages in Locke's *Two Treatises on Government*. Like Aristotle and Machiavelli, this English thinker combined literary pursuits with practical affairs, although it must be said that his first-hand experience with politics is not to be compared with that of the Italian or the Greek.

Both the origin and end of the state Locke finds in the roots of property. "To avoid these inconveniences which disorder men's property in the state of nature," he writes, "men unite into societies, that they may have the united strength of the whole society to secure and defend their properties and may have standing rules to bound it, by which every one may know what is his. . . . The reason why men enter into society is the preservation of their property, and the end why they choose and authorize a legislature is that there may be laws made and rules set as guards and fences to the properties of all the members of the society." As the origin of the state is to be found in the requirements of property owners, so is the end of the state to be sought in the same source. "The great and chief end, therefore, of men's uniting into commonwealths and putting themselves under government is the preservation of their property."

As the preservation of property is the origin and end of the state, so it gives the right of revolution against any government or authority that invades property. Such is the economic foundation of the ethics of revolt. "The supreme power cannot take from any man part of his property without his consent." If perchance this is done, the owners of property, the people, have the right to cast off the old form of government and to establish a new one that will observe the ends of civil society. This will not be undertaken, of course, for light and transient reasons, but when a long train of abuses menaces the privileges of property and person, the right of revolution may be exercised. (pp. 25-7)

> *Charles A. Beard, "The Doctrines of the Philosophers," in his* The Economic Basis of Politics, *Alfred A. Knopf, 1922, pp. 9-45.*

JOHN DEWEY　　(essay date 1926)

[*Dewey was one of the most celebrated American philosophers of the twentieth century and the leading philosopher of pragmatism after the death of William James. Dewey gave his pragmatic philosophy the name "instrumentalism." Like James's pragmatism, Dewey's instrumentalism is an action-oriented mode of speculation which judges ideas by their practical results, especially in furthering human adaptation to changing circumstances. Dewey criticized the detached pursuit of truth for its own sake, advocating a philosophy with the specific aim of seeking improvements in various spheres of human life. The author of a number of learned and popular works, including* Democracy and Education *(1916),* Philosophy and Civilization *(1931), and* Logic: The Theory of Inquiry *(1938), he strongly influenced contemporary education and political theory. In the following excerpt from an essay originally published in 1926, Dewey challenges the traditional interpretation of Locke's epistemology.*]

TWO
TREATISES
OF
𝕲𝖔𝖇𝖊𝖗𝖓𝖒𝖊𝖓𝖙:
In the former,
The *false Principles*, and *Foundation*
OF
Sir *ROBERT FILMER*,
And his FOLLOWERS,
ARE
𝕯𝖊𝖙𝖊𝖈𝖙𝖊𝖉 and 𝕺𝖛𝖊𝖗𝖙𝖍𝖗𝖔𝖜𝖓.
The latter is an
ESSAY
CONCERNING THE
True Original, Extent, and End
OF
Civil Government.

LONDON,
Printed for *Awnſham Churchill*, at the *Black Swan* in *Ave-Mary-Lane*, by *Amen-Corner*, 1690.

Title page of the first printing of Two Treatises of Government, *1690.*

According to the ordinary interpretation, Locke explicitly set forth a distinction between ideas as mental and natural objects as physical, while he held that all knowledge of the latter is by means of the former. He thus forced the question of knowledge to take this form: How can ideas which are mental truly represent or know objects which are radically different in kind from themselves? The difficulty of the question was accentuated because Locke divided ideas into two kinds, one of which resembled the objects while the other possessed no likeness to them. I am far from denying that the tenor of Locke's teaching points towards the positions just stated, or that it was practically inevitable that subsequent students of Locke should have been led to them as conclusions. But in this paper I wish to set forth, from a study of Locke himself, the conviction that Locke did not start out with any such conception; that it has a historical source which it is quite possible to point out; and that if Locke had avoided becoming entangled with traditional conceptions which are inconsistent with his own positive teachings, he might have developed an empirical theory of knowledge which would neither contain nor suggest the epistemological problem referred to above.

What is significant and original in Locke is his insistence that knowledge consists in the perception of a *relation*. It is true that he defines this as a relation between ideas. But it is also true that Locke was in no sense the originator of the doctrine that the object of knowledge is an idea; such was the teaching of the schools, using idea not to denote anything mental or psychical, but to signify "form," "species." And officially and intentionally Locke did not depart from this conception: by idea he means, as he says, simply "the immediate object of the mind in thinking"—thinking being used in the Cartesian sense to denote the act of being aware of. It is an *object* of mind; it is the real object as it becomes the object of awareness; it is not a state or content of mind, any more than it was with the scholastics. Where Locke departs from scholastic and classic theory is in holding that knowledge is not the apprehension of form or idea as such, but is the apprehension of a relation between forms or ideas.

But Locke was also obviously influenced by the new physical science, by Boyle, Newton, and other representatives of the new physics. Now this new physics had no use for species and forms in the classic sense. It substituted minute corpuscles mathematically or quantitatively defined. Let one deny the metaphysical reality of species and forms (ideas) in the old sense and still retain that part of the old theory which holds that the form or idea is the immediate object of the mind in knowing, and one enters upon a course which is full of snares and inconsistencies—as Locke found to his cost and to the perverting of pretty much all English theories of knowledge, psychological and epistemological, since his day.

But this is not the whole of the story. If knowledge is perception of relations, and if knowledge is to have to do with real natural existence, then Locke should have concluded that existence, as the subject matter of knowledge, is inherently relational. But Locke did not have the courage of his convictions; or rather he did not have the perspicacity of his convictions; he did not see what they implied. He retained the old notion of separate, independent substances, each of which has its own inner constitution or essence. Knowledge which grasps only relations—such as were the staple of the new physics—cannot grasp an inner essence, which remains accordingly hidden and mysterious. In final analysis, the opposition between the inner constitution and essence (which Locke retained from prior meta-

physics) and the relations which are knowable (his own contribution) is the source of the opposition which we are familiar with as the Lockian contrast between idea and object.

Nor is this quite the whole of the story. In the older metaphysics causation meant an operating and compelling force, emanating from substances and by some mysterious influence producing change in other substances. Clearly a relational theory of knowledge calls for quite a different notion of causation, if it is to have any place at all in the structure of knowledge. Any thoroughgoing acknowledgement of the implications of the relational theory of knowledge would soon have arrived at the conclusion that causality signifies simply the relation of orderly seriality among events. In this case the discovery that certain qualities (like colors) are "caused" by material corpuscles in conjunction with organic physiological structures would have been simply to discover one interesting and important succession in a single and homogeneous order of natural events. It would not have implied a mysterious power in physical objects to produce "ideas" in something totally different, namely, mind. But Locke retained the old conception of causation as well as of independent substances. In consequence he is constantly forced to move in the direction of the doctrine that the order of ideas is of one sort of existence and that of things (substances) is of another kind, while they are yet so related that the order of independent substances is the causally productive source of the order of ideas, while the latter is cognitively representative of the former, and the sole evidence of its existence. Here are all the materials of the epistemological problem, and if Locke did not make the implications explicit, his successors soon did so.

The usual statement of Locke's position concerning primary and secondary qualities fails to convey it in Locke's own terms. The Lockian terms are concerned with distinction of qualities in respect to *substances*, not in respect to being physical and mental, or objective and subjective. He makes a threefold distinction of qualities, not a dual one. The first kind corresponds in form to the traditional "essential" attributes, though differing radically in content. And this fact locates his primary contradiction. For his statement of the concrete nature of what he terms primary qualities is such as absolutely to destroy the classic distinction between essence, properties, accidents, and relations. Primary qualities are according to him such as "are utterly inseparable from the body in what state soever it be; such as . . . it constantly keeps." Like essence in classic thought they make it what it is; they constitute its formal cause. But instead of being such affairs as stoniness, humanity, etc., together with, in the case of physical substances, certain "sensible forms," they are "solidity, extension, figure, and mobility." Physical substances according to him are particles or corpuscles whose nature or essence is to have such properties. Since such properties, however, are not absolute but relational, he was in reality doing away with the old notion of substances, and along with it destroying the old notion of formal constitutive essence.

His secondary qualities are almost frankly relational in the modern sense of relational. They are powers in substances to produce by means of their primary qualities certain effects in us, such effects as colors, sounds, smells, tastes, etc. It is, be it noted, the power to produce which is called secondary, not the effects themselves. Then there is a "third sort," namely, the power of the primary properties to produce changes in other things—such as the power of fire by its primary qualities of bulk, texture, and motion of particles to produce a new consistency in wax. More explicitly, it is the ''power that is in any body by reason of the particular constitution of its primary qualities, to make such a change in the bulk, figure, texture and motion of *another body,* as to make it operate on our senses differently from what it did before.''

Taken strictly and literally, then, there is first a distinction between properties which are inherently, always and absolutely, in the substance, without which it cannot exist at all, and others which characterize a connection with other things, and which do not exist except where acting and being acted upon are found. Of the latter there are two sorts. There are those which designate power to produce effects like softness, weight, or acceleration in other things, and those which designate power to produce qualities like pain, griping, color, noise, taste, by acting upon the senses of an organic body. In both cases, the distinction depends upon maintaining a fixed separation between intrinsic essential properties and relational extrinsic ones. And, as before noted, the properties selected by Locke as intrinsically constitutive apart from acting and being acted upon, namely, bulk, figure, motion, and situation, are precisely the properties which in physical science are now treated as relational, not absolute.

The extent to which Locke retained the formal conceptions of substance and essence, while assigning to them a concrete content which negated the traditional meanings, is clear enough in his treatment of substance. Nominally he reduces it to an unknown substrate, which is a step toward eliminating it in its classic sense. But he retains the conception that things have essential natures. Thus, while he holds empirical (or ''nominal'') essences to be abstract ideas employed for the purpose of sorting (classifying) and discriminating, he never questions the existence of *real* essences. They are the ''constitution of the insensible parts of a body upon which'' the sensible qualities depend. Essence is the *''foundation* of all those qualities which are the ingredients of our complex idea.'' Or, more formally, ''by this real essence I mean the real constitution of anything, which is the foundation of all those properties which are combined in and are found constantly to coexist with the nominal essence; that particular constitution which everything has within itself, *without any relation to anything without it.''* Scores of passages could be quoted to the effect that this ultimate and intrinsic constitution is that upon which *all* the properties of things depend and from which they flow. ''What is that texture of parts, that real essence, that makes lead and antimony fusible, wood and stones not?'' ''It is true every substance that exists has its peculiar constitution, whereon depend those sensible qualities and powers we observe in it.'' ''By what right is it that fusibility comes to be a part of the essence signified by the word gold, and solubility but a property of it? or why is its color part of its essence, and its malleableness but a property? That which I mean is this, that these all being but properties, *depending on its real constitution,* and nothing but powers, either active or passive in relation to other bodies, no one has authority to determine the signification of the word gold (as referred to such a body existing in nature) more to one collection of ideas as found in that body than to another.'' In his chapters on knowledge he is constantly referring to the ''real constitution of the minute parts on which their qualities do depend''; ''the real constitution of substances whereon our simple ideas depend and which really is the cause of the strict union of some of them with one another, and the exclusion of others.''

The customary account of Locke misrepresents him by treating secondary qualities as something found in the mind, while to Locke . . . they signify the power of certain properties of substance to produce certain effects ''in us''—to employ his favorite and ambiguous phrase. . . . Locke follows the classic tradition which opposes ''relations'' to essence as the extrinsic to the intrinsic. The stock example of relation is ''quantity'' which varies without alteration of essence; a thing may be more or less, greater or smaller, without ceasing to be what it is; hence, quantity is an ''accident.'' Like every accident or nonessential change, it depends upon matters outside the thing itself; it is a relation, not a property, since not flowing from essence. While following this tradition, Locke also associates relation with comparison. ''When the mind so considers one thing that it does as it were bring it to and set it by another, and carries its view from one to the other; this is, as the words import, relation and respect; and the denominations given to positive things intimating that respect, and serving as marks to lead the thought beyond the subject itself denominated, to something distinct from it are what we call relatives; and the things so brought together, related.'' Examples are whiter in contrast with white; husband in contrast with man; father and son; servant, captain, enemy, patron; bigger and less; cause and effect, etc. And he remarks, ''Change of relation may be without any change in the subject.'' Caius remains Caius, although he ceases to be father when his son dies. Also we have clear ideas of the relation when the ideas of the things related are ''obscure and imperfect.'' This fact is of great significance in connection with mathematics and morals as demonstrative sciences.

Relations are thus opposed by Locke to the intrinsic constitution of a thing and also to the properties which directly depend upon this essence. And what is more important for our present purposes it is also marked off from what he terms ''connexion,'' both ''necessary connexion'' and ''real coexistence'' or as he frequently terms it ''going together.'' (pp. 205-11)

The traditional and current theory is that the difficulty with which Locke labors is the epistemological dilemma: things which we immediately know are mental, and we know physical or ''objective'' things only by the intervention of these mental things, while these mental things are themselves the effect of physical things. Given these premises there is certainly an epistemological problem distinct from any metaphysical or cosmological problem. But Locke's own theory is that we know essences of substances only through their powers, and powers only through their effects (which, as we have directly to do with them, he terms ideas of sensation or sensible qualities); and as we are not able to trace any *necessary* connection between the effects and their operative efficacious causes, we have no certain knowledge of the connection of the effects with one another. That is, we can know *in general* that the essence of things is the bulk, contexture, figure, and number of particles which have the power of communicating motion, but we cannot know the particular properties which produce in any particular case the particular effect or quality which is immediately present or with which we are in contact. The difficulty is not that primary qualities are physical while secondary are mental, but that we cannot ascertain the *necessary connection* which physically exists between causative powers and their effects. (p. 215)

[The] difficulty is that our organs of perception are not fitted to yield effects which are comparable in subtlety and minuteness to the real structure or constitution of things, and hence we can never establish the detailed and specific necessary connections that exist between causes and effects. For that reason, *and for that reason alone,* we cannot make universal and necessary statements, or attain knowledge (certainty) regarding the relations of the effects (ideas) to one another. (p. 216)

If Locke had held that the limits and uncertainty of our propositions about physical things were due to the fact that we know by means of ideas which are different in kind from the things, it would have been the easiest thing in the world for him to say so. But that to which he actually assigns the limitations of our physical knowledge is that "the *connexion between most simple ideas* is unknown." In his own words, knowledge of such connection is "very narrow and scarce any at all," for the "simple ideas whereof our complex ideas of substances are made up are, for the most part, such as carry with them in their own nature, no visible necessary connexion or inconsistency with any other simple ideas." (p. 217)

[Locke's discussion of the "Extent of Human Knowledge" and "Univeral Propositions" in *An Essay concerning Human Understanding*] is noteworthy for the explicit distinction it makes between the internal essence and the properties that flow directly from it and the properties that are due to "extrinsical causes." "Put a piece of gold anywhere by itself, separate from the reach and influence of all other bodies, it will immediately lose all its color and weight, and perhaps malleableness too; which for all I know would be changed into a perfect friability." Certainly Locke does not intend to imply that weight is a "subjective" or "mental" state, but that it depends upon connection with other things—namely, gravitation. Hence the passage is particularly instructive as to what is signified by "secondary" qualities in general. As he summarizes the matter: "Things however absolute and entire they seem in themselves, are but retainers to other parts of nature for that which they are most taken notice of by us." In this passage Locke seems almost on the verge of denying the very existence of ultimate disconnected things, a denial which would have radically altered his whole conception of knowledge, but he immediately returns to the idea of the absolute, intrinsic essence of things as that which, so to say, *ought* to be known, but which cannot be known, because qualities due to connections with other things so overlay them. (pp. 218-19)

[The] fact that Locke applies exactly the same logic to the matter of the perception of degree of likeness among *secondary qualities* seems to be crucially conclusive. Different degrees (shades) of color depend upon the size, position, number, and motion of minute insensible corpuscles. Therefore they may be *really* different although they are *sensibly* alike to us. We cannot *know* (have certainty) as to the degrees of similarity existing between two whitenesses. "Not knowing, therefore, what number of particles, nor what motion of them, is fit to produce any precise degree of whiteness, we cannot *demonstrate* the certain equality of any two degrees of whiteness; because we have no certain standard to measure them by, nor means to distinguish every the least real difference." This passage in itself completely refutes the current notion that Locke's secondary qualities are states of consciousness or of mind. If they were, their appearance would be their being; if they were alike in "consciousness" they would *be* alike. It is safe to issue a challenge to anyone who holds the traditional interpretation to explain this passage.

It is no part of the present enterprise to set forth just what Locke's positive theory of knowledge becomes when his theory of existence is made to square with his theory of knowledge. It is plain, however, that unless existences are in some aspect or phase connected instead of disconnected, and that unless the connectedness of things (or things in their connectedness)

is the proper object of knowledge, there is an unbridgeable gap between things and any knowledge which operates, as Locke's does, in terms of the perception of connections. It is enough for our present purpose that Locke repeatedly sets forth the gist of what his theory becomes when revised. "Ideas" are so connected together in experience that they serve with varying degrees of probability to point to and distinguish the complex interconnected wholes of which an "idea" ia a part. A certain yellowness enables us to distinguish gold from silver, a taste wine from water, and so on. And this function, as he repeatedly states, answers all our purposes: in fact, as he says in one passage, it would probably prove embarrassing if we could detect the inner essence, while other things remain as they now are. In short, it is enough if the connectedness of things is such as to render possible the relationship of *implication* and the act of *inference*. Berkeley put his finger on the point when he said [in his *Principles of Human Knowledge*]: "The connexion of ideas does not imply the relation of cause and effect, but only of a mark or sign with the things signified."

With this substitution, a distinction between those qualities which Locke calls secondary and those which he calls primary remains of value, though the Lockian interpretation is altered. Primary qualities cease to be the counterparts of traditional essential attributes and the efficacious causes of secondary; they are those qualities of things which serve as the most accurate, dependable, and comprehensive signs; the qualities most important and most available for reasoning in the *implication* relation. Sweetness has turned out to be a much less valuable *sign* than is the "bulk, number and texture" of extended parts. (pp. 219-20)

John Dewey, "Substance, Power, and Quality in Locke," in Freedom and Experience: Essays Presented to Horace M. Kallen, *edited by Sidney Hook and Milton R. Konvitz, Cornell University Press, 1947, pp. 205-20.*

GEORGE SANTAYANA   (lecture date 1932)

[*Santayana was a Spanish-born philosopher, poet, novelist, and literary critic who was for the most part educated in the United States, taking his undergraduate and graduate degrees at Harvard University, where he later taught philosophy. His earliest published work was* Sonnets, and Other Verses (1894). *Although Santayana is regarded as no more than an adequate poet, his facility with language distinguishes his philosophical works. Written in an elegant, nontechnical prose, Santayana's earliest major philosophical study is the five-volume* Life of Reason (1905-06), *which applies a materialist viewpoint to the study of society, religion, art, and science, and, along with* Scepticism and Animal Faith (1923) *and the four-volume* Realms of Being (1927-40) *puts forth the view that while reason undermines belief in anything whatever, an irrational animal faith suggests the existence of a "realm of essences" leading to the human search for knowledge. Late in his life Santayana stated that "reason and ideals arise in doing something that at bottom there is no reason for doing." "Chaos," he wrote earlier, "is perhaps at the bottom of everything." In the following excerpt from a paper read before the Royal Society of Literature on the tercentenary of John Locke's birth, Santayana probes Locke's natural philosophy.*]

A good portrait of Locke would require an elaborate background. His is not a figure to stand statuesquely in a void: the pose might not seem grand enough for bronze or marble. Rather he should be painted in the manner of the Dutch masters, in a sunny interior, scrupulously furnished with all the implements of domestic comfort and philosophic enquiry: the Holy Bible open majestically before him, and beside it that other revelation—the terrestrial globe. His hand might be pointing to a microscope set for examining the the internal constitution of a beetle: but for the moment his eye should be seen wandering through the open window, to admire the blessings of thrift and liberty manifest in the people so worthily busy in the marketplace, wrong as many a monkish notion might be that still troubled their poor heads. From them his enlarged thoughts would easily pass to the stout carved ships in the river beyond, intrepidly setting sail for the Indies, or for savage America. Yes, he too had travelled, and not only in thought. He knew how many strange nations and false religions lodged in this round earth, itself but a speck in the universe. There were few ingenious authors that he had not perused, or philosophical instruments that he had not, as far as possible, examined and tested; and no man better than he could understand and prize the recent discoveries of "the incomparable Mr Newton". Nevertheless, a certain uneasiness in that spare frame, a certain knitting of the brows in that aquiline countenance, would suggest that in the midst of their earnest eloquence the philosopher's thoughts might sometimes come to a stand. Indeed, the visible scene did not exhaust the complexity of his problem; for there was also what he called "the scene of ideas", immaterial and private, but often more crowded and pressing than the public scene. Locke was the father of modern psychology, and the birth of this airy monster, this half-natural changeling, was not altogether easy or fortunate.

I wish my erudition allowed me to fill in this picture as the subject deserves, and to trace home the sources of Locke's opinions, and their immense influence. Unfortunately, I can consider him—what is hardly fair—only as a pure philosopher: for had Locke's mind been more profound, it might have been less influential. He was in sympathy with the coming age, and was able to guide it: an age that confided in easy, eloquent reasoning, and proposed to be saved, in this world and the next, with as little philosophy and as little religion as possible. Locke played in the eighteenth century very much the part that fell to Kant in the nineteenth. When quarrelled with, no less than when embraced, his opinions became a point of departure for universal developments. The more we look into the matter, the more we are impressed by the patriarchal dignity of Locke's mind. Father of psychology, father of the criticism of knowledge, father of theoretical liberalism, god-father at least of the American political system, of Voltaire and the Encyclopaedia, at home he was the ancestor of that whole school of polite moderate opinion which can unite liberal Christianity with mechanical science and with psychological idealism. He was invincibly rooted in a prudential morality, in a rationalised Protestantism, in respect for liberty and law: above all he was deeply convinced, as he puts it, "that the handsome conveniences of life are better than nasty penury". Locke still speaks, or spoke until lately, through many a modern mind, when this mind was most sincere; and two hundred years before Queen Victoria he was a Victorian in essence.

A chief element in this modernness of Locke was something that had hardly appeared before in pure philosophy, although common in religion: I mean, the tendency to deny one's own presuppositions—not by accident or inadvertently, but proudly and with an air of triumph. (pp. 1-4)

In Locke the central presuppositions, which he embraced heartily and without question, were those of common sense. He adopted what he calls a "plain, historical method", fit, in his own words, "to be brought into well-bred company and polite conversation". Men, "barely by the use of their natural faculties", might attain to all the knowledge possible or worth having. All children, he writes, "that are born into this world, being surrounded with bodies that perpetually and diversely affect them" have "a variety of ideas imprinted" on their minds. "External material things as objects of Sensation, and the operations of our own minds as objects of Reflection, are to me", he continues, "the only originals from which all our ideas take their beginnings." "Every act of sensation", he writes elsewhere, "when duly considered, gives us an equal view of both parts of nature, the corporeal and the spiritual. For whilst I know, by seeing or hearing, . . . that there is some corporeal being without me, the object of that sensation, I do more certainly know that there is some spiritual being within me that sees and hears."

Resting on these clear perceptions, the natural philosophy of Locke falls into two parts, one strictly physical and scientific, the other critical and psychological. In respect to the composition of matter, Locke accepted the most advanced theory of his day, which happened to be a very old one: the theory of Democritus that the material universe contains nothing but a multitude of solid atoms coursing through infinite space: but Locke added a religious note to this materialism by suggesting that infinite space, in its sublimity, must be an attribute of God. He also believed what few materialists would venture to assert, that if we could thoroughly examine the cosmic mechanism we should see the demonstrable necessity of every complication that ensues, even of the existence and character of mind: for it was no harder for God to endow matter with the power of thinking than to endow it with the power of moving. (pp. 5-7)

[The] important philosophical question is the one raised by the other half of Locke's natural philosophy, by optics and the general criticism of perception. How far, if at all, may we trust the images in our minds to reveal the nature of external things?

On this point the doctrine of Locke, through Descartes, was also derived from Democritus. It was that all the sensible qualities of things, except position, shape, solidity, number and motion, were only ideas in us, projected and falsely regarded as lodged in things. In the things, these imputed or secondary qualities were simply powers, inherent in their atomic constitution, and calculated to excite sensations of that character in our bodies. This doctrine is readily established by Locke's plain historical method, when applied to the study of rainbows, mirrors, effects of perspective, dreams, jaundice, madness, and the will to believe: all of which go to convince us that the ideas which we impulsively assume to be qualities of objects are always, in their seat and origin, evolved in our own heads.

These two parts of Locke's natural philosophy, however, are not in perfect equilibrium. *All* the feelings and ideas of an animal must be equally conditioned by his organs and passions, and he cannot be aware of what goes on beyond him, except as it affects his own life. How then could Locke, or could Democritus, suppose that his ideas of space and atoms were less human, less graphic, summary, and symbolic, than his sensations of sound or colour? The language of science, no less than that of sense, should have been recognised to be a human language; and the nature of anything existent collateral with ourselves, be that collateral existence material or mental, should have been confessed to be a subject for faith and for hypothesis, never, by any possibility, for absolute or direct intuition. (pp. 8-10)

There were other presuppositions in the philosophy of Locke besides his fundamental naturalism; and in his private mind probably the most important was his Christian faith, which was not only confident and sincere, but prompted him at times to high speculation. He had friends among the Cambridge Platonists, and he found in Newton a brilliant example of scientific rigour capped with mystical insights. Yet if we consider Locke's philosophical position in the abstract, his Christianity almost disappears. In form his theology and ethics were strictly rationalistic; yet one who was a Deist in philosophy might remain a Christian in religion. There was no great harm in a special revelation, provided it were simple and short, and left the broad field of truth open in almost every direction to free and personal investigation. A free man and a good man would certainly never admit, as coming from God, any doctrine contrary to his private reason or political interest; and the moral precepts actually vouchsafed to us in the Gospels were most acceptable, seeing that they added a sublime eloquence to maxims which sound reason would have arrived at in any case.

Evidently common sense had nothing to fear from religious faith of this character; but the matter could not end there. Common sense is not more convinced of anything than of the difference between good and evil, advantage and disaster; and it cannot dispense with a moral interpretation of the universe. Socrates, who spoke initially for common sense, even thought the moral interpretation of existence the whole of philosophy. He would not have seen anything comic in the satire of Molière making his chorus of young doctors chant in unison that opium causes sleep because it has a dormitive virtue. The virtues or moral uses of things, according to Socrates, were the reason why the things had been created and were what they were; the admirable virtues of opium defined its perfection, and the perfection of a thing was the full manifestation of its deepest nature. Doubtless this moral interpretation of the universe had been overdone, and it had been a capital error in Socrates to make that interpretation exclusive and to substitute it for natural philosophy. Locke, who was himself a medical man, knew what a black cloak for ignorance and villainy Scholastic verbiage might be in that profession. He also knew, being an enthusiast for experimental science, that in order to control the movement of matter—which is to realise those virtues and perfections—it is better to trace the movement of matter materialistically; for it is in the act of manifesting its own powers, and not, as Socrates and the Scholastics fancied, by obeying a foreign magic, that matter sometimes assumes or restores the forms so precious in the healer's or the moralist's eyes. At the same time, the manner in which the moral world rests upon the natural, though divined, perhaps, by a few philosophers, has not been generally understood; and Locke, whose broad humanity could not exclude the moral interpretation of nature, was driven in the end to the view of Socrates. He seriously invoked the Scholastic maxim that nothing can produce that which it does not contain. For this reason the unconscious, after all, could never have given rise to consciousness. Observation and experiment could not be allowed to decide this point: the moral interpretation of things, because more deeply rooted in human experience, must envelop the physical interpretation, and must have the last word.

It was characteristic of Locke's simplicity and intensity that he retained these insulated sympathies in various quarters. A further instance of his many-sidedness was his fidelity to pure intuition, his respect for the infallible revelation of ideal being, such as we have of sensible qualities or of mathematical relations. In dreams and in hallucinations appearances may de-

ceive us, and the objects we think we see may not exist at all. Yet in suffering an illusion we must entertain an idea; and the manifest character of these ideas is that of which alone, Locke thinks, we can have certain "knowledge". (pp. 13-16)

This sounds like high Platonic doctrine for a philosopher of the Left; but Locke's utilitarian temper very soon reasserted itself in this subject. Mathematical ideas were not only lucid but true: and he demanded this truth, which he called "reality", of all ideas worthy of consideration: mere ideas would be worthless. Very likely he forgot, in his philosophic puritanism, that fiction and music might have an intrinsic charm. (p. 17)

[In Locke's view, the] actual existence of mind was evident: you had only to notice the fact that you were thinking. Conscious mind, being thus known to exist directly and independently of the body, was a primary constituent of reality: it was a fact on its own account. Common sense seemed to testify to this, not only when confronted with the "I think, therefore I am" of Descartes, but whenever a thought produced an action. Since mind and body interacted, each must be as real as the other and, as it were, on the same plane of being. Locke, like a good Protestant, felt the right of the conscious inner man to assert himself: and when he looked into his own mind, he found nothing to define this mind except the ideas which occupied it. The existence which he was so sure of in himself was therefore the existence of his ideas.

Here, by an insensible shift in the meaning of the word "idea", a momentuous revolution had taken place in psychology. Ideas had originally meant objective terms distinguished in thought—images, qualities, concepts, propositions. But now ideas began to mean living thoughts, moments or states of consciousness. They became atoms of mind, constituents of experience, very much as material atoms were conceived to be constituents of natural objects. Sensations became the only objects of sensation, and ideas the only objects of ideas; so that the material world was rendered superfluous, and the only scientific problem was now to construct a universe in terms of analytic psychology. Locke himself did not go so far, and continued to assign physical causes and physical objects to some, at least, of his mental units; and indeed sensations and ideas could not very well have other than physical causes, the existence of which this new psychology was soon to deny: so that about the origin of its data it was afterwards compelled to preserve a discreet silence. But as to their combinations and reappearances, it was able to invoke the principle of association: a thread on which many shrewd observations may be strung, but which also, when pressed, appears to be nothing but a verbal mask for organic habits in matter. (pp. 18-20)

[Locke] was restive in his orthodoxy and timid in his heresies; and like so many other initiators of revolutions, he would be dismayed at the result of his work. In intention Locke occupied an almost normal philosophic position, rendered precarious not by what was traditional in it, like the categories of substance and power, but rather by certain incidental errors—notably by admitting an experience independent of bodily life, yet compounded and evolving in a mechanical fashion. But I do not find in him a prickly nest of obsolete notions and contradictions from which, fledged at last, we have flown to our present enlightenment. In his person, in his temper, in his allegiances and hopes, he was the prototype of a race of philosophers native and dominant among people of English speech, if not in academic circles, at least in the national mind. If we make allowance for a greater personal subtlety, and for the diffidence and perplexity inevitable in the present moral anarchy of the world, we may find this same Lockian eclecticism and prudence in the late Lord Balfour: and I have myself had the advantage of being the pupil of a gifted successor and, in many ways, emulator, of Locke, I mean William James. So great, at bottom, does their spiritual kinship seem to me to be, that I can hardly conceive Locke vividly without seeing him as a sort of William James of the seventeenth century. And who of you has not known some other spontaneous, inquisitive, unsettled genius, no less preoccupied with the marvellous intelligence of some Brazilian parrot, than with the sad obstinacy of some Bishop of Worcester? Here is eternal freshness of conviction and ardour for reform; great keenness of perception in spots, and in other spots lacunae and impulsive judgments; distrust of tradition, of words, of constructive argument; horror of vested interests and of their smooth defenders; a love of navigating alone and exploring for oneself even the coasts already well charted by others. Here is romanticism united with a scientific conscience and power of destructive analysis balanced by moral enthusiasm. Doubtless Locke might have dug his foundations deeper and integrated his faith better. His system was no metaphysical castle, no theological acropolis: rather a homely ancestral manor house built in several styles of architecture: a Tudor chapel, a Palladian front toward the new geometrical garden, a Jacobean parlour for political consultation and learned disputes, and even—since we are almost in the eighteenth century—a Chinese cabinet full of curios. It was a habitable philosophy, and not too inharmonious. There was no greater incongruity in its parts than in the gentle variations of English weather or in the qualified moods and insights of a civilised mind. Impoverished as we are, morally and humanly, we can no longer live in such a rambling mansion. It has become a national monument. On the days when it is open we revisit it with admiration; and those chambers and garden walks re-echo to us the clear dogmas and savoury diction of the sage—omnivorous, artless, loquacious—whose dwelling it was. (pp. 23-6)

> George Santayana, "Locke and the Frontiers of Common Sense," in his Some Turns of Thought in Modern Philosophy: Five Essays, *Charles Scribner's Sons, 1933, pp. 1-47.*

BASIL WILLEY (essay date 1934)

[*Willey is an English academic whose numerous studies of English literature and culture have earned him his colleagues' high regard. The author of over fifty works, he is perhaps best known for his pioneering books of intellectual history, among them* The Seventeenth Century Background: Studies in the Thought of the Age in Relation to Poetry and Religion *(1934),* The Eighteenth Century Background: Studies on the Idea of Nature in the Thought of the Period *(1940), and* Nineteenth Century Studies: Coleridge to Matthew Arnold *(1949). In the following excerpt from* The Seventeenth Century Background, *he surveys Locke's place among his contemporaries, noticing, among other issues, his subject's political and religious opinions and his attitude toward poetry.*]

The Newtonian world-picture, and Locke's picture of the mind, came to be, in the eighteenth century, the normal possession of the educated and enlightened of Europe. Locke, in particular, has been described [by Alfred Cobban in his *Edmund Burke and the Revolt Against the Eighteenth Century* (1929)] as 'the writer whose influence pervades the eighteenth century with an almost scriptural authority'. This remark is doubtless truer of Locke's political writings than of his philosophy, for as a recent editor [A. S. Pringle-Pattison] of the ***Essay Concerning Human Understanding*** has said, 'the subsequent course of European philosophy consists largely of a series of attempts to

clear up the ambiguities of Locke's terminology and to surmount the difficulties created for him by his presuppositions'. Nevertheless it was Locke who determined the direction of this 'subsequent course', and he may truly be called, after Descartes, the founder of modern philosophy. For Addison, and the men of letters in general, he was 'the philosopher', somewhat as Aristotle had been for the schoolmen. The supremacy which Milton held in heroic poetry, and Newton in physics, belonged in philosophy to Locke. Moreover, his authority was not confined to this one sphere; indeed, the prestige of his philosophical work was itself ascribable to the wide acceptance of his views on political liberty and religious toleration. As the philosophic vindicator of the Glorious Revolution he was, unlike Hobbes, in the position to supply his generation with precisely the doctrine most congenial to them. In celebrating the final triumph of Whig principles over the Stuarts, Locke founded the 'liberal' tradition of political thought which was vigorous in the eighteenth century, and inspired both the American and French Revolutions. Locke's authority was behind the eighteenth century belief in the inalienable rights of the human individual as such, and in the 'natural' and 'original' liberties of man.

> Man being born, . . . with a title to perfect freedom and uncontrolled enjoyment of all the rights and privileges of the law of nature . . . no one can be put out of this estate and subjected to the political power of another, without his own consent.
>
> **[Treatise of Civil Government]**

The 'State of Nature', in Locke, is so far from resembling the 'ill condition' described by Hobbes, that it approximates rather to the Eden of the religious tradition, or the golden age of the poets. After Locke, this conception becomes an expression of the current faith that, on the whole, *things if left to themselves are more likely to work together for good than if interfered with by meddling man.* To this conception of 'Nature' as a system of divine laws whose workings, if unimpeded by governmental or other interference, will produce the greatest happiness of the greatest number, must be ascribed the *laissez-faire* economics of later times, and the confidence in the virtues of unrestricted competition in industry. In Locke's political theory the thing to be explained was, not by what fortunate device men escaped from the State of Nature, but what motives could ever have induced them to desert their Eden. The explanation he gives is highly characteristic. In the state of nature, in spite of all its advantages, *Property* was insecure, and it was to remedy this defect that men entered into the Social Contract. Locke is never more completely the spokesman of the Whig oligarchy than in his insistence on the protection of property as the characteristic function of government. The 'Rights of Man', as yet, are the rights of Proprietors. Locke is the father of nineteenth century as well as eighteenth century 'liberalism'.

In his religious writings, too . . . , he gave his age just what it was ready to receive, a reasoned plea for toleration and a demonstration of the Reasonableness of Christianity. It was Locke's appointed task to work up into a system all the assumptions about God, Nature and Man which, as the seventeenth century storm-clouds drew off, seemed to most men to stand firm and unquestionable in the light of common day. Locke is like Milton in numerous ways—in his Puritan upbringing, in his passion for liberty, in his rational piety, in his feeling for human dignity, in his views on education, in his sense of the limits of human knowledge, in his acceptance of scripture; but he is a Milton without the garland and the singing-robes. It is wholly in the cool element of prose that Locke lives and moves. The passionate sense of life as perilous, glorious or tragic which inspired Milton to prophecy, whether in prose or in verse, has all departed; instead, there is a feeling of security, of confidence in the rationality of the universe, in the virtuousness of man, in the stability of society, and in the deliverances of enlightened common sense; while underneath are the everlasting arms. The things that were most real to Locke were also the things that were most real to the majority of his readers for several generations. The very limitations of his mind fitted him to be the accepted thinker of an age which had lost the taste for spiritual exploration. There is a safeness in Locke's mental habits which made him a fit guide for readers of the *Spectator;* when he comes to a speculative precipice he does not peer over it with dread or fascination, but gives it a glance and returns promptly to the path of common sense.

Locke's prose style is the best index of his mind, and the mind of his age as well. Like Wren's architecture, it is harmonious, lucid and severe, rising occasionally into a dome of manly eloquence. The prose of Browne, Milton or even Hobbes looks Gothic by the side of it. In reading Locke we are conscious of being in the presence of a mind which has come to rest in the 'philosophic' world-view. There is no more of the metaphysical flicker from world to world, none of the old imagery struck out in the heat of struggle or in the ardour of discovery. Locke writes philosophy in the tone of well-bred conversation, and makes it his boast to have discarded the uncouth and pedantic jargon of the schools. His air is that of a gentleman who, along with a group of like-minded friends, proposes to conduct a disinterested enquiry into truth. The very ease of his prose betokens a mind at rest in its own assumptions, and reveals how fully Locke could count on these being also the assumptions of his readers. His vocabulary is almost wholly abstract and uncoloured; what he offers us is always the reasoning of a grave and sober man, not the visions of enthusiasm or the fictions of poetry. (pp. 265-69)

I have ventured to compare Locke with Milton; but a comparison, say, of their respective essays on Education reveals, together with many ideas held in common, an instructive difference in tone and aim—the difference, one might perhaps say, between Renaissance and Augustan ethics. Both believe in education for life and not for learning's sake only; and both believe that an incredible syllabus may be got through 'between twelve and twenty, less time than is now bestowed in pure trifling at grammar and sophistry.' But whereas Milton aims at inspiring his pupils with 'high hopes of living to be brave men, and worthy patriots, dear to God and famous to all ages', and 'infusing into their young breasts such an ingenuous and noble ardour, as would not fail to make many of them renowned and matchless men', Locke, with the general aim of producing a 'sound mind in a sound body', has more particularly in view the 'breeding' of a 'gentleman's son' rather than the rearing of heroes or saints. He discourses of the things that are 'convenient and necessary to be known by a gentleman'; and we feel that we are nearer to Lord Chesterfield than to Milton when Locke tells us that 'it is necessary in this learned age' for a gentleman to study natural philosophy 'to fit himself for conversation', and when he prescribes dancing-lessons as the cure for clownishness. Milton's heroic tone is absent; and it will suffice for Locke's ideal pupil, whose lot is cast in a less warlike age, to conduct himself in accordance with the dictates of Reason, Religion and Good Breeding. (pp. 270-71)

[What, if anything, did Locke's] influential philosophy mean for poetry? Most of us to-day consider the arts to hold some-

thing of a central position amongst the activities of human existence, and it is hardly to be supposed that a system of thought which affected the outlook of several generations can have had no relevance whatever for poetry. Locke himself seems to have taken no interest in art, and the few references he makes to poetry are of a disparaging kind. This fact alone is significant, and suggests part of the answer to our question. Philosophers of earlier and of later ages, particularly those of the nineteenth century, have thought it necessary to find a place in their systems for the 'imaginative' way of approaching truth, and some have given it the very highest credentials. But seventeenth century philosophers as a whole, and Locke above all, did not feel this necessity. . . . Locke summed up in his work the doctrines and assumptions of the seventeenth century, and his great influence imposed them bodily upon the eighteenth as unquestionable truths. That the things which were most real to Locke—his metaphysically-certified God, his outer world of geometrical atoms, and his inner world of mathematical ideas—were not the realities of poetry, will perhaps be generally allowed, suspicious though we rightly are of all romantic presuppositions about what is poetic. Locke's philosophy is the philosophy of an age whose whole effort had been to arrive at 'truth' by exorcising the phantasms of the imagination, and the truth-standards which the eighteenth century inherited through him involved the relegation of the mind's shaping-power to an inferior status. What Locke himself thought of 'the imagination', and of 'poetry', as he understood these terms, can be illustrated from his remarks on 'wit' and 'judgment'. The mind, though passive in perception becomes active in all the subsequent processes of reflection, which include compounding, comparing, and abstracting from the ideas that sensation has impressed upon it. Our complex ideas so formed are 'real' when they correspond to an actual state of affairs in the 'real' world; or again, they are real if they are mathematical, that is to say, if they are *wholly* the 'workmanship of the mind', and are thus exempted, by their abstract nature, from having any reference to external 'things'. Other mental compounds are 'fantastic', 'chimerical' fictions of our fancies. These may indeed be allowed for purposes of pleasure, but no philosopher can regard them as having any serious importance. 'Wit', for Locke, as for Hobbes and Dryden, consists in a certain 'quickness of parts', whereby the contents of memory—the storehouse of impressions—are readily available when needed. Men who have 'a great deal of wit and prompt memories', however, are not usually distinguished for the 'clearest judgment' or 'deepest reason'. For wit consists in a facility for assembling or combining any ideas which may seem to have some congruity with each other,

> thereby to make up pleasant pictures and agreeable
> visions in the fancy.

Wit is completely irresponsible, concerning itself not a jot with the 'truth' or 'reality' of its conceits. Judgment, on the other hand, proceeds by a method exactly contrary—by the method, in fact, which it is Locke's whole purpose to recommend. It carefully distinguishes one idea from another, wherever the least difference is discernible, so as to avoid being 'misled by similitude' into mistaking one thing for another. Locke emphasises the radical opposition between this method and that of 'wit'; it is evidently a matter of importance to him to 'place' poetry as unambiguously as he can:

> This is a way of proceeding quite contrary to metaphor and allusion, wherein for the most part lies that *entertainment and pleasantry of wit* which strikes so lively on the fancy, and therefore so acceptable to

all people, because its beauty appears at first sight, and there is required *no labour of thought to examine what truth or reason there is in it.*

The mind is content to be amused with 'the agreeableness of the picture', and the 'gaiety of the fancy'; its pleasure would be spoiled by the application of the 'severe rules of *truth and good reason,* whereby it appears that *it consists in something that is not perfectly conformable to them'.* And for what was not conformable to 'truth and good reason' Locke could not be expected to have a very high regard. We get a glimpse of his true feelings about poetry in his ***Thoughts Concerning Education,*** where he declares that if a child has a poetic vein, the parents, so far from cherishing it, 'should labour to have it stifled and suppressed as much as may be'. The air of Parnassus may be pleasant, but its soil is barren.

Thus do all charms fly 'at the touch of cold philosophy'. I do not wish to suggest, however, that the ascendancy of Locke, or the wide acceptance of his standards of truth, made every sort of poetry impossible. We of this generation have less cause than our predecessors to undervalue the poetic output of the eighteenth century. Conformity to truth and good reason is never a wholly bad principle, even for poets; and we owe to it much first-rate satire, as well as a work like the *Essay on Man.* What the cold philosophy did destroy was the union of heart and head, the synthesis of thought and feeling, out of which major poetry seems to be born. There were, it is true, elements in Locke's oddly-composite system which later proved of unexpected service to poetry. The doctrine which derived all our knowledge from the senses was capable of serving Wordsworth, who imbibed it through Hartley, as a philosophic sanction for his own most deep-rooted instincts, and furnished him with at least a foundation for his conscious poetic theory. Wordsworth was working in the spirit and tradition of Locke when he rejected gaudy and inane phraseology and devoted his powers to the task of making verse 'deal boldly with substantial things'. And in a sense, moreover, Locke's 'new way of knowing by ideas', his insistence that all we can contemplate is mind-stuff, contained the implication (though Locke would not have welcomed it) that 'mind is incorrigibly poetical'. But all this could as yet mean to the average intelligent man of letters is illustrated by Addison in one of his papers on 'Chearfulness'. Concerned, as always, to put a favourable interpretation upon everything, Addison finds in the limitation of our knowledge to 'ideas' a source of satisfaction rather than of humiliation. If the material world, he says, had appeared to us 'endow'd only with *those real Qualities which it actually possesses,* it would have made but a very joyless and uncomfortable Figure'. A kindly Providence, therefore, has given matter the power of producing in us a whole series of delightful 'imaginary' qualities, to the end that man might 'have his Mind cheared and delighted with agreeable Sensations'. In indulging in the Pleasures of the Imagination, therefore, we are doing something not unworthy of a rational being, and something, moreover, which has the approval of Heaven.

But, of course, much more than this was required before there could arise a theory of the imagination adequate to the dignity of poetry, and much had to be added to Locke's sensationalism before it could be pressed into the service of the creative power. Above all, there was required the conviction that the 'inanimate cold world' of the mechanical philosophy was not the whole reality, that there was a closer bond between the mind and nature than the old dualism could conceive, and the 'Truth'

was not given to the naked Reason, but was constituted, in moments of impassioned vigilance, by the whole soul of man

> Working but in alliance with the works
> Which it beholds.

(pp. 290-95)

Basil Willey, "John Locke," in his The Seventeenth Century Background: Studies in the Thought of the Age in Relation to Poetry and Religion, *Columbia University Press, 1934, pp. 264-95.*

BERTRAND RUSSELL (essay date 1945)

[*A respected and prolific author, Russell was an English philosopher and mathematician known for his support of humanistic concerns. Two of his early works,* Principles of Mathematics *(1903) and* Principia Mathematica *(1910-1913), written with Alfred North Whitehead, are considered classics of mathematical logic. His philosophical approach to all his endeavors discounts idealism or emotionalism and asserts a progressive application of his "logical atomism," a process whereby individual facts are logically analyzed. Russell's humanistic beliefs often centered around support of unorthodox social concerns, including free love, undisciplined education, and the eradication of nuclear weapons. His staunch pacifism during World War I led to a six-month imprisonment and began a history of political and social activism which culminated when, at the age of eighty-nine, he was again jailed for his active participation in an unruly demonstration advocating unilateral nuclear disarmament. After the incident Russell stated: "What I want is some assurance before I die that the human race will be allowed to continue." Regarding Russell, biographer Alan Wood wrote: "He started by asking questions about mathematics and religion and philosophy, and went on to question accepted ideas about war and politics and sex and education, setting the minds of men on the march, so that the world could never be quite the same as if he had not lived." In recognition of his contributions in a number of literary genres, Russell was awarded the Nobel Prize in literature in 1950. In the following excerpt from his* History of Western Philosophy *(1945), in which he approaches philosophy "not as the isolated speculations of remarkable individuals, but as both an effect and a cause of the character of the various communities in which different systems flourished," Russell surveys Locke's theory of knowledge and his conception of the state of nature and natural law.*]

Locke's philosophy, as it appears in the [*Essay concerning Human Understanding*] has throughout certain merits and certain demerits. Both alike were useful: the demerits are such only from a *theoretical* standpoint. He is always sensible, and always willing to sacrifice logic rather than become paradoxical. He enunciates general principles which, as the reader can hardly fail to perceive, are capable of leading to strange consequences; but whenever the strange consequences seem about to appear, Locke blandly refrains from drawing them. To a logician this is irritating; to a practical man, it is proof of sound judgement. Since the world is what it is, it is clear that valid reasoning from sound principles cannot lead to error; but a principle may be so nearly true as to deserve theoretical respect, and yet may lead to practical consequences which we feel to be absurd. There is therefore a justification for common sense in philosophy, but only as showing that our theoretical principles cannot be quite correct so long as their consequences are condemned by an appeal to common sense which we feel to be irresistible. The theorist may retort that common sense is no more infallible than logic. But this retort, though made by Berkeley and Hume, would have been wholly foreign to Locke's intellectual temper.

A characteristic of Locke, which descended from him to the whole Liberal movement, is lack of dogmatism. Some few certainties he takes over from his predecessors: our own existence, the existence of God, and the truth of mathematics. But wherever his doctrines differ from those of his forerunners, they are to the effect that truth is hard to ascertain, and that a rational man will hold his opinions with some measure of doubt. This temper of mind is obviously connected with religious toleration, with the success of parliamentary democracy, with *laissez-faire,* and with the whole system of liberal maxims. Although he is a deeply religious man, a devout believer in Christianity who accepts revelation as a source of knowledge, he nevertheless hedges round professed revelations with rational safeguards. On one occasion he says: "The bare testimony of revelation is the highest certainty," but on another he says: "Revelation must be judged by reason." Thus in the end reason remains supreme. (pp. 606-07)

What Locke means by "reason" is to be gathered from his whole book. There is, it is true, a chapter called "Of Reason," but this is mainly concerned to prove that reason does not consist of syllogistic reasoning, and is summed up in the sentence: "God has not been so sparing to men to make them barely two-legged creatures, and left it to Aristotle to make them rational." Reason, as Locke uses the term, consists of two parts: first, an inquiry as to what things we know with certainty; second, an investigation of propositions which it is wise to accept in practice, although they have only probability and not certainty in their favour. "The grounds of probability," he says, "are two: conformity with our own experience, or the testimony of other's experience." The King of Siam, he remarks, ceased to believe what Europeans told him when they mentioned ice. (pp. 607-08)

Locke is, as a rule, contemptuous of metaphysics. *A propos* of some speculation of Leibniz's, he writes to a friend: "You and I have had enough of this kind of fiddling." The conception of substance, which was dominant in the metaphysics of his time, he considers vague and not useful, but he does not venture to reject it wholly. He allows the validity of metaphysical arguments for the existence of God, but he does not dwell on them, and seems somewhat uncomfortable about them. Whenever he is expressing new ideas, and not merely repeating what is traditional, he thinks in terms of concrete detail rather than of large abstractions. His philosophy is piecemeal, like scientific work, not statuesque and all of a piece, like the great Continental systems of the seventeenth century.

Locke may be regarded as the founder of empiricism, which is the doctrine that all our knowledge (with the possible exception of logic and mathematics) is derived from experience. Accordingly the first book of the *Essay* is concerned in arguing, as against Plato, Descartes, and the scholastics, that there are no innate ideas or principles. In the second book he sets to work to show, in detail, how experience gives rise to various kinds of ideas. (pp. 609-10)

Our ideas are derived from two sources, (*a*) sensation, and (*b*) perception of the operation of our own mind, which may be called "internal sense." Since we can only think by means of ideas, and since all ideas come from experience, it is evident that none of our knowledge can antedate experience.

Perception, he says, is "the first step and degree towards knowledge, and the inlet of all the materials of it." This may seem, to a modern, almost a truism, since it has become part of educated common sense, at least in English-speaking countries. But in his day the mind was supposed to know all sorts of things *a priori,* and the complete dependence of knowledge upon perception, which he proclaimed, was a new and revolutionary doctrine. Plato, in the *Theaetetus,* had set to work to refute the identification of knowledge with perception, and from his time onwards almost all philosophers, down to and including Descartes and Leibniz, had taught that much of our most valuable knowledge is not derived from experience. Locke's thorough-going empiricism was therefore a bold innovation. (p. 610)

Empiricism and idealism alike are faced with a problem to which, so far, philosophy has found no satisfactory solution. This is the problem of showing how we have knowledge of other things than ourself and the operations of our own mind. Locke considers this problem, but what he says is very obviously unsatisfactory. In one place we are told: "Since the mind, in all its thoughts and reasonings, hath no other immediate object but its own ideas, which it alone does or can contemplate, it is evident that our knowledge is only conversant about them." And again: "Knowledge is the perception of the agreement or disagreement of two ideas." From this it would seem to follow immediately that we cannot know of the existence of other people, or of the physical world, for these, if they exist, are not merely ideas in any mind. Each one of us, accordingly, must, so far as knowledge is concerned, be shut up in himself, and cut off from all contact with the outer world.

This, however, is a paradox, and Locke will have nothing to do with paradoxes. Accordingly, in another chapter, he sets forth a different theory, quite inconsistent with the earlier one. We have, he tells us, three kinds of knowledge of real existence. Our knowledge of our own existence is intuitive, our knowledge of God's existence is demonstrative, and our knowledge of things present to sense is sensitive. . . . (pp. 611-12)

In the next chapter, he becomes more or less aware of the inconsistency. He suggests that some one might say: "If knowledge consists in agreement of ideas, the enthusiast and the sober man are on a level." He replies: "Not so where ideas agree with things." He proceeds to argue that all *simple* ideas must agree with things, since "the mind, as has been showed, can by no means make to itself" any simple ideas, these being all "the product of things operating on the mind in a natural way." And as regards complex ideas of substances, "all our complex ideas of them must be such, and such only, as are made up of such simple ones as have been discovered to coexist in nature." Again, we can have no knowledge except (1) by intuition, (2) by reason, examining the agreement or disagreement of two ideas, (3) "by sensation, perceiving the existence of particular things." . . .

In all this, Locke assumes it known that certain mental occurrences, which he calls sensations, have causes outside themselves, and that these causes, at least to some extent and in certain respects, resemble the sensations which are their effects. But how, consistently with the principles of empiricism, is this to be known? We experience the sensations, but not their causes; our experience will be exactly the same if our sensations arise spontaneously. The belief that sensations have causes, and still more the belief that they resemble their causes, is one which, if maintained, must be maintained on grounds wholly independent of experience. The view that "knowledge is the perception of the agreement or disagreement of two ideas" is the one that Locke is entitled to, and his escape from the paradoxes that it entails is effected by means of an inconsistency so gross that only his resolute adherence to common sense could have made him blind to it. (p. 612)

No one has yet succeeded in inventing a philosophy at once credible and self-consistent. Locke aimed at credibility, and achieved it at the expense of consistency. Most of the great philosophers have done the opposite. A philosophy which is not self-consistent cannot be wholly true, but a philosophy which is self-consistent can very well be wholly false. The most fruitful philosophies have contained glaring inconsistencies, but for that very reason have been partially true. There is no reason to suppose that a self-consistent system contains more truth than one which, like Locke's, is obviously more or less wrong. (p. 613)

• • • • •

[Just after] the Revolution of 1688, Locke wrote his two *Treatises on Government,* of which the second especially is very important in the history of political ideas. (p. 617)

Locke begins his second *Treatise on Government* [*An Essay concerning the True Original, Extent, and End of Civil Government*] by saying that, having shown [in his first *Treatise*] the impossibility of deriving the authority of government from that of a father, he will now set forth what he conceives to be the true origin of government.

He begins by supposing what he calls a "state of nature," antecedent to all human government. In this state there is a "law of nature," but the law of nature consists of divine commands, and is not imposed by any human legislator. It is not clear how far the state of nature is, for Locke, a mere illustrative hypothesis, and how far he supposes it to have had a historical existence; but I am afraid that he tended to think of it as a stage that had actually occurred. Men emerged from the state of nature by means of a social contract which instituted civil government. This also he regarded as more or less historical. But for the moment it is the state of nature that concerns us.

What Locke has to say about the state of nature and the law of nature is, in the main, not original, but a repetition of medieval scholastic doctrines. (p. 623)

In Locke's theory of government, I repeat, there is little that is original. In this Locke resembles most of the men who have won fame for their ideas. As a rule, the man who first thinks of a new idea is so much ahead of his time that every one thinks him silly, so that he remains obscure and is soon forgotten. Then, gradually, the world becomes ready for the idea, and the man who proclaims it at the fortunate moment gets all the credit. So it was, for example, with Darwin; poor Lord Monboddo was a laughing-stock.

In regard to the state of nature, Locke was less original than Hobbes, who regarded it as one in which there was war of all against all, and life was nasty, brutish, and short. But Hobbes was reputed an atheist. The view of the state of nature and of natural law which Locke accepted from his predecessors cannot be freed from its theological basis; where it survives without this, as in much modern liberalism, it is destitute of clear logical foundation.

The belief in a happy "state of nature" in the remote past is derived partly from the biblical narrative of the age of the patriarchs, partly from the classical myth of the golden age. The general belief in the badness of the remote past only came with the doctrine of evolution.

The nearest thing to a definition of the state of nature to be found in Locke is the following:

> Men living together according to reason, without a common superior on earth, with authority to judge between them, is properly the state of nature.

This is not a description of the life of savages, but of an imagined community of virtuous anarchists, who need no police or law-courts because they always obey "reason," which is the same as "natural law," which, in turn, consists of those laws of conduct that are held to have a divine origin. (For example, "Thou shalt not kill" is part of natural law, but the rule of the roads is not.) (pp. 624-25)

[It appears] that, where most men are in the state of nature, there may nevertheless be some men who do not live according to the law of nature, and that the law of nature provides, up to a point, what may be done to resist such criminals. In a state of nature, we are told, every man can defend himself and what is his. "Who so sheddeth man's blood, by man shall his blood be shed" is part of the law of nature. I may even kill a thief while he is engaged in stealing my property, and this right survives the institution of government, although, where there is government, if the thief gets away I must renounce private vengeance and resort to the law.

The great objection to the state of nature is that, while it persists, every man is the judge in his own cause, since he must rely upon himself for the defence of his rights. For this evil, government is the remedy, but this is not a *natural* remedy. The state of nature, according to Locke, was evaded by a compact to create a government. Not any compact ends the state of nature, but only that of making one body politic. The various governments of independent States are now in a state of nature towards each other.

The state of nature, we are told in a passage presumably directed against Hobbes, is not the same as a state of war, but more nearly its opposite. After explaining the right to kill a thief, on the ground that the thief may be deemed to be making war upon me, Locke says:

> And here we have the plain "difference between the state of nature and the state of war," which, however some men have confounded, are as far distant, as a state of peace, good-will, mutual assistance and preservation, and a state of enmity, malice, violence and mutual destruction are from one another.

Perhaps the *law* of nature must be regarded as having a wider scope than the *state* of nature, since the former deals with thieves and murderers, while in the latter there are so such malefactors. This, at least, suggests a way out of an apparent inconsistency in Locke, consisting in his sometimes representing the state of nature as one where every one is virtuous, and at other times discussing what may rightly be done in a state of nature to resist the aggressions of wicked men.

Some parts of Locke's natural law are surprising. For example, he says that captives in a just war are slaves by the law of nature. He says also that by nature every man has a right to punish attacks on himself or his property, even by death. He makes no qualification, so that if I catch a person engaged in petty pilfering I have, apparently, by the law of nature, a right to shoot him.

Property is very prominent in Locke's political philosophy, and is, according to him, the chief reason for the institution of civil government:

The great and chief end of men uniting into commonwealths, and putting themselves under government, is the preservation of their property; to which
in the state of nature there are many things wanting.

The whole of this theory of the state of nature and natural law
is in one sense clear but in another very puzzling. It is clear
what Locke thought, but it is not clear how he can have thought
it. Locke's ethic . . . is utilitarian, but in his consideration of
"rights" he does not bring in utilitarian considerations. Something of this pervades the whole philosophy of law as taught
by lawyers. *Legal* rights can be defined: broadly speaking, a
man has a legal right when he can appeal to the law to safeguard
him against injury. A man has in general a legal right to his
property, but if he has (say) an illicit store of cocaine, he has
no legal remedy against a man who steals it. But the lawgiver
has to decide what legal rights to create, and falls back naturally
on the conception of "natural" rights, as those which the law
should secure. (pp. 626-27)

[We may] identify "natural law" with moral rules in so far as
they are independent of positive legal enactments. There must
be such rules if there is to be any distinction between good
and bad laws. For Locke, the matter is simple, since moral
rules have been laid down by God, and are to be found in the
Bible. When this theological basis is removed, the matter becomes more difficult. But so long as it is held that there is an
ethical distinction between right actions and wrong ones, we
can say: Natural law decides what actions would be ethically
right, and what wrong, in a community that had no government;
and positive law ought to be, as far as possible, guided and
inspired by natural law. (p. 628)

> *Bertrand Russell, "Locke's Theory of Knowledge"*
> *and "Locke's Political Philosophy," in his* A History
> of Western Philosophy, and Its Connection with Po-
> litical and Social Circumstances from the Earliest
> Times to the Present Day, *Simon & Schuster, 1945,*
> *pp. 604-17, 617-40.*

HUNTINGTON CAIRNS   (essay date 1949)

[*An American lawyer, educator, editor, and author, Cairns was
an expert in both the law and the fine arts. He has been described
by several writers as a Renaissance man, as he directed his studies
toward a variety of intellectual disciplines, interweaving them
with the common thread of his rationalist philosophy. The author
of works on tax law, French literature, the social sciences, and
the visual arts, Cairns is perhaps best known for his many writings
on legal history, including* Legal Philosophy from Plato to Hegel
(1949), *a work described by the leading German jurist Hans
Kelsen as especially successful in illustrating a coherent connection between society and the law. In the following excerpt from
this work, Cairns describes Locke's conception of prepolitical
society, chiefly as it is reflected in* Two Treatises of Government
and An Essay concerning Human Understanding.]

Locke hoped in his political theory, at the core of which was
his idea of law, to find, as a basis for the State, some sagacious
principle the self-evident virtues of which would be plain to
practical men. He was an intelligent man with a large experience in constitutional affairs who wrote on philosophical subjects. But his dominant impulse was not philosophical: he was
fearful of the unfamiliar. "Our business here is not to know
all things," he wrote, "but those which concern our conduct."
His philosophy was thus a philosophy of the middle area; he
began with the familiar, and for the most part did not pass
beyond it in either of the two directions in which speculative
inquiry moves. He did not attempt, in one direction, to justify

the primary ideas on which his whole system rested. On this
subject he took for granted the thought of his time. Thus,
although his connections with the Cambridge Platonists were
close, he nevertheless undertook an examination of the nature
and extent of knowledge without any prior inquiry into the
character of reality, a procedure entirely foreign to their practices and, indeed, to that of philosophy generally. He also failed
to move very far in the other direction, towards a consideration
of the consequences of the propositions established in his system. This is not a matter of much importance, provided indicia
are present in the system which will enable readers to draw
the necessary conclusions themselves. But on significant issues
Locke has too frequently halted his speculation at a point which
does not permit readers to draw conclusions. Thus Locke argued that government is established by society, and may therefore be disestablished by it. But who is to judge when the
government has betrayed its trust to the extent necessary to
justify an act of revolution? Locke answers, "the people." But
by what means is this judgment to be taken? By a plebiscite?
Rioting in the streets? An act of revolution itself? Locke does
not provide the answer to the question, nor is it possible to
deduce it from the propositions of his system.

By avoiding abstractness at one end and complexity at the
other, Locke kept his philosophical position free of elements
which are held to discourage popular interest. It may be remarked, however, that the wide acceptance at various times
of certain theological systems which embraced those elements
to a high degree might have indicated that the foundations of
this supposition needed examination. At any rate, not the least
of the interest we have in Locke's philosophy today is due to
its vast influence on practical affairs. . . . Nevertheless, altogether apart from their problematical future, Locke's ideas
deserve study as a typical way of approach to the problems of
the legal order. It is not the approach of the philosophical
specialist, who can exclude nothing from his purview, but that
of the temperate sagacious man, whose efforts are directed to
things which seem to him really to matter.

Locke's first step in the development of his theory of law was
to deny, in accordance with his general philosophical position,
that the law of nature was innate. He argued that a rule of
conduct imposes a duty; but what a duty is cannot be understood
without a law, and a law cannot be known, or supposed, without a lawmaker, or without reward and punishment. It is therefore impossible for a rule of conduct to be innate (that is,
imprinted on the mind as a duty) without supposing the ideas
of God, law, obligation, punishment, and a life after death,
also to be innate. But these ideas are so far from being innate,
that it is not every studious man, much less every one that is
born, in whom they are to be found clear and distinct. However,
because Locke denies an innate law, he must not be thought
as holding there are nothing but positive laws. He believes
there is a great difference between something imprinted on our
minds at the outset and something that we, being ignorant of,
may attain to the knowledge of by the due application of our
natural faculties. Thus, he believes they equally forsake the
truth who, running into the contrary extremes, either affirm an
innate law, or deny that there is a law knowable by the light
of nature, that is, without the help of positive revelation.
(pp. 335-37)

Locke's next step is to invoke the conception of a state of
nature. This condition he defines for men as "a state of perfect
freedom to order their actions, and dispose of their possessions
and persons as they think fit, within the bounds of the law of

Nature, without asking leave or depending upon the will of any other man.'' This conception is a strict deduction from the proposition which he lays down with respect to political power, the self-evident validity of which he takes for granted and which he consequently advances no arguments to sustain: ''Political power . . . I take to be a right of making laws, with penalties of death, and consequently all less penalties for the regulating and preserving of property, and of employing the force of the community in the execution of such laws, and in the defence of the commonwealth from foreign injury, and all this only for the public good.'' Locke's idea of political power is thus a formal one. He finds in the law-making function the single element which distinguishes the power of the state from that of a father over his children, a master over his servant, a husband over his wife, and a lord over his slave. In spite of the large element of truth in Locke's assertion, we must recognize that as a complete factual description of political authority it is inadequate. It enables him to distinguish the State from the family and from economic organizations. But if, as Ratzenhofer and Small have done, we choose to look at the social process as one of a conflict of group interests, we arrive at a conception of political power as an arrangement of combinations by which mutually repellant forces are brought into some measure of concurrent action. In the performance of that function law is an important, but not the only, tool. Conciliation, propaganda, war, and many other devices, are instruments to that end. Locke's premise should therefore be understood as valid only for the purposes of his argument, and inasmuch as one of his conscious and valid techniques was the employment of such abstractions, it is fair to assume that he meant it to be taken in that manner.

Thus Locke arrived at a conception of a state of nature on purely rational grounds; he did not appeal to the thought of the Middle Ages, to the Roman lawyers, to the Stoics or to Aristotle as authorities upon which to base it. He argued merely that political power is the right to make law and to punish for the public good. Take away that power and men have perfect freedom to order their actions within the bounds of the law of nature. As a strictly formal argument—apart from the introduction of the idea of natural law, in which Locke is anticipating himself—no exception can be taken to it. However, the argument must not be understood as asserting an actual historical condition. Locke himself was fully aware of the force—and the limitations—of that criticism by his opponents. ''It is often asked as a mighty objection,'' he remarks, thus anticipating his modern critics, 'where are, or ever were, there any men in such a state of Nature?'' To show that the conception is not entirely fictitious he suggests that the actual state of nature in his sense exists between independent princes and rulers, and between men of different societies who bargain with each other in a place where there is no government, *e.g.* between a Swiss and an Indian who bargain for truck in the wilds of America. ''They are perfectly in a state of Nature in reference to one another,'' he remarks, ''for truth and keeping of faith belong to men as men and not as members of society.'' However, he implies that these two examples are really superfluous, inasmuch as he wishes to affirm that all men are naturally in a state of nature, and remain so until they make themselves members of a political society.

Locke next asserts that all men in a state of Nature are equal by nature, and it is at this precise point that his argument breaks down. He here evokes a studied ambiguity of statement which makes it impossible to ascertain with any confidence his true meaning; but his proposition falls if taken in either of its two possible interpretations. Locke's actual words are: men are naturally in ''a state also of equality, wherein all the power and jurisdiction is reciprocal, no one having more than another, there being nothing more evident than that creatures of the same species and rank, promiscuously born to all the same advantages of Nature, and the use of the same faculties, should also be equal one amongst another, without subordination or subjection, unless the lord and master of them all should by any manifest declaration of his will, set one above another, and confer on him, by an evident and clear appointment, an undoubted right to dominion and sovereignty.'' This statement, if taken formally, in accordance with Locke's argument up to this point, means that no man in a society which is not politically organized has any political authority over any other man. As such, the statement is a truism, and we are at once in the dilemma supposed by Hobbes: Where there is no political authority, the right of all men to things, is in effect no better than if no man had right to anything. But even within the framework of Locke's argument there is a deeper objection. If he intends his assertion to be taken in a formal sense, then he has reached an impasse. His objective is to pass from a state of nature to a state of politically-organized society; but this he cannot accomplish on his hypothesis if the inhabitants of his society remain formally equal. Thus, when he comes to make the transition he does so by making those inhabitants ''biased by their interest,'' ''ignorant'' in their knowledge of it, refuse to allow the application of the law of nature to themselves, ''partial,'' motivated by ''passion'' and ''revenge,'' ''negligent,'' and most important of all, without power to back their rights. Now in Locke's formal system the equality of the members should be self-executing; if it is not, there is no equality. But if the equality is self-executing, in Locke's system the condition would have been an idyllic one, and Locke's imaginary beings would never have consented to the substitution for it of a political society.

But Locke's assertion can be understood in a different sense, one which is equally invalid but which has the virtue of allowing the argument to progress. It also seems to be the sense in which he meant it, if we judge by the subsequent development of his thought. It can be taken to mean that in a state of nature the physical and mental differences among men are so slight that no man can claim authority over another because of them. This is Hobbes' argument, and in Locke's case it can be understood in either an ethical or an empirical sense. We may dismiss the empirical meaning at once—that men would not in fact claim that authority could be predicated on their differences—since Locke's subsequent argument seems to show that he meant it to be taken ethically. Furthermore, Locke could not safely at this stage base his argument on what men would or would not do in fact in a state of nature; he would have to admit on historical grounds that they both would and would not make such claims. He therefore argues:

> The state of Nature has a law of Nature to govern it, which obliges every one, and reason, which is that law, teaches all mankind who will but consult it, that being all equal and independent, no one ought to harm another in his life, health, liberty or possessions; for men being all the workmanship of one omnipotent and infinitely wise Maker; all the servants of one sovereign master, sent into the world by His order and about His business; they are His property, whose workmanship they are made to last during His, not one another's pleasure. And, being furnished with like faculties, sharing all in one community of Nature, there cannot be supposed any such subordina-

tion among us that may authorize us to destroy one another, as if we were made for one another's uses, as the inferior ranks of creatures are for ours.

In its ethical significance, as distinguished from its theological, the doctrine is an anticipation of Kant's maxim that we ought to treat every man as an end, never as a means only. This asserts that every man is the judge of his own good; and no man, and therefore no government, can impose another good upon him. But this would make government impossible unless everyone acquiesced in the good established by the government for the community. The doctrine of Locke and Kant is the modern democratic doctrine of individualism, but it plainly needs restatement in order to fit the facts of that type of government.

We are therefore at the stage in Locke's argument at which he has abandoned his method of conscious abstraction. Henceforth, his discussion is on an ethical or an empirical level, and may thus be tested by criteria, such as the historical, which would be inappropriate had he continued his initial method. In this respect he stands in sharp contrast to a philosopher such as Leibniz, who constructed two theories of law, one formulated on a set of ideal postulates, the other empirical and based on the facts of positive law.

Locke's state of Nature, as we have seen, was governed by a law of Nature, the basis of which was established both theologically and ethically. The law of Nature, which was known through reason, was at bottom the rule of self-preservation, which was generalized by Locke to include the preservation of all members of the society. "Every one as he is bound to preserve himself," he wrote, "so by the like reason, when his own preservation comes not in competition, ought he as much as he can to preserve the rest of mankind." In terms as concrete as Locke thought it advisable to make them, this meant that no one ought to harm another in his life, health, liberty or possessions. From this it followed, in Locke's view, that the execution of the law of Nature was in every man's hands. Not only may a man punish for the injury done him, but others may assist in that process, because an injury is social as well as personal. Nevertheless, the punishment must not be arbitrary, but must be proportionate to the transgression, that is to say, will be such as will serve for reparation and restraint.

Apparently Locke was concerned over his proposal that every man in a state of Nature had a right to punish and to be the executioner of the law of Nature. He referred to it specifically as a "strange doctrine," as indeed it was, and he attempted to bolster it by two arguments. The first argument we have already noticed: that an offence is a trespass against the whole society; and since every man has a right to preserve mankind in general, every man therefore has a right of punishment. His second argument bore upon a principle of English law that had just been established. By what right, Locke asked, except on his argument, can a State punish an alien for a crime committed in its country? It is certain, he says, that the laws of a State, by virtue of any sanction they receive from the promulgated will of the legislature, do not reach a stranger. Therefore, if by the law of Nature every man does not have a power to punish offences against it, Locke does not see how the magistrates of any community can punish an alien of another country, since in reference to him, they can have no more power than what every man naturally may have over another.

It is curious that Locke should have advanced such an argument, since the question of the liability of an alien for violations of the local criminal law had recently been settled on another ground by the English courts. Moreover, the argument contradicts a position Locke was to assume later on in the *Treatise*. . . . Locke was well acquainted with the rule established by [contemporary cases concerning alien liability], because he stated it approvingly in section 122 of the *Treatise*. "Thus we see," he writes, "that foreigners, by living all their lives under another government, and enjoying the privileges and protection of it . . . are bound, even in conscience, to submit to its administration as far forth as any denizen." This rule is binding, in Locke's opinion, upon the alien in conscience because the alien, through the enjoyment of the government's protection, has given his tacit consent to obey the rules of the government.

Locke defined a state of nature as a society of "men living together according to reason without a common superior on earth, with authority to judge between them." This grouping of men is a society, but it is not political, its members possess natural rights, and the ordering of the group is regulated by natural law. There are also certain institutions in the society which are antecedent to the organization of political society: executive power to punish, property, money, war, slavery, the family, religion, education, inheritance, and other elements. Thus Locke's prepolitical society contains all the institutions, some of which are surplusage, for the necessary functioning of a society. He omits, in fact, only one institution—the state, or sovereign governmental group—which is customarily found in societies. (pp. 339-46)

Yet, in Locke's view . . . , the state of nature in reality is such an intolerable one that its inhabitants, however free, are willing to quit it. Every man's life, liberty and property are constantly exposed to invasion by others; the rules of justice and equity are only partially obeyed; and his condition generally is full of fears and continual dangers. Men therefore agree with other men to unite into a community for their comfortable, safe and peaceable living, and when they have so consented to make one community a government, they are thereby presently incorporated, and make one body politic, in which the majority have a right to act and conclude the rest.

Thus, political society is established by the freely given consent of the men who are to be members of that society. Every individual has the natural right to be free from any superior power on earth, and not to be under the will or legislative authority of other men, but to have only the law of nature for his will. He may, however, abrogate that right by consenting to form a political society. When he forms that society he surrenders his power to preserve his property—that is, his life, liberty and estate—against the injuries and attempts of other men, and he surrenders also his power to judge of and punish breaches of the law. At the moment of the formation of political society these natural powers pass to it. In Locke's opinion the possession of these powers by a society constitutes the sole criterion by which to judge whether it is politically organized or not. (pp. 346-47)

Two mistaken assumptions are at the basis of Locke's account of the transition from prepolitical to political society, one that he could predict how men would actually behave in a prepolitical society; and the other, that he could determine how men ought to behave at all times and everywhere. As for the first, it was a matter of necessity for Locke to establish that conditions resulting from human behavior in the state of nature would be so unsatisfactory that men would be instigated or compelled to form a political society; otherwise mankind would never abandon their liberty to the extent required to submit to a government. But how men will behave in the theoretical circumstances established for them by Locke is clearly beyond the limits of present knowledge to predict. In its abstract form the problem is analogous to a much simpler one in mathematics which is still unsolved—the problem of three bodies. Newton was able to account for the motions of a single planet revolving about its primary; but the determination for a particular time of the positions and motions of three mutually gravitating bodies when their positions and motions are known for some other time, is still so complex a matter that its full solution has never been accomplished. The social sciences are not even at the stage at which they can handle the problem of two bodies. Two men, sworn enemies, are turned loose on an uninhabited island; one is stupid and weak, the other strong and intelligent. Who can conjecture which will survive? We know further that many communities have existed in an even more rudimentary state of nature than the imaginary one constructed by Locke and were not under any apparent compulsion to form a government. (pp. 347-48)

Nevertheless, in its essence, Locke's method of approach contains a large element of truth. He began by asking a legitimate question, *i.e.*, one for which there exists some possibility of an answer: What is the origin of government? He endeavored to answer the question conjecturally through abstract reasoning, and, from such material as was available in the seventeenth century, empirically. In all this his methods, abstractly considered, do not differ essentially from those employed in such a work as Lowie's *The Origin of the State,* which exhibits the most refined of modern techniques. Locke's error, however, lay in the fact that he lost sight of his objective. His objective, unlike Lowie's, was not to discover the origin of government, but to prove a political theory. He was therefore compelled to introduce elements, such as ethical norms and the idea of necessity, in a manner which distorted his inquiry and led him to erroneous results if judged historically. But that he was on the right track, apart from his political distortions, the most approved methods of contemporary ethnology are ample evidence. (pp. 350-51)

> Huntington Cairns, "Locke," in his Legal Philosophy from Plato to Hegel, *1949, pp. 335-61.*

LEO STRAUSS (essay date 1952)

[*A well-known German-born American scholar, philosopher, and political theorist, Strauss was noted for his lucid and insightful interpretations of standard political theories. Credited by one observer with "keeping the study of the political classics alive," Strauss demonstrated the relevance of such thinkers as Plato, Niccolò Machiavelli, Thomas Hobbes, and Locke to present-day political dilemmas. Strauss is perhaps best known for* Die religionskritik Spinozas als grundlage seiner Bibelwissenschaft *(1930; Spinoza's Critique of Religion, 1965), Thoughts on Machiavelli (1959), and What is Political Philosophy? and Other Studies (1959). In the following excerpt from another work, he discusses Locke's doctrine of nature and of natural right in his* Second Treatise of Government.]

Locke's notion of natural law appears to be much closer to the traditional view as restated by Hooker than to the revolutionary view of Hobbes. Closer inspection would show that this appearance is deceptive and must be traced to Locke's peculiar caution. To indicate with utmost brevity the main point, Locke says on the one hand that, in order to be a law, the law of nature must not only have been given by God and be known to have been given by God, but it must in addition have as its sanctions divine "rewards and punishments, of infinite weight

and duration, in another life." On the other hand, however, he says that reason cannot demonstrate that there is another life. Only through revelation do we know of the sanctions for the law of nature, or of "the only true touchstone of moral rectitude." Natural reason is therefore unable to know the law of nature as a law. Yet Locke contends that there is "a law knowable by the light of nature, that is, without the help of positive revelation." If there is to be such a law this law must therefore consist of a set of rules whose validity does not presuppose life after death or belief in a life after death. (p. 475)

[Locke] cannot have recognized any law of nature in the proper sense of the term. This conclusion stands in shocking contrast to what is generally thought to be his doctrine, and especially the doctrine of the *Second Treatise.* Before turning to an examination of the *Second Treatise,* we beg the reader to consider the following facts: The accepted interpretation of Locke's teaching leads to the consequence [stated by J. W. Gough; see Additional Bibliography] that "Locke is full of illogical flaws and inconsistencies," of inconsistencies, we add, which are so obvious that they cannot have escaped the notice of a man of his rank and his sobriety. Furthermore, the accepted interpretation is based on what amounts to a complete disregard of Locke's caution, of a kind of caution which is, to say the least, compatible with "so involving one's sense that one cannot easily be understood" and with "going with the herd in one's outward professions." Above all, the accepted interpretation does not pay sufficient attention to the character of the *Treatise*; it somehow assumes that the *Treatise* contains the philosophic presentation of Locke's political doctrine, whereas it contains in fact only its "civil" presentation. In the *Treatise,* it is less Locke the philosopher than Locke the Englishman who addresses not philosophers, but Englishmen. It is for this reason that the argument of that work is based partly on generally accepted opinions, and even to a certain extent on Scriptural principles: "The greatest part cannot know, and therefore they must believe," so much so, that even if philosophy had "given us ethics in a science like mathematics, in every part demonstrable, . . . the instruction of the people were best still to be left to the precepts and principles of the gospel."

Yet however much Locke may have followed tradition in the *Treatise,* already a summary comparison of its teaching with the teachings of Hooker and of Hobbes would show that Locke deviated considerably from the traditional natural law teaching and followed the lead given by Hobbes. There is indeed only one passage in the *Treatise* in which Locke explicitly notes that he deviates from Hooker. But the passage draws our attention to a radical deviation. After having quoted Hooker, Locke says: "But I, moreover, affirm that all men are naturally in (the state of nature)." He thus suggests that according to Hooker some men were in fact, or accidentally, in the state of nature. Actually, Hooker had not said anything about the state of nature: the whole doctrine of the state of nature is based on a break with Hooker's principles, i.e., with the principles of the traditional natural law doctrine. Locke's notion of the state of nature is inseparable from the doctrine "that in the state of nature everyone has the executive power of the law of nature." He states twice in the context referred to that this doctrine is "strange," i.e., novel. (pp. 477-78)

[The] law of nature will not be effective in this world and hence not be a true law, if it is not effective in the state antedating civil society or government, in the state of nature: even in the state of nature everyone must be effectively responsible to other human beings. This however requires that everyone in the state of nature have the right to be the executioner of the law of nature: "the law of nature would, as all other laws that concern men in this world, be in vain, if there were nobody that in the state of nature had a power to execute that law." The law of nature is indeed given by God, but its being a law does not require that it be known to be given by God, because it is immediately enforced, not by God or by the conscience, but by human beings.

The law of nature cannot be truly a law if it is not effective in the state of nature. It cannot be effective in the state of nature, if the state of nature is not a state of peace. The law of nature imposes on everyone the perfect duty of preserving the rest of mankind "as much as he can," but only "when his own preservation comes not in competition." If the state of nature were characterized by habitual conflict between self-preservation and the preservation of others, the law of nature which "willeth the peace and preservation of all mankind" would be ineffectual: the higher claim of self-preservation would leave no room for concern with others. The state of nature must therefore be "a state of peace, good-will, mutual assistance, and preservation." This means that the state of nature must be a social state: in the state of nature all men "make up one society" by virtue of the law of nature, although they have no "common superior on earth." Inasmuch as self-preservation requires food and other necessities, and scarcity of such things leads to conflict, the state of nature must be a state of plenty: "God has given us all things richly." The law of nature cannot be a law if it is not known; it must be known and therefore it must be knowable in the state of nature.

After having drawn or suggested this picture of the state of nature especially in the first pages of the *Treatise,* Locke demolishes it as his argument proceeds. The state of nature which at first glance seems to be the golden age ruled by God or good demons, is literally a state without government, "pure anarchy." It could last forever, "were it not for the corruption and viciousness of degenerate men," but unfortunately "the greater part" are "no strict observers of equity and justice." For this reason, to say nothing of others, the state of nature has great "inconveniences." Many "mutual grievances, injuries and wrongs . . . attend men in the state of nature"; "strife and troubles would be endless" in it. It "is full of fears and continual dangers." It is "an ill condition." Far from being a state of peace, it is a state in which peace and quiet are uncertain. The state of peace is civil society; the state antedating civil society is the state of war. (pp. 479-81)

The state of nature would be a state of peace and good-will if men in the state of nature were under the law of nature. But "nobody can be under a law which is not promulgated to him." Man would know the law of nature in the state of nature if "the dictates of the law of nature" were "implanted in him" or "writ in the hearts of mankind." But no moral rules are "imprinted in our minds," or "written on [our] hearts" or "stamped upon [our] minds" or "implanted." Since there is no *habitus* of moral principles, no *synderesis* or conscience, all knowledge of the law of nature is acquired by study: to know the law of nature, one must be "a studier of that law." The law of nature becomes known only through demonstration. The question, therefore, is whether men in the state of nature are capable of becoming studiers of the law of nature. "The greatest part of mankind want leisure or capacity for demonstration. . . . And you may as soon hope to have all the day-labourers and tradesmen, and spinsters and dairy-maids, perfect mathematicians, as to have them perfect in ethics this way."

Yet a day laborer in England is better off than a king of the Americans, and "in the beginning all the world was America, and more so than it is now." "The first ages" are characterized by "negligent and unforeseeing innocence" rather than by habits of study. The condition in which man lives in the state of nature—"continual dangers" and "penury"—makes impossible knowledge of the law of nature: the law of nature is not promulgated in the state of nature. Since the law of nature must be promulgated in the state of nature if it is to be a law in the proper sense of the term, we are . . . forced to conclude that the law of nature is not a law in the proper sense of the term.

What then is the status of the law of nature in Locke's doctrine? What is its foundation? There is no rule of the law of nature which is innate, "that is, . . . imprinted on the mind as a duty." This is shown by the fact that there are no rules of the law of nature, "which, as practical principles ought, do continue constantly to operate and influence all our actions without ceasing [and which] may be observed in all persons and all ages, steady and universal." However, "Nature . . . has put into man a desire of happiness, and an aversion to misery; these, indeed, are innate practical principles": they are universally and unceasingly effective. The desire of happiness, and the pursuit of happiness to which it gives rise, are not duties. But "men . . . must be allowed to pursue their happiness, nay cannot be hindered." The desire of happiness and the pursuit of happiness have the character of an absolute right, of a natural right. There is then an innate natural right while there is no innate natural duty. To understand how this is possible one merely has to reformulate our last quotation: pursuit of happiness is a right, it "must be allowed," because "it cannot be hindered." It is a right antedating all duties for the same reason which, according to Hobbes, establishes as the fundamental moral fact the right of self-preservation; man must be allowed to defend his life against violent death because he is driven to do so by some natural necessity which is not lesser than that by which a stone is carried downward. Being universally effective, natural right, as distinguished from natural duty, is effective in the state of nature: man in the state of nature is "absolute lord of his own person and possessions." Since the right of nature is innate whereas the law of nature is not, the right of nature is more fundamental than the law of nature and is the foundation of the law of nature.

Since happiness presupposes life, the desire for life takes precedence of the desire for happiness in case of conflict. This dictate of reason is at the same time a natural necessity: "the first and strongest desire God planted in men, and wrought into the very principles of their nature, is that of self-preservation." The most fundamental of all rights is therefore the right of self-preservation. While Nature has put into man "a strong desire of preserving his life and being," it is only man's reason which teaches him what is "necessary and useful to his being." And reason—or rather reason applied to a subject to be specified presently—is the law of nature. Reason teaches that "he that is master of himself and his own life has a right, too, to the means of preserving it." Reason further teaches that since all men are equal in regard to the desire, and hence to the right, of self-preservation, they are equal in the decisive respect, notwithstanding any natural inequalities in other respects. From this Locke concludes, just as did Hobbes, that in the state of nature everyone is the judge of what means are conducive to his self-preservation, and this leads him, as it did Hobbes, to the further conclusion that in the state of nature "any man may do what he thinks fit." No wonder therefore that the state of nature is "full of fears and continual dangers." But reason teaches that life cannot be preserved, let alone enjoyed, except in a state of peace: reason wills peace. Reason wills therefore such courses of action as are conducive to peace. Reason dictates accordingly that "no one ought to harm another," that he who harms another—who therefore has renounced reason—may be punished by everyone and that he who is harmed may take reparations. These are the fundamental rules of the law of nature on which the argument of the *Treatise* is based: the law of nature is nothing other than the sum of the dictates of reason in regard to men's "mutual security" or to "the peace and safety" of mankind. Since in the state of nature all men are judges in their own cases and since therefore the state of nature is characterized by constant conflict that arises from the very law of nature, the state of nature is "not to be endured": the only remedy is government or civil society. Reason accordingly dictates how civil society must be constructed and what its rights or bounds are: there is a rational public law or a natural constitutional law. The principle of that public law is that all social or governmental power is derivative from powers which by nature belong to the individuals. The contract of the individuals actually concerned with their self-preservation—not the contract of the fathers qua fathers nor divine appointment nor an end of man that is independent of the actual wills of all individuals—creates the whole power of society: "the supreme power in every commonwealth [is] but the joint power of every member of the society."

Locke's natural law teaching can then be understood perfectly if one assumes that the laws of nature which he admits are, as Hobbes put it, "but conclusions, or theorems concerning what conduces to the conservation and defense" of man over against other men. And it must be thus understood since the alternative view is exposed to the difficulties which have been set forth. The law of nature, as Locke conceives of it, formulates the conditions of peace or, more generally stated, of "public happiness" or "the prosperity of any people." There is therefore a kind of sanction for the law of nature in this world: the disregard of the law of nature leads to public misery and penury. But this sanction is insufficient. Universal compliance with the law of nature would indeed guarantee perpetual peace and prosperity everywhere on earth. Failing such universal compliance, however, it may well happen that a society which complies with the law of nature enjoys less of temporal happiness than a society which transgresses the law of nature. For in both foreign and domestic affairs, victory does not always favor "the right side": the "great robbers . . . are too big for the weak hands of justice in this world." There remains however at least this difference between those who strictly comply with the law of nature and those who do not, that only the former can act and speak consistently: only the former can consistently maintain that there is a fundamental difference between civil societies and gangs of robbers, a distinction to which every society and every government is forced to appeal time and again. In a word, the law of nature is "a creature of the understanding rather than a work of nature"; it is "barely in the mind," a "notion," and not "in the things themselves." This is the ultimate reason why ethics can be raised to the rank of a demonstrative science.

One cannot clarify the status of the law of nature without considering the status of the state of nature. Locke is more definite than Hobbes in asserting that men actually lived in the state of nature or that the state of nature is not merely a hypothetical assumption. By this he means in the first place that men actually lived, and may live, without being subject to a common superior on earth. He means furthermore that men living in that condition, who are studiers of the law of nature, would know how to set about remedying the inconveniences of their condition, and to lay the foundations for public happiness. But only such men could know the law of nature while living in a state of nature who have already lived in civil society, or rather in a civil society in which reason has been properly cultivated. An example of men who are in the state of nature under the law of nature would therefore be an elite among the English colonists in America rather than the wild Indians. A better example would be that of any highly civilized men after the breakdown of their society. It is only one step from this to the view that the most obvious example of men in the state of nature under the law of nature is that of men living in civil society in so far as they reflect on what they could justly demand from civil society or on the conditions under which civil obedience would be reasonable. Thus it becomes ultimately irrelevant whether the state of nature understood as a state in which men are subject only to the law of nature and not to any common superior on earth, was ever actual or not.

It is on the basis of Hobbes's view of the law of nature that Locke opposes Hobbes's conclusions. He tries to show that Hobbes's principle—the right of self-preservation—far from favoring absolute government, requires limited government. Freedom, "freedom from arbitrary, absolute power," is "the fence" to self-preservation. Slavery is therefore against natural law except as a substitute for capital punishment. Nothing which is incompatible with the basic right of self-preservation, and hence nothing to which a rational creature cannot be supposed to have given free consent, can be just; hence civil society or government cannot be established lawfully by force or conquest: consent alone "did or could give beginning to any lawful government in the world." For the same reason Locke condemns absolute monarchy or, more precisely, "absolute arbitrary power . . . of any one or more" as well as "governing without settled standing laws." In spite of the limitations which Locke demands, the commonwealth remains for him, as it was for Hobbes, "the mighty leviathan": in entering civil society, "men give up all their natural power to the society which they enter into." Just as Hobbes did, so Locke admits only one contract: the contract of union which every individual makes with every other individual of the same multitude, is identical with the contract of subjection. Just as Hobbes did, so Locke teaches that by virtue of the fundamental contract, every man "puts himself under an obligation to everyone of that society to submit to the determination of the majority, and to be concluded by it"; that, therefore, the fundamental contract establishes immediately an unqualified democracy; that this primary democracy may by majority vote either continue itself or transform itself into another form of government; and that the social contract is therefore in fact identical with a contract of subjection to the "sovereign" (Hobbes) or to the "supreme power" (Locke) rather than to society. Locke opposes Hobbes by teaching that wherever "the people" or "the community," i.e., the majority, have placed the supreme power, they still retain "a supreme power to remove or alter" the established government, i.e., they still retain a right of revolution. But this power (which is normally dormant) does not qualify the subjection of the individual to the community or society. On the contrary, it is only fair to say that Hobbes stresses more strongly than does Locke the individual's right to resist society or the government whenever his self-preservation is endangered.

Locke would nevertheless have been justified in contending that the mighty leviathan, as he had constructed it, offered a greater guarantee for the individual's self-preservation than Hobbes's Leviathan. The individual's right of resistance to organized society, which Hobbes had stressed and which Locke did not deny, is an ineffectual guarantee for the individual's self-preservation. Since the only alternative to pure anarchy—to a condition in which everyone's self-preservation is in continual danger—is that "men give up all their natural power to the society which they enter into," the only effective guarantee for the rights of the individuals is that society be so constructed as to be incapable of oppressing its members: only a society, or a government, thus constructed is legitimate or in accordance with natural law; only such a society can justly demand that the individual surrender to it all his natural power. According to Locke the best institutional safeguards for the rights of the individuals are supplied by a constitution that, in practically all domestic matters, strictly subordinates the executive power (which must be strong) to law, and ultimately to a well-defined legislative assembly. The legislative assembly must be limited to the making of laws as distinguished from "extemporary, arbitrary decrees"; its members must be elected by the people for fairly short periods of tenure and therefore be "themselves subject to the laws they have made"; the electoral system must take account of both numbers and wealth. For although Locke seems to have thought that the individual's self-preservation is less seriously threatened by the majority than by monarchic or oligarchic rulers, he cannot be said to have had an implicit faith in the majority as a guarantor of the rights of the individual. In the passages in which he seems to describe the majority as such a guarantor, he is speaking of cases in which the individuals' self-preservation is threatened by tyrannical monarchic or oligarchic rulers, and wherein therefore the last and only hope for the suffering individual obviously rests on the dispositions of the majority. Locke regarded the power of the majority as a check on bad government and a last resort against tyrannical government; he did not regard it as a substitute for government or as identical with government. Equality, he thought, is incompatible with civil society. The equality of all men in regard to the right of self-preservation does not obliterate completely the special right of the more reasonable men. On the contrary, the exercise of that special right is conducive to the self-preservation and happiness of all. Above all, since self-preservation and happiness require property, so much so that the end of civil society can be said to be the preservation of property, the protection of the propertied members of society against the demands of the indigent—or the protection of the industrious and rational against the lazy and quarrelsome—is essential to public happiness or the common good. (pp. 481-88)

> Leo Strauss, "On Locke's Doctrine of Natural Right," in The Philosophical Review, Vol. LXI, No. 4, October, 1952, pp. 475-502.

RICHARD I. AARON   (essay date 1955)

[*Aaron is a Welsh academic and philosopher. The author of several works on epistemology, he is perhaps best known for* The Nature of Knowing *(1930) and* Knowing and the Function of Reason *(1971). In the following excerpt from his exposition of Locke's writings, Aaron discusses Locke's thoughts on education and religion.*]

Locke realized the supreme importance of education. 'Of all the men we meet with, nine parts of ten are what they are, good or evil, useful or not, by their education.' He himself had been led to inquire into the subject as the consequence of

his interest in Edward Clarke's family. When in exile in Holland he wrote long letters to Clarke instructing him how best to educate his son. Later, in 1693, he gathered the drafts of these letters together and after modifying them in certain particulars published them as *Some Thoughts concerning Education*. In reading the book it is well to remember that he is dealing with a limited problem: How best to educate the son of the squire who will one day be squire himself. He has before his mind young Edward Clarke, who showed little promise of great scholarship, or of greatness of any kind, but was plainly destined to live the life of the average English gentleman of good birth. Locke believed in the individual method in education, as he himself informs us. The details of educational procedure should vary with the idiosyncrasies of each pupil. And here he is outlining a system of education for Edward Clarke in particular, with the hope that its general principles will hold for the education of the normal boy of the squire class.

First, Locke deals with the health of the body. Children when young are not to be coddled and spoilt, but their bodies are to be gradually hardened to withstand external changes. Their clothes should be light and loose-fitting. They should spend much of their time in the open and be given sufficient exercise. Locke recommends cold baths and leaky shoes as aids in the process of hardening. Sleep, 'the great cordial of nature', should not be neglected. Children should be given little meat and no strong drinks, and regular habits should be established. They should be permitted to romp and play to their heart's content. The theory that children should be seen, but not heard, finds little support in Locke's pages. Their 'gamesome humour, which is wisely adapted by nature to their age and temper, should rather be encouraged, to keep up their spirits, and improve their strength and health, than curbed or restrained: and the chief art is to make all that they have to do sport and play too'. In this way, by obedience to rules of health, the body may be made strong and active.

In respect to the education of the mind, the first thing to emphasize, in Locke's opinion, is that a sound mind does not mean merely a well informed mind. A pupil may know all the scholastic philosophy, may write perfect Greek and Latin exercises, and yet be badly educated. Character, Locke thinks, is indeed more important than learning. Virtue, wisdom, good breeding—these are the marks of the sound mind. Learning is secondary. First comes the good life, based, as Locke thinks, on a knowledge of God. Then comes wisdom, not crafty cunning, but sagacity and prudence in the conduct of one's affairs. Thirdly, good breeding, which Locke neatly defines as 'not thinking meanly of ourselves nor of others', not being 'sheepishly bashful' on the one hand, nor 'negligent and disrespectful in one's carriage' on the other.

Now virtue, wisdom, and good breeding cannot be taught directly as one teaches the multiplication table. And certainly they cannot be enforced. Nothing is more dangerous and nothing in the long run more ineffective than an attempt to compel a child against its will to a certain mode of life. Compulsion at best can only succeed in breaking the child, and so unfitting it for life. 'Dejected minds,' says Locke, 'timorous and tame and low spirits are hardly ever to be raised and very seldom attain to any thing'. The successful teacher does not need to compel; and the use of force, for instance, in corporal punishment is a sign of failure on the teacher's part. A good teacher will teach much by example and by suggestion. Children, of course, with their readiness to emulate others, learn quickly from the example of others. For this reason, they should be reared in the company of virtuous, wise, and well-mannered men and women. Speaking generally, children should be as frequently as possible in the company of their parents, and although occasionally a maid may have greater virtue than her mistress—and then it is best to leave the child to the maid— in general a mother should rear her own offspring. On the difficult question of whether a child should be sent away to school or not, Locke thinks that in the majority of cases it is best for the child to remain at home in the care of its parents for as long as possible. It is foolish 'to hazard one's son's innocence and virtue for a little Greek and Latin'. It is true that the child away from home will learn manliness and self-reliance more quickly, although this may develop into 'a forward pertness' not consonant with good manners. But these virtues can be learnt at home in a well regulated household, and it is easier there to learn the further lesson which boys find difficult to learn, that, whilst courage is good, cruelty is always evil. Accordingly, Locke would recommend for most gentlemen's sons an education at home carried forward under the watchful eye of the parent, but with a tutor from outside to help in the work.

The tutor will have to be carefully chosen, for much depends on the right choice. By precept, and even more by example, he will teach the child to control and discipline itself. He will discourage the desire for pleasure, never restraining forcibly, but carefully refraining from encouraging the natural desire for pleasure present in every child. For instance, he will not reward a good act with the gift of a sugar plum, lest the pleasure of winning the reward fill the child's mind. Wherever possible, and as soon as possible, he will appeal to the rational element. He will treat his pupil as a rational creature and encourage him to reason for himself and to see the rationality and wisdom of the conduct suggested to him. Rules should be as few as possible, although it is well that these few should be obeyed.

In this way will virtue, wisdom, and good breeding best be taught. In addition, the child needs a stock of useful knowledge. And here the method of teaching is all-important. For the young child, at least, learning must be made another form of playing. Children cannot learn under compulsion; restraint paralyses them. The skilful teacher knows how to impart his information in so interesting a fashion that the children learn with the same zest as they play. He finds an ally in the natural curiosity of childhood. Children are very curious; they are full of questions about the things they see and hear. 'They are travellers newly arrived in a strange country, of which they know nothing: we should, therefore, make conscience not to mislead them.'

The child should first be instructed in its own tongue so that it speaks, reads, and writes that tongue correctly. Then as soon as possible it should begin to learn another language, for instance, the English child might learn French. In a year or two Latin also should be taught, and taught by the conversational or direct method. (Children should not begin with exercises in Latin grammar. Let the teacher talk to them in Latin and let them learn to read the language fluently, and then it will be time enough to turn to grammar.) When they have gained some mastery over these languages, Locke cannot recommend the practice of his age that pupils should then spend the rest of their time learning other ancient languages, Greek, Hebrew, and Arabic, together with rhetoric and logic. He recommends instead geography, history, and anatomy, subjects which require little reasoning powers but some memorizing. At the same time a beginning should also be made with the study of more

abstract inquiries, arithmetic, geometry, and astronomy. Later, the growing youth should learn a little civil law and a little ethics. And his education might be completed with an introduction into the various hypotheses in natural philosophy, both physical and metaphysical. He will not, of course, be a specialist in any of these subjects. His knowledge will be general and not very deep. But it will be enough for his needs.

For recreation, after more serious study, Locke will turn his pupil's mind to the arts and the crafts. The young gentleman, however, is not to take these too seriously. The enjoyment of poetry, for instance, is pleasant and so is its writing, but it is an art not to be encouraged in a young man. No father is anxious to see his son a poet: 'For it is very seldom seen that any one discovers mines of gold or silver in Parnassus. 'Tis a pleasant air, but a barren soil.' Towards music Locke is somewhat more sympathetic, although he thinks proficiency at a musical instrument hardly worth the time taken to acquire it. Moreover, it engages a young man 'in such odd company'. 'Men of parts and business' do not commend it. Nevertheless, some recreation is certainly necessary. Locke thinks sport rather a waste of time. His own recommendation is that young men, even young gentlemen, should learn a trade, such as gardening or carpentry, in their leisure hours. Finally, he thinks travel good, although not at the usual age, that is between sixteen and twenty-one. A youth travels for one of two purposes: to learn a foreign tongue, or to make acquaintance with men of note abroad and to understand the political and social conditions in which they live. For the first purpose the usual age for travel is much too late, and for the second it is too early.

No book of Locke's is more readable than his *Some Thoughts concerning Education*. Most of its teaching has long since become part of the generally accepted educational theory of this country, although in many places practice still lags behind theory. In his own day, however, to judge from the evidence to hand, it must have been regarded as highly heretical. His contemporaries must have been surprised by his assertion that the teacher's first task was to create character; while his suggestions that logic and rhetoric could be neglected, and geography, history, and anatomy substituted in their place, that English should be studied as thoroughly as Latin and that Greek could be entirely omitted from the curriculum, must have been regarded as revolutionary in the extreme. But the pleasant, fresh style of the work, its forcefulness, and, at the same time, its general good sense, captured the imagination of men and also appealed to their intellect. *Some Thoughts concerning Education* is a very definite step forward in educational theory and few other English books have influenced educational thought so deeply.

Religion was Locke's dominating interest in the closing years of his life. The works he wrote on religious topics in that last decade, the *Reasonableness of Christianity* and its *Vindications*, together with the commentaries on the *Epistles,* make up a volume larger than the [*Essay concerning Human Understanding*] itself. (pp. 287-92)

[Locke] advocated toleration. He was not, of course, the first to argue for toleration. On paper at least the battle was wellnigh won before Locke wrote. The plea for freedom in religion was a plea with which Englishmen had long been acquainted, and by Locke's time it was obvious to the discerning that religious toleration was not only a primary necessity for the spiritual health of the individual, but that it also increased the national strength. It made for understanding and for an inner unity, even at the cost of sacrificing uniformity in worship. Moreover, the economic advantages to be gained from toleration, as the instance of Holland made abundantly clear, were many. But it was not upon arguments such as these that Locke based his case, although they were doubtless in his mind. He tried rather to prove his point by arguing from the essential nature of a religious community on the one hand, and from the inevitable limitation of man's knowledge on the other.

Locke's main arguments are three in number. In the first place, from its very nature no church has a right to persecute, nor has it a right to use the civil power for this purpose. A church is a 'voluntary society of men'. To that extent it is, in Locke's view, analogous to a state, but it differs from the state in one important respect. When a state comes into being the individuals composing it give up their own power of executing punishment, and entrust this power to the state. Now when individuals join a church they do not give it any powers of this sort. A church has no power to use force; whereas a state has. But the state has no right to use its force in religious matters. The purely religious sphere is not political. The care of the citizen's body and of his property is the proper concern of the civil magistrate, but no one, neither God nor man, has entrusted the care of the citizen's soul to him. Accordingly, a church has no right to persecute through its own agents, nor again has it a right to persecute through the civil power.

In the second place, it is most unlikely that any church or any individual man possesses the full truth about human life and destiny. And this very limitation makes intolerance at once unjustifiable. For when two men genuinely disagree after a sincere search for truth, what possible justification can there be for intolerance and persecution on the part of one of these men? Surely no man has a right to persecute another because this other fails to see eye to eye with him. The persecuted party may be nearer the truth than the persecuting. All over Europe in Locke's day the differing sects persecuted each other. Not more than one of them could possess the full truth, and the extreme probability was that none of them possessed it fully. And yet one had the incongruous spectacle of men 'punished in Denmark for not being Lutherans, in Geneva for not being Calvinists, and in Vienna for not being Papists'. It will be time enough to be intolerant when the full truth is known.

But, thirdly, even though we did know the truth, little could be gained by intolerance. The use of force may certainly secure an empty outward conformity, but such conformity does not carry with it inward conviction. It breeds hypocrisy and false religion. Persuasion and example are the true weapons of a church. Persecution is not one of them. Intolerance is not merely evil; it is also ineffective.

These are the arguments upon which Locke bases his pleas for toleration. He demands complete freedom for the individual in religious matters, and makes but one exception. If an individual as the result of his religion does positive harm either to another individual or to the state, then he cannot be permitted to practise his religion. For instance, a religion having human sacrifice as part of its ritual could not be tolerated in any modern community. Locke includes as instances of this exceptional case two groups to whom he would not grant toleration. Atheists cannot be trusted, not having the proper basis for morality, namely, a belief in God. They are, consequently, very likely to do harm to their fellow citizens, and so should not be tolerated. Again, some religions demand from their believers allegiance to a foreign potentate. Locke instances the case of the Mahometans, although it is clear that he has Roman Catholics most in mind. The state can only permit such religions at

considerable risk to itself. In all cases, however, where the state intervenes and suppresses, it does so not on religious grounds (for in this purely religious sphere it has no rights whatsoever) but on political and social grounds only.

But while Locke advocated toleration in the religious life, he could not but regret the disunion and schism which he saw around him. His ideal was a broad, comprehensive church which could contain within itself men of different opinions. He was convinced that the Latitudinarian position was sound, that belief in one or two essential tenets of the Christian religion should be sufficient for membership. Locke had been brought up a Calvinist, but under the influence of Latitudinarians, Cambridge Platonists, and Remonstrants in Holland he adopted a position in theology more consonant with the liberalism and rationalism of his politics. This becomes apparent in his *Reasonableness of Christianity.*

This book is the outcome of a critical study of the Gospels. Locke approached Holy Scripture with the reverence of a believing Christian, but this did not prevent him from studying it in an intelligent manner. In his historical and critical approach to the Scriptures Locke is a worthy forerunner of Schleiermacher; he is a pioneer of modern Biblical criticism, as is shown both by the *Reasonableness of Christianity* and even more by his commentaries on the Epistles of St. Paul. The introductory essay to the commentaries, *An Essay for the Understanding of St. Paul's Epistles by consulting St. Paul Himself,* is an exceedingly able plea for the critical method in the study of the *Epistles.*

Locke bases his thesis in the *Reasonableness of Christianity* upon an appeal to Scriptures, studied in the same careful and intelligent manner. He argues that if we read the Bible carefully we shall find that the theologians with their endless creeds and dogmas, their mysteries innumerable, and their tiresome articles, confuse the issue. Christianity in its essentials is a rational creed, natural and simple. It demands of the believer, first, that he should believe in Christ the Messiah, one sent from God to reveal his true nature; secondly, that he should live in accordance with the Christian morality, the morality based on this new revelation of God. These are the essentials, and anyone who fulfils these is a Christian. The theologian's creeds, the priest's elaborate ritual, do not make a Christian. Christianity is something simpler, although it may very well be more difficult. 'Lustrations and processions are much easier than a clean conscience and a steady course of virtue; and an expiatory sacrifice, that atoned for the want of it, is much more convenient than a strict and holy life.' (pp. 293-96)

Locke is radical and yet conservative; he is a rationalist and yet he finally puts his faith on what is not reason. . . . Reason alone is inadequate. It is inadequate in the sphere of religion, just as it is inadequate in the sphere of natural science. There we have to wait on sense-experience. And it seems as if Locke recognizes in religion also a religious experience, a feeling and an intuition of God, Pascal's knowledge of 'the heart', which supplements reason. In the *Essay* Locke distinguishes between the revelation which comes from God through reason and that which comes through His Spirit. For beings constituted as we are, children of the twilight, the former is not enough. And it is dangerous to erect a faith on it alone—as dangerous as it is to deduce a science of nature *a priori.* Locke does not analyse this second kind of knowledge, this consciousness of the presence of God in our life. He hardly ever talks of it. But he makes it none the less clear that it is an essential element in religion. (p. 300)

And when we pass from the particular problems of Christian theology to the final problem of theology itself, that of the being and nature of God, it is clear that Locke does not expect reason to provide the full solution in this case either. He thinks we can prove God's *existence* by reason, and offers a proof in IV.x of the *Essay*. That proof . . . is not beyond suspicion. But it is obvious in reading it that it is an attempted rationalization of what is already believed. Locke believes first, and then seeks rational justification for his belief in the cosmological argument. Why does Locke believe? His education and the custom of the age clearly account in some part for this fact. But the belief plays too great a part in his philosophy to be attributed entirely to these sources. Locke, no doubt, did feel that a First Cause was essential, and he also felt that we ourselves needed explaining. Surely the cause of 'cogitative beings' must itself be 'cogitative'. The First Cause must be Spirit. Again, the order in the universe—however we account for its disorder and its evil—is too great to allow us to suppose that it is the result of an accidental 'concourse of atoms', it must surely be the work of an intelligent Creator. Moreover, man is not merely cogitative, he is also moral; and although Locke never presents us with an adequate analysis of the moral consciousness, he does vaguely feel something of what Kant made clear later, that morality (if we interpret it in the Kantian way) necessitates

the being of God. Of all this and more Locke was aware. Yet one cannot but feel that his real ground for believing was no rational argument of any kind. It was the knowledge of God 'through His Spirit', this deep intuition of his presence. The piety and deep religious feeling of Locke's works forcibly suggest such a view.

As to the nature of God Locke has little to say. We cannot hope to know him fully as he is. We frame an idea of him as best we may, a complex idea, framed, as all complex ideas are framed, from ideas of sensation and reflection. We think of all the qualities that are worth possessing and attribute these to God—not, however, as they are to be found amongst us, but as they are in their perfection. God is one, enduring from eternity to eternity; in him is all true pleasure and happiness; he is omniscient, wholly good, and omnipotent. But ours is no positive idea of God. When we say that God is good what we mean is that he is better than anyone else, that his goodness is greater than the greatest goodness we have yet known. When we say that he is wise we mean that his wisdom surpasses all the wisdom we know positively. It is no positive conception. Our complex idea of God must fall far short of the reality; in his true nature he must be very different from our best conception of him. That this is so is not to be wondered at if we recall our ignorance even of finite things, even of our own selves. It is not strange if the infinite is almost wholly hidden from us. God is incomprehensible. And yet, Locke thinks, we are aware of him as a powerful presence in our life, and in this knowledge find strength and peace. (pp. 300-01)

Richard I. Aaron, in his John Locke, Oxford at the Clarendon Press, *Oxford, 1955, 323 p.*

MAURICE CRANSTON   (essay date 1961)

[*Cranston is an English academic, scholar, biographer, and political theorist who frequently studies human rights issues, political philosophy, the life and works of Jean-Jacques Rousseau, and the political New Left. The author of several critical and historical works, he won the 1958 James Tait Black Memorial Prize for his* John Locke: A Biography *(1957). In the following excerpt from a later work, he discusses Locke's epistemology and assesses his contribution to modern thought.*]

[John Locke] was never a man of artistic and literary taste. David Hume was once said to have looked like 'a turtle-eating alderman instead of a refined philosopher'; Locke, who had the looks Hume lacked, wrote like a water-drinking local councillor, his style ungainly, his idioms commercial, his imagination puritanical, his humour laboured, his interests wholly practical. 'What is the *use*', he asked, 'of poetry?'

He was a great materialist, in a sense, and an important sense. Our modern Western world has been made by scientists, merchants, statesmen, industrialists; Locke was the first philosopher to expound their view of life, to articulate their aspirations and justify their deeds. No philosopher has exercised a greater influence. And yet it could be said—and has been said—that Locke was not a philosopher at all. But to say this is only to say that Locke was not a metaphysician; and he was certainly not one, in the sense that Leibniz or Spinoza, his contemporaries, were metaphysicians. Locke offered no all-embracing system to explain the nature of the universe. On the contrary, he tried to show that the human understanding is so limited that such comprehensive knowledge is beyond men's powers to reach. Where philosophy is concerned Locke did not give the answers; he achieved greatness rather in his formulation of

A note, written in shorthand in 1677, in which Locke outlines his method of translating selections from Pierre Nicole's Essais de morale.

the problems. He set out, as no one had done before, the questions philosophy should deal with, and also the ways of dealing with them; he gave epistemology, the theory of knowledge, its method.

Two powerful streams in seventeenth century thought, the semi-sceptical rational theorising of Descartes, and the *ad hoc* scientific experimenting of Bacon and the Royal Society came together in Locke. Their union was not perfect, because the streams were so different, but his mind was the meeting point, a point which marked a new beginning, not only in philosophy, but in the way in which men thought about the world. Locke, one might almost say, had the first modern mind. Descartes, though more original than Locke, was still in many ways a medieval thinker; his philosophy was still attached to theology. Even Gassendi, who anticipated much of Locke, did not quite leap free. Locke made the break; he separated philosophy from theology, and set the proper study of philosophy within the boundaries of man's experience: 'Our portion', he wrote, 'lies only here in this little spot of earth, where we and all our concernments are shut up.'

Yet Locke was not a sceptic, and in his capacity as theologian he had thoughts of his own about God to expound. He quarrelled with bishops and the orthodox of most denominations. He maintained that a Christian need believe no more than the single proposition 'that Christ is the Messiah'; but to that minimal creed he clung with the firmest assurance. He had a quiet and steady faith in the immortality of the soul, and in the prospects of happiness in the life to come. He had no belief in miracles; and no patience with people who had mystical experiences or visions of God, and he detested religious enthusiasm, but in his own unemotional way he was, like Newton, a deeply religious man. (pp. 7-8)

In the Epistle to the Reader, printed at the beginning of his *Essay Concerning Human Understanding,* Locke says that in an age of such 'master builders' as Boyle and Sydenham and Huygenius and 'the incomparable Mr. Newton' it is, for him, 'ambition enough to be employed as an under-labourer in clearing the ground a little and removing some of the rubbish that lies in the way of knowledge' [see excerpt dated 1690]. Despite this modest explanation of his purpose Locke is generally, and rightly, believed to have done much more. He provides, among other things, the first modern philosophy of science. A recurrent word—perhaps the most important word—in the *Essay* is a Cartesian one, 'idea'. Locke's use of the word is curious. He does not merely say that we have ideas in our minds when we think; he says that we have ideas in our minds when we see, hear, smell, taste, or feel. The core of his epistemology is the notion that the objects of perception are not *things,* but ideas which are derived in part from things in the external world, but which also depend to some extent on our own minds for their existence. Locke defines an 'idea' as the 'object of the understanding' whether it is notion, an entity, or an illusion, perception being for him a 'species of understanding'.

Locke opens his *Essay* with an attack on what was in his time the established opinion that certain ideas are innate. He claims that they have been thought to be innate only because people cannot remember when they first learned them. Locke's belief is that we are born in total ignorance, and that even our theoretical ideas of identity, quantity and substance are derived from experience. He says that a child gets ideas of black and white, of sweet and bitter before and not after it gets an idea of abstract principles such as identity or impossibility. 'The sense at first let in particular ideas, and furnish the yet empty cabinet. . . .' Afterwards the mind abstracts these theoretical ideas, and so 'comes to be furnished with ideas and language, the materials about which to exercise the discursive faculty'. In the child's development, 'the use of reason becomes daily more visible as these materials that give it employment increase'.

Locke has thus to defend the belief that everything which he calls an idea is derived from sensation, though he admits that the idea may also be produced by what he calls reflection—'remembering, considering, reasoning, etc.'. He classifies ideas as simple and complex. Simple ideas are those which the mind receives passively. Complex ideas are produced by the exercise of the mind's own powers. It is in his chapters on 'simple ideas' that Locke sets out the main lines of his theory of perception. Most people, if asked what it is that they see, smell, hear, taste or touch would answer 'things', though they might add 'but sometimes illusions, chimeras, mirages, which are not real things'. They would probably maintain that there are two elements in an act of perception: the observer and the object. Locke differs from this plain view in two respects: first he claims that what we perceive is always an idea, as distinct from a thing; secondly, he claims that there are not two but three elements in perception, the observer, the idea, and the object which the idea represents.

The reasoning which leads Locke to this conclusion is not difficult to appreciate. We look at a penny. We are asked to describe it. It is round, brown, and of modest dimensions. But do we really see just this? We look again and what we see is elliptical, not circular; in some lights it is golden, in others black; close to the eye it is large; seen from afar it is tiny. The actual penny, we are certain, cannot be *both* circular and elliptical, both golden all over and black all over. So we may be led to agree that there must be something which is the one and something which is the other, something which changes, and something which does not change, the elliptical 'penny' we see and the real circular penny, or, in Locke's own words, the 'idea' in the mind of the observer and the material 'body' itself.

Locke's theory of perception is both easily defended and easily attacked. It is easily defended in the twentieth century on the basis of what is said by many physicists about the structure of the universe and by many physiologists about the mechanism of perception. The penny we give a child is something that looks brown, feels warm, tastes sharp on the tongue. The penny we give to the scientist is described as a congeries of electrons and protons. He tells us that certain light-waves strike the retina of the observer's eye, while waves of other kinds strike nerve terminals of other sorts: and these processes produce those modifications of the neurological system which we call 'seeing', 'feeling' or 'tasting' a penny. Neither the electrons nor the protons, neither the waves outside nor the modifications inside are brown or warm or astringent. The scientist thus eliminates what Locke called the *secondary* qualities—colour, taste, sound; and these are precisely those qualities which Locke said depended for their existence on the mind of the observer. At the same time, science seems to accept the objective existence of the qualities which Locke called *primary,* and which he thought of as belonging to material bodies themselves: namely impenetrability, extension, figure, mobility and number. These are the qualities with which scientists are accustomed to deal. Nor is Locke's distinction between primary and secondary qualities acceptable only to scientists. Most people would probably be willing to agree that they could imagine an object divested one by one of its qualities of taste and smell and so forth, but they could not imagine a body divested of impenetrability, or shape or size or position in space: for a body without primary qualities would not exist at all.

But if there is much to be said for Locke's epistemology, there is also much to be said against it. If we are aware in our perceptual experience only of ideas which represent objects, and never of objects themselves, there can be no means of knowing what, if anything, is represented by those ideas. The human predicament, according to Locke's account of it, is that of a man permanently imprisoned in a sort of diving bell, receiving some signals from without and some from within his apparatus, but having no means of knowing which, if any, of these signals come from outside and hence no means of testing the authenticity of any of the signals. Man cannot therefore have any definite knowledge whatever of the external world.

In the later chapters of the *Essay* the author puts an even heavier emphasis on human ignorance. Our knowledge, Locke says, 'is not only limited to the paucity and imperfections of the ideas we have, and which we employ about it', it is something still more circumscribed. Our knowledge of identity and diversity in ideas extends only as far as our ideas themselves; our knowledge of their co-existence extends only a little way because knowledge of any necessary connection between primary and secondary qualities is unattainable. However, with the area of certainty thus diminished, Locke does not deny us the possibility of an assurance which falls short of perfect knowledge. We can have *probable* knowledge; even when we cannot have certain knowledge. Moreover, unlike most of his successors among empiricist philosophers, Locke admits the existence of substance. He says that substance is somehow present in all things, even though we do not see or feel it. What we see and feel are the primary and secondary qualities. Substance is what stands under and props up those qualities. Beyond that Locke says the subject must necessarily remain a mystery. . . . (pp. 23-6)

The *Essay Concerning Human Understanding* is a very English book both in its merits and its faults. Its tone is at once moral and pragmatic, its style is homely rather than elegant, its construction informal and even amateurish. The 'pursuit of Truth' the author says, 'is a duty we owe to God . . . and a duty we owe also to ourselves'; utility is at one with piety. Truth, as Locke defines it, is the 'proper riches and furniture of the mind'; but he does not claim to have added to that stock, but rather to have shown the conditions under which the mind could acquire its proper riches and furniture. . . . (p. 27)

In the preface to the English edition of the first *Letter for Toleration* is a sentence which reads: 'Absolute liberty, just and true liberty, equal and impartial liberty is the thing we stand in need of.' Many people have supposed these words to be Locke's, and Lord King used them as an epigraph for his biography of the philosopher, but in fact the words were written by William Popple, the translator of the *Letter*.

Locke did *not* believe in absolute liberty, any more than he believed in absolute knowledge. Locke wanted as much knowledge as possible; and he thought the way to achieve as much as possible of each was to face the fact that both were limited and then to find out what the limitations were. Once men recognised that certain information could be had only in one or two fields, they could go on to acquire a great deal of probable information in other fields. Hence the seeming paradox of Locke's attempt in his *Human Understanding* to show

how much men can know by demonstrating how little they can know.

Locke's political writings are less elaborately argued than his *Human Understanding,* but his technique is much the same. By demonstrating the liberty that men cannot have, Locke shows the liberty that men can have. The limits of liberty are set by the nature of political societies as such, by the necessity of protecting the life, property, and freedom of each from invasion by any other, and protecting the safety of all from common enemies. Once those limitations are understood, no other limitations need be borne, indeed no other limitations *should* be borne. Locke set men on the road to the greatest possible liberty by the method he used to set them on the road to the greatest possible knowledge—by teaching them the impossibility of the absolute. (pp. 32-3)

> *Maurice Cranston, in his* Locke, *The British Council, 1961, 38 p.*

MICHAEL V. DePORTE (essay date 1974)

[*An American educator who specializes in Restoration and eighteenth-century English literature, DePorte is also the author of several studies of the early history of abnormal psychology. In the following excerpt, he delineates Locke's views of the origin and progress of mental illness, chiefly as revealed in his journals and* An Essay concerning Human Understanding.]

[No philosopher of his age] was better qualified to write about afflictions of the mind than was Locke. He had been trained as a physician and had enjoyed the friendship of both Willis and Sydenham. Recently the medical notations made in the journals he kept from 1675 to 1698 have been published by Kenneth Dewhurst [see Additional Bibliography] and they reveal an interest in abnormal psychology long antedating the appearance of the *Essay Concerning Human Understanding* in 1690. Many of Locke's later ideas about irrationality can, in fact, be seen to evolve from an entry he made in July of 1676 while traveling about France for his health:

> Query whether mania be not putting together wrong ideas and so making wrong propositions from them, not withstanding the reason be right? But madness is a fault in the faculty of reasoning.

Locke was raising the question, which [Robert] Burton too had raised, of whether mental illness affected the imagination or the understanding. Burton, after judiciously citing authorities on both sides, concluded that the defect "is first in *imagination, and afterwards in reason*" (*Anatomy . . .*). Indeed this was the usual conclusion of Christian writers; they were anxious to preserve the sanctity of reason—which as part of the rational soul was thought to be immaterial—by blaming its errors on defects in the lower faculties. Possibly such considerations influenced Locke, for a year later he had second thoughts:

> Madnesse seems to be nothing but a disorder in the imagination, and not in the discursive faculty; for one shall find amongst the distracted, those who phansy them selves kings, &c, who discourse and reason right enough upon the suppositions and wrong phansies they have taken.

Everyday experience confirmed such a hypothesis, he argued, as when one enters a street with which he is only half familiar at a point different than he had expected, and thus finds all his reasonings about the location of things to be inaccurate. Locke noted that once one had formed a wrong opinion of something—the layout of the street, say—it was difficult to correct it. He concluded that great care should therefore be taken "that the first impressions we setle upon our minds be conformable to the truth and to the nature of things, or else all our meditation and discourse there upon will be noe thing but perfect raveing." The following week Locke returned to the problem again and, as if wishing somehow to preserve the antithesis of his original query, suggested that "where a man argues right upon wrong notions or termes he does like a madman, where he makes wrong consequences he does like a foole." Theologically the resolution was safe since fools were considered to be marked out by God, not stricken by disease. One was *born* a fool; one *became* mad.

Out of these entries came the distinction in the *Essay* between idiots and madmen, which in the eighteenth century was to be one of the most frequently quoted observations on insanity. Madmen, he said, "do not appear to have lost the faculty of reasoning, but having joined together some ideas very wrongly, they mistake them for truths; and they err as men do that argue right from wrong principles. For by the violence of their imaginations, having taken their fancies for realities, they make right deductions from them." It is significant that Locke does not, as many of his first readers must have expected him to do, go on to say that imagination deceives the intellect at the behest of the passions; he says only that the imaginations of madmen contain ideas falsely connected. His concept of imagination is somewhat clarified by a long entry in the journals on the difference between it and memory. Locke supposes that whereas memory furnishes the mind with ideas of things encountered in experience, ideas which "like painting after the life come always short," the imagination is free to join ideas together into wholly new combinations; it is a "picture drawne in our mind without reference to patterne," a picture which cannot be diminished by comparison to any object in the real world." The ideas of imagination are "usually very bright and clear," but should they come to be drawn with such boldness and intensity that they make impressions on the mind as strong as those of external objects on the senses, then, he contends, a man will mistake them for reality and go mad. Locke is convinced that the natural freedom and vivacity of imagination enable it at times to dominate the other faculties of the mind, but he is forced to confess himself at a loss to tell "how it comes thus to be let loose."

The problem is not discussed in the first edition of the *Essay*, but it evidently weighed on Locke's mind, for in 1700, near the close of his life, he added a chapter on the association of ideas which proposed a revolutionary solution. He had said before that ideas might be rightly or wrongly connected in the imagination and that the latter might be the case in the imaginations of madmen; now he sets out to explain why ideas should come to be wrongly connected in the first place, and concludes that it is "wholly owing to *chance* or *custom*":

> This strong combination of ideas, not allied by nature, the mind makes in itself either voluntarily or by chance; and hence it comes in different men to be very different, according to their different inclinations, education, interests, &c. *Custom* settles habits of thinking in the understanding, as well as of determining in the will, and of motions in the body: all which seems to be but trains of motions in the animal spirits, which once set a going, continue in the same steps they have been used to; which, by often treading, are worn into a smooth path, and the motion in it becomes easy, and as it were natural.

So it was that ideas not naturally related might, by being simultaneously experienced over long periods of time, "come to be so united in some men's minds, that it is very hard to separate them; they always keep company and the one no sooner at any time comes into the understanding, but its associate appears with it; and if they are more than two which are thus united, the whole gang always inseparable, show themselves together." . . . Hence the fear many men have of the dark often stems from the association they make between the idea of darkness and that of evil spirits or ghosts as a result of superstitious tales they heard in childhood. Similarly, one might have a horror of entering a particular room because many years before he saw a friend die in it, or suffered through a long illness there. While such irrational associations are common and seldom taken for symptoms of madness, Locke maintains that madness arises in exactly the same way, and differs from ordinary folly only in degree; the man who associates his idea of self with his idea of God and then proclaims himself lord of the universe errs in the same way as the one who associates sickness with a room.

Locke's theory of mental illness is revolutionary for its complete rejection of the traditional concept of the passions in revolt against reason. It is education and environment, rather than fear or lust or rage, which warp the imagination and deceive reason, and Locke takes care to underscore the point. He insists that there can be no absolute dichotomy between sanity and insanity: all "opposition to reason . . . is really madness," he writes, and "there is scarce a man so free from it, but that if he should always, on all occasions, argue or do as in some cases he constantly does, would not be thought fitter for Bedlam than civil conversation." Thus far the passage reads like a restatement of Hobbes' assertion that the passions are degrees of madness when they tend to evil, but in the next sentence, Locke makes clear that his point is altogether different: "I do not here mean when he is under the power of an unruly passion, but in the steady calm course of his life." . . . (pp. 19-23)

By minimizing the role of passion and stressing the importance of education, Locke in effect removes mental disease from the province of the moralist. So long as madness is viewed as a failure of will, or even as a failure to take proper care of the body, the madman can be held accountable for his condition and judged as a sinner; once it is seen as the result of unfortunate experiences over which he has no control, madness must be considered unavoidable, and man to have no power over his sanity. Furthermore, if every "opposition to reason" is madness, and madness out of our hands, can we honestly be thought able to correct any error of judgment or conduct whatever? Such a theory would seem subversive of Christian and secular ethics alike, since it implies the impossibility both of free will and of moral regeneration. That Locke was aware of these implications is doubtful; the only indication that he might have wished to avoid providing a new psychological basis for determinism is his remark about the mind forming unnatural associations "either voluntarily or by chance." The notion of voluntary association is, however, never developed; the examples he gives of wrong association all suggest that it is something which happens to the mind, rather than something the mind imposes upon itself. Locke even goes so far as to deny men the power to free themselves from a wrong association once it has settled in the mind; it may fade with time, but "while it lasts, it is not in the power of reason to help us." . . . It is probable that he did not make a greater effort to check the deterministic tendency of his argument because his attention was fixed elsewhere. Locke was not attempting a comprehensive theory of behavior and motivation; he was attempting to account for the phenomenon of error. He wished first . . . to reveal the extent to which men were liable to err in their private judgments, and second, to stress the importance of education by showing the far-reaching effects of early experience on the mind. Those who had charge of children he urged "diligently to watch, and carefully to prevent the undue connexion of ideas." . . . But the deterministic implications are there nonetheless, and in the curious spectacle of a chapter written to help men reform, yet showing how much they are at the mercy of environment, we perhaps have the germ of the paradox which Basil Willey sees as characteristic of the later associationists, Hartley, Priestly, and Godwin (and which is indeed characteristic of many modern revolutionary movements), namely, "that belief in Necessity should have been part of the creed of those who were the most ardent exponents of political, intellectual, and religious liberty," and who most vehemently argued the possibility of change. (pp. 23-4)

> *Michael V. DePorte, "Abnormal Psychology in England: 1660-1760," in his* Nightmares and Hobbyhorses: Swift, Sterne, and Augustan Ideas of Madness, *The Huntington Library, 1974, pp. 3-54.*

KATHLEEN M. SQUADRITO　(essay date 1979)

[*An American academic who studies the history of modern philosophy, epistemology, and metaphysics, Squadrito is the author of several studies of Locke's writings, most notably* Locke's Theory of Sensitive Knowledge *(1978) and* John Locke *(1979). In the following excerpt from the last-named work, she describes Locke's treatment of language and essence in* An Essay concerning Human Understanding, *noting his philosophical approach to words, ideas, and the classification of species.*]

In the introduction to the [*Essay concerning Human Understanding*], Locke indicates that his purpose is two-fold; to inquire into the origin, certainty, and extent of human knowledge, and to determine the grounds and degrees of belief, opinion, and assent. His examination into the foundations of knowledge is a study of questions such as the following: What types of things can the human mind know? What is the nature of the objects of knowledge? How do we come to know? For example, what is the role of sense-perception and reason in knowledge? Do we have any knowledge prior to experience? What kind of evidence is relevant to the truth of different sorts of statements? (p. 27)

Locke refers to the method by means of which he intends to discover the origin and extent of knowledge as the "historical, plain method," the term "historical" meaning factual or descriptive. A good deal of the *Essay* is simply a descriptive account of the human mind or intellect as it is engaged in gaining knowledge of different objects, an examination that we would today regard as psychological rather than scientific or philosophical. Locke complains that previous philosophers failed in their quest for knowledge because they did not bother to consider the capacities of the human mind. He regards an analysis of the nature of knowledge as necessary because, he says, "nobody, that I had met with, had, in their writings, particularly set down wherein the act of knowing precisely consisted. . . . If I have done any thing new, it has been to describe to others more particularly than had been done before, what it is their minds do, when they perform that action which they call knowing."

From the outset Locke insists that he does not intend to provide new methods of attaining certainty or of extending our knowledge; his interest is in things that are knowable, and his aim is to clear away misconceptions that stand in the way of obtaining knowledge. He intends the *Essay* to provide a foundation upon which others can build. Locke remarks that in an age of such masters as Boyle and Newton "it is ambition enough to be employed as an under-labourer in clearing the ground a little, and removing some of the rubbish that lies in the way to knowledge" [see excerpt dated 1690]. (pp. 29-30)

For Locke, words are by far the most significant instruments of knowledge. There is so close a connection between ideas and words, he says, "that it is impossible to speak clearly and distinctly of our knowledge, which all consists in propositions, without considering, first, the nature, use, and signification of language." Not only is there a very close connection between ideas and words, there is an intimate connection between ideas, words, and things. Locke reports that words, in their primary or immediate signification, stand for or represent nothing but the ideas in the mind of the speaker who uses them. By being signs they become instruments whereby people communicate their conceptions and express to one another their thoughts, imaginations, or ideas. A point worth noting is that words are not adopted by people as signs for their ideas by any *natural* connection that exists between articulate sounds and ideas, but rather, by a voluntary imposition whereby "words are made arbitrarily the mark of ideas." That it is by "*a perfect arbitrary imposition* is evident," Locke claims, for words "often fail to excite in others (even that use the same language) the same ideas we take them to be signs of." The relation of representation holding between words and ideas is that of signification. Any proposition to the effect that *A* is the sign of *B* cannot be known to be true on Locke's empiricist principles unless both *A* and *B* have been experienced in conjunction. One would have no reason for supposing that words and ideas are related as sign and thing signified unless both are observed. If only words are experienced they cannot, according to Locke, be signs of ideas; in effect, he says, they would "have no signification at all." (p. 39)

[The] representative relation obtaining between words and ideas is arbitrary. The sign "man," for example, does represent the idea a person has of man because the idea, for Locke, is known directly or immediately, the sign is voluntarily or arbitrarily assigned to it. Words, being voluntary signs, cannot, he says, "be voluntary signs imposed by" a person "on things he knows not." In order to know exactly what idea a word represents, or is the "sign of," one must first know or have the idea the word signifies, or, at least know an idea that resembles it in many respects. According to Locke, until a person has some ideas of his own, he "cannot suppose them to correspond with the conceptions of another man; nor can he use any signs for them; for thus they would be the signs of he knows not what, which is in truth to be the signs of nothing."

Although words immediately signify nothing but ideas in the mind of a speaker, Locke contends that communication depends on referring words to two other things. First, people take words to be marks of ideas in the minds of other people with whom they communicate. Second, because we do not speak barely of our own imagination, but of things as they really are, we often suppose words to stand also for the reality of things.

Locke goes on to point out the importance of general terms. It is not enough for the perfection of language in increasing our knowledge that sounds can be made signs of ideas; those signs must also be understood to comprehend several particular things. In the example used above, the sign "man" does not represent any particular idea of an individual thing, but signifies many different ideas or individual things of the same kind. Locke assumes at the outset that all things that exist are particulars. The universal character of scientific knowledge that Locke is so much interested in depends on general ideas; for the most part, Locke is not concerned with particular things, but with particular *kinds* of things, e.g., with man, and not with Sue, John, or Linda. Words are general when they are used for signs of general ideas, and are thus applicable indifferently to many particular things. Ideas are general when they are framed by the mind as the representatives of many particulars. Universality, Locke contends, "belongs not to things themselves, which are all of them particular in their existence, even those words and ideas which in their signification are general." That existence is limited to particulars is a fundamental axiom in Locke's philosophy; he naturally places the burden of proof on those who contend otherwise. Locke shows little interest in discussing the traditional philosophical problem of universals. The closest he comes to it is in his analysis of natural kinds. His interest is in the question "What do general words signify?" His answer is that they signify a *sort* or kind of thing by being signs of abstract ideas.

Locke's analysis of natural kinds has recently been recognized as an important aspect of his theory of knowledge. His doctrine, to be found in book 3 of the *Essay,* is a radical attack on the Aristotelian-Scholastic view of species or natural kinds, a view that Locke finds unscientific as well as dangerous to religious and social tolerance. By distinguishing nominal from real essence he seeks to replace the traditional view of kinds by one that he believes to be more in accord with the actual classifying procedures used in everyday life and science. The question he is concerned with is the basis for classifying things into various species. Why, for example, do we call one particular thing a horse and another a mule? How are kinds determined? Must we take into account any facts about the word? About human beings? About language?

Negatively, Locke argues against two bases for kind determinations; each concerns real essence. He points out that the expression "real essence" can be used in two different ways. In one sense the term is used in reference to particular substances, e.g., a particular man, horse, or gold nugget; in the other sense it is used to refer to particular sorts or kinds of substances, e.g., gold. When Locke speaks of the real essence of a particular substance, he is referring to the internal constitution of its insensible parts, i.e., the atomic constitution of the object. It is on this real essence that a particular substance's sensible qualities such as color, shape, weight, etc. depend. In Locke's opinion, human knowledge is limited to the observable or sensible qualities of bodies only; the real essence is considered unknown. Although the real essence of particular things cannot be discovered or known, Locke believes the idea of such an essence to be perfectly respectable; it is said to be the proper original meaning of the word "essence." That every individual substance has a real, internal, specific constitution, i.e., a real essence, he thinks beyond doubt.

When Locke uses the expression "real essence" in the second sense, as referring to sorts or species of substances, he has in mind the traditional Scholastic doctrine of genus and species as well as the doctrine of Platonic forms in which all natural existing things are said to be cast and to partake. He considers this idea of essence to be so much rubbish; the notion of "sortal

substances" having themselves real essences is said to be totally unintelligible, wholly useless and unserviceable to any part of our knowledge. Locke firmly believes that scientific progress had been hampered by the uncritical acceptance of the doctrine of substantial forms. The doctrine of substantial forms, taken as a theory about natural kinds, is not characterized by Locke in any great detail. He is content to point out a few of its salient features. The proponents of this doctrine suppose that individual things become of this or that species by virtue of partaking of a certain or fixed number of real essences, i.e., forms. According to this traditional view, people *discover* species; we are supposedly led to find particular things and their characteristics divided by nature or God into real and objective kinds. The primary focus of Locke's attack is precisely this idea that nature, not persons, makes classes or species. That nature "prefixes unmovable boundaries" of species is an assumption he goes to great lengths to dispose of. He admits to having a general idea of insensible particles of matter, but he denies that anyone has any idea whatsoever of substantial forms except the idea of the sound "form."

Locke advances several arguments against the Scholastic view of species. I will mention only the most important. In the first place, let us suppose that our senses were more acute than they presently are. Would it be possible to perceive, as it is in the proper sense of the term, this supposed essence of a species of things? One of Locke's reasons for rejecting the traditional account of kinds lies in his negative answer to this question. Such an essence is necessarily unobservable. Locke constantly asks us to consider how anyone could possibly tell one species from another if species were determined by unobservable and unknown forms; this he thinks impossible. Further, if the traditional doctrine were true, a certain state of affairs would have to obtain in the world. The condition Locke has in mind is the existence of precisely determinate or clear-cut boundaries of things to be met with in nature. The doctrine is considered factually false for the very reason that there are no such clearcut states of affairs. There are border-line cases or states of affairs best designated as "indeterminancy" in nature itself.

Locke reasons that if the traditional view were true, then there could not be the confusion and debates concerning classification that are most certainly found among the advocates of that view; by knowing the real essence one would be capable of determining without the least bit of hesitation whether a given thing were of this or that species. Champions of the traditional doctrine contradict their own tenets by basing their decisions concerning questionable cases on observable properties of bodies, the most common of which Locke takes to be shape. The case he quotes concerning the abbot of St. Martin can be used to illustrate the point. When the abbot was born, Locke recounts, "he had so little of the figure of a man, that it bespake him rather a monster. It was for some time under deliberation, whether he should be baptized or not. However, he was baptized, and declared a man provisionally (till time should show what he would prove)." To Locke's mind such doubts undermine the traditional view of kinds. As a child the abbot was nearly excluded from the species of human beings because of his shape. Locke surmises that "a figure of little more oddly turned" would have been executed "as a thing not to be allowed to pass" for a person. He insists that absolutely no reason can be given why a rational soul could not have been lodged inside such a body.

Locke's positive thesis is that the human understanding makes species or kinds of things. It does so in this way. In imagination one strips off from among the simple observable qualities which characterize a particular thing just those in respect to which it differs from things that resemble it closely in other respects. The product of this process of abstraction is a general idea of a sort or kind of thing in which all the qualities common to a set of resembling objects are combined. Locke uses the phrase "nominal essence" to signify this man-made abstract idea. It is an idea of qualities found together in objects that resemble one another, objects that fall under the same general name, e.g., "person," "horse," etc. The nominal essence of persons might, for example, include such properties as the power of speaking, the power of laughing, upright posture, abstract reasoning, two legs, and so forth. No single property on such a list can be considered essential to persons. Locke would not rule a person out of the species of human beings simply because the person had only one leg. For Locke classification of things into kinds does rest, in part, on a conventional or arbitrary basis. The choice of simple ideas included in a nominal essence, as well as the number of such ideas, is to a large extent determined by the interests of the classifier. Locke points out that "he that annexes the name man to a complex idea, made up of sense and spontaneous motion, joined to a body of such a shape, has thereby one essence of the species man; and he that . . . adds rationality, has another essence of the species he calls man; by which means the same individual will be a true man to the one which is not so to the other."

Kind determinations are not totally arbitrary. Species of things may be conventional in the sense that individual minds make kinds, but even though they may disagree as to the essence of a certain species, there *are* objective criteria by which people sort things into kinds. It is not a matter of "say what you like, you cannot be mistaken." Locke makes this quite clear with the following considerations: (1) Nominal essences must to some degree conform to what exists in nature "or else men's language will be like that of Babel; and every man's words, being intelligible only to himself, would no longer serve for conversation and the ordinary affairs of life, if the ideas they stand for be not some way answering the common appearances and agreement of substances as they really exist." (2) "To the making of any nominal essence, it is necessary . . . that the ideas whereof it consists have such a *union* as to make but one idea," i.e., "the mind, in making its complex ideas of substances, only follows nature. . . . Nobody joins the voice of a sheep with the shape of a horse; nor the color of lead with the weight and fixedness of gold, to be the complex ideas of any real substances; unless he has a mind to fill his head with chimeras, and his discourse with unintelligible words."

Locke's view of kinds is objective in the sense that the foundation of the essence of a sort of natural substance is the "similitude of things." Sorting of things into kinds is the work of the human understanding, but this sorting is possible only because things are more or less similar with regard to their observable qualities. Certain ways of classifying things are more reasonable and objective than others. Locke points out that for practical purposes our nominal essences of substances usually consist of only a small number of observed qualities in things, that we usually take the qualities of shape and color for "presumptive ideas of several species." He goes on to say that this serves well enough only for "gross and confused conceptions and inaccurate ways of talking and thinking." For the most part, the general names we use "receive their birth and signification from ignorant and illiterate people, who sorted and denominated things by those sensible qualities they found in them. . . . Locke points to a more objective notion of kinds

to be found in science. Science cannot give us a more objective notion of kinds in the sense of basing its descriptions upon the discovery of real essences, but it comes close to this ideal and does give us a more objective notion in the sense of detailed examinations of observable qualities. It requires, says Locke, "much time, pains, and skill, strict inquiry, and long examination to find out what, and how many, those simple ideas are, which are constantly and inseparably united in nature, and are always to be found together in the same subject."

Because scientists do not have a method adequate for discovering the real nature or essence of things, Locke's theory of knowledge culminates in skepticism with respect to the physical world. He considers the advocacy of this type of skepticism extremely important for several reasons, the foremost reason being that in the absence of such skepticism, there is a likelihood of dogmatism in considering the nature or essence of mind, spirit, matter, God, etc. For example, Locke considers empirically unverifiable the Cartesian claim that the mind is a spiritual or thinking substance. We simply do not know the essence of mind; it is quite possible that the mind is nothing but a material substance. Because the way we perceive the world is determined by our theoretical concepts, i.e., nominal essences, it is possible that these concepts are not reliable indicators of the real nature of material bodies. Locke's doctrine of natural kinds, with minor modifications, compares favorably with that advanced by many contemporary philosophers. (pp. 39-45)

The current interest in linguistic philosophy has led to the discovery of the significance of the third book of the *Essay*. Essentially, the third book concerns language and its relation to philosophical problems. Like many contemporary philosophers, Locke contends that many apparently philosophical problems are easily resolved by paying close attention to language. "I am apt to imagine," he says, "that were the imperfections of language, as the instrument of knowledge, more thoroughly weighed, a great many of the controversies that make such a noise in the world, would of themselves cease." Locke was also one of the first philosophers to insist that scientific classification of natural substances is arbitrary. The existence of borderline cases was enough to convince him that natural properties could not constitute criteria for determining what species a particular object should be classified under. Because particulars of the same species do not share a common essence, Locke was led to draw one of the most important distinctions to be found in the century's literature. The distinction between real and nominal essence that is presented in book 3 is still a topic of debate in philosophical circles. (p. 125)

Kathleen M. Squadrito, in her John Locke, *Twayne Publishers, 1979, 153 p.*

ELDON J. EISENACH (essay date 1981)

[*Eisenach is an American educator and scholar who concentrates his studies on the works of John Stuart Mill, Thomas Hobbes, and John Locke. In the following excerpt from his* Two Worlds of Liberalism: Religion and Politics in Hobbes, Locke, and Mill *(1981), he discusses Locke's philosophy of good and evil, pleasure and pain, and reward and punishment.*]

In his *Essay Concerning Human Understanding*, Locke discusses how men come to learn rules which define good and evil. In that discussion, he makes no distinction in principle between the processes of learning pure or corrupt sets of rules, or between learning rules in a traditional society or in a state of nature. What his discussion does show, however, is that learning in a state of nature would yield far different rules and opinions than learning as it has taken place heretofore in history.

When Locke had discussed speculative religious faith in his [first *Letter concerning Toleration*], he had argued that faith promising eternal reward terminated simply in the understanding. This termination meant that belief concerning life after death could not directly affect specific actions and thus could not be the cause of any other man's injury. This is simply a fact. True or not, however, past societies generated and enforced rules concerning professions of belief even though belief itself could motivate no "injurious" consequences. Thus, absurd and unjust rules can teach absurd and unjust morality. Locke's epistemology rests on pleasure and pain. He who has power to enforce rules defines good and evil. Opinions of good and evil determine our wills and our actions.

Will is the power to act or to refrain from action. Action, in turn, is motivated by a desire to seek pleasure or avoid pain.

> A power to direct the operative faculties to motion or rest in particular instances is that which we call the will. That which in the train of our voluntary actions determines the will to any change of operation is some present uneasiness, which is, or at least is always accompanied with, that of desire.

In contrast to the desire to seek pleasure, desire to avoid pain is always a motivating factor and always causes "uneasiness," because "a total freedom from pain always makes a *necessary* part of our happiness." It is inappropriate in this context to speak of freedom of the will, for so long as man has the capacity to move and to desire he *must* will. Not freedom, but power, is the appropriate term: "For desire being nothing but an uneasiness in the want of an absent good, in reference to any pain felt, ease is that absent good." "Uneasiness of desire" is that which "immediately determines the will." Since power is always relational, he who, "has the power or not the power to operate is that alone which is or is not free."

To move from this general theory of human action to Locke's theory of how men learn definitions of what is good and evil depends on an understanding of that most slippery of concepts, "uneasiness." Men will desire what they "think" is a good. But in Locke's definition, will can only be known by the act, the only proof that a person has willed. Thus, to say that "the will operates on the understanding," or that the understanding operates on the will, is not to speak properly. A proper formulation of the relationship between acting (willing) and learning takes us into the language of pain and pleasure, punishment and reward, misery and happiness.

> Now, because pleasure and pain are produced in us by the operation of certain objects either on our minds or our bodies and in different degrees, therefore, what has an aptness to produce pleasure in us is that we call *good*, and what is apt to produce pain in us we call *evil*.

Since Locke has already shown that not "all good, even seen and confessed to be so, necessarily move[s] every particular man's desire" but only that "taken to make a necessary part of his happiness," punishment in some form is a necessary part of the efficacy of teaching rules that define moral good and evil. In Locke's formulation, punishment is necessary both in learning the rules and then in being "willing" to adhere to them. Good and evil generally "are nothing but pleasure or pain, or that which occasions pleasure or pain to us." Moral good or evil, therefore,

[is] only the conformity or disagreement of our voluntary actions to some law, whereby good or evil is drawn on us from the *will and power of the lawmaker;* which good and evil, pleasure or pain, attending our observance or breach of the law by the decree of the lawmaker, is that we call reward and punishment.

For Locke—and only here does he differ significantly from Hobbes—moral rules are taught in a diffused set of contexts which mete out punishment. Locke's perception of rules and rule learning is at once central to his system and notoriously lacking a determinate source. For Locke, rules of good and evil are simultaneously articulated by divine law, the civil law, and the "law of opinion"; therefore, they are "taught" respectively by revelation, by government, and by public opinion. Here . . . Locke has built a bridge spanning the separate jurisdictions of church and state and of faith and reason.

In the *Essay* Locke sees moral good and evil as being defined and enforced by church, government, and society; each realm possesses a unique set of rewards and punishments. His primary purpose in making these distinctions is to explain the origin in men of ideas of moral relationships, given the sensible reality of uneasiness in the mind or pain in the body when the rules are violated. On the purely descriptive level, Locke argues that the knowledge of moral relationships and, therefore, of good and evil is "taught" to men through these three mechanisms.

Such a description does not raise the problem of reasonable assent or reasonable tests for assent to these rules. Nor does such a description raise the possibility of conflict among rules. The important element is the power to punish their breach. The source of power behind civil law is the physical power of the magistrate; in most cases that source is easily known. The source of power behind the law of opinion is the power of the "public" to distribute reputations and thus affect the distribution of wealth, power, and happiness. This source is somewhat indeterminate because opinion is segmented and often divided, even though its effects are palpable. The source of power behind the divine law is God. This source is most powerful and most indeterminate, because the use of this power cannot be proven. Only belief in a future judgment, and opinion regarding the standards for judgment, stand behind divine law.

In the *Essay* Locke makes no attempt to rank either these three sets of rules or the relative efficacy of their sanctions. Both in the [*Letters concerning Toleration*] and in [*On the Reasonableness of Christianity, as Delivered in the Scriptures*], however, he strongly suggests that political life in history merges rule-sets and sanctioning power into the power of the despotic king. The king and his priestly allies enforce divine law through the agency of an intolerant church; he and his dependents distribute reputations and rewards, thus dominating opinion and manners; he and his hangman sanction civil law—indeed, sanction all laws, for despotism claims power over faith, reason, opinion, and interest. And no matter how harshly the despot metes out pain, he is obeyed so long as religious belief supports his power: "The view of heaven and hell will cast a slight upon the short pleasures and pains of the present state." The historical success of despotism proves that men are enslaved by their own false religious beliefs, not that the despot's physical power is unchallengeable. Because the power backing divine law is not of this world, the causes of despotic power are also the source of its overthrow. The claim by civil authority or dominant opinion that certain rules are direct commands of God is a claim always open to challenge. And if men believe that politically enforced rules are contrary to divine law and that obedience to the former is breach of the latter, civil war and political revolution result.

The *Essay* contains no discussion of despotism, no guarantee that men will learn the right moral relationships, and no promise that correct knowledge of right moral relationships is discoverable through reason alone. The *Essay* claims only that faith and reason have "distinct provinces" which bar the right of magistrates to command faith. An enormous gap exists between man's history and the teachings of philosophy. This gap reflects the paradox that divine punishment is the most powerful and the least determinate sanction and that divine law is the most obligatory and the least known. The Bible as written revelation contains evidence from the past of determinate divine punishment and positive divine law. But God does not act supernaturally in the present epoch; Christ's coming demands that reason search out the laws of God as they operate in a world without visible signs of grace: a state of nature. This is the historical setting of the [*Second Treatise of Government*] and the justification for Locke's hope that law, moral opinion, and religion can be integrated by reason and not by the despot. Natural law taught by the pains and pleasures in a state of nature is at once divine command, the sum of individual desires, and, ultimately, the model for civil law.

Seen solely through the lens of Locke's formal epistemology, the search for natural laws in a state of nature is an exercise in futility: all men are born entrapped in webs of extant powers and are taught good and evil by self-interested men. Locke's exercise would seem as futile as the first half of Hobbes's *Leviathan:* the discussion of toleration by Locke and his interpretation of Scripture would suggest that his discoveries from state-of-nature reasoning—like Hobbes's civil philosophy—is dependent on prophecy for relevance in history. This conclusion is not fully warranted. The *Second Treatise* is not only an account of man's natural faculties played out in a timeless natural environment. Locke's state of nature has its own history—albeit a natural history—and the obligations learned in the state of nature are also learned in this history. Even in the *Essay* Locke suggests that adopted as well as natural desires and acquired habits, and also natural wants, inexorably teach man in history lessons which run counter to the disutilities sanctioned by prevailing laws, opinion, and religious belief. The *Second Treatise* contains a history of this acquisition, a history culminating in the present age.

The fact that the *Second Treatise* contains two somewhat contradictory states of nature has often been remarked. The logical tensions between the two are treated here as more properly viewed as tensions between a logic of nature and a logic of materialist history. Viewed this way, Locke's discussion of punishment—especially the right of every man in the state of nature to punish crime with death—takes on new meaning. Locke asserts that this natural right is given to men by nature's God and then shows why man would never exercise that right until a particular stage was reached in his history. The political import of this tension is that Locke's natural history includes a history of political sovereignty and despotism. The right to kill thieves includes the right to destroy rulers who wrongfully take property by force. To ask of the *Second Treatise* when in history the need to kill despots arose is to ask also when men in history began to question the legitimacy of paternalistic and theocratic political authority. The answer in the *Second Treatise* is not "when Christ appeared," but perhaps when property and markets and inequality did. Answers to questions of this type can never be entirely satisfactory, if only because the

Second Treatise is such a limited production in the repertoire of Locke. No understanding of either these questions or their possible answers can be gained, however, if we begin with some "light of nature" sparked by the wand of a benevolent deity—unless we are to believe that this treatise is Locke's only published fairy tale. (pp. 89-93)

> *Eldon J. Eisenach, "John Locke," in his* Two Worlds of Liberalism: Religion and Politics in Hobbes, Locke, and Mill, *The University of Chicago Press, 1981, pp. 73-113.*

PETER SIMPSON (essay date 1985)

[*In the following excerpt, Simpson compares Locke's and René Descartes's opinions concerning the existence of innate knowledge.*]

Before I proceed to my argument . . . , I ought to make one thing clear. My interest in the views of Descartes and Locke in this paper is philosophical, not historical. That is to say I intend to compare and contrast them with respect to content and reasoning and I am not concerned with how they were in fact compared or contrasted by the individuals in question. So, in particular, I leave aside the fact that when Locke attacks the doctrine of innate ideas he does not so much have Descartes in mind, as rather certain English thinkers. (p. 15)

It seems clear from a perusal of the writings of Descartes and Locke that what principally divides them is that the former does, while the latter does not, accept the existence of innate knowledge. Locke indeed devotes the first book of the [*Essay concerning Human Understanding*] to an attack on such knowledge, and empiricism, the doctrine he developed, is basically the claim that all knowledge is acquired by experience and cannot, as rationalists thought, be spun out of innate principles in the mind. (p. 16)

One may divide Locke's criticism of innate ideas into a negative and a positive part; the negative part attempts to refute the reasons advanced for innate knowledge, while the positive part gives reasons against such knowledge. As regards the first division, the major argument that Locke maintains is used to support innate knowledge is drawn from universal consent; but, says Locke, there is no knowledge that all men consent in, and even if there were it would not thereby be proved innate unless one also showed that no other explanation would do.

Further, the various shifts and qualifications resorted to to explain the apparent lack of universal consent, namely (a) that the knowledge is in all men, but implicitly, (b) that use of reason is required first before the knowledge becomes actual, (c) that the knowledge is admitted as soon as proposed, are all inadequate. As regards (a), "implicit knowledge" either means that the mind is capable of possessing such knowledge or it means nothing, for to say that the mind has knowledge it does not know is nonsense; but being capable of coming to know applies to everything we know and so will prove all knowledge innate if it proves any to be so, and this Locke's opponents do not want to admit. As regards (b), use of reason, how can reasoning be required for knowledge which, as innate, must be regarded as existing prior to reasoning? And anyway, some men who clearly can reason do not know those principles said to be innate. Moreover, since the only sense the phrase "use of reason" can bear is that it refers to knowledge that is not known or taken notice of before one comes to the use of reason, and since this is true of all knowledge, it will again follow that all knowledge is innate, and this is more than the proponents of this argument want to admit. The same criticism will apply also to (c), knowledge recognized on first proposing, for many things are known on first proposing that have not been accorded the title of innate. One can, therefore, summarize this destructive side of Locke's criticism as follows: supposed innate knowledge does not have what is held to be the sign of innateness, namely universal consent, and all efforts to overcome this difficulty fail altogether, or if they prove anything prove all knowledge to be innate including what it is generally admitted is not so.

Locke's positive criticism draws attention to evidence that argues the opposite of innateness. First, he says, the knowledge that is actually first in time for us is of particulars, universals being only understood afterwards when one has learnt the difficult task of abstraction. But all supposed innate principles are universal and so, far from being first, as they ought to be if they are innate, must be last of all. Second, the ideas that occur as the terms in these principles are not present in the minds of all men, and, being universal, must follow the particulars that are visibly first for us, so they cannot be innate either; and neither, therefore, can the principles that use them be innate. Third, no sense can be given to the notion that there is knowledge in a mind which it has never yet perceived, for any idea that the mind has never perceived was, says Locke, never in the mind, and whatever idea is in the mind is either a present perception or was so and is now preserved in the memory.

Turning now to Descartes, he makes a division of ideas into innate, adventitious and factitious, but he regards this division as provisional and, in fact, it turns out that though there are differences between these types of ideas all of them must, in the end, be considered innate.... [Descartes] includes the following among those ideas he provisionally calls innate: a thing, a truth, a thought. He gives these reasons for considering them innate. First, when one examines a piece of wax, the idea of this as a thing, or as an enduring and self-identical object, cannot be derived from sensation because all the sensible qualities may change while the wax yet remains the same piece of wax; so it must be innate. Second, it is possible to form in one's thought clear conceptions of an infinity of geometrical figures that one has never perceived through the senses, and, further, these conceptions are quite different in character from sensible impressions and images because while one can form a clear conception of a chiliagon, say, as a thousand-sided figure, one can by no means form a clear sensible image of one; therefore these ideas too must be innate. Third, the ideas of God and the soul cannot be sensible or derived from sensible ideas because there is nothing sensible about either of them. Fourth and finally, there are universal principles such as "Things equal to the same thing are equal to each other" which cannot be derived from something particular such as sensible ideas are.

If one views these arguments together, one may say that what Descartes is basically doing is adverting to certain facts about our knowledge that point to a difference in kind between sensations and imaginations on the one hand and thoughts on the other, or between what one may call sensible ideas and intellectual ones. But (and this is significant) he regards it as sufficient to point this out to be able immediately to conclude that intellectual ideas cannot be derived from sensible ones, and must therefore be innate.

As regards those sensible ideas which Descartes provisionally classified as adventitious, these also, he maintains, must be acknowledged as innate. This is because of certain convictions he has about the nature of physical things, for he holds that bodies are just extended things capable of motion and that all that is really in the senses when stimulated by external bodies is corporeal movements and nothing else. Consequently the sensible ideas we actually experience, as colours, sounds, tastes and so on, which clearly have no likeness to the corporeal movements, cannot be derived from them and must be innate in the mind so that they can be envisaged by the mind on the occasion of the relevant stimulus. Finally, as regards those ideas provisionally classified as factitious, since these are just made up of other ideas, they too must be acknowledged as innate, at least with respect to their materials.

Such, then, is a brief summary of the reasonings of Descartes and Locke about innate knowledge. Now I do not intend to examine each argument in detail (that would take too long and is, anyway, not necessary for my purpose), but a general remark is here in order. What is particularly noteworthy is that, in the case of Locke, his attention is principally directed to the observable phenomena about the state and growth of knowledge among men and he pays little attention to the precise character of that knowledge. The reverse, however, is true of Descartes, for what tends to impress him and make him opt in favour of innate ideas is that the content of our knowledge is such that it cannot be accounted for in purely empirical terms. It is worth pointing out that a similar motivation lies behind the thinking of others who have adopted a theory of the innate-knowledge type. One thinks, for example, of Chomsky with his generative grammar that underlies all languages and is genetically inherited, for he holds language-ability to be too complex to have been acquired by experience alone; one thinks also of Kant who felt compelled to posit, if not innate knowledge, at least innate forms of knowledge, or *a priori* concepts to explain the universality and necessity of the propositions of science. One is tempted to suggest that in proportion as one concentrates on those aspects of the question that impressed Descartes, on the one hand, or Locke on the other, so one will incline accordingly for or against belief in some kind of innate knowledge.

What I wish to do now, having summarized the arguments, is to examine how far and in what ways it is, in theory, possible to construct a defense for the position of each against the criticisms of the other. (pp. 16-18)

Descartes need not be much embarrassed by Locke's negative criticism because he does not appeal to universal consent in support of his position. In fact such consent might appear to him unattainable in existing conditions because of the way men's thought is corrupted, in his view, during the long period of their immature and undiscriminating youth. The practice of the method of doubt is an absolute preliminary to genuine knowledge and not all men are capable of that, so it would be unreasonable to expect them all to assent to the same things. Further, as Descartes is prepared to say that all knowledge is innate he would escape all the objections that Locke makes on this score.

The first two parts of Locke's positive criticism would cause Descartes as little trouble. Since he regards all knowledge as innate, it hardly matters which parts of it are recognised first. But, anyway, it is only reasonable to expect that beings whose life, from its very beginning, is lived so much in the senses, should become conscious first of the part of their innate knowledge that concerns sensible particulars. In fact, the predominating influence that such ideas have over men's thinking just reinforces, for Descartes, the need for a proper method to overcome it.

The only argument of Locke's that might cause a problem for Descartes is the final one that it makes no sense to talk of knowledge that is not known, as one does if one says that all knowledge is innate but yet brought to consciousness only after time and learning. Descartes' response on this point would be to the effect that innate knowledge is such that one can draw it out of one's mind, not that one is always conscious of it, so he might well argue that there is no contradiction involved since one is not talking of knowledge that is not known but about ideas that have a two-fold manner of existence: first unconsciously, when they are not known, and second consciously, when they are. In other words "being in the mind" does not mean "being known" as Locke maintains.

Nevertheless, even if one says this, one must recognize that there is a difference between the unconscious knowledge that has been learnt but is not being reflected on, and knowledge that is supposed to be possessed unconsciously but has never yet been learnt. The former knowledge can be brought to mind more or less at will, but the latter cannot. . . . [I] think it is here that Descartes' position is most vulnerable. When one considers the role that experience as a matter of fact plays in the generation of our knowledge (and in this respect, at any rate, Locke's reflections are very much to the point), Descartes' thesis, despite all he has to say in favour of it, seems somehow out of line.

Turning now to Locke and in what way his position could be defended against Descartes, there is first of all Descartes' reason for making sensible or adventitious ideas innate. Locke had similar materialist views to Descartes and likewise believed that all that was real in things was corpuscles and their motions; his classic division into primary and secondary qualities reflects that belief. Why then is his conclusion different since he accepts the premise? There is some evidence that Locke did feel the force of Descartes' argument here, for he says that it is God who "annexes" sensible ideas to such and such motions in the sense organs. How far Locke was aware of the significance of this remark is unclear, but what it effectively amounts to is the admission that the motions by themselves are incapable of causing the ideas and that it is necessary to have recourse to some other cause, God, to account for them. Certainly there is, for Locke, no discoverable connection (and so no discoverable connection of causality) between motions and bodies, or primary qualities, on the one hand, and tastes and sounds etc., or secondary qualities, on the other.

It is clear from this that, if not as explicit on this point as Descartes, Locke evidently felt its force sufficiently to speak as if God rather than the corporeal motions was the cause; the motions would at best be occasions for divine activity. And if this is so, then the question at issue reduces to the manner of this divine activity: does God implant the ideas once for all in the nature of the soul, to be made conscious on the occasion of the appropriate stimulus, or does he implant them afresh each time? Descartes takes the former view, and, if "annex" can be pressed, so, it seems, would Locke: thus they would hardly differ from each other at all.

In this light Locke would turn out to be almost as much a believer in innate knowledge as Descartes. Certainly he would be more a believer than those he attacks in his *Essay,* for they only posited some innate knowledge, but Locke would virtually be saying that all knowledge is innate, at least all sensible

knowledge. This is a paradoxical result for it seems to overturn Locke's empiricism completely. In fact it does not so much destroy empiricism as bring to light its precise nature. Locke's thesis will not be much affected if sensible ideas turn out to be innate rather than received from without, for what he is principally contending for is that all knowledge is derived from sensible knowledge (whether directly in the case of outer sensation or indirectly in the case of inner reflection), and whatever the origin of sensible knowledge, the dependence of other knowledge on it would remain unaffected. (pp. 18-20)

It is at this point that one must consider Descartes' arguments that we do have knowledge, intellectual knowledge, that is not derived from sensible knowledge and differs from it in kind. Locke does not directly confront such arguments, but he does say enough about the generation of our knowledge for us to be able to judge how defensible against them his attempt to show that it is all derived from the ideas of experience would be. The important tests concern his explanations of such things as substance, infinity, and abstract ideas.

As regards substance it is difficult to regard Locke's position as anything other than inconsistent. It is, according to him, not a distinct, positive idea and is not derived from sensation or reflection; it is a relative idea, a "something I know not what." Locke seems to attribute the origin of this idea to an inner compulsion of thinking which does not allow us to suppose ideas can exist without a subject or support for them. Now this, interestingly, brings him close to Descartes for whom substance is an innate intellectual idea that is necessarily present in the mind's thinking. Moreover, the idea of substance, if one is going to talk about a something that supports other ideas (its "accidents"), can be thought in separation from those accidents, and as such it is a distinct idea. In fact, as Descartes' wax example helps to show (and as his scholastic teachers would have argued), substance is the idea of the thing itself, considered, however, without consideration of its qualities; it is thus a positive idea as well, the idea of the thing as taken under the aspect of self-subsistence, as opposed to the ideas of its qualities, its shape, or colour, which are ideas of the thing as taken under the aspect, not of its existing purely and simply, but of its existing in a certain way, as round or white. Locke does not take this line, and principally, one supposes, because substance understood in this way is not reducible to any impressions or images of sensation. But if so, he would have been more consistent to have followed Hume and refused to admit the idea of substance at all. If Locke would have been unhappy about such an extreme answer and felt it necessary to posit substance as a genuine part of the idea of a physical object, then one must say that he has in effect made an important concession in favour of Descartes, for it becomes difficult, if not impossible, to regard substance as an idea of purely empirical origin.

Similar problems arise with respect to the idea of infinity. Here again, says Locke, we have no positive idea, only a negative one that is positive insofar as it includes some determinate size or length and negative insofar as it includes the idea of an indeterminate amount more. In the whole of Locke's discussion, judging by the argumentation and the examples used, there is a persistent confusion of the notion of infinity with the image of something infinite. Locke only succeeds in showing that we can form no image of an infinite thing (which is perhaps a truth too obvious to justify the amount of space devoted to it), and he leaves out altogether any mention of the notion of infinity, of the "what it is" of infinity. Aristotle defines the infinite as that of which there is always something more (and in this he is followed by Aquinas), which seems clear and positive enough. Locke's failure to take notice of this illustrates the basic thrust of his empiricism, for his implicit argument (which accounts for the confusion just mentioned) is that if infinity is an idea derived from the senses it must be analyzable in terms of the immediate sensible data, namely sensible qualities and images. His empiricism, in other words, amounts to the claim not just that knowledge is derived from sensible experience, but that it is reducible to those very sensible impressions.

This talk of sensible impressions and images reminds one of Descartes' remarks concerning the chiliagon when he distinguishes between thought and imagination. He argues, and correctly, that there must be a difference between these two, for while we have a very clear conception of what chiliagons and other many-sided figures are, that is of their specific nature, we can form no clear image of them. Now Locke is prepared to talk of natures and essences, but what he means by them is just a collection of simple ideas of images to which a single name is given; he does not mean an intellectual concept as Descartes does.

That this amounts to a deficiency in Locke's thought is further illustrated by what he says of abstract ideas. We arrive at these, in his opinion, by removing from the several particulars we perceive—Peter, James, Mary, Jane—what is peculiar to each and retaining what is common to all—man. Abstract ideas are thus particular ideas narrowed down, or partial ideas of more complex ones. Berkeley's celebrated attack on this view, is convincing: no idea whatever can be without characteristics that make it a particular [see excerpt dated 1734]. This criticism is correct when "idea" means, as it does in this context, a sensible image, but if one is talking about intellectual concepts, not images, as Descartes is when he mentions universals, the same objection does not arise, for these are understood as not being bound by particularity.

Having examined and compared these arguments, it remains to consider what they tell us about the differences between Descartes and Locke. I think it can quite readily be seen that the point at issue between them is not the existence or non-existence of innate knowledge but the difference between imagining and sensing, on the one hand, and thinking (or what Descartes calls pure intellection), on the other. Locke's distinctive thesis, and indeed what empiricism basically amounts to, is the denial that there is any such difference, or in other words the reduction of thought in effect to imagination. This is true despite the fact that Locke posits reflection as a source of knowledge in addition to sensation, for this really makes no difference since not only do the ideas of reflection arise from the mind's perception of its own operations about sensible ideas, but this reflection is itself said to be a kind of inner sensation, and so is, in principle, no different in its cognitive character from sensation proper. Nevertheless, as the examples of substance and abstract ideas indicate, Locke is not as thorough-going as his reductive thesis requires him to be. He seems to have remained aware, possibly because of his closeness to the scholastic tradition, of elements of thought with which his thesis does not square, but which he felt it was somehow necessary to fit in. Despite this, however, his successor, Berkeley, had no doubt about the bearing of that thesis. For him what Locke meant by "idea" was "sensible image" as is clear from his attack on Locke's abstract ideas. Hume is even more explicit about the reduction of thought to imagination, declaring that all knowledge resolves itself into impressions, that is immediate sensible experience, and ideas, that is their "faint images in thinking and reasoning"; it was he, above all, who carried empiricism to its sceptical, but logical, extreme.

To return to Descartes, all he in effect does is to point to aspects of thought that show it to be quite distinct from sensation, or to be at a higher cognitive level; and with respect to none is it possible for Locke to give a really satisfactory reply. If this analysis is correct, then it means that the real point at issue between the empiricism of Locke and the rationalism of Descartes is not, as appears on the surface, about the origin of thought, but about its nature. The question that divides them is not so much "Where does knowledge come from, experience or the innate resources of the mind?" as rather "What is the nature of thought—is it, or is it not, distinct in kind from sensation and imagination?" It is worth asking why this latter question gets transformed into the former. A look at the general form of the reasoning employed by each thinker will help to reveal the answer.

The general form of Descartes' reasoning (disregarding the argument about the origin of sensible ideas which is not relevant here) is as follows: thoughts are quite different from sensations or images, therefore they cannot be derived from them but must be innate. The general form of Locke's reasoning is conversely: no knowledge is innate but it all comes from sensible experience (the argument of the first book of the *Essay*), therefore it is all sensible knowledge or reducible to such knowledge, that is, to sensations and images. Now once this general form is exposed, it can be seen that there is a common assumption that lies behind both these arguments. If Descartes believes that the difference between thought and sensation means that the former cannot be derived from the latter, this can only be because he is taking for granted the additional premise that if thought is sense-derived it must ultimately be the same as sensation; and if Locke believes that the derivation of knowledge from sensible experience means it must all be sensible knowledge, this can only be because he is taking for granted the same additional premise, namely that if all knowledge (including thought) is sense-derived it must ultimately be the same as sensation. This conditional premise can be expressed more fully thus: if all knowledge is conveyed to the mind through the senses, it must be sensible knowledge or reducible to such knowledge. Now there are two ways to argue from a conditional premise; one either asserts the antecedent and concludes by asserting the consequent, or one denies the consequent and concludes by denying the antecedent. Locke and Descartes only differ from each other about innate knowledge as completely as they do because Locke adopts the former procedure while Descartes adopts the latter. (pp. 20-3)

Peter Simpson, "The Nature and Origin of Ideas: The Controversy over Innate Ideas Reconsidered," in International Philosophical Quarterly, *Vol. XXV, No. 97, March, 1985, pp. 15-30.*

RUSSELL KIRK   (essay date 1986)

[An American historian, political theorist, novelist, journalist, and lecturer, Kirk is one of America's most eminent conservative intellectuals. His works have provided a major impetus to the conservative revival that has developed since the 1950s. The Conservative Mind (1953), one of Kirk's early books, describes conservatism as a living body of ideas "struggling toward ascendancy in the United States"; in it Kirk traces the roots and canons of modern conservative thought to such important predecessors

as Edmund Burke, John Adams, and Alexis de Tocqueville. Kirk has also been a trenchant critic of the decline of academic standards in American universities: Decadence and Renewal in the Higher Learning *(1978), in particular, is a forceful denunciation of the "academic barbarism" which he states has replaced the traditional goals of higher education—wisdom and virtue—with the fallacious ones of "utilitarian efficiency" and innovative forms of education. The result, in Kirk's view, is that "the higher learning in America is a disgrace." Kirk's detractors have sometimes been skeptical of the charges he levels against liberal ideas and programs, accusing him of simplistic partisanship. His admirers, on the other hand, point to the alleged failure of liberal precepts— in particular those applied in the universities—as evidence in support of Kirk's ideas and criticism. In the following excerpt, Kirk argues that Locke's influence on the framers of the Constitution of the United States was not a seminal one.]*

For decades, the typical American school textbook in history— supposing that the textbook's author touches at all upon the intellectual background of the Constitution—has asserted that the great name of Locke commanded the minds both of the signers of the Declaration of Independence and of the framers of the Constitution. But nowadays most people have learned how wretched a production is the typical textbook in American history; we have become aware that many textbook authors borrow from other textbooks, rather than turning to genuine historical sources.

A good many names, some of them political philosophers, appear in the pages of *The Federalist,* the series of essays that secured the ratification of the Constitution. Yet the name of John Locke does not appear in any of those papers, written by Madison, Hamilton, and Jay. Nor is any reference to Locke to be found in Madison's *Notes of Debates in the Federal Convention.* Does not the hard fact of these omissions seem significant to the textbook writers and the textbook companies' editors? Or may it be that the people who prepare American school manuals do not trouble themselves with the facts? (pp. 561-62)

[In] truth John Locke did not fix American political convictions, in the eighteenth-century or the nineteenth; he was merely one of a number of important political thinkers who contributed to the climate of political opinion about the time of the Declaration and Constitution.

As Daniel Boorstin, the ablest of our present American historians, has written in several of his books, the genius of American politics consists in the American habit of refraining from abstract doctrine and theoretical dogma. Moreover, the fundamental American political institutions already had taken form before 1776—and America's economic and social patterns, too. John Locke had very little to do with that complex of institutions and customs; his one attempt at shaping America, his *Fundamental Constitutions of Carolina,* was totally ignored by the colonists. In America, as in England, Locke's writings were employed as an apology for what already had come into being—not as a grand design for emulation.

Ideas take root only if the soil of society has been prepared for them by circumstances. Locke's ideas in some degree influenced Americans, but did not dominate their minds; his ideas took on flesh in America only so far as they accorded with social arrangements and customs already flourishing there.

Let us test this hypothesis by examining succinctly Locke's writings. Although his *Two Treatises on Civil Government,* published in 1690 (but probably written for the most part some years earlier), purport to be abstract discourses on the origin

and character of society, in truth they amount to an explanation of the English political experience over many centuries. *Civil Government* is a kind of apology for the Revolution of 1688. A Marxist might argue that *Civil Government* is an ideological tract: that is, a propaganda veil for the defense of certain economic interests, in this instance the interests of William III, the Whig magnates, and the landed classes generally. Locke's eagerness to protect "property" or "estate," and to establish it as one of three natural rights, seems to justify the application of "ideology" here, as Marx defined that sinister term.

Locke's objectives in the practical politics of the closing years of the seventeenth-century may be stated quite simply: to secure the Protestant ascendancy; to advance the interest of the commercial classes, which Locke identified with England's national economic interest; and to sustain what Disraeli much later would call a "Venetian constitution" for England, with the royal authority subordinated to the influence of the great Whig landed proprietors.

These objectives Locke—who was no democrat—shores up with a body of political theory. Political sovereignty belongs to the people, Locke argues—and not, by implication, to the king. The people delegate their power to a legislative body, Parliament, but they may withdraw that power on occasion. The executive authority, derived from the legislative, is dependent upon Parliament. That ought to be the constitution of England, Locke believed; and the Whig magnates with whom he was associated did establish such a constitution in 1688-1689.

Despite Locke's conformity to the Church of England, these ideas somewhat resemble the theories of certain Puritan writers and politicians on either side of the Atlantic. In New England, between 1642 and 1660, the Puritan colonists had governed themselves on such principles—although they had found it necessary to submit to Stuart authority at the Restoration. The Massachusetts Declaration of Laws and Liberties of 1649 obviously was not inspired by Locke; one may say that Locke, rather, was the inheritor of Puritan claims.

It is Locke's aspiration to prove that government is the product of free contract; that governors hold their authority only in trust; and that when trust is violated, a people rightfully may exercise their strength to undo tyranny—although only under unendurable provocation. These arguments explain and defend the Revolution of 1688, but also they purport to explain the nature of a long struggle for balanced government in England, from the thirteenth-century onward. For the principle of parliamentary control of royal succession had been maintained successfully when Henry of Bolingbroke was crowned; and one finds the principle of resistance to tyranny in the pages of Hooker's *Laws of Ecclesiastical Polity.*

In most matters, Locke was not an original thinker, but rather a synthesizer or popularizer. In moral philosophy, he endeavored to harmonize the findings of seventeenth-century science with Christian doctrine. Similarly, in politics he sought to work the opinions of earlier philosophers into a system consonant with historical experience and the new needs of his country.

Society is the product of a voluntary contract among men equal in a state of nature, Locke writes, to secure better the rights that are theirs by nature—life, liberty, property. Locke has much more to say about estate, or real property, than about life and liberty. Several times he declares that "the reason why men enter into society is the preservation of their property." This argument appealed strongly to colonial Americans, a very high proportion of the white inhabitants owning some sort of real property.

But can Locke's idea of the social compact be taken seriously in the twentieth-century? Certainly no cultural anthropologist of 1986 regards Locke's state of nature as ever having existed, nor subscribes to the notion of any formal social compact ever having been concluded by any primitive folk. For that matter, how much private property do primitive societies have to protect? Locke's conract theory—which Locke took literally himself—is one of several postulates that he fails to establish satisfactorily; as a reply to Hobbes, it now seems ludicrously insufficient.

Only sixty years later, David Hume would make mincemeat of Locke's theory that men, at any remote period, ever joined themselves into a formal concert for their common welfare. The historical origins of the state, Hume would point out, are nothing like Locke's primitive voluntary union: force and conquest, in England as elsewhere, have occurred recently or in some remote period, and have resulted in the forming of a state—although afterward most states are not held together by force alone.

So, too, Edmund Burke implied (though, like Locke, he stood for the Whig party) when, nearly a century after Locke, he advised his generation to "draw a sacred veil" over the remote origins of the state. Perhaps Locke's "law of nature" is not applicable to natural, primitive man, but rather to civilized Englishmen, whose impulses and appetites have been chastened by Christian teaching.

In some of his other writings, Locke seems to contradict certain of his own assertions in the *Second Treatise on Civil Government.* He denies, for instance, the existence of innate ideas. This denial endangers his political postulate that men possess by nature an understanding of how life, liberty, and property are the equal rights of all. If no ideas are innate, how can there subsist the "self-evident truths" which the Declaration of Independence would proclaim?

The *Second Treatise,* then, cannot be accepted as a literal historical account of the origins of society. Nor is Locke's particular understanding of natural law tenable today. Despite Locke's frequent quoting of Richard Hooker, Locke did not really follow that acute divine in his theory of natural law, and still less did he follow Hooker back to Aquinas and other Schoolmen. As Locke's most recent scholarly biographer, Maurice Cranston, points out, Locke's notion of "natural law" was a Renaissance understanding, derived from Pufendorf and other secularists of the German school [see Additional Bibliography]. (pp. 563-65)

Locke's other principal work, his *Essay Concerning Human Understanding,* was taken in its time as a contribution to philosophy that never would die. In this famous book the thesis of Locke is that the mind of every human individual at birth, resembles a blank tablet, on which experience marks a series of impressions. These impressions gradually are formed into general ideas. No innate ideas exist, says Locke in *Human Understanding*: all that an infant inherits from his forefathers, or receives from God, is the *means* for giving significance to separate impressions.

As *Civil Government* was meant to demonstrate the sufficiency of individual interest and private judgment in politics, so *Human Understanding* was intended to establish an individualism of the mind. This essay opened the way for the empiricism of

the eighteenth-century: everything in heaven and earth must come under the critical scrutiny of private judgment. It would be easy for the Deists, and for the skeptics who went beyond deism, to apply the theories of Locke to their own innovating impulses. Locke was neither Deist nor thoroughgoing skeptic, but he did intend *Human Understanding* to be a weapon, especially against the Catholics, whose fortresses of Authority and Tradition would tremble before him.

Large though the influence of his chief philosophical work has been for nearly three centuries, there remain few people today who would defend the whole of his argument. Some would go beyond Locke, all the way to untrammeled materialism, denying that even the capabilities for comparing, distinguishing, judging, and willing are innate. Others, pointing to the wealth of inquiry into the mysteries of human nature since the end of the seventeenth-century, would remark that Locke does not take into account those operations of the mind that lie below the level of consciousness; nor those that lift man, by mystical means or by poetic and mathematical insights, to a condition transcending the limits of pure reason. Yet other critics remark that Locke could know nothing about genetic inheritance, the science of genetics not having been dreamed of in Locke's age. Some such misgivings about Locke's first principles may be discerned among men of the Revolutionary and Constitutional eras in North America—that is, among those thoughtful Americans who had read Locke carefully, rather than receiving his concepts at second or third hand. (It is worth noting that *Civil Government* was not printed in America until 1773.) By 1776, and still more by 1787, John Locke's books were dusty enough.

And yet one continues to encounter, even in works of reference, the delusion that somehow John Locke was the real author of the Constitution of the United States. Consider the following passage from the brief article on Locke in *The Columbia Viking Desk Encyclopedia* (1953): "The state, he held, was formed by social contract and should be guided by belief in natural rights. This was in essence a plea for democracy, which bore fruit in the U.S. Constitution."

Now John Locke expressly denounced the notion of democracy in 1669; democracy is not mentioned in the Constitution of the United States, and indeed most of the framers went to considerable pains to make sure that the general government would not be a democracy; there is not one word in the Constitution about social contracts and natural rights. The Constitution is not a theoretical document at all, and the influence of Locke upon it is negligible—although Locke's phrases, at least, crept into the Declaration of Independence (despite Jefferson's awkwardness about confessing the source of "life, liberty, and the pursuit of happiness"). (pp. 567-68)

A character in one of James Thurber's comic stories suggests that had there been no Voltaire, it would not have been necessary to invent one. I do not say that about John Locke; but I do suggest that he did not make the Glorious Revolution or foreordain the Constitution of the United States. The Revolution of 1776, like the Revolution of 1688, presumably would have occurred even if Locke, like his Cambridge friends, had devoted himself lifelong to the study of Plato, eschewing politics. And the Constitution of the United States would have been framed by the same sort of men, and defended by Hamilton, Madison, and Jay, had Locke in 1689 lost the manuscripts of his *Treatises on Civil Government* while crossing the narrow seas with the Princess Mary. (p. 571)

Russell Kirk, "The Constitution of the United States Was Not Written by Locke," in The World & I, *Vol. 1, No. 11, November, 1986, pp. 561-71.*

ADDITIONAL BIBLIOGRAPHY

Allison, Henry E. "Locke's Theory of Personal Identity: A Re-examination." *Journal of the History of Ideas* XXVII, No. 1 (January-March 1966): 41-58.
  Analyzes the origin and influence of Locke's theory of personal identity.

Anderson, F. H. "On Interpreting Locke." *The University of Toronto Quarterly* IV, No. 4 (July 1935): 524-33.
  Laudatory reading of *An Essay concerning Human Understanding,* extolling Locke's wisdom, intellectual honesty, and permanence.

Armstrong, Robert L. "John Locke's 'Doctrine of Signs': A New Metaphysics." *Journal of the History of Ideas* XXVI, No. 3 (July-September 1965): 369-82.
  Compares Locke's metaphysics with that of his predecessors and contemporaries.

Ashcraft, Richard. *Revolutionary Politics and Locke's "Two Treatises of Government."* Princeton: Princeton University Press, 1986, 624 p.
  Reconstructs the intellectual and practical context of Locke's political thought.

Attig, John C. *The Works of John Locke: A Comprehensive Bibliography from the Seventeenth Century to the Present.* Westport, Conn.: Greenwood Press, 1985, 185 p.
  Comprehensive list of all major editions and translations of Locke's works, from the first printings to the most recent ones.

Axtell, James L. Introduction to *The Educational Writings of John Locke: A Critical Edition with Introduction and Notes,* pp. 3-97. Cambridge: Cambridge University Press, 1968.
  Surveys Locke's educational writings, placing them in the context of seventeenth- and eighteenth-century thought.

Ayers, M. R. "Mechanism, Superaddition, and the Proof of God's Existence in Locke's Essay." *The Philosophical Review* XC, No. 2 (April 1981): 210-51.
  Contends that, in arguing in *An Essay concerning Human Understanding* against the orthodox proofs of a simple, immaterial, and naturally immortal soul, Locke is neither thoughtless, recklessly inconsistent, nor unsystematic.

Barfield, Owen. *Poetic Diction: A Study in Meaning,* third edition, pp. 26ff. Middletown, Conn.: Wesleyan University Press, 1973.
  Accuses Locke of treating simple ideas as though they were bare precepts in *An Essay concerning Human Understanding.*

Briggs, Peter M. "Locke's *Essay* and the Tentativeness of *Tristram Shandy.*" *Studies in Philology* LXXXII, No. 4 (Fall 1985): 493-520.
  Explores Laurence Sterne's use of Lockean ideas in *The Life and Opinions of Tristram Shandy, Gentleman.*

Butler, Melissa A. "Early Liberal Roots of Feminism: John Locke and the Attack on Patriarchy." *American Political Science Review* 72, No. 1 (March 1978): 135-50.
  Discusses Locke's comments on marriage, education, and female preaching.

Christophersen, H. O. *A Bibliographical Introduction to the Study of John Locke.* 1930. Reprint. New York: Burt Franklin, 1968, 134 p.
  Useful primary and secondary bibliography of works by and about John Locke.

Coleridge, Samuel Taylor. "Lecture XIII: Descartes, Spinosa, Liebnitz, Locke, Kant, Schelling." In his *The Philosophical Lectures of Samuel Taylor Coleridge,* edited by Kathleen Coburn, pp. 368-91. London: Pilot Press, 1949.

Coleridge's notes for an 1819 lecture comparing Locke's philosophy with that of his precursors, contemporaries, and successors.

Colman, John. *John Locke's Moral Philosophy.* Edinburgh: Edinburgh University Press, 1983, 282 p.
  Comparative study of Locke's writings on moral philosophy, especially *Two Treatises of Government, Essays on the Law of Nature,* and *An Essay concerning Human Understanding.*

Cox, Richard H. *Locke on War and Peace.* Oxford: Oxford University Press, Clarendon Press, 1960, 220 p.
  Comprehensive critical survey of Locke's opinions about war, slavery, and toleration.

Cranston, Maurice. *John Locke: A Biography.* New York: Macmillan, 1957, 496 p.
  The standard biography of Locke, based on its subject's personal papers, letters, and miscellaneous manuscripts.

Curti, Merle. "The Great Mr. Locke: America's Philosopher, 1783-1861." *The Huntington Library Bulletin,* No. 11 (April 1937): 107-51.
  Comments on Locke's influence on American political thought, chiefly as reflected in the writings of the American Founding Fathers and other early American thinkers.

Dewhurst, Kenneth. *John Locke (1632-1704), Physician and Philosopher: A Medical Biography, with an Edition of the Medical Notes in His Journals.* London: Wellcome Historical Medical Library, 1963, 331 p.
  Explores, through the study of his medical notes, methods of treatment, and clinical observations, Locke's contribution to seventeenth-century English medicine.

Dunn, John. *The Political Thought of John Locke: An Historical Account of the Argument of the "Two Treatises of Government."* Cambridge: Cambridge University Press, 1969, 290 p.
  Rigorous study of the meaning and argument of *Two Treatises of Government.*

———. *Locke.* Oxford: Oxford University Press, 1984, 97 p.
  Concise, comprehensive, and authoritative introduction to Locke's life and works.

Emerson, Ralph Waldo. Notebook entry for 9 September 1830. In his *The Journals and Miscellaneous Notebooks of Ralph Waldo Emerson, Vol. III, 1826-1832,* edited by William H. Gilman and Alfred R. Ferguson, pp. 197-98. Cambridge: Harvard University Press, Belknap Press, 1963.
  Maintains that the "history of John Locke or of Isaac Newton is [a] far more important part of the stock of knowledge . . . than the whole history of Poland or Hungary."

Engell, James. "Empiricism in Earnest: Hobbes and Locke." In his *The Creative Imagination: Enlightenment to Romanticism,* pp. 11-21. Cambridge: Harvard University Press, 1981.
  Argues that Locke's notion of complex ideas anticipated later developments in the psychology of the imagination.

Farr, James. "The Way of Hypothesis: Locke on Method." *Journal of the History of Ideas* XLVIII, No. 1 (January-March 1987): 51-72.
  Examines Locke's views of the human understanding by studying his invocation of "hypotheses" and "method."

Franklin, Julian H. *John Locke and the Theory of Sovereignty: Mixed Monarchy and the Right of Resistance in the Political Thought of the English Revolution.* Cambridge: Cambridge University Press, 1978, 146 p.
  Describes and explains Locke's role in developing a modern theory of political sovereignty.

Frye, Northrop. "Blake's Case against Locke." In *English Literature and British Philosophy,* edited by S. P. Rosenbaum, pp. 119-35. Chicago: University of Chicago Press, 1971.
  Describes *An Essay concerning Human Understanding*'s negative effect on the poet William Blake.

Gough, J. W. *John Locke's Political Philosophy: Eight Studies.* Oxford: Oxford University Press, Clarendon Press, 1950, 204 p.

Surveys Locke's political philosophy, focusing on such issues as natural law, individual rights, government by consent, sovereignty, and Locke's theory of property.

Hartz, Louis. *The Liberal Tradition in America: An Interpretation of American Political Thought Since the Revolution.* New York: Harcourt, Brace and Co., 1955, 329 p.

Scattered references to Locke, investigating his role in the development of an American concept of a liberal society.

Hefelbower, S. G. *The Relation of John Locke to English Deism.* Chicago: University of Chicago Press, 1918, 188 p.

Examines the impact of Locke's philosophy on seventeenth- and eighteenth-century liberal religious movements.

Helm, Paul. "John Locke and Jonathan Edwards: A Reconsideration." *Journal of the History of Philosophy* VII, No. 1 (January 1969): 51-61.

Contends that, while *An Essay concerning Human Understanding* was a major factor in Jonathan Edwards's philosophical development, "it is too much to say that his philosophy was Locke-inspired."

Kendall, Willmoore. *John Locke and the Doctrine of Majority-Rule.* 1941. Reprint. Urbana: University of Illinois Press, 1959, 141 p.

Historical survey of Locke's doctrine of majority rule.

Lamb, Charles. "Letter CLX: To William Wordsworth, 26 April 1816." In his *Letters of Charles Lamb,* edited by Alfred Ainger, Vol. I, pp. 304-6. London: Macmillan, 1888.

Anecdotal account of the present state of English literature, claiming that there is "not as much metaphysics in thirty-six of the people in [the accounts office of the East India Company] as there is in the first page of Locke's *Treatise on the Human Understanding.*"

Landesman, Charles. "Locke's Theory of Meaning." *Journal of the History of Philosophy* XIV, No. 1 (January 1976): 23-35.

Close analysis of Locke's theory of meaning in the third book of *An Essay concerning Human Understanding.*

Landor, Walter Savage. "On Tucker's Treatise concerning Civil Government, in Opposition to Locke." In his *The Poetical Works of Walter Savage Landor,* edited by Stephen Wheeler, Vol. III, p. 442. Oxford: Oxford University Press, Clarendon Press, 1937.

Censures *A Treatise concerning Civil Government* (1781) by Josiah Tucker, Dean of Gloucester, maintaining, "Thee, meek Episcopacy! shall kings unfrock / Ere Tucker triumph over sense and Locke."

Locke Newsletter I—(1970—).

An annual publication containing articles, notices, and criticisms in English, French, German, and Italian on the many facets of Locke's life, works, and influence.

Mackie, J. L. *Problems from Locke.* Oxford: Oxford University Press, Clarendon Press, 1976, 237 p.

Discusses *An Essay concerning Human Understanding,* focusing on the questions: "What sort of world can we claim to know about?"; "Can we defend our claims to knowledge?"; and "About what, and how, can we talk meaningfully?"

McLaverty, James. "From Definition to Explanation: Locke's Influence on Johnson's Dictionary." *Journal of the History of Ideas* XLVII, No. 3 (July-September 1986): 377-94.

Traces the influence of Locke's philosophy on the concept of explanation underlying Samuel Johnson's *Dictionary of the English Language* (1755).

MacLean, Kenneth. *John Locke and English Literature of the Eighteenth Century.* New Haven: Yale University Press, 1936, 176 p.

Delineates *An Essay concerning Human Understanding*'s influence on eighteenth-century English literature.

Macpherson, C. B. "Locke: The Political Theory of Appropriation." In his *The Political Theory of Possessive Individualism: Hobbes to*

Locke, pp. 194-262. Oxford: Oxford University Press, Clarendon Press, 1962.

Explores Locke's theory of property rights and his notions of class differentials.

Mason, M. G. "The Literary Sources of John Locke's Educational Thoughts." *Pædagogica Historia* V, No. 1 (1965): 65-108.

Surveys the origin and development of Locke's opinions concerning education.

Miller, Perry. "The Rhetoric of Sensation." In his *Errand into the Wilderness,* pp. 167-83. Cambridge: Harvard University Press, Belknap Press, 1956.

Studies *An Essay concerning Human Understanding*'s influence on the eighteenth-century American sermonist Jonathan Edwards.

Pickering, Samuel F., Jr. *John Locke and Children's Books in Eighteenth-Century England.* Knoxville: University of Tennessee Press, 1981, 286 p.

Historical study of eighteenth-century English children's literature, maintaining that, by providing a "theoretical umbrella for all seasons," Locke's works profoundly influenced eighteenth-century thought and education.

Post, David M. "Jeffersonian Revisions of Locke: Education, Property-Rights, and Liberty." *Journal of the History of Ideas* XLVII, No. 1 (January-March 1986): 147-57.

Discusses the Jeffersonian Republicans' reworking of prevalent Lockean beliefs about political liberty.

Powys, Llewelyn. "John Locke." *The Saturday Review of Literature* XVI, No. 8 (19 June 1937): 3-4, 12.

Approaches Locke as a champion of tolerance, stressing his writings' importance in "our present turbulent epoch."

Quintana, Ricardo. *Two Augustans: John Locke, Jonathan Swift.* Madison: University of Wisconsin Press, 1978, 148 p.

Approaches Locke and Swift as two outstanding Augustan figures who represent their age's temper and frame of mind.

Riley, Patrick. "How Coherent is the Social Contract Tradition?" *Journal of the History of Ideas* XXXIV, No. 4 (October-December 1973): 543-62.

Examines Locke as a social contract theorist.

Rossiter, Clinton. *Seedtime of the Republic: The Origin of the American Tradition of Political Liberty,* pp. 33ff. New York: Harcourt, Brace & World, 1953.

Numerous brief references to the role of Locke's works in shaping the political thought of the American Founding Fathers.

Ryan, Alan. "The 'New' Locke." *The New York Review of Books* XIII, No. 9 (20 November 1969): 36-40.

Discusses the mid-twentieth-century image of Locke's historical importance as a thinker.

Sorley, W. R. "John Locke." In *The Cambridge History of English Literature,* Volume VIII: *The Age of Dryden,* edited by A. W. Ward and A. R. Waller, pp. 375-98. New York: G. P. Putnam's Sons, 1912.

Explicates Locke's theory of knowledge in *An Essay concerning Human Understanding,* commenting as well on Locke's religious, political, and economic ideas.

Strauss, Leo. "Locke's Doctrine of Natural Law." *American Political Science Review* 52, No. 2 (June 1958): 490-501.

Describes Locke's early essays on natural law, focusing on the question, Is the natural law based on speculative principles?

Tarbet, David W. "Lockean 'Intuition' and Johnson's Characterization of Aesthetic Response." *Eighteenth-Century Studies* 5, No. 1 (Fall 1971): 58-79.

Attributes Samuel Johnson's aesthetic convictions to his reading of Lockean philosophy.

Tarlton, Charles D. "A Rope of Sand: Interpreting Locke's *First Treatise of Government.*" *Historical Journal* 21, No. 1 (March 1978): 43-73.

Refutes the standard critical opinion of Locke's *First Treatise of Government*.

Thompson, Cameron. "John Locke and New England Transcendentalism." *The New England Quarterly* XXXV, No. 4 (December 1962): 435-57.
    Examines the "pivotal role" of Locke's writings in the development of New England transcendentalism.

Thomson, James. "The Summer." In his *The Seasons*, edited by James Robert Boyd, pp. 97-103. New York: A. S. Barnes & Burr, 1860.
    Poetic account, written between 1726 and 1728, of humankind's greatest achievements, describing Locke as the one who "made the whole internal world his own."

Ware, Charlotte S. "The Influence of Descartes on John Locke: A Bibliographical Study." *Revue Internationale de Philosophie* IV (1950): 210-30.
    Compares René Descartes's philosophy with Locke's, noting especially Locke's method of composing *An Essay concerning Human Understanding* and his general interest in French philosophy.

Weston, Peter J. "The Noble Primitive as Bourgeois Subject." *Literature and History* 10, No. 1 (Spring 1984): 59-71.
    General survey of seventeenth- and eighteenth-century opinion concerning the noble savage, containing a brief Marxist reading of *An Essay concerning Human Understanding* and *Two Treatises of Government*.

Yolton, Jean S., and Yolton, John W. *John Locke: A Reference Guide*. Boston: G. K. Hall, 1985, 294 p.
    Annotated bibliography of writings about Locke, from the earliest appraisals to 1982.

Yolton, John W. *John Locke and the Way of Ideas*. Oxford: Oxford University Press, 1956, 235 p.
    Introduces Locke's philosophy, tracing the reception given to and influence of his theory of knowledge.

————, ed. *John Locke, Problems and Perspectives: A Collection of New Essays*. Cambridge: Cambridge University Press, 1969, 278 p.
    Excellent, wide-ranging collection of critical essays on various aspects of Locke's life and work.

————. *Locke and the Compass of Human Understanding: A Selective Commentary on the "Essay."* Cambridge: Cambridge University Press, 1970, 234 p.
    Comments on *An Essay concerning Human Understanding*, focusing on Locke's science of nature.

————. *Locke: An Introduction*. Oxford: Basil Blackwell, 1985, 162 p.
    Excellent and comprehensive introduction to Locke's writings by a leading Locke scholar.

Charles-Louis de Secondat, Baron de la Brède et de Montesquieu

1689-1755

French political philosopher, historian, essayist, and fiction writer.

Montesquieu is renowned for his pioneering scholarship in the realms of political science, sociology, jurisprudence, and history. In his monumental work, *De l'esprit des lois (The Spirit of Laws)*, he essayed an objective, comparative approach to these disciplines which has become the basis of modern studies in social science. As an original theorist, Montesquieu exercised an inestimable influence on the development of political thought, both in Europe and in North America, where his doctrine of the separation of powers was incorporated into the American Constitution.

Montesquieu was born Charles-Louis de Secondat to a wealthy aristocratic family at Château La Brède, near Bordeaux. In 1700 he was sent to the Collège de Juilly, an Oratorian school noted for its progressive curriculum. Five years later, he undertook legal studies at the University of Bordeaux, receiving his degree in 1708. He passed the next few years in Paris, though little is known of his activities there. With his father's death in 1713, Charles-Louis was summoned back to La Brède, where he soon afterward married Jeanne Lartigue and became a councillor in the Bordeaux *parlement*, a regional judiciary/political body. In 1716 Charles-Louis's uncle, the Baron of Montesquieu, died, bequeathing to his nephew his title, estate, and position as one of the deputy presidents (*président à mortier*) of the *parlement*. (Henceforth, Montesquieu was often referred to by the respectful title of ''president.'') However, Montesquieu's magisterial career was less important to him than his membership in the newly formed Academy of Bordeaux, dedicated to the exploration of scientific and philosophical studies. Montesquieu occasionally wrote and delivered dissertations to the academy, though none of his extant essays from this period is today considered especially noteworthy. *Lettres persanes (Persian Letters)*, his first published work, appeared in 1721 and was an immediate and enormous success. Although the work was published anonymously, the author's identity was soon discovered, and Montesquieu began to spend increasingly more time in Paris to enjoy his fame in the capital's literary and social circles. Montesquieu's second published work, *Le temple de Gnide (The Temple of Gnidus)*, was similarly well received by his contemporaries, but has since been widely dismissed as, in Kingsley Martin's words, ''a fashionable study in polite pornography.''

In 1726 Montesquieu sold his office in the Bordeaux *parlement*—a common and acceptable practice at the time. Back in Paris, he sought election to the prestigious French Academy. Ostensibly because he did not fulfill the Academy's requirement of Parisian residence (but more likely, biographers surmise, because some members of the society found the satirical criticism of French culture in *Persian Letters* politically and theologically suspect) the election proceedings were stymied, and Montesquieu did not take his place in the Academy until 1728. Only a few months after acceding to his hard-won position, he embarked on a three-year journey which took him to Austria, Italy, Germany, Holland, and (in the company of

English statesman Philip Dormer Stanhope, Earl of Chesterfield) England. His sojourn in England is of primary importance to Montesquieu's work, for his observations of and reflections on the British political system comprise a seminal part of the political philosophy he later expressed in *The Spirit of Laws*.

After returning to France, Montesquieu resided for the most part at La Brède (though he made frequent trips to Paris), working on his major political works: first, *Considérations sur les causes de la grandeur des Romains et de leur décadence (Considerations on the Causes of the Grandeur and the Decadence of the Romans)*, and later, *The Spirit of Laws*. The latter was the result of twenty years' labor; Montesquieu read a vast number of scholarly tomes for his research and at one point apparently employed six secretaries simultaneously to aid him in his gargantuan task. In 1748 the finished work was published and Montesquieu almost immediately found himself in a maelstrom of controversy, as a flurry of pamphlets—both of praise and of condemnation—ensued. Montesquieu himself entered the fray in 1750 with his *Défense de ''L'esprit des loix''*. Much of the furor arose from Montesquieu's supposed religious heresy, for *The Spirit of Laws* treats all faiths, including Christianity, in a sociopolitical rather than a theological context. Within France official sanctions against *The Spirit of Laws* were considered but not imposed, though in 1751 the work was placed on the Papal Index of Prohibited Books, despite Montesquieu's efforts to propitiate the censors. Montesquieu died in Paris at age sixty-nine.

Although best known for his theoretical *The Spirit of Laws*, Montesquieu is also celebrated as the author of *Persian Letters*. This important fictional work consists entirely of imaginary correspondence, most of it between the two principal characters, Usbek and Rica, and their friends, wives, and servants. As Persians touring Europe, Usbek and Rica are cast in the role of interested, amused, frequently puzzled, and sometimes appalled commentators on European (and particularly French) society. Their descriptions of their sojourn in Paris and the life—social, political, religious, moral, and cultural—of its inhabitants afford Montesquieu the opportunity for ironic criticism and wry satire. C. A. Sainte-Beuve has remarked upon the "audacity" and "irreverence" of *Persian Letters*, for Montesquieu's satire castigated even the king and the pope. Interspersed among the letters satirizing French follies are several letters between Usbek and the members of his Persian seraglio—his many wives and their eunuch guardians. Urbane and rational as Usbek the social commentator seems, Usbek the master of the harem is, critics have observed, quite a different man. In accordance with Persian custom, Usbek's wives are confined always within the seraglio walls, forbidden to see or be seen by any man other than Usbek himself, but still Usbek is tormented by suspicion and dread of his wives' infidelity and haunted by fears that his harem-warden eunuchs will betray him. Ultimately, Usbek's fears are realized, as his favorite wife claims her freedom in the only way possible to her: suicide.

The significance of *Persian Letters* was long thought to lie solely in its satirical sections; the seraglio intrigue was considered merely a titillating subplot inserted to please licentious tastes and thus to sell more copies of the book. Recent critics, however, have discerned in the subplot a political allegory: the seraglio is a despotic state, Usbek a tyrant, ruling through force and intimidation, but always subject to the fear of insurrection. Modern commentators have also noted with interest the feminist sympathy implied by the plight of the harem women; while not all critics are willing, with Pauline Kra, to call *Persian Letters* a "feminist manifesto," many agree that Montesquieu showed more sensitivity to the issue than was common among writers of his era. *Persian Letters*, for both its satire of European culture and its seraglio subplot, is today viewed as a charming and entertaining but nonetheless serious counterpart to Montesquieu's nonfiction work.

As its title indicates, *Considerations on the Causes of the Grandeur and the Decadence of the Romans* is an interpretive history of the Roman empire. Many commentators have characterized *Considerations* as an embryonic *The Spirit of Laws*, for here Montesquieu essayed his method of basing political theorizing on historical and cultural interpretation. In this work he sought to determine the underlying sociopolitical causes of Rome's decline, which he attributed to the state's betrayal, following the republican period, of its own ruling principles of virtue and civil liberty. Edward Gibbon, whose multivolume *History of the Decline and Fall of the Roman Empire* (1776-88) is considered the classic treatment of the subject, acknowledged his debt to Montesquieu in his *Memoirs of My Life and Writings* (1796), claiming that his "delight was in the frequent perusal of Montesquieu whose energy of style, and boldness of hypothesis were powerful to awaken and stimulate the Genius of the Age."

Montesquieu is generally credited with being the first political scientist as well as the first sociologist, though these terms did not come into usage until many years after his death. His claim to the former title consists in his attempts to derive political principles from empirical data rather than from philosophical abstractions. Scholars note that while previous political theorists had by and large begun from idealistic premises—what *ought* to be in the political realm—Montesquieu based his study on observation of existing political realities—what actually *is*. Montesquieu is hailed as a forerunner of sociology because in *The Spirit of Laws* he was the first to study the effects, individually and cumulatively, of social and environmental phenomena on human behavior. *The Spirit of Laws* purposes to investigate how laws arise, what factors influence them, and how legislators might best formulate and implement just and appropriate laws. The book is much more than a treatise on jurisprudence, however. Montesquieu defined laws as "the necessary relationships which derive from the nature of things," and *The Spirit of Laws* represents a sustained analysis of that very "nature of things," resulting in an ambitious blend of political science, sociology, philosophy, and history. The scope of the work is indeed far-reaching, as Montesquieu believed that laws and political systems could not be profitably studied in isolation, but must be seen in a wider, sociocultural context. *The Spirit of Laws* thus evaluates the relation of law and legislation to a multitude of physical and cultural variables: climate; the size of a government's territory; the morals, customs, and *esprit générale* (general spirit or national character) of a culture; its religion; and its economic and commercial customs.

From his basis in empirically determined data, Montesquieu moved to philosophical theorizing. Although in his preface to *The Spirit of Laws* Montesquieu himself named the subject matter of his book "infinite" and requested that his readers "approve or condemn the book entire, and not a few particular phrases," inevitably certain themes of the work have commanded special critical attention over the years. One of the most important of these aspects is Montesquieu's definition of the three types of government and their ruling principles: he identified the democratic republic, the monarchy, and the despotic state, ruled, respectively, by guiding principles of virtue, honor, and fear. The citizens of a republic, Montesquieu argued, maintain their system of government by the voluntary exercise of political virtue, and, as the absence of social class distinctions in an ideal republican model ensures that all are equal in wealth and status, so all bend their efforts toward civic betterment rather than toward individual gain. Most commentators agree that while Montesquieu clearly admired the republican model, his preference was for the monarchy, in which the concept of honor is the guide and impetus to public life. In a monarchy, sharp distinctions of social class dominate the system. The citizens of each class, motivated by a desire to act in such a way that honor and profit—both political and material—redound to their class, keep the system in a state of perpetual (and to Montesquieu, politically healthy) competition and tension. This tension keeps the government stable, as it does not permit any one class or individual to accrue too much power. That any one sector should have absolute power was anathema to Montesquieu, as is evident from his writings on despotic states. Like the monarchy, the despotism is headed by a single individual, but differs in that the tyrant's power is unchecked by any competing forces. As in the republic, all citizens of a despotic state are equal in wealth and influence, but the absolute sway of the potentate, whose arbitrary commands are law, renders the ruling principle and motivation of the citizens not virtue, but rather simple fear of the tyrant.

Montesquieu did not contend that existing political systems did or could embody perfectly the models he set forth; the models were intended as archetypes, of which actual governments, due to varying circumstances, could well be adulterated versions. Furthermore, Montesquieu recognized the changing nature of political systems: a republic might easily ripen into a monarchy, for example, or a monarchy degenerate into a despotic state.

Scholars agree that Montesquieu clearly had in mind his preferred monarchical model—and, more specifically, his perception of the constitutional monarchy of Britain—when he wrote Book XI, chapter six of *The Spirit of Laws,* which outlines his famous doctrine of the separation of powers. Here Montesquieu laid out the plan of three branches of government—executive, legislative, and judicial—each of which is to act as a counterbalance to and check upon the power of the others. That Montesquieu based this system on an erroneous perception of Britain's parliamentary government, attributing to it a more well-defined balance of power than it actually possessed at that time, does not, scholars contend, vitiate the brilliance of his thesis.

The Spirit of Laws had a profound impact on the development of political thought in the eighteenth century. In France, Montesquieu's emphasis on the primacy of human reason, the efficacy of scientific pursuit, the desirability of political liberty, and a rationalist approach to religion, accorded well with the temper of the times. But although Montesquieu embraced many of the philosophical ideals of the French Enlightenment, he was censured by the more radical elements of the movement for failing to carry his ideas far enough. Voltaire, for example, though he shared many beliefs with Montesquieu and on occasion defended his work from detractors, objected that *The Spirit of Laws* was too conservative: that it neglected to advocate the sweeping political reform Voltaire deemed necessary. Montesquieu's direct influence on the French Revolution is indeterminable. Assuredly his name and ideas were cited by Revolutionary writers, but Montesquieu's wariness of sudden political change and his defense of the aristocratic class of which he was himself a member, clearly mark him as a man at odds with the Revolution's republican fervor. The rest of eighteenth-century Europe also felt the influence of Montesquieu to some degree, most notably England, where *The Spirit of Laws* was translated almost immediately and where it was discussed and frequently quoted in Parliamentary debates. Horace Walpole exemplified enthusiastic English opinion in a 1750 letter in which he wrote that he considered *The Spirit of Laws* "the best book that ever was written—at least I never learned half so much from all I ever read."

It is Montesquieu's influence on eighteenth-century America, however, that is of most interest to many historians and scholars. To what extent did Montesquieu's theories of government, particularly his doctrine of the separation of powers, influence the drafting of the American Constitution? Paul Merrill Spurlin has done extensive research on the question, combing early American documents—including books, periodicals, pamphlets, texts of speeches and of private correspondence, library catalogues, and lists of college curricula—for references to Montesquieu and his work. Such references are myriad, and Spurlin has concluded: "By 1787 the *Spirit of Laws* had become an 'American' classic." While post-colonial early American response to Montesquieu was by no means universally or consistently favorable (Thomas Jefferson, though he had once copied lengthy extracts from *The Spirit of Laws* into his commonplace book, later expressed his ambivalence in letters describing the work as "a book of paradoxes," whose value was "equivocal on the whole"), Montesquieu was quoted extensively and cited as an authority by such prominent American statesmen as John Adams, Alexander Hamilton, and James Madison. Madison himself defined the central importance of Montesquieu to the Founding Fathers in a 1788 newspaper article discussing the doctrine of the separation of powers. Wrote he: "If [Montesquieu] be not the author of this invaluable precept in the science of politics, he has the merit at least of displaying and recommending it most effectually to the attention of mankind."

Modern commentators unanimously concur that *The Spirit of Laws* is an important and influential book, but they do not deny its shortcomings. Foremost among these is the essay's inadequate organization: the inability of its structural arrangement to support the immensity of its subject matter. Franz Neumann has noted that "initial bewilderment . . . is the inevitable fate of every reader of *The Spirit of the Laws.*" Other faults of the book include its occasional factual inaccuracies, its ambiguous language, and its logical inconsistencies: though Montesquieu strove to produce political science based on empirical data rather than theoretical political philosophy alone, at times this method falters, as his facts fail to support his conclusions or are too obviously conjured from obscure sources for the sole purpose of fitting a conclusion that Montesquieu favored. (In connection with the last fault, Samuel Johnson once remarked irascibly that "whenever [Montesquieu] wants to support a strange opinion, he quotes you the practice of Japan or of some other distant country, of which he knows nothing.") Nonetheless, as George Saintsbury has maintained: "His instinct in political science [is] so sure, that even the falsity of his premises frequently fails to vitiate his conclusions. He has known wrong, but he has thought right." In fine, the faults of *The Spirit of Laws* are deemed of negligible importance when considered in the context of Montesquieu's tremendous innovation and achievement.

"The reader who has digested [*The Spirit of Laws*] has lived a rare intellectual experience." The truth of such an assessment as J. Robert Loy's has been granted for over two hundred years. In *The Spirit of Laws,* Montesquieu coupled innovative scientific procedures with thoughtful interpretive theorizing to create a work notable for both its methods and its conclusions. His contributions to the disciplines of political science, sociology, comparative jurisprudence, and history are considered immense, and his impact on the development of constitutional government incalculable.

PRINCIPAL WORKS

Lettres persanes. 2 vols.   (fictional letters)   1721
  [*Persian Letters,* 1722]
Le Temple de Gnide (prose poem) 1724; published in *Bibliothèque française*
  [*The Temple of Gnidus,* 1765]
Traité des devoirs   (essay)   1725
De la politique   (essay)   1725
Réflexions sur le caractère de quelques princes et sur quelques événements de leur vie   (essays)   1731-33
Considérations sur les causes de la grandeur des Romains, et de leur décadence   (essay)   1734
  [*Reflections on the Causes of the Grandeur and Declension of the Romans,* 1734; also published as *Considerations on the Causes of the Grandeur and the Decadence of the Romans,* 1894]

De l'esprit des loix; ou, Du rapport que les loix doivent avoir avec la constitution de chaque gouvernement, les moeurs, la climat, la religion, le commerce, &tc., à quoi d'auteur a ajouté des recherches nouvelles, sur les loix romaines touchant les successions, sur les loix françoises, & sur les loix féodales ... 2 vols. (essay) 1748; also published as *Esprit des lois,* 1858
[*The Spirit of Laws,* 1750]

Défense de "L'esprit des loix" (essay) 1750

The Works of M. de Secondat, Baron de Montesquieu. 3 vols. (essays, fictional letters, romances, and correspondence) 1800

*Voyages de Montesquieu. 2 vols. (travel journals) 1894-96

†Pensées et fragments inédits de Montesquieu. 2 vols. (journal) 1899-1901

Correspondance de Montesquieu. 2 vols. (letters) 1914

*This work consists of fragments of travel journals written between 1728 and 1731.

†This work consists of notes kept by Montesquieu throughout his adult life.

JOHN OZELL (essay date 1722)

[*Ozell was the first English translator of* Persian Letters. *In the following excerpt from his introduction, he warmly commends the work.*]

I Here present the English Reader with the most diverting as well as instructive Book that France has produced these many Years. It is wrote with a Strength of Reasoning, a Freedom of Thought, and a Vein of just Humour, which that Nation was hardly thought capable of: and which is most surprising, not-withstanding the supposed impossibility of such an Attempt, the Author has found a new Sett of Characters never before represented in Europe. He has opened to us a Scene of Action which all the Curiosity of our most famous Travellers cou'd never pierce into, and given us so natural an Idea of the Manners of the Seraglio, the Thoughts and Passions of a number of Women confined for the Pleasures of a single Man, and the Notions and cast of Mind of the Eunuchs whose whole Lives are spent in guarding and watching them, that one wou'd almost believe the Letters to be Genuine.

If ever the Translation of a French Book was necessary in a Country where that Language is so much understood as in England, it is this, which in many places is so obscure, that tho' I think I have had a tolerable experience in this Tongue, yet without much Thought and even sometimes consulting of Friends, I own I cou'd not have reach'd the Sense. The Author, hurried away by the fire of his Wit, and the multitude of Thoughts crowding in upon him, cou'd not so well attend to Perspicuity of Expression. But if we often forgive an Author his want of Thought when his Language is smooth, sure we may pardon the darkness of Style in a Work where the Thoughts make us so full amends!

I shall not pretend to inform the Public of the Name of the Author; if I knew it I wou'd bury it in eternal Silence. He has threaten'd us with so severe a Penalty if we enquire him out, namely, that of being silent from the moment he is discovered, that the World would have no great Obligation to any body's

impertinent Curiosity, that shou'd make them pay for so trifling an information with so invaluable a Loss. (pp. iii-v)

> *John Ozell, "Advertisement," in* Persian Letters, Vol. I, *by Charles de Secondat, Baron de Montesquieu, translated by John Ozell, 1722. Reprint by Garland Publishing, Inc., 1972, pp. iii-vi.*

CHARLES DE SECONDAT, BARON DE MONTESQUIEU (essay date 1748)

[*In the following reprint of his preface to the first edition of* The Spirit of Laws, *Montesquieu describes his intentions in the work and his hopes for its reception.*]

If amidst the infinite number of subjects contained in this book there is anything which, contrary to my expectation, may possibly offend, I can at least assure the public that it was not inserted with an ill intention: for I am not naturally of a captious temper. Plato thanked the gods that he was born in the same age with Socrates: and for my part I give thanks to the Supreme that I was born a subject of that government under which I live; and that it is His pleasure I should obey those whom He has made me love.

I beg one favour of my readers, which I fear will not be granted me; this is, that they will not judge by a few hours' reading of the labour of twenty years; that they will approve or condemn the book entire, and not a few particular phrases. If they would search into the design of the author, they can do it in no other way so completely as by searching into the design of the work.

I have first of all considered mankind; and the result of my thoughts has been, that amidst such an infinite diversity of laws and manners, they were not solely conducted by the caprice of fancy.

I have laid down the first principles, and have found that the particular cases follow naturally from them; that the histories of all nations are only consequences of them; and that every particular law is connected with another law, or depends on some other of a more general extent.

When I have been obliged to look back into antiquity, I have endeavoured to assume the spirit of the ancients, lest I should consider those things as alike which are really different; and lest I should miss the difference of those which appear to be alike.

I have not drawn my principles from my prejudices, but from the nature of things.

Here a great many truths will not appear till we have seen the chain which connects them with others. The more we enter into particulars, the more we shall perceive the certainty of the principles on which they are founded. I have not even given all these particulars, for who could mention them all without a most insupportable fatigue?

The reader will not here meet with any of those bold flights which seem to characterise the works of the present age. When things are examined with never so small a degree of extent, the sallies of imagination must vanish; these generally arise from the mind's collecting all its powers to view only one side of the subject, while it leaves the other unobserved.

I write not to censure anything established in any country what-soever. Every nation will here find the reasons on which its maxims are founded; and this will be the natural inference, that to propose alternations belongs only to those who are so happy as to be born with a genius capable of penetrating the entire constitution of a state.

It is not a matter of indifference that the minds of the people be enlightened. The prejudices of magistrates have arisen from national prejudice. In a time of ignorance they have committed even the greatest evils without the least scruple; but in an enlightened age they even tremble while conferring the greatest blessings. They perceive the ancient abuses; they see how they must be reformed; but they are sensible also of the abuses of a reformation. They let the evil continue, if they fear a worse; they are content with a lesser good, if they doubt a greater. They examine into the parts, to judge of them in connection; and they examine all the causes, to discover their different effects.

Could I but succeed so as to afford new reasons to every man to love his prince, his country, his laws; new reasons to render him more sensible in every nation and government of the blessings he enjoys, I should think myself the most happy of mortals.

Could I but succeed so as to persuade those who command, to increase their knowledge in what they ought to prescribe; and those who obey, to find a new pleasure resulting from obedience—I should think myself the most happy of mortals.

The most happy of mortals should I think myself could I contribute to make mankind recover from their prejudices. By prejudices I here mean, not that which renders men ignorant of some particular things, but whatever renders them ignorant of themselves.

It is in endeavouring to instruct mankind that we are best able to practise that general virtue which comprehends the love of all. Man, that flexible being, conforming in society to the thoughts and impressions of others, is equally capable of knowing his own nature, whenever it is laid open to his view; and of losing the very sense of it, when his idea is banished from his mind.

Often have I begun, and as often have I laid aside, this undertaking. I have a thousand times given the leaves I had written to the winds: I, every day, felt my paternal hands fall. I have followed my object without any fixed plan: I have known neither rules nor exceptions; I have found the truth, only to lose it again. But when I once discovered my first principles, everything I sought for appeared; and in the course of twenty years, I have seen my work begun, growing up, advancing to maturity, and finished.

If this work meets with success, I shall owe it chiefly to the grandeur and majesty of the subject. However, I do not think that I have been totally deficient in point of genius. When I have seen what so many great men both in France, England, and Germany have said before me, I have been lost in admiration; but I have not lost my courage: I have said with Correggio, "And I also am a painter." (pp. xxi-xxii)

> *Charles de Secondat, Baron de Montesquieu, in a preface to* The Spirit of Laws, *translated by Thomas Nugent, revised edition, Encyclopaedia Britannica, Inc., 1955, pp. xxi-xxii.*

THOMAS GRAY   (letter date 1749)

[*Gray is widely considered the most important poet of mid-eighteenth-century England. His "Elegy Written in a Country Churchyard" (1751), noted for its eloquent evocation of the natural world and its profound contemplation of death, greatly influenced such Romantic poets as Samuel Taylor Coleridge and Percy Bysshe Shelley. Gray is also esteemed as a consummate letter writer; in addition to gracefully expressed sentiment and perspicuous observation of life, his letters, according to R. W. Ketton-Cremer, "contain some of the most intelligent literary criticism of the time." In the following excerpt from a letter written in 1749, Gray reports admiringly on a new book he has read:* The Spirit of Laws]

You ask for some Account of Books. [The] principal I can tell you of is a work of . . . Montesquieu's, the Labour of 20 Years. [It] is called, *L'Esprit des Loix*. [He] lays down the Principles on which are founded the three Sorts of Government, Despotism, the limited Monarchic, & the Republican, & shews how from thence are deducted the Laws & Customs, by which they are guided and maintained: the Education proper to each Form, the influences of Climate, Situation, Religion, &c: on the Minds of particular Nations, & on their Policy. the Subject (you see) is as extensive as Mankind; the Thoughts perfectly new, generally admirable, as they are just, sometimes a little too refined: in short there are Faults, but such as an ordinary Man could never have committed: the Style very lively & concise (consequently sometimes obscure) it is the Gravity of Tacitus (whom he admires) temper'd with the Gayety & Fire of a Frenchman. (pp. 195-96)

> *Thomas Gray, in a letter to Thomas Wharton on March 9, 1749, in his* The Letters of Thomas Gray, *Vol. I, edited by Duncan C. Tovey, revised edition, George Bell and Sons, 1909, pp. 192-96.*

FRANÇOIS MARIE AROUET DE VOLTAIRE   (letter date 1751)

[*A French philosopher and man of letters, Voltaire was a major figure of the eighteenth-century European Enlightenment, a movement in which reason and empiricism markedly superseded reliance on prescription, faith, and authority. As a man of diverse and intense interests, Voltaire wrote prolifically on many subjects and in a variety of genres, always asserting the absolute primacy of personal liberty—be it intellectual, social, religious, or political. Consequently, Voltaire opposed religious traditions and political organizations that he believed thwarted or curtailed individual freedom. Voltaire's most valuable contribution to literature is usually considered to be his invention of the philosophical* conte, *or tale, in which the story is a vehicle for an ethical or philosophical message: the most famous of these* contes *is the highly regarded* Candide (1759). *In the following excerpt from a letter dated 1751, Voltaire offers his opinion of Montesquieu.*]

I would have hoped [Montesquieu's *L'esprit des lois*] had been as methodical and true as it is full of wit and great maxims, but such as it is, it has seemed useful to me. The author always thinks and causes others to think; "he is a formidable antagonist" as Montaigne put it; his imagination causes mine to rush forth. Mme. Du Deffand was right to call his book *De l'esprit sur les lois* ["Of Wit on the Laws"]; it seems to me that it cannot be better defined. It must be confessed that few people have as much wit as he, and his lofty boldness must please all who think freely. It is said that he had only been attacked by slaves of prejudice; it is one of the merits of our century that these slaves are not dangerous. These wretches would like the rest of the world to be strangled by the same chains they are. (p. 164)

> *François Marie Arouet de Voltaire, in a letter to Charles-Emmanuel de Crussol, Duc d'Uzès on September 14, 1751, in his* The Selected Letters of Voltaire, *edited and translated by Richard A. Brooks, New York University Press, 1973, pp. 163-64.*

LORD CHESTERFIELD   (essay date 1755)

[*An English statesman and diplomat, Philip Dormer Stanhope, fourth earl of Chesterfield is best known today for the letters he wrote to his son instructing the young man in the niceties of gentlemanly deportment in polite society. Collected and published in 1774 as* Letters to His Son on the Fine Art of Becoming a Man of the World and a Gentleman, *the letters are celebrated for their engaging wit and candor. Chesterfield befriended Montesquieu on the latter's trip to England and the two remained friends until Montesquieu's death. In the following obituary notice, which appeared in the* London Evening Post *in February, 1755, Chesterfield eulogizes his friend.*]

On the tenth of this month, died at Paris, universally and sincerely regretted, Charles Secondat, Baron de Montesquieu, and *Président à Mortier* of the Parliament at Bourdeaux. His virtues did honour to human nature; his writings, to justice. A friend to mankind, he asserted their undoubted and inalienable rights with freedom, even in his own country, whose prejudices in matters of religion and government he had long lamented, and endeavoured, not without some success, to remove. He well knew, and justly admired, the happy constitution of this country, where fixed and known laws equally restrain monarchy from tyranny, and liberty from licentiousness. His works will illustrate his name, and survive him as long as right reason, moral obligation, and the true spirit of laws, shall be understood, respected, and maintained. (pp. 308-09)

> *Lord Chesterfield, in a letter to the editor of the "London Evening Post" in February, 1755, in* Letters of Lord Chesterfield, *Oxford University Press, London, 1929, pp. 308-09.*

JEAN JACQUES ROUSSEAU   (essay date 1762)

[*Rousseau was a French philosopher, essayist, and novelist who has often been called "the father of Romanticism" because of the influence he exerted on William Wordsworth and Percy Bysshe Shelley in England and on Johann von Schiller and Immanuel Kant in Germany. Though he was by no means a literary critic in the strict sense, his ideas of individual freedom, of the supremacy of emotion over reason, of the goodness of the primitive human being as opposed to the civilized one, and of the benefits of "natural" education, permeate late-eighteenth- and the whole of nineteenth-century literature. The most significant aspect of Rousseau's philosophy was his renunciation of the Christian doctrine of original sin; he argued that evil emanated not from religious transgression but from civilized society, which through its institutions corrupts the individual and removes him or her from a natural state of goodness. In such areas as education, which Rousseau discussed in his popular* Émile (1762; *Emilius; or, An Essay on Education, 1763), he contended that instruction should proceed according to a child's curiosity, by stimulating his or her intelligence, rather than by the imposition of cut-and-dried notions. Though many of Rousseau's ideas were not new, his significance lies in the fact that he presented them concretely and forcefully at a receptive moment of transition in European history. His work of political philosophy,* Du contrat social (1762; *A Treatise on the Social Compact; or, the Principles of Politic Law, 1764) outlines a relationship between government and governed whereby the former acts in the service of the collective will of the latter. In the following excerpt from this work, Rousseau disagrees with Montesquieu's theories of republican government.*]

Taking the word "democracy" in its strict sense, perhaps there never did, and never will, exist such a government. It is against the natural order that the greater number should govern, and the smaller number be governed. It cannot be imagined that the chief part of the people should be always assembled for the discharge of public affairs, and it is evident that commissioners cannot be appointed to govern without the form of administration changing.

In fact, I believe it may be laid down as a principle that, when the functions of government are divided among a number of tribunals, the fewer in number will sooner or later acquire the greatest authority, if it were for no other reason than because affairs will be transacted with greatest ease and expedition in fewest hands, which naturally brings them control of affairs.

Besides, how many circumstances must conspire to make such a government possible! First, the State must be a very small one, where the people can easily assemble, and where each citizen can easily know all the others; there must, in the second place, be great simplicity of manners to prevent a multiplicity of affairs and those tedious discussions which are the consequence of them; and there must also be much equality in the rank and fortunes of all the citizens, or there will not be equality of rights and authority for long; finally there must be little or no luxury, for whether luxury be considered as the effect of riches, or as the incitement to covet them, it corrupts at once both the wealthy and the poor, the one by its possession, the other by the desire of possessing; it betrays the nation into effeminate softness, and debases it by vanity; and it takes away all the citizens from the State by making them subservient to each other, and all the slaves of opinion.

This is the reason why a celebrated author [Montesquieu] has made virtue the principle on which a republic must be founded; because all these circumstances could never subsist without her ruling influence. But this fine genius has not only omitted making the necessary distinctions, but he is not always exact, and sometimes obscure, and he did not perceive that, the sovereign authority being everywhere the same, the same principle must prevail in every well-formed State, though in a greater or less degree, according to its form of government. (pp. 59-60)

If there were a nation of gods they might be governed by a democracy. So perfect a government will not agree with men. (p. 60)

> *Jean Jacques Rousseau, "Treats of Political Laws, That Is, of the Form of Government: Of Democracy," in his* The Social Contract: An Eighteenth-Century Translation, *revised edition, edited by Charles Frankel, Hafner Publishing Company, 1947, pp. 59-60.*

OLIVER GOLDSMITH   (essay date 1774)

[*Goldsmith was one of the most important writers of the Augustan age. He distinguished himself during his lifetime as an expressive narrative poet, but has since been acclaimed for the novel* The Vicar of Wakefield (1766), *which pioneered the device of protagonist as narrator, and the drama* She Stoops to Conquer (1773), *which has been credited with ushering in a new era of robust comedy to an eighteenth-century theater overwhelmed by sentimentalism. In the following excerpt from the second edition (1774) of his* An Enquiry into the Present State of Polite Learning in Europe, *Goldsmith highly praises Montesquieu.*]

[There are] many among the French who do honour to the present age, and whose writings will be transmitted to posterity with an ample share of fame. (p. 32)

Montesquieu, a name equally deserving fame with [Voltaire]. The *Spirit of Laws* is an instance how much genius is able to lead learning. His system has been adopted by the literati; and yet, is it not possible for opinions equally plausible to be formed upon opposite principles, if a genius like his could be found to attempt such an undertaking? He seems more a poet than a philosopher. (p. 33)

Oliver Goldsmith, "Of Polite Learning in France," in his The Works of Oliver Goldsmith: Enquiry into the Present State of Polite Learning, the Citizen of the World, Vol. II, edited by Peter Cunningham, John Murray, 1854, pp. 30-6.

JEREMY BENTHAM (essay date 1781-85)

[An English philosopher, Bentham was the foremost theorist and proponent of utilitarianism in the eighteenth and early nineteenth centuries. His Introduction to the Principles of Morals and Legislation (1789) carried his theory of ethical utilitarianism ("It is the greatest happiness of the greatest number that is the measure of right and wrong") into the legislative realm: Bentham believed that as the quantitative and qualitative value of pleasure and pain could be accurately measured, so the rightness of laws could be evaluated, practically and scientifically, by ascertaining the extent to which they conduce to human happiness. In the following excerpt from an entry written sometime between 1781 and 1785 in his commonplace book, Bentham predicts eventual oblivion for Montesquieu's reputation and The Spirit of Laws.]

When the truths in a man's book, though many and important, are fewer than the errors; when his ideas, though the means of producing clear ones in other men are found to be themselves not clear, that book must die: Montesquieu must therefore die: he must die, as his great countryman, Descartes, had died before him: he must wither as the blade withers, when the corn is ripe he must die, but let tears of gratitude and admiration bedew his grave. O Montesquieu! the British constitution, whose death thou prophesiedst, will live longer than thy work, yet not longer than thy fame. Not even the incense of [the illustrious Catherine] can preserve thee.

Locke—dry, cold, languid, wearisome, will live for ever. Montesquieu—rapid, brilliant, glorious, enchanting, will not outlive his century.

I know—I feel—I pity—and blush at the enjoyment of a liberty which the birth-place of that great writer, (great with all his faults,) [forbade him to enjoy.]

I could make an immense book upon the defects of Montesquieu—I could make not a small one upon his excellencies. It might be worth while to make both, if Montesquieu could live. (p. 143)

Jeremy Bentham, "Extracts from Commonplace Book," in his The Works of Jeremy Bentham, Vol. X, William Tait, 1843, pp. 141-47.

JOHN ADAMS (essay date 1787)

[Pamphleteer, lawyer, statesman, and second president of the United States, Adams helped draft the American Declaration of Independence and was, according to Thomas Jefferson, "the pillar of its support" on the congressional floor. Essentially a conservative whose political philosophy placed him between Alexander Hamilton's federalism and Jefferson's agrarianism, Adams set out his approach to government in such works as A Dissertation on Canon and Feudal Law (1768) and A Defence of the Constitutions of Government of the United States of America (3 vols., 1787-88). In the following excerpt from this work, Adams contests elements of Montesquieu's theory of the ruling principles of states.]

Montesquieu's *Spirit of Laws* is a very useful collection of materials; but is it too irreverent to say that it is an unfinished work? He defines a republican government to be "that in which the body, or only a part of the people, is possessed of the supreme power." This agrees with Johnson's definition, "a state in which the government is more than one." "When the body of the people," says Montesquieu, "in a republic, are possessed of the supreme power, this is called a democracy; when the supreme power is lodged in the hands of a part of the people, it is then an aristocracy." And again, "it is the nature of a republican government, that either the collective body of the people, or particular families, should be possessed of the sovereign power." "In a popular state, virtue is the necessary spring of government. As virtue is necessary in a popular government, so it is necessary also under an aristocracy. True it is, that in the latter it is not so absolutely requisite."

Does this writer mean that honor and fear, the former of which he calls the principle of monarchy, and the latter of despotism, cannot exist in a republic? or that they are not necessary? Fear, surely, is necessary in a republican government; there can be no government without hopes and fears. Fear then, in truth, is at least one principle in every kind of government, in the simplest democracy as well as the simplest despotism. This arrangement, so exact and systematical in appearance, and which has been celebrated as a discovery of the principles of all government, is by no means satisfactory, since virtue and honor cannot be excluded from despotisms, nor fear nor virtue from monarchies, nor fear nor honor from republics; but at least it is apparent that in a republic, constituted as we propose, the three principles of fear, honor, and virtue, unite and produce more union among the citizens, and give greater energy to the laws.

But not to enlarge on this, let us proceed to the inquiry, what is virtue? It is not that classical virtue which we see personified in the choice of Hercules, and which the ancient philosophers summed up in four words,—prudence, justice, temperance, and fortitude. It is not Christian virtue, so much more sublime, which is summarily comprehended in universal benevolence. What is it then? According to Montesquieu, it should seem to be merely a negative quality; the absence only of ambition and avarice; and he thinks that what he thus advances is confirmed by the unanimous testimony of historians. But is this matter well considered? Look over the history of any republic, and can you find a period in it, in which ambition and avarice do not appear in very strong characters, and in which ambitious men were not the most popular? In Athens, Pisistratus and his successors were more popular, as well as ambitious, than Solon, Themistocles than Aristides, &c. In Rome, under the kings, the eternal plots of the nobles against the lives of the kings, to usurp their thrones, are proofs of an ardent and unbridled ambition. Nay, if we attentively examine the most virtuous characters, we shall find unequivocal marks of an ardent ambition. The elder Brutus, Camillus, Regulus, Curius, Æmilius, Cato, all discover an ambition, a thirst of glory, as strong as that of Cæsar; an honorable ambition, an ambition governed by justice, if you will; but an ambition still. But there is not a period in Athenian or Roman annals, when great characters did not appear actuated by ambition of another kind; an unjust and dishonorable ambition; such as Pisistratus, Themistocles, Appius Claudius, &c.; and these characters were always more popular than the others, and were supported chiefly by plebeians, not senates and patricians. If the absence of avarice is necessary to republican virtue, can you find any age or country in which republican virtue has existed? That single characters, or a few among the patricians, have existed, who were exempt from avarice, . . . [may be] admitted; but that a moment ever existed, in any country, where property was enjoyed, when the body of the people were universally or even generally exempted from avarice, is not easy to prove. Every page of the history of Rome appears equally marked with ambition and avarice; and the only difference appears in the means and objects. In some periods the nation was extremely poor, in others immensely rich; but the passions existed in all; and the Roman soldiers and common people were forever quarrelling with their most virtuous generals, for refusing to indulge their avarice, by distributing the spoils among them, and for loving the public too well, by putting the booty into the public treasury.

Shall we say then that republican virtue is nothing but simple poverty; and that poverty alone can support such a government? But Montesquieu tells us, virtue in a republic, is a love of the republic; virtue in a democracy, is a love of the democracy; and why might he not have said, that virtue in a monarchy is a love of the monarchy; in a despotism, of the despot; in a mixed government, of the mixture? Men in general love their country and its government. Can it be proved that Athenians loved Athens, or Romans, Rome, more than Frenchmen love France, or Englishmen their island?

There are two principal causes of discrimination; the first is, the greatness or smallness of the state. A citizen of a small republic, who knows every man and every house in it, appears generally to have the strongest attachment to it, because nothing can happen in it that does not interest and affect his feelings; but in a great nation, like France or England, a man is, as it were, lost in the crowd; there are very few persons that he knows, and few events that will much affect him; yet you will find him as much attached to his circle of friends and knowledge as the inhabitant of the small state. The second is, the goodness or badness of the constitution, the climate, soil, &c. Other things being equal, that constitution, whose blessings are the most felt, will be most beloved; and accordingly we find, that governments the best ordered and balanced have been most beloved, as Sparta, Athens, Carthage, Rome, and England, and we might add Holland, for there has been, in practice and effect, a balance of three powers in that country, though not sufficiently defined by law. Moral and Christian, and political virtue, cannot be too much beloved, practised, or rewarded; but to place liberty on that foundation only would not be safe; but it may be well questioned, whether love of the body politic is precisely moral or Christian virtue, which requires justice and benevolence to enemies as well as friends, and to other nations as well as our own. It is not true, in fact, that any people ever existed who loved the public better than themselves, their private friends, neighbors, &c., and therefore this kind of virtue, this sort of love, is as precarious a foundation for liberty as honor or fear; it is the laws alone that really love the country, the public, the whole better than any part; and that form of government which unites all the virtue, honor, and fear of the citizens, in a reverence and obedience to the laws, is the only one in which liberty can be secure, and all orders, and ranks, and parties, compelled to prefer the public good before their own; that is the government for which we plead.

The first magistrate may love himself, and family, and friends better than the public, but the laws, supported by the senate, commons, and judges, will not permit him to indulge it; the senate may love themselves, their families, and friends, more than the public, but the first magistrate, commons, and judges,

uniting in support of public law, will defeat their projects; the common people, or their representatives, may love themselves and partial connections better than the whole, but the first magistrate, senate, and judges, can support the laws against their enterprises; the judges may be partial to men or factions, but the three branches of the legislature, united to the executive, will easily bring them back to their duty. In this way, and in no other, can our author's rule be always observed, "to avoid all who hate the commonwealth, and those who are neutral and indifferent about it."

Montesquieu adds, "a love of democracy is that of equality." But what passion is this? Every man hates to have a superior, but no man is willing to have an equal; every man desires to be superior to all others. If the meaning is, that every citizen loves to have every other brought down to a level with himself, this is so far true, but is not the whole truth. When every man is brought down to his level, he wishes them depressed below him; and no man will ever acknowledge himself to be upon a level or equality with others, till they are brought down lower than him.

Montesquieu subjoins, "a love of the democracy is likewise that of frugality." This is another passion not easily to be found in human nature. A passion for frugality, perhaps, never existed in a nation, if it ever did in an individual. It is a virtue; but reason and reflection prove the necessity and utility of this virtue; and, after all, it is admired and esteemed more than beloved. But to prove that nations, as bodies, are never actuated by any such passion for frugality, it is sufficient to observe that no nation ever practised it but from necessity. Poor nations only are frugal, rich ones always profuse; excepting only some few instances, when the passion of avarice has been artfully cultivated, and has become the habitual national character; but the passion of avarice is not a love of frugality.

Is there, or is there not, any solid foundation for these doubts? Must we bow with reverence to this great master of laws, or may we venture to suspect that these doctrines of his are spun from his imagination? Before he delivered so many grave lessons upon democracies, he would have done well to have shown when or where such a governement existed. Until some one shall attempt this, one may venture to suspect his love of equality, love of frugality, and love of the democracy, to be fantastical passions, feigned for the regulation and animation of a government that never had a more solid existence than the flying island of Lagado. (pp. 205-10)

John Adams, "Marchamont Nedham: Errors of Government and Rules of Policy," in his The Works of John Adams, Vol. VI, *Charles C. Little and James Brown, 1851, pp. 161-216.*

EDMUND BURKE (essay date 1791)

[Burke was an Irish-born English statesman, philosopher, and critic. Throughout his career in Parliament he aligned himself with such causes as the abolition of the slave trade, taxation reform for the American colonies, and removal of political restrictions on Catholics in Ireland. Burke's political thought at no point sanctioned radical innovation, and among his most renowned works is a condemnation of anarchic underpinnings and practices of the French Revolution, Reflections on the Revolution in France *(1790). In addition to his distinction as a political thinker, Burke wrote a pioneering work in the field of aesthetics,* A Philosophical Inquiry into the Origin of Our Ideas of the Sublime and the Beautiful *(1756), and in 1759 founded the* Annual Register, *a yearly review of important events. In the following excerpt*

from his Appeal from the New to the Old Whigs *(1791), Burke cites the magnitude of Montesquieu's achievement in* The Spirit of Laws.]

Rational and experienced men tolerably well know, and have always known, how to distinguish between true and false liberty, and between the genuine adherence and the false pretence to what is true. But none, except those who are profoundly studied, can comprehend the elaborate contrivance of a fabric fitted to unite private and public liberty with public force, with order, with peace, with justice, and, above all, with the institutions formed for bestowing permanence and stability, through ages, upon this invaluable whole.

Place, for instance, before your eyes such a man as Montesquieu. Think of a genius not born in every country or every time: a man gifted by Nature with a penetrating, aquiline eye,—with a judgment prepared with the most extensive erudition,—with an Herculean robustness of mind, and nerves not to be broken with labor,—a man who could spend twenty years in one pursuit. Think of a man like the universal patriarch in Milton (who had drawn up before him in his prophetic vision the whole series of the generations which were to issue from his loins): a man capable of placing in review, after having brought together from the East, the West, the North, and the South, from the coarseness of the rudest barbarism to the most refined and subtle civilization, all the schemes of government which had ever prevailed amongst mankind, weighing, measuring, collating, and comparing them all, joining fact with theory, and calling into council, upon all this infinite assemblage of things, all the speculations which have fatigued the understandings of profound reasoners in all times. Let us then consider, that all these were but so many preparatory steps to qualify a man, and such a man, tinctured with no national prejudice, with no domestic affection, to admire, and to hold out to the admiration of mankind, the Constitution of England. And shall we Englishmen revoke to such a suit? Shall we, when so much more than he has produced remains still to be understood and admired, instead of keeping ourselves in the schools of real science, choose for our teachers men incapable of being taught,—whose only claim to know is, that they have never doubted,—from whom we can learn nothing but their own indocility,—who would teach us to scorn what in the silence of our hearts we ought to adore? (pp. 211-12)

> Edmund Burke, "Appeal from the New to the Old Whigs," in The Works of the Right Honourable Edmund Burke, Vol. 4, *John C. Nimmo, 1887, pp. 57-215.*

JAMES MADISON   (essay date 1792)

[*Madison was an American statesman and the fourth president of the United States. He earned the sobriquet "Father of the Constitution" for his leading role in the Federal Constitutional Convention of 1787 and for his impassioned championship of the resulting document. Also the primary chronicler of the Convention's deliberations, Madison wrote* Journal of the Federal Convention, *published posthumously in 1840. In the following excerpt from an essay written in 1792, Madison discusses what he considers the merit of Montesquieu's theory of the ruling principles of governments.*]

No government is perhaps reducible to a sole principle of operation. Where the theory approaches nearest to this character, different and often heterogeneous principles mingle their influence in the administration. . . .

Montesquieu has resolved the great operative principles of government into fear, honor, and virtue, applying the first to pure despotisms, the second to regular monarchies, and the third to republics. The portion of truth blended with the ingenuity of this system sufficiently justifies the admiration bestowed on its author. Its accuracy, however, can never be defended against the criticisms which it has encountered. Montesquieu was in politics not a Newton or a Locke, who established immortal systems—the one in matter, the other in mind. He was in his particular science what Bacon was in universal science. He lifted the veil from the venerable errors which enslaved opinion, and pointed the way to those luminous truths of which he had but a glimpse himself. (p. 474)

> James Madison, "Spirit of Governments," in his Letters and Other Writings of James Madison: 1829-1836, Vol. IV, *J. B. Lippincott & Co., 1865, pp. 474-75.*

[FRANCES JEFFREY]   (essay date 1809-10)

[*A Scottish literary critic, Jeffrey cofounded the* Edinburgh Review *in 1802 and served as its editor until 1829. Considered an exacting but fair critic, he was praised by William Hazlitt for his "great range of knowledge" and "incessant activity of mind." In the following excerpt, Jeffrey succinctly dismisses* The Spirit of Laws.]

[Montesquieu is] an author who frequently appears profound when he is only paradoxical, and seems to have studied with great success the art of hiding a desultory and fantastical style of reasoning in imposing aphorisms and epigrams of considerable effect. It is impossible to read the *Esprit des Loix,* without feeling that it is the work of an indolent and very ingenious person, who had fits of thoughtfulness and ambition, and had meditated the different points which it comprehends at long intervals, and then corrected them as he best could, by insinuations, metaphors, and vague verbal distinctions. (p. 464)

> [Francis Jeffrey], "Correspondance de Madame du Deffand et de Mademoiselle de Lespinasse," in The Edinburgh Review, *Vol. XV, October, 1809 - January, 1810, pp. 458-85.*

LORD MACAULAY   (essay date 1827)

[*Macaulay was a distinguished mid-nineteenth-century English historian, essayist, and politician. For many years he was a major contributor of erudite, highly opinionated articles to the* Edinburgh Review. *Besides these essays, collected in* Critical and Historical Essays *(1843), his most enduring work is his five-volume* History of England from the Accession of James II *(1849-61), which despite criticism of its strong bias toward the Whig political party is admired for its consummate rhetorical and narrative prose. According to Richard Tobias, Macaulay was a writer who "feared sentiment and preferred distance, objectivity, dispassionate vision. Yet withal, he was a brilliant writer who . . . is still capable of moving a reader by sheer verbal excitement." In the following excerpt from an essay originally published in the* Edinburgh Review *in 1827, Macaulay attacks Montesquieu's philosophical method and writing style.*]

Montesquieu enjoys, perhaps, a wider celebrity than any political writer of modern Europe. Something he doubtless owes to his merit, but much more to his fortune. He had the good luck of a Valentine. He caught the eye of the French nation, at the moment when it was waking from the long sleep of political and religious bigotry; and, in consequence, he became a favourite. The English, at that time, considered a Frenchman who talked about constitutional checks and fundamental laws as a prodigy not less astonishing than the learned pig or the musical infant. Specious but shallow, studious of effect, indifferent to truth, eager to build a system, but careless of collecting those materials out of which alone a sound and durable system can be built, the lively President constructed theories as rapidly and as slightly as card-houses, no sooner projected than completed, no sooner completed than blown away, no sooner blown away than forgotten. . . . Montesquieu errs, because he has a fine thing to say, and is resolved to say it. If the phænomena which lie before him will not suit his purpose, all history must be ransacked. If nothing established by authentic testimony can be racked or chipped to suit his Procrustean hypothesis, he puts up with some monstrous fable about Siam, or Bantam, or Japan, told by writers compared with whom Lucian and Gulliver were veracious, liars by a double right, as travellers and as Jesuits.

Propriety of thought, and propriety of diction, are commonly found together. Obscurity and affectation are the two greatest faults of style. Obscurity of expression generally springs from confusion of ideas; and the same wish to dazzle at any cost which produces affectation in the manner of a writer, is likely to produce sophistry in his reasonings. . . . The style of Montesquieu, on the other hand, indicates in every page a lively and ingenious, but an unsound mind. Every trick of expression, from the mysterious conciseness of an oracle to the flippancy of a Parisian coxcomb, is employed to disguise the fallacy of some positions, and the triteness of others. Absurdities are brightened into epigrams; truisms are darkened into enigmas. It is with difficulty that the strongest eye can sustain the glare with which some parts are illuminated, or penetrate the shade in which others are concealed. (pp. 313-15)

> *Lord Macaulay, "Machiavelli," in his* Critical, Historical and Miscellaneous Essays, *Vol. 1, Sheldon and Company, 1862, pp. 267-320.*

C. A. SAINTE-BEUVE   (essay date 1852)

[Sainte-Beuve is considered the foremost French literary critic of the nineteenth century. Of his extensive body of critical writings, the best known are his "lundis"—weekly newspaper articles which appeared every Monday morning over a period of two decades, in which his knowledge of literature and history was evident. While Sainte-Beuve began his career as a champion of Romanticism, he eventually formulated a psychological method of criticism. Asserting that the critic cannot separate a work of literature from the artist and from the artist's historical milieu, Sainte-Beuve considered an author's life and character integral to the comprehension of his work. This perspective led to his classification of writers into what he called "familles d'esprits," or "families of the mind." Though he usually treated his subjects with respect, he dealt harshly with several, notably François Chateaubriand and Honoré de Balzac. In the twentieth century, Sainte-Beuve's treatment of Balzac provoked the ire of Marcel Proust and inspired Contre Sainte-Beuve *(1954;* By Way of Sainte-Beuve, *1958), in which Proust contested the validity of Sainte-Beuve's analytical method. Other twentieth-century critics praise Sainte-Beuve's erudition and insight but question his biographical approach. They consider him a historian of manners, a psychologist, and a moralist. In the words of René Wellek, "Sainte-Beuve should be described as the greatest representative of the historical spirit in France," who, at his best, "preserves the delicate balance needed to save himself from relativism or overemphasis on external conditions." In the following excerpt from a "lundi" originally pub-*

lished in 1852, Sainte-Beuve discusses Persian Letters, Considerations, *and* The Spirit of Laws.]

The *Lettres Persanes* is one of three great books of Montesquieu's life—for in truth he wrote but three: these *Lettres*; his admirable work, *Le Grandeur et la Décadence des Romains*, which is only a detached episode in advance of his third and last great book, *L'Esprit des Lois*. The manner of these three works differs, but not as much as one would think. The basis of the ideas differs still less. The book on the Romans is the one in which the writer restrains himself most; he is master of himself from first to last; his tone is firm, lofty, simple, and wholly on the level of the majesty of the People-king. In the *Esprit des Lois,* he often mingles, one hardly knows how, epigram with grandeur. In the *Lettres Persanes*, Montesquieu, then young, sports and takes his pleasure; but gravity is found in his play; the greater part of his ideas are there in the germ,— better, indeed, than in the germ, they are developing. He is more indiscreet than he is later; and it is in this sense principally that he is less mature. He will retain most of his ideas, but, in his future works, he will not produce them in the same way; he will reflect them differently, and will speak of them only with gravity, feeling more and more the grandeur of the social institution, and desiring the ennobling of human nature. (pp. 117-18)

That which gives the *Lettres Persanes* their date and the stamp of the Regency, is the touch of irreverence and libertinism, which comes in to lighten the background and season the book to the taste of the day. . . . The *Lettres Persanes,* with all their defects, is one of the books of genius which our literature has produced.

Usbek and Rica, two friends, two Persians of rank, leave their country and make a journey to Europe. Usbek, the principal personage, has a harem at Ispahan, and on leaving Persia he commits it to the care of the Grand Eunuch, a black man, whom he reminds, from time to time, of his strict injunctions. In this harem are women whom he loves exceedingly, and the author would not be sorry to interest us in this romantic topic, very choice in its Asiatic taste and carefully studied. He succeeded, no doubt, in doing so at that date—1721; the libertine, or, to speak correctly, the licentious part of the *Lettres Persanes,* the perpetual details of eunuchs, passions, practices, and almost of utensils, on which the imagination of readers could dwell with pleasure, required a society that enjoyed the novels of Crébillon *fils*. To-day, this part seems to us artificial, dead; and, if it were longer, intolerably wearisome. What pleases us, and what we seek in these *Lettres,* is Montesquieu himself, slightly disguised among his various personages, and judging, under that transparent mask, the manners and customs, the ideas—in short, the whole social life of his youth.

Rica is a satirist, Parisian from the first day, and painting with a jest the eccentricities and absurdities of the queer characters who pass before his eyes, and with whom he gets along very well. Usbek, more serious, resists and reasons; he takes up questions, he propounds and discusses them in letters which he addresses to the theologians of his own country. The art of the work, and what, through the apparent mixture, shows the talent of composition, is that, side by side with a harem letter, there will be one on free-will. An ambassador from Persia to Muscovy writes a half-page to Usbek about the Tartars, which might be a chapter in the *Esprit des Lois*. Rica, on the one hand, writes the cleverest criticism on the chatter of Frenchmen and on the talkers with nothing to say in society; on the other, Usbek discusses God and justice in a very noble and far-reaching letter. The idea of justice, independent in itself, is therein explained under the true principles of the social institution. Montesquieu (for it is he who speaks here, as he spoke in his own name to the end of his life), tries to establish in what respect that idea of justice does not depend on human conventions: "If it did so depend," he adds, "it would be a terrible truth that we should have to conceal from ourselves."

Montesquieu goes farther. He tries to render the idea and the worship of justice independent of all existence higher than man; he goes so far as to say, through the mouth of Usbek: "If there were no God, we ought always to love justice; that is to say, we should make efforts to resemble that Being, of whom we have so lofty an idea, and who, if he existed, would necessarily be just. Free as we may be from the yoke of religion, we cannot be free from that of equity."

Here we touch the very foundation of Montesquieu's thought, and of all his habitual mental procedure; let us not be weak or wavering, let us not hesitate to expose the truth in its nudity. He says still further:

> Even if the immortality of the soul is an error, I should be sorry not to believe it: I own that I am not so humble as the atheists. I do not know what they think, but, for my part, I do not choose to barter the idea of my immortality for that of the beatitude of to-day. I am glad to believe myself as immortal as God himself. Independently of revealed ideas, metaphysical ideas give me a very strong hope of my eternal happiness which I do not choose to renounce.

In these words we have the measure of Montesquieu's belief and his noble desire: even in the expression of that desire, the supposition glides in that "even if the thing did not exist" it would be best to believe in it. I do not blame that homage rendered, in any case, to the elevation and the idealisation of human nature; but I cannot help remarking that it is taking and accepting the ideas of justice and of religion on the political and social side and not potentially in themselves. Montesquieu, when, by degrees, he freed himself from the irony of the *Lettres Persanes,* came more and more to respect the objects of human veneration and conscience. Not that I think he entered into them with more personal feeling, for in the midst of his most majestic parts a sort of barrenness is felt. He has ideas, but he has not, it has been remarked, civic feelings. A sort of life is lacking, a tie that binds: we feel the powerful brain, but not the heart. I think it incumbent on me to note, if not this weak side, at least this cold side of a great man. (pp. 118-22)

All the questions of the day under the Regency are touched upon in the *Lettres Persanes*—the dispute of the ancients and moderns, the revocation of the Edict of Nantes and its effects, the quarrel concerning the Bull *Unigenitus,* and so forth; the author serves the spirit of the day by mingling his views with it; the reign of Louis XIV is sharply attacked with a backward thrust. In the famous episode of the Troglodytes, Montesquieu relates, after his manner, his dream of Salenté. In the portraits of the Farmer-general, the Director, the Casuist, the Man *à bonnes fortunes,* the Gambling Wife, Montesquieu equals La Bruyère in recollection. He resembles him also in language, but without intending it. His own language, while it is quite as new, is perhaps less complicated; it has a clearness and a singularly picturesque quality. . . . The whole style is clear, pungent, full of wit, a little thin and sharp, occasionally incorrect.

But Montesquieu has certain free and easy ideas as to style. "A man who writes well," he thinks, "does not write as other people write, but as *he* writes; and often it is when he speaks ill that he speaks well." He writes, therefore, in his own manner; and that manner, always refined and lively, becomes strong and proud and rises higher with his topics. . . . [He] liked and even delighted in a style of imagery or of picturesque comparisons to elucidate his thought: for example, wishing to make Rica say that the husband of a pretty woman in France, if he is worsted at home, takes his revenge on the wives of others:

> "This title of husband of a pretty woman," he writes, "which is so carefully concealed in Asia, is borne in France without uneasiness. Men feel they have opportunity to find compensation everywhere. A prince consoles himself for the loss of a fortress by capturing another; when the Turks took Bagdad from us did we not take the fortress of Kandahar in Mongol-Tartary from them?"

Exactly in the same manner Montesquieu, in the *Esprit des Lois,* describing an English Utopian who, having under his eyes the image of true liberty, goes about imagining quite another liberty in his book, says: "He built Chalcedonia, having the shores of Byzantium before his eyes." In Montesquieu's thought, at the moment when we least expect it, suddenly the summits glow.

Amid the audacity and the irreverence of the *Lettres Persanes,* a spirit of prudence is observable in Usbek's pen. While discussing questions so well and occasionally letting daylight into them, Usbek (and here, perhaps, is a contradiction that Montesquieu failed to avoid), continues to remain faithful to the laws of his country and to his religion. "It is true," he says, "that, by a caprice that comes more from the nature than from the mind of men, it is sometimes necessary to change certain laws, but the case is rare; and when it does occur, it should be touched with a *trembling hand.*" Rica himself, light-hearted jester, remarking that in courts of justice when judgment is to be pronounced the votes of the majority are taken, adds, by way of epigram: "But they say they have found by experience that it would be better to take those of the minority; and that is natural enough, for there are very few just minds, and all the world agrees that there are quantities of unjust ones." This is enough to show that the mind that dictated the *Lettres Persanes* would never push things to extremity on the side of reform and popular revolution.

After touching upon questions which belong properly to the philosophy of history, after expressing astonishment that Frenchmen should have abandoned the old laws made by their first kings in the assemblies of the nation, and, having thus reached the threshold of the great work he no doubt foresaw in the future, Montesquieu resumes his laughter over many subjects, and when he has laughed enough he stops short. The *Lettres Persanes,* having exhausted the picture and the satire of present manners and morals, turns to the romantic: Usbek receives news that his harem, profiting by his absence, has made a revolution; all are in rebellion, flying at each other's throats, and killing one another. It is a voluptuous and delirious conclusion, a "fire and blood" end, that has nothing relating to us in it. All this sensual part is dry and hard, showing that Montesquieu's imagination lay solely in the direction of historical and moral observation. Once more I remark that there is in the *Lettres Persanes,* from beginning to end, and viewed as a whole, a resemblance to the novels of Crébillon *fils.* (pp. 124-28)

In Montesquieu's great work [*Considérations sur les Causes de la Grandeur des Romains et de leur Décadence*] the artist counts for much; many things are said in it which are open to doubt. The author-artist is there in presence of his subject, of his vast study; he wants a law, he searches for it, and sometimes he creates it. From the accumulation of texts and notes which he has brought before him, and which press upon him and almost overwhelm him, he frees himself, he chooses his course; his work springs up. Boldly, sometimes painfully, he begins his *Considérations* and his perspective; he fashions them to suit himself. Was it not he who, in the privacy of his own study, said: "Histories are false facts composed on true facts."

And did he not say, still further: "In history we see men painted in noble portraits, but we do not find them to be what we see them." How is it, then, when the spirit of history alone is sought? Men are seen at too great a distance; the human stuff which the statesman should consider too often disappears in Montesquieu. (p. 133)

Montesquieu joined to [the useful] an idea of the beautiful. He had a sacred pattern within him; he raised a temple, and the crowd flocked to it. But did he not set up in it certain idols?

Let us lay aside regrets, and accept respectfully the unique and regal form of his *Considérations,* which is peculiarly his own; a form born of a mind so lofty and so firm, and bearing the imprint of a mould which, with all the fine accessories that characterised it, will not be met with again. (pp. 133-34)

[*Considérations*] has remained the most classic and perfect of his works; the only one, indeed, that seems to have been cast in a single mould like a statue.

The works of Montesquieu are nothing else than the philosophic summing up and the ideal review of his studies; no one reasons better than he on history when he has closed the book that contains the narrative. He expresses the thought in it; he gives it continuity, connectedness, counsel; and that which makes the beauty of what he says is the manner in which it is put forth. He advances with a firm step, by a series of vivid and compact reflections, which, as a whole, have the grand air; his wit is also quick, brief, and is aimed high.

This style of seeing and speaking was marvellously well suited for application to the Romans. To judge of the book of *Considérations* which he gave to them, we should have to examine what had been said before him on that subject, and render to Machiavelli, Saint-Évremond, Saint Réal, that which is their due; and as for form we should have to place the historic discourses of Montesquieu side by side with those of Bossuet.

The nature of Montesquieu's mind is so completely that of reasoning upon history, that he does it where there is no call for it, and where the grounds are insufficient; as, for instance, on the beginnings of Rome. Before making reflections on what he had read, he ought to have asked himself whether the historians spoke the truth; there was criticism to be made on the books and on the traditions that were semi-fabulous. Montesquieu does not make it. From the statement that Romulus took the shield of the Sabines, which was large, in place of the small shield he had hitherto used, Montesquieu jumps to the conclusion that a certain custom and a certain policy was in practice among the Romans to borrow from the vanquished whatever they had that was better than their own.

It is not until the period of Hannibal and the Punic wars, that Montesquieu's thought develops with ease, and that he commands his whole subject. Chapter VI, on the policy of the Romans, and on their conduct at the submission of other peoples, is a masterpiece, in which prudence and majesty are combined;

the grand style begins here, never to cease again. In speaking of the Romans, Montesquieu's language becomes like Latin; it takes a character of firm conciseness that brings it near to the language of Tacitus or Sallust; there is study, profound combination, effort, as with Sallust, to attain to propriety of expression in words, and to conciseness; also to make the image, as in Tacitus, both magnificent and brief, and to imprint on the whole diction something grave and august.

No one has entered more fully than Montesquieu into the ideal of the Roman genius; he is, by inclination, favourable to the Senate, and something of a patrician of the ancient Republic. It should be remarked that he who spoke so admiringly of Alexander, Charlemagne, Trajan, and Marcus Aurelius is less generous on the subject of Cæsar; at any rate, he does not speak of him as if he were under a sort of enchantment, as he does of those other great mortals. He is angry with him for having been the potential instrument of the great transformation of the Roman world. Montesquieu (if we except the *Lettres Persanes*) always used noble words in relation to Christianity, and, as he advanced in life, he more and more accepted and, so to speak, espoused its benefits in all that concerned civilisation and humanity. Nevertheless, he had for pure Roman nature anterior to all Christian influence, for the stoical Roman nature, a predilection that he never concealed. The suicides of Cato and Brutus inspired him with reflections in which there is, perhaps, a sort of classic idolatry, and even some prestige. . . . (pp. 134-37)

Montesquieu divined many things, ancient or modern; about those even of which he had seen the least in his day—free government, civil wars, imperial government. One might make a piquant extract of such predictions or allusions taken from his works. Let us beware of that method which draws to self a great mind and turns it from its broad and special path. In all that Montesquieu foresaw and divined, one thing is lacking to make him wholly himself, and to complete the education of his genius,—he did not foresee the revolution. (p. 137)

I desired to read Machiavelli in comparison with Montesquieu; the latter is the true refutation, or, at any rate, the true corrective. With Machiavelli, we are always closer to natural corruption, to primitive cupidity; Machiavelli distrusts himself; Montesquieu does not. It was Machiavelli who said that there is in all men a hidden, vicious inclination, which awaits only the opportunity to show itself, and needs all civil laws, supported by force of arms, to repress it. Men, according to him, never do right unless they cannot do otherwise: "And when they have that choice, and the liberty to do evil with impunity, they never fail to cause confusion and disorder everywhere." Machiavelli is convinced that, although men may seem to change in the course of a given state of things, fundamentally they do not change, and, certain occasions returning, we find them absolutely the same. Montesquieu is not wholly convinced of that truth. At the opening of the *Esprit des Lois,* he goes so far as to say that the first men supposed to be savages and children of nature, were, above all, timid, and wanted *peace:* as if physical cupidity, want, and hunger, the blind consciousness that all youth has of its own force, and "that rage for domination innate in the human heart," would not engender from the very first, conflict and warfare. This criticism is fundamental, and bears, as I think, on the whole of the *Esprit des Lois.* Montesquieu grants too much, not only outwardly, but secretly in his own mind, to the decorum of human nature. This defect in Montesquieu is infinitely honourable, but a real defect, none the less. Admirable explainer and classifier of the past and of those accomplished things that have no present consequences, he is likely to lead into error those who take him at his word about the future. Born under a mild government, living in the midst of an enlightened society, where the memory of factions was far-distant, and the despotism that repressed them was no longer present, or, at any rate, not felt, he lightly adjusted humanity to his desire. He forgot what Richelieu had known, and what he had had to do, and Louis XIV also, at the beginning of his reign. He had need . . . of a revolution (were it only such a Fronde as Pascal saw) to refresh his idea of the reality of human nature, that idea which is so easily covered up in calm and civilised epochs.

Machiavelli, on the contrary (let us not forget this in a comparison of the two geniuses), lived at an epoch and in a country where there were daily, for individuals as well for cities, thirty ways of being destroyed and of perishing. Such a state of society naturally keeps men on the alert, and gives prudence to all.

I return to the *Considérations*, from which I have wandered. Divided between the old Romans of the resistance and the Roman who first passed the Rubicon, Montesquieu does not understand Cæsar to the same degree that he understands other great men; he follows him with a sort of regret. Montesquieu had so lived in idea among those old Romans, that he had an opinion upon them, a direct, personal impression, which he produces sometimes in quite a naïve manner. Speaking of the triumvir Lepidus, sacrificed by Octavius: "We are very glad," he exclaims, "to see the humiliation of this Lepidus. He was the most wicked citizen in the Republic."—*We are very glad:* Montesquieu, when writing, lets many of these familiar expressions escape him, showing his intimacy with his great subjects; there is something abrupt and unexpected, like his own conversation, in these chapters. He says of Alexander: "Let us talk about him at our ease." Elsewhere he says: "I request the reader to pay a little attention"—I see in this the sort of gesture of an eager man who is full of his subject, who fears in talking to let something escape him, and so grasps the arm of his listener.

Sometimes the gesture is grander, less familiar; the orator rises: "Here we must give ourselves the spectacle of things human" . . . and he goes on to enumerate in a manner worthy of Bossuet all that labour of the Roman people and their Senate—the wars undertaken, the blood shed, so many triumphs, so much wisdom and courage, all to serve finally "to glut the happiness of five or six monsters." The whole passage is pure Bossuet.

There is a main point, nevertheless, on which Montesquieu differed from Bossuet. Both believed in a sovereign counsel in human things; but Bossuet assigns that counsel to God and Providence, who has His secret purpose and object. Montesquieu assigns it elsewhere:

> [It is not] fortune that rules the world; we can ask the Romans, who had a continual succession of prosperity so long as they governed themselves on a certain plan, and an uninterrupted succession of reverses when they conducted themselves on another plan. There are general causes, whether moral or physical, which act in each monarchy, raising it, maintaining it, or flinging it down. All events are subject to these causes; and, though the chances of a battle, which is a particular cause, may have ruined a State, there was a general cause, which brought about that this State should perish by a single battle. In a word: the main procedure sweeps along with it all special incidents.

Montesquieu's whole philosophy of history lies in those words; and we must agree that in what concerns the Romans, judging things after the event, he seems to be right. The Romans certainly do lend themselves wonderfully to the application of this linked system: we might even say, in truth, that they came into the world expressly that Montesquieu might "consider" them.

And yet, even if we do not assign directly to Providence itself, as Bossuet does, the counsel and law of the world of history, it seems to me very difficult and very perilous to find it in this succession and linking together of events in which Montesquieu flatters himself he has discovered it. Machiavelli, on this point, seems to me wiser and nearer the truth than Montesquieu when he reminds us, even in the midst of his reflections, how much of chance—that is, of causes to us unknown—there is in the origin and in the accomplishment of the facts of history and the life of empires. Here, again, Montesquieu suffers from living in his study and never seeing history make itself before him. Otherwise, he would oftener have said to himself: "On what small things do great things hinge!" (pp. 138-42)

No one will expect me to assume the airs of a critic in speaking of the *Esprit des Lois:* many volumes would be needed for such criticism, and the work would have to be taken book by book, chapter by chapter. . . . Montesquieu can be stopped at every step on his general divisions of government, on the principle he assigns to each of them, on climates and the influence he attributes to them, on the quotations with which he strews his work. If often happens that he quotes incorrectly and for effect, as Chateaubriand has done later; that happens to men of imagination who make use of erudition without binding themselves down to it or mastering it. They take note, as they read, of witty or salient passages, and later, when composing, they take infinite pains to turn their royal road past their illustrative note, which may sometimes be merely a lively anecdote. Montesquieu makes too much use of classic incidents and the petty equivocal examples they afford him. What is it to us, I ask, how Arribas, King of the Molossians, modified an absolute government? Why should we know whether such or such police measures were adopted by the Epidamnians, and what conclusions could we reasonably draw from them?

The frequent breaks in the *Esprit des Lois,* the cutting up into chapters—composed, sometimes, of a single sentence—also show either a certain hesitation in arrangement, or a certain pretension to authority. . . . All said, however, the book remains a work of genius; chapters like those on Alexander and on Charlemagne compensate us for everything; chapters like those on the Constitution and, especially, on the political morals of England, are discoveries in the world of history. We feel at every turn in Montesquieu one of those rapid, penetrating minds which are the first to stir a mass, and then enlighten it.

I have stated the radical defect that I believe is in Montesquieu's statesmanship: he puts the average of humanity, considered in its natural data, rather higher than it is. It is not ill that a legislator should impel men, even by means of a little illusion, to the use of all their faculties and all their virtue; but he ought to know under what inward conditions that is possible, and take his precautions in consequence. Montesquieu not only does not acquaint his reader with this, he does not acquaint himself. In picturing the government of England as so noble (which he had, nevertheless, seen closely with all its shadows), he seems never to have asked himself what effect his pictures might have in France. He certainly did not wish for the ruin of the monarchy, even that of Louis XV; he considered it tempered by the parliaments, and reformable in itself: "I have not, by nature," he said, "a disapproving spirit"; and he was far indeed from having a revolutionary one. Very different from Jean-Jacques, he desired that every man, after reading him, should have "new reasons to love his duty, his prince, his country, and the laws"; and yet he shows nowhere the slightest anxiety as to the result of the comparison he presents to the imagination of his compatriots. In the *Esprit des Lois,* Montesquieu seems to forget that Frenchmen remain what he saw and described them to be in the *Lettres Persanes;* and, though he speaks continually, with virtuous conviction, of moderate government, he does not sufficiently tell himself under his breath that such moderation is not one of the qualities that can be transplanted. (pp. 147-50)

Jean-Jacques Rousseau, who feared no revolution, might be bold and foolhardy; but Montesquieu, who does not desire one, was he sufficiently foresighted? or Let us take the *Esprit des Lois* for what it is: a work of thought and civilisation. What is finest in it is the man behind the book. We must not ask of that book more method, more continuity, more precision, and more practicality in detail, more sobriety in imagination and in erudition, more practical counsels than are actually in it; we should see the characteristics of moderation, patriotism, and humanity that the writer wrought into all his noble words and into many of his magnanimous utterances. It is in this sense that he has reason to speak of the "majesty" of his topic, and to add: "I do not think I have totally lacked genius." Everywhere, and in those noble portions so often quoted, we feel the man who desires true liberty, the true virtue of the citizen; things of which he had seen no perfect pattern among moderns, the idea of which he had formed for himself in his study and before the busts of the ancients.

The *Esprit des Lois* is a book which now is of no other use than that noble, perpetual use of carrying the mind into high historic regions, and giving birth to a vast array of fine discussions. In the order and practice of free and moderate governments men will continue to find in it general inspiration and memorable texts. As for its oracles, those who want them may seek them. The circle of things human, which has so many turns and twists, and of which we can never say that it is closed for ever, seems many a time to have given both right and wrong to Montesquieu. Very clever and very confident would he be who could see the confirmation of any certain order announced by him, and not eternal vicissitude. (pp. 151-52)

C. A. Sainte-Beuve, "Montesquieu (1689-1755)," in his Portraits of the Eighteenth Century: Historical and Literary, Vol. I, *translated by Katharine P. Wormeley, G. P. Putnam's Sons, 1905, pp. 109-56.*

EMILE DURKHEIM   (essay date 1892?)

[A French academic and philosopher, Durkheim was instrumental in the establishment of twentieth-century sociology. Through his founding of the first sociological review, Année sociologique, *and in his several sociological studies, he propounded his thesis that social phenomena can be examined scientifically and objectively; as he described it: "Sociological method rests wholly on the basic principle that social facts must be studied as things; that is, as realities external to the individual." Durkheim is credited with steering social theory from the nineteenth-century emphasis on the individual to the modern concept of "collective consciousness" or culture. In the following excerpt from an essay probably first published in 1892, he explicates Montesquieu's theories of societal classification as outlined in* The Spirit of Laws.]

Montesquieu did not classify societies, but rather the ways in which they are governed. Consequently he simply took over the traditional categories with slight modifications. He distinguished three types: the republic—which includes aristocracy and democracy—monarchy, and despotism. Comte criticized him sharply for discarding the plan set forth at the beginning of the book and reverting to an Aristotelian conception, but if we examine the work more closely, we shall see that the resemblance to Aristotle is only apparent.

For one thing, his classification is not, like Aristotle's, based on the number of rulers. Montesquieu regards democracy and aristocracy as varieties of one and the same type, though in the former all the citizens participate in government and in the latter only a small number. But though power is in the hands of a single person in both monarchy and despotism, these forms are not only dissimilar but even antagonistic. Many critics have called this distinction confused and ambiguous, and the charge would be justified if it were true that Montesquieu considered only the political regimes of societies. But his range of vision is far wider, for as he describes them the three types of society differ not only in the number of their rulers and in the administration of public affairs, but in their entire nature.

This becomes apparent as soon as we see how he distinguishes them from each other. Aristotle and his followers derive their classification from an abstract notion of the state, but Montesquieu's is based on phenomena themselves. He derives his three types not from any a priori principle, but from a comparison of the societies known to him from his study of history, from travelers' accounts, or from his own travels. And indeed the meaning he attaches to the terms escapes us unless we first find out what nations he is referring to.

He gives the name "republic" not to all societies administered by all or a part of their members, but to the Greek and Italic city-states of antiquity and the great Italian cities of the Middle Ages. However, he is chiefly concerned with the ancient city-states, and whenever he refers to the republican form, it is clear that he has in mind Rome, Athens, and Sparta. This explains why he assigns both democracy and aristocracy to the category of republics. Since both these forms were to be found in the ancient city-states and in some instances one even succeeded the other in the same nation, it was not possible to separate them completely. (pp. 24-5)

As for monarchy, he finds this social structure only among the large nations of modern Europe. He demonstrates that it could not have been known to the peoples of antiquity and that it made its first appearance when the Germans invaded and partitioned the Roman empire. He knew, of course, that the Greeks and Latins had long been ruled by kings, but the nature of their regime struck him as something very different from true monarchy. As for despotism, although in a sense it can grow out of any political form through corruption, he believes that it had a natural existence only in the Orient. He has in mind the Turks, the Persians, and several other Asiatic peoples, to which should be added the nations of northern Europe. But can anyone doubt that the ancient city-states, the oriental kingdoms, and the modern European nations represent three totally distinct types of society?

Montesquieu distinguishes the three types of society not only because they are governed differently but also because they differ in the number, arrangement, and cohesion of their component parts.

The republican form flourished in small cities and never suc-ceeded in spreading beyond their narrow limits; the ancient cities are examples of this form. The despotic state, on the other hand, is found in large societies that spread over vast areas—the Asiatic nations for example. The monarchic state is of medium size, and though it has a larger population than the republic, it has fewer subjects than the despotic.

Moreover, the structures of these various societies are not the same, nor are their members united by the same ties. In a republic, particularly in a democracy, the citizens are all equal and even alike. The city-state appears to be a kind of block made up of homogeneous components, none superior to the others. All are equally zealous for the common weal. Those who occupy positions of authority are not above the others, for they hold office only for a given time. Even in private life there is little difference between them. Indeed, it is the principle of the republic, or at least the aim for which it strives, that no man's personal resources should too far exceed those of his fellow citizens; for though it is difficult to attain absolute equal-ity, the laws of every republic form a barrier to excessive differences in fortune, and such equality would be impossible without restrictions on individual wealth. The means of all men must be modest if they are to be more or less equal. "Since every individual ought here to enjoy the same happiness and the same advantages," says Montesquieu, "they should con-sequently taste the same pleasures and form the same hopes, which cannot be expected but from a general frugality."

In such a state, private fortunes play no important role in the lives and thinking of individuals, who are preoccupied rather with the common welfare. Hence, the chief source of the dif-ference among men is eliminated. Even private life is much the same for all; the modest status of all citizens, which is established by law, eliminates almost all stimulus to commerce, which can hardly exist without a certain inequality. Thus the activity of all persons is approximately the same. They till a piece of land, which is of the same size for all, and from this they derive their subsistence. In short, there is no division of labor among the members of the body politic, unless we apply the term to the rotation of public office.

All this is eminently a picture of democracy. As for aristocracy, Montesquieu regards it as a debased form of democracy (the more it resembles a democracy, the more perfect it is), and we can therefore leave it out of account.

It is easy to imagine what the unanimous will of the citizens can accomplish in such a society. The idea of the nation is uppermost in men's minds. Since there is practically no private property, the individual is indifferent to personal profit. There are no antagonistic parties to create disunity among citizens. This is the *virtue* that Montesquieu regards as the basis of the republic. He is referring not to ethical virtue but to the political virtue that resides in love of country and leads men to place the interests of the state above their own. The term lends itself to criticism, for it is ambiguous, but Montesquieu's use of it should not surprise us. Do we ourselves not apply it to any moral attitude that sets limits to excessive self-interest?

In a republic, at all events, all citizens necessarily share this attitude, since everyone is "socially minded"—if we may use the term—and in view of the general frugality self-love has nothing to feed on. That part of the individual consciousness which is an expression of society and which is the same in all persons is broad and powerful. The part which relates to the individual and his personal affairs is weak and limited. The citizens do not have to be spurred on by an external force, but by a natural impulse subordinate their own interests to those of the state.

The nature of monarchy is quite different. Here, all the func-tions of private as well as public life are divided among the various classes of citizens. Some engage in farming, others in trade, still others in the various arts and crafts. Some make the laws, others execute them either as judges or governors, and no one is permitted to deviate from his role or infringe upon that of others. Thus monarchy cannot be defined by the power of a single person. Montesquieu adds that even if a society is ruled by one individual, it should not be called a monarchy unless it has fixed laws according to which the king governs and which he may not modify arbitrarily. This implies that there are established orders which limit his power. Though he is superior to them, they must have a power of their own and must not be so far below the ruler as to be unable to resist him. For if there were no barrier to the prince's authority, there could be no law limiting his will, since the laws themselves would be entirely dependent on it. It is this principle that distinguishes monarchy from other political regimes. *Division of labor*, which does not exist in the republic, tends toward its maximum development in the monarchy. Monarchical society may be compared to a living organism, each of whose parts performs a specific function in accordance with its nature.

This explains why Montesquieu considers political freedom to be peculiar to monarchy. The classes—or, to use a contem-porary term, the *organs*—of the social body limit not only the authority of the prince, but each other as well. Since each is prevented by the others from growing too powerful and ab-sorbing all the powers of the organism, it is free to develop its special nature, but in moderation. We are now in a position to understand the role played by the famous theory of the division of powers in Montesquieu's thinking. It is merely a particular form of the principle that the various public functions should be performed by different persons. If Montesquieu at-taches so much importance to the distribution of authority, it is not in order to eliminate all disagreement between the various powers, but rather in order to foster such rivalry that none among them will be able to rise above the others and reduce them to insignificance.

The social tie in a monarchy cannot be the same as in a republic. Since each class is concerned with a limited area of social life, it sees nothing beyond the function it performs. Men's minds are imbued with the idea of their class rather than that of their country. Each order has only one objective, which is not the common weal but self-aggrandizement. Even the private in-dividual is chiefly concerned with his own interests. While under the republic, the equality of all citizens inevitably results in a general frugality, the diversity of status characteristic of monarchy arouses ambition. Where there are varying degrees of rank, honor, and wealth, each individual has before his eyes persons with a standard of living superior to his own and grows envious. Thus the members of society disregard the general welfare in favor of their personal interests, so that the condi-tions making for the *virtue* which is the foundation of the republic are lacking. But this very diversity of the component parts makes for cohesion. The ambition that fosters rivalry among classes and individuals also leads them to perform their particular functions as well as possible. They therefore work unconsciously for the common good, though to their own minds they are promoting only their personal interests. Emulation results in a harmony between the different elements of society.

Montesquieu calls this stimulus to public life in a monarchy *honor*. He uses the term to designate the particular ambitions of individuals or classes which make men strive to attain as high a status as possible. Such an attitude is possible only if men have a certain concern for dignity and freedom. Thus *honor* is not without its greatness, but it may give rise to excessive self-love and can easily become a failing. In several passages, Montesquieu speaks with a certain severity of *honor* and of monarchic customs in general. However, he does not mean to disparage monarchy. These shortcomings spring solely from the development of private enterprise and the greater freedom enjoyed by individuals in the pursuit of their interests. *Virtue*, to his mind, is so rare and difficult to attain that the prudent ruler will use it with the utmost caution. This wise organization of society, which without requiring virtue impels men to great undertakings, is so admirable in Montesquieu's opinion, that he readily forgives it certain imperfections.

I shall say little of despotism, for Montesquieu himself seems to have been less concerned with it. This form of government stands midway between the societies we have been discussing. A despotism is either a variety of monarchy in which all the orders have been abolished and there is no division of labor, or a democracy in which all the citizens except the ruler are equal, but equal in a state of servitude. Thus it has the aspect of a monster, in which only the head is alive, having absorbed all the energies of the organism. The principle of social life in such a society can be neither *virtue*, because the people do not participate in the affairs of the community, nor *honor*, because there are no differences of status. If men adhere to such a society, it is from passive submission to the prince's will, that is, solely from *fear*.

The foregoing suffices to make it clear that Montesquieu distinguished definite types of society. This would be still more evident if we went into detail, for they differ not only in structural principles but in all aspects of life. Customs, religious practices, the family, marriage, the rearing of children, crimes and punishments, are not the same in a republic, a monarchy, and a despotism. Montesquieu seems even to have been more interested in the differences between societies than their similarities.

The reader may wonder why, if Montesquieu actually classified and described types of society, he defined and named them as he did. He distinguishes them and names them, not on the basis of division of labor or the nature of their social ties, but solely according to the nature of the sovereign authority.

These different points of view are not incompatible. It was necessary to define each type in terms of its essential property from which the others follow. At first sight, the form of government seems to meet this condition. No aspect of public life is more apparent, more evident to all. Since the ruler is at the summit, so to speak, of society and is often, not without reason, referred to as the "head" of the nation, everything is thought to depend on him. Furthermore, Montesquieu's predecessors had not yet discovered any other aspect of social phenomena that could serve as a principle of classification, and despite the originality of his approach it was hard for him to break entirely with their point of view.

This explains why he classified societies according to form of government. To be sure, this method is subject to many objections. The form of government does not determine the nature of a society. . . . [The] nature of the supreme power can be modified while the social structure remains unchanged, or con-

versely it can remain identical in societies which differ in the extreme. But the error lies in the terms rather than the realities, for apart from the political regime Montesquieu mentions many other characteristics by which societies can be differentiated.

If we overlook his terminology, we shall probably find nothing more truthful or more penetrating in the entire work than this classification, the principles of which are valid even today. (pp. 26-33)

Emile Durkheim, "Montesquieu's Classification of Societies," in his Montesquieu and Rousseau: Forerunners of Sociology, *translated by Ralph Manheim, The University of Michigan Press, 1960, pp. 24-35.*

L. LÉVY-BRUHL (essay date 1899)

[*A French philosopher, sociologist, and anthropologist, Lévy-Bruhl stressed ethical relativism and championed the need for comparative scientific examination of moral systems in his* Ethics and Moral Science *(1902). He also wrote several studies of primitive society and thought, including* Primitive Mentality *(1922) and* The Soul of the Primitive *(1928). In the following excerpt from another work, he outlines both the innovations and the limitations of* The Spirit of Laws.]

L'Esprit des Lois is a grand, lofty, and enigmatic title. It is interpreted, at least partially, by the sub-title: "Of the relation which the laws should bear to the constitution of each government, to manners, climate, religion, trade, etc.," although the unfinished enumeration leaves some perplexity in our minds. It is nothing less than a political and social philosophy, conceived after a new plan, and Montesquieu was quite justified in choosing as the motto of his book: *Prolem sine matre creatam* ["Progeny without mother born"].

His predecessors, to whom he alludes in his preface [see essay dated 1748], had not the same object in view. Some, as Grotius and Puffendorf, treated especially the theory of the law of nations. Others, like Hobbes, spoke as philosophers on the origin of society and the nature of the state; or, like more and other Utopian dreamers of the sixteenth century, set up an ideal city in contrast to the real states they had before their eyes. Harrington, Algernon Sidney, and Locke, had written entirely from an English point of view. Locke's two treatises *On Civil Government* go back to first principles only in so far as it was necessary to vindicate the Revolution of 1688 and the conditions imposed upon the prince of Orange, afterwards William III.

The work of Montesquieu is entirely different. It deals with political realities, and takes its materials from history and from observed facts; herein Montesquieu stands apart from the dreamers, but he differs also from Locke in not devoting his attention to the practical, or at least immediate, application of his theories. His aim is to study, as a philosopher, and in a strictly methodical way, that body of realities which was afterwards to become the subject of social science or sociology. Thus the *Esprit des Lois* is, properly speaking, neither a philosophy of politics, nor a philosophy of history, nor a philosophy of law, nor a philosophy of political economy; for none of these sciences is there considered by itself, but all of them are studied in their natural relations so as to deduce the principles which are common to them. Montesquieu's originality consists in having fully perceived in the various series of social phenomena that solidarity by which each of these contributes to limit the others, and is in its turn limited by them. For instance, if the government of a country is a monarchy, the laws concerning education, luxury, trade, the condition of women, the liberty of citizens, etc., will necessarily be adapted to that political form; in a republican country they will be different. Social phenomena are thus subject to fixed attendant conditions, and can form only definite systems.

In a word, there are *laws of laws:* the political, civil, and penal *laws* of any society are regulated, in their nature, their development, and even their form, by natural laws, that is, according to Montesquieu's celebrated definition, by the necessary relations derived from the nature of things. A profound thought, which tends to nothing less than subjecting to scientific form and method a vast domain hitherto neglected or regarded as inaccessible. A profound thought also, to seek the manifestation of those ''laws of laws'' in the mutual dependency of the various orders of social phenomena. Montesquieu thus assumes a point of view superior to that of the jurist, the historian, and the politician, and from which he overlooks them all. He shows, by means of history, how laws are modified in accordance with political forms,—and in accordance with not only these, but also with the climate, the nature of the soil, the facilities for trade, etc. This was already a remarkable attempt towards a sociologic synthesis. Well could Montesquieu speak of the ''majesty'' of his subject. The conception is a fine one, and we may easily understand that it should have produced a deep impression at the time of its appearance.

The performance, unfortunately, did not equal the conception. It undoubtedly has great merits. Despite a subject so austere and so unfamiliar to the very great majority of his readers, Montesquieu succeeded in not seeming dull to his contemporaries. He avoids the danger of being a doctrinaire and the no less formidable one of seeming partisan. He really looks upon all this political and social material with the eyes of a philosopher. Uneven as the work is, it is full of things both new and striking, which command attention, and bear the impress of vigorous thought. All this is true, but, it must be confessed, it does not prevent *L'Esprit des Lois* from being but a poor fulfillment of the beautiful plan stated in the preface and the first chapters. There are several reasons for this incongruity. Some are in the very nature of the subjects; others, in the character and spirit of Montesquieu himself.

Auguste Comte has clearly shown that Montesquieu's attempt could not have been successful, because it was premature. In order that scientific sociology might be established, it was essential that biology should be sufficiently advanced: for social phenomena, although not reducible to physiological phenomena, are yet closely united with the latter. In order to study social phenomena to any purpose, it is indispensable to be already reasonably well acquainted with the laws of the development of the human race and of its organic, intellectual, and moral functions: laws which biology alone can discover. Now, at the time when Montesquieu wrote, biology as a science did not exist; hardly had chemistry, on which biology, in its turn, is immediately dependent, begun to be a science. It was therefore inevitable that Montesquieu should be unacquainted with the method which would have been suitable for the science of which he had conceived the idea; that he should seek a model among the methods of sciences already existing in his time, i.e., among the mathematical and physical sciences; and, as such a method is wholly unsuited to the investigation of sociologic laws, that there should be a sort of perpetual contradiction between Montesquieu's right *apprehension* of the subject he treats, and the wrong *method* he applies to it.

That Montesquieu knew and admired the method of Descartes is beyond doubt. . . . Montesquieu therefore really places, as Descartes does, the essential part of method in the system which derives the particular from the universal, the complex from the simple, the consequence from the principle, in short, in deduction.

In fact, however, nothing is less deductive than *L'Esprit des Lois.* The reader will rather think himself in the presence of something badly put together, fragmentary, and desultory. This impression is somewhat lessened as we look closer, but it does not disappear altogether. It may be so vivid that competent judges (not to mention Voltaire himself) have gone so far as to compare Montesquieu to his fellow-countryman Montaigne, and to say that these two Gascons, though extremely witty and deeply skilled in the art of style, were unacquainted with the art of composition. This is going too far, at least as regards Montesquieu; nevertheless, the mere fact of its having been possible, without any absurdity, to draw a comparison between Montaigne and a writer who piqued himself upon following the Cartesian method is significant enough. Shall we say that Montesquieu wished, at any cost, to avoid monotony, to keep awake the reader's interest, and to puzzle him by the curious arrangement of books and chapters? This may be, but a deeper reason may explain the condition of Montesquieu's book. If it is wanting in continuity, it is because the deductive reasoning, on the one hand, and the facts on the other hand, do not connect. The deduction remains purely abstract, and the facts, of which Montesquieu collected such a vast number, and the importance of which he duly felt, have nothing to do with the demonstration. Montesquieu usually infers a consequence from a given principle by reasoning alone. For instance, from the notion of a despotic or republican government, he infers the condition of women to be thus and so. In support of his conclusion, he quotes indifferently either a law in China, or one among the ancient Greeks, or an anecdote borrowed from the Travels of Chardin. He does not perceive that a fact thus set apart from its surroundings has no scientific or sociologic value whatever.

Montesquieu therefore lacked a method enabling him to treat of sociological facts in the proper way. How can we wonder at this, when sociologists in our days have not yet been able to agree on their method? And yet they have before their eyes the comparative method employed in biology, which has given such favorable results, but which was unknown in the time of Montesquieu. As he had no idea of this comparative method (the only one applicable, however, when we study organic beings), he conceives social facts to be of the nature of physical phenomena, which are the same in all times and places. A given physical experiment, being performed under the same conditions must give the same result, be it in London, in Paris, or in Pekin. From this beginning, Montesquieu thinks himself justified in borrowing his examples indifferently from Tacitus or Confucius. He arrives in this manner at the abstract idea of mankind as always and everywhere like unto itself, an idea which continued to prevail during the eighteenth century in France, though it was opposed by the celebrated theory of the influence of climate, a theory of which Montesquieu himself is the author.

Thus, if Montesquieu often seems to lack system, it is not for want of endeavor to acquire it. One might even reproach him with being too systematic (for instance, in his theory of constitutions) had he not, fortunately, a taste for facts. In him the historian and the keen observer of political things happily compensate for the philosopher badly prepared to build a sociologic system. The original conception of the whole belongs to the latter; but it was the former who wrote the more permanent parts of **L'Esprit des Lois.** (pp. 30-4)

L. Lévy-Bruhl, "Montesquieu," in The Open Court, *Vol. XIII, No. 512, January, 1899, pp. 28-35.*

OLIVER WENDELL HOLMES   (essay date 1900)

[*A prominent and distinguished American jurist, Holmes was a justice of the U.S. Supreme Court from 1902 to 1932. Like Montesquieu, he advocated an empirical, sociological approach to jurisprudence. Holmes believed that "the first call of a theory of law is that it should fit the facts," stating in his book* The Common Law *(1881): "The life of the law has not been logic: it has been experience." In the following excerpt from an essay originally published as the introduction to a 1900 edition of* The Spirit of Laws, *Holmes defines Montesquieu's unique importance, characterizing him as "a precursor . . . in so many ways."*]

"There is no new thing under the sun." It is the judgment of a man of the world, and from his point of view it is true enough. The things which he sees in one country he sees in another, and he is slightly bored from the beginning. But the judgment is quite untrue from the point of view of science or philosophy. From the time of Pericles to now, during the whole period that counts in the intellectual history of the race, the science or philosophy of one century has been different from that of the one before, and in some sense further along. By a corollary easy to work out, we have the paradox that the books which are always modern, the thoughts which are as stinging to-day as they were in their cool youth, are the books and thoughts of the men of the world. Ecclesiastes, Horace, and Rochefoucauld give us as much pleasure as they gave to Hebrew or Roman or the subject of Louis XIV. In this sense it is the second rate that lasts. But the greatest works of intellect soon lose all but their historic significance. The science of one generation is refuted or out-generalized by the science of the next; the philosophy of one century is taken up or transcended by the philosophy of a later one; and so Plato, St. Augustine, and Descartes, and we almost may say Kant and Hegel, are not much more read than Hippocrates or Cuvier or Bichat.

Montesquieu was a man of science and at the same time a man of the world. As a man of science he wrote an epoch-making book. And just because and in so far as his book was a work of science and epoch-making, it is as dead as the classics. The later investigations which it did so much to start have taken up what was true in it and have refuted what needed refutation, and without the need of controversy they have killed many pale shoots of fancy and insufficient knowledge simply by letting in light and air. For a beginner to read Montesquieu with the expectation that there he is to find his understanding of the laws of social being, would be as ingenuous as to read Plato at eighteen expecting to find in him the answers to the riddles of life when they begin to perplex and sadden the mind of youth. He would learn a good deal more from Lecky. Montesquieu is buried under his own triumphs, to use his own words with a different application.

But Montesquieu also was a man of the world and a man of *esprit.* That wit which deals with the daily aspect of life and offers trenchant solutions in two or three lines is a dangerous gift. It hardly is compatible with great art, and Flaubert is not without reason when he rails at it in his letters. It is no less dangerous to great thinking, to that profound and sustained insight which distrusts the dilemma as an instrument of logic, and discerns that a thing may be neither A nor not A, but the

perpendicular, or, more plainly, that the truth may escape from the limitations of a given plane of thought to a higher one. Montesquieu said that Voltaire had too much *esprit* to understand him. Nevertheless, Montesquieu had enough of it to have sustained the *Saturday Review* when Maine and Fitzjames Stephen or Venables were its contributors, and as a man of wit he still is fresh and pleasant reading. When one runs through the *Lettres Persanes* one feels as he does after reading Swift's *Polite Conversation,* struck with a wondering shame at the number of things he has been capable of feeling pleased with himself for saying, when they had been noted as familiar two hundred years before. He is in the realm of the ever old which also is the ever new, those middle axioms of experience which have been made from the beginning of society, but which give each generation a fresh pleasure as they are realized again in actual life. There is a good deal more than this, because Montesquieu was a good deal more than a man of the world, but there is this also in which we escape from the preliminary dulness of things really great.

We find the same thing in the *Esprit des Lois,* and one might read that work happily enough simply as literature. One may read it also as a first step in studies intended to be carried further and into later days. But to read it as it should be read, to appreciate the great and many-sided genius of the author and his place in the canonical succession of the high priests of thought, one must come back to it in the fulness of knowledge and the ripeness of age. To read the great works of the past with intelligent appreciation, is one of the last achievements of a studious life. (pp. 250-53)

Montesquieu the ladies' man, Montesquieu the student of science, Montesquieu the lover of travel both real and fictitious, Montesquieu the learned in the classics and admirer of that conventional antiquity that passed so long for the real thing in France—all these Montesquieus unite in the *Esprit des Lois,* as is pointed out most happily by Faguet, whose many-sided and delicate appreciation of the author I read just as I was writing this sentence. The book, he says, is called *Esprit des Lois;* it should have been called simply *Montesquieu.* (p. 261)

It would be out of place to offer an analysis of [*Esprit des Lois*], and it would take a larger book to contain all the thoughts which it suggests. The chapters on the feudal law are so far separable from the rest that it had been thought a mistake of Montesquieu to add them. The modern student naturally would turn to Roth or whatever still later man may displace Roth. With regard to the main body of the work, one might say that it expressed a theory of the continuity of the phenomenal universe at a time when, through no fault of the author, its facts were largely miraculous. He was not able to see history as an evolution, he looked at all events as if they were contemporaneous. Montesquieu's Rome was the Rome of fable uncritically accepted. His anthropology was anecdotic. His notion of a democracy suggests a Latin town meeting rather than the later developments in the United States and France. He made the world realize the influence of the climate and physical environment—which in our day furnished the already forgotten Buckle a suggestive chapter—but had not the data to be more than a precursor.

His England—the England of the threefold division of power into legislative, executive and judicial—was a fiction invented by him, a fiction which misled Blackstone and Delolme. (pp. 262-63)

It is worth remarking that, notwithstanding his deep sense of the inevitableness of the workings of the world, Montesquieu

Montesquieu's home, Château La Brède.

had a possibly exaggerated belief in the power of legislation, and an equally strong conviction of the reality of abstract justice. But it is vain to attempt to criticise the book in detail. Indeed, it is more important to understand its relation to what had been done before than to criticise. There is not space even to point out how many seeds it sowed. Montesquieu is a precursor, to repeat the word, in so many ways. He was a precursor of political economy. He was the precursor of Beccaria in the criminal law. He was the precursor of Burke when Burke seems a hundred years ahead of his time. The Frenchman tell us that he was the precursor of Rousseau. He was an authority for the writers of *The Federalist*. He influenced, and to a great extent started scientific theory in its study of societies, and he hardly less influenced practice in legislation, from Russia to the United States. His book had a dazzling success at the moment, and since then probably has done as much to remodel the world as any product of the eighteenth century, which burned so many forests and sowed so many fields. (pp. 263-64)

> Oliver Wendell Holmes, "Montesquieu," in his Collected Legal Papers, *1920. Reprint by Peter Smith, 1952, pp. 250-65.*

GEORGE McLEAN HARPER   (essay date 1901)

[*An American educator and critic, Harper wrote* Masters of French Literature *(1901) and* William Wordsworth: His Life, Works and Influence *(1916). In the following excerpt from the former work, he discusses* Persian Letters, Considerations, *and* The Spirit of Laws, *assessing Montesquieu's importance both to his era and to posterity.*]

Montesquieu, the first great French writer belonging to the eighteenth century, except Saint-Simon, is the prototype of all who followed him. . . . He was the forerunner of Voltaire, and even more certainly of Rousseau. It is remarkable how much can now be discerned in him that we find more fully developed in the next generation. Fortunately for his peace, Montesquieu's genius was not fully appreciated in his lifetime. It is doubtful whether posterity also has not underestimated him. Though not so potent, he is perhaps a finer spirit than Voltaire, and in the line of political speculation a greater writer. His prose suffers little by comparison with Voltaire's. Indeed, in some respects it rather gains, because it has certain graces which Voltaire's style lacks. There is no hardness, crudity, or haste in Montesquieu. He is always elegant, and even leisurely, seeking to produce a cumulative and permanent effect. His ambition is always artistic completeness. In this he reminds us constantly of the writers of the preceding reign. It is a great achievement to have been in spirit a forerunner of the new era, while preserving in form the superior finish of the older and more gracious generation. If he yet leaves us cold, if he fails to enthrone himself in our affections or to stir our enthusiasm, he shares in this the fate of every other eighteenth-century French writer except Saint-Simon and Rousseau. (pp. 111-12)

The *Lettres persanes* are vastly entertaining, and must have been more so when they first appeared. One can enjoy them for their own sake, for their fine observations, their subtle irony, their urbane style. It is not and was not necessary to see in them a serious attack on the institutions of Montesquieu's time. It was possible to regard them as a good-natured, genial criticism, and the government, after some hesitation, chose to take this view. But when we think of the serious, thorough-going work their author afterwards performed, it seems likely he intended the *Lettres persanes* to mean all they now appear to imply. Whatever diversity of opinion might exist as to their political import, their literary value received prompt acknowledgment. . . . (pp. 113-14)

[*Considérations sur la Cause de la Décadence des Romains*] is not a large book, but covers the subject. It was impossible to treat of national aggrandizement and decline, without reference, direct or indirect, to the exalted state of France under Louis XIV., and to the symptoms of weakness which had multiplied so alarmingly under the Regent. And here we come upon the other influence which, next to the example of England, most affected French political thought throughout the first three-quarters of the eighteenth century. This was the example, apt or fanciful, of the ancient Greek and Roman commonwealths. Solon and Lycurgus, the Horatii, Cincinnatus, Brutus, and Cicero were names to conjure with. The Latin classics, particularly, were very familiar to the average educated Frenchman of that day. Those passages which celebrate liberty and the Republic were regarded with reverence, and from them French authors were accustomed to draw most of their political illustrations, so that Montesquieu's *Considérations* was in line with the taste of his age. Its originality lay in the application, more or less plainly indicated, which Montesquieu made of these old examples. The work was a specimen of real philosophy of history, useful to his contemporaries because bravely facing the issues of the time, and a permanent contribution to literature because greatly conceived and admirably written. (pp. 116-17)

L'Esprit des Lois is one of the first and noblest contributions in modern times to the science of comparative jurisprudence. Primitive as is its method, narrow as is its statistical range, the conclusions reached are singularly numerous and sound. It is pervaded with the breath of genius. None but a deep and comprehensive mind, endowed with a veritable instinct for observing relationships, could have made so many successful generalizations on so small a basis of facts. With a rather loose arrangement, the ideas are yet very clearly presented. It is a book which contains the results of much reading and more thinking. Each page seems the product, the secretion, of a lifetime. A vast and complicated subject is reduced to a simplicity which, though perhaps illusory, is certainly fascinating.

Even in this calm, scientific work, the outcome of an orderly and studious life, we can plainly discern the revolutionary bias. By the mere fact that he showed Frenchmen the possibility of living under law in some other than a despotic *régime*, Montesquieu awakened longings for a change. But he went further. He states that there are three forms of government,—despotic, monarchical, and republican, and defines them thus: "The republican government is that in which the people as a whole, or only a part of the people, possess the sovereign power; the monarchical, that in which only one person governs, but by fixed and established laws; whereas in the despotic government

a single person, without law and without restraint, determines all things by his will and his caprice." Full of respect and admiration for the republics of antiquity and the constitutional government of England, and employing as his chief argument their success and the happiness of their subjects, he hesitates between monarchy and republic, but never falters in his impeachment of despotism, which we must remember was the French form. And the most brilliant part of the book, where his faculty of divination has freest play, is the chapter on the English People and the chapter on the French Monarchy. He does justice to the English character and constitution, magnificent justice for a Frenchman, and such as no other of his countrymen has ever done before or since, not excepting even Taine. And, finally, I do not know any subtler characterization of the French spirit than this: Society life under the monarchy "is the school of what is called *honor*, the universal master who shall be everywhere our guide. Three things we observe there and find constantly mentioned: that our virtues should be touched with a certain nobleness, our morals with a certain freedom, our manners with a certain politeness. The virtues exhibited in this society are always less what one owes to others, than what one owes to one's self; they are not so much a response to an appeal from our fellow-citizens, as a mark of distinction between us and them. In this society men's actions are judged not as good, but as handsome; not as just, but as great; not as reasonable, but as extraordinary. When honor can point to something noble in them, it becomes the judge, and renders them legitimate, or the sophist, and justifies them."

As may be inferred even from these citations, Montesquieu was both a destructive critic and a constructive critic. He attacked abuses; but on almost every page, especially of *L'Esprit des Lois,* he proposes as a substitute for despotism the institution of a limited monarchy. He acquaints us, therefore, in advance with the double aspect of the Revolution, with the revolutionary analysis and the revolutionary synthesis. (pp. 118-21)

George McLean Harper, "The Revolutionary Analysis—Saint-Simon and Montesquieu," in his Masters of French Literature, *1901. Reprint by Books for Libraries Press, 1968; distributed by Arno Press, Inc., pp. 87-121.*

EDWIN PRESTON DARGAN (essay date 1907)

[*Dargan was an American educator and author whose works include* Honoré de Balzac: A Force of Nature *(1932) and* Anatole France *(1937). In the following excerpt from his study of Montesquieu's literary aestheticism, he surveys the author's works.*]

I should find [the] key, or leading principle [of Montesquieu's literary doctrine], in his opposition of thought and amusement. The majority of his views seem derivatory from this contrast. Those that are not come from a second subsidiary opposition, allied or confused with the first, between restrained classic art and original expression.

Let us see if such systematizing will hold.

That he makes thought the main issue appears from his desire not to "faire lire, mais de faire penser" ["cause to read, but to cause to think"], from his exaltation of Reason as the divinest faculty, from his usual admiration of those writers who were the greatest thinkers. Works of thought are *ouvrages d'esprit* ["works of soul"].

That he makes of amusement a main issue appears from his statement that we ordinarily read for pleasure alone, from his allowance of *esprit* ["wit"] and the *salon* style, of gallantry and salaciousness. Works of pleasure are *belles-lettres*.

How often does he conciliate the two motives? The lower will be subordinated to the higher, pleasure to thought. This is seen in his suggestion of researches for *savants*, "et un trait de galanterie" ["and a dash of gallantry"] for the rest; and more brilliantly in his Invocation to the Muses to lead to wisdom and truth *through* pleasure. If he allows the means to obscure the end, both in detailed development and in execution, that will be perfectly human.

From his devotion to the supreme idea comes his view of suggestiveness in thought, akin to an appeasing of the higher curiosity, to the use of compressed diction; thence also proceed his causal conception of history, his love of knowledge and study, his care for the spirit rather than the form of laws. Here primarily come into play his principles of order and *suite* ["coherent continuance"].

His hesitancy as to pleasure, his more or less reluctant yielding to its calls, become manifest not only in frequent discussions of women, wit and gallantry, but in his opposition of truth and the *bon mot*, his view of the limits of satire and epigram. The qualities of variety, uniformity, curiosity and surprise, mystery and *naïveté*, are largely chosen because of their pleasurable appeal.

The subsidiary contrast, that between genius and "manner," or individualism and classicism, will likewise include much. His standpoint here similarly fluctuates, according as to whether or not he esteems a point of style so powerfully and reasonably classic to be indisputably good form. Otherwise genius will prevail, and art is only artificiality and emptiness.

Accordingly, he believes in a delicate literary treatment of the sciences, in a measured use of true antithesis, in using while imitating nature. But loud is his denunciation of rhetoric and figures, of hampering pedants, and of senseless, tasteless critics. Genius is its own arbiter. A work not of genius is worthless. And simple genius—to complete the cycle—is thought.

Things of a pure abstract beauty hardly concern him. Contrast and charm are the only qualities falling strictly here. Imagination and sentiment are briefly dismissed, though he will not have the latter ridiculed. Literature may be addressed to the soul; but of his division he has chosen that type "dont le sujet consiste dans le raisonnement [of which the subject consists in reasoning"].

Briefly surveying his works, it will readily be seen that the principle of amusement obtained in his earlier years. Reserving for a moment the *Lettres persanes,* let us consider his contributions to the art of fiction.

None of these show much narrative ability; but they do show, each and all, a compromise with the disposition to the ornate, the elaborate, the artificial, which theoretically he so heartily rejects. The *Temple de Gnide* and the *Voyage à Paphos* were written to please a princess; and throughout they evince the flattest concessions to the *salon* taste—which was also that of the hothouse.

The *Temple de Gnide* with its pretty conceits, its faded figures and images, its false nature and its *art suspect* ["doubtful art"], is evidently designed to satisfy the délicatesse de got" [delicacy of taste"] which he found at court. It has no note of real feeling,

no vitality, no appeal save that of the *curiosa felicitas* ["nice felicity of expression"] and of voluptuous suggestion. Its descriptions of nature are tame and trite to a degree; neither here nor elsewhere has Montesquieu shown vividness or pictorial power in representing the outdoor world. Its plot is rambling, revealing already its author's lack of constructive ability. This is best excused by considering this production with the *Voyage à Paphos* as connected and incomplete sketches.

Such are the evident weaknesses of the method. Perhaps there is compensating gain. For certainly, insipid, cold and tasteless as is most of the *Temple,* it is yet *spirituel* ["witty"] and pleasant in places. There is some picturesque force and imagination in the account of the cavern of Jealousy, in the still-life view of the Sybarites. There is some daintily *malin* ["roguish"] charm in the *tableaux* of the Gods, in the closing scene with Thémire—the charm of a Boucher allegory. Better than either are the fair pages of fine prose, modeled and moulded into a rigid and polished beauty, as of *beau marbre* ["fine marble"]—the still cold beauty of the perfect classic phrase. Then, too, no one can deny the presence of that harmony which he claimed for himself.

Cephise et l'Amour is a pretty and *provoquant jeu d'esprit* ["provacative witticism"]. Not so much can be said for the *Voyage à Paphos,* which is wearisome, silly and the worst of these productions. It is the apex of passionless gallantry, tribe ornament and stale mythology.... He has ... rebuked the throwing of flowers; but in these tales he throws them with both hands; and they are palpably artificial flowers.

The principle of a lower pleasure, then, seems inadequate for literary purposes. It is interesting in this same *genre,* to compare with these stories the *Arsace et Isménie* of his later years. This tale is fully as poorly constructed, has still the *clinquant* ["glitter"] and the appeal to the passions. But thought has now been added to amusement. There is both brilliancy and profundity in reflection, a restrained richness in style, a simpler and more interesting manner of relation. It is more nearly a philosophic apologue. The high light of humanity and idealism appearing at the end of his life shines brightly here, and— *chose étrange*—["strange to say"]—thereby is it even given to him to display in his last story more of sentiment than elsewhere, more movement and a purer passion.

One point must be touched on, in connection with Montesquieu's avowed preference of gallantry to grossness.... When it comes to gallantry, there is a coldness in his most passionate scenes that is quite repulsive. His Galateas are all statuesque and his ardors rhetorical and his transports unconvincing. The *fade* ["stale"] language of compliment and the vagueness of the classic vocabulary help in this effect. He is at his best in the agreeably *malin* scenes, dependent on suggestion or *rouerie* ["trickery"], as in the *Gnide* and in certain episodes of the *Lettres persanes*.

That masterpiece, "le plus profond des livres frivoles" ["the most profound of frivolous books"], shows what is on the whole a happy compromise between the two principles. The desire to please perforce compounds with the irresistible idea, determined to have its way. "Manner," which is now a brilliant style, and genius have found a common ground. Libertinism, some critics would have it, and story-telling, form but a cloak, a foil for thoughtful discussion. The last part of the book turns preponderatingly to the consideration of grave questions, social and artistic, political and economic, religious and historical: the *Esprit des Lois* is already announced.

Yet there can be no doubt that in the mind of Montesquieu, as in that of his contemporaries and in that of impartial posterity, the lighter elements, whether of the Oriental *trame* ["plot"], the sparkling epigrams and portraits, the delightful tone, the perfect grace and vividness of the style, play at least as considerable a part as any doctoral discussion. What really makes the **Lettres persanes** is its brilliancy, its *esprit* in the fullest sense of the word.

The reign of this quality comes as supplementary to, as supplanting indeed, that of feminism. It appears in many guises: as simple brilliancy or style of statement; as epigrammatic subtlety *à la* Rochefoucauld or as more abiding apothegm, shading into the Orphic and the prophetic utterance; as humorous exaggeration, paradoxical in both senses, and as deft irony; as realistic drollery, colloquial repartee, even poor puns; as excoriating satire and biting ridicule.

Just here it may be well to take account of one or two influences. . . . [A] striking analogy may be traced—whether or not an influence may be predicated—between the Dean of Dublin and the President, between the **Lettres Persanes** and *Gulliver's Travels*. . . . That contention, plausible though dangerous as all such speculations are, would, however, if sustained, help forward the present argument.

All that is now submitted is that there are distinct analogies, in conception and satiric treatment, between the points of view ascribed to Gulliver and to the Persians. There is the same perfectly straightforward and almost serious handling of very familiar European things as from a foreigner's naïve standpoint. There is the same realism of detail, the same jocose appreciation of what would strike the foreigner as remarkable. Few Frenchmen have endeavored to convey, certainly nowhere else has Montesquieu succeeded in conveying that humor which is so peculiarly Swiftian: that tone of simple description which hardly takes the reader into its confidence, which baffles him by minuteness in fact, by solemnity in statement, which appalls him by the satire of its ultimate truth. Only, Swift is the elder and more terrible, having far more of gloom and disheartenment than the Frenchman cared to attain.

This much by way of illustration for a certain phase of our author's wit. Another phase—and this time La Bruyère is the precursor—is to be found in the delicate cameo, the finely touched laughable portraits, which so deliciously enliven the **Persanes.** In this connection, it may be remarked that Montesquieu's belief in painting types instead of individual characters is well wrought out in his own creation. Every portrait is as typical as Molière—and as inoffensive.

With his leading characters, he is hardly so happy. . . . [His] Bajazets would be very weak if considered solely as faithful pictures of Oriental potentates. It may be argued, as he has argued, that their occidentalization, proceeding rapidly throughout the book, would naturally progress with the length of their stay in Europe. His "Turks" become passable Christians. But, in truth, Usbek and Rica, it has often been said, were manufactured as two mouthpieces of two Montesquieus; and their individual characterization concerned him but little.

An allied point is that of the Oriental coloring. This he obtained, in his opinion, by luxurious harem descriptions, by the employment of exalted language. . . . Yet several of his fine passages have the Oriental warmth as a *raison d'être*. As a rule, however, there is a suggestion of irony in the very magnificence and ampollosity of this made-to-order vocabulary. Hyperbole, to which as a Gascon he was sufficiently addicted,

comes here into play. The "figured language" in general, which even Usbek would abjure in itself, the flowery language of compliment are made to contribute their part. With all this, it is of course no real Orient that he depicts, however well it may have satisfied the Regency.

Hyperbole is not the only figure which Montesquieu uses in his normal style. There are epithets and oratorical climaxes. There is the dexterous use of detail, making a sort of synecdoche which gives much vividness. There is, most important of all, his fondness for antitheses.

The great principle of contrast, in its larger relations, has been put to masterly use by Montesquieu. In this very work, there is as essential point of departure, the contrast, evidently designed by the author, between the Persian point of view and the European setting. Again, the **Romains** is one long sustained antithesis between the *Grandeur* and the *Décadence* of that nation. One may also find, in the **Sylla et Eucrate,** a contrast between the historical brutality of the hero and the dramatic, rhetorical way in which his character is presented. In the **Lettres persanes,** once more, it is the recurring contrast of grave and gay that piques our interest. It may then be conceded that the President could aptly apply the fecund principle in the large.

But how when it comes to details, to such things as parallelism and antithesis? (pp. 184-91)

When parallelism and sentence-balancing, things beautiful in themselves, become wearisome from repetition, when the antithetical purpose is nakedly evident and its artifice manifest, the principle has clearly gone to seed. The reader stands in a pained attitude of attention, ready to pounce on the next antithesis. He does not have long to wait. He is pleased by what promises to be a gentle and fruitful contrast—he finds himself involved, bemused in a threefold and fourfold antithesis, continuing through an involved sentence, and perhaps balanced by a corresponding sentence to form a perfectly antithetical paragraph. This, of course, is an extreme case. But it is rare that Montesquieu stops with one simple word-antithesis. That would have been too palpably easy.

It has seemed worth while to enlarge on this figure, and its extensions, since it is the most prominent technical element in our writer's style. Its abuse is related to his protests against uniformity and does not conspicuously make for variety. The latter quality is, however, gained for the **Lettres persanes** by the different subjects and tones which characterize successive letters.

As to the construction of the book, it properly has none. The sketchy harem imbroglio is hardly a very strong *chaîne* ["chain"]. The lack of constructive ability, which Montesquieu has elsewhere so signally evidenced, makes less difference here on account of the very nature of letters. He may wander at his own sweet will to any subject and proceed with any development, without seriously marring the symmetry of such a work. There is no beginning, no particular conduct of plot, and a hurried ending—which, however, is sufficiently well brought about.

The episodes, which are certainly distinct stories, are interesting enough. The best seems the story of the Troglodytes, wherein may be partly realized his ideal of antique simplicity.

The style is rather *sec* and brilliant than flowing. The "asthmatic" sentences seem like successive *étapes* ["stages"], whose point of junction is nowhere. There are few connectives. An event or separate fact is frequently stated in each phrase. This shows already the lack of care for transitions, which will be a later reproach.

There is uniformity again when he begins periods with the same words several times in succession. This is a favorite habit, and with this go the long linked peroratory sentences, with climactic finishes. A more serious reproach is that of occasional crudity, cacophony, bad grammar and obscurity.

When all this has been said—and most of this is not in reprehension—it remains that our author has forged himself a polished and trenchant instrument, flexible for defense, sharp-edged and piercing in attack. (pp. 193-94)

What contributes to this beauty of expression, as much as his grace and finished manner, is the concentrated and powerful force of his vocabulary. Not only is this most striking, but most suggestive, containing many a *nuance,* many a felicity and, it must be admitted, many a piece of preciosity. He not only "creates" his diction at need, but is constantly in the habit of exercising a "gentle pressure" on words to make them give up all that they have of significance and connotation. He has, of course, his favorite expressions, his hyperboles and Gasconisms. But only in the *Romains* does he surpass the *Persanes* for concision, force and elegance of diction.

In this *chef-d'oeuvre* of historical writing—*multum in parvo*—he has merged two historical methods, the philosophic and the panoramic or dramatic. If at one moment he seems somewhat spectacular, at the next he is engaged mainly in marshalling causes, and always his attitude is in the best sense human and "popular." This he has kept as legacy from his previous worldly influences. *Esprit* and feminism have vanished. But there is still the classic compulsion to throw his thoughts into a shape that may be understood and honored by an audience not specially trained. Both idea and expression are brought within the reach of all, without losing in nobility or impairing the general tone—a reproach which has justly been made against the *Esprit des Lois.*

The result of the method has been a masterly piece of writing, no less delightful than thoughtful, no less instructive than artistic. It is a very perfect welding of thought and form, and as such would seem to unite the two kinds of books. It is true that in the last part, one becomes somewhat confused and weary, less perhaps from Montesquieu's fault than from the nature of the subject, as he is forced to wander amid the chaotic ruins of the two Empires. But as a complete product, let us note what is now the fully established reign of the general Idea in his mental processes and output.

It is largely because he has been able to grasp the leading principles of every period that he has succeeded in presenting, in such little space, a clear coördinated view of the whole history of Rome. The work is saved from sketchiness by its aim, which is not narrative. Yet, in order to avoid too abstract and dry a treatment, he has relieved his philosophic view with illustrations and figures of an extraordinary force, with magnificent and climactic periods, with a suggestive concision, illuminative and felicitous. In his abstracting of the essence from incidents and events, he puts forth generalities which do not glitter but impress. His thought remains on the heights and so does his expression.

For this grave and lofty survey of an empire's course is clad in a style, equally grave, noble and at times sublime. At its best it is a stately and harmonious organ-roll, here sonorous in quality, there marked by a proud and dignified phrase, like

his own Roman Stoics. This indeed is a fine outcome of his classicism; a contained and finished modern development of the best Latin prose. Such an effect, however, is seen rather as an inspiring or as a chastening element, than in a way to vitiate and weaken his own individual expression.

Classicism again appears and conspicuously in his choice of vocabulary—and here is the point of union with the *Lettres persanes.* There is the same power of compression and of *nuances;* but his "creation" of diction here is rather along the line of Latinisms. He turns words, if every so slightly, from their modern to their antique signification, thus recoining them with the Roman stamp.

The concision extends to sentences; which are again almost too *serrés* ["condensed"] and compact. They have at times something of a telegraphic effect, tending to the interjectional, seeming more like notes and jottings. The paragraphs, too, are not infrequently *hachés* ["choppy"] and brief, consisting of a single sentence and having each the air of a separate treatise. Again there is the lack of transitions. Wherever the *Romains* shows aridity and lacks *entrain* ["animation"], over-concision is likely to be the fault.

The paragraphs are marked by another peculiar trait. Their succession is not always thoroughly logical. They hardly succeed one another so much as they grow out in separate stems— each following the former, not as arising from its whole thought, but as suggested by some special thought back in the body of the predecessor. The movement is rather inward than onward. There is thus frequently a feeling of unpleasant suspense and entanglement, without the sense of mental progress.

Such things cannot seriously mar the beauty of the whole. The *Grandeur et Décadence* has well gained its place among the world's Little Masterpieces. It is one of the prime products of classicism, alike by its supremacy of thought and its beauty of form.

It has been too much the fashion to regard this work merely as an antechamber or annex to the spacious halls of the *Esprit des Lois.* The *Romains* is quite capable of standing on its own merits; and needs perhaps less defence than its more imposing and celebrated rival.

When it comes to the *Esprit des Lois,* one's impulse is first to throw up the hands in bewilderment and stupefaction; and, secondly, to apologize for presenting cold and categorical conclusions, which it would take hundreds of pages adequately to prove. This work represents Montesquieu in his fourth stage. He has passed through his eras of worldly frivolity, of the union of that and brilliant speculation, of a combined classical and philosophical conception of history. He has now placed himself with tolerable absoluteness on the side of thought, of erudition; and vast scholastic labors supplant the careful hours formerly devoted to artistic finish. (pp. 194-97)

From the literary standpoint, and the present standpoint is necessarily that, the *Esprit des Lois* is a colossal failure. Or, if preferred, it is a *succès d'estime.* This statement is not made without due regret and all circumspection.

For, to consider closely his "delicate treatment," the literary condiments which he has insinuated into the work, which he has *added* not interfused, represent only a compromise with his condemned principle of ornament. He has made a hasty, ill-advised and inartistic return to the *ressorts* ["springs"] of *esprit* and licentiousness, which marked the *Persanes.* Only now, such condiments are more poorly prepared; and they are markedly out of place in a serious work of jurisprudence and government. Further, he has attempted to relieve his subject, by the insertion of chance *colifichets* [''trinkets''], by writing very short chapters, which sometimes contain nothing at all, by a quantity of supernumerary *faits divers* [''news items'']. His belated return to the principle of pleasure, to a desire to amuse, becomes *gauche* and inharmonious in its manifestations.

One might pardon all this, were it not for the main offense against literary presentation that ruins the book: it is lamentably lacking in construction. It is a chaotic mass of good things gone astray. He offends against his every dogma of order and *suite*. There is no coördinate principle binding the whole; and his own hypothetical arrangements are clearly not carried out. (pp. 197-98)

It might also be said that even if some scheme, both broad and ingenious enough, were found and manipulated to fit the turns and twists of the *trame's* eccentric development, even then the literary offense is not nullified; for in a work of this size, the arrangement should be more evidently logical and patent, not requiring the ingenuity of a problem-solver to grasp its divisions.

Granted the confusion, its explanation is not far to seek: the three or four souls and principles which made Montesquieu are each wrestling for the predominance, the victory going to none; and in such a vast field, with so enormous an array of material, he has not succeeded in ordering and mastering his forces. There is no vantage-point, sufficiently lofty for either author or reader to obtain a *coup-d'oeil* of his chaos. (pp. 198-99)

His material overcame him in another way; that is, with reference to style. In contrast to his previous works, the pedestrian quality of this becomes at times marked. He plods on, frequently amid arid wastes, and the aridity penetrates to the founts of inspiration. Consequently, there is the effect of reading a note-book, interjectional jottings that are not artistically expanded and linked.

Yet there are certainly oases. There is usually the old clearness in detail, the careful choice of vocabulary. And there is occasionally the old brilliancy, profundity, strength and charm of statement. (p. 199)

Episodes and interludes may have their value; familiar personal expressions may have their charm; but it is as a whole that the work must be judged. For the scholarly part of it, there can be no doubt that he shows his love of study and vast knowledge. . . .

This work is not a masterpiece of literature in the same sense that the *Romains* and the *Lettres persanes* are just that. It may be a masterpiece of jurisprudence, political science, or even of legal and economic history. But a masterpiece of literature, if literature is an art, the *Esprit des Lois* can hardly be esteemed. (p. 200)

It remains to decide whether or not he was a man of letters and an artist. For the first, his intimate knowledge of the profession, his evident vocation for it, seems to point in a different direction from his plainly expressed dislike and distrust thereof. His contempt for mere authors, for poets and critics especially, his condemnation of books, are not in favor of a high reverence for his calling. He was more or less ashamed of his *métier*. He was too much of an aristocrat to be a thorough *littérateur*. Yet his lifelong devotion, his absorption in his task declare the vocation, whether or not he would admit it. He was a man of letters *malgré lui* [''in spite of himself''].

That of itself hardly tends to prove him an artist. What further militates against this conception, is his lack of imagination and sentiment, of a feeling for beauty, poetry and nature. For doctrine, he interests himself in abstractions, in the plastic arts, he loves antiquity; but the first is the intellectual, analytical interest, the second is the taste rather of the cultured amateur, not of the *connaisseur,* and for the third he recognized sufficiently well that the Romans were not poetically sensible nor artistically supreme. For practice, his corrections and care of vocabularly, his best and most brilliant sentences, passages, figures and finish, would pronounce him of the craft; but powerlessness of construction, of narration, descent in tone and a fondness for paste jewels leave one in doubt. . . . If there can be an art wholly of the head, concerned with the creation and manipulation of ideas, he has achieved that art. Its accomplishment brought him nearer the lyric transport than anything he has known.

He was an artist in so far as a cultivated gentleman, in so far as a thinker of great and catholic intelligence is bound to have some appreciation of artistic matters. He is a creator of ideas and a verbal artist of a rare order. But an artist in the subtle, manifold, perfect sense of the word, he was not, and could never be. (pp. 202-03)

> *Edwin Preston Dargan, in his* The Aesthetic Doctrine
> of Montesquieu: Its Application in His Writings, *1907.*
> *Reprint by Burt Franklin, 1968, 203 p.*

GEORGE SAINTSBURY (essay date 1910-11)

[*Saintsbury has been called the most influential English literary historian and critic of the late nineteenth and early twentieth centuries. He adhered to two distinct sets of critical standards: one for the novel and the other for poetry and drama. As a critic of novels, he maintained that ''the novel has nothing to do with any beliefs, with any convictions, with any thoughts in the strict sense, except as mere garnishings. Its substance must always be life not thought, conduct not belief, the passions not the intellect, manners and morals not creeds and theories. . . . The novel is . . . mainly and firstly a criticism of life.'' As a critic of poetry and drama, Saintsbury was a radical formalist who frequently asserted that subject is of little importance and that ''the so-called 'formal' part is of the essence.'' René Wellek has praised Saintsbury's critical qualities: his ''enormous reading, the almost universal scope of his subject matter, the zest and zeal of his exposition,'' and ''the audacity with which he handles the most ambitious and unattempted arguments.'' In the following excerpt from an essay originally published sometime during 1910 or 1911, Saintsbury discusses Montesquieu's work, reputation, and lasting importance, both literary and philosophical.*]

In the guise of letters written by and to two Persians of distinction travelling in Europe, Montesquieu not only satirized unmercifully the social, political, ecclesiastical and literary follies of his day in France, but indulged in a great deal of the free writing which was characteristic of the tale-tellers of the time. But what scandalized grave and precise readers naturally attracted the majority, and the *Lettres persanes* were very popular, passing, it is said, through four editions within the year, besides piracies. Then the vogue suddenly ceased, or at least editions ceased for nearly nine years to appear. It is said that a formal ministerial prohibition was the cause of this, and it is not improbable; for, though the regent and Guillaume Dubois must have enjoyed the book thoroughly, they were both shrewd enough to perceive that underneath its playful exterior there lay a spirit of very inconvenient criticism of abuses in church and state. The fact is that the *Lettres persanes* is the first book of what is called the Philosophe movement. It is amusing to find Voltaire describing the *Lettres* as a "trumpery book," a "book which anybody might have written easily." It is not certain that, in its peculiar mixture of light badinage with not merely serious purpose but gentlemanlike moderation, Voltaire could have written it himself, and it is certain that no one else at that time could.

The reputation acquired by this book brought Montesquieu much into the literary society of the capital, and he composed for, or at any rate contributed to, one of the coteries of the day the clever but rather rhetorical *Dialogue de Sylla et d'Eucrate,* in which the dictator gives an apology for his conduct. For Mlle de Clermont, a lady of royal blood, a great beauty and a favourite queen of society, he wrote the curious prose-poem of the *Temple de Gnide.* This is half a narrative, half an allegory, in the semi-classical or rather pseudo-classical taste of the time, decidedly frivolous and dubiously moral, but of no small elegance in its peculiar style. A later *jeu d'esprit* of the same kind, which is almost but not quite certainly Montesquieu's, is the *Voyage à Paphos,* in which his warmest admirers have found little to praise. (p. 85)

[The *Considérations sur les Causes de la Grandeur et de la Décadence des Romains* is said] by competent authorities to have been the most enduringly popular and the most widely read of all its author's works in his own country, and it has certainly been the most frequently and carefully edited. Merely scholastic criticism may of course object to it, as to every other book of the time, the absence of the exactness of modern critical inquiry into the facts of history; but the virtue of Montesquieu's book is in its views, not in its facts. It is (putting Bossuet and Giovanni Vico aside) almost the first important essay in the philosophy of history. The point of view is entirely different from that of Bossuet, and it seems entirely improbable that Montesquieu knew anything of Vico. In the *Grandeur et décadence* the characteristics of the *Esprit des lois* appear with the necessary subordination to a narrower subject. Two things are especially noticeable in it: a peculiarity of style, and a peculiarity of thought. The style has a superficial defect. The page is broken up into short paragraphs of but a few lines each, which look very ugly, which irritate the reader by breaking the sense, and which prepare him to expect an undue and ostentatious sententiousness. On the other hand, the merits of the expression are very great. It is grave and destitute of ornament, but extraordinarily luminous and full of what would be called epigram, if the word epigram had not a certain connotation of flippancy about it. It is a very short book; for, printed in large type with tolerably abundant notes, it fills but two hundred pages in the standard edition of Montesquieu's works. But no work of the century, except Turgot's second Sorbonne *Discourse,* contains, in proportion to its size, more weighty and original thought on historical subjects, while Montesquieu has over Turgot the immense advantage of style. (pp. 87-8)

The *Esprit des lois* represents the reflections of a singularly clear, original, and comprehensive mind, corrected by forty years' study of men and books, arranged in accordance with a long deliberated plan, and couched in language of remarkable freshness and idiosyncrasy. . . . Speaking summarily, the first part, containing eight books, deals with law in general and with forms of government; the second, containing five, with military arrangements, with taxation, &c.; the third, containing six, with manners and customs, and their dependence on climatic conditions; the fourth, containing four, with economic matters; and the fifth, containing three, with religion. The last

five books, forming a kind of supplement, deal specially with Roman, French, and feudal law. The most noteworthy peculiarity of the book to a cursory reader lies in the section dealing with effects of climate, and this indeed was almost the only characteristic which the vulgar took in, probably because it was easily susceptible of parody and *reductio ad absurdum.* The singular spirit of moderation which distinguishes its views on politics and religon was indeed rather against it than in its favour in France, and Helvétius, who was as outspoken as he was good-natured, had definitely assigned this as the reason of his unfavourable judgment. On the other hand, if not destructive it was sufficiently critical, and it thus raised enemies on more than one side. It was long suspected, but is now positively known, that the book (not altogether with the good-will of the pope) was put on the Index, and the Sorbonne projected, though it did not carry out, a regular censure. To all these objectors the author replied in a masterly *défense* [*Défense de "L'esprit des loix"*]; and there seems to be no foundation for the late and scandalous stories which represent him as having used Mme de Pompadour's influence to suppress criticism. The fact was that, after the first snarlings of envy and incompetence had died away, he had little occasion to complain. Even Voltaire, who was his decided enemy, was forced at length to speak in public, if not in private, complimentarily of the *Esprit,* and from all parts of Europe the news of success arrived. (pp. 89-90)

The literary and philosophical merits of Montesquieu and his position, actual and historical, in the literature of France and of Europe, are of unusual interest. At the beginning of the next century the vicomte de Bonald classed him with Racine and Bossuet, as the object of a "relgious veneration" among Frenchmen. But Bonald was not quite a suitable spokesman for France, and it may be doubted whether the author of the *Esprit des lois* has ever really occupied any such position in his own country. For a generation after his death he remained indeed the idol and the great authority of the moderate reforming party in France. Montesquieu is not often quotable or quoted, at the present day, and the exact criticism of our time challenges the accuracy of his facts. Although he was really the founder, or at least one of the founders, of the sciences of comparative politics and of the philosophy of history, his descendants and followers in these sciences think they have outgrown him. In France his popularity has always been dubious and contested. It is a singular thing that for more than a century there was no properly edited edition of his works, and nothing even approaching a complete biography of him, the place of the latter being occupied by the meagre and rhetorical *Éloges* of the last century. According to his chief admirers, he is hardly read at all in France to-day, and they attempt to explain the fact by confessing that Montesquieu, great as he is, is not altogether great according to French principles. It is not only that he is an Anglo-maniac, but that he is rather English than French in style and thought. He is almost entirely dispassionate in politics, but he lacks the unswerving deductive consistency which Frenchmen love in that science. His wit, it is said, is quaint and a little provincial, his style irregular and in no definite *genre.*

Some of these things may be allowed to exist and to be defects in Montesquieu, but they are balanced by merits which render them almost insignificant. It is on his three principal works that his fame does and must rest. Each one of these is a masterpiece in its kind. It is doubtful whether the *Lettres persanes* yield at their best either in wit or in giving lively pictures of the time to the best of Voltaire's similar work, though they are more unequal. There is, moreover, the great difference between Montesquieu and Voltaire that the former is a rational reformer, and not a mere *persifleur* ["banterer"] or *frondeur* ["censurer"], to whom fault-finding is more convenient than acquiescence for showing off his wit. Of course this last description does not fully or always describe Voltaire, but it often does. It is seldom or never applicable to Montesquieu. Only one of Voltaire's own charges against the book and its author must be fully allowed. He is said to have replied to a friend who urged him to give up his habit of sneering at Montesquieu, "Il est coupable de lèse-poésie" ["He is guilty of wronging poetry"], and this is true. Not only are Montesquieu's remarks on poetry childish (he himself occasionally wrote verses, and very bad ones), but he is never happy in purely literary appreciation. The *Considérations* are noteworthy, not only for the complete change of style (which from the light and mocking tone of the *Lettres* becomes grave, weighty and sustained, with abundance of striking expression), but for the profundity and originality of the views, and for the completeness with which the author carries out his plan. These words—except, perhaps the last clause—apply with increasing force to the *Esprit des lois*. The book has been accused of desultoriness, but this arises, in part at least, from a misapprehension of the author's design. At the same time, it is impossible to deny that the equivocal meaning of the word "law," which has misled so many reasoners, has sometimes misled Montesquieu himself. For the most part, however, he keeps the promise of his sub-title ["concerning the Relationship which Laws Must Have with the Constitution of Each Government, Manners, Climate, Religion, Commerce, etc., to which the Author Has Added New Researches on Roman Laws Pertaining to Successions, French Laws, and Feudal Laws"] . . . with fidelity, and applies it with exhaustive care. It is only in the last few books, which have been said to be a kind of appendix, that something of irrelevancy suggests itself. The real importance of the *Esprit des lois,* however, is not that of a formal treatise on law, or even on polity. It is that of an assemblage of the most fertile, original and inspiriting views on legal and political subjects, put in language of singular suggestiveness and vigour, illustrated by examples which are always apt and luminous, permeated by the spirit of temperate and tolerant desire for human improvement and happiness, and almost unique in its entire freedom at once from doctrinairism, from visionary enthusiasm, from egotism, and from an undue spirit of system. As for the style, no one who does not mistake the definition of that much used and much misused word can deny it to Montesquieu. He has in the *Esprit* little ornament, but his composition is wholly admirable. Yet another great peculiarity of this book, as well as of the *Considérations,* has to be noticed. The genius of the author for generalization is so great, his instinct in political science so sure, that even the falsity of his premises frequently fails to vitiate his conclusions. He has known wrong, but he has thought right. (pp. 90-2)

George Saintsbury, "Montesquieu," in his French Literature and Its Masters, *edited by Huntington Cairns, Alfred A. Knopf, 1946, pp. 84-93.*

EUGEN EHRLICH (essay date 1916)

[*An Austrian jurist, Ehrlich was a leading theorist of the sociology of law. His writings support his belief that law has its foundation in social phenomena. In the following excerpt, he assesses Montesquieu's chapter on the English constitution in* The Spirit of Laws.]

[The chapter of *L'Esprit des Lois* entitled "De la Constitution d'Angleterre" is one of Montesquieu's] chief titles to glory and perhaps more than any other is destined to immortality.

The arrangement of this chapter is very like that of the chapter . . . in which he treats of the influence of the political constitution upon the character of a nation. There is no doubt that it is founded entirely on observation of the working of the British constitution. Yet there is still no mention of Great Britain except in the title and in a few words at the end of the chapter. The question with which he is concerned is not the frame of the British constitution, but how the constitution of a free people must be framed. And he examines the principles of this constitution "where liberty will appear as in a mirror" only because, to quote his words in the preceding chapter, "there exists a nation in the world which has political liberty for the direct object of its constitution." Here, too, he intends a general law embodied in a special case.

The chapter in question sets forth the famous doctrine of the balance of powers. The three branches of government—legislation, administration, and judicature—must be intrusted by the constitution to different bodies and must be kept in perfect equilibrium in order to make impossible any arbitrary discretion on the part of an officer of state; the legislative power being confined to the settlement of general rules and to control of the executive power on general lines without regard to any special case; the executive power being limited to foreign politics and military affairs; and the judicial power having for its only task the decision of lawsuits and criminal prosecutions on the basis of statutory law. In this way each power is checked by the two others and all oppression and extortion is obviated. And as the person who wields military force might not care too much for constitutional checks when planning an assault upon liberty, Montesquieu imagines a military organization which makes the army quite inefficient at home without paying much respect to its efficiency abroad.

Accordingly liberty, in the opinion of Montesquieu, means the condition of society in which it is not restricted by government beyond limits determined by legislation, which in turn, in accordance with the views on representative government which he entertains, is in functional connection with society. The judicial power also, though in a different way, is intrusted to delegates of society. This doctrine has been thoroughly disputed, and in fact it is in part vague and incomplete and it does not avoid contradictions. In the first place, we are told that the legislative power merely states general rules, enacts statutes, and settles the budget, but it does not interfere with special cases. As the executive power is concerned only with affairs of international law, and the judicial power with affairs of civil law, we might assume that the executive power had nothing to do with domestic affairs. But there is plenty of domestic business which cannot be provided for by general rules and cannot be dispatched by judges. We must inquire for the department which is to manage it. Subsequently Montesquieu seems to suppose that the executive power has for its function the execution of statutes and ordinances made by the legislature. And he says that the ministers charged by the king with this duty of executing them are accountable to the legislative power therefor. But the executive power goes beyond the boundaries of its competency described in the first instance. Finally there is a great deal of governmental business which does not consist in the execution of statutes, and as it is not connected with any expense independent of the budget, there is no hint in Montesquieu which power has to do with it. These are the most striking inconsistencies in Montesquieu's exposition, but we may easily find much more of the same description.

There are two inaccuracies in point of fact. The balance of power imagined by Montesquieu really never existed either in Great Britain or elsewhere. The English Parliament was at first only a court of justice. It never became an exclusively legislative and controlling body. It has still at present executive and judicial work to perform and it had much more of this work in the time of Montesquieu. Much of the authority of the king and consequently of the Cabinet in Great Britain, and moreover the authority of some boards may with good reason be considered legislative; the king in the past was a judge also and has never been deprived by law of this function, some judicial power being still exercised by his officers. Courts in Great Britain and elsewhere are not restricted to the application of statutes as Montesquieu maintains in consequence of his misconception of the judicial function. British judges find law themselves and settle rules of judicial law. Thus in the sense of Montesquieu they are legislating.

Because of these and some other deficiencies which have been pointed out, especially by German scholars, the theory of Montesquieu does not hold ground in the scientific world. But after all, Montesquieu saw more and deeper than his learned critics. It is precisely the merit of Montesquieu that from the embarrassing perplexity of state institutions he disentangled the elements of the fundamental functions they subserved, and singled out the concrete bodies by which those fundamental functions were exercised in Great Britain in his time. State authorities, magistrates, officers, boards, may arise for governmental purposes, may appropriate and usurp in the long run very disparate jurisdictions, and still there are the needs of governmental business, the tendencies of social life, which determine them in their growth, and the insight of a genius will distinguish in their intricacy the great lines of development and point out the forces driving in a certain direction.

That is exactly what Montesquieu did. He observed the three branches of governmental power which must necessarily exist in any state, be they actually alloted as they may. He saw the general tendency to separate them and attribute them to different boards or bodies. He perceived the importance of disconnecting and balancing them for the individual welfare and the freedom of the people. He understood the very meaning of parliamentary control and of the responsibility of the Cabinet. In all this he cared much more to delineate the essential traits than to accurately set forth the details. In order to bring out the true direction of the movement he neglected the secondary forces which might produce accidental deviations. In this turn of his mind he is essentially French. What is not plain is not French. (*Ce qui n'est pas clair n'est pas français.*) Certainly he had a great predecessor in Locke, but it is just his additions and omissions which give general bearing to his teachings, whereas Locke's statements apply only to the British constitution. In this part of his book, which we must recognize as a masterpiece, Montesquieu proved himself a profound and keen observer, capable not only of seeing what had grown, but of foreseeing what was growing. Palpably the British constitution has since followed in the way at which he hinted. At present it corresponds to his description much more than it did at the time when he wrote. The framers of the constitution of the United States adopted a great part of his teaching, especially with respect to the balance of powers. The constitution of the first French republic and that of the Restoration were largely influenced by his doctrine. But most of all the constitution of

Belgium, the model of written constitutions in Europe and other parts of the world in the nineteenth century, shows the same influence. Thus the eleventh chapter of the eleventh book of *L'Esprit des Lois* became an event in the world's history. (pp. 592-95)

Eugen Ehrlich, "Montesquieu and Sociological Jurisprudence," in Harvard Law Review, *Vol. 29, No. 6, 1916, pp. 582-600.*

C. E. VAUGHAN (essay date 1921?)

[*An English educator, Vaughan edited the political writings of eighteenth-century thinkers Jean Jacques Rousseau and Edmund Burke. In the following excerpt, he assesses Montesquieu's contributions as a political theorist and historian and examines the method of* The Spirit of Laws.]

[Of] all the political works produced in Europe during the half century before the Revolution, the only one which can stand comparison with the *Contrat social* is *Esprit des lois*. Where indeed, in the whole range of political literature, shall we find a book more solidly argued? the materials of which are gathered from a wider field, or more firmly welded together? Are there many books, we may even ask, whose ultimate principles are at once so simple and so fruitful, or whose influence upon those who form public opinion in these matters has been wider and more salutary? (p. 254)

That in man's political life all things are relative, that 'all law consists in relations'—this . . . is the central idea of the whole treatise. (p. 288)

From this central idea radiates a whole web of consequences. . . . That the whole life of a nation is woven of one piece, and therefore that it is impossible to make sweeping changes in one direction without laying the train for a thousand changes, unforeseen and perhaps undesired, in other directions also; that in this vast tissue of relations—relations of physical surrounding, of material needs, of historical antecedent, of national character original or acquired, of expediency, of Right, of justice, of religion natural or positive—one strand is perpetually liable to run athwart the others, one relation to find itself in conflict, more or less deadly, with the others, and therefore that there is constant need for adjusting the one to the others:—these are perhaps the most significant of the inferences which Montesquieu draws from his fundamental principle, and which he drives home with an abounding wealth of historical illustration. To these must be added one further inference which, though nowhere distinctly stated, is yet . . . implied in the whole tenor of his argument: the inference that the present is the child of the past, that the life of a nation at any one moment is a growth determined by all that has gone before.

It is manifest that the first and third of these inferences follow a line of thought very different from that of the second. The two former belong to the contemplative and conservative strain of Montesquieu's nature; the latter to that which he had in common with the practical statesman, perhaps even with the reformer. And it is in the conflict between these two strains that the main difficulty of interpreting him has always been found to consist.

Up to a certain point, no doubt, the two strains may be said to run parallel, certainly not counter, to each other. And this is particularly the case when it is the problems of the statesman, rather than the historian, that Montesquieu has in view. 'Wisdom,' said Burke, and it is the wisdom of the statesman he is speaking of, 'wisdom does not create materials; her pride is in their use.' And Montesquieu would heartily have echoed the assertion. The relations with which the statesman has to deal, he urges in effect, are given ready to his hands: given either in the inherent nature of man, or in his physical surroundings, or in the traditions and bias which he has inherited from the past. And it is the business of the statesman to make the best of them: to discern which of them at the moment is the most important for his purpose; which of them must, for the moment, be subordinated to the others; to which of them, in his final choice, he ought to give the greatest weight. To adjust the balance between the diverse elements of a nation's life, to distinguish how far it is necessary to bow to the 'empire of climate,' how much must be given to the material needs of the community, how much to the traditions which have come down from the past, how much to the claims of expediency, how much to those demands of justice which, just because they are the least ponderable, are the most apt to be thrust into the background: to judge of the relative worth of each of these—and that, not only in the abstract, but as they are under the particular circumstances in which he is called upon to act—that, to Montesquieu as to Burke, is the chief, if not the only, task of the statesman; the chief, if not the only, test of his wisdom and capacity.

With the necessary changes, that is true also of the historian: of the historian, that is, such as Montesquieu conceived him; such as he was himself in that part of *Esprit des lois*—and it is by far the greater part—in which he is not first and foremost a political philosopher. What the statesman does for the present and the near future, that the historian who accepts the ideal of Montesquieu strives to do for the past. Looking back upon the past, he sets himself to discover what have been the 'relations' at work in the formation of a given institution, a given national character, a given tradition, a given law, a given course of conduct. Among the various relations which have contributed to any such result, he will endeavour to pick out those which have played the leading part, which have given to the whole its 'distinguishing colour and discriminating effect.' In proportion as he does so, he will have watched national life and character in the making; by dint of intense study and imaginative insight, he will have witnessed the shaping of laws, customs and policies; he will have divined the motives by which the human agents who took park in the process were in the main determined; even when he conceives mistakes to have been made, he will yet be able to account for them, to lay his finger upon the reasons, plausible or otherwise, which have led to their commission.

This is what Montesquieu himself attempted, and in great measure achieved, in *Esprit des lois;* and in so doing, he revolutionised not only the methods, but also the ideas, both of political philosophy and of history. He redeemed history from the mere record of facts to the study of causes and of motives. He warned the political philosopher that the life of the community depends at least as much upon historical causes as on the working of abstract ideas; and that, until those ideas have taken flesh in a given national will and bowed themselves to the concrete conditions of a given national life—that is, until they have submitted to qualification by all the other 'relations' which combine to form that life—he can neither say that they wield any effective influence upon the affairs of men nor expect the historian, whose task it is to interpret the actual facts and struggles of the past, very seriously to reckon with them. Thus, by the same stroke, he made history rational and the historical

method a vital necessity to political philosophy. Thanks to his teaching—as, more indirectly, to that of Vico before him—both studies were henceforth to be dominated by the idea of growth, of organic development. For, whether fully realised or no, this is among the conceptions which lie at the root of his whole theory. All that he left to his successors was to lift that conception into clearer consciousness, to work it out with ever increasing fullness.

It is the chief blot on Montesquieu's achievement that he never thought out this question to its final issue: that, believing the present to be determined by the past, he never clearly recognised that, the present being different from the past, such determination necessarily carries with it the idea of growth; still less, that in such matters, growth is only another name for development or progress. This means that his conception of 'law' was coloured rather by physical than by biological associations: that it was mechanical rather than organic. And what is the result of this upon his handling of human action? It is obvious that the more mechanical a law is, the less is the freedom it leaves to the human agents it controls. And those who have been the most ready to bring the life of the community under such laws have seldom wholly escaped from the danger of treating men as machines. In their zeal for general tendencies, they have too often forgotten that it is the men who make the tendencies, at least as much as the tendencies the men. So far as regards the past, Montesquieu is saved by his keen perception that the relations in which man finds himself are infinitely various and that his first duty has always been to discriminate and to judge between them. But when he comes to the problems of his own day, can it be said that he shows the same even-handed justice? Like many of those whose studies are concerned mainly with the past, he is hardly to be cleared of allowing the past to tyrannise over the present: of denying to his own generation that spontaneity, that freedom of action, which he had conceded to its forerunners. And this discrepancy, latent in Montesquieu himself, becomes glaring in some of his successors. What in him is no more than a markedly, but not immoderately, conservative bias—a 'disposition to preserve,' so far as may be, the order inherited from the past—is in them, above all in Burke, little better than a gospel of stagnation.

That Montesquieu himself, like the majority of those who have heartily welcomed the historical method, was strongly, if not consistently, conservative in temper, is evident at a glance. He was so in matters of politics; witness his oft-repeated insistence that, all the elements of national life combining to form one integral whole, it is impossible to tamper with any one of them without endangering all the rest; witness also his disposition—sometimes severely checked, however—to accept the accomplished fact as necessarily rational and to build upon it a general principle of wide, if not universal, application accordingly: in other words, as Rousseau complains, to 'establish the right by the fact.' He was so, which was less to be expected, even in matters of religion; witness the letter [to Warburton in May, 1754] in which he complains of Bolingbroke for 'discharging his blunderbuss against Christianity,' especially the significant question with which it closes: 'What motive can there be for attacking revealed religion in England, where it has been so completely purged of all hateful prejudices that it cannot do any harm and, on the contrary, may do an infinite amount of good?' At first sight, this may seem to sit strangely on the author of *Lettres persanes;* it shows, however—what, after all, was to be looked for—that, with him, the preoccupations of the statesman counted for more than the disinterested search for truth.

That, like many of his disciples, he turned the organic whole-ness of the communal life into something of a fetish, that he exaggerated the importance of doing nothing to destroy the 'general spirit,' the traditional character, of a nation, unless where there is some flagrant injustice to be remedied, is not to be denied. And this means that he would always have been opposed to sweeping changes: in particular, that he would have had nothing to say to the French Revolution, at any rate from the moment when the royal authority, as tempered by that of the Estates, and the independence, as distinguished from the 'hateful prejudices,' of the Church became avowed objects of attack. It is hard to believe that he would not have joined, from the very bottom of his heart, in Burke's fervid lament that 'the age of chivalry was gone,' that the spirit of honour—that hon-our which, in his view, was the 'vital principle' of the French nation, the fine flower of French breeding—had received its death-blow from the Revolution. (pp. 289-92)

Constitutional blindness, the bias of a naturally conservative temperament, was one cause of Montesquieu's distaste for sweeping change. But . . . there was another cause which lay more in his own power. He had never worked out his principles to what, in the light of subsequent speculation and subsequent experience, we can now see to be their logical result. The idea of progress had therefore hardly more weight with him than it had with most of his contemporaries; and change, so far from being the rule in his scheme of national life, was the rare, perhaps the lamentable, exception.

Yet, if he failed to pursue to the end the line of thought which he had opened out, that must not be reckoned seriously against him. It is the fate of almost all those who have thrown new and fruitful ideas upon the world. And who can deny that he had, in the fullest measure, the quality which goes hand in hand with this defect? the power of spontaneous intuition which bids defiance to all rules and prescriptions, the flashes of insight which, in an instant, forestall the toilsome reasoning of years? And, as there seems to be much misapprehension on this point—he has been praised for strict adherence to a particular method, he has been blamed for a significant lack of all method—we shall do well to ask ourselves where exactly the truth is to be found.

The method attributed to him by some zealous admirers is the inductive method. That, however, to say the least of it, is altogether too high-sounding a term to describe the method of *Esprit des lois.* The mass of materials from which the author distilled, or with which he illustrated, his conclusions was far too vast, the conclusions themselves are far too tentative, to justify any claim so formidable as this. And Montesquieu him-self, we may be very sure, would have been the last man in the world to make it. The truth is that any such claim, if it does more than justice to his scientific precision, does infinitely less than justice to his sagacity and his genius for divination.

It does more than justice to his precision: since with all history, ancient and modern, for his field of enquiry, how was it pos-sible that he should apply the tests—the successive processes of exclusion and the like—demanded by even the loosest forms of induction? How was it possible that he should use that field as more than a storehouse of illustration for truths which he had reached by quite other—and, if we choose to say so, less scientific—methods: by deduction from his central principles or, more often perhaps, by pure introspection, lit up by his own inimitable sagacity and power of divination? Is it not evident that, judged by the inductive standard, his method, so far from satisfying the demands of Bacon, or indeed any other

advocate of the art, hardly gets beyond the way of 'simple enumeration' which all alike agree in despising? The only part of his work in which he can be said even remotely to approach the way of induction is that in which, confining his view to a carefully limited field, he sets himself to consider the vicis-situdes of the law of succession among the Romans and the Salic Franks, or the customs which regulated the fines for homicide and the whole framework of feudal society, among the Franks, the Burgundians and the Lombards. And this . . . is an excrescence, and an excrescence which, however admi-rable in itself, has little relation, either in manner or in method, to the main body of his work.

That Montesquieu himself would have repudiated the claim put forward by these unwary disciples is tolerably clear. 'I have laid down principles,' he says in his Preface, 'and have seen the details conform to them, as of their own accord. I have satisfied myself that the history of every nation follows natu-rally from these general principles; that each particular law is closely bound up with other laws, or depends upon a higher law more general yet' [see essay dated 1748]. Is this, it may be asked, the language of one who believed himself to be working by the inductive method? Does it not rather suggest a conclusion exactly the reverse? How else could a man express himself, if he wished to say that his conclusions, though freely checked by the facts of experience and history, were in their origin rather of reason than of 'experiment': in other words, that they were reached, in the main, not by induction, but by deduction?

It is, of course, true that his 'general principles' themselves owed much to a historical learning which, for his own time at any rate, was exceptionally wide and deep. It is probable, however, that, so far from being built up methodically—and if terms are to have any meaning, induction must mean that—they had formed themselves by a process of half-unconscious reflection, and 'of their own accord,' in his mind; and that the conscious process only began when, having formulated them provisionally, he hastily reviewed the vast stores of his knowl-edge in the light of them; modifying and even rejecting them, in case of need; but far more often, we may well believe, maintaining them and enforcing them with the illustrations which 'of their own accord' thronged into his memory. It is in this sense, and not in any alleged adherence to the inductive rigours, that he may be rightly said to have followed—indeed, with due allowance for the claims of Vico, to have introduced—the historical method into political philosophy.

But, if some critics have claimed too much method for *Esprit des lois,* there is no doubt that others have credited it with too little. To contrast the stately order of the seventeenth-century writers—Bossuet, for example—with the more popular appeal, the more discursive manner, of their successors in the next century, is sound enough. Between the *Variations du Pro-testantisme* and the 'six thousand pamphlets of Voltaire,' or the rapid improvisations of Diderot, the contrast holds good, and it is significant. But there are exceptions to the rule; Rous-seau is one of them, and Montesquieu is another. And to range the latter with Voltaire and Diderot, to assert that his methods, like theirs, were those of the pamphleteer, to describe him as writing a chapter or two on one subject and then darting off to write one or two more on quite another, is surely something of a libel. That, in style as in other things, Montesquieu was the child of his century, that he has much of the lightness, the point, the epigram of Voltaire himself, is perfectly true; though even here there are many qualifications. It is true, again, that his immediate theme is constantly changing, that he is seldom minded to pursue any one theme to its minutest details. How should it not be so, when the subject he had chosen was so wide and the issues it raised so many-sided and so various? But apart from the purely historical chapters—and even those are, at bottom, entirely relevant—who can say that any one of the themes he discusses was not essential to his purpose? who can deny that, through the inevitable diversity of his divisions and subdivisions, there runs a thread of the most orderly connection? Bossuet himself, had he ever been moved to preach from so pregnant a text, could hardly have acquitted himself in more logical fashion. (pp. 292-95)

> *C. E. Vaughan, "The Eclipse of Contract: Vico, Montesquieu," in his* Studies in the History of Political Philosophy Before and After Rousseau: From Hobbes to Hume, Vol. I, *edited by A. G. Little, 1925. Reprint by Russell & Russell, 1960, pp. 204-302.*

HUNTINGTON CAIRNS   (essay date 1935)

[*An American lawyer and literary critic, Cairns is the author of* Law and the Social Sciences *(1935) and* Legal Philosophy from Plato to Hegel *(1949). Hans Kelsen has written of Cairns: "Although there is an essential relationship between philosophy and jurisprudence, there are only a very few scholars who are masters of both. Huntington Cairns is one of the few." In the following excerpt from* Law and the Social Sciences, *Cairns investigates Montesquieu's sociological definition of law.*]

Montesquieu's *The Spirit of Laws,* Brunetière has written [in *Études critiques sur l'histoire de la littérature française* (1894)], "is the wraith of a great monument, but the monument has never existed." Montesquieu's failure to investigate systematically the ideas he put forth was the result of the application of a method which he had deliberately adopted. "To write well," he said [in his *Pensées*], "it is necessary to skip intermediate ideas, enough not to be tiresome, not too many for fear of not being understood." There can be no question that Montesquieu carried this method to too great an extreme; that he skipped too many intermediate but clarifying ideas. As a consequence, *The Spirit of Laws* is a brilliant and suggestive book; it may even be, as it has been called from the point of view of literature, the greatest book of the eighteenth century; but as an adequately reasoned, unambiguous exposition of Montesquieu's political ideas it falls far short of what is desirable. Nevertheless, for all its lack of orderly analysis, it is the fountainhead of the sociological approach to law.

Montesquieu's central ideas on the problem of the nature of law are set forth in the three brief chapters with which the book begins. "Laws, in their widest meaning," he writes with evident care, "are the necessary relations arising from the nature of things." This definition has brought upon Montesquieu's head much severe criticism, as much for its obscurity as because of its departure from accustomed modes of thought. Destutt de Tracy said flatly, "a law is not a relation and a relation is not a law"; and Helvetius added, laws are not relations, but the result of relations. But such statements do not give much help in attempting to reach Montesquieu's meaning. It has often been claimed for Montesquieu, and indeed he makes the claim for himself, that *The Spirit of Laws* was a work of surpassing originality; certainly of the writers concerned with social questions, from Locke to Condillac to Bentham, Montesquieu was the one least influenced by the mechanistic philosophy of the period. He did not, however, entirely escape its influence and I believe that, in his definitions of

laws, whether he was aware of it or not, he was influenced by what may be called the Newtonian world-view. By defining laws as relations he was synthesizing the thought of his century. He meant nothing more by his definition than that, as he writes in his preface, the infinite diversity of laws and manners are not solely conducted by the caprice of fancy [see essay dated 1748]. In other words, he has anticipated in the identical language, the now widely held conception of a scientific law as a relation between events, or, in more popular terms, as the assertion of cause and effect. Montesquieu included in his definition of laws both physical laws and positive laws. But positive laws are not altogether the product of external causes as is the case with physical laws; they are determined in large part by human reason, and Montesquieu therefore states that positive law in general is human reason. Nevertheless, he holds that positive laws should be so framed that they should be in relation to the characteristics of each nation; the role of human reason, in other words, should be minimized and laws should be framed so far as possible *as if* they were determined by the nation's characteristics. (pp. 131-33)

This is the heart of Montesquieu's conception of law. It is also the statement of the sociological conception of law; it recognizes and takes account of the influence of social conditions on the legal process. Montesquieu's definition of law as a relation contains an important element of truth, even if it is not sufficiently precise to be of much utility. Under its broad terms customary rules would be law as well as the rules of positive law. Montesquieu, however, in the high position from which he surveyed the characteristics of the peoples of the world perhaps meant to include customary rules under the term law, and we need have no quarrel with him on that account. His contribution lies in the fact that he was the first to see clearly, if not altogether adequately, that laws are not the arbitrary products of reason but are largely the result of the social forces obtaining in the community. (pp. 133-34)

Many of the geographico-political correlations put forward by Montesquieu are regarded to-day with distrust, but in view of the scanty material available at that time this is at bottom no criticism of him; but his basic proposition—that in the study of the social process geographical and other environmental factors must be considered—is firmly established and any inquiry which ignores it is incomplete. (p. 147)

> *Huntington Cairns, "Sociology," in his* Law and the Social Sciences, *Harcourt Brace Jovanovich, 1935, pp. 124-68.*

F. T. H. FLETCHER   (essay date 1939)

[*An English educator, Fletcher is the author of* Montesquieu and English Politics *(1939) and* Pascal and the Christian Mystical Tradition *(1953). In the following excerpt from the former work, he examines the bases and implications of Montesquieu's historical method in* The Spirit of Laws.]

Montesquieu's historical method is generally understood to mean the relating of particular laws to the special historical causes which gave rise to them. It is therefore opposed to the metaphysical method of Locke, which seeks the sanction of particular laws in first principles anterior to human history. In so far as Montesquieu's method influenced legal inquiry in Great Britain, it cannot be denied that it was through this simple interpretation of it. Yet we find Bentham reproaching Montesquieu with 'pseudo-metaphysical sophistry', as though the *Esprit des Lois* were a mere tissue of abstract theory. Whence could this wide diversity in the interpretation of Montesquieu arise?

In the first place, it can quite easily be shown that Montesquieu was not a pure empiricist. Though his constant purpose is to relate laws and institutions to their particular historical causes, these causes themselves are represented as mere aspects of national spirit—of honour in monarchies, of virtue in republics, of fear in despotic states. These 'principles', as he calls them, arise in their turn from a blending of a constant, 'human Reason', with variable physical circumstances. The ultimate ground of human law, therefore, even in Montesquieu, may be said to be outside history.

Again, Montesquieu's method was by no means purely inductive. It is true that he usually starts from particular 'facts' and then extracts from them a general principle. By a sufficiently vast correlation of such 'facts' and of the particular principles which emerge from them, he is enabled by his inductive process to reach those very broad generalisations which he calls the 'principles' of the leading types of government. But thereafter the method becomes deductive. (pp. 71-2)

If Montesquieu's historical method consists neither in 'pseudo-metaphysical sophistry' nor in a crass empiricism, did it merely study present laws and institutions as the result of a long and slow evolution? Doubtless it did not, since evolution implies development in time, and everyone agrees that Montesquieu shamefully neglects the time-dimension. As Justice O. W. Holmes puts it, 'He was not able to see history as an evolution; he looked at all events as if they were contemporaneous' [see excerpt dated 1900]. Indeed, one of the stock objections to his methods is that, in order to discover the 'spirit' of civilised and modern institutions, he adduces historical evidence from sources indiscriminately distributed over time and space.

Here perhaps is the key to the riddle. The novelty of Montesquieu's historical method really consists in its neglect of the very thing considered most fundamental to history—Time. To 'human Reason', that spiritual constant which was the ultimate ground of all law, Time could obviously mean nothing: here is the true metaphysical basis of Montesquieu's legal apologetic. . . . Thus does he bridge the gap between vital and supervital activities. The bridge itself is composed of a number of general 'principles', which he calls virtue, moderation, honour and fear. Though absolute on one side—that of the changeless human reason—on the other side, by virtue of their contact with finite living forms and societies, these principles share the propensity of living organisms to decay. . . . Montesquieu's sense of the perishability of his principles upon the human side is best illustrated by the adjectives with which he feels obliged to qualify them: thus, by virtue he claims to mean only political virtue, and by honour he means 'false honour'.

Montesquieu's true historical method therefore appears to consist in setting all those human experiences preserved by history, that have left their mark on laws and institutions, side by side, instead of before and after. He sees history spread out flat before him, and arranged in a certain pattern, the designer of which he calls 'human Reason'. The leading *motifs* in that pattern are his general principles—virtue, moderation, honour, fear—and all those phenomena which come into contact with these *motifs* are coloured, distorted, or in some way affected by them. The general arrangement of the pattern is determined by such things as climate, soil, situation, race, government, etc., which together constitute the material or physical mould into which the intellectual pattern is run. Doubtless this method

had already been applied before in a promiscuous and uncomprehending way: Montesquieu's unique genius consists in applying it over an almost unlimited area of human experience, and hence in placing every legal phenomenon in its complete human context. The supreme value of the method is that it permits the observer to see particular historical data in an entirely new setting, and hence to perceive relationships between things which, through their separation in time or space, must otherwise have remained unrelated. By applying the method over a sufficiently wide area of experience, and comparing similar 'relationships' in whatever time or place each to each, the general 'spirit' governing them all can be revealed. Besides, then, placing legal philosophy upon a base as broad as human life, this method serves to reveal the nature of the human spirit itself. Before such a conception of law as this, the objections of those who condemn Montesquieu's undue respect for travellers' unreliable reports fade like mist before the sun. Had he relied upon nothing, or little, else, his generalisations would indeed have been valueless. But his general scheme is altogether too solid, too massive, to be invalidated by a few possible blemishes or inaccuracies. In spite of Voltaire's gibe, in no case would the suppression of a datum from Siam, Japan or Bantam nullify a single principle which Montesquieu advances. Other things might, but not these. Moreover, it has been shown that Montesquieu sometimes deliberately spurned the well-authenticated modern instances of his historical sources, and preferred curious, obscure, or unknown examples of his own finding to point the same lesson. Perhaps in such cases he desired to make his ideas appear more original than they really were; possibly he took a romantic delight in adducing oddities of human experience, for there was something of the *collectionneur* [''collector''], as well as of the artist and philosopher, in Montesquieu.

The other leading objection levelled against Montesquieu as to the general disorderliness of his book, becomes almost frivolous. Looked at in the way suggested above, the work appears almost too neat, too schematic and orderly; but in order for it to appear so, it must indispensably be looked at as a whole. (pp. 72-5)

It is clear that Montesquieu's method, whether it be qualfied by the epithet 'historical' or not, included the process of relating any given institution to its present environment, past history, future usefulness, and to eternal truth insofar as this can be known through human reason or intuition. It asserts the solidarity of past, present and future, through the dissolution of Time itself in a constant, invariable, timeless solvent which is the human spirit itself. Hence we may be led to comprehend what Montesquieu understood by the 'spirit of law'. The form or body of law is its letter, the diverse and perishable shape impressed upon it by temporal circumstances. The spirit of law is its inward reason, its essential life. (p. 75)

> *F. T. H. Fletcher, in his* Montesquieu and English Politics (1750-1800), *Edward Arnold & Co., 1939, 286 p.*

FRANZ NEUMANN   (essay date 1949)

[*Neumann was a German-born lawyer, political scientist, and educator whose most significant work is* Behemoth: The Structure and Practice of National Socialism *(1942), a Marxist analysis of Nazism. In the following excerpt from his comprehensive introduction to a 1949 edition of* The Spirit of Laws, *Neumann explicates all but Books XI and XII of the work.*]

[Montesquieu's] great contribution is that of a political scientist who, standing in the tradition of Aristotle, undertook to analyze governments on a cosmic scale and to derive from historical observations a system of politics. Let us admit at the outset that this enterprise failed, as it necessarily must. The scope was too big, the task too huge for his abilities. Promise and performance are not in proportion. The facts are frequently wrong, the interpretation often not warranted by the facts, the logic often faulty, and the language ambiguous. Yet with all these reservations, there remains the work of an original thinker, who uncovered thought structures and historical processes which prepared the way for, and still nourish, political scientists and historians. The *Esprit des Lois* may not be a great book on the level of the works of Plato, Aristotle, Marsilius, Hobbes, Rousseau, and Hegel, but it is an extraordinarily stimulating book whose riches have remained neglected because of the attention given to one of the most doubtful of his discoveries: the separation of powers as the instrument of securing political liberty. (p. xxix)

In the opening statement of *The Spirit of the Laws,* Montesquieu defines laws generally as "the necessary relations resulting from the nature of things." This definition has been held to be either meaningless or tautological, expressing either a complete relativism or the acceptance of an objective standard of justice. Those who actually read Chapter I and compare it with Persian Letter No. 84 will, I believe, invariably come to the conclusion that Montesquieu expressed his conviction that justice exists as an objective rule, and that its validity, therefore, is not dependent upon human actions. Justice is the supreme criterion of the laws. But since society "is far from being so well governed as the physical" world, it followed for him that no human society is capable of fully realizing objective justice. It is for this reason also . . . that Montesquieu did not believe in an ideal solution of the conflict between might and right. If one accepts this interpretation, then his discussions of the various types of political society are all oriented toward finding an approximation to the standard of justice by taking into account all factors that shape society.

The impossibility of realizing the standard of justice in civil societies is due to civil society itself. In contrast to Hobbes, Spinoza, and Locke, the entry of man into civil society marks for Montesquieu the beginning of a state of war. Man in the state of nature is weak. His entry into the civil society makes him strong, and it is this newly gained strength that produces conflict—within the state and between states. This conception, although it still has all the marks of natural law, is in our view extraordinarily fruitful. It is here that Montesquieu stands with Helvétius, Holbach and Rousseau: society itself becomes an agent of history. Consequently the structure of society must be examined.

It is essential for Montesquieu to distinguish between the nature of governments and the constitutive principles of the different societies. The "nature" is defined in a fairly traditional manner, namely by the number of the rulers. A republic is governed by the people or a part of it; a monarchy by a monarch ruling through established laws; despotic government by a single person ruling arbitrarily. The republic thus comprises democracy and aristocracy. That this classification is not very convincing is obvious, and has often been said. Since in a democracy it is the people that rule, the most crucial concern of a democracy is the determination of suffrage. In the definition of the nature of monarchy, his political prejudices mar his scientific objectivity. The term "monarchy" is arbitrarily defined as rule through intermediate powers, the "most natural" of them being the aristocracy. The history of England, e.g., proves that a monarchy which destroys aristocratic privileges destroys itself. Parlements must, in addition, be the depositories of royal laws. This chapter has thus to be read in conjunction with the elaborate historical discussions on the origin of feudalism, and is, in the form of an objective analysis, a simple political tract against Dubos and the royal thesis. Democracy, aristocracy, and monarchy are for him "moderate" forms which are sharply distinguished from despotism.

Quite different from the nature of government is the structure of society, the ideal type, what he calls the "principles" of government, and what Jefferson correctly translated as the "energetic principles." There are, for a democracy, virtue; for aristocracy, moderation; for monarchy, honor; for despotism, fear. The principles are thus the "ought" of the government. A democracy must thus have laws and constitutions conforming to the principle of virtue, which is love for the republic, for equality, and sobriety; respect for laws and the acting according to them. It is thus more the Machiavellian virtue than Christian virtues. It is in Jefferson's words the "*amor patriae,*" and implies the same idea of identification of individual interests and general will that Rousseau made the cornerstone of his democratic doctrine. It is that virtue that Robespierre was prone to invoke whenever it suited his purpose. Quite logically, compulsory "public employment" in government and army follows from the principle of democracy but not from that of a monarchy. Quite in line with Rousseau, yet sharply differing from him, equality becomes, consequently, essential for democracy. This equality is, however, essentially one of frugality rather than, as with Helvétius, the equal share of abundance. Again, the caution inherent in Montesquieu compelled him to reiterate his general conviction that a perfect and pure democracy being impossible, only an approximation to this ideal is attainable, so that perfect equality being impossible and undesirable, democratic legislation should merely prevent excessive differences in wealth and private power. This, to him, is quite difficult. For democracy is usually the political form of a commercial civilization which, however, leads to the "acquisition of vast riches." The corrective is contained in the very nature of commerce which stimulates "frugality, economy, moderation, labor, prudence, tranquility, order and rule." This is an almost accurate description of the puritan conception of civil society.

Moderation, as the principle of an aristocratic society, is a principle to be applied by the aristocratic ruling class against itself and, through it, against the people. Self-discipline of the aristocracy is essential for its preservation; this self-discipline should prevent them from engaging in commerce, should compel them to abide by the laws and to chain their pride. The material basis for moderation is the happy medium between excessive poverty and excessive wealth.

Honor, as the principle of a monarchy, is objectively the respect of the monarch for the laws and the intermediate institutions through which his executive power should be exercised. Richelieu's conception of monarchy is thus not that of monarchy but of despotism. Without nobility, therefore, no monarchy can be a true monarchy; monarchy must look to its appearances, as well as to its laws and intermediate institutions.

Fear, the constitutive principle of despotism, is a simple principle, its end being tranquillity. But that tranquillity is not peace, "it is only the silence of towns which the enemy is ready to invade." It is maintained by the army.

These principles cannot be mixed. In view of the later discussion of the English government, this statement is surprising and is hardly compatible with his blending of democracy and aristocracy.

Book V, then treats in detail and in the usual haphazard and repetitious manner the type of legislation corresponding to the principle of government. Books VI and VII are special applications of Book V. In the three approved types of government, laws, in general, should protect life and property of the citizen. Life and property are best preserved by rational law and a rational administration. Three types of law administration emerge: The Kadi justice—Pasha jurisprudence—as the one marginal case (for despotic governments); an independent judiciary applying rigid and fixed rules—the other marginal case for republics; and a combination of individual and differentiated creation of law for particular cases—with the application of fixed rules—for the monarchy. Despotism, by its very principle, cannot know law. Law-making and its execution are thus one and the same. The closer a government comes to a republic, "the more the manner of judging becomes settled and fixed," while a monarchy has to combine both elements in view of the hierarchic structure of society which requires particular laws for the various strata. The dichotomy—fixed rule and its application—implies, consequently, a division of functions between legislation (or monarchical power) and the judiciary. In a monarchy, at least, the independence of the judiciary is to be secured by the venality of judicial offices. His humanitarian spirit is clearly revealed in his discussion of crime and punishment, his insistence on moderation and on a fitting proportion between crime and punishment, and his rejection of informers and of torture.

It is my conviction that Book VI contains insights into legal sociology which anticipate Max Weber's famous treatise, and which have found but little attention.

"The corruption of each government generally begins with that of its principles." Democracy suffers corruption either by excessive equality or by its total loss. Aristocracy corrupts through arbitrary use of power, and monarchy by the abrogation of the intermediary powers. Despotic government will destroy itself by its own inner logic, while in all other types correction can prevent corruption.

All this is a mere repetition and by no means a very logical demonstration of the value of his own typology. But while the logic is faulty, the meaning is quite clear. There is a sharp dividing line between despotism and all other forms of government. There is not and cannot be a defense of despotism, but all other forms may, provided they fulfill the conditions set out below, be made to work. But even despotism is rationally understandable in backward countries or where climate makes man accept this form of rule.

Montesquieu insists that "it is natural to a republic to have only a small territory. Otherwise it cannot long subsist," and for a monarchy to have a "moderate extent." While this view may suit Rousseau's construction of direct democracy, it hardly follows from Montesquieu's own analysis of democratic government. He became a victim of his philosophy of history, as expressed in his *Considerations*.

Democracy and aristocracy thus find themselves in a quandary. "If a republic is small, it is destroyed by a foreign power; if it be large, it is ruined by an internal imperfection." Consequently, a monarchy is better. But since he was well aware that such a statement could not possibly stand the test of ex-

perience, he gave the republics another chance: the confederation. Confederations, without abolishing the internal strength of the republics derived from smallness, give them external strength through association. External security is, of course, the business of the army. Generally, defensive wars alone are justified by the law of nations; an offensive war only if it is objectively necessary for the preservation of the nation's integrity. Conquest is permissible but subject to the law of nature, of reason, to political law, and to "the law derived from the nature of the thing itself." As against Grotius, who, however, is not mentioned by name, self-interest of the conqueror and humanitarian considerations require moderation in the treatment of conquered people.

Montesquieu now introduces the factor of space (climate and soil) into the discussion of the nature and principles of government. If, as he claims, character and passions vary according to climate, the laws ought to take these external factors into account. It is undoubtedly true that Montesquieu did not invent the idea that climate conditions had some bearing upon the structure of society. Bodin in his *Six Books of the Republic,* and Chardin's *Les Voyages de Chevalier Chardin en Perse et autres lieux de l'Orient* had undoubtedly directed attention to the problem. But if Montesquieu for this reason is to be a plagiarizer, then almost all scholars are plagiarizers. Montesquieu tried, unsuccessfully to be sure, to determine scientifically the exact role of the factor of space in political science. That he did not attempt to derive political conditions exclusively or even primarily from climatic conditions is clear to everyone who takes the trouble of reading what he wrote. He was not a geopolitician. In his *Pensées et Fragments* is found the first formulation of a theory.

Climate operates more directly on the lower stage of development than on the higher—a statement that will hardly be challenged. If history is man's attempt to control nature, clearly then, in the lower stage of civilization, the blind forces of nature had a more direct effect on society and politics than in the higher forms where man could begin to emancipate himself from them. What Montesquieu did not state, and where Vico had a much deeper insight, is that the increasing control of nature by man is not necessarily accompanied by an increasing freedom of man, but may result in a relapse into serfdom. But Montesquieu stated the problem correctly. He was, in spite of his pessimism and relativism, a believer in justice and thus held to the view that political freedom ought to be the result of man's increasing power over nature. He may be blamed for his lack of realism, but not for his convictions. It may readily be admitted that the discussion of the influences of climatic conditions is primitive. He tries to establish a direct, causal relationship between climate, the physiological condition of man, his character, and the structure of political society. He thus sees direct, causal relationships between climate, slavery, the relation of the sexes, and the forms of political control.

Climate influences are modified by differences in the quality of the soil. Statements like "Thus monarchy is more frequently found in fruitful countries, and a republican government in those which are not so," are clearly untenable. But other observations on the relations between the character of the space and the character of a nation, and, consequently, its political organization, still have great value—e.g., mountain dwellers and liberty; and the character of the American space on Indian tribes, etc.

Book XIX then contains an admittedly unsystematic attempt at determining the interrelationships among the principles of government, the "general spirit" of a nation, its morals and customs. The general spirit corresponds to some degree to the *Volksgeist* ["national spirit"] of the German historical school. It is the integration of all the various external and internal elements that shape the character of a nation. It is, as one would say today, an attempt to develop the principles of a cultural anthropology. This very conception of an integrated culture naturally strengthened his conservatism; it made him reluctant to recommend change, especially change from without by legislation. Change is to be the result of a process. Laws affect merely the actions of the citizen, but laws do not exhaust the controls of man's behavior: manners control the actions of man (as opposed to citizen), customs regulate the exterior behavior of man, manners his internal behavior. These various types of social regulations should not be confused, but they are interrelated and a change of one affects the others.

One would be disappointed if one were to expect valid generalizations on these interrelationships. Shrewd observations are, as usual, mingled with quite untenable historical statements.

Books XX to XXV present such difficulties to a systematic analysis that no attempt at it will be made. He was, indeed, "carried away by a torrent" in discussing commerce, its natural conditions, its influence upon society, and its relation to political forms and religion. The general rule is: "A nation in slavery labors more to preserve than to acquire; a free nation, more to acquire than to preserve." The general rule is followed by a general observation: "It is not those nations who have need of nothing that must lose by trade; it is those who have need of everything. It is not such people as have a sufficiency within themselves but those who are most in want that will find an advantage in putting a stop to all commercial intercourse." This general principle is implemented by a number of concrete statements interspersed with the usual historical references: such as the need for competition which creates "a just value on merchandises"; the desirability of free trade and undesirability of monopolistic trading practices, hence the need for restraint on trade (as the Navigation Act of 1660) in order to help commerce.

There follows suddenly Religion as the subject of Books XXIV and XXV. The intrinsic connection between "religion, commerce, and liberty" is realized in England. To guard himself against the obscurantists he was careful to insist that he was dealing with religion "not [as] a divine but as a political writer. I may [therefore] here advance things that are not otherwise true." He is, consequently, not concerned with the truth or falsity of a religious doctrine, but with its social and political function. He correlates despotic government and Mohammedanism, and moderate states and Christianity, Catholicism being more adequate for monarchies, protestantism more for republics. We must forbear to discuss his sociology of religion in the light of the works of Brooks Adams, Max Weber, Tawney, but we can readily see that he had, indeed, sociological insights which, although badly formulated, are quite a testimony to his sociological method. From what has been said about his character, it will not surprise that his greatest admiration is for the Stoics and that toleration is demanded as a vital political principle. . . . (pp. xxxix-xlvii)

Books XXVII, XXVIII, XXX, and XXXI add fragmentary observations which are not related to the rest of *The Spirit of the Laws*. Book XXVII deals with the origin and the changes of the Roman law of Succession. It is quite impossible to see that this mere antiquarian analysis has any bearing on anything heretofore discussed. But in Books XXVIII, XXX, and XXXI

the history and development and theory of the civil and feudal laws of France receive a more extended treatment than any other subject of *The Spirit of the Laws*. . . . (pp. xlvii-xlviii)

In the body of the *The Spirit of the Laws* there are two books (XXVI and XXIX) which ought to stand at the beginning of the work and whose actual place can be explained only by the length of time spent on the composition of his work and his reluctance to change radically the order of his work. Book XXVI distinguishes the following several layers of law: law of nature; divine law (that of religion); canon law (religious policy); law of nations (civil law of the universe); general political law (sum of human wisdom); particular political laws; law of conquest; civil law (protection of life and liberty against attack by other citizens); domestic law (family law). These layers do not form (as in the Thomistic philosophy) a hierarchy. There exists rather a division of functions among them, meaning that a particular social phenomenon should be regulated by a corresponding layer of law and not by a law that is not related to the phenomenon. Laws of inheritance, e.g., should not be governed by natural law but by political and civil law. This division of functions might even cut across a unified social institution. The family could thus be the object of religious law—namely, as to its form and nature—and of civil law—namely, as to the consequences of marriage. One may, with justice, reject the nine-fold division of laws as arbitrary, although I believe it to have a very good meaning, but we are compelled to admit the intrinsic soundness of this approach. We would, if we could go deeper into the problem, show that Montesquieu, although not giving us a systematic analysis, yet foreshadows a dual development in legal science: the legal theory of German idealism culminating in Kant's rigid division of morality and legality, and the sociological theory of law initiated by Bentham. This includes the general survey of *The Spirit of the Laws*, except for Books XI and XII. . . . The understanding of his work is frequently rendered difficult by the intrusion of many historical references, the bulk coming from the classics. His scholarship in the use of sources is decidedly second-rate, even if eighteenth century standards are applied. Many are wrong, others totally irrelevant, their great number, instead of helping, merely obscure the meaning. But the general significance of these books is clear, and the approach new. The positive suggestions are at least as numerous as the errors, and the fact that many of his ideas have not been examined at all is a testimony to discontinuity of modern scholarship. (pp. xlviii-xlix)

Franz Neumann, in an introduction to The Spirit of the Laws *by Baron de Montesquieu, edited by Franz Neumann, translated by Thomas Nugent, Hafner Publishing Company, 1949, pp. ix-lxiv.*

LOUIS ALTHUSSER   (essay date 1959)

[*Althusser is a French philosopher and essayist. A Marxist, he subscribes to the doctrine of historical materialism, the theory that the material economic foundation of a society gives rise to its ideas and social institutions. In Althusser's view, historical materialism is the science of history, whereas other historical theories are ideological in nature. In the following excerpt from an essay originally published in French in 1959, Althusser discerns cohesiveness in Montesquieu's political theories and unity in* The Spirit of Laws.]

'I have first of all considered mankind; and the result of my thoughts has been, that, amidst such an infinite diversity of laws and manners, they were not solely conducted by the caprice of fancy. I have laid down the first principles, and have found that the particular cases apply naturally to them; that the histories of all nations are only consequences of them; and that every particular law is connected with another law, or depends on some other of a more general extent' [see essay dated 1748]. Such is Montesquieu's discovery: not *particular ingenuities* but universal first principles making intelligible the whole of human history and *all its particulars:* 'When once I had discovered my first principles, everything I sought for appeared.' . . . (p. 43)

What then are the principles which make history intelligible in this way? Once posed, this question raises a number of difficulties which directly involve the *make-up* of the *Spirit of Laws.* Montesquieu's great work . . . does not indeed have the expected arrangement. First of all, from Book I to Book XIII, it contains a theory of governments and of the different laws that depend either on their natures or on their principles: in other words, a *typology,* which appears very abstract, although it is crammed with historical examples, and seems to constitute a whole isolated from the rest. . . . After Book XIII we seem to enter another world. Everything should have been said about the governments, their types being known, but here we have the climate (Books XIV, XV, XVI, XVII), then the quality of the soil (Book XVIII), then manners and morals (Book XIX), and commerce (Books XX, XXI), and money (Book XXII), and population (Book XXIII) and finally religion (Books XXIV, XXV), which each in turn determine the laws whose secret has apparently already been provided. And to cap the confusion, four Books of history, one discussing the development of the Roman laws of succession (Book XXVII), three expounding the origins of feudal laws (Books XXVIII, XXX, XXXI), and between them one Book on the 'manner of composing laws' (Book XXIX). Principles which claim to provide order for history ought at least to put some of it in the treatise which expounds them.

Where indeed are they to be found? The *Spirit of Laws* seems to be made up of three parts added on to one another, like ideas which have come up and that one does not want to lose. Where is the clear unity we expected? Should we seek Montesquieu's 'principles' in the first thirteen Books, and thus owe him the idea of *a pure typology of the forms of government,* the description of their peculiar dynamic, the deduction of laws as a function of their nature and principle? Suppose we agree. But then all the material about climate and the various factors, then the history, seem interesting certainly, but additional. Are the true principles on the contrary in the *second part,* in the idea that the laws are determined by different factors, some material (climate, soil, population, economy), others moral (manners and morals, religion)? But then what is the concealed argument linking these determinant principles with the first ideal principles and the final historical studies? Any attempt to maintain the whole in an impossible unity, the ideality of the types, the determinism of the material or moral environment, and the history, falls into irresoluble contradictions. Montesquieu could be said to be torn between a mechanistic materialism and a moral idealism, between atemporal structures and a historical genesis, etc. Which is a way of saying that if he did make *certain* discoveries, they are only linked by the disorder of his book, which proves against him that he did not make *the particular* discovery he thought he had made.

I should like to try to combat this impression and reveal between the different 'truths' of the *Spirit of Laws* the *chain that links them to other truths* discussed in the Preface [to *The Spirit of Laws*].

The first expression of Montesquieu's new principles is to be found in the few lines which distinguish between the *nature* and the *principle* of a government. Each government (republic, monarchy, despotism) has *its nature* and *its principle.* Its *nature* is 'that by which it is constituted,' its *principle* the passion 'by which it is made to act.' . . . (pp. 43-4)

What is to be understood by the *nature* of a government? The *nature* of the government answers the question: *who holds power? how does the holder of power exercise that power?* Thus, the *nature* of republican government implies that the body of the nation (or a part of the nation) has sovereign authority. The *nature* of monarchical government, that one alone governs, but by fixed and established laws. The *nature* of despotism, that one alone governs, but with neither laws nor rules. The retention and mode of exercise of power—all this remains purely legal, and when all is said and done, *formal.*

The *principle* takes us into life. For a government is not a pure form. It is the concrete form of existence of a society of men. For the men subject to a particular type of government to be precisely and lastingly subject to it, the mere imposition of a political form (*nature*) is not enough, they must also have a disposition to that form, a certain way of acting and reacting which will underpin that form. As Montesquieu puts it, there has to be a specific *passion.* Each form of government necessarily desires its own passion. The republic wants virtue, monarchy honour, and despotism fear. The principle of a government is drawn from its form, for it is a 'natural' derivation of it. But this consequence is less its *effect* than its *precondition.* Take the example of the republic. The *principle* of the republic, virtue, answers the question: *on what condition can there be a government which gives power to the people and makes it exercise that power by the laws?*—On the condition that the citizens are *virtuous,* i.e. sacrifice themselves to the public good, and, in all circumstances, prefer the fatherland to their own passions. The same for monarchy and despotism. If the *principle* of the government is its *spring, that which makes it act,* that is because it is, as the life of the government, quite simply its condition of existence. The republic will only 'go,' to coin a phrase, on virtue, just as some motors will only go on petrol. Without virtue the republic will fall, as will monarchy without honour, despotism without fear.

Montesquieu has been accused of formalism because of his way of defining a government by its *nature,* which does indeed consist of a few words of pure constitutional law. But it is forgotten that *the nature of a government is formal for Montesquieu himself, so long as it is separated from its principle.* One should say: in a government a nature without a principle is inconceivable and non-existent. Only the *nature-principle totality* is conceivable, because it is real. And this totality is no longer formal, for it no longer designates a purely juridical form, but a political form engaged in its own life, in its own conditions of existence and survival. Although defined in one word, virtue, honour, fear, these conditions are highly concrete. Like passion in general, the passions may seem abstract, but *as principles they express politically the whole real life of the citizens.* The virtue of the citizen is his entire life devoted to the public good: this passion, dominant in the State, is, in one man, all his passions dominated. With the principle it is the concrete life of men, public and even private, that enters into the government. The *principle* is thus the intersection of the *nature* of the government (its political form) with the real life of men. It is thus *the point and aspect in which the real life of men has to be resumed in order to be inserted into the form of a government*. The principle is the concrete of that abstract, the nature. It is their unity, it is their totality, that is real. Where is the formalism?

This point will be conceded. But it is decisive if we are to grasp the full extent of Montesquieu's *discovery*. *In this idea of the totality of the nature and the principle of a government, Montesquieu is in fact proposing a new theoretical category,* one which gives him the key to an infinity of riddles. Before him political theorists had certainly tried to explain the multiplicity and diversity of the laws of a given government. But they had done little more than outline a logic of the *nature* of governments, even when they were not, as in most cases, satisfied by a mere description of elements *without any inner unity*. The immense majority of laws, such as those that determine education, division of lands, degree of property, techniques of justice, punishments and rewards, luxury, the condition of women, the conduct of war, etc, were excluded from this logic, because their *necessity* was not understood. Montesquieu here majestically closes this old debate, by *discovering and verifying in the facts the hypothesis that the State is a real totality and that all the particulars of its legislation, of its institutions and its customs are merely the effect and expression of its inner unity.* He submits these laws, which seem fortuitous and irrational, to a profound logic, and relates them to a single centre. I do not claim that Montesquieu was the first to think that the State should of itself constitute a *totality*. This idea is already lurking in Plato's reflection and we find it again at work in the thought of the theoreticians of natural law, at any rate in Hobbes. But before Montesquieu this idea only entered into the constitution of an *ideal* State, without lowering itself to the point of making *concrete* history intelligible. With Montesquieu, the totality, which was an *idea*, becomes a scientific *hypothesis*, intended to *explain the facts*. It becomes the fundamental category which makes it possible to think, no longer the reality of an ideal state, but the concrete and hitherto unintelligible diversity of the institutions of human history. History is no longer that infinite space in which are haphazardly scattered the innumerable works of caprice and accident, to the discouragement of the understanding, whose only possible conclusion is the insignificance of man and the greatness of God. This space has a structure. *It possesses concrete centres to which are related a whole local horizon of facts and institutions: the States. And at the core of these totalities, which are like living individuals, there is an inner reason, an inner unity, a fundamental primordial centre: the unity of nature and principle.* (pp. 45-8)

Here, however, formalism is still lying in wait for us. For it may well be that this category of the totality constituted the unity of the first Books of the *Spirit of Laws*. But it may be said that it is restricted to them, and that it is marked by the error of these first Books: that it concerns *pure models*, a truly republican republic, a truly monarchical monarchy and a truly despotic despotism only. In 'Reflections on the Preceding Chapters', Montesquieu says: 'Such are the principles of the three sorts of government: which does not imply, that, in a particular republic, they actually are, but that they ought to be, virtuous: nor does it prove, that, in a particular monarchy, they are actuated by honour; or, in a particular despotic government, by fear; but that they ought to be directed by these principles, otherwise the government is imperfect.' Is this not to prove that *an idea which is only valid for pure models and perfect political forms* has been taken for a category applicable to all existing governments? Is it not to relapse into a theory of essences and into the ideal trap which was precisely what

was to be avoided? Whereas one must, *as a historian*, necessarily explain *a certain* very imperfect republic or monarchy, not a *pure* republic or monarchy? If the totality is only valid for the purity, what use is the totality in history, which is impurity itself? Or, and this is the same aporia, how can one ever think history in a category attached in essence to pure atemporal models? We have come back to the difficulty of the disparity of the *Spirit of Laws:* how to unite the beginning and the end, the pure typology and the history?

I believe we should be careful not to judge Montesquieu by one sentence, but, as he forewarns us, take his work as a whole, without separating what he says in it from what he does. It is indeed very remarkable that this theoretician of pure models never (or hardly ever) in his work gives any but *impure* examples. Even in the history of Rome, which is for him truly the most perfect experimental subject, a kind of 'pure substance' of historical experimentation, the ideal purity only had one moment, at the beginning, for all the rest of the time Rome lived in political impurity. It would surely be incredible if Montesquieu were unaware of such a contradiction. It must be that he does not think he is contradicting his principles, but that he is giving them a more profound meaning than they are attributed. I believe in fact that the category of the *totality* (and the *nature-principle* unity which is its core) is indeed a universal category, one which does not concern just the perfect adequacies: republic-virtue, monarchy-honour, despotism-fear. Manifestly, Montesquieu considers that *in any State, whether it is pure or impure, the law of this totality and its unity is supreme*. If the State is pure, the unity will be an *adequate* one. But if it is impure, it will be a *contradictory* one. . . . To say, as Montesquieu does, that a government which loses its principle is a lost government means quite clearly that the nature-principle unity is also supreme in the *impure* cases. If it were not, it would be impossible to understand how this broken unity could break its government.

Hence it is a strange mistake to doubt that Montesquieu has a sense of history, or to suspect that his typology diverted him from a theory of history, that he wrote books on history through a distraction which led him away from his principles. This mistake is no doubt rooted primarily in the fact that Montesquieu did not share the already widespread and soon to be dominant ideology, the belief that history has an end, is in pursuit of the realm of reason, liberty and 'enlightenment.' *Montesquieu was probably the first person before Marx who undertook to think history without attributing to it an end*, i.e. without projecting the consciousness of men and their hopes onto the time of history. This criticism is thus entirely to his credit. *He was the first to propose a positive principle of universal explanation for history;* a principle which is not just *static*: the totality explaining the diversity of the laws and institutions of a given government; but also *dynamic*: the law of the unity of nature and principle, a law making it possible to think the development of institutions and their transformations in real history, too. In the depth of the countless laws which come and go, he thus discovered a *constant connection* uniting the nature of a government to its principle; and at the core of this constant connection, he stated the inner variation of the relation, which, by the transitions of the unity from adequacy to inadequacy, from identity to contradiction, makes intelligible the changes and revolutions in the concrete totalities of history. (pp. 48-50)

'The force of the principles draws everything to it.' Such is the grand lesson of Book VIII, which opens with the sentence,

'The Corruption of each government generally begins with that of the principles.' Corruption (and thus the impure state I have been discussing) constitutes a sort of experimental situation which makes it possible to penetrate the indivisible nature-principle unity and decide *which is the decisive element of the opposition.* The result is that it is definitely the principle that governs the nature and gives it its meaning. 'When once the principles of government are corrupted, the very best laws become bad, and turn against the state: but, when the principles are sound, even bad laws have the same effect as good.' 'A State may alter two different ways; either by the amendment, or by the corruption, of the constitution. If it has preserved its principles, and the constitution changes, this is owing to its amendment; if, upon changing the constitution, its principles are lost, this means that it has been corrupted.' This clearly shows the transition from the case of the experimental situation of corruption to the general case of any modification (to the good as well as to the bad) in the nature of the State. Thus it really is the principle which is, in the last resort, the cause of the development of forms and their meanings. To the point that the classic image of form and content (form being what informs, effectivity itself) has to be inverted. It is the principle that is, in this sense, the true form of that apparent form, the nature of the government. 'There are very few laws which are not good, while the State retains its principles. Here I may apply what Epicurus said of riches: "It is not the liquor, but the vessel, that is corrupted".' (pp. 52-3)

Of course, this does not exclude *the effectivity of the nature on the principle,* but within certain limits. Otherwise it would be difficult to understand how Montesquieu could have imagined laws intended to preserve or reinforce the principle. The urgency of these laws is simply a confession of their *subordinate* character: they are only active in a domain which may escape them not only for a thousand accidental and external reasons, but also and above all for the fundamental reason that it reigns over them and decides even what they mean. There are thus limit situations in which laws that are intended to *provide manners and morals* are powerless against manners and morals themselves, and rebound against the end they were supposed to serve—the manners and morals rejecting laws opposed to their own goals. However hazardous a comparison it may be, and one that I put forward with all possible precautions, the type of this *determination in the last instance by the principle,* determination which nevertheless farms out a whole zone of subordinate effectivity to the *nature* of the government, can be compared with the type of determination which Marx attributes *in the last instance to the economy,* a determination which nevertheless farms out a zone of subordinate effectivity to *politics.* In both cases it is a matter of unity which may be harmonious or contradictory; in both cases this determination does nonetheless cede to the determined element a whole region of effectivity, but subordinate effectivity.

Hence this interpretation reveals a real unity between the first and last parts of the **Spirit of Laws,** between the typology and the history. But there remains one difficulty: the so varied second part, which introduces climate, soil, commerce, religion—surely it represents new principles, and heteroclite ones, which clash with the unity I have just demonstrated?

Let us first run through the new determinant factors suggested to us. Before climate (Book XIV), there is another important element, referred to on several occasions, and particularly in Book VIII: *the dimensions of the State.* The nature of a government depends on the geographical extent of its empire. A minute State will be republican, a moderate State monarchic and an immense State despotic. Here is a determination that seems to overthrow the laws of history, since geography decides its forms *directly.* Climate reinforces this argument, since this time it is the temperature of the air that distributes the empires, despotisms beneath violent skies, moderate governments beneath tender ones, and decides in advance which men will be free and which slaves. We learn that 'The empire of the climate is the first, the most powerful of all empires', but at the same time that this empire can be conquered by well-conceived laws leaning on its excesses to protect men from its effects. A new cause then appears: *the nature of the soil* occupied by a nation. According to whether it is fertile or arid, the government there will be a government of one man or of many; according to whether is is mountainous or a plain, a continent or an island, liberty or slavery will be found to triumph there. But here again the causality invoked can be counteracted: 'Countries are not cultivated in proportion to their fertility, but to their liberty.' But here are the *manners and morals (moeurs)* or general spirit of a nation, which add their effectivities to the others; then commerce and money, and finally religion. It is hard to avoid an impression of disorder, as if Montesquieu wanted to exhaust a series of principles he has discovered separately and then heaped together for want of any better order. 'Mankind are influenced by various causes; by the climate, by the religion, by the laws, by the maxims of government, by precedents, morals and customs.' The unity of a profound law has turned into a plurality of causes. The totality is lost in a list.

I do not want to make it look as if I hoped to save Montesquieu from himself by forcing this disorder to appear as an order. But I should like to suggest briefly that in this disorder we can often glimpse something approaching an order which is not foreign to what has so far been established.

What is indeed remarkable in the majority of these factors, which either determine the very nature of the government (e.g. geographical extent, climate, soil) or a certain number of its laws, is the fact that they only act on their object *indirectly.* Take the example of the climate. The torrid climate does not produce the despot just like that, nor does the temperate the monarch. The climate only acts on the *temperament* of men, by way of a nice physiology which dilates or contracts the extremities and thereby affects the global sensitivity of the individual, imprinting on him peculiar needs and leanings, down to his style of conduct. It is *the men thus constituted and conditioned* who are apt for particular laws and governments. 'It is the variety of wants, in different climates, that first occasioned a difference in the manner of living, and thus gave rise to a variety of laws.' The *laws* produced by the climate are thus the *last effect* in a whole chain, whose *penultimate link,* the *product* of the climate and the cause of the laws, is the 'customary life' (*manière de vivre*) which is the outside of the 'manners and morals' (*moeurs*). Look at the *soil:* if fertile lands are good for the government of one man alone, that is because the peasant there is too busy and too well-paid by his efforts to raise his nose from the ground and his pence. *Commerce:* it does not act directly on the laws but via the intermediary of the manners: 'Wherever there is commerce, there we meet with agreeable manners'—hence the peaceful spirit of commerce, its suitability to certain governments, its repugnance for others. As for *religion* itself, it seems to be part of another world than these completely material factors, but it acts nonetheless in the same way: by giving a nation ways of living the law and practising morality; it only concerns government through the behaviour of citizens and subjects. It is its mastery of fear that makes the Mahometan religion so apt for despotism: it provides it with slaves, ripe for slavery. It is its mastery of morality that makes the Christian religion accord so well with moderate government: 'We owe to Christianity, in government, a certain political law; and in war, a certain law of nations.' Thus just when they are acting on the government and determining certain of its essential laws, all these causes, apparently so radically disparate, converge *on a common point:* the customs, morals and manners of being, feeling and acting that they confer on the men who live within their empire.

From their conjunction arises what Montesquieu calls *the spirit of a nation.* He does write: 'Mankind are influenced by various causes; by the climate, by the religion, etc.,' but only so as to conclude: 'from whence is formed a general spirit of the nation.' (pp. 53-6)

Hence it is the *result:* the manners and morals, the general spirit of a nation, which determines either the form of the government or a certain number of its laws. The question then arises, *is this not an already familiar determination?* Indeed, remember what I have said of the *principle* of a government and of the depths of the concrete life of men it expresses. Considered not from the viewpoint of the *form* of the government, i.e. of its political exigencies, but from the viewpoint of its *content,* i.e. of its origins, *the principle is really the political expression of the concrete behaviour of men,* i.e. of their manners and morals, and spirit. Of course, Montesquieu does not say in so many words that the manners and morals or spirit of a nation constitute the very essence of the *principle* of its government. But he does set out from principles as the pure forms of the government: their truth appears in their corruption. When the *principle* is lost, it is clear that *manners and morals effectively take the place of principle:* that they are its loss or salvation. Take the republic, abandoned by virtue: there is no longer any respect for magistrates there, nor for old age, nor even for . . . husbands. 'No longer will there be any such things as manners, order, or virtue.' It would be hard to say more clearly that the *principle* (virtue) is simply the expression of the *manners.* . . . How can it be doubted that the manners and morals, vaster and more extensive than the principle, are nonetheless its real foundation and seat, when the same dialectic can be seen outlined between the manners and morals and the laws as between the principles and the nature of a government? (pp. 56-7)

I know that counter-quotations will be used against me and that I shall be accused of giving Montesquieu the benefit of the doubt. However, it seems to me that all the reservations one might express turn on no more than a single point: the ambiguity of the concepts of *principle* and *manners and morals.* But I believe that this ambiguity is *real* in Montesquieu himself. I should say that it expresses simultaneously his wish to introduce the utmost clarity and necessity into history, but also in some sense his inability—not to speak of his *choice.* For if the region of the *nature* of a government is always perfectly sharply defined, if the dialectic of the nature-principle unity and contradiction, and the thesis of the primacy of principle, both emerge clearly from his examples, the concept of principle and the concept of manners and morals remain vague.

I said that the principle expresses the condition of existence of a government, and has the real life of men as its concrete background. The parallel causalities of the second part of the **Spirit of Laws** reveal to us the components of this real life, i.e.

the real material and moral conditions of the existence of a government—and summarize them in the manners and morals which come to the surface in the *principle.* But it is hard to see the transition from the manners and morals to the principle, from the real conditions to the political exigencies of the form of a government, which come together in the *principle.* The very terms I used, such as *the manners being expressed in the principles,* betray this difficulty—for this *expression* is in some sense torn between its origin (the manners and morals) and the exigencies of its end (the form of the government). All Montesquieu's ambiguity is linked to this tension. He did feel that the necessity of history could only be thought in the unity of its forms and their conditions of existence, and in the dialectic of that unity. But he grouped all these conditions, *on the one hand in the manners and morals,* which are indeed produced by real conditions, but whose concept remains vague (the synthesis of all these conditions in the manners and morals is no more than cumulative); and *on the other hand in the principle,* which, divided between its real origins and the exigencies of the political form it has to animate, *leans too often towards these exigencies alone.*

It will be said that this contradiction and this ambiguity are inevitable in a man who thinks in the concepts of his period and cannot transcend the limits of the then established knowledges, simply interrelating what he knows, and unable to seek in the conditions he is describing a deeper unity, which would presuppose a complete *political economy.* That is true. And it is already remarkable that Montesquieu should have defined and designated in advance in a brilliant conception of history an as yet obscure zone barely illuminated by a vague concept: the zone of *manners and morals (moeurs),* and behind it the zone of *the concrete behaviour of men in their relations with nature and with their past.*

But within him another man than the scientist took advantage of this ambiguity. The man of a political party which needed precisely the pre-eminence of the forms over their principles, and wanted there to be *three kinds of government,* in order that, protected by the necessities of climate, manners and morals, and religion, it could make its *choice* between them. (pp. 58-60)

Louis Althusser, "Montesquieu: Politics and History, The Dialectic of History," in his Politics and History: Montesquieu, Rousseau, Hegel and Marx, *translated by Ben Brewster, NLB, 1972, pp. 43-60.*

ROBERT SHACKLETON   (essay date 1961)

[*Shackleton was an English academic and scholar. In the following excerpt from a work considered by many the definitive critical biography of Montesquieu, he explicates Montesquieu's treatment of religious themes in his work and outlines the author's personal beliefs.*]

Montesquieu's views on the source of religious sentiment are summed up in the second chapter of Book XXV of *L'Esprit des lois.* In the eighteenth century there were several discussions of this problem ranging from the intelligent analyses of Fontenelle and the Président de Brosses, to the naïve hypotheses of Montesquieu's own disciple Boulanger. Montesquieu's personal contribution is a valuable one.

He lists seven different reasons for adherence to a religion, and more specifically for adherence to the Christian religion: pleasure at our own intelligence in having selected a non-idolatrous faith (or in other words, intellectual vanity); the gratification afforded to our senses and emotions by the ceremonies of religion; the pride we feel in being able to regard ourselves as selected individuals; the frequency of occupation imposed on us by religious practices; the satisfaction given to our natural tendency to hope and to fear by the belief in heaven and in hell; the attractiveness of the morality taught by the Church . . . ; and finally, the great appeal made by the magnificence and wealth of the visible Church, even to those who can but contrast it with their own poverty.

If the elements of religion evoke in this way a response in men's hearts and minds, religious institutions also can be explained similarly. All civilized peoples live in houses: what is more reasonable than to believe that God, too, must have his house, larger and more magnificent than the houses of individuals? What is more natural than that the temple should be deemed to offer immunity from pursuit to those who seek asylum there? Proper care for the temple, and adequate attention to the worship of God, require more constant application than ordinary men can give: what more reasonable, then, than to create a caste of priests who will devote themselves exclusively to the cult of God? If there are many priests, what more sensible than to appoint a pontiff to preside over them?

These are general and universal causes of religion; but there are also local and particular causes. Religion is in important measure dependent on the political and social background, on existing political institutions and traditions, on *moeurs* ["manners and customs"]. So a country which has a tradition of liberty, like England, will find either that there is great indifference in the matter of religion, or that there are a large number of rival religious sects. So a despotically governed land, inadequately provided with laws, will need another sanction and will rely greatly for this purpose on religion. So, since the organization of a religion must bear some analogy to the system of government of the State, it will be found that the people of the south will embrace more readily Roman Catholicism, while those of the north will turn to Protestantism, preferring Lutheranism if they are governed by princes, and Calvinism if they live in republics. As political institutions are themselves in part determined by climate, so too does climate influence religions. Montesquieu here abstains, as he abstained when discussing the general influence of climate, from producing a rigorous and systematic theory like that of Charron; he contents himself with examples of its effect on feasts, taboos, and practices: food growing more readily in the south, leisure is more easily socially practicable, and the number of feast days may be greater; the meat of the pig being extremely rare in Arabia, it is expedient that its consumption should be forbidden; hot climates make frequent bathing in rivers salutary, and Islam and Hinduism have therefore vested it with religious significance. There are two cases in the writings of the President where he assigns accidental causes to theological doctrine itself, coming nearer here than elsewhere to full psychological determination. He asserts that Moslems see in their daily lives so many examples of the unforeseen and the extraordinary, caused by the arbitrary civil power which oppresses them, that they are perforce driven to believe in the rigid control of external fate; while Christians, living under moderate governments which are controlled by human prudence, believe that their own actions also are so controlled and that their wills are free. The other example is afforded by metempsychosis, which Montesquieu suggests was invented in the hot climate and parched countrysides of India, in order to protect from slaughter the few cattle which can live there, by teaching that human souls have passed into their bodies.

Montesquieu was not a builder of systems. He did not write what was later, with Hume, to be known as the natural history of religion. But in his examples, his *obiter dicta,* and his occasional generalizations, he produces the elements of such a history. In enumerating the causes of religion he is not fired with a desire to discredit it. He does not see religion as the invention of dishonest priests; it is not a fraud. Herein he differs from men like D'Holbach, who regarded organized religion as an imposture, and were anxious first to discredit religion, and then to extirpate it. Montesquieu was concerned to explain it; to understand rather than to judge was his aim as it is necessarily the aim of the historian.

An important consequence arises from this. If it is the historian's duty to discover the causes of religion, as of other institutions, it is the statesman's duty to respect these causes. Montesquieu . . . never wholly abandoned the principle of Spinoza, that that which is has a right to continue to be, and he cannot avoid applying that principle to religion. (pp. 337-40)

Pierre Bayle, in his *Pensées diverses sur la comète,* had devoted one of his monumental digressions to an examination of the relative merits of atheism and idolatry; approaching this problem from the social point of view, he had argued in favour of atheism, claiming that ideas of morality existed independently of religious faith. Montesquieu dissents from this contention. He insists that all religions have social and moral consequences, and in Book XXIV especially he sets out to examine them. . . . He considers also the Christian religion, but hastens to protect himself against censure by saying that he writes only as a political writer and not as a theologian.

His first attack on Bayle takes the form of a declaration that even if it were useless for the subjects in a State to have a religion, it would still be expedient that the prince, standing above all earthly sanctions, should be placed under this restraint. . . . But the moderating consequences of religion are not less desirable on the part of the people than on that of their ruler. Spinoza had claimed that even the superstitions of the Turks were useful; and Montesquieu enumerates the merits of Islam as well as those of Christianity. Though the faith of Mahomet tends to favour despotism, since it is a fear added to the fear which is the principle of that government, it may help to temper some of its evils, perhaps by modifying the will of the prince, perhaps by modifying the penal code.

The effect of Christianity is different. It opposes despotism. It has improved the lot of human beings in many parts of the world, in Ethiopia, in spite of the climate, as well as in Europe. Its principles, if followed, would be infinitely stronger than honour, virtue—the purely human virtue of the republic—and fear. The effect of Christianity has sometimes been harmful: Lucretius's lamentation over the ills which religion has inspired can sometimes be justly applied even to the Christian religion; witness the crippling effect on commerce of the Church's condemnation of usury. But for good or for ill the historical significance of Christianity is seen by Montesquieu as transcendently great, and in no case more pregnant with consequence or more praiseworthy than in its effect on slavery: Plutarch in his life of second King of Rome declares that when men were governed by Saturn there was neither master nor slave. Christianity, says the President, has in our lands brought back that age.

The social and historical importance of Christianity, as of other religions, is a result of its moral teaching and not of its articles of belief. Montesquieu agrees with most of the thinkers of the

Enlightenment in prizing morality more highly than faith. . . . For Montesquieu the value of morality is more evident than the truth of doctrine, and religions can be compared more easily in point of morality than in respect of their faith. The moral inferiority of Islam to Christianity is immediately obvious. In those countries which do not enjoy Christianity, it is imperative that religion should accord with morality. Three examples of non-Christian religions which do this are given by Montesquieu: the simple moral faith of the inhabitants of Pegu in Burma; that of the Jewish sect of the Essaeans; and the Stoics, in praise of whom Montesquieu extracts a paragraph from his *Traité des devoirs* of many years before, adding to it a sentence eulogizing Julian the Apostate. The social utility of religion, proclaims the President in as many words, is irrelevant to the truth of its doctrine; false doctrines may be useful, true and sacred doctrines may be harmful in social life.

An early paragraph in the *Pensées* gives a simple analysis of duty as it arises from religion. God has given laws to men, and these laws are of two sorts: moral precepts and sacred precepts. The first of these are based on the necessity of pre-serving society, of in some cases simply on their own ease of execution; sacred precepts are either based on eternal reason, such as the injunction to love God; or they are arbitrary and relate to ceremonial. This strange mixture of Spinozism and orthodoxy, coeval roughly with the *Traité des devoirs,* does not represent the final attitude of Montesquieu. In *L'Esprit des lois,* using the Catholic terminology of precept and counsel, he in-sists that precepts should be given by the civil law. It is the function of religion to give the more general and the more elevated guidance, to point to ideals rather than to prescribe sanctions. . . . Man-made rules are concerned rather with the possible and the expedient. (pp. 341-44)

In considering the religion of any individual two separate things must be considered: external practice and internal conviction. (p. 349)

Montesquieu's external profession was of loyalty to the Roman Church. . . . The background of Montesquieu's life was that of an orthodox Roman Catholic, with one striking and almost startling exception: his wife was a Calvinist and remained to the end of her days loyal to her original faith.

The first thing that must be said about the religious conviction of Montesquieu is that he believes firmly in the existence of God. This belief he holds early in his life and late in his life. . . . A long discussion in the *Pensées* . . . contains vigorous argu-ments for the existence of God. It is true that some of them are based on the psychological utility of the idea of God, as a consolation when men think of death; what is at issue, however, is not whether Montesquieu's reasons for belief were beyond logical reproach, but whether he believed, and this passage leaves no possibility of doubt. His belief in God was the foun-dation of his notions, as they then existed, of morality. The hopes and fears of mankind are derived from the existence of God, and if God were proved not to exist, the whole economy of the human mind would be destroyed. Nor is this belief the passing fancy of the young man dallying with metaphysics. (pp. 350-51)

That is not to say, however, that he had a firm Christian con-viction. (p. 352)

It is in deism that is to be found the real religious belief of Montesquieu.

Many definitions of deism have been given, but in *L'Esprit des lois* Montesquieu gives his own. Plato, he says, declared im-pious alike those who deny the existence of the gods, those who admit their existence but maintain that they are uncon-cerned with earthly events, and those who think the gods can be appeased by sacrifices. . . . This deistic sentiment is com-pletely consonant with the personal religion of Montesquieu, who unites it with an ecumenical outlook when he asserts that God is a monarch to whom all nations bring tribute, each with its own religion. (pp. 352-53)

One element in the religious outlook of Montesquieu . . . is the belief to which he clung more tenaciously than to any other, and in support of which he engaged to the limit his powers of eloquence. This is his belief in the necessity of religious tol-eration, a belief which he shared with Voltaire, and which he held more consistently than did Rousseau. It has been said that a man's support for religious toleration varies inversely with the vigour of his own religious conviction. Montesquieu does nothing to disprove such a contention.

Before his travels he deplored already the revocation of the Edict of Nantes and the massacre of Saint Bartholomew. The ideal of liberty which his stay in England revealed to him included, as it did for Voltaire, liberty of conscience; and no Spinozist acceptance of the right of the existing to exist ever destroyed the integrity of his belief in religious toleration: God must be honoured, not avenged. The principle of toleration must be accepted by the State, and imposed on all religions found within the State's frontiers. In a moment of unfounded optimism he had written, soon after his travels, that the Jews were now saved, and superstition would not return, and that their persecution had ended. He was wrong. Persecutions con-tinued in his lifetime, and an *auto-da-fé* at Lisbon inspired Montesquieu's most impassioned piece of writing. This is an open letter, styled *Très Humble Remontrance,* to the Inquisitors of Spain and Portugal. It constitutes the thirteenth chapter of Book XXV of *L'Esprit des lois.* In this letter a Jew appeals to the Inquisitors to spare his race. Their sole error is to have remained faithful to the creed which the Christians of the pre-sent day believe once to have been the true creed. . . . Christians appeal to the blood of martyrs to prove the divine mission of their faith; but they have become themselves the Diocletians of their day. . . . The age they live in is an age of enlightenment greater than has been known before; but in time to come men will look back and consider the persecutions which were then practised. By the persecutors, the reputation of the age will be for ever tarnished. They, and with them their contemporaries, will be viewed with hatred. This remonstrance, a useless doc-ument, says Montesquieu . . . , is comparable with the *Ar-eopagitica* and with the *Declaration of the Rights of Man.* It reveals the principal and inviolable article of Montesquieu's faith. (pp. 354-55)

Robert Shackleton, in his Montesquieu: A Critical Biography, *Oxford University Press, 1961, 432 p.*

DAVID KETTLER   (essay date 1964)

[*Kettler is a German-born American educator and political sci-entist whose studies are concentrated in exploring the links be-tween social science and moral philosophy. In the following ex-cerpt, he addresses the theme of love in* Persian Letters.]

Among students of political philosophy, Montesquieu is chiefly honored as author of *The Spirit of the Laws.* His earlier im-portant work, *The Persian Letters,* is more often cited than read and is considered primarily as a collection of fragments, some of which may be useful for clearing up some disputed point or other in the interpretation of the *magnum opus*. In these notes I propose to treat it as a meaningful whole—as a book which in fact has the theme which it purports to have, the theme of love and its relation to social institutions. This is not an altogether novel approach, even among political scientists. . . . Nevertheless, I believe that Montesquieu's conception of love is sufficiently important and the implications of his conception sufficiently interesting, so that a closer analysis will not be redundant.

In brief, I will argue that Montesquieu treats love as a decisive manifestation of humanity. The lover is more truly human than other men; his potentialities as man are then more fully realized. Both virtue and wisdom are opened to him in this happy state. But love is not always possible. In fact, it is truer to say that almost never can men find true love, for the *institutions of society* deprive man of the capability for love. This is a crucial point; Montesquieu tells us not only that social conditions may preclude the fruition of love, but that men's perception of themselves and others is so decisively influenced by the habits they acquire in society that the very emotion of love will be denied them, or be transformed into a parody of that love which fulfills man. A proper treatment of the theme of love, then, requires more than an examination of the immediate and personal feelings of individuals; it requires also a study of the social context in which individuals move, the conditions which will affect both the character and fate of love. In this way, the writer or artist who truly understands love, whose sensibilities are developed, becomes at once a student of social reality and, perforce, a social critic. Furthermore, since no one himself incapable of love can know it, he shares at once the blessing and curse of the lover in a corrupted society. He alone can feel and know truly, but he must also be alone—a stranger and outcast in society. This last, on the role of the artist, is implicit rather than explicit in Montesquieu's work. . . . [This] much emerges clearly: for Montesquieu, the theme of love is intimately tied to the problems of society, and specifically, to the problem of dehumanization.

What, then, is Montesquieu's conception of true love? In the first place, its object is frankly sexual. Montesquieu breaks decisively with the classical and Christian philosophical traditions, as well as with what I understand to be the dominant tradition in serious literature. Man's love is not directed toward Platonic ideas or the Christian God; its object is woman. Nor is love for woman sublimated into an ephemeral adulation; it seeks sexual gratification. There is nothing necessarily heinous in the life of the passions. When Montesquieu seeks to ascertain the quality of love in a society, he first directs his attention to the relationship between the sexes. He investigates the emotions attendant to courtship and marriage.

But obviously, not all sexual passion is true love, which involves fidelity and respect also. The lover must direct his desire solely at the object of his love, and remain steadfast in his dedication. (Incidentally, this does not rule out polygamy automatically. There is nothing in this which precludes love of more than one. The point is that the lover does not follow random sexual inclinations.) Steadfastness, however, is not a sufficient condition for true love. The lover must respect his beloved, value her feelings and intelligence. She is no mere sexual object. Love implies at least the possibility of reciprocity and an essential equality between men and women. The love which enhances humanity presupposes a modicum of humanity, and this is at the mercy of society. (pp. 658-59)

In the *Persian Letters,* Montesquieu tests the equality of love in two social contexts, the Persian seraglio and the Parisian *haut-monde,* adding some comments on Russia and Spain, as well as a tale of true love between brother and sister. Except for the last, all appearances of love disintegrate either under close scrutiny or under the pressure of the environment. They are illusory or doomed not because of "fate" or individual failings, but because social circumstances forbid them reality.

Seraglio love fails, despite its guarantee of gratification and at least external fidelity, because the seraglio rests on the principle of terror, force and general denial of individual dignity. Usbek, the master of the seraglio, admits "It is not so much that I love them: in this respect, I find in myself an insensible mood which leaves me empty of desires. In the well-stocked seraglio where I lived, I anticipated love and destroyed it by [the act of] love itself; yet, out of my very coldness, springs up a secret jealousy that consumes me." His love is little more than pride of possession. The objects which he possesses will be more valuable if they are beautiful, and more enjoyable if they love him. They are not human. The sole exception is his feeling for Roxana which has the element of desire because she has fought him, but it cannot be love because she too must be treated as a slave in the discipline of the seraglio. He is a humane and cultured man, who would rather persuade than terrorize, but his situation denies him the opportunity—and presumably the capacity—to love. Usbek is, then, after all not so different from the eunuchs whom at times he pities. For them, desire has been transformed into lust for power and bitter hatred. And if one should seek love despite his impotence, he must experience bitter frustration. But Usbek's situation parallels this exactly. They are all caught up in the logic of the system.

In some ways, the victims fare better than their master or his ministers. At least, the physical pleasure of gratifying real desires is not denied them. For Zachi, a former favorite of great beauty, this is almost enough. Yet if she can be contented in her slavery, she cannot be truly human. In punishment for some minor transgression she is spanked by a eunuch, and relates: "My soul, at first annihilated by shame, was rediscovering the feeling of its own existence and was growing indignant, at which time my cries made the vaults of my apartment resound. I could be heard beseeching mercy from the most abject of all humans." A self-awareness so located and so manifested betokens a complete dehumanization. Zelis, another wife, is less degraded. She consoles herself with her husband's fears, priding herself on his dependence on the wives. In many ways, she is the counterpart of the eunuchs. But the facts of power deprive her of this consolation. She shares Zachi's fate, and her sadistic pleasure turns into a hatred which must destroy her. Destruction is also the necessary punishment for Roxana, the most fortunate of the wives. By whatever chance, she is the one person in the seraglio capable of love. She bestows it adulterously, with good cheer and hate deceiving Usbek. When she is discovered, and her lover slain, she kills herself, flaunting her freedom to her husband. The iron law of the seraglio is summarized in Zelis' last letter to Usbek: "You have degraded your soul and become inhuman." At best, this inhumanity may take the form of the happy assemblage of mares serviced by an angelic and superpotent stud, as set forth in Rica's idyllic tale; at worst, it will take the form of total terror described in glowing terms by the Black Eunuch. Love enters the seraglio only by accident, and those who can partake of it must die. Rule based on fear must destroy the humanity of both ruler and ruled.

But a society characterized by relative freedom and equality may crush humanity as well as a slave state. This emerges from Montesquieu's survey of love in France. As the seraglio promised much because of its sensuality and fidelity, France promises much because of the independence and equality of women there. But despite Rica's decision to remain, the import of Montesquieu's judgment is that love is impossible there too. Life is so artificial—directed by mode, opinion and pretense—that men do not trust their feelings for real love. Love becomes a matter of love-affairs, pursued for the sake of reputation as gallant and lady of mode. Rica jibes: "Here, a husband who loves his wife is a man who has not enough merit to make himself loved by another woman; who abuses the necessity of the law to make up for the charms he lacks." "A husband, who would want to be the only one to possess his wife would be considered a perturber of the public happiness, and a madman who would want to enjoy the light of the sun by himself, to the exclusion of all others." In interpreting such passages as these, there is always the risk of killing an exaggeration meant merely to amuse and sell books, but I do not believe that the risk is too great in this instance. Montesquieu sought to do all those things, but he also paints a consistent and widely detailed picture of a polished society in which men have lost self-respect, and with all conceivable freedom cannot arrive at a human condition of love.

Not only the lionized adulterer signals the bankruptcy of French marital institutions. Montesquieu also has Rica deride the legal structure of marriage (he says of a domestic relations court: "Love makes this court resound: here, nothing is spoken of but angered fathers, seduced daughters, unfaithful lovers, and unfortunate husbands.") And, more seriously, he has Usbek analyze the Christian laws forbidding divorce in order to point out that this cuts the sexual core out of marriage by compelling parties who have no love for one another to remain married. French love is sterile rather than impotent, and it does not achieve the level of true love—again, not because of the individual faults of the would-be lovers, but because the habits engendered by a whole way of life and the demands made by the system preclude a human life.

In the romance of *Apheridon and Astarte,* a story told Usbek by one of his correspondents, Montesquieu presents a picture of true love. The pair are brother and sister, permitted by their religion to marry. The brother must surmount many obstacles to gain his sister who had been converted to Mohammedanism and placed in a seraglio (the seraglio of a eunuch, in fact). The first step is her reconversion to Zoroastrianism. Love achieves this task; she says to him: "You are loved, my brother, and by a Zoroastrian. I struggled long: But, O Gods! how love lifts difficulties! How relieved I am! I can no longer set bounds to my love; its very excess is legitimate." With truth revealed to her by the power of love, she throws herself wholeheartedly into a plan for her abduction. All obstacles are overcome and complications resolved, and the two live happily as man and wife.

This story is, in many ways, indistinguishable from countless tales of romance. Yet, if our analysis of the book is correct, its appearance there may tell much about Montesquieu's conception of love. First, it is an incestuous love: perhaps it is only between brother and sister that the equality and intimate respect requisite for true love can appear. (Montesquieu declared elsewhere that he could not believe that incest was a sin.) What is almost equally striking is that the brother and sister are *strangers* to the society in which they love. They belong to a small remnant of the original inhabitants of Persia, and are now outsiders. In their flight after marriage they wander far through the world, helped everywhere by other outsiders—either Guebres, like themselves or, in one crucial case, by an Armenian merchant. (Montesquieu remarks elsewhere on the separateness of the Armenians' state.) With some trepidation, one might push this analysis further to suggest that it is significant that the "outsiders" in each case are the original natives. Is it farfetched to infer that Montesquieu intends to suggest the irony of love becoming an outcast in human life to which it is natural? But it is not necessary to push this point to see that something significantly new is here emerging. That lovers live in a world of their own has been standard fare for comedies, and the basic framework of tales of love. The difference in Montesquieu's treatment is that the aloneness of the lovers has a social definition and is as much a condition for their love as of it. (pp. 659-61)

The striking thing is that this view of love leads at one and the same time to careful attention to social reality, and to the most bitter rejection of that reality in the name of humanity. As a real human potentiality which exists in some form, however distorted, in every man, love, when used as a criterion of social organization, raises in the most immediate way the relationship between actuality and potentiality, between real and ideal. I do not maintain that this is completely worked out in Montesquieu. In fact, his realism in this work is very incomplete, even in contrast with Schiller. Rica and Usbek limit their examination of French society pretty much to the upper strata, and there is far less awareness of the total social picture (including the economic) than in Montesquieu's later theoretical work. Similarly, the seraglio is not really placed in its social context, except for a few sketchy remarks on the general spirit of Persian society. But the questions are asked. This is the crucial breakthrough.

Montesquieu's critique of the dehumanization of society eventuates in pessimism rather than radical reform. For him it is probably impossible ever to devise social institutions which will not take a significant toll of that full freedom and respect essential to a full humanity. All that can be done is to prevent further degradation. Perhaps some institutions are less harmful than others; it is clear, for example, that the terroristic rule of the seraglio is more destructive than the flighty freedom of French society—but it is equally clear that the previous experiences of men limit their capability of surviving in a different situation. This is the problem to which Montesquieu addresses himself in the *Spirit of the Laws.* Hence it is not surprising that the conception of love plays no further role in his work. The search for love has enabled him to define his basic problem. Having discovered true love to be an accidental phenomenon on the margin of modern society, he abandons it as a tool of analysis or as a goal to be sought. To evaluate society by the criterion of love reveals too much. More relative criteria are needed to discern the possible. (p. 661)

David Kettler, "Research Notes: Montesquieu on Love, Notes on 'The Persian Letters'," in The American Political Science Review, *Vol. LVIII, No. 3, September, 1964, pp. 658-61.*

J. ROBERT LOY (essay date 1968)

[*An American educator and critic, Loy specializes in French literature of the eighteenth and twentieth centuries. In the following excerpt, he comments on Montesquieu's importance to both social science and literature.*]

Montesquieu wrote, when all is said, three books; he was not prolific in the age of Voltaire, Rousseau, and Diderot. Yet his name elicits and should elicit some reaction from every commonly cultured Occidental.

The Persian Letters stands as a literary landmark and influences thinking about the novel for a good part of the century. It can be read with pleasure today, but the book scarcely coincides with the modern reader's notion of the novel. The study on the Romans [*Considerations on the Causes of the Grandeur and Decadence of the Romans*] filled an important need in Montesquieu's intellectual formation and provided a pleasant compendium of Roman history for his contemporaries. But it has been superseded many times over by more methodical histories and by better informed studies that have taken advantage of continuing research. The modern student of history would turn to it only after having finished Gibbon and that feat, in itself, remains doubtful. The great work on the laws [*The Spirit of Laws*] is again and most indubitably a landmark, but at the risk of attack for cynicism, it may be doubted that more than a handful of social scientists in any given academic institution have read it in its entirety. All of this is not to belittle the reputation of a great man. But let us try to be honest in our estimate of why greatness still attaches to his name.

It will seem ungracious, at the very least, to voice here a regret, a regret as unreasonable as the criticisms levied against Montesquieu by his contemporaries for not having written *The Spirit* as they would have done. The regret is simply that Montesquieu spent twenty years on his great work and then stopped writing, never returning to the rich vein in him so clearly demonstrated by the *Persian Letters*. Or, to put it in another fashion, the literary man cannot but regret that Montesquieu's faltering vision saw his future solely in scholarship and not in the novel. For had he worked in that direction (discounting the *Temple of Gnidus,* which even he knew was a momentary detour), he would no doubt have added important titles to a century already rich with *La Nouvelle Héloise, Candide,* and *Le Neveu de Rameau,* to mention the fictional achievements of only the *philosophes.* But such regret is surely wrong-headed and perhaps, on the contrary, we should be grateful that the man who wrote the *Spirit* was the same man who *might have written* a great novel—and that for a very good reason. The reader who has digested *The Spirit* has lived a rare intellectual experience. He has just as surely missed much if he has not looked into the travel-notes and the *Pensées,* that heteroclite collection of aphorisms, character sketches, and intimate reflection. They are eminently human and that is the very good reason one must be grateful that their author wrote *The Spirit.* Dry as dust as much of *The Spirit* material might have been, Montesquieu's personality still comes through.

[This] very fact has been and continues to be one of the chief sources of criticism of his work. . . . It must be seen, rather, it seems to me, as a particular reason for the lasting quality of the *Spirit.* For Montesquieu never forgot for one moment that what he was really talking about was a man—men living together to be sure, but fundamentally a man. However important it has since become that social scientists should emulate the objectivity of their confrères in the natural sciences, this single facet, the humanity of Montesquieu, is still the first to catch the eye of the modern reader. For him, the science of society was predicated upon the knowledge and comprehension of the human being, and who says comprehension says sympathy. If Montaigne, in that eminently French way of uncomplicated self-analysis, could hope to know himself, Montesquieu would

seem to progress along the same road by proposing to extrapolate social self from a multitude of historical selves. Ste.-Beuve, that usually penetrating and sagacious judge of men, writers, and thinkers, somehow underestimates Montesquieu's essential honesty and credits him with the illusion that his eighteenth-century colleagues had criticized him for. "I have stated the radical defect that I believe is in Montesquieu's statesmanship; he puts the average of humanity, considered in its natural data, rather higher than it is" [see excerpt dated 1852]. If Montesquieu put that humanity higher, he did so advisedly. How blind the extraordinary vision of Ste.-Beuve can become on occasion is even more apparent in the following estimate of Montesquieu as "one of those gods who are benefactors of humanity without human tenderness."

Montesquieu's historical method was, of course, not eventually aimed at presenting a series of psychological sketches, however much the individual human being remained his measure. He hoped, like many other historians of his day, to use the past in order to enlighten the future. That was normal and natural and one of the accepted uses of history. But Montesquieu uses history in two other ways that characterize his peculiar method immediately. If the study of historical civilizations gave him valuable information on various systems of social living and, hence, a realization of the basic relativity obtaining in human affairs, he nonetheless continued to impose on that experience the conviction that there could be an absolute discerned in the relative. However varied in detail, each historical society had to disclose eventually a common Reason at work. He was to be harshly criticized for such thinking, which seemed to most of his readers to confuse the inductive with the deductive. . . . Yet he persisted in supposing that diversity itself continued to reveal a natural reason behind all social organization. Secondly, once he had, as he puts it, found his principles, he is careful not to fix them adamantly for all time. For his vision of the historical process is a dynamic one, conscious of change, development, and the on-going process. "Its function," remarks Fletcher, "is not historical but prophetic." Thus, even his theory of check and balance and the separation of powers could never have been stated in the static formalization of a De Lolme. Nor, with all of his advised hope for human progress as more and more could be known of the spirit behind social organization, could he have accepted Auguste Comte's later conviction that progress was a one-way street; he had been, since the Troglodytes, too aware of ever-imminent regression. Indeed he had warned his prize society, the English, of such dangers in terms which became meaningful to most late eighteenth-century English thinkers. Thus Bentham, who dismisses Montesquieu all too easily because he did not show that legislation was a simple matter (i.e., so long as it set its sights irrevocably on utilitarianism) might, posthumously and in the spirit world, have been dismissed by Montesquieu, who was ever conscious of the difficulty of balancing all possible determinants to arrive at just legislation. Montesquieu would first have wanted to know "useful for whom?" and thereby he returns us to one of the basic intentions of his twenty-year work. "Several people," he writes in his notes, "have examined which is better: monarchy, aristocracy or the popular state. But, as there are an infinity of kinds of monarchy, aristocracy and popular state, the question thus stated is so vague that one would have to possess very little logic to want to treat it."

The Reason behind diversity and relativity, the natural law behind the positive, Montesquieu had sought to clarify in those first concentrated pages (the metaphysical pages, as his adverse critics will have it). Years of meditation go into that famous definition—general enough to be universal, specific enough to accommodate the diversity of positive laws: laws are relationships deriving from the nature of things. Curiously, Montesquieu does not insist much in his work on the applicability of that definition to so-called laws of science: gases, volumes, planetary movement, etc. And yet he must have seen his definition as applicable to both human law and scientific law, both somehow emerging from an overriding natural law. Here is where Goldsmith [see excerpt dated 1774] and others so easily see the poet in Montesquieu: given other times and other concerns, Montesquieu's *Spirit* might have become *De Rerum Natura* or *La Divina Commedia*. (pp. 157-60)

[Were] Montesquieu to write his study today, he would no doubt suffer the disdain of his colleagues in many disciplines who would not choose to bite off so much. All that is very well and understandable in a world that has made specialization a necessity, or attempted to convince us that it is a necessity. Yet Montesquieu, feeling his way where none had gone before in precisely his tracks, insisted upon treating of the spirit behind the law, thus involving himself in history, philosophy, psychology, anthropology, geography, economics, linguistics, sociology, political science, demography, etc. and all the resultant branches of intermarriage like economic geography, sociology of knowledge, linguistic anthropology, and the like. Foolish (from the modern point of view) he no doubt was, but then, very brave, too. . . . (p. 161)

It will appear to some sophomoric to reduce the reasons for Montesquieu's great contribution to Western thought to just two; let it appear so. If we leave aside the details (all of them instructive), Montesquieu is telling us that (1) laws all spring from the nature of things, no matter how far removed therefrom some specific laws may appear and (2) that, although there is somewhere, and ill-understood as yet, a common spirit of all law, the specific laws, of various kinds and nature, are all relative rather than absolute, and relative to so many determinants that our work of clarification, even in the twentieth century, has only begun. Thus, we are wrong to suppose that the English constitution was the end point of Montesquieu's search. It just happened that, at that time, the English constitution with its separation of powers seemed to have achieved the greatest share of liberty. It is liberty that is important and the key to his long studies, not the British constitution. . . . A constitution for Montesquieu, then, is not *per se* sacrosanct but rather represents the most developed form of safeguard against the ever-threatening cycle of the Troglodytes. Clearly, for Montesquieu, the best constitution was that one which allowed for change within its existing form. For supposing that the principle did not change, the constitution would continue to reflect that principle through numerous specific and temporary interpretations of the document. If the principle were to change (political virtue in the case of the United States) then the constitution would be less than worthless, and would lead to situations analogous to those in Roman history where the republic labored in vain to tie old laws (and customs) to decadent principle. A constitution, then, is not sacred, but it should be durable while allowing for interpretation; the only other alternative is anarchy. Better continual change that can be read into the existing constitution than violent revolution and chaos.

Whether future social scientists will continue to claim Montesquieu as colleague or precursor remains to be seen. That his broad venture strikes some of them as superficial can be no surprise, given the broadened field of knowledge in those sci-ences. . . . But the humanist must beg leave to essay the conclusion that Montesquieu was one of the last scientists of society to cling to his conviction during every waking hour that the all was in the all and that the spirit behind the law, as behind every social discipline, was by definition human. The science of society was to Montesquieu the science of man, in all his varied aspects and only the all could keep in communication with the many-faceted complications of human life—physical and mental. He would have been the first to deplore the necessity for specialization; he would have been the first to encourage a constant meeting point, man, for the specialists. (pp. 162-64)

That is why, weary to the bone and almost completely blind toward the end, his "soul" continued "to be seized by everything." That is why on many scores, he passes in his enthusiasm to moments when his critical sense wavers; that is why a good part of the details of his insistence on physical and climatic determinants has been discounted, although the basic idea has been further developed by many: Mme de Staël, Herder, Ratzel, Vidal de la Blache, Miss Churchill Simple, etc. That is why our hearts fill with a kind of pride in another human mind that was seized with the basic injustice of slavery and cognizant of the abuses of colonialism, back there in the eighteenth century when normal souls did not allow themselves to be aroused by such long established institutions; institutions, let Montesquieu continue to remind us, are not necessarily the nature of things.

Finally, that is why we are privileged and delighted to have record of some of the things that seized Montesquieu's soul yet never quite belonged in *The Spirit*. Even when he is wrong, he is delightful. . . . (pp. 164-65)

> *J. Robert Loy, in his* Montesquieu, *Twayne Publishers, Inc., 1968, 191 p.*

ARAM VARTANIAN   (essay date 1969)

[*Vartanian is an American educator and critic of eighteenth-century French literature. In the following excerpt, he parallels the erotic element of* Persian Letters *with its political message.*]

While almost any fantasied thought may be made to yield a hidden erotic meaning, the reverse of such a procedure is admittedly unfamiliar. Yet there is no reason why a literally erotic fiction, especially in an artistic context, should not on occasion symbolize a veiled *non-erotic* content—to the point even of prefiguring some abstract idea with which its author might be philosophically obsessed. A study of the *Lettres persanes* from such a perspective will show that the real motive behind Montesquieu's inclusion of the *roman du sérail* ["fiction of the seraglio"] in its pages was the clarification that it brought, by analogy, to certain political truths which, for him, were essential. The place of the novelistic material in the structure of the work indicates that, very likely, Montesquieu regarded it as the proper framework for the presentation of his philosophical criticism. About forty letters, or one fourth of the total number, concern the *roman de sérail,* and these, being concentrated mostly at the beginning and at the end, are distributed so as to suggest that they are the "introduction" and the "conclusion" of the *Lettres persanes* as a whole. Despite this, the tendency of many critics has long been to judge the harem intrigue in the *Lettres persanes* as mainly a frivolous or enticing *hors d'oeuvre,* concocted to heighten the book's appeal for the wide and mixed public whom Montesquieu wished to reach, but otherwise as not particularly deserving of "serious" interest. Such critics have often assumed, with all the unimaginativeness of a prejudice, that anything erotic in a work of intellectual significance must somehow be irrelevant, trivial, or, at best, only tastelessly decorative. This, however, would be to overlook the quite positive role played by erotic themes and elements in the development and expression of much "enlightened thought" in the French eighteenth century. The seraglio fiction of the *Lettres persanes,* whatever its piquancy, was not merely a sauce spread over the philosophical food offered by the author: it constituted the substance itself of that food. In the *Réflexions* which prefaced the 1754 edition of the *Lettres persanes,* Montesquieu stated that a "chaîne secrète" linked together the letters of the entire correspondence; but he did not say what this connecting thread was, nor how the underlying unity of the work was to be understood. The author's own vagueness on this important point has permitted, in recent years, several different opinions to be formed about the meaning of the Oriental fiction in the *Lettres persanes,* and about its relationship to the social satire and philosophical doctrines present in the major portion of the book. There seems to be agreement, at least, that the "chaîne secrète" ought to be sought in the Oriental fiction of the *Lettres persanes.* While I do not believe that a single thematic "chain" could neatly explain the work as a whole (which, by its very character, remains heterogeneous), the erotico-political parallelism in the *Lettres persanes* may be regarded as one aspect of its basic coherence.

The oft-cited episode of the Troglodytes has been considered as the key political lesson in the *Lettres persanes,* indicating Montesquieu's early and deep sympathy with liberalism. Actually, the story of Usbek's harem approaches the same lesson from the opposite side, complementing thereby the Troglodyte parable. While the latter shows the likely prosperity and well-being of a free society, the former, by an inverse logic, exposes the inner contradiction, fatal instability, and final ruin of despotism. For the seraglio is so obviously the symbolic miniature—the domestic analogue—of the socio-political structure of the Oriental state, that it would be hard to say how Montesquieu could better have imagined a fictional quintessence of the Persian despotism which, more broadly, is itself the subject behind the *roman du sérail.* In the privacy of the harem, as in its public counterpart, the central fact is the complete subordination of the will and convenience of everyone to the pleasure and whim of a single master. Moreover, such a system of universal self-denial, running counter to the natural egoism of human beings, can be maintained only by means of an equally universal system of police constraints, such as the confinement and discipline of the seraglio, the incessant spying of the eunuchs, and a pervasive atmosphere of terror. All this—and a good deal more that may easily be surmised—amounts, of course, to a classic image of the despotic type of government which Montesquieu was to describe in the *Esprit des lois* as functioning by its fundamental use of the "principe de la crainte" ["principle of fear"].

In a sense, the seraglio analogy may be said to offer an even deeper insight into the workings of despotism than will later be apparent in the *Esprit des lois.* For it indicates that something more ingenious and perverse than simple fear is required to support so "unnatural" an order as the subjugation of all by one. This something is the special role attributed to the corps of eunuchs, who make up in effect the administrative apparatus—the civil service—without whose mediating position between Usbek and his wives, that is, between the ruler and the people, the fragile balance of the despotic state could not be

long preserved. We shall see presently what is, in relation to the mechanics of such a government, the meaning of the particular sexual character of its faithful eunuchs. But even their extraordinary zeal as agents of oppression would be insufficient to keep peace in the seraglio, if still another method of asserting control were not employed. This is the steady stream of propaganda, which tediously assures Usbek's wives that their condition is in their own best interest; that they are bound by the tenderest and purest of passions to their lord and master; and that all the seemingly cruel or frustrating features of the seraglio-*régime* are merely measures to make their happiness complete and permanent. . . . The dependence of the harem on a methodical falsification of reality—as seen no less in the tissue of propagandist deception than in the psychophysical anomaly of the eunuch himself—might suggest already that Montesquieu, in resorting as a novelist to a symbolic representation of despotism, perceived better the deviousness of thought and the perversion of feeling that were peculiar to it, than he succeeded in doing later by studying the same phenomena with the analytical intelligence of the political scientist.

Of more specific interest, however, is the prevalence of the erotic element in the parallelism evident between the organization of the *sérail* and that of the *état despotique* ["despotic state"]. The *sérail* represents, unlike monogamous marriage, an effort totally to eroticize life. In the *Lettres persanes,* it is this commanding erotic aim that not only defines the basic political struggle of the harem, but expresses what, in that struggle, is or is not ultimately in harmony with Nature, that is, with human realities. Against the "unnaturalness" and "inhumanity" of despotic rule, sexuality thus becomes the guarantor of all those sound instincts which, *malgré tout* ["after all"], can neither be hoodwinked, sidetracked, intimidated, nor suppressed by the apparatus of lies and terror. Like an *a priori* and immutable law, its natural "clairvoyance" enables Usbek's wives to see through and to defy the web of political mystification and subjection in which they are caught. It is their dissatisfaction as *women,* more than anything else, that "enlightens" them, because the grand illusion on which the seraglio is founded—an illusion that will be thoroughly dispelled by the course of events—is the presumed passiveness of feminine sexuality, the *pudeur vertueuse* ["virtuous modesty"] about which Usbek likes so fatuously to prate. The latter has been away from Ispahan only a short time, when he receives from Fatmé, one of his wives, a letter of bitter complaint, which corrects any mistaken notion he might still wish to harbor about the sexual feelings of women. . . . The same idea, namely, that a similarity of erotic desire implies fundamentally the same rights for both sexes, finds expression also in the interpolated tale of Ibrahim's wife, who is rewarded with a seraglio *à l'inverse* in the Moslem paradise; in the "Histoire d'Aphéridon et d'Astarté," where a woman, whom fate has made the wife of a eunuch, abjures her marriage and flees with the person she loves; and in the anecdote about the Hindu woman who refuses to commit suttee, on learning that she will only be reunited in the after-life with her old and impotent husband. All these digressive episodes in the *Lettres persanes,* intended obviously to throw further light on the *roman du sérail,* serve to show that love in a woman is not an attitude of passive self-denial, but, as for the man, an egotistical "volonté de jouir" ["will to enjoy"]; and that the ideal (preached by men) of a "pure and virtuous love," which is expected to sacrifice sexual self-assertion to social convenience and order, is in reality only a trap leading to her enslavement.

The touchstone of eroticism thus lays bare the preposterous and unviable character of a government dedicated to the proposition of general non-enjoyment. The erotic factor in the *Lettres persanes* comes to express, by the same token, both the individual will to freedom and the need, in a well-run society, to identify as nearly as possible the interests of the state with the gratification of each of its members. When this maxim is thoroughly violated by those in power, the infallibility (as it were) of the sexual instinct becomes the source of a revolutionary energy that threatens to overthrow the entire system. Usbek's wives are all—in ways that each expresses with a distinct tonality in her letters of reproach to him—potential subverters of the seraglio-state; they are all secretly rebellious in the least ambivalent sense possible, that is, in their flesh and blood. It is this crucial truth that bursts forth and finds its consummation in the final revolt and vengeance of Roxane. Her frank declaration of independence—which is at once erotic and political in meaning—may be read as the author's concluding comment on the natural human basis of a liberal polity, and indeed as the conclusion to the work in general. . . . With the downfall of Usbek's *despotisme domestique* ["domestic despotism"], the dynamics of sexuality illustrate a political truth that Montesquieu was to affirm in the famous dictum of the *Esprit des lois:* "Le principe du gouvernement despotique se corrompt sans cesse, parce qu'il est corrompu par sa nature" ["The principle of the despotic government corrupts itself ceaselessly, because it is corrupt by nature"]. The *roman de sérail* was, more than twenty-five years earlier, the eroticized dramatization of this essential idea. (pp. 23-7)

The eunuch, who literally no less than figuratively is the negation of sexuality, has an unusually large place in the *Lettres persanes,* his role being in fact motivated by its whole scheme of erotico-political parallelism. To assure the operation of a system as unnatural and inhuman as the seraglio-state, it is necessary to depend on a no less "denatured" and "de-humanized" group of civil servants. . . . We shall suggest that Montesquieu's almost obsessive interest in the eunuch-type was owing to the fact that the latter summed up perfectly his attitudes of revulsion and condemnation towards despotism itself. The "erotic alienation" of the eunuch, with all its psychic and social implications, became for him the profoundly true symbol of the degradation and perversity of despotic power.

It is evident that a system of government demanding the surrender of the self-interest of all to that of one person could not be upheld by the effective power of the latter, since no single person could be that powerful. An intermediary group is needed— a "party bureaucracy"—ready to execute promptly the dictates of the despot, and, what is no less important, able to remain absolutely loyal, blindly obedient to him in everything. The eunuch-administrator of the seraglio-state, who conforms exactly to these requirements, has in fact, by the surrender of what (next to life itself) is most precious to him, surrendered his human identity to another; for the existential meaning of the eunuch is that of one "cut off," not only anatomically speaking, but cut off from Nature, from humanity, and from himself. This extremely high price paid by the eunuch is, however, part of a bargain; for in alienating his will to that of his master, he expects to be a master in his own turn and to share in the despot's exercise of power. In the peculiar depersonalization of the eunuch, Montesquieu has expressed the basic transaction—the terms of the *pacte despotique* ["despotic pact"]—on which such a political system must be established. The eunuch is central to the *Lettres persanes* because he is the *moyen d'être* ["means of existence"] of despotism.

Thanks to the pact, the eunuch does indeed become a little despot. But his power is intrinsically meaningless; for the en-

joyment of power in the seraglio-state can have only one valid meaning—that of sexual pleasure. The eunuch has made a senseless bargain. He has sold his soul . . . to his master, and received in return only the semblance of power, but none of its substance. He is in fact quite powerless—literally *impuissant* ["impotent"]—to share in any of the real gratifications of the despotic system that he must, ironically, serve to perpetuate. If Usbek's wives are the unwilling victims of the harem, the eunuchs, caught in a Tantalus-like situation, are its willing dupes. For while they have given up, irreversibly, all claim to erotic freedom, they have not lost all desire for such freedom. Nature cannot be entirely silenced even when it is mutilated. Paradoxically, it is the vestige of the erotic instinct in the eunuch that points up the fraudulence and absurdity of the *pacte despotique.* . . . The eunuch is thus witness to the sterile duplicity of despotism; his emasculation is depicted by Montesquieu as the horrible sign—the shameful emblem—of the loss risked by all those who imagine that they can enter into a mutually profitable collaboration with despotic power. For in the last analysis the eunuch, a non-person, is only an object, allowed to exist as an expendable instrument of the despot's will. . . . To the extent that the eunuch has come to symbolize, in the *Lettres persanes,* the very "soul" of the soulless system to which he is indispensable, the work may be said to elaborate a particularly caustic satire on despotism itself, which in the reader's mind becomes inseparable from the emotional complex of disgust, contempt, horror, and derision that he reserves for its unique representatives.

But what about the despot himself, for whose sole benefit, presumably, the harem-state exists? It is clear enough that Usbek, despite his position of unchecked power, is portrayed by Montesquieu in a posture of increasing vulnerability and distress as the story unfolds. Once removed from the *sérail d'Ispahan,* his suspicions and insecurity are in proportion to what he suspects, privately, to be the resentment and disloyalty of his wives. The *harem,* like any despotic government, has no inner principle of stability or cohesion; it is, as Usbek well realizes, a fragile structure that can be held together only by carefully applied pressures from without, which require the despot's presence. Usbek's sufferings during his absence from Persia are not the sufferings of love, nor even of desire; he is tormented by the untenability of his position, which the optic of time and distance magnify and threaten to expose painfully for what it is. . . . For the despot shares, in a decisive sense, the impotence of his eunuchs. Since he is unable to satisfy *all* his wives, he is unable to satisfy any of them and cannot elude the consequences of such a failure. This dilemma is made plain in Letter CXIV, which argues that the practice of a plurality of wives, far from attesting the potency of the head of the harem, has the opposite effect of rendering him in fact "powerless," the victim of his own ascendancy. . . . The very character of the seraglio-government makes it impossible for the "master" ever to master the situation. It is, patently, the erotic context into which the contradictions of despotic power have been translated in the *Lettres persanes* that permits Montesquieu to show, as against its seeming absoluteness, the inward fragility of that power. When wheedling propaganda fails to restore order to the harem, Usbek reverts to threats of dire punishment and works himself by stages into a fit of tyrannical rage. We are impressed, however, less by the magnitude of the terror that he unleashes, than by his inability to exert any real control over events in Ispahan. As the seraglio-state collapses under the stress of its inner deficiencies, demonstrating in the process the self-destructiveness of its *principe,* Usbek (who has meanwhile acquired, thanks to his travels abroad,

Montesquieu's library at Château La Brède.

some philosophical insight into the origin of his misfortunes) recognizes at last the truth about the ultimate failure of despotism—its failure, that is, even for the despot. . . . In order to make Usbek's defeat and despair seem complete, Montesquieu refuses to him any obvious escape or consolation in his predicament; we are led to believe that his conduct in (of all places) Paris has been one of continence during the unlikely period of more than seven years! In spite of this, he cringes at the thought of resuming his former place at the head of the *sérail*. . . . Usbek's demoralization reaches its climax as he compares his fate, unfavorably, with that of his eunuchs: "Rebut indigne de la Nature humaine, esclaves vils dont le coeur a été fermé pour jamais à tous les sentiments de l'amour, vous ne gémiriez plus sur votre condition si vous connoissiez le malheur de la mienne" ["Vile outcast of human nature, base slaves whose hearts have been forever closed to all feelings of love, you would lament no more over your condition if you knew the unhappiness of my own"]. Such an anguished cry, within the framework of the novel's erotic symbolism, needs no comment: *C'est tout dire* ["I needn't say more"]. (pp. 27-31)

> Aram Vartanian, "Eroticism and Politics in the 'Lettres Persanes'," in The Romanic Review, Vol. LX, No. 1, February, 1969, pp. 23-33.

NEAL WOOD (lecture date 1969)

[*Wood is an American educator whose works include* Communism and British Intellectuals (1959). *In the following excerpt, he ex-* amines Montesquieu's theories of the necessity for social conflict in political systems.]

[Attention] should be given to the relationship between [Montesquieu's] concept of human nature and his theory of domestic conflict. It is not surprising that he should place the clash of interest and party strife at the center of his political considerations because his psychology gives primacy to the passions. They constitute the main motive force of the human machine, a point made clear by the *Pensées* and the unpublished essay on causes. "All the vices and the human virtues," Montesquieu contends, "are ordinarily the effect of a certain condition of the machine." The different constitution of the human mechanism produces the different force of the passions, which vary in kind and intensity from individual to individual. The combination of passions peculiar to each determines the whole of his life, accounting for the great variety of human behavior. With his well-known theories of climate and of manners, Montesquieu allows for regularities and uniformities in human behavior dependent upon psychology and physical and social environment. The ordering of a commonwealth must rest upon an understanding of the nature and the force of the passions, and of the cardinal fact that for each individual, preservation of self is the major motive in behavior. Montesquieu does not mean self-love in any narrow sense, for it may lead us to suicide or to benevolent actions out of sympathy for the predicament of others, the very source of all social action. Perhaps, because of his conception of the psyche as a crucible of energy-seeking release, Montesquieu condemns the life of ascetic withdrawal. The ideal life is one of vigor and productive activity. Passions must find outlets and be safely canalized by the intervention and interaction of laws and manners in order to invigorate and strengthen the social order.

The internal dissensions, largely responsible for the Roman citizens' liberties, cannot be viewed in isolation from the passions which had set those same citizens on the road to world conquest. Montesquieu develops his brief reference to the importance of conflict in [letter 136 of *Persian Letters*] beginning with the following opening remark in the eighth chapter of the [*Consideration on the Causes of the Greatness of Romans and Their Decline*]:

> While Rome conquered the world, a secret war was going on within its walls. Its fires were like those of volcanoes which burst forth whenever some matter comes along to increase their activity.

After citing the familiar example of the plebes and patricians, and referring to the government of England, he concludes that a free government is always "subject to agitation." In the following chapter he reasons that Rome's expansionism, not social dissension, was the main factor in her decline. Conflict was inevitable because citizen-soldiers, so courageous and vigorous in the defense of the city from external foes, could not completely transform their conduct into moderation in domestic matters. Boldness in war and timidity in peace are simply too much to ask of such a hardy race. Indeed, if a republic is characterized by internal tranquility, then we may be sure that the citizens have lost their liberty and vigor. Two kinds of harmony in a commonwealth must be distinguished. The first is that of the Romans: while the parts at one level are in opposition, at a higher level they cooperate for the common good. As do Aristotle and Polybius before him, Montesquieu employs the familiar analogy of musical harmony. However, he gives the musical allusion new content, because his concept of the common good entails the security and happiness of the citizens, the satisfaction of their desires instead of an absolute moral end. The second harmony is that which exists under an oriental despot, and which consists of an almost absolute quiet, the solitude of "dead bodies buried next to the other." At another level, however, analysis reveals a fundamental cleavage not only between ruler and ruled, the oppressor and the oppressed, but also between each individual, so atomized has despotic society become. Unlike a republic, dissension in a despotic state will prove disastrous for the regime; rather than working to reform or change a particular law, the dissenters will unseat the despot, creating a power vacuum to be filled by another despot.

Fourteen years afterwards in *The Spirit of the Laws*, Montesquieu turns from Rome to the analysis of conflict in England. In passing, he repeats his principle that a healthy democratic republic thrives on conflict, although aristocratic republics like ancient Sparta and modern Venice do not. Then in the nineteenth book he analyzes party conflict in England. The connection between this section and the comments on Roman dissension would seem self-evident, but few commentators specifically refer to it. (pp. 300-03)

By designating the parties as "court" and "country," instead of by the more traditional, but for the period less accurate "Tory" and "Whig," Montesquieu proves to be an acute observer of English political life. He begins by attempting to relate the nature of the English parties to the basic separation of governmental powers between the executive and the legislative, already explained in the eleventh book. Depending upon his particular interests, a citizen is free to indicate a preference for one of the two powers, and to align himself either with the monarch or the parliament. Passions are given free reign in England; two parties, the court and country, are in constant struggle. When one party becomes too strong support may shift to the other. English politics would seem to consist of a constant circulation of supporters from one party to another, according to the power relations of the moment. Individuals may be political friends and associates one day, and enemies the next, which means that although political friendships are enfeebled, extreme political hatreds are appreciably reduced. Both sovereign and subject are in a never-ending state of political insecurity. On one day the sovereign may have to award and share confidences with individuals and groups who were his opponents of yesterday. The political friends of an individual may at any time become his opponents. All of this produces a general uneasiness, but with the salutary consequence that each individual is extremely watchful of his own liberties. A domestic threat such as the violation of a fundamental law will rally support behind the legislative, while a danger from abroad will increase the strength of the court. In what is unquestionably an allusion to the Glorious Revolution, Montesquieu feels that when both a domestic threat and a foreign danger occur simultaneously a revolution may take place which would alter neither the constitution nor the form of government.

The discussion of English parties is of fundamental significance. Montesquieu has provided the first effort of a political theorist, crude as it may be, to analyze a party system and to relate it to the basic structure of government. Again, he tries to explain the moderation of English politics and the stability of English government by showing that the very party system itself performs an integrating role by the reduction of extreme forms of political behavior. And finally he holds that the continuous free play of the parties is the best guarantee of the Englishman's liberties. Politics becomes a function of individual passions as they are manifested in the great social arena of clashing interests. The frenetic movement of the party struggle keeps every citizen alert, prevents indolence and social stagnation, and enhances the strength and vitality of English society.

What we have here considered in the thought of . . . Montesquieu is, in fact, the emergence of a new concept of society. Paradoxically, it is a view of society as necessarily involving asocial as well as social elements, just as man was considered to be both an asocial and a social being. The social element is necessary for men to live together; the asocial element is crucial, however, if man is to become more than an unreflective automaton of habit and tradition, as Hegel put it somewhere, a clock wound up and left to run down. Civilization implies reform and the self-conscious reflection necessary for reform. Indeed, civilization entails perpetual conflict between the old and the new in a kind of dialectical process. When this process is lacking, civilization itself is absent. Men only lifted themselves out of the primeval slime to become more than stupid, unimaginative brutes, because some individuals stood in opposition to their fellows. Modern liberalism with all its defects, has at least labored valiantly to defend the principle of opposition and conflict, particularly in the realms of thought, speech, and association. Once the principle of questioning authority and commonly accepted ends and of opposition to the established is no longer cherished or recognized, the human spirit is stifled and perishes, and society in the sense of the civilized withers away. . . . The thinkers who perhaps contributed most to this perspective in early modern Europe are Machiavelli,

Sidney, and Montesquieu. Nor can the influential example of the English social and political experience be overlooked. If contemporary bureaucratic capitalism and communism are not to dehumanize and destroy men, more attention will have to be given to the nature of conflict and to the ways and means by which our common life can be enriched by conflict. (pp. 304-07)

Neal Wood, "The Value of Asocial Sociability: Contributions of Machiavelli, Sidney and Montesquieu," in Machiavelli and the Nature of Political Thought, edited by Martin Fleisher, Atheneum, 1972, pp. 282-307.

ROBERT F. O'REILLY (essay date 1973)

[O'Reilly is an American educator who studies French literature of the eighteenth and twentieth centuries. In the following excerpt, he investigates Montesquieu's views of women and of sexual equality.]

In the *Essai sur les causes qui peuvent affecter les esprits et les caractères* Montesquieu used scientific evidence as a basis for conclusions on sexual inequality in much the same manner as experiments with the sheep's tongue would lead to theories on climate and human nature in *L'Esprit des lois*. In both cases his final decisions reveal social myths rather than any clear knowledge of physiology. He suggested in the *Essai sur les causes* a fatalistic view of temperamental differences at puberty, vaguely reminiscent of Freud's definition of the feminine with passivity and the masculine with activity. . . . Noting that two flows occur at puberty, he compared the effect of the menses on female character with the influence of semen on male character. The passive receptivity of the female is juxtaposed to the activity of the male. Female anatomy by nature of the hollowness of the uterine cavity is conceived as possessing 'fibres plus molles, plus lâches, plus flexibles, plus délicates que les hommes' ["fibers more soft, more slack, more flexible, more delicate than men"]. Montesquieu's choice of vocabulary is, of course, a purely subjective description of femininity. The male 'liqueur,' on the other hand, contains an extraordinary activity which we can assume, though it is not specifically stated, bestows on the male those opposite qualities generally acknowledged to be masculine.

In view of the female's passive nature, Montesquieu could explain the broad range of character traits that he associated with an easily modifiable and changeable feminine constitution. He was imbued with the Christian concept of woman's dual nature. Sometimes he idealized her as a Beatrice-like character, a guiding inspiration, who could yield up the best in man. But most often he imagined her as an Eve-like figure, the eternal temptress of man, possessing an unsettled and violent disposition and threatening to destroy man's tranquility and happiness. Montesquieu used this latter idea of feminine temperament to explain and justify the treatment of women under various forms of patriarchal rule in republics, monarchies, and despotic governments.

In the *Lettres persanes* and in the *Pensées* Montesquieu had already formed a firm opinion of women. They were ridiculous, frivolous, and addlepated; their successes in society and at Court depended on physical charms, stubbornness and unreasonableness, and they were easily susceptible to vanity and passion.

In the *Lettres persanes* women are studied in various poses. In some instances they are abstract examples of the results of un-

natural restraints on human nature. Letters 4 and 147 mention lesbianism as an extreme to which Usbek's wives are driven to release frustrated sexual energies, and Roxane's suicide symbolizes the defiance of human nature in the face of repression. At another level Montesquieu portrayed the female's sexually promiscuous tendencies which he felt to be an inherent inclination of all women. In France where women enjoyed greater freedom and greater social mobility, feminine inconstancy was expressed regularly, though less obtrusively than in the orient where sexual drives were always turbulent though contained by the harem system and where infidelities were all the more blatant because of their infrequency (letter 55). Letters 3 and 7 indicate already Montesquieu's serious belief (to be developed in *L'Esprit des lois*) in the extraordinary lubricity of eastern women and in the necessity for their confinement. At still another level western ladies are satirized as vain and coquettish (letter 55), frivolous and ridiculous in their conversations and customs (letters 63 and 110), and changeable in their tastes and fashions (letter 99).

Between the writing of the *Lettres persanes* and the work on *L'Esprit des lois*, Montesquieu's notions concerning women seem to have been confirmed through his experiences with life at Court, Chantilly, Bellébat, and in the salon of mme de Lambert and during his participation in the great salons of the day, especially that of mme de Tencin. During this socially active period of his life, he wrote two insipidly stylized tales expressly for the delectation of women, *Le Temple de Gnide* and *Le Voyage à Paphos*. These stories celebrate the cults of love and physical beauty, the two subjects he felt women were eminently capable of understanding. The *Histoire véritable* or *Le Métempsychosiste* (c. 1731-1738) is another accurate barometer of Montesquieu's attitude towards women. Being a woman is portrayed as a humiliating and debilitating stage during the soul's transmigration from the world of animals to the world of men. . . . The same weaknesses of the *beau sexe* found in these stories, in the *Lettres persanes,* and in the *Pensées* are restated more succinctly and with greater conviction in *L'Esprit des lois*.

In *L'Esprit des lois* public morality is treated as a powerful social force. Montesquieu's concern for safeguarding a woman's 'pudeur naturelle' ["natural modesty"] was prompted in part by his opinion that the degree of female chastity was organically related to the type of government. . . . (pp. 146-49)

In considering republics where 'la pureté des moeurs est une partie de la vertu' ["moral purity is a part of the virtue"], Montesquieu had the historical examples of Greece and Rome where tribunals and magistrates had rigorously supervised and controlled the conduct of women. . . . Public prostitution is depicted as a threat to the guiding principle of virtue in a republic and is represented as symptomatic of the drift towards the sexually freer monarchy. . . . (pp. 149-50)

Montesquieu's recommendations that republican legislators institute laws regulating female conduct to preserve the purity of a republic was an invitation to the domestic enslavement of women. . . .

Montesquieu's restrictions on women in republics and despotic governments are separated only by the method. In despotic governments women are restrained by the practice of the harem since temperamental qualities threaten the absolutism and forced tranquillity which are among the aims of despots. . . . (p. 150)

Montesquieu had illustrated what happens in a poorly managed harem in the *Lettres persanes*. While the master is absent, discipline declines, wives acquire too much freedom, and the feminine personality explodes, disrupting the seraglio. *L'Esprit des lois* summarizes similar dangers posed by women unless their freedom is severely restricted. . . . (pp. 150-51)

It was only in monarchies that Montesquieu did not recommend strict controls over women. However, he surrendered nothing to the ladies by advocating greater freedom. Feminine nature could be profitably exploited to the advantage of men and of the state since woman's inherent vanity introduced a competitive situation, disastrous for republics and despotic governments but beneficial to the economy and principle of 'honneur' in a monarchy. . . . (p. 151)

The importance of Montesquieu's concept of human nature and especially of feminine nature has not been sufficiently emphasized as an important factor urging him to favour monarchy over despotic and republican governments. Monarchy provided the most realistic and most natural framework within which men could express their competitive and ambitious inclinations, where women could manifest with minimum restraint their intrinsic penchant for vanity, luxury, and intrigue, and where both sexes could contribute to the advancement of the state.

Because of his disparaging remarks on female character and his observations on her passive physical nature, it is not surprising that Montesquieu never hesitated to affirm the natural right of patriarchy. The Troglodyte episode in the *Lettres persanes* provides an early example of the patriarchal state. The powerful position of the male as father, legislator, and monarch is portrayed as the nucleus of the family structure which reflects a larger social complex (letters 11-14). . . . A comparison of fathers with the creator of the universe gives a rather imposing sanction to male dominance in the family and in the state. . . . (pp. 151-52)

Such high praise for patriarchy resulted in a predictably low opinion of matriarchy. Montesquieu had a knowledge of historical matriarchal societies as early as the *Lettres persanes* where the cults of Isis in Egypt and that of Semiramis in Babylonia are mentioned (letter 38). He disapproved of such female oriented societies because he felt they ran contrary to nature. They are depicted as having encouraged harmful incestuous relationships, but basically they are criticized by the circular argument that they are not patriarchies.

The *Pensées* and *L'Esprit des lois* support the idea that the male receives his first mandate to rule because of his superior physical strength. In the *Pensées* patriarchal power is an obligation which the stronger parent has of protecting his young. . . . *L'Esprit des lois* stresses, also, the father's duty to provide nourishment for his children. . . . (pp. 152-53)

Montesquieu's questionable natural laws were partly contingent on his assumption that the historical practice of maintaining patriarchy through marriage was correct and proper. . . . In a restatement of his ideas on patriarchy in *L'Esprit des lois* Montesquieu indicates some measure of sexual equality at the animal level, an idea which would appear to dispute the male's absolute right to rule through superior strength. . . . However, the equality of animals in nature does not obtain for human beings in society. . . . Montesquieu offers no satisfactory justification why the male rather than the female should govern with nature's blessing. The true bias of his perspective is revealed when the discussion is transferred to a social context. Ignoring the implications of equality and freedom in the natural state, Montesquieu accepts unflinchingly the bondage that society and its man-made laws have established for women in

favour of arbitrary laws of marriage, the family, and the patriarchy. . . . (pp. 153-54)

In *L'Esprit des lois* Montesquieu's theory of climate dovetails readily with his conception of woman's physical and psychological inferiority. This particular drift of the climate theory was already implicit in the *Lettres persanes,* where letters 20 and 26 portrayed the harem as a necessary refuge for the weaknesses of oriental women, and attempted to rationalize the confinement of women through the traditional argument of the inherent frailness of females. Montesquieu's thoughts on the turbulent passions of oriental women had been conditioned especially through his reading of Chardin's *Voyages en Perse.* Thus the infidelities and revolt of Usbek's wives should be understood as a natural expression of oriental temperament as well as the protest of freedom-seeking individuals.

Despite a general condemnation of despotic government and despite a censure of polygamy as harmful to the interests of both sexes, Montesquieu regarded despotism as a reasonable phenomenon with a natural basis. Despotism and 'esclavage domestique' ["domestic slavery"] were the logical results of the effects of climate on individuals and of the necessity of confining women. Montesquieu justified polygamous practices through his observations that women in warm climates often reach puberty sooner, marry earlier, and burn out faster than women in cold climates, whose charms are more enduring and therefore more satisfying for one husband over a longer period of time. His ideal harem was intended to preserve morality, to re-establish a semblance of family unity, and above all to modify the effects of climate in favour of what he felt was the higher natural law of virtue and chastity.

Even though he shows an apparent impatience with those who examine the origins of society, Montesquieu felt the need, also, to speak out in the *Lettres persanes,* in the *Pensées,* and in *L'Esprit des lois* on the condition of the sexes in the state of nature. His theoretical position of the independence of women remained consistent with his attitude on the natural equality of all men and his objection to slavery of any sort. He was steadfast in the belief that the male's natural authority extended only to his offspring and that women ought to be exempted from male domination. (pp. 154-56)

Montesquieu was solidly fixed in a traditional belief in male superiority. Almost unwittingly he sought a natural basis for patriarchal prerogatives despite his best intentions of maintaining a fundamental freedom for women. His masculine prejudices overwhelmed the dictates of his reason. Hypotheses on natural equality remained timid, tentative, and unconvincing by comparison with his strong conviction that nature had determined woman's inferiority and subservience through her anatomy, beauty, and emotions. It is difficult, if not impossible, to see how Montesquieu's claims for the social equality and independence of women could ever be reconciled with his position of the preeminence of male dominated societies. Montesquieu seemed aware of this very problem when he implied that women in monarchies achieved only a relative approximation of freedom . . . as contrasted to women under despotic governments. As the natural state yields to the social, Montesquieu's attitude on woman's rightful role in the family and in the State becomes increasingly problematic since the seeds of patriarchal rule and its inevitable inequities are already inherent in the male's mandate to govern his children in nature. (p. 156)

Robert F. O'Reilly, "Montesquieu: Anti-Feminist,"
in Studies on Voltaire and the Eighteenth Century,
Vol. 102, 1973, pp. 143-56.

THOMAS L. PANGLE (essay date 1973)

[*In the following excerpt, Pangle examines Montesquieu's treatment of religion in* The Spirit of Laws.]

Religion in general, and the Christian religion in particular, advances an authoritative claim to give guidance in all spheres of human life. Anyone who reflects in a comprehensive way about politics and who gives any credence to this claim must accord to religion a paramount place in his reflections. Montesquieu shows at the very outset, by the place of the word "religion" in the full title of *The Spirit of the Laws,* that he does not accord it this paramount place. He indicates that the relation of the laws to religion will be treated only after several other important relations have been treated. . . . Nevertheless, we might have gathered from the title that religion would occupy a place of considerable importance, coming prior to commerce and other topics.

In fact the relation of the laws to religion is the last particular relationship discussed. Montesquieu turns to a thematic discussion of religion only after he has presented the bulk of his teaching; in the twenty-three preceding books where that presentation has been made, religion has played a very minor role. These observations suggest that for Montesquieu religion does not contribute substantially to an understanding of what good political life requires. They might even suggest that, except in the virtuous republic and in despotism, religion is of little practical use. It would then seem that religion must be treated at some length only because "belief" stands as a massive political fact which we cannot ignore but which cannot much help us: "The prejudices of superstition are superior to all other prejudices, and its reasons to all other reasons. . . . In the case of what Montesquieu calls "today's" Christian religion . . . the fact of widespread belief in this religion's particular "prejudices" poses a considerable obstacle to sound politics and economics.

Montesquieu's presentation of the relation of the laws to religion is divided into two books. In the first his intention is to show which *dogmas* are more advantageous; in the second, he discusses what are the best arrangements of religious *institutions* within a state. The teaching of the second book is largely a consequence of the first.

The manner in which Montesquieu introduces his reflections on the advantages and disadvantages of the various religious beliefs and practices confirms our impression that religion makes no contribution to political theory. Montesquieu says that in this work he will not discuss theology. Although he is aware that "there may be things which would not be entirely true except in a human manner of thinking," he has not "considered them in their relation to more sublime truths." The likely possibility of a contradiction between rational and revealed political truth is unimportant. Religion is to be judged by standards derived from "human thought" and "the happiness in this life.". . . (pp. 249-51)

This posture might well seem to imply a "ceding of the interests of true religion to the interests of politics." Anticipating or drawing attention to this difficulty, Montesquieu denies such a consequence. But he can make this denial only by implicitly contradicting himself and denying the possibility he mentioned

previously of a divergence between human and "sublime" truth. His assertion that the political principles following from Christian teaching are identical with the principles of rational political science is supported only by the argument that since Christianity wants men "to love one another," or to be charitable, it must "without a doubt" also want the best laws among men. The uncharacteristic rhetorical phrase "without a doubt" would not be needed were the demonstration truly indubitable; Montesquieu's argument, of course, simply begs the question of whether Christianity does not call for a sacrifice of some "happiness in this life" for the sake of "felicities of the other life." Montesquieu shows by his contradiction and by his inept argument that despite his explicit claim to the contrary he does in fact "cede the interests of the true religion to the interests of politics." What *is* true, however, is Montesquieu's claim that he wishes to "unite" the two interests. In these two books on religion, in contrast to the preceding books, Montesquieu does no more than allude to the threats Christianity poses to propagation and commercialism; having already pointed to these threats earlier, his policy here is one of reinterpreting Christianity so as to make it harmless. Montesquieu proceeds to show what are acceptable or beneficial religious dogmas from a purely political point of view and then assumes that Christianity holds those dogmas and no others. By this he seems to show through example what should be the policy of a legislator in a Christian country who wishes to follow his teaching.

After his introductory chapter, Montesquieu enters the subject matter by piously defending all religion against the famous, or notorious, argument of Pierre Bayle. Bayle was the first political philosopher who openly advocated the possibility and desirability of an atheistic society. By defending religion, Montesquieu lends respectability to his own position. At the same time, and more important, he seems to show that the inference we were led to by his earlier silence about religion is wrong: for Montesquieu religion almost always serves a beneficial political function. What Montesquieu emphasizes most, however, is the advantage of religion in principalities where it can check the power of the supreme ruler. . . . One would have to say that Montesquieu is at least less emphatic about the value of religion in well-balanced political systems. And he does admit that "religion is sometimes abused"; he is therefore unwilling to take on himself the task of proving that every man and every people should have religion. . . . We are at this point led to wonder whether no religion may not be preferable to a bad religion among certain peoples, especially well-governed peoples. . . . It becomes important, then, to know what constitutes bad religion, or an "abuse" of religion. And after having seen Montesquieu's defense of religion in general, we expect him to show us next the relative merits of various religions, starting from the best or most advantageous as a standard.

In the next chapters he does indeed turn from a discussion of all religions, including idolatrous ones, to a praise of Christianity. But this praise is at first rather weak. Christianity is praised only as preferable to the modern alternative, Islam, and especially because of its restraining effect in despotic regions. Christianity moderates absolute rule better than Islam because of the "softness" of its teachings. . . . (pp. 251-53)

We are thus kept in suspense as to whether Christianity is an advantageous religion in all regimes. . . . Montesquieu finally answers our doubts, praising highly the contribution Christianity makes to good citizenship. His praise is framed as an answer to another impious attack by Bayle. Again his role as defender of the faith gives him respectability; but at the same time his introduction of the objection of Bayle, "this great man," serves to introduce serious doubts about the political soundness of Christianity. His method of answering these doubts shows his essential agreement with them. In order to refute Bayle, Montesquieu shows himself compelled to radically reinterpret the traditional distinction between the "laws" of the Christian religion and its "counsels." The laws, which alone are absolutely binding, include everything conducive to good citizenship, and nothing more. Everything pertaining to "perfection," to the other world, to "the heart," everything which cannot be applied to "the universality of men," must cease to be considered a "law" and be relegated to the status of a "counsel" which is by no means absolutely binding. . . . Thus understood, Christianity is advantageous and forms the standard for judging the political advantage of all other religions.

The chapter praising and redefining "Christianity" is followed by a chapter praising a "false" pagan religion because its precepts were devoted to the "laws of morality" (by which Montesquieu here seems to mean the principles of reciprocal justice necessary for any society). Montesquieu follows this with a brief chapter implicitly praising a Jewish sect on similar grounds; finally, he turns to a praise of the pagan Stoics (including the apostate Julian) and a condemnation of the contemplative life. It becomes clear that what constitutes a good religion is merely its enforcement of the rules necessary for maintaining a social bond within a regime, and no more. . . . This understanding of religion implies that insofar as the laws and customs of a people are politically sound, religion should simply reinforce adherence to them; where the political institutions are defective, the ruler should emphasize those elements of the religious prescriptions which can remedy the defects; where religion itself promotes antisocial behavior, the laws must try, without contradicting the religious teachings, to substitute motives for useful behavior. . . . In addition, religion, as an institution of "the legislator," should, like all other political institutions, conform to the physical environment. . . . (pp. 253-55)

In his praise of non-Christian religions, Montesquieu makes no more than vague allusions to their specific doctrines about divinity. Two of them deny any after-life (the religion of the Essenes and of the Stoics); the third (that of Pegu), which seems to have instilled as much "softness and compassion" as Christianity, was extremely undogmatic and tolerant. Montesquieu seems by these examples to teach that the less doctrine about divinity the better. In the best case, religion will deemphasize all but moral-political precepts. In later chapters Montesquieu discusses how various transcendent or spiritual doctrines may be interpreted so as to bring them into harmony with the needs of men, who are "made to conserve themselves . . . and to do all the activities of society." The general principle governing these chapters is that "it is less the truth or falsity of a dogma which renders it useful or pernicious to men in the civil state than the use or abuse one makes of it." (p. 255)

Montesquieu thus indicates the lines along which Christianity is to be reinterpreted in order to make it harmonize with the needs of the commercial republic. Like Locke, Montesquieu promotes a new understanding of the "reasonableness of Christianity." Nothing reveals more clearly Montesquieu's refusal simply to bow to the "general spirit of a nation" than his opposition to the religion so deeply entrenched in the manners, morals, customs, and traditions of every European nation.

The reasons for Montesquieu's policy of "uniting" politics and religion rather than opposing religion openly as Bayle had done include more than a concern for his own safety and the respectability of his work. In the next book, when discussing the reasons for tolerance of religion by government authority, Montesquieu takes up thematically the question of how best to "change religion." He argues at first that it is bad to change or destroy the dominant religion because such a radical change in the way of life will unsettle men's opinions about everything and create the threat of revolutionary upheaval. But in the next chapter he implies that this prudential prohibition applies only to changes carried out swiftly and through force or violence. The proper way to change religion is by tempting men. . . . Christianity will be overcome by making men "forget" everything which is at a tension with securing "the commodities of life." All that is required on the part of "political writers" like Montesquieu is to show the way to an understanding of Christianity which is not in conflict with devotion to commerce and comfort; the inherent attractions of these things will do the rest.

Montesquieu's discussion in Book XXV of the proper institutional place of the religious "cult" within the political order follows strictly from this understanding of the proper dogmas. He begins by drawing our attention to the effects of two extreme postures toward religion: both the pious man and the atheist are preoccupied with religion, the one because he loves it and the other because he fears it. The purpose of Book XXV as a whole is to combat both extremes, to make men neither pious nor atheistic but simply "lukewarm" or indifferent. All Montesquieu's recommendations tend toward reducing to a minimum the role of religion in the life of the citizenry.

He speaks first of the motives which attract men to religion. One must understand these motives in order to know how to placate them, how to limit religion to what is necessary to it and keep from it what is not necessary. According to Montesquieu, men are led to religion primarily by "hope and fear," that is, by the passions which are the primary motives for all human activity. Vanity is often the motive which leads men to choose one religion over another. But men are also attracted by a certain universal love of morality. Montesquieu is silent about motives of gratitude or awe or recognition of beauty and order; neither does he mention the motive of anger or revenge (contrast Plato *Laws*). However that may be, the motives Montesquieu does recognize imply that religion requires a rather considerable external cult, including property and splendid adornments. . . . The wealth of the church can and should be kept within limits; the legislator best achieves this through "indirect means." . . . (pp. 255-58)

Besides restrictions on the material wealth and power of the church, the other most important limitation is the enforcement of toleration and the discouragement of proselytizing. But toleration should be extended only to existing religions; religious freedom is not itself the aim of toleration. Peace, freedom from religious strife and discordant preoccupation with religion, is the proper end of the legislator. . . .

Montesquieu's treatment of religion becomes somewhat bolder in Book XXV. On the one hand his discussion of the institutions of religion induces him to speak more concretely about the Catholic Church. On the other hand, and more important, he contradicts his original disavowal of an intention to enter on any theological speculation: he goes so far as to suggest that the argument for limitations on gifts to the church can be based on the "natural light," the natural theology, of the pagan philosopher in Plato's *Laws*. In the book which follows (Book XXVI), Montesquieu will go still further, entering into a discussion of the central theme of Christian political theology, the relation between divine, natural, and human law. Despite the initial pretense of avoiding theology, it in fact proves impossible to speak comprehensively about politics without confronting Christian theology. . . . (p. 258)

Thomas L. Pangle, in his Montesquieu's Philosophy of Liberalism: A Commentary on "The Spirit of the Laws," *The University of Chicago Press, 1973, 336 p.*

RUSSELL KIRK (essay date 1974)

[*An American historian, political theorist, novelist, journalist, and lecturer, Kirk is one of America's most eminent conservative intellectuals. His works have provided a major impetus to the conservative revival that has developed since the 1950s. The* Conservative Mind (1953), *one of Kirk's early books, describes conservatism as a living body of ideas "struggling toward ascendancy in the United States"; in it Kirk traces the roots and canons of modern conservative thought to such important predecessors as Edmund Burke, John Adams, and Alexis de Tocqueville. Founder of the conservative quarterlies* Modern Age *and the* University Bookman, *Kirk has long been a trenchant critic of the decline of academic standards in American universities. His* Decadence and Renewal in the Higher Learning (1978), *in particular, is a forceful denunciation of the "academic barbarism" which he states has replaced the traditional goals of higher education—wisdom and virtue—with the inferior ones of "utilitarian efficiency" and innovative forms of education. The result, in Kirk's view, is that "the higher learning in America is a disgrace." Kirk's detractors have sometimes been skeptical of the charges he levels against liberal ideas and programs, accusing him of simplistic partisanship. His admirers, on the other hand, point to the alleged failure of liberal precepts—in particular those applied in the universities—as evidence of the incisiveness of Kirk's ideas and criticism. In the following excerpt, Kirk examines the nature and extent of Montesquieu's influence on eighteenth-century America.*]

In any era, public opinion tends to heed especially those important writers who are contemporary with that particular age. Or, to speak more precisely, the leading public men of any age are influenced deeply by important books published during their own formative years. They read those books when they are young, not long after the books have been published; a generation later, the opinions expressed in such books often are reflected in the actions of leading men who had studied them closely when, aged fifteen to twenty-five years, they were seeking for first principles. In Britain and America especially, it is usual enough for some three decades to elapse before the ideas of a powerful writer result in changed public policy or altered consciences—though in some countries, notably France, well-expressed ideas may move society more quickly (not necessarily to society's unqualified advantage). It was so with the thought of Jonathan Edwards; it was so with the thought of Montesquieu, Hume, Blackstone, and Burke.

At the Constitutional Convention in 1787, no man would be more frequently cited and quoted than Charles Louis de Secondat, Baron de Montesquieu. . . . All of Montesquieu's writings were eagerly read, in youth, by many of the men who signed the Declaration of Independence and drew up the Constitution of the United States; others absorbed Montesquieu's ideas at second hand through Blackstone's *Commentaries on the Laws of England*. Even when done into English, Montesquieu's style is pithy and vigorous: most books that move public

opinion achieve their purpose as much by their rhetoric as by their logic.

Montesquieu's works soon were to be found in every British country house; they were almost as frequently encountered on the library shelves of educated Americans. . . . Montesquieu, eminently an urbane gentleman, became essential reading for all urbane gentlemen—or persons wishing to become urbane eighteenth-century gentlemen—on either side of the Atlantic. (p. 350)

There are many aspects to Montesquieu's thought, but for our purposes . . . it is well to emphasize Montesquieu on the nature of law, on the influence of custom and habit (as opposed to the notion of a "social contract"), and on the separation of powers in government. These concepts of his were received so sympathetically in America (and in Britain) that to Montesquieu often has been attributed far more influence upon the Constitution of the United States than was exerted by any other political philosopher.

Montesquieu's ascendancy over English and American minds was not gained because he was a radical innovator: he was nothing of that sort. On the contrary, Montesquieu expressed better than could any Englishman or American of his day the very principles in which most thinking Englishmen and Americans already believed. He had resided for two years in England, and was an ardent admirer of the English constitution. His understanding of the nature of law confirmed Englishmen and Americans in their affection for their own jurisprudence and legal institutions; his discussion of the power of custom and habit in shaping society agreed with the prescriptive politics of the English-speaking peoples; his advocacy of the separation of powers sustained the political experience of Britain and the colonies. Upon Englishmen and Americans, his influence was conservative.

It would be somewhat otherwise in France, where Montesquieu's praise of the English constitution would produce demands for reconstruction of the French political structure upon the English model. Those who so read Montesquieu were disappointed in the event. For as Montesquieu himself made clear, one country's historic experience cannot be transported to a different land, and customs and habits cannot be altered by positive law—they can only be distorted. In France, the early ideals of many revolutionaries, Mirabeau among them, were connected with the English pattern of politics. But the Revolution, as it ran its course, redoubled the very defects—centralization especially—which Montesquieu had assailed obliquely in the France of the Old Regime; what emerged from the French Revolution did not resemble either the English constitution or Montesquieu's general model of a constitution with separation of powers and local liberties. Somewhat wistfully, Montesquieu had desired French reform—but no revolution. In America, his great book would help in the recovery of order after a revolution.

To live under law is natural for man, said Montesquieu, and reasonable. Although the mass of laws bewilders most people, actually laws form a pattern, relating to one another and connecting all the concerns of society. In essence, laws are relationships: the necessary bonds between man and man, among classes, joining communities in common interests. Laws relate men to the circumstances under which a society exists. True, all law has its root in general truths: "Law is human reason, inasmuch as it governs all the inhabitants of the earth; the political and civil laws of each nation ought to be only the particular cases in which this human reason is applied.'' But those particular cases vary in many ways.

Although law is reasonable, Montesquieu continues, we cannot expect it to assume a universal pattern. For men's circumstances vary mightily one from another—affected by climate, by soil, by extent of a country, by historic experience, by customs and habits, by strategic situation, by commerce and industry, by religion, by a multitude of other influences. Therefore every people develop their own particular laws, and rightly so. Montesquieu is a ''relativist'' in believing that there is no single ''best'' body of laws or pattern of politics.

Nevertheless, Montesquieu does not deny the existence of natural law; in effect, he affirms the concept of natural law that had come down from Plato and Cicero and Aquinas and Hooker. ''Before laws were made, there were relations of possible justice. To say that there is nothing just or unjust but what is commanded or forbidden by positive laws, is the same as saying that before the describing of a circle all the radii were not equal.'' Positive law should conform to the principles of natural justice.

On those principles, Montesquieu was the first political philosopher to oppose human slavery, root and branch. He set his face against a different concept of ''natural law''—against the seventeenth-century legal theories of the Dutch jurist Hugo Grotius, who had argued that one of the laws of nature is this: that a conqueror has the right to slaughter or perpetually enslave a whole people whose armies he has defeated. This would deny, said Montesquieu, the natural law of preservation of life; it would be contrary to the political law of the survival of communities; contrary, indeed, to even the conqueror's self-interest. What is ruinous to society cannot be natural law. Although Montesquieu was a witty critic of the Church in his age, at bottom his understanding of natural law is religious.

For Montesquieu, the highest achievement of any country's law is the enlargement of personal freedom. Law and freedom are not opposed; for there cannot be freedom without law, only violent anarchy; and without freedom, law is despotic, obeyed only out of fear. Law does restrain men from injuring others and themselves, but it did not come into existence merely to establish a despotic authority.

Here Montesquieu drubs Thomas Hobbes. ''The natural impulse or desire which Hobbes attributes to mankind of subduing one another, is far from being well founded. The idea of empire and dominion is so complex, and depends so much on other notions, that it could never be the first that would occur to human understandings.'' Laws, rather, are the beneficial rules by which we contrive to live in community, the products of human wisdom to satisfy general human wants.

So Montesquieu rejects Hobbes' theory of a social compact formed out of fear, requiring total submission to Leviathan; also he rejects, less explicitly, John Locke's theory of a social compact formed to shelter life, liberty, and property. (Despite much writing about Locke's influence upon Montesquieu, actually Montesquieu disagrees with the great Whig more often than he agrees; he may have learned as much from the Tory Bolingbroke, with whom he was personally acquainted.) Montesquieu does not believe in the necessary existence of any social compact at all.

For political and civil laws are not abstractly ordained or agreed upon at any one moment in history: instead, laws slowly grow out of men's experience with one another—out of social customs and habits—as, one may add, the common law of England developed. ''When a people have pure and regular manners, their laws become simple and natural.'' In this argument, Montesquieu draws extensively upon the laws of the Romans, as well as upon his own observations in his time.

It is not because of some conscious artificial early agreement that men live under law. Human communities, even on a tiny scale, cannot exist without at least rudimentary laws; man is not really man, not fully human, until he lives by law. Montesquieu, as the first historian of modern times to seek for philosophical meaning in the course of human events, cast the notion of the social compact into eclipse.

Let us look at laws, especially those fundamental laws called constitutions, more realistically. Forms of government arise out of complex combinations of circumstances and experiences; and governments are reflections of a nation's laws, rather than the source of laws. We can no more expect a universal pattern of government than we can expect identical positive laws in every country. Montesquieu discerns three general patterns of government, nevertheless: the republic, the monarchy, and the despotism. The republic is sustained by the citizens' virtue, the monarchy by the king's honor, and the despotism (like that of the Ottomans) by the subjects' fear. Ordinarily a people do not *choose* one constitutional form or another: they find themselves necessarily under the sort of government which is suited to their social circumstances. In a sense, any people obtain the kind of government they desire—or, at any rate, the kind of government which their history and their conditions of existence have brought upon them.

Still, it does not follow that all governments are equal in merit. What governments most successfully reconcile the claims of order and the claims of freedom? Here Montesquieu admires the constitution of the Roman Republic, as described by Polybius, before foreign conquests and luxury worked corruption; and he finds the best government of his age in the constitutional monarchy of England, where the subject enjoyed personal and civic freedom. Once France, too, had been like England in some sort, a true monarchy balanced by a degree of representative government: but Louis XIII and his minister Cardinal Richelieu had ruined French freedom, so that in Montesquieu's time the French state was sinking toward despotism, a centralized state apparatus excluding from real participation the nobles, the clergy, and the people.

How did old Rome and modern England maintain an ordered freedom, liberty under law? Why, so far as institutions are concerned, by the devices of separation of powers and of checks and balances. Power can be restrained only by counterbalancing power, Montesquieu reasoned. No man, and no political body or office, ought to possess unchecked power. For the sake of personal liberty and free community, power ought to be divided and hedged. Might this slow the actions of the state? Well, be it so, Montesquieu thought: freedom is better than haste.

Although the concept of the separation of powers and the concept of checks and balances are related, they are not identical. By the separation of powers is meant the apportioning of authority to different branches of government: to the executive branch, to the legislative, to the judicial. Checks and balances to prevent the arbitrary employment of power may work *within* a government of separated powers, or they may be applied to a ''mixed government'' of classical times, or to some other form of government. Checks and balances upon power may be exerted by non-political bodies, among them the Church and the university. Montesquieu desired both separation of powers and the development of checks and balances. His plan is the precise opposite of Hobbes'. Representative parliaments, competent local governments with established usages, and the claims of conscious social classes all are restraints upon Leviathan.

In England, Montesquieu saw a successful separation of powers: the king as executive, the Parliament as representative assembly (incorporating check and balance through its two houses, Lords and Commons), the courts as an independent judiciary. (Although in theory modern Britain does not separate the executive power from the legislative, actually this separation still exists: the power formerly possessed by the king now is possessed by the cabinet, which is not simply a committee of Parliament.)

In France, an independent judiciary survived to Montesquieu's time; but from Louis XIV onward, and indeed earlier, executive and legislative had been merged in the French state, so that the Parlement of Paris and the lesser French *parlements* had ceased to function as representative assemblies. Even the independence of judges was more secure in England than in France, having been guaranteed by the Bill of Rights in 1689. In France, nearly all checks upon the power of king and court had vanished by the time Montesquieu wrote. That harsh concentration of power would be the primary cause of the French Revolution.

Even separation of powers and effective checks and balances, Montesquieu feared, might not suffice to ensure continuity of law and evenhanded justice. Somewhere there ought to exist a "depository" or guardian of laws, protecting the fundamental laws, the constitution of a country. He thought the nobility not intelligent enough for this function; he was not clear as to how any political body could undertake this task impartially. What Montesquieu desired would not take form until some decades after his death; and then it would be called the Supreme Court of the United States.

This has been only a summary description of the temperate wisdom of Montesquieu. Because his principles of politics found their best embodiment in eighteenth-century England, his reputation in that realm stood high. And it is not difficult to understand why Montesquieu was far more popular with Americans than he was either with the French masters of the Old Regime or with the rash French reformers who brought on the Revolution.

For Montesquieu's understanding of the nature of law was shared by the Americans. They recognized religious and moral sanctions behind positive law; they had been brought up in the English juridical principles and practices of common law and equity, which clearly had developed out of a people's experience in community; they looked upon law as the protector of freedom. The Americans knew that their own society was not the product of a single formal social compact; it was in part an inheritance from British social development, and in part the consequence of their own peculiar geographical, economic, and political circumstances; it had grown accidentally or providentially, rather than being created out of an abstract general agreement. They understood very well indeed the benefits of separation of powers and of checks and balances: in every colony, the governor held executive power, the assembly representing the freeholders controlled legislation, and the courts were independent. (In Virginia, the county courts even resembled Montesquieu's "depository of laws.")

Thus Montesquieu, who never saw America, provided philosophical and historical justifications for the framework of ordered liberty that the Thirteen Colonies experienced in the latter half of the eighteenth century. In effect, Montesquieu was America's apologist. His books acquired authority among Americans because his principles and deductions were sustained by American experience of political reality. Montesquieu's federalism, detesting centralization, struck a sympathetic chord; his warning against the decay of constitutional monarchy into despotism would furnish the American Patriots with arguments against the policies of George III.

Montesquieu's moderation did something to moderate the passions of the American Revolution. His exposition of the rule of law helped to point the way, for American leaders after the War of Independence, toward a frame of government which would be neither oppressively central nor weakly confederate, but something new (or at least eclectic) in political contrivances. More important still, his aphorisms directly assisted in the triumph of the separation of powers within both general and state governments, and in the reinforcement of elaborate checks and balances at every level of the American political structure. Montesquieu had little expectation of reforming or renewing the political forms of France under Louis XV; perhaps he would have been astounded to find that across the Atlantic his books had encouraged republican virtue. Political virtue, Montesquieu had written, is eagerness to serve the commonwealth. That eagerness in America had been augmented by much reading of Montesquieu.

France, through all its violent changes of regime after 1789, would grow steadily more arbitrary and centralized in government. England's separation of powers and political equilibrium were changing even as Montesquieu wrote. But in the Constitution of the United States there would be fulfilled practically the polity sketched by Montesquieu, with freedom and order balanced on the scales. (pp. 351-58)

Russell Kirk, "Eighteenth-Century Intellects," in his The Roots of American Order, *Open Court, 1974, pp. 347-91.*

MARK HULLIUNG   (lecture date 1979)

[*Hulliung is the author of a 1976 study of Montesquieu,* Montesquieu and the Old Regime (*see Additional Bibliography). In the following excerpt from an essay originally delivered as a lecture in 1979, he takes issue with several aspects of the Montesquieu scholarship he encountered while conducting research for his book.*]

Anyone who writes an interpretive book on Montesquieu premised on the assumption that the secondary literature may well be more an obstacle than an aid in the search for truth is under an obligation to explain where and why he believes so many able scholars have gone wrong. My purpose in the present essay is to honor my duty to the secondary literature by taking it to task.

The literature on Montesquieu is possibly the least satisfactory body of interpretive works dealing with a major political thinker. Taken in the large, the mass of books, essays, and articles written on Montesquieu is so wanting that even at this late date his powerful claim to membership in the ranks of the greatest political theorists remains inadequately acknowledged. When scholars call out the honor roll of the foremost political minds, Plato to Marx, the name Montesquieu either is omitted or is included as an act of magnanimity. Truth be told, the Montesquieu of the secondary literature, even when sympathetically portrayed, is more fitting company for, say, Harrington, an influential second-rater, than for the likes of Rousseau or Hegel, thinkers who are their own history by virtue of their preeminent intellectual accomplishments. And if Montesquieu's intellectual stature has been so seriously misjudged, we should not be surprised to find that his ideological convictions have also been misunderstood, his intentions misread, and his thought obscured by a secondary literature, passed from generation to generation, which contains as many layers of cumulative error as of cumulative knowledge.

Neither an exhaustive book-by-book critique of the secondary literature nor a bibliographical essay will be attempted here, but rather a paper organized around various "fallacies" of Montesquieu interpretation. (pp. 327-28)

Aristocratic Liberal or Feudal Reactionary? Was Montesquieu an "aristocratic liberal" or was he a "feudal reactionary"? Much ink has been spilled over this question—enough to testify that the majority of Montesquieu's interpreters believe the essence of his ideological commitments, his *parti pris*, is surely contained in one or another of these alternatives. (p. 328)

Despite the animosity which has highlighted their debate, the proponents of the "aristocratic liberal" and "feudal reactionary" theses, viewed from a distance, are strikingly similar, strikingly wrong, and wrong for the same reasons. Brothers under the skin, they have stood together, and now it is time for them to fall together. Each assumes, incorrectly, that Montesquieu favored virtually all aspects of the old regime except absolute monarchy: in either interpretation Montesquieu figures as the enthusiastic supporter of aristocracy, of feudalism, of "intermediary bodies." Against these views it is necessary to object that Montesquieu attacked all of the old order, its social as well as its political structure. A country that failed to break the power of its First and Second Estates, he warned, was likely to go the way of Spain—the way of Inquisition, of economic stagnation. Conversely, a country which did break the power of its intermediary bodies, and of its absolute monarch as well, would be following in the footsteps of England, the most free and progressive of nations. Montesquieu's thought does indeed "express" the old regime, as we have so often heard; it does so, however, not passively but through actively analyzing and explaining the old order; it does so, furthermore, through indicting and offering an enlightened alternative to the pre-revolutionary status quo.

"Aristocratic liberal" or "feudal reactionary"? Montesquieu was neither, and we are unlikely to do him justice until we delete both this question and the methodological assumptions which underlie it, namely, that the social history of ideas is either unimportant or impossible to write, or else is all-important and is properly written by discovering the social situation which a set of ideas "reflects." So long as our choice is "materialism" or "idealism," reductionism or platonic abstraction, the interpretive process is bound to yield disappointing results. A different tactic must be pursued. Henceforth encounters with the thoughts of a great mind should be undertaken in the realization, contra Marx, that ideas can be "reflections on" rather than "reflexes of the life process"; whence it will follow that we should stop working inward from the social world to thought which reputedly "mirrors" it, and start working outward from thought to the social world it apprehends. The history of ideas will then enrich, but not disappear into, social history. Ideas will not be isolated from their social context, nor will their logical, analytical, or revelatory

powers be neglected. The twin pitfalls of "idealism" and "materialism" will be averted.

The Comparative Study of Societies and Polities. Most students of Montesquieu's pioneering efforts in the use of comparative method argue one point above all: his objective in juxtaposing images of oriental and occidental countries was to sing the praises of the Robe, Sword, and clergy. Monarchy in the West, according to him, was one-man rule underwritten by the corporate bodies and privileged social groups—the "intermediary powers"—of feudal society: the estates, parlements, provincial assemblies, and semi-autonomous cities. Eastern monarchy, in dramatic contrast, was one-man rule in the absence of feudalism and hence in the presence of fear, purge, and social chaos. The message is unmistakable: succeed in subtracting feudalism from the French monarchy, Richelieu, and you will have created a despotic desert in the Western world. Once again we have Montesquieu presented as the champion of the old regime.

But Montesquieu was far from believing that the retention of intermediary bodies was sufficient reason for rejoicing, or their expulsion sufficient reason for despairing. Not at all: intermediary bodies had been removed from the English monarchy with admirable consequences, and retained by the Spanish monarchy with disastrous consequences, he insisted. The England which Montesquieu presented to the world as a pattern country was not, as has usually been maintained, a constitutional monarchy combined with intermediary bodies; it was constitutional monarchy, undeniably, but without intermediary bodies: "The English, to favor their liberty, have abolished all the intermediate powers of which their monarchy was composed." Not for want of clarity on Montesquieu's part has his position been misconstrued: "Abolish the privileges of the lords, the clergy, and cities in a monarchy, and you will soon have a popular state, or else a despotic government." Again and again commentators have called our attention to the words "despotic government" in the foregoing quotation while ignoring the words "popular government" and their explicit referent, Montesquieu's beloved England. If a purge of intermediary bodies can lead to the worst of possibilities, despotism, it can also lead to the best, England's "system" of liberty. An aristocracy that was no longer a feudal nobility, a clergy tolerant, liberal, and removed from the political assemblies, an entrepreneurial ethic suffused throughout all social ranks—such were the benefits England reaped upon entering a post-feudal, post-old regime era of history.

Spain's significance as a pattern country equal in importance to England in Montesquieu's thought has gone unnoticed in the secondary literature—and this is spite of his lifelong fascination with Iberian affairs. Drawing attention to the Spaniards was for Montesquieu a means of complementing his comments on the British. If England's was the glory that potentially awaited a Western monarchy that crushed its feudal bodies, then Spain's was the degradation that threatened a monarchy whose feudal bodies continued to flourish. Inquisition, economic retardation, political weakness, and national decline were the fruits of Spain's tenacious clerical and aristocratic estates. Not an imported tyranny of exotic origin but rather a homegrown despotism—a despotism caused by the retention not the overthrow of feudal society—was what plagued Spain and menaced France. Montesquieu's comparative method yielded a vision of society and politics drastically at odds with the old regime—and drastically at odds with the opinions attributed to him by his interpreters.

Precisely why Montesquieu's findings as a comparative analyst have been slighted or misunderstood is not easy to determine.

A certain relative neglect of the topic of comparative method can, however, be suggested as a tendency among students of the political classics. The theory of the social contract arouses much more interest today, doubtless because many contemporary political theorists are moral philosophers in search of ethical concepts that can be adapted to current dilemmas. Problems of political science are not their concern. Others do care about political science and its historical roots, but usually they assume that the social sciences did not exist before the French Revolution. That leaves Montesquieu nowhere.

Poor fellow, he does not even enjoy the consolation of good prospects, and especially not when it comes to an appreciation of his comparative method. At a time such as ours when there are those, armed with computers, who are eager to revive the nineteenth-century positivist quest for cross-cultural laws, it is perhaps inevitable that their critics (Alasdair MacIntyre, Peter Winch, for example) should revive the nineteenth-century historicist claim that each nation is unique and comparison impossible. Montesquieu, however, knew nothing about positivism or historicism, but a great deal about Aristotle's *Politics,* including the comparative logic of genus and species which the master applied to Greek constitutions. An infusion of the concept of "feudalism" into the Aristotelian logic of *per genus et differentiam* was Montesquieu's intent. Applied to the West, feudalism supplied the generic term of comparative analysis, the common denominator; comparability of Western nations was assured because they were, differences notwithstanding, so many statements of the historical logic of feudalism. Applied to East and West, feudalism supplied the term which differentiated types of royal absolutism, the oriental variety being unchecked, the occidental checked, by corporate bodies.

Neither the most outspoken contemporary advocates of comparative method, the neo-positivists, nor its most outspoken opponents, the neo-historicists, belong to the classical, Aristotelian world of ideas Montesquieu inhabited. His intellectual tradition is before theirs in time, between theirs in argumentation—comparative generalizations, yes, global laws, no— and feasibly above theirs in good sense. Together, the neo-positivists and neo-historicists block our awareness that another way once existed, with Aristotle and Montesquieu as its foremost representatives. (pp. 329-32)

Economics. As an economist, Montesquieu's reflections were far-reaching and highly significant. Numbered among his accomplishments were contributions to formal economic theory, the sociology of economics, and international political economy. His suggestion that interest rates are decided by the supply and demand of money; his radical argument that economic progress is the special preserve of modern republics with open, liberal, and democratic societies; his appreciation of laissez-faire, both in its enlightening influence on domestic politics, and in its Janus-faced impact on international relations, where it curtails the violence of states but ruins poor nations—such are representative examples of his discoveries in different branches of economic thought.

Obviously any comprehensive interpretation must come to grips with Montesquieu the economist; and yet scholars such as Mathiez, Althusser, Neumann, and Ford write almost as if Montesquieu never scribbled a line on economics. Not surprisingly, these are the same scholars who decipher Montesquieu's political commitments by pointing to his social class. Now they compound their initial error. If Montesquieu by virtue of his aristocratic status was the defender of aristocratic society, it follows that he could not have had much to say about economics, the science of the rising bourgeoisie. . . .

Not all of Montesquieu's interpreters have ignored his economic writings; rather the pattern has been one in which scholars of each generation have had to rediscover Montesquieu the economist—they have had, time and again, to begin at the beginning. (p. 335)

Politics and Morals. Like a thirsty man in sight of a well, Montesquieu's interpreters have raced to Book I of the *Esprit des lois,* hoping to quench their thirst for knowledge of what he had to say about "is" and "ought," empirical and normative. Whatever moral judgments the later Books contain are then referred back to Book I, and Montesquieu is graded for consistency and inconsistency. Despite the brevity of Book I's statements on natural law, despite the blatant contradiction between its a priori definition of justice on the one hand and Montesquieu's epistemological skepticism and cultural relativism on the other, Book I continues to enjoy a privileged position in the secondary literature on Montesquieu. It is time for Book I to suffer a demotion.

Every one knows Montesquieu wanted to believe, contra Hobbes, in a justice superior to human conventions, those notorious carriers of evil. As early as the *Traité des devoirs* he may be seen advocating the anti-Hobbesian notion of transcendental justice which eventually found its way into Book I of the *Lois.* A direct plea via natural law philosophy for a more just and humane world was, then, characteristic of Montesquieu. It was not, however, the only characteristic of Montesquieu's moral thought, nor the most significant. In the *Traité* he was already visibly dissatisfied with a moralistic morality, as can be seen in the section entitled "De la politique." Here emerged the Montesquieu of the future. Rather than plead the cause of justice, he sought to disprove the cause of injustice; that is, he set out to destroy from within the reason of state ideology, which, judging actions solely by consequences, suspended all considerations of justice. Out to prove that injustice is poor policy, Montesquieu quickly transformed his treatise on duties into a demonstration of the political inutility of "la politique," the "science of ruse and artifice." Machiavellism, he argued with the aid of historical examples, simply did not measure up to Machiavellian standards. It did not work.

Over the course of his subsequent writings Montesquieu doggedly continued his indirect assault on injustice. In the *Persian Letters* he demonstrated that a despotic society, a society thoroughly unjust, was disastrous for every last one of its members, not excepting the despot. In the *Considerations* he argued that the corruption of the Roman republic was the consequence of its unjust imperialism. Then followed the *Spirit of the Laws* in which he maintained that the injustice of monarchical imperialism led to consequences antithetical to the intentions of its perpetrators. Indeed, the best way to pursue power was to follow the program of Enlightenment: trade instead of guns, constitutional government, laissez-faire, social welfare. By the time Montesquieu had finished deliberately confounding the terminologies of freedom and power, no one could discern the difference between them.

Of course, an over-emphasis on the significance of Book I is not the only reason interpreters have misunderstood the links Montesquieu drew between politics and morals. Equally blameworthy and responsible is their insistence on viewing him through the lenses of the philosophies of a later day. (pp 337-38)

''Montesquieu the positivist,'' ''Montesquieu the historicist''—these phrases tell us very little about Montesquieu but a great deal about the methods of his interpreters. To wit, such formulas suggest that his modern readers, often overly eager for generalization, generalize improperly. Interpreters read history backwards, tearing Montesquieu out of his context and congratulating him for discoveries—the founding of positivism or historicism—he never made nor had any interest in making. They over-state his break with the past by fixating on his supposed links with intellectual traditions which succeeded him, while systematically ignoring those traditions which preceded him and gave him intellectual nourishment. (p. 339)

Properly situated, Montesquieu is neither a positivist *ex nihilo*—the first cause uncaused of later positivist thinkers—nor is he a significant link in an unbroken transmission of natural law philosophy through the ages. Rather, he is part of the tradition of classical, Aristotelian political science, and of its sporadic, discontinuous revival in early modern Europe, notably by Machiavelli, Bodin, and Harrington.

Improper generalizations are not the only obstacle to an appreciation of Montesquieu. An absence of generalization, or a bias against generalization, may well be the pattern of future research. Atonement for past mistakes, as is so often the case, may lead to the rise of new errors, the reverse side of the old. The danger is that books on Montesquieu may henceforth be graded as scholarly and proper to the extent they lack the generalizations which render findings meaningful. Unhistorical books written on topics in intellectual history (studies of ''perennial questions''), books containing histories of relationships between thinkers who were scarcely aware of one another (studies of ''influence''), books telling stories of intellectual goings-on that never happened (studies of ''anticipation'') have been very common in the discipline of intellectual history; and in Quentin Skinner's telling critiques they have received their just deserts. Should, however, Skinner's attacks inadvertently signal the rise of a new generation of erudites without purpose or vision, Montesquieu among others will suffer. Conceivably, more and more will be said about less and less in his works. Skinner, the self-conscious thinker, may have unwittingly paved the way for the dominance of unselfconscious thinkers, mere chroniclers.

Nearest at hand, a generalization-killing fear of treating Montesquieu's thought as a whole easily follows from Skinner's strictures. The assumption of unity in the works of political philosophers is arbitrary, Skinner has complained. Generalization is thereby attained, but falsely so, since the various works of a given philosopher were spread out over a lifetime and written with different purposes in mind. Surely Skinner's point is well taken, but we must be on guard against substituting an a priori assumption of disunity for the previous assumption of unity. In Montesquieu's case the chronological, work-by-work approach is not mandatory and can be pernicious; applied to him, Skinner's critique run wild would lead to an unnecessary dismemberment of the *Oeuvres complètes*. For Montesquieu's thought truly is a whole. Already in the *Persian Letters* his thought is mature: the model of oriental despotism is fully articulated; the civic nature of the ancient republic receives brief but definite mention; monarchy is linked with aristocratic ''honor'' and luxury; England is saved and Spain is damned. Much, of course, can be learned by studying the *Persian Letters, Considerations,* and *Spirit of the Laws* one by one, in isolation from one another; but many of the finest riches of Montesquieu's mind can only be experienced by empathy with the

amazing persistence and unity of his vision. His lifelong dedication to the refutation of injustice through covert means is a case in point.

Lastly, the process of seeing Montesquieu's work as a whole confers this benefit: it acts as a check against interpretations of particular works. Every so often one hears, for instance, that Roxane's rebellion at the end of *Persian Letters* is a premonition of the French Revolution. Would it not be more accurate to understand her suicide as an early statement of the lesson Montesquieu taught most systematically in the *Spirit of the Laws,* that oriental despotism can sustain nothing of worth and is inimical even to the interests of the despot? (pp. 339-40)

Whatever our concern as we read the classics of political thought, Plato to Marx, whether we approach them as historians, as moral philosophers, or as political scientists, generalizations that matter are waiting to be made if only we will make them. (p. 441)

Mark Hulliung, ''Montesquieu's Interpreters: A Polemical Essay,'' in Studies in Eighteenth-Century Culture, *Vol. 10, 1981, pp. 327-45.*

PAULINE KRA (essay date 1984)

[*Kra is a Polish-born American educator and critic. In the following excerpt, she studies Montesquieu's attitude toward women and their sociopolitical status.*]

Montesquieu in his writing on women brought to the forefront the empiricism, relativism, pragmatism, and breadth of vision that are characteristic of his thought. Discarding the notion of the natural inferiority of woman, he explored the multiplicity of factors that affect her condition and studied the effect of circumstances on feminine character and behavior. The scope of his inquiry embraced women from ancient Persia, Greece, and Rome to contemporary Europe, from the Oriental seraglio to the French court. In this broad historical and geographic perspective, he examined the variety of customs and institutions that regulate the relationships between the sexes and the many forms of interaction, from the harmony that may exist in an incestuous union to the alienation that may result from the indissoluble Catholic marriage. Relativism and pragmatism account for the complexity of his position and for the apparent inconsistencies that have given rise to widely divergent assessments of his attitude. He has been traditionally considered a feminist but has also been branded a misogynist and antifeminist. He placed himself outside the theoretical debate on the equality of the sexes when he attributed to a ''gallant philosopher'' the feminist arguments derived from Poulain de La Barre. Yet his own analysis of customs and institutions gave empirical support to the feminist ideas and to the demands for the improvement of the status of women. (p. 272)

In the *Esprit des lois* and in the *Pensées*, Montesquieu examines the influence of physical, moral, economic, social, and political factors on the potential of women, their role in society, and types of family structure. He rejects absolute norms based on a universal concept of the nature of woman, but in evaluating existing institutions, he gives preference to those that provide the greatest degree of freedom and equality for women. In every case where he states a general practice based on reason and experience, he mentions also exceptions and alternative forms. The subject of women figures prominently in the books on morals and sumptuary laws under the various forms of government, domestic slavery in relation to climate, the national character, population, religion, and jurisprudence.

Montesquieu considered the feminine character to be a function of physiology, physical environment, and social conditioning. In the *Essai sur les causes qui peuvent affecter les esprits et les caractères,* he stated that physiological differences between the sexes result in differences of character. The menstrual cycle produces changes in mood and because of different anatomical configuration and hormonal balance, the fibers of women are softer, more delicate, and more flexible than those of men. Yet, unlike Malebranche and others he did not conclude that the organic differences result in inferior aptitudes.

He regarded beauty as an essential feminine attribute, but he pointed out that the ascendancy it gives depends on climate and that appearance is modified by environment. The degree of power that women derive from beauty depends on its chronological coincidence with the development of reason. Though he recognized empirically the importance of beauty, Montesquieu was aware that its criteria are imaginary and relative to country and time. In the present state of affairs, he remarked, women do well to be as pretty as possible, but it would be good if they were all equally beautiful or equally ugly to do away with the pride of beauty and the despair of ugliness.

He explains various negative personality traits as the result of conditioning. . . . [He] notes that male domination stifles the talents of women. Similarly, the falsehood of women is due to their dependent status. The greater the dependence, the greater the falsehood, just as higher taxes increase the amount of smuggling. Greed is a sign of weakness, but women are often greedy out of vanity and desire to show that money is spent on them. Women talk more than men because they lack serious occupation. The silly behavior of girls and their eagerness to marry are clearly stated to be the result of the way they are treated; constrained and condemned to triviality, they do not dare use their faculties, and marriage alone gives women freedom and access to pleasures.

The attraction between the sexes, Montesquieu maintained, is a fundamental law of nature, but it is variously modified in humans by ways of thinking, character, passions, concern for beauty, and fear of pregnancy or of a large family. The relative importance attached to the physical and emotional aspects of love varies also with time and place.

Rejecting universal norms, he showed that marriage customs as well depend on a variety of factors; they are developed in ways that are not always natural or reasonable, and there is nothing in the nature of woman that relegates her permanently to a subordinate position. In primitive families, men had authority over their children but not over their wives. It was indeed the incompatibility between the obedience that a daughter owed her father and the equal status held by the wife that gave rise to the repugnance for incestuous marriages. The Egyptians submitted to the authority of their wives in honor of the goddess Isis and enjoyed the servitude so much that they took care of the house and left outside affairs to women. Scythian women revolted against marriage as slavery and founded the Amazon empire. If the Amazons or the Egyptians had continued their conquests, men would live in submission and one would have to be a philosopher to maintain that another arrangement was more natural. If, on the other hand, Islam had conquered the earth, women would be everywhere behind bars.

An essential idea in Montesquieu's analysis of the relationships between the sexes is that their relative ascendancy depends on physical causes determined by climate. Nature gave man physical strength and reason; it endowed woman with beauty and reason. Women are weakest in hot climates, where their beauty wanes before their rational faculties are fully developed. Their dependence makes it easy for men to move from one woman to another and leads to the institution of polygamy. In temperate climates, on the other hand, there is greater equality between the sexes because women mature later, their beauty lasts longer, and they have more reason and knowledge at the time they marry. In cold climates, women have the additional advantage of superior reasoning because unlike men they do not drink. The monogamous marriage, which represents "a kind of equality between the sexes," prevails therefore in the colder climates.

He discarded universal norms of family structure and the traditional notion that the wife must by nature be subordinate to her husband. It is unnatural, he wrote, for women to rule over the household, as they did among the Egyptians; but he did not deny the possibility of equal sharing of authority. In a major departure from traditional views, he argued vigorously against the exclusion of women from political life and succession to the throne. It had been contended in the Aristotelian tradition that because of her weakness woman should not take any part in the running of the state. Montesquieu declared that, on the contrary, her very weakness may be a source of political virtues of gentleness and moderation needed for good government. While successful women rulers had been viewed before him as exceptions, he puts forth the reigns of Elizabeth I and Catherine II as proof of woman's ability to govern in a variety of political systems. Significantly, the chapter on feminine rule is placed at the end of a book that examines the forms of legal subjection imposed on women under the various regimes. He interpreted the salic law as a measure adopted for economic reasons, rather than out of discrimination against women. Yet he admired women who placed devotion to their husbands above political ambition. He praised the greatness of Queen Ulrica Leonora of Sweden who abdicated in favor of her husband; and in *Arsace et Isménie,* the heroine steps down from the throne, entreating her subjects to accept the man she loves as their master.

Montesquieu's view of marriage is pragmatic and independent of the theological definition he satirized in the *Lettres persanes.* In his analysis, matrimony is simply the basic social structure necessary for procreation and the survival of the species. Unlike in animals, where the female suffices to assure the survival of the young, the more prolonged physical and moral nurturing in humans requires the efforts of both parents. Marriage is the convention that designates the father. But though matrimony is the prevailing institution among civilized peoples, he notes at the outset that there are other ways of assigning parental responsibility; among the Garamantes, a nomad people of Africa, the father was designated on the basis of resemblance. He condemned illegitimate relations on the pragmatic grounds that they do not contribute to propagation, because the father does not fulfill his natural obligation and the unwed mother finds too many obstacles to bringing up the children alone.

The extensive study of polygamy is part of his analysis of the effect of climate on social and political institutions. He demonstrates that hot climate promotes conditions favorable to polygamy and to the sequestration of women, but he is critical of the manner in which one sex takes advantage of physical circumstances to enslave the other. There is every reason to believe his claim that he explained the reasons for the practice of polygamy but did not approve of it. Through numerous statements and arguments, he condemned the plurality of wives and parodied the opinion that the treatment of women should be determined by climate. In an ironic chapter, he enumerates, on the one hand, the crimes, horrors, poisonings, and assassinations perpetrated under the effect of hot climate by the women of Goa; and on the other, he portrays with equal exaggeration the moderation and purity of morals in temperate climates. He parodies also the oriental contention that women have so many duties to fulfill in the family that they must be sheltered from all outside concerns.

The one traditional universal norm Montesquieu upheld is that of the chastity of women. Feminine continence, he maintained, is a law of nature reflected in the scorn that all nations attach to incontinence. The loss of virtue in a woman is a major flaw that entails overall psychological degradation and corruption. Moreover, public incontinence is harmful to society because it does not contribute to propagation and weakens the stability of marriages; the decline in the number of marriages reduces the fidelity of those who have been contracted.

The distinctive aspect of Montesquieu's writing on women is his extensive analysis of the relationships between their condition and the political, social, religious, and economic structures. He demonstrated that the status of women and their morals are closely linked to the political regime. They have least freedom under the two extremes of despotism and republic. Under despotism, the protection of morals is entrusted to harem walls and the enslavement of women is part of the general climate of servitude. In the republic, women are free under the law but captives of austere moral restraints. It is the monarchy that allows the greatest degree of freedom for women and requires least purity of morals. Noting the disadvantages of extreme moral rigor of ancient republics, he showed a clear preference for the relative freedom prevailing under monarchy. In Greek republics, he observed, the effective preservation of feminine chastity was accompanied by rampant homosexuality. In England, leading separate lives, women are modest and timid, while men throw themselves into debauchery. The decline of virtue under the corrupting influence of court is regrettable, but it is compensated for by the positive influence of women.

In the chains of causality that characterize the *Esprit des lois,* feminine behavior appears as the result of conditions imposed by climate, political regime, customs, and laws. The one book in which woman's traits and behavior appear as a cause at the beginning of the chain is Book XIX on the *esprit général.* The book demonstrates that where woman acts within a parameter of freedom her role has positive effects on the development of national character, the arts, the economy, and political institutions. The French monarchy is used in this context as a case study for the demonstration of the benefits that result from free association between the sexes. Men and women, Montesquieu contended, realize their potential best in an atmosphere of freedom for both sexes. Allowed to extend their activities outside the home, women make a major contribution to the development of sociability, manners, and politeness. They promote the refinement of taste and the progress of arts, commerce, and industry. The positive civilizing influence of women is brought out also by the example of Russia, where reforms were resisted so long as women were kept in seclusion but European customs and manners were eagerly adopted when Peter I liberated the Russian women and brought them to court. Feminine vanity, tastes, and passions provided the necessary impetus for change.

The Russian example serves to show, in addition, that the liberation of women leads to greater political freedom. It is the absence of women from public life in despotic countries that safeguards the tranquillity and the stagnation that are essential for the preservation of the regime. The free interaction between the sexes, on the other hand, produces social ferment that disrupts despotic rule. Montesquieu deplored the corruption of morals, the loss of gravity, and the folly, but he viewed the overall effect of women's participation as favorable to political freedom and progress of civilization.

In his appraisal of civil laws regarding marriage, divorce, adultery, and abortion, he advocated measures that would give greater freedom and equality to women. He regarded marriage as a contract that is intended to serve the good of society and that should fall, therefore, under the jurisdiction of civil rather than canon law. The Catholic prohibition of divorce is, in his opinion, harmful to both sexes, to growth of population, and to the institution of marriage itself. Divorce, on the other hand, is generally useful to the state and to the spouses, though it does not always serve the best interests of the children. Mutual incompability, he maintained, is the most compelling and sufficient reason for divorce. He judged tyrannical the law that gave the right of repudiation to the husband but not to the wife, and he even suggested that under polygamy the right of repudiation should be given only to the woman in order to counteract the man's authority within the household. The chapters on repudiation and divorce are placed significantly at the end of the book on polygamy, just as the chapters on the liberation of slaves conclude the book on slavery.

He condemned as contrary to natural law a series of civil statutes that tyrannized women. Yet, in dealing with adultery, he denied women the equality granted to them by the church. While the church demanded fidelity equally from both spouses, Montesquieu followed the spirit of contemporary jurists who punished the infidelity of the wife but condoned it in the husband. He criticized, however, excessively severe punishment of adultery. As a counterpart to marriages of convenience, he recalled with admiration the custom of the Samnites that assorted young people on the basis of their courage, beauty, and virtue.

Since depopulation was one of his major concerns, he cited at great length Roman laws designed to increase the number of marriages and children, and he suggested that similar laws were necessary again in Europe. His approach to abortion was equally pragmatic. He deplored as harmful to population the practice of abortion for cosmetic reasons among savages, but he considered abortion a legitimate means of population control in areas of inadequate food supply. In support of this measure, he referred to Aristotle who recommended induced miscarriage for population control. He also recalled that on the American continent Indian women resorted to abortion as a protest against the cruelty of the colonizers.

One of the logical outcomes of Montesquieu's vast analysis of relationships among physical, moral, and political factors is the total rejection of fundamental traditional notions about woman: that she is, by nature, physically and mentally inferior and that she should, therefore, have subordinate status in the family, be relegated to the home, and be excluded from public office. He recognized differences between the sexes but did not conclude that woman's physiology results in inferior psychology. He also objected to the principle that woman's participation in society and the qualities that she developed were inexorably limited by her physical traits. He maintained that the distinctive characteristics of the sexes are enhanced by separation but become flexible in civilized society when men and women interact freely and women participate in life outside the home. There are statements in his work on women's weaknesses and vices that, taken out of context, may be construed as antifeminist, but the negative characteristics are never presented as inherent in the nature of women or as traits that cannot be overcome. The *Lettres persanes* argue clearly against enslavement, subordination, and ideological humiliation. They proclaim feminine intellectual independence and liberation from the walls, the veil, and the male conception of women's role. The *Esprit des lois* continues to expose the irrationality of male views and the injustice and destructiveness of conditions imposed on women. Montesquieu vindicated woman's right to political rule and advocated legal reforms in her favor. Through the study of polygamy, he attacked servitude motivated by climate, politics, and male selfishness. His strongest defense of women is the book on the national character, which demonstrates the social, cultural, economic, and political benefits of women's freedom. He agreed with contemporary feminists that feminine potential and its fulfillment depend on opportunity, and he enriched their arguments with his own empirical approach. Ahead of his time, Montesquieu created an awareness of the complexity of the factors that modify the relationships between the sexes, of the many forms they may take, and of their ongoing evolution. (pp. 278-84)

> Pauline Kra, *"Montesquieu and Women,"* in French Women and the Age of Enlightenment, *edited by Samia I. Spencer, Indiana University Press, 1984, pp. 272-84.*

DAVID CARRITHERS   (essay date 1986)

[*An American educator, Carrithers is a member of both the American Political Science Association and the American Society for Eighteenth-Century Studies. In the following excerpt, he traces the roles of determinism and voluntarism in Montesquieu's historical writing.*]

Given Montesquieu's obvious profundity in the area of philosophical history, surprisingly little attention has been bestowed on his minor historical writings. Two particular treatises stand out as likely candidates for analysis if our understanding of his historical thought is to be enlarged. These are *De la politique* (1725) and *Réflexions sur le caractère de quelques princes et sur quelques événements de leur vie* (1731-33). Neither of these works was explicitly intended as a discourse on historical causation per se, but both of them nonetheless included important philosophical statements about the nature of historical change. Both deserve analysis if one seeks to discover whether the roots of Montesquieu's determinism in his history of Rome [*Considérations sur les causes de la grandeur des Romains, et de leur décadence*] are discernible earlier and whether he applied this determinist theory to other historical settings besides Rome.

De la politique deserves substantially more attention than it has received. There has been no extended analysis of its contents, and as yet there is no English translation. Originally, it was composed as the concluding chapters of the *Traité des devoirs* (1725), a work revealing Montesquieu's deep concern, midway through the 1720s, with natural law theory stressing absolutes of justice to which positive laws should conform.... Mon-

tesquieu discussed in his *Traité des devoirs* three sorts of duties: duties to God, duties to oneself, and duties to one's fellow man. He concluded that the duties associated with our ontological condition have a higher priority than those duties associated with being a citizen of this or that country. Hence we should put our obligations to mankind ahead of more parochial attachments.

Not surprisingly, what is now known as *De la politique* bears a close thematic relation to the earlier portions of the *Traité des devoirs* of which it was once the concluding part. Whereas the first twelve chapters of that work dealt with justice abstractly and philosophically, Montesquieu turned in the two concluding chapters to the concrete world of historical experience. His express purpose was not the presentaton of any particular philosophy of history. Unlike his later work on Rome, *De la politique* presented no unifying statements suggesting that historical accidents are controlled by general causes. Rather, he merely flirted briefly with a determinist orientation in analyzing events in seventeenth-century England and early eighteenth-century France, while stressing the influence of unpredictable human behavior in other historical settings.

De la politique was cast essentially as an anti-Machiavellian tract. Montesquieu's purpose was to register a plea for simple, straightforward, honest statecraft that does not violate fundamental principles of justice. His disenchantment with politics considered as political cunning and duplicity was then at its height, and *De la politique* attacks what he perceived as widespread and immoral Machiavellianism in statecraft and international diplomacy. Rather than attacking the prevalent doctrine of *raison d' état* on abstract moral grounds, however, which he concluded would "convince everyone but influence no one," he chose to focus upon the real, empirical world of recorded human history in order to demonstrate the futility of self-serving, immoral statecraft.

Montesquieu suggests two different reasons for this futility, and the contrasting orientation of these explanations suggests an unmistakable tension, at this stage in his historical thought, between two contrasting historical explanations:

> Most effects come about from such unusual circumstances or depend on causes so imperceptible and remote that they defy prediction.

The mention of "unusual circumstances" clearly refers to the unpredictable world of accident and caprice. Such unpredictable occurrences make history a jumble of accident piled on accident. Stress on "imperceptible and remote" causes, on the other hand, bespeaks a view of history stressing necessity rather than chance.

Not surprisingly, the most determinist, and hence the most sensational, passages of *De la politique* are the best known. They are in fact almost the only ones that are ever quoted by secondary commentators. The most frequently cited passage presents, with a notably determinist twist, one of Montesquieu's early formulations of the doctrine of the *esprit général*:

> In all societies, which are really groupings of minds, a common character takes shape. This collective soul takes on a manner of thinking which is the effect of a chain of infinite causes that multiply and combine from century to century. Once the tone is set and has permeated the society, it alone governs and all that sovereigns, magistrates, and peoples are able to do or plan, whether they seem to go against this tone or follow it, is always in relation to it; and it dominates until the society is totally destroyed.

Major political events, Montesquieu here suggests, however they may appear to the merely casual observer, are the necessary result of the influence of a complex chain of causes resulting in what he will later label a society's *esprit général*. And lest his argument remain an abstraction, he introduced two historical examples in *De la politique* to prove his point: England in the period of civil war in the seventeenth century and France during the regency of Louis XV in the early eighteenth century.

Far from being a chance event uninfluenced by the dominant tone, or ''general spirit,'' of the times in England, the antimonarchical opposition to Charles I in mid-seventeenth-century England was well nigh inevitable once Henry VIII had freed England from the papal yoke. ''Literally everyone,'' Montesquieu wrote, ''thought he had increased his power by becoming head of his own church as well as dispenser of the spoils of the old. But not so.'' Freeing England from the theological domination of Rome gave rise to an uncontrollable spirit of liberty that soon degenerated into fanaticism and frenzy. The consequence for Charles I, roughly a century later, was that his power was fated to be radically curtailed however he might have acted. . . . No absolute English monarch would have fared any better since it was not Charles's actions but rather the underlying disposition of general causes that rendered his position untenable. A trace of the old attitude of respect for royalty remained in the reigns of Edward, Mary, and Elizabeth, Montesquieu contended, but by the seventeenth century it had been completely eroded. Hence the troubles Charles I (executed in 1649) faced in the English Civil War were a foregone conclusion.

Montesquieu also demonstrated the determinist grip a dominant ''tone'' can exert by referring to France in the period of the regency of Louis XV. In spite of the extraordinary nature of the events that occurred in that period, the general ''tone'' was such, Montesquieu contended, that even had those in power been entirely different, and even had entirely different policies been adopted, the general course of events would have been unaffected:

> The disposition of the people, the circumstances surrounding the government, the general situation of the country, the interests of different groups were such that the end result would have been the same regardless of the causes at work or the ruler in power.

This is an extraordinary thesis. (pp. 67-70)

To arrive at a proper understanding of the overall philosophy of history expressed in *De la politique*, the determinist passages . . . must be considered along with contrasting passages that attribute the primary role of shaping history to the chance actions of individuals. A substantial number of little noticed passages within *De la politique* maintain that the record of history is a complex and unpredictable web of chance occurrences uninfluenced by overriding general causes. At one point, in fact, Montesquieu contends that, far from being deterministically controlled by causes antecedent to the event in question, history is as riddled with accidental influences and occurrences as is an individual human life. When we turn to history, he writes, ''we discover momentous, unforseen events everywhere we look,'' momentous events that literally transform the contours of history and are clearly the product of unpredictable accident rather than some inexorable cunning of history.

In terms of sheer volume of texts, Montesquieu actually spends substantially more time in *De la politique* demonstrating the

thesis of historical accident than arguing on behalf of historical determinism. His first example, chronologically speaking, of the role of chance in history was the reign of Heraclius, Byzantine emperor from 610 to 641. Heraclius was clever but not sufficiently so to foresee what his fate would be as a result of a great and unpredictable historical accident. He believed the Avars and the Persian Sassanid dynasty posed the most substantial threat to his rule, and he therefore devoted himself to making peace with the Avars and subduing the Persians. Unbeknownst to him, however, a great, unanticipated intrusion of human will into history was brewing in Mecca, where in 613 the prophet Mohammed began preaching. Heraclius, Montesquieu commented, had probably not even heard of the town of Mecca; and yet the great historical accident of the birth of Mohammed—an accident from the vantage point of Montesquieu, if not from the viewpoint of the Islamic faithful—was soon to devastate his empire. No one—least of all Heraclius—foresaw the rapid expansion of Islam. It was one of these ''unusual circumstances'' that statesmen, no matter how cunning, cannot foresee and hence cannot forestall or overcome. (p. 71)

Clearly, close attention to *all* of *De la politique* reveals a Montesquieu who was just as fascinated by the capricious nature of history as by the contrasting idea of causal currents advancing events toward predetermined ends. Had he been a fully committed determinist, he would have consistently argued that Machiavellian duplicity and cunning are always ineffective because dominant tones and general causes render the accidental acts of key historical actors of minimal influence. He was not prepared, however, to advance this as a general, all-encompassng thesis valid in all historical contexts.

Like *De la politique*, Montesquieu's *Réflexions sur le caractère de quelques princes et sur quelques événements de leur vie* deserves fuller examination than it has received. There is at present no English translation, and most students of Montesquieu pay the work little heed. As was the case with *De la politique*, the *Réflexions* was not explicitly intended as a philosophical statement concerning history. Since the work consists of sketches of the lives of various influential princes, however, Montesquieu cannot help but make important judgments about the relation of these individuals to the flow of history around them. Hence a philosophical viewpoint about history emerges. The *Réflexions* were originally conceived as part of a larger, uncompleted work to be called *Le Prince*, or *Les Princes*. A fragment of this larger work preserved in the *Pensées* reveals that the overall emphasis of the work was to have been, as in the case of *De la politique*, the need for morality in politics, particularly on the part of rulers. (p. 72)

Using a comparative method and discussing two rulers at a time, after the model of Plutarch, Montesquieu discussed the careers of Charles XII of Sweden (1682-1718), Charles, Duke of Burgundy (1433-1477), Tiberius (42 B.C.-A.D. 37), Louis XI of France (1423-1483), Philip II of Spain (1527-1598), Pope Paul III (1468-1549), Pope Sixtus V (1521-1590), the Duke of Mayenne (1554-1611), Cromwell (1599-1658), Henry III of France (1551-1589), and Charles I of England (1600-1649). In contrast to his treatise on Roman history composed during the same time period, Montesquieu by no means adopted a determinist stance in this work. In fact one finds an important shift away from determinism in the analysis of Charles I as compared to the earlier *De la politique*. Whereas Montesquieu had earlier stressed the historical forces arrayed against Charles, he now stressed Charles's own actions as the main source of the problems he faced. Admittedly, Montesquieu began his re-analysis of Charles I with a text that sounds distinctly determinist:

> There are certain circumstances in which men of the least ability can govern succesfully; there are others where the greatest geniuses are shaken: sometimes the art of ruling is the easiest art in the world, and sometimes it is the most difficult.

This statement clearly stresses the importance of the underlying allure, or disposition of things, and thinking back to *De la politique,* one would expect Montesquieu once again to treat Charles I as a victim of irreversible historical tides. Instead, however, Montesquieu takes a different tack altogether, placing the blame for Charles's disastrous failures squarely on his own shoulders. He says absolutely nothing about a dominant anti-monarchical tone stemming from Henry VIII's break with Rome, which so increased the general desire for liberty that any absolute monarch would have been doomed to failure. Instead he focuses on Charles's imperfections. (p. 73)

The significance of this shift in emphasis from the determinism of *De la politique* to the voluntarism of the *Réflexions* should not be underestimated. Clearly, the determinist leanings evident in *De la politique* did not develop into a doctrinaire position. Montesquieu backed away from inflexible determinism in the *Réflexions* even with regard to that very monarch who had earlier been his chief example of the role of determinism in history. Charles I, Montesquieu now contended, was himself responsible for the animosity he faced. He was weak, superstitious, biased, alternatively too bold and too timid, and much more concerned with pleasing his courtesans than his subjects. The result was that his subjects' initial hatred turned soon to scorn. Charles's personal defects, then, rather than the general antimonarchical tone discussed in *De la politique,* are the reason for the fate he met at the hands of the Puritans. (p. 74)

In Montesquieu's *Réflexions* only one brief passage in a discussion of Charles XII of Sweden even hints at a determinist philosophy of history. Charles XII's colorful and daring career proved a popular subject for eighteenth-century writers—Voltaire's *Historie du Charles XII* (1731) is the preeminent example—and readers of the *Espirit des lois* will recall that Montesquieu later included a chapter on Charles XII in Book X of that work. Seeds of the later treatment of Charles XII are clearly present in the *Réflexions.* In both instances Montesquieu made statements that seem at first to evoke the earlier determinism of portions of *De la politique* but prove instead to be implanted within general arguments moving in a decidedly voluntarist direction contending that Charles XII was himself the architect of the misfortunes that befell him.

In the *Réflexions* Montesquieu compared Charles XII to Charles, Duke of Burgundy, and remarked of them both:

> These princes are also similar in that they continually rebelled against their destiny.

Certainly the idea of rebelling against one's destiny seems to suggest irreversible tides of history that can only be ineffectually opposed. If one is fated to be doled out a given historical result, resistance to the dictates of history would seem to be futile. Close analysis of Montesquieu's text, however, reveals that this was not actually his meaning. He actually stops short of depicting an historically determined fate that made Charles a prisoner of forces beyond his control. Precisely as Voltaire had done, Montesquieu stressed defects of Charles's character, above all, as the reason for his misguided decision to wage the disastrous battle of Pultova.... Montesquieu remarked:

> In most cases, when a monarch is killed on the battlefield it is a result of chance; but the military conduct of Charles XII . . . made such a death inevitable.

Clearly what Montesquieu was arguing is that death became a necessity for Charles XII—[Letter 127 in *Persian Letters*] reveals he was fully aware Charles died not at Pultova but in battle in Norway in 1718—because he insisted on engineering military campaigns which other generals would have eschewed as foolhardy. Charles's eventual death, then, was "a necessity" only because of his consistent tendency to deny rational odds of survival. (pp. 75-6)

What, then, can we conclude concerning Montesquieu's philosophy of history based on the works we have considered? Certainly it is safe to say that, as of 1725, when he composed *De la politique,* he had not yet chosen between accident and necessity as the primary force of history. He was willing to consider both possibilities as having some validity depending on the particular historical setting. Furthermore, by 1731-1733, when he composed the *Réflexions sur le caractère de quelques princes,* his emphasis had shifted from the determinism of portions of *De la politique* to the unpredictable actions of political leaders. Prior, then, to the *Considérations sur les causes de la grandeur des Romains et de leur décadence,* Montesquieu had not emerged as anything resembling a dogmatic determinist. He had toyed with determinism but had certainly not discovered a *système* to be articulated over and against all other theories of historical interpretation.

How, then, do we account for the distinctively determinist orientation of Montesquieu's philosophical sketch of Roman history? Perhaps the most plausible explanation is that, however much chance occurrences and circumstances seem to predominate in some periods of history, there does seem to have been an overriding logical sequence to Roman historical development. If one were ever tempted towards a determinist reading of history, Rome would be the example triggering that response. And Roman history, furthermore, was sufficiently distant in time from the eighteenth century to enable Montesquieu to discern a logical development in events that certainly would have escaped such a perception among those living through them or commenting on them in close proximity.

Certainly Montesquieu's Roman history cannot be characterized as embodying an actual transformation in his historical thought. Rather, Roman materials simply brought to the fore determinist sentiments traceable to *De la politique.* the Roman history does present, however, his most doctrinaire stance on determinism as a mode of historical explanation. Not only Rome, he writes, but "every monarchy" was subject to general causes controlling even what seem to be accidents. Merely suggesting such a broad applicability of the determinist formula, however, is very different from demonstrating it. Had he tried to do so, he would likely have had a difficult time, since the historical writings we have examined reveal a Montesquieu who very strongly believed that the course of European history up to his day had been very substantially affected by the upredictable decisions, actions, and blunders of those European rulers who had quite literally *made* the history of their day.

It is also true that the search for monistic explanations, which became something of an obsession in the nineteenth century, was not part of Montesquieu's outlook. He would almost certainly have allowed his broad statement concerning "every monarchy" to be tempered by the facts. He clearly never aimed for the sort of rigid, dogmatic systematization that a nineteenth-century intellectual might have demanded of himself. He did not set out to be a philosopher of history in the modern manner of a Marx, a Spengler, or a Toynbee. "Philosopher of history" is a phrase he would not have accepted. He was rather a student of history who sometimes made philosophical statements about the content of history. Therefore one does not encounter a finished *système* in his works. He did not attempt to impose a dogmatic inflexible system on all of recorded history.

Furthermore, even Montesquieu's determinist pronouncements do not always preclude a realm of influence for accidents. He never denied that those events that triggered this or that necessary sequence of events did not have points of origin that were accidental rather than predetermined. There was no hint, for example, in his analysis in *De la politique* of the historical causation of Charles I's problems, that Henry VIII's break with Rome was itself a predetermined event. Another monarch, we are left to assume, might have followed a different course. Nor did Montesquieu contend that a given determinist flow of history, when and where it existed, could never be altered. What he maintained instead is that changes in that dominant, historically-conditioned tone will not be predicted or seen ahead of time. Such changes, he asserted, will "depend either on causes so remote that they seem no more capable of influencing the course of events than many others, or on a minor effect hidden by a great cause which produces other great, readily apparent effects, while holding in store the minor effect until it erupts, sometimes three centuries later." And what makes a hidden cause suddenly or finally erupt may itself be accidental. Hence the role of the unpredictable cannot be dismissed even within the context of some of Montesquieu's determinist thinking. We must be wary, therefore, of one-sided readings of Montesquieu's philosophy of history.

Surely the overall historical philosophy of Montesquieu's Roman history was determinist. Focusing exclusively on that work, however, cannot help but lead to a distortion of the true complexity of his historical thought. A foray into his less studied historical writings demonstrates that he possessed a rich awareness of the many twists and turns events can take depending on the decisions made by influential historical actors. At the same time, however, Montesquieu's appreciation of the underlying general causes at work in *Roman* history enabled him to look . . . to the realm of structural history which focuses on the underlying constellation of forces influencing a given historical development. Hence Montesquieu was clearly an important contributor to the movement attempting to make history something more than "an undecipherable hieroglyphic." He sensed the need to move beyond the level of mere chronicle to ask not just what happened but why. Only when this question was asked could historical studies come of age.

To see rhyme and reason within a given series of events, however, was not equivalent to perceiving transcendent meaning in history. Montesquieu could discover that a certain series of historical happenings were set in motion by general causes without jumping to the conclusion that the overall pattern of events served some teleological goal or end. He discerned no "plan" in history akin to Kant's contention in his *Idea for a Universal History from a Cosmopolitan Point of View* (1784) that Nature's historical intention for man was "the development of all the capacities which can be achieved by mankind" and the attainment of "a perfectly just civic constitution." Montesquieu neither retained Bossuet's teleological stress on Divine providence nor envisioned, as did many among his intellectual contemporaries, its replacement by a teleological

stress on incessant progress based on scientific advance. He was part of that movement striving to "free history from the domination of final causes and lead it back to the real empirical causes." In spite of his substantial interest in natural science, he did not join the ranks of those prophesying infinite progress as nature was subjected more and more to man's control. He would have considered the progressivist vision of a Turgot or a Condorcet in his own century, or of a Saint Simon or a Comte in the next, a subjective, unwarranted gloss. Far from being a believer in infinite progress, Montesquieu was, as Gilbert Chinard demonstrated [in an essay included in *Studies in the History of Culture* (1942)], a "historical pessimist," whether spinning out the circularity of moral progress in the Troglodyte cycle in the *Lettres persanes,* or dwelling on the contemporary decline of Spain, Italy, and Poland in the same work, or delineating the historical inevitability of Rome's decline, or predicting the eventual demise, even of England, toward the end of his famous Book XI, chapter 6 of the *Esprit des lois,* setting out the main components of English liberty. Insofar as he was willing to indulge in sweeping speculation, Montesquieu believed not in endless upward advance but in the likelihood of birth, rise, and decline as epitomized by the example of Rome. And this means he was closer in spirit to Fénelon, Diderot, D'Alembert, Condillac, Raynal, Grimm, Dubos, and Vico than to the French prophets of progress.

What is important about Montesquieu's contribution to historiography is that he understood better than most of his contemporaries that history is not just a record of man's impress on events. If great men sometimes shape history, it is also true that sometimes the cumulative weight of past events coalesces into a general cause inclining a given society in one direction rather than another so that the role of particular individuals is reduced to a near nullity. As Gibbon, too, was aware, Montesquieu perceived that these general causes sometimes overpower secondary causes and predispose events toward one historical outcome rather than another. As Raymond Aron aptly observed [in *Main Currents in Sociological Thought: Montesquieu, Comte, Marx, Tocqueville, and the Sociologists and the Revolution of 1848* (1968)], Montesquieu was trying to replace "incoherent diversity" in the social universe with "a conceptual order," having concluded that "beyond the chaos of accidents, there are underlying causes which account for the apparent absurdity of things." Hence Montesquieu can be interpreted as the Kepler, or Newton of the social world. If nature had been shown to be subject to rationalistic explication, so too might the world of man be made to give up its secrets to a suitably perspicacious philosophe. For Montesquieu to have advanced historical studies by means of this keen insight must certainly be judged a substantial achievement. (pp. 77-80)

David Carrithers, "Montesquieu's Philosophy of History," in Journal of the History of Ideas, *Vol. 47, No. 1, January-March, 1986, pp. 61-80.*

JEFFREY HADDEN   (essay date 1987)

[*Hadden is an associate editorial page editor at the* Detroit News. *During 1987 he contributed a series of articles on the background of the framing of the United States Constitution. In the following excerpt, he demonstrates Montesquieu's continuing influence on American constitutional law.*]

On July 7, 1986, the U.S. Supreme Court struck down a portion of the Gramm-Rudman-Hollings Deficit Reduction Act. The court ruled that the section of the law in question violated the constitutional doctrine of the separation of powers between the legislative, executive, and judicial branches of the federal government. The court held that Congress was improperly giving itself the power to administer one of its own laws.

Chief Justice Warren Burger, writing for the court's majority, said that "even a cursory examination of the Constitution reveals the influence of Montesquieu's thesis that checks and balances were the foundation of a structure of government that would protect liberty." The former chief justice was referring to Charles Louis de Secondat, baron de La Brede et de Montesquieu, whose separation of powers theory was contained in his *The Spirit of the Laws,* published in 1748.

It should be noted that the Founders saw checks and balances as something quite different from the separation of powers. But as the court's ruling on the deficit reduction act indicates, Montesquieu's separation of powers doctrine continues to influence American constitutional law, as it did at the time of the constitutional convention.

Madison, in *The Federalist No. 47,* refers to "the celebrated Montesquieu" as "the oracle who is always consulted and cited on this subject." But, according to several scholars, Montesquieu's theory of the separation of powers was based on his *misunderstanding* of the British government.

Montesquieu wrote in his *Spirit of the Laws* that "it is necessary from the very nature of things that power should be a check to power . . . When the legislative and executive powers are united in the same person . . . there can be no liberty." Again, he continued, "there is no liberty if the judiciary power be not separated from the legislative and executive."

Montesquieu's doctrine of the separation of powers was derived from his observations of British government during a visit to England in 1729-31. He conceived of the British government as divided into distinct branches, with the king, the House of Lords, and the House of Commons having unique powers and serving distinct functions, with each acting as a check upon the other. In referring to the judicial function, Montesquieu was really discussing independent juries—not judges.

But reality contradicted Montesquieu's theory as applied to the British government. Even 250 years ago, though the king was far more powerful than today's figurehead monarch, he didn't dare veto parliamentary legislation and his ability to select ministers was limited to approval by Parliament. He had to exercise what Montesquieu conceived of as executive power by indirection, through patronage and bribes.

Nor did Commons necessarily serve as a check upon the House of Lords. Some of the members of Lords controlled dozens of votes in Commons. And Lords acted then and still serves as an ultimate court.

Though his political science was faulty, Montesquieu exerted an enormous influence on American constitutional thought, primarily, however, by confirming American experience. The American colonies prior to the Revolution were the scene of repeated struggles between royal governors and colonial assemblies. Americans had become used to the idea of a divergence of interest between executives and legislative bodies, and most of their discussions were about arriving at a proper balance of power between these two branches.

As for courts, they were, at the time, as Alexander Hamilton later wrote in *The Federalist No. 78,* "the least dangerous branch." Lay juries during most of the 18th century had more power than did judges in the colonies.

Consequently, though the Framers delineated three separate and distinct branches of government, as historian Forrest McDonald notes, they left the Supreme Court and other federal courts at the mercy of Congress.

> Jeffrey Hadden, *"Montesquieu's Mistake Preserves Liberty,"* in The Detroit News, *May 4, 1987, p. 10A.*

ADDITIONAL BIBLIOGRAPHY

Catlin, George. "The American and French Revolutions: Montesquieu, Jefferson, Burke and Paine." In his *The Story of the Political Philosophers,* pp. 300-41. New York: Whittlesey House, 1939.
    Describes the development and influence of Montesquieu's political theories.

Chamley, P. E. "The Conflict between Montesquieu and Hume: A Study of the Origins of Adam Smith's Universalism." In *Essays on Adam Smith,* edited by Andrew S. Skinner and Thomas Wilson, pp. 274-305. Oxford: Clarendon Press, 1975.
    Outlines points of agreement and of conflict in the sociopolitical theories of Montesquieu and David Hume.

Collins, J. Churton. "Montesquieu in England." In his *Voltaire, Montesquieu and Rousseau in England,* pp. 117-81. London: Eveleigh Nash, Fawside House, 1908.
    Investigation of Montesquieu's sojourn in England. Collins concludes: "It was in England that the ideas embodied in both these masterpieces [*Considerations* and *The Spirit of Laws*] took definite from, in England that they found stimulus and inspiration, from England that they drew nutriment."

Crisafulli, Alessandro S. "Parallels to Ideas in the *Lettres Persanes.*" *PMLA* LII, No. 2 (June 1937): 773-77.
    Tracks correspondences between Montesquieu's ideas in *Persian Letters* and the thought of Nicolas de Malebranche, Gottfried Wilhelm von Leibniz, and Anthony Ashley Cooper, Earl of Shaftesbury. Crisafulli contends that "there are between Montesquieu and these three writers some relationships of ideas which may imply influence."

————. "Montesquieu's Story of the Troglodytes: Its Background, Meaning, and Significance." *PMLA* LVIII, No. 2 (June 1943): 372-92.
    Close examination of the Troglodyte allegory in *Persian Letters.* Crisafulli contends that the episode "shows Montesquieu in the process of discovering, in the social conduct peculiar to certain political and economic conditions, two kinds of predominant motives that, when fully elaborated, precisely defined and labelled, becomes in the *Esprit des lois* the democratic principle of 'vertu' and the monarchical principle of 'honneur'."

Devletoglou, Nicos E. "Montesquieu and the Wealth of Nations." *The Canadian Journal of Economics and Political Science* 29, No. 1 (February 1963): 1-25.
    Examines aspects of Montesquieu's economic theory.

Ebenstein, William. "Montesquieu." In his *Introduction to Political Philosophy,* pp. 142-47. New York: Rinehart & Co., Inc., 1952.
    Outlines the main tenets of Montesquieu's political philosophy in *The Spirit of Laws,* stressing the author's unique qualities.

Hamilton, Alexander [Publius, pseud.]. "No. IX: The Union As a Safeguard against Domestic Faction and Insurrection." In *The Federalist: A Commentary on the Constitution of the United States, Being a Collection of Essays Written in Support of the Constitution Agreed upon September 17, 1787, by the Federal Convention,* by Alexander Hamilton, John Jay, and James Madison, edited by Henry Cabot Lodge, pp. 45-51. New York: G. P. Putnam's Sons, 1902.

Reprints a significant document in *The Federalist* in which Hamilton extensively quotes from *The Spirit of Laws* to buttress his argument for creating an American confederate republic.

Hampson, Norman. "Montesquieu" and "Montesquieu, Rousseau, and the Revolutionary Generation." In his *Will & Circumstance: Montesquieu, Rousseau and the French Revolution*, pp. 3-25, 55-64. Norman: University of Oklahoma Press, 1983.
Overview of Montesquieu's work with particular attention to *The Spirit of Laws*. Hampson also analyzes the impact of Montesquieu's theories on leaders of the French Revolution.

Havens, George R. "Montesquieu and America." In his *The Age of Ideas: From Reaction to Revolution in Eighteenth-Century France*, pp. 140-56. New York: Henry Holt and Co., 1955.
Account of the Founding Father's political debates and decisions, with particular reference to how they were influenced by *The Spirit of Laws*. Havens concludes: "Without the aid of Montesquieu's *Spirit of Laws*, the uncertain task of drawing up the new constitution would certainly have been more difficult, perhaps even impossible, in the midst of the violent struggle between divergent opinions."

Hulliung, Mark. *Montesquieu and the Old Regime*. Berkeley and Los Angeles: University of California Press, 1976, 258 p.
Study of Montesquieu as a catalytic force for radical political change. Hulliung contends that Montesquieu "was a foremost detractor of the old regime" and that he "dreamed of nothing less than a national republic and a democratic society in France which could displace monarchical politics and an aristocratic society."

Hume, David. Letter to Rev. Hugh Blair. In his *The Letters of David Hume*, Vol. II, edited by J. Y. T. Greig, pp. 133-34. Oxford: Clarendon Press, 1932.
Letter of 1 April 1767, in which Hume describes *The Spirit of Laws* as a work of "considerable Merit, notwithstanding the Glare of its pointed Wit, and notwithstanding its false Refinements and its rash and crude Positions."

Jefferson, Thomas. *The Writings of Thomas Jefferson: Being His Autobiography, Correspondence, Reports, Messages, Addresses, and Other Writings, Official and Private*, Vol. V, edited by H. A. Washington, pp. 532ff. New York: Derby & Jackson, 1853?
Three letters mentioning Montesquieu, dated 12 August 1810, 16 September 1810, and 26 January 1811. Jefferson's correspondence reflects his ambivalence toward Montesquieu; he says of *The Spirit of Laws*: "I had, with the world, deemed Montesquieu's work of much merit, but saw in it, with every thinking man, so much of paradox, of false principle and misapplied fact, as to render its value equivocal on the whole."

Jones, W. T. "Charles Louis de Secondat, Baron de Montesquieu." In his *Masters of Political Thought*, Vol. 2: *Machiavelli to Bentham*, edited by Edward McChesney Sait, pp. 217-47. Boston: Houghton Mifflin Co., 1949.
Explication (buttressed by frequent quotation from Montesquieu) of important aspects of *The Spirit of Laws*, including Montesquieu's general concept of law, his divisions of political systems and the ruling principles of each, and his thoughts on education and taxation.

Keener, Frederick M. "The Spirit of the *Lettres persanes*, and of Enlightened Characterization" and "The Generation and Progress of Usbek's Ideas in the *Lettres persanes*." In his *The Chain of Becoming, The Philosophical Tale, the Novel, and a Neglected Realism of the Enlightenment: Swift, Montesquieu, Voltaire, Johnson, and Austen*, pp. 127-53, 154-93. New York: Columbia University Press, 1983.
Two essays on *Persian Letters*. The first compares the work with Jonathan Swift's *Gulliver's Travels* in order "to fathom the points of contrast beneath the similarities"; the second approaches the meaning of the book through an analysis of the character of Usbek.

Keohane, Nannerl O. "Virtuous Republics and Glorious Monarchies: Two Models in Montesquieu's Political Thought." *Political Studies* 20, No. 4 (December 1972): 383-96.

Maintains that Montesquieu conceived of his political models of the republic and the monarchy as "Weberian ideal-types: conceptions abstracted from empirical reality which any particular republic or monarchy might be expected to approximate but never fully embody."

Lowell, Edward J. "Montesquieu." In his *The Eve of the French Revolution*, pp. 126-53. Boston: Houghton Mifflin Co., 1892.
Surveys *Persian Letters*, *Considerations*, and *The Spirit of Laws*, paraphrasing the most important and innovative ideas contained in each.

Madison, James [Publius, pseud.]. "No. XLVII: The Particular Structure of the New Government and the Distribution of Power among Its Different Parts." In *The Federalist: A Commentary on the Constitution of the United States, Being a Collection of Essays Written in Support of the Constitution Agreed upon September 17, 1787, by the Federal Convention*, by Alexander Hamilton, John Jay, and James Madison, edited by Henry Cabot Lodge, pp. 299-307. New York: G. P. Putnam's Sons, 1902.
Reprint of a 1788 defense of the American Constitution against detractors who feared that it did not sufficiently contradistinguish and define the three branches of American government. Madison repeatedly cites Montesquieu as his authority on the subject of the separation of powers.

Martin, Kingsley. "The British Constitution." In his *French Liberal Thought in the Eighteenth Century: A Study of Political Ideas from Bayle to Condorcet*, rev. ed., edited by J. P. Mayer, pp. 147-69. London: Turnstile Press, 1954.
Explains and critiques aspects of *The Spirit of Laws* and delineates Montesquieu's influence on his peers.

Merry, Henry J. *Montesquieu's System of Natural Government*. West Lafayette, Ind.: Purdue University Studies, 1970, 414 p.
Comprehensive study of Montesquieu's political theory. Merry writes that his purpose is "to explain that Montesquieu's work embodies a systematic analysis of the complex interactions of political life, that he finds the central psychological spirit of a nation in the conflicts of social classes and social forces, and that *L'Esprit des lois*, like many recent studies of political systems, makes the interrelationship of governmental institutions, political infrastructures, and sociological environment, the focal point of both the method of inquiry and the theory of government."

Oake, Roger B. "Montesquieu's Religious Ideas." *Journal of the History of Ideas* 14, No. 4 (October 1953): 548-60.
Proposes to "illustrate [Montesquieu's] general view of human nature by an analysis of his treatment of man's religious activity."

———. "Montesquieu's Analysis of Roman History." *Journal of the History of Ideas* 16, No. 1 (January 1955): 44-59.
Study of Montesquieu's historical methods and conclusions in *Considerations*.

Perkins, Merle L. "Montesquieu on National Power and International Rivalry." *Studies on Voltaire and the Eighteenth Century* 238 (1985): 1-95.
Aims "to evaluate with greater attention to their international implications the great themes of Montesquieu's philosophic and political thought." Ranging over the complete oeuvre, Perkins's study emphasizes Montesquieu's personal perspectives in the formulation of his ideas and the relation of those ideas to eighteenth-century currents of thought.

Price, E. H. "Voltaire and Montesquieu's Three Principles of Government." *PMLA* LVII, No. 4 (December 1942): 1046-52.
Recapitulation and explication of Voltaire's criticism of *The Spirit of Laws*, concluding: "Voltaire felt that the principles in the *Esprit des lois* were too theoretical and too remote from the problems of human betterment."

———. "Montesquieu's Historical Conception of the Fundamental Law." *The Romanic Review* 38, No. 3 (October 1947): 234-42.
Argues that Montesquieu "saw legal fundamentals changing to keep pace with history."

Rogers, Katharine M. "Subversion of Patriarchy in *Les Lettres persanes*." *Philological Quarterly* 65, No. 1 (Winter 1986): 61-78.

> Excellent study of Montesquieu's attitude toward feminism. Rogers argues that while Montesquieu remained largely bound by conventional patriarchal assumptions in his own life and in *The Spirit of Laws*, he nonetheless advocated radical feminism in the fictional *Persian Letters*.

Shackleton, Robert. "Montesquieu and Machiavelli: A Reappraisal." *Comparative Literature Studies* 1, No. 1 (1964): 1-13.

> Assembles biographical and textual evidence to prove that Montesquieu knew well and was influenced by Niccolò Machiavelli's work.

Shanley, Mary Lyndon, and Stillman, Peter G. "Political and Marital Despotism: Montesquieu's *Persian Letters*." In *The Family in Political Thought*, edited by Jean Bethke Elshtain, pp. 66-79. Amherst: University of Massachusetts Press, 1982.

> Examines the domestic tyranny inherent in the seraglio intrigue of *Persian Letters*, relating this to Montesquieu's theory of familial despotism.

Shklar, Judith N. "Putting Cruelty First." *Daedalus* 111, No. 3 (Summer 1982): 17-27.

> Interesting theoretical query (using Montesquieu and Michel de Montaigne as examples) of the ethical and logical implications of a belief system which assumes human cruelty to be the greatest moral wrong.

Sorel, Albert. *Montesquieu*. Translated by Gustave Masson. London: George Routledge and Sons, 1887, 190 p.

> Biography offering critical appraisals of both major and minor works.

Spurlin, Paul Merrill. *Montesquieu in America: 1760-1801*. University, La.: Louisiana State University Press, 1940, 302 p.

> Seminal study of the impact of Montesquieu's political philosophy on eighteenth-century America. Spurlin has extensively researched textual evidence of the dissemination of Montesquieu's writings in America and American opinion of the author as expressed in the many references to him in early documents. Spurlin concludes that, with respect to the idea of the separation of powers, political liberty, and political virtue, Montesquieu served as "guide and mentor to a free and proud people essaying a new form of government."

———. "Montesquieu and the American Constitution." In his *The French Enlightenment in America: Essays on the Times of the Founding Fathers*, pp. 86-98. Athens: University of Georgia Press, 1984.

> Condensed and definitive statement of Spurlin's thesis in his *Montesquieu in America*. He declares: "[Montesquieu's] doctrine that made tripartition of powers the sine qua non of liberty helped give a definite and permanent form to American constitutional thought."

Todorov, Tzvetan. "The Morality of Conquest." *Diogenes*, No. 125 (Spring 1984): 89-102.

> Applies the political philosophies of Montesquieu and Michel de Montaigne to the issue of the morality of the Spanish conquest of Mexico and Peru, comparing the two writers' beliefs.

Walter, E. V. "Policies of Violence: From Montesquieu to the Terrorists." In *The Critical Spirit: Essays in Honor of Herbert Marcuse*, edited by Kurt H. Wolff, Barrington Moore, Jr., and others, pp. 124-49. Boston: Beacon Press, 1967.

> Traces the influence of Montesquieu's perspective of political sociology on the theories of government held by French revolutionaries Robespierre and Saint-Just.

Frances (Chamberlaine) Sheridan

1724-1766

Irish novelist, dramatist, and poet.

Sheridan is chiefly remembered as the author of *Memoirs of Miss Sidney Bidulph,* a novel redolent of the eighteenth-century vogue of sentimentalism (particularly as exemplified by the novels of Samuel Richardson) yet unique in its rendering of theme and characterization. Like Richardson's work, *Sidney Bidulph* and its sequel, *Conclusion of the Memoirs of Miss Sidney Bidulph,* are written in epistolary style, are largely concerned with the issue of sexual morality, and have as their literary goal the evocation of pathos. At the same time, Sheridan is considered unique in her treatment of the themes of ethical dilemma and the consequences of an individual's moral choices, innovative in her recognition of the effect of the past on the present, and noteworthy for her achievement of a degree of realistic characterization rare in eighteenth-century fiction.

Frances Chamberlaine was born in Dublin. A childhood accident left her lame, making it difficult for her to walk more than a short distance unaided. According to Alicia Le Fanu, Sheridan's granddaughter and principal biographer, Frances's father the Reverend Philip Chamberlaine so strongly disapproved of literacy in women that Frances received no formal education, but her brothers surreptitiously taught her reading and writing as well as Latin and botany. She put this tutoring to good use, writing a romance, *Eugenia and Adelaide,* while yet in her teens. Tradition has it that Frances met her future husband as the result of writing a poem. Thomas Sheridan, as manager of the Theatre Royal in Smock Alley, Dublin, was embroiled in a controversy following a seemingly minor disagreement between himself and actor Theophilus Cibber. During the public debate over the incident, Frances published in Sheridan's defense a poem called "The Owls" and also a prose pamphlet, whereupon Sheridan arranged a meeting with his defender. The two were married in 1747 and eventually had six children, among them the famous dramatist Richard Brinsley Sheridan.

In the 1750s the Sheridans moved to London, where Thomas became involved in a number of theatrical and literary ventures and where the couple became acquainted with such leading literary figures as Richardson and Samuel Johnson. Sheridan showed her manuscript of *Eugenia and Adelaide* to Richardson, who encouraged her to write a longer, more fully developed work. The result was *Memoirs of Miss Sidney Bidulph,* which was published to great acclaim in 1761, bearing a dedication to Richardson. Two years later Sheridan's first play, *The Discovery,* was presented with similar success at Drury Lane by theater manager and actor David Garrick, with Garrick and Thomas Sheridan playing the leading male roles. Later in 1763, Sheridan's *The Dupe* was performed, but the play failed. The following year, plagued by financial difficulties despite their varied endeavors, the Sheridans were forced to move to Blois, France in order to escape their creditors. There Sheridan wrote the sequel to *Sidney Bidulph,* a play entitled *A Journey to Bath,* and another novel, *The History of Nourjahad.* Sheridan intended this novel to be the first in a series of instructive moral tales, but her death prevented the completion of more than the single work. She died at Blois in 1766.

The work considered Sheridan's finest by her contemporaries and by modern critics alike, *Memoirs of Miss Sidney Bidulph* is deemed a curious mixture of imitation and originality. The novel's plot is fairly standard sentimental fare: the young Sidney, learning that her betrothed, Faulkland, has seduced another woman and fathered a child by her, refuses to marry him on the advice of her mother, who was herself jilted on her wedding day by a conscience-stricken groom in circumstances similar to Faulkland's. Sidney marries another. After she is widowed, Faulkland renews his suit to her, but though she still loves him, Sidney holds fast to her moral course and even prevails upon Faulkland to wed the woman she believes he has wronged, Miss Burchell. Years later, Sidney discovers that Miss Burchell, a "female libertine," was the instigator in the original seduction, a fact which to her mind absolves Faulkland of moral guilt in the affair. Meanwhile, Faulkland discovers his wife with a lover and shoots and apparently kills her, then refuses to flee the country to save himself until Sidney agrees to marry him at last. The marriage knows no happiness, however—is in fact never consummated—for it soon develops that Faulkland's wife is very much alive. Faulkland himself is shortly afterward found dead, apparently by his own hand.

Eighteenth-century reviewers were quick to note the similarity between *Sidney Bidulph* and Richardson's novels, particularly *Clarissa; or, The History of a Young Lady* (1747-48) and *The History of Sir Charles Grandison* (1753-54). Like these works,

Sheridan's novel tells, in a series of letters, a highly affecting and emotional tale on the themes of sexual misconduct and moral rectitude. Yet Sheridan's story of long-suffering love, heightened by the pathos of missed opportunities and tragic misunderstandings, is not resolved as Richardson's are, with a happy ending in one case and a promise of heavenly reward in the other. Such a departure was viewed by some early critics as a dereliction of the novelist's duty to "encourage and promote Virtue," as the *Monthly Review* remarked, adding tersely that "the Author seems to have had no other design than to draw tears from the reader by distressing innocence and virtue, as much as possible." Nonetheless, early reviewers praised the believability of Sheridan's characters as well as the moving pathos of their situation; indeed, the emotional impact of the plot is in large measure attributable to the realistic and sympathetic characterization. Johnson's comment to Sheridan attests both to the effectiveness of the novel's realism and pathos and to the eighteenth-century disapproval of virtue failing to receive its just reward in literature: "I know not, Madam, that you have a right, upon moral principles, to make your readers suffer so much." Apparently readers of *Memoirs of Miss Sidney Bidulph* had no objection to suffering, though, for the novel enjoyed a tremendous popular success in England and especially on the Continent.

The novel's initial fame, though impressive, was not enduring, for as the sentimental vogue fell into disfavor, so did *Sidney Bidulph* fade into obscurity. In recent years, however, the novel has attracted the attention of several critics who have discerned in the work issues of greater subtlety and import than had been noted by earlier commentators. Scholars now claim that Sheridan broadened Richardson's concern with sexual morality to include a full-scale investigation of the implications of any attempt to live one's life according to a single, ruling moral principle. To modern critics, the validity of Sidney's moral stance appears ambiguous because she adheres to a moral course of action which is in fact based on a mistaken assumption. The moral probity of her cause is compromised by Faulkland's relative innocence of any wrongdoing, so that her refusal to marry him seems to some commentators to be less a noble course than a stubborn one. It has been suggested that Sidney's motives are not pure, that she basks in self-denial, unnecessarily subjecting herself and Faulkland to years of unhappiness which could have been avoided had she resolved to determine the truth of the matter. As Robert Hogan and Jerry C. Beasley have stated the issue: "It is difficult to know whether Mrs. Sheridan meant the reader to believe that Sidney is denied fulfillment because she made the wrong decision at last and married Falkland . . . , or because she ruined both their lives by being too scrupulously pious and conventional and by delaying the right decision for too long."

Sheridan's treatment of time in *Sidney Bidulph* and its sequel has also piqued critical interest, for the insistent effect of the past upon the present is evident throughout the two works. Sidney's adamant refusal to marry Faulkland is initially fostered by her mother, whose own oddly similar past experience has colored her—and through her, Sidney's—perception of the situation. This phenomenon of events from the past recurring, with slight variations, in the present, becomes even more pronounced in *Conclusion of the Memoirs of Miss Sidney Bidulph*. Here, Sidney's two daughters and Faulkland's son are the principals in an ill-fated love triangle strongly reminiscent of the Sidney-Faulkland-Miss Burchell drama. Margaret Doody has explained: "For Sheridan, past and present lapse into one another, conflate. Memory takes precedence of experience. It is

as if consciousness lapses into intervals of dreamlike, if vivid, activity, only to awaken and return to some inevitable and more solid (if terrible) recurrence of the past, which is reality."

The fluidity of time is also a motif in Sheridan's last novel, *The History of Nourjahad*. A moral fable, *Nourjahad* tells of a young Persian noble who, granted his wishes for immortality and unlimited wealth, lives a life of dissipation, eventually comes to see the error of his ways, and repents. The novel takes a surprising turn when it develops that Nourjahad's "lifetime" has in reality been only fourteen months, that the entire episode has been an illusion crafted by his friend the sultan to show him the folly of his desires.

Of Sheridan's plays, only the first, *The Discovery,* proved a success at any time. Lighthearted but intricately plotted, *The Discovery* is a comedy of courtship and marriage. Although popular with eighteenth-century audiences, it has not met with much approval since. In the twentieth century, Aldous Huxley attempted to adapt it to suit the tastes of modern audiences, but his efforts were unsuccessful. Burdened, as critics agree it is, by contrived actions and excessive sentimentality, *The Discovery* yet has a "saving grace," according to Hogan and Beasley, in that "it is written with uncommon fluency, so that even the more tedious parts of the plot and the more lachrymose revelations of feeling flow smoothly." On the whole, however, to modern commentators, Sheridan's plays are noteworthy less for their own merits than for their occasional anticipation of her more famous son's plays. The clearest example of Sheridan's influence on Richard Brinsley Sheridan's work is found in *A Journey to Bath* in the character of Mrs. Tryfort, whose eccentricities of language evidence her as the inspiration for the notorious Mrs. Malaprop of *The Rivals*.

Sheridan's work is at once recognizably the product of her time and its influences and uniquely her own: although allied to the Richardsonian sentimental school, Sheridan's best novels are ultimately testaments to their author's original imagination and talent. *Sidney Bidulph* and its sequel are respected today as probing studies of the implications of adopting a moral cause and as investigations of the pivotal role of the past in human destiny.

(See also *Dictionary of Literary Biography,* Vol. 39: *British Novelists, 1600-1800.*)

PRINCIPAL WORKS

A Letter from a Young Lady to Mr. Cibber (prose) 1743
"The Owls: A Fable Addressed to Mr. Sheridan, on the Late Affair in the Theatre" (poetry) 1743; published in journal *Dublin News Letter*
Memoirs of Miss Sidney Bidulph, Extracted from Her Own Journal. 3 vols. (novel) 1761
The Discovery (drama) 1763
The Dupe (drama) 1763
Conclusion of the Memoirs of Miss Sidney Bidulph. 2 vols. (novel) 1767
The History of Nourjahad (novel) 1767
*Eugenia and Adelaide. 2 vols. (novel) 1791
†A Journey to Bath (drama) 1902; published in *Sheridan's Plays: Now Printed as He Wrote Them. And His Mother's Unpublished Comedy, "A Journey to Bath"*
The Plays of Frances Sheridan (dramas) 1984

*This work was written probably in 1739.

†This work, of which only a fragment survives, was written in 1764.

THE CRITICAL REVIEW (essay date 1761)

[*In the following excerpt from a review of* Memoirs of Miss Sidney Bidulph, *the anonymous critic praises Sheridan as an affecting, if imitative, novelist.*]

If a copy drawn with the most exquisite skill, and heightened with the nicest touches of art, can be allowed merit equal to a justly admired original, the **Memoirs of Miss Bidulph** may deservedly claim a place in our esteem with the histories of Clarissa and Sir Charles Grandison. They are characterised by the same elegant fluency of narrative, the same interesting minuteness, inimitable simplicity, delicacy of sentiment, propriety of conduct, and irresistible pathos, which render them indisputably the best models in this species of writing, perhaps the most engaging, persuasive, and difficult of any other. . . . It is sufficient proof of the difficulty of this method of writing, that the ingenious inventive lady, to whom the **Memoirs of Miss Bidulph** are attributed, hath not been able to avoid imitation. Her heroine is a type of Miss Clarissa Harlowe, involved like her in a passion which she cannot gratify consistently with the dictates of filial duty, and rigid female delicacy. Faulkland is a composition of features borrowed from Grandison and Lovelace: possessed of the strict honour, the steadiness and integrity of the former, he sometimes delights in the stratagem of the latter. (pp. 186-87)

All the situations are highly interesting, because the passions are strongly engaged in the fate of characters rendered so eminently amiable, noble, and heroic. The reflections are equally just and natural; some of the characters are new, and all of them admirably sustained. Not a single impropriety of thought or expression occurs in the course of three volumes; but the whole flows easy, chaste, natural, simple, and beyond measure affecting and pathetic. In a word, as we entertain the highest opinion of the genius, delicacy, and good sense of Mrs. S——, we cannot but wish she may continue to exert those talents, so honourable to herself, so useful, so entertaining to society, and particularly so beneficial to the republic of letters. (pp. 197-98)

> *A review of "Memoirs of Miss Sidney Bidulph," in* The Critical Review, *Vol. XI, March, 1761, pp. 186-98.*

THE MONTHLY REVIEW, LONDON (essay date 1761)

[*In the following excerpt, the anonymous critic questions whether* Memoirs of Miss Sidney Bidulph *promotes virtue. The same query arises in the* Monthly Review's *criticism of* Conclusion of the Memoirs of Miss Sidney Bidulph *(see excerpt dated 1767).*]

It is the opinion of a distinguished French Writer, that *Romance* is the last physic that can be administered to a corrupt people. Nothing can be more certain, than that a nation absorbed in luxury will pay very little regard to sermons, or professed treatises of morality, and that the most probable means for a moral writer to catch the attention of those who are in most want of his instruction, is to mix up the medicine with some pleasant *vehicle,* so that the patient may imbibe the salutary parts without disgust, and enjoy their effect without perceiving their operation.

Two of our countrymen (and only two) have succeeded in this design. Mr. Richardson's works, in particular, constitute the best and most applicable system of morality, for young people, that ever appeared in any language. In his history of Clarissa, the most virtuous character is apparently the greatest sufferer; but notwithstanding that, the moral is extremely evident: Clarissa, tho' severely persecuted by her implacable relations, was nevertheless guilty of a flagrant error in putting herself into the power of a professed libertine; and all her future misfortunes are no more than the natural consequences of her indiscretion: but, in the Romance now before us [**Memoirs of Miss Sidney Bidulph**], the Author seems to have had no other design than to draw tears from the reader by distressing innocence and virtue, as much as possible. Now, tho' we are not ignorant that this may be a true picture of human life, in some instances, yet, we are of opinion, that such representations are by no means calculated to encourage and promote Virtue. (p. 260)

We had prepared a few slight criticisms on this performance; but being assured that it is the work of a Lady, we shall only add, that, in our opinion, it is, upon the whole, greatly superior to most of the productions of her *brother* Novelists. (p. 266)

> *A review of "Memoirs of Miss Sidney Bidulph," in* The Monthly Review, *London, Vol. XXIV, April, 1761, pp. 260-66.*

MRS. FRANCES SHERIDAN (letter date 1765)

[*In 1765, Sheridan (then living in France) gave the manuscript of* A Journey to Bath *to her friends the Victors, who, knowing that Sheridan wanted the play produced at Drury Lane, submitted it to the theater's manager, David Garrick. Mrs. Victor relayed to Sheridan Garrick's appraisal—which was decidedly negative— and Sheridan refuted his criticisms in a letter to Mrs. Victor, from which the following excerpt is taken. (For Garrick's response to Sheridan's defense of her play, see the excerpt dated 1765.)*]

Thank Mr. Garrick in my name for delivering his sentiments so frankly; it shows, at least, that he has some opinion of my philosophy, though he has none of my genius. I thank you for transmitting them to me so faithfully; and must now in my turn beg you will be so kind as to let him know what I have to say on the subject.

It is but a disagreeable task to defend one's own writing, but in the present case I think my honour at stake, and that I am bound to justify myself to you and Mr. Victor, for having put (as it appears upon the face of the evidence) a worthless stranger under your care, with no other recommendation than that of its own natural parent, and who, upon trial, has had so unfavourable a verdict returned, that perhaps you may condemn the poor culprit according to law, to return from whence it came, and thence to the place of execution (the fire), without vouchsafing it a second hearing.

I have the utmost deference for Mr. Garrick's opinion; I think extremely well of his wit, and still better of his discernment in judging what will, or will not succeed with the public; and for his abilities in his own profession, you know how highly I rate them: yet notwithstanding all this, and that I live too at present in a Roman Catholic country, I allow not infallibility to mortal man. People of the best understandings may differ widely in their sentiments of one and the same thing: we have all a certain perception which, for want of another name, goes by the general one of taste, and which if the subject to be decided on does not hit, we are apt sometimes to withhold the suffrage of our judgments, and to confound one with the other, though they are in fact distinct things, however one (to be perfect) ought to be founded on the other. (pp. 16-17)

There are four heavy accusations laid against [*A Journey to Bath*]: any one of which being sufficient to weigh the stripling down, I think it a maternal duty to exculpate my child, as far as it is in my power, from so many complicated faults, more especially as these vices have not been acquired by evil communications, but were born with it, and consequently take their rise originally from myself.

Imprimis, the play is without fable; secondly, all the scenes are detached; thirdly, there is nothing to interest the audience; and lastly, it has no humour. Tell Garrick I have thrown my gauntlet down, and am going to defend myself.

To the first charge, I plead not guilty, and will maintain that the fable is fully sufficient to build a series of events upon,—that there is as much as most of our comedies have, and more than in many which have been well received.

For the second, I cannot pretend to say (contrary to the opinion of so good a master of his art) whether the scenes are laid with that rigorous exactness that theatrical architecture may require; but thus much I will venture to assert, that their succession is regular and natural, and that they all tend to the main purpose of the drama, which is comprised in the two or three last lines of the play.

For the third objection, perhaps, I may be singular in my opinion; but I own, I do not think it absolutely necessary to interest the passions in a comedy; in a tragedy it is indispensable; but if the Comic Muse can excite curiosity enough to keep up the attention of the audience, she has, in my mind, acquitted herself of her duty; and I think this seems to be the general style of some of our most entertaining comedies, and the one in question, I should hope, is not entirely void of this merit; as the fate of an unworthy project against two innocent young people, artfully carried on, on one side, by a designing pair, and ridiculously supported, on the other, by an absurd pair, is not decided till the very last scene.

As for the fourth charge, I shall leave it as I found it; for unless I were to use Bayes's expressions, I should be at a loss for words to defend it—I promised you but pleasantry, and if I have utterly failed in that, I am more unfortunate than I expected to be. Just give me leave to add, what I think will not be denied me, that there is a good moral, and some character, in this piece. The latter of these two articles seems to be growing fast out of fashion: the late writers treating the taste of the times as physicians do the stomachs of their sick patients, which, finding [too] weak for substantial food, they supply with slops. But the reason of this is obvious: our present race of poets not abounding with invention of their own, have taken stories they found ready to their hand, which never having been intended for representation, the authors did not think themselves tied down to rules with which the stage ought not to dispense; yet I thought that Mr. Garrick, who himself knows so well how to support this grand requisite of dramatic works, would willingly have encouraged every effort which had the least pretensions to merit of this kind. (pp. 17-18)

> *Mrs. Frances Sheridan, in a letter to Mrs. Victor on November 16, 1765, in* The Private Correspondence of David Garrick with the Most Celebrated Persons of His Time, Vol. I *by David Garrick, Henry Colburn and Richard Bentley, Publishers, 1831, pp. 16-18.*

DAVID GARRICK   (letter date 1765)

[*An English actor, dramatist, and theater manager, Garrick was one of the most important theatrical innovators of the eighteenth*

century. His immense popularity as an actor was largely due to his natural acting style, a sharp contrast to the declamatory style customary in his day. His contribution as a dramatist consists primarily of farces such as The Lying Valet *(1741) and* Miss in Her Teens *(1747). As manager of the Drury Lane Theatre, he introduced to the English stage several improvements in the technical aspects of production. In the following excerpt, Garrick answers—via a letter to Mrs. Victor—Sheridan's defense of* A Journey to Bath *(see excerpt dated 1765).]*

I am got into a Scrape—to have a gauntlet thrown down to me by a Lady! & one who can Use her weapons with such skill too! I wish myself a good deliverance!—let what will be the Consequence, I must not turn my back upon a female Challenger.

As I have not the Comedy [*A Journey to Bath*], I must be very short and general in my answer; & give an account only of the particular Effect it had upon Me—that there were Characters in the play I allow'd but I thought, they were not well employ'd: I felt the scenes languid for want of an interesting fable, & that Spirit of dialogue of Vis comica ["comic force"], which was to be found in many Scenes of the *Discovery*.

Mr Smith's criticism in the *Rehearsal,* that the *Plot stands still,* might I think be apply'd in some measure to the play in question. But I am sure, that Mrs Sheridan (who is so unlike Bayes in Every thing else) will never agree with Him in this—that *a Plot is only good to bring in fine things*—How could Mrs Sheridan imagine that I wanted the passions to be interested? I should as soon expect to have my laughter rais'd in a tragedy—I said indeed that the Comedy wanted interest, but not of ye *Passions*—I meant a Comic interest, resulting from ye various humours of the Characters thrown into spirited action & brought into interesting Situations, naturally arising from a well-constructed fable or Plot—This, with a good moral, deduc'd from ye whole, is all I wish or look for in a *Comedy.*

Mrs Sheridan hints, (if I mistake not, for I read her letter but once) that I judge of these matters by some peculiar (I am affraid she means confin'd) notions of my own—perhaps I may—I can only judge with those materials for judging which I have—but if I am not entertain'd & interested in reading a play, I judge, and I think naturally enough, that it will not have the desir'd Effect upon an Audience, & I might say for Myself that hitherto I have been tolerably lucky in my guesses—it was my opinion that the *Discovery* would have success, and that the *Dupe* wd fail of it, upon the Stage—

When You write to Mrs Sheridan, I beg that You would present my best Compts to her & assure her, that there is no Manager more sincerely encourages Comedy in general than I do, or is more desirous of Shewing his regard to her's in particular than [I am]. (pp. 478-79)

> *David Garrick, in a letter to Mrs. Benjamin Victor c. November 16(?), 1765, in his* The Letters of David Garrick: Letters 335-815, Vol. II, *edited by David M. Little and George M. Kahrl, Cambridge, Mass.: The Belknap Press, 1963, pp. 478-79.*

THE MONTHLY REVIEW   (essay date 1767)

[*In the following excerpt from an anonymous review of* Conclusion of the Memoirs of Miss Sidney Bidulph, *the critic assesses the moral effect of the novel. For a similar appraisal of* Memoirs of Miss Sidney Bidulph, *see the excerpt from the* Monthly Review *dated 1761.*]

In our account of [*Memoirs of Miss Sidney Bidulph*], we observed that the chief design of the lady to whom it is supposed the public are obliged for this ingenious romance, seems to have been *to draw tears from the reader, by distressing innocence and virtue as much as possible* [see the excerpt from the *Monthly Review* dated 1761]. In this design Mrs. S. appears to have persisted to the final conclusion of her work; and, in the perusal of [*Conclusion of the Memoirs of Miss Sidney Bidulph*], we have *felt* that she wanted not power to effect her purpose: for, indeed, the catastrophe of the *Arnold family* is a tale so extremely affecting and tender, that the reader who can peruse it without plenteously shedding tears over the distressful pages, must, surely, possess an heart of iron. But, as we have intimated in the former account of these *Memoirs,* it is much to be questioned if such pictures of human life, however justly they may be copied from nature, are well adapted to serve the cause of virtue: but this is a remark which we shall leave to the sagacity of our Readers.

A review of "Conclusion of the Memoirs of Miss Sydney Bidulph," in The Monthly Review, *London, Vol. XXXVII, September, 1767, p. 238.*

JAMES BOSWELL   (essay date 1791)

[*A Scottish biographer, diarist, and man of letters, Boswell is one of the most colorful and widely read figures in eighteenth-century British literature. He is esteemed for his pictorial documentation of life in such works as* Journal of a Tour to the Hebrides *(1785),* London Journal *(unpublished until 1950), and the masterpiece for which he has been labeled the greatest of British biographers:* The Life of Samuel Johnson, LL.D. *(1791). In this immensely readable and memorable work, Boswell vivified the genre of biography through his pioneering combination of life history with anecdote, observation, and the literary techniques of dialogue, theme, and plot. In addition to the* Life, *Boswell's staggering production of journals and letters, many undiscovered until recent years, heighten his reputation as an engagingly introspective writer. A friend of the Sheridans, Boswell wrote two prologues for* The Discovery, *both rejected by Frances. In the following excerpt from the* Life, *Boswell remarks on the moral quality of* Memoirs of Miss Sidney Bidulph *and relates a comment by Johnson concerning the book.*]

Mrs. Sheridan was a most agreeable companion to an intellectual man. She was sensible, ingenious, unassuming, yet communicative. I recollect, with satisfaction, many pleasing hours which I passed with her under the hospitable roof of her husband, who was to me a very kind friend. Her novel, entitled *Memoirs of Miss Sidney Biddulph,* contains an excellent moral, while it inculcates a future state of retribution; and what it teaches is impressed upon the mind by a series of as deep distress as can affect humanity, in the amiable and pious heroine who goes to her grave unrelieved, but resigned, and full of hope of "heaven's mercy." Johnson paid her this high compliment upon it: "I know not, Madam, that you have a right, upon moral principles, to make your readers suffer so much." (pp. 240-41)

James Boswell, *in extract in his* The Life of Samuel Samuel Johnson, *Vol. 1, J. M. Dent & Sons Ltd, 1976, pp. 240-41.*

ALICIA LE FANU   (essay date 1824)

[*Sheridan's granddaughter, Le Fanu is the author of the only full-length biography of Sheridan. In the following excerpt from this work, she surveys Sheridan's works.*]

At the early age of fifteen, [Frances's] talent for literary composition evinced itself. Notwithstanding his aversion to writing, and writing ladies, Dr. Chamberlaine could not refuse his housekeeper paper to keep the house accounts, and a portion of this paper (ill-coloured and coarse, it is true) Miss Fanny thought it no robbery to appropriate to the far nobler purpose of writing a romance, in two volumes, entitled *Eugenia and Adelaide.* This novel, which remained in MS. till published (after her decease, and without the author's name) by Dilly, displays unquestionable proofs of a fertile imagination and inventive skill; indeed, the whole style and story may be said to breathe the freshness of fifteen—the happy period at which the novel was written. The plot, as the name imports, is a double one, containing two complete stories, each in its way interesting and attractive. That of Eugenia is full of Spanish imbroglio, and highly susceptible of comic heightening. It was, in fact, at a subsequent period, adapted for the stage in the form of a comic drama, by the author's eldest daughter, Mrs. Lefanu, of Dublin; and was represented with success at the theatre of that metropolis.

If the story of Eugenia is more animated and sprightly, that of Adelaide is more tender and pathetic. It possesses a deeper and more powerful interest, and is wound up with a degree of skill truly surprising in so young a writer. The episodical characters introduced evince still further the invention and resources she already possessed; and some allusions to the historical events of the period with which she has connected her narrative, bear witness alike to the extent of her reading, and the accuracy of her discrimination. (pp. 7-8)

The *Memoirs of Miss Sidney Biddulph* were published, March 1761, and the book became an immediate and permanent favourite.

Notwithstanding the high praise bestowed by Richardson on her *Eugenia and Adelaide,* it is but justice to observe, that bright and auspicious dawn of fame scarcely taught her to expect the full and steady radiance which afterwards distinguished her meridian celebrity.

In that juvenile performance, "Love, only Love," inspired the rich, romantic page, whether it dwelt upon the fully delineated sufferings of Adelaïde and Eugenia, or the episodical sketches of Clara and Raphael, Cynthia, Violante, and Isidore. Though the adventures and surprises were varied and interesting, the moral improvement was not proportionably great.

In *Sidney Biddulph,* the offspring of her maturer years, on the contrary, Love was reduced to his subordinate place, and made subservient to the triumph of wedded constancy, and the exercise of the domestic duties and affections. (pp. 110-11)

Among Mrs. Sheridan's contemporaries, none admired her novel more warmly than Dr. Johnson, whose compliment to her upon its publication has been more frequently repeated than any other. "I know not, Madam! that you have a right, upon moral principles, to make your readers suffer so much" [see excerpt by Boswell dated 1791]. (p. 113)

As it stands, the observation of Dr. Johnson includes but half its praise, and might convey to the minds of some readers an erroneous impression; for the fact is, that *humour,* as well as *pathos,* forms a leading quality in the novel of *Sidney Biddulph.* (p. 114)

An old master of the art [Smollett] has aptly defined a novel to be "a large diffused picture, comprehending the characters of life, disposed in different groups, and exhibited in various attitudes, for the purposes of a uniform plan and general concurrency, to which every individual figure is subservient.'' He adds—

> But this plan cannot be executed with propriety, probability, or success, without a principal person to attract the attention, unite the incidents, unwind the clue of the labyrinth, and at last close the scene by virtue of his own importance.

If this definition be admitted to be correct, *Sidney Biddulph* may, without fear of contradiction, be pronounced to afford one of the best specimens of a well-written novel—the fable faultless—the incidents well prepared—the characters all conducive to the catastrophe—and even the hero himself a personage of some importance to the plot.

Orlando Faulkland, in addition to all those qualities which most interest and please, possesses that rarest attribute of heroes and heroines, either in or out of books, a fund of humour and entertainment. This greatly increases the sympathy he inspires, when that fine mind is for ever overclouded by calamity.

The only defects of Faulkland's character are, a warm impetuosity of feeling, and an imprudent hastiness of temper, the consequences of which he has reason to deplore to the latest period of his existence.

Mrs. Sheridan's novel is not (like many otherwise excellent compositions) an entertaining gallery of portraits, but of portraits to which the painter has assigned little employment, or at best a forced one. *Her* figures, on the contrary, are exhibited each in the attitude in which their predominant humour and character would most naturally place them, and which is best calculated to elucidate the progress of the story.

Thus, in the character of Lady Biddulph, the heroine's mother, her peculiar prejudices and modes of thinking, are not only very effectively described and accounted for in themselves, but they *bear upon* the story in a manner the most important, as, ''had 'she' been less stern,'' she would have read, or listened to Faulkland's justification, and all the miseries occasioned by her well-meaning, but provoking obstinancy, would have been prevented.

While the few foibles of Lady Biddulph occasion, sometimes amusement, and sometimes regret, the sterling virtues of her heart command unmingled praise. We discern the superior penetration and latent playfulness of Sidney's mind, leading her sometimes to indulge in a smile at the unconquerable prejudices of her ''dear literal parent,'' but at the same chastised by that reverential awe and filial deference, which at the time in which the events are supposed to take place, formed the first principle inculcated in female education.

The character of Sidney Biddulph, the heroine, is one unfortunately almost forgotten in the regions of romance—That of a woman, young, beautiful, and engaging, of a disposition equally removed from the extremes of levity or austerity—amiable without artifice, virtuous without prudery, and pious without pretension. Sidney is neither a bigot nor a freethinker, neither insipid nor volatile. She is no female philosopher, who could find in science or study a compensation for the disappointment of the finest affections of her heart; neither is she a tall, pale, gigantic heroine, full six feet high, without her stilts, whose lofty person is an emblem of her loftier mind, and each of whose maxims deserves to become a universal aphorism. In one word, she is—reader, have you lately met with such a one?—*unaffected*.

Simple, artless, and unpretending,

> She frowns *no* goddess, and she moves *no* queen.

Yet she is highly informed, possesses a cultivated mind, and rich intellectual resources. Sidney introduces herself to the reader with native cheerfulness, the result of innocence, and tender sensibilities, corrected by delicacy. We enjoy, *with* her, the few and brief hours of happiness alloted to her, and sympathize with equal warmth in the unmerited afflictions that succeed them. (pp. 114-18)

The religious sentiments interspersed throughout the work, breathe a strain of piety so fervent and sincere, that they cannot fail to excite a responsive sympathy in every serious mind.

The incidents and sudden turns of fortune are so various and surprising, that it is impossible for the reader, the most practised in that style of composition, to foresee or calculate upon them; at the same time, every step, every event is prepared and accounted for, in a manner so natural, that it is difficult to resist the illusion which frequently recurs, that we are reading a real history.

The interest never flags a moment, but on the contrary goes on rising, with the force of dramatic composition, to the closing scenes, which should be read in solitude, and with the door locked to prevent interruption; for the mind hangs suspended in breathless anxiety upon the catastrophe, which is worked up with that strong, increasing, deepening, nervously agitating interest, that affords to the novel reader the most delightful exercise of the feelings of sympathy and curiosity.

And this effect is produced without any elaborate effort, any over-strained endeavours to rouse the passions. (pp. 119-20)

On the fifth of February, 1763, the comedy of *The Discovery* was presented to the public. The first night of its representation must have been one of fearful anxiety to Mrs. Sheridan. Notwithstanding the success of *Sidney Biddulph,* her uncertainty must have been great respecting the reception of this, her first dramatic attempt. (p. 222)

On this trying occasion Mrs. Sheridan had all the support that a just confidence in her own powers, united to the highest domestic encouragement, could give her. (p. 223)

The strong characters of Lord Medway and Mrs. Knightly, and the humorous ones of Sir Anthony Branville, Sir Harry, and Lady Flutter, could not, she felt assured, fail of being relished and justly appreciated by the tasteful and discriminating part of the audience in the pit and boxes. . . . (p. 225)

The Discovery continued to be acted with success for a considerable part of the winter; and Mrs. Sheridan's fame and profit increased proportionably.

Of this comedy, as I have already mentioned the leading characters, it is unnecessary to say much.

The plot is deep and interesting; and the truly tremendous and startling ''Discovery'' most artfully concealed until the final development. The imperious character of Lord Medway finely contrasts with the gentleness of his lady; and the really frigid temper and affected raptures of the romantic old knight, Sir Anthony Branville, who makes love according to the antiquated rules of chivalry, and esteems a task or a penance set him by his mistress as a favour, were rendered irresistibly ludicrous and effective by the inimitable acting of Garrick. But still a great portion of the amusement certainly rests upon the two characters of Sir Harry and Lady Flutter. These claim the merit, almost singular in the modern drama, of perfect originality in the conception. The quarrels and "makings-up" of this school-boy and school-girl pair; their mutual reproaches and recriminations, which are in the best style of Sheridan's comic dialogue; their dangerous reference to the interested arbitration of Lord Medway; and their final and heartfelt reconciliation, present altogether such a "picture of youth," as was rarely traced by any other pen, in a manner equally true to nature. (pp. 226-27)

If *The Discovery* has, in modern times, been comparatively laid aside, this may partly be attributed to the want of an adequate representative of Sir Anthony Branville, and partly to the large drafts drawn upon Mrs. Sheridan's muse by succeeding dramatic writers. In Holcroft's *Road to Ruin*, the filial self-devotion of Harry Dornton is copied, without acknowledgment, from that of Colonel Medway; and in his most lachrymose comedy, *The Deserted Daughter*, the character of Lady Anne Mordent is a compound of Lady Easy in *The Careless Husband*, and Lady Medway in *The Discovery*. (pp. 228-29)

[*The Dupe*] was pronounced by several of the best judges to be possessed of equal merit with [*The Discovery*], and sanguine expectations were entertained of its ultimate success: but, like Goldsmith's *Good-natured Man*, which was ill-received by the audience that had welcomed with smiles his first effort, *She Stoops to Conquer*, *The Dupe* was fated to experience the mutability of public opinion. . . . (p. 235)

In the space of two years [Mrs. Sheridan] conceived and executed the beautiful oriental tale of *Nourjahad*, and added two additional volumes to the novel of *Sidney Biddulph*, which were not published till after her decease. To the two last volumes of *Sidney Biddulph* may be applied much of the criticism which was made upon the first part.

We meet our old acquaintances Sidney and Sir George again: with only those differences which we should observe in different portraits taken of the same individuals in youth or middle life. The additional personages introduced chiefly consist of the younger Faulkland, son of Orlando, the Audleys, the venerable Price (who was only introduced in the preceding volumes), and the sweet characters of Mrs. Arnold's two daughters.

By many persons the second part of *Sidney Biddulph* was preferred to the first; as the production of a person who had acquired more extensive views of life, and a greater insight into character. Her talent for portrait-painting had certainly improved. . . . (pp. 289-90)

But it is in the deathbed of the pious and suffering heroine, in the closing scene of Sidney's eventful life, that the author sets her seal upon the whole, and illustrates her finely expressed moral, that it is in a future state of retribution alone, we can hope for an explanation of the ways of Providence, and that there we shall see all apparently unequal dispensations justified, and all seeming inconsistencies reduced to rule. When every worldly comfort vanishes from the sufferer's view, we see Religion, like a distant star, shining to light the pure and unpretending saint, to receive the rich reward long laid up for her virtues in Heaven. Though the last moments of Sidney are accompanied by every circumstance of bitterness that the ingratitude of those she loved, and the disappointment of her fondest hopes could impart, yet we find her firm and collected, and at the same time divested of none of her wonted tenderness. After a scene of most affecting pathos . . . , she is in the midst of some affectionate injunctions to her remaining family, when the sudden and awful, yet blessed transition from life to death,

or rather from a living death to life, is thus powerfully and impressively described.

> She stopped short, as if interrupted by some sudden and extraordinary emotion; a fine colour flushed at once into her face, and her eyes, which were before sunk and languishing, seemed in an instant to have recovered all their fire. I never saw so animated a figure; she sprung forward with energy, her arms extended, her eyes lifted up with rapture, and with an elevated voice she cried out, "I come!" Then, sinking down softly on her pillow, she closed her eyes, and expired without a sigh.
>
> (pp. 292-94)

Alas! she who could so well describe the last moments of expiring excellence, was shortly to be summoned from every tie that renders life endearing, to receive the reward of her own.

Mrs. Sheridan's last work was the oriental tale of *Nourjahad*. The plan was suggested to her mind one sleepless night, when from reflecting upon the inequality in the conditions of men, she was led to consider that it is in the due regulation of the passions, rather than on the outward dispensations of Providence, that true happines or misery depends; and she conceived the idea of the probable condition of a human being of violent and perverse disposition, supposing his wealth to be inexhaustible, and his days extended to infinity. In fancy she beheld this being, possessed of the two greatest apparent goods, riches and immortality, yet devoid of any inward principle to restrain the unbounded indulgence of his passions. Nourjahad finds in those gratified, yet still importunate passions, his tormentors, and the two blessings he had impatiently coveted transformed into insupportable evils. As this idea acquired form and consistency, Mrs. Sheridan represented it as entering her mind like a kind of vision or dream, between sleep and waking; and though this account is very extraordinary, persons of a fertile and poetical imagination themselves, will see nothing impossible in it. (pp. 294-96)

Alicia Le Fanu, in her Memoirs of the Life and Writings of Mrs. Frances Sheridan, *G. and W. B. Whittaker, 1824, 435 p.*

THE MONTHLY REVIEW   (essay date 1824)

[In the following excerpt from an unsigned review of Alicia Le Fanu's 1824 biography of Sheridan, the critic compares Memoirs of Miss Sidney Bidulph *with the novels of Samuel Richardson.]*

[Some] of us can remember the great popularity which [the *Memoirs of Miss Sidney Biddulph*] acquired, and the great avidity with which it was read: for in the circulating libraries it retained an undisputed supremacy long after its appearance, and even down to a period comparatively recent. It is a novel in the true Grandison school. The same exactness of detail, the same pains to make us thoroughly acquainted with the character and situation of the personages with whom we are occupied, and occasionally something of that prolixity with which merely preparatory scenes are depicted, and which have too often the effect of exhausting the reader's attention before he arrives at the momentous passages in which some important passion is brought into play, or some measure is adopted which decides the destiny of the piece,—these characteristics are in a great degree common both to the master and his disciple. In *Sidney Biddulph*, as in *Clarissa Harlowe*, though with less copiousness of description, (much of which we can afford to spare in Richardson,) we are let into the domestic privacies of the characters, in a manner which inspires a powerful conviction of their reality:—we form one of the party, and take a share in those pleasing though often wearisome chit-chats, which, leading to no consequence, and sometimes retarding the progress of the story, insensibly impart to us a sincere sympathy for all that befalls the individuals to whom we are introduced. Yet, in other particularities of the school, Mrs. Sheridan manifests little or no resemblance to Richardson. Of the stiff and unnatural air of some of his virtuous characters, which injured the moral effect of his pieces nearly as much as the brilliant and engaging qualities with which he endowed several of his most vicious personages, nothing is to be seen in the *Memoirs of Miss Sidney Biddulph:* while in knowledge of the human heart and in a powerful pathos, the latter work nearly equals the best production of Richardson. The fable also is well managed, and the incidents lead gradually and necessarily to the catastrophe, which is sufficiently melancholy. Dr. Johnson, a warm admirer both of the lady and her book, exclaimed, in allusion to the pathetic close of it, "I know not, Madam, that you have a right, upon moral principles, to make your readers suffer so much!" [see excerpt by Boswell dated 1791] Altogether, Sidney Biddulph, though not likely to regain her former popularity, or to resist the setting in of so many new tides of taste and new modes of composition as have prevailed since her days, is justly intitled to a place in our libraries: and her mournful tale can never be read without improving the heart that it softens. (pp. 257-58)

> *"Miss Lefanu's Memoirs of Mrs. F. Sheridan," in*
> The Monthly Review, *London, Vol. CIV, July, 1824, pp. 257-65.*

ALDOUS HUXLEY (essay date 1925)

[*Known primarily for his dystopian novel* Brave New World *(1932), Huxley was an English novelist of ideas. The grandson of noted Darwinist T. H. Huxley and the brother of scientist Julian Huxley, he was interested in many fields of knowledge, and daring conceptions of science, philosophy, and religion are woven throughout his fiction. Huxley published an altered version of* The Discovery, *removing from the play those eighteenth-century elements which he felt were distasteful to modern audiences. In the following excerpt from the introduction to that publication, Huxley discusses the juxtaposition of eighteenth-century sentimentalism and refinement in the play.*]

Mrs. Sheridan wrote at a time when the eighteenth-century public was discovering the joys of sentiment. The Man of Feeling haunted polite society; cloudily sublime, Macpherson's Ossian went stalking, in defiance of Dr. Johnson, through the best drawing-rooms. It was the age of landscape gardening, when people of refined taste erected ruined abbeys at the end of winding walks or built across artificial rivers a broken Gothic bridge leading from nowhere to nowhere else. Parallel with the polished and sophisticated literature which we are accustomed, without much historical justification, to think of as being typically and exclusively *dix-huitième* ["of the eighteenth century"], there grew up in the second half of the century a literature of sentiment—but of a sentiment so crude, high-flavoured, and raw that we are astonished that palates accustomed to the delicacy and refined aroma of the other literature could tolerate it. The explanation is simple: too much reasonable refinement was becoming tedious in the end. Having thirsted, people were now making themselves drunk. When it is a matter of satisfying a craving, a strong bootlegger's brew

is as efficacious as a fragrant Burgundy—more efficacious indeed.

Mrs. Sheridan's *Discovery* is a specimen at one and the same time of the eighteenth-century refinement, polish, and acuteness, and of eighteenth-century emotional crudity. It is at once high comedy and low sentiment. Passages which for grace and fidelity to life are hardly to be matched in eighteenth-century comedy, are succeeded by scenes of the most jejune and conventional sentimentality. These passages, which seem to us, accustomed as we are to the refinements introduced into the literature of sentiment by a century and a half of constant literary experiment, so boring and even positively repulsive, were clearly most moving to Mrs. Sheridan's contemporaries. Garrick declared that *The Discovery* was one of the best comedies he ever read, and its success on the stage was considerable. Tastes have changed, and though we can endorse the high opinions of her contemporaries with regard to considerable parts of Mrs. Sheridan's play, we cannot, with the best will in the world, put up with the sentimental remainder. (pp. v-vi)

> *Aldous Huxley, in an introduction to* The Discovery: A Comedy in Five Acts *by Frances Sheridan, adapted by Aldous Huxley, George H. Doran Company, 1925, pp. v-vii.*

THE TIMES LITERARY SUPPLEMENT (essay date 1927)

[*In the following excerpt from an unsigned review of* The History of Nourjahad, *the critic praises the novel for its unique ingenuity.*]

Mrs. Sheridan, the author of the *Memoirs of Sidney Bidulph,* a novel which had a great success in its time, and the mother of the famous Sheridan, was a contemporary of Dr. Johnson and lived in the full tide of the eighteenth century. *Nourjahad* was her last work, published posthumously. It is praised by Croker in his edition of Boswell's life: "Her last work is perhaps her best—*Nourjahad, an Eastern Tale*: in which a pure morality is inculcated with a great deal of fancy and considerable force." It was intended to be the first of a series of moral tales; but as to the pure morality there is nothing very remarkable about it and nothing which went beyond the average sentiments of the age. It is, in fact, a homily upon the vanity of human wishes, that rather trite subject upon which so much excellent rhetoric and seasonable argument was wont to be employed. Mrs. Sheridan's power of rhetoric and of persuasion by force of words rather than by force of imagination is well below that of Dr. Johnson, who had a liking for this subject and indeed could grow really poetical about it. At the end of Mrs. Sheridan's story the hero is exhorted

> never to suppose that riches can secure happiness;
> that the gratification of the passions can satisfy the
> human heart; or that the immortal part of our nature
> will suffer us to taste unmixed felicity, in a world
> which was never meant for our final place of abode.

Though these sentiments are expressed with reasonable eloquence they have often been better expressed and with a more persuasive sincerity. But this moral is so little a part of the story that it seems with Mrs. Sheridan to be little more than a convention—and it is indeed doubtful whether the moral properly follows from the fable. It is her fancy which is remarkable, and all the more remarkable for her time.

In an age when there are few channels, and these often narrow, along which the imagination may go, if a writer's imagination does find an outlet along some rather unexpected channel, the

effect is often more pleasing than an equally powerful imagination moving along the same channel in an age when there
are many broad channels of this sort open. Perhaps this is
because the writer's consciousness of audacity has a more potent effect upon his works and upon his readers than actual
audacity. Not that the East is a very unexpected channel for
eighteenth-century imagination; for Rasselas moralized in the
East, and Voltaire succeeded in making the East about as much
use to the imagination as the wigs of his actors. The contrasts
of the East, the extremes of luxury and misery which were
supposed to obtain there, were of great use to moralists and
to writers of tragedy. But Mrs. Sheridan wrote a real Arabian
Night. The story begins in a rather ordinary way. Nourjahad
wishes under provocation that he had boundless riches and a
life as long as that of the earth. If he had this he would renounce
the expectation of paradise. A young man of surpassing beauty
miraculously appears to him and grants him these wishes; and
it only remains for the hero to discover that riches can never
secure happiness and that immortality has its inconveniences.
But these discoveries are attended with many adventures more
suitable to the *Arabian Nights* than to *Rasselas,* and there is
an unexpected and remarkable end to the story. We must not
give the plot of the story away, and we will therefore only
quote from ''H.V.M.'s'' preface: ''The *dénouement* comes as
a genuine surprise even to the practised reader'' [see entry by
H. V. Marrot in Additional Bibliography]. It is indeed a genuine surprise, for the practised reader is accustomed to the
language of the moral tale:

> Rash mortal, replied the shining vision, reflect once
> more before you receive the fatal boon; for once
> granted you will wish perhaps, and wish in vain to
> have it recalled.

The practised reader knows very well that Nourjahad will wish
to have the fatal boon recalled, for it has so often happened
before. He will expect to go away from the tale edified and
soothed, or perhaps doubting whether it is quite true that if he
were offered three wishes he would so inevitably wish for a
black pudding on his wife's nose. It is therefore the more
pleasing to find an ingenious plot, more ingenious than that of
most detective stories, and a variety of remarkable adventures,
and yet still to find the language of the moral tale, sometimes
rather stilted and even ridiculous, for mortals are always rash
and boons are always fatal. But this diction is at any rate always
free, if not from the commonplaces of the eighteenth century,
at any rate from the commonplaces of to-day; and it is this
diction which makes such moral tales, even without adventures
and plot, consistently readable and amusing.

"A Moral Tale," in The Times Literary Supplement,
No. 1341, October 13, 1927, p. 710.

B. G. MacCarthy (essay date 1947)

[*In the following excerpt, MacCarthy evaluates the strengths and
weaknesses of* Memoirs of Miss Sidney Bidulph *and comments
on its feminine viewpoint.*]

By far the best writer of the school of sensibility was Mrs.
Frances Sheridan whose *Miss Sydney Bidulph* is in the direct
line of succession from Richardson. Richardson, indeed, encouraged Mrs. Sheridan as a writer, and he it was who arranged
for the publication of this novel. Its reception amply justified
the enthusiasm which Richardson had expressed when he first
read it in manuscript. (pp. 64-5)

The [novel's] *motif* of endless misfortunes suggests the influence of Madame Riccoboni; and the many-volume convention
was an added reason for the undue protraction of the story.
Indeed the necessity for spinning out the plot appears to have
been chiefly responsible for the divagation and discursiveness
which are too apparent in this novel. Condensed, it would have
gained greatly in strength. Mrs. Sheridan could have omitted
her adventitious stories and shortened her sub-stories. She frequently made the mistake of concentrating interest on what
should have been merely incidental. For example, when Sydney repeats the account given her by Sir George of Faulkland's
deed in Ireland, her narrative is far too detailed. Mrs. Sheridan
ignored the fact that Faulkland's past adventures are far less
exciting than his present distracted state.

There are many interesting aspects in *Miss Sydney Bidulph.*
There is a stressing of sensibility and endurance. Each of these
qualities increases the other, and both unite to wring the heart
of the heroine. Still, Sydney neither goes mad nor falls into a
decline, but survives until her daughters are of marriageable
age. Another point worth noting is that, in general, Mrs. Sheridan subscribes to the accepted standards of feminine status
and behaviour, and yet, in some respects, most strikingly presents the feminine point of view. In fact, the pivotal point of
this story essentially represents a woman's judgment on an
issue which, until that time, had not been raised in fiction.
Before Mrs. Sheridan, women writers had not required that
the hero should be guiltless of seducing innocence. In *Miss
Sydney Bidulph* this claim is made, but a single standard of
morality is not applied. Faulkland is exonerated when it is
discovered that Miss Burchell was guilty before she met him.
Mrs. Sheridan does not judge immorality *per se,* but only in
relation to its victim. Nevertheless, it was an advance on the
code of gallantry and on the code of casual sexual adventure
which sheltered women were supposed to take for granted in
their men-folk.

But it was not merely in moral outlook that Mrs. Sheridan
struck a feminine note. In her presentation of a woman's mind,
with its characteristic moods and impulses, there is much that
indicates a woman's insight. When the excellent Lord V—
pays court to Sydney's daughter, Cecilia, she will have none
of him, and makes short work of every argument which a family
friend makes in his favour. Yes, he is handsome, very accomplished, extremely well-bred and perfectly good-tempered: his
morals are unexceptionable.

> She turned her eyes at me with so arch a look, that
> I could scarce refrain from laughing. 'I know nothing
> to the contrary, Madam,'—'Has he not a fine es-
> tate?'—'I do not want money, Mrs. B—.'—'Of a
> considerable family, and noble rank?'—'I desire not
> titles either.'—'What then *do* you desire, Cecilia?'—
> 'Only to please myself;' and she shook her little head
> so, that all the powder and the curls in her hair fell
> about her face . . . And yet she has her hours of
> sadness. 'For what, my dear?'—'Oh, you'll know
> all in time,' in a low voice, as she curtseyed to take
> her leave; and down she flew like a lapwing.

Cecilia has vivacity, charm and depth; she is a 'bewitching
little gypsy,' in marked contrast to her sister Dolly who is a
young woman of the greatest sensibility. Dolly is far too full
of maidenly delicacy. She is too grave, too prone to tears and
swoons. Both sisters love young Faulkland. Dolly feeds on her
emotions which so rend her that, when Faulkland's dislocated
shoulder is being set, she faints away twice although she is in
a distant part of the house. On the contrary, Cecilia candidly

avows her love to Faulkland—surely the first woman in fiction thus to take the initiative. "'I always thought you loved me,'" said she, "yet, Faulkland, you should have spoken first, and spared me the pains of extorting a confession from you.'" (pp. 66-8)

But Faulkland, in a moment of pity for Dolly, has already given her his vows. Now he engages himself to Cecilia whom he really loves. Their marriage ceremony is interrupted by Dolly's distraught reproaches, and Faulkland fights and kills the man who has played on his weakness and used him as a catspaw. This is the end of Audley, a most interesting villain with a sense of humour. Audley is determined to marry either Cecilia or Dolly, because both have splendid fortunes. Personally he prefers Cecilia because she is spirited. (pp. 68-9)

But Cecilia loves Faulkland, so Audley concentrates his energies on winning this bread-and-butter miss, undeterred by the fact that he has a wife already. He kidnaps her and releases her unharmed, hoping that the compromising circumstances will force her to marry him. His death cuts the tangle he has so cunningly devised. . . .

Truly excellent is the hypocritical account which he gives Dolly of his efforts to persuade her relatives that she was constrained by illness to spend the night in his house. Poor Dolly is innocent, but he has spread too clever a net. His arguments, his deceptions, his sophistries, his deliberate forcing of her into a corner until there appears no possibility of escape except through lies and a patched-up marriage with him—here is a fine crescendo of subtle and cynical villainy. (p. 69)

Though Mrs. Sheridan owed much to Richardson's influence and something to French sensibility, these debts are merely incidental—not more than any author owes to the literary atmosphere of his period. *Sydney Bidulph* is an original, vivid, and charming book. It is, above all, human. Mrs. Sheridan never forgets that she is dealing with people of flesh and blood; and (as with her description of Lady Grimston) she can make them live before our eyes. (p. 70)

B. G. MacCarthy, "The Novel of Sentiment and of Sensibility," in her The Female Pen: The Later Women Novelists, 1744-1818, *Cork University Press, 1947, pp. 31-86.*

ROBERT HOGAN AND JERRY C. BEASLEY (essay date 1984)

[*Hogan is an American playwright, editor, and critic. Beasley is an American educator and essayist. In the following excerpt from their edition of Sheridan's plays, they survey the author's works.*]

Sidney Bidulph is for the most part a very conventional sentimental novel, though it studiously avoids a happy ending and the easy option of virtue rewarded. It is difficult to know whether Mrs. Sheridan meant the reader to believe that Sidney is denied fulfillment because she made the wrong decision at last and married Falkland, the reformed libertine and apparent murderer, or because she ruined both their lives by being too scrupulously pious and conventional and by delaying the right decision for too long. Possibly the ambiguity was deliberate, for the author certainly proved herself capable of real subtleties of character and situation in her other works. At any rate, *Sidney Bidulph*, though overly long and too often strained, is a genuinely moving work, something after the tragic manner of Richardson's *Clarissa*. Dr. Johnson spoke feelingly of its power when he said to Mrs. Sheridan, "I know not, Madam, that you have a right, upon moral principles, to make your

readers suffer so much" [see excerpt by Boswell dated 1791]. It should also be said that Frances' story is on the whole more tough-minded and honest in its representation of human emotions than that most celebrated of eighteenth-century tales of sensibility, Henry Mackenzie's *The Man of Feeling,* published ten years after Frances Sheridan's work first appeared. Less estimable novels than *Sidney Bidulph* have been considered minor classics.

Sidney Bidulph remains a work extremely good for its own day. If it does not seem quite worth resuscitating for ours, it nevertheless had one important influence, and that was upon the achievement of the author's most notable son. The book does have its comic as well as its pathetic touches, and Richard Brinsley Sheridan seems to have used suggestions from it in both *The Rivals* (the characters of Faulkland and Julia Melville, for example) and *The School for Scandal* (Lady Teazle, Sir Oliver, and the two Surface brothers, Joseph the hypocrite and Charles the good-natured ne'er-do-well). *Sidney Bidulph* was the most conspicuous literary achievement yet produced by a Sheridan, and it heralded the long series of noteworthy works by which members of this remarkable family would distinguish themselves during the next several generations. (pp. 20-1)

The Discovery is a multiplotted piece concerning happy marriage and the question of what-boy-gets-what-girl. There are three, or possibly four, such plot strands, all intricately connected with each other. By far the best of these is the one involving Sir Harry Flutter and his wife, an attractive and naive young married couple who constantly quarrel over trivialities. Their early dialogues are as charmingly amusing as anything to be found in eighteenth-century comedy, and this brilliant beginning is the main interest of the first half of the play. Unfortunately, the Flutters have nothing significant to do in the second half, and the play suffers somewhat.

Another plot line concerns the curmudgeonish father, Lord Medway, who wants to marry his children well as a means of redeeming his own wasted fortunes. He offers his beautiful daughter Louisa, whose character bears hints of the Lydia Languish of *The Rivals,* to the pedantic-romantic old fool Sir Anthony Branville, although she loves this buffoon's young and presentable offstage nephew. Lord Medway meanwhile persuades his son to wed the clever and wealthy widow Mrs. Knightly, the former object of Sir Anthony's ridiculous addresses, instead of her lovely sister Miss Richly, to whom the youth has pledged his eternal adoration. Mrs. Sheridan imparts real freshness to her development of this hackneyed domestic conflict through several effective comic scenes, the most successful of which center on Sir Anthony and Mrs. Knightly. Sir Anthony is hardly a comic creation of the first rank, but he was good enough for Garrick to sense and exploit his possibilities. The greatest actor of the age must have enjoyed playing this verbal and social bungler, whose eccentricities of language and manner almost always delight while they display impressive skill and ingenuity on the part of the author. Mrs. Knightly is interesting, but troublesome. She is not one but three separate characters, and this multischizophrenia is not the result of any insight by Frances into abnormal psychology but simply an answer to the necessities of her many-stranded plot. For one plot, Mrs. Knightly is a witty woman-of-the-worldish Millamant, and these scenes are carried off with some panache. For another plot, she is one of Cinderella's nasty-tempered older sisters. Although this complex of contradictions is acceptable enough, Mrs. Knightly's incarnation as the crushed and reformed devious female is not, for it dulls the brightness of her character and is finally just unconvincing.

Whatever coherence there may be among the various plot strands of the play is imparted by making Lord Medway in each instance the villain. For four acts, Frances paints him effectively as wastrel and middle-aged late-Restoration rake. A mere twisting of circumstances radically changes him in the end—it is, like Mrs. Knightly's reformation, a purely theatrical device; and the Lord Medway of Act V is a creature of the theater rather than of reality. The "discovery" that provides the twist and leads to the comic ending of the play is the revelation that Mrs. Knightly is Lord Medway's daughter. Naturally, she cannot marry Medway's son, her own brother. In a gesture of goodwill, then, she persuades Sir Anthony to renew his court to her. Both Medway children are released from the bondage of their chastened father's wishes, and there is the promise of happiness for all. This elaborate contrivance, of course, is a hoary stock device, but in this play it even remains undramatized, for the discovery occurs between Acts IV and V.

Despite such a trite and awkwardly handled resolution, and despite large dollops of eighteenth-century sentiment, *The Discovery* is nowhere so maudlin as parts of plays by Steele and Lillo, and it has nothing quite so stilted as portions of Julia's dialogue in *The Rivals*. In fact, a saving grace of the play is that it is written with uncommon fluency, so that even the more tedious parts of the plot and the more lachrymose revelations of feeling flow smoothly by. A chief glory of Richard Brinsley Sheridan's three great comic plays is a consciousness of language that is comic by its divergence from a civilized norm. Among dramatists of the time, perhaps only Fielding and Goldsmith approached Dick Sheridan in the consummate use of quirky, mangled language. But much more than a hint of this same gift was there in the comedies of his mother. Lord Medway's first-act injunction to Sir Harry about how to control his wife really comes down to what kind of language Sir Harry should use. And the language of spleen and anger, with all of its inadequate silliness, is scarcely less brilliantly employed in Sir Anthony and Jack Absolute than it is in Sir Harry and Lady Flutter. In sum, the finest parts of Frances Sheridan's play, mostly contained in the first half, are as good as anything in all but the best of eighteenth-century comic drama. And two of the greatest comedies of the period, *The Rivals* and *The School for Scandal*, owe more than a little to *The Discovery*.

Emboldened by the success of her first play, Frances completed a second, called *The Dupe*, during the middle months of 1763. This new work was staged at Drury Lane by George Colman (Garrick being away in France) toward the end of the year, beginning on December 10. This time, however, the play failed, receiving only three performances, and it seems never to have been revived. Sam Whyte [in his *Miscellanea Nova* (1810)] and Alicia Le Fanu both attribute the failure to "the theatrical cabals of a popular actress." The reason, however, may partly reside in the work itself. Certain scenes seem written more for psychology than for theater, and the manner is sometimes talky and novelistic. Still, there are definite theatrical qualities of both characterization and language. Frances' most theatrical character is Mrs. Friendly, a sympathetic and pleasant middle-aged woman who is hopelessly given to brainless, aimless talk full of inconsequential and maddeningly boring detail. Whenever Mrs. Friendly has something of import to say, it is so burdened with superfluous facts that her hearers are reduced to exasperation. This engaging featherhead, in both her character and her speech, seems taken directly from life. She has been limned with little theatrical broadening, but she is a theatrical delight.

Some other characters are nearly as fine. The rakish, middle-aged curmudgeon Sir John Woodall, his unscrupulous mistress Mrs. Etherdown, her disreputable accomplice Sharply, and the quick-tongued servant Rose—all are products of Mrs. Sheridan's genuine wit and real sensitivity to manners and language. The play's flabby verbosity, however, comes close to undermining the strengths of its several crisp characterizations, some good theatrical scenes, and a plot that is tighter and less awkwardly contrived than that of *The Discovery*. This prosiness, together with the author's generally unsentimental treatment of love and marriage and her avoidance of conventional morality, may have cost *The Dupe* any chance of a long run on the stage. As closet drama it enjoyed somewhat greater success. The London and Dublin editions (both 1764) seem to have sold briskly, and Mrs. Sheridan's London publisher, the exemplary Andrew Millar, made such profits that he was able to send her £100 beyond the copyright money—surely this remittance from the honest Millar was prompted in part by his compassion for the disappointment he knew Frances must have been feeling over the failure of her play upon the stage. Millar believed, rightly, that *The Dupe* deserved better than the rejection it had endured at Drury Lane, and indeed it is worthy of better than the utter neglect it has suffered in our own day. (pp. 23-5)

[Frances' third comedy, *A Journey to Bath*,] was submitted to Drury Lane apparently through Benjamin Victor, Thomas' old deputy manager at Smock-Alley who was now Garrick's treasurer. Garrick did not like it; and, when Mrs. Victor communicated his reasons to Frances, she wrote back at once [see excerpt dated 1765], obviously as irked as she was polite. Frances devoted the latter part of the letter to a refutation of Garrick's objections, one by one, and these pages constitute her fullest extant discussion of any of her works. . . . (p. 25)

A large anthology could probably be made of such letters from disappointed dramatists, and it is to Frances' credit that she, for the most part, avoids taking a strident tone. However, such letters, no matter how mild or how ferocious, are practically always futile—as, indeed, Mrs. Sheridan's was. Garrick's response, addressed to Mrs. Victor, is courteous, even friendly, but unmistakably firm [see excerpt dated 1765]. (p. 26)

No copy of *A Journey to Bath* in its entirety exists, but from the three-act fragment that survives we can glean enough evidence to make some assessment of the merits of Frances' and Garrick's divergent opinions. Frances seems wrong on one point and Garrick on another, but both were really in agreement that comedy should be laughing, not weeping, and that the play had well-developed characters. Indeed, one must go further and say that *A Journey to Bath* contains the freshest, most diversified collection of characters that Frances had yet created. Even her young hero and heroine have individualizing, humanizing traits not always found in such roles. The villains, Lord Stewkly and Lady Filmot, are no monsters but are urbanely plausible. And the character roles include a supercilious snob, a vulgar parvenu, a pompous politician, a sycophantic landlady, and, in Mrs. Tryfort, a widow with such absurd pretensions to polite learning that she became the pattern for Dick Sheridan's immortal Mrs. Malaprop.

To the character roles, Frances attached peculiarities of language that are both neatly apt and finely comic. Mrs. Surface, the lodginghouse keeper who tries to keep in with everybody, has a droll scene based on the confusions arising from hypocrisies of language. The language of Sir Jeremy Bull is beautifully contrasted with that of his brother, Sir Jonathan. Sir Jeremy is a family-proud egotist who has served in Parliament, and his remarks are like pronouncements—orotund, obscure, pretentious, and long-winded. Sir Jonathan is a sweet, straightforward, credulous man whose conversation is garrulously friendly and sunnily simple. In Lady Bell Aircastle, we have the language of snobbery, and in Mrs. Tryfort such an ingenious misapplication of words that Dick Sheridan later simply appropriated her best *mal mots* ["malapropisms"] and burnished them a bit. Garrick went quite astray in thinking that Frances' dialogue was uncomic, for *A Journey to Bath* is the most cunningly written of all her plays.

Insofar as we can tell, however, from the extant three acts, Garrick was on much surer ground when he charged that "the scenes were languid for want of an interesting fable." Several scenes are in themselves comically effective, but the main intrigue is built up in so leisurely a manner, and with such a want of thrust, that the play ambles. Even the big scene at the end of Act III, to which all of the action has been tending, is treated somewhat lifelessly. Dick's *The Rivals* is, by contrast, composed of one bold-relief comic situation after another. Whether Frances actually managed to rise to a strongly done, climactic comic situation in her last acts, we cannot say. But even with her paleness of plot, we can say that *A Journey to Bath* contains better characterization and better writing than her previous plays, and that its pattern was developed by her son into one of the great comedies of the English stage. (pp. 27-8)

Over the years, several of Frances' works have appeared posthumously—the juvenile *Eugenia and Adelaide,* the sequel to *Sidney Bidulph,* and *The History of Nourjahad.* The *Sidney* sequel is not so long as the original, but is nonetheless a substantial 125,000 words. In it, the heroine has retired to the country and raised her two daughters as well as Orlando Falkland, the son of her old lover. Told again in the form of letters, the story is basically that of the children, and Sidney only takes the center of the stage at the end of the novel, with her death. The plot concerns a love triangle, a minor seduction, a major seduction, an interesting study of near madness, and a narrowly averted marriage. The structure is tighter, more exciting, and rather more melodramatic than that of the first part. The characterization of the three young principals is rather stiff, but some of the conniving minor figures are excellent. The style is predictably fluent and supple, but the moral tone seems to have hardened into conventionality. For instance, after a minor character, Theodora Williams, has been seduced through little fault of her own other than naiveté, Frances draws this conclusion:

> There was nothing now to be done but to remove her from the scene of her misfortune, and accordingly we yesterday sent her down to the country to the house of the lady whom she is to serve; where the poor creature may pine away the rest of her life in sorrow. . . .

At the end, after most of the characters (particularly the women) have suffered and suffered and suffered, Sidney dies, the pattern of a heroic and impeccably virtuous woman. In this continuation of her first published novel, Frances Sheridan's technique has improved, especially in the staging of dramatic scenes, but her moral view has become a good deal less interesting. . . .

The History of Nourjahad appeared a year after Frances' death. It was written as the first in a projected series of moral tales exploiting the current interest in Oriental exotica, and so it is longer than a story and shorter than a novel. *Nourjahad* features a childlike arbitrariness of values, of situations, and of lucid expression that draws it closer to a fable than to a conventional work of fiction. Some quite familiar qualities of conventional

novelistic fiction, however, it does possess. Its plot is developed, complicated, and so successfully surprising in its denouement that a critic must not divulge it. Its main personage, Nourjahad, is simple but well defined, and his character is made plausibly to change and grow. But overall the story is more abstract than circumstantial. The generalized rather than realistic Persian setting helps to create this effect, as does the fairy-tale device that impels the plot. And both qualities, of course, contribute to the prime excellence of the work, namely its charm. (p. 30)

Admirers of Johnson's *Rasselas* (1759) will recognize certain echoes of her old friend's work in Frances Sheridan's tale, while those who have read *Vathek* (1786) may be surprised by how close William Beckford came to repeating the outlines of the plot of *Nourjahad.* But Frances' last book can stand on its own without benefit of reference to these more familiar props of literary history. Its story is so good, its details so inventive, and its telling so uncluttered that *Nourjahad* really deserves the kind of attention usually lavished upon a minor classic. If Frances had been able to write a number of companion pieces, as she proposed, her place in English literature would have been secured long ago. In modern times, *Nourjahad* has been once rediscovered and reprinted, and might well be again. The style of the work could be slightly less cluttered with eighteenth-century mannerisms, but on the whole Mrs. Sheridan's prose is as clear and clean as Swift's and would provide no barrier to the pleasure of a child or intelligent adult today. *Nourjahad* is not a great lost masterpiece, but it is a worthy conclusion to the all too brief career of a very talented lady. (p. 31)

> Robert Hogan and Jerry C. Beasley, "Introduction: Frances Sheridan, Her Family and Career," in The Plays of Frances Sheridan *by Frances Sheridan, edited by Robert Hogan and Jerry C. Beasley, University of Delaware Press, 1984, pp. 13-31.*

GERARD A. BARKER   (essay date 1985)

[*In the following excerpt, Barker compares the principal characters of* Memoirs of Miss Sidney Bidulph *with those of Samuel Richardson in his* The History of Sir Charles Grandison *(1753-54).*]

An examination of Grandison's descendants must begin with the one significant but neglected novel to have been written by a member of Richardson's circle of admirers—*Memoirs of Miss Sidney Bidulph*. . . . [Its author, Frances Sheridan,] was encouraged by Richardson's praise of *Eugenia and Adelaide* (an unpublished novel written when she was fifteen) "to try her powers in a work of higher importance and greater length." The resulting novel, dedicated to "the Author of *Clarissa* and *Sir Charles Grandison*" as a "tribute due to exemplary Goodness and distinguished Genius," clearly shows her acknowledged master's influence. As the *Critical Review* observed,

> If a copy drawn with the most exquisite skill, and heightened with the nicest touches of art, can be allowed merit equal to a justly admired original, the *Memoirs of Miss Bidulph* may deservedly claim a place in our esteem with the histories of Clarissa and Sir Charles Grandison [see excerpt dated 1761].

Like Sir Charles, Orlando Faulkland is a "nonpareil," whom Sir George Bidulph, Sidney's brother, calls "the best *behaved* young man I ever saw," while Ned Warner, her cousin, claims he "never saw his equal either in mind or person." Sidney, on the other hand, is more reminiscent of Clarissa Harlowe than of Harriet Byron, and for good reason. (pp. 53-4)

Frances Sheridan, though she "considered Richardson as her master . . . had the good sense and judgment," according to her granddaughter [Alicia Le Fanu], "to be conscious of his defects." . . . Not only would she have recognized the shortcomings of *Grandison* but she would also have found *Clarissa* a much more congenial model to draw upon. The difficulty for her, as well as for succeeding novelists, was to complement her heroine with an acceptable Lovelace. Richardson's antagonist must have seemed an immoral and hence dangerous literary representation to a woman who insulated her daughters from "all such books as are not calculated, by their moral tendency, expressly for the perusal of youth" . . . and who at the time of her death was working on "a series of instructive moral fictions" . . . , only the first of which, *The History of Nourjahad,* was completed. But even without such scruples, her sheltered upbringing as a clergyman's daughter had hardly prepared Mrs. Sheridan for creating a Lovelace, let alone realizing his point of view. Indeed, among English novelists, only Holcroft, some thirty years later, succeeded in recreating Richardson's archrake.

Sir Charles Grandison, on the other hand, though didactically a much more appealing choice, is prevented by his very perfection from offering a heroine the kind of challenge and self-conflict that would demonstrate her nobility. He can only provide someone like Harriet an opportunity to give him up magnanimously for another woman. Under the circumstances, Mrs. Sheridan hit upon a solution that would allow her to have the best of both worlds: she patterned Faulkland, with some qualifications, after Grandison but created a chain of circumstances that misleads Sidney into believing him a virtual Lovelace. This enables the heroine to demonstrate her exemplary character by renouncing the man she loves, though his comparative innocence increases the pathos of her decision and saves her from the aspersions Clarissa was exposed to for having been capable of loving an immoral man.

Just as in *Grandison,* published only seven years before *Bidulph,* the lovers' union is impeded by the hero's prior entanglement with another woman, though with one important difference: while Sir Charles's problem stems from having become engaged to Clementina before he knew Harriet, Orlando's dilemma arises from having been enticed, before he has actually met Sidney, into going to bed with Miss Burchell, who as a consequence becomes pregnant. (pp. 54-5)

Sir Charles Grandison, though he is also popular with the opposite sex and claims to be impetuous, is too cautious and vigilant to allow himself to be tempted. . . . And even on those rare occasions when Grandison's situation approximates Faulkland's, his self-command . . . falters. When Miss Obrien, the steward's beautiful young niece who, like Miss Burchell, has a scheming aunt, attempts to entice Sir Charles, he remains . . . perfectly impassive, just as earlier he had proved himself immune to Olivia's tempting offers of "probatory Cohabitation."

Grandison's so-called failings never, in fact, produce the harm and regrets they lead to in others. They are . . . "sprinkle[d]" into Sir Charles's character lest he should appear "a *faultless monster,*" they are confessed and alluded to, but they are never allowed to spawn consequences that affect the action of the novel. Though he fears, for example, the violence of his temper, there is little . . . to justify his concern. Far from being a blemish, his supposed violent temper results in personal triumph because it demonstrates his self-conquest. In Faulkland's case, on the other hand, we are not only told that "when provoked, no tempest is more furious," but dramatically shown the dire consequences of his irascibility: lashing an inept footman "with his whip across the shoulders" for causing Sidney to fall off her horse is instrumental in leading her to reject him, for it results in the vindictive servant's stealing and sending Sidney the letter in which Miss Burchell informs Faulkland of her pregnancy.

If this makes Faulkland a more believable character than his predecessor, it also dramatically demonstrates the constraint Richardson had worked under in his last novel. (pp. 55-6)

In the final analysis, it is their difference in function, rather than a greater concern for realism on the part of Frances Sheridan, that makes Faulkland the more credible character. Far from being himself an exemplary hero and the center of the novel, his primary purpose is to support and enhance Sidney's exemplary role. The novel, though a thousand pages long, thus tells us next to nothing about Faulkland's past, his childhood, or his family—details given to us at great length about Grandison. His attractiveness and nobility of character, borrowed from Sir Charles, are designed not so much to encourage emulation as to aggrandize Sidney's act of self-denial when she comes to reject him. At the same time, his principal weaknesses, impetuosity and irascibility, clearly affect the action of the novel, helping to impel it forward to its tragic conclusion.

When we first meet Faulkland, however, such differences are hardly noticeable. On the contrary, his courtship of Sidney recalls Sir Charles's wooing of Harriet in the sixth volume of *Grandison.* Like his predecessor, he is sensitive to the woman's vulnerable social and economic position. Though Sidney nervously asks Cecilia, her confidante, "can you conceive any thing more distressing than the situation of a poor girl, receiving the visit of a man, who, for the first time, comes professedly as her admirer?", Faulkland's tact and delicacy soon relieve her of her anxiety. . . . Moreover, just as Sir Charles generously refuses to let Harriet's relations increase her dowry and directs Mr. Deane, her godfather, to arrange the settlements, so likewise is Faulkland reluctant to allow Sir George to mention Sidney's "expectations" and insists "upon leaving the appointment of her settlement" to her mother and brother. Nor is he less humane and tenderhearted than Grandison. As Lady Bidulph, Sidney's mother, "conveniently" discovers, he has arranged to let his coachman's children be raised in his own town house to relieve the father's anxiety after his wife's death.

But if such touches are reminiscent of Richardson's hero, the woman Faulkland courts is no Harriet Byron. Although both heroines are great beauties, nearly the same age, and visiting London for the first time after having been raised in the country, they differ temperamentally, reflecting divergent authorial functions. Harriet, whose main purpose is to enhance the hero's exemplary stature, exults in her love of Sir Charles despite receiving no encouragement from him. Indeed, not only does she soon dislike "all other men," but also would "rather have his pity, than the love of any other man." Sidney, almost at times sensing her exemplary role, is less fervent, more cautious in her responses. Although prepossessed in Faulkland's favor after Sir George's glowing report and worried lest he "be snapped up before he comes to town," she is nevertheless not prepared to love without reciprocal affection. . . . (pp. 56-8)

After having met Faulkland and been obviously attracted to him, she self-consciously strikes a sardonic note to offset the enthusiastic tone she finds herself falling into:

Now you'll expect I should describe him to you, perhaps, and paint this romantic hero in the glowing colours of romantic exaggeration. But I'll disappoint you—and tell you, that he is neither like an Adonis nor an Apollo—that he has no hyacinthine curls flowing down his back; no eyes like the suns, whose brightness and majesty strikes the beholders dumb; nor, in short, no rays of divinity about him; yet he is the handsomest man that I ever saw.

Although it is only in her dreams that Harriet indulges in the kind of "exaggeration" Sidney ridicules, her description of Sir Charles is, nevertheless, at times unabashedly romantic. . . . (pp. 57-8)

Sidney, on the other hand, can only call Faulkland "the most amiable of men," though conceding, "if my heart were (happily for me it is not) *very* susceptible of tender impressions, I really believe I should in time be absolutely in love with him. Yet, even though she soon prefers him "over all the rest of his sex," she is nevertheless convinced that "if any unforeseen event were to prevent my being his, I am sure I should bear it, and behave very handsomely." As an exemplary heroine, Sidney must love with prudence and self-restraint, despite her suitor's fervor and sincerity. . . . Ironically, the situation in *Grandison* is thus reversed since it is now the heroine rather than the hero who loves with such discretion and restraint that it is Faulkland, where before it was Harriet, who is kept in suspense. Indeed, even after Sidney announces her acceptance of her suitor, she flippantly hides the depth of her feelings behind a façade of self-interest. . . . (p. 59)

The stage is now set for Sidney to prove just how exemplary a heroine she can be. Though she obviously loves Faulkland, she readily follows her mother's wishes to give him up once his relationship with Miss Burchell is exposed. . . . No doubt her decision appears virtuous, inspired as it is by filial obedience and high principles of conduct. One might even liken her act to what Clarissa would have done without the threat of marriage to Solmes hanging over her: "she never would have married Mr. Lovelace," Richardson insists, "because of his immoralities, had she been left to herself." Yet Faulkland is no Lovelace but only becomes one in the imagination of Lady Bidulph, who, having been jilted on her wedding day by a bridegroom overcome with guilt for having broken a prior engagement, is too easily prejudiced against Faulkland to listen to his explanation, calling him Miss Burchell's "destroyer."

Thus Sidney's supposedly heroic act of self-denial, that which initiates her and Faulkland's eventual tragedies, has a hollow ring to it. "We can see," wrote one reviewer [in the *London Magazine* in 1761], "that they [Sidney's tribulations] arose from want of knowledge of the world, from a too easy credulity, from *innocence that suspecteth not.*" Her decision is based not on reasonable grounds but stems from a misunderstanding originating with Lady Bidulph and credulously accepted by Sidney, though she is usually an astute observer of her mother's shortcomings. . . . (pp. 59-60)

Whether Sidney would have married Faulkland if she had known the negligible degree of his culpability toward Miss Burchell is a question left deliberately ambiguous. By the time Sidney knows the truth, other factors have arisen to prevent a union. Sheridan seems to skirt around the problem of male chastity, a particularly touchy question for an eighteenth-century woman novelist, by casting Faulkland's principal apologist in an unsympathetic light. Sir George Bidulph, we soon discover, is a vain, often tactless and even heartless young man, who, Sidney

claims, is prepossessed in his friend's favor because, like Clarissa's brother, he "would sacrifice every consideration to aggrandize his family." Thus his spirited defense of Faulkland (an implicit though probably unintentional criticism of Sir Charles Grandison), which recalls Mrs. Haywood's defense of Trueworth, is effectively blunted:

The *best* men, said he confidently, may fall into an error; and if you expect to find a man intirely free from them, you look for what is not possible in human nature.

Once Sidney has rejected him and married Mr. Arnold in obedience to her mother's wishes rather than her own preference, Faulkland tries tactfully to avoid meeting her, though still watching over her "with the disinterested zeal of a guardian spirit." . . . So impeccable is his conduct, in fact, that when Sidney is trapped in a burning theater, he comes to her rescue only when he realizes that her own party has deserted her. He is the ideal lover—out of sight but standing in the wings, ready to help when the need arises. It is a situation Sir Charles is unlikely to find himself in because, except when Clementina's religious scruples finally get the better of her, women never reject him, thus debarring him from exhibiting the kind of disinterested love Faulkland attains.

When Arnold is enticed away from his wife by Mrs. Gerrarde, the same scheming aunt of Miss Burchell who had earlier lured Faulkland into her niece's embrace, Sheridan's hero is so far from rejoicing over or encouraging a situation that might regain him Sidney's love that he takes it upon himself to carry Mrs. Gerrarde off "in hopes to restoring, to the most amiable of women, a besotted husband's heart." Deluding her into believing he loves her, he takes Mrs. Gerrarde to France and persuades her to write to Arnold, informing her lover that she has left him out of remorse for having alienated him from his wife, whom she has wrongfully maligned. After the letter has been sent, he admits to his astonished and enraged companion that "*love* has had no share in my conduct," and to make certain she can no longer endanger Sidney's marriage, bribes and wheedles her into wedding M. Pivet, who, unbeknown to her, is Faulkland's valet and has pledged to prevent his wife from corresponding with anyone in England.

He accomplishes these maneuvers with an aplomb and relish worthy of Lovelace, calling himself "the first of politicians, the greatest of negotiators!" . . . "Faulkland," the *Critical Review* observed, "is a composition of features borrowed from Grandison and Lovelace: possessed of the strict honour, the steadiness and integrity of the former, he sometimes delights in the stratagem of the latter." That, of course, is the hybrid that Richardson, under Lady Bradshaigh's prodding, had so diligently striven for in his last novel. Indeed, Faulkland's deft manipulation of Mrs. Gerrarde recalls Sir Charles's handling of Lady Beauchamp. Like his prototype, he shrewdly determines his adversary's temperament in order to exploit her weakness. . . . (pp. 60-2)

But whereas Sir Charles is simply acting out his role as a do-gooder—helping out his friend Edward Beauchamp, Faulkland offers eloquent testimony of the selflessness of his love by his efforts to reconcile Arnold to his wife, prepared, he affirms, to risk his own life to save Sidney's husband "from ruin." Grandison's love for Miss Byron never undergoes such a trial; on the contrary, it is Harriet who must play the disinterested role of supporting Sir Charles's expected marriage to Clementina. Faulkland's triumph is, moreover, all the greater because, despite needing to make Mrs. Gerrarde believe him infatuated with her, he manages to "avoid all approaches which usually forerun the catastrophe of an amour." Overcoming such a temptation from "one of the finest women in England" redeems him, cancelling out his earlier lapse with her niece.

With the success of Faulkland's stratagem, Sidney gains an opportunity, like Pamela or Amanda in Vanbrugh's *The Relapse* (1696), to demonstrate her exemplary qualities as a wife by joyfully welcoming her erring husband back: "I exult in his restored affections, and love him a thousand times better than I ever did." When only a few months later, Arnold dies from a fall off his horse, Faulkland's hopes revive, but the truth is that he understands the woman he has so steadfastly loved as little as she understands him.

All along, Sidney has gloried in the belief that her passions could be kept in check and, if necessary, subdued by her judgment. It is an assumption that Clarissa also clings to, though to her sorrow discovers to be illusive, but one that Sidney has no trouble maintaining. When she is under parental pressure to marry Arnold, she admits to Cecilia: "I knew a man once that I liked better—but fie, fie upon him! I am sure I ought not to like him, and therefore I will not." (pp. 62-3)

It is the "merit" of having virtuously sacrificed her first love that has nourished that self-esteem which she now sees threatened by Faulkland's renewed proposal. Thus, even after Miss Burchell has confessed her own guilt and Faulkland's comparative innocence, Sidney can still reject him in the belief that he knowingly "paid the price of her innocence to the wicked aunt" when actually, as she later discovers, he was ignorant of Mrs. Gerrarde's intention of repaying him with her niece's favors. Urging him instead to marry Miss Burchell, whose advocate she has promised to become, Sidney attempts to raise Faulkland to the same heights of self-denial she herself basks in.... (p. 64)

Although, when Faulkland first courts her, she assures her confidante that she is not "so prepossessed in his favour, as to suppose him a phoenix," ironically, that is precisely what she is now asking him to become. And her wish to give him up by turning him into an exemplary hero, another Sir Charles Grandison, comes all the easier because his passionate love has all along alarmed her, made her fearful of the expectation his fervency implied. "I would not," she exclaims, "have my heart devoured by such a flame as her's [Miss Burchell], for the whole world." She cannot, in fact, help being disgusted by the intensity of Miss Burchell's love, though her antipathy is tinged with envy.... (pp. 64-5)

Ironically, because she wants to admire Faulkland rather than physically desire him, he must be persuaded to accept the purely sensual love Miss Burchell offers. It is essentially a struggle of egos, less subtle than that which takes place in the sixth volume of *Grandison* but more far-reaching in its consequences. Unable to win her, Faulkland finally succumbs to Sidney's entreaties....

But Sidney's triumph is short-lived, for she is soon forced to recognize that she has needlessly sacrificed Faulkland at the altar of her misdirected idealism. Coming across his candid letter to Sir George, written long ago from Bath, which her prejudiced mother had refused to read through, she becomes fully convinced "of Mr. Faulkland's honour" as well as Miss Burchell's "folly." However, while this discovery increases the pathos of her position, it also tends to weaken for us Faulkland's stature in the novel. The man who so deftly manipulated Mrs. Gerrarde has become the victim of the situation rather than its master, because having insisted on idolizing the woman he loves into what he calls the "arbitress of my fate," he has allowed her to mislead him into the arms of Miss Burchell. (p. 65)

[Sidney] comes to accept her harsh destiny, believing, as Mrs. Norton assures Clarissa, that she has been singled out as a divine example: "I have been set up as a mark, my Cecilia; let me fulfil the intention of my Maker, by shewing a perfect resignation to His will."

But how can we reconcile such claims with the novel's clearly expressed moral that it is folly to interpret man's earthly fortunes as an expression of divine judgment? It is, in fact, to demonstrate this doctrine that Sidney must come to be seen as "a woman of most exemplary virtue, [who] was, through the course of her whole life, persecuted by a variety of strange misfortunes." As a now aged Cecilia points out,

> to all human appearance, [she] *ought* at least to have been rewarded even here—but her portion was affliction. What then are we to conclude, but that God does not estimate things as we do?

It may, of course, be argued that, under the circumstances, Sidney's reactions are perfectly natural, that they, in fact, demonstrate the psychological realism of Sheridan's characterization. But it is hard to believe that she would allow her heroine, who in every other respect is consistently exemplary in her conduct (even to the point of stretching the bounds of credibility), to fall prey to the very error the novel was supposedly designed to condemn. More likely, Sheridan's professed moral, like Richardson's condemnation of poetic justice in the "Postscript" to the third edition of *Clarissa,* was little more than a pretext or afterthought for justifying her heroine's interminable misfortunes. If so, it proved to be of little benefit in placating the *Monthly Review* [see excerpt dated 1761]:

> the Author seems to have had no other design than to draw tears from the reader by distressing innocence and virtue, as much as possible. Now, tho' we are not ignorant that this may be a true picture of human life, in some instances, yet, we are of opinion, that such representations are by no means calculated to encourage and promote Virtue.

Dr. Johnson, on the other hand, told Frances Sheridan, "I know not, Madam, that you have a right, upon moral principles, to make your readers suffer so much" [see excerpt by Boswell dated 1791]. That Johnson's often quoted utterance should be taken by Boswell and his contemporaries as a "high compliment" tells us much about the audience Sheridan was writing for as well as the reason for her novel's considerable success. The age, as its sentimental drama and fiction attest, was inordinately fond of pathos; and Sheridan, who embarked on her novel out of financial necessity . . . , was determined to exploit that popularity. Since the pathos is all the greater if the heroine is innocent of the cause of her suffering, **Bidulph** was meant to become, in its simplest terms, a novel of virtue in distress, combining "propriety of conduct" and "irresistible pathos," terms with which the *Critical Review* had voiced its praise.

Both qualities are in evidence in the closing scenes of the novel.... Resigned now to "His will," Sidney writes to Faulkland, "beseeching him to forget her, as they were never more to meet." But, of course, he cannot share her fortitude, only admire it: "*Her* heroic soul is still unmoved, and above the reach of adversity. Happy Mrs. Arnold—What a vain fool was I to think that such a mind as *hers* could be subdued."

His tribute, coming shortly before his death (presumably at his own hands), closes Faulkland's role in the novel. While he cannot "survive this last blow," she endures and supposedly triumphs through what Cecilia describes as "a resignation . . . heightened by religion into an almost saintlike meekness and humility."

If Sidney's stance recalls Clarissa, the character of Faulkland suggests how Richardson's prototypal hero could be adapted to the needs of the feminine novel. Rejected, deceived, discredited where Grandison was adored and aggrandized, he helps to establish and enhance the heroine's exemplary nature. Sharing Sir Charles's tact, refinement, and benevolence but falling short of his preeminence, Faulkland comes to assume a distinctly supportive role opposite the heroine, heralding a new kind of Grandisonian hero. (pp. 67-8)

> Gerard A. Barker, "Sheridan's Orlando Faulkland: 'To Suppose Him a Phoenix'," in his Grandison's Heirs: The Paragon's Progress in the Late Eighteenth-Century English Novel, *University of Delaware Press, 1985, pp. 53-69.*

MARGARET ANNE DOODY (essay date 1986)

[*Doody is an American critic, novelist, and dramatist. Her academic work is primarily concerned with literature of the eighteenth century. In the following excerpt, she examines the two parts of* Memoirs of Miss Sidney Bidulph *and* Nourjahad, *seeing in them a manifestation of feminine insights, especially regarding the nature of time.*]

[Throughout the course of **Miss Sidney Bidulph**, nothing] has stayed constant—as [the] denouement, with its melodramatic whirlwind of ironies, intends to prove. The girl who seemed so obsessively in love threw away that love once she had it. The man who at one point seemed Grandisonian in perfection becomes an innocent murderer, a crazed sufferer, a miserable suicide. Virtue is not rewarded, even by personal development. Moral decisions based on high principles of honor and the nicest scruples turn out wrong. All judgments err. Impressions are unstable; judgments of prudence are, after all, founded on assumptions and impressions, and these may betray.

Through Cecilia and her editor, Frances Sheridan assures us several times of her moral; Sidney's constant afflictions "may serve to show that it is not *here* that true virtue is to look for its reward." But we may ask if that is *the* moral, the only or even the central theme illustrated by the extraordinary story.

What is Frances Sheridan doing? She seems perhaps to be betraying the cause of women, and even of morality—those causes that Richardson said were the same. In some ways the novel seems to be an answer back to *Sir Charles Grandison;* we have here a quasi-rake vindicated as a Grandisonian man, and that Grandisonian figure in turn reduced to chaos and self-destruction. Women assert, as Richardson advised, their detestation of rakes, and lo! that detestation is, in the particular instance, misplaced. The cause of women against rakes and rakishness, against the prevailing male ethos to which women are by custom expected to accede, is valiantly supported by Lady Bidulph and her daughter, but their crusade against the double standard comes to grief. Their new and singular feminine code ceases to be for Sidney (if indeed it ever was for her) simply and self-evidently valid. Sisterhood, and the responsibility of women to and for each other against a doctrine of male exploitation of women, seem right. Yet sisterhood comes on the rocks in the association with Miss Burchell,

whose own piratical code has nothing of the generosity of sisterhood, though she is quick to notice her advantage in dealing with the magnanimous Bidulphs. Miss Burchell, one of the best drawn and most interesting characters in the novel—though we see her only from a distance—is a wonderfully mixed character, capable of being variously interpreted. She is herself an exploiter; she uses others ruthlessly and has no allegiance to inconvenient truth. Yet her "love" for Faulkland seems in some sense real, if only kind of monomania with a romantic tinge—though the selfish romanticism, like the "tears and languishments," is both genuine and theatrical. She had a claim on Faulkland and used it to advantage, in effect turning the tables by getting him "into trouble," though he would have had no trouble in shunting her off if it weren't for the Bidulph women. Miss Burchell was able to manipulate a (false) position as Woman wronged, acting for the eyes of the Bidulph women the role of Woman as Eternal Victim. Confronted by a woman who is extremely feminine but not womanly, the Bidulph ladies do not know what to make of her. They proceed by assumption, and, in Lady Bidulph's case, by enthusiasm *partly* arising from self-vindication. Miss Burchell made herself into a kind of cliché that the women (particularly Lady Bidulph) can accept because it is so recognizable.

Yet, as the novel of course shows, there is no satisfactory alternative to the Bidulph women's romantic code, to their "feminism," in the world as it is. Sir George, bluff, bossy and insensitive, is right, but only accidentally. He adheres to his own accepted masculine code, propped up by society in general, and his judgment is always crude. His views allow no room for women, and little for morality; that his attitudes don't make for happiness or virtue is illustrated in his own life. He can only reveal the truth about Miss Burchell (too late) because he slept with her, and then was disgusted and disturbed to find he had been used by "a sly rake in petticoats." (We may choose not to trust entirely his account of that affair; he says that he wearied of Miss Burchell, but we are, I think, free to wonder if she didn't tire of him first.) Society of course exacts no penalty of Sir George for his concupiscence, and he is free to marry the "virtuous," stupid, and miserly Lady Sarah; he can bear being tied for life to an ignorant shrew only because he has in general such a low opinion of women. Mr. Arnold, who so disapproved of Sidney's reading Horace, illustrates all the limitations of the male world that allows women neither freedom nor intelligence. His low opinion of women does not prevent his being made a fool of by a woman who can size him up and flatter him, drawing out the silly and empty fellow who lurked behind the rigid exterior.

The masculine views of women and sex do not make for sexual or emotional happiness for either men or women. The novel satirizes the crudity of masculine views, and of the world's views of family life, sexuality, and society's claims. It makes us feel that it *is* time someone took a feminist stand against the restrictions and debasements, time that someone worked through these limitations. That is what the Bidulph women try to do. But their new "feminist" view is also shown as limited by human fallibility. It is something to have characters—in the world and in a novel—who are capable of living according to a moral idea, of making a moral problem the center of life. Then, Frances Sheridan wants us to acknowledge, it must also be seen that this higher feminine understanding, these moral views, have their own limitations which in turn must be transcended in a larger comprehension. Above all, it must be seen that all moral life is intensely fragile, that even the highest decisions are founded partly on guesswork and prejudice, and that ''worthy'' acts have another side. Sidney's high-principled endeavor to assist Miss Burchell to marriage with Faulkland arises from a mixture of motives, and has its reverse side. (To some readers it has seemed as crazily obsessed and absurd as Miss Burchell's incessant hoping.) Principles themselves are founded on shaky judgments and beliefs, and, if we had known the effect in advance, our ''prudent'' actions would have been prudently different. It can, one observes, even be argued that Sidney, not Miss Burchell, is the final cause of Faulkland's death; the novel is constructed so that we can ask that question too (it would have been easy enough to engineer the ending so that Faulkland died in a duel). We never know quite how to place our shots—as illustrated in the night scene with the pistols. Sidney's letter to Faulkland, prudent, heartfelt, high-principled, struck the final blow.

The women's world is a real world, with both good and evil in it. Like Grimston Hall, it is not a sanctuary, and must not be made into an illusory perfection. In some respects—to the puzzlement of readers then and now—Frances Sheridan has, in what looks like a feminist novel, taken us beyond feminism, opening out the complexities that arise in human life whenever human beings try to do right. To wish to be right is a noble wish, but it may be as unreasonable as more worldly wishes.

Yet the debate over the cause of women, over sexual morality, or even over the real nature of morality is only part of the novel's subject. What seems to interest Frances Sheridan above all is the effect of the past on the present. Her whole novel, in both parts, is constructed (if that is the right word) around the idea that no act exists singly, in itself. The past never ceases, a past action is never cleared out of the way; the past never stops having an effect on the present. In a novel that pays so much attention to the idea of principle as abstract moral axiom guiding action, it is interesting to note the counteracting attention to the sources or origins of action—but one meaning of ''principle'' is fundamental basis or ultimate cause. In the novel the two meanings of ''principle'' intersect, creating tensions or ironies. The whole of *Miss Sidney Bidulph* circles about and repeatedly returns to the original experience of Lady Bidulph on her abortive wedding day. Lady Bidulph as a young woman did not make the primary decision (it was made for her, done to her); her decision is a reaction internalizing a meaning in what was done to her. She turned rejection into active sacrifice, elaborating a moral motif suggested by her wretched bridegroom into a governing law. The Bidulph women in general, and Sidney most especially, rarely initiate important action; their strength is that of reaction. Refusing to take initiative, they also refuse to be mere passive objects of the percussion of experience. They have a talent for transmuting experience into law. It may be that Sheridan saw this as at once the strength and the weakness of the female in her time, cut off from the power of original action and the force of positive law in the external social world. Emotionally reacting, woman turns into private lawmaker and lawgiver; her laws are transmissible, but only in company with emotional responses.

The original action or reaction of Lady Bidulph is a predetermining event. Her decision sets up in herself and later in her family currents of thought, patterns of action, that affect the lives of a number of people in the next two generations. Lady Bidulph, having accomplished her heroic and disastrous mission, dies, but the effects of all her acts, including primarily her original response to her original problem, remain. People die, but the past does not die.

It is doubtless this interest in the influence of the past that led Frances Sheridan to continue her novel in a second part, which appeared in 1767 (the year of her death). This second novel traces the effect of previous acts and responses on a third generation. The central characters here are Sidney's daughters, Dolly and Cecilia, and Faulkland's son, the next Orlando Falkland (for some reason the name ''Faulkland'' is throughout the second part spelled without the ''u''). As far as I know, *Miss Sidney Bidulph* is the only English novel before Elizabeth Inchbald's *A Simple Story* (1791) to deal with the interlocking life of two generations, with parents the heroes of the first half of the story and those parents' children the central characters in the second. *Miss Sidney Bidulph,* like *A Simple Story,* may well have been an influence on *Wuthering Heights.* I believe also that the second part of *Sidney Bidulph* was an influence on Jane Austen's *Mansfield Park.* (pp. 342-46)

What is most noticeable about the second part of *Miss Sidney Bidulph* is not its pathos, or its plots, or the witty machinations of the Audleys. Its most signal quality is the reiterated presence of the past. There are constant allusions to the history and deeds of the preceding two generations. . . . In an endeavor not to repeat what they consider the mistakes of the past generation, lively Cecilia and weak Orlando bring about new misery. Yet the new misery is parallel to the old. The old decisions and the old actions and reactions are the final causes of renewed unhappiness, to which the Audleys merely contribute as ignorant external agents. Cecilia unwittingly commits the ''sin'' which her grandmother and her mother had struggled so strenuously to avoid. She takes another woman's man—in this case, a man ''belonging'' to a literal sister. The shy and intensely emotional Dolly was not physically but emotionally seduced, and betrayed by her belief in a promise of marriage. She is a victim—or she casts herself in that role. But this victim who prevents the marriage of lovers is also unwittingly cast in the role of Miss Burchell, the interrupter of joy. The past refuses to die.

The undying past is transmitted partly through heredity. Young Orlando visibly inherits the qualities of both parents, in a confused mixture that makes for the lack of ''strong lines in his soul.'' He has his father's impatience and susceptibility, and his mother's softness, tears and languishments, ''insinuating address,'' and dishonesty. The Arnold girls, too, take after both parents, inheriting in uneven mixtures both Sidney's romantic principles and sensibility, and Mr. Arnold's dogged self-will. They may be new actors on the scene, and they think that they improvise, but they also inherit old roles with temperaments that prove inescapable.

The past is also transmitted in the conditions it creates. Out of the past came both the estrangement of Sidney and Faulkland, and their lasting attachment. Out of the past came thus the Bidulphs' and Arnolds' involvement with the young Orlando. The past sets up psychological patterns; Sidney's reluctance to see any sexual attachment between her girls and Orlando has psychological rather than objective material causes; young Orlando is at once her lover returned, and the child that she never had by Orlando (which would make marriage to her daughters appear to her unconscious mind as a form of incest). Most important, out of the past came the self-consciousness of the characters about right and wrong, fear of old failure, and caution about self-denying decisions that lead to misery, as well as a continuing penchant for self-denial. The past repeats itself with every attempt to escape it.

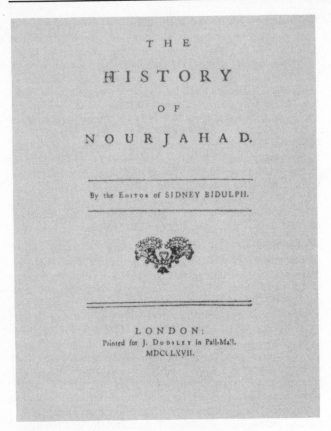

Title page of the first edition of The History of Nourjahad, *1767.*

The investigation of past and present was Sheridan's contribution to the novel as a genre. She took much from Richardson, who is good on families, but even Richardson never presented this tight patterning of generational interrelation. For Sheridan, past and present lapse into one another, conflate. Memory takes precedence of experience. It is as if consciousness lapses into intervals of dreamlike, if vivid, activity, only to awaken and return to some inevitable and more solid (if terrible) recurrence of the past, which is reality. It is no wonder that a critic [in a 1761 review in the *London Magazine*] of part 1 of *Miss Sidney Bidulph* worried lest "the too popular doctrine of predestination seems here to be encouraged." There is some kind of predestination at work, though it seems less Providential than psychological, and less psychological than visionary. Actions are related to powerful "spots of time" which are conditioning but not redemptive.

The elements that I have extrapolated from *Miss Sidney Bidulph* appear in full force in Mrs. Sheridan's Oriental tale, *The History of Nourjahad.* Published anonymously in 1767, this tale was written at the same time as the continuation of *Miss Sidney Bidulph*. According to Sheridan's granddaughter [see excerpt dated 1824], the idea of the tale came to its author after a sleepless night spent "reflecting upon the inequality in the conditions of men" and the dependence of happiness or misery upon "the due regulation of the passions, rather than on the outward dispensations of Providence." (pp. 348-51)

The story of Nourjahad teaches "the folly of unreasonable wishes" (the subtitle of the tale in a children's version), as well as the unreason of letting appetite triumph over humanity.

Like so much Augustan literature, this tale preaches the need of acknowledging limitations and mortality in order to be fully human. Nourjahad's fantasies resemble Gulliver's ecstatic imaginings when he first hears of the immortal Struldbruggs in book 3 of *Gulliver's Travels*—that work by another Irish writer, a friend of Frances Sheridan's father-in-law. Nourjahad also bears a marked relationship to *Rasselas,* without resembling Johnson's story—there are, for instance, erotic elements completely absent in Johnson's work.

If *Nourjahad* is an Augustan piece, it is also a Romantic one; its influence can be felt in the exoticism of *Vathek* (1784), and in the fantastic elements in stories by William Godwin and Mary Shelley, authors who are also interested in the movement of time and in the psychological effects of peculiar immortalities.

What is really significantly new about Frances Sheridan's tale is its playing with time. Nourjahad experiences two time spans at once—but he is aware only of the longer one. His illusory protracted experience seems in duration and complexity more like real human life than does his saner existence, the shorter "real time" operated in by Schemzeddin. Nourjahad is for instance, made to experience, comically, the vicissitudes of fashion; when he tries to create yet another seraglio, after his forty-year sleep, he can find no girls to his taste—where, oh where, are the beauties of yesteryear? Cadiga the old informs him that "the taste for beauty is quite altered since that time: You may assure yourself that none will be offered to your acceptance that will exceed these. Were I and my companions, whom you once so much admired, to be restored to our youth again, we should not now be looked upon: such is the fantastic turn of the age."

Perhaps only a woman could have thought of this, but it should be pointed out that *Nourjahad* is consistent in maintaining a masculine point of view, just as it is consistent—and respectful—in its use of Mohammedanism. The main characters are male (women have only a subordinate walk-on part to play in the narrative) and masculine views, ambitions, and sexuality are sympathetically treated. This marks a change from *Miss Sidney Bidulph,* in which female experience and views are paramount, though in both novels the male characters are led to discover the power and importance of heterosexual love which mingles friendship and affection with erotic desire . . . the eighteenth-century ideal. Both novels, however, show a sympathy with men of strong sex drives who are tempted into excess. Nourjahad, given the license of the Persian seraglio, can discover his true love, Mandana, without suffering as Faulkland does for other adventures. And of course, Mandana, given the license of her position as member of a seraglio, does not worry about seduction nor in the conclusion stick at any scruples or "punctilio" regarding Nourjahad's connections with Cadiga & Co. It is noticeable that the excessively indulgent hero of the moral tale wins his true love, for all his debauchery, while the more virtuous hero of the romantic novel remains eternally denied consummation with his beloved, who is likewise his Nemesis as well as guardian genius.

What goes wrong in *Miss Sidney Bidulph* would seem at first glance to go even more wrong in *Nourjahad,* but in the latter work the road of excess leads not only to the palace of wisdom, but also to happiness and fulfillment. Nourjahad's unreasonable wishes only *appear* to wreak havoc for a time; morally, they are easily identifiable and corrigible. *Miss Sidney Bidulph* too is a story of unreasonable wishes, but the most unreasonable wishes are precisely the moral ideals. Lady Bidulph's—and Sidney's—wishes to do right, to behave with heroic justice to other women and, like the sultan, to mete out just returns to lascivious men, are destined for unsuccess. Only life's experience over time can prove to the would-be doer of right the disparity between external reality and private judgment. The true difficulty of doing right can be known only over a lifetime, just as the true difficulty of achieving pleasure can be proved to Nourjahad only after what seems a span of two generations' worth of time. Nourjahad can have a second chance; Sidney cannot.

Yet, until the end and the surprise turning of the closure with the sudden revelation of the sultan's trick, Nourjahad's experience is very like Sidney's after all. Both characters learn melancholy, and find everything they have hoped and worked for with apparent prudence slipping through their fingers. Experience changes them; indeed, perhaps Nourjahad's processes of psychological change are deeper and more interesting than Sidney's. Yet they cannot escape the consequences of the past, in external situation and in internal condition. A reviewer in the *Monthly Review* had doubts about *Miss Sidney Bidulph,* wondering whether such pictures of unhappiness could have a moral end: "It is much to be questioned if such pictures of human life, however justly they may be copied from nature, are well adapted to serve the cause of virtue" [see excerpt dated 1767]. *Nourjahad* met more unreserved critical admiration because its overt morality is simpler, more acceptable and cheerful than that of the long novel. Yet we can doubt whether morality—or rather, the "moral"—interested Sheridan primarily. In both the somber-shaded novel and the optimistic tale similar themes can be traced.

As I have indicated, Sheridan's new contribution in both narratives is found in her handling of *time*. In the apparently realistic *Miss Sidney Bidulph* as in the dreamlike and dream-originated *Nourjahad*, time proceeds in a spiral, or rather a helix, doubling back on itself. In both, the inner meaning of a series of actions or happenings can be understood only by circling back to an original point or time, a point of departure. Sidney's (and her daughters') periods of activity and pseudo-decision (moral and social activity) are as vivid, lengthy and ironic as Nourjahad's pleasure seeking. The major decisive actions of characters in *Miss Sidney Bidulph* (for example, Sidney's first rejection of Faulkland, her marriage to Arnold, Dolly's interruption of her sister's wedding) take place in dreamlike states. These "realities" seem like illusions; they scatter and reform, as in a lapse of consciousness, and they return like recurring dreams. However far the Bidulph women may seem to advance in time (and they do proceed from cradle to grave in moral time) the characters all return, as if subject to reiterated and inevitable sleep of reason, to the condition in which individual desires or decisions are blotted out. Progressive time is annihilated.

The whole narrative of *Miss Sidney Bidulph* can be seen metaphorically in the light of what *Nourjahad* is literally—the story of a continuing consciousness (in this case a kind of group consciousness which endures through three generations of women) doomed to "the temporary death of sleep," as well as to the sleep of death. Which is more real—the activity or the dreamlike return to reenactment? Consciousness itself cannot triumph over the reiterated fate—the past—which makes almost every character succumb in a deathly reversion to Lady Bidulph's story. Characters awaken after this lapse and find everything altered, and yet after they have tried to cope with the disorienting and puzzling new conditions, they are still eventually doomed to fall again into that lacuna in time. They are constantly immobilized and rendered oblivious at that a-temporal point to which all their actions, however ambitious or frenetic, tend. Time is conflated in *Miss Sidney Bidulph,* as it is more happily in *Nourjahad.* The past is simultaneous with the present. But in *Nourjahad,* the past time, the time the sultan knows, the "real" time, is redemptive, whereas in *Miss Sidney Bidulph* the past can never be redeemed, and cannot heal or be healed.

Sheridan's view of time and the effect of the past is a somber one, however cheerfully she tried to render it at the end of *Nourjahad.* And in the Oriental tale, too, the most vivid effects concern the hero's fatiguing immortality of error, stuck at age twenty-three over a period of sixty years, and his bewilderment after each fit of oblivion. That Sheridan's views are somber does not mean that they are unattractive. Her handling of time is quite exciting, and it brings something new to fiction. I believe that her works were an influence on the Brontës' novels. One of her later, indirect, inheritors is Virginia Woolf (one thinks of *The Years*). Sheridan's novels were translated into French, and may have had an effect on the French novel; perhaps ultimately, indirectly and among many other influences, her novel was to affect *A La Recherche du Temps Perdu.*

Yet I believe too that that grave sense of time, and the sense of helplessness in relation to time and the past, are feminine insights, or at least in the eighteenth century could have been expressed only by a female writer. Such insights, that is, could have been expressed only by a sensibility with a deep knowledge of the meaning of powerlessness, and of lack of control over fate, as well as a comprehension of the hardship involved in encountering the outside world with moral ideals, or with warm desires. It is in her larger aesthetic view of the nature of time, rather than in particular opinions about female education or sexual morality, that Sheridan is truly a "feminist," and her treatment of time is her contribution—not only to feminism but to the Novel at large—that is, to humanism and humane experience. (pp. 353-56)

> *Margaret Anne Doody, "Frances Sheridan: Morality and Annihilated Time," in* Fetter'd or Free? British Women Novelists, 1670-1815, *edited by Mary Anne Schofield and Cecilia Macheski, Ohio University Press, 1986, pp. 324-58.*

ADDITIONAL BIBLIOGRAPHY

Chew, Samuel P., Jr. "*The Dupe:* A Study in the 'Low'." *Philological Quarterly* XVIII, No. 1 (January 1939): 196-203.
    Discusses *The Dupe* as portraying situations and dialogue considered coarse by eighteenth-century audiences. Chew quotes contemporary printed reactions to the play.

M[arrot], H. V. Introduction to *The History of Nourjahad,* by Frances Sheridan, pp. v-ix. London: Elkin Mathews & Marrot, 1927.
    Biographical sketch of Sheridan combined with a brief assessment of *The History of Nourjahad.* Marrot writes: "Its morality is never laboured: the reader has the sensation of drawing his own moral without the distraction of any objectionable sermonising by the author. If all works of moral application were as tactfully written as this, morality in art would not be at such a discount."

Reeve, Clara. "Evening X: Hortensius, Sophronia, Euphrasia." In her *The Progress of Romance, through Times, Countries, and Manners,* Vol. II, pp. 22-49. 1785. Reprint. New York: Facsimile Text Society, 1930.

Discussion, in fictional dialogue form, of the merits of *Memoirs of Miss Sidney Bidulph*. The participants in the conversation render differing judgments: one avows that "this book is a great favorite of mine, the Story is admirably told, and the language is so easy and natural, that every thing seems real in it, and we sorrow as for a well known and beloved friend," while another objects to the novel on moral grounds, stating: "I do really think that books of a gloomy tendency do much harm in this country, especially to young minds; they should be shewn the truth through the medium of chearfulness, and led to expect encouragement in the practice of the social duties, and rewards for virtuous actions."

Russell, Norma H. "Some Uncollected Authors XXXVIII." *The Book Collector* 13, No. 2 (Summer 1964): 196-205.
    Comments on Sheridan's major works and the circumstances surrounding the composition, publication, or production of each.

Wilson, Mona. "The Mother of Richard Brinsley Sheridan." In her *There Were Muses*, pp. 27-49. London: Sidgwick & Jackson, 1924.
    Anecdotal biography of Sheridan, with brief commentary on contemporary reaction to *Memoirs of Miss Sidney Bidulph*, *The Discovery*, *The Dupe*, *A Journey to Bath*, and *The History of Nourjahad*.

Johan Herman Wessel

1742-1785

Dano-Norwegian dramatist, poet, and short story writer.

A prominent figure in late eighteenth-century Norwegian literary life, Wessel wrote what is widely considered some of the finest humorous verse in Scandinavian literature. He championed writing that adhered to classical values, yet he scorned neoclassical trends toward pretentious diction, contrived plots, and dramatic hyperbole. Wessel is best remembered for his versified drama *Kierlighed uden strømper (Love without Stockings)*, a hilarious parody of then-fashionable Danish imitations of French and Italian tragedies which effectively destroyed that trend and reinvigorated the national theater of Denmark.

Born into a clergyman's family in Vestby, near Christiania (now Oslo), Wessel received his early education at home. He attended the Latin grammar school in Christiania during his teens; then, in 1761, he enrolled in the humanities program at the University of Copenhagen, the cultural citadel of both Denmark and Norway. He attended the university for perhaps ten years, but never received an advanced degree, though he demonstrated unusual talent for languages and a penchant for European and English literature. For the rest of his life, Wessel remained in the Danish capital where, for his wit and conviviality, he became a celebrated conversationalist and coffeehouse habitué. He did not begin his literary career until 1772, when he helped found *Det Norske Selskab* (The Norwegian Society), an informal conversational group of intellectuals and writers who upheld the Latin and Greek classics as the models upon which to base their own work. That same year Wessel established himself as a brilliant verse dramatist with *Love without Stockings*, a work most probably inspired by the recent successful production of Johan Nordahl Brun's *Zarine* (1772), which Wessel and others recognized as a poor Scandinavian adaptation of Voltaire's tragedy *Zaire* (1732). With *Love without Stockings*, which Frederik Winkel Horn has regarded as "a standing protest against all affectation and bombast in art," Wessel attained the artistic height of his career, for though he later published two additional tragicomedies, both elicited only passing recognition. He also published a few collections of poetry—primarily songs, epigrams, and occasional verse of a lighthearted nature—which provided entertainment for a season, but did little to further his literary reputation. Because of the slight compensation his works afforded him, Wessel lived meagerly, sustaining himself primarily by teaching modern languages. For a short time during the mid-1770s he edited the humorous weekly *Votre serviteur, otiosis,* to which he contributed a number of verse tales in the manner of Jean de La Fontaine's *Fables choisies mises en vers* (1668-94; *Fables,* 1734), but with a decidedly nonmoralistic, playful cast. In 1779 Wessel obtained the position of translator to the royal theater, but the post did little to improve his precarious finances. During his last years Wessel drank heavily—the sole visible sign, according to scholars, of an underlying melancholy spirit which tinged his poetry. Wessel died impoverished but nationally famous at age forty-three from typhoid fever.

Scholars record that Wessel, though an ardent enthusiast for and theorist of fine literature, was an indolent writer who left but a small corpus of work. Only a fraction of this work has been translated into English—a fact which has, no doubt, contributed to the scarcity of critical appraisals of Wessel's writings by English-speaking commentators. All Wessel scholars, though, rank *Love without Stockings* as the author's greatest work and accordingly devote their discussions largely, if not entirely, to it. The mock tragedy concerns the wedding day of a tailor's apprentice named Johan von Ehrenpreis. Discovering that he lacks a pair of white stockings, and after considerable pondering and poeticizing on the respective value of love and virtue, he steals a pair from a rival suitor. Following the discovery of the theft, the play concludes with a heroic oration by Johan, who then atones for his crime by committing suicide; his betrothed, Grete, quickly does the same, as do the other main characters, completing the farce. Much of the comical power of *Love without Stockings* is sustained, according to scholars, by the incongruity between the characters' insipid natural speech and their continual, laughably flawed attempts to couch their motives and actions in grandiloquent, classical verse similar to that of many great tragic figures of dramatic literature. Although Wessel primarily directed his satire at derivative, poetically overblown Danish productions, it has been recognized that, as Harald Beyer has expressed it, Wessel's is "a satire on all poetic artificiality, all false solemnity, on big words that cover small actions, and on bourgeois vulgarization of the fate motif." For its many memorable epigrams and high parodic humor, the work ranks, in the words of Edmund Gosse, as "one of the masterpieces of Danish literature."

Wessel is also esteemed—especially among Scandinavian readers—as a consummate writer of comic verse tales, of which "Smeden og bageren" ("The Smith and the Baker") is his most famous. In a noteworthy insight, Frederika Blankner asserts that his tales "display a comic vein of the first order, not free, however, from a pessimistic sarcasm which reveals him fundamentally as a tragic and melancholy spirit." The remainder of Wessel's poetry is marked by levity, clever phrasing, and occasional ridicule of unrefined or blustering artistry.

Despite his obscurity in world literature, Wessel is deemed a prominent figure in Dano-Norwegian writing. He stands as one of the few highly imaginative talents of his time, an era when the Copenhagen stage was slowly recovering after the loss of the first great Danish dramatist, Ludvig Holberg. Beyer summarizes Wessel's literary contribution thus: "He was not a poet of deep feelings or ideas, or a prophet with philosophic or patriotic passions. But he was a genius in a miniature field, that of the epigram and the parody. His special talent was that of the biting wit, whose happy improvisations . . . have become enduring parts of Dano-Norwegian literature."

PRINCIPAL WORKS

Kierlighed uden strømper (drama) 1772
  [*Love without Stockings* (partial translation); published in journal *The New Monthly Magazine and Humorist*, 1852]
Epilog (poetry) 1774
"Smeden og bageren" (versified short story) 177?; published in journal *Votre serviteur, otiosis*
  ["The Smith and the Baker"; published in *Denmark, Past and Present*, 1902]
Anno 7603 (poetry) 1785

Johan Herman Wessels samtlige skrivter. 2 vols. 1787 (dramas, poetry, and versified short stories)
Johan Herman Wessels digte (poetry) 1936

EDMUND W. GOSSE (essay date 1879)

[*A distinguished English literary historian, critic, and biographer, Gosse wrote extensively on seventeenth- and eighteenth-century English literature. His commentary in* Seventeenth-Century Studies *(1883),* A History of Eighteenth Century Literature *(1889),* Questions at Issue *(1893), and other works, is generally regarded as sound and suggestive. He is also credited with introducing the works of the Norwegian dramatist Henrik Ibsen and other Scandinavian writers to English readers. In the following excerpt, Gosse discusses the artistic state of the Copenhagen Royal Theatre in the 1770s and assesses the impact of* Love without Stockings *on Danish drama.*]

In 1771, the Royal Theatre [of Copenhagen] entered upon a fresh and fortunate epoch. It became a pensioner of Government, and at the same time received its first important enlargement. This crisis was simultaneous with two events of literary importance. One was the production of the lyrical dramas of Johannes Ewald, the poet who composed the well-known national hymn,

King Christian stood by the high mast,

and who composed, lying on his back in bed, dying, like Heine, by inches, some of the masterpieces of Danish dramatic literature; and the other was the production of a single play so unique in its character that it is worth while to pause a few minutes to discuss it. In the course of fifty years, no poet had risen up whose talents in any way fitted him to carry on the war against affectation that Holberg had fought so bravely and so successfully. The comedies of that author, however, still kept the stage, and the particular forms of folly satirised by them had long ago died and faded into thin air. But affectation has a thousand hydra-heads, and if a Hercules annihilate one, there are nine hundred and ninety-nine left. The craving after German support and German fashion was indeed dead in 1772, but another fearful craving had taken its place, a yearning after the stilted and beperiwigged chivalry that passed for good manners and good taste in France, or rather on the French heroic stage. To act in real life like the heroes of the tragedies of Voltaire was the universal bourgeois ideal in Copenhagen, and to write as much as possible in alexandrines the apex of good taste. Zaire was the model for a romantic Danish lady. This rococo taste had penetrated to the theatre, where the nobility and the court had introduced it after the death of Holberg. Voltaire had been translated and imitated with great popular success; and when the Royal Theatre was opened anew after its enlargement, a native tragedy [*Zarine*] by the court poet, Nordahl Brun, was performed on the opening night. This production, which out-Alzired *Alzire*, was the finishing touch given to the exotic absurdity. A young man, who had hitherto been known only as the president of a kind of club of wits, rose up and with one blow slew this rouged and ruffled creature. His name was Wessel, and the weapon he used was a little tragedy called ***Love without Stockings***. The title was quite *en règle; Love without Hope, Love without Fortune, Love without Recompense,* all these are familiar; and why not ***Love without Stockings***? The populace thronged to see this novelty, and Zaire and Zarine and all the other fantastic absurdities faded away

in a roar of universal laughter. ***Love without Stockings*** is in some respects unique in literature. The only thing I know that is in any way parallel to it is Lord Buckingham's *Rehearsal;* and it differs from that inasmuch as that, while the *Rehearsal* parodies certain individual pieces of Dryden and others, Wessel's play is a parody of a whole class of dramas. ***Love without Stockings***! Cannot one love without possessing stockings? Certainly not, answers Wessel; at all events, not in the age of knee-breeches. And out of this thought he develops a plot wholly in accordance with the arbitrary rules of French tragedy, with the three unities intact, with a hero and his friend, a heroine and her confidante, with a Fate that pursues the lovers, with their struggle against it, their fall and tragic death. And the whole is worked out in the most pathetic alexandrines, and with a pompous, ornate diction. At the same time, while he adheres strictly to the rules of French tragedy, he does so in such a manner as to make these rules in the highest degree ridiculous, and to set the faults of this kind of writing in the very plainest light. The wedding-day of the two lovers has arrived; all is ready, the priest is waiting, the bride is adorned, but alas! the bridegroom, who is a tailor, has no stockings, or, at all events, no white ones. What can he do? Buy a pair? But he has no money. Borrow a pair of his bride? On the one hand, it would not be proper; on the other, his legs are too thin. But his rival is rich, is the possessor of many pairs of white stockings; the lover fights a hard battle, or makes out that he does, between virtue and love—but love prevails, and he steals a pair. Adorned in them he marches off to the church with his bride, but on the way the larceny is discovered, and the rival holds him up to public disgrace. For one moment the hero is dejected, and then, recalling his heroic nature, he rises to the height of the situation and stabs himself with a pocket-knife. The bride follows his example, then the rival, then the confidante, then the friend; and the curtain goes down on a scene in the approved tragic manner. The purity of the language, and the exactitude with which not only the French dramas, but the Italian arias then so much in vogue, were imitated, secured an instant success for this parody, which took a place that it has ever since retained among the classics of its country. The French tragedy fell; an attempt to put Nordahl Brun's *Zarine* on the boards again was a signal failure, and the painted Muse fled back to her own Gallic home. The wonderful promise of ***Love without Stockings*** was scarcely fulfilled. Wessel wrote nothing more of any great importance, and in a few years both he and Ewald were dead. The death-blow, however, that the first had given to pompous affectation, and the stimulus lent by the second to exalted dramatic writing, brought forward several minor writers, whose very respectable works have scarcely survived them, but who helped to set Danish literature upon a broad and firm basis. (pp. 144-47)

Edmund W. Gosse, "Denmark: The Danish National Theatre," in his Studies in the Literature of Northern Europe, *C. Kegan Paul & Co., 1879, pp. 134-56.*

FREDERIK WINKEL HORN (essay date 1884)

[*In the following excerpt, Horn examines the intent and effect of* Love without Stockings *and concludes with a brief assessment of Wessel's career.*]

Wessel's great parody, the tragedy called ***Kjærlighed uden Strömper*** (***Love without Stockings***), [was] written throughout in the style of the pseudo classical tragedies, in Alexandrines, with here and there an air inserted. From beginning to end there was a scrupulous and most ridiculous regard for the prescribed "unities." Wessel availed himself of the conventional, stereotyped apparatus of the above mentioned dramas, that is to say of the hero and heroine, the rival of the former and the betrothed. The action likewise consists chiefly in the conflict between virtue and love; in short, the whole play is a faithful copy of his models, and a parody has seldom been more skilfully planned or executed with more precision. The contents of the play are briefly the following: Grete, the female lover, has in a dream received a terrible warning that she "will never be married unless the wedding takes place that very day." But her bridegroom, the tailor-apprentice Johan von Ehrenpreis, is unable to lead her to the altar on this day because he lacks stockings and he cannot present himself on an occasion so solemn in ordinary boots. But Grete is determined to have the wedding, and so her friend Mette suggests to Johan the idea that he steal a pair of stockings from his rival, Mads, whose prospects for obtaining Grete himself have been noticeably improved by Johan's lack of stockings. After a terrible inward struggle between love and virtue, love conquers, and Johan becomes a thief. Grete has evil forebodings, but Johan indignantly refuses to countenance them as unworthy of both her and himself, and everything promises well when Mads and his friend Jesper discover the theft and charge Johan with it in the presence of his bride. Johan is unwilling to outlive the disgrace and stabs himself, and Grete follows his example. Then Mads kills himself from grief at the loss of his beloved, and his friend Jesper follows him faithfully. Finally Mette, too, follows suit and kills herself simply because she does not care to be the only survivor, and thus the play terminates as tragically as could well be desired.

The effect of the drama depends on the contrast between the ludicrous action of the most insignificant persons and the grand plot planned according to all the rules of art, on the one hand, and on the other a pretentious diction which struts about in high buskins, and which, at every moment, forgets its own assumed part, while the natural utterances of these persons with their coarse phrases and insipid figures of speech obtrude themselves even in the midst of their grandest speeches. The poet has accomplished his difficult task in a most satisfactory manner and filled his play to the brim with fun and humor, and while he never exaggerates, he betrays no anxiety lest he should give too loose reins to his sallies.

The chief literary-historical value of Wessel's parody consists in his attack on the affected French taste, and this value is not lessened by the circumstance that he probably borrowed his idea from an older English play, *The Rehearsal*, which was written in 1672 by the duke of Buckingham, and which ridiculed the pseudo-classical style of the dramatic literature, for the Danish parody is vastly superior. It obtains its high, imperishable value by its universal character, and though it was primarily written for the purpose of ridiculing certain favorite Danish plays, it is at the same time aimed at the essentially false tendency of art in Wessel's time, and is, on the whole, a standing protest against all affectation and bombast in art.

Wessel's tragical parody did not at once produce the effect intended by the poet, for the public did not thoroughly comprehend the significance of the satire, which ran through the whole play. The cheerful and vivid style did not fail to please, but people were perplexed in regard to the purpose of the drama, and did not know whether to laugh or to cry, a fact which gives us a fair idea of the overstrained character of the plays which were at that time offered to the public and which were listened to with all seeming gravity. The affected man-

nerism, with its sham, plaintive pathos, still held its own on the stage for some time, though Wessel by his striking parody gave the impulse to its final banishment.

Wessel was not a very prolific writer, and his complete works fill only one moderately sized volume. In addition to the drama mentioned, he wrote two other plays, which, however, have no value whatever. But we have from his pen a few pithy, lyrical poems, among which the **"Ode to Sleep"** is a gem of the first order. Still more important are some of his humorous narrations in verse, published in the weekly paper, *Votre Serviteur, Otiosis,* which he edited for a short time. Some of these remain unequalled in Danish literature both in form and comical effect. (pp. 217-20)

> Frederik Winkel Horn, ''The Age of Enlightenment (1750-1800),'' in his History of the Literature of the Scandinavian North from the Most Ancient Times to the Present, *translated by Ramus B. Anderson, revised edition, S. C. Griggs and Company, 1884, pp. 205-27.*

ILLIT GRØNDAHL   (essay date 1923)

[In the following excerpt, Grøndahl discusses Wessel's career, noting literary and biographical highlights.]

The time immediately following Holberg was not a great one in Dano-Norwegian literary history. Thought and taste in the Western countries had deviated somewhat from that which Holberg in his youth had admired, taken up, and taught. When, after the accession of the new King, Frederick V., the theatre in Copenhagen was reopened in 1747, Holberg had resumed writing comedies; but the *festivitas* ["pleasantry"] of the works of his prime was no longer there. The dainty rococo drama came to be the fashion, and made Holberg appear rough and coarse. Later on, an aftermath of the French classical tragedy, with Voltaire and translations of his plays, in its turn came into vogue. Literary interests, lacking original substance, turned towards questions of form. In accordance with the social turn of the time there sprang up literary clubs which were to take care of intellectual life. (p. 35)

[In] February 1772 the tragedy *Zarine* crossed the stage.... The writer, a young Norwegian, Johan Nordahl Brun . . . , was praised up to the skies. At last the pearl of poetry seemed to have been found, and the natural occupation of our writers to be the production of tragedy. It was in reality nothing but a homely imitation of the French tragedies, hardly French in outward form and with no intimation of the French *esprit* throughout its eighteen long monologues. It had all the apparatus with which its model was necessarily provided. The hero and heroine poured their troubles and endless struggles between virtue and passion into the patient ever-open ears of their confidants and confidantes. So also with regard to the three unities of time, place, and action the play was perfect. This perfection of orthodox arrangement, together with the thinness of the material, made this play the most excellent substratum for a parody—and a parody there did come, a most astounding one, which not only overwhelmed with laughter poor *Zarine*, but made importation and imitation of classical tragedy perilous for all futurity.

Kierlighed uden Strømper (***Love without Stockings***), a tragedy, was written in March 1772, immediately after the production of Brun's *Zarine*, published anonymously in September 1772 and performed in March 1773. The heroes and heroines of this tragedy are not kings and queens, nor Greeks and Romans, but just common people. Their speech, however, is kingly and delivered on stately Alexandrines. With perfect mastery the author has spun the tragic and comic together and balances surely and gracefully on his line; the beautiful simplicity of the diction surpasses everything in our joint literatures. Northern wit is generally supposed to be more related to boxing than to fencing; but this is all swift and agile wrist play, with rapid gleams of the point, and a feeling of strength in reserve.

What was work for Holberg is here evidently play; but if Holberg is difficult to render in a foreign tongue, *Kierlighed uden Strømper,* where the comic effect lies so much more in the outer form, is certainly no easier.

> Thou never wilt be wed if it be not to-day.

Those are the portentous words of the demon in the ear of the heroine Grete, as she is taking her morning nap; and with this opening line we have at once given the unity of time, inaugurating the tragedy. The unity of action is ensured by centring the whole play around the fact that her lover's, the tailor Johan von Ehrenpreis's, white stockings—*de rigueur* for the wedding—are nonexistent. The unity of place is kept throughout, the same room being at one moment Grete's kitchen-parlour, at another the closet where Johan's stout rival, Mads, can give vent to his feelings in fiery monologue. In there he pulls his great chest when he has to examine it, in company with his confidant, Jesper, with regard to a reluctantly suspected theft. Over this spot have to pass, in the course of one fatal day, the events that lead to the tragic end of *Love without Stockings.* All the paraphernalia of true tragedy are there in full order. Grete has her confidante, Mette, as Mads has his Jesper. The tailor hero has none of his own, but a share in each of the others. In truly tragic fashion he is tossed between virtue and fearful temptation: Can he steal his rival's stockings—the only way out of the difficulty? The action is carried on in the orthodox way by dreams, intuitions, and faintings, with intricate reasoning and high-tuned pathos, the mental strife being interrupted by confidential nudges as to what, as a hero or heroine, one is supposed to do next. Now and again the players relieve their pent-up feelings through the safety-valve of an appropriate *aria,* to which further effect was added by the Italian composer Scalabrini's theatre-music. Here is a faint echo of Mads's ardent declaration to himself and to Jesper of his feelings towards Grete:

> On my heart's hearthstone is lighted
> a tempestuous passion's flame.
> At both ends it is ignited,
> and god Cupid lit the same.
> He who sees the smoke uprising
> —for my *aria* is the smoke—
> won't be far wrong in surmising:
> "That fire there's no need to poke!"

Grete, under the pressure of the double attention of the rivals, and the misgivings which steadily advancing Fate inspires, gets into such a state of utter depression that she cannot even enjoy her pea-soup, which Mette can witness is her favourite dish. At last Fate forces Johan, after proper protestation, and, worse luck, at a moment when Virtue is on top, to steal the pair of white stockings—and from now events speed on to an unheard-of catastrophe, in which *all* the acting persons, one after the other, after passing round the portentous bowl of peas for one last feed, stab themselves. Faithful Jesper, the last to stand on the scene, finishes off the peas, picks up the one common knife

and, before following the example of the others, addresses to the surviving spectators the heartfelt wish:

> May you, when *you're* in love, be never out of stockings!

We may now ask, as Copenhagen did, when the piece first appeared in print: "Who is the author?" The *Critical Journal* remarks in its review that the author "is said to be one Mr. Wessel, a Norwegian." After twelve years in the capital he was not further known. (pp. 39-41)

The Norwegian Society was Wessel's home. It was the soil in which his talent lived and grew, and he enriched and vitalized it in return. Through it his vigorous common sense and discerning criticism permeated to the wider Danish society and in time to his native Norway. No one could be annoyed with Wessel's fun. Holberg gave stinging blows, but Wessel turned one upside down, and set one on one's feet again so smartly that one did not know exactly what had happened. He was the indefatigable jester of the Society—a trifler, maybe, but a splendid one. As he wrote underneath his portrait:

> This man seemed born for bagatelles,
> nor did he ever do much else.

His wit lived after him in Copenhagen, and may be at least in part responsible for that excessive tendency to trifling with which the Danes are sometimes charged. (pp. 43-4)

Wessel's further dramatic productions, one or two comedies which he pulled himself together to write, hardly count. Of the better one, *Lykken bedre end Forstanden,* we cannot admit the intimation of the title that the luck was better than the wits. Two serious productions of his ["**Epilog**" and "**Anno 7603**"] are respectable specimens of 18th-century didactic poetry.

From 1776 to 1778 Wessel suffered from a painful disease which broke down his strength and nearly quenched his spirits. In the following time he succumbed more and more to the habit of drink, and developed a deep melancholy and indifference with regard to life, and an increased loathing for all activity. After he had in 1779 in vain applied for a situation as controller of Customs at Kristiania, a Bergen man, Bredal's successor as director of the Danish stage, gave him a small post as translator at the theatre. Encouraged by the prospects of a regular income, Wessel married a Norwegian girl without means. He seems to have expected to get a nurse, and she to be provided for by marrying the well-known writer; they were both mistaken.

Though generally depressed and silent he would, when stimulated by a visit or over a friendly cup, be reanimated and throw his improvisations liberally about. Eventually he began to edit a humorous weekly, *Votre Serviteur* (Otiosis—For Idlers). But this was too plainly wit coined out for cash—mostly adaptations from English and other foreign authors. Manuscript did not flow freely in, and though *Votre Serviteur* craned its letters and strained its lines, the reader was often cut off with some such valedictory advice:

> When you are tired of rhyming, then,
> Rhymer, like me put down the pen!

This Idler journal contains some of Wessel's genial trifles, versified stories which are to this day a relieving feature in the Norwegian schoolboy's curriculum of literature. In "**The Fork**"— an imitation of Matthew Prior's "The Ladle"—Jupiter and Mercury visiting the earth find everything in such excellent order

> that Jupiter exclaims
> —these were his very words:
> "Pope has but told the truth,
> this is the best of earths."

Here also is found his jovial song, **"Good and Ill in Every Nation,"** at the end of which he praises the *"brave Nordmand"* for his love of his native land, warning him at the same time against the belief that there live men and women only in England and there.

Wessel has been compared as a stylist to the French fabulist, La Fontaine, with whom he certainly had in common indolence, volatility, and other temperamental qualities. But Wessel produced a form of his own for his peculiar *vis comica* ["comic power."] He throws his clever verse into everyday language; it does not sing, it talks. Wessel is a constant improviser, while La Fontaine was always the careful artist. La Fontaine treats the moral of his fable with apparent gravity; he is a moralist and accepted as good reading for the young. Wessel invariably treats the whole thing as exquisite nonsense, and only tags on a moral to dispose of any lingering suspicion of moral intent. In the story of **"The Smith and the Baker,"** the village blacksmith has killed the tailor, for which crime an old baker is hanged in his stead, considering that the village has two bakers and only one blacksmith. Moral:

> For death be constantly prepared: it may
> be lurking where you think it miles away.

Wessel reflected, with his fun, Holberg's more indignant scorn of all asceticism—the renouncement of being human, in order to escape from, rather than master, the human passions. We may, perhaps, be touching something deeply Norwegian underlying both men's view of what the elder one termed the "undefinable animal" by defining it for them:

> Man, tragic skeleton! Alway afresh
> appearing in the comedy of flesh!

In his last verses, written a few months before his death, Wessel lowers his flag and gracefully hands over his mantle to the young Dane Jens Baggesen, who had just published a collection of comical tales; Baggesen in his turn declared that he had married Wessel's Muse when she became a widow. (pp. 44-6)

> *Illit Grøndahl, "Johan Herman Wessel and 'Det Norske Selskab',"* in Chapters in Norwegian Literature *by Illit Grøndahl and Ola Raknes, 1923. Reprint by Books for Libraries Press, 1969, pp. 35-51.*

THEODORE JORGENSON   (essay date 1933)

[*In the following excerpt, Jorgenson analyzes Wessel's character and work.*]

Johan Nordahl Brun and Johan Herman Wessel are the leading figures of Norwegian cultural life during the second half of the eighteenth century. The contrast between these two men is vividly set forth by professor Francis Bull:

> The former healthy and spontaneous, a lover of nature, a man of powerful instincts and of a mental life characterized by simplicity, a man possessing a voice and a laughter which resounded far off, a lover of power gripped by the sweep of life, imposing to the point of offense, ambitious and eager to fight, always aglow either with enthusiasm or with anger on behalf

of country, religion, or self; a social personality and an active leader by nature, always taking himself seriously, never in possession of the least desire to laugh at himself. And the other (Wessel) pale and sickly, a city personality, a boheme without contact with nature, an unassuming intellectualist who found comfort in the sparkling wine and happiness in the world of the mind, in books and in conversation, an outsider who had none of the ambitious desire to run the competitive race, but with an ironic smile at himself and others observed life and human beings, a linguistic artist without equal and a humorist who had the rare capacity of being witty without carrying a sting, a man who fights neither for nor against anyone or anything except when art and good taste are in danger.

(p. 177)

As a literary man [Wessel] was distinctly an intellectualist. His wit and his pleasant irony gleamed and glittered in spirited conversations at Madame Juel's or when stirred by some ungenuine and incongruous situation in literature. Life did not furnish him with poetic impulses. He could not directly express the blackness of despair which he felt. His smile is in reality a mask to hide his tears. The greatness of his art is found in a classic use of language and in a unique humor. Like Holberg his work was largely negative. From Wessel's time on imitation and pretense must pass muster before his good-natured irony, but creative, in the sense of Johannes Ewald and Wergeland, he was not.

Wessel's conversational ability and scintillating wit made him the central figure in many a gathering of the Norwegian Student Society. His literary debut was made in 1772 with what also proved to be his masterpiece, *Love Without Stockings*. The occasion for a parody of this kind was the forthcoming of such dramas as Bredal's *The Throne of Sidon,* Fasting's *Hermione,* and Brun's *Zarine.* Wessel tells in the manner of heroic dramas of the tailor Johan von Ehrenpreis, who, lacking the proper stockings for his own wedding, is the victim of a terrific mental anguish which causes not only him but four others involved to commit suicide. The comic element arises from the fact that the simple tailor uses the language and the exalted thought of the conventionalized noble hero. Brilliant wit created in this initial work a large number of epigrammatic sayings which became the common property of people throughout the Scandinavian kingdoms.

Beside his one great parody Wessel is known chiefly for his comic narrative poems. Many of these, especially **"The Smith and the Baker"** and **"The Murder of the Dog,"** are familiar to every school boy in Norway and have passed in the culture of the country to a central place from which they can never be removed. (pp. 178-79)

> *Theodore Jorgenson, "The Growth of National Feeling,"* in his History of Norwegian Literature, *The Macmillan Company, 1933, pp. 157-80.*

ELIAS BREDSDORFF   (essay date 1951)

[*A Danish-born author who resides in England, Bredsdorff has written numerous studies of English, American, and Scandinavian literature. In addition, he has served as editor of* Scandinavica: An International Journal of Scandinavian Studies *since 1962. In the following excerpt, Bredsdorff summarizes Wessel's achievement in drama and verse.*]

[Johan Herman Wessel], a poet of Norwegian extraction, was a Bohemian and an idler, whose name is immortal in Danish literature as one of its greatest humorists. His dramatic work, *Love without Stockings* (*Kærlighed uden Strømper*), the only long work he ever had the energy to write, is undoubtedly one of the most comic tragedies in literature, but one must read it in the original Danish, for it hardly lends itself to translation. Like Holberg's *Peder Paars* it is written in alexandrines, and as in *Peder Paars* the irony depends upon the putting of ordinary characters into a heroic setting; but Wessel's tragedy is far more elegant and light in its form than Holberg's satire, and it is written in graceful alexandrines, which Holberg's certainly were not. *Love without Stockings* must be seen against the background of the dramatic fashion of Wessel's time, when Holberg's comedies had been superseded by Danish imitations of Italian operas and French tragedies. These were heroic plays about the conflict between Love and Virtue, culminating in a series of suicides. It was against the unnaturalness of these dramas, and especially of the tragedies written by his compatriots Niels Krog Bredal and Johan Nordahl Brun, that Wessel directed his ridicule, when he wrote the tragedy in which with great artistic skill he out-Heroded Herod. (p. 54)

Wessel wrote *Love without Stockings* for fun, simply because it amused him, but it was such a success that it put an end to imitations of French and Italian classicism in Danish drama.

Of Wessel's light humorous poems and versified narratives, many have been loved and admired by generation after generation. His verse story, **"The Blacksmith and the Baker"** (**"Smeden og Bageren"**), is a good example of these sauntering verses, in which Wessel, with a great many amusing digressions, tells an anecdote. The moral in **"The Blacksmith and the Baker"**—for these stories usually have a humorous moral—is that if, for some reason you cannot hang the man who committed the crime, you can always hang someone else. Wessel's small impromptus are quick-witted and nimble; he was a master of brief humorous verse. His little poem in *Aftenposten* may serve as an example:

Dare I compose *The Post* a stanza
on how to deal with influenza?
Crush cloves at morning in a cup,
mix them in mead, and drink it up.

If long before the evening greet us
your cough don't get its full quietus,
then you may strike a vengeful note:
"Go, cut, Sir Leech, your lying throat!"

(pp. 55-6)

Elias Bredsdorff, "Danish Literature in the 18th Century," in An Introduction to Scandinavian Literature from the Earliest Time to Our Day *by Elias Bredsdorff, Brita Mortensen, and Ronald Popperwell, Cambridge at the University Press, 1951, pp. 46-62.*

HARALD BEYER (essay date 1952)

[*In the following excerpt from an essay originally published in 1952, Beyer assesses the nature of Wessel's literary talent, commenting on the parodic intent of* Love without Stockings *and concluding with a balanced estimate of Wessel's literary productions.*]

In its best years, around 1780, the [Norwegian Society (*Det norske Selskab*)] had as many as 120 members, of whom about a dozen were writers. But only one was a really notable talent, Johan Herman Wessel. He was not a poet of deep feelings or ideas, or a prophet with philosophic or patriotic passions. But he was a genius in a miniature field, that of the epigram and the parody. His special talent was that of the biting wit, whose happy improvisations in the circle of friends have become enduring parts of Dano-Norwegian literature. (pp. 106-07)

If one were to find a basic idea in his poetry, it would be this: why bother? This is the burden of his jesting verse to be placed on his own gravestone:

He drank with zeal, was seldom happy,
His shoes were leaky as a sieve.
He couldn't be bothered to do any work,
At last he didn't bother to live.

He expresses the same idea in many ways. He makes a comparison with his brother, the mathematician Caspar Wessel: "He traces maps and reads the law. He is as diligent as I am lazy." But he also says it indirectly in one of his comic tales: "Listen," said Jupiter, "I can't be bothered. . . ." It was said in Copenhagen that no one could pronounce the words "why bother" with such energy as Wessel. The only good serious poem we have from his hand is a passionate defense of sleep.

Like his great Scandinavian contemporaries, Bellman and Ewald, Wessel was no success as a citizen, being intemperate, slovenly, and irresponsible, a bohemian who burned out at an early age. His great and overpowering passion was his love of good poetry. However kindly and tolerant he might be in private life, he was contemptuous of writing that seemed to him stilted, obscure, or false. He was influenced by English and French literature, and while he admired the classical French tragedy, he can scarcely have been fond of its pseudoclassical imitations, like Voltaire's *Zaïre*. His major work is a parody on just this kind of writing, the unforgettable *Love Without Stockings* (*Kierlighed uden Strømper*). This carries on the tradition of Holberg's *Peder Paars*, but like that poem it has a wider significance than that of the purely literary parody.

It is a satire on all poetic artificiality, all false solemnity, on big words that cover small actions, and on bourgeois vulgarization of the fate motif. His hero Johan is the victim of a cruel fate: on his wedding day his stockings are stolen. He cannot marry without them, and fate has announced that unless he is married that very day, he will never be married. Johan is a most unheroic hero, being only a tailor's apprentice, but his sweetheart's confidante Mette says to him that it doesn't matter how cowardly he really is, just so he says the words that heroes say. Then everyone will think he is a hero. Nor does it matter if he steals himself a pair of stockings, if only he first goes through the motions of a debate between virtue and temptation, like every other hero on the stage. It does not even matter that he happens to steal while virtue has the upper hand. Johan is typed as the tailor of humorous tradition, with skinny legs and bad complexion from his unhealthy occupation. He is cowardly and fussy, more concerned with outward than inward qualities, and his fine customers have taught him to speak in elaborate turns of phrase.

All the characters are desperately attempting to live up to the requirements of classical tragedy, but fail at every turn. Johan's rival Mads is a rougher character than he. His difficulty is that he cannot add, he confuses furies and graces, and worries about living up to the role of tragic hero. Grete, the heroine, is a natural enough girl, but contorts herself trying to play the part of a heroine. Her plebeian taste for peas, herring, and pork, and her habit of immoderate swearing give the lie to all her social pretenses. There are also two confidantes, one female and one male, who frequently discuss how they are to manage things so that they will have the properly heroic touch. The characters all take themselves with inordinate seriousness, which makes them irresistibly comic. Their speeches are a charming mixture of high-flown rhetoric and everyday banalities. They sing parodic arias, with lines like these: ''In my heart's fire-place there burns a resined brand of love which is lighted at both ends.''

The plot is pure mechanics and conspicuous at all times, while the characters are marionettes marched around by fate. The action is restricted to a single day and place: Grete has her fatal dream, the lovers and the confidantes meet, Mads's trunk is examined and the theft discovered, the peas are eaten, and they all die—in the same room. This does not necessarily mean that Wessel rejected the classical unities of time and place, but he did show how artificial and unreal they could become.

The rest of his writing consists of epigrams and comic tales, all in verse. These are pure wit, without pretension to serious ideas. They point a finger of scorn at stupidity, or jest with a friend's qualities, including his own, as in the verse quoted above. His model in the tales was the Frenchman La Fontaine. His verse has a coquettish air, quick and elegant, with an unexpected twist at the end which is underscored by a surprising rhyme. (pp. 107-09)

> *Harald Beyer, ''Holberg's Successors,'' in his* A History of Norwegian Literature, *edited and trans-lated by Einar Haugen, New York University Press, 1956, pp. 105-12.*

ADDITIONAL BIBLIOGRAPHY

Bach, Giovanni, and Blankner, Frederika. ''The Age of Enlightenment or Rationalism and the First Signs of Cultural Independence.'' In *The History of the Scandinavian Literatures,* edited and translated by Frederika Blankner, pp. 22-5. 1938. Reprint. Port Washington, N.Y.: Kennikat Press, 1966.

> Contains a brief estimation of Wessel.

Burchardt, C. B. ''Outlines of Norwegian Literature from the Death of Holberg to the Appearance of Ibsen and Bjornson.'' In his *Norwegian Life and Literature: English Accounts and Views, Especially in the 19th Century,* pp. 81-96. London: Oxford University Press, 1920.

> Includes an account of the Norwegian Society, crediting the ''graceful humour and the simplicity of expression'' of *Love without Stockings* with establishing Wessel as ''by far the most brilliant writer of the circle.''

Bushby, Mrs. [Anna S.]. ''A Survey of Danish Literature, from the Earliest Period to the Present Time: Part II.'' *The New Monthly Magazine and Humorist* XCV, No. CCCLXXVII (May 1852): 40-54.

> Favorably appraises *Love without Stockings,* reprinting selected translated passages from the drama.

Gosse, Sir Edmund. ''The Poetry of Denmark: Introduction.'' In *The Oxford Book of Scandinavian Verse: XVIIth Century—XXth Century,* edited by Sir Edmund Gosse and W. A. Craigie, pp. 3-20. Oxford: Clarendon Press, 1925.

> Praises *Love without Stockings* as ''one of the masterpieces of Danish literature.''

Wu Ch'eng-en

1500?-1582?

Chinese novelist, poet, essayist, and short story writer.

Wu is widely, though not conclusively, identified as the author of *Hsi-yu chi (The Journey to the West),* a long seriocomic religious allegory which scholars rank among the few indisputably great Chinese classical novels. Inspired by the imaginative lore surrounding the true story of a renowned seventh-century Buddhist monk's pilgrimage to India, *The Journey to the West* details the numerous adventures of the sage Tripitaka and his entourage during their travels. The novel, one of the richest and most cherished works in all Chinese literature, is a lengthy narrative informed by Taoist, Buddhist, and Confucian teachings, and enlivened by a wide variety of classical poetic forms and boldly imaginative, Rabelaisian episodes.

Although many details of Wu's life and career remain uncertain, a short outline may be given. Born in Huia-än, Kiangsu province, Wu was the son of an educated but unmoneyed merchant and his concubine. He received a sound education at the village school and early displayed a penchant for reading popular fantastic tales. Around 1526 he entered Lung Ch'i College and quickly gained a reputation as an original, accomplished writer of traditional poetry and essays and as a scholar of Chinese classical literature. About this time Wu compiled a collection of the favorite T'ang tales he recalled from childhood reading, and cast them in the *ch'uan-chi* form of compact, semipoetic prose embroidered with esoteric allusion. Only his preface to this collection has survived. (Scholars stress the importance of this literary undertaking, though, as an early exercise in fiction writing.) Wu soon turned to other literary genres, however; regarded by his professors and literary elders as a precocious young scholar, he was often sought from this time on to write prefaces and commendatory poems to adorn the works and embellish the reputations of many higher-ranking acquaintances. Unfortunately, Wu never passed the triennial provincial examinations—requisite civil service tests which measured academic proficiency but often failed to recognize creativity and originality—though he tried several times. He was thus barred from assuming all but minor official posts.

In 1544, some ten years after his graduation from Lung Ch'i, Wu was honored for his assiduous scholarship and exemplary writings—which at this point comprised primarily poems, prefaces, and social essays, (all later collected in his *Wu Cheng'en shih-wen chi*)—by being named that year's Tribute Student for the Huai-än Prefectural College. This temporary position, which served to enhance Wu's financial position and academic standing, enabled him to reside in both Nanking and Beijing as a National University scholar. From roughly 1545 to 1552 Wu studied in Beijing; it was here that he met several prominent scholars and writers of the time. In 1554 Wu removed to the southern capital of Nanking, where many of his friends had been gathering to form a casual literary and artistic coterie. It is believed that during the four or five years he spent there he wrote many of his extant celebrative works of verse and honorary essays. About 1559 it appears that Wu returned to Huai-än to lecture and to assist a friend in compiling and editing an anthology of poems. For the remainder of his life Wu continued to write, travel, and teach, holding two minor official posts as well. It is probable that *The Journey to the West* was in near-

final manuscript form as early as 1570, though neither it nor his collected works was published until several years after his death.

Not surprisingly, English-language scholarship of Wu has focused almost exclusively on his novel, his only work yet translated into English. Although the first, partial translation of *Hsi-yu chi* was not published until 1943, in China this novel has reigned as a classic since its first appearance in 1592. Undoubtedly, its long popularity is due to its close link to the very roots of China's strong mythic tradition, for since the time of Tripitaka's eighteen-year journey from T'ang China to Buddhist centers of wisdom in India to collect scriptures and return them to the emperor, legends of his quest have risen and embedded themselves in Chinese culture. Glen Dudbridge has documented how these numerous oral and early written sources tended to consolidate episodes, themes, and characters. With such a large and complex network of antecedent materials, it is extremely difficult to ascertain the role each narrative played in forming Wu's novel; nevertheless it has been demonstrated that *Hsi-yu chi* is most closely affined in plot, characterization, and theme to a twenty-four-act Yüan drama of the same title. A subject of ongoing speculation is exactly how the historical Tripitaka (named Hsüän-tsang in the novel) came to acquire his four supernatural companions: Pigsy, Sandy, the dragon-horse, and in particular, Monkey. While originally serving as mere embellishments to the central legend, these characters evolved to assume especial significance in Wu's novel for their symbolic value in completing the five-element Chinese cosmos of earth, water, fire, wood, and metal. Collectively traveling the circular path of unity, separation, and ultimate unity, the five archetypal characters support Wu's dominant theme of spiritual self-perfection, thus forming an important subtext of the novel, as noted by Chang Ching-erh.

The framework of the 100-chapter novel can be divided into three major sections. In chapters 1-7, the character Wu-K'ung, or Monkey, is introduced and his life traced from his birth, maturation, and attainment of celestiality through to his fall from the heavens because of sin; chapters 8-12 describe Hsüän-tsang's early years; and chapters 13-100 narrate the actual journey of the pilgrims. The placement of Monkey's story at the beginning bespeaks the centrality of this figure; for it is Monkey, despite his comedic antics, who exemplifies the calm awareness, harmony with one's environment, and closeness to blissful emptiness that approximate the state of supreme Buddhistic spirituality. Helen A. Kuo has written, "Although the story of Monkey is fantastic and luminous nonsense, it is sparkling entertainment, and there is a profound teaching in every single incident, the teaching of sanctity and purity and simplicity of heart and soul." James S. Fu has elaborated, "The quest of Monkey through the Mountain of Flowers and Fruit, the pilgrimage, and the mountain again is from the innocent world of 'emptiness,' through the experienced world of 'forms,' and back to 'emptiness' again. It goes in a circle because in the world of experience, the quest is to restore the lost world of innocence." Although pervaded by religious teachings, Wu's novel is far removed from simple didactic narrative. The inherent humor of its many fantastic episodes, for which the author has been compared to the French humanist-satirist François Rabelais, has charmed Chinese audiences for centuries. Wu is deemed to have possessed a fine sense of the extent to which comedy and myth could support the serious overtures of his novel, which include keen satire of hypocritical religious beliefs, particularly those of the then morally corrupt Taoist school. As had several enlightened late-medieval Chinese writers, Wu proposed as a curative a synthesis of the best teachings of the three major schools—Buddhist, Taoist, and Confucian.

In the West, scholarship of *The Journey to the West* is still in its infancy, though such pioneering studies as Anthony C. Yu's preface to his four-volume English-language translation of the work have opened several areas for further investigation. But while interpretive critics continue to uncover a wealth of complex, interrelated themes, the popular appeal of the novel remains in its sheer entertainment value, mythic connections, and rich evocation of the themes of outward quest and inward, personal development. Favorably compared in this to the Western classics *Don Quixote* and *The Adventures of Huckleberry Finn,* and widely praised for its abundant humor, adventure, romance, poetry, and religious wisdom, *The Journey to the West* has captured the imaginations of Oriental and Occidental readers alike, and is considered one of the best and most memorable of all Chinese classical novels.

PRINCIPAL WORKS

She-yan hsien-sheng ts'un-kao (poetry, essays, and prose) 1590?; also published as *Wu Ch'eng-en shih-wen chi* [revised edition], 1958

*Hsi-yu chi (novel) 1592; revised edition, 1954
   [*Monkey* (partial translation), 1943; also translated as *The Journey to the West.* 4 vols. 1977-83]

*Known as the Shih-te t'ang text, this is the earliest extant edition of Wu's 100-chapter masterwork. Although numerous successive editions of this novel have appeared, the original text—along with that of the authoritative 1954 edition—served as the two principal sources for Anthony C. Yu's translation, *The Journey to the West.*

LU HSUN   (essay date 1924)

[Many critics consider Lu Hsun the leader of China's cultural revolution. He spearheaded the move to write in the popular language rather than the classical, which had been the standard for generations, and his penetrating stories attacking China's old tradition contributed immeasurably to that country's cultural upheaval. Although Lu Hsun was never formally a communist, and his devotion to communist philosophy is still debated, he has consistently been idolized by leftist writers throughout the world. According to Mao Tse-tung, Lu Hsun "was not only a great man of letters but a great thinker and revolutionary." In the following excerpt from an essay originally published in 1924, he favorably considers The Journey to the West, *noting its independence of Buddhist, Confucian, and Taoist teachings.]*

[Wu Ch'eng-en] was an intelligent and witty scholar, well read and fond of a jest, who wrote several works of fiction and enjoyed quite a reputation in his lifetime. . . . We lack detailed information about his life, but know that he was a good poet. His poems were "restrained but clear, learned and profound." Indeed he was the best poet in Huaian during the Ming dynasty. Since he died a poor man and had no son, most of his writings were lost. Chiu Cheng-kang made a collection in five books

of some of them, which Wu Yu-chin included among the works of Shanyang scholars. The *Shanyang County Records* edited in the Tung Chih period (1862-1874) omitted the information that Wu Cheng-en had written stories and novels, and his *Pilgrimage to the West* was left out of the bibliography. So Wu's fame was forgotten and few readers knew that he was the author of the novel. (pp. 210-11)

Though the skeleton plot [of *Pilgrimage to the West*] already exists in the Yang Chih-ho version, the language is crude and the book hardly a proper novel. Wu Cheng-en, however, was a brilliant man of wide learning and he drew upon many sources including the stories about Hua-kuang and Chen-wu in *The Four Romances of Wandering Saints,* the earlier plays and chantefable about Tripitaka, miraculous happenings in the Tang dynasty tales, as well as satires based on current events. He rewrote and embellished the old version to such an extent that he produced what was virtually a new book. For example, the fight between Erh-lang and Monkey in Yang's version comes to some three hundred words only, whereas Wu Cheng-en makes it ten times as long. First he describes how the two opponents change their forms: Monkey transforms himself into a sparrow, an egret, a fish, a water snake, while the god changes into a kite, a stork, a cormorant and a crane. Then Monkey becomes a bustard and the god, scorning to contend with such a low creature, takes his own form again and knocks the bird off a cliff with his catapult. (pp. 211-12)

But the most daring flights of fancy occur in the eighty-one perils such as the battle with the Rhinoceros Monster, the fight between the real and the false Monkey, and the battle of the Flaming Mountain, where the most miraculous and fantastic changes take place. The first two episodes appear in Yang's version also; the last, which borrows the Princess of the Iron Fan from a play and *Prince Hua-kuang,* and which includes the Ox Monster mentioned by name only in Yang's version, is even more strange and exotic. (p. 214)

Since Wu Cheng-en had a sense of humour, when describing supernatural beings or miracles he often slips in amusing touches, ascribing to the monsters human feelings and worldly wisdom. For instance, when Monkey is defeated by the Rhinoceros Monster and loses his gold-tipped wand, he asks the Jade Emperor for reinforcements.

> The Four Heavenly Masters reported this to the court and Monkey was led to the steps where he bowed and said: "Excuse me for troubling you, old man, but I am helping a monk to find sutras in the West and I've had more than my share of trouble on the way. I won't go into that now. But since we came to Gold-Helmet Mountain a Rhinoceros Monster has dragged my monk into its cave—I don't know whether it means to eat him steamed, boiled or baked. When I went to fight it, the monster proved so powerful that it took away my wand and I couldn't beat it. Since it said it knew me, I suspect it is some fallen angel. So I have come to report this, and I hope you will be kind enough to order an investigation and send troops to conquer it. I await your answer in hope and trepidation." Then with a deep bow he added: "I beg to submit my humble report."
>
> Saint Ko who was standing beside him burst out laughing. "What has humbled the proud Monkey all of a sudden?"
>
> "Nothing has humbled me all of a sudden," retorted Monkey. "But I have lost my job. . . ."

Various appraisals of this novel were written in the Ching dynasty, including Chen Shih-pin's *The True Exposition of the Pilgrimage* with a preface by Yu Tung dated 1696, Chang Shu-shen's *The Correct Interpretation of the Pilgrimage* with a preface dated 1748, and Liu Yi-ming's *The Original Significance of the Pilgrimage* with a preface dated 1810. These critics argued that the book dealt with Confucian, Taoist or Buddhist philosophy, delving into its hidden meaning in detail and at great length. Actually, although Wu Cheng-en was a Confucian scholar, he wrote this book for entertainment. Its theme was not Taoism either, for the whole novel contains a few casual references only to the five elements; and the author was clearly no Buddhist, for the last chapter has some fantastic and utterly fanciful names of Buddhist sutras. Since there had long been talk about the common origin of the three religions, it was natural that a literary work should present readers with both Buddha and Lao Tzu, Buddhist concepts as well as Taoist, and that Buddhists, Taoists or Confucians alike should recognize their own philosophical views there. If we insist on seeking some hidden meaning, the following comment by Hsieh Chao-chih is quite adequate: "The *Pilgrimage to the West* is purely imaginary, belonging to the realm of fantasy and miraculous transformations. Monkey symbolizes man's intelligence, Pigsy man's physical desires. Thus Monkey first runs wild in heaven and on earth, proving quite irrepressible; but once he is kept in check he steadies down. So this is an allegory of the human mind, not simply a fantasy." The author himself wrote:

When the monks discussed the tenets of Buddhism and the purpose of the pilgrimage . . . Tripitaka remained silent, simply pointing at his heart and nodding again and again. The monks did not understand him . . . and he said: "It is the mind that gives birth to monsters of every kind, and when the mind is at rest they disappear. I made a vow to Buddha in Huasheng Monastery and I must keep my word. I am determined to go on this pilgrimage to seek Buddha in the Western Paradise and obtain the true sutras so that our Dharma-wheel will turn again and our empire may for ever be secure."

(pp. 216-18)

Lu Hsun, "Ming Dynasty Novels about Gods and Devils (continued)," in his A Brief History of Chinese Fiction, *translated by Yang Hsien-Yi and Gladys Yang, Foreign Languages Press, 1959, pp. 209-19.*

HU SHIH (essay date 1942)

[*A leading twentieth-century Chinese philosopher, diplomat, historian, and literary scholar, Hu was instrumental in launching a literary revolution in 1917 which succeeded in establishing spoken Chinese as a far more suitable medium than the heavily adorned, belle-lettres language then employed for both scholarly and creative writing. Hu is also recognized for his concurrent studies of vernacular classics and Chinese linguistic history. In Wu studies he is often cited for his untranslated 1923 essay "Hsi-yu-chi k'ao-cheng," in which he asserted Wu's authorship of* Journey to the West *and attempted to liberate the novel from the many allegorical interpretations which had been placed upon it by Taoist, Buddhist, and Confucian scholars. In the following excerpt from his 1942 introduction to Arthur Waley's abridged English version of the novel, Hu briefly discusses these and other critical issues.*]

I was very fond of strange stories when I was a child. In my village-school days, I used to buy stealthily the popular novels and historical recitals. Fearing that my father and my teacher might punish me for this

and rob me of these treasures, I carefully hid them in secret places where I could enjoy them unmolested.

As I grew older, my love for strange stories became even stronger, and I learned of things stranger than what I had read in my childhood. When I was in my thirties, my memory was full of these stories accumulated through years of eager seeking.

I have always admired such writers of the T'ang Dynasty as Tuan Ch'eng-shih and Niu Sheng-ju, who wrote short stories so excellent in portrayal of men and description of things. I often had the ambition to write a book (of stories) which might be compared with theirs. But I was too lazy to write, and as my laziness persisted, I gradually forgot most of the stories which I had learned.

Now only these few stories, less than a score, have survived and have so successfully battled against my laziness that they are at last written down. Hence this Book of Monsters. I have sometimes laughingly said to myself that it is not I who have found these ghosts and monsters, but they, the monstrosities themselves, which have found me!

Although my book is called a book of monsters, it is not confined to them: it also records the strange things of the human world and sometimes conveys a little bit of moral lesson. . . .

Thus wrote Wu Ch'êng-ên in his preface to a book of short stories written in the classical language. This collection has been lost; but this preface, fortunately preserved in his *Collected Writings* [*Wu Ch'êng-ên Shih-wen chi*], tells us much about the future author of *Monkey* or *Hsi Yu Ki.* It tells of his boyhood delight in the strange stories and historical recitals written in the living tongue of the people. It reveals his life-long ambition to write a great book of stories about ghosts and monsters which was to rival the stories by the famous writers of T'ang, and which, though primarily about monsters, did not exclude the strange things of our human world and might also convey "a little bit of moral lesson."

All this he might have written of the *Monkey,* had he cared to write a preface to it under his own name. He had apparently grown dissatisfied with his monster stories composed in the classical style in imitation of the T'ang writers. At long last, he decided to carry out his great literary ambition by writing a greater book of monsters in the language of the "vulgar" literature of his time. But it was such a great disgrace for a man of literary reputation to produce a novel in the vulgar tongue that the story was published anonymously. And nothing in the two volumes of his Collected Writings (discovered in the Imperial Palaces and reprinted by the Palace Museum Library, 1930) gives the slightest hint of his connection with the book. Just as he in his early boyhood could only enjoy the novels and stories in secret hiding places, so he in his old age had to conceal the authorship of his great masterpiece in anonymity. (pp. 1-2)

The anonymity of the authorship of *Monkey* was so complete that for over three centuries the general reading public actually believed that the story was written by the Taoist Patriarch Chiu Ch'u-ki (1148-1227) who in 1219 was invited by Genghis Khan to visit him in Central Asia and who left a record of his travels under the title *Hsi Yu Ki (Record of a Journey to the West),* which is still regarded as a valuable contribution to the geographical knowledge of the time. It was the similarity in title and the seemingly allegorical character of the novel which were largely responsible for the erroneous attribution of authorship.

But to the people of Huai-an, the birthplace of Wu Ch'êng-ên, the authorship of the story was apparently well-known in the sixteenth and seventeenth centuries. The local history (gazetteer) of Huan-an, compiled in 1625, definitely recorded that the novel *Hsi Yu Ki* was written by him. This is the first Chinese novel of which the authorship is now authentically established.

The story is originally in one hundred chapters which may be divided into three main parts:

    I. The Story of the Monkey (chapters, 1-7)
    II. The Story of Hsuan Tsang and the Origin of the Mission to India (chapters 8-12)
    III. The Pilgrimage to India (chapters 13-100)

Mr. Waley's version in thirty chapters has translated Part I and Part II almost entirely, his chapter divisions corresponding exactly to the first twelve chapters in the original. From Part III, Mr. Waley has translated only Chapters 13-15 (XIII-XV), 18-19 (XVI-XVII), 22 (XVIII), 37-39 (XIX-XXI), 44-46 (XXII-XXIV), 47-49 (XXV-XXVII), and 98-100 (XXVIII-XXX).

It will be noted that Mr. Waley has here translated only thirty of the one hundred chapters in the original and has left out in particular the second half (chapters 50-97) of the book. Of the thirty-four episodes after the conversion of the three disciples, Waley has selected four: (1) the Story of the Kingdom of Crow-Cock (XIX-XXI), (2) the Story of the Three Taoist Demons in the Cart-Slow Kingdom (XXII-XXIV), (3) the River That Leads to Heaven (XXV-XXVII), and (4) the Final Calamity Caused by the White Turtle (XXIX).

Recollection of my own boyhood favorites in the book makes me feel a little regret that my friend Waley has not included in this translation such exceedingly exciting episodes as the Three Demons of the Lion Camel Mountain (74-77) or the Battles With the Red Boy (40-42), or such charmingly entertaining episodes as the Dharma-Destroying Kingdom (84-85), the Monkey Playing the Medico at the Vermilion-Purple Kingdom (68-69), or the Story of the Mandrake Fruit (24-26). I cannot help expressing the wish that at a more propitious time Mr. Waley may be moved to include a few of these episodes in his most admirable and most delightful translation.

But in spite of these few mildly regretted omissions, Mr. Waley has on the whole exercised excellent critical judgment in his selection of the episodes. I agree with most of his omissions, and heartily approve his method of "omitting many episodes, but translating those that are retained almost in full." His rendering of dialogue is truly masterful both in preserving its droll humor and retaining its rich proverbial form. Only a careful comparison with the original text can fully appreciate the translator's painstaking effort in these directions.

Freed from all kinds of allegorical interpretations by Buddhist, Taoist, and Confucianist commentators, *Monkey* is simply a book of good humor, profound nonsense, good-natured satire and delightful entertainment. It has delighted millions of Chinese children and adults for over three hundred years, and thanks to Mr. Waley, it will now delight thousands upon thousands of children and adults in the English-speaking world for many years to come. (pp. 3-5)

Hu Shih, in an introduction to Monkey *by Ch'êng-ên Wu, translated by Arthur Waley, 1943. Reprint by Grove Press Inc., 1958, pp. 1-5.*

LIU TS'UN-YAN (essay date 1967)

[*Liu is the author of the only full-length English-language biography of Wu. In the following excerpt, Liu examines* The Journey to the West, *with reference to Wu's untranslated works.*]

To give a fair and overall assessment of Wu Ch'êng-ên's contribution to Chinese literature is difficult, for he was a prolific writer and his interests were manifold. To the literary critics of his own age, such as Li Wei-chên . . . ,

> his classical pieces do not necessarily follow the path opened up by the Later Seven Masters, although he was very much familiar with Hsü Tzŭ-yü [Hsü Chung-hsing], one of the Seven Masters, and they had many poems responding to each other. Wu writes what is in his mind, without embellishments. His tone is mild and relaxed, with no feeling of abruptness or harshness. Behaviour and judgment are brought before our ears and eyes without a forced and kaleidoscopic presentation. His classical poems are comparable to those of [Ch'ien Ch'i, Liu Chang'ch'ing, Yüan Chên, and Po Chü-i] . . . of the T'ang dynasty, and his essays can be likened to those of [Lu-ling (Ou-yang Hsiu) and Nan-fêng (Tsêng Kung)] . . . of the Sung period. The textural fabric of his parallel prose is very like that of [Su Tuan-ming (Su Shih)] . . . and the short lyrical verses among his *tz'ŭ* poems greatly resemble the works found in the Collection of the *Tz'ŭ* Poems Along the Flowery Path and the Collection of the *Tz'ŭ* Poems from a Thatched Hall. He was skilled in harmonizing the musical tunes, and spinning hemp into yarn. His parallel prose and *tz'ŭ* poems are both suitable for solo chanting, and for setting to music. For these he had special talent.

But my appreciation is rather of his popular writings. The *Hsi-yu Chi*, as one of Wu's literary works, is recorded in the early editions of the FC [*Huai-an Fu-chih*] along with his *Collected Works*, but it was deleted from both the FC and the Local Gazetteer of the Shan-yang District . . . from the middle of the 19th century. Very few readers of the novel knew who was its real author. (pp. 64-5)

In the 19th century, Ting Yen . . . was the first one to discover from the early Ch'ing editions of the FC that Wu Ch'êng-ên was the author of the *Hsi-yu Chi*. As a scholar who was also a native of Shan-yang, he was even able to point out that 'Wu has made use of a large amount of native dialectal expressions which are characteristic of our speech'. This has been partially verified in some of the annotated modern editions, including the 1954 edition published by the Tso-chia Ch'u-pan Shê. . . . This edition, using the 1592 Shih-tê T'ang . . . edition as its basis, and collating it against six later editions, is perhaps the best one available for studying the typographical evolution of this novel. (pp. 66-7)

The Preface to the Records of the Inscriptions on the Tripods Cast by Emperor Yü tends to give us some hint that its author had a gift for telling fictitious and wonderful tales with a satirical vein, a gift he may have inherited from his father. Hu Shih has pointed out that in Wu's writings there is an **"Êrh-lang Sou-shan-t'u Ko"** . . . or **"A Song on a Painting Depicting the God Êrh-lang Hunting in the Surrounding Country with His Followers"** (*Wu Ch'eng-en Shih-wen Chi* . . .) which may have something to do with the attitude of the novel's author. It is true that in this long poem the author expresses his discontent with his lot, and denounces the existing evils, but is it merely a coincidence that the God Êrh-lang is also playing an active part in the novel in which he has had a life-and-death combat with Monkey when the latter plays havoc in heaven and even that the term *sou-shan* . . . , which means searching for wild animals or game around the hills, is used several times in the novel (Chs. 6, 28, 92). As a matter of fact, the painting referred to in Wu's poem had been done some fifty years before he inscribed this poem, and the term *sou-shan* can be found in some earlier works dealing with the same subject such as the *tsa-chü* play *Hsi-yu Chi* . . . by Yang Ching-hsien . . . , a late Yän playwright.

To compare some of the *tz'ŭ* poems used in the novel with the **Collected Works** may to some extent place this matter in a new light. Generally speaking, although some of the poems found in the novel are rather vulgar, and may have been directly taken from its prototype works, there are still quite a lot of *shih* or *tz'ŭ* poems which are better quality and deserve serious study. The fact that a large number of *tz'ŭ* poems on different musical tunes appear in the novel is already a noteworthy feature. All of the musical tunes of the *tz'ŭ* poems found in Chapter 10 of the novel . . . are also found in [*Wu Ch'eng-en Shih-wen Chi*]. . . . (pp. 67-8)

In Chapter 64 of the novel, the author indulges himself in poetry to such an extent that his love for it can no longer be ignored. He makes Monk Hsüan-tsang be surrounded by a group of scholarly spirits who are transformed from pine-tree, cypress, Chinese juniper and bamboo to discuss the art of versification with him in the moonlight, attended by an extremely beautiful young lady and two maids who are again spirits of apricot, cassia and *la-mei* . . . (*Chimonanthus fragrans*) respectively. The skeleton of this story is derived from previous works, such as Chapter 37 of the *Hsi-yu Chi* in the Four Romances of the Wandering Saints, but the poetic descriptions and the poems are Wu's own. In praising a poem composed by Hsüan-tsang, the Tripitaka Master, one of the spirits, Grandad Wiping-off the Clouds Fu-yün Sou . . . , says, "Only your work, Sacred Monk, is equivalent to that of the golden period of T'ang times!" . . . This sounds quite similar to the literary theories of the Later Seven Masters, if not of Wu Ch'êng-ên himself! (p. 69)

[The] prototypes of **Hsi-yu Chi** are mainly the *Hsi-yu Shih-o Chuan* and the *Hsi-yu Chi* in the Four Romances of Wandering Saints. But even at the present time some scholars may still hold the same view as Hu Shih and Sun K'ai-ti who believed that these two works were abridged editions of Wu Ch'êng-ên's huge work. I would be the last person to disparage Wu's elaborate masterpiece, in which he utilized existing materials merely as his framework. The labour he exerted, and the size of his writing are ten times greater than the crude models he used. Without his imagination and literary technique the story of the Monkey and of Tripitaka's pilgrimage to the West would still be buried in oblivion among piles of doggerel and tasteless writings that an average reader would disdain to touch. (p. 81)

Wu Ch'êng-ên's world-famous novel has been accredited with great merit not only because of its artistic style, and combination of literary delineation with colloquial expressions, but also because of its stringent social criticism and satire which reflect uncompromisingly the rotten and corrupt politics of his days. We know that Emperor Shih-tsung was a ruler who indulged excessively in Taoist worship. Taoist priests were made ministers at his court. The art of love was learned openly by the upper classes and intellectuals. Recipes for aphrodisiacs were often presented to the throne by ministers and high officials seeking to achieve high rank. This was the decadent age in which the *Chin-p'ing-mei* was written. It was against this

background that in his **Hsi-yu Chi**, Wu Ch'êng-ên created several original stories in which not only Taoist high-priests form his main targets of derision, but he also directly criticizes the Taoist teaching of practising the art of love as a means to obtain longevity "like dragging up the moon from the depth of water":

> The Patriarch Subodhi said, "Then, how about teaching you the process of 'Moving'?" "What do you mean by it"? asked the Monkey. "There are many forms of exercises," said the Patriarch, "such as Gathering the *Yin* to Patch up the *Yang*, Drawing a Bow and Trampling the Catapult, Rubbing the Navel to pass Long Breath. There are also the Preparation of Recipes, the Burning of Reeds and Making up a Tripod, Taking of Red-lead, Melting the Autumn-stone and Drinking of A Young Mother's Milk." "Would these practices make me immortal?" asked the Monkey. The Patriarch said, "To hope for that through such practices, would be like dragging up the moon from the depth of water." (Chapter 2)

Both the "red-lead" (menses) and the "autumn-stone" (crystallized urine) here are technical terms in Taoist works on aphrodisiacs. Another passage, when Pigsy describes his own "technique" to Monkey who pursues him down to his grotto, runs:

> My breath goes up to the Mud-pill Palace on my head, and down to the Jetting-spring Spots which are the soles of my feet. By keeping my saliva running under my tongue, known as the Flowery-pool, my Cinnabar-field is kept always warm. I am skilled in matching the Baby with an Amazed Maid; when the Lead and the Mercury are combined, the sun and moon will be discerned. In the Eight Trigrams, *li* is a dragon and *k'an* a tiger; to bring them to harmony is a great feat. The Spirit Turtle of mine is able enough to exhaust the blood of the Silky Fowl. (Chapter 19)

Here again we find some esoteric terms which have implied meanings known only to the initiated. What we can say here is that the Mud-pill Palace . . . is the top of the head, the Jetting-spring Spots . . . are two spots on the flats of the feet. The place under the tongue in the mouth is called Flowery-pool . . . , while the Cinnabar-field . . . is alleged to be a spot three inches below the navel. The Baby . . . and the Amazed Maid . . . are two elliptical terms for lead and mercury in alchemical preparation. It is not difficult to understand that the Turtle here is another name for the male organ, while the Silky Fowl . . . represents vaguely the female part as a whole. Therefore, the description here is nothing but the art of love as taught by the Taoist priests. In answer to what can be called Pigsy's brag, Monkey simply retorts "You have sinned for raping a girl!"

Though in his conventional writings Wu sometimes used Taoist terms to praise others, in the novel he did not hide his deep resentment for such degenerate practices which encourage debauchery and moral laxity. . . . I have collected statistics from the novel which show that in the whole work some forty Taoist terms have been used of which one term appears from one time to more than ten times at the most. The reason why Wu used so many Taoist terms in a novel apparently of Buddhist influence is perhaps that the author himself was an advocate of the amalgamation of the Three Teachings. This can be verified by the words of Monkey, who tells the king, the ministers, the monks and the common people of the Kingdom of Cart-slow that "We hope you would see the point of amalgamation of the Three Teachings: you should have equal respect for the *samgha*, the Taoist priests, and you should also nourish and educate your intelligent youth.'' (Ch. 47) At the end of the novel, when the scriptures have been given to the Tripitaka Master Hsüan-tsang, the Tathāgata tells him, ''The efficacy of these scriptures is beyond description. They are not only a revealing mirror of our Doctrine, but also the source of all Three Teachings.'' (Ch. 98) But there is no testimony supporting this view in his incomplete *Collected Works*. (pp. 81-3)

Whether it has been duly revised or not, the *Hsi-yu Chi* of Wu Ch'êng-ên has added immensely to the heritage of Chinese literature. Today we may know very little about the background of the novel, still less about the life of its author. . . . However, there is little doubt that every Chinese child would greedily grab a copy of this voluminous work for his pastime. From it he would learn to struggle against difficulties and darkness, just as some four hundred and fifty years ago its imaginative author surreptitiously read in a shelter the vernacular works to which he had access. In it we find the inspiration of a great writer who failed to distinguish himself in his official career. (p. 86)

Liu Ts'Un-Yan, in his Wu Ch'êng-ên: His Life and Career, *E. J. Brill, 1967, 97 p.*

C. T. HSIA   (essay date 1968)

[*Hsia is considered one of the foremost scholars of classical Chinese literature. In the following excerpt, he studies characterization in* The Journey to the West, *presenting an extended appreciation of the novel's most spiritually advanced pilgrim, Monkey.*]

George Steiner has brilliantly observed that the major characters in Tolstoy and Dostoevsky, when confronted with personal problems of crucial moral importance, often recite and discuss passages from the New Testament, which in turn keynote and illuminate the meaning of the novels in which these characters appear. In *Hsi yu chi* the Heart Sutra is a subject of repeated discussion between Tripitaka and Monkey and serves the same novelistic function.

Though Tripitaka seems to have gained immediate illumination upon receiving the sutra and recites it constantly afterwards, its transcendent teaching that ''form is emptiness and the very emptiness is form'' is so far beyond his mortal understanding that every calamity that befalls him demonstrates anew his actual incomprehension. During pauses between adventures, therefore, it is Monkey with his far superior spiritual understanding that repeatedly asks his master to heed the sutra. Thus, in chapter 43, he makes another attempt,

> ''Reverend master, you have forgotten the verse, 'No eye, ear, nose, tongue, body, mind.' Of all of us who have forsaken the world, our eyes should not see color, our ears should not hear sound, our nose should not smell, our tongue should not taste, our body should not feel cold and heat, and our mind should not harbor vain illusions: this is known as 'routing the six thieves.' Now your mind is constantly occupied with the task of seeking the scriptures, you are afraid of the monsters and unwilling to give up your body, you beg for food and move your tongue, you are fond of sweet smells and titillate your nose, you listen to sounds and excite your ear, you see things around you and strain your pupils. Since you have welcomed these six thieves on your own invitation, how can you hope to see Buddha in the Western Paradise?''

Tripitaka is often aware of Monkey's superior understanding. In chapter 93, when Pigsy and Sandy laugh at Monkey's pretensions as a Zen master because he has again reminded their master to heed the Heart Sutra, Tripitaka upbraids the two less discerning disciples, ''Sandy and Pigsy, don't talk so foolishly. What Monkey comprehends is the wordless language. This is true comprehension.'' Measured against the standard of non-attachment upheld by Monkey, therefore, Tripitaka's every manifestation of fear and credulity, of fanatical obsession with correct conduct and peevish concern over his creaturely comforts is as much part of a deliberate comedy as the obviously gross behavior of Pigsy.

But Tripitaka is not only enslaved by his senses; his humanitarian pity—the most endearing trait about him—is itself a form of enslavement. Upon joining Tripitaka, Monkey's first act is to slay the six thieves—Eye, Ear, Nose, Tongue, Mind, Body—an allegorical event indicative of his superior detachment in comparison with the other pilgrims. But Tripitaka is horrified because, among his other frailties, he is still obsessed with love and compassion for phenomenal beings. This episode causes the first temporary rift between master and disciple, and Monkey is later twice punished with dismissal, following his seemingly merciless killing of first a demon in pathetic human disguise and then a number of brigands. From the viewpoint of popular Buddhism, Tripitaka has on all occasions followed the command not to kill, but because the novel inculcates the kind of Buddhist wisdom which excludes even the finest human sentiments as a guide to salvation, he is seen as a victim of perpetual delusion and can never make the same kind of spiritual progress as the hero of a Christian allegory. The novel, however, ultimately demonstrates the paradoxical character of this wisdom in that its nominal hero is granted Buddhahood at the end precisely because he has done nothing to earn it. To consciously strive for Buddhahood would again have placed him under bondage.

Monkey (Sun Wu-k'ung or Sun Aware of Vacuity), who repeatedly warns Tripitaka of his spiritual blindness, is, of course, the real hero of the book. He has already assumed the role of Tripitaka's protector on the road in the Sung *shih-hua*, and many of his deeds familiar to the reader of the 100-chapter novel must have appeared in the Yuan version, in however sketchy a fashion. But it is Wu Ch'eng-en who has enlarged upon these deeds and consistently defined his hero's character in terms of his spiritual detachment, his prankish humor, his restless energy, and his passionate devotion to his master. (pp. 128-30)

Monkey was hatched from a stone egg, under the influence of the sun and moon. Like many other Chinese novels, *Hsi yu chi* begins at the beginning, with the creation myth. In this regard, Monkey's discontent with a pastoral mode of life and his ambition to seek power and knowledge can be seen as signs of a conscious striving upward—from inanimate stone to animal shape with human intelligence to the highest spiritual attainment possible. Until this striving is deflected into the Buddhist path of obedient service following his humiliating defeat in the palm of Buddha, Monkey is but the smartest of all the monsters who share with him this unquenchable desire for evolution. In his brilliant reinterpretation of the novel in Communist terms, Chang T'ien-i, a great short-story writer of the pre-Communist period, boldly allies Monkey with all the eventually captive or destroyed monsters in their aspect of revolt against the powers of heaven jealous of their aspirations. In this light, Monkey's later career can only be viewed as that of an apostate who systematically kills or subdues his former comrades to serve the interests of a heavenly bureaucracy. But Chang T'ien-i's view (first expressed in an article in 1954) has understandably provoked unanimous protest from Communist critics who believe that it not only maligns Monkey but also discredits the whole purpose of the journey: it would be far better to regard the monsters as the ''enemies of the people'' and Monkey as their friend and savior.

These critics are right insofar as Monkey is too mischievous and spirited an animal to be always contemplating his quest. Even in his rebellious phase, he differs from the other monsters and from Ravana and the Satan of *Paradise Lost* in his ability to view himself in a humorous light and his actual detachment from whatever business he is engaged in. He is never too solemn even when fighting a whole battalion of heavenly troops. Without his sense of humor, Monkey would have become a tragic hero or else shared the fate of the other monsters. With his sense of humor, he can turn from rebel to Buddha's obedient servant without forfeiting our sympathy. This sense of humor, however coarsely and at times cruelly expressed at the expense of his companions and enemies, implies his ultimate transcendence of all human desires to which Pigsy remains a prey and from which Tripitaka barely detaches himself by his vigilant exercise of self-control. It is consonant with the Buddhist insistence on detachment that laughter should be adopted as the ultimate mode of viewing the world. In the novel, therefore, comedy mediates between myth and allegory. Monkey is at once a hero of boundless energy and an eloquent spokesman for the esoteric doctrine of emptiness (quite rightly, traditional commentators have regarded him as the mind or intelligence in the allegoric scheme of the novel). But to the end he retains the comic image of a mischievous monkey whose very zeal and mockery become an expression of gay detachment.

If Monkey is always the spirit of mischief when he is in command of a situation, there are occasions, nevertheless, when he impresses us with his passionate sorrow and anger. If humanitarian pity remains an endearing trait of Tripitaka, then, with all his superior understanding and mocking detachment, Monkey is also the antithesis of Buddhist emptiness in his passionate attachment to the cause of the journey and to his master. At times one gets the feeling that he is the only serious pilgrim, perpetually harassed by the mistrust and indolence of his fellow pilgrims and the indifference and malice of the deities above. Even Kuan-yin, who succors the pilgrims on numerous occasions, appears to Monkey to be at times patently cruel in tormenting them needlessly. In chapter 35, after Monkey has with great difficulty captured two powerfully armed demons, he learns to his consternation that the demons in their original shapes, together with their weapons, are actually the property of Lao Tzu and that it is with the deliberate intention of testing the pilgrims that Kuan-yin has borrowed them from him:

> Hearing this, the Great Sage thought to himself, ''This Bodhisattva is a double-crosser. Formerly, after she had restored my freedom, she asked me to protect Tripitaka on the western journey to get the scriptures. I told her then that the journey would be very hard, and she promised that during dangers she would personally come to my rescue. Now she has incited demons to harm us and her words are not trustworthy. No wonder she will remain a spinster all her life!''

But it is his master Tripitaka who causes him the greatest anguish. Monkey is completely loyal to him, but the latter, who listens to the envious Pigsy, frequently mistrusts him. . . . In chapter 27, after Monkey has finally killed a demon who

has thrice assumed human shape to deceive the pilgrims, the enraged Tripitaka gives him a note of dismissal, saying, ''Monkey-head, take this as proof that I no longer want you as my disciple. If I ever see you again, may I be instantly condemned to the Avici Hell!'' Monkey, who has killed the demon to protect his master, takes it extremely hard . . . : (pp. 134-36)

> Swallowing his resentment, he parted from his master and soon he was borne aloft on the somersault cloud, on his way back to the Water-Curtain Cave of the Flower and Fruit Mountain. Riding all alone, he was extremely miserable. Suddenly his ears caught the sound of waters. Looking down, the Great Sage knew that it was the noise made by the rising tide in the Eastern Ocean. He was again reminded of Tripitaka and could not hold his tears from falling over his cheeks. He stopped the cloud and stood there for a while and then went on . . . saying to himself, ''I have not been on this route for five hundred years!'' . . . That Monkey then made a big leap over the Eastern Ocean and soon he was at the Flower and Fruit Mountain. He got off his cloud and looked around him. On the mountain were neither flowers nor grass. Mountain hazes had vanished, peaks and cliffs had fallen, and forest trees were all charred. Do you know how this could have happened? At the time when, after his riot in heaven, Monkey had been handed over to the upper realm, the Illustrious God Erh-lang had come with the seven brothers of Mount Mei and burned the mountain. The Great Sage now became twice as despondent as before.

It is this passionate devotion to his home, to Tripitaka and his cause, that sets Monkey apart from the rest of the pilgrims. Above and beyond his mythic and comic roles, he shows himself as an endearing person subject to misunderstanding and jealousy and given to frequent outbursts of genuine emotion. He, too, belies his superior attainment in Buddhist wisdom with his incorrigible humanity. (pp. 137-38)

> C. T. Hsia, '''Journey to the West','' in his The Classic Chinese Novel: A Critical Introduction, Columbia University Press, 1968, pp. 115-64.

ANTHONY C. YU (essay date 1977)

[*A prominent American scholar of Oriental literature, Yu is best known for his editorship and translation of the four-volume* The Journey to the West. *In the following excerpt from his extensive introduction to this translation, he considers the poetry, myth, and Buddhist allegory in the novel.*]

It is not without reason that the author of [*Journey to the West*] has been ranked by C. T. Hsia as ''one of the most skilled descriptive poets in all Chinese literature,'' for much of the descriptive verse in this narrative is marked by extraordinary realism, vivid delineation, and vivacious humor. . . . [What] the reader meets again and again in these poems is an enthralling spectacle of exquisite details. Indeed, if judged by some of the traditional norms of Chinese lyric poetry, most of the poems of *The Journey to the West* might be considered inferior products because of their graphic and, occasionally, unadorned diction. The language is often too explicit, too direct, too bold, to be evocative or suggestive—that quality of metaphorical elusiveness which most Chinese lyric poets cherish and seek to incorporate into their verse.

What is scorned by tradition, however, may turn out to be a poetic trait of special merit in the *Hsi-yu chi*. For what the author has sought to express in these poems is hardly the kind of lyricism suffused with symbolic imageries so characteristic of the earlier poetry of reclusion, nor is he attempting to achieve the subtle fusion of human emotion and nature which has been the constant aim of many of the T'ang and Sung poets. Most of all, he is not trying to enlist the service of the lyrical tradition to realize the ancient ideal of "expressing serious intent" (*shih yen chih*), and that is why none of these descriptive poems can be said to be the bearer of profound moral ideas or weighty philosophical substances. Rather, what the author of the *Hsi-yu chi* seeks to convey to us seems to be the overpowering immediacy of nature, with all its fullness and richly contrasting variety, as it is often experienced by the main characters in the narrative. (pp. 24-6)

In an essay on *The Journey to the West* published recently in a volume titled *Ssŭ-pu ku-tien hsiao-shuo p'ing-lun . . . (Criticism of Four Classic Novels)*, a committee on literature at the Normal University of Shanghai has pinpointed the distinctive feature of this work: "In the first place, what distinguishes the *Hsi-yu chi* from most other fiction of antiquity is that it is a novel of the supramundane." Few readers will dispute such a remark on what is certainly the prima facie character of this epic narrative on Buddhist pilgrimage. It is surprising, however, that the bulk of modern criticism has not made any serious investigation into the significance of the supramundane, the mythic, and, indeed, the religious themes and rhetoric that pervade the entire work. (p. 33)

Although the story of *The Journey to the West* is based upon the historical pilgrimage of Hsüan-tsang, it is quite remarkable how extensively the themes and rhetoric of Taoism appear in every part of the work. By Taoism, I mean the concepts, ideas, and practices traceable to the *Tao Tsang* (The Taoist Canon), while fully acknowledging that many such elements codified and preserved for religious or non-religious reasons in this collection are no more than folk beliefs and rituals. As so many students of Chinese culture have come to realize, Taoism as a distinct philosophical movement or religious tradition is notoriously difficult to define. My pragmatic proposal here is made strictly in order to facilitate critical analysis, for the pervasive use of Taoist vocabularies in *The Journey to the West*'s titular couplets, in hundreds of its narrative and descriptive poems, and in various parts of the prose narration to illumine the significance of certain episodes, is quite without parallel in classic Chinese fiction. True, the *Fêng-shên yen-i* (Investiture of the Gods) surpasses even the *Hsi-yu chi* in its dramatization of the enormous celestial pantheon, the many sacred sites, and the weapons of stupendous magic power; the *Chin P'ing Mei* may contain concise transcriptions of a number of Taoist masses and rituals; and in the *Dream of the Red Chamber*, as Plak's study has brilliantly shown, there is some subtle interplay between *yin-yang* and *wu-hsing* theories and the development of characters and action in the novel. None of these works, however, is comparable to *The Journey to the West*, in which Taoist elements serve, not merely as a means of providing choric commentary on incidents and characters in the narrative, but frequently as an aid to reveal to the reader the true nature of the fellow pilgrims, to help define their essential relationships, and to advance the action of the narrative itself. Though the numerous literary antecedents to this novel clearly reveal an extended tradition wherein the story of the Buddhist pilgrim-monk becomes progressively assimilated to popular myths and legends, many of them originating from popular Taoism, it remains for the author of the hundred-chapter version to give shape and coherence on an unprecedented scale to this tradition by endowing the Buddhist Hsüan-tsang

with four supernatural disciples, the divine status of three of whom is attained through their efforts in alchemical self-cultivation. Indeed, as one examines the story of the pilgrims developed through spagyric themes and rhetoric in the narrative, one may come to the conclusion that the journey to the West also takes on the appearance of an allegorical pilgrimage in self-cultivation. (pp. 36-7)

Their supernatural character and their magical powers, on which the master pilgrim [Tripitaka] must so heavily depend, thus do not stem from their association with Buddhism. Rather, it is their success in internal alchemy, in making the inward elixir of immortality, as it were, that qualifies Sun Wu-k'ung, Chu Wu-nêng, and Sha Wu-ching to be the proper guardians of the mortal monk. The reason their assistance is needed is that the pilgrimage itself is believed to be so filled with hazards and perils that human help and companionship for the scripture pilgrim will not suffice. Already in chapter 8, when the Boddhisattva Kuan-yin is sent by Sākyamuni to seek a scripture pilgrim in the Land of the East, she is given special treasures by Buddha to present to the candidate for his protection. She is also told to persuade any monster possessing great magical power whom she meets on her way to become the disciple of the scripture pilgrim. Her journey to China, which in essence becomes a proleptic journey to the West with the order of events and geographical direction partially reversed, results in four celestial renegades' being made into disciples and thus prepares the reader for subsequent developments in the narrative. When the fictive Hsüan-tsang later departs from the capital of Ch'angan, he is quickly divested of his human assistants. At the mountain significantly named the Two Frontiers, which in the structure of the narrative marks the pilgrim's departure from the mundane territory of T'ang China and his entrance into the mythic realm of the journey infested by wild beasts, monsters, and demons, Hsüan-tsang is told by a human hunter who has come to his aid during his first ordeal that he must proceed alone, for the tigers and wolves beyond that mountain are not submissive to the hunter (chap. 13). It is, in fact, at that critical moment that Hsüan-tsang encounters Monkey, who will prove to be his most resourceful and trustworthy disciple. This meeting also initiates the fulfillment of the poetic prophecy announced by the god the night before when he rescues the monk from a band of animal spirits:

> I am the planet Venus from the West,
> Who came to save you by special request,
> Some pupils divine will come to your aid.
> Blame not the scriptures for hardships ahead.

The contrast between the limited strength of the human hunter and the fantastic power of Wu-k'ung is dramatically underscored by the episode immediately following the latter's release from the Wu-hsing Mountain. When master pilgrim and disciple encounter another ferocious tiger on their way, Monkey disposes of the beast with one stroke of his rod, causing

> its brain to burst out like ten thousand red petals of peach blossoms, and the teeth to fly out like so many pieces of white jade. So terrified was our Ch'ên Hsüan-tsang that he fell off his horse. "O God! O God!" he cried, biting his fingers. "When Guardian Liu [the hunter] overcame that striped tiger the other day, he had to do battle with him for almost half a day. But without even fighting today, Sun Wu-k'ung reduces the tiger to pulp with one blow of his rod. How true is the saying, 'For the strong, there's always someone stronger!'" [chap. 14]

This note of Hsüan-tsang's reliance on supernatural assistance is sounded again when, some time later, his white horse—his last link to the ordinary human world—is devoured by the Dragon prince exiled at the Eagle Grief Stream. Kuan-yin, who has been asked by Wu-k'ung to come to subdue the dragon, explains to the frustrated disciple:

> I went personally to plead with the Jade Emperor to have the dragon stationed here so that he could serve as a means of transportation for the scripture pilgrim. Those mortal horses from the Land of the East, do you think that they could walk through ten thousand waters and a thousand hills? How could they possibly hope to reach the Spirit Mountain, the land of Buddha? Only a dragon-horse could make that journey! [chap. 15]

To recognize the mighty resources of the disciples is to understand why Tripitaka is portrayed in such a manner in the *Hsi-yu-chi.* For no one familiar with the work has failed to notice to what degree this Hsüan-tsang differs from the heroic figure drawn from history and hagiography. With studied irony, the author seems to delight in demeaning the popular religious hero. Joyless and humorless, the fictive Tripitaka is dull of mind and peevish in spirit, his muddle-headedness matched only by his moral pusillanimity. As someone who is supposedly committed to the life of *pravraj (ch'u-chia,* a life of having forsaken the family), he is singularly attached to bodily comforts, complaining more than once about the cold and hunger inflicted by the journey. The slightest foreboding of ill or danger terrifies him; the most groundless kind of slander at once shatters his confidence in his most trustworthy follower, Sun Wu-k'ung, who has never failed to come to his rescue. Though he does win admiration from his disciple on a few occasions by his dogged resistance to sexual temptation, most of his encounters with evil, whether in human or supernatural form, find him impotent and paralyzed by fear, never revealing, even at the journey's end, that he has gained any moral or spiritual insight from his experience. It is this characteristic in Tripitaka that elicits an interesting observation from Hsia [see excerpt dated 1968], who writes:

> From the viewpoint of popular Buddhism, Tripitaka has on all occasions followed the command not to kill, but because the novel inculcates the kind of Buddhist wisdom which excludes even the finest human sentiments as a guide to salvation, he is seen as a victim of perpetual delusion and can never make the same kind of spiritual progress as the hero of a Christian allegory. The novel, however, ultimately demonstrates the paradoxical character of this wisdom in that its nominal hero is granted Buddahood at the end precisely because he has done nothing to earn it. To consciously strive for Buddhahood would again have placed him under bondage.

As far as Tripitaka is concerned, Hsia's point is well taken, for Tripitaka's achievement does little to merit his final exaltation. However, the weakness of his character, it may be argued, does not necessarily imply that "the finest human sentiments" are not desirable or that they have little value in the religious vision of the work. On the contrary, Tripitaka's frail and fallible character is deliberately magnified by the author in order to stress his absolute need for his supernatural companions and, most especially, for the protective guidance of Sun Wu-k'ung. (pp. 42-4)

Turning now to the discussion of Buddhist elements in the *Hsi-yu chi,* we may begin with the rather puzzling phenomenon that the narrative presents surprisingly few details traceable to specific Buddhist sources, despite the fact that its story is built on the historical pilgrimage undertaken by one of the most famous Buddhist personalities in Chinese history. (p. 52)

Although there may be no systematic exposition of one particular Buddhist doctrine in the narrative comparable to the kind of explicit presentation of Calvinistic thinking on predestination and atonement found in Book Three of Milton's *Paradise Lost,* certain themes and figures do receive consistent development.

The first such theme is the emphasis on the compassionate power of Buddha himself. Because of the immense appeal of the character of Sun Wu-k'ung, many modern critics, especially those who favor a more political interpretation of the narrative, have found it rather difficult to accept Monkey's subjugation in chapter 7, let alone the use of the golden fillet later as a means of gaining continuous control over him by inflicting unbearable pain once recalcitrant behavior is detected. The "conversion" of Monkey in this view is a basic flaw in the narrative, and what we see of him after his release from the Wu-hsing Mountain in chapter 14, as a faithful guardian of the cowardly and ineffectual Buddhist pilgrim, seems to contradict the magnificent heroic character whose defiance and love of independence we have come to cherish and admire in the first seven chapters.

That such a view fails to do full justice to the complexity of the narrative should also be apparent. For, although Buddha and his divine followers do constitute part of the entire celestial hierarchy (the other part being made up of what may be called Taoist divinities), and in this sense the Buddhist pantheon may seem, in Arthur Wright's words, "a victim of its own adaptability," there are nonetheless some subtle differentiations in the narrative concerning the two groups of deities. Whereas the bureaucratic pretension and incompetence of both groups become frequent targets of the author's biting satire, the wisdom and mercy of Buddha—characteristics hardly shared by any of the Taoist deities, least of all by the Jade Emperor—are constantly emphasized. Unlike the historical pilgrimage of Hsüan-tsang, which had its origin in the profound religious vision of the human monk, the journey of the narrative really begins with the Buddha's benevolent intention to impart the sacred Tripitaka to the inhabitants of the East. During the celestial assembly in chapter 8, this is the declaration of Buddha: "Those who reside in the South Jambūdvīpa, however, are prone to practice lechery and delight in evil-doing, indulging in much slaughter and strife. . . . However, I have three baskets of true scriptures which can persuade man to do good. . . . This will provide a source of blessings great as a mountain and deep as the sea." To be sure, this motive of Buddha is severely questioned by Sun Wu-k'ung later; when defeated by the Lion, the Elephant, and the Garuda Monsters, he wonders why Buddha, instead of asking someone to go through such ordeals to fetch the scriptures, does not send them to the East in the first place (chap. 77). But Wu-k'ung's anguished query represents only a momentary lapse of faith; his unreserved commitment to the journey and to what it seeks to accomplish is, in fact, what sustains the pilgrims through all those overwhelming difficulties. For the meaning of the journey, as it is developed in the narrative, is not confined to the benefits of acquiring sacred scriptures for the people of T'ang China. On a more personal and profound level, the journey signifies for the pilgrims a new beginning, a freely given opportunity for self-rectification. It is in this way that the theme of the journey as a protracted process of merit-making complements and magnifies the theme of Buddha's mercy.

I pointed out earlier how the distinctive characteristic of three of Tripitaka's disciples is to be found in their status as immortals, as beings who have succeeded in the way of alchemical self-cultivation. One further observation must now be added: they are not just immortals with great magic power, they are also delinquent ones. All three of them, together with the dragon-horse, have been condemned for certain misdeeds. The widespread fame of Monkey stems from the turmoils he caused in Heaven; Pa-chieh, Sha Monk, and the dragon-horse were punished and exiled to the earth below for getting drunk and insulting Ch'ang O, the legendary beauty of the Lunar Palace, for breaking crystals during a solemn banquet, and for setting fire to his father's palace and thereby destroying some precious pearls. The modern reader of the *Hsi-yu chi* may be offended by the harshness of their sentences, but it is no less clear that the author's intention is not so much to dwell on their misery, deserved or not, as to emphasize their preservation for a ''higher'' purpose. Thus it is that the narrator, after Monkey has been imprisoned by Buddha beneath the Wu-hsing Mountain, closes the chapter with the poetic commentary:

> Prideful of his power once the time was ripe,
> He [i.e., Monkey] tamed dragon and tiger, exploiting wily
>   might. . . .

As Kuan-yin carries out Tathāgata's instruction to persuade any monster with great magical power she may meet on her way to find a scripture pilgrim in the East (chap. 8) to become one of the pilgrim's guardians, all four disciples-to-be of Tripitaka are told by the Bodhisattva to wait for this special emissary from T'ang China. For their willingness to journey to the West with him and their faithful service will win for Sun Wu-k'ung, Chu Wu-nêng, Sha Wu-ching, and the dragon sufficient merit to atone for their past crimes. This motif is repeatedly heard in the narrative, of which one conspicuous example is when the dragon joins the pilgrimage in chapter 15 after Kuan-yin arrives at the Eagle Grief Stream. ''The Bodhisattva went up to the little dragon and plucked off the shining pearls hanging around his neck. . . . After Pilgrim had heard all these kind words, he thanked the Bodhisattva of Great Mercy and Compassion.''

It is important for us to note that in the admonition of the Bodhisattva to both the dragon and Wu-k'ung, the journey promises not merely a restoration of their previous divine status, but in fact a higher plane of attainment. This may be part of the reason, too, why Wu-k'ung is made to say to Wu-nêng during their first meeting in chapter 19, ''It's old Monkey who turned from wrong to right, who left the Taoist to follow the Buddhist. I am now accompanying the royal brother of the Great T'ang Emperor in the Land of the East, whose name is Tripitaka, Master of the Law.'' By her words of encouragement and her additional gift of magic power to Monkey, which will indeed prove to be life-saving in a later crisis (chap. 70), the Bodhisattva Kuan-yin of the narrative thus reveals her character to be consistent with a long established tradition, which venerates Avalokiteśvara as one who enlightens and who delivers her followers from all kinds of perils and pains. In her person and in her action, the compassionate power of Buddha extends not only to the disciples of Tripitaka but also to someone like the Bear Monster of chapter 17, whose life she spares in order that he might become a mountain guardian of Potalaka, thus winning for herself the spontaneous compliment of Monkey: ''truly a salvific and merciful goddess, who will not hurt a single sentient being!''

It may be asked at this point what sort of merit the disciples do succeed in making during their lengthy journey. The most

obvious answer to this question must be, of course, their success in overcoming the marauding hordes of demons and monsters along the way which seek to harm the pilgrim monk. (pp. 54-6)

The journey to obtain scriptures in the Western Heaven is, for Tripitaka and his disciples, also the piacular journey of return to Buddha, and like the Odysseus of the Homeric poem, the scripture pilgrim must pass through appalling obstacles for past offenses against the gods.

It is only when we perceive the religious significance of the journey that we can understand more adequately the relation among the five pilgrims. That the defenseless and hapless monk of the narrative has need of his four supernatural companions in order to traverse ''the thousand hills and ten thousand waters'' is very much self-evident. On the other hand, the person and the sacred mission of Tripitaka is also stressed by the author as the means by which the hubristic tendencies of someone like Sun Wu-k'ung are curbed as his mighty and hardwon abilities are converted to serve a less self-centered and self-serving purpose. Both the human monk and his powerful companion must ''work out their salvation'' on the basis of mutual reliance. . . . (pp. 58-9)

[What] Tripitaka has to offer to his four disciples is the occasion by which their antinomian and anarchic tendencies are checked and reoriented toward the good of the human community, and by which their peculiar strengths and talents (even Chu Pa-chieh can serve as a ''super bulldozer'' for plowing a way through eight hundred miles of thorns and prickles in chapter 64 and through the Rotted-tree Alley in chapter 67) may be put to serve a noble cause. To elaborate these deeper meanings of the journey, the author has made striking use of the rhetoric of two religious traditions. In accordance with folk Taoism, the emphasis is on integration, for the essence of self-cultivation, as Andrew Plaks has succinctly observed, ''lies in the subordination of the individual Self to a larger vision of totality'' [see Additional Bibliography]. To all four of his imprisoned followers Tripitaka offers the opportunity of finding renewal and release through the subordination of their selves ''to the Selfhood of the pilgrimage.'' But the vision of the spagyrical arts, to quote Plaks further, ''leads directly to the illusion that the self-contained world of the individual mind [and, one might add, the individual body as well] can stand alone, since it can encompass the entire universe with its ken.'' It is to modify such a vision, I believe, that the narrative also places such strong emphasis on the Buddhist concepts of the maturation of good stock . . . (*kuśalamūla*), and the accumulation of merits . . . (*punyam-karoti*), conditions which are socially beneficent and are to be achieved through mutual dependence and communal effort. That is why in the climactic moment of their journey, when the pilgrims finally arrive at the shores of salvation after having been ferried across the Cloud-Transcending Stream by the Buddha of the Light of Ratnadhvaja in a bottomless boat, and having seen in midstream the ''proof'' of their liberation through the shedding of their ''old bodies'' or shells, we are allowed to witness this important conversation between master and disciple.

> When Tripitaka realized what had happened, he turned quickly to thank his three disciples. Pilgrim said: ''We two parties need not thank each other, for we are meant to support each other. We are indebted to our master for our liberation, through which we have found the gateway to the making of merit, and fortunately we have achieved the right fruit. Our master also has to rely on our protection so that he may be

firm in keeping both law and faith to find this happy deliverance from the mortal stock'' [chap. 98].

This segment of *The Journey to the West,* when read within the context of the entire narrative, should help us see that the submission of the disciples to the master pilgrim, and through him to the claims of Buddhism, is not simply a matter of passive acquiescence to a hateful policy of pacification as some critics have suggested when they compare the disciples to the one hundred and eight heroes of the *Shui-hu chuan* (The Water Margin). In this latter novel, the surrender to the political powers that be indeed marks the disintegration and decline of the gallant brigands, but for Sun Wu-k'ung, Chu Wu-nêng, Sha Wu-ching, and the Dragon Prince, the decision to undertake the journey to the West is also the beginning of their discovery of self-fulfillment and a freedom that does not destroy. (pp. 61-2)

> Anthony C. Yu, in an introduction to The Journey to the West, Vol. 1 by Ch'êng-ên Wu, *edited and translated by Anthony C. Yu, The University of Chicago Press, 1977, pp. 1-62.*

JAMES S. FU (essay date 1977)

[*In the following excerpt, Fu analyzes* The Journey to the West *as a quest romance, comparing it with the Western novels* Don Quixote *and* Huckleberry Finn.]

In the first chapter of Aristotle's *Poetics,* there could have been a place for fiction, but it was then without a name in his deductive classification. *Don Quixote, Hsi-yu chi (Journey to the West),* and *Huckleberry Finn,* the three novels which we plan to discuss in this study, all represent a re-creation of the basic action of romance, the quest. By romance here we mean not merely a tale of love or adventure but a representation of both the dark force of *yin* and the bright force of *yang.* It includes at once the visions of faith and doubt, humour and horror, order and disorder, and in the Buddhist terms, 'form and emptiness'. The quest represents an 'archetypal pattern' deeply rooted in our daily dreams and deeds. No matter how great a change may take place in society, the romance of the quest will inspire us again and again, into looking for new hopes and desires to feed on, and, like 'the hunger of imagination' in Dr. Johnson's *Rasselas,* breaking through the boundary of even a paradise. (p. 1)

Hsi-yu chi is a cosmic comedy with myth as its husk and humour as its kernel. It would be humourless to propose a rigid definition for humour, which seems as elusive as faith in Buddhism; to strive too self-consciously for enlightenment as Tripitaka does in his quest for the scriptures would only lead to illusions. For our purpose here, however, we shall use 'humour' in two related senses: first, as the peculiar traits of our personality like the four humours; and then as the sense of humour, a genial tolerance of the incongruities in life, and a sympathetic attitude toward the errors of man. We shall see how a harmony of the four humours can ripen into a mellow sense of humour, and can thus achieve the ever-quivering happy mean, not by avoiding the extremes, but by reconciling the conflicting elements. Therefore, the sense of humour is like faith and love, which can sustain the quest of the self for immortality. There are three equally significant parallel lines running simultaneously through *Hsi-yu chi.* The top level is the divine world, the middle is the human world, and the bottom is the animal world. The divine world is marked by epic destiny, and by humour of a gentle smile and permeating com-

passion; the human world is marked by sentimental seeking, fretting and sweating; and the animal world is marked by pastoral relaxation, and by hearty laughter and unbound fantasy. In order to restore the divine aspects of humanity, the poet and the pilgrim first have to return to the animal world. As the story goes on, the top and the bottom levels meet and merge in fantasy and compassion, and thus encircle the human quest, uplifting it to a divine comedy.

Hsi-yu chi is like an ancient Chinese dragon, in which beast, bird, and fish unite into one organism, having at once three levels of living experience. Its style and structure represent an asymmetrical metamorphosis, bursting from the tension of the double plane of meaning. In the baroque structure of *Don Quixote* and *Huckleberry Finn,* there is tension of such a double perspective. In the three novels, the plot of almost any episode may simultaneously be used for a serious and a humorous tale. The three authors' vision of life includes both the grotesque *yin* and the sublime *yang.* In his plot, Wu Ch'eng-en has made imaginative use of the Buddhist transmigration of souls, where the animal, the human, and the divine can grow into one another. For instance, both Monkey and Pigsy are powerful gods, but Pigsy very often complains that the small luggage he carries on the way is too heavy; and in chapter 41, Monkey is almost drowned when he is overwhelmed by his love for Tripitaka. In chapter 76, Monkey, in the disguise of a demon-messenger from hell, frightens Pigsy out of his wits, and thus squeezes from Pigsy the little money the latter has saved for himself; and in chapter 77, even Buddha becomes the relative of the Garuda-monster. In the wheel of karma, the comic ego can become the mythic god, while a dragon can be malign or benign, or can grow from evil into good. The magic in *Don Quixote* and the morality in *Huckleberry Finn* are also presented as a deep inner change of attitude.

Since the three novels represent the archetypal quest, the focus of interest is always cast on Don Quixote and Sancho, Huck and Jim, and the five pilgrims. Among the pilgrims, the story of the Dragon-horse has a 'primitive' plot. It is a primitive force made domestic, which carries Tripitaka, the civilized monk, to the goal, whereas the domestic hack of Don Quixote, Rocinante, carries its master into the wilderness. The story of Sandy has a 'stoical' plot. In Chinese literature, there is the recurring pattern of rebel-exile-recluse-creator, which corresponds with the archetypal pattern in universal myth, childhood-obscurity-maturity. The metamorphic self is always a rebel-child groping for his true character in obscurity. David Daiches well said that in James Joyce art is regarded as moving from the personal lyrical form, through the narrative form, to the impersonal dramatic form, where the artist, like God the Creator, remains within and beyond his creation. The artist must become an exile in order that he may be as objective as God. In the three novels, like the knight and his squire, the two fugitives, and the five pilgrims, the three narrators are all obscure exiles. Sandy, with his objective contemplation and his sullen complexion, is the closest character to the author as a humorist, who has to remain grave while making other people laugh.

The stories of Tripitaka in *Hsi-yu chi,* Tom Sawyer in *Huckleberry Finn,* and the duke and duchess in *Don Quixote* have 'sentimental' plots. The stories of Monkey, Don Quixote and Huck have 'epic' plots, while the stories of Pigsy, Sancho and Jim have 'pastoral' plots. By pastoral here is meant a figure for a condition in which the characters understand life in relation not so much to civilized society as to the basic patterns of nature. The pastoral plot is often introduced as an interlude in an epic when the hero faces the crisis of choice, and appeals to nature for revelation. The core of action in the three novels lies in the tension and the unity of the epic aspiration and the pastoral retreat, while the unity of the two makes the 'simple' plot. What Schiller called the 'naive' or the 'simple' is nature itself, while the 'sentimental' is to yearn for nature as a sick person yearns for health. Tripitaka is a holy monk in a civilized society, but a weakling in the wilderness; all the other pilgrims are primitive forces and animal spirits protecting the poor human being, who has so rashly and firmly plunged into nature to restore his lost faith. Like Everyman, Tripitaka has to go through the pilgrimage step by step on the Dragon-horse, thus giving a concrete human context to the miraculous actions of his disciples, who always surround him to protect him. He is the 'centre of indifference' around which revolves a world full of vital actions and laughter. (pp. 1-4)

At the heart of *Hsi-yu chi* throbs the Mahayana (the Big Vehicle) Buddhist *Heart Sutra,* compact with the elemental forces of *yin* and *yang,* which contradict yet complement each other. The unifying theme of the novel lies in the transcendental teaching of the *Heart Sutra,* which has become a Chinese folk saying: 'Form is emptiness and the very emptiness is form.' The abstract 'Word' of Buddha has become concrete 'Flesh' since the pilgrims have to live it through their daily experience of the quest. In the mythic tradition of Chinese fiction, *Hsi-yu chi* begins at the beginning, with the creation myth followed closely by the birth of Monkey, which illuminates the identification of 'form' and 'emptiness'. He is born out of a static rock, and rapidly grows into a lively symbol of dynamic action and transformation. He grows so swiftly from the elemental into the immortal that even immortality cannot stop his growth. He is soon bored by the secure prison-paradise in heaven, falls from heavenly grace, and thus takes part in the painful quest in the human world, to be united with his fellow pilgrims and especially his *alter ego,* Pigsy. (pp. 8-9)

Hsi-yu chi has incorporated the Chinese folk belief of the three religions: Taoism, Confucianism, and Buddhism. As a 'travelling monk' and a former disciple of the Ch'an Patriarch, Subodhi, Monkey is the mouthpiece of Ch'an Buddhism, which is a form of developed Mahayana Buddhism. It was under tremendous Taoist influence that Confucius formulated the golden mean, while his ideal of self-realization suggests the spirit of quest. At the heart of the novel throbs the *Heart Sutra,* the very essence of Mahayana Buddhism. The novel opens and closes with the terms and the imagery of *The Book of Changes,* which is the foundation of Taoism. In addition, the mutually changing forces of *yang* and *yin* correspond well with 'form and emptiness' in the novel, while the five elements . . . are closely related to the harmony of humours, and thus to the happy mean and to the achievement of the goal of the quest.

In the life of Tripitaka, the *Heart Sutra* has played a decisive role in sustaining his faith in the trying pilgrimage. The sutra, like his disciples, is a spiritual companion appointed for his protection on his perilous journey. In the novel, the sutra has become Flesh like the Word in the Bible, since the pilgrims have re-enacted it through their daily experience. According to C. T. Hsia [see excerpt dated 1968], 'George Steiner has brilliantly observed that the major characters in Tolstoy and Dostoevsky, when confronted with personal problems of crucial moral importance, often recite and discuss passages from the New Testament, which in turn keynote and illuminate the meaning of the novels in which these characters appear. In

Hsi-yu chi the *Heart Sutra* is a subject of repeated discussion between Tripitaka and Monkey and serves the same novelistic function.' Though a Buddhistic sutra, it is compact with the elemental forces of *The Book of Changes,* the Dionysian *yin* and the Apollonian *yang.* To indicate the original oneness of the dual modes, it is full of paradoxes such as the saying, 'All *dharmas* are marked with emptiness, they are neither produced nor stopped, neither defiled nor immaculate, neither deficient nor complete.' Such paradoxes are essential to the double perspective of significance in the novel, and to the creation of the contradictory yet complementary characters like Monkey and Pigsy. (p. 76)

Don Quixote, Monkey, and Huck belong to the 'simple' heroes of the quest; they become mythic figures in world literature because of the basic simplicity of their character. They are seldom preoccupied with themselves, and hence are free from self-love, which is a dead end, for real love has to involve other people, and we can have love and faith only in what is apart from us. Hamlet, Tripitaka, Tom Sawyer, Gulliver, and Ahab are solitary lovers of their egos. The living core of Don Quixote's spirit becomes a dead code for Tom Sawyer in the beginning of *Huckleberry Finn.* Don Quixote and Huck show a profound veneration for tradition like the Church. Monkey's revolt is the result of a perpetual evolution. Actually, he has a profound respect for real authorities like Buddha, Kuan-yin, and even his rival Erh-lang. He likes to tease self-centered people like Lao Tzu and Tripitaka in the novel. Hamlet, Tripitaka, Tom Sawyer, and Ahab often depend upon other people, yet they are also tyrannous and intolerant to them. The jokes of Tom, the dreams of Hamlet, the mistakes of Tripitaka, the neuroses of Gulliver, and the obsession of Ahab are all a meaningful upsurge of their repressed unconscious, and of their egoistic vanity.

The imagination of Monkey can melt the golden fillet on his head. The imagination of Don Quixote can turn the barber's brass basin into Mambrino's helmet. Being ready for chivalrous action, Don Quixote can sally forth with a helmet repaired with cardboard, and let a hack like Rocinante lead him into adventures. The beginning of *Don Quixote* at a village of no recalled name is a mythic opening to the end of most personal novels (*Bildungsroman*) like *Rene, The Sorrows of Young Werther,* and *Catcher in the Rye.* The sentimental, irresponsible, young hero has to learn by renunciation and self-knowledge to live humbly for a cause, which is the beginning of a new quest. Huck is a boy much younger than Rene and Werther, but he unconsciously assumes the responsibility of an adult, and intuitively carries out the mission of the liberation of a mythic hero, a black Christ like Jim.

The metamorphic self is a fool-seer, a sinner-redeemer, and a picaro-pilgrim, for there is pastoral wandering in his epic striving and vice versa. In their rambling Monkey and Pigsy open the quest to new adventures and bring forth the common redemption of other people as well as the self-realization of the pilgrims. Besides, for the self to transform from a fool into a seer, mutual love among the questers is necessary. The isolated ego can have no metamorphosis at all. . . . [In] the baroque structure of the three novels, the centre of gravity leans toward the solid base of reality. At the end of the three novels, it is Sancho who urges his dying master to go on their immortal quest; it is Pigsy whom Buddha finds most difficult to convert from a lusty man into a buddha; and we wonder how Huck can go on his idyllic journey without Jim. The quest of Huck and Jim, unlike that of Ahab or Gulliver, shows us that freedom is found in love rather than in self-love. Because of the active love in the free spirit of quest, the self is transformed in the glory of serving other people. (pp. 82-4)

At the end of **Hsi-yu chi** the author of the novel does not sacrifice the character so as to round off the plot. Buddha finally lets Monkey's challenging spirit and Pigsy's animal appetite grow beyond the plot of apotheosis, for he promotes Monkey to be the Buddha Victorious in Strife, and Pigsy to be Cleaner of the Altar, who can enjoy all the offerings of the people whenever there is a Buddhist ceremony. Right after the author's hint that Pigsy should have a poorer appetite, he shows himself still a hearty eater.

According to Plato's idea of the ridiculous, Pigsy is comic for lacking self-knowledge in regard to his wealth, beauty, and wisdom. Still, the self in its metamorphoses cannot have a definite self-knowledge. Both the metamorphic self and the comic spirit are like God or Buddha in always having new identity or no identity. As a poor, ugly fool, the self can laugh at the world of 'vanities', and remain faithful to the ideal. With his constantly changing identity, the self can keep integral his infantile innocence despite his continuous involvement in the world of experience. Pigsy not only can keep himself intact in going through the vicissitudes of the quest, but can see himself transform before his own eyes, and can act in accordance with his new persona.

At the end of the novel, Monkey consoles Tripitaka on the loss of a small portion of the scriptures, and tells him that the scriptures are incomplete like the universe. Buddha himself has also told the pilgrims that the blank scriptures are the real scriptures. Monkey is attracted to Pigsy because Pigsy often tells us that he is the most incomplete among the pilgrims. Being the youngest folk figure in the novel, he is the most potential questing hero, and attracts the most attention from the audience. Such a fool is thus the archetypal quester, whereas the form of the novel as a literary genre is precisely the fool's quest for self-knowledge. A fool like Pigsy often suffers for his desire for food, sex, and money, the basic needs of human nature. The fool is thus representative in his humour and humanity because he suffers most for our common sin. (pp. 84-5)

The quest of Monkey through the Mountain of Flowers and Fruit, the pilgrimage, and the mountain again is from the innocent world of 'emptiness', through the experienced world of 'forms', and back to 'emptiness' again. It goes in a circle because in the world of experience, the quest is to restore the lost world of innocence. At the end of *Four Quartets*, T. S. Eliot said, 'We shall not cease from exploration / And the end of all our exploring / Will be to arrive where we started / And know the place for the first time.' When the raft of Huck and Jim drifts down the river, their life is open and 'naked'. They are freest in the process of their quest for freedom. Having helped Jim in restoring his freedom, Huck at last runs away from 'sivilization' to keep his own spirit free. To return from the official life to the pastoral life is a recurring theme in Chinese literature. The epic quest in the three novels, both Chinese and Western, is indeed idyllic; the perpetual process of the quest is identified with its goal of paradise. Therefore, the novel, as the embodiment of the quest, ought to have no end. In the novel as a whole, the process is always more important than the end. The characters often break through the plot, and thus open the story to new dimensions.

Since 'form is emptiness', it is crucial for us to distinguish between appearance and the ideal as antithesis to reality, and

between death and immortality as opposite to life. As we know, striving, with all its blundering, is indispensable to salvation. That is why Pigsy and Sancho have to follow Monkey and Don Quixote, though with much grumbling. Furthermore, only in striving can we perceive the difference between the damnation of Satan and the nirvana of Buddha. Since being perfect is an unattainable goal, the followers of Satan despair and kill all the actions to become perfect, but the followers of Buddha still have faith and heal all the mistakes caused by the striving to become perfect. As a pilgrim, Pigsy cannot let himself go so far as a picaro because Monkey always draws him back to follow the direction of the quest.

Pigsy and Sancho offer comic relief and pastoral retreat to the epic quest, but they indeed need the quest. Faith is not absurd, for there is no safe way to salvation, and thus the quest is never in vain. We can see at last that Pigsy and Sancho do have deep faith in the quest. . . . (pp. 90-1)

To tell the truth, Monkey prefers the process of the quest to the paradise lost and regained. As his alter ego, Pigsy, has told us, nothing can be sweeter to Monkey than to evoke and to subdue the monsters. When all songs and stories end, the rest is silence; and a paradise tends to become a prison when it loses the support of the constant questing spirit. The basic paradox of the quest is that it can transform its perpetual process into its unattainable goal. It can identify the colourful 'form' with the transparent 'emptiness', and it can let the metamorphic self from the earthy base reach the spiritual height of the selfless buddha. As usual, the quest brings the metamorphic self into the midst of trials, where the victor with faith can achieve an impersonal height to transcend the self from the trials.

The quest moves in accordance with the phenomena of nature like the changing of the seasons. When the force of *yin* reaches its limit, it becomes the force of *yang* and vice versa, in order to maintain the harmony and the rejuvenation of nature. In the same manner, the metamorphic self moves to and fro between life and death to reach immortality. It goes by the 'centripetal force' to seek its true identity, and thus it goes spirally up to reach the top of the mountain of purgatory. There it finds a green world of innocence, a Thunder-clap Temple of human imagination, for the Holy Mountain is in the human mind. From the temple at the top of the Holy Mountain, the pilgrims bring the inspiring words of Buddha to the world, and by the 'centrifugal force' they move down the spiral mountain. After the people of the world have received the scriptures, the pilgrims go back to the Holy Mountain to become buddhas. As a result, the spiral quest can reach a changing centre of nowhere by the 'centripetal force' of the self, and can also encompass a cosmic cycle of everywhere by the 'centrifugal force' of service. The cosmic cycle is like the perpetual process, while the ever changing centre is like the unattainable goal of the cyclic quest. (p. 92)

All three novelists have a profound sympathy for the questing heroes. Still, they are too wise to condemn the world through which their heroes have to go. They are content to let the world judge itself; their Olympian laugh and love are not to escape from life, but to accept reality as it is. Their compassion illuminates the impersonal objectivity of the creator, while their irony goes beyond pity and terror and leads us toward the joy of a transcendent anonymity. Like the spirit of the scriptures, their creative attitude can keep us free from the sentimental fixation which revolves around the beauty of 'forms' in art and life. (p. 98)

James S. Fu, in his Mythic and Comic Aspects of
the Quest: 'Hsi-yu chi' as Seen through 'Don Quixote' and 'Huckleberry Finn', *Singapore University
Press, 1977, 125 p.*

CHANG CHING-ERH (essay date 1980)

[*In the following excerpt, Chang, through a comprehensive overview of the novel's episodic structure, stresses the thematic importance of the elements water, fire, metal, wood, and earth and
the cycle of initial unity, separation, and final unity in* The Journey
to the West.]

The theory of the five elements was a system of thought devised
by the Chinese thinker in ancient times to view the materialistic
phenomena of nature. The interaction of the five elements—
water, fire, metal, wood and earth—designates the five primordial essences in a state of constant flux and incessant movement. For our present purpose it suffices to know that the theory
involves two orders: mutual production and mutual conquest.
According to the former water produces wood, wood produces
fire, fire produces earth, earth produces metal, and metal produces water. And as stated by the latter water conquers fire,
fire conquers metal, metal conquers wood, wood conquers
earth and earth conquers water. . . . The mutual production and
mutual conquest of these elements which effect the successive
transformations and causal relationships of all things in the
universe are not passively stagnant, but powerfully constitute
an endless cycle in an active way.

The five elements were said to have taken its origin from the
yin . . . and the *yang*. . . . These two forces in turn took their
source at Tao. . . . Before it divided, Tao was whole, complete
and traceless; it was in a state of Chaos or Great Mist. It was
then rent as a result of its constant flowing into the *yin-yang*
forces, which drawing apart became the five elements. When
in due course the *yin-yang* forces and the five elements grew
merged into one, the split Tao would return to its original state.
The *Hsi-yu chi*, like many other Chinese folk novels, begins
with the creation myth to expound the cyclical transformation
of the universe. This is what its first verse passage says:

> Before Chaos split, Heaven and Earth were in
>   confusion,
> Being vast and void, nothing was discernible.
> When P'an Ku sundered the Great Mist,
> Creation began, and the pure were separated from
>   the impure.
> All things in between Heaven and Earth were created
>   to adore the supreme Benevolence.
> The ten thousand creatures were shaped and led to
>   goodness.
> Those who would know creation's work in myriads
>   of years,
> Must read *The Story of Deliverances on the Westward
>   Journey*. . . .

The three stages described above are unity, separation and
unity: the process from the state of Chaos or Great Mist to the
creation of the world and all things is the process from unity
to separation, and the process from creation and production to
the Journey's end, then, is the one from separation to unity. . . .
As the movement from instability toward stability constitutes
the legitimate plot of a story, it is only natural that the scheme
of the novel concerned is placed upon the transition from separation to unity, a transition which involves the adjustment of
the five elements represented by the questers of True Scriptures.

The term, *wu-hsing* . . . (five elements), occurs approximately
thirty times throughout the *Hsi-yu chi*. But the five elements
respectively as [*shui* (water), *huo* (fire), *chin* (metal), *mu* (wood),
and *t'u* (earth)] . . . are innumerable. They are usually found
in titular couplets and verse passages. The couplet which sums
up the incidents of a chapter tells us that Monkey is associated
with metal, Pigsy with wood and Sandy with earth; from the
verse passage interlaced in the narrative we know Tripitaka
embodies water and Monkey incarnates fire. An example for
illustration can be cited from chapter 57, where the T'ang
monk, having expelled Monkey, feels for a moment unbearably
parched. Then the verse passage that follows reads: "Earth
and wood struggle in vain while metal and water sever.'' . . .
Here water apparently designates Tripitaka. Actually the often-
mentioned term, "heart-monkey," already connotes the association of Monkey with metal and fire: the "monkey" comes
to be connected with metal in the cycle of the Twelve Animals,
while the "heart" is the viscus that corresponds to fire.

A further perusal of the text will demonstrate that these five
elements are not arbitrarily assigned to the pilgrims, but in
agreement with their character traits. Tripitaka, nicknamed
"River Float," is described as soft and meek as water, timorous, sentimental and muddle-headed. Monkey has a fiery
disposition, impetuous, boastful and quick-witted on the one
hand, and proud, capricious, stubborn, and courageous on the
other. Pigsy is said to be stupid as a stick, lewd, greedy and
slanderous. Finally Sandy is mild as the noblest element earth,
a peace-maker, a harmonizer and a nourisher, distinguished
among other things for its generative as well as productive
power. Their character traits are easy to be recognized; they
are, in the words of E. M. Forster, "flat characters." Though
interpretators of the *Hsi-yu chi* have seldom pointed out the
correspondence of these, they have nevertheless elaborately
analyzed the character traits of the pilgrims, wherefore we shall
not further enter into details here.

The popular 100-chapter *Hsi-yu chi,* in which the legend of the
Journey takes a definite shape and receives a full treatment, is
allegedly based upon the version published in 1592 by the *Shih-
tê t'ang* . . . of Nanking. Its entire arrangement of incidents,
like the *Odyssey, Adventures of Huckleberry Finn* or the picaresque novel, is episodic. Its episodes succeed each other
chronologically without strongly emphasized causality. Each
of them, which consists of half a chapter at least (i.e. the two
episodes in chapter 13) and seven chapters at most (i.e. chapters
1-7), makes up a very self-contained unit. The action of the
entire narrative is of course complete, so is it true with that of
each episode in it. Yet if we make a close examination of its
tone and atmosphere expressed, we can discover its framework
designed dramatically according to certain natural stages and
its seemingly veiled theme threading the novel from beginning
to end.

Let us now take the first, and also the most typical, episode
of the *Hsi-yu chi* (chapters 1-7) as an example for illustration.
This episode, whose plot revolves around its central character,
Monkey, is intended to portray the unifying process of the two
antagonistic elements, metal and fire. Monkey was born from
an immortal "rock" on the Flower-Fruit Mountain worked
upon by the pure essences of the "sun" and the "moon." The
sun and the moon are heavenly "fires," while the rock is the
consolidated material that consists principally of "minerals."
Thus he has aggregated in his body fire and metal at birth albeit
they are not purified yet. As soon as he sees the world, he
"astonishes" the Jade Emperor by flashing two beams of me-

tallic light from his eyes. After he has drunk water, the light grows dim, and his original nature becomes gradually merged. This is the first time that water conquers fire. He finds the Water-Curtain Cave for his fellow monkeys, and having suddenly realized one day during his carefree existence the uncertainty of life and the threat of death, decides to quest for immortality (chapter 1). After a long wandering search, he comes to the Holy-Terrace Mountain where he learns the secret of life. And here ends the exposition of the episode.

Hardly has he returned to the Flower-Fruit Mountain when his fiery temper and steely stubbornness begin to break out, thereby causing the action to accend. First he slays the Demon of Havoc, burns down her Water-Viscera Cave (chapter 2), carries away military equipments by magic from the Ao-lai Country, demands a weapon and garments from the Dragon Kings, and then in a drunken dream disposes two summoners and crosses out all the names of the monkeys on the Life-and-Death Records in the Palace of Shadows (chapter 3). The rising action is suspended for a moment when the Planet Venus suggests a means of pacification. Before long, however, it continues to mount up with Monkey's rebellious return to the earth, calling himself "Great Sage, Equal of Heaven" and repeatedly defeating the heavenly troops that come to arrest him. Again at the Planet Venus' suggestion of a peaceful solution the narrative movement slackens once more. Monkey is given the title of the "Sage" (chapter 4), and soon afterwards appointed supervisor of the Peach Garden. Yet he "astounds" the Jade Emperor for the second time by eating the Peaches of Immortality, drinking the nectar prepared for a celestial feast and purloining the Elixir of Longevity. Highly enraged the Emperor forthwith dispatches a hundred thousand heavenly soldiers to pursue him (chapter 5). The action continues to rise to a very high pitch until Monkey is defeated by Erh-lang through the help of Lao Tzŭ's magical snare (chapter 6) and, after the vain attempts of execution, pushed into the Crucible of the Eight Trigrams. There he is, contrary to expectation, tempered into "fiery eyes and metallic pupils." His former self consisted of a "stone" body with fine "fire" in it; but now the stone is purified and fire refined. The two mutually conquering elements are miraculously united into one to give forth an extremely invincible force. So when he jumps out of the Crucible, his magical power, having become much greater than ever before, almost turns heaven upside down. The Emperor, in great "consternation," appeals to the Patriarch Buddha for an immediate measure. The action reaches its turning point when Buddha comes. After a little wager, the self-conceited Monkey is humiliated under the Mountain of the Five Elements. At the Great Banquet for Peace, with which ends the episode, the cosmos restores its peace and perfect order.

It must have been noted that the Jade Emperor is "astounded" or "consternated" thrice throughout the episode. We might thus divide the action into three stages. The atmosphere is gradually intensified until it reaches the crucial moment at the third time. Between these stages of action there are suspensions, rises and falls. Thus viewed the episode can be said to be a very complete piece of short story. Though named "Aware-of-Emptiness," Monkey fails ironically to grasp its real intent, and becomes true to it. His pride and arrogance, if judged solely from this episode, indicate the propensity of a tragic hero. To achieve his unquenchable desire for longevity he needs, and is in effect given an opportunity to exert through Buddha's mercy, further efforts.

Dr. Hu Shih divides the *Hsi-yu chi* into three parts [see excerpt dated 1942]: Part I includes chapters 1-7; Part II embraces chapters 8-12; and Part III consists of the rest of the novel. The novel structurally considered, however, the episode discussed above and those episodes contained in chapters 8-12 should be regarded as its exposition on the ground that they are meant to introduce the pilgrims separately and state the motivation of the quest for the True Scriptures. Chapters 8-12, which comprise five episodes at least, relate how the Bodhisattva Kuan-yin, under the orders of Tathāgata, comes to the East to find an appropriate scripture pilgrim and prepares for the future encounters of the five elements (chapter 8), how Ch'en Kuang-lei and his wife meet with their misfortunes, how Tripitaka revenges his father's murderers (chapter 9), how Wei Chêng executes the Dragon King of the Ching River in a dream (chapter 10), how the T'ang emperor T'ai-tsung tours the Region of Death, how Liu Ch'üan voluntarily presents melons and fruits to the Kings of Hades (chapter 11), how Tripitaka responds to the imperial commission to procure the Scriptures (chapter 12), and the like. Contrary to the brisk tempo of the first episode created by Monkey's restless energy, magical virtuosity and supernatural tricks performed specially in his battle with Erh-lang, these episodes, which revolve primarily around the element water together with the poetic debate between fisherman and woodcutter as well as the melancholy atmosphere of the Underworld, are slow in pace, murky in tone and, as matters of details are too many, loose in structure.

As the exposition of the novel, the episodes in chapters 1-12 suggest, aside from the incentive of the quest, the fact that since the creation of the universe the five elements have been separated. The first of their unifications starts at the moment when Tripitaka leaves Ch'ang-an (chapter 13), and is attained when Sandy joins the pilgrimage (chapter 22). It is worthy of note that in this process of unification the five elements come to the scene in accordance with the mutually conquering order. Water respresented by Tripitaka appears first, whereas the embodiment of earth, Sandy, comes into view last. Water is granted the primacy because it is the "source of the five elements." As the "mother of the five elements," earth presents itself last to provide harmony, peace and nourishment on the journey. Thus paradoxically mutual antagonism also means mutual agreement. Since conflict is the soul of every piece of literary work, this mutually conquering order is the best way to arouse interest and suspense.

The action of the novel begins to rise with Tripitaka's departure from the Capital City, proceeds through the episodes of the Two-Forked Ridge (chapter 13), the Double-Frontier Mountain (chapter 14), the Eagle-Grief Stream (chapter 15), the Kuan-yin Hall (chapter 16), the Black-Wind Mountain (chapter 17), the Cloudy-Paths Cave (chapter 18) and makes a temporary stop when he receives the Heart Sutra from the Zen master of the Crow-Nest (chapter 19). Then it resumes its ascendancy in his passage through the Yellow-Wind Ridge (chapters 20-21) and the Flowing-Sand River (chapter 22). It again comes to a temporal rest at chapter 23, where the lascivious Pigsy, tempted by beauty and wealth, makes a fool of himself in a scene of comic relief. Soon thereafter the action persists to move upward as the pilgrims arrive at the Five-Village Temple (chapters 24-26), and drastically reaches a climactic moment when Tripitaka, deceived by the Cadaver Demon and instigated by the envious Pigsy, chastises Monkey for cruelty (chapter 27). Shortly after Monkey's dismissal, Tripitaka stumbles mistakenly into the Wave-Moon Cave (chapter 28), seized and then released. A moment later, Sandy is taken prisoner (chapter 29), the master transformed into a ferocious striped tiger, and the Dragon Horse defeated (chapter 30). The five elements are scattered.

Two illustrations from an early edition of The Journey to the West, *published about 1600.*

When Monkey is called back to defeat the monster, they are united again (chapter 31).

In the episode of the Lotus-Flower Cave (chapters 32-35), the pilgrims meet with unexpected catastrophe once again. But the poetic scene of the Treasure-Wood Temple (chapter 36) at once relieves the tension, and momently suspends the tempo. When the Ghost King visits Tripitaka at night (chapter 37) with a weird moan of dark wind flickering the lamp and blowing about the ashes, the peaceful atmosphere vanishes. The action gains its gradual ascendancy in the episodes of the Fire-Cloud Cave (chapters 40-42), the Black River (chapter 43), the Cart-Slow Kingdom (chapters 44-46), the Heaven-Reaching River (chapters 47-49), the Golden-Helmet Mountain (chapters 50-52), the Son-and-Mother River (chapter 53), the Women Kingdom of Western Liang (chapter 54) and the Lute Cave (chapter 55). For all the unforeseen disasters encountered and the inordinate anguish experienced, the pilgrims are progressively improving their relations. Their joint efforts enable them to survive the ordeals. Once when they are in the neighborhood of the Roaring Mountain, Sandy earnestly advises Tripitaka not to recite the headache spell. Another time, at the approach of the Black River, it is Sandy again that sincerely remonstrates with Pigsy to endure hardship. Sandy and Monkey keep themselves in the foreground to confront their formidable adversaries at the Black River and the Son-and-Mother River. Antagonistic as they are, Monkey (metal) and Pigsy (wood) brave the Scorpion in united

action. And it is exclusively Monkey's dharma power that defeats the fatal challenge of the demonic Taoists at the Cart-Slow Kingdom. Needless to say, Monkey's mighty resources are duly discovered and appreciated by his fellow pilgrims. Even the timid master, who is easily frightened by any inkling of danger, joins the contest of meditation of his own accord at the Cart-Slow Kingdom. Thus despite their repeated antagonism, fire (Monkey) and water (Tripitaka) practically cooperate for this once. After the episode of the Golden-Helmet Mountain, Tripitaka reposes his full trust in Monkey. Thus the pilgrims seem to have entertained so far intimate relations with one another.

Nevertheless the following incident proves otherwise. When Monkey disposes in seemingly cold blood of several brigands (chapter 56), an internal strife is engaged. Each of the pilgrims feels discontented and irritated. Their relation reaches its nadir. Then fire and water are at serious variance for the second time, again resulting in Monkey's banishment (chapter 57). After the turmoil created by the two Monkeys (chapter 58), the five elements come together once more. The incident at the Flaming Mountain (chapters 59-61) purposes to reconcile fire and water, while what happen at the Ritual-Festival Kingdom (chapters 62-63) and the T'uo-lo Village (chapter 67) are intended to portray the agreement of metal and wood. It is Pigsy that opens the road at the Ridge of Thorns (chapter 64) and clears away the dirt of the Pulpified-Persimmon Alley (chapter 67). All these incidents do contribute greatly to the unification of the five elements. Meanwhile we find in between them the idyllic interlude of the Wood-Deity Temple (chapter 64) moving at a leisurely pace. Yet this is only the lull before the impending storm; what instantly follows is the pilgrims' confrontation of dire difficulties at the counterfeit Thunderclap Temple (chapters 65-66). All the deities that come to their rescue are encompassed with perils. Monkey's might proves to be of no avail, and pierced with grief he cannot but sigh despondently and shed helpless tears. Then there succeed two scenes, which mix comicality in seriousness: one of them is the playful disposal of a Red Python at the T'uo-lo Village by Monkey and Pigsy together, while the other happens at the Vermillion-Purple Kingdom, where Monkey plays the Medico to check the King's disease and lovesickness, Pigsy and Sandy serving as pharmacists to compound medicine with the urine reluctantly contributed by the Dragon Horse (chapters 68-69). Again the situation becomes intense as master and disciples come upon a series of calamities at the Monoceros Mountain (chapters 70-71), the Gossamer-Entangling Cave (chapter 72) and the Yellow-Flower Temple (chapter 73). The action is now progressively building up to the unprecedented critical time in the entire narrative.

The challenge of the monsters of the Lion-Camel Cave is the greatest one with which the pilgrims are ever faced on their way to the Western Paradise. When they are drawing near the Cave, the Planet Venus appears in disguise to forebode the danger ahead. Then Monkey scares most of the little demons away by psychological warfare (chapter 74). However [his identity] is unluckily discovered and he is trapped in the *Yin-yang* magical bottle. After a tremendous exercise of efforts, he is able to effect his narrow escape by piercing open a small hole on it (chapter 75). Though he has succeeded in the subdual of Green-hair Lion and the Yellow-tusk Elephant, all the pilgrims are nevertheless tricked and trapped. Monkey gets away singly, but the rumour has it that Tripitaka is eaten alive. In his despondence he appeals to Buddha, who promises to intervene and, with overwhelming powers, turns the scale (chapter 77). As has been pointed out, each of the episodes in the *Hsi-yu chi* is almost always self-contained. For this reason we can find a number of climaxes in it. The most conspicuous among them are the thrice interventions of Buddha in person to subjugate the wily Monkey (chapter 7), the counterfeit Monkey (chapter 58) and the Garuda Monster (chapter 77). When these monsters are acting lawlessly, heaven and earth are thrown into violent confusion. Once Buddha comes to interfere, the universe returns to its regular order in no time. It is the peripety for the five elements to be re-united. Of the three crises, Monkey's rebel, dramatic as it is, is the smallest in scale. Since the two Monkeys are roughly equal in their feats, the disturbance they have caused becomes more serious. In comparison the havoc raised by the Garuda Monster turns out to be the most serious since its magical power is much greater than Monkey's, that the situation is awkwardest for him, and that the universe becomes the most chaotic. It is worthy of note further that this episode is placed at the three fourth of the entire narrative; to a master hand of fiction, this is exactly the most appropriate spot for climax. Though there are yet adverse circumstances lying ahead, the intensity is being gradually alleviated.

The rest of the events are meant to depict the increasing understanding and mutual trust among the pilgrims. Learning that the King of the Bhikshu Country wishes to eat his heart and liver, the consternated Tripitaka is compelled to follow Mon-

key's ruse to exchange their appearances (chapters 78-79), an exchange which suggests change of positions as well as the elements they are embodied. Despite Monkey's repeated warning when they are pursuing the road in a dark pine forest, the saintly monk takes a she-monster in disguise along, and as a result is twice trapped in the Bottomless Cave (chapters 81-83). In the ensuing combat of Monkey and Pigsy against the Rat Monster there is a mixture of danger and humor. Again Tripitaka is captured at the foot of the Mist-Hiding Mountain. Realizing that his master is in mortal danger, Monkey becomes so sad as to shed tears when Pigsy advises him not to. Once when Pigsy wailed over the master's fate at the Yellow-Wind Mountain (chapter 24), Monkey told him to spirit up; but now Monkey is bewailing himself. Thus metal (Monkey) and wood (Pigsy) also change positions. Such incidents are significant in that these hostile elements—fire and water, metal and wood—are becoming conjoined.

Twice in front of the Interlocking-Ring Cave (chapters 84-86), the Leopard Monster tries to cheat the disciples by starting a rumour that Tripitaka was eaten alive. Formerly under the circumstances Pigsy would invariably move a break-up of the group. But now all of them in one mind swear to avenge their master. The pilgrims are closely knit. Monkey assumes the central role in the admonition for good deeds, which brings torrential rain to the Phoenix-God Country (chapter 87), as well as the rejection of marriage proposal at the T'ien-chu Kingdom (chapters 93-95). The three disciples together are active in the impartment of martial arts to the three princes of the Jade-Flower District (chapter 84), in the battle engaged at the Leopard-Head Mountain (chapters 89-90), and in the combat at the Blue-Dragon Mountain (chapters 91-92). While Monkey enjoys the confidence of his master and brothers, Tripitaka [is] loved and respected by his disciples. After the ordeal they suffer at the Copper-Platform Prefecture (chapters 96-97), they eventually arrive at the Holy Mountain. Tripitaka forsakes his earthly frame, crossing the Cloud-Transcending Stream in a bottomless boat, and surmounts his mortal fate (chapter 98). The dénouement of the novel comes when master and disciples through mutual support and reliance are rewarded with final exaltation in the presence of Buddha (chapter 99), and are harmonized (chapter 100). After such a prolonged process of adjustment the five elements represented by Tripitaka, Monkey, Pigsy and Sandy are ultimately united into one.

Seen from the above analysis, the stages of unity, separation and unity as the underlying structure of the *Hsi-yu chi* can be applied not only to the larger scheme of the novel, but almost always to each of the episodes therein, except that the unity at the end of the entire narrative designates a return to the state of Chaos, whereas the unity within each episode refers to the temporally renewed harmony of the pilgrims. (pp. 170-80)

At first glance the *Hsi-yu chi* seems to be structureless. Yet when we weigh the intensity of tone and atmosphere presented in each of its episodes, we can trace its natural stages of development. Like most of the structurally close-knit fiction, it consists of an exposition (chapters 1-12), ascending action (chapters 13-73), climax (chapters 74-77), falling action (chapters 78-98) and dénouement (chapters 99-100). There are rhythmic waves of poetic scenes to relax the tension as well as intensifying atmospheres to build up the climactic moment. All these are closely associated with the relations of the five elements. Meanwhile threading through the entire narrative is the theme of "emptiness" which is made manifest in the course of "awareness." *Everyman,* a representative of the ecclesiastic drama of the medieval period, dramatizes the self-saving of the soul by virtuous deeds; its moral teaching, however, is too obvious and too weighty. Again John Bunyan's *The Pilgrim's Progress*, which deals with man's journey through life to heaven or hell in novel form, is allegorically shallow and morally preoccupied. Because of the superb skill of its author, the didactic overtone of the *Hsi-yu chi* is drastically reduced. We may read it in different attitudes. If we reject it for its interest in the "six ways of reincarnation" as well as the idea of the "correspondence between heaven and man," we are biased in our judgement. If, on the other hand, we accept it only for its combination of beauty with absurdity, of profundity with nonsense, we are lacking in refined taste. An appropriate attitude is to appreciate with wisdom, apart from the lyrical beauty, epic grandeur, and verbal humour woven in the fabric of the narrative, the superb manipulation of its theme and structure. Needless to say this is what our author has satisfactorily achieved, and this again is what the *Hsi-yu chi* depends upon to command the interest and admiration of all time. (p. 186)

> *Chang Ching-erh, "The Structure and Theme of the 'Hsi-yu chi'," in* Tamkang Review, *Vol. XI, No. 2, Winter, 1980, pp. 169-88.*

DORE J. LEVY (essay date 1984)

[*In the following excerpt, Levy compares the translations of Wu's novel by Arthur Waley and Anthony C. Yu and offers a general evaluation of the work's literary significance.*]

The mystery of the anonymous author of *The Journey to the West* has never quite been solved. The most likely candidate to emerge is Wu Ch'eng-en, a minor official under the Ming dynasty with a modest reputation as a poet and perhaps a greater one as a satirist, but his authorship has not been proven conclusively. This kind of anonymity is a feature of other important works of Chinese fiction. It seems strange that authors of such remarkable works should remain resolutely obscure. It is as if Ariosto could not finally be identified as the author of *Orlando Furioso,* or as if Fielding had published *Tom Jones* anonymously and without being identified as the author by any of his contemporaries. It is true that the *hsiao-shuo* or novel in China was regarded in the early stages with the same kind of suspicion as its European counterpart. Certainly the Chinese model displays a similar vernacular idiom and ironic intent, and perhaps anonymity ensured the novelist greater freedom of expression. Whatever the author's actual identity, we are in the presence of a polymath of Chinese learning, a virtuoso of literary composition, and an absolutely wicked wit. (pp. 508-09)

One of the most distinctive features of the Chinese novel in general and *The Journey to the West* in particular is the frequent occurrence of poems in the narrative, not just as poetic speeches and rhetorical descriptions, but as an integral part of the flow of the prose narrative. This is both the result of literary conventions responding to the flexibility of the Chinese poetic language, and a demonstration of the author's literary virtuosity. *The Journey to the West* contains some 750 poems in its hundred chapters, representing almost every poetic genre in Chinese literature. These act in the service of the narrative as a whole, enriching the description, the action, and the dialogue.

The use of poetic narrative is a unique and delightful feature of Chinese fiction, but one that has posed problems for Western audiences and translators. Even Waley, whose own poetic genius so enhanced his translations of Chinese and Japanese poetry, shied away from the poetry in *Monkey*. Yu has plunged gamely into the enterprise, and while he cannot always project the subtle nuances of the poetic forms, he has succeeded in producing an integrated and satisfying text with all the poems intact. This fidelity adds immeasurably to our ability to appreciate a work of literature so different from anything in our own tradition.

Another distinctive aspect of the novel which is intimated in Waley's abridgement but can only be fully appreciated in the complete version is the underlying allegorical structure of *The Journey to the West.* We can recognize simple elements of the allegory in *Monkey,* such as personifications and the nature of the pilgrimage itself. The complete novel, however, participates in an intentional mode of composition similar to that which characterizes such works as Dante's *Commedia* and Spenser's *The Faerie Queene;* that is, the functioning of symbols, action, and language in a text in such a way as to project complex patterns of meaning beyond the literal level of the text. The author does utilize many of the more obvious conventions of allegorical composition: personifications and symbolic names (the Many-eyed Fiend, Demon Lord of a Hundred Eyes, gives a lesson on the perils of perception in Chapter 73), symbolic iconography (Pa-chieh's mighty muckrake), and chapter titles, many of which are epigrams which indicate the significance of the chapters' contents. These features provide a concrete apparatus which serves to guide the reader on the pilgrimage. There is also, as might be expected, a plethora of technical and symbolic Buddhist terminology, but in addition, the text responds to the intellectual climate of the author's time in the integration of Taoist and Confucian elements in the pilgrims' spiritual universe. In short, Buddhism provides the framework of the mission, which in its fulfillment embraces the diversity of all Chinese thought. The journey is a physical symbol of the process of karma and redemption, and an allegory in which spiritual processes dominate over ascetic or alchemical ones; indeed, over institutionalized spiritual seeking of any kind. The signficance of this process extends well beyond the boundaries of the text in time and space, and transcends the cultural context of the work with direct ease. (pp. 509-10)

Waley's *Monkey* and Yu's *The Journey to the West* represent radically different approaches to the novel and to the enterprise of translation, but considered together provide provocative insights into the evolution of our understanding of Chinese fiction. The shortcoming of *Monkey* is that it seems, by the episodes selected and their mode of presentation, to cater to a popular notion of the novel rather than representing the novel itself. In this, Waley was conforming to the views of a new generation of Chinese critics opposed to the traditional, complex interpretations of the work. Dr. Hu Shih, one of this century's most influential proponents of Chinese language reform and the introduction of Chinese literature to the West, was delighted with Waley's abridgement, since it conformed to his preference for considering the novel in terms of the popular tradition. In his introduction to the first American edition of *Monkey,* Hu wrote, "Freed from all kinds of allegorical interpretations by Buddhist, Taoist, and Confucian commentators, *Monkey* is simply a book of good humor, profound nonsense, good-natured satire and delightful entertainment" [see excerpt dated 1942]. . . . Hu's pronouncement is misleading in precisely the way *Monkey* is misleading. *The Journey to the West* is no more a "folk novel" than Boccaccio's *Decameron* is a collection of "folk tales." Both have generous helpings of material from folk traditions, but this material is integrated into larger contexts, elegantly and subtly structured. By rejecting a major part of the traditional interpretations, Hu and Waley risked rejecting a major part of the novel, and ultimately its integrity as a work of art. *Monkey* is delightful but limited. It captures the fun, but does not touch the profundity.

Yu's first commitment is to render as faithfully as possible the entire text, but he also carries with him the constant awareness of the gap between this translation and the original. (p. 514)

Yu's literary scruples and personal enthusiasm occasionally combine to produce some rather self-conscious effects, and in striving to reflect the exuberance and variety of the original he occasionally produces a semantic misfit. For instance, in Chapter 54, the pilgrims attend an uproarious royal betrothal banquet supposedly in Tripitaka's honor. Pa-chieh is in his element, and when running dry hollers, "Bring some big steins! After we drink a few more steins, each of us will attend to our business." . . . The Chinese *kuang* is actually a cup made of horn, and while Pa-chieh is never elegant in his manners, this palace is not a beer-garden. Similarly, bandits block the pilgrims' way in Chapter 97 and threaten, "Quickly give us some toll money, and your lives will be spared! If only half a no escapes from your mouth, each of you will face the cutlass." . . . The Chinese *tao* is the most general word for handheld blade, and considering that the pilgrims are probably several hundred miles from the nearest ocean, another kind of blade might have been more appropriate. There are also a few jarring patches of informal usage which are questionably justified by the Chinese and produce effects in English more nonsensical than nonchalant.

Such observations pale in the face of the marvelous flow of the text as a whole. Even with worse faults than these, a complete translation must be regarded as actually more faithful to the original than any abridgement. Yu's translation is infinitely more faithful than any previous version in form, content, and even spirit. In addition, his textual notes are careful and comprehensive, dealing with esoterica and "in-jokes" with equal clarity. Yu has made his translation as useful to scholars of Chinese literature as it is accessible to non-specialists, although for the sake of both one could wish for a glossary of names and the unavoidable Sanskrit and Pali terms, as it is often impossible to remember them and discouraging to hunt for them in the notes.

Literary translation is one of the most constructive forms of cultural embassy. Professor Yu has produced a translation which allows the *The Journey to the West* to take its place as a masterwork of prose fiction for the consideration of Western literary scholars as well as Far Eastern enthusiasts. Exotic and magical as the journey is, the underlying heroic and spiritual themes are not limited to its fantastic context. As a work of allegory, *The Journey to the West*'s structure of multiple senses informs an oddly-assorted pilgrimage with wisdom, humor, and humanity. As a work of fiction, this quest provides, in the words of Tripitaka's favorite textual companion, the *Heart Sutra*, "O what an awakening!" (pp. 514-15)

> *Dore J. Levy, "A Quest of Multiple Senses: Anthony C. Yu's 'The Journey to the West'," in* The Hudson Review, *Vol. XXXVII, No. 3, Autumn, 1984, pp. 507-15.*

PAUL V. MARTINSON (essay date 1985)

[*In the following excerpt, Martinson studies the interplay and thematic religious significance of comedy, symbol, and allegory in* The Journey to the West.]

While a work of fiction, [*The Journey to the West*] is also a major work in Chinese religious literature. Not only does the prehistory of this novel present a long and complicated background of oral narration with roots that sink deep into folk religion, much of this background now no longer recoverable, its posthistory also is long and complex. Perhaps no fictional writing in China has had a more profound socioreligious impact on the Chinese mind than has this novel. It is a high-water mark both in Chinese literary history and in Chinese socioreligious history. (p. 378)

At the risk of oversimplifying a terribly complex work I suggest that its religious import can be summarized as affirmation of the values of vitality, emptiness, and integrity conveyed to us in the three modes of fantasy, comedy, and allegory. (p. 379)

Attention to the detail of phenomena in the novel is overpowering. These phenomena belong to either the natural or the fantastic world. The hitherto, to my knowledge, unstudied theriology of the novel is a prime example of the latter. In the case of the former, while on this fantastic journey our attention is forever drawn to the exuberant detail of the natural world.

Poetry plays a particularly important role here. One of the marked achievements of [Anthony C. Yu's] translation is its rendering of the considerable poetic segments of the novel. The narrative is served in a variety of ways by this poetry— it furthers narrative, it comments on action and character, and above all it describes. Only the reader of the novel can appreciate this latter. The author "must be considered one of the most skilled descriptive poets in all Chinese literature." All this contributes to a sense of the "overpowering immediacy of nature." . . . (p. 380)

But if the sensuous richness of nature is ever before us, even more so is the phantasmagoria of exotic monsters and unearthly places. The extensive attention devoted to these monsters has one fundamental rationale—these monsters are all symbols of the quest for vitality. The pervasive themes of Taoist alchemy, the permutations of yin and yang as well as of the hexagrams of the *I-ching,* and the attention accorded throughout the novel to eating of all kinds—whether the gluttony of a Pa-chieh (one of the pilgrims) or the cannibalism of the less kindly monsters, all are a part of this vital quest.

In the internal alchemy of Taoism the "emphasis is upon integration" . . . or, rather, vital integration. To state it broadly, the goal is to prevent the outflow, and therefore loss, of vital energies, so as to rather cultivate them, as well as to appropriate energies from without, that by means of the integration of these a vital center of energy might take form and enable one to transcend the limitations of a less vital existence.

These monsters depict the upsurge of nature toward ever-increased vitality. This upsurge is ambiguous: on the one hand, it is an upsurge toward the human form of existence, regardless of whether the beastly origin is chthonic or celestial; yet, on the other, it seeks a transcendence of the limits of the human condition, particularly the conditions of weakness and mortality. As to the former aspect of this upsurge, there is no evidence of a movement from the human to the monstrous, an important theme in Western theriology.

Most of the monsters encountered are in pseudo-human form, though at the moment of supreme crisis they are often unable to maintain the integration of energies this requires and collapse back into their monstrous or, in many cases, their original animal or vegetable form. Yet, the alchemic goal is to overcome this potential for collapse.

Pilgrim Sun symbolizes the ambiguity of this upsurge well. Originally a stone atop a mountain, this stone was energized by the confluent forces of the universe. Gradually, it began to transcend its stony limits, split open, and yielded a fantastic stone monkey. But this monkey, having become a king of monkeys, soon enough laments his mortal state. He then begins his own minor pilgrimage and goes out in quest of a Taoist master. Eventually he learns the various arts of internal alchemy that will later be put to good use in the major pilgrimage of the novel. While he never becomes more than a demi-human, his powers are enormous. His ambition, however, vaults higher yet. After an effort to take heaven by storm, and arrogating to himself the title "Great Sage Equal to Heaven, " he is subdued by the Buddha and encased under the Five Phases mountain, formed by cosmic energies. It is from this mountainous mass that he is later rescued by the pilgriming Hsuan-tsang. From that point on this restless, energetic demi-human monkey is subordinated to the very human quest of Hsuan-tsang, a quest for final enlightenment. This subordination to the human pilgrim is the redeeming element in Pilgrim Sun's erstwhile, and ultimately self-destructive, quest for ever-increasing vitality.

This vital upsurge, best exemplified in the boisterous energy of the monsters and the singular attention to the alchemical arts of Taoism, obviously has its limits. Fantasy turns into comedy when it meets up with the Buddhist doctrine of emptiness.

Clearly the Buddhist concept of emptiness is essential to this entire fictional construction. Despite the cavalier treatment of history, the fact of Hsuan-tsang's (or Tripitaka, which is how I shall refer to him below) historic trek inevitably imbues the novel with a certain subliminal seriousness and purpose. Yet, strangely, it is not the sutras acquired at the end of the journey that are important, but the sutra acquired by oral recitation at the commencement of the journey—the transmission of the *Heart Sutra* by the Crow's Nest Ch'an (Zen) Master. On encountering him Tripitaka anxiously queries how far to Buddha's abode. Assured by the Ch'an Master that it is very far indeed, he presents the oral recitation to the disquieted Tripitaka with the comment that, "All those mara ["evil"] hindrances along the way are hard to dispel. . . . When you meet these mara hindrances, recite the sutra and you will not suffer any injury or harm." . . . Although we are told more than once that Tripitaka was enlightened about the truth of emptiness and form, and despite the fact that he constantly meditates on it, his actual and utter incomprehension of the emptiness of all phenomena is patent throughout. It is Pilgrim Sun who alone comprehends its meaning and who must continually instruct Tripitaka, though to no avail. Had Tripitaka comprehended he could have made the journey alone; indeed, he would have arrived at his destination instantly.

Since the doctrine of emptiness reduces all phenomena to appearance only, everything can be taken in a lighthearted manner. This is the supreme achievement of Pilgrim Sun, whose religious name is Wu-k'ung ("awake to emptiness"). Humor and impiety are his hallmark. No sooner had the Crow's Nest Ch'an Master returned to his high perch than Wu-k'ung uses his rod to try and knock the nest down, claiming that some comments of the Ch'an Master had been insulting to them. Whenever it seems the novel might take a serious turn, Wu-k'ung is there to return it to the ridiculous, or, if he is uncharacteristically serious, others will perform that task. Everything becomes the proper subject for mockery—and this

includes not only the continual political satire of the novel but the mockery of all celestial beings, all holy rites—whether orthodox, heterodox, or whatever. Even Kuan-yin and the Buddha are not spared some degree of mockery.

Pilgrim Sun is the ultimate comedian, and he exploits all occasions for their satiric and comic worth. Nevertheless, Pa-chieh (tamed hog monster in the entourage named "eight commandments," the other two being Sha Monk and the white horse, both of watery origins) and Tripitaka are fit comic characters in their own right, but only by default. Pa-chieh is so ugly, so clumsy, so naive, so slothful, so crude, and so driven by his appetites that his every act arouses laughter. Tripitaka is so serious, yet so fearful, so preoccupied with his own petty comforts, so peevish, and so religiously "straight" that one can only chuckle. To see him sit in stiff embarrassment as female demons make their advances and his bald head turns red is cause enough for mirth.

By means of this comic mode every moment in the novel becomes a moment that transcends the phenomenal. Hsia surely grasps the central meaning of this comic quality when he writes: "It is consonant with the Buddhist insistence on detachment that laughter should be adopted as the ultimate mode of viewing the world. In the novel, therefore, comedy mediates between myth and allegory" [see excerpt dated 1968]. And, thus, we laugh our way through the story.

At a number of points we have already trespassed on the domain of allegory. The fantastic and the comic both attend to the particular. The fantastic leads us ever deeper into the inexhaustible fecundity of particulars—one exotic beast follows another. The comic examines each particular for its specific incongruity, so that every incident, every detail, is subject to its own unique humor. But allegory is very different from these two. Allegory marshals the particulars to serve the purposes of the typical. Particulars lose their uniqueness as they become likened to some other set of particulars, and the reader begins to discern significant congruities.

The most obvious allegorical element is the idea of pilgrimage itself. As we have already seen, the pilgrimage proper, which is a quest for scriptures, and the alchemical quest of the monsters are in continual counterpoint. This double quest is what makes the novel possible.

At the same time, it is no mere onward pilgrimage; it is also inward. (pp. 380-83)

In this light, the figure of Tripitaka takes on new significance. He is not simply the dim-witted priest puffing along on a seemingly hopeless trek; he is rather a symbol of human consciousness refracted into its various modes: Tripitaka symbolizes moral purpose; Pa-chieh symbolizes craving and love of the domestic life; Pilgrim Sun symbolizes intelligence, ambition, impetuosity, and so forth; the nefarious monsters, of course, symbolize the underlying attachment to life. All of these are at war with one another in our state of primal ignorance.

These psychological symbolisms are often made quite explicit. At one point Pilgrim Sun meets up with an exact replica of himself. Not even Kuan-yin, or the Buddha himself, let alone his companions, can discern the true from the false. In fact, both are Wu-k'ung. This split in his personality follows yet another banishment of him from the journey by Tripitaka because of his irrepressible rascality. We hardly need to read the explanation: "Thus the Great Sage Sun harbored feelings of hostility, while Pa-chieh and Sha Monk, too, were swayed by enmity. In fact, master and disciples, as they followed the main road westward, only appeared to be cordial.'' . . . The reader, of course, is led to ask whether Wu-k'ung is going ultimately to be the rebellious (spurious) or the submitting (true) mind. The novel is replete with such psychological allegory.

It is at this point that the pervasive alchemical imagery of the novel has its most important and complex role to play. It has always been recognized that this is so. ''The Taoist elements serve . . . frequently as an aid to reveal to the reader the true nature of the fellow pilgrims, to help define their essential relationships, and to advance the action of the narrative itself.'' . . . Yu, both in the introduction and in the notes, has aided us immensely in the decipherment, one of his most impressive contributions to the critical interpretation of this novel. Yet for all its obtrusiveness, enigmas remain. More work needs to be done. (pp. 383-84)

More than any other, Sun Wu-k'ung sums up the triple meaning of the fantastic, the comic, and the allegorical. It is, we might say, by allegory that he is saved. To keep him subdued, Kuan-yin sealed a golden fillet about his head which, when Tripitaka recited a secret spell, would slowly crush his head. Thus ''the Monkey of the Mind'' is subdued, and thus his successful acquisition of vitality while yet an untamed monster, together with his comic insight into reality, make possible the successful pilgrimage of an all too peevish and petty human monk through phenomena to reality. The due reward of all five in the troupe is to be canonized at the last.

This monumental work, now made available in its entirety in translation, awaits the scholarly attention that is its due. Without it our study and interpretation not only of the literary but also of the religious mind of Chinese civilization will be impoverished, and we ourselves will be the losers. (p. 385)

Paul V. Martinson, ''Buddhist Pilgrim, Immortal Beast,'' in The Journal of Religion, *Vol. 65, No. 3, July, 1985, pp. 378-85.*

DORE J. LEVY (essay date 1987)

[*In the following excerpt, Levy compares Wu's depiction of female-dominated society in* The Journey to the West *with that of Edmund Spenser in* The Faerie Queene.]

Edmund Spenser's *The Faerie Queene* and *The Journey to the West* (a Chinese *hsiao-shuo*, or work of prose fiction, in 100 chapters dating from the end of the sixteenth century) have provocative similarities beyond the contemporaneity of their authors and the close dates of publication of the versions we read today. The greatest of their similarities is that both narratives are long works of sustained allegory; that is, both works participate in an intentional mode of composition where symbols, action, and language all function to project complex patterns of meaning beyond the literal level of the text. They are also bound by a theme of quest and by a sense of physical and spiritual progression on the part of the protagonists, which is achieved through their endurance of a series of adventures and trials. Culturally unrelated though the heroes are, and diverse as are the aims of their quests, the impulse to build a sense of progression toward spiritual perfection through trials and experience is the same in both texts. It is a fundamental aspect of allegorical narrative.

These texts offer many episodes that correspond strikingly in terms of subject matter or form of adversity met by the protagonists. The episodes to be examined in this essay are the adventures in the kingdoms of women encountered by Artegall (the hero of Book V of *The Faerie Queene*) and by Tripitaka and his disciples in *The Journey to the West*. These are societies in which women assume roles typical of men in familiar social structures, including or perhaps especially military and governmental positions. There are significant differences in the premises on which these two kingdoms are founded. Radigone is a city in which men are subjugated by vengeful and rebellious women who are Amazonian warriors. Hsi-liang nu-kuo (''The Women's Kingdom of Western Liang'') is a country mysteriously without men, the women performing all public and domestic tasks and reproducing magically by drinking the water of the Child-and-Mother River (*Tsu-mu ho*). There are also differences in the positions of these episodes in their respective narratives, which influence their significance and interpretation. In both works, however, for male protagonists in an allegorical search for themselves, women without men are a challenge to the order of society, and to individual senses of identity. Countries of women also challenge female protagonists in both works, and for many of the same reasons. The societies of women must be understood by the heroes and heroines before they can fully understand the role of sexuality in the natural order, and its importance to their own role in society. In terms of the positions of these episodes in the quests of the protagonists, the degree to which males or females can cope with the untypical order is an indication of their spiritual maturity.

Incidental parallels between the two countries of women in *The Faerie Queene* and *The Journey to the West* abound. The countries of women themselves, dream visions, men stopped in mid-journey by aggressive females unaccustomed to acknowledging male authority, men's embarrassment in female roles (Artegall's dress and apron, Tripitaka's and Pa-chieh's pregnancies), are highly suggestive but perhaps coincidental similarities of action or motif. The thematic parallels which underlie the two quests may be more significant: weakness and failure of personal resources in moments of crisis, the need for outside help and the sense to know when it is needed, the need to ''fight fire with fire'' to overcome adversity either by ruse or by strength, and the didactic import of the encounters for the future of the quest. What the heroes learn from their adventures in the countries of women may be different, but is this because there is actually something different to be learned, or because what the heroes are capable of learning at the given stages of their quests is different? We should bear in mind that both adventures are midway trials, incidental to the pursuit of larger quests. Therefore, although these experiences have important ramifications for the protagonists, they are but part of an education which, when completed, will naturally bring them to the fulfillment of their quests.

The subject of Book V of *The Faerie Queene* is Justice. The quest set for Artegall, the champion of Justice, reflects the necessity of combining right with might, and of knowing what their proper combinations may be, in order to achieve this most difficult of social goals. (pp. 218-20)

In Artegall's world, justice should *not* be blind but should exercise great powers of discernment. In this Artegall shows promise, forcing Sir Sangliere to bear his shame before him in the form of his lady's severed head, restoring the horse Brigadore . . . to his master Guyon, and settling the property dispute between the brothers Bracidas and Amidas. (pp. 220-21)

The powers of discernment and the ability to distinguish true from false, so fundamental to Artegall's quest, are equally important to the pilgrims in *The Journey to the West (Hsi-yu chi)*. Here these abilities are also tested by opportunities for self-delusion, self-restraint, and sexual temptation. The chapters about the Women's Kingdom of Western Liang, 53-55, are organized as three discrete episodes in the three stages of their journey through the region. This is by no means the pilgrims' only trial by sexual temptation. In Chapter 23, long before their arrival in the Women's Kingdom, Pa-chieh, the second disciple of Tripitaka, is befooled by a lovely and wealthy widow and her three bewitching daughters. In this case, the temptresses are really virtuous boddhisattvas who have taken these seductive forms in order to test the worldly detachment of the pilgrims. Pa-chieh fails miserably in upholding his priestly vows, and is hung upside down in a tree in a magic net he mistakes for a wedding garment. Most of the supernatural temptresses, however, are wicked and potentially harmful. Because Tripitaka's lofty spiritual attainments have given him powers and protection beyond the lot of ordinary mortals, the demons seek to eat a piece of his flesh or to draw out his semen (virtuously unspilled through ten incarnations), so that they may absorb his essence and attain immortality. The "White-bone Demon" (*Pai-ku fu-jen*) in Chapter 27 disguises herself as a child, a lovely maiden, an old woman, and finally a distinguished-looking old man to lull the pilgrims' suspicions and give her a chance for a bite of perfected flesh. In Chapters 72-74 all the pilgrims are frustrated by a bevy of seven spider spirits who embarrass Tripitaka, elude Sun Wu-kung (better known as "Monkey" from Waley's abridged translation of the same name), and divert Pa-chieh (Waley's "Pigsy") in their communal bath. Tripitaka is often sought as a "husband" by scheming demons, and it is these advances made with "honorable" intentions that are most difficult to resist. The Apricot Fairy, a tree spirit who snuggles up to Tripitaka under the moon on Bramble Ridge in Chapter 64, is so susceptible to his poetry and so flatters him with her praise that the T'ang monk nearly comes to grief. The Jade Hare in Chapters 93-95 kidnaps the princess of the Kingdom of India and takes her place, seeking to obtain Tripitaka as a husband by precisely the same method employed by his own mother in choosing his father in Chapter 9; namely, by tossing an embroidered ball down onto the hat of the first man in the street who catches her fancy. In this case, of course, the false princess has carefully manipulated the pilgrims into danger, and only by the wily intelligence of Sun Wu-kung is the rightful princess restored, and the not entirely reluctant Tripitaka set back on the path to enlightenment.

Even without these later trials, by the time the pilgrims reach the Women's Kingdom they are not inexperienced with sexual temptation. The adventures here surprise them by teaching that relations between men and women are not confined to sexual relations, and so to treat all women in these terms is to fall into error as serious as other lapses in judgment. Certainly this episode contains the most and greatest variety of women in the book. Different aspects of the monks' inevitably clichéd attitudes toward women are examined in the three episodes. In his commentary edition of *The Journey to the West,* Chang Shu-shen interprets the three chapters as allegories of diverse problems of "appetite":

> This episode, taken in its entirety, may be examined in three parts. The first section is the Child-and-Mother River, which tells of errors of "drinking." The second section is the country of Western Liang,

which examines errors of "eating." The third section is [about] the Cave of the Lute, and this chapter combines the preceding ideas . . . Now, although the original purpose of eating and drinking is to preserve life, *this* kind of ["eating and drinking"] may, on the contrary, injure life. It is almost a matter of knowing that one has a mouth and a stomach but not knowing that they have a place in the larger pattern of things, from which [knowledge] one could avoid error.

(pp. 225-27)

Tripitaka and his disciples have already been warned about the Women's Kingdom of Western Liang in Chapter 48, when Old Man Ch'en tells them tales of the land beyond the Heaven-Reaching River (*T'ung ti'ien ho*). Unfortunately, here forewarned is not forearmed. The chapter title informs the reader to expect "female troubles" as soon as they enter the borders: "The Zen Master, taking food, was demonically conceived; Yellow Hag brings water to dissolve the perverse pregnancy." The Buddhist pilgrims' lack of experience in dealing with females is immediately apparent, as their powers of discernment do not avail against the hazards of a women's country. When Tripitaka and the ever-greedy Pa-chieh succumb to a cool draught from the Child-and-Mother River, even Pilgrim Sun attributes their subsequent morning sickness to chill. Their horror upon discovering their true condition is made more ironic by the implications for their priestly vows as well as for their manhood: Buddhist monks adhere to strict injunctions against consuming flesh and the taking of life. Their unwitting error implies the former, and their desperation for a cure the latter. The earthy proprietress of the Male Reception House (*Ying-yang kuan-tzu*) informs them that the only cure is water of the Abortion Stream (*Lo-t'ai ch'uan*) from the Child Destruction Cave (*P'o-erh tung*) in the Male-Undoing Mountain (*Lieh-yang shan*). Obviously, "undoing the male element" (*lieh-yang*) will undo a pregnancy, although when the pregnant one happens to be male, it suggests a lack of sensitivity toward the need for male restraint in a land where there are no men at all. Even "those who have left the family" have not left behind the need for sympathy and understanding for the rest of the social order. (pp. 227-28)

Tripitaka and Pa-chieh must take only a small sip of the antidote, enough to dissolve the agonizing pregnancy but not so much as to dissolve their original vital organs. Tripitaka's and Pa-chieh's pregnancies are like Artegall's dress and apron; all are physical symbols of loss of male identity and power. At the end of these ordeals, a sense of the importance and security of masculinity, even to a monk, is restored. Buoyed along by a new sense of male selfhood, the pilgrims advance to the capital city of the Women's Kingdom.

Unfortunately, this newly-realized masculine potency is not yet linked with reciprocal respect for the role of the feminine in society. To his acute embarrassment, Tripitaka attracts women in droves on the streets. Chang Shu-shen's introductory remarks to Chapter 54 state the issue here as one of proportion:

> Hsi-liang is a rich place, and the subjects of the Women's Kingdom are people of various appetites. The preceding chapter described "thirst" in order to illustrate that [what seem to be] small injuries may actually be great ones. This chapter described "hunger" and shows that what [seem to be] trifling offenses may indeed be grave ones. (my translation)

The arrival of the pilgrims is announced to the queen, who interprets this occurence in terms of a dream which seemed to foretell the coming of the T'ang monk. The queen regards Tripitaka's arrival as a sign from Heaven that she is to establish the natural order, based on male fertility rather than magic, in her kingdom by voluntarily ceding her throne to the man, becoming his wife and raising a family. . . . (pp. 228-29)

The pilgrims have no ready response to the queen's innocent and, except for the fact that her proposed bridegroom is a monk, perfectly proper offer of marriage. Tripitaka finds himself dreadfully embarrassed and unable to refuse, unable even to respond on his own behalf. Pilgrim then devises an elaborate ruse to deceive the queen by first seeming to comply with her wishes, then escaping from the wedding procession by means of his magic of immobilization. Pilgrim justifies his plan by saying, "For one thing, their lives will be preserved, and for another, your primal soul will not be hurt. This is a plot of Fleeing the Net by a False Marriage. Isn't it a doubly advantageous act?" Although the queen and her subjects are not demons at all, the pilgrims, except perhaps for Pa-chieh, feel threatened by the community and by their own unknown susceptibilities. Pa-chieh, a champion of domesticity before he became a monk, and having far more experience in such matters, gladly offers himself to the queen in place of his master. When he is delicately refused because of his frightening ugliness, he replies, in effect, "Who on earth gives a hoot if a man is *ugly*?" The queen, of course, is no more experienced than Tripitaka when it comes to understanding the facts of life.

If Pa-chieh's sexual appetites are to be denied, at least his master's apparent acquiescence allows him to gratify his appetite for food at the magnificent betrothal feast. The T'ang monk, however, finds it increasingly difficult to maintain his equilibrium. The queen is ravishingly beautiful, and discreet and respectful as well. She loves the monk and trusts him on sight, increasing his discomfiture as he reflects upon the deception he will perpetrate. The pilgrims mean to satisfy their appetite for food, at any rate, without making any return for the hospitality shown them and fully intending to break faith with trusting people. Even "those who have left the family" are expected to keep their promises to other members of society, when such agreements have been entered in good faith.

When the queen and her entourage, decoyed out of the city by Pilgrim's plan, realize that Tripitaka means to go on with his disciples after all, the queen protests vigorously in terms of the contract they have entered:

> "Royal brother darling," she cried, "I'm willing to use the wealth of my entire nation to ask you to be my husband. Tomorrow you shall ascend the tall treasure throne to call yourself king, and I am to be your queen. You have even eaten the wedding feast. Why are you changing your mind now?"

Pa-chieh bellows abuse to her in reply, as though his rejection had given him a "truer" vision of the queen, "How could we monks marry a powdered skeleton like you! Let my master go on his journey!" Apparently as a result of breaking his troth with the honorable queen, a terrible female demon appears at the moment of the pilgrims' escape and demands that Tripitaka fulfill his obligations with *her*. . . . (pp. 229-30)

The timorous monk is borne away by this whirlwind of malevolent female energy, which will give new dimensions to his fear of the feminine while it instills in him new sympathy for the role of the feminine in his own order. The T'ang monk and his disciples are victims of their own imaginations; in other words, when they underestimate the queen's capacity for understanding and treat her like a demon, a real she-demon ap-

pears to satisfy their dread. The fact that the pilgrims in the Women's Kingdom lay their plans as if the threat to them were purely sexual is also a symptom of their larger insensitivity. Pilgrim Sun, especially, might have been expected to discern the true nature of the inhabitants of the Women's Kingdom, as he is clever at sensing a "baleful aura" (*ch'i-se hsiung-wu*), and has often read the signs of danger rightly in the past. Perhaps their many encounters with demons have given the pilgrims great insight into ways to baffle and conquer them, but they have far less experience with dealing equitably with mortals from their master's order. (p. 231)

Tripitaka, at least, is filled with regret when comparison with the female demon reveals the truth of the queen to him: ". . . this fiend is not like the queen. The queen, after all, is a human being whose action is governed by propriety. This fiend is a monster spirit most capable of hurting me." He finds himself in the Cave of the Lute (*P'i-p'a tung*) in the Toxic Foe Mountain (*Tu-ti shan*). According to Chang Shu-shen, the *p'i-p'a*, (also known as the "moon lute" because of its round shape) is the key to the nature of Tripitaka's trial with this demon. He quotes an admonitory remark from the Analects of Confucius: "The music of the *p'i-p'a* is also licentious and wayward." This reference also demonstrates that here, as in Book V of *The Faerie Queene*, the issue of equity is crucial to an understanding of this trial. The term *pu-cheng*, here translated as "wayward," also means "unorthodox" or "unjust." In the eyes of Chang Shu-shen, the question of *cheng pu-cheng* ("orthodox or unorthodox" or "just or unjust") in behavior is the center of this passage in the education of the pilgrims. Tripitaka and his disciples are caught between the religious order of Buddhism, which has encouraged them in their search for self-enlightenment, and the social order, which actually demands more of the self, a sort of insight and generosity not really a part of the pilgrims' view of the secular world up to this point in the text.

Pilgrim Sun enters the cave in the form of a bee to reconnoiter. Tripitaka is pale from the demon's "poison" but puts (for him) an unusually cheerful face on the situation. He humors her at dinner by politely offering her preferred viands (buns filled with human flesh) to her. She teases him for insisting on vegetarian food, when he eagerly took "water pudding" from the Child-and-Mother River a couple of days ago, probably speaking the confusion in the monk's own mind. Tripitaka, however, has mastered his bewilderment. He sees through the demon's seductions and while he cannot repulse her, he steadfastly refuses to consent.

Pilgrim challenges the female fiend, but the fight ends badly for him when she mysteriously stings him on the head, the seat of his power—one of his most common epithets is "Mind Monkey" (*hsin hou*)—and his pride. This female victory over the Mind Monkey is a sort of emasculation, a blow to the mind felt as a blow to the body. He is totally unprepared for the excruciating pain of the sting, and is completely unmanned. Pa-chieh is repaid for jeering at the previously impervious Pilgrim's hurt the next day, when he is stung on the seat of *his* shortcomings: his mouth.

Tripitaka is actually managing to keep his equilibrium better than are his disciples. To their surprise, he resists all seductions and all threats; finally, the fiend trusses him up and throws him in a heap at the foot of her bed. Even then, she can hardly believe his resolve: "You mean to tell me that you don't want to get married and still want to go and seek scriptures?" At the disciples' moment of greatest frustration, or impotence,

Kuan-yin appears as an old woman carrying a bamboo basket. Pilgrim immediately recognizes her and implores her aid. Chang Shu-shen remarks that at least Pilgrim does not miss this reality, although he may not have always recognized Kuan-yin in the past: "He does not err in the greater matters, but then the Boddhisattva has manifested herself to him before." Kuan-yin reveals the original nature of the demon to them: she is actually a celestial scorpion who attained great spiritual power from listening to the chanting of the Buddha, but then had the temerity to sting his left hand. Even the Buddha was discomfited by that sting. Kuan-yin admits that she herself cannot touch her; compassion is not the proper response to this fiend. She refers the disciples to the Mao Star, Star Lord of the constellation Orion, as the proper master of the scorpion.

The Mao Star in his original form is a cock, and he dispatches the monster scorpion in two clucks. She reverts to her true form, and Pa-chieh cheerfully crushes her body to powder. (pp. 231-32)

While there are many possible interpretations of the significance of the appearance of a figure like the Mao Star at this particular point, it is less important to determine a one and only correct interpretation than to appreciate the texture of meaning when many possible significances are brought to bear on the text simultaneously. Here, in fact, many aspects of the Lord of Orion are operating at once, on the literal level of the text, and allegorically. The interplay of the Mao Star's spiritual and practical potencies is humorous and provocative. The context of *The Journey to the West* is admittedly fantastic, but like *The Faerie Queene*, the text itself conveys and binds together earthly and exalted wisdom.

The Mao Star returns to the sky with suitable thanks, and the disciples allow the scorpion's servants, who were enslaved by her from the Women's Kingdom, to return to their homes. Tripitaka is released, and Pilgrim sets fire to the Cave of the Lute and destroys it as utterly as Pa-chieh destroyed the body of its owner. The relieved pilgrims proceed, momentarily secure that the sinister fires and demons in their hearts which rendered them so vulnerable in this country are thus completely destroyed as well.

The incidental parallels between *The Faerie Queene* and *The Journey to the West* help to illuminate the underlying concerns which show strong thematic affinity between the two texts. Patently allegorical in intention, these texts have extraordinary unity in their interpretation of the meaning of the traumatic episodes in the countries of women. For instance, in both *The Faerie Queene* and *The Journey to the West* the protagonists' overriding concern is the completion of their quests, and the particular adventure is but part of the progress of the quest as a whole. Where Britomart wishes for Artegall to continue on his quest, the queen of the Women's Kingdom wishes to detain the man she loves. In terms of structure, the queen is parallel to the detaining Radigund, while Kuan-yin is the deliverer to whom the quest is as important as it is for the questors.

In facing unfamiliar situations, all the male protagonists fall victim to their ignorant misinterpretation of appearances, thus considerably increasing the danger of the obstacles encountered. Artegall foolishly assumes that Radigund is "like" Britomart; Tripitaka inverts this error by seeing the innocent queen as a succubus. As a result in both cases the true representatives of the heroes' expectations must appear, to be compared with their apparent counterparts and thus reveal their true nature. (pp. 233-34)

In both *The Faerie Queene* and *The Journey to the West,* when the false is weighed against the true, the true is always finally manifest. On the level of the plot, this emphasizes the necessity of knowing an obstacle's true form or nature in order to overcome it. Knowledge of the reason for Radigund's rage should have implied the weakness that would overthrow her, as the disclosure of the harpy's scorpion nature at the Cave of the Lute pointed to the power which could overthrow *her*. Allegorically, this is often presented as a problem of *vision*; the heroes falter when they are unable to apprehend the true character of a creature confronting them or the real implications of a situation.

Questions of justice and equity in personal and social relations are posed in both narratives, and a need to achieve self-awareness and knowledge in order to integrate social and personal concerns is implied. It is often the case that apparently external obstacles are actually manifestations of tendencies within the self. The fact that even the most illusion-ridden obstacles seem to have palpable existence suggests both lack of vision and self-knowledge, without which the heroes cannot complete their quests. In many cases, the name of the obstacle reveals its nature to the astute reader of allegory, and points to a way around it. If Tripitaka and Pa-chieh had bothered to ask the name of the Child-and-Mother River, they might not have been so eager to drink of it.

Ultimately, the lessons of an allegorical adventure, however fantastic or humorous, are intended for the reader. The explicitly fictional contexts of *The Faerie Queene* and *The Journey to the West* seem removed from any audience, but in fact the ironic points of view of their narrators bridge the gap between text and reader, and awaken the reader to the underlying purpose of the narratives. In the progress of an extended allegory, the interpretation or resolution of discrete episodes is fulfilled in the sum of all parts: a moral and spiritual education. The allegorist sets the quest for the reader as well as the protagonists to follow and the final enlightenment—or joke—is for the reader. The countries of women flummox the minds and senses of males and females alike, but their agonies and burlesques should be considered in the larger structure of human development which underlies both *The Faerie Queene* and *The Journey to the West.* In each case, from the standpoint of the work as a whole, the challenges of the countries of women transcend the battle of the sexes, to exemplify the fundamental issues of equity in human relations. The key to both episodes is the power of discernment in the face of illusion. Truth is revealed as individuals are able to reject the images before them, seeing beyond particular events to the larger social questions that the events both embody and conceal. Thus while the demands of justice may seem harsh, it is precisely the need to consider the significance of events beyond their immediate context which is crucial to the betterment, indeed the survival, of humanity. (pp. 234-35)

Dore J. Levy, "Female Reigns: 'The Faerie Queene' and 'The Journey to the West'," in Comparative Literature, *Vol. 39, No. 3, Summer, 1987, pp. 218-36.*

ADDITIONAL BIBLIOGRAPHY

Dudbridge, Glen. The *"Hsi-yu chi": A Study of Antecedents to the Sixteenth-Century Chinese Novel.* Cambridge: Cambridge University Press, 1970, 219 p.

Definitive study of the large heritage of oral, folkloric, dramatic, and religious source material upon which is based the Monkey-Tripitaka legend in *The Journey to the West*.

Hegel, Robert E. "The Tower of Myriad Mirrors." In his *The Novel in Seventeenth-Century China*, pp. 142-66. New York: Columbia University Press, 1981.

An analysis of satire and personal identity in *Hsi-yu pu* (1641; *The Tower of Myriad Mirrors*) containing several lengthy references to *The Journey to the West* as the inspiration for the seventeenth-century narrative.

Hsia, T. A. "The *Hsi yu pu* as a Study of Dreams in Fiction." In *Wen-lin: Studies in the Chinese Humanities*, edited by Chow Tse-tsung, pp. 239-46. Madison: University of Wisconsin Press, 1968.

Focuses on dream motifs in *Hsi yu pu* and stresses the essential differences between this work and its progenitor, *Journey to the West*.

Kao, Karl S. Y. "An Archetypal Approach to *Hsi-yu chi*." *Tamkang Review* V, No. 2 (October 1974): 63-97.

Using C. T. Hsia's essay (see excerpt dated 1968) as a point of departure, explores the mythic levels on which *The Journey to the West* functions.

Kuo, Helen A. "*Monkey*: A Chinese Folk Novel." *The New York Times Book Review* (14 March 1943): 6.

Favorable review of *Monkey*. Kuo writes: "With its rich beauty and lilting gayety *Monkey* is one of those books that should be read for pleasure as well as for instruction."

Liu Ts'un-yan. "The Prototypes of *Monkey (Hsi yu chi)*." *T'oung Pao* LI (1964): 55-71.

Study of the sources of *The Journey to the West*. Liu places particular emphasis on *T'ang Tripitaka Master's Pilgrimage to the West* (printed during the Wan-li reign of the Ming Dynasty, 1573-1619) as a primary narrative influence on Wu's novel.

Plaks, Andrew H. "Allegory in *Hsi-yu Chi* and *Hung-lou Meng*." In *Chinese Narrative: Critical and Theoretical Essays*, edited by Andrew H. Plaks, pp. 163-202. Princeton: Princeton University Press, 1977.

Documents numerous allegorical structures in *The Journey to the West* which underline the novel's major themes.

Wakeman, Frederic, Jr. "The Monkey King." *The New York Review of Books* XXVII, No. 9 (29 May 1980): 28-31.

Brief character analysis of Monkey.

Waley, Arthur. "The Real Tripitaka." In his *The Real Tripitaka and Other Pieces*, pp. 9-130. New York: Macmillan Co., 1952.

Historical account of the original Tripitaka's monastic career.

Yu, Anthony C. "Two Literary Examples of Religious Pilgrimage: The *Commedia* and *The Journey to the West*." *History of Religions* 22, No. 2 (February 1983): 202-30.

Traces similarities and differences in Dante's and Wu's approaches to such concerns as sin, atonement, and redemption in their respective works of religious pilgrimage.

Appendix

The following is a listing of all sources used in Volume 7 of *Literature Criticism from 1400 to 1800*. Included in this list are all copyright and reprint rights and acknowledgments for those essays for which permission was obtained. Every effort has been made to trace copyright, but if omissions have been made, please let us know.

THE EXCERPTS IN LC, VOLUME 7, WERE REPRINTED FROM THE FOLLOWING PERIODICALS:

The Academy, v. LVI, March 18, 1899.

American Mercury, v. VI, October, 1925. Copyright 1925, renewed 1953, by American Mercury Magazine, Inc.

The American Political Science Review, v. LVIII, September, 1964. Copyright, 1964, by The American Political Science Association. Reprinted by permission of the publisher.

Blackwood's Edinburgh Magazine, v. XXIV, December, 1828; v. XXXIX, June, 1836.

The Boston Gazette, March 1, 1773.

Bulletin of The New York Public Library, v. 68, March 1964. Reprinted by permission of the publisher, The New York Public Library.

The CEA Critic, v. 43, November, 1980. Copyright © 1980 by the College English Association, Inc. Reprinted by permission of the publisher.

CLA Journal, v. VII, March, 1964; v. X, December, 1966. Copyright, 1964, 1966 by The College Language Association. Both used by permission of The College Language Association.

Comparative Literature, v. 39, Summer, 1987 for "Female Reigns: 'The Faerie Queene' and 'The Journey to the West'" by Dore J. Levy. © copyright 1987 by University of Oregon. Reprinted by permission of the author.

The Contemporary Review, v. L, July-December, 1886.

The Critical Review, v. XI, March, 1761.

The Dedham Historical Register, v. II, January, 1891.

The Detroit News, April 20, 1987; May 4, 1987. Copyright 1987, The Detroit News, Inc., A Gannett Newspaper. Both reprinted by permission of the publisher.

Aaron, Richard I. From *John Locke*. Second edition. Oxford at the Clarendon Press, Oxford, 1955.

Adams, John. From *A Defence of the Constitutions of Government of the United States of America*. Hall and Sellers, 1787.

Adams, John. From a letter in *The Works of John Adams, Second President of the United States, Vol. I*. Edited by Charles Francis Adams. Little, Brown and Company, 1856.

Albee, Ernest. From *A History of English Utilitarianism*. Swan Sonnenschein & Co., Ltd., 1902.

Aldridge, Alfred Owen. From *Jonathan Edwards*. Washington Square Press, 1964. Copyright, ©, 1964 by Washington Square Press. All rights reserved. Reprinted by permission of Washington Square Press, a division of Simon & Schuster, Inc.

Althusser, Louis. From *Montesquieu, Rousseau, Marx: Politics and History*. Translated by Ben Brewster. Verso, 1982. Originally published as *Politics and History: Montesquieu, Rousseau, Hegel and Marx*. NLB, 1972. © NLB, 1972. Reprinted by permission of Verso.

Angoff, Charles. From *A Literary History of the American People: From 1607 to the Beginning or the Revolutionary Period, Vol. 1*. A. A. Knopf, 1931.

Anscombe, G. E. M. From *The Collected Philosophical Papers of G. E. M. Anscombe: From Parmenides to Wittgenstein, Vol. 1*. University of Minnesota Press, 1981. © in this collection G. E. M. Anscombe 1981. All rights reserved. Reprinted by permission of the publisher.

Ashbee, C. R. From an introduction to *The Treatises of Benvenuto Cellini on Goldsmithing and Sculpture*. By Benvenuto Cellini, translated by C. R. Ashbee. E. Arnold, 1898.

Babbitt, Irving. From *Democracy and Leadership*. Houghton Mifflin Company, 1924. Copyright 1924 by Irving Babbitt. Renewed 1951 by Esther Babbitt Howe and Edward S. Babbitt. All rights reserved. Reprinted by permission of National Humanities Institute.

Barker, Gerard A. From *Grandison's Heirs: The Paragon's Progress in the Late Eighteenth-Century English Novel*. University of Delaware Press, 1985. © 1985 by Associated University Presses, Inc. Reprinted by permission of the publisher.

Beard, Charles A. From *The Economic Basis of Politics*. Knopf, 1922. Copyright 1922 by Alfred A. Knopf, Inc. Renewed 1950 by Miriam Beard Vagts and William Beard. Reprinted by permission of the Literary Estate of Charles A. Beard.

Beattie, James. From *An Essay on the Nature and Immutability of Truth, in Opposition to Sophistry and Scepticism*. A. Kincaid & J. Bell, 1770.

Bentham, Jeremy. From *The Works of Jeremy Bentham, Vol. X*. William Tait, 1843.

Berkeley, George. From *A Treatise concerning the Principles of Human Knowledge*. J. Pepyat, 1710.

Berlin, Isaiah. From *The Age of Enlightenment: The Eighteenth Century Philosophers*. Edited by Isaiah Berlin. Houghton Mifflin, 1956. Copyright © 1956, renewed 1984 by Isaiah Berlin. All rights reserved. Reprinted by permission of the author.

Beyer, Harold. From *A History of Norwegian Literature*. Edited and translated by Einar Haugen. New York University Press, 1956.

Birrell, Augustine. From *The Collected Essays & Addresses of the Rt. Hon. Augustine Birrell: 1880-1920, Vol. 2*. J. M. Dent & Sons Ltd., 1922.

Borges, Jorge Luis. From "'Jonathan Edwards' (1703-1758)," translated by Richard Howard and César Rennert in his *Selected Poems: 1923-1967*. Edited by Norman Thomas Di Giovanni. Delacorte Press/Seymour Lawrence, 1972. English translations, copyright © 1968 by Emecé Editores, S.A., and Norman Thomas Di Giovanni. All rights reserved. Published by arrangement with Delacorte Press/Seymour Lawrence.

Boswell, James. From *The Life of Samuel Johnson, LL.D., Vol. 1*. Charles Dilly, 1791.

Boswell, James and Samuel Johnson. From *The Life of Samuel Johnson, LL.D.* Vol. 2. By James Boswell. Charles Dilly, 1791.

Boufflers, Comtesse de, Hyppolyte De Saujon. From a letter in *The Life of David Hume*. By Ernest Campbell Mossner. Second edition. Oxford at the Clarendon Press, Oxford, 1980. © Oxford University Press 1980. All rights reserved. Reprinted by permission of Oxford University Press.

Braudy, Leo. From *Narrative Form in History and Fiction*. Princeton University Press, 1970. Copyright © 1970 by Princeton University Press. Reprinted by permission of the publisher.

Bredsdorff, Elias. From ''Danish Literature in the 18th Century,'' in *An Introduction to Scandinavian Literature from the Earliest Time to Our Day*. By Elias Bredsdorff, Brita Mortensen, and Ronald Popperwell. Cambridge at the University Press, 1951.

Buckle, Henry Thomas. From *History of Civilization in England*. J. W. Parker and Son, 1857.

Burckhardt, Jacob. From *The Civilization of the Renaissance in Italy*. Translated by S. G. C. Middlemore. The Phaidon Press, 1944.

Burke, Edmund. From *An Appeal from the New to the Old Whigs*. P. Byrne, 1791.

Burton, John Hill. From *Life and Correspondence of David Hume, Vol. 1*. William Tait, 1846.

Cairns, Huntington. From *Law and the Social Sciences*. Harcourt Brace Jovanovich, 1935.

Cairns, Huntington. From *Legal Philosophy from Plato to Hegel*. Johns Hopkins Press, 1949. Copyright 1949, The Johns Hopkins Press. Renewed 1976 by Huntington Cairns. Reprinted by permission of the publisher.

Cervigni, Dino S. From *The ''Vita'' of Benvenuto Cellini: Literary Tradition and Genre*. Longo Editore, 1979. © copyright A. Longo Editore. Reprinted by permission of the publisher.

Cherry, Conrad. From *The Theology of Jonathan Edwards: A Reappraisal*. Anchor Books, 1966. Copyright © 1966 by C. Conrad Cherry. All rights reserved. Reprinted by permission of Doubleday, a division of Bantam, Doubleday, Dell Publishing Group, Inc.

Chesterfield, Lord. From *Letters of Lord Chesterfield*. Oxford University Press, London, 1929.

Cobban, Alfred. From *Edmund Burke and the Revolt against the Eighteenth Century: A Study of the Political and Social Thinking of Burke, Wordsworth, Coleridge and Southey*. The Macmillan Company, 1929.

Colden, Cadwallader. From a letter in *Collections of the New-York Historical Society for the Year 1868*. New-York Historical Society, 1868.

Coleridge, Samuel Taylor. From *Biographia Literaria; or, Biographical Sketches of My Literary Life and Opinions*. Kirk and Mercein, 1817.

Coleridge, Samuel Taylor. From letters in *Coleridge on the Seventeenth Century*. Edited by Roberta Florence Brinkley. Duke University Press, 1955. Copyright © 1955 by Duke University Press, Durham, N.C. Renewed 1983 by Roberta C. Cox. Reprinted by permission of the publisher.

Courtney, C. P. From *Montesquieu and Burke*. Basil Blackwell, 1963. © Basil Blackwell & Mott, Ltd., 1963. Reprinted by permission of the author.

Cranston, Maurice. From *Locke*. The British Council, 1961. © Profile Books Ltd. 1961. Reprinted by permission of Profile Books Limited.

Dargan, Edwin Preston. From *The Aesthetic Doctrine of Montesquieu: Its Application in His Writings*. J. H. Furst Company, 1907.

DePorte, Michael V. From *Nightmares and Hobbyhorses: Swift, Sterne, and Augustan Ideas of Madness*. Huntington Library, 1974. Copyright © 1974 Henry E. Huntington Library and Art Gallery. Reprinted by permission of the publisher.

Dickinson, John. From a letter in *The Writings of John Dickinson: Political Writings, 1764-1774, Vol. 1*. Edited by Paul Leicester Ford. The Historical Society of Pennsylvania, 1895.

Doody, Margaret Anne. From ''Frances Sheridan: Morality and Annihilated Time,'' in *Fetter'd or Free? British Women Novelists, 1670-1815*. Edited by Mary Anne Schofield and Cecilia Macheski. Ohio University Press, 1986. Copyright © 1986 by Ohio University Press. All rights reserved. Reprinted by permission of the publisher.

Durkheim, Emile. From *Montesquieu and Rousseau: Forerunners of Sociology*. Translated by Ralph Manheim. University of Michigan Press, 1960. Copyright © by The University of Michigan 1960. Reprinted by permission of the publisher.

Hogan, Robert and Jerry C. Beasley. From "Introduction: Frances Sheridan, Her Family and Career," in *The Plays of Frances Sheridan*. By Frances Sheridan, edited by Robert Hogan and Jerry C. Beasley. University of Delaware Press, 1984. © 1984 by Associated University Presses, Inc. Reprinted by permission of the publisher.

Holbrook, Clyde A. From *The Ethics of Jonathan Edwards: Morality and Aesthetics*. University of Michigan Press, 1973. Copyright © by The University of Michigan 1973. All rights reserved. Reprinted by permission of the publisher.

Holmes, Oliver Wendell. From *Collected Legal Papers*. Harcourt, Brace and Howe, 1920.

Hopkins, Samuel. From a preface to *The Life and Character of the Late Reverend, Learned, and Pious Mr. Jonathan Edwards*. S. Kneeland, 1765.

Horn, Frederik Winkel. From *History of the Literature of the Scandinavian North: From the Most Ancient Times to the Present*. Translated by Rasmus B. Anderson. Revised edition. S. C. Griggs and Company, 1884.

Hsia, C. T. From *The Classic Chinese Novel: A Critical Introduction*. Columbia University Press, 1968. Copyright © 1968 Columbia University Press. Reprinted by permission of the author.

Hsun, Lu. From *A Brief History of Chinese Fiction*. Translated by Yang Hsien-Yi and Gladys Yang. Foreign Languages Press, 1959.

Hume, David. From *An Abstract of a Book Lately Published, Entituled, "A Treatise of Human Nature"* C. Borbet, 1740.

Hume, David. From *The Letters of David Hume, Vol. I*. Edited by J. Y. T. Greig. Oxford at the Clarendon Press, Oxford, 1932.

Hunter, Robert. From a dedication to *Androboros*. N.p., 1714.

Huxley, Aldous. From an introduction to *The Discovery: A Comedy in Five Acts*. By Frances Sheridan, adapted by Aldous Huxley. George H. Doran Company, 1925. Copyright 1925, renewed 1952, by Aldous Huxley. Reprinted by permission of the Literary Estate of Aldous Huxley and The Hogarth Press.

Huxley, Thomas H. From *Hume*. N.p., 1878.

Jefferson, Thomas. From *The Complete Jefferson*. Edited by Saul K. Padover. Duell, Sloan & Pearce, Inc., 1943. Copyright 1943, renewed 1971 by Saul K. Padover. All rights reserved. Reprinted by permission of E. P. Dutton/Hawthorn Books, a division of NAL Penguin Inc.

Jefferson, Thomas. From *The Jefferson Papers*. Massachusetts Historical Society, 1906.

Johnson, Samuel. From an excerpt in *The Life of Samuel Johnson, LL.D.* By James Boswell. Charles Dilly, 1791.

Jorgenson, Theodore. From *History of Norwegian Literature*. The Macmillan Company, 1933.

Kant, Immanuel. From an introduction to *Prolegomena to Any Future Metaphysics*. Edited and translated by Lewis White Beck. Liberal Arts Press, 1951. Copyright 1950 by Macmillan Publishing Company. Renewed 1978 by Lewis White Beck. Reprinted with permission of Macmillan Publishing Company.

Kirk, Russell. From *Edmund Burke: A Genius Reconsidered*. Arlington House, 1967. Copyright © 1967 by Arlington House, Inc. All rights reserved. Used by permission of the publisher.

Kirk, Russell. From *The Roots of American Order*. Open Court, 1974. Copyright © 1974 by Pepperdine University. All rights reserved. Reprinted by permission of the author.

Kra, Pauline. From "Montesquieu and Women," in *French Women and the Age of Enlightenment*. Edited by Samia I. Spencer. Indiana University Press, 1984. Copyright © 1984 by Indiana University Press. All rights reserved. Reprinted by permission of the publisher.

Kuklick, Bruce. From *Churchmen and Philosophers: From Jonathan Edwards to John Dewey*. Yale University Press, 1985. Copyright © 1985 by Yale University. All rights reserved. Reprinted by permission of the publisher.

Laird, John. From *Hume's Philosophy of Human Nature*. E. P. Dutton and Company Inc. 1932.

Laski, Harold J. From *Political Thought in England: Locke to Bentham*. Henry Holt and Company, 1920.

Le Clerc, Jean. From "Le Clerc's Character of Locke," in *The Life and Letters of John Locke*. Edited by Lord King. G. Bell & Sons, 1884.

Learned, William Law. From a preface to *The Private Journal of a Journey from Boston to New York in the Year 1704*. By Sarah Kemble Knight, edited by William Law Learned. Frank H. Little, 1865.

Lefanu, Alicia. From *Memoirs of the Life and Writings of Mrs. Frances Sheridan*. G. and W. B. Whittaker, 1824.

Lewis, C. S. From *Miracles: A Preliminary Study*. G. Bles, The Centenary Press, 1947. Copyright C. S. Lewis 1947, 1960. Renewed 1974 by Arthur Owen Barfield and Alfred Cecil Harwood. All rights reserved. Reprinted by permission of G. Bles, The Centenary Press, an imprint of William Collins Sons & Co. Ltd.

Lewisohn, Ludwig. From *Expression in America*. Harper & Brothers, Publishers, 1932. Copyright 1932 by Harper & Brothers. Renewed 1959 by Louise Lewisohn. Reprinted by permission of the grandchildren of Ludwig Lewisohn.

From an introduction to *The Life of Benvenuto Cellini, a Florentine Artist, Vol. I*. By Benvenuto Cellini, translated by Thomas Nugent. Whittaker, Treacher, and Arnot, 1828.

Locke, John. From *An Essay concerning Human Understanding*. Thomas Basset, 1690.

Lodge, Edmund. From *Portraits of Illustrious Personages of Great Britain, Vol. IX*. Harding and Lepard, 1835.

Lowell, Robert. From *Lord Weary's Castle*. Harcourt Brace Jovanovich, 1946. Copyright 1946, 1974 by Robert Lowell. Reprinted by permission of Harcourt Brace Jovanovich, Inc.

Loy, J. Robert. From *Montesquieu*. Twayne, 1968. Copyright 1968 by Twayne Publishers. All rights reserved. Reprinted with the permission of Twayne Publishers, a division of G. K. Hall & Co., Boston.

Lucas, F. L. From *The Art of Living, Four Eighteenth-Century Minds: Hume, Horace Walpole, Burke, Benjamin Franklin*. Cassell & Co. Ltd., 1959. © F. L. Lucas 1959. Reprinted by permission of Mrs. F. L. Lucas. In Canada by Macmillan Publishing Company.

MacCarthy, B. G. From *The Female Pen: The Later Women Novelists, 1744-1818*. Cork University Press, 1947.

MacCunn, John. From *The Political Philosophy of Burke*. Longmans, Green and Co., 1913.

Macpherson, C. B. From *Burke*. Hill and Wang, 1980. Copyright © 1980 by C. B. Macpherson. All rights reserved. Reprinted by permission of Farrar, Straus and Giroux, Inc.

Madison, James. From *Letters and Other Writings of James Madison: 1829-1836, Vol. IV*. J. B. Lippincott & Co., 1865.

Mansfield, Harvey C., Jr. From an introduction to *Selected Letters of Edmund Burke*. By Edmund Burke, edited by Harvey C. Mansfield, Jr. University of Chicago Press, 1984. © 1984 by The University of Chicago. All rights reserved. Reprinted by permission of the publisher and the author.

Mates, Julian. From "Robert Hunter (fl. 1714-1734)," in *American Writers before 1800: A Biographical and Critical Dictionary, G-P*. Edited by James A. Levernier and Douglas R. Wilmes. Greenwood Press, 1983. Copyright © 1983 by James A. Levernier and Douglas R. Wilmes. All rights reserved. Reprinted by permission of Greenwood Press, Inc., Westport, CT.

Maugham, W. Somerset. From *The Vagrant Mood: Six Essays*. Heinemann, 1952. Copyright 1950 by W. Somerset Maugham. Reprinted by permission of Doubleday, a division of Bantam, Doubleday, Dell Publishing Group, Inc.

McGinley, Phyllis. From "The Theology of Jonathan Edwards," in *Times Three*. The Viking Press, 1961. Copyright © 1957 by Phyllis McGinley. Renewed 1985 by Patricia Hayden Blake. Reprinted by permission of Viking Penguin Inc.

Meserve, Walter J. From *An Emerging Entertainment: The Drama of the American People to 1828*. Indiana University Press, 1977. Copyright © 1977 by Indiana University Press. All rights reserved. Reprinted by permission of the publisher.

Meserve, Walter J. and William R. Reardon. From an introduction to *Satiric Comedies*. Edited by Walter J. Meserve and William R. Reardon. Indiana University Press, 1969. Copyright © 1969 by Indiana University Press. All rights reserved. Reprinted by permission of the publisher.

Mill, John Stuart. From *A System of Logic: Ratiocinative and Inductive*. N.p., 1843.

Miller, Perry. From *Jonathan Edwards*. Sloane, 1949. Copyright 1949 by William Sloane Associates, Inc. Renewed 1977 by Mrs. Perry Miller. Abridged by permission of William Morrow & Company, Inc.

Montesquieu, Charles de Secondat, Baron de. From *The Spirit of Laws*. Translated by Thomas Nugent. Revised edition. G. Bell and Sons, 1902.

Moses, Montrose J. From *The American Dramatist*. Third Edition. Little, Brown, 1925. Copyright, 1911, 1917, 1925, by Little, Brown, and Company. Renewed 1953 by Leah H. Moses. All rights reserved. Reprinted by permission of the Literary Estate of Montrose J. Moses.

Mumford, Lewis. From "Hume: Nihilistic Atomism," in *Interpretations and Forecasts, 1922-1972: Studies in Literature, History, Biography, Technics, and Contemporary Society*. Harcourt Brace Jovanovich, 1973. Copyright 1944, 1973 by Lewis Mumford. Reprinted by permission of Harcourt Brace Jovanovich, Inc.

Neumann, Franz. From an introduction to *The Spirit of the Laws*. By Baron de Montesquieu, edited by Franz Neumann, translated by Thomas Nugent. Hafner Publishing Company, 1949.

Norris, John. From *Christian Blessedness; or, Discourses upon the Beatitudes of Our Lord and Saviour Jesus Christ*. S. Manship, 1690.

Ozell, John. From "Advertisement," in *Persian Letters, Vol. I*. By Charles de Secondat, Baron de Montesquieu, translated by John Ozell. J. Tonson, 1722.

Paine, Thomas. From *The Rights of Man, Part 1*. J. S. Jordan, 1791.

Pangle, Thomas L. From *Montesquieu's Philosophy of Liberalism: A Commentary on "The Spirit of the Laws."* University of Chicago Press, 1973. © 1973 by The University of Chicago. All rights reserved. Reprinted by permission of the publisher and the author.

Parkin, Charles. From *The Moral Basis of Burke's Political Thought: An Essay*. Cambridge at the University Press, 1956.

Parrington, Vernon Louis. From *Main Currents in American Thought: The Colonial Mind, 1620-1800, Vol. I*. Harcourt Brace Jovanovich, 1927. Copyright 1927, 1930 by Harcourt Brace Jovanovich, Inc. Renewed 1955, 1958 by Vernon L. Parrington, Jr., Louise P. Tucker and Elizabeth P. Thomas. Reprinted by permission of the publisher.

Peirce, Charles S. From *Values in a Universe of Chance: Selected Writings of Charles S. Peirce (1839-1914)*. Edited by Philip P. Wiener. Doubleday & Company, Inc., 1958. Copyright © 1958, renewed 1986, by Philip P. Wiener. All reserved. Reprinted by permission of Philip P. Wiener.

Price, John Valdimir. From *David Hume*. Twayne, 1969. Copyright 1968 by Twayne Publishers. All rights reserved. Reprinted with the permission of Twayne Publishers, a division of G. K. Hall & Co., Boston.

Priestley, Joseph. From *Letters to a Philosophical Unbeliever, Part I*. R. Cruttwell, 1780.

Prior, Matthew. From *Dialogues of the Dead and Other Works in Prose and Verse*. Edited by A. R. Waller. Cambridge at the University Press, 1907.

Quinn, Arthur Hobson. From *A History of the American Drama: From the Beginning to the Civil War*. Second edition. F. S. Crofts & Co., 1943, Irvington, 1979. Copyright 1923, 1943, 1951 by Arthur Hobson Quinn. Renewed 1970 by Arthur Hobson Quinn, Jr. All rights reserved. Reprinted by permission of Irvington Publishers, Inc. and the Literary Estate of Arthur Hobson Quinn.

Reid, Christopher. From *Edmund Burke and the Practice of Political Writing*. St. Martin's Press, 1958, Gill & Macmillan, 1985. © Christopher Reid, 1985. All rights reserved. Used with permission of St. Martin's Press, Inc. In Canada by Gill & Macmillan, Ltd.

Reid, Thomas. From *An Inquiry into the Human Mind on the Principles of Common Sense*. N.p., 1764.

Rousseau, Jean Jacques. From *The Social Contract: An Eighteenth-Century Translation*. Edited by Charles Frankel. Revised edition. Hafner Publishing Company, 1947.

Rousseau, Jean Jacques. From a letter in *The Life of David Hume*. By Ernest Campbell Mossner. Second edition. Oxford at the Clarendon Press, Oxford, 1980. © Oxford University Press 1980. All rights reserved. Reprinted by permission of Oxford University Press.

Russell, Bertrand. From *A History of Western Philosophy, and Its Connection with Political and Social Circumstances from the Earliest Times to the Present Day*. Simon & Schuster, 1945, G. Allen and Unwin Ltd., 1946. Copyright 1945, 1972, by Bertrand Russell. Reprinted by permission of Simon & Schuster, Inc. In Canada by Unwin Hyman Ltd.

Saint-Beuve, C. A. From *Portraits of the Eighteenth Century: Historical and Literary, Vol. I*. Translated by Katharine Wormeley. G. P. Putnam's Sons, 1905.

Saintsbury, George. From *A History of Criticism and Literary Taste in Europe from the Earliest Text to the Present Day: Modern Criticism, Vol. III*. William Blackwood & Sons Ltd., 1904.

Saintsbury, George. From "Montesquieu," in *Encyclopaedia Britannica*. The Encyclopaedia Britannica Company, 1910-11.

Sanctis, Francesco de. From *History of Italian Literature, Vol. 2*. Translated by Joan Redfern. Harcourt Brace Jovanovich, 1931. Copyright 1931, 1959 by Harcourt Brace Jovanovich, Inc. Reprinted by permission of the publisher.

Santayana, George. From *Some Turns of Thought in Modern Philosophy: Five Essays*. Charles Scribner's Sons, 1933.

Scheick, William J. From *The Writings of Jonathan Edwards: Theme, Motif, and Style*. Texas A & M University Press, 1975. Copyright © 1975 by William J. Scheick. All rights reserved. Reprinted by permission of the publisher.

Schlegel, Friedrich von. From *Lectures on the History of Literature: Ancient and Modern*. Translated by J. G. Lockhart. W. Blackwood, 1818.

Schmidgall, Gary. From *Literature as Opera*. Oxford University Press, 1977. Copyright © 1977 by Oxford University Press, Inc. Reprinted by permission of the publisher.

Seelye, John. From *Prophetic Waters: The River in Early American Life and Literature*. Oxford University Press, 1977. Copyright © 1977 by John Seelye. Reprinted by permission of Oxford University Press, Inc.

Shackleton, Robert. From *Montesquieu: A Critical Biography*. Oxford University Press, 1961. © Oxford University Press 1961. Reprinted by permission of Oxford University Press.

Sheridan, Mrs. Frances. From a letter in *The Private Correspondence of David Garrick with the Most Celebrated Persons of His Time, Vol. I*. By David Garrick. Henry Colburn and Richard Bentley, Publishers, 1831.

Shih, Hu. From an introduction to *Monkey*. By Ch'êng'ên Wu. Translated by Arthur Waley. John Day, 1943. Copyright 1943 by Harper & Row, Publishers, Inc. All rights reserved. Reprinted by permission of Harper & Row, Publishers, Inc.

Smith, Adam. From a letter in *An Enquiry Concerning Human Understanding*. By David Hume. N.p., 1777.

Smith, Norman Kemp. From *The Philosophy of David Hume: A Critical Study of Its Origins and Central Doctrines*. Macmillan and Co., Limited, 1941.

Spengemann, William C. From *The Adventurous Muse: The Poetics of American Fiction-1789-1900*. Yale University Press, 1977. Copyright © 1977 by Yale University. All rights reserved. Reprinted by permission of the publisher.

Squadrito, Kathleen M. From *John Locke*. Twayne, 1979. Copyright 1979 by G. K. Hall & Co. All rights reserved. Reprinted with the permission of G. K. Hall & Co., Boston.

Stanford, Ann. From "Images of Women in Early American Literature," in *What Manner of Woman: Essays on English and American Life and Literature*. Edited by Marlene Springer. New York University Press, 1977. Copyright 1977 by New York University. Reprinted by permission of the publisher.

Stanlis, Peter J. From *Edmund Burke and the Natural Law*. The University of Michigan Press, 1958.

Stephen, Sir Leslie. From *History of English Thought in the Eighteenth Century, Vols. I and II*. Smith, Elder & Co., 1876.

Sterne, Laurence. From *The Life and Opinions of Tristram Shandy, Gentleman, Vol. II*. Second edition. R. & J. Dodsley, 1760.

Strauss, Leo. From *Natural Right and History*. University of Chicago Press, 1953. Copyright 1953 by The University of Chicago. Renewed 1981 by Miriam Strauss. All rights reserved. Reprinted by permission of the publisher.

Symonds, John Addington. From *Renaissance in Italy: The Fine Arts, Vol. III*. Smith, Elder & Co., 1877.

Symonds, John Addington. From an introduction to *The Life of Benvenuto Cellini, Vol. I*. By Benvenuto Cellini, translated by John Addington Symonds. John C. Nimmo, 1888.

Trevor-Roper, H. R. From "Hume as a Historian," in *David Hume: A Symposium*. Edited by D. F. Pears. Macmillan, 1963. Copyright © Macmillan & Co. Ltd. 1963. Reprinted by permission of Macmillan, London and Basingstoke.

Ts'Un-Yan, Liu. From *Wu Ch'êng-ên: His Life and Career*. Brill, 1967. Copyright 1967 by E. J. Brill. All rights reserved. Reprinted by permission of the publisher.

Turnbull, Ralph G. From *Jonathan Edwards: The Preacher*. Baker Book House, 1958.

Twain, Mark., S. L. From a letter to Reverend J. H. Twichell in February, 1902, in *Mark Twain's Letters, Vol. II*. Edited by Albert Bigelow Paine. Harper & Row, 1917.

Van Doren, Carl. From an introduction to *Benjamin Franklin and Jonathan Edwards: Selections from Their Writings*. By Benjamin Franklin and Jonathan Edwards, edited by Carl Van Doren. Charles Scribner's Sons, 1920. Copyright, 1920, by Charles Scribner's Sons. Renewed 1948 by Carl Van Doren. Reprinted with the permission of Charles Scribner's Sons, an imprint of Macmillan Publishing Co.

Van Dyke, John C. From an introduction to *Memoirs of Benvenuto Cellini*. By Benvenuto Cellini, translated by John Addington Symonds. D. Appleton and Company, 1898.

Vaughan, C. E. From *Studies in the History of Political Philosophy Before and After Rousseau: From Hobbes to Hume, Vol. I*. Edited by A. G. Little. Manchester University Press, 1925.

Voltaire. From *Letters concerning the English Nation*. Translated by John Lockman. C. Davis and A. Lyon, 1733.

Voltaire, François Marie Arouet de. From *The Selected Letters of Voltaire*. Edited and translated by Richard A. Brooks. New York University Press, 1973. Copyright © 1973 by New York University. Reprinted by permission of the publisher.

Voltaire, François Marie Arouet de. From an extract of a review of "History of England," in *The Life of David Hume*. By Ernest Campbell Mossner. Second edition. Oxford at the Clarendon Press, Oxford, 1980. © Oxford University Press 1980. All rights reserved. Reprinted by permission of Oxford University Press.

Walpole, Horace. From an autographed signed letter to Mary Berry on May 26, 1791. Reprinted by permission of The Pierpont Morgan Library, New York.

Webb, Thomas E. From *The Intellectualism of Locke: An Essay*. W. McGee & Co., 1857.

Wesley, John. From *The Works of John Wesley, Vol. VII*. Wesleyan Conference Office, 1872.

Wesley, John. From *The Works of John Wesley: Letters, Essays, Dialogs and Addresses, Vol. X*. Wesleyan Conference Office, 1872.

Whately, Richard. From *Historic Doubts Relative to Napoleon Bonaparte*. N.p., 1819.

White, Trentwell Mason and Paul William Lehmann. From *Writers of Colonial New England*. The Palmer Company, Publishers, 1929.

Willey, Basil. From *The Seventeenth Century Background: Studies in the Thought of the Age in Relation to Poetry and Religion*. Columbia University Press, 1934.

Wilson, Woodrow. From *Mere Literature, and Other Essays*. Houghton Mifflin Company, 1896.

Winship, George Parker. From an introduction to *The Journal of Madam Knight*. By Sarah Kemble Knight. Small, Maynard & Company, 1920. Reprinted by permission.

Winslow, Ola Elizabeth. From *Jonathan Edwards, 1703-1758: A Biography*. Macmillan, 1940. Copyright, 1940, renewed 1967, by Ola Elizabeth Winslow. All rights reserved. Reprinted with permission of Macmillan Publishing Company.

Wood, Neal. From "The Value of Asocial Sociability: Contributions of Machiavelli, Sidney and Montesquieu," in *Machiavelli and the Nature of Political Thought*. Edited by Martin Fleisher. Atheneum, 1972. Copyright © 1972 by Martin Fleisher. All rights reserved. Reprinted with the permission of Atheneum Publishers, an imprint of Macmillan Publishing Company.

Wollstonecraft, Mary. From *A Vindication of the Rights of Men*. J. Johnson, 1790.

Wynne, John. From a letter in *The Life and Letters of John Locke*. Edited by Lord King. G. Bell & Sons, 1884.

Yandell, Keith E. From "Hume on Religious Belief," in *Hume: A Re-Evaluation*. Edited by Donald W. Livingston and James T. King. Fordham University Press, 1976. © copyright 1976 by Fordham University Press. All rights reserved. Reprinted by permission of the publisher.

Yu, Anthony C. From an introduction to *The Journey to the West, Volume One*. By Ch'êng-ên Wu, edited and translated by Anthony C. Yu. University of Chicago Press, 1977. © 1977 by The University of Chicago. All rights reserved. Reprinted by permission of the publisher.

Literary Criticism Series
Cumulative Author Index

This index lists all author entries in the Gale Literary Criticism Series and includes cross-references to other Gale sources. For the convenience of the reader, references to the *Yearbook* in the *Contemporary Literary Criticism* series include the page number (in parentheses) after the volume number. References in the index are identified as follows:

Bradbury, Ray(mond Douglas)
      1920-............ CLC 1, 3, 10, 15, 42
   See also CANR 2
   See also CA 1-4R
   See also SATA 11
   See also DLB 2, 8
   See also AITN 1, 2

Bradley, David (Henry), Jr.
      1950-......................CLC 23
   See also CA 104
   See also DLB 33

Bradley, Marion Zimmer
      1930-......................CLC 30
   See also CANR 7
   See also CA 57-60
   See also DLB 8

Bradstreet, Anne 1612-1672 .... LC 4
   See also DLB 24

Bragg, Melvyn 1939-..............CLC 10
   See also CANR 10
   See also CA 57-60
   See also DLB 14

Braine, John (Gerard)
      1922-1986..............CLC 1, 3, 41
   See also CANR 1
   See also CA 1-4R
   See also DLB 15
   See also DLB-Y 86

Brammer, Billy Lee 1930?-1978
   See Brammer, William

Brammer, William 1930?-1978.....CLC 31
   See also obituary CA 77-80

Brancati, Vitaliano
      1907-1954.................TCLC 12
   See also CA 109

Brancato, Robin F(idler) 1936-.....CLC 35
   See also CANR 11
   See also CA 69-72
   See also SATA 23

Brand, Millen 1906-1980 ....CLC 7
   See also CA 21-24R
   See also obituary CA 97-100

Branden, Barbara 19??-..... CLC 44 (447)

Brandes, Georg (Morris Cohen)
      1842-1927.................TCLC 10
   See also CA 105

Branley, Franklyn M(ansfield)
      1915-......................CLC 21
   See also CANR 14
   See also CA 33-36R
   See also SATA 4

Brathwaite, Edward 1930-.........CLC 11
   See also CANR 11
   See also CA 25-28R
   See also DLB 53

Brautigan, Richard (Gary)
      1935-1984.........CLC 1, 3, 5, 9, 12,
                               34 (314), 42
   See also CA 53-56
   See also obituary CA 113
   See also DLB 2, 5
   See also DLB-Y 80, 84

Brecht, (Eugen) Bertolt (Friedrich)
      1898-1956..........TCLC 1, 6, 13
   See also CA 104

Bremer, Fredrika 1801-1865 ..... NCLC 11

Brennan, Christopher John
      1870-1932.................TCLC 17
   See also CA 117

Brennan, Maeve 1917-.............CLC 5
   See also CA 81-84

Brentano, Clemens (Maria)
      1778-1842..................NCLC 1

Brenton, Howard 1942- ....CLC 31
   See also CA 69-72
   See also DLB 13

Breslin, James 1930-
   See Breslin, Jimmy
   See also CA 73-76

Breslin, Jimmy 1930- .... CLC 4, 43
   See also Breslin, James
   See also AITN 1

Bresson, Robert 1907-............CLC 16
   See also CA 110

Breton, André 1896-1966..... CLC 2, 9, 15
   See also CAP 2
   See also CA 19-20
   See also obituary CA 25-28R

Breytenbach, Breyten
      1939-............... CLC 23, 37
   See also CA 113

Bridgers, Sue Ellen 1942-..........CLC 26
   See also CANR 11
   See also CA 65-68
   See also SAAS 1
   See also SATA 22

Bridges, Robert 1844-1930........ TCLC 1
   See also CA 104
   See also DLB 19

Bridie, James 1888-1951 .... TCLC 3
   See also Mavor, Osborne Henry
   See also DLB 10

Brin, David 1950- .... CLC 34 (133)
   See also CA 102

Brink, André (Philippus)
      1935-.................... CLC 18, 36
   See also CA 104

Brinsmead, H(esba) F(ay)
      1922-......................CLC 21
   See also CANR 10
   See also CA 21-24R
   See also SATA 18

Brittain, Vera (Mary)
      1893?-1970.................CLC 23
   See also CAP 1
   See also CA 15-16
   See also obituary CA 25-28R

Broch, Hermann 1886-1951...... TCLC 20
   See also CA 117

Brock, Rose 1923-
   See Hansen, Joseph

Brodsky, Iosif Alexandrovich 1940-
   See Brodsky, Joseph
   See also CA 41-44R
   See also AITN 1

Brodsky, Joseph
      1940-...............CLC 4, 6, 13, 36
   See also Brodsky, Iosif Alexandrovich

Brodsky, Michael (Mark)
      1948-......................CLC 19
   See also CANR 18
   See also CA 102

Bromell, Henry 1947-..............CLC 5
   See also CANR 9
   See also CA 53-56

Bromfield, Louis (Brucker)
      1896-1956.................TCLC 11
   See also CA 107
   See also DLB 4, 9

Broner, E(sther) M(asserman)
      1930-......................CLC 19
   See also CANR 8
   See also CA 17-20R
   See also DLB 28

Bronk, William 1918-.............CLC 10
   See also CA 89-92

Brontë, Anne 1820-1849.......... NCLC 4
   See also DLB 21

Brontë, Charlotte
      1816-1855.................NCLC 3, 8
   See also DLB 21
   See also DLB 39

Brontë, (Jane) Emily
      1818-1848..................NCLC 16
   See also DLB 21, 32

Brooke, Frances 1724-1789 .... LC 6
   See also DLB 39

Brooke, Henry 1703?-1783 .... LC 1
   See also DLB 39

Brooke, Rupert (Chawner)
      1887-1915.................TCLC 2, 7
   See also CA 104
   See also DLB 19

Brooke-Rose, Christine 1926- ......CLC 40
   See also CA 13-16R
   See also DLB 14

Brookner, Anita
      1938-............ CLC 32, 34 (136)
   See also CA 114

Brooks, Cleanth 1906- ....CLC 24
   See also CA 17-20R

Brooks, Gwendolyn
      1917-.............. CLC 1, 2, 4, 5, 15
   See also CANR 1
   See also CA 1-4R
   See also SATA 6
   See also DLB 5
   See also CDALB 1941-1968
   See also AITN 1

Brooks, Mel 1926-...............CLC 12
   See also Kaminsky, Melvin
   See also CA 65-68
   See also DLB 26

Brooks, Peter 1938-......... CLC 34 (519)
   See also CANR 1
   See also CA 45-48

Brooks, Van Wyck 1886-1963......CLC 29
   See also CANR 6
   See also CA 1-4R
   See also DLB 45

Brophy, Brigid (Antonia)
      1929-................CLC 6, 11, 29
   See also CAAS 4
   See also CA 5-8R
   See also DLB 14

Brosman, Catharine Savage
      1934-......................CLC 9
   See also CA 61-64

Broughton, T(homas) Alan
1936- ....CLC 19
See also CANR 2
See also CA 45-48

Broumas, Olga 1949- ....CLC 10
See also CANR 20
See also CA 85-88

Brown, Claude 1937- ....CLC 30
See also CA 73-76

Brown, Dee (Alexander) 1908- .....CLC 18
See also CANR 11
See also CA 13-16R
See also SATA 5
See also DLB-Y 80

Brown, George Mackay 1921-.......CLC 5
See also CANR 12
See also CA 21-24R
See also SATA 35
See also DLB 14, 27

Brown, Rita Mae 1944- .... CLC 18, 43
See also CANR 2, 11
See also CA 45-48

Brown, Rosellen 1939- ....CLC 32
See also CANR 14
See also CA 77-80

Brown, Sterling A(llen)
1901- .... CLC 1, 23
See also CA 85-88
See also DLB 48

Brown, William Wells
1816?-1884.................. NCLC 2
See also DLB 3, 50

Browne, Jackson 1950-............CLC 21

Browning, Elizabeth Barrett
1806-1861............... NCLC 1, 16
See also DLB 32

Browning, Tod 1882-1962 ....CLC 16
See also obituary CA 117

Bruccoli, Matthew J(oseph)
1931- .... CLC 34 (416)
See also CANR 7
See also CA 9-12R

Bruce, Lenny 1925-1966..........CLC 21
See also Schneider, Leonard Alfred

Brunner, John (Kilian Houston)
1934-..................... CLC 8, 10
See also CANR 2
See also CA 1-4R

Brutus, Dennis 1924-.............CLC 43
See also CANR 2
See also CA 49-52

Bryan, C(ourtlandt) D(ixon) B(arnes)
1936-.........................CLC 29
See also CANR 13
See also CA 73-76

Bryant, William Cullen
1794-1878.................. NCLC 6
See also DLB 3, 43

Bryusov, Valery (Yakovlevich)
1873-1924.................. TCLC 10
See also CA 107

Buchanan, George 1506-1582 .... LC 4

Buchheim, Lothar-Günther
1918-.........................CLC 6
See also CA 85-88

Buchwald, Art(hur) 1925- ....CLC 33
See also CA 5-8R
See also SATA 10
See also AITN 1

Buck, Pearl S(ydenstricker)
1892-1973.............CLC 7, 11, 18
See also CANR 1
See also CA 1-4R
See also obituary CA 41-44R
See also SATA 1, 25
See also DLB 9
See also AITN 1

Buckler, Ernest 1908-1984........CLC 13
See also CAP 1
See also CA 11-12
See also obituary CA 114

Buckley, William F(rank), Jr.
1925-.................. CLC 7, 18, 37
See also CANR 1
See also CA 1-4R
See also DLB-Y 80
See also AITN 1

Buechner, (Carl) Frederick
1926-..................CLC 2, 4, 6, 9
See also CANR 11
See also CA 13-16R
See also DLB-Y 80

Buell, John (Edward) 1927-.......CLC 10
See also CA 1-4R
See also DLB 53

Buero Vallejo, Antonio
1916-................... CLC 15, 46
See also CA 106

Bukowski, Charles
1920-.................CLC 2, 5, 9, 41
See also CA 17-20R
See also DLB 5

Bulgakov, Mikhail (Afanas'evich)
1891-1940............... TCLC 2, 16
See also CA 105

Bullins, Ed 1935-............. CLC 1, 5, 7
See also CA 49-52
See also DLB 7, 38

Bulwer-Lytton, (Lord) Edward (George Earle
Lytton) 1803-1873 .... NCLC 1
See also Lytton, Edward Bulwer
See also DLB 21

Bunin, Ivan (Alexeyevich)
1870-1953................... TCLC 6
See also CA 104

Bunting, Basil
1900-1985.......... CLC 10, 39 (297)
See also CANR 7
See also CA 53-56
See also obituary CA 115
See also DLB 20

Buñuel, Luis 1900-1983 ....CLC 16
See also CA 101
See also obituary CA 110

Bunyan, John (1628-1688)..........LC 4
See also DLB 39

Burgess (Wilson, John) Anthony
1917-.....CLC 1, 2, 4, 5, 8, 10, 13, 15,
                                   22, 40
See also Wilson, John (Anthony) Burgess
See also DLB 14
See also AITN 1

Burke, Edmund 1729-1797 .... LC 7

Burke, Kenneth (Duva)
1897-..................... CLC 2, 24
See also CA 5-8R
See also DLB 45

Burney, Fanny 1752-1840 .... NCLC 12
See also DLB 39

Burns, Robert 1759-1796........... LC 3

Burns, Tex 1908?-
See L'Amour, Louis (Dearborn)

Burnshaw, Stanley
1906-............CLC 3, 13, 44 (456)
See also CA 9-12R
See also DLB 48

Burr, Anne 1937-..................CLC 6
See also CA 25-28R

Burroughs, Edgar Rice
1875-1950.................. TCLC 2
See also CA 104
See also DLB 8
See also SATA 41

Burroughs, William S(eward)
1914-..........CLC 1, 2, 5, 15, 22, 42
See also CANR 20
See also CA 9-12R
See also DLB 2, 8, 16
See also DLB-Y 81
See also AITN 2

Busch, Frederick 1941-...... CLC 7, 10, 18
See also CAAS 1
See also CA 33-36R
See also DLB 6

Bush, Ronald 19??-......... CLC 34 (523)

Butler, Octavia E(stelle) 1947-......CLC 38
See also CANR 12
See also CA 73-76
See also DLB 33

Butler, Samuel 1835-1902 .... TCLC 1
See also CA 104
See also DLB 18, 57

Butor, Michel (Marie François)
1926-............. CLC 1, 3, 8, 11, 15
See also CA 9-12R

Buzzati, Dino 1906-1972..........CLC 36
See also obituary CA 33-36R

Byars, Betsy 1928-................CLC 35
See also CLR 1
See also CANR 18
See also CA 33-36R
See also SAAS 1
See also SATA 4, 46
See also DLB 52

Byatt, A(ntonia) S(usan Drabble)
1936-.........................CLC 19
See also CANR 13
See also CA 13-16R
See also DLB 14

Byrne, David 1953?-.............CLC 26

Byrne, John Keyes 1926-
See Leonard, Hugh
See also CA 102

Byron, George Gordon (Noel), Lord Byron
1788-1824............... NCLC 2, 12

Caballero, Fernán 1796-1877 .... NCLC 10

Catton, (Charles) Bruce
    1899-1978....................CLC 35
    See also CANR 7
    See also CA 5-8R
    See also obituary CA 81-84
    See also SATA 2
    See also obituary SATA 24
    See also DLB 17
    See also AITN 1

Caunitz, William 1935-....... CLC 34 (35)

Causley, Charles (Stanley)
    1917-.........................CLC 7
    See also CANR 5
    See also CA 9-12R
    See also SATA 3
    See also DLB 27

Caute, (John) David 1936-........CLC 29
    See also CAAS 4
    See also CANR 1
    See also CA 1-4R
    See also DLB 14

Cavafy, C(onstantine) P(eter)
    1863-1933.................TCLC 2, 7
    See also CA 104

Cavanna, Betty 1909-..............CLC 12
    See also CANR 6
    See also CA 9-12R
    See also SATA 1, 30

Cayrol, Jean 1911- ....CLC 11
    See also CA 89-92

Cela, Camilo José 1916-........ CLC 4, 13
    See also CA 21-24R

Celan, Paul 1920-1970 .... CLC 10, 19
    See also Antschel, Paul

Céline, Louis-Ferdinand
    1894-1961........ CLC 1, 3, 4, 7, 9, 15
    See also Destouches, Louis Ferdinand

Cellini, Benvenuto 1500-1571 .... LC 7

Cendrars, Blaise 1887-1961.......CLC 18
    See also Sauser-Hall, Frédéric

Cervantes (Saavedra), Miguel de
    1547-1616.....................LC 6

Césaire, Aimé (Fernand)
    1913-.................... CLC 19, 32
    See also CA 65-68

Chabrol, Claude 1930-............CLC 16
    See also CA 110

Challans, Mary 1905-1983
    See Renault, Mary
    See also CA 81-84
    See also obituary CA 111
    See also SATA 23
    See also obituary SATA 36

Chambers, Aidan 1934-...........CLC 35
    See also CANR 12
    See also CA 25-28R
    See also SATA 1

Chambers, James 1948-
    See Cliff, Jimmy

Chandler, Raymond
    1888-1959................TCLC 1, 7
    See also CA 104

Channing, William Ellery
    1780-1842.................NCLC 17
    See also DLB 1, 59

Chaplin, Charles (Spencer)
    1889-1977....................CLC 16
    See also CA 81-84
    See also obituary CA 73-76
    See also DLB 44

Chapman, Graham 1941?-
    See Monty Python
    See also CA 116

Chapman, John Jay
    1862-1933.................. TCLC 7
    See also CA 104

Chappell, Fred 1936- ....CLC 40
    See also CAAS 4
    See also CANR 8
    See also CA 5-8R
    See also DLB 6

Char, René (Emile)
    1907-..................CLC 9, 11, 14
    See also CA 13-16R

Charyn, Jerome 1937- .... CLC 5, 8, 18
    See also CAAS 1
    See also CANR 7
    See also CA 5-8R
    See also DLB-Y 83

Chase, Mary Ellen 1887-1973 ....CLC 2
    See also CAP 1
    See also CA 15-16
    See also obituary CA 41-44R
    See also SATA 10

Chateaubriand, François René de
    1768-1848..................NCLC 3

Chatterji, Saratchandra
    1876-1938................. TCLC 13
    See also CA 109

Chatterton, Thomas 1752-1770....... LC 3

Chatwin, (Charles) Bruce
    1940-.........................CLC 28
    See also CA 85-88

Chayefsky, Paddy 1923-1981.......CLC 23
    See also CA 9-12R
    See also obituary CA 104
    See also DLB 7, 44
    See also DLB-Y 81

Chayefsky, Sidney 1923-1981
    See Chayefsky, Paddy
    See also CANR 18

Cheever, John
    1912-1982...... CLC 3, 7, 8, 11, 15, 25
    See also SSC 1
    See also CANR 5
    See also CA 5-8R
    See also obituary CA 106
    See also CABS 1
    See also DLB 2
    See also DLB-Y 80, 82
    See also CDALB 1941-1968

Cheever, Susan 1943-.............CLC 18
    See also CA 103
    See also DLB-Y 82

Chekhov, Anton (Pavlovich)
    1860-1904................ TCLC 3, 10
    See also CA 104

Chernyshevsky, Nikolay Gavrilovich
    1828-1889.................. NCLC 1

Cherry, Caroline Janice 1942-
    See Cherryh, C. J.

Cherryh, C. J. 1942-.............CLC 35
    See also DLB-Y 80

Chesnutt, Charles Waddell
    1858-1932.................. TCLC 5
    See also CA 106
    See also DLB 12, 50

Chesterton, G(ilbert) K(eith)
    1874-1936................ TCLC 1, 6
    See also SSC 1
    See also CA 104
    See also SATA 27
    See also DLB 10, 19, 34

Ch'ien Chung-shu 1910-...........CLC 22

Child, Lydia Maria 1802-1880 .... NCLC 6
    See also DLB 1

Child, Philip 1898-1978 ....CLC 19
    See also CAP 1
    See also CA 13-14

Childress, Alice 1920-........ CLC 12, 15
    See also CLR 14
    See also CANR 3
    See also CA 45-48
    See also SATA 7, 48
    See also DLB 7, 38

Chislett, (Margaret) Anne
    1943?-................. CLC 34 (144)

Chitty, (Sir) Thomas Willes 1926-
    See Hinde, Thomas
    See also CA 5-8R

Chomette, René 1898-1981
    See Clair, René
    See also obituary CA 103

Chopin, Kate (O'Flaherty)
    1851-1904................ TCLC 5, 14
    See also CA 104
    See also DLB 12

Christie, Agatha (Mary Clarissa)
    1890-1976........... CLC 1, 6, 8, 12,
                                  39 (436)
    See also CANR 10
    See also CA 17-20R
    See also obituary CA 61-64
    See also SATA 36
    See also DLB 13
    See also AITN 1, 2

Christie, (Ann) Philippa 1920-
    See Pearce, (Ann) Philippa
    See also CANR 4

Chulkov, Mikhail Dmitrievich
    1743-1792.....................LC 2

Churchill, Caryl 1938- ....CLC 31
    See also CA 102
    See also DLB 13

Churchill, Charles 1731?-1764 .... LC 3

Chute, Carolyn 1947- .... CLC 39 (37)

Ciardi, John (Anthony)
    1916-1986........CLC 10, 40, 44 (374)
    See also CAAS 2
    See also CANR 5
    See also CA 5-8R
    See also obituary CA 118
    See also SATA 1, 46
    See also DLB 5
    See also DLB-Y 86

Cimino, Michael 1943?- ....CLC 16
    See also CA 105

Deutsch, Babette 1895-1982.......CLC 18
See also CANR 4
See also CA 1-4R
See also obituary CA 108
See also DLB 45
See also SATA 1
See also obituary SATA 33

Devkota, Laxmiprasad
1909-1959................ TCLC 23

De Vries, Peter
1910-.......CLC 1, 2, 3, 7, 10, 28, 46
See also CA 17-20R
See also DLB 6
See also DLB-Y 82

Dexter, Pete 1943-.......... CLC 34 (43)

Diamond, Neil (Leslie) 1941-.......CLC 30
See also CA 108

Dick, Philip K(indred)
1928-1982............. CLC 10, 30
See also CANR 2, 16
See also CA 49-52
See also obituary CA 106
See also DLB 8

Dickens, Charles 1812-1870..... NCLC 3, 8
See also SATA 15
See also DLB 21

Dickey, James (Lafayette)
1923-.......... CLC 1, 2, 4, 7, 10, 15
See also CANR 10
See also CA 9-12R
See also CABS 2
See also DLB 5
See also DLB-Y 82
See also AITN 1, 2

Dickey, William 1928-......... CLC 3, 28
See also CA 9-12R
See also DLB 5

Dickinson, Peter (Malcolm de Brissac)
1927-.................... CLC 12, 35
See also CA 41-44R
See also SATA 5

Didion, Joan 1934- .... CLC 1, 3, 8, 14, 32
See also CANR 14
See also CA 5-8R
See also DLB 2
See also DLB-Y 81, 86
See also AITN 1

Dillard, Annie 1945-.............CLC 9
See also CANR 3
See also CA 49-52
See also SATA 10
See also DLB-Y 80

Dillard, R(ichard) H(enry) W(ilde)
1937-.....................CLC 5
See also CANR 10
See also CA 21-24R
See also DLB 5

Dillon, Eilís 1920- ....CLC 17
See also CAAS 3
See also CANR 4
See also CA 9-12R
See also SATA 2

Dinesen, Isak 1885-1962....... CLC 10, 29
See also Blixen, Karen (Christentze
Dinesen)

Disch, Thomas M(ichael)
1940-.................... CLC 7, 36
See also CAAS 4
See also CANR 17
See also CA 21-24R
See also DLB 8

Disraeli, Benjamin 1804-1881 ..... NCLC 2
See also DLB 21

Dixon, Paige 1911-
See Corcoran, Barbara

Döblin, Alfred 1878-1957....... TCLC 13
See also Doeblin, Alfred

Dobrolyubov, Nikolai Alexandrovich
1836-1861.................... NCLC 5

Dobyns, Stephen 1941-.............CLC 37
See also CANR 2, 18
See also CA 45-48

Doctorow, E(dgar) L(aurence)
1931-...........CLC 6, 11, 15, 18, 37,
44 (166)
See also CANR 2
See also CA 45-48
See also DLB 2, 28
See also DLB-Y 80
See also AITN 2

Dodgson, Charles Lutwidge 1832-1898
See Carroll, Lewis
See also YABC 2

Doeblin, Alfred 1878-1957...... TCLC 13
See also CA 110

Doerr, Harriet 1910-........ CLC 34 (151)
See also CA 117

Donaldson, Stephen R. 1947-.......CLC 46
See also CANR 13
See also CA 89-92

Donleavy, J(ames) P(atrick)
1926- .... CLC 1, 4, 6, 10, 45
See also CA 9-12R
See also DLB 6
See also AITN 2

Donnadieu, Marguerite 1914-
See Duras, Marguerite

Donnell, David 1939?-....... CLC 34 (155)

Donoso, José 1924- ....CLC 4, 8, 11, 32
See also CA 81-84

Donovan, John 1928- ....CLC 35
See also CLR 3
See also CA 97-100
See also SATA 29

Doolittle, Hilda 1886-1961
See H(ilda) D(oolittle)
See also CA 97-100
See also DLB 4, 45

Dorn, Ed(ward Merton)
1929-.................... CLC 10, 18
See also CA 93-96
See also DLB 5

Dos Passos, John (Roderigo)
1896-1970..... CLC 1, 4, 8, 11, 15, 25,
34 (419)
See also CANR 3
See also CA 1-4R
See also obituary CA 29-32R
See also DLB 4, 9
See also DLB-DS 1

Dostoevski, Fedor Mikhailovich
1821-1881............... NCLC 2, 7

Doughty, Charles (Montagu)
1843-1926................ TCLC 27
See also CA 115
See also DLB 19, 57

Douglass, Frederick
1817-1895................. NCLC 7
See also SATA 29
See also DLB 1, 43, 50

Dourado, (Waldomiro Freitas) Autran
1926-....................CLC 23
See also CA 25-28R

Dowson, Ernest (Christopher)
1867-1900................ TCLC 4
See also CA 105
See also DLB 19

Doyle, (Sir) Arthur Conan
1859-1930............... TCLC 7, 26
See also CA 104
See also SATA 24
See also DLB 18

Dr. A 1933-
See Silverstein, Alvin and Virginia
B(arbara Opshelor) Silverstein

Drabble, Margaret
1939-.......... CLC 2, 3, 5, 8, 10, 22
See also CANR 18
See also CA 13-16R
See also DLB 14

Dreiser, Theodore (Herman Albert)
1871-1945............... TCLC 10, 18
See also SATA 48
See also CA 106
See also DLB 9, 12
See also DLB-DS 1

Drexler, Rosalyn 1926-.......... CLC 2, 6
See also CA 81-84

Dreyer, Carl Theodor
1889-1968...................CLC 16
See also obituary CA 116

Drieu La Rochelle, Pierre
1893-1945................ TCLC 21
See also CA 117

Droste-Hülshoff, Annette Freiin von
1797-1848................. NCLC 3

Drummond, William Henry
1854-1907................ TCLC 25

Drummond de Andrade, Carlos 1902-
See Andrade, Carlos Drummond de

Drury, Allen (Stuart) 1918-........CLC 37
See also CANR 18
See also CA 57-60

Dryden, John 1631-1700 .... LC 3

Duberman, Martin 1930-...........CLC 8
See also CANR 2
See also CA 1-4R

Dubie, Norman (Evans, Jr.)
1945-......................CLC 36
See also CANR 12
See also CA 69-72

Du Bois, W(illiam) E(dward) B(urghardt)
1868-1963................ CLC 1, 2, 13
See also CA 85-88
See also SATA 42
See also DLB 47, 50

Dubus, André 1936- .... CLC 13, 36
See also CANR 17
See also CA 21-24R

Ducasse, Isidore Lucien 1846-1870
See Lautréamont, Comte de

Duclos, Charles Pinot 1704-1772 ..... **LC 1**

Dudek, Louis 1918- .... **CLC 11, 19**
See also CANR 1
See also CA 45-48

Dudevant, Amandine Aurore Lucile Dupin
1804-1876
See Sand, George

Duerrenmatt, Friedrich 1921-
See also CA 17-20R

Duffy, Maureen 1933- .... **CLC 37**
See also CA 25-28R
See also DLB 14

Dugan, Alan 1923- .... **CLC 2, 6**
See also CA 81-84
See also DLB 5

Duhamel, Georges 1884-1966 .... **CLC 8**
See also CA 81-84
See also obituary CA 25-28R

Dujardin, Édouard (Émile Louis)
1861-1949 .... **TCLC 13**
See also CA 109

Duke, Raoul 1939-
See Thompson, Hunter S(tockton)

Dumas, Alexandre (Davy de la Pailleterie)
(*père*) 1802-1870 .... **NCLC 11**
See also SATA 18

Dumas, Alexandre (*fils*)
1824-1895 .... **NCLC 9**

Dumas, Henry (L.) 1934-1968 ...... **CLC 6**
See also CA 85-88
See also DLB 41

Du Maurier, Daphne 1907- ..... **CLC 6, 11**
See also CANR 6
See also CA 5-8R
See also SATA 27

Dunbar, Paul Laurence
1872-1906 .... **TCLC 2, 12**
See also CA 104
See also SATA 34
See also DLB 50, 54

Duncan (Steinmetz Arquette), Lois
1934- .... **CLC 26**
See also Arquette, Lois S(teinmetz)
See also CANR 2
See also CA 1-4R
See also SAAS 2
See also SATA 1, 36

Duncan, Robert (Edward)
1919- .... **CLC 1, 2, 4, 7, 15, 41**
See also CA 9-12R
See also DLB 5, 16

Dunlap, William 1766-1839 .... **NCLC 2**
See also DLB 30, 37

Dunn, Douglas (Eaglesham)
1942- .... **CLC 6, 40**
See also CANR 2
See also CA 45-48
See also DLB 40

Dunn, Elsie 1893-1963
See Scott, Evelyn

Dunn, Stephen 1939- .... **CLC 36**
See also CANR 12
See also CA 33-36R

Dunne, John Gregory 1932- .... **CLC 28**
See also CANR 14
See also CA 25-28R
See also DLB-Y 80

**Dunsany, Lord (Edward John Moreton Drax
Plunkett)** 1878-1957 .... **TCLC 2**
See also CA 104
See also DLB 10

Durang, Christopher (Ferdinand)
1949- .... **CLC 27, 38**
See also CA 105

Duras, Marguerite
1914- ..... **CLC 3, 6, 11, 20, 34 (161),**
40
See also CA 25-28R

Durban, Pam 1947- .... **CLC 39 (44)**

Durcan, Paul 1944- .... **CLC 43**

Durrell, Lawrence (George)
1912- .... **CLC 1, 4, 6, 8, 13, 27, 41**
See also CA 9-12R
See also DLB 15, 27

Dürrenmatt, Friedrich
1921- .... **CLC 1, 4, 8, 11, 15, 43**
See also Duerrenmatt, Friedrich

Dwight, Timothy 1752-1817 ...... **NCLC 13**
See also DLB 37

Dworkin, Andrea 1946- .... **CLC 43**
See also CANR 16
See also CA 77-80

Dylan, Bob 1941- .... **CLC 3, 4, 6, 12**
See also CA 41-44R
See also DLB 16

East, Michael 1916-
See West, Morris L.

Eastlake, William (Derry) 1917- ..... **CLC 8**
See also CAAS 1
See also CANR 5
See also CA 5-8R
See also DLB 6

Eberhart, Richard 1904- .... **CLC 3, 11, 19**
See also CANR 2
See also CA 1-4R
See also DLB 48
See also CDALB 1941-1968

Eberstadt, Fernanda
1960- .... **CLC 39 (48)**

**Echegaray (y Eizaguirre), José (María
Waldo)** 1832-1916 .... **TCLC 4**
See also CA 104

Eckert, Allan W. 1931- .... **CLC 17**
See also CANR 14
See also CA 13-16R
See also SATA 27, 29

Eco, Umberto 1932- .... **CLC 28**
See also CANR 12
See also CA 77-80

Eddison, E(ric) R(ucker)
1882-1945 .... **TCLC 15**
See also CA 109

Edel, Leon (Joseph)
1907- .... **CLC 29, 34 (534)**
See also CANR 1
See also CA 1-4R

Eden, Emily 1797-1869 .... **NCLC 10**

Edgar, David 1948- .... **CLC 42**
See also CANR 12
See also CA 57-60
See also DLB 13

Edgerton, Clyde 1944- .... **CLC 39 (52)**
See also CA 118

Edgeworth, Maria 1767-1849 ..... **NCLC 1**
See also SATA 21

Edmonds, Helen (Woods) 1904-1968
See Kavan, Anna
See also CA 5-8R
See also obituary CA 25-28R

Edmonds, Walter D(umaux)
1903- .... **CLC 35**
See also CANR 2
See also CA 5-8R
See also SATA 1, 27
See also DLB 9

Edson, Russell 1905- .... **CLC 13**
See also CA 33-36R

Edwards, G(erald) B(asil)
1899-1976 .... **CLC 25**
See also obituary CA 110

Edwards, Gus 1939- .... **CLC 43**
See also CA 108

Edwards, Jonathan 1703-1758 .... **LC 7**
See also DLB 24

Ehle, John (Marsden, Jr.)
1925- .... **CLC 27**
See also CA 9-12R

Ehrenbourg, Ilya (Grigoryevich) 1891-1967
See Ehrenburg, Ilya (Grigoryevich)

Ehrenburg, Ilya (Grigoryevich)
1891-1967 .... **CLC 18, 34 (433)**
See also CA 102
See also obituary CA 25-28R

Eich, Guenter 1907-1971
See also CA 111
See also obituary CA 93-96

Eich, Günter 1907-1971 .... **CLC 15**
See also Eich, Guenter

Eichendorff, Joseph Freiherr von
1788-1857 .... **NCLC 8**

Eigner, Larry 1927- .... **CLC 9**
See also Eigner, Laurence (Joel)
See also DLB 5

Eigner, Laurence (Joel) 1927-
See Eigner, Larry
See also CANR 6
See also CA 9-12R

Eiseley, Loren (Corey)
1907-1977 .... **CLC 7**
See also CANR 6
See also CA 1-4R
See also obituary CA 73-76

Ekeloef, Gunnar (Bengt) 1907-1968
See Ekelöf, Gunnar (Bengt)
See also obituary CA 25-28R

Ekelöf, Gunnar (Bengt)
1907-1968 .... **CLC 27**
See also Ekeloef, Gunnar (Bengt)

Ekwensi, Cyprian (Odiatu Duaka)
1921- .... **CLC 4**
See also CANR 18
See also CA 29-32R

Author Index

Kazan, Elia 1909- .... CLC 6, 16
See also CA 21-24R

Kazantzakis, Nikos
1885?-1957................ TCLC 2, 5
See also CA 105

Kazin, Alfred 1915-..... CLC 34 (555), 38
See also CANR 1
See also CA 1-4R

Keane, Mary Nesta (Skrine) 1904-
See Keane, Molly
See also CA 108, 114

Keane, Molly 1904-................CLC 31
See also Keane, Mary Nesta (Skrine)

Keates, Jonathan 19??-..... CLC 34 (201)

Keaton, Buster 1895-1966 ....CLC 20

Keaton, Joseph Francis 1895-1966
See Keaton, Buster

Keats, John 1795-1821 .... NCLC 8

Keene, Donald 1922-........ CLC 34 (566)
See also CANR 5
See also CA 1-4R

Keillor, Garrison 1942-............CLC 40
See also Keillor, Gary (Edward)
See also CA 111

Keillor, Gary (Edward)
See Keillor, Garrison
See also CA 117

Kell, Joseph 1917-
See Burgess (Wilson, John) Anthony

Keller, Gottfried 1819-1890 ...... NCLC 2

Kellerman, Jonathan (S.)
1949-................ CLC 44 (225)

Kelley, William Melvin 1937- ......CLC 22
See also CA 77-80
See also DLB 33

Kellogg, Marjorie 1922-............CLC 2
See also CA 81-84

Kemal, Yashar 1922- .... CLC 14, 29
See also CA 89-92

Kemelman, Harry 1908-............CLC 2
See also CANR 6
See also CA 9-12R
See also DLB 28
See also AITN 1

Kempe, Margery 1373?-1440?....... LC 6

Kendall, Henry 1839-1882 ...... NCLC 12

Keneally, Thomas (Michael)
1935-......CLC 5, 8, 10, 14, 19, 27, 43
See also CANR 10
See also CA 85-88

Kennedy, John Pendleton
1795-1870................ NCLC 2
See also DLB 3

Kennedy, Joseph Charles 1929-
See Kennedy, X. J.
See also CANR 4
See also CA 1-4R
See also SATA 14

Kennedy, William
1928-............CLC 6, 28, 34 (205)
See also CANR 14
See also CA 85-88
See also DLB-Y 85

Kennedy, X. J. 1929- .... CLC 8, 42
See also Kennedy, Joseph Charles
See also DLB 5

Kerouac, Jack
1922-1969......CLC 1, 2, 3, 5, 14, 29
See also Kerouac, Jean-Louis Lebrid de
See also DLB 2, 16
See also DLB-DS 3
See also CDALB 1941-1968

Kerouac, Jean-Louis Lebrid de 1922-1969
See Kerouac, Jack
See also CA 5-8R
See also obituary CA 25-28R
See also CDALB 1941-1968
See also AITN 1

Kerr, Jean 1923-................CLC 22
See also CANR 7
See also CA 5-8R

Kerr, M. E. 1927-............ CLC 12, 35
See also Meaker, Marijane
See also SAAS 1

Kerrigan, (Thomas) Anthony
1918-................ CLC 4, 6
See also CANR 4
See also CA 49-52

Kesey, Ken (Elton)
1935-............ CLC 1, 3, 6, 11, 46
See also CA 1-4R
See also DLB 2, 16

Kesselring, Joseph (Otto)
1902-1967................CLC 45

Kessler, Jascha (Frederick)
1929-................CLC 4
See also CANR 8
See also CA 17-20R

Kettelkamp, Larry 1933-.........CLC 12
See also CANR 16
See also CA 29-32R
See also SAAS 3
See also SATA 2

Kherdian, David 1931-.......... CLC 6, 9
See also CAAS 2
See also CA 21-24R
See also SATA 16

Khlebnikov, Velimir (Vladimirovich)
1885-1922................ TCLC 20
See also CA 117

Khodasevich, Vladislav (Felitsianovich)
1886-1939................ TCLC 15
See also CA 115

Kielland, Alexander (Lange)
1849-1906................. TCLC 5
See also CA 104

Kiely, Benedict 1919- .... CLC 23, 43
See also CANR 2
See also CA 1-4R
See also DLB 15

Kienzle, William X(avier)
1928-....................CLC 25
See also CAAS 1
See also CANR 9
See also CA 93-96

Killens, John Oliver 1916-.........CLC 10
See also CAAS 2
See also CA 77-80
See also DLB 33

Killigrew, Anne 1660-1685.......... LC 4

Kincaid, Jamaica 1949?- ....CLC 43

King, Francis (Henry) 1923- ....CLC 8
See also CANR 1
See also CA 1-4R
See also DLB 15

King, Stephen (Edwin)
1947-................ CLC 12, 26, 37
See also CANR 1
See also CA 61-64
See also SATA 9
See also DLB-Y 80

Kingman, (Mary) Lee 1919- ....CLC 17
See also Natti, (Mary) Lee
See also CA 5-8R
See also SATA 1

Kingsley, Sidney 1906- ...... CLC 44 (229)

Kingston, Maxine Hong
1940-................ CLC 12, 19
See also CANR 13
See also CA 69-72
See also DLB-Y 80

Kinnell, Galway
1927-......CLC 1, 2, 3, 5, 13, 29
See also CANR 10
See also CA 9-12R
See also DLB 5

Kinsella, Thomas 1928- ..... CLC 4, 19, 43
See also CANR 15
See also CA 17-20R
See also DLB 27

Kinsella, W(illiam) P(atrick)
1935-.................... CLC 27, 43
See also CA 97-100

Kipling, (Joseph) Rudyard
1865-1936............... TCLC 8, 17
See also CA 20, 105
See also YABC 2
See also DLB 19, 34

Kirkup, James 1927-...............CLC 1
See also CAAS 4
See also CANR 2
See also CA 1-4R
See also SATA 12
See also DLB 27

Kirkwood, James 1930- ....CLC 9
See also CANR 6
See also CA 1-4R
See also AITN 2

Kizer, Carolyn (Ashley)
1925-................ CLC 15, 39 (168)
See also CAAS 5
See also CA 65-68
See also DLB 5

Klausner, Amos 1939-
See Oz, Amos

Klein, A(braham) M(oses)
1909-1972....................CLC 19
See also CA 101
See also obituary CA 37-40R

Klein, Norma 1938-...............CLC 30
See also CLR 2
See also CANR 15
See also CA 41-44R
See also SAAS 1
See also SATA 7

Klein, T.E.D. 19??-.......... CLC 34 (70)
See also CA 119

Rice, Tim 1944-
  See Rice, Tim and Webber, Andrew Lloyd
  See also CA 103

Rice, Tim 1944- and
  Webber, Andrew Lloyd
  1948-.......................CLC 21

Rich, Adrienne (Cecile)
  1929-..........CLC 3, 6, 7, 11, 18, 36
  See also CANR 20
  See also CA 9-12R
  See also DLB 5

Richard, Keith 1943-
  See Jagger, Mick and Richard, Keith

Richards, I(vor) A(rmstrong)
  1893-1979................ CLC 14, 24
  See also CA 41-44R
  See also obituary CA 89-92
  See also DLB 27

Richards, Keith 1943-
  See Richard, Keith
  See also CA 107

Richardson, Dorothy (Miller)
  1873-1957..................TCLC 3
  See also CA 104
  See also DLB 36

Richardson, Ethel 1870-1946
  See Richardson, Henry Handel
  See also CA 105

Richardson, Henry Handel
  1870-1946..................TCLC 4
  See also Richardson, Ethel

Richardson, Samuel 1689-1761.......LC 1
  See also DLB 39

Richler, Mordecai
  1931-..........CLC 3, 5, 9, 13, 18, 46
  See also CA 65-68
  See also SATA 27, 44
  See also DLB 53
  See also AITN 1

Richter, Conrad (Michael)
  1890-1968....................CLC 30
  See also CA 5-8R
  See also obituary CA 25-28R
  See also SATA 3
  See also DLB 9

Richter, Johann Paul Friedrich 1763-1825
  See Jean Paul

Riding, Laura 1901- .... CLC 3, 7
  See also Jackson, Laura (Riding)

Riefenstahl, Berta Helene Amalia 1902-
  See Riefenstahl, Leni
  See also CA 108

Riefenstahl, Leni 1902-...........CLC 16
  See also Riefenstahl, Berta Helene Amalia

Rilke, Rainer Maria
  1875-1926..............TCLC 1, 6, 19
  See also CA 104

Rimbaud, (Jean Nicolas) Arthur
  1854-1891..................NCLC 4

Rio, Michel 19?? ....CLC 43

Ritsos, Yannis 1909- ....CLC 6, 13, 31
  See also CA 77-80

Rivers, Conrad Kent 1933-1968 .....CLC 1
  See also CA 85-88
  See also DLB 41

Roa Bastos, Augusto 1917-........CLC 45

Robbe-Grillet, Alain
  1922-..... CLC 1, 2, 4, 6, 8, 10, 14, 43
  See also CA 9-12R

Robbins, Harold 1916-............CLC 5
  See also CA 73-76

Robbins, Thomas Eugene 1936-
  See Robbins, Tom
  See also CA 81-84

Robbins, Tom 1936- .... CLC 9, 32
  See also Robbins, Thomas Eugene
  See also DLB-Y 80

Robbins, Trina 1938- ....CLC 21

Roberts, (Sir) Charles G(eorge) D(ouglas)
  1860-1943..................TCLC 8
  See also CA 105
  See also SATA 29

Roberts, Kate 1891-1985 ....CLC 15
  See also CA 107
  See also obituary CA 116

Roberts, Keith (John Kingston)
  1935-......................CLC 14
  See also CA 25-28R

Roberts, Kenneth 1885-1957 ..... TCLC 23
  See also CA 109
  See also DLB 9

Robinson, Edwin Arlington
  1869-1935..................TCLC 5
  See also CA 104
  See also DLB 54

Robinson, Henry Crabb
  1775-1867.................NCLC 15

Robinson, Jill 1936-..............CLC 10
  See also CA 102

Robinson, Kim Stanley
  19??- .... CLC 34 (105)

Robinson, Marilynne 1944- ....CLC 25
  See also CA 116

Robinson, Smokey 1940- ....CLC 21

Robinson, William 1940-
  See Robinson, Smokey
  See also CA 116

Robison, Mary 1949-..............CLC 42
  See also CA 113, 116

Roddenberry, Gene 1921- ....CLC 17

Rodgers, Mary 1931- ....CLC 12
  See also CANR 8
  See also CA 49-52
  See also SATA 8

Rodgers, W(illiam) R(obert)
  1909-1969....................CLC 7
  See also CA 85-88
  See also DLB 20

Rodríguez, Claudio 1934-..........CLC 10

Roethke, Theodore (Huebner)
  1908-1963...... CLC 1, 3, 8, 11, 19, 46
  See also CA 81-84
  See also CABS 2
  See also SAAS 1
  See also DLB 5
  See also CDALB 1941-1968

Rogers, Sam 1943-
  See Shepard, Sam

Rogers, Will(iam Penn Adair)
  1879-1935..................TCLC 8
  See also CA 105
  See also DLB 11

Rogin, Gilbert 1929-.............CLC 18
  See also CANR 15
  See also CA 65-68

Rohan, Kōda 1867-1947........ TCLC 22

Rohmer, Eric 1920-...............CLC 16
  See also Scherer, Jean-Marie Maurice

Roiphe, Anne (Richardson)
  1935-..................... CLC 3, 9
  See also CA 89-92
  See also DLB-Y 80

Rolfe, Frederick (William Serafino Austin
  Lewis Mary) 1860-1913..... TCLC 12
  See also CA 107
  See also DLB 34

Rolland, Romain 1866-1944...... TCLC 23
  See also CA 118

Rölvaag, O(le) E(dvart)
  1876-1931.................TCLC 17
  See also DLB 9

Romains, Jules 1885-1972 ....CLC 7
  See also CA 85-88

Romero, José Rubén
  1890-1952.................TCLC 14
  See also CA 114

Ronsard, Pierre de 1524-1585........LC 6

Rooke, Leon 1934-....... CLC 25, 34 (250)
  See also CA 25-28R

Rosa, João Guimarães
  1908-1967...................CLC 23
  See also obituary CA 89-92

Rosen, Richard (Dean)
  1949- .... CLC 39 (194)
  See also CA 77-80

Rosenberg, Isaac 1890-1918...... TCLC 12
  See also CA 107
  See also DLB 20

Rosenblatt, Joe 1933- ....CLC 15
  See also Rosenblatt, Joseph
  See also AITN 2

Rosenblatt, Joseph 1933-
  See Rosenblatt, Joe
  See also CA 89-92

Rosenthal, M(acha) L(ouis)
  1917-......................CLC 28
  See also CANR 4
  See also CA 1-4R
  See also DLB 5

Ross, (James) Sinclair 1908- ....CLC 13
  See also CA 73-76

Rossetti, Christina Georgina
  1830-1894.................. NCLC 2
  See also SATA 20
  See also DLB 35

Rossetti, Dante Gabriel
  1828-1882.................. NCLC 4
  See also DLB 35

Rossetti, Gabriel Charles Dante 1828-1882
  See Rossetti, Dante Gabriel

Rossner, Judith (Perelman)
  1935-................... CLC 6, 9, 29
  See also CANR 18
  See also CA 17-20R
  See also DLB 6
  See also AITN 2

Rostand, Edmond (Eugène Alexis)
1868-1918................... **TCLC 6**
See also CA 104

Roth, Henry 1906-.......... **CLC 2, 6, 11**
See also CAP 1
See also CA 11-12
See also DLB 28

Roth, Philip (Milton)
1933-......**CLC 1, 2, 3, 4, 6, 9, 15, 22, 31**
See also CANR 1
See also CA 1-4R
See also DLB 2, 28
See also DLB-Y 82

Rothenberg, Jerome 1931-..........**CLC 6**
See also CANR 1
See also CA 45-48
See also DLB 5

Roumain, Jacques 1907-1944 .... **TCLC 19**
See also CA 117

Rourke, Constance (Mayfield)
1885-1941................... **TCLC 12**
See also CA 107
See also YABC 1

Roussel, Raymond 1877-1933 .... **TCLC 20**
See also CA 117

Rovit, Earl (Herbert) 1927-........**CLC 7**
See also CA 5-8R
See also CANR 12

Rowson, Susanna Haswell
1762-1824................... **NCLC 5**
See also DLB 37

Roy, Gabrielle 1909-1983...... **CLC 10, 14**
See also CANR 5
See also CA 53-56
See also obituary CA 110

Różewicz, Tadeusz 1921- .... **CLC 9, 23**
See also CA 108

Ruark, Gibbons 1941-..............**CLC 3**
See also CANR 14
See also CA 33-36R

Rubens, Bernice 192?- .... **CLC 19, 31**
See also CA 25-28R
See also DLB 14

Rudkin, (James) David 1936- ......**CLC 14**
See also CA 89-92
See also DLB 13

Rudnik, Raphael 1933-.............**CLC 7**
See also CA 29-32R

Ruiz, José Martínez 1874-1967
See Azorín

Rukeyser, Muriel
1913-1980..........**CLC 6, 10, 15, 27**
See also CA 5-8R
See also obituary CA 93-96
See also obituary SATA 22
See also DLB 48

Rule, Jane (Vance) 1931-..........**CLC 27**
See also CANR 12
See also CA 25-28R

Rulfo, Juan 1918-1986 ....**CLC 8**
See also CA 85-88
See also obituary CA 118

Runyon, (Alfred) Damon
1880-1946................... **TCLC 10**
See also CA 107
See also DLB 11

Rush, Norman 1933-........ **CLC 44 (91)**

Rushdie, (Ahmed) Salman
1947-.................... **CLC 23, 31**
See also CA 108, 111

Rushforth, Peter (Scott) 1945-......**CLC 19**
See also CA 101

Ruskin, John 1819-1900........ **TCLC 20**
See also CA 114
See also SATA 24

Russ, Joanna 1937-..............**CLC 15**
See also CANR 11
See also CA 25-28R
See also DLB 8

Russell, George William 1867-1935
See A. E.
See also CA 104

Russell, (Henry) Ken(neth Alfred)
1927-....................**CLC 16**
See also CA 105

Rutherford, Mark 1831-1913 .... **TCLC 25**
See also DLB 18

Ruyslinck, Ward 1929-............**CLC 14**

Ryan, Cornelius (John)
1920-1974...................**CLC 7**
See also CA 69-72
See also obituary CA 53-56

Rybakov, Anatoli 1911?- ....**CLC 23**

Ryder, Jonathan 1927-
See Ludlum, Robert

Ryga, George 1932-..............**CLC 14**
See also CA 101

Sabato, Ernesto 1911-........ **CLC 10, 23**
See also CA 97-100

Sachs, Marilyn (Stickle) 1927-......**CLC 35**
See also CLR 2
See also CANR 13
See also CA 17-20R
See also SAAS 2
See also SATA 3

Sachs, Nelly 1891-1970...........**CLC 14**
See also CAP 2
See also CA 17-18
See also obituary CA 25-28R

Sackler, Howard (Oliver)
1929-1982...................**CLC 14**
See also CA 61-64
See also obituary CA 108
See also DLB 7

Sade, Donatien Alphonse François, Comte de
1740-1814................... **NCLC 3**

Sadoff, Ira 1945- ....**CLC 9**
See also CANR 5
See also CA 53-56

Safire, William 1929- ....**CLC 10**
See also CA 17-20R

Sagan, Carl (Edward) 1934- ......**CLC 30**
See also CANR 11
See also CA 25-28R

Sagan, Françoise
1935-............. **CLC 3, 6, 9, 17, 36**
See also Quoirez, Françoise

Sahgal, Nayantara (Pandit)
1927-........................**CLC 41**
See also CANR 11
See also CA 9-12R

Sainte-Beuve, Charles Augustin
1804-1869................... **NCLC 5**

Sainte-Marie, Beverly 1941-
See Sainte-Marie, Buffy
See also CA 107

Sainte-Marie, Buffy 1941- ....**CLC 17**
See also Sainte-Marie, Beverly

Saint-Exupéry, Antoine (Jean Baptiste Marie Roger) de 1900-1944 .... **TCLC 2**
See also CLR 10
See also CA 108
See also SATA 20

Sait Faik (Abasıyanık)
1906-1954................... **TCLC 23**

Saki 1870-1916................. **TCLC 3**
See also Munro, H(ector) H(ugh)

Salama, Hannu 1936- ....**CLC 18**

Salamanca, J(ack) R(ichard)
1922-..................... **CLC 4, 15**
See also CA 25-28R

Salinas, Pedro 1891-1951........ **TCLC 17**
See also CA 117

Salinger, J(erome) D(avid)
1919-.................**CLC 1, 3, 8, 12**
See also CA 5-8R
See also DLB 2
See also CDALB 1941-1968

Salter, James 1925-...............**CLC 7**
See also CA 73-76

Saltus, Edgar (Evertson)
1855-1921................... **TCLC 8**
See also CA 105

Saltykov, Mikhail Evgrafovich
1826-1889................. **NCLC 16**

Samarakis, Antonis 1919-..........**CLC 5**
See also CA 25-28R

Sánchez, Luis Rafael 1936- ....**CLC 23**

Sanchez, Sonia 1934-..............**CLC 5**
See also CA 33-36R
See also SATA 22
See also DLB 41

Sand, George 1804-1876.......... **NCLC 2**

Sandburg, Carl (August)
1878-1967....... **CLC 1, 4, 10, 15, 35**
See also CA 5-8R
See also obituary CA 25-28R
See also SATA 8
See also DLB 17

Sandburg, Charles August 1878-1967
See Sandburg, Carl (August)

Sanders, Lawrence 1920-..........**CLC 41**
See also CA 81-84

Sandoz, Mari (Susette)
1896-1966...................**CLC 28**
See also CANR 17
See also CA 1-4R
See also obituary CA 25-28R
See also SATA 5
See also DLB 9

Saner, Reg(inald Anthony)
1931-........................**CLC 9**
See also CA 65-68

Sansom, William 1912-1976...... **CLC 2, 6**
See also CA 5-8R
See also obituary CA 65-68

Theroux, Alexander (Louis)
1939- .... CLC **2, 25**
See also CANR 20
See also CA 85-88

Theroux, Paul
1941- .... CLC **5, 8, 11, 15, 28, 46**
See also CANR 20
See also CA 33-36R
See also DLB 2
See also SATA 44

Thibault, Jacques Anatole Francois
1844-1924
See France, Anatole
See also CA 106

Thiele, Colin (Milton) 1920- ....CLC **17**
See also CANR 12
See also CA 29-32R
See also SAAS 2
See also SATA 14

Thomas, Audrey (Grace)
1935- .... CLC **7, 13, 37**
See also CA 21-24R
See also AITN 2

Thomas, D(onald) M(ichael)
1935- .... CLC **13, 22, 31**
See also CANR 17
See also CA 61-64
See also DLB 40

Thomas, Dylan (Marlais)
1914-1953................. TCLC **1, 8**
See also CA 104, 120
See also DLB 13, 20

Thomas, Edward (Philip)
1878-1917................. TCLC **10**
See also CA 106
See also DLB 19

Thomas, John Peter 1928-
See Thomas, Piri

Thomas, Joyce Carol 1938- ....CLC **35**
See also CA 113, 116
See also SATA 40
See also DLB 33

Thomas, Lewis 1913- ....CLC **35**
See also CA 85-88

Thomas, Piri 1928- ....CLC **17**
See also CA 73-76

Thomas, R(onald) S(tuart)
1913- .... CLC **6, 13**
See also CAAS 4
See also CA 89-92
See also DLB 27

Thomas, Ross (Elmore)
1926- .... CLC **39** (246)
See also CA 33-36R

Thompson, Francis (Joseph)
1859-1907................. TCLC **4**
See also CA 104
See also DLB 19

Thompson, Hunter S(tockton)
1939- .... CLC **9, 17, 40**
See also CA 17-20R

Thompson, Judith 1954- ..... CLC **39** (250)

Thomson, James 1834-1882...... NCLC **17**
See also DLB 35

Thoreau, Henry David
1817-1862.................. NCLC **7**
See also DLB 1

Thurber, James (Grover)
1894-1961............CLC **5, 11, 25**
See also SSC 1
See also CANR 17
See also CA 73-76
See also SATA 13
See also DLB 4, 11, 22

Thurman, Wallace 1902-1934 ..... TCLC **6**
See also CA 104

Tieck, (Johann) Ludwig
1773-1853.................. NCLC **5**

Tillinghast, Richard 1940- ....CLC **29**
See also CA 29-32R

Tindall, Gillian 1938- ....CLC **7**
See also CANR 11
See also CA 21-24R

Tocqueville, Alexis (Charles Henri Maurice Clérel, Comte) de
1805-1859.................. NCLC **7**

Tolkien, J(ohn) R(onald) R(euel)
1892-1973....... CLC **1, 2, 3, 8, 12, 38**
See also CAP 2
See also CA 17-18
See also obituary CA 45-48
See also SATA 2, 32
See also obituary SATA 24
See also DLB 15
See also AITN 1

Toller, Ernst 1893-1939 .... TCLC **10**
See also CA 107

Tolson, Melvin B(eaunorus)
1900?-1966...................CLC **36**
See also obituary CA 89-92
See also DLB 48

Tolstoy, (Count) Alexey Nikolayevich
1883-1945.................. TCLC **18**
See also CA 107

Tolstoy, (Count) Leo (Lev Nikolaevich)
1828-1910.............TCLC **4, 11, 17**
See also CA 104
See also SATA 26

Tomlin, Lily 1939-...................CLC **17**

Tomlin, Mary Jean 1939-
See Tomlin, Lily

Tomlinson, (Alfred) Charles
1927-.............. CLC **2, 4, 6, 13, 45**
See also CA 5-8R
See also DLB 40

Toole, John Kennedy
1937-1969....................CLC **19**
See also CA 104
See also DLB-Y 81

Toomer, Jean
1894-1967............CLC **1, 4, 13, 22**
See also SSC 1
See also CA 85-88
See also DLB 45, 51

Torrey, E. Fuller 19??- ...... CLC **34** (503)

Tournier, Michel 1924-...... CLC **6, 23, 36**
See also CANR 3
See also CA 49-52
See also SATA 23

Townshend, Peter (Dennis Blandford)
1945-................... CLC **17, 42**
See also CA 107

Trakl, Georg 1887-1914 .... TCLC **5**
See also CA 104

Traven, B. 1890-1969......... CLC **8, 11**
See also CAP 2
See also CA 19-20
See also obituary CA 25-28R
See also DLB 9

Tremain, Rose 1943-.............CLC **42**
See also CA 97-100
See also DLB 14

Tremblay, Michel 1942-...........CLC **29**

Trevanian 1925-..................CLC **29**
See also Whitaker, Rodney
See also CA 108

Trevor, William
1928-..................CLC **7, 9, 14, 25**
See also Cox, William Trevor
See also DLB 14

Trifonov, Yuri (Valentinovich)
1925-1981....................CLC **45**
See also obituary CA 103

Trilling, Lionel
1905-1975..............CLC **9, 11, 24**
See also CANR 10
See also CA 9-12R
See also obituary CA 61-64
See also DLB 28

Trogdon, William 1939-
See Heat Moon, William Least
See also CA 115

Trollope, Anthony 1815-1882 ..... NCLC **6**
See also SATA 22
See also DLB 21, 57

Trotsky, Leon (Davidovich)
1879-1940.................. TCLC **22**
See also CA 118

Troyat, Henri 1911- ....CLC **23**
See also CANR 2
See also CA 45-48

Trudeau, G(arretson) B(eekman) 1948-
See Trudeau, Garry
See also CA 81-84
See also SATA 35

Trudeau, Garry 1948-............CLC **12**
See also Trudeau, G(arretson) B(eekman)
See also AITN 2

Truffaut, François 1932-1984 ......CLC **20**
See also CA 81-84
See also obituary CA 113

Trumbo, Dalton 1905-1976 ....CLC **19**
See also CANR 10
See also CA 21-24R
See also obituary CA 69-72
See also DLB 26

Tryon, Thomas 1926- .... CLC **3, 11**
See also CA 29-32R
See also AITN 1

Ts'ao Hsüeh-ch'in 1715?-1763........ LC **1**

Tsushima Shūji 1909-1948
See Dazai Osamu
See also CA 107

Tsvetaeva (Efron), Marina (Ivanovna)
1892-1941.................... TCLC **7**
See also CA 104

Tunis, John R(oberts)
1889-1975....................CLC **12**
See also CA 61-64
See also SATA 30, 37
See also DLB 22

Tuohy, Frank 1925- ....CLC 37
  See also DLB 14

Tuohy, John Francis 1925-
  See Tuohy, Frank
  See also CANR 3
  See also CA 5-8R

Turco, Lewis (Putnam) 1934- ......CLC 11
  See also CA 13-16R
  See also DLB-Y 84

Tutuola, Amos 1920-........CLC 5, 14, 29
  See also CA 9-12R

Twain, Mark
  1835-1910.............TCLC 6, 12, 19
  See also Clemens, Samuel Langhorne
  See also DLB 11

Tyler, Anne
  1941-...... CLC 7, 11, 18, 28, 44 (311)
  See also CANR 11
  See also CA 9-12R
  See also SATA 7
  See also DLB 6
  See also DLB-Y 82

Tyler, Royall 1757-1826.........NCLC 3
  See also DLB 37

Tynan (Hinkson), Katharine
  1861-1931................. TCLC 3
  See also CA 104

Unamuno (y Jugo), Miguel de
  1864-1936................TCLC 2, 9
  See also CA 104

Underwood, Miles 1909-1981
  See Glassco, John

Undset, Sigrid 1882-1949........ TCLC 3
  See also CA 104

Ungaretti, Giuseppe
  1888-1970.............CLC 7, 11, 15
  See also CAP 2
  See also CA 19-20
  See also obituary CA 25-28R

Unger, Douglas 1952- ....CLC 34 (114)

Unger, Eva 1932-
  See Figes, Eva

Updike, John (Hoyer)
  1932-......CLC 1, 2, 3, 5, 7, 9, 13, 15,
                       23, 34 (283), 43
  See also CANR 4
  See also CA 1-4R
  See also CABS 2
  See also DLB 2, 5
  See also DLB-Y 80, 82
  See also DLB-DS 3

Uris, Leon (Marcus) 1924-...... CLC 7, 32
  See also CANR 1
  See also CA 1-4R
  See also AITN 1, 2

Ustinov, Peter (Alexander)
  1921-......................CLC 1
  See also CA 13-16R
  See also DLB 13
  See also AITN 1

Vaculík, Ludvík 1926- ....CLC 7
  See also CA 53-56

Valenzuela, Luisa 1938- ....CLC 31
  See also CA 101

Valera (y Acalá-Galiano), Juan
  1824-1905................. TCLC 10
  See also CA 106

Valéry, Paul (Ambroise Toussaint Jules)
  1871-1945............... TCLC 4, 15
  See also CA 104

Valle-Inclán (y Montenegro), Ramón (María)
  del 1866-1936 .... TCLC 5
  See also CA 106

Vallejo, César (Abraham)
  1892-1938.................. TCLC 3
  See also CA 105

Van Ash, Cay 1918- .... CLC 34 (118)

Vance, Jack 1916?-..............CLC 35
  See also DLB 8

Vance, John Holbrook 1916?-
  See Vance, Jack
  See also CANR 17
  See also CA 29-32R

Van Den Bogarde, Derek (Jules Gaspard
  Ulric) Niven 1921-
  See Bogarde, Dirk
  See also CA 77-80

Vanderhaeghe, Guy 1951- ....CLC 41
  See also CA 113

Van der Post, Laurens (Jan)
  1906-........................CLC 5
  See also CA 5-8R

Van Dine, S. S. 1888-1939...... TCLC 23

Van Doren, Carl (Clinton)
  1885-1950................ TCLC 18
  See also CA 111

Van Doren, Mark
  1894-1972................ CLC 6, 10
  See also CANR 3
  See also CA 1-4R
  See also obituary CA 37-40R
  See also DLB 45

Van Druten, John (William)
  1901-1957.................. TCLC 2
  See also CA 104
  See also DLB 10

Van Duyn, Mona 1921- .... CLC 3, 7
  See also CANR 7
  See also CA 9-12R
  See also DLB 5

Van Itallie, Jean-Claude 1936- ......CLC 3
  See also CAAS 2
  See also CANR 1
  See also CA 45-48
  See also DLB 7

Van Peebles, Melvin 1932-...... CLC 2, 20
  See also CA 85-88

Vansittart, Peter 1920-............CLC 42
  See also CANR 3
  See also CA 1-4R

Van Vechten, Carl 1880-1964......CLC 33
  See also obituary CA 89-92
  See also DLB 4, 9

Van Vogt, A(lfred) E(lton)
  1912-.......................CLC 1
  See also CA 21-24R
  See also SATA 14
  See also DLB 8

Varda, Agnès 1928-..............CLC 16
  See also CA 116

Vargas Llosa, (Jorge) Mario (Pedro)
  1936-....CLC 3, 6, 9, 10, 15, 31, 42
  See also CANR 18
  See also CA 73-76

Vassilikos, Vassilis 1933- .... CLC 4, 8
  See also CA 81-84

Vazov, Ivan 1850-1921......... TCLC 25

Verga, Giovanni 1840-1922....... TCLC 3
  See also CA 104

Verhaeren, Émile (Adolphe Gustave)
  1855-1916................ TCLC 12
  See also CA 109

Verlaine, Paul (Marie)
  1844-1896.................. NCLC 2

Verne, Jules (Gabriel)
  1828-1905.................. TCLC 6
  See also CA 110
  See also SATA 21

Very, Jones 1813-1880 .... NCLC 9
  See also DLB 1

Vian, Boris 1920-1959 .... TCLC 9
  See also CA 106

Viaud, (Louis Marie) Julien 1850-1923
  See Loti, Pierre
  See also CA 107

Vicker, Angus 1916-
  See Felsen, Henry Gregor

Vidal, Eugene Luther, Jr. 1925-
  See Vidal, Gore

Vidal, Gore
  1925-........CLC 2, 4, 6, 8, 10, 22, 33
  See also CANR 13
  See also CA 5-8R
  See also DLB 6
  See also AITN 1

Viereck, Peter (Robert Edwin)
  1916-.......................CLC 4
  See also CANR 1
  See also CA 1-4R
  See also DLB 5

Vigny, Alfred (Victor) de
  1797-1863.................. NCLC 7

Villiers de l'Isle Adam, Jean Marie Mathias
  Philippe Auguste, Comte de,
  1838-1889.................. NCLC 3

Vinge, Joan (Carol) D(ennison)
  1948-.......................CLC 30
  See also CA 93-96
  See also SATA 36

Visconti, Luchino 1906-1976.......CLC 16
  See also CA 81-84
  See also obituary CA 65-68

Vittorini, Elio 1908-1966 ..... CLC 6, 9, 14
  See also obituary CA 25-28R

Vizinczey, Stephen 1933- ....CLC 40

Vliet, R(ussell) G. 1929-...........CLC 22
  See also CANR 18
  See also CA 37-40R
  See also obituary CA 112

Voigt, Cynthia 1942-..............CLC 30
  See also CANR 18
  See also CA 106
  See also SATA 33, 48

Voinovich, Vladimir (Nikolaevich)
  1932-.......................CLC 10
  See also CA 81-84

Von Daeniken, Erich 1935-
  See Von Däniken, Erich
  See also CANR 17
  See also CA 37-40R
  See also AITN 1

Webb, Sidney (James) 1859-1947 and
   Webb, Beatrice (Potter) 1858-1943
  See Webb, Beatrice (Potter) and Webb,
   Sidney (James)

Webber, Andrew Lloyd 1948-
  See Rice, Tim and Webber, Andrew Lloyd

Weber, Lenora Mattingly
   1895-1971.....................CLC 12
  See also CAP 1
  See also CA 19-20
  See also obituary CA 29-32R
  See also SATA 2
  See also obituary SATA 26

Wedekind, (Benjamin) Frank(lin)
   1864-1918...................TCLC 7
  See also CA 104

Weidman, Jerome 1913-...........CLC 7
  See also CANR 1
  See also CA 1-4R
  See also DLB 28
  See also AITN 2

Weil, Simone 1909-1943.........TCLC 23
  See also CA 117

Weinstein, Nathan Wallenstein 1903?-1940
  See West, Nathanael
  See also CA 104

Weir, Peter 1944- ....CLC 20
  See also CA 113

Weiss, Peter (Ulrich)
   1916-1982................ CLC 3, 15
  See also CANR 3
  See also CA 45-48
  See also obituary CA 106

Weiss, Theodore (Russell)
   1916-.................. CLC 3, 8, 14
  See also CAAS 2
  See also CA 9-12R
  See also DLB 5

Welch, James 1940-........... CLC 6, 14
  See also CA 85-88

Welch, (Maurice) Denton
   1915-1948................. TCLC 22

Weldon, Fay
   1933-......... CLC 6, 9, 11, 19, 36
  See also CANR 16
  See also CA 21-24R
  See also DLB 14

Wellek, René 1903-...............CLC 28
  See also CANR 8
  See also CA 5-8R

Weller, Michael 1942-...........CLC 10
  See also CA 85-88

Weller, Paul 1958-...............CLC 26

Wellershoff, Dieter 1925- ....CLC 46
  See also CANR 16
  See also CA 89-92

Welles, (George) Orson
   1915-1985....................CLC 20
  See also CA 93-96

Wells, H(erbert) G(eorge)
   1866-1946............TCLC 6, 12, 19
  See also CA 110
  See also SATA 20
  See also DLB 34

Wells, Rosemary 19??-............CLC 12
  See also CA 85-88
  See also SAAS 1
  See also SATA 18

Welty, Eudora (Alice)
   1909-..........CLC 1, 2, 5, 14, 22, 33
  See also SSC 1
  See also CA 9-12R
  See also CABS 1
  See also DLB 2
  See also CDALB 1941-1968

Werfel, Franz (V.) 1890-1945 ..... TCLC 8
  See also CA 104

Wergeland, Henrik Arnold
   1808-1845..................NCLC 5

Wersba, Barbara 1932- ....CLC 30
  See also CLR 3
  See also CA 29-32R
  See also SAAS 2
  See also SATA 1

Wertmüller, Lina 1928- ....CLC 16
  See also CA 97-100

Wescott, Glenway 1901-..........CLC 13
  See also CA 13-16R
  See also DLB 4, 9

Wesker, Arnold 1932-........ CLC 3, 5, 42
  See also CANR 1
  See also CA 1-4R
  See also DLB 13

Wesley, Richard (Errol) 1945-......CLC 7
  See also CA 57-60
  See also DLB 38

Wessel, Johan Herman
   1742-1785.....................LC 7

West, Jessamyn 1907-1984...... CLC 7, 17
  See also CA 9-12R
  See also obituary SATA 37
  See also DLB 6
  See also DLB-Y 84

West, Morris L(anglo)
   1916-..................... CLC 6, 33
  See also CA 5-8R

West, Nathanael
   1903?-1940..............TCLC 1, 14
  See Weinstein, Nathan Wallenstein
  See also DLB 4, 9, 28

West, Paul 1930- .... CLC 7, 14
  See also CA 13-16R
  See also DLB 14

West, Rebecca 1892-1983..... CLC 7, 9, 31
  See also CA 5-8R
  See also obituary CA 109
  See also DLB 36
  See also DLB-Y 83

Westall, Robert (Atkinson)
   1929-........................CLC 17
  See also CANR 18
  See also CA 69-72
  See also SAAS 2
  See also SATA 23

Westlake, Donald E(dwin)
   1933-.................. CLC 7, 33
  See also CANR 16
  See also CA 17-20R

Whalen, Philip 1923-.......... CLC 6, 29
  See also CANR 5
  See also CA 9-12R
  See also DLB 16

Wharton, Edith (Newbold Jones)
   1862-1937..............TCLC 3, 9, 27
  See also CA 104
  See also DLB 4, 9, 12

Wharton, William 1925-....... CLC 18, 37
  See also CA 93-96
  See also DLB-Y 80

Wheatley (Peters), Phillis
   1753?-1784....................LC 3
  See also DLB 31, 50

Wheelock, John Hall
   1886-1978...................CLC 14
  See also CANR 14
  See also CA 13-16R
  See also obituary CA 77-80
  See also DLB 45

Whelan, John 1900-
  See O'Faoláin, Seán

Whitaker, Rodney 1925-
  See Trevanian
  See also CA 29-32R

White, E(lwyn) B(rooks)
   1899-1985......... CLC 10, 34 (425),
                         39 (369)
  See also CLR 1
  See also CANR 16
  See also CA 13-16R
  See also obituary CA 116
  See also SATA 2, 29
  See also obituary SATA 44
  See also DLB 11, 22
  See also AITN 2

White, Edmund III 1940-.........CLC 27
  See also CANR 3
  See also CA 45-48

White, Patrick (Victor Martindale)
   1912-............CLC 3, 4, 5, 7, 9, 18
  See also CA 81-84

White, T(erence) H(anbury)
   1906-1964....................CLC 30
  See also CA 73-76
  See also SATA 12

White, Walter (Francis)
   1893-1955................ TCLC 15
  See also CA 115

White, William Hale 1831-1913
  See Rutherford, Mark

Whitehead, E(dward) A(nthony)
   1933-........................CLC 5
  See also CA 65-68

Whitemore, Hugh 1936-..........CLC 37

Whitman, Walt 1819-1892........ NCLC 4
  See also SATA 20
  See also DLB 3

Whitney, Phyllis A(yame)
   1903-........................CLC 42
  See also CANR 3
  See also CA 1-4R
  See also SATA 1, 30
  See also AITN 2

Whittemore, (Edward) Reed (Jr.)
   1919-........................CLC 4
  See also CANR 4
  See also CA 9-12R
  See also DLB 5

Whittier, John Greenleaf
   1807-1892..................NCLC 8
  See also DLB 1

LC Cumulative Nationality Index

AMERICAN
Bradstreet, Anne 4
Edwards, Jonathan 7
Eliot, John 5
Knight, Sarah Kemble 7
Munford, Robert 5
Wheatley, Phillis 3

CHINESE
P'u Sung-ling 3
Ts'ao Hsueh-ch'in 1
Wu-Ching-tzu 2
Wu Ch'eng-en 7

DANO-NORWEGIAN
Holberg, Ludvig 6
Wessel, Johan Herman 7

ENGLISH
Andrewes, Lancelot 5
Arbuthnot, John 1
Behn, Aphra 1
Brooke, Frances 6
Bunyan, John 4
Burke, Edmund 7
Chatterton, Thomas 3
Churchill, Charles 3
Cleland, John 2
Collier, Jeremy 6
Collins, William 4
Congreve, William 5
Davys, Mary 1
Day, Thomas 1
Defoe, Daniel 1
Dryden, John 3
Fielding, Henry 1
Fielding, Sarah 1
Goldsmith, Oliver 2
Gray, Thomas 4

Haywood, Eliza 1
Hunter, Robert 7
Jonson, Ben 6
Julian of Norwich 6
Kempe, Margery 6
Killigrew, Anne 4
Locke, John 7
Manley, Mary Delariviere 1
Marvell, Andrew 4
Parnell, Thomas 3
Pope, Alexander 3
Prior, Matthew 4
Richardson, Samuel 1
Sheridan, Frances 7
Smart, Christopher 3
Spenser, Edmund 5
Sterne, Laurence 2
Swift, Jonathan 1
Walpole, Horace 2
Winchilsea, Anne Finch,
  Lady 2
Wollstonecraft, Mary 5
Young, Edward 3

FRENCH
Boileau-Despréaux, Nicolas 3
Crébillon, Claude Prosper
  Jolyot de (fils) 1
Duclos, Charles Pinot 1
La Fayette, Marie-Madelaine,
  Comtesse de 2
Lesage, Alain-René 2
Malherbe, François de 5
Marivaux, Pierre Carlet de
  Chamblain de 4
Marmontel, Jean-François 2
Montesquieu, Charles-Louis,
  Baron de 7
Perrault, Charles 2

Prévost, Antoine François,
  Abbé 1
Rabelais, François 5
Ronsard, Pierre de 6
Scudéry, Madeleine de 2

GERMAN
Beer, Johann 5
Grimmelshausen, Johann Jakob
  Christoffel von 6
Moritz, Karl Philipp 2
Schlegal, Johann Elias 5

IRISH
Brooke, Henry 1

ITALIAN
Ariosto, Ludovico 6
Boiardo, Matteo Maria 6
Cellini, Benvenuto 7
Goldoni, Carlo 4
Tasso, Torquato 5

MEXICAN
Juana Inés de la Cruz 5

RUSSIAN
Chulkov, Mikhail
  Dmitrievich 2

SCOTTISH
Boswell, James 4
Buchanan, George 4
Burns, Robert 3
Hume, David 7
Smollett, Tobias 2

SPANISH
Cervantes, Miguel de 6

LC Cumulative Title Index

493

"Comme on voit sur la branche" **6**:425, 435

Comparative Histories of Heroes **6**:282

Comparative Histories of Heroines **6**:282

"Complaint" (Marvell)
   See "The Nymph Complaining for the Death of her Faun"

"Complaint" (Young)
   See "The Complaint; or, Night Thoughts"

"The Complaint; or, Night Thoughts" **3**:462, 464, 466-78, 480-84, 486-89, 491-500

"The Complaint; or, Night Thoughts: Night the Eighth" **3**:464, 466, 498-99

"The Complaint; or, Night Thoughts: Night the Fifth" **3**:464, 466, 480, 491

"The Complaint; or, Night Thoughts: Night the First" **3**:491, 498

"The Complaint; or, Night Thoughts: Night the Fourth" **3**:464, 465, 478, 491, 498-99

"The Complaint; or, Night Thoughts: Night the Ninth" **3**:464, 466, 498-99

"The Complaint; or, Night Thoughts: Night the Second" **3**:464, 480, 491

"The Complaint; or, Night Thoughts: Night the Seventh" **3**:464, 466, 498

"The Complaint; or, Night Thoughts: Night the Sixth" **3**:466, 498

"The Complaint; or, Night Thoughts: Night the Third" **3**:465, 472, 491

Complaints (Spenser)
   See *Complaints: Containing Sundrie Small Poemes of the Worlds Vanitie*

Complaints: Containing Sundrie Small Poemes of the Worlds Vanitie **5**:311-12

A Compleat History of England **2**:342, 344

La Comtesse de Tende **2**:138-39, 144, 149-50, 152, 157-59, 165-67, 169

"Concerning Humour in Comedy"
   See "Letter Concerning Humour in Comedy"

Concerning the End for Which God Created the World **7**:93, 95, 101-03, 117-18, 121

Conclusion of the Memoirs of Miss Sidney Bidulph **7**:371, 378, 383-84

The Conduct of the Minority **7**:47

"The Conference" **3**:150-52, 155-56, 160, 163

Les confessions du Comte de *** **1**:187-88, 190-93, 198

Conjectures
   See *Conjectures on Original Composition in a Letter to the Author of Sir Charles Grandison*

Conjectures on Original Composition in a Letter to the Author of Sir Charles Grandison **3**:474, 479, 481-82, 484, 489, 492-96, 499

"Le connaisseur" **2**:214, 221

"The Connoisseur"
   See "Le connaisseur"

The Conquest of Granada by the Spaniards **3**:179, 208, 221, 232

Conquistata
   See *Di Gerusalemme conquistata*

Considerations on the Causes of the Grandeur and the Decadence of the Romans
   See *Considérations sur les causes de la grandeur des Romains, et de leur décadence*

Considerations sur le goût **1**:188

Considérations sur les causes de la grandeur des Romains, et de leur décadence **7**:309-12, 319, 321-25, 332, 342, 347, 356-57, 360, 362

Considérations sur les moeurs de ce siècle **1**:184-85, 187-88, 191, 199

Considerations upon Two Bills **1**:489

"The Consolation"
   See "The Complaint; or, Night Thoughts: Night the Ninth"

"Consolation" (Malherbe)
   See "Consolation à Du Perier"

"Consolation à Du Perier" **5**:168, 170

"Consolation au Président de Verdun" **5**:171

"Consolation to Monsieur Du Perier on the death of his daughter"
   See "Consolation à Du Perier"

The Consolidator **1**:162

"Constantia" **1**:62

"Conte" (Marmontel) **2**:220

"Contemplations" **4**:85-6, 90-3, 95-6, 100-04, 108, 112

The Contending Brothers **1**:63

Contes de Ma Mère l'Oye
   See *Histoires ou contes du temps passé*

Contes moraux **2**:208-15, 220-22, 224

Continuation (Ronsard)
   See *Continuation des amours*

Continuation des amours **6**:425-26, 431
   See also *Continuations*

"Continuation of the Yellow Millet"
   See "Hsu huang-liang"

Continuations (Ronsard) **6**:425, 427

"Contre les bûcherons de la forêt de Gastine" **6**:417

"The Conversation" **4**:459

Conversations **6**:324

Conversations sur divers sujets **2**:293-94, 303, 307

"Conversion of St. Paul" **3**:403

"The Convert's Love" **3**:255

"The Copernican System" **3**:127

"Corn Rigs" **3**:87

"The Coronet" **4**:396, 403, 426, 437-38, 443

The Correspondence of Swift **1**:449

El cortesan o l'uomo di mondo **4**:249

Corylo **5**:56

"The Cottar's Saturday Night" **3**:48, 50, 52, 54-6, 65, 67, 72, 77, 79, 81, 83-5, 93, 102-04

"The Cotter's Saturday Night"
   See "The Cottar's Saturday Night"

The Counterfeit Bridegroom; or, The Defeated Widow **1**:33

The Countess of Dellwyn **1**:273, 278

"Country Churchyard"
   See "Elegy Written in a Country Churchyard"

"The Country Lass" **3**:85

Courage
   See *Die Erzbetrugerin und Landstortzerin Courasche*

Courasche
   See *Die Erzbetrugerin und Landstortzerin Courasche*

Court Intrigues
   See *The Lady's Pacquet of Letters Broke Open*

"The Court of Equity"
   See "Libel Summons"

The Court of the King of Bantam **1**:34, 38, 45-6, 48

The Cousins **1**:97

The Covent-Garden Tragedy **1**:239

"The Coy Mistress"
   See "To His Coy Mistress"

"The Crawlin' Ferlie"
   See "To a Louse, on Seeing One on a Lady's Bonnet at Church"

The Craze for the Summer Resort
   See *Le smanie della villeggiatura*

"The Cricket"
   See "Tsu-chih"

Crispin, rival de son maître **2**:182, 201

"The Critic and the Writer of Fables" **3**:443, 457

Critique de l'Opera **2**:259

The Cry: A New Dramatic Fable **1**:270, 273

The Cub at Newmarket, A Letter to the People of Scotland **4**:50, 52-3

"Culex" **5**:312
   See also *Complaints: Containing Sundrie Small Poemes of the Worlds Vanitie*

"Cupid and Ganymede" **4**:461

"Cymon and Iphigenia" **3**:184, 205, 213, 243

"Cynthia" **6**:322

Cynthia's Revels **6**:300, 302, 306, 308, 311, 335-36, 342

"Les daimons" **6**:407, 411, 422, 424

"Daintie Davie" **3**:56

"Damon the Mower" **3**:410-11, 441-42

The Danish Comedy's Funeral
   See *Den danske comoedies ligbegængelse*

Dannemarks og Norges beskrivelse **6**:266, 281

Dannemarks riges historie **6**:266, 278, 281-82

"Daphnaida" **5**:312-13

"Daphnis and Chloe" **4**:408-10

"The Daughter of the Yen Family"
   See "Yen Shih"

"David" **3**:255

David Simple, Volume the Last **1**:270, 278-79
   See also *The Adventures of David Simple*

"The Day of Judgement" **1**:522, 524

"The Dean of the Faculty" **3**:96

"Death and Daphne" **1**:459

"Death and Doctor Hornbook" **3**:50, 82, 87, 90

"The Death and Dying Words of Poor Mailie" **3**:57, 71, 90

"Death of a Favorite Cat"
   See "Ode on the Death of a Favourite Cat, Drowned in a Tub of Gold Fishes"

"Death of the Lord Protector"
   See "Poem upon the Death of O. C."

The Debauchee **1**:33

"Deborah" **3**:255

"The Dedication" (Churchill)
   See "Fragment of a Dedication to Dr. W. Warburton, Bishop of Gloucester"

"Dedication of *Examen Poeticum*" **3**:214

"The Dedication of the *Aeneis*" **3**:242

"The Dedication of the Sermons to William Warburton, Bishop of Gloster"
   See "Fragment of a Dedication to Dr. W. Warburton, Bishop of Gloucester"

"Dedication to Dr. W. Warburton"
   See "Fragment of a Dedication to Dr. W. Warburton, Bishop of Gloucester"

The Life of Samuel Johnson, LL. D.
4:18-19, 21-6, 30, 36-7, 39-41, 46-8, 50, 53-4, 56-60, 65-71, 75, 77-9
Life of the Late Jonathan Wild the Great
See *The Life of Mr. Jonathan Wild the Great*
Life's Progress through the Passions; or, The Adventures of Natura **1**:291
Limberham; or, The Kind Keeper **3**:222, 229-30
"Lines by Ladgate" **3**:119
"Lines to Sour-Faced Gila" **5**:146
"Lines Written in Mezeray"
See "Written in the Beginning of Mezeray's History of France"
"Lisetta's Reply" **4**:461, 466
Little Female Academy
See *The Governess; or, Little Female Academy*
"Little Red Riding Hood"
See "Le petit chaperon rouge"
"Little T. C."
See "The Picture of Little T. C. in a Prospect of Flowers"
The Lives of Cleopatra and Octavia **1**:273
The Lives of the Scholars
See *Ju-lin wai-shih*
"Livret de Folastries" **6**:417, 431
Loa a los años del rey **5**:159
Loa en las huertas donde fue a divertirse la Excelentísima Señora Condesa de Paredes, Marquesa de la Laguna **5**:159
La locandiera **4**:262, 264, 267, 273-74
The Logick Primer
See *The Logick Primer, Some Logical Notions to Initiate the Indians in Knowledge of the Rule of Reason; and to Know How to Make Use Thereof*
The Logick Primer, Some Logical Notions to Initiate the Indians in Knowledge of the Rule of Reason; and to Know How to Make Use Thereof **5**:132, 134-35
London Journal (Boswell)
See *Boswell's London Journal*
"Longing for Heaven" **4**:85, 112
"A Long Story" **4**:301, 312, 315-17, 333-34
"Lord Daer"
See "Meeting with Lord Daer"
The Lost Lover; or, A Jealous Husband **1**:315
"Louse on the Lady's Bonnet"
See "To a Louse, On Seeing One on a Lady's Bonnet at Church"
"Love-Begotten Daughter"
See "A Poet's Welcome to His Love-Begotten Daughter"
"Love Disarm'd" **4**:459
Love for Love **5**:66, 68, 70-1, 74, 76, 78-9, 81, 83, 84, 86-90, 92, 94, 96-101, 105-06, 109, 111
Love in Excess; or, The Fatal Enquiry **1**:284-85, 290, 292, 295-300
"Love in Fantastic Triumph Sat" **1**:31, 38
Love in Several Masques **1**:250
Love Letters between a Nobleman and His Sister **1**:34, 43, 48
Love Letters to a Gentleman **1**:38
"The Love of Fame"
See "The Universal Passion; or, The Love of Fame"
"A Lover's Anger" **4**:460
The Lovers Watch **1**:41

Love, the Greater Labyrinth
See *Amor es más laberinto*
Love Triumphant **3**:230
Love without Stockings
See *Kierlighed uden strømper*
"Lucia" **3**:472
"Lucius" **4**:455
The Luckey Chance; or, An Alderman's Bargain **1**:27-9, 34, 37, 40-1, 47-8
The Lucky Mistake **1**:32, 46, 51-2
Lucretia
See *Den vægelsindede*
"Lung-fei hsiang Kung" **3**:350
"Lu p'an" **3**:350
"Le lutrin" **3**:16-17, 19, 21-2, 24, 29, 37-43
Lycidus **1**:41
The Lying-in Room
See *Barselstuen*
Lykken bedre end Forstanden **7**:390
"La Lyre" **6**:427-28
"MacFlecknoe; or, A Satire upon the Trew-Blew-Protestant Poet, T. S." **3**:189, 192, 199, 205, 212, 222, 231, 242
"Macphersons' Farewell" **3**:60
The Madness of Roland
See *Orlando furioso*
La madre amorosa **4**:260
Magazin zur Erfahrungsseelenkunde **2**:236
The Magic Bird's Nest
See *Das wunderbarliche Vogelnest [I and II]*
The Magnetic Lady **6**:306, 311, 314, 327, 339
Mahomet **1**:162
The Maiden Queen
See *Secret Love; or, The Maiden Queen*
"Mailie's Dying Words and Elegy"
See "The Death and Dying Words of Poor Mailie"
"Le maître chat; ou, Le chat botté" **2**:254, 257-58, 260, 266-71, 280-81, 284
Malpiglio **5**:407
Mamusse wunneetupanatamwe Up-Biblum God Naneeswe Nukkone Testament Kah Wonk Wusku Testament **5**:124, 126-28, 130-32, 134
The Mandrake
See *Das Galgen-Männlin*
"Man Naturally God's Enemies" **7**:98
"Manne, Womanne, Syr Rogerre" **4**:214, 229, 231, 237, 239-43
Manon Lescaut
See *Histoire du Chevalier des Grieux et de Manon Lescaut*
"A Man's a Man for A' That"
See "Is There for Honest Poverty"
"Man's Injustice toward Providence" **3**:451
"Man Was Made to Mourn" **3**:48, 52, 67, 74, 87
Maria
See *The Wrongs of Woman; or, Maria*
Marian: A Comic Opera, in Two Acts **6**:107-09
Marianne
See *La vie de Marianne; ou, Les aventures de Mme La Comtesse de***
Maria; or, the Wrongs of Woman
See *The Wrongs of Woman; or, Maria*
"Le mari sylphide" **2**:212
Marriage-á-la-Mode **3**:208, 210, 214, 222, 230-33

Marriage as Retribution
See *Hsing-shih yin-yuan chuan*
The Marriage Contract **1**:63
Martin Mar-All
See *Sir Martin Mar-All; or, The Feign'd Innocence*
El mártir de Sacramento **5**:158
Mary: A Fiction **5**:426-28, 442-43, 453, 460-61
"Mary Blaize" **2**:74
"Mary in Heaven"
See "To Mary in Heaven"
"Mary Morison" **3**:71, 78, 87
Mascarade **6**:259, 269, 277
Maskarade
See *Mascarade*
The Masked Ladies
See *De usynlige*
"Mask of Semele" **5**:72
Masque of Beauty **6**:338
Masque of Blacknesse **6**:321, 337-38
The Masque of Queens **6**:315, 337, 339
Masquerades
See *Mascarade*
Masques **6**:323
Le massere **4**:264-66
Master Gert Westphaler; or, The Very Loquacious Barber
See *Mester Gert Westphaler; eller, Den meget talende barbeer*
"The Match" **4**:403, 408
"The Medall. A Satire Against Sedition" **3**:187, 199, 222, 234-35, 240
Medea
See *Medea Euripidis poetae tragici Georgio Buchanano Scoto interprete*
Medea Euripidis poetae tragici Georgio Buchanano Scoto interprete **4**:134-35
Medico olandese **4**:259
"Meditations" (Bradstreet)
See "Meditations Divine and Moral"
"Meditations Divine and Moral" **4**:96-7, 99-100, 114
"Meditations upon an Egg" **4**:182
See also *Divine Emblems; or, Temporal Things Spiritualized*
"Meeting with Lord Daer" **3**:71, 86
Melampe **6**:259, 277
Melampus
See *Melampe*
"Memoir" (Boswell) **4**:61
Mémoire d'un honnête homme **1**:343-44
Mémoires (Goldoni)
See *Mémoires de M. Goldoni, pour servir à l'histoire de sa vie, et à celle de son théâtre*
Mémoires de ma vie (Perrault) **2**:277, 283
Les Mémoires de M. de Montcal **1**:335, 337
Mémoires de M. Goldoni, pour servir à l'histoire de sa vie, et à celle de son théâtre **4**:255, 262-64, 268, 275
Mémoires d'un homme de qualité
See *Mémoires et aventures d'un homme de qualité*
Mémoires d'un honnête homme
See *Mémoire d'un honnête homme*
Mémoires d'un père pour servir à l'instruction de ses enfans **2**:208-12, 221, 223
Mémoires et aventures d'un homme de qualité, qui s'est retiré du monde **1**:327, 329, 333-37, 343-44, 347, 351-52, 356